ELEMENTS OF COMMON LAW MURDER

***Actus Reus* (Voluntary Act)**
Voluntary act of killing another person

***Mens Rea* (General Intent)**
Express or implied malice aforethought

Circumstance
1. Victim a "reasonable" person or human being
2. All persons except alien enemies in times of war

Criminal Harm

ELEMENTS OF MATERIAL SUPPORT TO TERRORIST ORGANIZATIONS

***Actus Reus* (Voluntary Act)**
1. Provide support or resources ***or***
2. Attempt to provide support or resources ***or***
3. Conspire to provide support or resources

Mens Rea
Knowingly commit *Actus Reus*

Circumstance
Designated foreign terrorist organization

Criminal Conduct
Material support to terrorist organizations

Criminal Law

12TH EDITION

JOEL SAMAHA

Horace T. Morse Distinguished Teaching Professor
University of Minnesota

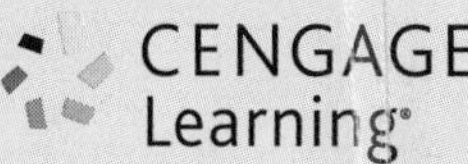

Australia • Brazil • Mexico • Singapore • United Kingdom • United States

***Criminal Law,* Twelfth Edition**
Joel Samaha

Product Director: Marta Lee-Perriard

Senior Product Manager:
Carolyn Henderson Meier

Associate Content Developer: Julia White

Product Assistant: Valerie Kraus

Senior Marketing Manager: Kara Kindstrom

Senior Content Project Manager:
Christy Frame

Managing Art Director: Andrei Pasternak

Senior Manufacturing Planner: Judy Inouye

Text Researcher: Kanchana Vijayarangan,
Lumina Datamatics

Production Service/Compositor: Cenveo®
Publisher Services

Text and Cover Designer: Diane Beasley

Cover Image: alancrosthwaite/istockphoto

Library of Congress Control Number: 2015949002

Student Edition:
ISBN: 978-1-305-57738-1

Looseleaf Edition:
ISBN: 978-1-305-66017-5

Cengage Learning
20 Channel Center Street
Boston MA 02210
USA

Printed in the United States of America
Print Number: 01 Print Year: 2015

FOR MY STUDENTS

About the Author

Professor Joel Samaha teaches Criminal Law and Criminal Procedure and, until 2014, Introduction to Criminal Justice at the University of Minnesota. He is both a lawyer and a historian whose primary interest is crime control in a constitutional democracy. He received his BA, JD, and PhD from Northwestern University. Professor Samaha also studied under the late Sir Geoffrey Elton at Cambridge University, England. He was named the College of Liberal Arts Distinguished Teacher in 1974. In 2007, he was awarded the title of University of Minnesota Distinguished Teaching Professor and inducted into the Academy of Distinguished Teachers.

Professor Samaha was admitted to the Illinois Bar in 1962, where he practiced law briefly in Chicago. He taught at UCLA before going to the University of Minnesota in 1971. He has taught both television and radio courses in criminal justice and co-taught a National Endowment for the Humanities seminar in legal and constitutional history. At the University of Minnesota, he served as chair of the Department of Criminal Justice Studies from 1974 to 1978.

In addition to *Law and Order in Historical Perspective* (1974), an analysis of law enforcement in pre-industrial English society, Professor Samaha has transcribed and written a scholarly introduction to a set of local criminal justice records from the reign of Elizabeth I. He has also written several articles on the history of criminal justice, published in the *Historical Journal, American Journal of Legal History, Minnesota Law Review, William Mitchell Law Review*, and *Journal of Social History*. In addition to *Criminal Law*, he has written two other textbooks, *Criminal Procedure*, now in its ninth edition, and *Criminal Justice*, now in its seventh edition.

Brief Contents

Contents

CHAPTER 10

Crimes Against Persons II: Sex Offenses, Bodily Injury, and Personal Restraint 380

CHAPTER 11

Crimes Against Property 430

CHAPTER 12

Crimes Against Public Order and Morals 484

CHAPTER 13

Crimes Against the State 518

Preface

Criminal Law was my favorite class as a first-year law student at Northwestern University Law School in 1958. I've loved it ever since, a love that has only grown from teaching it at least once a year at the University of Minnesota since 1971. I hope my love of the subject comes through in *Criminal Law*, which I've just finished for the twelfth time. It's a great source of satisfaction that my modest innovation to the study of criminal law—the text-casebook—has endured and flourished. *Criminal Law*, the text-casebook, brings together the description, analysis, and critique of general principles with excerpts of cases edited for nonlawyers.

Like its predecessors, *Criminal Law*, Twelfth Edition, stresses both the general principles that apply to all of criminal law and the specific elements of particular crimes that prosecutors have to prove beyond a reasonable doubt. Learning the principles of criminal law isn't just a good mental exercise, although it does stimulate students to use their minds. Understanding the general principles is an indispensable prerequisite for understanding the elements of specific crimes. The general principles have lasted for centuries. The definitions of the elements of specific crimes, on the other hand, differ from state to state and over time because they have to meet the varied and changing needs of new times and different places.

That the principles have stood the test of time testifies to their strength as a framework for explaining the elements of crimes defined in the fifty states and in the U.S. criminal code. But there's more to their importance than durability; it's also practical to know and understand them. The general principles are the bases both of the elements that prosecutors have to prove beyond a reasonable doubt to convict defendants and of the defenses that justify or excuse defendants' criminal conduct.

So *Criminal Law*, Twelfth Edition, rests on a solid foundation. But it can't stand still, any more than the subject of criminal law can remain frozen in time. The more I teach and write about criminal law, the more I learn and rethink what I've already learned; the more "good" cases I find that I didn't know were there; and the more I'm able to include cases that weren't decided and reported when the previous edition went to press.

Of course, it's my obligation to incorporate into the twelfth edition these now-decided and reported cases, and this new learning, rethinking, and discovery. But obligation doesn't describe the pleasure that preparing now twelve editions of *Criminal Law* brings me. It's thrilling to find cases that illustrate a principle in terms students can understand and that stimulate them to think critically about subjects worth thinking about. It's that thrill that drives me to make each edition better than the last. I hope it will make my students—and you—more intelligent consumers of the law and social reality of criminal law in the U.S. constitutional democracy.

Organization/Approach

The chapters in the text organize the criminal law into a traditional scheme that is widely accepted and can embrace, with minor adjustments, the criminal law of any state and/or the federal government. The logic of the arrangement is first to cover the general part of the criminal law—namely, principles and doctrines common to all or most crimes—and then the special part of criminal law—namely, the application of the general principles to the elements of specific crimes.

Chapters 1 through 8 cover the general part of criminal law: the sources and purposes of criminal law and criminal punishment; the constitutional limits on the criminal law; the general principles of criminal liability; the defenses of justification and excuse; parties to crime; and incomplete crimes.

Chapters 9 through 13 cover the special part of the criminal law: the major crimes against persons; crimes against homes and property; crimes against public order and morals; and crimes against the state.

Criminal Law has always followed the three-step analysis of criminal liability (criminal conduct, justification, and excuse). *Criminal Law* brings this analysis into sharp focus in two ways. First, the chapter sequence: Chapters 3 and 4 cover the general principles of criminal conduct (criminal act, criminal intent, concurrence, and causation). Chapter 5 covers the defenses of justification, the second step in the analysis of criminal liability. Chapter 6 covers the defenses of excuse, the third step. So the chapter sequence mirrors precisely the three-step analysis of criminal liability.

Criminal Law also sharpens the focus on the three-step analysis by means of the two kinds of *Elements of Crime* art. First are criminal conduct crime boxes, consisting of a voluntary criminal act triggered by criminal intent. Second are bad result crimes, consisting of a voluntary criminal act, criminal intent, and causing a criminal harm.

The design of these boxes is consistent throughout the book. The elements boxes go right to the core of the three-step analysis of criminal liability, making it easier for students to master the essence of criminal law: applying general principles to specific individual crimes.

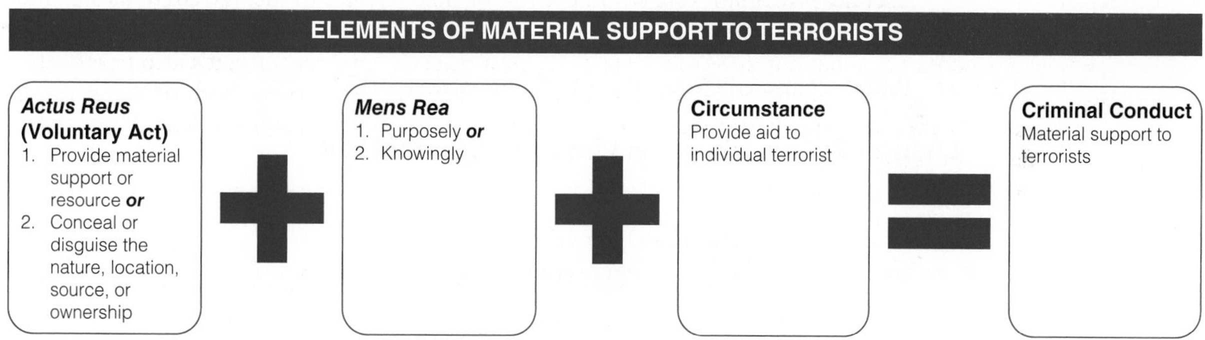

Changes to the Twelfth Edition

Criminal Law, Twelfth Edition, includes new case excerpts; an increased selection of relevant legal and social science research; a rich collection of examples to illustrate main points; new chapter-opening vignettes to enhance student relevancy; and numerous new "You Decide" to give students an opportunity to prepare for on-the-job challenges.

For the first time, we have included the "Criminal Law in Focus" feature to highlight current topics of interest in criminal law, such as relevant excerpts from the U.S. Criminal Code, a comparison of the insanity defense myths and reality, and the Oregon Death with Dignity Act. We have also included a running glossary to define terms as each chapter progresses—a tool we think students will find invaluable.

Additionally, the Twelfth Edition includes entirely new sections, including some on such high-profile topics as the ban on carrying concealed guns in churches, mandatory life without parole for juveniles, the duty to intervene in criminal omissions, physician-assisted suicide, "homegrown" (U.S. born and/or longtime resident non–U.S. born) terrorists, and more.

Throughout the book are also new charts and tables, and all retained graphics are updated to reflect the most recent information available. Here are the highlights of the changes in each chapter.

Chapter 1, Criminal Law and Punishment in U.S. Society: An Overview

NEW

- **Vignette** "Did he 'intend' to cause bodily harm?"
- **Introduction** "Overcriminalization and mass incarceration" Two hot button issues that affect two aspects of CL12, namely criminal law and punishment
- **Figure** "Arrests 2013"
- **Text** Link the general discussion of the breadth and depth of criminal law and punishment to specific chapters in the book.
- **Subsections**
  - "Informal Discretionary Law Making" In practice, police, prosecutors, and judges are a source of law making in the vast number of minor crimes, such as drug offenses and disorderly conduct covered in Chapters 2 and 12.
  - "The Era of Mass Imprisonment, 1970s–Present" Develops the point that U.S. has 5% of world population and 25% of prisoners.
  - "Empirical Evaluation of Criminal Law Theories" Contains the latest empirical research on retributionists and deterrence theories.
- **You Decide** "Was the 'law making' of the police and prosecutor ethical?"
- **Case Excerpt** *Carole Anne Bond v. United States* (2014) "Was the arsenic a 'chemical weapon?'"

REVISED

- **Table** "Selected Crimes and Arrest Statistics, 2013"

Chapter 2, Constitutional Limits on Criminal Law

NEW

- **Vignette** "Violation of Doctors' Right to Free Speech?"
- **You Decide** "Did the longer sentence violate the ban on *ex post facto* laws?"
- **Subsections**
  - "The Rule of Lenity"
  - "Proving Guilt in Criminal Cases"
- **Case**
  - *Commonwealth v. William P. Johnson and Commonwealth v. Gail M. Johnson* (2014) "Is cyberharassment free speech?"
  - *Woollard v. Gallagher* (2013) "Does the 'good and substantial reason' requirement violate the Second Amendment?"

REVISED

- **Subsection**
  - "Right to 'Bear Arms'"
  - "Prison Sentences"

Chapter 3, The Criminal Act: The First Principle of Criminal Liability

NEW

- **Vignette** "Did They Have a 'Legal' Duty to Act?"
- **Section** "Sleep Driving"

- **Case Excerpts**
  - — *State v. Newman* (2013) "Did 'sleep driving' nullify the voluntary act requirement?"
  - — *People v. Levy* (2011) "Did his conduct 'include a voluntary act'?"
  - — *Williams v. State* (2013) "Did she possess cannabis with the intent to sell, manufacture, or deliver it?"
- **You Decide**
  - — "Is 'sleep sex' a voluntary act?"
  - — "Did he kill during 'insulin shock'?"

Chapter 4, The General Principles of Criminal Liability: *Mens Rea*, Concurrence, Ignorance, and Mistake

NEW

- **Section** "Failure of Proof 'Defenses': Ignorance and Mistake"
- **Subsections**
  - — "Ignorance of Law"
  - — "Mistake of Fact"
  - — "A General Ignorance of Mistake 'Defense'"
  - — "Morality and Ignorance of the Law: Empirical Findings"
- **Case Excerpts**
  - — *State v. Fleck* (2012) "Did he intend to inflict bodily harm?"
  - — *State v. Bauer* (2014) "Did he cause the gunshot wounds?"
  - — *State v. Jacobson* (2005) "Did he qualify for a *failure of proof defense*?"
- **Criminal Law in Focus**
  - — "Definitions of the Three Kinds of Criminal Liability"
  - — "MPC Levels of Culpability"
  - — "Ignorance or Mistake: Model Penal Code, Section 2.04"
- **You Decide**
  - — "Which court's decision established the most ethical public policy regarding the control of HIV?"
  - — "Who's entitled to the mistake of law defense?"

REVISED

- "*Mens Rea*" Major rewrite includes:
  - — **Major Subsection Rewrites**
    - ▪ "Criminal Intent"
    - ▪ "General and Specific Intent"

Chapter 5, Defenses to Criminal Liability I: Justifications

NEW

- **Vignette** Battered woman defense
- **Subsections**
  - — "Cohabitant Rule" Exception to Retreat Rule
  - — "Battered Women Who Kill Their Abusers" Major expansion of the battered woman syndrome and the defense that grew out of it. Also statistics on domestic partner violence
- **Case Excerpt** *State v. Batie* (2015) "Did she start the fight with her husband?"

- **Criminal Law in Focus**
  - "Reasonableness and the Battered Woman: *Donna Lee Bechtel v. Oklahoma*"
  - "Alabama Criminal Code Consent Law"
- **You Decide**
  - "Do the new castle laws protect the right to defend or provide a license to kill?"
  - "Was burglary the lesser evil?"
  - "Can she consent to being assaulted?"
  - "Can he consent to being shot?"

REVISED

- **Sections**
  - "Proving Defenses" Rewritten to clarify differences between perfect and imperfect defenses and how to prove them.
  - "Choice of Evils" Rewritten to clarify and improve the elements and history of the "general defense of necessity."
- **Case Excerpt** *State v. Stewart* (1988) Major addition to dissent to expand on battered woman defense evidence.

Chapter 6, Defenses to Criminal Liability II: Excuses

NEW

- **Vignette** *Myers III v. State*
- **Case Excerpts**
  - *Myers III v. State* (2015) "Was he guilty but mentally ill?"
  - *State v. Belew* (2014) "Were his 'hidden wounds' an excuse for shooting police officers?"
- **Criminal Law in Focus**
  - "The Insanity Defense: Popular Myths and Empirical Reality"
  - "Competence and Sanity: Critical Differences"
  - "Juveniles Tried as Adults"
  - "Duress Statutes in Three States"
- **Figure** "Percent of Afghanistan/Iraq War Vets Suffering from PTSD, Depression, and Traumatic Brain Injuries (TBI)"
- **You Decide**
  - "Is it ethical policy to try an eight-year-old for murder?"

REVISED

- **Sections**
  - "The Insanity Defense" Revision to update and focus on the myth (fakers get away with murder) and reality (defendants hardly ever plead insanity, and of those practically none succeed).
  - "The Defense of Entrapment" Update history to include modern totalitarian government, including Moammar Ghadafi and Kim Jong-un.
  - "Syndrome Defenses" Substantial new material, including empirical findings on PTS effects on defense as it applies to the "hidden wounds" of returning Afghanistan and Iraq War veterans.

Chapter 7, Parties to Crime and Vicarious Liability

NEW

- **Vignette** "Was She an Accomplice?"
- **Criminal Law in Focus** "Common Law Parties to Crime"
- **Case Excerpts** *City of Waukesha v. Boehnen* (2015) "Was the owner criminally liable for selling liquor to minors?"
- **You Decide** "Is it wise public policy to make parents guilty for their children's crimes?"

Chapter 8, Inchoate Crimes

NEW

- **Vignette** *State v. Damms*
- **Criminal Law in Focus**
  - — "The Line between 'Preparation' and 'Attempt'"
  - — "1. Did They Get 'Very Near' to Robbing the Clerk?" and "2. Was It 'Preparation' or 'All But the Last Act'?"
  - — "Why Prosecute Organized Crime under RICO?"
- **Case Excerpts**
  - — *Dabney v. State* (2004) "Did he attempt to commit burglary?"
  - — *State v. King* (2015) "Did he intend to kill?"
  - — *Griffin v. Gipson* (2015) "Did he conspire to commit murder?"
- **You Decide** "Should both women be treated equally?"

Chapter 9, Crimes Against Persons I: Murder and Manslaughter

NEW

- **Section** "Kinds and Degrees of Murder"
- **Vignette** *State v. Snowden*
- **Criminal Law in Focus**
  - — "Stages of Fetal Development in Feticide Statutes"
  - — "Proving 'Premeditation' and 'Deliberation'"
  - — "Inherently Dangerous to Life in the Abstract Felonies"
  - — "Four 'Adequate' Provocations"
  - — "Provocation Jury Instruction"
  - — "Model Penal Code Homicide Sections"
  - — "Oregon Death with Dignity Act"
- **Figure** "Violent Crimes, 2013"
- **You Decide**
  - — "Is partial birth abortion murder?"
  - — "Was beating him to death with a baseball bat atrocious first-degree murder?"
  - — "Murder or manslaughter?"
  - — "Should doctor-assisted suicide be considered murder?"

Chapter 10, Crimes Against Persons II: Sex Offenses, Bodily Injury, and Personal Restraint

NEW

- **Vignette** "Did he commit a felony sex offense?"

- **Section**
  - "Does 'No' Always Mean 'No'?"
  - "The Kahan *Berkowitz* Experiment"
- **Case Excerpt**
  - *State in the Interest of S.M.I.* (2012) "Did he force her to have sexual intercourse?"
  - *State v. Triestman* (2010) "Did he commit criminal sexual contact?"
- **You Decide**
  - "Is criminal law the best response to promote ethical domestic violence public policy?"
  - "Should cyberbullying be a crime?"
- **Table**
  - "Perceived Offender Characteristics in Rape and Sexual Assault Victimizations Against Females Ages 18–24 (by post-secondary enrollment status of victim), 1995–2013"
  - "Rape or Sexual Assault Victimizations Against Females Ages 18 to 24 (reported and not reported to police and reasons for not reporting, by post-secondary enrollment status), 1995–2013"
- **Revised**
- **Major Section Rewrite** "Criminal Sexual Conduct Statutes" Added new material on grass roots movement that swept the country and produced a revolution in rape law, especially date rape

Chapter 11, Crimes Against Property

NEW

- **Vignette** "Was it theft?"
- **Subsection** "The Dark Net" Focuses on "...a part of the Internet most people have never gone to because it's an encrypted, hidden underworld that's home to pornography, black markets, trolls, criminals and extremists."
- **Case Excerpt**
  - *People v. Lai Lee* (2009) "Was it purse snatching or shoplifting?"
  - *State v. Rolon* (2012) "Did he rob or steal from the victim?"
  - *Flores-Figueroa v. U.S.* (2009) "Did he 'knowingly' use someone else's identification cards?"
  - *U.S. v. Ulbricht* (2015) "Is he a libertarian hero or calculating drug lord?"
- **Criminal Law in Focus**
  - "Madoff Forfeiture Order"
  - "'Purse Snatching' vs. 'Robbery'"
  - "MPC Criminal Mischief Provision"
  - "Grading Burglary"
  - "Aggravated Identity Theft"
  - "The Silk Road in Operation"
- **Figure** "Total Losses, 2012"
- **Table** "National Estimates of Intentionally Set Fires and Losses in Residential Buildings"

REVISED

- **Major Section Revision** "Cybercrimes"

Chapter 12, Crimes Against Public Order and Morals

NEW

- **Section** "Minor Offenses: Public Order or Cash Cows?" An investigation of whether police practices promote public order or only generate income for city governments. The section homes in on the Ferguson MO PD and the US DOJ's reports: one clearing Officer Darren Wilson of shooting Michael Brown and the other condemning the FPD's use of minor city offenses (jaywalking) to pay for the city government's operation.
- **Case Excerpt** *U.S. Department of Justice v. Civil Rights Division* (2015) "Investigation of the Ferguson Police Department"
- **Criminal Law in Focus**
  - "Model Penal Code Elements of Special Disorderly Conduct Sections"
  - "Many Conservatives Are Blowing It on the DOJ Ferguson Report"

REVISED

- **Major Section Revisions**
  - "Violent Video Games" Especially empirical research on the scientific link between violent video games and criminal behavior.
  - "Prostitution" Reduce coverage of the history of prostitution, and of the "double standard" for johns and sex workers.
- **Figure** "Total Prostitution Arrests, 2013"

Chapter 13, Crimes Against the State

NEW

- **Vignette** Social media and cybercrime
- **Case Excerpt** *U.S. v. Asher Abid Khan* (2015)
- **Criminal Law in Focus**
  - "Selected Provisions and Definitions of Terrorism in the United States Code"
  - "U.S. Criminal Code 'Material Support and Resources' Provisions"
- **You Decide**
  - "Did they commit sabotage?"
  - "Which *should* be banned as 'material support and resources' to terrorists?"

REVISED

- **Major Section Revision** "'Material Support and Resources' to 'Terrorists' and Terrorist Organizations"
- **Section**
  - "The History of the Espionage Act" Streamlined, including other rarely prosecuted crimes against the state.
  - "The Espionage Act Today" Updated to include espionage cases and punishments up to 2015.

SUPPLEMENTS

Resources for Instructors

- **MindTap Criminal Justice** MindTap from Cengage Learning represents a new approach to a highly personalized, online learning platform. A fully online learning solution, MindTap combines all of a student's learning tools—readings, multimedia, activities, and assessments—into a singular Learning Path that guides the student through the curriculum. Instructors personalize the experience by customizing the presentation of these learning tools for their students, allowing instructors to seamlessly introduce their own content into the Learning Path via "apps" that integrate into the MindTap platform. Additionally, MindTap provides interoperability with major Learning Management Systems (LMS) via support for open industry standards and fosters partnerships with third-party educational application providers to provide a highly collaborative, engaging, and personalized learning experience.
- **Online Instructor's Resource Manual** The instructor's manual, which has been updated and revised by Valerie Bell of Loras College to the Twelfth Edition, includes learning objectives, key terms, a detailed chapter outline, a chapter summary, discussion topics, student activities, and media tools. The learning objectives are correlated with the discussion topics, student activities, and media tools.
- **Online Test Bank** Each chapter's test bank contains questions in multiple-choice, true/false, completion, and essay formats, with a full answer key. The test bank is coded to the learning objectives that appear in the main text and includes the page numbers in the main text where the answers can be found. Finally, each question in the test bank has been carefully reviewed by experienced criminal justice instructors for quality, accuracy, and content coverage so instructors can be sure they are working with an assessment and grading resource of the highest caliber.
- **Cengage Learning Testing Powered by Cognero** This assessment software is a flexible, online system that allows you to import, edit, and manipulate test bank content from the *Criminal Law* test bank or elsewhere, including your own favorite test questions; create multiple test versions in an instant; and deliver tests from your LMS, your classroom, or wherever you want.
- **PowerPoint® Lectures** Helping you make your lectures more engaging while effectively reaching your visually oriented students, these handy Microsoft PowerPoint® slides outline the chapters of the main text in a classroom-ready presentation. The PowerPoint® slides are updated to reflect the content and organization of the new edition of the text and feature some additional examples and real-world cases for application and discussion. The PowerPoint® slides were updated for the current edition by Valerie Bell of Loras College.

Resources for Students

- **MindTap Criminal Justice** MindTap from Cengage Learning represents a new approach to a highly personalized, online learning platform. A fully online learning solution, MindTap combines all of a student's learning tools—readings, multimedia, activities, and assessments—into a singular Learning Path that guides the student through the curriculum. Instructors personalize the experience by customizing the presentation of these learning tools for their students, allowing instructors to seamlessly introduce their own content into the Learning Path via "apps" that integrate into the MindTap platform. Additionally, MindTap provides interoperability with major Learning Management Systems (LMS) via support for open industry standards and fosters partnerships with third-party educational application providers to provide a highly collaborative, engaging, and personalized learning experience.

ACKNOWLEDGEMENTS

Criminal Law, Twelfth Edition (like the other eleven), didn't get to you by my efforts alone; I had a lot of help. I'm grateful for all those who have provided feedback over the years. Many thanks also to Senior Product Manager Carolyn Henderson Meier and Associate Content Developer Julia White; they and others at Cengage Learning have helped me at every stage of the book.

Additionally, I would like to thank the following reviewers of the Eleventh Edition for providing invaluable feedback and direction for this revision:

- Seth A. Dupuis, *Springfield Technical Community College*
- Keith E. Johnson, *Mansfield University of Pennsylvania*
- Daniel Hebert, *Springfield Technical Community College*
- Andrew Kozal, *Northwest State Community College*
- Emily Renzelli, *West Virginia University*

Derek Volke. For five years Derek has enriched my life. First as my student. Second as my TA in all three courses that I've taught at the University of Minnesota—Introduction to Criminal Justice, Criminal Law, and Criminal Procedure. Third, he's been indispensable assistant in preparing *Criminal Law*, Twelfth Edition. The **Learning Objectives, Marginal Key Terms**, and the **Chapter Summaries** are utterly and invaluably his. I can't count the number of times throughout the manuscript where he added comments like "I think students might understand this better if you worded it this way...." "I think this should be a *key term*; otherwise students might miss its significance." "I'm glad you changed this; I think it'll be easier for students to understand now." I accepted *all* of Derek's suggestions. The result—*Criminal Law*, Twelfth Edition, for the first time was written with the active participation of a student who used it as a student, and dealt with students' problems understanding it, when he was a TA. This isn't to say we "dumbed down" and "spoon-fed" students. We just made a serious effort to write difficult matter in clear, straightforward prose.

What would I do without Doug and Steve? Doug takes me there and gets me here and everywhere, day in and day out, days that now have stretched to 17 years. And my old and dearest friend Steve, who from the days when he watched over our Irish Wolfhounds in the 1970s, to now decades later when he keeps "Frankie" the Standard Poodle, "Kitty" the OSH, me, and a lot more around here in order. And both Steve and Doug do it all while putting up with what my beloved mentor at Cambridge, the late Sir Geoffrey Elton, called my "mercurial temperament." Only those who really know me can understand how I can try the patience of Job! Friends and associates like these have given *Criminal Law*, Twelfth Edition, whatever success it enjoys. As for its faults, I own them all.

Joel Samaha
Minneapolis

Learning Objectives

1 To know the dual nature of the social reality of U.S. criminal law and understand how it reflects both our criminal law and punishment imaginations.

2 To understand the differences between criminal and noncriminal sanctions, and to know the purposes of each.

3 To understand the various ways to classify crimes and appreciate the legal and social ramifications of these labels.

4 To identify, describe, and understand the main sources of criminal law.

5 To define and understand what behavior deserves criminal punishment and to understand the social consequences of the era of mass imprisonment.

6 To know and understand that the main theories of criminal punishment center on either retribution or prevention and to appreciate the large, complex body of empirical research supporting each.

7 To understand the text-case method and how to apply it to the study of criminal law.

1 Criminal Law and Punishment in U.S. Society

An Overview

Chapter Outline

Did he "intend" to cause bodily harm?

A man knew he was HIV positive. Despite doctors' instructions about safe sex and the need to tell his partners before having sex with them, he had sex numerous times with three different women without telling them. Most of the time, he used no protection, but, on a few occasions, he withdrew before ejaculating. He gave one of the women an anti-AIDS drug "to slow down the AIDS." None of the women contracted HIV.

LO1 "Every known organized society has, and probably must have, some system by which it punishes those who violate its most important prohibitions" (Robinson 2008, 1). This book explores, and invites you to think critically about, the answers to the two questions implied in Professor Robinson's quote:

1. What behavior deserves criminal punishment?
2. What's the appropriate punishment for criminal behavior?

To introduce you to some possible answers, read the brief summaries presented from real cases that we examine deeper in the remaining chapters. After you read each summary, assign the case to one of the five following categories:

1. Crime
2. Noncriminal wrong (tort)
3. Regulation
4. License
5. Lawful

These categories move across a spectrum of interference with the liberty, privacy, and property interests of individuals. These are precious rights in a free and democratic society. But, so is our need to feel safe and secure, and the need to protect us from others (and maybe even ourselves) who take or threaten to take them away from us. So, ask yourself, "How much does the behavior in the story threaten your need to feel safe and secure?" And, "Is it worth the loss your liberty, privacy, and property that all but option 5 will cost you?" Don't worry about whether you know enough about criminal law to decide which category the story belongs in. In fact, try to ignore what you already know; just choose the category you *feel* best fits the case:

1. ***Crime.*** If you put the case into this category, then grade it as very serious, serious, or minor. The idea here is to stamp it with both the amount of disgrace (stigma) you believe a convicted "criminal" should suffer and roughly the kind and amount of punishment you believe the person deserves.
2. ***Noncriminal Wrong.*** This is a legal wrong that justifies suing someone and getting money, usually for some personal injury. In other words, name a price that the wrongdoer has to pay to another individual, but don't stamp it "criminal" (Coffee 1992, 1876–77).
3. ***Regulation.*** Use government action—for example, a heavy cigarette tax to discourage smoking—to discourage the behavior (Harcourt 2005, 11–12). In other words, make the price high, but don't stamp it with the stigma of "crime."
4. ***License.*** Charge a price for it—for example, a driver's license fee for the privilege to drive—but don't try to encourage or discourage it. Make the price affordable, and attach no stigma to it.
5. ***Lawful.*** Let individual conscience and/or social disapproval condemn it, but create no legal consequences. (You should also choose this option if you believe society should *encourage* the behavior. A few students occasionally do.)

The Cases

Here are brief highlights from some of the cases you'll encounter in the remaining chapters.

1. A young man beat a stranger on the street with a baseball bat for "kicks." The victim died. (*Commonwealth v. Golston* 1977, "Atrocious Murder" in Chapter 9, p. 343)
2. A wife cheated on her husband for months. He begged his wife not to leave him. She replied, "No, I'm going to court, and you're going to have to give me all the furniture. You're going to have to get the hell out of here; you won't have nothing." Then, pointing to her crotch, she added, "You'll never touch this again, because I've got something bigger and better for it." Breaking into tears, he begged some more, "Why don't you try to save the marriage? I have nothing more to live for." "Never," she replied. "I'm never coming back to you." He "cracked," ran into the next room, got a

gun, and shot her to death. (*Commonwealth v. Schnopps* 1983, Chapter 9, "Voluntary Manslaughter," p. 360)

3. Two robbers met a drunk man in a bar, displaying a wad of money. When the man asked them for a ride, they agreed, drove him out into the country, robbed him, forced him out of the car without his glasses, and drove off. A college student, driving at a reasonable speed, didn't see the man standing in the middle of the road waving him down, couldn't stop, and struck and killed him. (*People v. Kibbe* 1974, Chapter 4, "Proximate Cause," p. 147)
4. A police officer followed James Newman's car and observed him making a left-hand turn without signaling or stopping, running a red light, and driving down the middle of a street, straddling the two traffic lanes. The officer activated his overhead lights to initiate a traffic stop and, in response, Newman pulled into a parking lot. Dr. Joshua Ramseyer, a certified neurologist and sleep medicine specialist, was prepared to testify that Newman was "sleep driving." He emphasized that activities performed while "sleep driving" are unconscious acts. He further noted that sleepwalking resulting in "sleep driving," while uncommon in the general population, is a well-established phenomenon. (*State v. Newman* 2013, 302 P.3d 435, Chapter 3, p. 102)
5. A neighbor told an eight-year-old boy and his friend to come out from behind a building and not to play there because it was dangerous. The boy answered belligerently, "In a minute." Losing patience, the neighbor said, "No, not in a minute; get out of there now!" A few days later, he broke into her house, pulled a goldfish out of its bowl, chopped it into little pieces with a steak knife, and smeared it all over the counter. Then he went into the bathroom, plugged in a curling iron, and clamped it onto a towel. (*State v. K.R.L.* 1992, Chapter 6, "The Excuse of Age," p. 224)
6. A young man lived in a ground-level apartment with a large window opening onto the building parking lot. At eight o'clock one morning, he stood naked in front of the window eating his cereal in full view of those getting in and out of their cars. (*State v. Metzger* 1982, Chapter 2, "Defining Vagueness," p. 45)
7. A man knew he was HIV positive. Despite doctors' instructions about safe sex and the need to tell his partners before having sex with them, he had sex numerous times with three different women without telling them. Most of the time, he used no protection, but, on a few occasions, he withdrew before ejaculating. He gave one of the women an anti-AIDS drug, "to slow down the AIDS." None of the women contracted the HIV virus. (*State v. Stark* 1992, Chapter 4, "MPC Mental Attitudes: Purpose," p. 135)
8. A woman met a very drunk man in a bar. He got into her car, and she drove him to her house. He asked her for a spoon, which she knew he wanted to use to take drugs. She got it for him and waited in the living room while he went into the bathroom to "shoot up." He came back into the living room and collapsed; she went back to the bar. The next morning she found him "purple, with flies flying around him." Thinking he was dead, she told her daughter to call the police and left for work. He was dead. (*People v. Oliver* 1989, Chapter 3, "Omissions as Acts," p. 116)

CRIMINAL LAW IN U.S. SOCIETY

"Nothing is certain," Ben Franklin said, "but death and taxes." Had he lived during our time, Franklin might have added a few other certainties—and almost assuredly among them would have been the concept of "crime." By this, I am not referring to the rate of violence and unlawful deprivations of property or privacy in the United States, which ebbs and flows from year to year and decade to decade, often coinciding with dips in the economy or spikes in the number of young males in the general population. Instead, it is the troubling phenomenon of continually adding new crimes or more severe punishments to the penal code, criminalizing, recriminalizing, and overcriminalizing all forms of conduct, much of it innocuous, to the point of erasing the line between tolerable and unacceptable behavior.

—Erik Luna (2004, 1)

social reality of U.S. criminal law the dual nature of U.S. criminal law divided into two categories: a small number of serious, core offenses and a large number of lesser crimes, or "everything else"

criminal law imagination the contributions of law, history, philosophy, the social sciences, and sometimes biology to explain the moral desires we wish to impose on the world

Professor Luna is referring to the social reality of U.S. criminal law, namely that there are two criminal laws. This dual nature of criminal law is the organizing theme and organization of your book. There's a small group of core offenses and a huge number of crimes we call "all the rest" (Professor Stuntz [2001] calls them "everything else" (512).)

Notice the number of arrests Table 1.1 keyed to the chapters in which they appear. Also, look at the revealing distribution of violent, property, and drug offense arrests depicted in Figure 1.1. They're the latest numbers available when your book went to press.

Table 1.1 and Figure 1.1 tell you a lot about criminal law in U.S. society. They reflect what we call the criminal law imagination in United States society. What do I mean by "criminal law imagination?" Conduct that reflects our "moral desires—visions of a moral order, yearnings for the comportment of others and ourselves," and which "*we seek to impose… on the world*" (Harcourt 2005, 10 emphasis added). (I borrowed and tailored the term *sociological imagination* coined by the American sociologist C. Wright Mills in 1959 to describe the type of insight offered by the discipline of sociology, namely to explain the nature of sociology and its relevance in daily life.)

TABLE 1.1 Selected Crimes and Arrest Statistics, 2013

SELECTED CRIMES	ARRESTS
Murder and nonnegligent manslaughter (Chapters 3, 4, 7, 8, 9)	10,231
Arson (Chapter 11)	10,509
Rape (Chapter 10)	16,863
Sex offenses (except rape and prostitution; e.g., offenses against chastity/morals) (Chapter 12)	57,925
Forgery and counterfeiting (Chapter 11)	60,969
Motor vehicle theft	64,566
Stolen property (buying, receiving, possessing)	92,691
Robbery (Chapter 11)	94,406
Weapons (illegal carrying, possessing, etc.) (Chapters 2, 3, 5, 6)	137,779
Fraud (Chapter 11)	143,528
Vandalism (Chapter 11)	201,168
Burglary (Chapter 11)	252,629
Liquor laws	354,872
Aggravated assault (attacks with intent to murder or inflict serious injury, usually with a weapon) (Chapters 6, 8)	358,860
Drunkenness	443,527
Disorderly conduct (disturb public peace, scandalize community, shock public sense of morality) (Chapter 12)	467,993
Driving under the influence (Chapters 2, 3)	1,166,824
Larceny-theft (Chapter 11)	1,231,580
Drug abuse violations (use, possess, sell, grow, manufacture, make narcotic drugs) (Chapters 2, 3, 12)	1,501,043
All other arrests	6,009,807
Total Arrests (selected + all other arrests)	**11,302,102**

Source: FBI Uniform Crime Report 2013 (Sept.), Table 29.

ARRESTS 2013

Figure 1.1

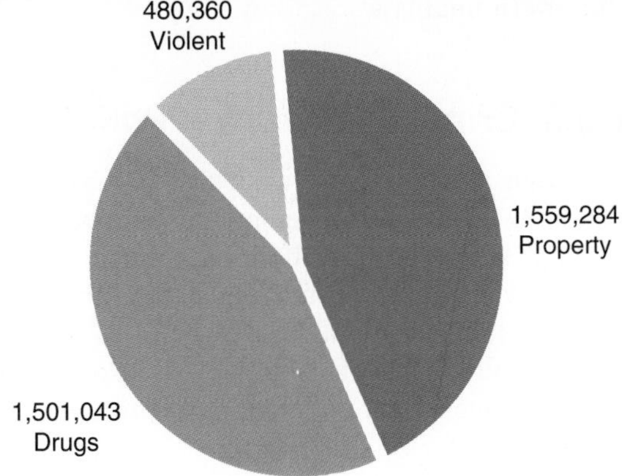

Source: FBI Uniform Crime Report 2013 (Sept.), Table 29.

The Core Felonies

LO1

The core offenses comprise the most serious crimes in two general categories:

- Felonies against persons, which are murder, manslaughter, rape, kidnapping, and robbery
- Felonies against property, which include all forms of felony theft, robbery, arson, and burglary (Chapter 11).

felonies against persons the core offenses of murder, manslaughter, rape, kidnapping, and robbery

felonies against property the core offenses of felonious theft, robbery, arson, and burglary

You've almost certainly heard of these ancient crimes. These are the "Index" crimes that the FBI tracks in its annual Uniform Crime Reports (UCR). Most people believe they're morally wrong and that those who commit them deserve criminal punishment. You probably agree. Analyzing the elements of these crimes and their punishment fill up most law school criminal law casebooks, law school criminal law courses, criminal law scholarship—and the book you're reading (Stuntz 2001, 512). All states and the federal government have criminal codes that both define in detail the elements the prosecution has to prove beyond a reasonable doubt to convict defendants, *and* prescribe hard punishment (a year or more in prison) for committing them. (We get to the punishment later.)

hard punishment a sentence of a year or more in prison

Notice several other points about the social reality of the handful of core felonies in U.S. criminal law:

1. There are far fewer core offenses and far fewer people committing them (see Table 1.1 and Figure 1.1) than in the rest of the criminal law.
2. Core offenses are ancient.
3. Most have remained remarkably stable in definition. Their elements are pretty much what they were when the judges created them and Blackstone (1769) wrote about them. (But see sex offenses and domestic violence in Chapter 10.)
4. The short list of them has not grown much since Blackstone's day either. (Motor Vehicle Theft is the only core offense in the FBI Index that was not one of the ancient felonies.)

The core offenses clearly fit within what Professor Bernard Harcourt (2005) calls our "carceral imagination." The word *carceral* refers to jail and prison. We call it the

punishment imagination crimes that fit within the criminal law imagination and that the law should punish by locking people up

punishment imagination, crimes that fit within the criminal law imagination *and* that the law *should* punish by locking up people. Now, let's turn to "all the rest" of the offenses that make up our criminal law.

LO1

"All the rest" of U.S. Criminal Law: The "Police Power"

police power all federal, state, and local governments' executive, legislative, and judiciary's power, including uniformed police officers, to carry out and enforce the criminal law

Most "everything else" offenses derive from what's known as the government's police power. Police power includes what you immediately imagined—uniformed police officers enforcing the criminal law. However, it extends much further to encompass all federal, state, and local governments' executive, legislative, and judiciary's acts to carry out the "broad public policies regarding public safety, public economy, public property, public morals, and public health" (Novak 1996, 49). It also arguably comprises all of the responsibilities of government listed in the Preamble to the U.S. Constitution:

- Form a more perfect union
- Establish justice
- Insure domestic tranquility
- Provide for the common defense
- Promote the general welfare
- Secure the blessings of liberty to ourselves and our posterity

LO1

HISTORY OF THE POLICE POWER

Sir William Blackstone (1769), in his *Commentaries on the Laws of England* (most educated eighteenth-century Americans read it), claimed that the king, as the "father of his people" (Blackstone, 169), held the police power. Under the head "public police and economy," here's how Blackstone defined the police power:

> By the public police . . . I mean the due regulation and domestic order of the kingdom: whereby the individuals of the state like the members of a well-governed family, are bound to conform their general behavior to the rules of propriety, good neighborhood, and good manners: and to be decent, industrious in their respective stations. (162)

During the spring of 1777, a few years after Blackstone's *Commentaries* appeared in print, the members of the Continental Congress (the body that coordinated the colonial resistance against Great Britain) were gathering in Philadelphia. They realized their cause was in grave danger. The war was going badly: New York had fallen to the British army. The Hessians and British Redcoats were about to cut off New England. And, the British army was planning to crush the rebellion utterly by taking Philadelphia.

The Revolutionary War generation fought for liberty. However, after the war, they quickly came to fear that their revolution had "unleashed widespread licentiousness, vice, and crime." They reacted to this fear in two ways. On the positive side, they called on private citizens to "invest liberty in virtue." Voluntary organizations "spread the gospel of Christian goodness and good citizenship." Second, they set aside their liberal ideas—individual autonomy, consent, and law—and

> called on local and state governments to limit or deny liberty to those individuals who *appeared* to endanger public peace. Legislatures, judges, and other officials responding by exercising the state's police power to detain, prosecute, and punish wrongdoers. (Kann 2008, 74; emphasis added)

In short, people fought and died to be free from King George III and his detested exercise of police power during the American Revolution, only to replace it with their own officials' exercise of the *same* police power. Historian William Novak (1996) has convincingly documented a "powerful government tradition devoted in theory and practice to the vision of a well-regulated society" in the century after the Revolution. He has also established that criminal law was a "key technology in morals and cultural policing" to maintain that regulation (150).

POLICE POWER AND PUBLIC MORALS

LO1

"No subject can more closely affect the interest of man considered as an individual, or in a more common and enlarged view, as a member of society, than those laws he may be subject to, and none more certainly than those that concern his liberty and life." So wrote Jacob Wheeler (1854, 1) in 1854, in the Preface to his history of criminal cases in the Courts of Justice of New York City. Wheeler took a decidedly sociological approach in the cases he collected. He promised his readers that he would focus on the "thousands and tens of thousands of complicated and important relations that grow out of property, liberty, and life" (6). Here's how he tied these social relations to morals crimes:

> Man is not only a social, but a reasonable being, not only rational, but moral, and, therefore, accountable. It is in this state we find him, and it is in this state that he is subject to those regulations mankind has adopted for their government, and that we shall attempt to deal with in the work before us.
>
> It is here where those salutary principles of criminal law operate with effect, admonishing, restraining, and punishing the foolish, the rash, and the wicked: binding the parts of society together in one bond of equal justice. (Wheeler 1854, 6; also quoted in Novak 1996, 150)

With this background, I believe you've got a good idea of how broad and deep our criminal law imagination is. Broad and deep as it is, our criminal law has its limits, as you learn in:

1. *Chapter 2*, the constitutional limits imposed by the protections of free speech, the right to possess and use guns; and due process rights to life, liberty, and property
2. *Chapter 3*, the principle of criminal liability voluntary act requirement
3. *Chapter 4*, the criminal intent requirement
4. *Chapter 5*, the justification defenses, such as self-defense and defense home
5. *Chapter 6*, the excuse defenses, such as insanity and age
6. *Chapter 7*, the limits imposed on criminal liability for others' behavior (accomplice) and relationships (vicarious liability)
7. *Chapter 8*, limits on uncompleted crimes—attempt, solicitation, and conspiracy
8. *Chapters 10–12*, limits imposed by definitions of crimes against persons, property, and public order and morals
9. *Chapter 13*, the limits to crimes of international and domestic terrorism, and to immigration crimes

I hope these—and all the other chapters—will help you to understand the criminal law and the social reality of the U.S. criminal law imagination. But, I hope our journey through the criminal law will encourage you also to adopt *Criminal Law's* critical approach. If you do, you can formulate your own criminal law imagination, namely how broad and deep it *should* be, as well as what it *is*.

CRIMES AND NONCRIMINAL LEGAL WRONGS

LO2

The opening case summaries demonstrate that criminal law is only one kind of social control called upon to respond to deviating from social norms. The norm is the other four categories mentioned in the beginning of the chapter (p. 4). And they *should* be, because criminal liability is the harshest and most expensive form of social control. But, criminal law is a last resort, a "very rough engine" of social control (Stephen 1883, 2:81).

torts private wrongs for which you can sue the party who wronged you and recover money

In this section, we concentrate on the noncriminal wrongs called **torts**, private wrongs for which you can sue the party who wronged you and recover money.

Crimes and torts represent two different ways our legal system responds to social and individual harm (Table 1.2). Before we look at their differences, let's look at how they're similar.

- Both are sets of rules telling us what we *can't* do ("Don't steal") and what we *must* do ("Pay your taxes").
- The rules apply to everybody in the community, and they speak on behalf of everybody, with the power and prestige of the whole community behind them.
- The power of the law backs up the enforcement of the rules. (Hart 1958, 403)

How are they different? Some believe that crimes injure the whole community, whereas torts harm only individuals. But that's not really true. Almost every crime is also a tort. Many crimes and torts even have the same name (there's a crime and a tort called "assault"). Other crimes are torts even though they don't have the same names; for example, the crime of murder is also the tort of wrongful death. In fact, the same killing sometimes is tried as murder and later as a civil wrongful death suit. One famous example is in the legal actions against the great football player O. J. Simpson. He was acquitted in the murder of his ex-wife and her friend in a criminal case but then lost in a tort case for their wrongful deaths.

Also, torts don't just harm other individuals; they can also harm the whole community. For example, breaches of contract don't just hurt the parties to the contract. Much of what keeps daily life running depends on people keeping their word when they agree to buy, sell, perform services, and so on.

Are crimes just torts with different names? No. One difference is that criminal prosecutions are brought by the government against individuals; that's why criminal

TABLE 1.2 Crimes and Torts: Similarities and Differences

CRIMES	TORTS (PRIVATE WRONGS)
Crimes originate from a list of "can'ts" and "musts."	Torts originate from a list of "can'ts" and "musts."
The list applies to everybody.	The list applies to everybody.
Crimes injure another individual and the whole community.	Torts injure another individual and the whole community.
Criminal prosecutions are brought by the state against individuals.	Private parties bring tort actions against other parties.
Convicted offenders pay money to the state or serve time in the custody of the state.	Defendants who lose in tort cases pay money to the plaintiff who sued.
Criminal conviction is the condemnation by the whole community, the expression of its "hatred, fear, or contempt for the convict."	The tort award compensates the plaintiff who brought the suit.
The state has to prove all elements of the crime by "proof beyond a reasonable doubt."	The burden on the plaintiff is to prove responsibility by a preponderance of the evidence.

cases always have titles such as "*U.S. v. Rasul*," "*People v. Menendez*," "*State v. Hepworth*," or "*Commonwealth v. Kim*" (the first name in the case title is what that government entity calls itself, and the second name, the defendant's, is the individual being prosecuted). Nongovernment parties bring tort actions against other parties who may or may not be governments.

A second difference is that injured plaintiffs (those who sue for wrongs in tort cases) get money (called *damages*) from defendants for the injuries they suffer. In criminal actions, defendants pay fines to the state and/or serve time doing community service, in jail, or in prison.

Perhaps the most important difference between torts and crimes is the conviction itself. It's "the expression of the community's hatred, fear, or contempt for the convict" (Hart 1958). Professor Henry M. Hart (1958) sums up the difference this way:

> [Crime] is not simply anything which a legislature chooses to call a "crime." It is not simply antisocial conduct which public officers are given a responsibility to suppress. It is not simply any conduct to which the legislature chooses to attach a criminal penalty. It is conduct which... will incur a formal and solemn pronouncement of the moral condemnation of the community. (405)

But you should understand that condemning *words* alone don't make crimes different from torts. Not at all. When the legislature defines a crime, it's issuing a threat—"Don't steal, or else..." "File your taxes, or else..." What's the "or else"? It's the threat of punishment, a threat that society will carry out against anyone who commits a crime.

In fact, so intimately connected are condemnation and criminal punishment that some of the most distinguished criminal law scholars say that punishment has two indispensable components, condemnation *plus* "hard treatment." According to Andrew von Hirsch, honorary professor of Penal Theory and Penal Law at the University of Cambridge, a prolific writer on the subject, and his distinguished colleague, Andrew Ashworth, the Vinerian Professor of Law at Oxford University, "Punishment conveys censure, but it does not consist solely of it. The censure in punishment is expressed through the imposition of a deprivation ('hard treatment') on the offender" (Von Hirsch and Ashworth 2005, 21).

If the threat isn't carried out when a crime is committed, condemnation is meaningless, or worse—it sends a message that the victim's suffering is worthless. Punishment has to back up the condemnation. According to another respected authority on this point, Professor Dan Kahan (1996), "When society deliberately forgoes answering the wrongdoer through punishment, it risks being perceived as endorsing his valuations; hence the complaint that unduly lenient punishment reveals that the victim is worthless in the eyes of the law" (598).

We'll come back to the subject of punishment later in this chapter, where we'll discuss its purposes more fully, and again in Chapter 2, where we'll discuss the constitutional ban on "cruel and unusual punishment." But here it's important to emphasize the intimate connection (often overlooked) between punishment and its place in the criminal law imagination itself.

Even on this important point of expression of condemnation backed up by punishment, the line between torts and crime can get blurred. In tort cases involving violence and other especially "wicked" circumstances, plaintiffs can recover not only compensatory damages for their actual injuries but also substantial punitive damages to make an example of defendants and to "punish" them for their "evil behavior" (Black 1983, 204).

compensatory damages damages recovered by tort plaintiffs for their actual injuries

punitive damages damages recovered by tort plaintiffs to punish the defendant for their "evil behavior"

Now that you've got some idea of what criminal wrongs are and how they differ from private wrongs, let's go inside criminal law to see how the law classifies crimes so we can make sense of the enormous range of behavior it covers.

CLASSIFYING CRIMES

LO3

***mala in se* (inherently evil) crimes** offenses that require some level of criminal intent

***mala prohibita* offenses** offenses that are crimes only because a specific statute or ordinance prohibits them

felonies crimes punishable by death or confinement in the state's prison for one year to life without parole

misdemeanors offenses punishable by fine and/or confinement in the local jail for up to one year

state criminal codes criminal law created by elected representatives in state legislatures

municipal codes criminal law created by city and town councils elected by city residents

U.S. Criminal Code criminal law created by the U.S. Congress

There are various ways to classify crimes, most of them with ancient roots. One scheme divides crimes into two categories: ***mala in se*** crimes and ***mala prohibita*** offenses. *Mala in se* (inherently evil) crimes require some level of criminal intent (discussed in Chapter 4). We don't need a law to tell us murder, rape, robbery, and stealing are crimes because they're inherently evil.

Mala prohibita offenses are crimes only because a specific statute or ordinance prohibits them. They include minor offenses, such as parking illegally, drinking in public, and the countless other minor offenses that don't require criminal intent, only a voluntary act (Chapter 3). Professor Wayne Logan (2001, 1409) calls them "the shadow criminal law of municipal governance." For a selection from Professor Logan's (1426–28) list, see the "Municipal Ordinances" section (p. 15).

The most widely used scheme for classifying crimes is according to the kind and quantity of punishment. **Felonies** are crimes punishable by death or confinement in the state's prison for one year to life without parole; **misdemeanors** are punishable by fine and/or confinement in the local jail for up to one year.

Notice the word "punishable"; the classification depends on the *possible* punishment, not the *actual* punishment. For example, Viki Rhodes pled guilty to "Driving under the Influence of Intoxicants, fourth offense," a felony. The trial court sentenced her to 120 days of home confinement. When she later argued she was a misdemeanant because of the home confinement sentence, the appeals court ruled that "a person whose felony sentence is reduced does not become a misdemeanant by virtue of the reduction but remains a felon" (*Commonwealth v. Rhodes* 1996, 532).

Why should the label "felony" or "misdemeanor" matter? One reason is the difference between procedure for felonies and misdemeanors. For example, felony defendants have to be in court for their trials; misdemeanor defendants don't. Also, prior felony convictions make offenders eligible for longer sentences. Another reason is that the legal consequences of felony convictions last after punishment. In many states, former felons can't vote, can't serve in public office, can't work in certain occupations and professions, and can't be attorneys. A felony conviction also can be a ground for divorce. This isn't true of misdemeanor offenders.

Now, let's turn from the classifications of crimes to the two divisions of criminal law: the general and special parts.

SOURCES OF CRIMINAL LAW

LO4

administrative agencies appointed participants in creating criminal law that assist the U.S. Congress

By far the most prevalent source of criminal law is found in **state criminal codes** created by elected representatives in state legislatures and **municipal codes** created by city and town councils elected by city residents.

There's also a substantial—and most rapidly growing—body of criminal law in the **U.S. Criminal Code** created by the U.S. Congress. These elected bodies frequently rely on **administrative agencies**, whose members are appointed, *not* elected by the voters, to "participate" in creating criminal law.

Criminal court opinions, especially state appeals courts, in fact create criminal law by *interpreting* state and municipal criminal codes. (Almost every case excerpt in your book is an edited version of an appellate court opinion. See pp. 29–30 later in this chapter.)

criminal court opinions create criminal law by interpreting state and municipal criminal codes

Criminal law enforcement agencies, namely police and prosecution, create criminal law too, especially in the "all the rest" crimes (p. 6 earlier) By means of informal discretionary law making, these professionals make decisions based on their education, training, and their experience that results in how the criminal law process works on a day-to-day basis.

criminal law enforcement agencies create criminal law through informal discretionary law making to decide how the criminal law process works on a day-to-day basis

Let's look at each of these sources in more detail.

State Criminal Codes

LO4

From time to time in U.S. history, reformers have called for the abolition of the common law crimes and their replacement with criminal codes created and defined by elected legislatures. The first criminal codes appeared in 1648, the work of the New England Puritans. The Laws and Liberties of Massachusetts codified (put into writing) the colony's criminal law, defining crimes and spelling out punishments.

codified written definitions of crimes and punishment enacted by legislatures and published

John Winthrop, the author of the code, stated the case for a code this way: "So soon as God had set up political government among his people Israel he gave them a body of laws for judgment in civil and criminal causes. . . . For a commonwealth without laws is like a ship without rigging and steerage" (Farrand 1929, A2).

Some of the codified offenses sound odd today (witchcraft, cursing parents, blasphemy, and idolatry), but others—for example, rape—don't: "If any man shall ravish any maid or single woman, committing carnal copulation with her by force, against her own will, that is above ten years of age he shall be punished either with death or some other grievous punishment" (5).

Another familiar codified offense was murder: "If any man shall commit any willful murder, which is manslaughter, committed upon premeditated malice, hatred, or cruelty not in a man's necessary and just defense, nor by mere casualty against his will, he shall be put to death" (6).

Hostility to English institutions after the American Revolution spawned another call by reformers for written legislative codes to replace the English common law. The eighteenth-century Enlightenment, with its emphasis on reason and natural law, inspired reformers to put aside the piecemeal "irrational" common law scattered throughout judicial decisions and to replace it with criminal codes based on a natural law of crimes. Despite anti-British feelings, reformers still embraced Blackstone's *Commentaries* (1769) and hoped to transform his complete and orderly outline of criminal law into criminal codes.

Reformers contended judge-made law was not just disorderly and incomplete; it was antidemocratic. They believed legislatures representing the popular will should make laws, not aloof judges out of touch with public opinion. Thomas Jefferson proposed such a penal code for Virginia (Bond 1950). The proposed code never passed the Virginia legislature, not because it codified the law but because it recommended too many drastic reductions in criminal punishments (Preyer 1983, 53–85).

There was also a strong codification movement during the nineteenth century. Of the many nineteenth-century codes, two codes stand out. The first, the most ambitious, and least successful, was Edward Livingston's draft code for Louisiana, completed in 1826. Livingston's goal was to rationalize into one integrated system criminal law, criminal procedure, criminal evidence, and punishment. Livingston's draft never became law.

The second, David Dudley Field's code, was less ambitious but more successful. Field was a successful New York lawyer who wanted to make criminal law more accessible, particularly to lawyers. According to Professors Paul Robinson and Markus Dubber (2004):

> Field's codes were designed to simplify legal practice by sparing attorneys the tedium of having to sift through an ever rising mountain of common law. As a result, Field was more concerned with streamlining than he was with systematizing or even reforming New York penal law. (3)

Field's New York Penal Code was adopted in 1881 and remained in effect until 1967, when New York adopted most of the Model Penal Code (described next in "The Model Penal Code (MPC)" section).

LO4 The Model Penal Code (MPC)

The codification movement gathered renewed strength after the American Law Institute (ALI) decided to "tackle criminal law and procedure" (Dubber 2002, 8). ALI was created by a group of distinguished jurists "to promote the clarification and simplification of the law and its better adaptation to social needs, to secure the better administration of justice, and to encourage and carry on scholarly and scientific legal work" (8). After its first look at criminal law and procedure in the United States, the prestigious group "was so appalled by what it saw that it decided that... what was needed was a fresh start in the form of model codes (8).

The Great Depression and World War II stalled the development of a model penal code. But after the war, led by reform-minded judges, lawyers, and professors, ALI was committed to replacing the common law. From the earliest of thirteen drafts written during the 1950s to the final version in 1962, in the Model Penal Code (MPC), ALI (1985) made good on its commitment to draft a code that abolished common law crimes.

Model Penal Code (MPC) proposed criminal code drafted by the American Law Institute and used to reform criminal codes

After its adoption in 1962, more than forty states changed their criminal codes. None adopted the MPC completely; but criminal law in all states, not just states that rewrote their codes, felt its influence (Dubber 2002, 6). More than 2,000 opinions from every state, the District of Columbia, and the federal courts have cited the MPC (7). Many of the case excerpts you encounter in this book are from those 2,000. Moreover, this book follows the general structure and analysis of the MPC, because if you understand the MPC's structure and analysis, you'll understand criminal law itself. You encounter many variations of MPC throughout the book. However, "If there is such a thing as a common denominator in American criminal law, it's the Model Penal Code" (Dubber 2002, 5).

Let's look briefly at the American Law Institute's Model Penal Code (MPC) definition of behavior that deserves punishment. It's the framework we use to guide our analysis of **criminal liability**, namely "conduct that unjustifiably and inexcusably inflicts or threatens substantial harm to individual or public interests" (ALI 1985, § 1.02(1)(a)).

criminal liability conduct that unjustifiably and inexcusably inflicts or threatens substantial harm to individual or public interests

Here's a breakdown of the words and phrases in the definition:

1. Conduct that
2. Unjustifiably and inexcusably
3. Inflicts or threatens substantial harm
4. To individual or public interests

The Elements of Criminal Liability boxes here illustrate these elements as they apply to criminal conduct crimes (rape as an example here); and "result crimes" (murder is

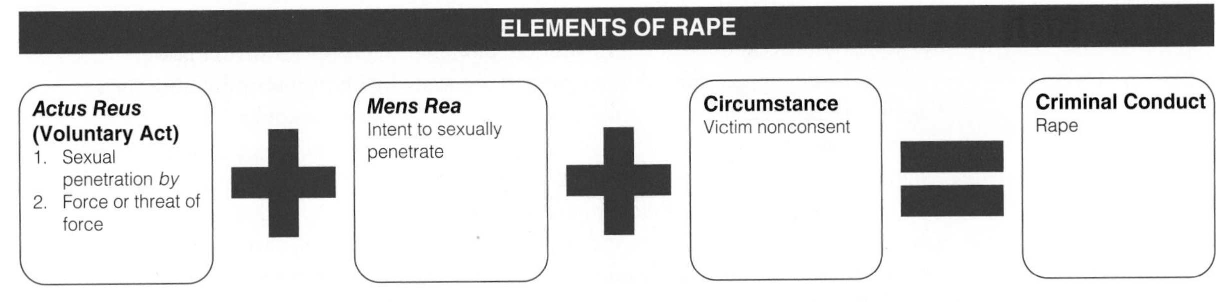

ELEMENTS OF FIRST-DEGREE MURDER (SPECIFIC INTENT)

Actus Reus* (Voluntary Act)** Killing another person + ***Mens Rea Intent to kill + **Circumstance** Premeditated, deliberate, or atrocious + **Causation** Factual *and* legal cause of death = **Criminal Harm** Death

the example here). There you have, in a nutshell, the elements of criminal liability in the states and the federal government that we elaborate on and apply to the definitions of individual crimes throughout the book. Let's turn next to another source of criminal law: municipal ordinances.

Municipal Ordinances

LO4

City, town, and village governments enjoy broad powers to create criminal laws, a power local governments are enthusiastically using in today's atmosphere of "zero tolerance" for drugs, violence, public disorder, and other "quality of life" offenses that violate community standards of good manners in public (Chapter 12). Municipalities have a "chorus of advocates" among criminal law reformers who've helped cities write a "new generation" of their old vagrancy and loitering ordinances that "cleanse" them of prior objections that they're unconstitutional and discriminatory (Logan 2001, 1418).

Municipal criminal lawmaking isn't new; neither is the enthusiasm for it. In his provocative book *The People's Welfare*, historian William Novak (1996) convincingly documents the "powerful government tradition devoted in theory and practice to the vision of a well-regulated society" from 1787 to 1877:

> At the heart of the well-regulated society was a plethora of bylaws, ordinances, statutes, and common law restrictions regulating nearly every aspect of early American economy and society. . . . These laws—the work of mayors, common councils, state legislators, town and county officers, and powerful state and local judges . . . taken together . . . demonstrate the pervasiveness of regulation in early American versions of the good society: regulations for public safety and security; . . . the policing of public space . . .; all-important restraints on public morals (establishing the social and cultural conditions of public order). (1–2)

Here's a sample from current ordinances collected by Professor Wayne Logan (2001):

> Pick-pocketing; disturbing the peace; shoplifting; urinating in public; disorderly conduct; disorderly assembly; unlawful restraint; obstruction of public space; harassment

> over the telephone; resisting arrest; obscenity; nude dancing; lewdness, public indecency, and indecent exposure; prostitution, pimping, or the operation of "bawdy" houses; gambling; graffiti and the materials associated with its inscription; littering; aggressive begging and panhandling; vandalism; trespass; automobile "cruising"; animal control nuisances; excessive noise; sale or possession of drug paraphernalia; simple drug possession; possession of weapons other than firearms; possession of basic firearms and assault-style firearms; discharge of firearms; sleeping, lying, or camping in public places; driving under the influence of drugs or alcohol; carrying an open container of alcohol; underage drinking; and public drinking and intoxication; vagrancy and loitering; curfews for minors; criminal assault and battery. (1426–28)

Municipal ordinances often duplicate and overlap state criminal code provisions. When they conflict, state criminal code provisions are supposed to trump municipal ordinances. A number of technical rules control whether they're in conflict, and we don't need to get into the details of these rules, but their gist is that unless state criminal codes make clear that they're preempting local ordinances, local ordinances remain in effect (*Chicago v. Roman* 1998).

In *Chicago v. Roman*, Edwin Roman attacked 60-year-old Anthony Pupius. He was convicted of the Chicago municipal offense of assault against the elderly and was sentenced to ten days of community service and one year of probation. However, the ordinance contained a mandatory minimum sentence of at least 90 days of incarceration. The city appealed, claiming that the sentence violated the mandatory minimum required by the ordinance. The Illinois Supreme Court overruled the trial court's decision. According to the court, the Illinois legislature can restrict Chicago's power to create crimes, but it has to pass a law specifically spelling out the limit. Because the legislature hadn't passed a law preempting the penalty for assaulting the elderly, Chicago's mandatory minimum had to stand.

The long list of ordinances Professor Logan found illustrates the broad power of municipalities to create local crimes. But, as the example of *Chicago v. Roman* indicates, the power of municipalities goes further than creating crimes; it includes the power to determine the punishment, too. They also have the power to enact forfeiture laws.

Under New York City's alcohol and other drug-impaired driver's law, thousands of impaired drivers have forfeited their vehicles (Fries 2001, B2). Another example: an Oakland, California, ordinance authorizes forfeiture of vehicles involved in "solicitation of prostitution or acquisition of controlled substances." The ordinance was passed after residents complained about individuals driving through their neighborhoods looking to buy drugs or hire prostitutes (*Horton v. City of Oakland* 2000, 372).

Don't get the idea from what you've just read that municipalities have unlimited powers to create crimes and prescribe punishments. They don't. We've already noted two limits—constitutional limits (which we discuss further in Chapter 2 and again in Chapter 12) and the power of states to preempt municipal criminal lawmaking and punishment. Municipalities also can't create felonies, and they can't prescribe punishments greater than one year in jail.

LO4 The U.S. Criminal Code

> Federal criminal law has exploded in size and scope and deteriorated in quality. It used to focus on inherently wrongful conduct: treason, murder, counterfeiting, and the like. Today, an unimaginably broad range of socially and economically beneficial

> conduct is criminalized.... More and more Americans who have worked diligently to abide by the law are being trapped and unjustly punished due to vague, overly broad criminal offenses. Congress must halt its overcriminalization rampage.
>
> —Heritage Foundation (2015)

According to a joint study conducted by the unabashedly conservative Heritage Foundation, and the equally committed liberal National Association of Criminal Defense Lawyers, there were over 4,450 crimes in the U.S. Criminal Code" in 2008. On top of these,

> scores of federal departments and agencies have created so many criminal offenses that the Congressional Research Service [the nonpartisan research arm of the U.S. Congress] itself admitted that it was unable to even count all of the offenses. The service's best estimate? "Tens of thousands." In short, Congress's own experts do not have a clear understanding of the size and scope of federal criminalization.

The U.S. Criminal Code covers more—and more trivial—conduct than most state and municipal codes! A huge number of federal offenses are minor regulation violations like tearing the tag off a mattress (Green 1997). Far more pervasive are fraud and misrepresentation offenses. The U.S. Criminal Code contains 100 separate misrepresentation offenses. Some make it a crime to lie; others scoop up not just lying but

> (a) ... whoever, in any matter within the jurisdiction of the executive, legislative, or judicial branch of the Government of the United States, knowingly and willfully—
>
> (1) falsifies, conceals, or covers up by any trick, scheme, or device a material fact;
>
> (2) makes any materially false, fictitious, or fraudulent statement or representation; or
>
> (3) makes or uses any false writing or document knowing the same to contain any materially false, fictitious, or fraudulent statement or entry;
>
> shall be fined under this title, imprisoned not more than 5 years or, if the offense involves international or domestic terrorism (as defined in section 2331), imprisoned not more than 8 years, or both. (U.S. Criminal Code, Title 18 § 1001)

In Professor Stuntz's (2001) words, "It is often said that ordinary lying is not a crime—a comment usually made by way of explaining the narrowness of the definition of perjury—but the statement is wrong; a good deal of ordinary lying fits within the definition of one or another federal felony" (517).

Administrative Agency Crimes

LO4

Both federal and state legislatures frequently grant administrative agencies the authority to make rules. One example is familiar to anyone who has to file a tax return. The U.S. Internal Revenue Service income tax regulations are based on the rule-making authority that Congress delegates to the IRS. Another example, this one from the state level: state legislatures commonly authorize the state highway patrol agencies to make rules regarding vehicle safety inspections. We call violations of these federal and state agency rules administrative crimes; they're a controversial but rapidly growing source of criminal law.

administrative crimes violations of federal and state agency rules that make up a controversial but rapidly growing source of criminal law

Informal Discretionary Law Making

LO4

The broad and deep reach of the state, municipal, and U.S. criminal code has led to a huge amount of law making by police and prosecutors. Here's how it works. There

YOU *DECIDE*

Was the "law making" of the police and prosecutor ethical?

It's a misdemeanor to drink in public parks in most cities, including Minneapolis. Yet when a gourmet group had a brunch in one of the city's parks, because they thought the park had just the right ambience in which to enjoy their salmon mousse and imported French white wine, not only did the police not arrest the group for drinking in the park, but the city's leading newspaper wrote it up as a perfectly respectable social event.

A public defender I knew wasn't pleased with these decisions. He pointed out that the police had arrested—and the prosecutor was at that moment prepared to prosecute—a Native American caught washing down a tuna fish sandwich with cheap red wine in another Minneapolis park. The public defender—a bit of a wag—noted that both the gourmet club and the Native American were consuming items from the same food groups.

This incident displays both the strengths and weaknesses of discretion. The legislature obviously didn't intend the statute to cover drinking of the type the gourmet club engaged in; arresting them would have been foolish. On the other hand, arresting and prosecuting the Native American might well have been discriminatory, a wholly unintended and unacceptable result of law enforcement that is discretionary and selective.

Question

- Do you believe this case involved unacceptable criminal law making? Back up your answer with details from the section "Informal Discretionary Law Making."

are too many minor crimes for police to arrest all suspects. Of course, in any case, there's no such thing as total criminal law enforcement. Police can't arrest all suspects, and prosecutors can't charge all suspects police arrest. There are simply too many. So, they're left with exercising their discretion. This means that the laws in the codes don't match the law as it's enforced. Law enforcers will "make" the law as it's actually enforced. In other words, the social reality of our criminal law is that law enforcers (police and prosecutors) will *create* the law as it operates in the real world.

Furthermore, the prosecutor's power to plea bargain, as a practical matter, turns the prosecutor into a judge. Here's how this works. Suppose a man breaks into a woman's apartment, stabs but doesn't kill her, rapes her, and takes her jewelry. This single event allows the prosecutor to threaten to charge the culprit with all four crimes, thereby increasing the possible minimum or maximum penalty under all sentencing regimes (Chapter 2). The prosecutor then can use the threat as a bargaining chip to get a guilty plea.

Both the power to charge and to plea bargain (and the power of the police not to arrest) the broad and deep criminal law lowers the cost of convicting criminal defendants. According to Professor Stuntz (2001),

> Substituting an easy-to-prove crime that is harder to establish obviously makes criminal litigation cheaper for the government. And the cost saving is substantial, since guilty pleas are much cheaper than trials, and defendants often respond to easily proved charges by pleading guilty. (520)

CRIMINAL LAW IN THE U.S. FEDERAL SYSTEM

Until now, we've referred to criminal law in the singular. That's inaccurate, and you'll see this inaccuracy repeated often in the rest of the book because it's convenient. But let's clear up the inaccuracy. In our federal system, there are 52 criminal codes, one for each of the 50 states, one for the District of Columbia, and one for the U.S. criminal code.

federal system 52 criminal codes, one for each of the 50 states, one for the District of Columbia, and one for the U.S. criminal code

The U.S. government's power is limited to crimes specifically related to national interests, such as crimes committed on military bases and other national property; crimes against federal officers; and crimes that are often difficult for one state to prosecute—for example, drug, weapons, organized and corporate crime, and crimes involving domestic and international terrorism (Chapter 13). The rest of criminal law, which is most of it, is left to the state codes. These are the crimes against persons, property, and public order and morals in the special part of the criminal law (Chapters 9–12).

So we have 52 criminal codes, each defining specific crimes and establishing general principles for the territory and people within it. And they don't, in practice, define specific crimes the same. For example, in some states, to commit a burglary, you have to actually break into and then enter a building. In other states, it's enough that you enter a building unlawfully, as in opening an unlocked door to a house the owners forgot to lock, intending to steal their new 3D TV inside. In still other states, all you have to do is stay inside a building you've entered lawfully—for example, hiding until after closing time in your college bookstore restroom during business hours, so you can steal your criminal law textbook and sneak out after the store closes (Chapter 11).

The defenses to crime also vary across state lines. In some states, insanity requires proof both that defendants didn't know what they were doing and that they didn't know it was wrong to do it. In other states, it's enough to prove either that defendants didn't know what they were doing or that they didn't know that it was wrong (Chapter 6). Some states permit individuals to use deadly force to protect their homes from intruders; others require proof that the occupants in the home were in danger of serious bodily harm or death before they can shoot intruders (Chapter 5).

Punishments also differ widely among the states. Several states prescribe death for some convicted murderers; others prescribe life imprisonment. Capital punishment states differ in how they execute murderers: by electrocution, lethal injection, the gas chamber, hanging, or even the firing squad. The death penalty is only the most dramatic example of different punishments. Less-dramatic examples affect far more people. For example, some states lock up individuals who possess small quantities of marijuana for private use; in other states, it's not a crime at all (Chapter 12).

This diversity among the criminal codes makes it clear there's no single U.S. criminal code. But this diversity shouldn't obscure the broad outline that's common to all criminal laws in the United States. They're all based on the general principles of liability that we touched on earlier in this chapter and that you'll learn about more in depth in Chapters 3 through 6. They also include the defenses of justification and excuse, which you'll learn about in Chapters 5 and 6.

The definitions of the crimes you'll learn about in Chapters 9 through 12 differ more, so there we'll take account of the major differences. But even these definitions resemble one another more than they differ. For example, "murder" means killing someone on purpose; criminal sexual assault includes sexual penetration by force; "robbery" means taking someone's property by force or threat of force; "theft" means taking, and intending to keep permanently, someone else's property. And the crimes against the state (Chapter 13) and other crimes in the U.S. Criminal Code don't recognize state lines; they apply everywhere in the country.

Now, let's turn to the other question in the big picture of American criminal law, the law of punishment and the criminal punishment imagination.

CRIMINAL PUNISHMENT IN U.S. SOCIETY

LO5 The United States has 5 percent of the world's population and 25 percent of the world's prisoners. That makes us the clear leader in world imprisonment rates (see Figure 1.2). These prisoners aren't distributed evenly across the population. Most of them come from city neighborhoods with the most concentrated disadvantage—poverty, unemployment, bad schools, high crime, single- (or no-) parent families, and little to no social agency support. They are mostly young, poorly educated, with little or no training and work experience. They often have suffered from other deficits. They entered prison in poor mental and physical health—substance abuse, mental illness, and risk for infectious diseases—alcohol and other drug addiction; mental and physical illness. And, most are not White.

LO5 The Era of Mass Imprisonment, 1970s–Present

How did this "era of mass incarceration" come to be, and why? We know when it began. It followed a period of great social and political upheaval that accompanied a steep rise in crime and urban riots during the 1960s. The era of mass imprisonment and steep rise in crime and violence accompanied a shift in political climate. That political culture turned to a series of policy choices across all branches and levels of government led to sending more people to prison, and keeping them there longer. All of these changes represented a consensus that supported prison as a key to crime control. But, is it?

After 40 years of rising incarceration rates, the rate for violent crime (the most-feared and enraging crimes) "rose, then fell, rose again, and then declined sharply" (National Research Council 2014, 3). The complicated connections among imprisonment, crime, sentencing policies, and the changes over time and place interact with each other. This makes estimating the social consequences of high imprisonment, *including*

Figure 1.2 WORLD IMPRISONMENT RATES, 2009

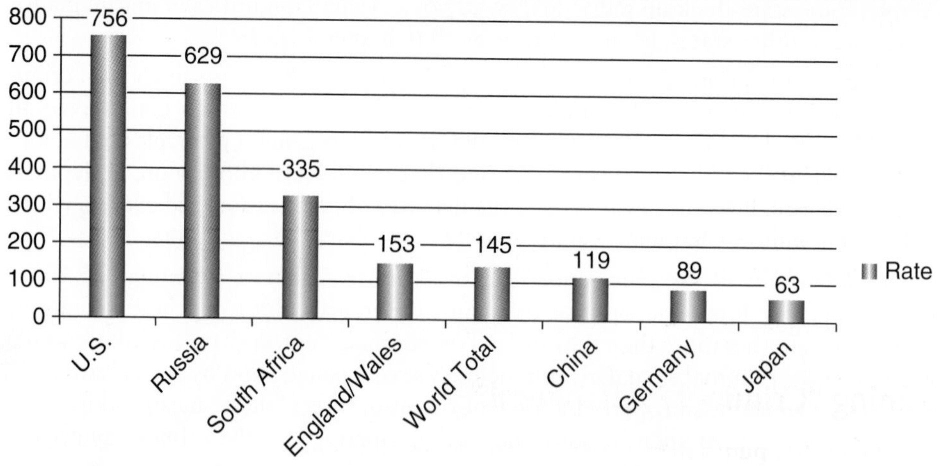

Source: Walmsley 2009.

its effects on crime, "extremely challenging." Nevertheless, for whatever reasons, most studies conclude that more prison *has* reduced crime. Unfortunately, the evidence doesn't tell clearly how much (4).

The most important consequence of mass imprisonment may be the massive expansion of the criminal justice system into the country's poorest communities. Most prisoners (about 90 percent) come home to the neighborhoods—sometimes to the same house—they left. There, their lives, not surprisingly, return to violence, joblessness, substance abuse, family breakup, and neighborhood disadvantage. It's hard to prove that their time in prison contributed to their difficulties after they came home. However, "there is little question that incarceration has become another strand in the complex combination of negative conditions that characterize high-poverty communities in U.S. cities" (6).

There's much more to this story of the *possible* negative consequences that mass imprisonment may have had not just on released prisoners, but on their families, their neighborhoods, cities, and beyond. But, there's enough of it here to make clear that mass imprisonment *may* have had unwanted social costs that outweigh its crime reduction benefits. That much is enough also to make clear that sound criminal punishment policies require both science *and* fundamental principles.

There wasn't much talk of principles during the 1960s and '70s when the rising violence and rapid social change fueled public fear and anger. Fear and anger against criminals was a powerful force arousing law-abiding people in *all* neighborhoods, perhaps most of all in poor neighborhoods where residents were most in danger of being victimized. Instead of principles, policy makers responded by locking up criminals as retribution, and to incapacitate them by getting them off the street.

Anger—even hate—aimed at criminals who prey or put in fear law-abiding people who work hard and play by the rules are certainly in order and definitely healthy. "It is morally right to hate criminals." (Stephen 1883, 2:81). But, it's equally necessary that in this age of mass imprisonment that we take care to limit this "very rough engine" of social control (80). Why? Because it can do lots of damage not just to prisoners, but to their families, neighborhoods, and to our whole society. Following four well-established and widely accepted principles can guide us in limiting the damages that always come with imprisonment and which mass imprisonment has aggravated. Here they are in the form of recommendations made by the National Research Council Committee on Causes and Consequences of High Rates of Imprisonment:

- *Proportionality*. Criminal offenses should be sentenced in proportion to their seriousness.
- *Parsimony*. The period of confinement should be sufficient but not greater than necessary to achieve the goals of sentencing policy.
- *Citizenship*. The conditions and consequences of imprisonment should not be so severe or lasting as to violate one's fundamental status as a member of society.
- *Social justice*. Prisons should be instruments of justice, and as such their collective effort should be to promote and not undermine society's aspirations for a fair distribution of rights, resources, and opportunities. (8)

Now, we're ready to turn our full attention to the *criminal punishment imagination*.

punishment intentionally inflicting pain or other unpleasant consequences on another person

Defining "Criminal Punishment"

LO5

In everyday life, **punishment** means intentionally inflicting pain or other unpleasant consequences on another person. It takes many forms. A parent grounds a teenager;

a club expels a member; a church excommunicates a parishioner; a friend rejects a companion; a school expels a student for cheating—all these are punishments in the sense that they intentionally inflict pain or other unpleasant consequences ("hard treatment") on the recipient.

criminal punishment penalties that meet four criteria: (1) inflict pain or other unpleasant consequences; (2) prescribe a punishment in the same law that defines the crime; (3) administered intentionally; (4) administered by the state

However, none of these is criminal punishment. To qualify as criminal punishment, penalties have to meet four criteria:

1. They have to inflict pain or other unpleasant consequences.
2. They have to prescribe a punishment in the same law that defines the crime.
3. They have to be administered intentionally.
4. The state has to administer them.

The last three criteria don't need explanation; the first does. "Pain or other unpleasant consequences" is broad and vague. It doesn't tell us what kind of, or how much, pain. A violent mental patient confined indefinitely to a padded cell in a state security hospital suffers more pain than a person incarcerated for five days in the county jail for disorderly conduct. Nevertheless, only the jail sentence is criminal punishment. The difference lies in the purpose of the confinement. Hospitalization aims to treat and cure the mental patient; the pain is a necessary but unwanted side effect, not the reason for the confinement. On the other hand, the pain of confinement in the jail is inflicted intentionally to punish the inmate's disorderly conduct.

This distinction between criminal punishment and treatment is rarely clear-cut. For example, the government may sentence certain convicted criminals to confinement in maximum-security hospitals; it may sentence others to prison for "treatment" and "cure." Furthermore, pain and pleasure don't always distinguish punishment from treatment. Shock treatment and padded cells inflict more pain than confinement in some minimum-security federal prisons with their "country club" atmospheres. When measured by pain, those who receive it may well prefer punishment to treatment. Some critics maintain that the major shortcoming of treatment is that "helping" a patient can lead to excessive measures, as it sometimes has, in such examples as massive surgery, castration, and lobotomy (Hart 1958, 403–405).

theories of criminal punishment ways of thinking about the purposes of criminal punishment

LO6 Theories of Criminal Punishment

Theories of criminal punishment refer to *thinking about* the *purposes* of criminal punishment. These theories have given rise to two schools that have battled for five centuries, maybe even for millennia: the retributionists and the preventionists (also called consequentialists).

retributionists inflicting on offenders physical and psychological pain ("hard treatment") so that they can pay for their crimes

preventionists punishment is only a means to a greater good, usually the prevention or at least the reduction of future crime

The "retributionists" insist that offenders can only pay for their crimes by experiencing the actual physical and psychological pain ("hard treatment") of having punishment inflicted on them. In other words, punishment justifies itself. Those on the prevention side of the divide, utilitarians, insist with equal passion that the pain of punishment can—and should—be only a means to a greater good, usually the prevention or at least the reduction of future crime. Let's look at each of these schools. Then we examine a challenge to this centuries' long criminal punishment imagination.

LO6 RETRIBUTION

Striking out to hurt what hurts us is a basic human impulse. It's what makes us kick the table leg we stub our toe on, or the bicycle we fall off. This impulse captures the idea of retribution, which appears in the texts of many religions. Here's the Old Testament version:

> Now a man, when he strikes down any human life, he is put to death, yes death! And a man, when he renders a defect in his fellow, as he has done, thus is to be done to him—break in place of break, eye in place of eye, tooth in place of tooth. (Fox 1995, 19–20; translating Leviticus 24:17)

Retribution looks back to past crimes and punishes individuals for committing them, because it's right to hurt them. According to the great Victorian English judge and historian of the criminal law Sir James F. Stephen (1883), the wicked deserve to suffer for their evil deeds:

> The criminal law proceeds upon the principle that it is morally right to hate criminals, and it confirms and justifies that sentiment by inflicting on criminals punishments, which express it. I think it highly desirable that criminals should be hated, that the punishments inflicted upon them should be so contrived as to give expression to that hatred. (2:81–82)

Retributionists contend that punishment benefits not just society, as Stephen emphasized, but criminals. Just as society feels satisfied by "paying back" criminals, giving criminals their "just deserts," offenders benefit by putting right their evil. Society pays back criminals by retaliation; criminals pay back society by accepting responsibility through punishment. Both paybacks are at the heart of retribution.

But retribution is right only if offenders choose between committing and not committing crimes. In other words, we can blame criminals only if they had these choices and made the wrong choice. So in the popular "Do the crime, do the time," what we really mean is, "You chose to do the crime, so you have to do the time." Their wrong choice makes them blameworthy. And their blameworthiness (the criminal law calls it their "culpability") makes them responsible (the criminal law calls it "liable"). So as culpable, responsible individuals, they have to suffer the consequences of their irresponsible behavior.

Retribution has several appealing qualities. It assumes free will, thereby enhancing individual autonomy. Individuals who have the power to determine their own destinies aren't at the mercy of forces they can't control. Retribution also seems to accord with human nature. Hating and hurting wrongdoers—especially murderers, rapists, robbers, and other violent criminals—appear to be natural impulses (Gaylin 1982; Wilson and Herrnstein 1985, ch. 19).

Retribution's ancient pedigree also has its appeal. From the Old Testament's philosophy of taking an eye for an eye, to the nineteenth-century Englishman's claim that it's right to hate and hurt criminals, to today's "three strikes and you're out" and "do the crime, do the time" sentences (Chapter 2), the desire for retribution has run strong and deep in both religion and criminal justice. Its sheer tenacity seems to validate retribution.

Retributionists, however, claim that retribution rests not simply on long use but also on two firm philosophical foundations, namely, culpability and justice. According to its proponents, retribution requires culpability. Only someone who intends to harm her victim deserves punishment; accidents don't qualify. So people who load, aim, and fire guns into their enemies' chests deserve punishment; hunters who fire at what they think is a deer and hit their companions who they should know are in the line of fire, don't. Civil law can deal with careless people (Chapter 4); the criminal law ought to punish only people who harm their victims "on purpose."

culpability only someone who intends to harm her victim deserves punishment; accidents don't qualify

justice depends on culpability; only those who deserve punishment ought to receive it

Retributionists also claim that justice is the only proper measure of punishment. Justice is a *philosophical* concept whose application depends on culpability. Culpability depends on blame; we can punish only those we can blame; we can blame only those who freely choose, and intend, to harm their victims. Therefore, only those who deserve punishment can justly receive it; if they don't deserve it, it's unjust. Similarly, justice is the only criterion by which to determine the quality and quantity of punishment (see "Disproportionate Punishments," in Chapter 2).

Opponents find a lot to criticize in retribution. First, it's difficult to translate abstract justice into concrete penalties. What are a rapist's "just deserts"? Is castration for a convicted rapist justice? How many years in prison is a robbery worth? How much offender suffering will repay the pain of a maimed aggravated assault victim?

Another criticism is that the urge to retaliate isn't part of human nature in a civilized society; it's the last remnant of barbarism. Retributionists can only assume that human nature cries out for vengeance; they can't prove it. So it's time for the law to reject retribution as a purpose for punishment. There's a substantial body of empirical research from psychology, anthropology, and biology contesting this "barbarism" argument. Instead, they maintain, "a wide variety of empirical studies indicate that people broadly share intuitions that serious wrongdoing should be punished and also share intuitions about the relative blameworthiness of different transgressions" (Robinson, Kurzban, and Jones 2007, 1636).

Determinists, which include many criminologists, reject the free-will assumption underlying retribution (Mayer and Wheeler 1982; Wilson and Herrnstein 1985). They maintain that conditions and forces beyond human control determine individual behavior. Social scientists have shown the relationship between social conditions and crime; the usual suspects are race, ethnicity, gender, age, neighborhood, education, and class.

deterrence the use of punishment to prevent or reduce future crimes

specific deterrence aims to reduce crime by inflicting the actual punishment to convince offenders not to commit crimes in the future

general deterrence aims to reduce crime by the threat of punishment to convince criminal wannabes in the general population to not commit a crime in the future

Psychiatrists point to subconscious forces beyond the conscious will's control that determine criminal conduct. A few biologists have linked violent crime to biological and biochemical abnormalities. Determinism undermines the theory of retribution because it rejects blame, and punishment without blame is unjust.

Another argument against retribution is the vast number of crimes that don't require culpability to qualify for criminal punishment (Diamond 1996, 34). This includes almost all the crimes outside the "core felonies" discussed earlier, and which we'll encounter again in Chapter 3 (drug and gun possession), Chapter 4 (negligent homicide and no-fault open bottle laws), and Chapter 12 (offenses against public order and morals). It includes some serious crimes, too—for example, statutory rape—where neither the consent of the victim nor an honest and reasonable mistake about the victim's age relieves statutory rapists from criminal liability (discussed in Chapter 10)—and several kinds of unintentional homicides (discussed in Chapters 4 and 9).

LO6 PREVENTION

Prevention (also called consequentialism) looks forward to the consequences of criminal conduct. It inflicts pain, not for its own sake, but to prevent (or at least reduce) future crimes. Punishment theorists break it down into three functions:

incapacitation prevents convicted criminals from committing future crimes by locking them up, or more rarely, by altering them surgically or executing them

1. Deterrence. Aims by specific deterrence, actual punishment to convince present offenders not to commit crimes in the future; and by general deterrence, the threat of punishment in the future, to convince criminal wannabes in the general population who haven't committed crimes from doing so.
2. **Incapacitation** prevents convicted criminals from committing future crimes by locking them up, or more rarely, by altering them surgically or executing them.

3. **Rehabilitation** (also called reformation) aims to prevent future crimes by changing individual offenders so that they *want* to play by the rules and support themselves and their families without committing future crimes.

rehabilitation aims to prevent future crimes by changing individual offenders so that they want to play by the rules and won't commit any more crimes in the future

Notice how all three forms of prevention inflict pain, not for its own sake, but to secure the greater good of preventing future crimes. Let's look at each of these forms of prevention.

LO6

DETERRENCE Jeremy Bentham, an eighteenth-century English philosopher and law reformer, promoted deterrence. Bentham was part of the intellectual movement called "the Enlightenment." At the Enlightenment's core was the notion that natural laws govern the physical universe and, by analogy, human society. One of these "laws," **hedonism**, is that human beings seek pleasure and avoid pain.

hedonism the natural law that human beings seek pleasure and avoid pain

A related "law," **rationalism**, states that individuals can, and ordinarily do, act to maximize pleasure and minimize pain. Rationalism permits human beings to apply natural laws mechanistically (according to rules) instead of having to rely on the discretionary judgment of individual decision makers.

rationalism the natural law that individuals can act to maximize pleasure and minimize pain, permitting human beings to apply natural laws mechanistically (according to rules) instead of having to rely on the discretionary judgment of individual decision makers

These ideas, almost insultingly oversimplified here, led Bentham to formulate **classical deterrence theory**. According to the theory, rational human beings won't commit crimes if they know that the pain of punishment outweighs the pleasure gained from committing crimes.

classical deterrence theory rational human beings won't commit crimes if they know that the pain of punishment outweighs the pleasure gained from committing crimes

Prospective criminals weigh the pleasure they hope to get from committing a crime now against the threat of pain they believe they'll get from future punishment. According to the natural law of hedonism, if prospective criminals fear future punishment more than they derive pleasure from present crime, they won't commit crimes. In short, they're deterred.

Supporters of deterrence argue that the **principle of utility**—permitting only the minimum amount of pain necessary to prevent the crime—limits criminal punishment more than retribution does.

principle of utility permits only the minimum amount of pain necessary to prevent the crime

English playwright George Bernard Shaw, a strong deterrence supporter, put it this way: "Vengeance is *mine* saith the Lord; which means it is not the Lord Chief Justice's" (Morris 1974). According to this argument, only God, the angels, or some other divine being can measure "just deserts." Social scientists, on the other hand, can determine how much pain, or threat of pain, deters crime. With this knowledge, the state can scientifically inflict the minimum pain needed to produce the maximum crime reduction.

Deterrence supporters concede that there are impediments to putting deterrence into operation. The emotionalism surrounding punishment impairs objectivity, and often, prescribed penalties rest more on faith than evidence. For example, the economist Isaac Ehrlich's (1975) sophisticated econometric study showed that every execution under capital punishment laws may have saved seven or eight lives by deterring potential murderers. His finding sparked a controversy having little to do with the study's empirical validity. Instead, the arguments turned to ethics—whether killing anyone is right, no matter what social benefits it produces. During the controversy over the study, one thoughtful state legislator told me that he didn't "believe" the findings, but if they were true, then "we'll just have to deep-six the study."

Critics find several faults with deterrence theory and its application to criminal punishment. According to the critics, the rational, free-will individual that deterrence supporters assumes exists is as far from reality as the eighteenth-century world that spawned the idea. Complex forces within the human organism and in the external environment, both of which are beyond individual control, strongly influence behavior (Wilson and Herrnstein 1985).

Furthermore, critics maintain that individuals and their behavior are too unpredictable to reduce to a mechanistic formula. For some people, the existence of criminal law is enough to deter them from committing crimes; others require more. Who these "others" are and what the "more" consists of hasn't been sufficiently determined to base punishment on deterrence. Besides, severity isn't the only influence on the effectiveness of punishment. Certainty and speed may have greater deterrent effects than severity (Andenaes 1983, 2:593).

Also, threats don't affect all crimes or potential criminals equally. Crimes of passion, such as murder and rape, are probably little affected by threats; speeding, drunk driving, and corporate crime are probably greatly affected by threats (Andenaes 1983, 2:596).

Finally, critics maintain that even if we could obtain empirical support for criminal punishment, deterrence is unjust because it punishes for example's sake. Supreme Court Justice Oliver Wendell Holmes offered this analogy: If I were having a philosophical talk with a man I was going to have hanged (or electrocuted) I should say, "I don't doubt that your act was inevitable for you but to make it more avoidable by others we propose to sacrifice you to the common good. You may regard yourself as a soldier dying for your country if you like. But the law must keep its promises" (qtd. in Howe 1953, 806).

Punishment shouldn't be a sacrifice to the common good; it's only just if it's administered for the redemption of particular individuals, say the retributionists. Punishment is personal and individual, not general and societal. Deterrence proponents respond that as long as offenders are in fact guilty, punishing them is personal; hence, it is just to use individual punishment for society's benefit.

LO6 INCAPACITATION Incapacitation restrains convicted offenders from committing further crimes. At the extreme, incapacitation includes mutilation—castration, amputation, and lobotomy—or even death in capital punishment. Incapacitation in most cases means imprisonment. Incapacitation works: dead people can't commit crimes, and prisoners don't commit them—at least not outside prison walls. Incapacitation, then, has a lot to offer a society determined to repress crime. The late criminologist James Q. Wilson (1975) put the case for incapacitation in its most favorable light:

> The chances of a persistent robber or burglar living out his life, or even going a year with no arrest, are quite small. Yet a large proportion of repeat offenders suffer little or no loss of freedom. Whether or not one believes that such penalties, if inflicted, would act as a deterrent, it is obvious that they could serve to incapacitate these offenders and, thus, for the period of the incapacitation, prevent them from committing additional crimes. (209)

Like deterrence and retribution, incapacitation has its share of critics. They argue that incapacitation merely shifts criminality from outside prisons to inside prisons. Sex offenders and other violent criminals can and do still find victims among other prisoners; property offenders trade contraband and other smuggled items. As you might imagine, this criticism finds little sympathy (at least among many of my students, who often answer this criticism with an emphatic, "Better them than me"). Of course, because almost all prisoners "come home," their incapacitation is always temporary.

LO6 REHABILITATION In his still widely and rightly acclaimed book *The Limits of the Criminal Sanction*, Herbert Packer (1968) succinctly summarized the aims of rehabilitation: "The most immediately appealing justification for punishment is the claim that it may be used to prevent crimes by so changing the personality of the offender that he will conform to the dictates of law; in a word, by reforming him" (50).

Rehabilitation borrows from the "medical model" of criminal law. In this model, crime is a "disease," and criminals are "sick" in need of "treatment" and "cure." According to rehabilitationists, the purpose of punishment is to "cure" criminal patients by "treatment." The length of imprisonment depends on how long it takes to cure the patient. Supporters contend that treating offenders is more humane than punishing them.

"medical model" of criminal law crime is a "disease," and criminals are "sick" in need of "treatment" and "cure"

Two assumptions underlie rehabilitation theory. The first is *determinism*; that is, forces beyond offenders' control cause them to commit crimes. Because offenders don't choose to commit crimes, we can't blame them for committing them.

Second, therapy by experts can change offenders (not just their behavior) so that they won't want to commit any more crimes. After rehabilitation, former criminals will control their own destinies. To this extent, rehabilitationists adopt the idea of free will and its consequences: criminals can choose to change their life habits; so society can blame and punish them.

The view that criminals are "sick" has profoundly affected criminal law—and generated acrimonious debate. The reason isn't because reform and rehabilitation are new ideas; quite the contrary is true. Victorian Sir Francis Palgrave (1837, 177) summed up a 700-year-old attitude when he stated the medieval church's position on punishment: it was not to be "thundered in vengeance for the satisfaction of the state, but imposed for the good of the offender; in order to afford the means of amendment and to lead the transgressor to repentance, and to mercy."

Sixteenth-century Elizabethan pardon statutes were laced with the language of repentance and reform; the queen hoped to achieve a reduction in crime by mercy rather than by vengeance. (Samaha 1978, 763) Even Jeremy Bentham, most closely associated with deterrence, claimed that punishment would "contribute to the reformation of the offender, not only through fear of being punished again, but by a change in his character and habits." (Bentham 1864, 338)

Despite this long history, rehabilitation has suffered serious attacks. First, and most fundamental, critics maintain that rehabilitation is based on false, or at least unproven, assumptions. The causes of crime are so complex, and the wellsprings of human behavior as yet so undetermined, that sound policy can't depend on treatment. Second, it makes no sense to brand everyone who violates the criminal law as sick and needing treatment (Schwartz 1983, 1364–73).

Third, critics call rehabilitation inhumane because the cure justifies administering large doses of pain. British literary critic C. S. Lewis (1953) argued:

> My contention is that good men (not bad men) consistently acting upon that position would act as cruelly and unjustly as the greatest tyrants. They might in some respects act even worse. Of all tyrannies a tyranny sincerely exercised for the good of its victims may be the most oppressive. It may be better to live under robber barons than under omnipotent moral busybodies.
>
> The robber baron's cruelty may sometimes sleep, his cupidity may at some point be satiated; but those who torment us for our own good, will torment us without end for they do so with the approval of their own conscience. They may be more likely to go to Heaven yet at the same time likelier to make a Hell of earth.
>
> Their very kindness stings with intolerable insult. To be "cured" against one's will and cured of states which we may not regard as disease is to be put on a level with those who have not yet reached the age of reason or those who never will; to be classed with infants, imbeciles, and domestic animals. But to be punished, however severely, because we have deserved it, because we "ought to have known better," is to be treated as a human person made in God's image. (224)

LO6 Empirical Evaluation of Criminal Law Theories

Beginning in the 1950s philosophers of law, legal scholars, historians, some biologists, and social scientists conducted empirical research to refine the retributionist and consequentialist theories of punishment. By 2010, they had produced a very impressive body of empirical research.

On the retributionists side, there are now moral retributivists, legal (or political) theorists, confrontational conception retributivists, empirical retributivists, communicative/penitential retributivists, expressivists, victim vindication theorists, virtue ethicists, vengeance retributivists, restorativists, and restitutionalists.

The consequentialists were refining their theories with equally impressive empirical research. There are hedonistic adaptionists, law and economics specialists, social influence deterrence experts, new rehabilitationists, and subjective experientialists.

In fact, the compiler of the lists in these two paragraphs, Professor Marc O. DeGirolami (2012), labeled their work "dizzyingly complex." (10) Acknowledging that this work is "important," he goes on to warn that this complexity has costs. We home in on one of these costs: The more complex and academic the research findings become, the less likely the people who create and sentence criminal offenders—legislators, sentencing commissions, judges, prosecutors, and defense attorneys—will pay attention to it.

THE TEXT-CASE METHOD

LO7 Now that you've got the big picture of criminal liability and punishment, the overarching principles that apply to all of criminal law, the sources of criminal law in a federal system, proving criminal conduct and the justifications and excuses to criminal liability, and the importance of discretionary decision making, it's time to take a closer look at the method this book uses to help you learn, understand, and think critically about criminal law.

This method is called the *text-case method*, and your book, *Criminal Law*, is called a *text-case book*, meaning that it's part text and part excerpts from criminal law cases specially edited for nonlawyers like you. The text part of the book explains the general principles of criminal law and the definitions of specific crimes. The case excerpts involve real-life crimes that apply the general information in the text to real-life situations.

The application of principles and definitions of crimes to the facts of specific cases serves two important purposes. First, it helps you understand the principles and the elements of specific crimes. Second, it stimulates you to think critically about the principles and their applications. I believe the combination of text and case excerpts is the best way to test whether you understand and can think about general concepts rather than just memorizing and writing them by rote. So, although you can learn a lot from the text without reading the case excerpts, you won't get the full benefit of what you've learned without applying and thinking about it by reading the case excerpts.

For most of my students (and from e-mails that you and professors send me), reading and discussing the case excerpts are their favorite parts of the book. That's good. Cases bring criminal law to life by applying the abstract general principles, doctrines, and rules described in the text to real events in the lives of real people. But keep in mind that judges write the reports of the cases from which the excerpts are taken. So don't be surprised to learn that they don't all write with college students or other nonlawyers in mind. Reading the excerpts may take some getting used to. This section is designed to help you get the most out of the cases.

The cases in this book are all excerpts, edited versions of the complete reports of the cases. In almost all the case excerpts, you'll read reports of the appeals of guilty verdicts, not transcripts of the criminal trial. A jury or trial court judge has already found a defendant guilty, or, more likely, the defendant has pleaded guilty in a trial court; the trial judge has entered a judgment of conviction; and the defendant has appealed the conviction.

Incidentally, you'll never read the appeal of an acquittal. Why not? In U.S. criminal law, a "not guilty" verdict is final and not subject to review. (There's an exception, *sort of*, to this rule, but we take it up in the first of the few case excerpts where the exception applies.)

Let's look at a few technical, but essential, points about the verdicts "not guilty" and "guilty." A "not guilty" verdict doesn't mean innocent; it means the government didn't prove its case beyond a reasonable doubt. Think of "not guilty" as "not legally guilty." A "guilty" verdict doesn't mean not innocent; it means the government proved its case beyond a reasonable doubt. Think of "guilty" as "legally guilty."

These differences aren't just technicalities. As you read the cases, remember that some of the legally guilty defendants you're reading about are factually innocent. The flip side is also true; some acquitted defendants are factually guilty. The number of factually guilty people who "got off" is probably less than many people believe ("Symposium: Wrongful Convictions and Systemic Reform" 2005).

Criminal cases start in trial courts. It's in the trial courts that the cases for the state and the defense are presented; where their witnesses and the physical evidence are introduced; and where the fact finders (juries in jury trials or judges in nonjury bench trials) decide what the "true" story is and whether the evidence all adds up to proof of guilt beyond a reasonable doubt. If there's reasonable doubt, the jury renders its "not guilty" verdict; the judge enters a judgment of acquittal; and, the case is over—for good. There's no appeal to an acquittal; the fact finders' not guilty verdict is always final.

If there's proof beyond a reasonable doubt, the fact finders render their "guilty" verdict; the judge enters a judgment of guilty—and the case might be over. Rarely (contrary to popular perception), defendants appeal judgments of guilt. These appeals go to appellate courts. (The case excerpts are drawn from the official reports of these courts' decisions.)

Most states and the federal government have two levels of appeals courts (see Figure 1.3): an intermediate court of appeals and a supreme court. The usual procedure

"not guilty" verdict doesn't mean "innocent"; it means that the government didn't prove its case beyond a reasonable doubt

"guilty" verdict legally, not necessarily factually, guilty; it means the government proved its case beyond a reasonable doubt

trial courts where the cases for the state and the defense are presented; their witnesses and the physical evidence are introduced; and the fact finders (juries in jury trials or judges in nonjury bench trials) decide what the "true" story is and whether the evidence all adds up to proof of guilt beyond a reasonable doubt

appellate courts in most states and the federal government, the two levels of appeals courts: an intermediate court of appeals and a supreme court

Figure 1.3

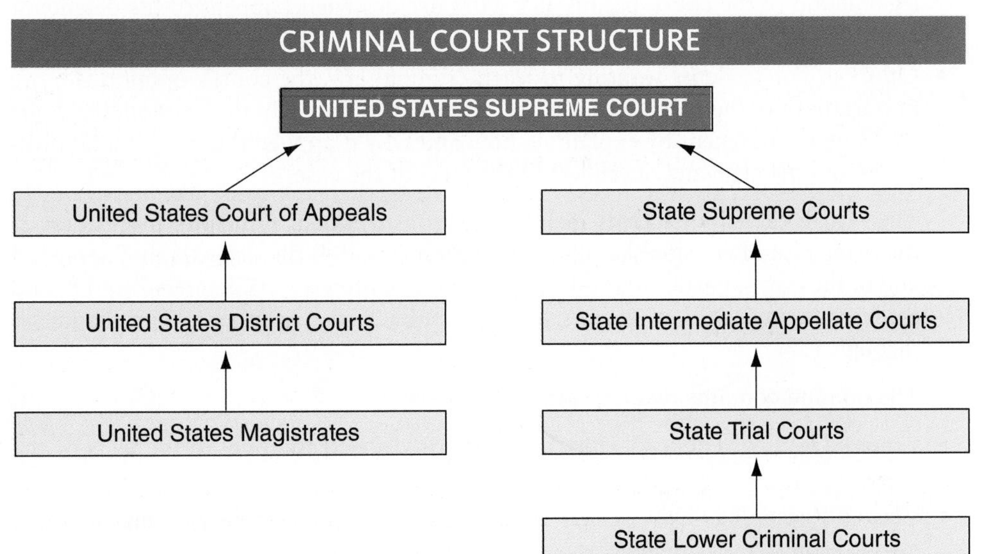

is to appeal first to the intermediate court of appeals and then to the state supreme court. In a tiny number of cases involving issues about the U.S. Constitution, the case may go to the Supreme Court of the United States (SCOTUS). We enter the picture in these appellate court case excerpts. Let's look at the parts of the appellate cases you'll be reading excerpts from.

LO7 The Parts of the Case Excerpts

Don't worry if reading cases intimidates you at first. Like students before you, you'll get the hang of it before long. To help you get the most out of the case excerpts, I've outlined the main parts of each case: the (1) title, (2) citation, (3) procedural history, (4) judge, (5) facts, (6) judgment, and (7) opinion.

- *Title*. The case title consists of the names of the parties, either appellants (the party appealing the case) and appellees (party appealed against) or petitioners (parties bringing a case in habeas corpus or certiorari) and respondents (parties petitioned against in habeas corpus and certiorari).
- *Citation*. The citation is like the footnote or endnote in any text; it tells you where to find the case. (See "Finding Cases" section, p. 35.)
- *Procedural History*. The case history is a brief description of the steps and judgments (decisions) made by each court that has heard the case.
- *Judge*. The name of the judge who wrote the opinion and issued the court's judgment in the case.
- *Facts*. The facts of the case are the critical starting point in reading and analyzing cases. If you don't know the facts, you can't understand the principle the case is teaching. One of my best law professors, Professor Hill, frequently reminded us: "Cases are stories with a point. You can't get the point if you don't know the story." He also gave us some helpful advice: "Forget you're lawyers. Tell me the story as if you were telling it to your grandmother who doesn't know anything about the law."

judgment the court's judgment (sometimes called the court's *decision*) is how the court disposes of the case

- *Judgment (Decision)*. The court's **judgment** (sometimes called the court's *decision*) is how the court disposes of the case. In the trial court, the judgments are almost always guilty or not guilty. In appeals courts, the judgments are affirmed, reversed, or reversed and remanded (sent back to the trial court). This is the most important legal action of the court, because it's what decides what happens to the defendant and the government.

opinion "the point of the story"; the court backs up its judgment by explaining how and why it applied the law (general principles and the elements of crimes) to the facts of the case

- *Opinion*. For students wanting to learn criminal law, the court's **opinion** is more important than the judgment: it's "the point of the story." In the opinion, the court backs up its judgment by explaining how and why it applied the law (general principles and the elements of crimes) to the facts of the case.

  The law in the case excerpts includes the constitutional principles in Chapter 2; the principles of criminal liability in Chapters 3 and 4; the defenses in Chapters 5 and 6; the law of parties to crime and incomplete offenses in Chapters 7 and 8; and the law of crimes against persons, property, public order, and the state in Chapters 9 through 13.

  The opinion contains two essential ingredients:

court's holding the legal rule the court has decided to apply to the facts of the cases

court's reasoning the reasons the court gives to support its holding

- **Court's Holding**. The legal rule the court has decided to apply to the facts of the cases.
- **Court's Reasoning**. The reasons the court gives to support its holding. In some cases, the justices write majority and dissenting opinions.

A **majority opinion**, as its name indicates, is the opinion of the majority of the justices on the court who participated in the case. The majority opinion lays out the law of the case.

majority opinion the law of the case; the opinion of the majority of the justices on the court who participated in the case

Although the majority opinion represents the established law of the case, dissenting opinions present a plausible alternative to the majority opinion. Dissents sometimes become the law in future decisions. For example, dissents in U.S. Supreme Court opinions of the 1930s became the law in the 1960s, and many of the dissents of the 1960s became law by the 1990s and remain the law as you're reading this.

Mostly in U.S. Supreme Court cases, you'll also see a **concurring opinion**. In concurring opinions, justices agree with the conclusions of either the majority or the dissenting opinion, but they have different reasons for reaching the conclusion.

concurring opinion agrees with the conclusions of either the majority or the dissenting opinion but provides different reasons for reaching the conclusion

Sometimes, enough justices agree with the *result* in the case to make up a majority decision, but not enough agree on the reasoning to make up a majority opinion. In these cases, there's a **plurality opinion**, an opinion that represents the reasoning of the greatest number (but less than a majority) of justices.

plurality opinion an opinion that represents the reasoning of the greatest number (but less than a majority) of justices

All of the differing perspectives in the opinions will stimulate you to think about all the topics in criminal law. They also clearly demonstrate that there's more than one reasonable way to look at important questions.

LO7

Briefing the Case Excerpts

To get the most from your reading of the case excerpts, you should write out the answers to the following questions about each. This is what we call "briefing" a case.

1. *Facts* State the facts in simple narrative form in chronological order. As Professor Hill said, "Tell me the story as if you were telling it to your grandmother." Then, select, sort, and arrange the facts into the following categories:
    a. *Acts of the defendant* List what the defendant did in chronological order. (Remember, there's no criminal case without a criminal act by the defendant.)
    b. *Intent of the defendant* required, if any. If none is required, say "none."
    c. *Circumstances* required, if any, by the statute defining the crime (such as age in statutory rape). If none is required, answer "none."
    d. *Causing a harmful result* if one is required. If none is required, say "none."
    e. *Justification and excuse (defense)* if any. If none, answer "none."
2. *The legal issue in the case* State the principle and/or element of a specific crime raised by the facts of the case.
3. *Arguments in the court's opinion to support the judgment* List the reasons the court gives for its decision. The court's opinion consists of how and why the court applies the principle, doctrine, and/or rule to the facts of the case.
4. *The court's judgment (decision)* The most common judgments are:
    a. *Affirmed.* The judgment (decision) of the lower court is upheld.
    b. *Reversed.* The judgment (decision) of the lower court is overturned.
    c. *Reversed and remanded.* The judgment (decision) of the lower court is overturned and sent the case back for further proceedings in accord with the appellate court's decision.

You can't answer all these questions in every case. First, the answers depend on the knowledge you accumulate as the text and your instructor introduce more principles, doctrines, and rules. Second, courts don't necessarily follow the same procedure in reviewing an appeal as the one outlined here. Third, not all of the questions come up in every case—except for one: What did the defendant do? That's because there's no criminal case without some action by the defendant (Chapter 3).

Developing the skills needed to sort out the elements of the case excerpts requires practice, but it's worth the effort. Answering the questions can challenge you to think not only about the basic principles, doctrines, and rules of criminal law but also about your own fundamental values regarding life, property, privacy, and morals.

Now that you've had a chance to read the description of the case-text method, let's give you the opportunity to apply the description to our first case excerpt. Here, the U.S. Supreme Court decided a case that touches on three topics from Chapter 1, overcriminalization, federalism, and criminal justice official discretionary law making.

CASE

*In **Bond v. U.S. (2014)**, Carol Anne Bond appealed her conviction in the U.S. District Court of Eastern Pennsylvania of possessing and using a chemical weapon and mail theft.*

Was the arsenic a "chemical weapon?"

Carol Anne Bond (Defendant/Petitioner) v. United States

134 S. Ct. 2077 (2014)

HISTORY

Carol Anne Bond (Defendant/Petitioner) was convicted in the U.S. District Court of Eastern Pennsylvania, of possessing and using a chemical weapon and mail theft, and she appealed. The Court of Appeals for the Third Circuit, affirmed. Bond petitioned the U.S. Supreme Court for a writ of certiorari. The Supreme Court reversed and remanded. The Court of Appeals again affirmed Bond's conviction. Bond petitioned for certiorari. The Supreme Court reversed and remanded again.

ROBERTS, CJ, JOINED BY KENNEDY, GINSBURG, BREYER, SOTOMAYOR, AND KAGAN, JJ.

The horrors of chemical warfare were vividly captured by John Singer Sargent in his 1919 painting *Gassed*. The nearly life-sized work depicts two lines of soldiers, blinded by mustard gas, clinging single file to orderlies guiding them to an improvised aid station. There they would receive little treatment and no relief; many suffered for weeks only to have the gas claim their lives. The soldiers were shown staggering through piles of comrades too seriously burned to even join the procession.

The painting reflects the devastation that Sargent witnessed in the aftermath of the Second Battle of Arras during World War I. That battle and others like it led to an overwhelming consensus in the international community that toxic chemicals should never again be used as weapons against human beings. Today that objective is reflected in the international Convention on Chemical Weapons, which has been ratified or acceded to by 190 countries.

The United States, pursuant to the Federal Government's constitutionally enumerated power to make treaties, ratified the treaty in 1997. Congress gave the Convention domestic effect in 1998 when it passed the Chemical Weapons Convention Implementation Act. See 112 Stat. 2681–856. The Act closely tracks the text of the treaty: It forbids any person knowingly "to develop, produce, otherwise acquire, transfer directly or indirectly, receive, stockpile, retain, own, possess, or use, or threaten to use, any chemical weapon." 18 U.S.C. § 229(a)(1). It defines "chemical weapon" in relevant part as "[a] toxic chemical and its precursors, except where intended for a purpose not prohibited under this chapter as long as the type and quantity is consistent with such a purpose." § 229F(1)(A). "Toxic chemical," in turn, is defined in general as "any chemical which through its chemical action on life processes can cause death, temporary incapacitation or permanent harm to humans or animals. The term includes all such chemicals, regardless of their origin or of their method of production, and regardless of whether they are produced in facilities, in munitions or elsewhere." § 229F(8)(A). Finally, "purposes not prohibited by this chapter" is defined as "[a]ny peaceful purpose related to an industrial, agricultural, research, medical, or pharmaceutical activity or other activity," and other specific purposes. § 229F(7). A person who violates section 229 may be subject to severe punishment: imprisonment "for any term of years," or if a victim's death results, the death penalty or imprisonment "for life." § 229A(a).

FACTS

Carol Anne Bond is a microbiologist from Lansdale, Pennsylvania. In 2006, Bond's closest friend, Myrlinda Haynes, announced that she was pregnant. When Bond discovered that her husband was the child's father, she sought revenge against Haynes. Bond stole a quantity of 10–chloro–10H–phenoxarsine (an arsenic-based compound) from her employer, a chemical manufacturer. She also ordered a vial of potassium dichromate (a chemical commonly used in printing photographs or cleaning laboratory equipment) on Amazon.com. Both chemicals are toxic to humans and, in high enough doses, potentially lethal. It is undisputed, however, that Bond did not intend to kill Haynes. She instead hoped that Haynes would touch the chemicals and develop an uncomfortable rash.

Between November 2006 and June 2007, Bond went to Haynes's home on at least 24 occasions and spread the chemicals on her car door, mailbox, and door knob. These attempted assaults were almost entirely unsuccessful. The chemicals that Bond used are easy to see, and Haynes was able to avoid them all but once. On that occasion, Haynes suffered a minor chemical burn on her thumb, which she treated by rinsing with water. Haynes repeatedly called the local police to report the suspicious substances, but they took no action. When Haynes found powder on her mailbox, she called the police again, who told her to call the post office. Haynes did so, and postal inspectors placed surveillance cameras around her home. The cameras caught Bond opening Haynes's mailbox, stealing an envelope, and stuffing potassium dichromate inside the muffler of Haynes's car.

Federal prosecutors naturally charged Bond with two counts of mail theft, in violation of 18 U.S.C. § 1708. More surprising, they also charged her with two counts of possessing and using a chemical weapon, in violation of section 229(a). Bond moved to dismiss the chemical weapon counts on the ground that section 229 exceeded Congress's enumerated powers and invaded powers reserved to the States by the Tenth Amendment. The District Court denied Bond's motion. She then entered a conditional guilty plea that reserved her right to appeal. The District Court sentenced Bond to six years in federal prison plus five years of supervised release, and ordered her to pay a $2,000 fine and $9,902.79 in restitution.

OPINION

In our federal system, the National Government possesses only limited powers; the States and the people retain the remainder. The States have broad authority to enact legislation for the public good—what we have often called a "police power." The Federal Government, by contrast, has no such authority and "can exercise only the powers granted to it."… For nearly two centuries it has been "clear" that, lacking a police power, "Congress cannot punish felonies generally." A criminal act committed wholly within a State "cannot be made an offence against the United States, unless it has some relation to the execution of a power of Congress, or to some matter within the jurisdiction of the United States."

…

In the Government's view, the conclusion that Bond "knowingly" "used" a "chemical weapon" in violation of section 229(a) is simple: The chemicals that Bond placed on Haynes's home and car are "toxic chemicals" as defined by the statute, and Bond's attempt to assault Haynes was not a "peaceful purpose." §§ 229F(1), (8), (7). The problem with this interpretation is that it would "dramatically intrude upon traditional state criminal jurisdiction," and we avoid reading statutes to have such reach in the absence of a clear indication that they do.…

…

It is appropriate to refer to basic principles of federalism embodied in the Constitution to resolve ambiguity in a federal statute. In this case, the ambiguity derives from the improbably broad reach of the key statutory definition given the term—"chemical weapon"—being defined; the deeply serious consequences of adopting such a boundless reading; and the lack of any apparent need to do so in light of the context from which the statute arose—a treaty about

(continues)

(continued)

chemical warfare and terrorism. We conclude that, in this curious case, we can insist on a clear indication that Congress meant to reach purely local crimes, before interpreting the statute's expansive language in a way that intrudes on the police power of the States.

We do not find any such clear indication in section 229. "Chemical weapon" is the key term that defines the statute's reach, and it is defined extremely broadly. But that general definition does not constitute a clear statement that Congress meant the statute to reach local criminal conduct.

In fact, a fair reading of section 229 suggests that it does not have as expansive a scope as might at first appear.... The chemicals in this case are not of the sort that an ordinary person would associate with instruments of chemical warfare.... The use of something as a "weapon" typically connotes "an instrument of offensive or defensive combat," or "an instrument of attack or defense in combat, as a gun, missile, or sword." But no speaker in natural parlance would describe Bond's feud-driven act of spreading irritating chemicals on Haynes's door knob and mailbox as "combat." Nor do the other circumstances of Bond's offense—an act of revenge born of romantic jealousy, meant to cause discomfort, that produced nothing more than a minor thumb burn—suggest that a chemical weapon was deployed in Norristown, Pennsylvania. Potassium dichromate and 10–chloro–10H–phenoxarsine might be chemical weapons if used, say, to poison a city's water supply. But Bond's crime is worlds apart from such hypotheticals, and covering it would give the statute a reach exceeding the ordinary meaning of the words Congress wrote.

... The Government would have us brush aside the ordinary meaning and adopt a reading of section 229 that would sweep in everything from the detergent under the kitchen sink to the stain remover in the laundry room. Yet no one would ordinarily describe those substances as "chemical weapons." The Government responds that because Bond used "specialized, highly toxic" (though legal) chemicals, "this case presents no occasion to address whether Congress intended [section 229] to apply to common household substances." That the statute *would* apply so broadly, however, is the inescapable conclusion of the Government's position: Any parent would be guilty of a serious federal offense—possession of a chemical weapon—when, exasperated by the children's repeated failure to clean the goldfish tank, he considers poisoning the fish with a few drops of vinegar.

We are reluctant to ignore the ordinary meaning of "chemical weapon" when doing so would transform a statute passed to implement the international Convention on Chemical Weapons into one that also makes it a federal offense to poison goldfish. That would not be a realistic assessment of congressional intent.

...

As the Government reads section 229, hardly a poisoning in the land would fall outside the federal statute's domain. Of course Bond's conduct is serious and unacceptable—and against the laws of Pennsylvania. But the background principle that Congress does not normally intrude upon the police power of the States is critically important. In light of that principle, we are reluctant to conclude that Congress meant to punish Bond's crime with a federal prosecution for a chemical weapons attack.

...

It is also clear that the laws of the Commonwealth of Pennsylvania (and every other State) are sufficient to prosecute Bond. Pennsylvania has several statutes that would likely cover her assault. And state authorities regularly enforce these laws in poisoning cases.

The Government objects that Pennsylvania authorities charged Bond with only a minor offense based on her "harassing telephone calls and letters," and declined to prosecute her for assault. But we have traditionally viewed the exercise of state officials' prosecutorial discretion as a valuable feature of our constitutional system. Here, in its zeal to prosecute Bond, the Federal Government has "displaced" the "public policy of the Commonwealth of Pennsylvania, enacted in its capacity as sovereign," that Bond does not belong in prison for a chemical weapons offense.... Bond's crime could hardly be more unlike the uses of mustard gas on the Western Front or nerve agents in the Iran–Iraq war.... There are no life-sized paintings of Bond's rival washing her thumb. And there are no apparent interests of the United States Congress or the community of nations in seeing Bond end up in federal prison, rather than dealt with (like virtually all other criminals in Pennsylvania) by the State.

...

In sum, the global need to prevent chemical warfare does not require the Federal Government to reach into the kitchen cupboard, or to treat a local assault with a chemical irritant as the deployment of a chemical weapon. There is no reason to suppose that Congress—in implementing the Convention on Chemical Weapons—thought otherwise.

...

The judgment of the Court of Appeals is reversed, and the case is remanded for further proceedings consistent with this opinion.

It is so ordered.

CONCURRENCES

SCALIA, J., joined by THOMAS and ALITO, JJ., CONCURRING

Somewhere in Norristown, Pennsylvania, a husband's paramour suffered a minor thumb burn at the hands of a betrayed wife. The United States Congress—"every where extending the sphere of its activity, and drawing all power into its impetuous vortex"—has made a federal case out of it. What are we to do?

It is the responsibility of "the legislature, not the Court,... to define a crime, and ordain its punishment." And, it is "emphatically the province and duty of the judicial department... say what the law is."

Today, the Court shirks its job and performs Congress's. As sweeping and unsettling as the Chemical Weapons Convention Implementation Act of 1998 may be, it is clear beyond doubt that it covers what Bond did; and we have no authority to amend it. So we are forced to decide—there is no way around it—whether the Act's application to what Bond did was constitutional. I would hold that it was not, and for that reason would reverse the judgment of the Court of Appeals for the Third Circuit.... Bond possessed and used "chemical[s] which through [their] chemical action on life processes can cause death, temporary incapacitation or permanent harm." Thus, she possessed "toxic chemicals." And, because they were not possessed or used only for a "purpose not prohibited," § 229F(1)(A), they were "chemical weapons." Ergo, Bond violated the Act. End of statutory analysis, I would have thought.

QUESTIONS

1. State the elements of the statute Carole Bond was convicted of violating.
2. List all of Carole Bond's acts and her intent relevant to deciding each of the elements of the crime.
3. Do you believe she violated the statute? Defend your answer.
4. Do you agree that Bond doesn't belong in prison for a chemical weapons offense? Explain your answer.
5. Who decided to charge Bond with the minor state offense of harassing phone calls and letters instead of the more serious federal chemical weapons offense? According to the Court who *should* decide? Do you agree? Disagree? Explain your answer.
6. Do you believe this case represents an example of federal government overcriminalization? (Review the discussion on page 17 of our text.)
7. In your opinion, does this statute violate the place of criminal law in our federal system of government? Explain.

Finding Cases

LO7

Knowing how to read and brief cases is important. So is knowing how to find cases. You may want to look up cases on your own, either in the library or in the rapidly expanding quantity of cases published on the Internet. These might include cases your instructor talks about in class, those discussed in the text, or the full versions of the case excerpts and the note cases following the excerpts. You may even want to look up a case you read or hear about outside of class.

case citation the numbers, letters, and punctuation that tell you where to locate the full case report; they follow the title of a case in the excerpts or in the bibliography at the end of the book

The case citation consists of the numbers, letters, and punctuation that follow the title of a case in the excerpts or in the bibliography at the end of the book. These letters and numbers tell you where to locate the full case report. For example, in *State v. Metzger*, just after the title of the case, "*State v. Metzger*," you read "319 N.W. 2d 459 (Neb. 1982)." Here's how to interpret this citation:

319 *means* Volume 319

N.W.2d *means North Western Reporter, Second Series*

459 *means* page 459

(Neb. 1982) *means* Nebraska Supreme Court in the year 1982

So if you're looking for the full version of *State v. Metzger*, you'll find it in Volume 319 of the *North Western Reporter, Second Series*, page 459. The *North Western Reporter, Second Series*, is the second series of a multivolume set of law books that publishes reports of cases decided by the supreme courts and intermediate appellate courts in Nebraska and several other states in the region. There are comparable reporters for other regions, including the Northeast (N.E.), Southern (So.), Southwest (S.W.), and Pacific (P.).

Case citations always follow the same order. The volume number always comes before the title of a reporter and the page always comes immediately after the title. The abbreviation of the name of the court and the year the case was decided follow the page number in parentheses. You can tell if the court was the highest or an intermediate appellate court by the abbreviation. For example, in Metzger, the court is the Nebraska Supreme Court. (If the Nebraska intermediate appeals court had decided the case, you'd see "Neb. App.")

Summary

LO1 The social reality of U.S. criminal law is that there are two criminal laws: (a) a small group of serious, core offenses and (b) a huge number of lesser crimes, or "everything else." This dual nature reflects the U.S. criminal law imagination, or the contributions of law, history, philosophy, the social sciences, and sometimes biology to explain the morals we want to impose on society. The social reality of U.S. criminal law also reflects our punishment imagination, or conduct that fits within the criminal law imagination and that should be punished by locking people up.

LO2 Criminal punishment is a special form of physical or psychological pain that goes beyond noncriminal sanctions (deserving of monetary award in torts), regulated behavior that laws formally discourage, licensed behavior (a price is charged), and lawful behavior that is subject to individual conscience and social disapproval.

LO3 Crimes can be classified in various ways. One scheme divides crime into two categories: *mala in se* and *mala prohibita*. *Mala in se* crimes are inherently evil and require some level of criminal intent. *Mala prohibita* offenses are crimes only because a specific statute or ordinance bans them. Another scheme, and the one that's most widely used, classifies crimes according to the kind and quantity of punishment. Felonies are crimes punishable by death or confinement in the state's prison for one year to life without parole, while misdemeanors are punishable by fine and/or confinement in the local jail for up to one year. These labels carry different legal and societal consequences.

LO4 Criminal law is established by elected representatives (e.g., state legislatures, city and town councils, U.S. Congress), administrative agencies (e.g., IRS tax regulations, vehicle safety standards of the state highway patrol), judges, and informal discretionary decision making by police, prosecutors, and other criminal justice professionals.

LO5 As criminal law is a rough engine of social control, criminal punishment is the most drastic reaction to unwanted behavior. Penalties must meet the following criteria to qualify as criminal punishment: they have to inflict pain or other unpleasant consequences, they have to prescribe a punishment in the same law that defines the crime, they have to be administered intentionally, and the state has to administer them. Although most studies conclude that more prison has reduced crime to some degree, the possible negative consequences of mass imprisonment may outweigh its crime reduction benefits.

LO6 Theories of criminal punishment are divided primarily into two schools of thought: retributionists and preventionists. Retributionists insist that offenders can only pay for their crimes through the "hard treatment" of having punishment inflicted on them, so the punishment justifies itself. Preventionists disagree, insisting that punishment should only be a means to do a greater good, usually the prevention or reduction of future crime. Each side of the divide has large, complex bodies of empirical research to support their theories of punishment.

LO7 This book, *Criminal Law*, is a "text-case book," meaning it contains two types of content. The text part of the book describes the principles of criminal law, while the accompanying case excerpts, edited for students and non-lawyers, allow you to apply those legal principles to real-life crimes and situations using the text-case method.

Key Terms

social reality of U.S. criminal law, p. 6
criminal law imagination, p. 6
felonies against persons, p. 7
felonies against property, p. 7
hard punishment, p. 7
punishment imagination, p. 8
police power, p. 8
torts, p. 10
compensatory damages, p. 11
punitive damages, p. 11
mala in se (inherently evil) crimes, p. 12
mala prohibita offenses, p. 12
felonies, p. 12
misdemeanors, p. 12
state criminal codes, p. 12
municipal codes, p. 12
U.S. Criminal Code, p. 12
administrative agencies, p. 12
criminal court opinions, p. 13
criminal law enforcement agencies, p. 13
codified, p. 13
Model Penal Code (MPC), p. 14
criminal liability, p. 14
administrative crimes, p. 17
federal system, p. 19
punishment, p. 21
criminal punishment, p. 22
theories of criminal punishment, p. 22
retributionists, p. 22
preventionists, p. 22
culpability, p. 23
justice, p. 24
deterrence, p. 24
specific deterrence, p. 24
general deterrence, p. 24
incapacitation, p. 24
rehabilitation, p. 25
hedonism, p. 25
rationalism, p. 25
classical deterrence theory, p. 25
principle of utility, p. 25
"medical model" of criminal law, p. 27
"not guilty" verdict, p. 29
"guilty" verdict, p. 29
trial courts, p. 29
appellate courts, p. 29
judgment, p. 30
opinion, p. 30
court's holding, p. 30
court's reasoning, p. 30
majority opinion, p. 31
concurring opinion, p. 31
plurality opinion, p. 31
case citation, p. 35

Learning Objectives

1 To understand and appreciate the reasons for the limits on criminal law and criminal punishment in the U.S. constitutional democracy.

2 To understand the principle of legality and the importance of its relationship to the limits of criminal law and punishment.

3 To appreciate the nature and importance of retroactive criminal lawmaking.

4 To know the criteria for identifying vague laws and to understand and appreciate their constitutional significance and consequences.

5 To understand and appreciate the rights defendants enjoy in criminal proceedings, the burden they have to support their affirmative defenses, and the requirement of the prosecution to prove guilt beyond a reasonable doubt.

6 To know, understand, and appreciate the limits placed on the criminal law and criminal punishment by the specific provisions in the Bill of Rights.

7 To understand and appreciate the constitutional significance and consequences of the principle of proportionality in criminal punishment and its relation to "cruel and unusual punishment."

8 To understand the importance of the right to trial by jury in the process of sentencing convicted offenders.

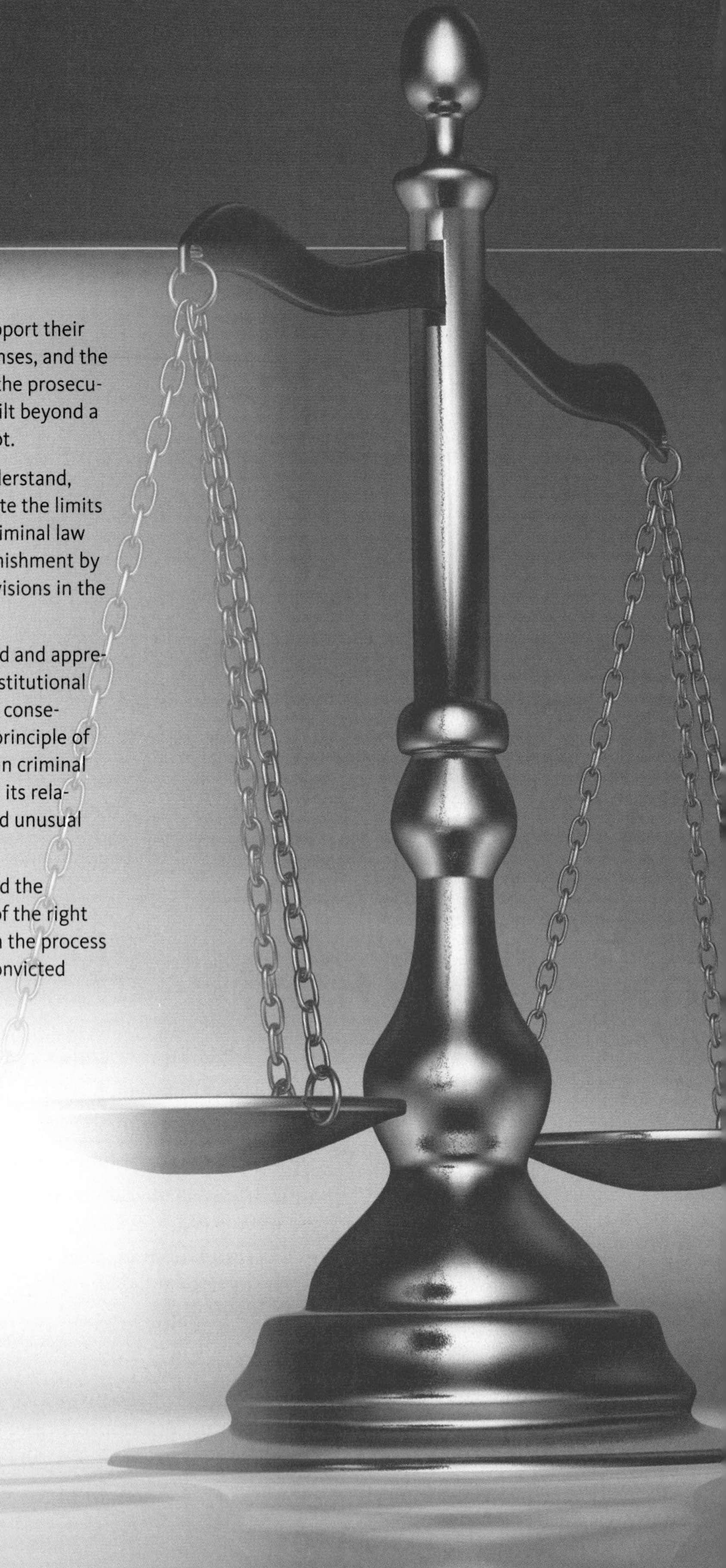

2 Constitutional Limits on Criminal Law

Chapter Outline

Violation of Doctors' Right to Free Speech?

The Woman's Right To Know Act obligates doctors (or technicians) to perform an ultrasound on any woman seeking an abortion at least four but not more than 72 hours before the abortion is to take place. The physician must display the sonogram so that the woman can see it, and describe the fetus in detail, "including the presence, location, and dimensions of the unborn child within the uterus and the number of unborn children depicted," as well as "the presence of external members and internal organs, if present and viewable." The physician also must offer to allow the woman to hear the fetal heart tone. The woman, however, may "avert her eyes from the displayed images" and "refuse to hear the simultaneous explanation and medical description" by presumably covering her eyes and ears.

LO1

The authors of the U.S. Constitution were suspicious of power, especially power in the hands of government officials. They were also devoted to the right of individuals to control their own destinies without government interference. But they were realists who knew that freedom depends on order, and order depends on social control. So they created a Constitution that balanced the power of government and the liberty of individuals. No one has expressed the kind of government the Constitution created better than James Madison (1787, 1961), one of its primary authors:

> If men were angels, no government would be necessary. If angels were to govern men, neither external nor internal controls on government would be necessary. In framing a government which is to be administered by men over men, the great difficulty is this: You must first enable the government to control the governed; and in the next place, oblige it to control itself. (349)

constitutional democracy the majority can't make a crime out of conduct protected by the fundamental rights in the U.S. Constitution

James Madison was describing the U.S. democracy—a **constitutional democracy**—not a pure democracy. In a pure democracy, the majority can have whatever it wants. In a constitutional democracy, the majority can't make a crime out of what the Constitution protects as a fundamental right. Even if 90 percent of the people want to make it a crime to say, "The president is a socialist," they can't. Why? Because the First Amendment to the U.S. Constitution guarantees the fundamental right of free speech.

A central feature of criminal law in a constitutional democracy is the limits it places on the government's power to create crimes and punish offenders. In this chapter, we focus on the limits imposed by the U.S. and state constitutions. But the idea of limited government power in criminal law and punishment is older than the U.S. Constitution; it has deep roots in English and American Colonial history. It begins more than 2,000 years ago with the ancient Greek philosopher Aristotle, who wrote in 350 BCE:

> He who bids the law rule may be deemed to bid God and Reason alone rule, but he who bids man rule adds an element of the beast; for desire is a wild beast, and passion perverts the minds of rulers, even when they are the best of men. The law is reason unaffected by desire. (qtd. in Allen 1993, 3)

rule of law the idea that government power should be defined and limited by laws

Almost 900 years later, in 1215, in the Magna Carta, King John promised his barons the **rule of law** when he agreed not to proceed with force against any free man, "except by the lawful judgment of his equals or by the law of the land." And in 1240, the great English jurist Bracton (1968) wrote that even the king ruled "under God and the law," and "it is a saying worthy of the majesty of a ruler that the prince acknowledges himself bound by the laws" (2:305–6).

THE PRINCIPLE OF LEGALITY

LO2

principle of legality no one can be convicted of, or punished for, a crime unless the law defined the crime and prescribed the punishment before the person engaged in the behavior that was defined as a crime

In criminal law, and in criminal punishment, there's an ancient proposition based on the principle of legality: "No crime without law; no punishment without law." This means that no one can be convicted of, or punished for, a crime unless the law defined the crime and prescribed the punishment *before* a person engaged in the behavior that was defined as a crime. It's called "the first principle of criminal law" (Packer 1968, 79); all other principles you learn about in this book are subordinate to it. And it applies even when following it allows morally blameworthy, dangerous people to go free without punishment. The basic idea of the principle is to let individuals know what the law prohibits, and what the punishment for its violation is (Singer and LaFond 2013, 7).

Let's look at three constitutional principles that fall within the scope of the principle of legality: the ban on *ex post facto* laws; the due process void-for-vagueness doctrine; and the rule of lenity in interpreting criminal laws and punishment.

The Ban on *Ex Post Facto* Laws

LO3

So fundamental did the authors of the Constitution consider a ban on retroactive criminal lawmaking, or *ex post facto* laws, that they raised it to constitutional status in Article I of the U.S. Constitution. Article I, Section 9, bans the *U.S. Congress* from enacting such laws; Article 1, Section 10, bans *state legislatures* from passing them. And most state constitutions include their own ban on retroactive statutes.

***ex post facto* laws** a retroactive law that does one of three things: (1) criminalizes an act that wasn't a crime when it was committed, (2) increases the punishment for a crime after the crime was committed, or (3) takes away a defense that was available to a defendant when the crime was committed

An *ex post facto* law does one of three things:

1. It criminalizes an act that wasn't a crime when it was committed.
2. It increases the punishment for a crime after the crime was committed. (The ban doesn't apply to reductions in punishment. So, for example, there's no ban on reducing the punishment for possessing marijuana from one year in prison to a fine.)
3. It takes away a defense that was available to a defendant when the crime was committed. (*Beazell v. Ohio* 1925, 169)

Statutes that make conduct criminal after the crimes take place are the clearest example of *ex post facto* laws. They're also the rarest because in modern times, legislatures never try to make them crimes. Equally clear, and equally rare, are statutes that change an element of a crime after it's committed—for example, raising the age of the victim in statutory rape from 16 to 21 or removing the "nighttime entry" element in a burglary statute. Statutes that increase punishment occur more often (LaFave 2003a, 110–11).

The *ex post facto* ban has two major purposes. One is to protect private individuals by ensuring that legislatures give them fair warning about what's criminal and that they can rely on that requirement. The second purpose is directed at preventing legislators from passing arbitrary and vindictive laws. ("Arbitrary" means legislation based on random choice or personal whim, not on reason and standards.)

YOU *DECIDE*

Did the longer sentence violate the ban on ex post facto *laws?*

LO3

Marvin Peugh and his cousin, Steven Hollewell, ran two farming-related businesses in Illinois. Grainery, Inc., bought, stored, and sold grain; Agri–Tech, Inc., provided farming services to landowners and tenants. When the Grainery began experiencing cash-flow problems, Peugh and Hollewell engaged in two fraudulent schemes. First, they obtained a series of bank loans by representing falsely the existence of contracts for future grain deliveries from Agri–Tech to the Grainery. When they failed to pay back the principal on these loans, the bank suffered losses of over $2 million. Second, they artificially inflated the balances of accounts under their control by "check kiting," or writing bad checks between their accounts. This scheme allowed them to overdraw an account by $471,000. They engaged in their illicit conduct in 1999 and 2000.

When their acts were uncovered, Peugh and Hollewell were charged with nine counts of bank fraud, in violation of 18 U.S.C. § 1344. While Hollewell pleaded guilty to one count of check kiting, Peugh pleaded not guilty and went to trial, where he testified that he had not intended to defraud the banks. The jury found him guilty of five counts of bank fraud and acquitted him of the remaining counts.

(continues)

Majority

SOTOMAYOR, J., JOINED BY KENNEDY, GINSBURG, BREYER, AND KAGAN, JJ.

At sentencing, Peugh argued that the *Ex Post Facto* Clause required that he be sentenced under the 1998 version of the Federal Sentencing Guidelines in effect at the time of his offenses rather than under the 2009 version in effect at the time of sentencing. Under the 1998 Guidelines, Peugh's sentencing range was 30 to 37 months, but the 2009 Guidelines assigned more severe consequences to his acts, yielding a range of 70 to 87 months. The District Court rejected Peugh's *ex post facto* claim and sentenced him to 70 months' imprisonment. The Seventh Circuit affirmed.

Majority

The Constitution forbids the passage of *ex post facto* laws, a category including every law that *changes the punishment*, and inflicts *a greater punishment*, than the law annexed to the crime, when committed. The touchstone of the inquiry is whether a given change in law presents a sufficient risk of increasing the measure of punishment attached to the covered crimes. Normally, a judge will use the Guidelines range as the starting point in the analysis and impose a sentence within the range. Appellate courts may presume a within-Guidelines sentence is reasonable, and may "consider the extent of the deviation" from the Guidelines as part of their reasonableness review (*Gall*, excerpt pp. 86–91). Common sense indicates that the federal system generally will steer district courts to more within-Guidelines sentences, and considerable empirical evidence suggests that the Guidelines have that effect. A retrospective increase in an applicable Guidelines range thus creates a sufficient risk of a higher sentence to constitute an *ex post facto* violation.

Dissent

THOMAS, J, JOINED BY ROBERTS, CJ, AND SCALIA, AND ALITO

The retroactive application of subsequently amended Guidelines does not create a "sufficient risk" of increasing a defendant's punishment for two reasons. First, the Guidelines do not constrain the discretion of district courts and, thus, have no legal effect on a defendant's sentence. Second, to the extent that the amended Guidelines create a *risk* that a defendant might receive a harsher punishment, that risk results from the Guidelines' persuasive force, not any legal effect. The Guidelines help district judges to impose sentences that comply with § 3553(a). The risk of an increased sentence is, in essence, the risk of a more *accurate* sentence—i.e., a sentence more in line with the statutory scheme's penological goals. Guideline changes that help district courts achieve such pre-existing statutory sentencing goals do not create a risk of an increased sentence cognizable under the *Ex Post Facto* Clause. We have never held that government action violates the *Ex Post Facto* Clause when it merely influences the exercise of the sentencing judge's discretion.

Today's opinion also demonstrates the unworkability of our *ex post facto* jurisprudence. Under our current precedent, whenever a change in the law creates a "risk" of an increased sentence, we must determine whether the risk is "sufficient," or sufficiently significant, to violate the *Ex Post Facto* Clause. Our analysis under that test has devolved into little more than an exercise in judicial intuition. I would return to the original meaning of the Clause as stated in Justice Chase's classic *Calder* formulation, under which laws of this sort are *ex post facto* only when they retroactively increase the punishment "annexed to the crime."

The Void-for-Vagueness Doctrine

LO4

void for vagueness the principle that statutes violate due process if they don't define a crime and its punishment clearly enough for ordinary people to know what is lawful

A law is void for vagueness if it forbids conduct and prescribes punishments in terms so uncertain that ordinary people have to guess at their meaning *before* they choose a course of action. (*Lanzetta v. New Jersey* 1939, 453)

The U.S. Supreme Court has ruled that vague laws violate the guarantees of two provisions in the U.S. Constitution. The Fifth Amendment to the U.S. Constitution guarantees that the *federal* government shall not deny any individual life, liberty, or property without due process of law. The Fourteenth Amendment provides that no *state* government shall deny any person life, liberty, or property without due process of law.

How do vague laws violate the due process guarantees? The reasoning behind the void-for-vagueness doctrine goes like this:

1. The Fifth and Fourteenth Amendments to the U.S. Constitution ban both federal and state governments from taking any person's "life, liberty, or property without due process of law."
2. Criminal punishment deprives individuals of life (capital punishment), liberty (imprisonment), or property (fines).
3. Therefore, failure to warn private persons of what the law forbids and/or allowing officials the chance to define arbitrarily what the law forbids denies individuals their life, liberty, and/or property without due process of law.

THE AIMS OF THE VOID-FOR-VAGUENESS DOCTRINE

LO4

The void-for-vagueness doctrine takes aim at two evils similar to those of the ban on *ex post facto* laws. First, void laws fail to give fair warning to private individuals as to what the law prohibits. Second, they allow arbitrary and discriminatory law enforcement. A famous case from the 1930s gangster days, *Lanzetta v. New Jersey* (1939), still widely cited and relied on today, is an excellent example of both the application of the doctrine and its purposes. The story begins with a challenge to this New Jersey statute:

> Any person not engaged in any lawful occupation, known to be a member of any gang consisting of two or more persons, who has been convicted at least three times of being a disorderly person, or who has been convicted of any crime, in this or in any other State, is declared to be a gangster.... Every violation is punishable by fine not exceeding $10,000 or imprisonment not exceeding 20 years, or both. (452)

The challengers attacking the statute for vagueness were Ignatius Lanzetta, Michael Falcone, and Louie Del Rossi. On June 12, 16, 19, and 24, 1936, the three challengers, "not being engaged in any lawful occupation"; "known to be members of a gang, consisting of two or more persons"; and "having been convicted of a crime in the State of Pennsylvania" were "declared to be gangsters."

The trial court threw out their challenge that the law was void for vagueness; they were tried, convicted, and sentenced to prison for "not more than ten years and not less than five years, at hard labor." The New Jersey intermediate appellate court and the New Jersey Supreme Court also threw out their challenges. But they finally prevailed when a unanimous U.S. Supreme Court ruled that the New Jersey statute was void for vagueness. Why?

> No one may be required at peril of life, liberty or property to speculate as to the meaning of penal statutes. All are entitled to be informed as to what the State commands or forbids; and a statute which either forbids or requires the doing of an act in terms so vague that men of common intelligence must necessarily guess at its meaning and differ as to its application violates the first essential of due process of law. (453)
>
> The phrase "consisting of two or more persons" is all that purports to define "gang." The meanings of that word indicated in dictionaries and in historical and sociological writings are numerous and varied. Nor is the meaning derivable from the common law, for neither in that field nor anywhere in the language of the law is there definition of the word. Our attention has not been called to, and we are unable to find, any other statute attempting to make it criminal to be a member of a "gang." (454–55)

fair notice in vague laws, isn't whether the defendant knows there's a law against the act but whether an ordinary, reasonable person would know that the act is a crime

Notice that the answer to the question, "What's fair notice?" in vague laws isn't subjective; that is, it's not what a particular defendant actually knows about the law. For example, the Court didn't ask what Lanzetta and his cohorts knew about the gangster ordinance: Were they aware it existed? Did they get advice about what it meant? Did their life experiences inform them that their behavior was criminal (Batey 1997, 4)?

That's because, according to the courts, the proper question, "What's fair notice in void-for-vagueness law?" is objective; namely, "Would an ordinary, reasonable person know that what he was doing was criminal?" Perhaps the best definition of objective fair warning is U.S. Supreme Court Justice Byron White's blunt phrase: "If any fool would know that a particular category of conduct would be within the reach of the statute, if there is an unmistakable core that a reasonable person would know is forbidden by the law, the enactment is not unconstitutional..." (*Kolender v. Lawson* 1983, 370–71).

Despite the importance of giving fair notice to individuals, the U.S. Supreme Court (1983) decided that providing "minimal guidelines to govern law enforcement" trumps notice to private individuals as the primary aim of the void-for-vagueness doctrine (*Kolender v. Lawson* 1983, 357). According to the Court:

> Where the legislature fails to provide such minimal guidelines, a criminal statute may permit a standardless sweep [that] allows policemen, prosecutors, and juries to pursue their personal predilections. (358)

And, quoting from an old case (*U.S. v. Reese* 1875), the Court in *Lawson* elaborated further on the choice to give priority to controlling arbitrary and discriminatory enforcement:

> It would certainly be dangerous if the legislature could set a net large enough to catch all possible offenders, and leave it to the courts to step inside and say who could be rightfully detained, and who should be set at large. This would, to some extent, substitute the judicial for the legislative department of government. (221)

Giving priority to controlling law enforcement is more realistic than giving fair notice to hypothetical reasonable, ordinary people. Police officers and prosecutors are more likely to read what's in the criminal statutes and know about the cases that interpret them. So it makes sense for courts to ask whether statutes clearly indicate to ordinary police officers and prosecutors what the law prohibits. Inquiries that seem "wrongheaded" when they're directed at guaranteeing fair notice to ordinary noncriminal justice experts become reasonable when they're examined to decide whether they're clear enough to limit arbitrary and discriminatory enforcement (Batey 1997, 6–7).

LO4 DEFINING VAGUENESS

Whether the emphasis is on notice to individuals or control of officials, the void-for-vagueness doctrine can never cure the uncertainty present in all laws. Why? "Condemned to the use of words, we can never expect mathematical certainty from our language" (U.S. Supreme Court Justice Thurgood Marshall, *Grayned v. City of Rockford* 1972, 110). It's not just the natural uncertainty of words that creates problems. It's also because the variety of human behavior and the limits of human imagination make it impossible to predict all the variations that might arise under the statutes. So, courts allow considerable leeway in the degree of certainty required to pass the two prongs of fair warning and avoidance of arbitrary law enforcement.

Furthermore, challengers face a strong presumption that statutes are constitutional. The Ohio Supreme Court summarized the heavy burden of proof challengers have to carry:

> The challenger must show that upon examining the statute, an individual of ordinary intelligence would not understand what he is required to do under the law. Thus, to escape responsibility... [the challenger] must prove that he could not reasonably understand that... [the statute] prohibited the acts in which he engaged.... The party alleging that a statute is unconstitutional must prove this assertion beyond a reasonable doubt. (*State v. Anderson* 1991, 1226–27)

CASE

*In **State v. Metzger** (1982), the Nebraska Supreme Court held that a Lincoln, Nebraska, city ordinance that made it a crime to "commit any indecent, immodest, or filthy act" was void for vagueness.*

Was his act "indecent, immodest, or filthy"?

State v. Metzger

319 N.W.2d 459 (Neb. 1982)

HISTORY

Douglas E. Metzger was convicted in the municipal court of the city of Lincoln, Nebraska, of violating § 9.52.100 of the Lincoln Municipal Code. The District Court, Lancaster County, affirmed the District Court judgment. Metzger appealed to the Nebraska Supreme Court. The Supreme Court reversed and dismissed the District Court's judgment.

KRIVOSHA, CJ.

FACTS

Metzger lived in a garden-level apartment located in Lincoln, Nebraska. A large window in the apartment faces a parking lot that is situated on the north side of the apartment building. At about 7:45 A.M. on April 30, 1981, another resident of the apartment, while parking his automobile in a space directly in front of Metzger's apartment window, observed Metzger standing naked with his arms at his sides in his apartment window for a period of five seconds. The resident testified that he saw Metzger's body from his thighs on up.

The resident called the police department, and two officers arrived at the apartment at about 8:00 A.M. The officers testified that they observed Metzger standing in front of the window eating a bowl of cereal. They testified that Metzger was standing within a foot of the window, and his nude body, from the mid-thigh on up, was visible.

The pertinent portion of § 9.52.100 of the Lincoln Municipal Code, under which Metzger was charged, provides as follows: "It shall be unlawful for any person within the City of Lincoln... to commit any indecent, immodest or filthy act in the presence of any person, or in such a situation that persons passing might ordinarily see the same."

OPINION

The... issue presented to us by this appeal is whether the ordinance, as drafted, is so vague as to be unconstitutional. We believe that it is. Since the ordinance is criminal in nature, it is a fundamental requirement of due process of law that such criminal ordinance be reasonably clear and definite.

The ordinance in question makes it unlawful for anyone to commit any "indecent, immodest or filthy act." We know of no way in which the standards required of a criminal act can be met in those broad, general terms. There may be those few who believe persons of opposite sex holding hands in public are immodest, and certainly more who might believe that kissing in public is immodest. Such acts cannot constitute a crime. Certainly one could find many who would conclude that today's swimming attire found on many beaches or beside many pools is immodest. Yet, the fact

(continues)

(continued)

that it is immodest does not thereby make it illegal, absent some requirement related to the health, safety, or welfare of the community.

The dividing line between what is lawful and what is unlawful in terms of "indecent," "immodest," or "filthy" is simply too broad to satisfy the constitutional requirements of due process. Both lawful and unlawful acts can be embraced within such broad definitions. That cannot be permitted. One is not able to determine in advance what is lawful and what is unlawful. We therefore believe that § 9.52.100 of the Lincoln Municipal Code must be declared invalid. Because the ordinance is therefore declared invalid, the conviction cannot stand.

We do not attempt, in this opinion, to determine whether Metzger's actions in a particular case might not be made unlawful, nor do we intend to encourage such behavior. Indeed, it may be possible that a governmental subdivision using sufficiently definite language could make such an act as committed by Metzger unlawful.

Reversed and dismissed.

DISSENT

BOSLAUGH, J., JOINED BY CLINTON AND HASTINGS, JJ.

The ordinance in question prohibits indecent acts, immodest acts, or filthy acts in the presence of any person. Although the ordinance may be too broad in some respects… the exhibition of his genitals under the circumstances of this case was, clearly, an indecent act. Statutes and ordinances prohibiting indecent exposure generally have been held valid. I do not subscribe to the view that it is only "possible" that such conduct may be prohibited by statute or ordinance.

QUESTIONS

1. State the exact wording of the offense Douglas Metzger was convicted of.
2. List all of Metzger's acts and any other facts relevant to deciding whether he violated the ordinance.
3. State the test the court used to decide whether the ordinance was void for vagueness.
4. According to the majority, why was the ordinance vague?
5. According to the dissent, why was the ordinance clear enough to pass the void-for-vagueness test?
6. In your opinion, was the statute clear to a reasonable person? Back up your answer with the facts and arguments in the excerpt and information from the void-for-vagueness discussion in the text.

LO4 The Rule of Lenity

rule of lenity the requirement of courts to resolve every ambiguity in a criminal statute in favor of the defendant

The **rule of lenity** requires courts to resolve every ambiguity in a criminal statute in favor of the defendant. This "venerable" rule (*U.S. v. R.L.C.* 1992, 305) dates back to 1820, when Chief Justice John Marshall described it as "perhaps not much less old than construction itself," *U.S. v. Wiltberger* 1820, 95). The rule has recently attracted critics who claim that courts don't follow the rule, they either just pay it lip service, or ignore it utterly. So, they say, "Good riddance." However, all seem to agree that courts have rendered the rule "impotent" (Notes 2006, 2420).

narrow lenity rule the requirement of courts to interpret ambiguous statutes in favor of defendants only in the core felony cases and other crimes requiring fault

Not so fast, concludes a careful review of U.S. Supreme Court decisions. The truth is (as so often seems the case) more nuanced. There's really a "new" and improved **narrow lenity rule**. It requires courts to interpret ambiguous statutes in favor of defendants only in the core felony cases and others requiring fault (see Chapters 1 and 4). In other words, the vast majority of cases don't get the benefit of the lenity rule. But, the ones that do get it deserve its protection. You should understand that this is not a rule the Supreme Court has explicitly adopted. However, it's one the reviewer argues urges the Court to create. (2441)

Proving Guilt in Criminal Cases

LO5

The Constitution also limits criminal law and punishment by means of a regime of procedures for proving defendants' guilt. Let's look first at how these procedures apply to proving criminal conduct, and next at how they apply to the defenses of justification and excuse. Then, we look at why the Constitution requires the government to jump these procedure hurdles in proving defendants' guilt, and why it requires defendants to share *some* of the burden for establishing the defenses of justification and excuse.

PROVING CRIMINAL CONDUCT

LO5

In every criminal case, the law requires satisfying the following conditions:

1. Every criminal defendant enjoys the **presumption of innocence**, from the time they're charged with crimes until they're convicted.
2. The prosecution has the **burden of proof** when it comes to the criminal act and intent. Defendants have no *legal* responsibility to cooperate with the government. They may stand in silence refusing to say a word. Prosecutors, judges, and juries can't use their silence against them.

presumption of innocence the prosecution has the burden of proof when it comes to proving the criminal act and intent

burden of proof to have to prove beyond a reasonable doubt "every fact necessary to constitute the crime charged"

proof beyond a reasonable doubt the highest burden of proof in the U.S. Criminal justice system reserved for criminal cases; the prosecution must prove every element of the crime charged to this standard

The government has to prove every element in the crime charged by a level of proof reserved for criminal cases: **proof beyond a reasonable doubt**. In the words of the U.S. Supreme Court, the government has to prove beyond a reasonable doubt "every fact necessary to constitute the crime charged" (*In re Winship* 1970, 363).

The Court in *Winship* offers two reasons for raising the two centuries old *proof beyond a reasonable doubt rule* to constitutional status. Conviction *might* cost defendants their lives, liberty, and property. And, they'll *definitely* face the stigma of a conviction, at least if they're convicted of the core felonies. In other words, in criminal cases, "the law tilts in favor of defendants; it prefers that some guilty go free rather than that innocent should be convicted." (Weinstein and Dewsbury 2006, 167)

This is, of course, the way the criminal law is supposed to operate; the social reality often doesn't match this scenario. In other words, law on the books is not the same as the law in day-to-day action. We have some thought-provoking empirical evidence to support that reality when it comes to proof beyond a reasonable doubt. Judge Jack B. Weinstein, a federal trial judge and his student law clerk Ian Dewsbury commented on some of this research on the reasonable doubt standard. They address the two questions regarding the tilt toward the defendant that proof beyond a reasonable doubt demands:

1. How high should the test of minimum probability be?
2. How can we put the test into words understandable to jurors or judges in trials without juries? (Weinstein and Dewsbury 2006, 167)

They believe that quantification is one way to state the standard: "Requiring a combined descriptive explanation and an explicit percentage would likely work well for thousands of jurors we have observed" (167).

These thousands of jurors represent enormous variations in background that affect their impressions of what the law is and should be, their evaluation of witness credibility, and the weight of the evidence. They should start with the assumption that before they hear any evidence, that there's close to "0% likely that the defendant (out of all the people in the universe) committed the crime charged." In practice, they start with a "considerably higher" (around 50 percent). Furthermore, if they believe there's not enough evidence presented to prove guilt, they'll assume that the defendant must be guilty because the prosecutor and investigators wouldn't have charged the defendant with the crime; the grand jury wouldn't have indicted her; and the judge wouldn't have "started up the machinery of selecting a jury and holding a trial." Also, if they identify with the defendant, a "few will almost certainly believe [he or she] did not commit any crime and is in the dock because of a trumped-up case." Finally, we can't ignore that "prejudice and life experience also cause enormous differences" in what amounts to reasonable doubt. (168)

Judge Weinstein used the following instruction to focus jurors' attention to the high standard of proof required to convict only the guilty and avoid convicting the innocent:

> The burden of proof on the government is beyond a reasonable doubt. Why do we have such a burden? The law prefers to see that guilty persons go free rather than an innocent be convicted.
>
> What is the height of the burden? That will vary. It may depend on your evaluation of the nature of the crime charged, the danger of letting the guilty go free, the great unfairness in convicting the innocent, and other factors you find appropriate. But you may not change the balance to convict on a lesser burden because of the particular gender, age, religion, place of origin, or other personal characteristics of the defendant.
>
> In general we can all agree that convicting the innocent is a great harm that should be avoided. That is why we have a presumption of innocence about which I've talked to you already. It is also one of the reasons why we require proof beyond a reasonable doubt. A reasonable doubt may arise from the evidence, the lack of evidence, or the nature of the evidence. Were I the trier of fact, I would require a probability of guilt of no less than 95%. But it is for you to decide how high the burden should be as long as it is much higher than the highest civil standard—"clear and convincing evidence," which itself is much higher than "more probable than not." (172–73)

affirmative defenses defendants have to "start matters off by putting in some evidence in support" of their defenses of justification and excuse

LO5 PROOF IN JUSTIFICATION AND EXCUSE DEFENSES

The defenses of justification (Chapter 5) and of excuse (Chapter 6) are called **affirmative defenses** because defendants present evidence. Of course, they don't have to present them because of their right not to help the government prove its case. But, to justify or excuse their conduct, they have some burden to help themselves. Affirmative defenses operate like this: Defendants have to "start matters off by putting in some evidence in support" of their justification or excuse (LaFave and Scott 1986).

burden of production to make defendants responsible for presenting evidence in their own justification or excuse defense

burden of persuasion defendants have to prove their justification or excuse defenses by a preponderance of the evidence

preponderance of the evidence more than 50 percent of the evidence proves justification or excuse

We call this the **burden of production**. Why put this burden on defendants? Because "We can assume that those who commit crimes are sane, sober, conscious, and acting freely. It makes sense, therefore, to make defendants responsible for injecting these extraordinary circumstances into the proceedings" (52).

The amount of evidence required "is not great; some credible evidence" is enough. In some jurisdictions, if defendants meet the burden of production, they also have the **burden of persuasion**, meaning they have to prove their defenses by a **preponderance of the evidence**, defined as more than 50 percent. In other jurisdictions, once defendants meet the burden of production, the burden shifts to the government to prove defendants weren't justified or excused (Loewy 1987, 192–204).

THE BILL OF RIGHTS AND THE CRIMINAL LAW

LO6

The ban on *ex post facto* laws, denial of due process, and equal protection of the laws are broad constitutional limits that cover all of criminal law. The Bill of Rights bans defining certain kinds of behavior as criminal. One is the ban on making a crime out of the First Amendment rights to speech, religion, and associations; another is the Second Amendment right to bear arms; and the third is the right to privacy, a right created by the U.S. Supreme Court, from an amalgam of parts of the Bill of Rights. Let's look at these three rights.

Right to "Freedom of Speech"

LO6

"Congress shall make no law abridging the freedom of speech," the First Amendment commands. The U.S. Supreme Court has expanded the ban beyond this already sweeping scope. First, the Court has expanded the meaning of "speech" by holding that the protection of the amendment "does not end with the spoken or written word" (*Texas v. Johnson* 1989, 404). It also includes **expressive conduct**, meaning actions that communicate ideas and feelings. So free speech includes wearing black armbands to protest war; "sitting in" to protest racial segregation; and picketing to support all kinds of causes from abortion to animal rights. It even includes giving money to political candidates.

expressive conduct nonverbal actions that communicate ideas and feelings

Second, although the amendment itself directs its ban only at the U.S. Congress, the U.S. Supreme Court has applied the ban to states since 1925 (*Gitlow v. New York*). Third, the Court has ruled that free speech is a fundamental right, one that enjoys preferred status. This means that the government has to provide more than a rational basis for restricting speech and other forms of expression. It has the much higher burden of proving that a compelling government interest justifies the restrictions.

Despite these broad prohibitions and the heavy burden the government faces in justifying them, the First Amendment doesn't mean you can express yourself anywhere, anytime, on any subject, in any manner. According to the U.S. Supreme Court, there are five categories of expression not protected by the First Amendment:

1. *Obscenity*. Material whose predominant appeal is to nudity, sexual activity, or excretion
2. *Profanity*. Irreverence toward sacred things, particularly the name of God
3. *Libel and slander*. Libels are damages to reputation expressed in print, writing, pictures, or signs; slander damages reputation by spoken words
4. *Fighting words*. Words that are likely to provoke the average person to retaliation and cause a "breach of the peace"
5. *Clear and present danger*. Expression that creates a clear and present danger of an evil, which legislatures have the power to prohibit (*Chaplinsky v. New Hampshire* 1942, 574)

Why doesn't the First Amendment protect these forms of expression? Because they're not an "essential element of any exposition of ideas, and are of such slight value as a step to truth that any benefit that may be derived from them is clearly outweighed by the social interest in order and morality" (*Gitlow v. New York* 1925, 572).

clear and present danger doctrine allows the government to punish words that "produce a clear and present danger of a serious substantive evil that rises far above public inconvenience, annoyance, or unrest"

These exceptions create an opportunity for the government to make these kinds of expression a crime, depending on the manner, time, and place of expression. For example, under the **clear and present danger doctrine**, the government can punish words that "produce a clear and present danger of a serious substantive evil that rises far above public inconvenience, annoyance, or unrest." So the First Amendment didn't save Walter Chaplinsky from conviction under a New Hampshire statute that made it a crime to call anyone an "offensive or derisive name" in public. Chaplinsky had called the marshal of the city of Rochester, New Hampshire, "a God-damned racketeer."

In perhaps the most famous reference to the doctrine, U.S. Supreme Court Justice Oliver Wendell Holmes wrote, "The most stringent protection of free speech would not protect a man in falsely shouting fire in a theatre and causing a panic" (*Schenck v. U.S.* 1919, 52).

void-for-overbreadth doctrine protects speech guaranteed by the First Amendment by invalidating laws written so broadly that the fear of prosecution creates a "chilling effect" that discourages people from exercising that freedom

The most difficult problem in making a crime out of speech and expressive conduct is when laws reach so far they that they include not just expression the Constitution bans but also expression it protects. The Court created the void-for-overbreadth doctrine to invalidate laws written so broadly that the fear of prosecution creates a "chilling effect" that discourages people from exercising their right to free speech. According to the Court, this "chilling effect" on the exercise of the fundamental right to freedom of expression violates the right to liberty guaranteed by the due process clauses of the Fifth and Fourteenth Amendments to the U.S. Constitution.

CASE

*In **Commonwealth v. William P. Johnson and Commonwealth v. Gail M. Johnson (2014),** Gail and William Johnson appealed their conviction of criminal harassment as applied to cyberharassment.*

Is cyberharassment free speech?

Commonwealth v. William P. Johnson and Commonwealth v. Gail M. Johnson

— N.E.3d—, 470 Mass. 300 (2014)

HISTORY

On December 1, 2011, a jury convicted the defendants of criminal harassment and convicted William of making a false report of child abuse. On the harassment charge, William was sentenced to two and one-half years in the house of correction, eighteen months to be served with the balance suspended until December 1, 2014, with probation conditions; on the charge of making a false report of child abuse, he was fined $1,000. Gail was sentenced to two years in the house of correction, six months to be served with the balance suspended until December 1, 2014, with probation conditions, and fined $1,000. We transferred the defendants' appeal to this court on our own motion.

CORDY, J. DELIVERED THE OPINION OF THE COURT, JOINED BY GANTS, C.J., AND SPINA, CORDY, BOTSFORD, DUFFLY, LENK, & HINES, JJ.

This case concerns the constitutionality of the criminal harassment statute, G.L. c. 265, § 43A(*a*), and its application to acts of cyberharassment among others. Specifically, we consider whether a pattern of harassing conduct that includes both communications made directly to the targets of the harassment and false communications made to third parties through Internet postings solely for the purpose of encouraging those parties also to engage in harassing conduct toward the targets can be constitutionally proscribed by the statute. We also consider whether, to the extent that this pattern of conduct includes speech, that speech is protected by the First Amendment to the United States Constitution or is unprotected speech integral to the commission of the crime.

FACTS

The victims, James "Jim" J. Lyons, Jr., and his wife, Bernadette, have lived on the same street as the defendants in Andover since around 2000. In 2003, the defendants acquired a tract of land abutting the Lyonses' property and intended to subdivide and develop it. The Lyonses, along with other neighbors, objected to the proposed development, and years of litigation ensued between the parties. By 2008, the relationship between the families had become strained and communication between them was infrequent.

Gerald Colton, a childhood friend of the Johnsons, did not know the Lyons family prior to 2008. Throughout the 1990s and early 2000s, William hired Colton to work as a handyman on an hourly basis and to identify lots for potential real estate development. If William later developed a lot Colton had identified, Colton would collect a finder's fee. Gerald Colton identified lots for William Johnson by placing his initials next to vacant lots on the sheets of the town of Andover's board of assessors. At trial, Colton admitted that his initials appeared to be next to the lot that later became the focus of litigation between the Johnsons and the Lyonses, but suggested that the initials had been forged.

In either late February or early March, 2008, William telephoned Colton and enlisted him to play a series of "pranks" on Jim. The ideas for these "pranks" were generated in several ways: (1) William would directly instruct Colton or convey ideas through Gail; (2) the Johnsons would provide information about the Lyons family to Colton so that he could use this information to harass them; or (3) the Johnsons would prompt Colton to think of ideas.

Over the course of thirty-five days in late March and early April, 2008, the defendants, directly and through Colton, engaged in a series of acts directed at the Lyons family. The Commonwealth alleged four separate acts of harassment in addition to the false report of child abuse, and Colton was called as its key witness at the trial.

The first alleged act occurred on March 18, 2008, when Colton posted from his computer an advertisement that appeared on the Internet site "Craigslist." The advertisement provided the Lyonses' home telephone number and address and stated that there were free golf carts available at this location on a "first come, first serve" basis. The Lyonses did not own any golf carts and had never used Craigslist. When Bernadette arrived home at 2:30 P.M. that same day, there were strangers in both her driveway and on the street near her home. These individuals informed her about the advertisement and explained that they were looking for golf carts. In total, about thirty to forty people arrived at the Lyonses' house that afternoon, causing Bernadette to be "scared" and "fearful."

When Jim arrived home later that evening, he telephoned the police, as Bernadette was in a state of "uneasiness" and Jim felt the incident was "really unusual" and "bizarre." Andover police Sergeant Chad Cooper responded and advised Jim to contact Craigslist to remove the advertisement and get the Internet Protocol address for the computer that posted it. In Sergeant Cooper's presence, Jim received numerous telephone calls from people inquiring about the golf carts. When William learned that the Craigslist advertisement had been removed, he asked Colton to "put it back up" and Colton complied. After reposting, Colton testified that he and William "laughed" about it and Colton said that he would post another advertisement.

The second alleged act occurred on March 19, when Colton posted a different Craigslist advertisement, selling "my late son's" motorcycle and directing interested parties to call Jim on his cellular telephone after 10 P.M. Colton then told William about the posting. That night, Jim received "non-stop" telephone calls regarding the advertisement, approximately twenty every ten minutes. Sergeant Cooper responded again. These late night calls continued for months after the posting.

The third alleged act occurred one week later on March 26, when Colton sent an electronic mail message (e-mail) to the Lyonses from a fictitious account. The subject of the e-mail read, "It's just a game for me," and the text stated, "Let The Games Begin!" The e-mail contained Jim and Bernadette's personal identifying information, including names, home telephone number and address, social security numbers, e-mail address, bank name and location, and Jim's date of birth and cellular telephone number. At the bottom, the e-mail stated: "Remember, if you aren't miserable, I aint happy! Let's Play." Colton testified that Gail had sent him an e-mail with the Lyonses' personal information.

The following evening, William arrived at Colton's home and told Colton that he wanted to call and "turn [Jim] in." William had a piece of paper with a hotline telephone number written on it and proceeded to use Colton's home telephone to call the Department of Children & Families (DCF) to file a false report alleging child abuse by Jim. William later telephoned Colton to report that a police cruiser and another vehicle were at the Lyonses' home.

(continues)

(continued)

Investigator Carrie Riley of the DCF testified that an after-hours "child abuse hotline" had received a call from someone using fictitious information and reporting that Jim was physically abusing his son. Riley and another investigator arrived at the Lyonses' home at 10:30 P.M. and said they had to examine their son. Jim testified that he and Bernadette were "panicked" and "frightened," but that, acting on the advice of their attorney, he awakened their son and permitted Riley to inspect him. Riley examined his body for marks and bruises. The DCF case was closed as the son denied any abuse and the investigators found no signs of it.

The fourth alleged act occurred on April 3, 2008, when Colton sent another anonymous e-mail to the Lyonses from another fictitious e-mail account. The subject line was "Brian," and the text read, "What have you done James?... or... Why James? You stole the innocence of a young man." Shortly thereafter, Jim received a letter by postal mail purportedly sent from an individual named "Brian." Brian claimed to have worked for Jim when he was fifteen years of age, accused Jim of sexually molesting him as a teenager, and threatened to press charges against him. Colton testified that William told Colton that he had sent the letter. (On cross-examination, Colton acknowledged that, in a 2008 statement, he told police that William showed him a copy of this letter in person while meeting with him somewhere near the Andover office of the Internal Revenue Service, and that, in a 2010 statement, he stated that William had called him and read aloud a "sick letter" that he had already sent to Jim.) Even though the allegations were false, reading the letter was "very tough" and "absolutely alarmed [Jim]."

Throughout this entire time period, Colton consistently kept in contact with both defendants, letting them know what he was doing or had done to the Lyons family. William and Gail acquiesced to Colton's conduct and encouraged him to do more.

OPINION

A criminal conviction under § 43A(*a*) requires proof that "(1) the defendant engaged in a knowing pattern of conduct or speech, or series of acts, on at least three separate occasions; (2) the defendant intended to target the victim with the harassing conduct or speech, or series of acts, on each occasion; (3) the conduct or speech, or series of acts, were of such a nature that they seriously alarmed the victim; (4) the conduct or speech, or series of acts, were of such a nature that they would cause a reasonable person to suffer substantial emotional distress; and (5) the defendant committed the conduct or speech, or series of acts, 'willfully and maliciously'" (citations omitted).

Although this court has previously construed the criminal harassment statute, it has not yet considered its application to the type of conduct at issue here. An analysis of whether the defendants' actions amounted to criminal harassment necessarily includes the consideration whether their conduct satisfied the statutory requirements and whether they engaged in constitutionally protected speech.

1. *Facial challenge*. William argues that § 43A(*a*) is both unconstitutionally overbroad and vague. He contends that the statute is dangerously susceptible of application to constitutionally protected speech and is so vague that it leaves the public uncertain as to the conduct it prohibits. His challenge fails on two accounts.

First, the claim is raised for the first time on appeal, and consequently is waived.

Second, the challenge fails because the statute is neither overbroad nor vague. William bears the burden of showing "'from the text of [the law] and from actual fact'... that substantial overbreadth exists" (citation omitted). As an initial matter, § 43A(*a*) is a statute directed at a course of conduct, rather than speech, "and the conduct it proscribes is 'not necessarily associated with speech.'" In particular, § 43A(*a*) specifically criminalizes "a knowing pattern of *conduct* or series of *acts*... directed at a specific person, which seriously alarms that person and would cause a reasonable person to suffer substantial emotional distress" (emphases added) because § 43A(*a*) "proscribes harassing and intimidating conduct, the statute is not facially invalid under the First Amendment."

Further, as the statute requires both malicious intent on behalf of the perpetrator and substantial harm to the victim, "it is difficult to imagine what constitutionally-protected speech would fall under these statutory prohibitions." Contrary to William's claim, the statutory elements such as "seriously alarms" "are not esoteric or complicated terms devoid of common understanding."

Together the component parts of the statute provide adequate notice and safeguards to prevent its application to protected speech. Contrary to William's claim that the statute leaves it to the hearer of the speech to determine what conduct is criminal, the Commonwealth must prove that a defendant knew he or she was engaged in a pattern of conduct that *intentionally* targeted a victim for the purpose of harassment with acts of such a nature that they would cause a reasonable person to suffer substantial emotional distress. This scienter requirement undermines William's claim that he could be liable under § 43A(*a*) if his actions were accidental and that putative harassers are at the mercy of a hearer's sensitivities. Moreover, William has offered no meaningful evidence to show that the statute has a real and substantial deterrent on protected speech or that it actually denies fair notice of what conduct is proscribed. The required elements are clearly delineated such that § 43A(*a*) leaves no putative harassers wondering what is prohibited. Accordingly, William's facial challenge to § 43A(*a*) fails.

2. *As-applied challenge.* The defendants' as-applied constitutional challenge also fails because the conduct in question was not protected speech, but rather a hybrid of conduct and speech integral to the commission of a crime. Accordingly, § 43A(*a*), as applied to the defendants, does not implicate constitutionally protected speech rights.

The defendants do not claim that creating fictitious Internet postings and sending a letter falsely accusing someone of a crime constitute legal conduct. Their conduct served solely to harass the Lyonses by luring numerous strangers and prompting incessant late-night telephone calls to their home by way of false representations, by overtly and aggressively threatening to misuse their personal identifying information, and by falsely accusing Jim of a serious crime. Where the sole purpose of the defendants' speech was to further their endeavor to intentionally harass the Lyonses, such speech is not protected by the First Amendment. "The [F]irst [A]mendment does not provide a defense to a criminal charge simply because the actor uses words to carry out his illegal purpose." The speech here was "integral to criminal conduct," serving only to implement the defendants' purpose to harass and cause substantial emotional distress to the Lyonses in violation of § 43A(*a*).

The defendants point to no lawful purpose of their "communications"... To the extent that any of the harassing contacts were composed of words, they were used "so close in time and purpose to a substantive evil as to become part of the ultimate crime itself." While the content of the speech in question certainly affected the Lyonses, much of the alarming impact was the product of the frightening number, frequency, and type of harassing contacts with which the defendants bombarded the Lyonses. In these circumstances, the application of § 43A(*a*) to the defendants fully withstands constitutional scrutiny.

Nonetheless, the defendants attempt to argue that they are entitled to a required finding of not guilty on the criminal harassment charge because none of their speech constituted "fighting words" which they contend was the only form of speech punishable at the time of the offense under our interpretation of the statute.... [We have held that]... "any attempt to punish an individual for speech not encompassed within the 'fighting words' doctrine (*or within any other constitutionally unprotected category of speech*) would of course offend our Federal and State Constitutions" (emphasis added).

These well-defined and limited categories of speech "are not protected because they are 'no essential part of any exposition of ideas, and are of such slight social value as a step to truth' that whatever meager benefit that may be derived from them is 'clearly outweighed' by the dangers they pose." Speech integral to criminal conduct is one such longstanding category that is constitutionally unprotected, directly applicable to the defendants' conduct here, and permissibly proscribed by § 43A(*a*). Accordingly, the denial of the defendants' motion for a required finding of not guilty on the basis that they engaged in protected First Amendment activity was not error.

3. *Sufficiency of evidence.* The defendants contend that there was insufficient evidence of their joint venture to criminally harass the victims, arguing that both the "directed at" and "seriously alarms" prongs of the statute were not met. In reviewing the sufficiency of the evidence, we consider the facts in the light most favorable to the Commonwealth, and determine whether any rational trier of fact could have found beyond a reasonable doubt all of the statutory elements.

a. *"Directed at" prong.* Section 43A(*a*) requires that the Commonwealth prove three or more predicate acts of harassment that were "directed at a specific person." The defendants argue that the Craigslist postings (two of the four acts supporting the harassment charge) were not directed at the victims, but were merely directed at the general public. This argument is without merit. As a factual matter, the jury clearly could have concluded that the "directed at" prong was met. While the defendants' methods were indirect, the false information in the Craigslist postings was intended solely to ensure that the victims

(continues)

(continued)

were harassed as a consequence by unwitting third parties contacting them at all hours of the night by telephone and showing up at their home. Essentially, the "sole immediate object" of the false advertisements was to create a marketplace for the guaranteed harassment of the victims.

The defendants… [contend] that statements made to a third party are not speech directed at a specific person. The Craigslist postings were the equivalent of the defendants recruiting others to harass the victims and the victims alone. The causation link is satisfied. The defendants cannot launder their harassment of the Lyons family through the Internet to escape liability.

b. *"Seriously alarms" prong*. Section 43A(*a*) also requires the Commonwealth to prove that the acts of alleged harassment "seriously alarmed" the victims. The serious alarm required under § 43A(*a*) is a "demanding, subjective element of harm" that must be satisfied by a victim's testimony rather than conjecture. Defendants argue that (1) the Commonwealth offered insufficient proof that the victims were seriously alarmed, and (2) the victims did not experience serious alarm separately for each act, as required, rather than cumulatively as the result of the pattern of harassing acts. We disagree with both contentions.

First, the Lyonses' subjective feelings of fear and anxiety were actual (not hypothetical), significant, and well documented at trial. As a general matter, Jim and Bernadette testified that they felt "bombarded," "attacked," and "very frightened" throughout the ordeal. Jim described the thirty-five-day "odyssey" in which the defendants would "torture [them]," stating that he was concerned about the safety of his family and himself: "They attacked my business. They attacked my family. And they tried to take my kids away from me." Bernadette described the situation as "very traumatic," stating that her family was in a "siege mentality where every day something was happening so [they] got afraid."

The Lyonses were sufficiently alarmed to call the police "right away" after the very first harassing act. Jim testified that the second act "stepped it up a notch" and made him feel "terrible," and that the correspondence that he received alleging sexual molestation was "very tough" and "absolutely alarmed" him. The police took notice of and corroborated Jim's testimony that the defendants' conduct took a substantial emotional toll on him.

The Lyonses' testimony of feeling frightened, tortured, and attacked more than meets the "seriously alarms" standard. The victims testified to an abundance of distressing and alarming conduct that amounted to a serious invasion of their emotional tranquility.

The evidence at trial was sufficient to support the verdict rendered by the jury.

Judgments affirmed.

QUESTIONS

1. List the facts relevant to whether Gail and/or William Johnson's were protected by the First Amendment.
2. Summarize the Commonwealth's arguments that the Johnsons' and their friend's conduct was cyberharassment.
3. Summarize the Johnsons' arguments that their conduct was protected speech.
4. In your opinion should it be cyberharassment or an exercise of First Amendment right?

LO6 Right to "Bear Arms"

> A well regulated Militia, being necessary to the security of a free State, the right of the people to keep and bear Arms, shall not be infringed.
>
> —U.S. Constitution, Amendment II

For most of our country's history, the Second Amendment was absent from the Supreme Court's agenda. When arguments based on the amendment reached the Court, they were ineffectual (Cook, Ludwig, and Samaha 2009, 16).

Outside the Court, however, there was a lot of excitement, generated by heated debate between gun rights and gun control activists, and by a booming Second Amendment scholarship produced by a growing number of constitutional law professors and historians. It caught legislators' attention, too. There were even "rumblings" among judges (Cook, Ludwig, and Samaha 2009, 16–17).

Then, in 2008, the U.S. Supreme Court case *District of Columbia v. Heller* became the "first successful Second Amendment challenge in the Court's history—a full 207 years after the Amendment was ratified" (Cook, Ludwig, and Samaha 2009, 17–18). Dick Heller, a D.C. special police officer, is authorized to carry a handgun while he's on duty at the Federal Judicial Center in Washington, D.C. He applied to the D.C. government for a registration certificate for a handgun that he wished to keep at home, to have it operable, and to "carry it about his home in that condition only when necessary for self-defense" (17–18).

The District of Columbia, not friendly to gun rights, as part of its gun control regime had two laws that stood in the way of Heller's application. One banned private citizens from possessing handguns (D.C. Gun Laws 2009, § 7–2502.01). The second required that registered gun owners (namely law enforcement officers), while at home, had to "keep any firearm in his possession unloaded and disassembled or bound by a trigger lock or similar device unless such firearm is kept at his place of business, or while being used for lawful recreational purposes within the District of Columbia" (§ 7-2507.02).

The D.C. government denied Heller's application. Heller filed suit in the U.S. District Court for the District of Columbia seeking, on Second Amendment grounds, an order to stop the D.C. government from:

1. enforcing the ban on registering handguns;
2. the licensing requirement insofar as it prohibits the carrying of a firearm in the home without a license; and
3. the trigger-lock requirement insofar as it prohibits the use of "functional firearms within the home." (*District of Columbia v. Heller* 2008, 2788)

The U.S. District Court dismissed Heller's complaint. The Court of Appeals for the D.C. Circuit reversed. The District of Columbia appealed, and the U.S. Supreme Court granted certiorari (2788). The Court (5–4) struck down both the D.C. code provision banning the possession of handguns and the one requiring that firearms in the home be kept nonfunctional even when necessary for self-defense. According to the majority, the core of the Second Amendment is "the right of law-abiding, responsible citizens to use arms in defense of hearth and home" (2821). And the two D.C. gun control provisions stand in the way of exercising this right.

Second Amendment "the right of law-abiding, responsible citizens to use arms in defense of hearth and home"

> The American people have considered the handgun to be the quintessential self-defense weapon. There are many reasons that a citizen may prefer a handgun for home defense: It is easier to store in a location that is readily accessible in an emergency; it cannot easily be redirected or wrestled away by an attacker; it is easier to use for those without the upper-body strength to lift and aim a long gun; it can be pointed at a burglar with one hand while the other hand dials the police. Whatever the reason, handguns are the most popular weapon chosen by Americans for self-defense in the home, and a complete prohibition of their use is invalid (2818).
>
> We must also address the District's requirement that firearms in the home be rendered and kept inoperable at all times. This makes it impossible for citizens to use them for the core lawful purpose of self-defense and is hence unconstitutional (2818).

After the decision, there was lots of ballyhooing about the triumph of the individual right to carry handguns. But the decision applied only to the District of Columbia, not to state and local governments. Two years later, in *McDonald v. City of Chicago* (2010), the Court made clear that the right recognized in *Heller* fully applied to state and local governments. *McDonald* (5–4) struck down a Chicago ordinance which mostly mimicked the D.C. ordinance.

According to the majority, "Like most rights, the right secured by the Second Amendment is not unlimited.... The right [is] not a right to keep and carry any weapon whatsoever in any manner whatsoever and for whatever purpose" (2816–17). It then provided a list of "presumptively lawful" examples, which it made clear was not "exhaustive." Here's the list:

1. Carrying concealed weapons
2. Felons possessing firearms
3. Mentally ill persons possessing firearms
4. Carrying firearms in sensitive places such as schools and government buildings
5. Laws imposing conditions and qualifications on the commercial sale of arms
6. Laws banning "dangerous and unusual weapons" not in common use, such as M-16 rifles and firearms used in the military (2817)
7. Laws that regulate "storage of firearms to prevent accidents" (2819–20)

Despite all the talk about limits, *Heller* is still an important decision for at least three reasons. First, it renders the first clause in the Second Amendment irrelevant: "A well regulated Militia, being necessary to the security of a free State...." Second, it doesn't rule out expanding the right beyond the narrow boundaries of *Heller* and *McDonald*. Third, and extremely important, it's a "litigation magnet" (Cook, Ludwig, and Samaha 2009, 22), largely because, "unfortunately, the [U.S. Supreme] Court declined to 'undertake an exhaustive historical analysis'... of the full scope of the Second Amendment" (*GeorgiaCarry.Org, Inc, v. Georgia* 2011, 1313).

Now 10 years out, the evidence points strongly to the lower courts as becoming ever more rapidly growing litigation magnets. The Law Center to Prevent Gun Violence, which tracks all Second Amendment court challenges to federal, state, and local gun laws, examined 900 federal and state cases after *Heller* until November 2012. (In November 2011, the number was 300.) The "Post-*Heller* lower court landscape" looks pretty much like "a flood of overwhelmingly unsuccessful challenges to federal, state, and local gun laws" (Law Center to Prevent Gun Violence 2014, 2). Let's look at the main points of the case outcomes. All these challenges arise because the Court in *Heller* and *MacDonald* didn't answer many questions about how the courts should flesh out the meaning of the right. For example, the Court didn't decide if, and if so how far does, the right extends outside the home. All we know from these cases is "Second Amendment rights are at their zenith within the home. What we do not know is the scope of that right beyond the home and the standards for determining" when and whether gun laws can regulate them (*Wollard v. Gallagher* 2013, 874). As of now, the most common approach is a two-pronged inquiry:

1. First, Does the challenged law "impose a burden on conduct falling within the Second Amendment's guarantee?" The answer frequently depends on history, namely whether "the conduct was understood to be within the scope of the right at the time of ratification." (*U.S. v. Chester* 2010, 680). If it wasn't, then the regulation is valid, and there's no need to proceed to the second question. (For the Supreme Court's list of "presumptively lawful" regulations, see above.)
2. Second, If it does impose a burden, is the burden "reasonably adapted to a substantial governmental interest?"

In our next court excerpt, the U.S. Fourth Circuit Court of Appeals reversed a Maryland state court decision striking down a Maryland statute that required gun permit applicants to demonstrate "a good and substantial reason to wear, carry, or transport a handgun as a reasonable precaution against apprehended danger."

CASE

*In **Woollard v. Gallagher (2013),** Raymond Woollard, a handgun owner, and a Second Amendment advocacy group sued state officials, alleging that Maryland's "good and substantial reason" for issuing a handgun violated the Second Amendment.*

Does the "good and substantial reason" requirement violate the Second Amendment?

Woollard v. Gallagher

712 F.3d 865 (2013, 4th Circuit Maryland)

HISTORY

Raymond Woollard, a handgun owner, and a Second Amendment advocacy group brought an action against state officials, alleging Maryland's requirement that an applicant demonstrate "good and substantial reason" for the issuance of a handgun permit violated the Second Amendment. The U.S. District Court for the District of Maryland granted the plaintiffs' motion and denied defendants' motion for summary judgment. The Defendants appealed. The U.S Fourth Circuit Court of Appeals reversed.

Judge KING wrote the opinion, in which Judge DAVIS and Judge DIAZ joined.

KING, CJ.

FACTS

On Christmas Eve, 2002, Woollard was at home with his wife, children, and grandchildren when an intruder shattered a window and broke into the house. The intruder was Kris Lee Abbott, Woollard's son-in-law. Abbott, who was high on drugs and intent on driving into Baltimore city to buy more, was looking for his wife's car keys. Woollard grabbed a shotgun and trained it on Abbott, but Abbott wrested the shotgun away. Woollard's son restored order by pointing a second gun at Abbott. Woollard's wife called the police, who took two-and-a-half hours to arrive.

Abbott, the son-in-law, received a sentence of probation for the Christmas Eve 2002 incident, but was subsequently incarcerated for probation violations. Woollard's 2006 permit renewal came shortly after Abbott was released from prison. In 2009, however, the Secretary (via the Handgun Permit Unit) and the Handgun Permit Review Board refused Woollard a second renewal because he failed to satisfy the good-and-substantial-reason requirement.

The Handgun Permit Review Board's decision of November 12, 2009, reflected that Woollard proffered solely the Christmas Eve 2002 incident in support of his request for a second renewal—i.e., as evidence that such a renewal was necessary as a reasonable precaution against apprehended danger—though he acknowledged that he had "not had any contact with his son-in-law in the seven years since the 2002 incident."

The decision also observed that, despite being advised that such proof was required in the circumstances of his renewal application, Woollard did not "submit documented threats or incidents that had occurred in the last three years," nor did he provide "documentation to verify threats occurring beyond his residence, where he can already legally carry a handgun." Accordingly, the Permit Review Board concluded that Woollard had "not demonstrated a good and substantial reason to wear, carry, or transport a handgun as a reasonable precaution against apprehended danger," and upheld the Permit Unit's denial of a second permit renewal. Instead of employing the state court appeal process provided by Maryland law, Woollard elected to join with Appellee Second Amendment Foundation in this federal action, challenging the constitutionality of the good-and-substantial-reason requirement and asserting jurisdiction under 28 U.S.C. §§ 1331 and 1343.

Under its permitting scheme, Maryland obliges "a person to have a permit issued before the person carries,

(continues)

(continued)

wears, or transports a handgun." (Md. Code Ann., Pub. Safety § 5-303). Such permits are not needed, however, by persons in numerous specified situations, including those who are wearing, carrying, and transporting handguns in their own homes and businesses or on other real estate that they own or lease.

Where a permit is mandated, a permitless person risks criminal penalties by "wear[ing], carry[ing], or transport[ing] a handgun, whether concealed or open, on or about the person" or "in a vehicle." Those penalties begin with imprisonment for a term of thirty days to three years, or a fine of $250 to $2500, or both.

...

In the present case, although the district court acknowledged "that one should venture into the unmapped reaches of Second Amendment jurisprudence 'only upon necessity and only then by small degree,'" the district court concluded that the individual right to possess and carry weapons for self-defense is not limited to the home.

We now know, in the wake of the Supreme Court's decision in *District of Columbia v. Heller*, that the Second Amendment guarantees the right of individuals to keep and bear arms for the purpose of self-defense. *Heller*, however, was principally concerned with the "core protection" of the Second Amendment: "the right of law-abiding, responsible citizens to use arms in defense of hearth and home." The *Heller* Court concluded that the District of Columbia's outright ban on the possession of an operable handgun in the home—proscribing "the most preferred firearm in the nation to keep and use for protection of one's home and family"—would fail to pass muster "under any of the standards of scrutiny that we have applied to enumerated constitutional rights." Otherwise, the Court recognized that "the right secured by the Second Amendment is not unlimited" and listed examples of "presumptively lawful regulatory measures," but declined to "clarify the entire field" of Second Amendment jurisprudence.

Two years after issuing its *Heller* decision, in *McDonald v. City of Chicago*, the Supreme Court recognized that "the Second Amendment right is fully applicable to the States," and reiterated *Heller's* holding "that the Second Amendment protects the right to possess a handgun in the home for the purpose of self-defense." Accordingly, a considerable degree of uncertainty remains as to the scope of the *Heller* right beyond the home and the standards for determining whether and how the right can be burdened by governmental regulation. What we know from *Heller* and *McDonald* is that Second Amendment guarantees are at their zenith within the home. What we do not know is the scope of that right beyond the home and the standards for determining when and how the right can be regulated by a government."

Like several of our sister circuits, we have found that a two-part approach to Second Amendment claims seems appropriate under *Heller*. Pursuant to our two-part *Chester* inquiry,

> [t]he first question is whether the challenged law imposes a burden on conduct falling within the scope of the Second Amendment's guarantee. This historical inquiry seeks to determine whether the conduct at issue was understood to be within the scope of the right at the time of ratification. If it was not, then the challenged law is valid. If the challenged regulation burdens conduct that was within the scope of the Second Amendment as historically understood, then we move to the second step of applying an appropriate form of means–end scrutiny.

Although the Supreme Court's cases applying the Second Amendment have arisen only in connection with prohibitions on the possession of firearms in the home, the Court's analysis suggests that the Amendment must have *some* application in the very different context of the public possession of firearms. Our analysis proceeds on this assumption." A handful of courts—most prominently the Seventh Circuit—have declared outright that the *Heller* right extends beyond the home. Other courts have ruled to the contrary, concluding that the *Heller* right is confined to the home. Notably, Maryland's highest court falls within the latter category.

We hew to a judicious course today, refraining from any assessment of whether Maryland's good-and-substantial-reason requirement for obtaining a handgun permit implicates Second Amendment protections. That is, we merely assume that the *Heller* right exists outside the home and that such right of

Appellee Woollard has been infringed. We are free to make that assumption because the good-and-substantial-reason requirement passes constitutional muster under what we have deemed to be the applicable standard—intermediate scrutiny.

...Intermediate scrutiny applies to laws that burden any right to keep and bear arms outside of the home. We assume that any law that would burden the fundamental, core right of self-defense in the home by a law-abiding citizen would be subject to strict scrutiny. But, as we move outside the home, firearm rights have always been more limited, because public safety interests often outweigh individual interests in self-defense. Because our tradition so clearly indicates a substantial role for state regulation of the carrying of firearms in public, we conclude that intermediate scrutiny is appropriate in this case.

The State has satisfied the intermediate scrutiny standard, in that it has demonstrated that the good-and-substantial-reason requirement for obtaining a Maryland handgun permit, as applied to Woollard, "is reasonably adapted to a substantial governmental interest."

We begin with the issue of whether the governmental interest asserted by the State constitutes a "substantial" one. The State explains that, by enacting the handgun permitting scheme, including the good-and-substantial-reason requirement, the General Assembly endeavored to serve Maryland's concomitant interests in protecting public safety and preventing crime—particularly violent crime committed with handguns. Such purpose is reflected in codified legislative findings that

1. the number of violent crimes committed in the State has increased alarmingly in recent years;
2. a high percentage of violent crimes committed in the State involves the use of handguns;
3. the result is a substantial increase in the number of deaths and injuries largely traceable to the carrying of handguns in public places by criminals;
4. current law has not been effective in curbing the more frequent use of handguns in committing crime; and
5. additional regulations on the wearing, carrying, and transporting of handguns are necessary to preserve the peace and tranquility of the State and to protect the rights and liberties of the public.

In these circumstances, we can easily appreciate Maryland's impetus to enact measures aimed at protecting public safety and preventing crime, and we readily conclude that such objectives are substantial governmental interests.

We thus turn to the question of whether the good-and-substantial-reason requirement, as applied to Appellee Woollard, is "reasonably adapted" to Maryland's significant interests. That is, we must decide if the State has demonstrated that there is a "reasonable fit" between the good-and-substantial-reason requirement and the governmental objectives of protecting public safety and preventing crime. Importantly, the State must show a fit that is "reasonable, not perfect." That test is satisfied if Maryland's interests are "substantially served by enforcement of the" good-and-substantial-reason requirement. There is no necessity either that the good-and-substantial-reason requirement "be the least intrusive means of achieving the relevant government objectives, or that there be no burden whatsoever on" Woollard's Second Amendment right.

The State has clearly demonstrated that the good-and-substantial-reason requirement advances the objectives of protecting public safety and preventing crime because it reduces the number of handguns carried in public. That is, limiting the public carrying of handguns protects citizens and inhibits crime by, inter alia:

- Decreasing the availability of handguns to criminals via theft (criminals often target victims "*precisely because* they possess handguns." "Criminals in Maryland are constantly looking for ways to arm themselves with handguns, including by stealing them from others. It is not uncommon for criminals to obtain these guns during street altercations."
- Lessening "the likelihood that basic confrontations between individuals would turn deadly." Incidents such as bar fights and road rage that now often end with people upset, but not lethally wounded, take on deadly implications when handguns are involved;
- Averting the confusion, along with the "potentially tragic consequences" that can result from the presence of a third person with a handgun during a confrontation between a police officer and a criminal suspect. Civilians without

(continues)

(continued)

sufficient training to use and maintain control of their weapons, particularly under tense circumstances, pose a danger to officers and other civilians;

- Curtailing the presence of handguns during routine police–citizen encounters ("If the number of legal handguns on the streets increased significantly, [police] officers would have no choice but to take extra precautions before engaging citizens, effectively treating encounters between police and the community that now are routine, friendly, and trusting, as high-risk stops, which demand a much more rigid protocol and a strategic approach.");
- Reducing the number of "handgun sightings" that must be investigated, *id.* ("Increasing the number of people legally carrying handguns in the streets will also force [police] officers to spend more resources responding to reports about handgun sightings and engaging handgun carriers to ensure they are doing so lawfully."); and
- Facilitating the identification of those persons carrying handguns who pose a menace, *id.* at 113 ("Police officers would also have a harder time identifying potential security risks if more people without good and substantial reason to carry a handgun were able to do so, making it more difficult to respond when necessary.").

At the same time that it reduces the number of handguns carried in public, however, the good-and-substantial-reason requirement ensures that those persons in palpable need of self-protection can arm themselves in public places where Maryland's various permit exceptions do not apply. Consequently, according to the State, the good-and-substantial-reason requirement "strikes a proper balance between ensuring access to handgun permits for those who need them while preventing a greater-than-necessary proliferation of handguns in public places that... increases risks to public safety."

We are convinced by the State's evidence that there is a reasonable fit between the good-and-substantial-reason requirement and Maryland's objectives of protecting public safety and preventing crime.

The good-and-substantial-reason requirement was inappropriately condemned by the district court for being a "rationing system," that "does no more to combat [threats to public safety] than would a law indiscriminately limiting the issuance of a permit to every tenth applicant." The court pointed out, inter alia, that the good-and-substantial-reason requirement "will not prevent those who meet it from having their guns taken from them." But we cannot substitute those views for the considered judgment of the General Assembly that the good-and-substantial-reason requirement strikes an appropriate balance between granting handgun permits to those persons known to be in need of self-protection and precluding a dangerous proliferation of handguns on the streets of Maryland. The duty of the courts is to ensure that the legislature's policy choice substantially serves a significant governmental interest. That is, the courts must be satisfied that there is a reasonable fit between the legislative policy choice and the governmental objective. Intermediate scrutiny does not require a perfect fit; rather only a reasonable one.

In summary, although we assume that Appellee Woollard's Second Amendment right is burdened by the good-and-substantial-reason requirement, we further conclude that such burden is constitutionally permissible. That is, under the applicable intermediate scrutiny standard, the State has demonstrated that the good-and-substantial-reason requirement is reasonably adapted to Maryland's significant interests in protecting public safety and preventing crime.

QUESTIONS

1. Summarize the facts relevant to deciding whether Maryland's "good-and-substantial-reason requirement" violates the Second Amendment.
2. Summarize Raymond Woollard's arguments that the requirement violated his Second Amendment rights.
3. Summarize the Court's arguments upholding the requirement against Woollard's challenge.
4. In your opinion, is the good-and-substantial-reason requirement "reasonably adapted to a substantial governmental interest"? Defend your answer.

THE RIGHT TO PRIVACY

LO6

Unlike the rights to free speech and to bear arms, which are spelled out clearly in the First and Second Amendments, you won't find the word "privacy" anywhere in the U.S. Constitution. Nevertheless, the U.S. Supreme Court has decided there is a **constitutional right to privacy**, a right that bans "all governmental invasions of the sanctity of a man's home and the privacies of life" (*Griswold v. Connecticut* 1965, 484).

constitutional right to privacy a right that bans "all governmental invasions of the sanctity of a man's home and the privacies of life"

fundamental right to privacy a right that requires the government to prove that a compelling interest justifies invading it

Not only is privacy a constitutional right, it's a fundamental right that requires the government to prove that a compelling interest justifies invading it. According to the Court (*Griswold v. Connecticut* 1965), the **fundamental right to privacy** originates in six amendments to the U.S. Constitution:

- The First Amendment rights of free speech, religion, and association
- The Third Amendment ban on the quartering of soldiers in private homes
- The Fourth Amendment right to be secure in one's "person, house, papers, and effects" from "unreasonable searches"
- The Ninth Amendment provision that "the enumeration in the Constitution, of certain rights, shall not be construed to deny or disparage others retained by the people"
- The Fifth and Fourteenth Amendments' due process right to liberty

This cluster of amendments sends the implied but strong message that we have the right to be let alone by the government. In the First Amendment, it's our beliefs and expression of them and our associations with other people that are protected from government interference. In the Third and Fourth Amendments, our homes are the object of protection. And, in the Fourth Amendment, it's not only our homes but our bodies, our private papers, and even our "stuff" that fall under its protection. The Ninth, or catchall, Amendment acknowledges we have rights not named in the Constitution. In other words, "specific guarantees in the Bill of Rights have penumbras, formed by emanations from those guarantees that help give them life and substance" (484).

According to the Court, privacy is one of these rights "not named in the Constitution." Based on this right, the Court struck down two Connecticut contraception statutes. The first statute provided:

> Any person who uses any drug, medicinal article or instrument for the purpose of preventing conception shall be fined not less than fifty dollars or imprisoned not less than sixty days nor more than one year or be both fined and imprisoned. (quoted in Griswold, 480)

The second provided:

> Any person who assists, abets, counsels, causes, hires or commands another to commit any offense may be prosecuted and punished as if he were the principal offender.

In several cases after *Griswold*, the Court decided several controversial cases based on the right to privacy (Table 2.1).

TABLE 2.1 The U.S. Supreme Court and the Right to Privacy from *Griswold* to *Lawrence*

CASE	DECISION
Griswold v. Connecticut, 381 U.S. 479 (1965)	Struck down laws (1) making it a crime for married couples to use contraceptives and (2) to counsel couples on birth control
Stanley v. Georgia, 394 U.S. 557 (1969)	Struck down a state law making it a crime for adults to possess pornography in the privacy of their homes
Eisenstadt v. Baird, 405 U.S. 438 (1972)	Invalidated a law banning distribution of contraceptives to unmarried persons
Roe v. Wade, 410 U.S. (1973)	Struck down a law banning abortions
Carey v. Population Services International, 431 U.S. 678 (1977)	Struck down a law banning the use or sale of contraceptive devices to persons under 16
Planned Parenthood v. Casey, 505 U.S. 833 (1991)	Struck down a law requiring a pregnant wife to notify her husband of her intention to abort the fetus
Lawrence v. Texas, 539 U.S.558 (2003)	Struck down a Texas statute making adult consensual same sex sodomy a crime

CASE

In ***Lawrence v. Texas* (2003),** *the U.S. Supreme Court struck down a Texas statute that made homosexual sodomy a crime.*

Do consenting adults have a right to privacy in their private sexual conduct?

Lawrence v. Texas

539 U.S. 558 (2003)

HISTORY

Defendants John Geddes Lawrence and Tyrone Garner were convicted in the County Criminal Court at Law No. 10, Harris County, Texas, of engaging in homosexual conduct. They appealed. On rehearing *en banc*, the Texas Court of Appeals affirmed. Certiorari was granted. The Supreme Court overruled its prior decision in *Bowers v. Hardwick* and held that the Texas statute making it a crime for two persons of the same sex to engage in certain intimate sexual conduct was unconstitutional, as applied to adult males who had engaged in a consensual act of sodomy in the privacy of their home.

KENNEDY, J., JOINED BY STEVENS, SOUTER, GINSBURG, AND BREYER, JJ.

Justice KENNEDY delivered the opinion of the Court.

FACTS

In Houston, Texas, officers of the Harris County Police Department were dispatched to a private residence in response to a reported weapons disturbance. They entered an apartment where one of the petitioners, John Geddes Lawrence, resided. The right of the police to enter does not seem to have been questioned. The officers observed Lawrence and another man, Tyron Garner, engaging in a sexual act. The two petitioners were arrested, held in custody overnight, and charged and convicted before a Justice of the Peace.

The complaints described their crime as "deviate sexual intercourse, namely anal sex, with a member of the same sex (man)." The applicable state law is Tex. Penal Code Ann. § 21.06(a) (2003). It provides: "A person commits an offense if he engages in deviate sexual intercourse with another individual of the same sex." The statute defines "deviate sexual intercourse" as follows:

> "(A) any contact between any part of the genitals of one person and the mouth or anus of another person; or
>
> "(B) the penetration of the genitals or the anus of another person with an object." § 21.01(1).

The petitioners were adults at the time of the alleged offense. Their conduct was in private and consensual.

OPINION

[The opinion is an excerpt taken from the Syllabus of the Court.]

Resolution of this case depends on whether petitioners were free as adults to engage in private conduct in the exercise of their liberty under the Due Process Clause.... Although the laws involved... here purport to do no more than prohibit a particular sexual act, their penalties and purposes have more far-reaching consequences, touching upon the most private human conduct, sexual behavior, and in the most private of places, the home. They seek to control a personal relationship that, whether or not entitled to formal recognition in the law, is within the liberty of persons to choose without being punished as criminals.

The liberty protected by the Constitution allows homosexual persons the right to choose to enter upon relationships in the confines of their homes and their own private lives and still retain their dignity as free persons.

...

The stigma the Texas criminal statute imposes, moreover, is not trivial. Although the offense is but a minor misdemeanor, it remains a criminal offense with all that imports for the dignity of the persons charged, including notation of convictions on their records and on job application forms, and registration as sex offenders under state law. Where a case's foundations have sustained serious erosion, criticism from other sources is of greater significance. In the United States, criticism of Bowers has been substantial and continuing, disapproving of its reasoning in all respects, not just as to its historical assumptions.

...

This case does not involve minors, persons who might be injured or coerced, those who might not easily refuse consent, or public conduct or prostitution. It does involve two adults who, with full and mutual consent, engaged in sexual practices common to a homosexual lifestyle. Petitioners' right to liberty under the Due Process Clause gives them the full right to engage in private conduct without government intervention. The Texas statute furthers no legitimate state interest which can justify its intrusion into the individual's personal and private life.

The judgment of the Court of Appeals for the Texas Fourteenth District is reversed, and the case is remanded for further proceedings not inconsistent with this opinion.

It is so ordered.

CONCURRING OPINION

O'CONNOR, J.

... Rather than relying on the substantive component of the Fourteenth Amendment's Due Process Clause, as the Court does, I base my conclusion on the Fourteenth Amendment's Equal Protection Clause. The Equal Protection Clause of the Fourteenth Amendment "is essentially a direction that all persons similarly situated should be treated alike."...

This case raises... [the] issue... whether, under the Equal Protection Clause, moral disapproval is a legitimate state interest to justify... a statute that bans homosexual sodomy, but not heterosexual sodomy. It is not.... We have never held that moral disapproval, without any other asserted state interest, is a sufficient rationale under the Equal Protection Clause to justify a law that discriminates among groups of persons.

Texas argues, however, that the sodomy law does not discriminate against homosexual persons. Instead, the State maintains that the law discriminates only against homosexual conduct. While it is true that the law applies only to conduct, the conduct targeted by this law is conduct that is closely correlated with being homosexual. Under such circumstances, Texas' sodomy law is targeted at more than conduct. It is instead directed toward gay persons as a class. "After all, there can hardly be more palpable discrimination against a class than making the conduct that defines the class criminal."...

DISSENT

SCALIA, J., JOINED BY REHNQUIST, CJ., AND THOMAS, J.

...Today's opinion is the product of a Court, which is the product of a law-profession culture, that has largely signed on to the so-called homosexual agenda, by which I mean the agenda promoted by some homosexual activists directed at eliminating the moral opprobrium that has traditionally attached to homosexual conduct.... It is clear from this that the Court has taken sides in the culture war, departing

(continues)

(continued)

from its role of assuring, as neutral observer, that the democratic rules of engagement are observed.

Many Americans do not want persons who openly engage in homosexual conduct as partners in their business, as scoutmasters for their children, as teachers in their children's schools, or as boarders in their home. They view this as protecting themselves and their families from a lifestyle that they believe to be immoral and destructive. The Court views it as "discrimination," which it is the function of our judgments to deter. So imbued is the Court with the law profession's anti-homosexual culture, that it is seemingly unaware that the attitudes of that culture are not obviously "mainstream"; that in most States what the Court calls "discrimination" against those who engage in homosexual acts is perfectly legal; that proposals to ban such "discrimination" under Title VII have repeatedly been rejected by Congress.

Let me be clear that I have nothing against homosexuals, or any other group, promoting their agenda through normal democratic means. Social perceptions of sexual and other morality change over time, and every group has the right to persuade its fellow citizens that its view of such matters is the best. That homosexuals have achieved some success in that enterprise is attested to by the fact that Texas is one of the few remaining States that criminalize private, consensual homosexual acts.

But persuading one's fellow citizens is one thing, and imposing one's views in absence of democratic majority will is something else. I would no more require a State to criminalize homosexual acts—or, for that matter, display any moral disapprobation of them—than I would forbid it to do so. What Texas has chosen to do is well within the range of traditional democratic action, and its hand should not be stayed through the invention of a brand-new "constitutional right" by a Court that is impatient of democratic change. It is indeed true that "later generations can see that laws once thought necessary and proper in fact serve only to oppress," and when that happens, later generations can repeal those laws. But it is the premise of our system that those judgments are to be made by the people, and not imposed by a governing caste that knows best.

...

I dissent.

JUSTICE THOMAS, DISSENTING.

I join Justice SCALIA's dissenting opinion. I write separately to note that the law before the Court today "is... uncommonly silly." If I were a member of the Texas Legislature, I would vote to repeal it. Punishing someone for expressing his sexual preference through noncommercial consensual conduct with another adult does not appear to be a worthy way to expend valuable law enforcement resources.

Notwithstanding this, I recognize that as a Member of this Court I am not empowered to help petitioners and others similarly situated. My duty, rather, is to decide cases agreeably to the Constitution and laws of the United States. And, I "can find neither in the Bill of Rights nor any other part of the Constitution a general right of privacy," or as the Court terms it today, the "liberty of the person both in its spatial and more transcendent dimensions."

QUESTIONS

1. State exactly what the Court decided regarding homosexual sodomy.
2. Summarize the majority opinion's argument supporting its decision.
3. Summarize Justice O'Connor's arguments in her concurring opinion.
4. Summarize Justice Scalia's arguments in his dissent.
5. Summarize Justice Thomas's arguments in his dissent.
6. Whose opinion do you support? Defend your answer.

EXPLORING FURTHER

Does the right to privacy protect pornography?

The Right to Privacy

Stanley v. Georgia, 394 U.S. 557 (1969)

FACTS

Federal and state law enforcement agents, armed with a search warrant, searched Eli Stanley's home for evidence of his alleged bookmaking activities. They didn't find evidence of bookmaking, but while they were searching his bedroom, they found three pornographic films. Stanley was charged, indicted, and convicted under a Georgia statute that made it a crime to "knowingly have(ing) possession of… obscene matter…." The Georgia Supreme Court affirmed the conviction. The U.S. Supreme Court reversed.

DECISION

According to the Court:

> Georgia contends that since obscenity is not within the area of constitutionally protected speech or press, the States are free, subject to the limits of other provisions of the Constitution, to deal with it any way deemed necessary, just as they may deal with possession of other things thought to be detrimental to the welfare of their citizens. If the State can protect the body of a citizen, may it not, argues Georgia, protect his mind?…
>
> In the context of this case—a prosecution for mere possession of printed or filmed matter in the privacy of a person's own home—is the… fundamental… right to be free… from unwanted governmental intrusions into one's privacy.
>
> The makers of our Constitution undertook to secure conditions favorable to the pursuit of happiness. They recognized the significance of man's spiritual nature, of his feelings and of his intellect. They knew that only a part of the pain, pleasure and satisfactions of life are to be found in material things. They sought to protect Americans in their beliefs, their thoughts, their emotions and their sensations. They conferred, as against the government, the right to be let alone—the most comprehensive of rights and the right most valued by civilized man. (quoting *Olmstead v. U.S.* [1928] and citing *Griswold v. Connecticut* [1965])

THE CONSTITUTION AND CRIMINAL PUNISHMENT

The Eighth Amendment to the U.S. Constitution commands that "cruel and unusual punishments" shall not be "inflicted." According to the U.S. Supreme Court, there are two kinds of cruel and unusual punishments: "barbaric" punishments and punishments that are disproportionate to the crime committed (*Solem v. Helm* 1983, 284).

LO7

"cruel and unusual punishments" "barbaric" punishments and punishments that are disproportionate to the crime committed

Let's look in turn at the "barbaric" and "disproportionate" dimensions of the Constitution's Eighth Amendment command.

Barbaric Punishments

barbaric punishments punishments considered no longer acceptable to civilized society

Barbaric punishments are punishments that are considered no longer acceptable to civilized society. At the time the Eighth Amendment was adopted, these included burning at the stake, crucifixion, breaking on the wheel, torturing, or lingering death (*In re Kemmler* 1890, 446); drawing and quartering, the rack and screw (*Chambers v. Florida* 1940, 227); and extreme forms of solitary confinement (*In re Medley* 1890, 160).

For more than a hundred years after the adoption of the Bill of Rights, no "cruel and unusual" punishment cases reached the U.S. Supreme Court because these medieval forms of execution weren't used in the United States. But, in 1885, the governor of the state of New York, in his annual message to the legislature, questioned the use of hanging as a method of execution:

> The present mode of executing criminals by hanging has come down to us from the dark ages, and it may well be questioned whether the science of the present day cannot provide a means for taking… life… in a less barbarous manner. (*In re Kemmler* 1890, 444)

The legislature appointed a commission to study the matter. The commission reported that electrocution was "the most humane and practical method [of execution] known to modern science (*In re Kemmler* 1890, 444)." In 1888, the legislature replaced the hangman's noose with the electric chair.

Shortly thereafter, William Kemmler, convicted of murdering his wife and sentenced to die in the electric chair, argued that electrocution was "cruel and unusual punishment." The U.S. Supreme Court disagreed. The Court said that electrocution was certainly unusual but not cruel. For the first time, the Court defined what "cruel" means in the Eighth Amendment. According to the Court, punishment by death isn't cruel as long as it isn't "something more than the mere extinguishment of life."

The Court spelled out what it meant by this phrase: First, death has to be both instantaneous and painless. Second, it can't involve unnecessary mutilation of the body. So, according to the Court, beheading is cruel because it mutilates the body. Crucifixion is doubly cruel because it inflicts a "lingering" death and mutilates the body (*In re Kemmler* 1890, 446–47).

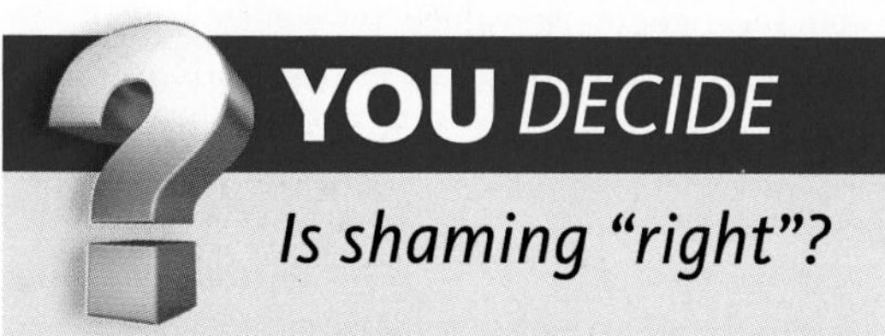

Is shaming "right"?

Shawn Gementera pilfered letters from several mailboxes along San Francisco's Fulton Street on May 21, 2001. A police officer who observed the episode immediately detained Gementera and his partner in crime, Andrew Choi, who had been stuffing the stolen letters into his jacket as Gementera anxiously kept watch. After indictment, Gementera entered a plea agreement pursuant to which he pled guilty to mail theft, and the government dismissed a second count of receiving a stolen U.S. Treasury check.

The offense was not Gementera's first encounter with the law. Though only twenty-four years old at the time, Gementera's criminal history was lengthy for a man of his relative youth, and it was growing steadily more serious. At age nineteen, he was convicted of misdemeanor criminal mischief. He was twice convicted at age twenty of driving with a suspended license. At age twenty-two, a domestic dispute led to convictions for driving with a suspended license and for failing to provide proof of financial responsibility. By age twenty-four, there was a conviction for misdemeanor battery. Other arrests and citations included possession of drug paraphernalia, additional driving offenses (most of which involved driving on a license suspended for his failure to take chemical tests), and, soon after his twenty-fifth birthday, taking a vehicle without the owner's consent.

On February 25, 2003, Judge Vaughn Walker of the United States District Court for the Northern District of California sentenced Gementera. The U.S. Sentencing Guidelines range was two to eight months' incarceration; Judge Walker sentenced Gementera to the lower bound of the range, imposing two months' incarceration and three years' supervised release. The court explained that, while it would have been strongly inclined to impose home confinement had Gementera's criminal history been better, the court felt that "given the unpromising road that the defendant has been following, that he needs to have a taste of federal custody, to be sure a brief one, but he needs to understand that if he continues on the course that he has set for himself at his age he's going to be facing a lot more serious charges in the future."

He also imposed conditions of supervised release. One such condition required Gementera to "perform 100 hours of community service," to consist of "standing in front of a postal facility in the city and county of San Francisco with a sandwich board which in large letters declares: 'I stole mail. This is my punishment.'"

"Gementera later filed a motion to correct the sentence by removing the sandwich board condition. Judge Walker modified the sentence after inviting both parties to present "an alternative form or forms of public service that would better comport with the aims of the court." In lieu of the 100-hour signboard requirement, the district court imposed a four-part special condition. Three new terms, proposed jointly by counsel, mandated that the defendant observe postal patrons visiting the "lost or missing mail" window, write letters of apology to any identifiable victims of his crime, and deliver several lectures at a local school. It also included a scaled-down version of the signboard requirement:

> The defendant shall perform 1 day of 8 total hours of community service during which time he shall either (i) wear a two-sided sandwich board-style sign or (ii) carry a large two-sided sign stating, "I stole mail; this is my punishment," in front of a San Francisco postal facility identified by the probation officer. For the safety of defendant and general public, the postal facility designated shall be one that employs one or more security guards. Upon showing by defendant that this condition would likely impose upon defendant psychological harm or effect or result in unwarranted risk of harm to defendant, the public or postal employees, the probation officer may withdraw or modify this condition or apply to the court to withdraw or modify this condition.

Gementera was ordered to surrender on March 31, 2003. On March 12, 2003, prior to his surrender, Gementera was arrested for possession of stolen mail.

Questions

Assume you're an advisor to the Criminal Law Committee in the California state legislature, which is considering legislation banning "shaming" punishments for selected crimes. You're asked to write a memorandum for the committee that answers the following questions and then recommends what, if any, legislation the committee should draft:

1. Do shaming punishments violate the Eighth Amendment ban on "cruel and unusual punishments"?
2. Assuming they don't, are they wise public policy? According to the dissent in *U.S. v. Gementera* (2004), "A fair measure of a civilized society is how its institutions behave in the space between what it may have the power to do and what it should do."
3. Recommend what, if any, legislation the committee should enact.
4. To prepare the memorandum, read the following:
   - *U.S. v. Gementera* (2004) (http://law.justia.com/cases/federal/appellate-courts/F3/379/596/475040/)
   - "Shame on You: Enough with Humiliating Punishments" by Jonathan Turley (http://www.washingtonpost.com/wp-dyn/content/article/2005/09/17/AR2005091700064.html)
   - "Can Shaming Punishments Educate?" by Stephen Garvey (http://scholarship.law.cornell.edu/cgi/viewcontent.cgi?article=1345&context=facpub)

Sources: *U.S. v. Gementera*, 379 F.3d 596 (2004); Turley 2005; Garvey 1998.

Disproportionate Punishments

principle of proportionality the punishment has to fit the crime

The principle of proportionality—namely, that the punishment should fit the crime—has an ancient history (see Chapter 1). The U.S. Supreme Court first applied proportionality as a principle required by the Eighth Amendment in *Weems v. U.S.* (1910). Paul Weems was convicted of falsifying a public document. The trial court first sentenced him to fifteen years in prison at hard labor in chains and then took away all of his civil rights for the rest of his life. The Court ruled that the punishment was "cruel and unusual" because it was disproportionate to his crime. *Weems* banned disproportionate punishments in federal criminal justice.

In extending the cruel and unusual punishment ban to state criminal justice in the 1960s, the Court in *Robinson v. California* (1962) reaffirmed its commitment to the proportionality principle. The Court majority ruled that a 90-day sentence for drug addiction was disproportionate because addiction is an illness, and it's cruel and unusual to punish persons for being sick. "Even one day in prison would be a cruel and unusual punishment for the 'crime' of having a common cold," wrote Justice Marshall for the Court majority (Chapter 3).

Let's look at the issues surrounding whether some modern forms of punishment are proportional punishments.

LO7 THE DEATH PENALTY: "DEATH IS DIFFERENT"

A majority of the U.S. Supreme Court has consistently agreed that the proportionality principle applies to death penalty cases. As the Court puts it, "death is different." There are numerous capital crimes where no one is killed; they include treason, espionage, kidnapping, aircraft hijacking, large-scale drug trafficking, train wrecking, and perjury that leads to someone's execution (Liptak 2003).

In practice, no one is actually sentenced to death for them, so it's difficult to tell whether the Court would rule that death is disproportionate to a crime where no one gets killed. With one exception—rape. In 1977, the Court heard *Coker v. Georgia*; it decided that death was disproportionate punishment for raping an adult woman.

In fact, it looked as if a majority of the Court was committed to the proposition that death is *always* disproportionate, except in some aggravated murders. That proposition held, but barely, in a bitterly contested case that reached the Court in 2008. In that case, our next case excerpt, the Court decided (5–4) that executing Patrick Kennedy was "cruel and unusual punishment" because it was disproportionate to his rape of his eight-year-old stepdaughter.

CASE

In ***Kennedy v. Louisiana*** **(2008),** *the Court decided that executing Patrick Kennedy was "cruel and unusual punishment" because it was disproportionate to his rape of his eight-year-old stepdaughter.*

Is the death penalty for child rape cruel and unusual?

Kennedy v. Louisiana

554 U.S. 407 (2008)

HISTORY

Patrick Kennedy was convicted of the aggravated rape of his eight-year-old stepdaughter under a Louisiana statute that authorized capital punishment for the rape of a child under 12 years of age and was sentenced to death. On his appeal, the Supreme Court of Louisiana affirmed. Kennedy petitioned for certiorari, which was granted. The U.S. Supreme Court reversed and remanded.

KENNEDY. J., JOINED BY STEVENS, SOUTER, GINSBURG, AND BREYER, JJ.

FACTS

At 9:18 A.M. on March 2, 1998, Patrick Kennedy called 911 to report that his stepdaughter, L. H., had been raped. When police arrived at Kennedy's home between 9:20 and 9:30 A.M., they found L. H. on her bed, wearing a T-shirt and wrapped in a bloody blanket. She was bleeding profusely from the vaginal area. Kennedy told police he had carried her from the yard to the bathtub and then to the bed. Once in the bedroom, Kennedy had used a basin of water and a cloth to wipe blood from the victim.

L. H. was transported to the Children's Hospital. An expert in pediatric forensic medicine testified that L. H.'s injuries were the most severe he had seen from a sexual assault in his four years of practice. A laceration to the left wall of the vagina had separated her cervix from the back of her vagina, causing her rectum to protrude into the vaginal structure. Her entire perineum was torn from the posterior fourchette to the anus. The injuries required emergency surgery.

At the scene of the crime, at the hospital, and in the first weeks that followed, both L. H. and Kennedy maintained in their accounts to investigators that L. H. had been raped by two neighborhood boys. L. H. was interviewed several days after the rape by a psychologist. She told the psychologist that she had been playing in the garage when a boy came over and asked her about Girl Scout cookies she was selling; then that the boy "pulled her by the legs to the backyard," where he placed his hand over her mouth, "pulled down her shorts," and raped her.

Eight days after the crime, and despite L. H.'s insistence that Kennedy was not the offender, Kennedy was arrested for the rape. The state's investigation had drawn the accuracy of Kennedy and L. H.'s story into question. Police found that Kennedy made two telephone calls on the morning of the rape. Sometime before 6:15 A.M., Kennedy called his employer and left a message that he was unavailable to work that day. Kennedy called back between 6:30 and 7:30 A.M. to ask a colleague how to get blood out of a white carpet because his daughter had "just become a young lady." At 7:37 A.M., Kennedy called B & B Carpet Cleaning and requested urgent assistance in removing bloodstains from a carpet. Kennedy did not call 911 until about an hour and a half later.

About a month after Kennedy's arrest, L. H. was removed from the custody of her mother, who had maintained until that point that Kennedy was not involved in the rape. On June 22, 1998, L. H. was returned home and told her mother for the first time that Kennedy had raped her. And on December 16, 1999, about 21 months after the rape, L. H. recorded her accusation in a videotaped interview with the Child Advocacy Center.

The state charged Kennedy with aggravated rape of a child under La. Stat. Ann. § 14:42 (West 1997 and Supp. 1998) and sought the death penalty. According to the statute, "aggravated" applies to anal or vaginal rape without the consent of the victim—when it's committed under any of 10 aggravating circumstances, one of which is when the victim was under 12 years of age at the time of the rape. The penalty for aggravated rape is life in prison at hard labor without parole, probation, or suspension of sentence. But, if the victim is under 12, the prosecutor asks for the death penalty: "The offender shall be punished by death or life imprisonment at hard labor without benefit of parole, probation, or suspension of sentence, in accordance with the determination of the jury."

The trial began in August 2003. L. H. was then 13 years old. She testified that she "woke up one morning and Patrick was on top of her." She remembered Kennedy bringing her "a cup of orange juice and pills chopped up in it" after the rape and overhearing him on the telephone saying she had become a "young lady." L. H. acknowledged that she had accused two neighborhood boys but testified Kennedy told her to say this and that it was untrue.

After the jury found Kennedy guilty of aggravated rape, the penalty phase ensued. The jury unanimously determined that Kennedy should be sentenced to death. The Louisiana Supreme Court affirmed. We granted certiorari.

OPINION

The Eighth Amendment's protection against excessive or cruel and unusual punishments flows from the basic precept of justice that punishment for a crime should be graduated and proportioned to the offense. Whether this requirement has been fulfilled is determined not by the standards that prevailed when the Eighth Amendment was adopted in 1791 but by the norms that currently prevail. The Amendment draws its meaning from the evolving standards of decency that mark the progress of a maturing society.

Capital punishment must be limited to those offenders who commit a narrow category of the most serious crimes and whose extreme culpability makes them the most deserving of execution. In these cases the Court has been guided by objective indicia of society's standards, as expressed in legislative enactments and state practice with respect to executions. Whether the death penalty is disproportionate to the crime committed depends as well upon the standards elaborated by controlling precedents and by the Court's own understanding and interpretation of the Eighth Amendment's text, history, meaning, and purpose.

(continues)

(continued)

The evidence of a national consensus with respect to the death penalty for child rapists, as with respect to juveniles, mentally retarded offenders, and vicarious felony murderers, shows divided opinion but, on balance, an opinion against it. Thirty-seven jurisdictions—36 States plus the Federal Government—have the death penalty. Only six of those jurisdictions authorize the death penalty for rape of a child. Though our review of national consensus is not confined to tallying the number of States with applicable death penalty legislation, it is of significance that, in 45 jurisdictions, Kennedy could not be executed for child rape of any kind.

There are measures of consensus other than legislation. Statistics about the number of executions may inform the consideration whether capital punishment for the crime of child rape is regarded as unacceptable in our society. These statistics confirm our determination from our review of state statutes that there is a social consensus against the death penalty for the crime of child rape.

Louisiana is the only State since 1964 that has sentenced an individual to death for the crime of child rape; and Kennedy and Richard Davis, who was convicted and sentenced to death for the aggravated rape of a 5-year-old child by a Louisiana jury in December 2007, are the only two individuals now on death row in the United States for a nonhomicide offense. After reviewing the authorities informed by contemporary norms, including the history of the death penalty for this and other nonhomicide crimes, current state statutes and new enactments, and the number of executions since 1964, we conclude there is a national consensus against capital punishment for the crime of child rape.

Objective evidence of contemporary values as it relates to punishment for child rape is entitled to great weight, but it does not end our inquiry. It is for us ultimately to judge whether the Eighth Amendment permits imposition of the death penalty. We turn, then, to the resolution of the question before us, which is informed by our precedents and our own understanding of the Constitution and the rights it secures.

It must be acknowledged that there are moral grounds to question a rule barring capital punishment for a crime against an individual that did not result in death. These facts illustrate the point. Here the victim's fright, the sense of betrayal, and the nature of her injuries caused more prolonged physical and mental suffering than, say, a sudden killing by an unseen assassin. The attack was not just on her but on her childhood. Rape has a permanent psychological, emotional, and sometimes physical impact on the child. We cannot dismiss the years of long anguish that must be endured by the victim of child rape.

It does not follow, though, that capital punishment is a proportionate penalty for the crime. The constitutional prohibition against excessive or cruel and unusual punishments mandates that the State's power to punish be exercised within the limits of civilized standards. Evolving standards of decency that mark the progress of a maturing society counsel us to be most hesitant before interpreting the Eighth Amendment to allow the extension of the death penalty, a hesitation that has special force where no life was taken in the commission of the crime.

It is an established principle that decency, in its essence, presumes respect for the individual and thus moderation or restraint in the application of capital punishment. We do not discount the seriousness of rape as a crime. It is highly reprehensible, both in a moral sense and in its almost total contempt for the personal integrity and autonomy of the female victim. Short of homicide, it is the ultimate violation of self. But the murderer kills; the rapist, if no more than that, does not. We have the abiding conviction that the death penalty, which is unique in its severity and irrevocability, is an excessive penalty for the rapist who, as such, does not take human life.

Consistent with evolving standards of decency and the teachings of our precedents we conclude that, in determining whether the death penalty is excessive, there is a distinction between intentional first-degree murder on the one hand and nonhomicide crimes against individual persons, even including child rape, on the other. The latter crimes may be devastating in their harm, as here, but in terms of moral depravity and of the injury to the person and to the public, they cannot be compared to murder in their severity and irrevocability.

The judgment of the Supreme Court of Louisiana upholding the capital sentence is reversed. This case is remanded for further proceedings not inconsistent with this opinion.

It is so ordered.

DISSENT

ALITO, J., JOINED BY ROBERTS, CJ., SCALIA AND THOMAS JJ.

The Court today holds that the Eighth Amendment categorically prohibits the imposition of the death penalty for the crime of raping a child. This is so, according to the Court, no matter how young the child, no matter how many times the child is raped, no matter how many children the perpetrator rapes, no matter how sadistic the crime, no matter how much physical or psychological trauma is inflicted, and no matter how heinous the perpetrator's prior criminal record may be. The Court provides two reasons for this sweeping conclusion: First, the Court claims to have identified "a national consensus" that the death penalty is never acceptable for the rape of a child; second, the Court concludes, based on its "independent judgment," that imposing the death penalty for child rape is inconsistent with "the evolving standards of decency that mark the progress of a maturing society." Because neither of these justifications is sound, I respectfully dissent.

I turn first to the Court's claim that there is "a national consensus" that it is never acceptable to impose the death penalty for the rape of a child. I believe that the "objective indicia" of our society's "evolving standards of decency" can be fairly summarized as follows. Neither Congress nor juries have done anything that can plausibly be interpreted as evidencing the "national consensus" that the Court perceives. State legislatures, for more than 30 years, have operated under the ominous shadow of the *Coker* dicta [cruel and unusual punishment to execute a man for raping an adult woman] and thus have not been free to express their own understanding of our society's standards of decency. And in the months following our grant of certiorari in this case, state legislatures have had an additional reason to pause. Yet despite the inhibiting legal atmosphere that has prevailed since 1977, six States have recently enacted new, targeted child-rape laws.

The Court is willing to block the potential emergence of a national consensus in favor of permitting the death penalty for child rape because, in the end, what matters is the Court's "own judgment" regarding "the acceptability of the death penalty." The Court's final—and, it appears, principal—justification for its holding is that murder, the only crime for which defendants have been executed since this Court's 1976 death penalty decisions, is unique in its moral depravity and in the severity of the injury that it inflicts on the victim and the public.

Is it really true that every person who is convicted of capital murder and sentenced to death is more morally depraved than every child rapist? Consider the following two cases. In the first, a defendant robs a convenience store and watches as his accomplice shoots the store owner. The defendant acts recklessly, but was not the triggerman and did not intend the killing. In the second case, a previously convicted child rapist kidnaps, repeatedly rapes, and tortures multiple child victims. Is it clear that the first defendant is more morally depraved than the second?

I have little doubt that, in the eyes of ordinary Americans, the very worst child rapists—predators who seek out and inflict serious physical and emotional injury on defenseless young children—are the epitome of moral depravity.

With respect to the question of the harm caused by the rape of child in relation to the harm caused by murder, it is certainly true that the loss of human life represents a unique harm, but that does not explain why other grievous harms are insufficient to permit a death sentence. The rape of any victim inflicts great injury, and some victims are so grievously injured physically or psychologically that life is beyond repair. The immaturity and vulnerability of a child, both physically and psychologically, adds a devastating dimension to rape that is not present when an adult is raped. Long-term studies show that sexual abuse is grossly intrusive in the lives of children and is harmful to their normal psychological, emotional and sexual development in ways which no just or humane society can tolerate.

The harm that is caused to the victims and to society at large by the worst child rapists is grave. It is the judgment of the Louisiana lawmakers and those in an increasing number of other States that these harms justify the death penalty. The Court provides no cogent explanation why this legislative judgment should be overridden. Conclusory references to "decency," "moderation," "restraint," "full progress," and "moral judgment" are not enough.

The party attacking the constitutionality of a state statute bears the "heavy burden" of establishing that the law is unconstitutional. That burden has not been discharged here, and I would therefore affirm the decision of the Louisiana Supreme Court.

(continues)

(continued)

QUESTIONS

1. According to the Court, why is death a disproportionate penalty for child rape? Do you agree? Explain your reasons.
2. Who should make the decision as to what is the appropriate penalty for crimes? Courts? Legislatures? Juries? Defend your answer.
3. In deciding whether the death penalty for child rape is cruel and unusual, is it relevant that Louisiana is the only state that punishes child rape with death?
4. According to the Court, some crimes are worse than death. Do you agree? Is child rape one of them? Why or why not?

The death penalty is disproportionate even for some murders. Let's look at two kinds: persons with developmental disabilities and juveniles who murder.

LO7 THE DEATH PENALTY FOR MENTALLY RETARDED MURDERERS

Thirty-five mentally retarded persons were executed between 1976 when the death penalty was reinstated and 2001 (Human Rights Watch 2002). The American Association on Intellectual and Developmental Disabilities (AAIDD) includes three elements in its definition of mental retardation:

1. The person has substantial intellectual impairment.
2. That impairment impacts the everyday life of the mentally retarded individual.
3. Retardation is present at birth or during childhood. (*Atkins v. Virginia* 2002, 308)

In *Atkins v. Virginia* (2002), the U.S. Supreme Court ruled that executing anyone who proved that the three elements in the AAIDD definition applied to them violated the ban on cruel and unusual punishment. The decision grew out of a grisly case. On August 16, 1996, Daryl Atkins and William Jones were drinking alcohol and smoking "pot." At about midnight, they drove to a convenience store to rob a customer.

They picked Eric Nesbitt, an airman from Langley Air Force Base, abducted him, took him in their pickup truck to an ATM machine, and forced him to withdraw $200. Then, they drove him to a deserted area. Ignoring his pleas not to hurt him, they ordered Nesbitt to get out of the car. Nesbitt took only a few steps when (according to Jones, who made a deal with prosecutors to testify against Atkins in exchange for a life instead of a death sentence), Atkins fired eight shots into Nesbitt's thorax, chest, abdomen, arms, and legs (338).

The jury convicted Atkins of capital murder. At the penalty phase of Atkins' trial, the jury heard evidence about his sixteen prior felony convictions, including robbery, attempted robbery, abduction, use of a firearm, and maiming. He hit one victim over the head with a beer bottle; "slapped a gun across another victim's face, clubbed her in the head with it, knocked her to the ground, and then helped her up, only to shoot her in the stomach" (339).

The jury also heard evidence about Atkins' mental retardation. After interviewing people who knew Atkins, reviewing school and court records, and administering a standard intelligence test, which revealed Atkins had an IQ of 59, Dr. Evan Nelson, a forensic psychologist concluded that Atkins was "mildly mentally retarded." According to Nelson, mental retardation is rare (about 1 percent of the population); it would automatically qualify Atkins for Social Security disability income; and that "of the over 40 capital defendants that he had evaluated, Atkins was only the second" who "met the criteria for mental retardation." Nelson also testified that "in his opinion, Atkins' limited intellect had been a consistent feature throughout his life, and that his IQ score of 59 is not an 'aberration, malingered result, or invalid test score'" (309).

In reversing the death sentence, the U.S. Supreme Court based its decision on a change in public opinion since its 1989 decision that it's not cruel and unusual punishment to execute retarded offenders (*Penry v. Lynaugh* 1989). How did the Court measure this change in public opinion? First, since 1989, nineteen states and the federal government had passed statutes banning the execution of mentally retarded offenders (*Atkins v. Virginia* 2002, 314). Second, it wasn't just the number of bans that was significant, it was "the consistency of the direction of the change":

> Given the well-known fact that anticrime legislation is far more popular than legislation providing protections for persons guilty of violent crime, the large number of States prohibiting the execution of mentally retarded persons (and the complete absence of States passing legislation reinstating the power to conduct such executions) provides powerful evidence that today our society views mentally retarded offenders as categorically less culpable than the average criminal.
>
> The evidence carries even greater force when it is noted that the legislatures that have addressed the issue have voted overwhelmingly in favor of the prohibition.
>
> Moreover, even in those States that allow the execution of mentally retarded offenders, the practice is uncommon. Some states, for example New Hampshire and New Jersey, continue to authorize executions, but none have been carried out in decades. Thus there is little need to pursue legislation barring the execution of the mentally retarded in those States.
>
> And it appears that even among those States that regularly execute offenders and that have no prohibition with regard to the mentally retarded, only five have executed offenders possessing a known IQ less than 70 since we decided *Penry*. The practice, therefore, has become truly unusual, and it is fair to say that a national consensus has developed against it. (315–16)

Third, executing retarded offenders doesn't serve the main purposes for having death sentences: retribution and deterrence. Mentally retarded offenders aren't as blameworthy or as subject to deterrence as people with normal intelligence because of their "diminished capacity to understand and process information, to learn from experience, to engage in logical reasoning, or to control their impulses" (319–20).

THE DEATH PENALTY FOR JUVENILE MURDERERS

LO7

The execution of juveniles began in 1642, when Plymouth Colony hanged 16-year-old Thomas Graunger for bestiality with a cow and a horse (Rimer and Bonner 2000). It continued at a rate of about one a year until Oklahoma executed Scott Hain on April 3, 2003, after the U.S. Supreme Court refused to hear his appeal.

Hain and a 21-year-old acquaintance killed two people in the course of a carjacking and robbery. He was a "deeply troubled" 17-year-old kid who dropped out of the seventh grade after repeating the sixth grade three times. As a teenager, Scott's father got him a job in a warehouse so he could steal stuff and give it to his father, who sold it. At the time of the carjacking murders, Scott was living on the street in Tulsa, drinking, and using other drugs daily, but he'd never committed a violent crime (Greenhouse 2003, A18).

Just a few months before the U.S. Supreme Court refused to hear Scott Hain's case, four Supreme Court justices (John Paul Stevens, David Souter, Ruth Bader Ginsburg, and Stephen Breyer) had called the death penalty for juveniles a "shameful practice," adding that "the practice of executing such offenders is a relic of the past and is inconsistent with the evolving standards of decency in a civilized society" (Greenhouse 2003, A18).

"evolving standards" test standards of decency that mark the progress of a maturing society

In *Trop v. Dulles* (1958), the Court first adopted the "evolving standards" test to decide whether sentences run afoul of the Eighth Amendment ban on "cruel and unusual punishments." The "evolving standards" refer to what the Court calls "evolving standards of decency that mark the progress of a maturing society."

In 1944, U.S. Army private Albert Trop escaped from a military stockade at Casablanca, Morocco, following his confinement for a disciplinary violation. The next day, Trop surrendered willingly. A general court martial convicted Trop of desertion and sentenced him to three years at hard labor, loss of all pay and allowances, and a dishonorable discharge. In 1952, Trop applied for a passport. His application was rejected on the ground that he had lost his citizenship due to his conviction and dishonorable discharge for wartime desertion. The Court decided the punishment was "cruel and unusual." Why? Because "the words of the Amendment are not precise, and their scope is not static. The Amendment must draw its meaning from the evolving standards of decency that mark the progress of a maturing society" (100–1).

The Court applied the "evolving standards of decency" approach in *Thompson v. Oklahoma* (1988) to ban the execution of juveniles under 16. But the next year, in *Stanford v. Kentucky* (1989), the Court ruled that executing juveniles between 16 and 18 didn't offend "evolving standards of decency." (After serving 14 years on death row, Stanford was granted clemency in 2003 and is now serving a life sentence.)

In 2005, the Court decided whether standards of decency had evolved enough since 1989 to be offended by executing Christopher Simmons for a carjacking murder he committed when he was seventeen (*Roper v. Simmons* 2005). By a vote of 5–4, the U.S. Supreme Court held that the Eighth and Fourteenth Amendments forbid the execution of offenders who were under the age of 18 when they committed their crimes. According to Justice Kennedy:

> When a juvenile offender commits a heinous crime, the State can exact forfeiture of some of the most basic liberties, but the State cannot extinguish his life and his potential to attain a mature understanding of his own humanity. (554)

The Court relied on "the evolving standards of decency that mark the progress of a maturing society" (561) to determine which punishments are so disproportionate as to be cruel and unusual. The Court argued that the majority of states' rejection of the death penalty for juveniles; its infrequent use in the states that retain the penalty; and the trend toward its abolition show that there's a national consensus against it. The Court determined that today our society views juveniles as categorically less culpable than the average criminal.

Justice Stevens, joined by Justice Ginsburg, wrote in a concurring opinion, that "if the meaning of... [the Eighth] Amendment had been frozen when it was originally drafted, it would impose no impediment to the execution of 7-year-old children today" (587).

Justice Scalia, joined by Justice Thomas and Chief Justice Rehnquist, dissented. Justice Scalia maintained that the Court improperly substituted its own judgment for the state legislature's. He criticized the majority for counting non–death penalty states toward a national consensus against juvenile executions. Scalia also objected to the Court's use of international law to support its opinion, claiming that "Acknowledgement of foreign approval has no place in the legal opinion of this Court..." (628).

LIFE WITHOUT PAROLE FOR JUVENILES

LO7

Does the proportionality principle extend to sentencing juveniles to life without parole for juveniles who don't kill? Over a strong dissent, the U.S. Supreme Court said yes (6–3) in *Graham v. Florida* (2010). Terrence Graham's parents were crack addicts when he was born. Terrence began drinking and smoking tobacco at nine and was smoking marijuana at 13. At 16, he and three other teenagers attempted to rob a barbecue restaurant. One, who worked in the restaurant, left the back door unlocked just before closing time. Graham and the other teenager, wearing masks, came through the unlocked door. The other masked accomplice hit the restaurant manager twice in the back of the head with a steel bar. When the manager started to yell at them, they fled in one of the accomplice's car. The manager had to get stitches for his head injury. No money was taken.

Graham was arrested for "armed burglary" and "attempted armed robbery" and was charged as an adult. Graham pleaded guilty to both charges. He wrote a letter to the trial court. In it, he said "this is my first and last time getting in trouble. I've decided to turn my life around. I made a promise to God and myself that if I get a second chance, I'm going to do whatever it takes to get to the NFL" (2). The judge sentenced Graham to a year in jail, followed by three years of probation.

Less than six months later, Graham participated in a home invasion robbery. Graham and two 20-year-old accomplices knocked on Carlos Rodriguez's door, forcibly entered, and held a pistol to his chest. For thirty minutes, while they held Rodriguez and his friend at gunpoint, they ransacked his house looking for money. They barricaded Rodriguez and his friend in a closet and left (3).

Later that same evening, the three attempted a second robbery. Bailey, one of the 20-year-olds, got shot during the attempt. Graham drove Bailey to the hospital in Graham's father's car, leaving him there with the other 20-year-old. As he drove away, a police officer signaled him to stop. Graham speeded up and drove away, crashing into a telephone pole. He tried to run away on foot but was caught. Three handguns were found in the car. The night he was arrested Graham was 34 days short of his eighteenth birthday (3).

Under Florida law, Graham could be sentenced to five years to life imprisonment. At his sentencing, the trial judge explained the sentence he was about to pronounce:

> Mr. Graham, as I look back on your case, yours is a really sad situation. You had a lot of people who wanted to try and help you get your life turned around including the court system, and you had a judge who took the step to try and give you direction. I don't know why you threw your life away.... But you did.... We can't do anything to deter you. So, if I can't do anything to get you back on the right path, then I have to start focusing on the community and trying to protect the community from your actions.... Given your escalating pattern of criminal conduct,... the only thing I can do now is try and to protect the community from your actions. (4–5)

The judge sentenced Graham to life imprisonment. In effect, this is a sentence to life without parole because Florida has abolished its parole system (of course, the governor might grant him clemency) (6).

Graham appealed. The U.S. Supreme Court reversed, holding that it's cruel and unusual punishment to sentence a juvenile offender to life without parole for a nonhomicide offense (1). Headed for the U.S. Supreme Court is a Wisconsin life without parole ("death in prison") case, *State v. Ninham* (2011), for an intentional murder committed by a juvenile when he was 14.

CASE

*In **State v. Ninham (2011),** the Wisconsin Supreme Court upheld Omer Ninham's "death in prison" sentence for the horrific intentional murder of 13-year-old Zong Vang. Ninham committed the murder when he was 14.*

Is it cruel and unusual punishment to sentence Omer Ninham to "death in prison"?

State v. Ninham

797 N.W.2d 451 (Wis. 2011)

HISTORY

Omer Ninham (Defendant) was convicted of first-degree intentional homicide and was sentenced to life in prison without possibility of parole. Ninham filed a motion for relief from his life sentence, seeking to allow for the possibility of parole. The Circuit Court denied the motion. Ninham appealed. The Supreme Court affirmed.

ZIEGLER, J.

FACTS

On September 24, 1998, around dusk, 13-year-old Vang was bicycling home along Webster Avenue in Green Bay, Wisconsin. Vang's older brother had sent Vang to the grocery store for tomatoes. Vang was returning home on his bicycle, carrying a plastic grocery bag filled with tomatoes, when he was approached by five juveniles: 14-year-old Ninham, 13-year-old Richard Crapeau (Crapeau), 13-year-old Jeffrey P., 14-year-old Amanda G., and 14-year-old Christin J.

Ninham and the other four juveniles did not know or recognize Vang. Moreover, by all accounts, Vang never said or did anything to provoke the five juveniles. Rather, at the time, Crapeau was upset with his mother and "wanted to fight or see a fight." Consequently, Crapeau said to Ninham, "Let's mess with this kid," and Ninham responded, "'I got your back,' meaning he would back [Crapeau] up in a fight." Ninham and Crapeau began by verbally taunting Vang, while the other three juveniles "egg[ed]" them on. Ninham and Crapeau's assaults escalated into physical attacks. Crapeau bumped into Vang's shoulder and yanked his bicycle away from him. Crapeau also grabbed Vang's grocery bag out of his hands and threw it in the direction of St. Vincent's Hospital, located along the same street. When Vang asked for his bicycle back, Ninham punched Vang, knocking him down.

Vang got up and started running towards the nearby St. Vincent's Hospital parking ramp. All five juveniles chased after Vang, eventually catching up to him on the top, or fifth floor, of the parking ramp. When they caught up to him, Crapeau punched Vang in the face. Vang repeatedly asked why they were trying to hurt him and pleaded with them to leave him alone. Instead, Ninham and Crapeau began pushing Vang back and forth between them, in a game Jeffrey P. referred to as "chicken." Ninham punched Vang in the chest as he pushed him back and forth. Ninham then pinned Vang by his wrists against the parking ramp's concrete wall. While Vang squirmed to get out of Ninham's grasp, Crapeau again punched Vang in the face. According to Crapeau, Vang was crying and screaming, "Let me go."

With Ninham still holding Vang by his wrists, Crapeau grabbed Vang's ankles. Ninham and Crapeau then began swinging Vang back and forth out over the parking ramp's concrete wall—a drop that measured nearly 45 feet to the ground. Vang was crying and screaming, begging Ninham and Crapeau not to drop him. While swinging Vang out over the wall, Crapeau let go of Vang's feet and told Ninham to "drop him." Ninham let go of Vang's wrists, and in Crapeau's words, Vang "just sailed out over the wall."

Vang landed on his back on the parking ramp's paved exit lane, 12 feet from the base of the ramp. Rescue personnel, dispatched at 8:03 P.M., detected a faint pulse from Vang. Vang was transported to St. Vincent's Hospital where physicians were unable to revive him. An autopsy revealed that Vang suffered a blunt impact to his head and trunk and died from craniocerebral trauma due to a fall from height.

Ninham and the other four juveniles never checked on Vang's condition and instead ran from the scene. Still, the Green Bay Police Department was able to focus its investigation on the five juveniles after some of them, in particular, Jeffrey P. and Amanda G., indicated to relatives and police that they knew who was responsible for Vang's death. In his statement to police, Jeffrey P. described how Ninham stood for several seconds looking over the edge of the wall at Vang below. Ninham then looked at Jeffrey P. and said, "Don't say nothing. Better not say shit."

The pre-sentence investigation (PSI) revealed that "Ninham emanates from an extremely dysfunctional family structure," in which both of his parents and several of his siblings engage in severe substance abuse and domestic violence. The PSI described Ninham as a "serious substance abuser" who snorted cocaine on a weekly basis and, since grade school, drank alcohol every day, often alone, and usually to the point of unconsciousness. The PSI also revealed that Ninham, a member of the Menominee Indian Tribe, claimed to have a newfound interest in Native American spirituality.

In addition, the PSI described the Vang family as devastated by the loss of their son and brother. Vang's parents indicated that they fled Laos and Thailand because they believed that the United States would be a safer and more prosperous country to raise their children; however, according to the Vangs, they fled evil only to discover it in a different place. Vang's parents further expressed that they had lost faith in the basic goodness of people and that their remaining children are fearful of leaving the safety of their home.

Relevant to this case, at the sentencing hearing, Vang's brother, Seng Say Vang (Seng Say), gave a statement on behalf of Vang's family and friends. Seng Say asked the circuit court to impose on Ninham the maximum sentence of life imprisonment without parole.... Seng Say then articulated to the circuit court a belief held by his family's Hmong culture:

> In our Hmong culture we believe that the spirit of a murdered person cannot be set free to go in peace until the perpetrators be brought to justice. Therefore, we ask the Court, who is the only one to have the power to set free the spirit of our beloved son, brother, and friend, Zong, to go in peace by bringing Omer Ninham and his accomplices to justice.

Ninham also spoke at sentencing. He told the circuit court that he was sorry about Vang's death, but "there wasn't nothing I could do. I wasn't there. I'm going to keep saying that until the day I die. I was not there, and that's the honest truth."

In imposing Ninham's sentence, the circuit court considered three primary factors: the gravity of the offense, the character of the offender, and the need to protect the public. First, the circuit court regarded the gravity of the offense as "beyond description" and indisputably "horrific." The circuit court noted that the offense has had an indescribable impact on Vang's family and friends and on the Green Bay community. Second, concerning the character of the offender, the circuit court "conceded for the sake of discussion that Omer Ninham is a child" but nevertheless described Ninham as "a frightening young man." The circuit court acknowledged that Ninham derives from a dysfunctional family but refused to let that excuse Ninham's conduct, explaining that Ninham is "a child of the street who knew what he was doing...." Third, the circuit court reasoned that the community needs to be protected from Ninham: "Society needs to know, and especially this community needs to know, that you can send your child to the grocery store and expect to see him again."

OPINION

First, we hold that sentencing a 14-year-old to life imprisonment without the possibility of parole for committing intentional homicide is not categorically unconstitutional. We arrive at our holding by applying the two-step approach employed by the United States Supreme Court, most recently in *Graham*, 130 S. Ct. 2011. First, we conclude that Ninham has failed to demonstrate that there is a national consensus against sentencing a 14-year-old to life imprisonment without parole when the crime is intentional homicide. Second, we conclude in the exercise of our own independent judgment that the punishment is not categorically unconstitutional.

In regard to Ninham's second argument, we conclude that his sentence of life imprisonment without the possibility of parole is not unduly harsh and excessive. Under the circumstances of this case, Ninham's punishment is severe, but it is not disproportionately so.

Third, we conclude that Ninham has not demonstrated by clear and convincing evidence that the scientific research on adolescent brain development

(continues)

(continued)

to which he refers constitutes a "new factor." While the studies themselves may not have been in existence at the time of Ninham's sentencing, the conclusions they reached were widely reported.

Fourth, we conclude that Ninham has not demonstrated by clear and convincing evidence that the circuit court actually relied upon the religious beliefs of Vang's family when imposing Ninham's sentence.

The decision of the court of appeals is affirmed.

DISSENT

ABRAHAMSON, CJ.

The Eighth Amendment cruel and unusual punishment issue before this court is easy to state and difficult to decide. The question before the court is the constitutionality of imposing a death-in-prison sentence on a 14-year-old juvenile boy who committed an intentional, brutal, senseless, grotesque, reprehensible murder of a 13-year-old innocent stranger.

In Wisconsin, both the adult offender and the juvenile offender (10 years old or older) who have committed first-degree intentional homicide are treated the same: the maximum penalty is a death-in-prison sentence, that is, life in prison without the possibility of parole. The circuit court need not impose this maximum sentence. It did in the present case.

A death-in-prison sentence is the most severe penalty authorized in Wisconsin. This penalty means that "whatever the future might hold in store for the mind and spirit of the young juvenile, he will remain in prison for the rest of his days. A death-in-prison sentence is an especially severe punishment, made harsher for a young juvenile 14 years old or younger because of the increased time and proportion of life that the juvenile will serve in prison.

I conclude, as has the United States Supreme Court (*Roper v. Simmons*, 543 U.S. 551 [2005]), that the differences between juveniles and adults mean that juvenile offenders "cannot with reliability be classified among the worst offenders." The three general differences are: (1) juveniles have a lack of maturity and an underdeveloped sense of responsibility resulting in impetuous and ill-considered actions and decisions; (2) juveniles are more susceptible to negative influences and outside pressures; and (3) the character of a juvenile is not as well formed as that of an adult.

Retribution is a legitimate penological goal, but retribution "must be directly related to the personal culpability of the criminal offender." The case for retribution is not as strong with a minor as with an adult." Accordingly, I conclude, that a juvenile cannot be sentenced to life without parole for a homicide committed when 14 years old or younger.

QUESTIONS

1. Summarize the majority's four reasons for deciding that Omer Ninham's sentence to life in prison without possibility of parole is not cruel and unusual punishment.
2. Summarize the dissent's reason for arguing that "death in prison" for a juvenile is cruel and unusual punishment.
3. The U.S. Supreme Court has agreed to hear the case in 2012. In your opinion, how should SCOTUS rule? Defend your answer.

LO7 PRISON SENTENCES

The consensus that the ban on cruel and unusual punishment includes a proportionality requirement in capital punishment doesn't hold when it comes to prison sentences. The important case of *Solem v. Helm* (1983) revealed that the U.S. Supreme Court was deeply divided over whether the principle of proportionality applied to sentences of imprisonment. The case involved Jerry Helm, whom South Dakota had convicted of six nonviolent felonies by 1975. The crimes included three third-degree burglaries, one in 1964, one in 1966, and one in 1969; obtaining money under false pretenses in 1972; committing grand larceny in 1973; and "third-offense driving while intoxicated" in 1975. A bare majority of five in the U.S. Supreme Court held that "a criminal sentence must be proportionate to the crime for which the defendant has been convicted" (290).

The split over the constitutional status of proportionality in prison sentences was revealed again when the constitutionality of three-strikes-and-you're-out laws reached the Court in 2003. Before we look at the Court's division, let's put three-strikes laws in some perspective. Three-strikes laws are supposed to make sure that offenders who are convicted of a third felony get locked up for a very long time (sometimes for life).

three-strikes laws intended to make sure that offenders who are convicted of a third felony get locked up for a very long time (sometimes for life)

The laws are controversial, and they generate passions on both sides. Supporters, such as Joanna Shepherd (2002), claim that "theory-based empirical results indicate that strike laws generally deter the crimes covered by the laws." According to these theory-based empirical results, Shepherd reports:

> During the first two years of the [California 3-strikes] legislation, approximately eight murders, 3,952 aggravated assaults, 10,672 robberies, and 384,488 burglaries were deterred in California; however, larcenies increased by 17,000 during this period. (159)

Opponents believe the harsh penalties won't have much effect on crime, and they'll cost states more than they can afford to pay (Turner et al. 1995, 75).

Despite controversy, three-strikes laws are (at least until recently) popular and widespread. Twenty-eight states have passed three-strikes laws. California's law, widely considered the toughest in the nation, includes a twenty-five-year-to-life sentence if you're "out" on a third strike. The law passed in 1994, after the kidnapping, brutal sexual assault, and murder of twelve-year-old Polly Klaas in 1993 (Ainsworth 2004, 1; Shepherd 2002, 161). A bearded stranger broke into Polly Klaas's home in Petaluma, California, and kidnapped her. He left behind two other girls bound and gagged. Polly's mother was asleep in the next room. Nine weeks later, after a fruitless search by hundreds of police officers and volunteers, a repeat offender, Richard Allen Davis, was arrested and, in 1996, convicted and sentenced to death.

Liberals and conservatives, Democrats and Republicans, and the public all jumped on the three-strikes bandwagon, taking it for granted these laws were a good idea. Why were they popular? Here are three reasons:

1. They addressed the public's dissatisfaction with the criminal justice system.
2. They promised a simple solution to a complex problem—the "panacea phenomenon."
3. The use of the catchy phrase "three strikes and you're out" was appealing; it put old habitual offender statute ideas into the language of modern baseball. (Benekos and Merlo 1995, 3; Turner et al. 1995)

What effects have three-strikes laws had? Everybody agrees that they incapacitate second and third-strikers while they're locked up. But incapacitate them from doing what? Some critics argue that most strikers are already past the age of high offending. Most of the debate centers on deterrence: Do the laws prevent criminals from committing further crimes? The conclusions, based on empirical research, are decidedly mixed: three-strikes laws deter crime; three-strikes laws have no effect on crime; three-strikes laws increase crime.

What happens if third-strikers are released early? This is what happened in California in 2012. In the 2012 November election, California enacted the Three Strikes Reform Act (Proposition 36 approved by 69 percent of California voters). The new law dialed back "the toughest sentencing law in the country." Severely overcrowded prisons, huge state budget problems, and growing concern over "mass incarceration" (see Chapter 1), combined to produce the strong victory for Proposition 36, and, as some say, its implementation's success (Mills and Romano 2014, 1). The new law allows prisoners whose third strike was a nonserious and nonviolent crime to seek early release. Between November 2012 and April 2014, California released 1,613 third-strike prisoners serving life sentences for nonviolent crimes. After 18 months the California Department of Corrections and Rehabilitation Data (CDCR) data showed a recidivism rate of 1.3 percent. The recidivism rate for other prisoners was 30 percent. CDCR defines recidivism as returning to prison for committing a new crime. Eligibility for release allows a Superior Court judge to resentence third-strikes prisoners unless they pose "an unreasonable risk of danger to public safety" (Mills and Romano 2014, 2).

David Mills and Michael Romano (2014) (Stanford Law School Three Strikes Project) maintain that these recidivism rates prove the reform's effectiveness:

> Prisoners released under Proposition 36 have been out of custody for an average of 9.2 months. Traditionally, the highest risk for recidivism is within the first 90 days of a prisoner's release. According to CDCR, over 75 percent of recidivists commit their new crime within 1 year of release. (2)

Not only do these numbers of released third-strikers "prove these judges right" about them posing no threat to public safety, say Mills and Romano," they're great for California's budget problems. "Proposition 36 has already saved California over $30 million dollars in prison costs and freed up valuable prison space for more dangerous criminals" (3).

Whatever the effectiveness of three-strikes laws may be, the U.S. Supreme Court has ruled they're constitutional, even if the justices can't agree on the reasons. This is clear from the Court's 5–4 decision in *Ewing v. California* (2003), upholding the constitutionality of California's three-strikes law.

CASE

In ***Ewing v. California*** **(2003),** *the Court upheld the constitutionality of California's three-strikes law.*

Is 25 years to life in prison disproportionate to grand theft?

Ewing v. California

538 U.S. 11 (2003)

HISTORY

Gary Ewing was convicted in a California trial court of felony grand theft and sentenced to 25 years to life under that state's three-strikes law. The California Court of Appeal, Second Appellate District, affirmed the sentence, and the State Supreme Court denied review. Certiorari was granted. The Supreme Court held that the sentence did not violate the Eighth Amendment's prohibition against cruel and unusual punishment.

O'CONNOR, J., JOINED BY REHNQUIST, CJ., AND SCALIA, KENNEDY, AND THOMAS, JJ.

FACTS

On parole from a 9-year prison term, petitioner Gary Ewing walked into the pro shop of the El Segundo Golf Course, in Los Angeles County, on March 12, 2000. He walked out with three golf clubs, priced at $399 apiece, concealed in his pants leg. A shop employee, whose suspicions were aroused when he observed Ewing limp out of the pro shop, telephoned the police. The police apprehended Ewing in the parking lot.

Ewing is no stranger to the criminal justice system. In 1984, at the age of 22, he pleaded guilty to theft. The court sentenced him to six months in jail (suspended), three years' probation, and a $300 fine. In 1988, he was convicted of felony grand theft auto and sentenced to one year in jail and three years' probation. After Ewing completed probation, however, the sentencing court reduced the crime to a misdemeanor, permitted Ewing to withdraw his guilty plea, and dismissed the case.

In 1990, he was convicted of petty theft with a prior and sentenced to 60 days in the county jail and three years' probation. In 1992, Ewing was convicted of battery and sentenced to 30 days in the county jail and two years' summary probation. One month later, he was convicted of theft and sentenced to 10 days in the county jail and 12 months' probation. In January 1993, Ewing was convicted of burglary and sentenced to 60 days in the county jail and one year's summary probation. In February 1993, he was convicted of possessing drug paraphernalia and sentenced to six months in the county jail and three years' probation. In July 1993, he was convicted of appropriating lost property and sentenced to 10 days in the county jail and two years' summary probation. In September 1993, he was convicted of unlawfully possessing a firearm and trespassing and sentenced to 30 days in the county jail and one year's probation.

In October and November 1993, Ewing committed three burglaries and one robbery at a Long Beach, California, apartment complex over a 5-week period. He awakened one of his victims, asleep on her living room sofa, as he tried to disconnect her video cassette recorder from the television in that room. When she screamed, Ewing ran out the front door. On another occasion, Ewing accosted a victim in the mailroom of the apartment complex. Ewing claimed to have a gun and ordered the victim to hand over his wallet. When the victim resisted, Ewing produced a knife and forced the victim back to the apartment itself. While Ewing rifled through the bedroom, the victim fled the apartment screaming for help. Ewing absconded with the victim's money and credit cards.

On December 9, 1993, Ewing was arrested on the premises of the apartment complex for trespassing and lying to a police officer. The knife used in the robbery and a glass cocaine pipe were later found in the back seat of the patrol car used to transport Ewing to the police station. A jury convicted Ewing of first-degree robbery and three counts of residential burglary. Sentenced to nine years and eight months in prison, Ewing was paroled in 1999.

Only 10 months later, Ewing stole the golf clubs at issue in this case. He was charged with, and ultimately convicted of, one count of felony grand theft of personal property in excess of $400. As required by the three-strikes law, the prosecutor formally alleged, and the trial court later found, that Ewing had been convicted previously of four serious or violent felonies for the three burglaries and the robbery in the Long Beach apartment complex.

As a newly convicted felon with two or more "serious" or "violent" felony convictions in his past, Ewing was sentenced under the three-strikes law to 25 years to life.

OPINION

When the California Legislature enacted the three-strikes law, it made a judgment that protecting the public safety requires incapacitating criminals who have already been convicted of at least one serious or violent crime. Nothing in the Eighth Amendment prohibits California from making that choice. To be sure, California's three-strikes law has sparked controversy. Critics have doubted the law's wisdom, cost-efficiency, and effectiveness in reaching its goals.

This criticism is appropriately directed at the legislature, which has primary responsibility for making the difficult policy choices that underlie any criminal sentencing scheme. We do not sit as a "superlegislature" to second-guess these policy choices. It is enough that the State of California has a reasonable basis for believing that dramatically enhanced sentences for habitual felons advances the goals of its criminal justice system in any substantial way.

Against this backdrop, we consider Ewing's claim that his three-strikes sentence of 25 years to life is unconstitutionally disproportionate to his offense of shoplifting three golf clubs. Ewing's sentence is justified by the State's public-safety interest in incapacitating and deterring recidivist felons, and amply supported by his own long, serious criminal record. To be sure, Ewing's sentence is a long one. But it reflects a rational legislative judgment, entitled to deference, that offenders who have committed serious or violent felonies and who continue to commit felonies must be incapacitated. The State of California was entitled to place upon Ewing the onus of one who is simply unable to bring his conduct within the social norms prescribed by the criminal law of the State.

We hold that Ewing's sentence of 25 years to life in prison, imposed for the offense of felony grand theft under the three-strikes law, is not grossly disproportionate and therefore does not violate the Eighth Amendment's prohibition on cruel and unusual punishments. The judgment of the California Court of Appeal is affirmed.

It is so ordered.

(continues)

(continued)

CONCURRING OPINION

SCALIA, J. CONCURRING IN THE JUDGMENT.

The Eighth Amendment's prohibition of cruel and unusual punishments was aimed at excluding only certain modes of punishment, and was not a guarantee against disproportionate sentences. Because I agree that petitioner's sentence does not violate the Eighth Amendment's prohibition against cruel and unusual punishments, I concur in the judgment.

CONCURRING OPINION

THOMAS, J. CONCURRING IN THE JUDGMENT.

In my view, the Cruel and Unusual Punishments Clause of the Eighth Amendment contains no proportionality principle. Because the plurality concludes that petitioner's sentence does not violate the Eighth Amendment's prohibition on cruel and unusual punishments, I concur in the judgment.

DISSENT

BREYER, J., JOINED BY STEVENS, SOUTER, AND GINSBURG, JJ.

A comparison of Ewing's sentence with other sentences requires answers to two questions. First, how would other jurisdictions (or California at other times, i.e., without the three-strikes penalty) punish the same offense conduct? Second, upon what other conduct would other jurisdictions (or California) impose the same prison term? Moreover, since hypothetical punishment is beside the point, the relevant prison time, for comparative purposes, is real prison time, i.e., the time that an offender must actually serve. Sentencing statutes often shed little light upon real prison time. That is because sentencing laws normally set maximum sentences, giving the sentencing judge discretion to choose an actual sentence within a broad range, and because many States provide good-time credits and parole, often permitting release after, say, one-third of the sentence has been served. Nonetheless, Ewing's sentence, comparatively speaking, is extreme.

As to California itself, we know the following: First, between the end of World War II and 1994 (when California enacted the three-strikes law), no one like Ewing could have served more than 10 years in prison. We know that for certain because the maximum sentence for Ewing's crime of conviction, grand theft, was for most of that period 10 years. From 1976 to 1994 (and currently, absent application of the three-strikes penalty), a Ewing-type offender would have received a maximum sentence of 4 years. And we know that California's "habitual offender" laws did not apply to grand theft. We also know that the time that any offender actually served was likely far less than 10 years. This is because statistical data show that the median time actually served for grand theft (other than auto theft) was about two years, and 90 percent of all those convicted of that crime served less than three or four years.

Second, statistics suggest that recidivists of all sorts convicted during that same time period in California served a small fraction of Ewing's real-time sentence. On average, recidivists served three to four additional (recidivist-related) years in prison, with 90 percent serving less than an additional real seven to eight years.

Third, we know that California has reserved, and still reserves, Ewing-type prison time, i.e., at least 25 real years in prison, for criminals convicted of crimes far worse than was Ewing's. Statistics for the years 1945 to 1981, for example, indicate that typical (nonrecidivist) male first-degree murderers served between 10 and 15 real years in prison, with 90 percent of all such murderers serving less than 20 real years. Moreover, California, which has moved toward a real-time sentencing system (where the statutory punishment approximates the time served), still punishes far less harshly those who have engaged in far more serious conduct. It imposes, for example, upon nonrecidivists guilty of arson causing great bodily injury a maximum sentence of 9 years in prison; it imposes upon those guilty of voluntary manslaughter a maximum sentence of 11 years. It reserves the sentence that it here imposes upon (former-burglar-now-golf-club-thief) Ewing for nonrecidivist, first-degree murderers.

As to other jurisdictions, we know the following: The United States, bound by the federal Sentencing Guidelines, would impose upon a recidivist, such as Ewing, a sentence that, in any ordinary case, would not exceed 18 months in prison. The Guidelines reserve a Ewing-type sentence for Ewing-type recidivists who currently commit murder, robbery (involving the discharge of a firearm, serious bodily injury, and about $1 million), drug offenses involving more than, for example, 20 pounds of heroin, aggravated theft of more than $100 million, and other similar offenses. The Guidelines reserve 10 years of real prison time (with good time)—less than 40 percent of Ewing's sentence—for Ewing-type recidivists who go on to commit, for instance, voluntary manslaughter, aggravated assault with a firearm (causing serious bodily injury and motivated by money), kidnapping, residential burglary involving more than $5 million, drug offenses involving at least one pound of cocaine, and other similar offenses. Ewing also would not have been subject to the federal three-strikes law, for which grand theft is not a triggering offense.

Justice SCALIA and Justice THOMAS argue that we should not review for gross disproportionality a sentence to a term of years. Otherwise, we make it too difficult for legislators and sentencing judges to determine just when their sentencing laws and practices pass constitutional muster. I concede that a bright-line rule would give legislators and sentencing judges more guidance. But application of the Eighth Amendment to a sentence of a term of years requires a case-by-case approach. And, in my view, like that of the plurality, meaningful enforcement of the Eighth Amendment demands that application—even if only at sentencing's outer bounds.

A case-by-case approach can nonetheless offer guidance through example. Ewing's sentence is, at a minimum, two to three times the length of sentences that other jurisdictions would impose in similar circumstances. That sentence itself is sufficiently long to require a typical offender to spend virtually all the remainder of his active life in prison. These and the other factors that I have discussed, along with the questions that I have asked along the way, should help to identify "gross disproportionality" in a fairly objective way—at the outer bounds of sentencing.

In sum, even if I accept for present purposes the plurality's analytical framework, Ewing's sentence (life imprisonment with a minimum term of 25 years) is grossly disproportionate to the triggering offense conduct—stealing three golf clubs—Ewing's recidivism notwithstanding.

For these reasons, I dissent.

QUESTIONS

1. List Gary Ewing's crimes, and match them to the three-strikes law.
2. Define "proportionality" as the plurality opinion defines it. Summarize how the majority applies proportionality to Ewing's sentence. How does Justice Scalia define "proportionality," and how does his application of it to the facts differ from the majority's? Summarize how the dissent applies the principle of proportionality to the facts of the case.
3. In your opinion, was Ewing's punishment proportional to the crime? Back up your answer with the facts of the case and the arguments in the opinions.
4. If Justice Thomas is right that the Eighth Amendment contains no proportionality principle, what is cruel and unusual punishment?

THE RIGHT TO TRIAL BY JURY AND CRIMINAL SENTENCING

LO8

Until 2000, the guidelines and mandatory forms of fixed sentencing created only possible cruel and unusual punishment problems. Beyond that, the U.S. Supreme Court took a hands-off approach to sentencing procedures, leaving it up to federal and state legislatures and judges to share sentencing authority and administration without interference from the Court. Then came *Apprendi v. New Jersey* (2000), called by two authorities (Dressler and Michaels 2006) "the first in a series of constitutional explosions that have rocked the world of criminal sentencing and caused fundamental alterations" in federal and state sentencing systems (366). (See the nearby Criminal Law in Focus for some of the leading cases.)

Charles C. Apprendi Jr. fired several .22-caliber bullets into a Black family's home; the family had recently moved into a previously all-White neighborhood in Vineland, New Jersey. Apprendi was promptly arrested and admitted that he was the shooter. Later, he made a statement—which he soon after retracted—that "even though he did not know the occupants of the house personally, 'because they are black in color he does not want them in the neighborhood'" (469).

Apprendi was convicted of possessing a firearm with an unlawful purpose, a felony in New Jersey, punishable by 5 to 10 years in prison. New Jersey also has a hate crime statute providing for an extended punishment of 10 to 20 years if the judge finds by a preponderance of the evidence that the defendant committed the crime with a "purpose to intimidate an individual or group of individuals because of race, color, gender, handicap, religion, sexual orientation or ethnicity" (469).

Apprendi argued that "racial purpose" was an element of the crime that the state had to prove beyond a reasonable doubt. New Jersey argued that the legislature had chosen to make "racial purpose" a sentencing factor. The U.S. Supreme Court (5–4) brought the Sixth Amendment right to trial by jury into the heart of criminal sentencing procedures with a sweeping rule (the **Apprendi rule**):

Apprendi rule other than the fact of prior conviction, any fact that increases the penalty for a crime beyond the prescribed statutory maximum must be submitted to a jury and proved beyond a reasonable doubt

> Other than the fact of prior conviction, any fact that *increases* the penalty for a crime beyond the prescribed statutory maximum must be submitted to a jury, and proved beyond a reasonable doubt. (490, emphasis added)

Between 2000 and 2005, the Supreme Court extended the *Apprendi* rule. In a series of 5–4 decisions made up of shifting member majority and dissenting justices, the Court stirred up uncertainty and anxiety about the effect of the rule on state and federal proceedings, particularly on the by now firmly established U.S. and state sentencing guidelines. In *Blakely v. Washington* (2004) 5–4, the Court struck down a Washington State statute that allowed judges to increase the length of prison time beyond the "standard range" prescribed in the Washington sentencing guidelines based on facts not proven to a jury beyond a reasonable doubt.

Major U.S. Supreme Court Trial by Jury Rights Cases

CASE	COURT DECISION
Apprendi v. New Jersey (2000) 5–4	Struck down New Jersey statute authorizing judges to increase maximum sentence based on facts judge found to be true by a preponderance of the evidence but not proof beyond a reasonable doubt Affirmed judge's authority to increase maximum based on prior convictions, or crimes defendants confess to, without jury finding there were prior convictions or defendants, or prior crimes defendants confessed to
Blakely v. Washington (2004) 5–4	Struck down Washington State statute that authorized judge to increase the length of prison time beyond the "standard range" in the Washington sentencing guidelines based on facts not proved beyond a reasonable doubt
U.S. v. Booker (2005) 5–4	Struck down provisions in the U.S. sentencing guidelines that allowed judges to increase individual sentences beyond the "standard range" based on facts not proved beyond a reasonable doubt to the jury Guidelines are advisory only but enjoy "a presumption of reasonableness"
Gall v. U.S. (2007) 7–2	Upheld a sentence of 36 months' probation imposed on a man who pleaded guilty to conspiracy to distribute ecstasy in the face of a recommended sentence of 30 to 37 months in prison Federal appeals courts may not presume that a sentence falling outside the range recommended by the Federal Sentencing Guidelines is unreasonable

In that case, after Ralph Blakely's wife Yolanda filed for divorce, he abducted her from the orchard on their farm home, bound her with duct tape, and forced her at knife-point into a wooden box in the bed of his pickup truck (300). When the couple's 13-year-old son Ralphy returned home from school, Blakely ordered him to follow in another car, threatening to harm Yolanda with a shotgun if Ralphy didn't do it. Ralphy escaped and sought help when they stopped at a gas station; Blakely continued on with Yolanda to a friend's house in Montana. He was finally arrested after the friend called the police (300).

The state charged Blakely with first-degree kidnapping. Then, in a plea agreement, the state reduced the charge to second-degree kidnapping involving domestic violence and use of a firearm. Blakely pleaded guilty, admitting the elements of second-degree kidnapping and the domestic violence and firearm allegations but no other relevant facts.

In Washington State, second-degree kidnapping is punishable by up to 10 years in prison. Washington's sentencing guidelines specify a "standard range" of 49 to 53 months for second-degree kidnapping with a firearm. A judge may impose a sentence above the standard range if she finds "substantial and compelling reasons justifying an exceptional sentence." In a plea agreement, the state recommended a sentence within the standard range of 49 to 53 months. After hearing Yolanda's description of the kidnapping, the judge rejected the state's recommendation and imposed an exceptional sentence of 90 months—37 months beyond the standard maximum. He justified the sentence on the ground that the petitioner had acted with "deliberate cruelty."

Faced with an unexpected increase of more than three years in his sentence, Blakely objected. The judge accordingly conducted a three-day bench hearing featuring testimony from Yolanda, Ralphy, a police officer, and medical experts. He concluded that

> Blakely used stealth and surprise, and took advantage of the victim's isolation. He immediately employed physical violence, restrained the victim with tape, and threatened her with injury and death to herself and others. He immediately coerced the victim into providing information by the threatening application of a knife. He violated a subsisting restraining order. (301)

The judge adhered to his initial determination of deliberate cruelty. Blakely appealed, arguing that this sentencing procedure deprived him of his federal constitutional right to have a jury determine beyond a reasonable doubt all facts legally essential to his sentence.

In *U.S. v. Booker* (2005), the Court applied the *Apprendi* rule to the U.S. sentencing guidelines. In Justice Stevens' words, writing for the five-member majority, "there is no distinction of constitutional significance" between the federal sentencing guidelines and the Washington sentencing guidelines in *Blakely*. Therefore, the Court held, judges can't increase defendants' sentence without proving beyond a reasonable doubt to a jury facts justifying the increase.

That raised a second question: What should be done instead? Four of the five justice majority would have continued sentencing according to the guidelines, except for cases that increased sentence lengths. In those cases, the government would have to "prove any fact that is required to increase a defendant's sentence under the Guidelines beyond a reasonable doubt" (284–85). But that's not what happened.

Justice Ginsburg, one of the five-member majority, broke with the majority on the remedy to join with the dissent to give them the majority on the remedy. What remedy? It had two parts:

> Sentencing guidelines would operate as they did before, but they're now advisory, not mandatory as they were before *Booker*. In the remedy majority's words, the new rule "requires judges to consider the Guidelines" but they don't have to follow them. (259)

Sentences are still subject to review by the U.S. Courts of Appeal. When they do, they have to consider whether the sentence is "unreasonable" in light of the guidelines and the general purposes of sentencing under federal law (261).

There was—and still is—much hand-wringing over where the Court is headed in its decisions on the right to trial by jury and sentencing and what implications it has for sentencing guidelines under state and federal law. But it's important not to exaggerate the impact of the *Apprendi* rule and its impact after *Blakely* and *Booker*. Remember, the rule applies only to cases in which judges increase sentences. According to a U.S. Sentencing Commission (2006) special report on the impact of *Booker*:

> The majority of federal cases continue to be sentenced in conformance with the sentencing guidelines. National data show that when within-range sentences and government-sponsored, below-range sentences are combined, the rate of sentencing in conformance with the sentencing guidelines is 85.9 percent. This conformance rate remained stable throughout the year that followed *Booker*. (vi)

Nevertheless, there's still great concern and uncertainty about what "advisory" and "unreasonable" mean in the remedy elements of *Booker*. The Court didn't seem to clear up very much in our next case excerpt, *Gall v. U.S.* (2007), the first case to apply the *Booker* rule.

CASE

In ***Gall v. U.S.* (2007),** *the five-member majority upheld the trial judge's sentence of Brian Michael Gall to 36 months of probation instead of a mandatory prison term.*

Did the probation sentence abuse the trial judge's discretion?

Gall v. U.S.

552 U.S. 38 (2007)

HISTORY

Brian Michael Gall (hereafter "Petitioner") was convicted, on his guilty plea, in the U.S. District Court for the Southern District of Iowa, of conspiracy to distribute ecstasy and was sentenced to 36 months of probation. The government appealed, challenging the sentence. The Eighth Circuit Court of Appeals remanded for resentencing. Certiorari was granted.

STEVENS, J., JOINED BY ROBERTS, CJ., AND SCALIA, KENNEDY, SOUTER, GINSBURG, AND BREYER, JJ.

FACTS

In February or March 2000, petitioner Brian Gall, a second-year college student at the University of Iowa, was invited by Luke Rinderknecht to join an ongoing enterprise distributing a controlled substance popularly known as "ecstasy." (Ecstasy is sometimes called "MDMA" because its scientific name is "methylenedioxymethamphetamine.") Gall—who was then a user of ecstasy, cocaine, and marijuana—accepted the invitation. During the ensuing seven months, Gall delivered ecstasy pills, which he received from Rinderknecht, to other conspirators, who then sold them to consumers. He netted more than $30,000.

A month or two after joining the conspiracy, Gall stopped using ecstasy. A few months after that, in September 2000, he advised Rinderknecht and other co-conspirators that he was withdrawing from the conspiracy. He has not sold illegal drugs of any kind since. He has, in the words of the District Court, "self-rehabilitated." He graduated from the University of Iowa in 2002, and moved first to Arizona, where he obtained a job in the construction industry, and later to Colorado, where he earned $18 per hour as a master carpenter. He has not used any illegal drugs since graduating from college.

After Gall moved to Arizona, he was approached by federal law enforcement agents who questioned him about his involvement in the ecstasy distribution conspiracy. Gall admitted his limited participation in the distribution of ecstasy, and the agents took no further action at that time. On April 28, 2004—approximately a year and a half after this initial interview, and three and a half years after Gall withdrew from the conspiracy—an indictment was returned in the Southern District of Iowa charging him and seven other defendants with participating in a conspiracy to distribute ecstasy, cocaine, and marijuana that began in or about May 1996 and continued through October 30, 2002.

The government has never questioned the truthfulness of any of Gall's earlier statements or contended that he played any role in, or had any knowledge of, other aspects of the conspiracy described in the indictment. When he received notice of the indictment, Gall moved back to Iowa and surrendered to the authorities. While free on his own recognizance, Gall started his own business in the construction industry, primarily engaged in subcontracting for the installation of windows and doors. In his first year, his profits were more than $2,000 per month.

Gall entered into a plea agreement with the government, stipulating that he was "responsible for, but did not necessarily distribute himself, at least 2,500 grams of [ecstasy], or the equivalent of at least 87.5 kilograms of marijuana." In the agreement, the government acknowledged that by "on or about September of 2000," Gall had communicated his intent to stop distributing ecstasy to Rinderknecht and other members of the conspiracy. The agreement further provided that recent changes in the guidelines that enhanced the recommended punishment for distributing ecstasy were not applicable to Gall because he had withdrawn from the conspiracy prior to the effective date of those changes.

In her presentence report, the probation officer concluded that Gall had no significant criminal history; that he was not an organizer, leader, or manager; and that his offense did not involve the use of any weapons. The report stated that Gall had truthfully provided the government with all of the evidence he had concerning the alleged offenses, but that his evidence was not useful because he provided no new information to the agents. The report also described Gall's substantial use of drugs prior to his offense and the absence of any such use in recent years. The report recommended a sentencing range of 30 to 37 months of imprisonment.

The record of the sentencing hearing held on May 27, 2005, includes a "small flood" of letters from Gall's parents and other relatives, his fiancé, neighbors, and representatives of firms doing business with him, all uniformly praising his character and work ethic. The transcript includes the testimony of several witnesses and the District judge's colloquy with the Assistant U.S. Attorney (AUSA) and with Gall. The AUSA did not contest any of the evidence concerning Gall's law-abiding life during the preceding five years but urged that "the Guidelines are appropriate and should be followed," and requested that the court impose a prison sentence within the guidelines range. He mentioned that two of Gall's co-conspirators had been sentenced to 30 and 35 months, respectively, but upon further questioning by the District Court, he acknowledged that neither of them had voluntarily withdrawn from the conspiracy.

The District judge sentenced Gall to probation for a term of 36 months. In addition to making a lengthy statement on the record, the judge filed a detailed sentencing memorandum explaining his decision, and provided the following statement of reasons in his written judgment:

> The Court determined that, considering all the factors under 18 U.S.C. 3553(a), the Defendant's explicit withdrawal from the conspiracy almost four years before the filing of the Indictment, the Defendant's post-offense conduct, especially obtaining a college degree and the start of his own successful business, the support of family and friends, lack of criminal

(continues)

(continued)

> history, and his age at the time of the offense conduct, all warrant the sentence imposed, which was sufficient, but not greater than necessary to serve the purposes of sentencing.

At the end of both the sentencing hearing and the sentencing memorandum, the District judge reminded Gall that probation, rather than "an act of leniency," is a "substantial restriction of freedom." In the memorandum, he emphasized:

> [Gall] will have to comply with strict reporting conditions along with a three-year regime of alcohol and drug testing. He will not be able to change or make decisions about significant circumstances in his life, such as where to live or work, which are prized liberty interests, without first seeking authorization from his Probation Officer or, perhaps, even the Court. Of course, the Defendant always faces the harsh consequences that await if he violates the conditions of his probationary term.

Finally, the District judge explained why he had concluded that the sentence of probation reflected the seriousness of Gall's offense and that no term of imprisonment was necessary:

> Any term of imprisonment in this case would be counter effective by depriving society of the contributions of the Defendant who, the Court has found, understands the consequences of his criminal conduct and is doing everything in his power to forge a new life. The Defendant's post-offense conduct indicates neither that he will return to criminal behavior nor that the Defendant is a danger to society. In fact, the Defendant's post-offense conduct was not motivated by a desire to please the Court or any other governmental agency, but was the pre-Indictment product of the Defendant's own desire to lead a better life.

The Court of Appeals reversed and remanded for resentencing. It held that a sentence outside of the guidelines range must be supported by a justification that "is proportional to the extent of the difference between the advisory range and the sentence imposed." Characterizing the difference between a sentence of probation and the bottom of Gall's advisory guidelines range of 30 months as "extraordinary" because it amounted to "a 100% downward variance," the Court of Appeals held that such a variance must be—and here was not—supported by extraordinary circumstances.

Rather than making an attempt to quantify the value of the justifications provided by the District judge, the Court of Appeals identified what it regarded as five separate errors in the District judge's reasoning: (1) He gave "too much weight to Gall's withdrawal from the conspiracy"; (2) given that Gall was 21 at the time of his offense, the District judge erroneously gave "significant weight" to studies showing impetuous behavior by persons under the age of 18; (3) he did not "properly weigh" the seriousness of Gall's offense; (4) he failed to consider whether a sentence of probation would result in "unwarranted" disparities; and (5) he placed "too much emphasis" on Gall's post-offense rehabilitation.

As we shall explain, we are not persuaded that these factors, whether viewed separately or in the aggregate, are sufficient to support the conclusion that the District judge abused his discretion. As a preface to our discussion of these particulars, however, we shall explain why the Court of Appeals' rule requiring "proportional" justifications for departures from the guidelines range is not consistent with our remedial opinion in *United States v. Booker*, 543 U.S. 220 (2005).

OPINION

While the extent of the difference between a particular sentence and the recommended Guidelines range is relevant, courts of appeals must review all sentences—whether inside, just outside, or significantly outside the Guidelines range—under a deferential abuse-of-discretion standard "failure to exercise sound, reasonable, and legal decision-making; an appellate court's standard for reviewing a decision that is asserted to be grossly unsound, unreasonable, illegal, or unsupported by the evidence" (Garner 2004, 11).

Because the Guidelines are now advisory, appellate review of sentencing decisions is limited to determining whether they are "reasonable" (*United States v. Booker*, 543 U.S. 220 [2005]), and an abuse-of-discretion standard applies to appellate review of sentencing decisions. A district judge must consider the extent of any departure from the Guidelines and must explain the appropriateness of an unusually lenient or harsh sentence with sufficient justifications.

An appellate court may take the degree of variance into account and consider the extent of a deviation from the Guidelines, but it may not require "extraordinary" circumstances or employ a rigid mathematical formula using a departure's percentage as the standard for determining the strength of the justification required for a specific sentence. Such approaches come too close to creating an impermissible unreasonableness presumption for sentences outside the Guidelines range.

The mathematical approach also suffers from infirmities of application. And both approaches reflect a practice of applying a heightened standard of review to sentences outside the Guidelines range, which is inconsistent with the rule that the abuse-of-discretion standard applies to appellate review of all sentencing decisions—whether inside or outside that range.

A district court should begin by correctly calculating the applicable Guidelines range. The Guidelines are the starting point and initial benchmark but are not the only consideration. After permitting both parties to argue for a particular sentence, the judge should consider all of 18 U.S.C. § 3553(a)'s factors to determine whether they support either party's proposal. The factors include

A. The court, in determining the particular sentence to be imposed, shall consider—
  1. the nature and circumstances of the offense and the history and characteristics of the defendant;
  2. the need for the sentence imposed—
    a. to reflect the seriousness of the offense, to promote respect for the law, and to provide just punishment for the offense;
    b. to afford adequate deterrence to criminal conduct;
    c. to protect the public from further crimes of the defendant; and
    d. to provide the defendant with needed educational or vocational training, medical care, or other correctional treatment in the most effective manner;
  3. the kinds of sentences available;
  4. the kinds of sentence and the sentencing range established for—
    a. the applicable category of offense committed by the applicable category of defendant as set forth in the guidelines—
      i. issued by the Sentencing Commission pursuant to section 994 (a)(1) of title 28, United States Code, subject to any amendments made to such guidelines by act of Congress (regardless of whether such amendments have yet to be incorporated by the Sentencing Commission into amendments issued under section 994 (p) of title 28); and
      ii. that, except as provided in section 3742 (g), are in effect on the date the defendant is sentenced; or
    b. in the case of a violation of probation or supervised release, the applicable guidelines or policy statements issued by the Sentencing Commission
  5. any pertinent policy statement issued by the Sentencing
  6. the need to avoid unwarranted sentence disparities among defendants with similar records who have been found guilty of similar conduct; and
  7. the need to provide restitution to any victims of the offense.

He may not presume that the Guidelines range is reasonable but must make an individualized assessment based on the facts presented. If he decides on an outside-the-Guidelines sentence, he must consider the extent of the deviation and ensure that the justification is sufficiently compelling to support the degree of variation. He must adequately explain the chosen sentence to allow for meaningful appellate review and to promote the perception of fair sentencing. In reviewing the sentence, the appellate court must first ensure that the district court made no significant procedural errors and then consider the sentence's substantive reasonableness under an abuse-of-discretion standard, taking into account the totality of the circumstances, including the extent of a variance from the Guidelines range, but must give due deference to the district court's decision that the § 3553(a) factors justify the variance. That the appellate court might have reasonably reached a different conclusion does not justify reversal.

On abuse-of-discretion review, the Eighth Circuit gave virtually no deference to the district court's decision that the variance was justified. The Circuit

(continues)

(continued)

clearly disagreed with the district court's decision, but it was not for the Circuit to decide de novo ("a court's nondiscretionary review of a lower court's factual or legal findings," Garner 2004, 865) whether the justification for a variance is sufficient or the sentence reasonable. On abuse-of-discretion review, the Court of Appeals should have given due deference to the district court's reasoned and reasonable decision that the § 3553(a) factors, on the whole, justified the sentence. Accordingly, the judgment of the Court of Appeals is reversed.

It is so ordered.

CONCURRING OPINION

SCALIA, J.

I join the opinion of the Court. The highly deferential standard adopted by the Court today will result in far fewer unconstitutional sentences than the proportionality standard employed by the Eighth Circuit. The door therefore remains open for a defendant to demonstrate that his sentence, whether inside or outside the advisory Guidelines range, would not have been upheld but for the existence of a fact found by the sentencing judge and not by the jury.

SOUTER, J.

After *Booker's* remedial holding, I continue to think that the best resolution of the tension between substantial consistency throughout the system and the right of jury trial would be a new Act of Congress: reestablishing a statutory system of mandatory sentencing guidelines, but providing for jury findings of all facts necessary to set the upper range of sentencing discretion.

DISSENT

THOMAS, J.

I would affirm the judgment of the Court of Appeals because the District Court committed statutory error when it departed below the applicable Guidelines range.

ALITO, J.

In reading the *Booker* opinion, we should not forget the decision's constitutional underpinnings. *Booker* and its antecedents are based on the Sixth Amendment right to trial by jury. The Court has held that (at least under a mandatory guidelines system) a defendant has the right to have a jury, not a judge, find facts that increase the defendant's authorized sentence (*Blakely v. Washington*, 542 U.S. 296 [2004]). It is telling that the rules set out in the Court's opinion in the present case have nothing to do with juries or fact-finding and, indeed, that not one of the facts that bears on petitioner's sentence is disputed. What is at issue, instead, is the allocation of the authority to decide issues of substantive sentencing policy, an issue on which the Sixth Amendment says absolutely nothing. The yawning gap between the Sixth Amendment and the Court's opinion should be enough to show that the *Blakely-Booker* line of cases has gone astray.

A sentencing system that gives trial judges the discretion to sentence within a specified range not only permits judicial fact-finding that may increase a sentence, such a system also gives individual judges discretion to implement their own sentencing policies. This latter feature, whether wise or unwise, has nothing to do with the concerns of the Sixth Amendment, and a principal objective of the Sentencing Reform Act was to take this power out of the hands of individual district judges.

The *Booker* remedy, however, undid this congressional choice. In curing the Sentencing Reform Act's perceived defect regarding judicial fact-finding, *Booker* restored to the district courts at least a measure of the policymaking authority that the Sentencing Reform Act had taken away. (How much of this authority was given back is, of course, the issue here.)

I recognize that the Court is committed to the *Blakely-Booker* line of cases, but we are not required to continue along a path that will take us further and further off course. Because the *Booker* remedial opinion may be read to require sentencing judges to give weight to the Guidelines, I would adopt that interpretation and thus minimize the gap between what the Sixth Amendment requires and what our cases have held.

Read fairly, the opinion of the Court of Appeals holds that the District Court did not properly exercise its sentencing discretion because it did not give sufficient weight to the policy decisions reflected in the Guidelines. Petitioner was convicted of a serious crime, conspiracy to distribute "ecstasy." He distributed thousands of pills and made between

$30,000 and $40,000 in profit. Although he eventually left the conspiracy, he did so because he was worried about apprehension. The Sentencing Guidelines called for a term of imprisonment of 30 to 37 months, but the District Court imposed a term of probation.

If the question before us was whether a reasonable jurist could conclude that a sentence of probation was sufficient in this case to serve the purposes of punishment set out in 18 U.S.C. § 3553(a)(2), the District Court's decision could not be disturbed. But because I believe that sentencing judges must still give some significant weight to the Guidelines sentencing range, the Commission's policy statements, and the need to avoid unwarranted sentencing disparities, I agree with the Eighth Circuit that the District Court did not properly exercise its discretion.

The court listed five considerations as justification for a sentence of probation: (1) petitioner's "voluntary and explicit withdrawal from the conspiracy," (2) his "exemplary behavior while on bond," (3) "the support manifested by family and friends," (4) "the lack of criminal history, especially a complete lack of any violent criminal history," (5) and his age at the time of the offense.

Two of the considerations that the District Court cited—the support manifested by family and friends and his age—amounted to a direct rejection of the Sentencing Commission's authority to decide the most basic issues of sentencing policy. In response to Congress's direction to establish uniform national sentencing policies regarding these common sentencing factors, the Sentencing Commission issued policy statements concluding that "age," "family ties," and "community ties" are relevant to sentencing only in unusual cases.

The District Court in this case did not claim that there was anything particularly unusual about petitioner's family or community ties or his age, but the Court cited these factors as justifications for a sentence of probation. Although the District Court was obligated to take into account the Commission's policy statements and the need to avoid sentencing disparities, the District Court rejected Commission policy statements that are critical to the effort to reduce such disparities.

The District Court relied on petitioner's lack of criminal history, but criminal history (or the lack thereof) is a central factor in the calculation of the Guidelines range. Petitioner was given credit for his lack of criminal history in the calculation of his Guidelines sentence. Consequently, giving petitioner additional credit for this factor was nothing more than an expression of disagreement with the policy determination reflected in the Guidelines range.

The District Court mentioned petitioner's "exemplary behavior while on bond," but this surely cannot be regarded as a weighty factor.

Finally, the District Court was plainly impressed by petitioner's "voluntary and explicit withdrawal from the conspiracy." As the Government argues, the legitimate strength of this factor is diminished by petitioner's motivation in withdrawing. He did not leave the conspiracy for reasons of conscience, and he made no effort to stop the others in the ring. He withdrew because he had become afraid of apprehension.

Because I believe that the Eighth Circuit correctly interpreted and applied the standards set out in the Booker remedial opinion, I must respectfully dissent.

QUESTIONS

1. Summarize the facts of the case.
2. Summarize the arguments of the majority opinion, applying the Sixth Amendment right to trial by jury.
3. Summarize the arguments of the concurring and dissenting opinions, applying the Sixth Amendment right to trial by jury.
4. Should the right to trial by jury apply to sentencing? Back up your answer with details from the facts and opinions of the Court.
5. In your opinion, what is the "fair" punishment Gall deserves? Back up your answer with details from the facts and opinions of the Court.

Summary

LO1 In our constitutional democracy, the power of the government is balanced against the liberty of individuals. The rule of law ensures criminality is not subject to passions of rulers of any type and helps protect the fundamental rights of individuals.

LO2, LO3 The principle of legality establishes: "No crime without law, no punishment without law." The principle of legality also prevents retroactive law making, ensuring that no one is punished for crimes that didn't exist at the time of the behavior.

LO4 Vague laws fail to give fair warning to individuals and law enforcement as to what conduct is lawful. The rule of lenity requires the courts to resolve ambiguities in criminal statues in favor of the defendant, especially in felony cases.

LO5 Defendants in criminal cases enjoy a presumption of innocence, and the prosecution has to prove every element of the crime charged beyond a reasonable doubt. Defendants who wish to use affirmative defenses bear the burden of production to put forth evidence supporting their justification or excuse defense.

LO6 The First Amendment ensures that people aren't criminally punished for their expressive behavior, and the Second Amendment protects against the government's ability to restrict the individual right to use handguns to protect ourselves in our homes. Though not explicitly in the Bill of Rights, there is a constitutional right to privacy that requires the government to prove that a compelling interest justifies invading it. All of these rights are limited to balance the power of the government against the rights of individuals.

LO7 The Eighth Amendment ensures that people aren't subject to cruel and unusual punishments. Barbaric punishments are punishments that are no longer considered acceptable in a civilized society, and the principle of proportionality requires that the punishment fits the crime.

LO8 The U.S. Supreme Court has ruled that the right to a jury trial also guarantees that no increase in sentencing can occur without the finding of all relevant facts by a jury. All sentences are still subject to review by the U.S. Courts of Appeal, and there is still contention surrounding departures from sentencing guidelines.

Key Terms

constitutional democracy, p. 40
rule of law, p. 40
principle of legality, p. 40
ex post facto laws, p. 41
void-for-vagueness doctrine, p. 42
fair notice, p. 44
rule of lenity, p. 46
narrow lenity rule, p. 46
presumption of innocence, p. 47
burden of proof, p. 47
proof beyond a reasonable doubt, p. 47
affirmative defenses, p. 48
burden of production, p. 48
burden of persuasion, p. 48
preponderance of the evidence, p. 48
expressive conduct, p. 49
clear and present danger doctrine, p. 49
void-for-overbreadth doctrine, p. 50
Second Amendment, p. 55
constitutional right to privacy, p. 61
fundamental right to privacy, p. 61
cruel and unusual punishments, p. 65
barbaric punishments, p. 65
principle of proportionality, p. 67
evolving standard test, p. 74
three-strikes laws, p. 79
Apprendi rule, p. 84

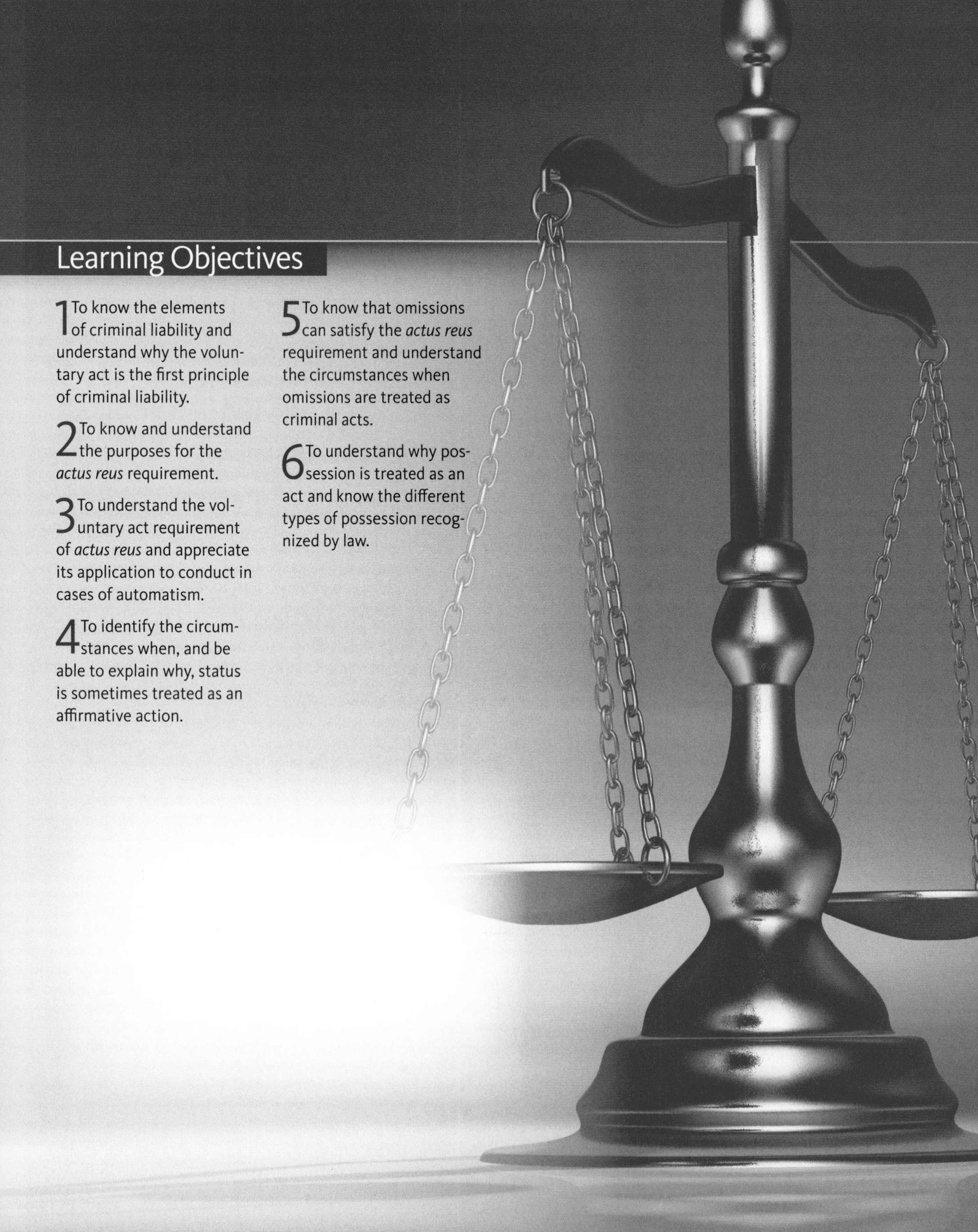

Learning Objectives

1 To know the elements of criminal liability and understand why the voluntary act is the first principle of criminal liability.

2 To know and understand the purposes for the *actus reus* requirement.

3 To understand the voluntary act requirement of *actus reus* and appreciate its application to conduct in cases of automatism.

4 To identify the circumstances when, and be able to explain why, status is sometimes treated as an affirmative action.

5 To know that omissions can satisfy the *actus reus* requirement and understand the circumstances when omissions are treated as criminal acts.

6 To understand why possession is treated as an act and know the different types of possession recognized by law.

3 The Criminal Act: The First Principle of Criminal Liability

Chapter Outline

Did They Have a "Legal" Duty to Act?

On the afternoon of November 15, when police and an ambulance crew arrived in response to a call by Helen and Walter Pestinikas, George Kly's dead body appeared emaciated, with his ribs and sternum greatly pronounced. Mrs. Pestinikas told police that she and her husband had taken care of Kly for $300 per month and that she had given him cookies and orange juice at 11:30 A.M. on the morning of his death. A subsequent autopsy, however, revealed that Kly had been dead at that time and may have been dead for as many as 39 hours before his body was found. The cause of death was determined to be starvation and dehydration. Expert testimony opined that Kly would have experienced pain and suffering over a long period of time before he died.

> No one should be punished except for something she does. She shouldn't be punished for what wasn't done at all; she shouldn't be punished for what someone else does; she shouldn't be punished for being the sort of person she is, unless it is up to her whether or not she is a person of that sort. She shouldn't be punished for being blond or short, for example, because it isn't up to her whether she is blond or short. Our conduct is what justifies punishing us. One way of expressing this point is to say that there is a voluntary act requirement in the criminal law.
>
> —RAYMOND R. CORRADO (1994, 1529)

The voluntary act requirement is called the "first principle of criminal liability." You'll learn why in this chapter. But, before we get to that, you need to be sure how the voluntary act requirement fits into the analytic framework of criminal liability

criminal liability "conduct that unjustifiably and inexcusably inflicts or threatens substantial harm to individual or public interests"

introduced in Chapter 1. Recall the definition of **criminal liability**: "conduct that unjustifiably and inexcusably inflicts or threatens substantial harm to individual or public interests" (ALI 1985, MPC § 1.02(1)(a), Chapter 1, p. 14).

Criminal liability falls only upon those whose cases progress through all the following analytic steps. We express them here as questions:

1. *Is there criminal conduct?* If there's no criminal conduct, there's no criminal liability. If there is, there might be criminal liability. To determine if there is, we proceed to the second question. (See this chapter on criminal acts; Chapter 2 on "the principle of legality;" Chapter 4 on criminal intent and causation.)
2. *Is the conduct justified?* If it is, then there's no criminal liability. If it isn't justified, there still might not be criminal liability. To determine if there is, we proceed to the third question. (See Chapter 5 on the defenses of justification.)
3. *Is the conduct excused?* If it is, then there's no criminal liability. (See Chapter 6 on the defenses of excuse.)

This scheme applies to *almost* everything you'll learn, not just in the rest of this chapter and Chapters 4 through 6. It also applies to the crimes covered in Chapters 7 through 13. Furthermore, the scheme applies whether you're learning about criminal liability under the federal government or the government of the state, city, or town where you live or attend school. It applies whether it's the common law, a criminal code, or the MPC being analyzed. (The "Elements of Crime" boxes that you'll find throughout the book illustrate the scheme.)

THE ELEMENTS OF CRIMINAL LIABILITY

LO1

elements of a crime to convict, the prosecution must prove beyond a reasonable doubt: (1) a criminal act (in all crimes), (2) criminal intent (in some crimes), (3) concurrence (in all crimes), (4) attendant circumstances (in some crimes), and (5) that criminal conduct caused a criminal harm (in bad result crimes only)

Criminal code authors have five building blocks at their disposal when they write the definitions of the thousands of individual crimes and defenses. These building blocks are the elements of a crime that the prosecution has to prove beyond a reasonable doubt to convict individual defendants.

Here's the list:

1. Criminal act (*actus reus*)
2. Criminal intent (*mens rea*)
3. Concurrence
4. Attendant circumstances
5. Bad result (causing a criminal harm)

These are illustrated in the Elements of Criminal Conduct Crimes box.

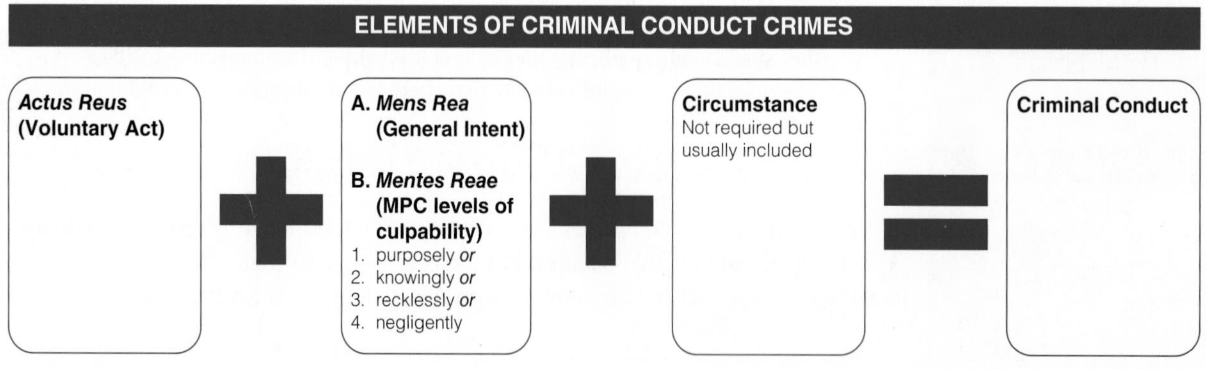

All crimes have to include a voluntary criminal act (*actus reus* or "evil act"; also referred to as the *physical element* in crime). That's why it's called the first principle of criminal liability. The vast majority of minor crimes against public order and morals (the subject of Chapter 12) include neither *mens rea* (criminal intent, often referred to as the mental element), nor the element of causation, nor conduct that causes a bad result (Chapter 4).

actus reus the requirement that all crimes have to include a voluntary criminal act, which is the physical element of a crime and the first principle of criminal liability

Serious crimes, such as murder (Chapter 9), sexual assault (Chapter 10), and robbery (Chapter 11); and theft and burglary (Chapter 11) include both a criminal act and a second element, the states of mind included in *mens rea* ("evil mind"). You'll learn more about *mens rea* in Chapter 4, and apply it to complicity crimes in Chapter 5 (accomplice and vicarious liability); Chapter 6 (the inchoate crimes attempt, conspiracy, and solicitation); and *most* but not all specific crimes in Chapters 8 through 13.

mens rea criminal intent, the mental element of a crime

We call crimes requiring a criminal act triggered by criminal intent **conduct crimes**. Let's look at burglary as an example of a criminal conduct crime. It consists of the act of breaking and entering a house, triggered by the *mens rea* of, say, intending to steal an iPhone 6+ once inside the house. The crime of burglary is complete whether or not the burglar actually steals the iPhone. So the crime of burglary is criminal conduct whether or not it causes any harm beyond the conduct itself.

conduct crimes requiring a criminal act triggered by criminal intent

criminal acts voluntary bodily movements

Don't confuse *criminal acts* with *criminal conduct* as we use these terms. **Criminal acts** are voluntary bodily movements (Holmes 1963, 45–47); **criminal conduct** is the criminal act triggered by *mens rea*. *Criminal liability* takes this one step further; it's criminal conduct that qualifies for punishment. Table 3.1 summarizes the differences among these important concepts.

criminal conduct a criminal act triggered by criminal intent (*mens rea*)

Crimes consisting of a criminal act and a *mens rea* include a third element, **concurrence**, which means that a criminal intent has to trigger the criminal act. Although concurrence is a necessary element that you have to know exists, you won't read much about it because it's practically never a problem to prove it in real cases.

concurrence the principle of criminal liability that requires that a criminal intent has to trigger the criminal act

It's a rare crime that includes only a criminal act. This is partly because without something more than an act, a criminal statute would almost certainly fail to pass the test of constitutionality (Chapter 2). For example, a criminal statute that made the simple act of "driving a car" a crime surely would be void for vagueness or for overbreadth; a ban on "driving while intoxicated" just as surely would pass the constitutional test (Dubber 2002, 44).

attendant circumstances element a "circumstance" connected to an act, an intent, and/or a bad result

That's why most of the offenses that don't require a *mens rea do* include what we call an **attendant circumstances element**. Circumstance elements are not acts, intentions, causes, or results; rather, they're facts or conditions connected with or relevant to acts, intentions, causes, or results. In our driving example, "while intoxicated" is the circumstance element connected to the act of "driving."

bad result crimes (result crimes) crimes that include all five elements: (1) a voluntary act, (2) the mental element, (3) circumstantial elements, (4) causation, and (5) a criminal harm

Some serious crimes include all five elements. In addition to (1) a voluntary act, (2) the mental element, and (3) circumstantial elements, they include (4) causation and (5) criminal harm. We call these crimes **bad result crimes** or, simply **result crimes**.

TABLE 3.1	Criminal Acts, Criminal Conduct, and Criminal Liability
Criminal act (also called *actus reus*)	The physical element of a crime; a bodily movement, muscular contraction
Criminal conduct	Criminal act + criminal intent (also called *mens rea*)
Criminal liability	Criminal conduct that qualifies for criminal punishment—namely, it's both unjustified and not excused

The Elements of Bad Result Crimes box illustrates these elements.

ELEMENTS OF BAD RESULT CRIMES

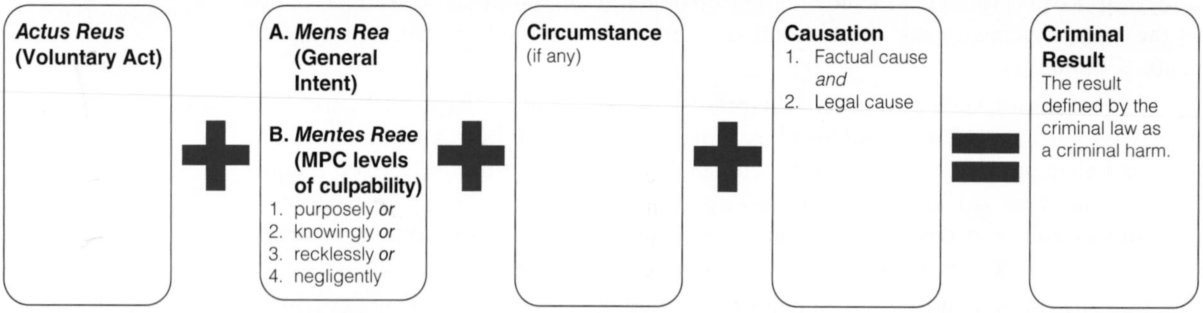

***Actus Reus* (Voluntary Act)**	+	**A. *Mens Rea* (General Intent)** **B. *Mentes Reae* (MPC levels of culpability)** 1. purposely *or* 2. knowingly *or* 3. recklessly *or* 4. negligently	+	**Circumstance** (if any)	+	**Causation** 1. Factual cause *and* 2. Legal cause	=	**Criminal Result** The result defined by the criminal law as a criminal harm.

criminal homicide conduct that causes another person's death

corpus delicti Latin for "body of the crime"; it refers to the body of victims in homicides and to the elements of the crime in other crimes

There are several result crimes (LaFave 2003b, 1:464–65; also see Chapter 1 on "core felonies"), but by far the most prominent in popular culture, and the one almost always included in criminal law books, is **criminal homicide**—conduct that causes another person's death (see Chapter 9). For example, first degree murder consists of (1) a lethal act (2) triggered by (3) the intent to kill, (4) which causes (5) someone's death.

This is a good time to review also what you learned in Chapter 2 about proving criminal behavior. But here, let's hone in on the commonly misunderstood and misused ***corpus delicti*** (Latin "body of the crime"). The misunderstanding arises from applying "body of the crime" only to the body of the victim in homicides. This is where the term *corpus delicti* most often appears. However, it also, more broadly, applies to the elements of conduct crimes (such as stealing someone's property in theft) and result crimes (such as burning a house in arson). You'll encounter these concepts again in Chapters 4 and 9 through 13.

Now, at last, it's time to turn to the main topic of the chapter: the requirement of a criminal act (*actus reus*).

THE CRIMINAL ACT (*ACTUS REUS*): THE FIRST PRINCIPLE OF LIABILITY

LO2

We punish people for what they *do*, not for who they *are*, or what they *intend*. You'll see this idea phrased variously, such as "we punish acts not status" or "we punish actions not intentions." However expressed, the phrase has to capture the idea of the first principle of criminal liability. So it's not a crime to wish your cheating boyfriend would die; to fantasize about nonconsensual sex with the person sitting next to you in your criminal law class; or to think about taking your roommate's wallet when he's not looking. "Thoughts are free," a medieval English judge, borrowing from Cicero, famously remarked.

Imagine a statute that makes it a crime merely to intend to kill another person. Why does such a statute strike us as absurd? Here are three reasons: First, it's impossible to prove a mental attitude by itself. In the words of a medieval judge, "The thought of man is not triable, for the devil himself knoweth not the thought of man." Second, a mental attitude by itself doesn't hurt anybody. Although the moral law may condemn you if you think about committing crimes, and some branches of Christianity may call thoughts "sins" ("I have sinned exceedingly in thought, word, and deed"), the criminal law demands *conduct*—a mental attitude that turns into action. So punishing the mere intent to kill (even if we could prove it) misses the harm of the statute's target—another's death (Morris 1976, ch. 1).

The third problem with punishing a state of mind is that it's terribly hard to separate daydreaming and fantasy from intent. The angry thought "I'm gonna kill you for that!" rarely turns into actual killing (or for that matter even an attempt to kill, discussed in Chapter 8), because it's almost always just a spur of the moment way of saying, "I'm really angry." Punishment has to wait for *enough* action to prove the speaker really intends to commit a crime (Chapter 8).

Punishing thoughts stretches the reach of the criminal law too far when it brings within its grasp a "mental state that the accused might be too irresolute even to begin to translate into action." The bottom line: we don't punish thoughts because it's impractical, inequitable, and unjust (Williams 1961, 1–2). Now you know why the first principle of criminal liability is the requirement of an act. This requirement is as old as our law. Long before there was a legal principle of *mens rea*, there was the requirement of a criminal act.

The requirement that intentions have to turn into deeds is called **manifest criminality**. It leaves no doubt about the criminal nature of the act. The modern phrase "caught red-handed" comes from the ancient idea of manifest criminality. Then, it meant catching murderers with the blood still on their hands; now, it means catching someone in any criminal act. For example, if bank customers see individuals entering the bank, drawing guns, threatening to shoot if the tellers don't hand over money, taking the money the tellers give them, and leaving the bank with the money, their criminality—the *actus reus* and the *mens rea* of robbery—is manifest (Fletcher 1978, 115–16).

manifest criminality the requirement that mental attitudes have to turn into actions for a "crime" to be committed

LO2

The *actus reus* requirement serves several purposes. First, acts help to prove intent. We can't see states of mind; we can only infer them from actions. Second, it reserves the harsh sanction of the criminal law for cases of actual danger. Third, it protects the privacy of individuals. The law doesn't have to pry into the thoughts of individuals unless the thinker crosses "the threshold of manifest criminality." Although simple to state as a general rule, much in the principle of *actus reus* complicates its apparent simplicity (Fletcher 1978, 117). We examine four complications: the voluntary act requirement; status or condition; criminal omissions; and criminal possession.

The "Voluntary" Act Requirement

LO3

Only voluntary acts qualify as *actus reus*. In the words of the great justice and legal philosopher Oliver Wendell Holmes, "An act is a muscular contraction, and something more. The contraction of muscles must be willed" (Holmes 1963, 46–47). Why do only voluntary acts qualify as criminal acts? The rationale consists of four logical steps:

1. Criminal law punishes people.
2. We can only punish people we can blame.
3. We can only blame people who are responsible for their acts.
4. People are responsible only for their voluntary acts.

The American Law Institute's (ALI) Model Penal Code's (MPC) widely adopted definition of "criminal act" provides: "A person is not guilty of an offense unless his liability is based on conduct that *includes* a voluntary act..." (emphasis added) (ALI 1985, § 2.01). (We'll call the MPC definition the **one-voluntary-act-is-enough rule.**) Notice that according to the MPC, even though a voluntary act is "an absolute requirement for criminal liability," it's not necessary that "every act up to the moment" the crime is completed be voluntary (LaFave 2010, 325).

one-voluntary-act-is-enough rule conduct that includes a voluntary act satisfies the voluntary act requirement

The *one-voluntary-act requirement* is the subject of our next case excerpt.

CASE

*In **State v. Burrell** (1992), the New Hampshire Supreme Court had to decide whether Marc Burrell's last act before the shooting death had to be voluntary.*

Did he fire the gun voluntarily?

State v. Burrell

609 A. 2d 751 (N.H. 1992)

HISTORY

Marc Burrell (defendant) was convicted of manslaughter after a jury trial in the Superior Court. Burrell appealed, arguing that the trial court committed an error in its jury instruction concerning the requirement under a New Hampshire statute that provides that conduct creating criminal liability must include a voluntary act. The New Hampshire Supreme Court affirmed the Superior Court.

THAYER, J.

FACTS

Douglas Saari and Joey Baglione made plans to have a few drinks at Baglione's house. Before going there, Saari, a minor, stopped at Burrell's house and asked Burrell to purchase beer. Burrell agreed and decided to accompany Saari to Baglione's. When they arrived, Baglione answered the door holding a .357 revolver. Inside the house were an AR-15 rifle, possibly a shotgun, a .44 revolver, and a .38 snub-nose revolver. The .357 and .44 revolvers were loaded.

During the afternoon the three drank beer and watched an X-rated movie. Baglione and Burrell played a form of Russian roulette with the .357 revolver. One bullet was placed in the chamber, the chamber was spun, one player placed the gun to his head with his finger on the trigger, and then the gun was examined to see whether the bullet would have been discharged if the trigger had been pulled. At some point in the afternoon, all three went out on Baglione's back porch and fired one or two rounds with the .44 revolver.

At trial, Saari testified that while Baglione was out of the room, Saari told Burrell that he was going to steal the .38 and placed it in the lining of his leather jacket. Burrell agreed to go along with Saari, and stated that he was going to steal the AR-15, the .44, and the .357. When Baglione returned, Burrell announced his intention to steal the weapons. Baglione said, "You're not going to steal those guns, so I'll stop you." Baglione ran out of the room, and returned with a shotgun. By then, Burrell had put down the AR-15, but kept the .44 in his belt and the .357 in his hand.

Saari testified that Baglione "came running out of the basement... and told [Burrell],... 'You're not going to steal those guns because I'll blow your f______ head off.'" Saari added that Baglione was not "serious... [and] he pumped the shotgun more than once, so I know it wasn't loaded." Saari then "looked at Burrell to see what his response was. And before I had time to do anything, he had shot in Baglione's direction" and hit him. Burrell dropped the gun, tried to call an ambulance, but panicked and went outside. At that time, Baglione's brother-in-law, Greg Eastman, arrived and called the ambulance. After the ambulance arrived, Eastman, Saari and Burrell went to the hospital.

At trial, Burrell testified that the fatal shooting did not occur when Baglione threatened him, but later in the afternoon while he and Baglione were preparing to take some of the guns back to a closet in Baglione's father's bedroom. Before storing the guns, Baglione told Burrell that his father always kept the .357 loaded.

Burrell testified that, after loading the .357 revolver, he was seated on the forward edge of the loveseat with his feet outstretched. Baglione passed in front of him from right to left. While Baglione was to his left, he sighted the gun on the hearth and put his finger on the trigger. He heard a noise and saw Baglione move from left to right in front of him. Thinking that they were going to collide, he jerked back and the gun went off. Burrell admitted on cross-examination that because of a lazy left eye, a problem he was aware of on the day of the shooting, he had great difficulty seeing anything to his left.

OPINION

In New Hampshire, "a person is not guilty of an offense unless his criminal liability is based on conduct that includes a voluntary act or the voluntary omission to perform an act of which he is physically capable."

RSA 626:1, I. Burrell does not dispute either the statutory requirement or the fundamental principle that criminal liability must be predicated upon conduct that includes a voluntary act. Burrell, however, contends that the court erred in failing to instruct the jury that it must find that Burrell's act of pulling the trigger was voluntary.

The trial court gave the jury the following instruction on the voluntary act requirement:

> A person is not guilty of an offense unless his criminal liability is based upon conduct that includes a voluntary act. A voluntary act is defined as conduct which is performed consciously as a result of effort or determination. To find Burrell guilty of an offense, any offense, you must find that the criminal liability is based upon conduct that includes a voluntary act. And although a voluntary act is an absolute requirement for criminal liability, you do not have to find that every single act in the circumstances presented to you was voluntary. It is sufficient to satisfy the requirement of a voluntary act if you find that Burrell's conduct causing the death of Joseph Baglione, Jr. included a voluntary act.

Burrell requested this instruction:

> A person is not guilty of an offense unless his criminal liability is based on conduct that includes a voluntary act. If you find Burrell's act of pulling the trigger of the handgun in this case not to have been a voluntary act, then you must find Burrell not guilty.

Burrell essentially asks this court to require the State to prove that Burrell's last act was voluntary in order to establish criminal liability. There is no support for this proposition in either the statute or in our case law. The statute only requires that Burrell's conduct that gives rise to criminal liability include a voluntary act. Although a voluntary act is absolutely necessary for criminal liability, there is no requirement that every act preceding the actual commission of the offense be voluntary. We hold that the trial court's refusal to instruct the jury that Burrell's act of pulling the trigger must have been a voluntary act was not error.

Affirmed.

QUESTIONS

1. State the facts relevant to deciding whether Marc Burrell "voluntarily" shot Joey Baglione.
2. State the court's definition of "voluntary act."
3. Summarize the court's reasons for holding that the trial judge wasn't required to give the jury instruction that Burrell asked for.
4. In your opinion, which is the better rule for determining whether an act is voluntary: (a) the last act has to be voluntary or (b) that conduct has to include a voluntary act? Defend your answer.

The MPC—and many state criminal codes—defines "voluntary," not by telling us what a voluntary act is, but by listing *involuntary* acts. The list usually includes movements during various forms of **automatism** (bodily movements while unconscious). The MPC also adds a fourth catchall: "a bodily movement that otherwise is not a product of the effort or determination of the actor, either conscious or habitual" (ALI 1985, § 2.01(2)).

automatism unconscious bodily movements

Let's look at two examples of automatism: acts during "sleep driving" and during epileptic seizures. Before we do, we need to make clear that there are two kinds of defenses that these examples of involuntary acts can trigger. The first are **fault-based defenses**, defenses based on creating a reasonable doubt about the prosecution's proof of a voluntary act. Fault-based defenses occur during the first step in our analytic framework of criminal liability (conduct that results from a voluntary act).

fault-based defenses defenses based on creating a reasonable doubt about the prosecution's proof of a voluntary act

The second kind of defenses is the *affirmative defenses* of excuse—insanity and diminished capacity. They take place *after* the prosecution has proved that the defendant's conduct caused the harm to the victim. (We discuss the affirmative defenses of excuse in Chapter 6.)

SLEEP DRIVING

LO3

Look first at the sleep driving issue in our next case excerpt.

CASE

*In **State v. Newman (2013),** James Robert Newman was convicted in the Circuit Court, Multnomah County, of felony driving under the influence of intoxicants (DUII), and he appealed.*

Did "sleep driving" nullify the voluntary act requirement?

State v. Newman

302 P.3d 435 (OR 2013)

HISTORY

James Robert Newman (Defendant) was convicted in the Circuit Court, Multnomah County, of felony driving under influence of intoxicants (DUII), and he appealed. The Oregon Court of Appeals affirmed. The Oregon Supreme Court allowed review, and reversed.

BALDWIN, J., JOINED BY BALMER, CJ, KISTLER, WALTERS, LINDER, AND BALDWIN. (BREWER, J. DID NOT PARTICIPATE.)

FACTS

"James Robert Newman (Defendant) met his friends for dinner one evening and, anticipating that he would drink alcohol at dinner, left his car parked by his apartment and walked to the restaurant. Thereafter, defendant's friends drove him home, and he went to sleep. Later that evening, a police officer followed defendant's car and observed defendant make a left-hand turn without signaling or stopping, run a red light, and drive down the middle of a street, straddling the two traffic lanes. The officer then activated his overhead lights to initiate a traffic stop and, in response, defendant pulled into a parking lot. The officer approached defendant's car, smelled a strong odor of alcohol, and observed defendant's bloodshot, watery eyes and slow, slurred speech. Defendant agreed to perform field sobriety tests and, after failing them, was taken into custody. At the police station, defendant consented to a Breathalyzer test, which revealed that he had a blood alcohol level of 0.15 percent."

Defendant was charged with felony DUII, reckless driving, and recklessly endangering another person. Before trial, the state filed a motion seeking to exclude as irrelevant testimony regarding defendant's sleepwalking disorder and his "sleep driving on the night in question." Defendant argued that evidence of his sleepwalking was relevant to negate the requirements for criminal liability under ORS 161.095—specifically, proof of a voluntary act with respect to the driving element of DUII. Defendant contended that he was not capable of performing the necessary volitional movements to consciously control his vehicle because he was asleep when the police stopped his vehicle.

As part of his offer of proof, defendant testified that he had sleepwalked within his apartment on a number of occasions in the past, but, to his knowledge, had not left his apartment while sleepwalking before this incident. A friend also provided testimony confirming defendant's sleepwalking behaviors. Defendant further testified that, after he went to sleep that evening, he had no recollection of leaving his apartment, getting behind the wheel of his car, or driving. Also, as part of defendant's offer of proof, Dr. Joshua Ramseyer, a physician certified in neurology and sleep medicine, provided expert testimony about the symptoms associated with parasomnia—a category of unwanted behavior that emerges during sleep. Within that category of sleep phenomenon, Dr. Ramseyer explained, exists somnambulism—which is also known as sleepwalking disorder. As Dr. Ramseyer explained:

> Sleep driving is thought of as being sort of a subtype of sleepwalking or an extension of sleepwalking. It's a motor behavior that occurs without consciousness... that comes out during sleep.... Just as someone's capable of sort of walking around the house, doing goal-directed behavior, such as eating, people can get behind the wheel, start up the car, and drive."

Dr. Ramseyer emphasized that activities performed while sleepwalking, such as "sleep driving," are unconscious acts. He further noted that sleepwalking resulting in "sleep driving," while uncommon in the general population, is a well-established phenomenon. If permitted to testify, Dr. Ramseyer would have rendered an expert opinion that defendant was "sleep driving" when stopped by police.

[The trial court excluded the sleepwalking evidence, and the Court of Appeals affirmed.] In this court, defendant again asserts that, for the purposes of DUII prosecutions, ORS 161.095(1) requires proof that a person committed the voluntary act of driving for criminal liability to attach. In defendant's view, evidence of his sleepwalking disorder and his condition on the night in question is relevant to the issue of whether his driving was voluntary, and thus should have been admitted. We allowed review to examine whether the trial court committed legal error in excluding defendant's "sleep driving" evidence.

OPINION

The relevant statutory provision defining felony DUII is set forth in the Oregon Vehicle Code as ORS 813.010. At the time that police officers stopped defendant, that statute provided, in pertinent part:

> (1) A person commits the offense of driving while under the influence of intoxicants if the person drives a vehicle while the person:
> (a) Has 0.08 percent or more by weight of alcohol in the blood of the person as shown by chemical analysis of the breath or blood of the person made under ORS 813.100, 813.140 or 813.150;
> (b) Is under the influence of intoxicating liquor, a controlled substance or an inhalant; or
> (c) Is under the influence of any combination of intoxicating liquor, an inhalant and a controlled substance.
>
> (4)... driving while under the influence of intoxicants, is a Class A misdemeanor and is applicable upon any premises open to the public.
> (5)(a) Driving while under the influence of intoxicants is a Class C felony if the current offense was committed in a motor vehicle and the defendant has been convicted, at least three times in the 10 years prior to the date of the current offense, of any of the following offenses....
> (A) Driving while under the influence of intoxicants....

ORS 813.010 sets forth two essential elements. A person commits the crime of DUII when the person (1) "drives a vehicle" (2) while "under the influence" of an intoxicating substance. As this court recently emphasized, the statute "prohibits driving under the influence of intoxicants." Thus, the focus of the DUII statute "is on the act of driving, and doing so while impaired."

When he was stopped, defendant admitted that he was intoxicated. He did not admit, however, that he had been consciously driving. He now contends, therefore, that he cannot be found criminally liable for driving his vehicle unless the voluntary act requirement of ORS 161.095(1) is met in this case. That statute requires a "voluntary act" as a "minimal requirement" for criminal liability:

> The minimal requirement for criminal liability is the performance by a person of conduct which includes a voluntary act or the omission to perform an act which the person is capable of performing.

Defendant thus contends that he should have been allowed to show that he was not engaged in a volitional act when driving because he was unconscious. The state responds that ORS 161.095(1) does not... require that the voluntary act be limited to the driving element of DUII.

The legislature has defined a "voluntary act" as used in ORS 161.095(1) to mean "a bodily movement performed consciously and includes the conscious possession or control of property." (ORS 161.085(2)). Applying that understanding to this case, defendant is not criminally liable under ORS 161.095(1) if he did not perform a bodily movement consciously.

Although the legislature has defined "voluntary act," it has not further defined what constitutes a "conscious" bodily movement. We have recognized that "conscious" is a word of common usage. Accordingly, we turn to the dictionary for further guidance to determine whether defendant's movements, if done while sleepwalking or "sleep driving," would be consciously performed.... Webster's Third New Int'l Dictionary 482 (unabridged ed. 2002) definition associates consciousness with a wakeful state and implies that a person in a state of sleep cannot execute a conscious action.

That understanding is consistent with the pertinent legislative history. The commentary accompanying

(continues)

(continued)

the 1971 substantive criminal code revisions explains that ORS 161.095(1)

> "enunciates the basic principle that, no matter how an offense is defined, the minimal requirement for criminal liability is conduct which includes a ' voluntary' act or omission. This excludes all 'involuntary' acts such as reflex actions, acts committed during hypnosis, epileptic fugue, etc."

That explanation discloses a legislative intent to exclude from the definition of voluntary acts any acts that are taken when a person is sleeping.

In drafting the criminal code's liability requirements, the legislature looked to analogous provisions of the Model Penal Code. Model Penal Code section 2.01 is the counterpart of ORS 161.095(1), and requires proof of volition to establish criminal liability. Section 2.01 provides examples of what is not a voluntary act. Those examples include a reflex or convulsion, a bodily movement during unconsciousness or sleep, conduct during or resulting from hypnosis, and movement that otherwise is not a product of the effort or determination of the actor. The commentary to section 2.01 clarifies that while "unconsciousness" may imply collapse or coma, there are "states of physical activity where self-awareness is grossly impaired or even absent"—i.e., what the commentary refers to as states of active automatism—that are subsumed within the meaning of the term. American Law Institute, Model Penal Code Comments § 2.01, 121 (Tentative *643 Draft No. 4 1955). The commentary explains that sleepwalking activity "should receive the same treatment accorded other active states of true automatism." Id. at 122. Thus, as the text and commentary suggest, the drafters of the Model Penal Code understood a person engaged in sleepwalking to lack the level of consciousness necessary for a volitional act.

Furthermore, the commentary to Model Penal Code section 2.01 states that criminal liability must be based on conduct that includes a voluntary act because

> the law cannot hope to deter involuntary movement or to stimulate action that cannot physically be performed; the sense of personal security would be short-lived in a society where such movement or inactivity could lead to formal social condemnation of the sort that a conviction necessarily entails. People whose involuntary movements threaten harm to others may present a public health or safety problem, calling for therapy or even for custodial commitment; they do not present a problem of correction.

We next address the state's argument that ORS 161.095(1) requires that the prosecution only prove that defendant engaged in "a voluntary act," which, in the state's view, does not require that the voluntary act be limited to driving for purposes of a DUII prosecution.... In the state's view,... the text requires only proof of a single voluntary act that connects to any of the elements of DUII.... The state points out that defendant voluntarily consumed alcohol resulting in his intoxication, and asserts that that conduct, which is linked to the intoxication element of DUII, satisfies the voluntary act requirement.

We disagree. Although intoxication is an element of the DUII offense, it is not the proscribed conduct; it is a condition necessary to establish the offense. The voluntary act that ORS 161.095(1) requires must be linked not to a condition but to proscribed conduct. That does not mean, however, that the only relevant voluntary act is the act of driving. The commentary to the Model Penal Code indicates that the voluntary act may occur prior to the proscribed act as long as it is related to it. That is to say, although a prior voluntary act may suffice, not merely any act, however tenuously related, is sufficient.

...

In this case, the jury was required to find that defendant engaged in a volitional act that led to the proscribed act of driving, but was permitted to consider evidence that defendant engaged in volitional acts other than the act of driving. For instance, the jury could have considered evidence that defendant engaged in the volitional act of drinking, if there were evidence that drinking led to the driving. However, the jury also could have concluded that defendant's "sleep driving" would have occurred without regard to whether he consumed alcohol and, thus, that defendant did not engage in a voluntary act which led to the act of driving,... or the omission to perform an act which the person is capable of performing.

However, the sufficiency of the evidence of a volitional act is not the issue on appeal. The issue presented is whether defendant was entitled to adduce evidence that he did not commit a voluntary act by driving on the night in question. The evidence defendant proffered was relevant to that issue. Sleepwalking disorder has been described as a condition that is distinct from the effects of intoxication. While sleepwalking can be induced by substances or medications, such a condition is diagnosed separately under the DSM–IV–TR as "Substance–Induced Sleep Disorder."

We conclude that the text, context, and legislative history of ORS 161.095(1) demonstrate a legislative intent to require that a defendant committed a voluntary act with respect to the driving element of DUII.

To summarize: We hold that the minimal voluntary act requirement of ORS 161.095(1) applies to the driving element of DUII in this case. Here, the trial court erred in not allowing defendant to adduce evidence that he was not conscious when he drove on the evening in question. The state was entitled to present evidence that defendant's drinking or other volitional act resulted in defendant driving his vehicle that evening. As noted, the state may also show a voluntary act with evidence that defendant had engaged in "sleep driving" prior to this incident and failed to take adequate precautions to remove access to his car keys.

As previously noted, the trial court concluded that defendant's sleepwalking evidence was irrelevant to any issue in controversy and therefore excluded the evidence. As this court has explained, evidence is relevant so long as it increases or decreases, even slightly, the probability of the existence of a fact that is of consequence to the determination of the action. Here, contrary to the trial court's ruling, defendant's proffered evidence was relevant as tending to show that defendant did not voluntarily drive his vehicle as required to establish liability for the offense of DUII. Thus, the trial court erred in excluding the evidence.

Nonetheless, this court will not reverse a trial court's erroneous decision to exclude evidence if the error is harmless. Here, defendant's "sleep driving" evidence tended to rebut an essential element of the state's case. Had a jury been allowed to hear that evidence, it may well have concluded defendant did not commit a voluntary act that led to his driving and acquitted him. It may well be that a jury would reject defendant's evidence as unconvincing. However, it is not for us to make this determination but rather a question for a jury to determine. Thus, we cannot say there is little likelihood that the error affected the verdict.

The decision of the Court of Appeals is reversed. The judgment of the circuit court is reversed, and the case is remanded to the circuit court for further proceedings.

QUESTIONS

1. List the facts relevant to deciding whether James Newman's conduct included a voluntary act.
2. Summarize the State's arguments that "sleep driving" didn't have to be voluntary.
3. Summarize Newman's argument that "sleep driving" was an involuntary act that negated the voluntary act requirement.
4. Summarize the Oregon Supreme Court's arguments for its decision.
5. In your opinion, should "sleep driving" disprove the element of *actus reus* generally? In this case? Defend your answer.
6. Do you believe someone can drive while they're sleeping? Explain your answer.

YOU *DECIDE*

Is "sleep sex" a voluntary act?

Bering 2011

Facts

Jan Luedecke, a 30-year-old landscaper, got drunk during a party in 2003 at a Toronto house and fell asleep on a couch. Sometime later, he approached a woman who was sleeping on an adjacent couch, put on a condom, and began sexual intercourse with her. The woman awoke to discover that her underwear had been removed and a glassy-eyed Luedecke was trying to rape her. She pushed him off, ran to the washroom, and returned to find him standing there bewildered.

(continues)

(continued)

Decision

At his trial in 2005, Luedecke was acquitted of sexual assault after University of Toronto psychiatry professor testified for the defense that Luedecke wasn't conscious of his actions. According to Dr. Shapiro, Luedecke was experiencing "sexsomnia" and was, therefore, not "consciously aware of his actions" during the assault. In February 2008, a Canadian provincial appellate court upheld Luedecke's acquittal.

EPILEPTIC SEIZURES

LO3

Experts agree that epileptic seizures and acts committed during the seizures are involuntary. But can epileptics be criminally liable because of voluntary acts before their seizures? (Kadish, Schulhofer, and Steiker 2007, 189) Voluntary acts that might create liability include choosing not to follow the laws of individual states.

The laws vary, but all 50 states restrict driver's licenses for persons who don't control their seizures with medication. Common restrictions include proof of being six months' free of active seizures and a physician's statement confirming that the seizures are controlled and that, if the person has a driver's license, he or she "will not present an unreasonable risk to public safety." According to the Epilepsy Therapy Project (2011a), being seizure free for 12 months "greatly reduces" the risk of traffic accidents of persons with epilepsy. Driving also "may be safe for some people with epilepsy after a shorter seizure-free period, depending on individual circumstances."

Circumstances that could make a person with epilepsy unsafe include missing even one dose of antiepileptic medication. Taking the medication at the wrong time is another of these circumstances. So is failing to heed the warning signs of oncoming seizures (auras). Auras vary significantly among individuals; they may occur right before a seizure, or several minutes, or even hours, before. Common warning signs that occur right before seizures include "changes in bodily sensations; changes in your ability to interact with things happening outside you; and changes in how familiar the outside world seems to you." Auras occurring hours before seizures include "depression, irritability, sleep disruption, nausea, and headache" (Epilepsy Therapy Project 2011b).

Our next case excerpt, *People v. Levy* (2011), a trial court convicted Ford Levy of reckless endangerment in the second degree, reckless driving, and speeding. The appeals court reversed and sent his case back for a new trial.

CASE

*In **People v. Levy (2011),** Ford J. Levy was convicted in the Justice Court of the Town of North Castle of reckless endangerment in the second degree, reckless driving, and speeding.*

Did his conduct "include a voluntary act"?

People v. Levy

936 N.Y.S.2d 835 (2011)

HISTORY

Ford J. Levy (Defendant) was convicted in the Justice Court of the Town of North Castle, Westchester County, of reckless endangerment in the second degree, reckless driving, and speeding. Levy appealed. The N.Y. Supreme Court, Appellate Term reversed and remanded for a new trial.

NICOLAI, P.J., LACAVA AND IANNACCI, JJ.

The People charged defendant with, among other things, reckless endangerment in the second degree (Penal Law § 120.20), reckless driving (Vehicle and Traffic Law § 1212) and speeding (Vehicle and Traffic Law § 1180[a]) after he allegedly rear-ended one vehicle, crossed the double yellow line on a two-lane road and collided with another vehicle while traveling at a high rate of speed. At a jury trial, defendant presented expert testimony that his erratic driving was likely caused by a temporal lobe seizure in his brain. Thereafter, defendant asked the Justice Court to charge the jury that, in order to find defendant guilty of the alleged offenses, he must have "acted voluntarily." The Justice Court refused to issue this charge, and the jury convicted defendant of the aforementioned offenses.

OPINION

"The minimal requirement for criminal liability is the performance by a person of conduct which includes a voluntary act" (Penal Law § 15.10). Penal Law § 15.00(2) defines a "voluntary act" as "a bodily movement performed consciously as a result of effort or determination." Neither "reflex actions, bodily movements during unconsciousness, hypnosis, [or] epileptic fugue" are subject to criminal liability. Furthermore, a court is required to instruct the jury on fundamental legal principles applicable to criminal cases in general and those material legal principles applicable to the particular case. When evidence at trial viewed in the light most favorable to the accused, sufficiently supports a claimed defense, the court should instruct the jury as to the defense, and must when so requested. A failure by the court to charge the jury constitutes reversible error.

In this case, defendant proffered expert testimony that he suffered from temporal lobe seizures and that these seizures could cause defendant to perform complex motor functions without any awareness of his actions both during and after each seizure. This testimony, when viewed in the light most favorable to the accused, along with defendant's request for the aforementioned jury charge, obligated the Justice Court to charge the jury accordingly. Its failure to do so constituted reversible error.

Additionally, the Justice Court improperly allowed the People to, in effect, constructively amend the accusatory instrument when it permitted them to argue in summation that defendant recklessly decided to drive his car because he should have known that he suffered from epilepsy. By the accusatory instruments relating to the charges of reckless endangerment in the second degree and reckless driving, the People limited the theory of their case to defendant's reckless "operation" of his vehicle during the accident.

In summation, however, the People proposed an alternative theory of liability when they asserted that defendant made a reckless "decision" to drive in the first place because he should have known that he suffered from epilepsy after his earlier accident. As the People asserted in their summation, "even if you believe defendant had a seizure, he shouldn't have been in a car, why, because you heard him testify that on December 1, 2008, he was in another accident in White Plains." The People's summation thereby provided the jury with the incorrect impression that they could convict defendant of reckless endangerment and reckless driving based on a theory that was at variance with the facts alleged in the accusatory instruments.

Accordingly, the judgments of conviction are reversed and the matter is remitted to the Justice Court for a new trial.

QUESTIONS

1. Do you believe there was enough evidence to send to a jury on whether Levy acted during an epileptic seizure? Explain your answer.
2. If you were a juror how much weight would you give to the expert's testimony? Explain your answer.
3. How important is it that Levy had an earlier accident? Explain.
4. Apart from the procedural question, does the prosecutor's argument that Levy "shouldn't have been in a car" have merit? Explain.

(continues)

(continued)

EXPLORING FURTHER

Voluntary Acts Prior to Involuntary Acts

Were his acts following exposure to Agent Orange voluntary?

State v. Jerrett, 307 S.E.2d 339 (1983)

FACTS

Bruce Jerrett terrorized Dallas and Edith Parsons—he robbed them, killed Dallas, and kidnapped Edith. At trial, Jerrett testified that he could remember nothing of what happened until he was arrested and that he had suffered previous blackouts following exposure to Agent Orange during military service in Vietnam. The trial judge refused to instruct the jury on the defense of automatism.

Did he act voluntarily? It's up to the jury said the appeals court.

DECISION

The North Carolina Supreme Court reversed and ordered a new trial:

Where a person commits an act without being conscious thereof, the act is not a criminal act even though it would be a crime if it had been committed by a person who was conscious. In this case, there was corroborating evidence tending to support the defense of unconsciousness. Defendant's very peculiar actions in permitting the kidnapped victim to repeatedly ignore his commands and finally lead him docilely into the presence and custody of a police officer lends credence to his defense of unconsciousness. We therefore hold that the trial judge should have instructed the jury on the defense of unconsciousness.

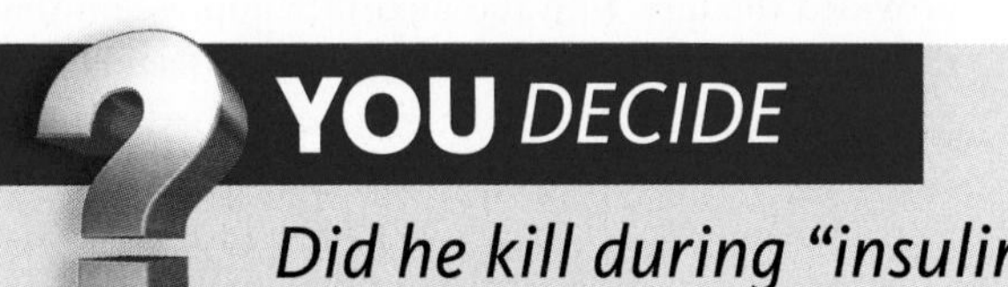

Did he kill during "insulin shock"?

State v. Moore

737 SE.2d 190 (2013 Ind.)

GEER, J., joined by STEPHENS and McCULLOUGH, JJ.

History

Acie Terry Moore was convicted of second-degree murder, and sentenced to the trial court sentenced defendant to a presumptive-range term of 146 to 185 months imprisonment. Moore appealed, arguing that the trial court should have instructed the jury on the defense of unconsciousness.

Facts

At about 9:00 P.M., Terry Moore was driving south on a two-lane paved road in Alamance County with a 50-mile-per-hour speed limit. At the same time, Mark McKinney was driving his truck north on the same road. Anthony Satterfield was riding a motorcycle directly behind Mr. McKinney's truck. Mr. Satterfield was followed by two more vehicles, one driven by Michael Rea and the second by Phillip Hagerman.

As defendant's truck approached Mr. McKinney's truck, Moore's truck crossed the double yellow center line into the wrong lane of travel. Mr. McKinney jerked the wheel of his truck to avoid colliding with defendant's truck. Defendant's truck, still in the wrong lane of travel, then struck Mr. Satterfield's motorcycle without braking. During the collision, the tire of defendant's truck severed

Mr. Satterfield's leg, the driver's side mirror on defendant's truck collided with Mr. Satterfield's helmet causing a large laceration on his forehead, and defendant's truck smashed the crank case on the motorcycle. Mr. Satterfield's body travelled approximately 100 feet before coming to rest.

After striking the motorcycle, defendant still did not brake, and his truck remained in the wrong lane of travel. Mr. Rea swerved his truck to the right to avoid colliding with defendant's truck. Defendant's truck travelled another 151 feet and then, again without braking, slammed into Mr. Hagerman's truck, snapping the rear axle of that truck and spinning the truck into a ditch. The left front tire of defendant's truck then deflated, and defendant's truck continued travelling for 168 feet off the highway into a field.

At trial, Moore's physician, Dr. Meindert Albert Niemeyer, testified as an expert in family medicine. According to Dr. Niemeyer, defendant has diabetes and a history of seizures and it was possible that hypoglycemia would cause a person like defendant to lose consciousness. He further testified that defendant's diabetes and low blood sugar could cause a state of "ketosis" in which defendant's body would produce "ketones" that can smell like alcohol.

Defendant's sister testified that when defendant does not "have good control over his diabetes," he gets disoriented and confused. She further testified that defendant has a history of seizures that caused him to "black out and stay out for a couple of minutes and then when he would come to he wouldn't know where he was at." On the night of the accident, defendant's sister was worried that defendant might have high blood glucose because he was acting tired and confused and had not eaten since early morning. Defendant's sister did not smell alcohol on defendant when he met her at the go cart track, and she would not have let defendant drive if she believed he had been drinking.

Defendant testified in his own defense, telling the jury that during the day on 14 August 2010, he mowed several lawns. Defendant ate breakfast early that morning, but did not eat anything for the remainder of the day. Although Trooper Norton testified that defendant told him on the night of the accident that he had taken his diabetes medication at about 5:30 A.M., defendant testified that he forgot to take his diabetes medication that morning. According to defendant, he drank a small amount of water and several sodas during the day. He also drank three 12- or 16-ounce beers at a friend's house that evening before driving to the go-cart track.

Opinion

The absence of consciousness not only precludes the existence of any specific mental state, but also excludes the possibility of a voluntary act without which there can be no criminal liability. Other courts have recognized "diabetic shock" and "epileptic black-outs" as sources of unconsciousness giving rise to the defense.

Evidence showing that the defendant was unconscious during commission of the crime only as a result of voluntary ingestion of alcohol or drugs will not warrant an instruction on the defense of unconsciousness. However, evidence of a defendant's voluntary consumption of alcohol does not render the defense of unconsciousness unavailable where there is additional evidence from which the jury could find the defendant's unconsciousness was caused solely by something other than the voluntary consumption of alcohol.

Here, Dr. Niemeyer, defendant's physician, testified that defendant is diabetic and has a history of seizures and that it is possible that defendant could pass out from hypoglycemia resulting from not taking diabetes medication, not eating during the day, not hydrating enough, and working outside during August temperatures. He further testified that defendant's diabetes and low blood sugar could cause defendant's body to produce "ketones" which can smell like alcohol. Defendant's sister testified that when defendant had a seizure, defendant would "black out" for a couple of minutes and be disoriented and forgetful. Defendant's sister explained in addition that when defendant "didn't have good control over his diabetes," defendant also became disoriented and forgetful.

Defendant testified that he forgot to take his diabetes medication on the day of the accident and ate breakfast early that morning but ate nothing else that day. The evidence showed that the accident occurred about 9:00 P.M. Defendant further testified that he mowed several yards that day, drank only a small amount of water and "a couple" sodas, and experienced nausea and a "burning sensation" in his eyes before the accident.

Regarding the accident, defendant testified that he "blacked out" and explained:

> I remember going into the curve and it just like—something just blanket over my head and I couldn't see nothing.... [A]ll I heard was something go bang, bang, bang. That's all I could hear but I couldn't see nothing.

(continues)

(continued)

Defendant also repeatedly testified that he was not drunk at the time of the accident.

Thus, taken in the light most favorable to defendant, the evidence permitted the jury to find that defendant was unconscious during the accident solely because of a hypoglycemic state, seizure disorder, or some combination of the two, and not as a result of his voluntary consumption of alcohol. The trial court, therefore, erred in failing to give an instruction on unconsciousness.

The State presented substantial evidence that defendant's voluntary intoxication caused defendant's mental state at the time of the accident. The State's evidence indicated that defendant had three to four beers in the middle of the afternoon at a bar. When he returned to the bar in the early evening, approximately two and a half hours prior to the collision, two witnesses saw defendant so intoxicated that he walked into a wall. When he got inside the bar, he fell off a bar stool. At the Alamance County Detention Center, on the night of the accident, defendant told the investigating officer that he was a "nine" on an intoxication scale of one to 10, with 10 being "completely drunk." Further, defendant performed poorly on four field sobriety tests and, in the investigating officer's opinion, defendant's physical and mental faculties were appreciably impaired by alcohol. Three other law enforcement officers and four civilian witnesses at the scene also observed defendant display signs of intoxication and many smelled an odor of alcohol on defendant. Defendant himself admitted drinking three 12- to 16-ounce beers that night.

Finally, chemical analysis showed that defendant had .18 grams of alcohol per 210 liters of breath at the time of the accident—a fact not explained by defendant's evidence. And, at trial, defendant testified: "Everybody drinks and drives. I was the one that just got caught."

Given this evidence, we cannot conclude that the jury would probably have reached a different verdict if properly instructed regarding the defense of unconsciousness.

No error.

Questions

1. List all the facts relevant to deciding whether Acie Terry Moore was conscious when he killed Anthony Satterfield.
2. If you were the prosecutor would you have decided to charge Moore with murder? Was the trial court right to refuse to instruct the jury on unconsciousness due to insulin shock? Defend your answer.
3. Assuming Moore was guilty, was the 12 to 15 year sentence proportionate to his crime? Defend your answer.

LO4 Status, *Actus Reus*, and the Constitution

status the character or condition of a person or thing

"Action" refers to what we do; status (or condition) denotes who we are. Most statuses or conditions don't qualify as *actus reus*. Status can arise in two ways. Sometimes, it results from prior voluntary acts—methamphetamine addicts voluntarily used methamphetamine the first time, and alcoholics voluntarily took their first drink. Other conditions result from no act at all, and individuals have no control over them. The most obvious examples are the characteristics we're born with: sex, age, sexual orientation, race, and ethnicity.

Is the voluntary act requirement a constitutional command? It's clear that, according to the general principle of *actus reus*, every crime has to include at least one voluntary act, but is the principle of *actus reus* a constitutional command? Twice during the 1960s, the U.S. Supreme Court considered this question.

In the first case, *Robinson v. California* (1962), Lawrence Robinson was convicted and sentenced to a mandatory 90 days in jail for violating a California statute making it a misdemeanor "to be addicted to" narcotics. Five justices agreed that punishing Robinson solely for his addiction to heroin was cruel and unusual punishment (see Chapter 2). The Court expressed the ban on status crimes in various ways: The California statute created a crime of personal condition, punishing Robinson for who he was (a heroin addict), not for what he did. The statute punished the sickness of heroin addiction—"even one day in prison would be a cruel and unusual punishment for the 'crime' of having a common cold"; the statute punished a condition that may be "contracted innocently and involuntarily" (667).

The decision that legislatures can't make status or personal condition by itself a crime brought into question the constitutionality of many old status crimes, such as being a prostitute, a drunkard, or a disorderly person. But what if these statutes include the requirement of some act *in addition to* the condition? That's where *Powell v. Texas* (1968) comes in. On December 19, 1966, Leroy Powell was arrested and charged under a Texas statute, which provided:

> Whoever shall get drunk or be found in a state of intoxication in any public place, or at any private house except his own, shall be fined not exceeding one hundred dollars. (517)

Powell was tried, found guilty, and fined $50. He appealed to the U.S. Supreme Court. His argument to the Court was that "the disease of chronic alcoholism" destroyed "his will power to resist drinking and appearing drunk in public." In other words, there was no voluntary act. So the statute, which "criminally punishes an ill person for conduct" he can't control, violates the ban on cruel and unusual punishment (*Powell v. Texas* 1968, Brief for Appellant, 6).

Texas, in its argument to the Court, relied on Powell's own witness, a nationally recognized psychiatrist, author, and lecturer on alcoholism, to make its case that Powell's being drunk in public was a voluntary act. From this and other expert testimony, Texas argued that although it's very tough, chronic alcoholics can become "chronic abstainers, although perhaps not moderate drinkers." In other words, with a lot of effort, they can stop themselves from taking the first, but not the second, drink of a "drinking bout." You might want to think about it this way: "barely" voluntary is good enough (*Powell v. Texas* 1968, Brief for Appellee, 8).

The U.S. Supreme Court's opinions reflected contrasting views on the critical question of how far the U.S. Constitution goes into the principle of *actus reus*. A plurality of four justices answered firmly: not one bit further than *Robinson v. California* took the principle. After making clear that the Constitution bans only pure status as a basis for criminal liability, Justice Thurgood Marshall, writing for the plurality, concluded:

> *Robinson* brings this Court but a very small way into the substantive criminal law. And unless *Robinson* is so viewed, it is difficult to see any limiting principle that would serve to prevent this Court from becoming, under the aegis of the Cruel and Unusual Punishment Clause, the ultimate arbiter of the standards of criminal responsibility, in diverse areas of the criminal law, throughout the country. (533)

Finally, the plurality invoked federalism to support its hands-off position regarding the principles of criminal liability:

> *Actus reus*, *mens rea*, insanity, mistake, justification, and duress have historically provided the tools for a constantly shifting adjustment of the tension between the evolving aims of the criminal law and changing religious, moral, philosophical, and medical views of the nature of man. This process of adjustment has always been thought to be the province of the States. (535–36)

Justice White wrote a separate opinion concurring in the plurality's judgment, because "Powell showed nothing more than that he was to some degree compelled to drink and that he was drunk at the time of his arrest. He made no showing that he was unable to stay off the streets on the night in question" (553–54).

Four dissenting justices were eager to bring the general principles of criminal liability fully under the protection of the U.S. Constitution. Writing for the dissent, Justice Fortas wrote:

> Powell is charged with a crime composed of two elements—being intoxicated and being found in a public place while in that condition. Powell was powerless to avoid drinking; that having taken his first drink, he had "an uncontrollable compulsion to drink" to the point of intoxication; and that, once intoxicated, he could not prevent himself from appearing in public places. (567–68)

Most criminal law books, and I'm sure most criminal law classes, spend lots of time and space on the Constitution and the general principles of criminal liability. At the time the cases were decided, there was great hope, and great fear (depending on your point of view), that an "activist" Supreme Court would use the "cruel and unusual punishment" ban and other provisions in the U.S. Constitution to write a constitutional doctrine of criminal liability and responsibility.

It never happened. Real cases in real courts since *Powell* have declined to bring the U.S. Constitution further into the principles of criminal liability than *Robinson* brought it in 1962. Legislatures define both the general principles of liability and the elements of specific crimes in their criminal codes. Courts interpret and apply the codes' provisions in decisions involving individual defendants.

OMISSIONS AS CRIMINAL ACTS

LO5

We support punishment for people who rape, murder, and rob because their affirmative actions caused harm. But what about people who stand by and do nothing while bad things are happening around them? As Professor George Fletcher (1978) describes these people, "They get caught in a situation in which they falter. Someone needs help and they cannot bring themselves to render it" (633). Can these failures to act satisfy the *actus reus* requirement? Yes, criminal omissions satisfy the voluntary act requirement, but only when there's a legal duty to the person in danger of harm.

criminal omission the failure to act when there's a legal duty to act

There are two kinds of criminal omission. One is the simple failure to act, usually the failure to report some information you're required by law to provide such as reporting an accident; reporting child abuse; filing an income tax return; registering a firearm; or notifying sexual partners of positive HIV status.

failure to report not providing information when you're legally required to

The other type of omission is the failure to intervene—that is, not actively preventing or interrupting injuries and death to persons or damage and destruction of property.

failure to intervene not actively preventing or interrupting injuries and death to persons or damage and destruction of property

Both omissions—failure to report and failure to intervene—are criminal omissions only if defendants had a legal duty (an obligation enforced by law), not just a moral duty, to act.

Technically speaking, a legal duty is an attendant circumstance element that the prosecution has to prove beyond a reasonable doubt. Legal duties are created in three ways:

legal duty an obligation created by a statute, contract, or special relationship, and enforceable by law

1. Statutes
2. Contracts
3. Special relationships

Statutes are the basis for legal duties to report—for example, the duty to file income tax returns, report accidents and child abuse, and register firearms. Individuals can also contract to perform duties; for example, law enforcement officers agree to "protect and serve." Failure to perform those duties can create criminal liability. The main special relationships are the:

- Parent–child relationship
- Doctor–patient relationship
- Employer–employee relationship
- Carrier–passenger relationship
- Husband–wife relationship (in some states)

Failure to perform **moral duties** (enforced by conscience, religion, and social norms) doesn't qualify as a criminal omission.

moral duties an obligation or norm created and enforced by society, conscience, and religion that's not enforceable by law

According to Professor Wayne LaFave (2010):

> Generally, one has no legal duty to aid another person in peril, even when that aid can be rendered without danger or inconvenience to himself. He need not shout a warning to a blind man headed for a precipice or to an absent-minded one walking into a gunpowder room with a lighted candle in hand. He need not pull a neighbor's baby out of a pool of water or rescue an unconscious person stretched across the railroad tracks, though the baby is drowning or the whistle of the approaching train is heard in the distance. A doctor is not legally bound to answer a desperate call from the frantic parents of a sick child, at least if it is not one of his regular patients. A moral duty to take affirmative action is not enough to impose a legal duty to do so. But there are situations which do give rise to legal duties. (331)

"Good Samaritan" doctrine imposes a legal duty to help or call for help for imperiled strangers

There are two approaches to defining a legal duty to rescue strangers or call for help. One is the **"Good Samaritan" doctrine**, which imposes a legal duty to help or call for help for imperiled strangers. While only a few jurisdictions follow the Good Samaritan approach, nearly all follow the approach of the **American bystander rule** (*State v. Kuntz* 2000, 951).

American bystander rule there's no legal duty to rescue or summon help for someone who's in danger, even if the bystander risks nothing by helping

According to the bystander rule, there's no legal duty to rescue or summon help for someone who's in danger, even if the bystander risks nothing by helping. So, although it might be a revolting breach of the moral law for an Olympic swimmer to stand by and watch a child drown, without so much as even placing a 911 call on her cell phone, the criminal law demands nothing from her.

Restricting criminal omissions to the failure to perform legal duties is based on three assumptions:

- First, individual conscience, peer pressure, and other informal mechanisms condemn and prevent behavior more effectively than criminal prosecution.
- Second, prosecuting omissions puts too heavy of a burden on an already overburdened criminal justice system.
- Third, criminal law can't force "Good Samaritans" to help people in need.

In our next case excerpt, the Pennsylvania Superior Court upheld a conviction for failure to act in *Commonwealth v. Pestinikas* (1992).

CASE

*In **Commonwealth v. Pestinikas** (1992), the Pennsylvania Superior Court upheld a conviction for failure to act based on a legal duty to act.*

Did the Pestinikases owe Joseph Kly a legal duty?

Commonwealth v. Pestinikas

617 A.2d 1339 (Pa. Sup. 1992)

HISTORY

Walter and Helen Pestinikas were convicted of third-degree murder in the Court of Common Pleas, Criminal Division, Lackawanna County. Each was sentenced to serve not less than five years or more than ten years in prison. Defendants appealed. The Superior Court, Nos. 375 and 395 Philadelphia 1989, affirmed.

WIEAND, J.

FACTS

Joseph Kly met Walter and Helen Pestinikas in the latter part of 1981 when Kly consulted them about pre-arranging his funeral. In March 1982, Kly, who had been living with a stepson, was hospitalized and diagnosed as suffering from Zenker's diverticulum, a weakness in the walls of the esophagus, which caused him to have trouble swallowing food. In the hospital, Kly was given food, which he was able to swallow and, as a result, regained some of the weight that he had lost.

When he was about to be discharged, he expressed a desire not to return to his stepson's home and sent word to the Pestinikases that he wanted to speak with them. As a consequence, arrangements were made for the Pestinikases to care for Kly in their home on Main Street in Scranton, Lackawanna County.

Kly was discharged from the hospital on April 12, 1982. When the Pestinikases came for him on that day they were instructed by medical personnel regarding the care that was required for Kly and were given a prescription to have filled for him. Arrangements were also made for a visiting nurse to come to the Pestinikases' home to administer vitamin B-12 supplements to Kly. The Pestinikases agreed orally to follow the medical instructions and to supply Kly with food, shelter, care, and the medicine he required.

The prescription was never filled, and the Pestinikases told the visiting nurse that Kly did not want the vitamin supplement shots and that her services, therefore, were not required. Instead of giving Kly a room in their home, the Pestinikases removed him to a rural part of Lackawanna County, where they placed him in the enclosed porch of a building, which they owned, known as the Stage Coach Inn. This porch was approximately 9 feet by 30 feet, with no insulation, no refrigeration, no bathroom, no sink, and no telephone. The walls contained cracks that exposed the room to outside weather conditions.

Kly's predicament was compounded by the Pestinikases' affirmative efforts to conceal his whereabouts. Thus, they gave misleading information in response to inquiries, telling members of Kly's family that they did not know where he had gone and others that he was living in their home.

After Kly was discharged from the hospital, the Pestinikases took Kly to the bank and had their names added to his savings account. Later, Kly's money was transferred into an account in the names of Kly or Helen Pestinikas, pursuant to which moneys could be withdrawn without Kly's signature. Bank records reveal that from May 1982, to July 1983, the Pestinikases withdrew amounts roughly consistent with the $300 per month Kly had agreed to pay for his care.

Beginning in August 1983, and continuing until Kly's death in November 1984, however, the Pestinikases withdrew much larger sums so that when Kly died, a balance of only $55 remained. In the interim, the Pestinikases had withdrawn in excess of $30,000.

On the afternoon of November 15, 1984, when police and an ambulance crew arrived in response to a call by the Pestinikases, Kly's dead body appeared emaciated, with his ribs and sternum greatly pronounced. Mrs. Pestinikas told police that she and her husband had taken care of Kly for $300 per month and that she had given him cookies and orange juice at 11:30 A.M. on the morning of his death.

A subsequent autopsy, however, revealed that Kly had been dead at that time and may have been dead for as many as 39 hours before his body was found. The cause of death was determined to be starvation and dehydration. Expert testimony opined that Kly would have experienced pain and suffering over a long period of time before he died.

At trial, the Commonwealth contended that after contracting orally to provide food, shelter, care, and necessary medicine for Kly, the Pestinikases engaged in a course of conduct calculated to deprive Kly of those things necessary to maintain life and thereby cause his death.

The trial court instructed the jury that the Pestinikases could not be found guilty of a malicious killing for failing to provide food, shelter, and necessary medicines to Kly unless a duty to do so had been imposed upon them by contract. The Court instructed the jury as follows:

> In order for you to convict the defendants on any of the homicide charges or the criminal conspiracy or recklessly endangering charges, you must first find beyond a reasonable doubt that the defendants had a legal duty of care to Joseph Kly.
>
> There are but two situations in which Pennsylvania law imposes criminal liability for the failure to perform an act. One of these is where the express language of the law defining the offense provides for criminal [liability] based upon such a failure. The other is where the law otherwise imposes a duty to act.
>
> Unless you find beyond a reasonable doubt that an oral contract imposed a duty to act upon Walter and Helen Pestinikas, you must acquit the defendants.

OPINION

The Pestinikases contend that this instruction was error. The applicable law appears at 18 Pa. C.S. § 301(a) and (b) as follows:

> (a) *General rule*. A person is not guilty of an offense unless his liability is based on conduct which includes a voluntary act or the omission to perform an act of which he is physically capable.
>
> (b) *Omission as basis of liability*. Liability for the commission of an offense may not be based on an omission unaccompanied by action unless:
>
> > (1) the omission is expressly made sufficient by the law defining the offense; or
> > (2) a duty to perform the omitted act is otherwise imposed by law.

Unless the omission is expressly made sufficient by the law defining the offense, a duty to perform the omitted act must have been otherwise imposed by law for the omission to have the same standing as a voluntary act for purposes of liability. It should, of course, suffice, as the courts now hold, that the duty arises under some branch of the civil law. If it does, this minimal requirement is satisfied, though whether the omission constitutes an offense depends as well on many other factors.

Consistent with this legal thinking, we hold that when the statute provides that an omission to do an act can be the basis for criminal liability if a duty to perform the omitted act has been imposed by law, the legislature intended to distinguish between a legal duty to act and merely a moral duty to act.

A duty to act imposed by contract is legally enforceable and, therefore, creates a legal duty. It follows that a failure to perform a duty imposed by contract may be the basis for a charge of criminal homicide if such failure causes the death of another person and all other elements of the offense are present. Because there was evidence in the instant case that Kly's death had been caused by the Pestinikases' failure to provide the food and medical care which they had agreed by oral contract to provide for him, their omission to act was sufficient to support a conviction for criminal homicide.

The Pestinikases argue that, in any event, the Commonwealth failed to prove an enforceable contract requiring them to provide Kly with food and medical attention. It is their position that their contract with Kly required them to provide only a place for Kly to live and a funeral upon his death. This obligation, they contend, was fulfilled.

Although we have not been provided with a full and complete record of the trial, it seems readily apparent from the partial record before us that the evidence was sufficient to create an issue of fact for the jury to resolve. The issue was submitted to the jury on careful instructions by the learned trial judge and does not present a basis entitling the Pestinikases to post-trial relief.

Affirmed.

(continues)

(continued)

DISSENT

MCEWEN, J.

The theory of the Commonwealth at trial was that the failure of the Pestinikases to fulfill the alleged civil contract to provide food, shelter, personal, and medical care to Mr. Kly was alone sufficient to support a finding of first and/or third degree murder. Section 301(b)(2) of the Crimes Code provides, in relevant part:

> Liability for the commission of any offense may not be based on an *omission unaccompanied by action* unless a duty to perform the omitted act is *otherwise imposed by law*. (emphasis added by the dissent; 18 Pa. C.S. § 301(b)(2))

The precise issue thus becomes whether the legislature intended that a "contractual duty" constitutes a "duty imposed by law" for purposes of ascertaining whether conduct is criminal. While I share the desire of the prosecutor and the jury that the Pestinikases must not escape responsibility for their horribly inhuman and criminally culpable conduct, I cling to the view that an appellate court is not free to reshape the intention or revise the language of the Crimes Code. Rather, our constitutional obligation is to implement the intent and comply with the direction of the legislature.

It is true that this Court has upheld convictions for endangering the welfare of children. However, all of the cases where liability is based upon a failure to act involved the parent–child relationship and the statutory imposition of duties upon the parents of minors. In the instant case, where there was no "status of relationship between the parties" except landlord–tenant, a failure to perform a civil contract cannot alone sustain a conviction for third degree murder. Thus, it is that I dissent.

QUESTIONS

1. List all the facts relevant to deciding whether the Pestinikases had a legal duty to Joseph Kly.
2. List all of the failures to act and voluntary acts that are relevant to deciding whether the Pestinikases failed to perform a legal duty to Mr. Kly.
3. Summarize the arguments regarding criminal omission of both the majority and dissenting opinions.
4. In your opinion, did the Pestinikases have a legal duty to Joseph Kly? Assuming they did have a legal duty, did they reasonably perform their duty? Back up your answer with facts and arguments in the case excerpt.

EXPLORING FURTHER

Omissions

1. Did she have a special relationship with the man in her house?

People v. Oliver, 258 Cal. Rptr. 138 (1989)

FACTS

Carol Ann Oliver met Carlos Cornejo in the afternoon when she was with her boyfriend at a bar. She and her boyfriend purchased jewelry from Cornejo. In the late afternoon, when Oliver was leaving the bar to return home, Cornejo got into the car with her, and she drove him home with her. At the time, he appeared to be extremely drunk.

At her house, he asked her for a spoon and went into the bathroom. She went to the kitchen, got a spoon, and brought it to him. She knew he wanted the spoon to take drugs. She remained in the living room while Cornejo "shot up" in the bathroom.

He then came out and collapsed onto the floor in the living room. She tried but was unable to rouse him. Oliver then called the bartender at the bar where she had met Cornejo. The bartender advised her to leave him and come back to the bar, which Oliver did.

Oliver's daughter returned home at about 5:00 P.M. that day with two girlfriends. They found Cornejo unconscious on the living room floor. When the girls were unable to wake him, they searched his pockets and found $8. They did not find any wallet or identification.

The daughter then called Oliver on the telephone. Oliver told her to drag Cornejo outside in case he woke up and became violent. The girls dragged Cornejo outside and put him behind a shed so that he would not be in the view of the neighbors. He was snoring when the girls left him there. About a half hour later, Oliver returned home with her boyfriend. She, the boyfriend, and the girls went outside to look at Cornejo. Oliver told the girls that she had watched him "shoot up" with drugs and then pass out.

The girls went out to eat and then returned to check on Cornejo later that evening. He had a pulse and was snoring. In the morning, one of the girls heard Oliver tell her daughter that Cornejo might be dead. Cornejo was purple and had flies around him. Oliver called the bartender at about 6:00 A.M. and told her she thought Cornejo had died in her backyard. Oliver then told the girls to call the police and she left for work. The police were called.

Oliver was convicted of involuntary manslaughter and appealed.

Did Oliver have a "special relationship" with Cornejo that created a legal duty? "Yes," said the appeals court.

DECISION

We conclude that the evidence of the combination of events which occurred between the time appellant left the bar with Cornejo through the time he fell to the floor unconscious established as a matter of law a relationship which imposed upon appellant a duty to seek medical aid. At the time appellant left the bar with Cornejo, she observed that he was extremely drunk, and drove him to her home. In so doing, she took him from a public place where others might have taken care to prevent him from injuring himself, to a private place—her home—where she alone could provide care.

2. Did he have a legal duty to his girlfriend's baby?

State v. Miranda 715 A.2d 680 (1998)

FACTS

Santos Miranda started living with his girlfriend and her two children in an apartment in September 1992. On January 27, 1993, Miranda was twenty-one years old, his girlfriend was sixteen, her son was two, and her daughter, the victim in this case, born on September 21, 1992, was four months old. Although he was not the biological father of either child, Miranda took care of them and considered himself to be their stepfather.

He represented himself as such to the people at Meriden Veteran's Memorial Hospital where, on January 27, 1993, the victim was taken for treatment of her injuries following a 911 call by Miranda that the child was choking on milk. Upon examination at the hospital, it was determined that the victim had multiple rib fractures that were approximately two to three weeks old, two skull fractures that were approximately seven to ten days old, a brachial plexus injury to her left arm, a rectal tear that was actively "oozing blood," and nasal hemorrhages.

The court determined that anyone who saw the child would have had to notice these injuries, the consequent deformities, and her reactions. Indeed, the trial court found that Miranda had been aware of the various bruises on her right cheek and the nasal hemorrhages, as well as the swelling of the child's head; that he knew she had suffered a rectal tear, as well as rib fractures posteriorly on the left and right sides; and that he was aware that there existed a substantial and unjustifiable risk that the child was exposed to conduct that created a risk of death.

The trial court concluded that despite this knowledge, the defendant "failed to act to help or aid the child by promptly notifying authorities of her injuries, taking her for medical care, removing her from her circumstances and guarding her from future abuses. As a result of his failure to help her, the child was exposed to conduct which created a risk of death to her, and the child suffered subsequent serious physical injuries."

Did Santos Miranda have a legal duty to "protect health and well-being" of the baby?

Yes, said the Connecticut Supreme Court.

DECISION

We conclude that, based upon the trial court's findings that the defendant had established a familial relationship with the victim's mother and her two children, had assumed responsibility for the welfare of the children, and had taken care of them as though he were their father, the defendant had a legal duty to protect the victim from abuse.

POSSESSION AS A CRIMINAL ACT

legal fiction pretending something is a fact when it's not, if there's a "good" reason for the pretense

Let's start this section by making clear that possession is not action; it's a condition (Dubber and Kelman 2009, 252). It's only by means of a legal fiction (pretending something is a fact when it's not, if there's a "good" reason for pretending) that the principle of *actus reus* includes possession.

According to Professor Markus Dubber (2001):

> Possession offenses have not attracted much attention. Yet, they are everywhere in American criminal law, on the books and in action. They fill our statute books, our arrest statistics, and eventually, our prisons. By last count, New York law recognized no fewer than 153 possession offenses; one in every five prison or jail sentences handed out by New York courts in 1998 was imposed for a possession offense. That same year, possession offenses accounted for over 100,000 arrests in New York State, while drug offenses alone resulted in over 1.2 million nationwide. (834–35)

In his criticism of the expansion of possession crimes, Professor Dubber (2001, 856–57) lists 38! And, he adds, "The list could go on and on." According to Dubber, "millions of people commit one of its variants every day.... Operating below the radars of policy pundits and academic commentators, as well as under the Constitution, possession does the crime war's dirty work."

Possession of weapons, illegal drugs, and drug paraphernalia are the most common possession crimes. The "good reason" for pretending possession is an act is the powerful pull of the idea that "an ounce of prevention is worth a pound of cure." Better to nip the bud of possession before it grows into an act of doing drugs or shooting someone. Also, most people get possession by their voluntary acts—for example, buying marijuana and putting it in their pocket. So their active acquisition brings about passive condition. But not always. Maybe a student who got a bad grade "planted" marijuana in my briefcase when I wasn't looking. Or, maybe you put your roommate's Ecstasy in your pocket to take it to the police station and turn it in.

actual possession physical control of banned items on my person, for example, marijuana in my pocket

constructive possession banned items not on my person but in places I control, for example, in my car or apartment

There are two kinds of possession: actual and constructive. Actual possession means items "on me," such as marijuana in my pocket. Constructive possession means items not on my person but in places I control, for example, my car or apartment (ALI 1985, 1:2, 24).

knowing possession items possessors are aware is either on their person or in places they control

mere possession items you possess but you don't know what they are

Possession, whether actual or constructive, can be either "knowing" or "mere." Knowing possession means possessors are aware of what they possess. So, if you buy crystal meth and know it's crystal meth, you have knowing possession. (Knowing doesn't mean you have to know it's a *crime* to possess crystal meth, only that you know the stuff you have *is* crystal meth.) Mere possession means you don't know what you possess. So if you agree to carry your friend's briefcase that you don't know is filled with stolen money, you've got mere possession of the money.

All but two states (North Dakota and Washington) require knowing possession. Also, almost all the cases in the court reports are constructive possession cases, and they're almost all drug and/or weapons cases.

CASE

*In **Williams v. State** (2013), Zamara Janice Williams was convicted in a jury trial in the Circuit Court, Hillsborough County, of possession of cannabis with intent to sell, manufacture, or deliver.*

Did she possess cannabis with the intent to sell, manufacture, or deliver it?

Williams v. State

110 So.3d 59 (FL App. 2013)

HISTORY

Zamara Janice Williams (Defendant) was convicted in a jury trial in the Circuit Court, Hillsborough County, of possession of cannabis with intent to sell, manufacture, or deliver. Defendant appealed. The Florida Court of Appeals reversed and remanded.

CASANUEVA, J.

FACTS

Tampa police officers Filippone and Cruz followed Zamara Janice Williams onto the interstate highway after they saw her drop off a passenger in the middle of 24th Avenue. They signaled to her to pull over because she was speeding and driving recklessly on the interstate and she complied, exiting the interstate and pulling into a parking lot. She was driving a rented compact hatchback with two passengers.

Even before the officers pulled up behind her in the parking lot, she had exited her vehicle and approached them in an extremely agitated state, telling the officers to just go ahead and give her the traffic citation. She was behaving in such an overwrought manner, amounting almost to having a panic attack and hyperventilating, that it took the officers several minutes to calm her before they could continue with the traffic stop. One officer testified that her heart was beating so furiously that he could see it pounding in her chest and offered to call emergency medical services (EMS), but she declined. The officers also testified that during this initial period of the stop, she was continually moving away from her vehicle and thus drawing them away with her; they had to keep bringing her back to her vehicle. As they stood near the driver's door, they perceived the strong odor of fresh marijuana that was emanating from the vehicle and traced it to a closed black bag behind the rear seat in the hatchback.

Based upon the odor of marijuana, the officers asked Ms. Williams for permission to search the car. She responded by saying that she did not think that there would be drugs in the car but consented to the search. Upon further investigation, the officers noted that the car was unkempt with paperwork bearing Ms. Williams' name strewn about. Inside the black bag they found a gallon ziplock bag containing almost a pound of fresh marijuana,[1] a smaller baggie containing several pieces of what appeared to be, and what were later confirmed to be, crack cocaine; an open box of sandwich bags; and two digital scales. No attempt was made to lift fingerprints from the black bag or any item from inside the bag. Although the car was rented in Ms. Williams' name, she was driving it, and her personal belongings were in the car, there was nothing on or in the black bag that tied it or the items inside it to her or anyone else.

Based on the above, the State charged Ms. Williams with three counts: possession of cannabis with intent to sell; possession of cocaine with intent to sell; and possession of drug paraphernalia. When Ms. Williams' defense counsel moved for judgment of acquittal at trial, the trial court denied the motion based on the strong odor of marijuana, the fact that the officers had found letters addressed to Ms. Williams in the car, and the fact that the car was rented in her name.

After the jury submitted a question that indicated its concern about interpreting constructive possession,[2] it returned a verdict of guilty of possession of

[1]When weighed, the FDLE found the amount of marijuana in the bag to be 413 grams or approximately 14.75 ounces.

[2]Specifically, the question the jury sent out was: "In evaluating constructive possession, when the person does not have exclusive possession, please define inferred or assumed, i.e., would stating that Zamara was aware of a smell, not necessarily what the smell was, be an inference or an assumption." The trial court's response to this question, with concurrence by both counsel, was: "All definitions and legal instructions permitted by law have been provided to you."

(continues)

(continued)

cannabis but not guilty of the cocaine and paraphernalia counts. The trial court sentenced Ms. Williams to four years' probation and she timely appealed.

OPINION

Because it was clear that Ms. Williams did not have exclusive possession of the black bag containing marijuana, as there were other persons in the car and she did not admit the bag was hers, the State was required to prove constructive possession with evidence beyond the fact that she was in near proximity to the black bag. When a defendant is not in exclusive possession of the vehicle where the contraband is found, the elements of knowledge and dominion and control may not be inferred or assumed but must be established through additional and independent proof. Therefore, the State's burden was to prove two elements: (A) that Ms. Williams knew of the presence of the contraband and (B) that she had the ability to exercise dominion and control over it. It is the latter element for which we find the State's evidence lacking.

The first element—knowledge of the presence of the marijuana in the black bag—that the State had to prove in order to convict Ms. Williams of constructive possession is satisfied here by the evidence of the strong odor of marijuana of which the officers were conscious when they approached her car. Additional evidence to support this first element is the reasonable inference that can be taken from Ms. Williams' extraordinary behavior when she was stopped. The officers testified that they had never before stopped anyone for a traffic violation and had the person react as Ms. Williams did. She was anxious and nervous to an unheard of degree, hyperventilating and having observable heart palpitations, causing the officers to fear for her health and to offer to send for EMS. Further, she continually tried to maintain a distance between herself and the officers and her car. The reasonable inference is that she knew there was marijuana in the car.

It is the second element—ability to exercise dominion and control—for which there was insufficient proof. Had Ms. Williams been the only person in the car when the officers stopped her, this element would have been satisfied and a jury question raised. But because Ms. Williams had two passengers with her, the State is not entitled to the benefit of an inference of dominion and control. The State is required to produce independent evidence pointing to her dominion and control of the black bag containing the marijuana.

. . .

Even under the lesser standard of proof by a preponderance of evidence in a violation of probation case, the State in *Hanania v. State*, 855 So.2d 92 (Fla.2d DCA 2003), failed to prove constructive possession of contraband. A law enforcement officer had stopped the car in which the defendant was a front seat passenger, and a narcotics dog alerted on the passenger's seat of the car. Upon his searching the car, the officer found a yellow manila envelope containing three baggies of suspected methamphetamine between the passenger's seat and the center console transmission column, an electronic scale in a recess under the dashboard, and an envelope containing marijuana addressed to the driver and owner of the car under the passenger seat. The defendant testified that he had only recently entered the car, about five blocks before the traffic stop, because the driver, an acquaintance of his, had agreed to give him a ride home from the store where they had met. The State argued that the defendant's proximity to the contraband was sufficient evidence of the conditions violated but this court disagreed because nothing in the record indicated that the defendant knew of the presence of the drugs or the scale or that he had the ability to exercise dominion and control over them.

Even though Ms. Williams was the driver of her car and the defendant in *Hanania* was a passenger, the present case is much like *Hanania* because there was no independent evidence linking either defendant to the contraband sufficient to convict other than mere proximity of contraband not in plain view.

The evidence presented at trial satisfied the first element—knowledge—that the State had to prove in order to overcome a motion for judgment of acquittal, but it did not establish that Ms. Williams was able to exercise dominion and control over the black bag that contained marijuana. Because the State failed to present sufficient evidence linking Ms. Williams to the contraband other than her mere proximity to it, the trial court erred in denying her motion for judgment of acquittal. Accordingly, we reverse the judgment and sentence for possession of marijuana. Because of the insufficient evidence supporting her conviction, on remand she must be discharged.

Judgment and sentence reversed and cause remanded with instructions to discharge Ms. Williams.

ALTENBERND, J., CONCURRING.

I agree that our outcome today is required by the precedent that is well explained in the court's opinion. Courts and legislatures around the country take different positions on this issue. If I were writing on a clean slate, I would be inclined to believe that a jury should be authorized to return a guilty verdict on a drug charge where the defendant is an operator of a motor vehicle and has actual knowledge that the vehicle contains illegal drugs that easily could be removed from the vehicle.

In this case, Ms. Williams was driving her small rental car fully aware that a bag containing a large quantity of marijuana was behind her in the hatchback area. This marijuana was either her marijuana, her passengers' marijuana, or marijuana jointly possessed by the driver and one or more of the passengers. Assuming the marijuana was not hers, she was in control of the car. She had the complete right before she entered the interstate to stop her car and order the criminal to exit the vehicle with the contraband. If she elected to continue to transport the contraband in this context, it seems to me that at a minimum she became a principal in the offense of possession and the jury was entitled to return this verdict.

QUESTIONS

1. Identify the two elements of constructive possession discussed by the court.
2. List the facts relevant to deciding whether Zamara Janice Williams constructively possessed marijuana.
3. Assume you're the prosecutor. Argue that Williams actually and constructively possessed marijuana. Back up your arguments with facts in the case.
4. Assume you're the defense attorney. Argue that Williams didn't physically or constructively possess marijuana.

YOU DECIDE

Did she possess alcohol?

Tracy Kastl, a juvenile, was found to be delinquent, convicted of being a minor in possession of alcohol, and her driver's license was suspended for one year. She appealed. The Arizona Supreme Court reversed and dismissed the case.

Facts

Tracy Kastl was one of five passengers in a vehicle that was parked in a parking lot in Waldron, Arkansas. Officers Johnny Smith and Ronnie Eisenhower of the Waldron City Police spotted beer cans beside the vehicle. They searched the vehicle with a flashlight and discovered a six pack of Coors Light beer lying on a "flat" in the hatch compartment of the vehicle behind Kastl. Randy Crowell, one of the passengers, admitted to purchasing the beer and claimed ownership.

The officers testified that Kastl did not have in her hand or lap any alcoholic beverage. The state contended that Kastl had "constructive possession" of the alcohol because it was in the vehicle in which she was an occupant.... The problem with joint occupancy arises because of the rule that when joint occupancy is the only evidence the State has, there must be some additional link between the accused and the contraband.... Tracy Kastl was clearly not in actual possession of the beer in this case.

The following was presented by the state to prove constructive possession of the beer by the appellant:

1. Beer cans were found lying between the vehicle in question and another parked vehicle;
2. A six-pack of Coors Light beer was found lying inside the vehicle in the hatch area behind Kastl, and according to Officer Eisenhower, all she would have had to have done was "just turn around and reached and grabbed it" [the beer]; and
3. Kastl had a smell of intoxicating alcohol about her person.

(continues)

(continued)

The state's evidence that there were beer cans beside the vehicle, that beer was found in the immediate proximity of Kastl in the vehicle, and that there was the smell of beer on her person are not sufficient evidence of constructive possession. The state has not proven the additional evidence necessary to link the appellant to possession of the beer.

Reversed and dismissed.

Dissent

I believe substantial evidence exists to support Kastl's conviction.... The state need not prove Kastl had actual possession of the contraband; constructive possession is sufficient.... The state can sufficiently link an accused to contraband found in an automobile jointly occupied by more than one person by showing additional facts and circumstances, indicating the accused's knowledge and control. One such circumstance is when the contraband is found on the same side of the car as the accused was sitting or in his or her immediate proximity. Here, it is undisputed that Tracy was seated in the immediate proximity of a six pack of beer. However, there are even more facts to show Tracy's knowledge and control of the beer or contraband seized in this case.

...The evidence shows:

1. Officers Smith and Eisenhower drove on to the lot where the car, in which Tracy was a passenger, was parked. There was a beer can by the car and one on the lot. The officers had been on the lot earlier and no beer cans were on it.
2. Five people were in the car, two young men in the front and Tracy and two young men in the rear seat. A six pack of beer was seen immediately behind the rear seat and the beer was within arm's reach of Tracy.
3. Several of the subjects were seen with open beer cans between their legs, although Tracy was not one of them.
4. Both officers smelled the odor of intoxicating beverage about Tracy's person.

The foregoing evidence speaks for itself. The trial judge could have reasonably inferred that Tracy had been drinking and that Tracy was within arm's reach of the six pack of beer found in the car. Some of the others in the car had open beer cans in their possession, and it is fair to infer occupants of the car had discarded two beer cans onto the lot—one of the cans was located immediately next to the car.

From this evidence, the trial judge, as fact finder, could have reasonably believed Tracy had knowledge and control of the beer located in the car. In fact, to have found and decided otherwise would, in my estimation, have ignored the obvious. The trial judge's decision should clearly stand.

Question

- Do you agree with the majority or the dissent? Support your answer with details from the case and from the "Possession as a Criminal Act" section in your text.

Summary

LO1 Criminal liability is criminal conduct that is without justification or excuse, and, therefore, qualifies for criminal punishment. There are five elements of a crime: (1) a criminal act, (2) criminal intent, (3) concurrence, (4) attendant circumstances, and (5) a bad result causing criminal harm. Conduct crimes require only the first three elements; bad result crimes require all five. The vast majority of minor crimes against public order and morals do not require criminal intent, concurrence, or a bad result. All crimes, however, must include a voluntary criminal act, which is the first principle of criminal liability.

LO2 The *actus reus* requirement serves several purposes: (1) it helps prove criminal intent, which can only be inferred from actions; (2) it reserves the harsh sanction of criminal law for cases of actual danger; and (3) it helps protect individual privacy by not punishing thoughts unless the thinker crosses the "threshold of manifest criminality."

Only voluntary acts, or *willed* muscular contractions, satisfy the *actus reus* requirement. Not every act leading up to the completed crime needs to be voluntary; the Model Penal Code's widely adopted definition of "criminal act" only requires a single act to be voluntary to impose criminal liability. Conduct during periods of automatism, such as sleep driving and epileptic seizures, do not qualify as voluntary acts. **LO3**

Status can arise in two ways: (1) it can result from a prior voluntary act, or (2) it can result from no act at all, such as sex, age, sexual orientation, race, and ethnicity. The Constitution bans pure status as a basis for criminal liability, but the U.S. Supreme Court hasn't expanded their interpretation of criminal liability and responsibility beyond what has traditionally been the decisions of the courts. **LO4**

Criminal omissions, or failures to act, consist of two types: (1) the failure to report some information you're required to, and (2) the failure to intervene to prevent injuries and death to persons or damage and destruction of property. Defendants can only be criminally liable for omissions if they had a legal duty, not just a moral duty, to act. **LO5**

Possession is not an action; it's a condition. The two main reasons for the legal fiction of possession as an action are: (1) to prevent future or more serious crime, and (2) most people get possession by their voluntary acts. There are different types of possession the law recognizes: actual, constructive, knowing, and mere. Actual possession refers to items on my person, while constructive possession refers to items in places I control. Knowing possession requires awareness of what you possess, while mere possession does not require that you know what you have. **LO6**

Key Terms

criminal liability, p. 96
elements of a crime, p. 96
actus reus, p. 97
mens rea, p. 97
conduct crimes, p. 97
criminal acts, p. 97
criminal conduct, p. 97
concurrence, p. 97
attendant circumstances element, p. 97
result crimes, p. 97
criminal homicide, p. 98
corpus delicti, p. 98
manifest criminality, p. 99
one-voluntary-act-is-enough rule, p. 99
automatism, p. 101
fault-based defenses, p. 101
status, p. 110
criminal omission, p. 112
failure to report, p. 112
failure to intervene, p. 112
legal duty, p. 112
moral duty, p. 113
"Good Samaritan" doctrine, p. 113
American bystander rule, p. 113
legal fiction, p. 118
active possession, p. 118
constructive possession, p. 118
knowing possession, p. 118
mere possession, p. 118

Learning Objectives

1 To understand and appreciate that most serious crimes require criminal intent and a criminal act.

2 To appreciate the long history of *mens rea* as a key element of criminal liability.

3 To appreciate the complexity of defining and proving *mens rea*, and to understand the difference between criminal intent and motive.

4 To understand that criminal liability, sometimes, is imposed without either objective or subjective fault (also known as strict liability).

5 To understand the difference between general and specific intent.

6 To understand and appreciate the differences in culpability among the Model Penal Code's (MPC's) four mental states: purposely, knowingly, recklessly, and negligently.

7 To understand the principle of concurrence and why it's important in criminal liability considerations.

8 To understand that the element of causation applies only to "bad result" crimes and to be able to differentiate factual cause from legal cause.

9 To understand that ignorance of facts and law can create a reasonable doubt that the prosecution has proved the element of criminal intent.

10 To appreciate the empirical research surrounding morality and ignorance of the law.

4 The General Principles of Criminal Liability: *Mens Rea*, Concurrence, Ignorance, and Mistake

Chapter Outline

Did He Intend to Give Them AIDS?

Calvin Stark tested positive for HIV, received extensive counseling about his infection, and was taught about "safe sex," the risk of spreading the infection, and the necessity of informing his partners before engaging in sexual activity with them. He disregarded the advice and engaged in unprotected sexual activity multiple times with each of three different women. He told the first victim he was HIV positive after the second time they had intercourse. He told the second victim he was HIV positive after they'd had sexual intercourse six times. The third victim and Stark had sexual relations throughout their brief relationship. It was "almost nonstop with him," "almost every night" during August 1989. Stark never wore a condom and never informed the victim he was HIV positive. When pressed, Stark denied rumors about his HIV status. The victim broke off the relationship because of Stark's drinking, after which Stark told her that he carried HIV and explained that if he had told her, she would not have had anything to do with him.

—State v. Stark (1992)

LO1

"I didn't mean to" captures a basic idea about criminal liability: a criminal act (*actus reus*) is necessary, but it's not enough for criminal liability—at least not liability for the most serious crimes. They include a mental element (*mens rea*) in addition to the criminal act. Why? Because it's fair and just to punish only people we can blame. We call this **culpability or blameworthiness**. Justice Holmes (1963, 4) put it this way: "Even a dog distinguishes between being stumbled over and being kicked."

culpability or blameworthiness the idea that it's fair and just to punish only people we can blame

Mens rea translated, in the singular, means "evil state of mind." In fact, as you'll learn in this chapter, there are several states of mind that can qualify as the mental element. The majority of states and the federal government apply a framework that began with the English common law (Chapter 1), which included general intent, specific intent, and strict liability. A substantial minority of states adopt the Model Penal Code (MPC) structure that consists of four states of mind, ranked according to the degree of their blameworthiness: purposely, knowingly, recklessly, and negligently. This book follows mainly (but not exclusively) the MPC structure. Because of the ranking by degree of blameworthiness, the MPC drafters preferred to call these mental states *levels* of culpability.

In addition to the mental state(s), we add two more elements essential to criminal liability: concurrence and causation. Concurrence refers to two connections: (1) In crimes of criminal conduct, criminal intent has to trigger the criminal act; (2) In result crimes, criminal conduct has to cause the bad result. The element of causation consists of two parts; the prosecution has to prove both beyond a reasonable doubt. Cause in fact (also called "factual cause" or "but for causation") consists of the objective determination that the defendant's act triggered a chain of events that ended as the harmful result, such as the death in a homicide. Cause in fact is necessary but not enough to satisfy the causation requirement; that requires legal cause. Legal cause consists of the subjective judgment that it's fair and just to blame the defendant for the bad result.

Last, we examine how ignorance and mistakes can create a reasonable doubt that the prosecution has proved criminal intent. Proving *mens rea*, and in result crimes, causation, isn't always enough to prove criminal liability. (Recall from Chapter 3 that result crimes include causing a criminal harm in addition to the conduct.) Sometimes, mistakes negate the *mens rea*. Let's turn first to the principle of *mens rea*, then to concurrence and causation, and finally to mistakes that negate *mens rea*.

MENS REA

LO1, LO2

> The contention that an injury can amount to a crime only when inflicted by intention is no provincial or transient notion. It is as universal and persistent in mature systems of law as belief in freedom of the human will and a consequent ability and duty of the normal individual to choose between good and evil. A relation between some mental element and punishment for a harmful act is almost as instinctive as the child's exculpatory, "I didn't mean to."
>
> —*Morissette v. United States* (1952, 250–51)

Mens rea, Latin for guilty mind, the mental element of a crime (also called "criminal intent," "evil mind," "mental attitude," or "state of mind") is an ancient idea. In *Laws* (348 BCE), Plato's last work, the philosopher lays out a sort of ancient Model Penal Code. His code rejected the voluntary and involuntary act distinction current in his day. In its place, he wrote a remarkably nuanced system of crimes based on levels of intent. Intentional crimes against persons and property are "maladies of the soul," to be cured "whenever they are curable."

mens rea Latin for guilty mind, the mental element (also called "criminal intent," "evil mind," "mental attitude," or "state of mind") in crime

> And so, if we can but bring a man to this—hatred of iniquity, and love of right—by acts we utter, through pain, through honor bestowed or disgrace inflicted, in a word, whatever the means we take, thus and only thus is the work of a perfect law effected.
>
> —*U.S. v. Cordoba-Hincapie* (1993, 487–88)

The result was a code that punished premeditated murder more severely than voluntary manslaughter (killing in the heat of passion); excluded unintended killings (see Chapter 9); and allowed defenses of insanity, infancy, and other forms of incapacity (see Chapter 8).

Fast forward about a millennium to the ancient English law based on liability without fault. Frederick Pollock and Frederic William Maitland (1898), the great Victorian scholars of medieval English law up to the reign of Edward I (1239), write about criminal homicide, "If once it be granted that a man's death was caused by the act of another, that other is liable, no matter what may have been his intentions" (264). But, even though they're writing about an era of liability without fault (see the section on "Strict Liability," p. 142), there were signs that, even in these years, the criminal law didn't entirely reject intent. Consider this passage you can relate to if you can get past its Victorian stiffness:

> It is hard for us to acquit the ancient law of that unreasoning instinct that impels the civilized man to kick, or consign to eternal perdition, the chair over which he has stumbled. But law that would not confess to sanctioning this instinct still finds grave difficulties in its way if it endeavors to detect and appreciate the psychical element in guilt and innocence. (266)

Another great *mens rea* scholar, Harvard Professor Francis B. Sayre (1932), pointed to two additional pieces of evidence that there was a *mens rea* requirement even though there was no *general* requirement of criminal liability. First, most *serious* crimes (the "core felonies" in Chapter 1) couldn't be committed without intent: murder, rape, robbery, burglary, and larceny (981). Second, defendants' punishments depended heavily on intent. From the earliest times, the criminal law in practice considered it "manifestly unjust" that a man who accidentally killed with no intention of doing harm should suffer the extreme penalty of death" (981–82).

According to Professor Sayre, the core felonies illustrate that

> [c]rime *in general* always has depended on and always will depend upon deep-lying ethico-psychological concepts. The early felonies were roughly the external manifestations of the heinous sins of the day. The point is not that morality first began to make its appearance in the law, but that an increasing and now conscious emphasis upon morality necessitated a new emphasis upon psychical elements in determining criminality. (989)

Joel Bishop's *Commentaries on the Criminal Law* (1907), the criminal law treatise most widely used by practicing lawyers from 1865 to 1912, put it simply: "An act and evil intent must combine to constitute a crime." (§206). This concept of *mens rea*, called general intent, refers to a "mind bent on moral wrongdoing" without further refinement (Sayre 1932, 1019). Fast forward again to a 2001 case where Senior U.S. District Court Judge and *mens rea* scholar Jack Weinstein reaffirmed the *mens rea* principle as the criminal law's "mantra." Summing up his extended passage, Judge Weinstein concludes that "Western civilized nations have long looked to the wrongdoer's mind to determine both the propriety and the grading of punishment" (*U.S. v. Cordoba-Hincapie* 1993, 489).

LO3 The Complexity of *Mens Rea*

Mens rea isn't just ancient; it's also complex. "No problem of criminal law ... has proved more baffling through the centuries than the determination of the precise mental element necessary to convict of any crime" (Sayre 1932, 974). Several reasons account for this bafflement. First, whatever it means, *mens rea* is difficult to discover and then prove in court. Second, courts and legislatures have used so many vague and incomplete definitions of the mental element.

Third, *mens rea* consists of several mental attitudes that range across a broad spectrum, stretching all the way from purposely committing a crime you're totally aware is criminal (stealing an iPod from an Apple store) to merely creating risks of criminal conduct or causing criminal harms—risks you're not the slightest bit aware you're creating (driving someone else's car with an open beer bottle you don't even know is in the car). We'll discuss these mental attitudes later in the chapter and in Chapters 9 through 13. For now, it's very important that you understand that intent in criminal law goes way beyond the dictionary definition of "intent," which refers to acting on purpose or deliberately.

Fourth, a different mental attitude might apply to each of the elements of a crime. So it's possible for one mental attitude to apply to *actus reus*, another to causation, another to the harm defined in the statute, and still another to attendant circumstance elements (ALI 1985, 1:2, 1:229–33).

As you learn about *mens rea*, you'll probably be confused by the multiple mental attitudes it includes; by the complexity and uncertainty surrounding the definitions of the multiple attitudes it encompasses; and by the practical problems of matching the attitudes to elements of the offense and then proving each one beyond a reasonable doubt. Maybe you can take some comfort in knowing that courts don't always get the definitions of mental states right, either. (Neither do I, and I've been thinking, talking, and writing about them since 1958!)

motive something that causes a person to act

We need to note one more complexity in *mens rea*: the relationship between mental attitude and motive. A **motive** is something that causes a person to act. Experts disagree over the difference between motive and intent. Probably for this reason, they clarify the difference with an example: if a man murders his wife for her money—his intent was to kill; his motive was to get her money.

It's often said that motive is irrelevant to criminal liability; good motive is no defense to criminal conduct, and a bad motive can't make legal conduct criminal. So if a wife poisons her husband because he's suffering from the unbearable pain of a terminal bone cancer, she's still guilty of murder. And if she wants him dead because she hates him and accidentally shoots him while they're deer hunting, she's not guilty even though she wanted him dead and she's glad he's out of the way.

Unfortunately, the relationship between motive and criminal liability is not so simple. The truth is that sometimes motive is relevant, and sometimes it's not. Greed, hate, and jealously are always relevant to proving the intent to kill. Compassion may well affect discretionary decisions, such as police decisions to arrest, prosecutors to charge, and judges to sentence, say, mercy killers.

Juries have sometimes refused to convict mercy killers of first-degree murder even though the intent to kill was clearly there (see Chapter 9). The murder case of Robert Latimer is a good example of this. Latimer could no longer stand the constant pain his 12-year-old daughter, Tracy, was suffering because of her severe and incurable cerebral palsy. She wore diapers, weighed only 38 pounds, and couldn't walk, talk, or feed herself. So he put Tracy into the cab of his pickup truck on the family farm and pumped exhaust into the cab of the truck. He told the police that he stood by, ready to stop if Tracy started to cry, but that she simply went quietly "to sleep. My priority was to put her out of her pain."

He pleaded not guilty to first-degree murder, but the jury found him guilty of second-degree murder. Despite the verdict of guilty on the lesser charge, many people in the town agreed with an 18-year-old high school student who said Latimer "did what he had to do for his daughter's sake. And that's the way a lot of people in town are feeling" (Farnsworth 1994, A6).

Motive is also important in some defenses. For example, it's a defense to the crime of escaping from prison if a prisoner breaks out to save her life from a rapidly spreading fire (the defense of necessity, see Chapter 5). Finally, motive is sometimes an element of a crime itself. For example, one of the attendant circumstances of burglary accompanying the act of breaking and entering someone else's property is "the purpose of committing a crime" once inside (see Chapter 11).

Let's look more closely at proving the *mens rea*, defining it, and classifying it, and the difficulties and complexities in doing all of these.

Proving "State of Mind"

LO3

You can't see a state of mind. Not even the finest instruments of modern technology can find or measure your attitude (Hall 1960, 106). Electroencephalograms can record brain waves, and X-rays can photograph brain tissue, but Chief Justice Brian's words are as true today as they were when he wrote them in 1477: "The thought of man is not triable, for the devil himself knoweth not the thought of man" (Williams 1961, 1). Three hundred years later, Sir William Blackstone put it simply: "A tribunal can't punish what it can't know" (Blackstone 1769, 21).

Confessions are the only direct evidence of mental attitude. Unfortunately, defendants rarely confess their true intentions, so proof of their state of mind usually depends on indirect (circumstantial) evidence. Acts and attendant circumstances are the overwhelming kind of circumstantial evidence. In everyday experience, we rely on what people do to tell us what they intend. For example, if I break into a stranger's house at night, it's reasonable to infer I'm up to no good. So by observing directly what I do, you can indirectly determine what I intend.

Criminal Intent

LO4

The list of terms used to define the mental element(s) that you'll run across in the case excerpts fit into three kinds of fault that satisfy the mental element in criminal liability (see Table 4.1). They are *subjective fault*; *objective fault*; and *criminal liability without fault.*

One is **subjective fault**, or fault that requires a "bad mind" in the actor. For example, suppose in your state, it's a crime to "receive property you know is stolen." You buy an iPod from another student who you know stole it. We call that bad state of mind "knowingly," which is more culpable than "recklessly" and less culpable than "purposely."

subjective fault fault that requires a "bad mind" in the actor

Subjective fault frequently is linked with immorality. You can see this connection in expressions in cases and statutes, such as "depravity of will," "diabolic malignity," "abandoned heart," "bad heart," "heart regardless of social duty and fatally bent on mischief," "wicked heart," "mind grievously depraved," or "mischievous vindictive spirit" (Dubber 2002, 50–51). Although these terms were typical of old laws and

TABLE 4.1 Mental Attitudes Used in the Alabama Code
"Intentionally"
"Willfully"
"Purposely"
"Designedly"
"Knowingly"
"Deliberately"
"Maliciously"
"With premeditation"
"Recklessly"
"Negligently"
"With culpable negligence"
"With gross negligence"
"With criminal negligence"
"Without due caution"
"Wickedly"
"Unlawfully"
"Wrongfully"

Source: Burnett v. State 1999, 575.

opinions, they're still in use in non-MPC jurisdictions, as you'll see in some of the case excerpts throughout the book.

objective fault requires no purposeful or conscious bad mind in the actor

The second kind of fault is objective fault, which requires no purposeful or conscious bad mind in the actor. For example, suppose it's a crime to "receive property you have reason to believe is stolen." You buy a new iPod in its original package for $10. You honestly don't know it's stolen. You *should* know it was stolen; a reasonable person *would* know it was stolen, and in fact it was stolen. So, even though you had no "bad" mind, you're held criminally accountable because you didn't live up to the norm of the average person.

Definitions of the Three Kinds of Criminal Liability

Specific intent. Actual intent to perform some act, along with a wish for the consequences that result from that act. Depending on the offense alleged, criminal prosecutors may need to prove that Defendant acted with specific intent.

General intent. Actual intent to perform some act, but without a wish for the consequences that result from that act. Depending on the offense alleged, prosecutors may need to prove that Defendant acted with general intent.

Strict liability. Strict liability exists when a defendant is in legal jeopardy by virtue of a wrongful act, without any accompanying intent or mental state. In criminal law, possession crimes and statutory rape are both examples of strict liability offenses.

Source: "Specific Intent," "General Intent," and "Strict Liability, *Legal Information Institute*, http://topics.law.cornell.edu/wex/.

The third kind of criminal liability, strict liability, requires neither subjective nor objective fault. Suppose a statute reads, "whoever receives stolen property" commits a crime. You buy an iPad for $45 that looks used, but you honestly and reasonably believe it wasn't stolen. It doesn't matter; under this statute, you're liable without either subjective or objective fault.

strict liability liability without either subjective or objective fault

It's easy enough to define and give examples of these three types of liability. It's also easy to rank them according to the degree of their culpability. Subjective "bad mind" fault is most blameworthy. Objective unreasonable risk creation is less blameworthy; some maintain it shouldn't even qualify as a criminal state of mind. No-fault liability requires the least culpability; it holds people accountable for their actions without regard to fault.

General and Specific Intent

LO5

We'll have more to say about mental fault and no fault shortly (also Chapters 7–13). But now, we have to examine two terms used by many courts and statutes.

General intent means the intent to commit the criminal act. Its general intent is general because it states the minimum requirement of *all* crimes—namely, that they have to include a voluntary act, omission, or possession (Chapter 3). It's the intent to commit whatever voluntary act, omission, or possession the criminal statute forbids. According to Professor LaFave's (2010), all crimes require "at least an intention to make the bodily movement that constitutes the act which the crime requires" (268). Unfortunately, courts and statutes use many synonyms for the general intent notion of *mens rea*. You can see this in these adjectives found in most ordinary dictionaries: "deliberate," "calculated," "conscious," "intended," "planned," "meant," "studied," "knowing," "willful," "purposeful," "purposive," "done on purpose," "premeditated," "preplanned," and "preconceived."

general intent the intent to commit the criminal act forbidden by statute

Specific intent applies only to *bad result* crimes. You might want to think of it as *general intent plus*, where "general intent" refers to the intent to commit the *actus reus* of the crime, and "plus" refers to the intent to cause a criminally harmful result. There are only a few specific intent crimes, most of them confined to the *core felonies*, most conspicuously murder (Chapter 9), aggravated assault (Chapter 10), and robbery and theft (Chapter 11).

specific intent the general intent to commit the *actus reus* of a crime plus the intent to cause a criminally harmful result

Our next case excerpt, *State v. Fleck* (2012), decides that one Minnesota assault statute is a general intent crime, and a second assault statute is a specific intent crime.

CASE

*In **State v. Fleck (2012),** Ronald Gene Fleck appealed his conviction by a jury of assault by intentionally inflicting, or attempting to inflict bodily harm upon another (assault-harm).*

Did he intend to inflict bodily harm?

State v. Fleck

810 N.W.2d 303 (Minn. 2012)

(continues)

(continued)

HISTORY

Ronald Gene Fleck (Defendant) was convicted by a jury in the District Court, Douglas County, of assault by the intentional infliction of or attempt to inflict bodily harm upon another (assault-harm). Fleck appealed. The Court of Appeals reversed and remanded. The State filed a petition for review. The Minnesota Supreme Court reversed and reinstated the conviction.

MEYER, J.

Ronald Gene Fleck lived with K.W. in Alexandria, Minnesota. When K.W. returned home in the early morning hours of January 23, 2009, Fleck was in the kitchen, drinking alcohol (according to K.W., Fleck had been drinking for "seven days straight"). As K.W. walked toward the bathroom, she heard Fleck call her name. When K.W. turned around, she saw Fleck with a large butcher knife. Fleck then stabbed K.W. once near her shoulder with an overhand motion. K.W. claimed that Fleck said something about "finishing her off" before he walked away. K.W. locked herself in the bathroom and called 911. Fleck then called his brother and sister-in-law, telling them about the stabbing and informing them that he was going to take his own life by ingesting sleeping pills.

Two officers from the Douglas County Sherriff's Department responded to the 911 call. On their arrival, the officers observed that Fleck was uncooperative and belligerent. Fleck told the officers he had taken 40 sleeping pills. Shortly after the officers arrived, Fleck became unresponsive and lost muscular control of his head and neck. Both Fleck and K.W. were taken to the hospital. At the hospital, Fleck was unresponsive and hospital tests revealed a blood alcohol level of 0.315.

Fleck was charged with second-degree assault with a dangerous weapon under Minn. Stat. § 609.222, subd. 1 (2010). Section 609.222 references Minn. Stat. § 609.02, subd. 10 (2010), which defines the offenses of assault-harm and assault-fear.[1] Before trial, Fleck gave written notice that he would be relying on intoxication as a defense, and specifically requested a voluntary intoxication jury instruction.

OPINION

The State contends that the language of Minn. Stat. § 609.075,[2] (Defense of Intoxication) should be interpreted as applying to specific-intent crimes, not to general-intent crimes. We agree. We next consider whether an assault-harm offense is a general-intent or specific-intent crime. We have on occasion made references to the offense of "assault" without expressly acknowledging that the Legislature has defined two distinct forms of assault. To ensure precision in our analysis, we begin with a discussion of the two distinct forms of assault recognized by the Legislature.

The first form of assault is assault-harm. A person commits the offense of assault-harm through "the intentional infliction of … bodily harm upon another." Minn. Stat. § 609.02, subd. 10(2). "Bodily harm" means "physical pain or injury, illness, or any impairment of physical condition." Minn. Stat. § 609.02, subd. 7 (2010).

The second form of assault is assault-fear. A person commits the offense of assault-fear through "an act done with intent to cause fear in another of immediate bodily harm or death." Minn. Stat. § 609.02, subd. 10(1). An assault-fear offense does not require a finding of actual harm to the victim. Instead, the assault-fear statute is violated when one engages in an act with the intent to cause fear in another of immediate bodily harm or death. In an assault-fear crime, the intent of Defendant, as contrasted with the effect upon the victim, becomes the focal point for inquiry. With the two forms of assault in mind, we consider the distinction between general-intent and specific-intent crimes.

When a statute simply prohibits a person from intentionally engaging in the prohibited conduct, the crime is considered a general-intent crime. General intent only requires an intention to make the bodily movement which constitutes the act which the crime requires…without proof that he meant to or knew that he would violate the law or cause a particular result.

Unlike a general-intent crime, a specific-intent crime requires an intent to cause a particular result. The phrase "with intent to" is commonly used by the Legislature to express a specific-intent requirement. The Legislature has defined the phrase "with intent to" as "the actor either has a purpose to do the

[1]The Minnesota Domestic Abuse Act defines domestic abuse to include two types of conduct, if committed against a family or household member by a family or household member: (1) physical harm, bodily injury, or assault, or (2) the infliction of fear of imminent physical harm, bodily injury, or assault.

[2]An act committed while in a state of voluntary intoxication is not less criminal by reason thereof, but when a particular intent or other state of mind is a necessary element to constitute a particular crime, the fact of intoxication may be taken into consideration in determining such intent or state of mind.

thing or cause the result specified or believes that the act, if successful, will cause that result." Minn. Stat. § 609.02, subd. 9(4) (2010).

The parties concede that an assault-fear offense under Minn. Stat. § 609.02, subd. 10(1), is a specific-intent crime. This concession is consistent with both the most common usage of the phrase "specific intent" and the Legislature's use of the phrase "with intent to." The definition of assault-fear requires the State to prove Defendant committed an act with an additional special mental element—specifically: "an act done *with intent to* cause fear in another of immediate bodily harm or death." Minn. Stat. § 609.02, subd. 10(1) (emphasis added). Because an assault-fear offense is a specific-intent crime, we conclude that the district court properly instructed the jurors that they could consider Fleck's voluntary intoxication in determining whether he intended to cause K.W. to fear immediate bodily harm or death.

The parties disagree on the issue of whether an assault-harm offense under Minn. Stat. § 609.02, subd. 10(2), is a general-intent or specific-intent crime. The State claims an assault-harm offense is a general-intent crime, while Fleck claims an assault-harm offense is a specific-intent crime. We conclude that assault-harm is a general-intent crime and, therefore, the district court did not err in concluding that assault-harm is not the type of crime that is subject to a voluntary intoxication jury instruction.

The Legislature defined assault-harm as "the intentional infliction of...bodily harm upon another." Minn. Stat. § 609.02, subd. 10(2). The forbidden conduct is a physical act, which results in bodily harm upon another. Although the definition of assault-harm requires the State to prove that Defendant intended to do the physical act, nothing in the definition requires proof that Defendant meant to violate the law or cause a particular result. If the Legislature intended to require an additional, special mental element, it could have defined assault-harm as "an act done with the intent to cause bodily harm to another." This is especially true because the Legislature used the phrase "with intent to" when defining assault-fear in the same statutory section. Consequently, we hold that assault-harm, as defined by Minn. Stat. § 609.02, subd. 10(2), is a general-intent crime. Therefore, the district court properly instructed the jurors that they could not consider Fleck's voluntary intoxication when determining whether Fleck was guilty of intentional infliction of bodily harm.

Reversed, judgment of conviction reinstated.

QUESTIONS

1. State all of the facts relevant to deciding whether Ronald Gene Fleck committed assault-threat and assault-harm.
2. How does the court define "general intent"?
3. How does the court define "specific intent"?
4. Explain the court's reasons for deciding that assault-fear is a specific intent crime and assault-harm is a general intent crime.
5. Why did the court have to decide question 2?
6. Does the court's opinion help you to understand *general intent* and *specific intent*? Defend your answer.

The Model Penal Code (MPC) Levels of Culpability

LO6

The multiple mental states, confusing terms, and varied meanings of criminal intent lay behind the Model Penal Code's (MPC's) provisions to make sense out of the confusing state of the law regarding criminal intent. According to Ronald L. Gainer (1988), former deputy attorney general of the United States:

> The Code's provisions concerning culpable mental states introduced both reason and structure to a previously amorphous area of American law. For centuries, the approach to mental components of crimes had been a quagmire of legal refuse, obscured by a thin surface of general terminology denoting wrongfulness. The archaic verbiage suggesting evil and wickedness was replaced by the drafters with concepts of purpose, knowledge, recklessness, and negligence, and the concepts were structured to apply separately to actions, circumstances in which actions took place, and results. (575)

The MPC's culpability provisions were arrived at only after enormous effort and heated debate among the leading legal minds, including judges, prosecutors, defense attorneys, and professors. As we look at the MPC's four mental states, we'll discuss how they're ranked according to their degree of culpability and how they're constructed to apply to the elements of (1) act, (2) mental state, (3) attendant circumstances, and (4) causation in "bad" result crimes. From most to least blameworthy, the MPC's four mental states are:

1. Purposely
2. Knowingly
3. Recklessly
4. Negligently

LO3 The MPC specifies that all crimes requiring a mental element (*most minor crimes and a few felonies don't*) have to include one of these degrees of culpability. Where codes don't specify a level of culpability, recklessness is the default state of mind. The MPC Levels of Culpability Box contains an edited version of the definitions.

CRIMINAL LAW IN FOCUS

MPC Levels of Culpability

MPC § 2.02. General Requirements of Culpability.

1. *Minimum Requirements of Culpability.* A person is not guilty of an offense unless he acted purposely, knowingly, recklessly or negligently with respect to each material element of the offense.
2. *Kinds of Culpability Defined*
   a. *Purposely.* A person acts purposely with respect to a material element of an offense when:
      i. if the element involves the nature of his conduct or a result thereof, it is his conscious object to engage in conduct of that nature or to cause such a result; and
      ii. if the element involves the attendance circumstances, he is aware of the existence of such circumstances or he believes or hopes that they exist.
   b. *Knowingly.* A person acts knowingly with respect to a material element of an offense when:
      i. if the element involves the nature of his conduct or the attendant circumstances, he is aware that his conduct is of that nature or that such circumstances exist; and
      ii. if the element involves a result of his conduct, he is aware that it is practically certain that his conduct will cause such a result.
   c. *Recklessly.* A person acts recklessly with respect to a material element of an offense when he consciously disregards a substantial and unjustifiable risk that the material element exists or will result from his conduct. The risk must be of such a nature and degree that, considering the nature and purpose of the actor's conduct and the circumstances known to him, its disregard involves a gross deviation from the standard of conduct that a law-abiding person would observe in the actor's situation.
   d. *Negligently.* A person acts negligently with respect to a material element of an offense when he should be aware of a substantial and unjustifiable risk that the material element exists or will result from his conduct. The risk must be of such a nature and degree that the actor's failure to perceive it, considering the nature and purpose of his conduct and the circumstances known to him, involves a gross deviation from the standard of care that a reasonable person would observe in the actor's situation. (ALI 1985, 1:2, 229)

Let's examine each level of culpability in more detail.

PURPOSELY

LO6

purposely the most blameworthy mental state requiring the actor's "conscious object" to be to commit crimes or cause criminal results

Purposely, the most blameworthy mental state, means what we mean by the everyday expression, "You did it on purpose." In MPC language, "purpose" means having the "conscious object" to commit crimes or cause criminal results. For example, in the criminal conduct crime of common law burglary, the burglar has to break into and enter a house for the very purpose (with the conscious object) of committing a crime after the burglar gets inside. In the bad result crime of murder, the murderer's purpose (conscious object) has to be to cause the victim's death.

In our next case excerpt, *State v. Stark* (1992), the Washington State Court of Appeals affirmed Calvin Stark's conviction because he purposely exposed his sexual partners to HIV.

CASE

*In **State v. Stark (1992),** the Washington State Supreme Court affirmed Calvin Clark's conviction because he purposely exposed his sexual partners to HIV.*

Did he expose his victims to HIV on purpose?

State v. Stark

832 P.2d 109 (Wash. App. 1992)

HISTORY

Calvin Stark was convicted in the Superior Court, Clallam County, Washington, of two counts of second-degree assault for intentionally exposing his sexual partners to the human immunodeficiency virus (HIV), and he appealed. The Washington Court of Appeals affirmed, and remanded the case for resentencing.

PETRICH, CJ.

FACTS

On March 25, 1988, Calvin Stark tested positive for HIV, which was confirmed by further tests on June 25 and on June 30, 1988. From June 30, 1988, to October 3, 1989, the staff of the Clallam County Health Department had five meetings with Stark during which Stark went through extensive counseling about his infection. He was taught about "safe sex," the risk of spreading the infection, and the necessity of informing his partners before engaging in sexual activity with them.

On October 3, 1989, Dr. Locke, the Clallam County Health Officer, after learning that Stark had disregarded this advice and was engaging in unprotected sexual activity, issued a cease and desist order as authorized by a Washington State statute. Stark did not cease and desist, and, consequently, on March 1, 1990, Dr. Locke went to the county prosecutor's office.... The prosecutor ... had Dr. Locke complete a police report. The state then charged Stark with three counts of assault in the second degree under RCW 9A.36.021(1)(e), which provides:

> A person is guilty of assault in the second degree if he or she ... with intent to inflict bodily harm, exposes or transmits human immunodeficiency virus....

Each count involved a different victim.

Count One. The victim and Stark engaged in sexual intercourse on October 27 and October 29, 1989. On both occasions, Stark withdrew his penis from the victim prior to ejaculation. The victim, who could not become pregnant because she had

(continues)

(continued)

previously had her fallopian tubes tied, asked Stark on the second occasion why he withdrew. He then told her that he was HIV positive.

Count Two. The victim and Stark had sexual relations on at least six occasions between October 1989 and February 1990. Stark wore a condom on two or three occasions, but on the others, he ejaculated outside of her body. On each occasion, they had vaginal intercourse. On one occasion Stark tried to force her to have anal intercourse. They also engaged in oral sex. When she told Stark that she had heard rumors that he was HIV positive, he admitted that he was and then gave the victim an AZT pill "to slow down the process of the AIDS."

Count Three. The victim and Stark had sexual relations throughout their brief relationship. It was "almost nonstop with him," "almost every night" during August 1989. Stark never wore a condom and never informed the victim he was HIV positive. When pressed, Stark denied rumors about his HIV status. The victim broke off the relationship because of Stark's drinking, after which Stark told her that he carried HIV and explained that if he had told her, she would not have had anything to do with him.

At the jury trial, the victim in count one testified to her contacts with Stark and the jury received Dr. Locke's deposition testimony regarding the Health Department's contacts with Stark. Stark did not testify. In the bench trial [trial without a jury], Dr. Locke testified. There the state also presented the testimony of one of Stark's neighborhood friends. She testified that one night Stark came to her apartment after drinking and told her and her daughter that he was HIV positive. When she asked him if he knew that he had to protect himself and everybody else, he replied, "I don't care. If I'm going to die, everybody's going to die." The jury found Stark guilty on count one.

A second trial judge found Stark guilty of the second and third counts at a bench trial. On count one, Stark was given an exceptional sentence of 120 months based on his future danger to the community. The standard range for that offense was 13 to 17 months. On counts two and three, Stark was given the low end of the standard range, 43 months each, to be served concurrently, but consecutively to count one.

OPINION

Stark contends that there is insufficient evidence to prove he "exposed" anyone to HIV or that he acted with intent to inflict bodily harm. Since Stark is undisputedly HIV positive, he necessarily exposed his sexual partners to the virus by engaging in unprotected sexual intercourse. The testimony of the three victims supports this conclusion.

The testimony supporting the element of intent to inflict bodily harm includes Dr. Locke's statements detailing his counseling sessions with Stark. With regard to the first victim, we know that Stark knew he was HIV positive, that he had been counseled to use "safe sex" methods, and that it had been explained to Stark that coitus interruptus will not prevent the spread of the virus. While there is evidence to support Stark's position, all the evidence viewed in a light most favorable to the State supports a finding of intent beyond a reasonable doubt. The existence of noncriminal explanations does not preclude a finding that a defendant intended to harm his sexual partners.

With regard to the later victims, we have, in addition to this same evidence, Stark's neighbor's testimony that Stark, when confronted about his sexual practices, said, "I don't care. If I'm going to die, everybody's going to die." We also have the testimony of the victim in count two that Stark attempted to have anal intercourse with her and did have oral sex, both methods the counselors told Stark he needed to avoid.

We affirm the convictions.

QUESTIONS

1. Identify all of the facts relevant to determining Stark's mental attitude regarding each of the elements in the assault statute.
2. Using the common law definition of "specific intent" and the Model Penal Code definitions of "purposely," "knowingly," "recklessly," and "negligently" and relying on the relevant facts, identify Stark's intention with respect to his acts.
3. Is motive important in this case? Should it be?

YOU DECIDE

Which court's decision established the most ethical public policy regarding the control of HIV?

The Trial Court

Dwight Ralph Smallwood was convicted of assault with intent to murder, reckless endangerment, and attempted murder. The trial court sentenced Smallwood to concurrent sentences of life imprisonment for attempted rape, 20 years' imprisonment for robbery with a deadly weapon, 30 years' imprisonment for assault with intent to murder, and five years' imprisonment for reckless endangerment. The court also imposed a concurrent 30-year sentence for each of the three counts of attempted second-degree murder. The conviction was based on evidence that Smallwood knew he had human immunodeficiency virus (HIV) when he raped three women.

The Court of Appeals

Smallwood appealed to Maryland's highest court, the Court of Appeals. The court held that the evidence that Smallwood knew he had human immunodeficiency virus (HIV) when he raped three women was insufficient to prove that he had the intent to kill. According to the court,

> We have no trouble concluding that Smallwood intentionally exposed his victims to the risk of HIV-infection. The problem before us, however, is whether knowingly exposing someone to a risk of HIV-infection is by itself sufficient to infer that Smallwood possessed an intent to kill.

The State in this case would allow the trier of fact to infer an intent to kill based solely upon the fact that Smallwood exposed his victims to the risk that they might contract HIV. Without evidence showing that such a result is sufficiently probable to support this inference, we conclude that Smallwood's convictions for attempted murder and assault with intent to murder must be reversed.

Instructions

1. Go to http://mdcourts.gov/opinions/cosa/1995/1678s94.pdf (March 1, 2015), and read the full opinion of the Court of Special Appeals of Maryland (Maryland's intermediate appeals court).
2. Then, go to http://www.mdcourts.gov/opinions/coa/1996/122a95.pdf (March 1, 2015), and read the Court of Appeals (Maryland's Supreme Court) full opinion in the case.
3. Did Smallwood intend to kill his victims or to spread the virus?
4. Does your answer depend at all on your position as to which interpretation of the law supports the most ethical public policy?

Source: *Smallwood v. State*, 680 A.2d 512 (Md. 1996).

KNOWINGLY

LO6

In the mental state of **knowingly**, the watchword is "awareness" (Dubber 2002, 65). In conduct crimes, awareness is clear—I'm aware that I'm taking an iPhone 6+; therefore, I'm taking it knowingly. (This doesn't mean you have to know your acts are crimes, just aware that you're taking a iPhone 6+.) It's a little different in bad result crimes. Here, the MPC says it's enough that I'm aware that it's "practically certain" my conduct will cause the bad result.

knowingly the mental state of awareness in conduct crimes and, in result crimes, awareness that it's "practically certain" that the conduct will cause the bad result

It's important for you to understand that knowledge is not the same as purpose or conscious objective. So a surgeon who removes a cancerous uterus to save a pregnant woman's life knowingly kills the fetus in her womb, but killing the fetus wasn't the purpose (conscious object) of the removal. Rather, the death of the fetus is an unavoidable consequence of removing the cancerous uterus.

In *State v. Jantzi* (1982), our next case excerpt, the Oregon Court of Appeals concluded that Pete Jantzi didn't knowingly assault Rex Anderson. You'll see just how complicated the application of "knowingly" to the facts of specific cases can get.

CASE

In ***State v. Jantzi* (1982),** *Pete Jantzi was convicted of knowingly committing second-degree assault, and he appealed.*

Did he "knowingly" assault with a knife?

State v. Jantzi

641 P.2d 62 (Or. App. 1982)

HISTORY

Pete Jantzi was convicted in the Circuit Court, Klamath County, of assault in the second degree, and he appealed. The Court of Appeals held that Defendant knew he had a dangerous weapon and that a confrontation was going to occur, but that he did not intend to stab the victim. Thus, Defendant acted "recklessly," not "knowingly," and should be convicted of assault in the third degree rather than assault in the second degree. Affirmed as modified; remanded for resentencing.

GILLETTE, J.

FACTS

Pete Jantzi (Defendant) testified and the trial court judge believed that he was asked to accompany Diane Anderson, who shared a house with Defendant and several other people, to the home of her estranged husband, Rex. While Diane was in the house talking with Rex, Defendant was using the blade of his knife to let the air out of the tires on Rex's van. Another person put sugar in the gas tank of the van.

While the Andersons were arguing, Diane apparently threatened damage to Rex's van and indicated that someone might be tampering with the van at that moment. Rex's roommate ran out of the house and saw two men beside the van. He shouted and began to run toward the men. Rex ran from the house and began to chase Defendant, who ran down a bicycle path. Defendant, still holding his open knife, jumped into the bushes beside the path and landed in the weeds. He crouched there, hoping that Rex would not see him and would pass by. Rex, however, jumped on top of Defendant and grabbed his shirt. They rolled over and Rex was stabbed in the abdomen by Defendant's knife. Defendant could not remember making a thrusting or swinging motion with the knife; he did not intend to stab Rex.

OPINION

The indictment charged that defendant "did unlawfully and knowingly cause physical injury to Rex Anderson by means of a deadly weapon, to-wit: knife, by stabbing the said Rex Anderson with said knife." ORS 163.175 provides that: A person commits the crime of assault in the second degree if he intentionally or knowingly causes physical injury to another by means of a deadly or dangerous weapon.

"Knowingly" is defined in ORS 161.085(8):

> "Knowingly" or "with knowledge" when used with respect to conduct or to a circumstance described by a statute defining an offense means that a person acts with an awareness that [his] conduct is of a nature so described or that a circumstance so described exists.

[According to the commentary to the New York Criminal Code that the Oregon Criminal Code was based on:]

> Under the formulations of the Model Penal Code (§ 2.02(2bii)) and the Illinois Criminal Code (§ 4–5(b)), "knowingly" is, in one phase, almost synonymous with "intentionally" in that a person achieves a given result "knowingly" when

> he "is practically certain" that his conduct will cause that result. This distinction between "knowingly" and "intentionally" in that context appears highly technical or semantic, and the New York Revised Penal Law does not employ the word "knowingly" in defining result offenses. Murder of the common law variety, for example, is committed intentionally or not at all. (Commentary § 15.05, New York Revised Penal Law)

[The trial court continued:]

> Basically, the facts of this case are: that Defendant was letting air out of the tires and he has an open knife. He was aware of what his knife is like. He is aware that it is a dangerous weapon. He runs up the bicycle path. He has a very firm grip on the knife, by his own admission, and he knows the knife is dangerous. It is not necessary for the state to prove that he thrust it or anything else. Quite frankly, this could have all been avoided if he had gotten rid of the knife, so he 'knowingly caused physical injury to Rex Anderson.' And, therefore, I find him guilty of that particular charge.

Although the trial judge found Defendant guilty of "knowingly" causing physical injury to Anderson, what he described in his findings is recklessness. The court found that defendant knew he had a dangerous weapon and that a confrontation was going to occur. The court believed that Defendant did not intend to stab Anderson. The court's conclusion seems to be based on the reasoning that because Defendant knew it was possible that an injury would occur, he acted "knowingly." However, a person who "is aware of and consciously disregards a substantial and unjustifiable risk" that an injury will occur acts "recklessly," not "knowingly."

We have authority, pursuant to ... the Oregon Constitution, to enter the judgment that should have been entered in the court below. Assault in the third degree is a lesser included offense of the crime of assault in the second degree charged in the accusatory instrument in this case. We modify defendant's conviction to a conviction for the crime of assault in the third degree.

Conviction affirmed as modified; remanded for resentencing.

QUESTIONS

1. List all of the facts relevant to determining Pete Jantzi's state of mind.
2. State the Oregon statute's mental element for assault.
3. State how, and explain why, Oregon modified the MPC definition of "knowingly."
4. In your opinion, did Jantzi knowingly assault Rex Anderson? Back up your answer with the facts of the case and the trial and appellate court's opinions.

RECKLESSLY

LO6

recklessly conscious creation of a "substantial and unjustifiable" risk of criminal harm

Reckless people know they're creating *risks* of criminal harm. But, they don't *intend*, or at least they don't *expect*, or don't care, if they cause harm itself. Recklessly (conscious risk creation) isn't as blameworthy as acting purposely or knowingly because reckless defendants don't act for the very purpose of doing harm; they don't even act knowing harm is practically certain to follow. But reckless defendants do know they're creating a risk of harm.

Criminal recklessness requires more than awareness of ordinary risks; it requires awareness of "substantial and unjustifiable risks." The MPC proposes that fact finders determine recklessness according to a two-pronged test:

1. *Was Defendant aware of how substantial and unjustifiable the risks that they disregarded were?* Under this prong, notice that even a substantial risk isn't by itself reckless. For example, a doctor who performs life-saving surgery has created a substantial risk. But the risk is justifiable because the doctor took it to save the life of the patient. This prong doesn't answer the important questions of how substantial and how unjustifiable the risk has to be to amount to recklessness. So the second prong gives guidance to juries.

2. *Does Defendant's disregard of risk amount to so "gross a deviation from the standard" that a law-abiding person would observe in that situation?* This prong requires juries to make the judgment whether the risk is substantial and unjustifiable enough to deserve condemnation in the form of criminal liability.

This test has both a subjective and an objective component. The first prong of the test is subjective. It focuses on this particular defendant's awareness, that is, it can't be compared to any other defendant's awareness or to a reasonable person's awareness. It requires measuring awareness case-by-case. The objective prong *does* compare, by measuring conduct according to how it deviates from what reasonable people do.

It should be clear to you by now that actual harm isn't the conscious object of reckless wrongdoers. In fact, most reckless actors probably hope they don't hurt anyone. Or, at most, they don't care if they hurt anyone. But the heart of their culpability is that, even with full knowledge of the risks, they act anyway. For example, in one case, a large drug company knew that a medication it sold to control high blood pressure had caused severe liver damage and even death in some patients; it sold the drug anyway. The company's officers, who made the decision to sell the drug, didn't want to hurt anyone (in fact, they hoped no one would die or suffer liver damage). They sought only profit for the company, but they were prepared to risk the deaths of their customers to make a profit (Shenon 1985, A1).

LO6

negligently the mental attitude that a person acts negligently with respect to a material element of an offense when he should be aware of a substantial and unjustifiable risk that the material element exists or will result from his conduct. The risk must be of such a nature and degree that the actor's failure to perceive it, considering the nature and purpose of his conduct and the circumstances known to him, involved a gross deviation from the standard of care that a reasonable person would observe in the actor's situation.

NEGLIGENTLY

Like acting recklessly, acting negligently is about creating risks. But acting recklessly refers to consciously creating risks; acting **negligently** refers to unconsciously (unreasonably) creating risks. Here's an example of a negligent wrongdoer: "Okay, so you didn't mean to hurt him, and you didn't even know the odds were very high you could hurt him, but you should have known the odds were very high, and you did hurt him." The test for negligence is totally objective—namely, that the actors should have known, even though in fact they didn't know, they were creating risks. Put another way, a reasonable person *would* have known she was creating the risk.

For example, a reasonable person would know that driving 50 miles an hour down a crowded street creates a risk of harm. The driver who *should* know what a reasonable person *would* know, but *doesn't*, is negligent. The driver who *knows* it but drives too fast *anyway* is reckless. Negligent defendants, like reckless defendants, have to create "substantial and unjustifiable risks"—risks that grossly deviate from the ordinary standards of behavior.

In our next case excerpt, *Koppersmith v. State* (1999), the Alabama Court of Appeals wrestled with the difficult task of drawing the line between recklessness and negligence.

CASE

*In **Koppersmith v. State (1999),** Gregory Koppersmith was charged with murder. He was convicted of reckless manslaughter and sentenced to 20 years in prison.*

Did he kill his wife recklessly or negligently?

Koppersmith v. State

742 So.2d 206 (Ala. App. 1999)

HISTORY

Gregory Koppersmith, the appellant, was charged with the murder of his wife, Cynthia ("Cindy") Michel Koppersmith. He was convicted of reckless manslaughter, a violation of § 13A-6–3(a)(1), Ala. Code 1975, and the trial court sentenced him to 20 years in prison. The Alabama Court of Appeals reversed and remanded.

BASCHAB, J.

FACTS

Gregory Koppersmith (appellant) and his wife were arguing in the yard outside of their residence. Cindy tried to enter the house to end the argument, but Greg prevented her from going inside. A physical confrontation ensued, and Cindy fell off of a porch into the yard. She died as a result of a skull fracture to the back of her head.

In a statement he made to law enforcement officials after the incident, Greg gave the following summary of the events leading up to Cindy's death. He and Cindy had been arguing and were on a porch outside of their residence. Cindy had wanted to go inside the house, but he had wanted to resolve the argument first. As she tried to go inside, Greg stepped in front of her and pushed her back. Cindy punched at him, and he grabbed her.

When Cindy tried to go inside again, Greg wrapped his arms around her from behind to stop her. Cindy bit him on the arm, and he "slung" her to the ground. He then jumped down and straddled her, stating that he "had her by the head" and indicating that he moved her head up and down, as if slamming it into the ground. When Cindy stopped struggling, he rolled her over and found a brick covered with blood under her head. Greg stated that, although Cindy fell near a flowerbed, he did not know there were bricks in the grass.

At trial, Greg testified that Cindy had tried to go into the house two or three times, but he had stopped her from doing so. During that time, she punched at him and he pushed her away from him. At one point, he put his arms around her from behind to restrain her, and she turned her head and bit him. When she bit him, he pulled her by her sweater and she tripped. He then "slung" her off of him, and she tripped and fell three to four feet to the ground. He jumped off of the porch and straddled her, grabbing her by the shoulders and telling her to calm down. When he realized she was not moving, he lifted her head and noticed blood all over his hands.

Greg testified that, when he grabbed Cindy from behind, he did not intend to harm her. He also testified that, when he "slung" her away from him off of the porch, he was not trying to hurt her and did not intend to throw her onto a brick. Rather, he stated that he simply reacted after she bit his arm. He also testified that he did not know there were bricks in the yard, that he had not attempted to throw her in a particular direction, and that he was not aware of any risk or harm his actions might cause.

Greg further testified that, when he grabbed and shook her after she fell, he did not intend to harm her, he did not know there was a brick under her head, and he did not intend to hit her head on a brick or anything else. Instead, he testified that he was trying to get her to calm down.

The medical examiner, Dr. Gregory Wanger, testified that the pattern on the injury to the victim's skull matched the pattern on one of the bricks found at the scene. He stated that, based on the position of the skull fracture and the bruising to the victim's brain, the victim's head was moving when it sustained the injury. He testified that her injuries could have been caused by her falling off of the porch and hitting her head on a brick or from her head being slammed into a brick.

The indictment in this case alleged that Greg Koppersmith "did, with the intent to cause the death of Cynthia Michel Koppersmith, cause the death of Cynthia Michel Koppersmith, by striking her head against a brick, in violation of § 13A-6–2 of the Code of Alabama (C.R.11)." Greg requested that the trial court instruct the jury on criminally negligent homicide as a lesser included offense of murder. However, the trial court denied that request, and it instructed the jury only on the offense of reckless manslaughter.

OPINION

Section 13A-6–3(a), Ala. Code 1975, provides that a person commits the crime of manslaughter if he recklessly causes the death of another person. A person acts recklessly with respect to a result or to a circumstance described by a statute defining an offense when he is aware of and consciously disregards a substantial and unjustifiable risk that the result will occur or that the circumstance exists. The risk must be of such nature and degree that disregard thereof constitutes a gross deviation from the standard of conduct that a reasonable person would observe in the situation.

(continues)

(continued)

"A person commits the crime of criminally negligent homicide if he causes the death of another person by criminal negligence" § 13A-6–4(a), Ala. Code 1975. A person acts with criminal negligence with respect to a result or to a circumstance which is defined by statute as an offense when he fails to perceive a substantial and unjustifiable risk that the result will occur or that the circumstance exists. The risk must be of such nature and degree that the failure to perceive it constitutes a gross deviation from the standard of care that a reasonable person would observe in the situation. A court or jury may consider statutes or ordinances regulating Defendant's conduct as bearing upon the question of criminal negligence.

The only difference between manslaughter under Section 13A-6–3(a)(1) and criminally negligent homicide is the difference between recklessness and criminal negligence. The reckless offender is aware of the risk and "consciously disregards" it. On the other hand, the criminally negligent offender is not aware of the risk created ("fails to perceive") and, therefore, cannot be guilty of consciously disregarding it. The difference between the terms "recklessly" and "negligently" is one of kind, rather than degree. Each actor creates a risk or harm. The reckless actor is aware of the risk and disregards it; the negligent actor is not aware of the risk but should have been aware of it.

Thus, we must determine whether there was any evidence before the jury from which it could have concluded that Greg did not perceive that his wife might die as a result of his actions. We conclude that there was evidence from which the jury could have reasonably believed that his conduct that caused her to fall was unintentional and that he was not aware he was creating a risk to his wife. He testified that, after she bit him, his reaction—which caused her to fall to the ground—was simply reflexive.

Greg also testified that he did not know there were bricks in the yard. Even in his statement to the police in which he said he was slamming her head against the ground, Greg said he did not know at that time that there was a brick under her head.

Finally, he stated that he did not intend to throw her onto a brick or harm her in any way when he "slung" her, and that he did not intend to hit her head on a brick or otherwise harm her when he grabbed and shook her after she had fallen.

Because there was a reasonable theory from the evidence that would have supported giving a jury instruction on criminally negligent homicide, the trial court erred in refusing to instruct the jury on criminally negligent homicide. Thus, we must reverse the trial court's judgment and remand this case for a new trial.

Reversed and remanded.

QUESTIONS

1. List all of the facts relevant to determining Koppersmith's mental state with respect both to his acts and the results of his actions.
2. In your opinion, was Koppersmith reckless or negligent? Support your answer with relevant facts.
3. Is it possible to argue that Koppersmith knowingly or even purposely killed his wife? What facts, if any, support these two states of mind?

LIABILITY WITHOUT FAULT (STRICT LIABILITY)

LO4 You've learned that criminal liability depends on at least some degree of blameworthiness when we're talking about serious crimes like the cases in the previous culpability sections. But there are enormous numbers of minor crimes where there's liability without either subjective or objective fault (see Chapter 12). We call this liability without fault strict liability, meaning it's based on voluntary action alone. Let's be blunt: strict liability makes accidental injuries a crime. In strict liability cases, the prosecution has to prove only that defendants committed a voluntary criminal act that caused harm. The U.S. Supreme Court has upheld the power of legislatures to create strict liability offenses to protect the "public health and safety," as long as they make clear they're imposing liability without fault (Chapter 3).

Supporters of strict liability make two main arguments. First, there's a strong public interest in protecting public health and safety. Strict liability arose during the industrial revolution when manufacturing, mining, and commerce exposed large numbers of the public to death, mutilation, and disease from poisonous fumes, unsafe railroads, workplaces, and adulterated foods and other products. Second, the penalty for strict liability offenses is almost always mild (fines, not jail time).

Critics say it's too easy to expand strict liability beyond offenses that seriously endanger the public. They're always wary of making exceptions to blameworthiness, which is central to the *mens rea* principle. It does no good (and probably a lot of harm) to punish people who haven't harmed others purposely, knowingly, recklessly, or at least negligently. At the end of the day, the critics maintain, a criminal law without blameworthiness will lose its force as a stern moral code.

In our next case excerpt, *State v. Loge* (2000), the Minnesota Supreme Court decided that Minnesota's legislature had created a strict liability open bottle offense.

CASE

In ***State v. Loge*** **(2000),** *Steven Loge was convicted of violating the "open bottle" law.*

Did the "open bottle law" create a strict liability offense?

State v. Loge

608 N.W.2d 152 (Minn. 2000)

HISTORY

Steven Mark Loge (Appellant) was cited for a violation of Minn. Stat. § 169.122, subd. 3 (1998), which makes it unlawful for the driver of a motor vehicle, when the owner is not present, "to keep or allow to be kept in a motor vehicle when such vehicle is upon the public highway any bottle or receptacle containing intoxicating liquors or 3.2 percent malt liquors which has been opened." Violation of the statute is a misdemeanor. Loge was convicted in the District Court, Freeborn County, and he appealed. The Court of Appeals affirmed, and Loge appealed to the Minnesota Supreme Court. The Supreme Court affirmed.

GILBERT, J.

FACTS

On September 2, 1997, Steven Loge borrowed his father's pickup truck to go to his evening job. Driving alone on his way home from work, he was stopped by two Albert Lea City police officers on County Road 18 at approximately 8:15 P.M. because he appeared to be speeding. Loge got out of his truck and stood by the driver's side door. While one officer was talking with Loge, the second officer, who was standing by the passenger side of the truck, observed a bottle, which he believed to be a beer bottle, sticking partially out of a brown paper bag underneath the passenger's side of the seat. He retrieved that bottle, which was open and had foam on the inside. He searched the rest of the truck and found one full, unopened can of beer and one empty beer can. After the second officer found the beer bottle, the first officer asked Loge if he had been drinking.

Loge stated that he had two beers while working and was on his way home. Loge passed all standard field sobriety tests. The officers gave Loge a citation for a violation of the open bottle statute.

(continues)

(continued)

At the trial Loge testified that the bottle was not his, that he did not know it was in the truck and had said that to one of the officers. The trial court found that one of the police officers "observed the neck of the bottle, which was wrapped in a brown paper sack, under the pickup's seat of the truck being operated by defendant." The trial court held that subdivision 3 creates "absolute liability" on a driver/owner to "inspect and determine whether there are any containers" in the motor vehicle in violation of the open bottle law and found Loge guilty. Loge was sentenced to five days in jail, execution stayed, placed on probation for one year, and fined $150 plus costs of $32.50.

Loge appealed the verdict. The Court of Appeals affirmed the decision of the trial court. The Court of Appeals held that proof of knowledge that the bottle was in the truck is not required to sustain a conviction. Loge's petition for further review was granted. The Attorney General then assumed responsibility for this case and filed a respondent's brief in which the Attorney General argues, contrary to the previous position of the state, that there is no knowledge requirement under subdivision 3.

OPINION

Loge is seeking reversal of his conviction because, he argues, the trial court and court of appeals erroneously interpreted subdivision 3 of the open bottle statute not to require proof of knowledge. Minnesota Statute § 169.122 reads in part:

> *Subdivision 1.* No person shall drink or consume intoxicating liquors or 3.2 percent malt liquors in any motor vehicle when such vehicle is upon a public highway.
>
> *Subdivision 2.* No person shall have in possession while in a private motor vehicle upon a public highway, any bottle or receptacle containing intoxicating liquor or 3.2 percent malt liquor which has been opened, or the seal broken, or the contents of which have been partially removed. This subdivision does not apply to a bottle or receptacle that is in the trunk of the vehicle if it is equipped with a trunk, or that is in another area of the vehicle not normally occupied by the driver and passengers if the vehicle is not equipped with a trunk.
>
> *Subdivision 3.* It shall be unlawful for the owner of any private motor vehicle or the driver, if the owner be not then present in the motor vehicle, to keep or allow to be kept in a motor vehicle when such vehicle is upon the public highway any bottle or receptacle containing intoxicating liquors or 3.2 percent malt liquors which has been opened, or the seal broken, or the contents of which have been partially removed except when such bottle or receptacle shall be kept in the trunk of the motor vehicle when such vehicle is equipped with a trunk, or kept in some other area of the vehicle not normally occupied by the driver or passengers, if the motor vehicle is not equipped with a trunk. A utility compartment or glove compartment shall be deemed to be within the area occupied by the driver and passengers.

An analysis of a statute must begin with a careful and close examination of the statutory language to ascertain and effectuate legislative intent. If the meaning of the statute is clear and free from all ambiguity, the letter of the law shall not be disregarded under the pretext of pursuing the spirit.

Minn. Stat. § 169.122, subd. 3 establishes liability for a driver when that driver "*keeps or allows to be kept*" [emphasis added] any open bottle containing intoxicating liquor within the area normally occupied by the driver and passengers. These two alternate concepts are separated by the disjunctive "or," not "and." Unlike the use of the word "and," "or" signifies the distinction between two factual situations. We have long held that in the absence of some ambiguity surrounding the legislature's use of the word "or," we will read it in the disjunctive and require that only one of the possible factual situations be present in order for the statute to be satisfied. Accordingly, we limit our opinion to the words "to keep."

In delineating the elements of the crime, we have also held that the legislature is entitled to consider what it deems "expedient and best suited to the prevention of crime and disorder." If knowledge was a necessary element of the open container offense, there would be a substantial, if not insurmountable, difficulty of proof. It is therefore reasonable to conclude that the legislature, weighing the significant danger to the public, decided that proof of knowledge under subdivision 3 was not required.

The legislature has made knowledge distinctions within its traffic statutes that also guide our interpretation. For example, with respect to marijuana in a motor vehicle, the Minnesota legislature has used language similar to the language found in section 169.122, subdivision 3 ("keep or allow to be kept") but added a knowledge requirement. An owner, or if the owner is not present, the driver, is guilty of a misdemeanor if he "*knowingly keeps or allows to be kept*" [emphasis added] marijuana in a motor vehicle. Minn. Stat. § 152.027, subd. 3 (1998). If the legislature had intended Section 169.122 to have a knowledge requirement, it could have added the word "knowingly," as the legislature did in Section 152.027.

Lastly, Loge argues that an interpretation excluding knowledge as an element could lead to absurd results. While it is true that the legislature does not intend a result that is absurd or unreasonable, we do not believe such a result exists here. Loge's conviction resulted from an officer standing outside the truck observing the open container of beer sticking partially out of a brown bag underneath the seat on the passenger side of the truck Loge was driving. By simply taking control of the truck, Loge took control and charge of the contents of the truck, including the open bottle, even if he did not know the open bottle was in the truck.

Affirmed.

DISSENT

ANDERSON, J.

I respectfully dissent. In its effort to reach a correct policy decision, the majority disregards our proper role as interpreters of the law. In doing so, the majority has preempted the legislature's function and assumed the mantle of policymaker.

I agree that under certain circumstances the legislature may provide that criminal liability attach without requiring any showing of intent or knowledge on the part of the person charged. Further, in the context of open containers of alcohol in motor vehicles, there is a credible argument that it is good public policy given the social and economic costs that result from the combination of alcohol and motor vehicles. But, all of that said, the majority's analysis simply does not demonstrate the requisite clear statement of legislative intent necessary to create criminal liability in the absence of a showing of knowledge or intent.

We have stated that when the legislature intends to make an act unlawful and to impose criminal sanctions without any requirement of intent or knowledge, it must do so clearly. Historically, our substantive criminal law is based upon a theory of punishing the vicious will. It postulates a free agent confronted with a choice between doing right and doing wrong and choosing freely to do wrong. § 169.122, subd. 3, simply lacks the requisite clarity to support the imposition of criminal liability without any showing of intent or knowledge.

The majority cannot avoid the implications of the term "allow" because it is convenient to do so. In other contexts, we have held that the inclusion of words like "permit" (a synonym of "allow") clearly indicates a legislative intent to require some level of knowledge or intent.

Under the majority's holding, we now will impose criminal liability on a person, not simply for an act that the person does not know is criminal, but also for an act the person does not even know he is committing. While the district court and the majority seem to assume that everyone who drives a motor vehicle knows that he or she is obligated to search the entire passenger compartment of the vehicle before driving on the state's roads, the law imposes no such requirement.

Most drivers would be surprised to discover that after anyone else used their vehicle—children, friends, spouse—they are criminally liable for any open containers of alcohol that are present, regardless of whether they know the containers are there. This also means that any prudent operator of a motor vehicle must also carefully check any case of packaged alcohol before transport and ensure that each container's seal is not broken. See Minn. Stat. § 169.122 (defining an open bottle as a container that is open, has the contents partially removed, or has the seal broken). Under the majority's interpretation, all of these situations would render the driver criminally liable under Minn. Stat. § 169.122. Without a more clear statement by the legislature that this is the law, I cannot agree with such an outcome.

QUESTIONS

1. What words, if any, in the statute indicate a *mens rea* requirement?
2. What *mens rea*, if any, do the words in the statute require?
3. Summarize the arguments that the majority of the court give to support this as a strict liability offense.
4. What arguments did the dissent give in response to the majority's arguments?
5. Do you agree with the majority or the dissent? Defend your answer.

CONCURRENCE

principle of concurrence some mental fault has to trigger the criminal act in conduct crimes and the cause in result crimes

The **principle of concurrence** means that some mental fault has to trigger the criminal act in conduct crimes and the cause in result crimes. So all crimes, except strict liability offenses, are subject to the concurrence requirement. In practice, concurrence is an element in all crimes where the mental attitude was formed with purpose, knowledge, recklessness, or negligence. Suppose you and your friend agree to meet at her house on a cold winter night. She's late because her car won't start. So she texts, "break front door lock, go in 2 keep warm." But once you're inside, you decide to steal her Blu-ray DVR. Have you committed breaking and entering?

No, because in crimes of criminal conduct, the principle of concurrence requires that a criminal intent (*mens rea*) triggers a criminal act (*actus reus*). You decided to steal her HDVR after you broke into and entered her house. Breaking and entering requires that the intent to commit the *actus reus* of breaking and entering set in the motion the act of breaking and entering your friend's house. That's how concurrence applies to breaking and entering, a crime of criminal conduct.

Now, let's look at an example of concurrence in murder, a crime causing a harm defined in the criminal code. Shafeah hates her sister Nazirah and plans to kill her by running over her with her Jeep Grand Cherokee. Coincidentally, just as Shafeah is headed toward Nazirah in her Cherokee, a complete stranger in an Audi A7 appears out of nowhere and accidentally runs over and kills Nazirah. Shafeah gets out of her Grand Cherokee, runs over to Nazirah's dead body, and gleefully dances around it. Although definitely a creepy thing to do, Shafeah's not a murderer because her criminal conduct (driving her Cherokee with the intent to kill Nazirah) didn't cause Nazirah's death. Concurrence here means the criminal conduct has to produce the criminal harm; the harm can't be a coincidence (Hall 1960, 185–90; see Chapter 11).

We won't say any more about concurrence, either here or in the remaining chapters. Not because it's not important. Quite the contrary, it's critical to criminal liability. But it's never an issue, at least not in real cases—not in the thousands of appellate court cases I've read over the years. And from what lawyers and trial judges I've known tell me, it's never an issue in the cases they try and decide. So for your purposes, know what it is, know it's a critical element of crimes requiring fault, and that's enough.

CAUSATION

causation holding an actor criminally accountable for the results of her conduct

Causation is about holding an actor criminally accountable for the results of her conduct. Causation applies only to criminal result crimes, the most prominent being criminal homicide (Chapter 9). But there are others, such as causing bodily harm in assault (Chapter 10), damage to property in malicious mischief (Chapter 11), and destruction of property in arson (Chapter 11). Like all elements of crime, prosecutors have to prove causation beyond a reasonable doubt.

Proving causation requires proving two kinds of cause:

1. Factual cause (also called "but for" cause or "cause in fact") of death, other bodily harm, and damage to and destruction of property
2. Legal cause (also called "proximate" cause) of death, other bodily harm, and damage to and destruction of property

Factual Cause

LO8

factual cause also called "but for" cause or "cause in fact"; if it weren't for an actor's conduct, the result wouldn't have occurred

Factual cause (also called "but for" cause or "cause in fact") is an empirical question of fact that asks whether an actor's conduct triggered a series of events that ended in causing death or other bodily harm; damage to property; or destruction of property.

In the cases and statutes, factual cause usually goes by the name "but for" cause or "cause in fact" (or if you want to be fancy and use its Latin name, *sine qua non* cause). "But for" cause means, if it weren't for an actor's conduct, the result wouldn't have occurred. Put another way, an actor's conduct triggered a chain of events that, sooner or later, ended in death or injury to a person or damage to and/or destruction of property. For example, I push a huge smooth round rock down a hill with a crowd at the bottom because I want to watch the crowd panic and scatter. The people see the rock and, to my delight, they scatter. Unfortunately, the rock hits and kills two people who couldn't get out of its path. My push is the cause in fact (the "but for") that kills the two people at the bottom. If I hadn't pushed the rock, they'd be alive. The MPC, Section 2.03(1), puts it this way: "Conduct is the cause of a result when it is an antecedent but for which the result in question would not have occurred."

Factual cause is an objective, empirical question of fact; that's why we call it factual cause. Proving factual cause in almost all real cases is as easy as the no-brainer example of pushing the rock. Proving "but for" cause is necessary, but it's not enough to satisfy the causation requirement. To be sufficient, the prosecution has to prove legal (also called "proximate" cause), too.

Legal ("Proximate") Cause

LO8

legal ("proximate") cause a subjective question that asks, "Is it fair to blame Defendant for the harm triggered by a chain of events her action(s) set in motion?"

Legal ("proximate") cause is a *subjective* question of fairness that appeals to the jury's sense of justice. It asks, "Is it *fair* to blame Defendant for the harm triggered by a chain of events her action(s) set in motion?" If the harm is accidental enough or far enough removed from Defendant's triggering act, there's a reasonable doubt about the justice of blaming Defendant, and there's no proximate cause.

Take our rock-pushing example, and change the facts. On the way down the hill, the rock runs into a tree and lodges there. A year later, a mild earthquake shakes the rock free and it finishes its roll by killing the victims at the bottom. Now, the no-brainer isn't a no-brainer anymore. Why? Because something else, facts in addition to my pushing, contributed to the deaths. We call this "something else" an intervening cause, an event that comes between the initial act in a sequence and the criminal result.

intervening cause an event that comes between the initial act in a sequence and the end result

Now, we've got our proximate cause problem: Is it fair to punish me for something that's not *entirely* my fault? As with factual cause, most legal (proximate) cause cases don't create problems, but the ones that do are serious crimes involving death, mutilation, injury, and property destruction and damage.

How do we (and the jury or judge in nonjury cases) determine whether it's fair to attribute the cause of a result to a defendant's conduct? The common law, criminal codes, and the MPC have used various and highly intricate, elaborate devices to help fact finders decide the proximate cause question. For our purposes, they're not too helpful. The best way to understand how fact finders and judges answer the fairness question is to look at how they decided it was fair to impute the bad result to actors' conduct in a real case. Our next case excerpt, *State v. Bauer*, provides us with an excellent example.

CASE

*In **State v. Bauer (2014)**, Douglas L. Bauer was charged with third-degree assault.*

Did he cause the gunshot wounds?

State v. Bauer

329 P.3d 67 (Wash. 2014)

HISTORY

Douglas L. Bauer (Defendant) was charged with third-degree assault. The Superior Court, Kitsap County, denied Bauer's motion to dismiss, but certified matter to the Court of Appeals. The Court of Appeals upheld the denial of motion to dismiss in a split decision. The Washington Supreme Court granted discretionary review, and reversed (5–1) the Court of Appeals.

Gonzalez, J., filed dissenting opinion.

McCLOUD, J, JOINED BY MADSEN, CJ, AND JOHNSON, OWENS, J. M. JOHNSON, J.P.T. JOHNSON, AND WIGGINS, JJ.

FACTS

On February 22, 2012, at about 1:30 P.M., the children at Armin Jahr Elementary School in Bremerton, Washington, were getting ready to go home for the day. As the teacher prepared to lead the children from the classroom to the school bus, she heard a loud pop. Looking around, the teacher saw one child bent over with blood on her hands. She summoned other staff, and before long they realized that the bloodied child had been shot.

A staff member noticed a backpack on TC's desk. It contained a gun. The backpack was identified as TC's backpack, and after the police arrived, TC was transported to a Youth Services Center for booking. Police later concluded that the gun, a Heckler & Koch .45 caliber pistol, had discharged "while still inside the backpack."

Police interviewed TC several times. TC explained that he had been visiting his mother and her boyfriend Bauer in their home for the past three years, since he was six years old. He asserted that ever since he first visited, he had seen multiple guns accessible throughout the house. TC said that his mother and Bauer told him the guns were all loaded.

According to TC, the weekend before the shooting, as he was leaving Bauer's house, he saw a gun on a bedroom dresser and "swiped the gun into his backpack." TC explained that he took the gun because some classmates had "told him they were going to have teenagers come and beat him up." He asserted that the shooting was accidental. TC pleaded guilty in juvenile court to reckless endangerment and was sentenced to probation and counseling.

Police also interviewed TC's mother and Bauer, along with TC's siblings. Their statements corroborate TC's statements that there were multiple unsecured and loaded guns around the house.

OPINION

CAUSATION IN CRIMINAL LAW IS DIFFERENT FROM CAUSATION IN TORT

The assault statute does not define the term "cause." Our court has ruled that "before criminal liability is imposed, the conduct of the defendant must be both the cause "cause in fact" and "legal cause" or "proximate cause," unless otherwise noted. "Cause in fact" refers to the "but for" consequences of an act—the physical connection between an act and an injury. "Legal causation, on the other hand, involves a determination of whether liability *should* attach as a matter of law given the existence of cause in fact. This court, in agreement with commentators and other jurisdictions, has observed that 'as to cause in fact, tort and criminal situations are exactly alike.'"

Legal causation, however, is different. Commentators and courts recognize that criminal law and tort serve different purposes and therefore have different principles of legal causation. With crimes, where the consequences of a determination of guilt are more drastic …, the wider doctrines of causation currently applied in tort law should not be extended to criminal law.

This court has never explicitly addressed whether "legal cause" is the same in both tort and criminal law. But a comparison of Washington criminal and tort cases shows that liability tends to extend further in tort cases. No appellate criminal case in Washington has found legal causation based on negligent acts similar to those in civil cases that were incapable of causing injury directly. For example, in *State v. Leech*, this court held that an arsonist "caused" the death of a fire fighter who responded to the arson fire, despite the fact that the fire fighter may have been negligent in his fire fighting. The arsonist, however, intentionally started the fire—clearly an intentional criminal act capable of causing harm in and of itself.

Bauer's act of gun ownership, in contrast, is not felonious or criminal. His decision to keep loaded weapons around the house is not, in itself, a crime in this state, either. The most analogous criminal case that we have found is from Iowa: *State v. Ayers*, 478 N.W.2d 606 (Iowa 1991). In that case, Ayers was a firearm vendor convicted of involuntary manslaughter for selling a gun to a minor. The minor accidentally shot and killed his girlfriend a few days later. The court held, "More is required than appears here to support a showing of proximate cause in a manslaughter case. The missing ingredient is a more direct connection between Ayers and the act which killed the young victim."

Neither party has identified a Washington case upholding criminal liability on facts like the ones on which the *Bauer* prosecution is based. This court has found no Washington case upholding such liability, either, where the accused did not actively participate in the immediate physical impetus of harm.

In light of the scholarly literature, our case law, and case law from foreign jurisdictions, we hold that "legal cause" in criminal cases differs from, and is narrower than, "legal cause" in tort cases in Washington.

LIABILITY DOES NOT ATTACH TO BAUER IN THIS CASE

As discussed above, there is no criminal case in Washington upholding criminal liability based on a negligent act that has such intervening facts as in this case between the original negligence and the final, specific, injurious result. More tellingly, even in analogous civil cases, we have declined to extend liability so far. For example, in *Sailor v. Ohlde*, this court addressed whether "the owner of an automobile who leaves the key in the ignition switch [can be civilly] liable for injury or damage caused by a stranger who enters upon private property and steals the automobile." We answered the question no.

[Several other cases are omitted here]

Finally, the Washington tort case most closely analogous to the one at hand, *McGrane v. Cline*, also supports our holding that Bauer is not liable for third degree assault in this case. In *McGrane*, a teenage daughter took the parents' firearm from their home, gave it to a friend, the friend used it to commit a robbery, and he fatally shot a third person during that crime. The Court of Appeals ruled that the parents were not civilly liable for that result.

Just as in *McGrane*, the firearm here was taken, without the owner's permission or knowledge, by a minor child and later used to cause serious harm. No criminal case in Washington has found liability on such attenuated facts as those in this case. Because legal causation in civil cases is broader and more flexible than it is in criminal cases, these civil cases compel the conclusion that legal causation is not satisfied as to Bauer in this case.

CONCLUSION

The legislature defined the crime of third degree assault to reach a person who "with criminal negligence, causes bodily harm to another person by means of a weapon or other instrument or thing likely to produce bodily harm." RCW 9A.36.031(1)(d). Bauer asserts that the State has failed to make a prima facie case that his conduct of leaving guns around his house loaded and accessible to invited children "caused" the bodily harm here. We agree. Although causation in fact is the same in criminal and civil cases, legal causation is not. Our case law suggests that legal causation does not extend as far in criminal cases as it does in tort cases, and even our civil cases do not extend liability as far as the State seeks to do in this case. We therefore reverse the decision of the Court of Appeals.

GONZÁLEZ, J. (DISSENTING).

Douglas Bauer kept multiple loaded guns unsecured throughout his house. These weapons were easily accessible to his girlfriend's minor children, including TC, a nine-year-old boy who frequently visited and sometimes stayed the night. Unsupervised, TC put one of Bauer's handguns into his backpack. Two days

(continues)

(continued)

later, that gun, still in TC's backpack, discharged in a classroom, seriously injuring one of TC's classmates. Bauer did not notice his handgun was missing until after the shooting.

The majority believes that because nine-year-old TC did not have permission to take the weapon and because two days elapsed between the taking and the subsequent shooting, Bauer's carelessness could not, as a matter of law, be the cause of the victim's serious injury. I disagree. The delay in Bauer noticing that his gun was missing is itself evidence of his negligence.

Though a jury may well find Bauer's actions to be too attenuated from the victim's injury to impose criminal liability as a matter of fact, whether criminal liability can attach as a matter of law is a policy question for the legislature. The legislature has made this policy judgment in RCW 9A.36.031(1)(d). It is neither unreasonable nor unwise to allow a jury to decide if it was the firearm owner's criminal negligence that caused the handgun to be brought to school, to be accidentally discharged, and to seriously injure the young victim. Since the majority believes otherwise, I respectfully dissent.

The issue before us is a novel one. As the majority notes, no Washington appellate court has weighed in on the lawful extent of legal cause in the context of the third degree assault statute. But that "this court has found no Washington case upholding ... liability ... where the accused did not actively participate in the immediate physical impetus of harm" is not a compelling argument against whether the legislature intended to criminalize this sort of carelessness. It is well settled that legal causation "rests on policy considerations as to how far the consequences of defendant's acts should extend. It involves a determination of whether liability *should* attach as a matter of law given the existence of cause in fact." In the context of criminal law, that question is for the legislature, and it has answered it.

Given scientific research on the topic, it is clear the legislative purpose of RCW 9A.36.031(1)(d) would be best served by letting a jury decide whether a firearm owner is liable for an unintended shooting that is the result of a young child picking up a carelessly stored handgun. In one study, scientists monitored numerous small groups of 8– to 12–year–old boys in a room that had two water pistols concealed in one drawer and an actual handgun concealed in another (Jackman, 1247–48).

The researchers limited the study to boys in this age range because they are "a high-risk group for unintentional fire-arm injury." The scientists found that 75 percent of the boys found the handgun within 15 minutes, 63 percent of these boys handled it, and 33 percent of them actually pulled the trigger enough to discharge the weapon. Overall, the "results suggest that 8– to 12–year–old boys cannot be trusted to refrain from handling a handgun if they encounter one outside the immediate supervision of an adult." Available at http://pediatrics.aappublications.org/content/107/6/1247.full.pdf (subscription required).

A different study, which measured the association of household firearm storage practices and the risk of unintentional and self-inflicted injuries associated with child or adolescent access to firearms in the home, also supports the conclusion that we should not preclude liability on legal causation grounds. *See* David C. Grossman et al., *Gun Storage Practices and Risk of Youth Suicide and Unintentional Firearm Injuries*, 293 JAMA 707, 708–10 (2005). There, researchers found that "storing household guns as locked, unloaded, or separate from the ammunition [was] associated with significant reductions in the risk of unintentional and self-inflicted firearm injuries and deaths among adolescents and children." In other words, and not surprisingly, this survey revealed that guns that were kept loaded, unsecured, and accessible to children were involved in accidents far more frequently than those that were not. Available at http://jama.jamanetwork.com/data/Journals/JAMA/4963/JOC32162.pdf.

Given both science and common sense, I find the legislature's inclusion of criminal negligence as a proper basis for an assault charge as permitting a jury to determine a handgun owner's liability in situations such as this. The jury would be able to consider all of the relevant circumstances, including the age and maturity of the child, the child's familiarity with firearms, and the precautions the firearm owner took or did not take to determine if the firearm owner's conduct amounts to criminal negligence. What the majority believes to be the intervening actions and attenuating circumstances in this case are the natural and foreseeable consequences of the very danger that Bauer's careless actions created.

TC's picking up the handgun and Bauer's failure to notice are not intervening causes in the ultimate injury. Like the majority, I do not believe "Bauer's act of gun ownership" or "his decision to keep loaded weapons around the house" is in itself criminal. But it need not be. Third degree assault predicated on criminal negligence does not require an underlying illegal act or an intentional act but merely criminal negligence that results in bodily harm. RCW 9A.36.031(1)(d). By its plain language, the purpose of the statute is to impose liability when injury is caused by criminal negligence, not criminal intent or felonious action.

A defendant can face liability for criminal negligence "when he or she fails to be aware of a substantial risk that a wrongful act may occur and his or her failure to be aware of such substantial risk constitutes a gross deviation from the standard of care that a reasonable person would exercise in the same situation." RCW 9A.08.010(1)(d). TC's actions are not distinct from Bauer's carelessness for legal causation purposes. When Bauer's gun ownership and method of storage is combined with the known presence of an unsupervised nine-year-old boy, especially when coupled with a failure to notice the unsecured weapon was missing, a jury, not a judge, should decide if this created a substantial risk that a wrongful act may occur.

Finding that TC's taking the gun without Bauer's permission was an intervening action, as the majority does, tacitly shifts the ultimate responsibility for the victim's injury to a nine-year-old child. Not only do I find this troubling in light of behavioral science, but also I agree with the legislature that "children of eight and under twelve years of age are presumed to be incapable of committing crime." RCW 9A.04.050. Though this presumption may be removed, and I do not seek to address the appropriateness of the liability imposed on TC, it is unsettling that TC, as a matter of law, will face more criminal culpability in this situation than Bauer.

At its core, this case comes down to considerations of sound policy. Bauer kept a loaded, unsecured handgun in a room that an unsupervised nine-year-old boy could access freely. Bauer also did not notice that this loaded weapon had been taken for two days as TC toted it in his backpack to and from school. Given that both science and common sense strongly suggest that Bauer was in the best position to prevent the injury to TC's classmate and that his conduct was its primary cause, I would not preclude Bauer's liability on legal causation grounds and would allow a jury to resolve the matter.

With these observations, I respectfully dissent.

QUESTIONS

1. List all of the facts relevant to deciding whether Douglas Bauer was the factual *and* legal (proximate) cause of TC's classmate's gunshot wounds.
2. Summarize the majority opinion's arguments that Bauer was not the proximate cause of the wounds.
3. Summarize the dissent's arguments that Bauer *was* the proximate cause of the wounds.
4. In your opinion, who has the stronger arguments, the majority or the dissent? Defend your answer.
5. In your opinion, how important *should* the studies cited by the dissent be in reaching the court's decision? Defend your answer.
6. In your opinion, was this a crime or a tragic accident? Defend your answer.

FAILURE OF PROOF "DEFENSES": IGNORANCE AND MISTAKE

LO9

Before we take up the complicated subject of the place of ignorance of law and mistake of facts in our criminal law regime, let's recap some basic points we've already covered, and say a few words about the defenses of justification (Chapter 5) and excuses (Chapter 6) which we'll take up in greater depth later.

1. All crimes have to include a voluntary act (*actus reus*, see Chapters 2 and 3).
2. Most crimes—and all serious crimes—include a mental element (see Chapter 1 and pp. 126–129 of this chapter).

3. In addition to the elements of *actus reus* and *mens rea*, a few serious crimes also require that criminal conduct cause a criminal harm (see previous section).
   a. General intent crimes only require that defendants intend to commit the voluntary act.
   b. Specific intent crimes require that defendants intend to cause the harmful result.
4. The prosecution has to prove every element in 1–3 beyond a reasonable doubt (see Chapter 2).

One other preliminary: Defendants don't *have to* prove anything. But they *may*. They can challenge the prosecution's case either before or after the prosecution rests its case. You don't need this book to tell you one way: Wait until the prosecution has rested its case and plead some justification (see Chapter 5; for example, self-defense) or excuse (see Chapter 6, insanity).

You might not be familiar with the other way: *Before* the prosecution rests its case, defendants can challenge the prosecution's case, like alibi, or mistaken eyewitness identification. Let's look at two others, namely *failure of proof defenses*, ignorance of the law and mistake of fact.

LO9

Ignorance of Law

ignorance maxim the presumption that defendants knew the law they were breaking

"Ignorance of the law is no excuse," is one of the most familiar maxims in criminal law. In law talk, the ignorance maxim means that everyone is presumed to know the law. Courts will decide particular cases as if defendants knew the law they were breaking, even though didn't in fact know it. For example, you believe that you don't have to come to a complete stop at a stop sign if there are no cars in or approaching the intersection. The law, as most of us know, is that you *always* have to stop. Most statutes and court opinions retain the *ignorance maxim* as the law, although the U.S. Supreme Court has taken some steps toward modifying the rule. (Alter et al. 2007, 821–23)

LO9

MISTAKE OF FACT

mistake of fact a defense to criminal liability whenever the mistake prevents the formation of any fault-based mental attitude—namely, purposely, knowingly, recklessly, or negligently

failure-of-proof defenses mistake defenses in which defendants usually present enough evidence to raise a reasonable doubt that the prosecution has proved the *mens rea* required for criminal liability

Unlike the *ignorance maxim*, you probably don't know that a mistake of fact *is* a defense whenever the mistake prevents the formation of the *mens rea* of the crime, namely, purposely, knowingly, recklessly, or negligently. Notice that the mistake of fact can't apply to strict liability because strict liability by definition is not fault-based. (See later, p. 153.)

Mistakes in this sense are sometimes called failure-of-proof defenses because defendants usually present enough evidence to raise a reasonable doubt that the prosecution has proved that they formed the *mens rea* required for criminal liability. We'll see examples of defenses that can be called either defenses of excuse or failures of proof of mental attitude in Chapter 6 (LaFave 2010, 298–300).

LO9

A General Ignorance or Mistake "Defense"

As we noted earlier, most criminal statutes and court opinion separate ignorance of law and mistake of fact, and reject ignorance of the law as a defense, but accept a mistakes of fact defense. But, a number of states have enacted the Model Penal Code's (MPC's) general provision on "Ignorance or Mistake" that applies to both law and facts. (See "Criminal Law in Focus" Box.)

Ignorance or Mistake

Model Penal Code, Section 2.04

1. Ignorance or mistake as to a matter of fact or law is a defense if:
   a. The ignorance or mistake negatives the purpose, knowledge, belief, recklessness or negligence required to establish a material element of the offense; or
   b. The law provides that the state of mind established by such ignorance or mistake constitutes a defense.
2. Omitted
3. A belief that conduct does not legally constitute an offense is a defense to a prosecution for that offense based upon such conduct when:
   a. The statute or other enactment defining the offense is not known to the actor and has not been published or otherwise reasonably made available prior to the conduct alleged; or
   b. He acts in reasonable reliance upon an official statement of the law, afterward determined to be invalid or erroneous, contained in (i) a statute or other enactment; (ii) a judicial decision, opinion or judgment; (iii) an administrative order or grant of permission; or (iv) an official interpretation of the public officer or body charged by law with responsibility for the interpretation, administration or enforcement of the law defining the offense.
4. The defendant must prove the defense arising under Subsection 3 of this section by a preponderance of the evidence.

Source: *Model Penal Code and Commentaries* 1985.

And, even if other statutes and courts don't adopt the MPC provision formally, they do so in practice. (See later, "Morality and Ignorance of the Law: Empirical Findings," pp. 156–158.)

To simplify matters for you, we follow the MPC's approach, which is that mistake matters when it prevents the formation of a mental attitude required by a criminal statute. To decide whether a mistake negates the mental element, we need to know what mental element the statute requires. Suppose it's a crime in your state for a bartender to sell alcoholic beverages to anyone under 21 for the purpose of supplying a minor with an alcoholic beverage. You're a bartender; you believe the customer you just sold to is 21 because she showed you a driver's license with a birth date more than 22 years prior to today's date. In fact, she's eighteen. Your mistake negates the mental element of purpose.

Suppose the statute says "recklessly supplies anyone under 21." You look at another customer's license; the date looks altered, but you're not sure. You say, "This date looks like it's been changed, but what the hell, I feel like living dangerously tonight" and sell her an orange blossom martini. She's 19. You're guilty, because you created a "substantial and unjustifiable risk" that she was under 21.

One final and important point about mistake; it doesn't work with strict liability crimes. Why? There's no mental element in strict liability offenses. In other words, the trail of mistake doesn't have to (in fact, it can't) lead to fault. To follow through with the bartender example, suppose the statute makes it a crime "to sell any alcoholic beverage to a person under 21." There's no mental element to negate, so it doesn't matter whether you sold it purposely, knowingly, recklessly, or negligently (or even accidentally, as we saw earlier in "Strict Liability," p. 142).

In our next case excerpt, *State v. Jacobson* (2005), Minnesota applied the MPC failure-of proof approach to mistake. The court held that "Jake" Jacobson could introduce his mistaken reliance on the advice of his lawyer to show that the state failed to prove beyond a reasonable doubt that Jacobson intended to commit election law fraud.

CASE

In ***State v. Jacobson*** **(2005),** *Richard Joseph Jacobson was charged with conspiracy to procure unlawful voting and conspiracy to commit forgery. The district court certified two questions to the court of appeals. The court of appeals held that evidence of Jacobson's mistake of law is admissible because it is relevant to whether he intended to break the law.*

Did he qualify for a *failure of proof defense*?

State v. Jacobson

697 N.W.2d 610 (Minn. 2005)

BLATZ, CJ.

HISTORY

This case comes to us on appeal from questions certified to the Minnesota Court of Appeals from the Dakota County District Court regarding two mistake of law defenses—reliance on advice of counsel and reliance on an official interpretation of the law. Richard Joseph Jacobson was charged with conspiracy to procure unlawful voting and conspiracy to commit forgery. At a pretrial hearing, the state brought a motion seeking to exclude evidence concerning an unrelated election law complaint and the response to that complaint by the Dakota County Attorney's Office. The district court granted the state's motion, barred Jacobson from asserting the defenses of reliance on advice of counsel and reliance on an official interpretation of the law, and certified two questions to the court of appeals. The court of appeals held that the defenses of good faith reliance on the advice of counsel and good faith reliance on an official interpretation of the law are "available defenses to a defendant charged with a specific intent crime" and that the district court prematurely concluded that any reliance was unreasonable. The court of appeals further held that Jacobson is entitled to present evidence of his reliance as part of his due process right to present a defense and explain his conduct. We hold that evidence of Jacobson's mistake of law is admissible because it is relevant to whether he intended to break the law—an element of the conspiracy charges.

FACTS

At the time of the events alleged in the complaint, Jacobson was the owner and operator of "Jakes," a strip club located at 15981 Clayton Avenue in Coates, Minnesota. For several years, Jakes has been the subject of substantial local legal controversy.[3] On October 11, 2002, the Dakota County Treasurer-Auditor's Office reported that it received 93 Minnesota voter registration cards and voter change of address cards listing 15981 Clayton Avenue, Coates, Minnesota—Jakes' address—as the voters' place of residence.[4] While the registrants signed the voter registration cards certifying that they "maintained residence at the address given on the registration form," Dakota County property tax records indicate that Jakes is a "bar/tavern" with four bathrooms and no bedrooms.

[3] On October 4, 2002, a federal district court filed an order closing Jakes. The federal district court specifically found that Jakes had previously been closed by federal court order for operating a sexually oriented business in violation of city ordinances and that, after the reopening of the business, the nature of the business continued to violate city ordinances.

[4] We note that Coates has a population of approximately 163 people. U.S. Census Bureau Fact Sheet, Census 2000 Demographic Profile Highlights, at http://factfinder.census.gov (last visited June 2, 2005). The record in this case reflects that the city is governed by a four-member city council and a mayor. In November 2002, two council seats and the mayor position were on the ballot. All three positions were contested.

On October 14, 2002, investigating officers executed a search warrant for Jakes and a vehicle registered to Jacobson. While inside Jakes, the officers found 13 blank voter registration forms and two completed voter registration cards listing 15981 Clayton Avenue, Coates, Minnesota, as the voters' place of residence. In the vehicle, officers found 26 blank voter registration forms and a highlighted copy of voter registration statutes. The officers found no evidence that anyone was residing at Jakes. Jacobson was subsequently charged with conspiracy to procure unlawful voting in violation of Minn. Stat. § 204C.14(e) (2004) and Minn. Stat. § 609.175 (2004), and conspiracy to commit forgery in violation of Minn. Stat. § 609.63, subd. 1(6) (2004), and § 609.175. Jacobson pleaded not guilty to the charges.

Subsequent to his pleas of not guilty, Jacobson filed a motion to dismiss on due process grounds. In connection with the motion, Jacobson submitted an affidavit stating that for the past several years he had retained an attorney, Randall Tigue, to attend to various civil matters. Jacobson averred that, in July 2002, Tigue showed him a copy of Minnesota's voting and election laws and a letter from Chief Deputy Dakota County Attorney Phillip Prokopowicz to Minneapolis Assistant Clerk and Director of Elections Suzanne Griffin.

The letter to Griffin, dated June 4, 2002, concerned possible violations of voter registration and election laws by Minneapolis police officers who registered to vote using their work addresses rather than their home addresses. The matter had been referred by the Hennepin County Attorney's Office to the Dakota County Attorney's Office, presumably because of a conflict of interest. In the letter, Chief Deputy Prokopowicz informed the city that the Dakota County Attorney's Office had concluded that there was no criminal wrongdoing by the police officers and thus the office was closing its investigation of the matter.[5] Jacobson asserted ... that "with Mr. Tigue's counsel and advice, and relying on a review of Minnesota's election laws and the letter by Mr. Prokopowicz," he and several of his employees "devised a plan to get people to register to vote using Jakes as a residence."

In response to Jacobson's assertions in his affidavit, the state filed a motion to exclude (1) "any documentation, testimony, or reference to an election law complaint made by [Suzanne] Griffin, Minneapolis Assistant City Clerk-Director of Elections, regarding alleged violations of voter registration election laws by various Minneapolis police officers" and (2) "any documentation, testimony, or reference to the disposition of the ... complaint by the Dakota County Attorney's Office." At the hearing on the state's motion to exclude, the state clarified that its motion included Tigue's testimony regarding Prokopowicz's letter, any advice Tigue may have given Jacobson based on the letter, and any reference to the advice.

Jacobson opposed the state's motion on five separate grounds. [Only three are relevant here.] He argued that the challenged evidence (1) was relevant to the issue of his intent; (2) was relevant to establish the defenses of reliance on the advice of counsel and reliance on an official interpretation of the law; ... and (5) had to be admitted to protect Jacobson's constitutional right to present a defense.

OPINION

Jacobson has been charged with conspiracy to procure unlawful voting and conspiracy to commit forgery. Under Minnesota law, conspiracy occurs when one "conspires with another to commit a crime" and requires proof that "in furtherance of the conspiracy one or more of the parties does some overt act." Minn. Stat. § 609.175, subd. 2. The state argues that the intent required under this statute is intent to commit the *underlying acts*. However, in explaining the intent required to establish conspiracy we have stated: "A conscious and intentional purpose *to break the law* is an essential element of the crime of conspiracy ...," *State v. Kuhnau*, 622 N.W.2d 552, 556 (Minn.2001) (emphasis added). Similarly, CRIMJIG 5.11 states that the actions of the conspirators "must be the result of a preconceived and mutual intention *to commit a crime*." 10 Minn. Dist. Judges Ass'n, *Minnesota Practice-Jury Instruction Guides, Criminal*, CRIMJIG 5.11 (4th ed. 1999) (emphasis added). We reaffirm our statement in *Kuhnau* and hold that the intent necessary to prove conspiracy is the intent to "break the law."

As a general rule, mistake or ignorance of the law is not a defense. It is assumed that all members of

(continues)

[5]After reading a Star Tribune article regarding the investigation of the Minneapolis police officers' possible violation of voter registration and election laws in which Prokopowicz was quoted, Tigue contacted the Dakota County Attorney's Office and requested a copy of any written opinion relating to the matter. In response, Prokopowicz sent him a copy of the letter he had written to the assistant city clerk. Jacobson stipulated that, with the exception of Tigue's written request for a copy of any written opinion on the police officer matter, there was no other contact with the county attorney's office regarding the registration or election laws or the legitimacy of Jacobson's plan.

(continued)

an ordered society are presumed either to know the law or, at least, to have acquainted themselves with those laws that are likely to affect their usual activities. But, a mistake of law "defense" has been recognized in limited circumstances when the mistake "negatives the existence of a mental state essential to the crime charged."

A mistake of law that negates the mental state of the charged offense is not a "defense" in the sense that the defendant carries the burden of persuasion. Rather the evidence relates to disproving or negating an element of the crime charged. In this circumstance, a mistake of law "defense" is actually an application of the principle that "the Due Process Clause protects the accused against conviction except upon proof beyond a reasonable doubt of every fact necessary to constitute the crime with which he is charged." *In re Winship* [Discussed in Chapter 2, pp. 47–48]

Here, Jacobson's mistake of law is relevant to negate the intent for the crime charged because conspiracy requires proof of a "conscious and intentional purpose to break the law." *Kuhnau*, 622 N.W.2d at 556. Thus, if Jacobson believed in good faith that it was legal to procure others to fill out voter registration cards listing Jakes as their residence, he would not have the requisite intent for conspiracy. We therefore hold that evidence relating to a defendant's misunderstanding of the law is admissible when relevant to whether the defendant had the intent required for the charged offense.

We now turn to the state's argument that, even if the "defenses" of reliance on advice of counsel and reliance on an official interpretation of the law exist in Minnesota, any reliance by a defendant must be reasonable in order to assert the defenses at trial. The state argues that Jacobson is precluded from using any evidence of his reliance at trial because the district court found that Jacobson's reliance on advice of counsel and on an official interpretation of the law was unreasonable. We disagree. As we stated above, the "defenses" at issue here are fundamentally evidentiary issues relating to the defendant's mental state. Because the existence of intent is a question of fact, it must be submitted to the jury.

We therefore hold that, on the record before us and based on the pending charges, Jacobson has a right to present evidence that he relied on Tigue's advice and on Chief Deputy Dakota County Attorney Prokopowicz's letter regarding the Minneapolis police officer matter. Our holding is grounded in constitutional law and our recognition that it is fundamental that criminal defendants have a due process right to explain their conduct to a jury. While the district court can impose limits on the testimony of a defendant, the limits must not trample on the defendant's right to a fair trial.

Affirmed.

QUESTIONS

1. List all of the facts relevant to deciding whether "Jake" Jacobson qualified for the *failure of proof defense* of mistake of law.
2. State the Minnesota Supreme Court's decision.
3. Summarize the court's arguments supporting its ruling that Jacobson was entitled to have the jury decide his *failure of proof defense*.
4. Recall that at the suppression hearing, the state argued that in a mistake of law claim, "there is no legal defense of [reliance on] advice of legal counsel, and that even if the defense of reliance on the advice of legal counsel and reliance on an official interpretation of the law exist as a general matter, the defenses could not be asserted in the instant case because these defenses require a showing that the defendant used due diligence and care." Which part of the court's decision is closest to your view? Defend your answer.

Morality and Ignorance of the Law: Empirical Findings

LO10

> This case stirs large questions—questions that go to the moral foundations of the criminal law. Whether postulated as a problem of *mens rea*, of "willfulness," of "criminal responsibility," or "scienter," the infliction of criminal punishment upon the unaware has long troubled the fair administration of justice.
>
> —*U.S. v. International Minerals & Chemical Corporation* (1971, 558)

These are U.S. Supreme Court Justice Potter Stewart's words, dissenting from a majority decision holding that a statute providing that "knowingly" shipping sulfuric acid "does not signal an exception to the general rule that ignorance of the law is no excuse. ... Where ... dangerous products are involved, the probability of regulation is so great that anyone who is aware that he is in possession or dealing with them must be presumed to be aware of the regulation" (558).

Researchers Adam L. Alter, Julia Kernochan, and John M. Darley (2007) contend that criminal law's moral authority depends on remaining "in step with the basic intuitions of the surrounding community." They tested this proposition empirically and published the results in "Morality Influences how People Apply the Ignorance of Law Defense." (Alter et al. 2007, 820. This section relies heavily on their research.) They acknowledge that morality consensus is tough to achieve in our "diverse and free society," and maintain that in a democracy, the majority should *not* always prevail.

Nevertheless, they contend that "conformity with community mores" *insofar as we can identify them* should shape criminal law. Research has convincingly demonstrated that the criminal law loses its force if people believe it's ineffective or doesn't deserve their respect. According to Professor Tom Tyler's important *Why People Obey the Law* (2006), people are more likely to obey the law under two circumstances: they believe the crime is morally wrong *and* that the law generally deserves respect. The law deserves respect when people *perceive* that its procedures are fair and impartial (41–68). Professor Janice Nadler (2005) has demonstrated that when a particular law violates a person's commonsense view of a just law, they're more likely to flout laws commonly encountered in everyday life, for example traffic laws and petty theft (1399).

In view of these findings, we should *measure* the mores we can clearly identify. "In that spirit, this article presents a group of four studies that provide the first empirical investigation of ... nonlawyers' moral intuitions about the interaction between the defense of legal ignorance and the defendant's broader course of conduct" (820).

Before we get to the studies, you need to keep in mind that the connection between moral intuitions and the ignorance of law rule wasn't urgent when it was created centuries ago. Why? Because at that time, it applied only to the core felonies—murder, rape, robbery, burglary, and theft (see Chapters 1, 9–11). These crimes were (and, of course, still are) widely known and accepted as wrong (*mala in se*). But, when it comes to the thousands if not tens of thousands and growing list of minor crimes and regulation violations (*mala prohibita*), in 50 states, the District of Columbia, and especially the even more rapidly growing U.S. Criminal Code (see Chapter 1), the "ignorance-of-law-is-no-excuse" rule is, frankly, preposterous. That leaves a huge number of offenses that vast numbers of people commit, who have no idea are crimes. And, if they *do* know, their moral sense tells them, "This may be against the law, but it's not wrong" (*mala prohibita*).

Now, let's turn to Alter and his colleagues' research findings. They explore how people think about ignorance of the law and about the morality of defendants' conduct. In minor crimes, nonlawyers might believe it's fair to allow defendants to claim they were ignorant of the law they were charged with violating. On the other hand, they might disapprove of the claim if they believe the defendant's conduct is immoral. They set out to test empirically nonlawyers' responses to claims of legal ignorance by moral, immoral, and morally neutral defendants (824). In all four studies, the results "suggest that

> people particularly disfavored immoral actors, whereas they were not particularly lenient toward moral actors. It was not the case that the moral actors alone were singled out for lenient treatment; instead, the immoral actors were generally convicted more often and given a harsher sentence than were either the moral or morally neutral actors. To the degree these that these results can be generalized, this suggests that participants resisted allowing a person who acted with wrongful intent to escape punishment even if he or she was genuinely ignorant of the laws proscribing that action. If,

on the other hand, a person committed an illegal act during the course of either moral or neutral behavior, then ignorance of the laws against those specific illegal acts was taken to provide a valid defense or at least a reason to mitigate the sentence for the offense. As we expected, the primary motivation behind laypeople's intuitions about the ignorance defense is a desire to punish the blameworthy, rather than an effort to reward the exceptionally good. In other words, laypeople seemed to want to prevent the ignorance defense from being used as a shield for the cynical wrongdoer. (843–44)

What are the implications for lawyers and judges that nonlawyers *intuitively* evaluate legal ignorance claims? According to Alter et al.,

> in contrast to the doctrine that ignorance *never* excuses ... laypeople view knowledge of illegality to be an aspect of moral wrongfulness that is relevant to criminal case outcomes across a variety of regulatory offenses, especially when the illegal act was part of a moral or neutral course of conduct with no wrongful motivation. Essentially, our respondents seemed intuitively to treat knowledge of illegality as an aspect of *mens rea*, or guilty mind. (846–47)

Now, let's look a little more closely at Study 3. Participants were 75 Princeton University psychology students (48 women) between 18 and 22 years old who participated for partial course credit. In all cases, the defendant attempted to enter the United States with $14,000, unintentionally violating customs regulations. In the moral condition, the defendant planned to buy medical equipment for sick kids in Europe. The immoral defendant intended to buy and export cheap heroin to Europe. The neutral defendant, the manager of a foreign construction company, planned to buy cheap U.S. concrete to use in his business. To examine participants' intuitions about how criminal law should respond to claims of ignorance, they were asked: (1) If they were a juror, would they vote to convict the defendant? and, (2) What would an appropriate sentence for the defendant?

Here's what they found:

Conviction Patterns

Participants perceived that

1. The moral actors were more moral than neutral actors and the immoral actors.
2. The neutral actors were more moral than the immoral actors.

Sentencing Patterns

1. Immoral defendants received harsher sentences than neutral defendants and moral defendants. (829–30)

YOU *DECIDE*

Who's entitled to the mistake of law defense?

Defendant 1

Mark is the head of a construction company in Europe. He learns that the price of a particular catalyst used to make reinforced concrete has recently plummeted in the United States, so he decides to fly to the United States to purchase US$14,000 worth of the catalyst. Mark places the $14,000 in an envelope in his suitcase, on top of his clothes.

At JFK Airport in New York, a customs officer randomly searches Mark's luggage and discovers the notes in his suitcase. The customs officer informs Mark that it is illegal to take more than $10,000 into the United States and that he will be charged with an offense under the Customs Act. Mark tells the customs officer that he was honestly not aware of the law, but he is still charged with the offense of attempting to import in excess of $10,000 into the United States.

Defendant 2

Mark is the head of a charity organization in Europe that purchases medical equipment for sick children's hospices. He learns that the price of several pieces of essential equipment in the United States has recently plummeted, so he decides to fly to the United States to purchase US$14,000 worth of equipment and have it shipped back to Europe. Mark places the $14,000 in an envelope in his suitcase, on top of his clothes.

At JFK Airport in New York, a customs officer randomly searches Mark's luggage and discovers the notes in his suitcase. The customs officer informs Mark that it is illegal to take more than $10,000 into the United States and that he will be charged with an offense under the Customs Act. Mark tells the customs officer that he was honestly not aware of the law, but he is still charged with the offense of attempting to import in excess of $10,000 into the United States.

Defendant 3

Mark is the head of a drug syndicate in Europe. He learns that the price of heroin in the United States has plummeted temporarily, that the sellers will only accept cash payments, and that the price will soon rise to its usual levels. Mark decides to fly to the United States to purchase US$14,000 worth of heroin. Mark places the $14,000 in an envelope in his suitcase, on top of his clothes.

At JFK Airport in New York, a customs officer randomly searches Mark's luggage and discovers the notes in his suitcase. The customs officer informs Mark that it is illegal to take more than $10,000 into the United States and that he will be charged with an offense under the Customs Act. Mark tells the customs officer that he was honestly not aware of the law, but he is still charged with the offense of attempting to import in excess of $10,000 into the United States.

Question

- Which of the three defendants is entitled to the defense of ignorance of law? Support your answer with the information in your text regarding *mens rea*, ignorance and mistake generally, and the empirical evidence on moral, neutral, and immoral defendants.

Summary

LO1 A criminal act (*actus reus*) is necessary, but not enough, for criminal liability for most serious crimes. They also include a mental element (*mens rea*), concurrence, and causation. These elements of crimes help us determine blameworthiness or culpability, meaning that it's only fair to punish people we can blame for their conduct.

LO2 *Mens rea*, Latin for "guilty mind," is an ancient concept. From the work of Plato to the present-day courts, criminal intent has been recognized and reaffirmed as the criminal law's "mantra."

LO3 *Mens rea* is the mental state, or criminal intent, that accompanies a criminal act (*actus reus*). This is different from a motive, which is something that causes a person to act. Motive isn't a required element of a crime, but it is sometimes relevant to criminal cases, such as murder. Confessions are the only direct evidence of mental attitude; proving criminal intent is difficult and usually relies upon inferences made from actions and attendant circumstances.

LO4 The long list of terms used to define *mens rea* fit into three different types of fault that satisfy the mental element of criminal liability: subjective fault, objective fault, and criminal liability without fault (strict liability). Subjective fault requires a "bad mind" in the actor; in the language of the MPC, it includes the mental states of "purposely" and "knowingly." Objective fault requires no purposeful or conscious "bad mind" in the actor; it includes the "negligently" and "recklessly" levels of culpability. Strict liability imposes criminal liability on the actor without either subjective or objective fault. Actors are held criminally accountable for accidents under strict liability.

LO5 General intent refers to the intent to commit the criminal act and is the minimum requirement for *all* crimes. Specific intent applies only to result crimes and refers to the general intent to commit the criminal act *plus* the intent to cause a harmful result.

LO6 The Model Penal Code (MPC) breaks down *mens rea* into four levels of culpability: purposely, knowingly, recklessly, and negligently. "Purposely" is the most culpable mental state and means that it was the actor's "conscious object" to commit crimes or cause criminal results. "Knowingly" refers to the actor's awareness that her conduct is "practically certain" to cause the bad result. The mental states of "recklessly" and "negligently" are focused on *risk creation* rather than a "bad mind" in the actor. Reckless actors *consciously* create a "substantial and unjustifiable" risk of harm. Negligent actors are the least culpable; they are *not* aware of the risks they create, but they *should* have known, and a reasonable person would have been aware of the risk of harm.

LO7 Concurrence means that some mental fault has to trigger the criminal act in conduct crimes and the cause in result crimes.

LO8 The element of causation applies only to "bad result" crimes. Like all elements of a crime, prosecutors have to prove causation beyond a reasonable doubt. Proving causation requires proving both kinds of cause: (1) factual or "but for" cause, and (2) legal or "proximate" cause.

LO9 Most statutes and court opinions retain the ignorance maxim as the law, but ignorance of facts and law can sometimes create a reasonable doubt that the prosecution has proved the element of criminal intent. Mistake is a defense whenever the mistake prevents the formation of the *mens rea* required by a criminal statute.

LO10 Empirical research shows support for a connection between morality and the ignorance of the law as a defense to criminal liability. The primary motivation behind peoples' intuitions about the ignorance defense is a desire to punish the blameworthy; they want to prevent the ignorance defense from being used as a shield for the most immoral actors.

Key Terms

culpability or blameworthiness, p. 126
mens rea, p. 126
motive, p. 128
subjective fault, p. 129
objective fault, p. 130
strict liability, p. 131
general intent, p. 131
specific intent, p. 131
purposely, p. 135
knowingly, p. 137
recklessly, p. 139
negligently, p. 140
principle of concurrence, p. 146
causation, p. 146
factual cause, p. 147
legal ("proximate") cause, p. 147
intervening cause, p. 147
ignorance maxim, p. 152
mistake of fact, p. 152
failure-of-proof defenses, p. 152

Learning Objectives

1 To know that defendants aren't criminally liable if their actions were justified or excused under the circumstances, and to understand how the affirmative defenses operate in justified and excused conduct.

2 To understand that self-defense limits the use of deadly force to those who reasonably believe that they're faced with the choice to kill or be killed right now.

3 To know and understand the four elements of self-defense.

4 To understand the retreat rule and its historic transformation that led to the stand-your-ground rule.

5 To know and understand the exceptions to the retreat rule, and to appreciate their impact on self-defense in cases of domestic violence.

6 To know and appreciate how self-defense has been expanded to include the defense of others, the home, and property.

7 To appreciate how the new "Castle Laws" are drastically transforming the law of self-defense, and to understand their application to self-defense cases.

8 To know that the choice-of-evils defense justifies the commission of a lesser crime to avoid an imminent threat of harm from a greater evil.

9 To know that the defense of consent is a justification defense based on the high value placed on individual autonomy in a free society.

5 Defenses to Criminal Liability I

Justifications

Chapter Outline

Following an annulment from her first husband and two subsequent divorces in which she was the petitioner, Peggy Stewart married Mike Stewart in 1974. Evidence at trial disclosed a long history of abuse by Mike against Peggy and her two daughters from one of her prior marriages.

In May 1986, Peggy left Mike and ran away to her daughter Laura's home in Oklahoma. On May 30, 1986, Mike called to say he was coming to get her. Peggy agreed to return to Kansas. As soon as they arrived at the house, Mike forced Peggy into the house and forced her to have oral sex several times.

The next morning, Peggy discovered a loaded .357 magnum. She testified she was afraid of the gun. She hid the gun under the mattress of the bed in a spare room. Later that morning, as she cleaned house, Mike kept making remarks that she should not bother because she would not be there long, or that she should not bother with her things because she could not take them with her. She testified she was afraid Mike was going to kill her.

Mike's parents visited Mike and Peggy that afternoon. Mike's father testified that Peggy and Mike were affectionate with each other during the visit. Later, after Mike's parents had left, Mike forced Peggy to perform oral sex. After watching television, Mike and Peggy went to bed at 8:00 P.M. As Mike slept, Peggy thought about suicide and heard voices in her head repeating over and over, "kill or be killed." At this time, there were two vehicles in the driveway and Peggy had access to the car keys. About 10:00 P.M., Peggy went to the spare bedroom and removed the gun from under the mattress, walked back to the bedroom, and killed her husband while he slept. She then ran to the home of a neighbor, who called the police.

LO1

criminal conduct a criminal act triggered by criminal intent

Proving **criminal conduct** (a criminal act triggered by criminal intent) is necessary to hold individuals accountable for the crimes they commit. But criminal conduct alone isn't enough to establish criminal liability. Recall that it's only the first of three requirements. First, we have to answer the question asked in Chapters 3 and 4, "Was there criminal conduct?" If there wasn't, the inquiry is over, and the defendant is free. If there was, we have to answer the question of this chapter, "Was the criminal conduct justified?" If it was, the inquiry ends, and the defendant goes free. If it wasn't justified, we have to go on to answer the third question (asked in Chapter 6), "Was the unjustified conduct excused?" If it wasn't, the defendant is criminally accountable for her criminal conduct. If it was, the defendant might, or might not, go free.

justification defenses defendants admit they were responsible for their acts but claim that, under the circumstances, what they did was right (justified)

excuse defenses defendants admit what they did was wrong but claim that, under the circumstances, they weren't responsible for what they did

The principles of justification comprise several traditional defenses to criminal liability and we discuss several in this chapter. In the **justification defenses**, defendants admit they were *responsible* for their acts but claim that, under the circumstances, what they did was *right* (justified). The classic justification is self-defense: kill or be killed. "I killed her. I'm responsible for killing her, but, under the circumstances, it was right to kill her." So, even if the government proves all the elements in the crime beyond a reasonable doubt, the defendant walks because she's not blameworthy.

In the **excuse defenses**, defendants admit what they did was *wrong* but claim that, under the circumstances, they weren't *responsible* for what they did (see Chapter 6). The classic excuse is insanity. "What I did was wrong, but I was too insane to know or control what I did. So, under the circumstances, I'm not responsible for what I did."

In addition to the traditional defenses of self and home, this chapter also examines, and asks you to think about, "the epochal transformation" in self-defense and the defense of homes represented by the new "castle doctrine" statutes (Suk 2008, 237). More than 40 states have either passed or proposed statutes that expand the right to use deadly force to protect self and home in two ways:

1. "They permit a home resident to kill an intruder, by presuming rather than requiring proof of reasonable fear of death or serious bodily harm."
2. "They reject a general duty to retreat from attack, even when retreat is possible, not only in the home, but also in public space." (238)

PROVING DEFENSES

LO1

affirmative defenses defendants have to "start matters off by putting in some evidence in support" of their justification or excuse defenses

perfect defenses defenses in which defendants are acquitted if they're successful

Justification and excuse are **affirmative defenses**, which operate like this: Defendants have to "start matters off by putting in some evidence in support" of their justification or excuse. (Review Chapter 2 on "Proving Guilt in Criminal Cases" p. 47.)

Most affirmative defenses are **perfect defenses**, which means that, if they're successful, defendants are acquitted. There's one major exception to this rule. Defendants who successfully plead the excuse of insanity don't "walk"—at least not right away. **Competency hearings** are special hearings to determine if these defendants are still insane. Most competency hearings decide they are, and so they're sent to maximum-security hospitals to be confined there until they regain their sanity. In most serious crimes, that's never (see Chapter 6).

Evidence that doesn't amount to a perfect defense might amount to an **imperfect defense**; that is, defendants are guilty of lesser offenses. For example, in *Swann v. U.S.* (1994), Ted Swann and Steve Crawford got into an argument while shooting baskets. Crawford's ball hit Swann in the stomach, where someone had recently stabbed him.

Crawford ordered Swann off the court. When Swann instead walked past him, ignoring the order, Crawford said, "You think you stabbed up now, just watch." Then, placing his hands to his side, Crawford appeared to be reaching for his back pocket. Swann, who had seen a bulge in Crawford's pocket, thought that he was reaching for a gun to kill him. Swann pulled his own gun from his waistband and shot Crawford twice in the head (929).

competency hearings special hearings to determine if defendants who have used the insanity excuse defense are still insane

The court ruled that Swann was entitled to a jury instruction on imperfect defense that would reduce the murder charge to manslaughter, because there was enough evidence for a jury to conclude that "Swann's belief that he was in imminent danger and that he had to use deadly force to repel that danger was in fact actually and honestly held but was in one or both respects objectively unreasonable" (930).

imperfect defense when a defendant fails in the full defense but is found guilty of a lesser offense

Even when the evidence doesn't add up to an imperfect defense, it might still show mitigating circumstances that convince judges or juries that defendants don't deserve the maximum penalty for the crime they're convicted of. For example, words, however insulting, can't reduce murder to manslaughter in most states, but they might mitigate a death sentence to life in prison without parole. So when a Black man killed a White man in a rage brought on by the White man's relentless taunting, "N....., n.....," [racial slurs] the killing was still murder, but the taunting mitigated the death penalty to life without parole (see Chapter 9).

mitigating circumstances circumstances that convince fact finders (judges or juries) that defendants don't deserve the maximum penalty for the crime they're convicted of

Now, let's look at five justification defenses: self-defense, the defense of others, the defense of home and property, the choice-of-evils defense, and consent.

SELF-DEFENSE

LO2

If you use force to protect yourself, your home or property, or the people you care about, you've violated the rule of law, which our legal system is deeply committed to (see Chapter 1). According to the rule of law, the government has a monopoly on the use of force; so when you use force, you're "taking the law into your own hands." With that great monopoly on force goes the equally great responsibility of protecting individuals banned from using force themselves.

Sometimes, the government isn't (or can't be) there to protect you when you need it. So necessity—the heart of self-defense—allows "self-help" to kick in. Self-defense amounts to a grudging concession to necessity. It's only good before the law when three circumstances come together:

1. The necessity is great.
2. It exists "right now."
3. It's for prevention only.

Preemptive strikes aren't allowed; you can't use force to prevent an attack that's going to take place tomorrow, or even this afternoon. Retaliation isn't allowed either; you can't use it to "pay back" an attack that took place last year or even this morning. In short, preemptive strikes come too soon and retaliation too late; they both fail the necessity test. Individuals have to rely on nonviolent means to prevent future attacks, and only the state can punish past attacks (Fletcher 1988, 18–19).

Now, let's examine the elements of self-defense. After that, we look at if and when self-defense claims are justifiable. Finally, we examine whether and when you can stand your ground against an imminent attack, or whether you have to retreat to escape harm.

LO2, LO3

Elements of Self-Defense

When can we ignore the government's monopoly on force and take the law into our own hands to defend ourselves? At common law, anyone who was subjected to an unprovoked attack could protect themselves by force from attacks that were going to happen right now. However, today, to justify the use of deadly force, the defender has to honestly and reasonably believe that she's faced with the choice of "kill, or be killed, right now!"

Self-defense consists of four elements:

1. *Nonaggressor*. The defender didn't start or provoke the attack.
2. *Necessity*. Defenders can use deadly force only if they reasonably believe it's necessary to repel an imminent deadly attack—namely, one that's going to happen right now.
3. *Proportionality*. Defenders can use deadly force only if the use of nondeadly force isn't enough to repel the attack. Excessive force isn't allowed.
4. *Reasonable belief*. The defender has to reasonably believe that it's necessary to use deadly force to repel the imminent deadly attack.

initial aggressor someone who provokes an attack can't then use force to defend herself against the attack she provoked

LO3

NONAGGRESSOR

Self-defense is available only against unprovoked attacks. So self-defense isn't available to an **initial aggressor**; someone who provokes an attack can't then use force to defend herself against the attack she provoked. With one exception: according to the **withdrawal exception**, if attackers completely withdraw from attacks they provoke, they can defend themselves against an attack by their initial victims.

withdrawal exception if initial aggressors completely withdraw from attacks they provoke, they can defend themselves against an attack by their initial victims

In the first case excerpt, Myah Evans Batie appealed her conviction for assaulting her husband. The trial court found that she failed to prove she was not the initial aggressor.

CASE

*In **State v. Batie** (2015), a jury convicted Myah Evans Batie of domestic violence against her husband.*

Did she start the fight with her husband?

State v. Batie

2015WL929478 (Ohio App. 2015)

STEWART, J. joined by KILBANE, PJ., and BOYLE, J.

HISTORY

On March 11, 2014, a jury convicted Myah Evans Batie of domestic violence in violation of R.C. 2919.25(A) with a prior conviction specification. The charge arose out of a physical altercation between Batie and her husband, where the husband called 911 for assistance. Batie appealed. The Ohio Court of Appeals affirmed.

FACTS

[On direct examination, Officer Todd Simpson testified as follows at Myah Evans Batie's trial:]

Q. And when you respond to a domestic violence call, is it your duty to determine who is the primary physical aggressor?

A. Yes, it is.

Q. Based on your conversation in speaking with the victim...outside, in speaking with the defendant inside, your observations, what did you conclude?

A. The observations of the evidence proved that Miss Batie—

Defense Counsel: Objection.

The Court: Overruled.

A. Miss Evans started the disturbance, continued and assaulted and injured her husband.

Q. And what was your basis for coming to that conclusion?

A. His bruising obviously on his face, the scratches, bite marks on his arm, and I think his leg.

OPINION

A claim of self-defense requires the defendant prove by a preponderance of the evidence that (1) she "was not at fault in creating the situation giving rise to the affray"; (2) that she "had a bona fide belief that she was in imminent danger of death or great bodily harm and that her only means of escape from such danger was in the use of such force;" and (3) "that she did not violate any duty to retreat or avoid danger."

The first prong of the test asks, in essence, whether the defendant was the initial aggressor. While the primary physical aggressor inquiry is not necessarily the same as whether a person was the initial aggressor, the primary aggressor question can nonetheless undermine a claim of self-defense. This is especially true when an officer's testimony goes beyond the primary aggressor inquiry and treads into the realm of who initiated the altercation. That is exactly what happened in this case.

A careful review of the record in this case establishes that Officer Simpson did opine on an ultimate issue in the domestic violence defense. When asked what conclusions he drew based on his observations, Simpson responded by saying that the observations of the evidence *proved* that Batie "started the disturbance, continued, and assaulted and injured," her husband (emphasis added). Simpson did not simply testify as to the reason why he treated Batie as the primary physical aggressor and choose to proceed with charging her—testimony that would otherwise be admissible. Rather, Simpson asserted that his observations proved Batie started the affray. This is exactly the type of improper testimony that must be omitted from trial, and we find that the trial court abused its discretion by allowing it.

Notwithstanding our determination that the trial court abused its discretion, we must nevertheless overrule the assignment of error because the testimony amounted to harmless error. Any error, defect, irregularity or variance which does not affect the substantial rights of the defendant shall be disregarded. The term "substantial rights" has been interpreted to require that the error be prejudicial—that is that it must have affected the outcome of the trial court proceedings.

Here, it cannot be said that allowing the testimony resulted in prejudice to the defendant. At trial, the state introduced numerous photographic exhibits detailing the extent of the husband's injuries. Many of these exhibits detailed what appeared to be numerous, severe, scratch marks down the length of the husband's face. The photos also depicted a large burn mark on his forearm—which corroborated the husband's testimony that Batie attacked him with a hot iron. Other photos depicted what appeared to be bite marks on the husband's upper arm, and pictures showing a bloody, swollen lip. Further, Simpson testified that when he arrived at the Batie household, the appellant did not have any visible marks on her that would indicate that her husband had been physical with her. In fact, the only evidence supporting Batie's claim that she was acting in self-defense, was her own trial testimony. Therefore, even if the trial court had excluded Simpson's improper testimony, it cannot be said that the exclusion would have had any effect on the outcome of the case.

Batie [also] argues that the jury's verdict was against the manifest weight of the evidence. In a manifest weight analysis, an appellate court reviews the entire record, weighs the evidence and all reasonable inferences, considers the credibility of witnesses and...resolves conflicts in the evidence. An appellate court may not merely substitute its view for that of the jury, but must find that the jury clearly lost its way and created such a manifest miscarriage of justice that the conviction must be reversed and a new trial ordered.

When analyzing a manifest weight challenge, appellate courts must give special deference to the conclusion reached by the trier of fact. Accordingly, reversal on manifest weight grounds is reserved for

(continues)

(continued)

the exceptional case in which the evidence weighs heavily against the conviction.

We cannot say that this is the exceptional case that warrants reversal because the jury clearly lost its way. While contradictory testimony was presented by both the victim and the defendant at trial, the pictures of the victim's injuries, together with the fact that Officer Simpson testified that there was not a mark on the appellant, is enough for a jury to conclude that Batie committed an act of domestic violence against her husband and was not acting in self-defense. Batie's second assignment of error is also overruled.

Judgment affirmed.

QUESTIONS

1. List all the facts relevant to deciding whether Myah Batie was the initial aggressor.
2. Summarize the court's arguments to support its decision.
3. According to the court, what's the difference between a "primary physical aggressor" and an "initial aggressor"?
4. Do you agree that Myah Batie was the original or primary aggressor? Defend your answer.
5. Explain how the court found Myah the primary aggressor, and therefore her husband was not guilty. Do you agree? Defend your answer.

LO3

NECESSITY, PROPORTIONALITY, AND REASONABLE BELIEF

necessity a defense that argues an imminent danger of attack was prevented

imminence requirement an element of self-defense requiring the danger to be "right now!"

Necessity refers to an imminent danger of attack. Simply put, it means, "The time for defense is right now!" When is "right now"? The majority view in the cases is: "right now" means "right now."

What if the danger of a deadly attack doesn't exist "at the moment" the defendant reasonably strikes in self-defense, because the threat of deadly harm will "inevitably and eventually come back"? Does "eventual" and "inevitable" satisfy the imminence requirement? Let's look at what happened to Xi Van Ha (*Xi Van Ha v. State* 1995).

Late in the evening, Buu Van Truong, a Vietnamese fisherman working in Alaska, attacked another fisherman, Xi Van Ha, with a hammer and threatened to kill Ha. At 1:30 P.M. the next day, Ha shot Buu in the back, killing him instantly. On appeal from a murder conviction, the Alaska Supreme Court affirmed the conviction. According to the court:

> There was sufficient evidence that a reasonable person in Ha's position would have feared death or serious physical injury from Buu. Buu had threatened Ha with death. Buu was a violent man who nursed grudges and who was likely to carry out his threat *someday* (emphasis added). Moreover, the evidence suggested that Buu came from a violent, criminal clan, and that Buu's relatives might very well help Buu carry out the threat—or might carry it out themselves if Buu was unable.
>
> In sum, Ha produced evidence to justify the remarks his attorney made during the defense opening statement: "A threat from Buu that he would kill you was as good, had as much weight, as a kiss on the cheek by a Mafia godfather. That's how deadly Buu's threats were. From knowing Buu, Ha knew that there was no escape. Buu comes from a family of thugs who have a reputation for violence and extortion. *Ha knew that he would have to deal with the family, or with Buu himself. Today, tomorrow, they would stalk him down*" (emphasis added).
>
> However, "*inevitable*" *harm is not the same as "imminent" harm. Even though Ha may have reasonably feared that Buu (or one of Buu's relatives) would someday kill him, a reasonable fear of future harm does not authorize a person to hunt down and kill an enemy* (emphasis added). (191)

Here's how U.S. Circuit Court Judge Frank Easterbrook, known for his pithy comments, put his argument against inevitable danger: "'later' and 'imminent' are opposites" (*U.S. v. Haynes* 1998, 1090).

CASE

*In **U.S. v. Haynes (1998),** the U.S. Seventh Circuit Court of Appeals held that a prisoner who was attacked wasn't in imminent danger.*

Can a sneak attack be self-defense?

U.S. v. Haynes

143 F.3d 1089 (C.A. 7 Wis. 1998)

HISTORY

Charles E. Haynes (Defendant-Appellant) entered a conditional plea of guilty in the United States District Court for the Western District of Wisconsin, to assault. Haynes appealed. The Court of Appeals affirmed.

EASTERBROOK J.

FACTS

Nelson Flores-Pedroso was playing dominoes after lunch in the cafeteria of the federal prison in Oxford, Wisconsin, when Charles Haynes emerged from the kitchen and poured scalding oil on his head. Severely burned over 18 percent of his body, Flores-Pedroso is disfigured for life. Haynes pleaded guilty to assault, and was sentenced to 33 months' imprisonment (consecutive to the ten-year term he was serving for a drug offense). The guilty plea reserved the right to argue on appeal that the district judge erred in foreclosing Haynes from arguing to the jury that the attack was justified as a measure of self-defense.

Self-defense? How can a sneak attack be self-defense? Haynes made an offer of proof that Flores-Pedroso was a bully who had a reputation for coercing smaller inmates (such as Haynes) to provide favors of all kinds—food, commissary items, and sex. About a month before the incident in the cafeteria, Flores-Pedroso began pressuring Haynes to use Haynes' position as a food preparer in the kitchen to do favors for him. Haynes refused, and in response Flores-Pedroso threatened to make Haynes his "bitch" (homosexual plaything).

For the next month staredowns and jostling occurred, while Flores-Pedroso kept up a stream of threats. One time Flores-Pedroso cornered Haynes in a bathroom, and Haynes thought that rape was imminent, but another inmate entered and Flores-Pedroso left.

A day before Haynes poured the oil, Flores-Pedroso picked up Haynes and slammed him to the ground within sight of a guard, who did nothing. On the day of the oil incident, Flores-Pedroso told Haynes that as soon as food service was closed for the afternoon he would "finish what he started." Haynes contends that he believed that he would be attacked as soon as he left the cafeteria, and that he struck first in order to protect himself.

OPINION

Under the law of the jungle a good offense may be the best defense. But although prisons are nasty places, they are not jungles—and it is the law of the United States rather than Hobbes' state of nature that regulates inmates' conduct. Haynes concedes that he never reported Flores-Pedroso to the guards or sought protection—protection a prison is constitutionally obliged to provide.

Haynes asserted in his offer of proof:

> He could not go to "the police"—a term used to describe the guards. If the guards elected to take him out of population, he would be forced to stay in administrative segregation which meant 24-hour-per-day lock-up. If his protective custody status resulted in a transfer, all the inmates of the receiving institution would know that he was in protective custody, for being victimized by another inmate and by being a "snitch," which would result in further victimization and perhaps invite an assault by not just one inmate, but several. If Haynes went to the guards and they did not believe him and left him in population, things would only get worse. He would certainly be attacked, not only by [Flores] Pedroso, but by others who labeled him a "snitch." Haynes did not believe he could go to the guards and help himself in any appreciable way.

(continues)

(continued)

In other words, Haynes did not fancy the prospect of administrative segregation, feared the consequences of appearing to be an informer, and decided that it was better to take matters into his own hands. What his claim of self-defense comes down to is the proposition that an inmate is entitled to attack and maim a prison bully even if there is ample time to report the threats and obtain protection from the guards.

The district court ruled that Haynes would not be allowed to argue self-defense or inform the jury about Flores-Pedroso's threats. The evidence and line of defense Haynes wanted to pursue, as the district court saw things, was just a request for jury nullification—a plea to jurors to let the Davids of federal prisons smite the Goliaths, to give the predators a taste of their own medicine, without legal consequences. The judge ruled that an inmate must use available, lawful options to avoid violence, even if they find those options unpalatable. Haynes asks us to hold that the existence of lawful alternatives is irrelevant to a claim of self-defense.

All doubts about the role of lawful alternatives to one side, it is hard to see how Haynes' offer of proof conforms to the normal understanding of self-defense: a use of force necessary to defend against an imminent use of unlawful force. Haynes was not faced with an imminent use of force by Flores-Pedroso. There was a threat of action later that afternoon, but Flores-Pedroso had made unfulfilled threats before, and anyway "later" and "imminent" are opposites.

A judge may, and generally should, block the introduction of evidence supporting a proposed defense unless all of its elements can be established. But we need not dwell on timing, because we agree with the district judge's reason: absence of lawful alternatives is an element of all lesser-evil defenses [see "Choice of Evils," on p. 192], of which self-defense is one. When A threatens B, and B hits A, the defense receives the name "self-defense." When A threatens C, and B hits A, the name is "defense of another."

But in all of these cases, the defense fails if the use of force was unjustified. This is the idea behind the "imminence" requirement (if the threat is not imminent, a retreat or similar step avoids injury) as well as the requirement that the object of the threat prefer a lawful response to an unlawful one.

Prisons collect violent persons who have little respect for the law, which makes them hard to control without the use of devices such as segregation that are unpleasant in their own right. If prisoners could decide for themselves when to seek protection from the guards and when to settle matters by violence, prisons would be impossible to regulate. The guards might as well throw the inmates together, withdraw to the perimeter, and let them kill one another, after the fashion of the movie *Escape from New York* (1981).

Perhaps Haynes was hoping that a jury would have this view of the right way to manage prisons. But it is not the view reflected in the United States Code or the United States Constitution. A prisoner who requests protection from the guards without success (or who lacks time to do so) may defend himself with force proportioned to the threat. But Haynes, who listened to Flores-Pedroso's menaces for a month without seeking help, had no conceivable justification for a preemptive strike. The district judge correctly barred Haynes from making his proposed defense.

Affirmed.

QUESTIONS

1. List the facts and circumstances relevant to deciding whether Charles Haynes was entitled to the defense of self-defense.
2. State the court's definition of "imminent" danger.
3. Summarize the court's arguments for ruling against imminent danger.

The most widely publicized self-defense cases involve individuals who need to kill to save their own lives, but self-defense covers more than this. It also includes killing someone who's about to kill a member of your family—or any innocent person for that matter.

Necessity doesn't limit you to killing someone who's going to kill either. You can also kill an attacker whom you reasonably believe is right now going to *hurt* you or someone else badly enough to send you or them to the hospital for the treatment of serious injury. This is what serious (sometimes called "grievous") bodily injury means in most self-defense statutes.

Some self-defense statutes go even further. They allow you to kill someone you reasonably believe is about to commit a serious felony against you that doesn't threaten either your life or serious bodily injury. These felonies usually include rape, sodomy, kidnapping, and armed robbery. However, the list also almost always includes home burglary and, sometimes, even personal property (discussed in the section "Defense of Home and Property" in this chapter).

What kind of belief does self-defense require? Is it enough that you *honestly* believed (1) that you were in imminent danger; (2) that you needed to use force to fend it off; and (3) that you needed to use the amount of force you used?

No. *Honest* (*subjective*) belief won't do. All statutes also include an *objective* element that requires that your beliefs are *reasonable*. In other words, a reasonable person in the same situation would have believed that the attack was *imminent* and that the *need* for force and the *amount* of force used were necessary to repel an attack.

In our next case excerpt *People v. Goetz* (1986), the 1980s' sensational "New York Subway Vigilante Case," the New York Court of Appeals examined these elements as applied to the defense against the armed robbery provision in New York's self-defense statute (Fletcher 1988, 18–27).

CASE

In ***People v. Goetz* (1986),** *Bernhard Goetz was indicted for criminal possession of a weapon, attempted murder, assault, and reckless endangerment.*

Did he shoot in self-defense?

People v. Goetz

497 N.E.2d 41 (N.Y. 1986)

HISTORY

Bernhard Goetz (defendant) was indicted for criminal possession of a weapon, attempted murder, assault, and reckless endangerment. The Supreme Court, Trial Term, New York County, dismissed the indictment and the People appealed. The Supreme Court, Appellate Division affirmed, and the People appealed. The Court of Appeals reversed and dismissed, and reinstated all the counts of the indictment.

WACHTLER, CJ

FACTS

On Saturday afternoon, December 22, 1984, Troy Canty, Darryl Cabey, James Ramseur, and Barry Allen boarded an IRT express subway train in the Bronx and headed south toward lower Manhattan. The four youths rode together in the rear portion of the seventh car of the train. Two of the four, Ramseur and Cabey, had screwdrivers inside their coats, which they said were to be used to break into the coin boxes of video machines.

Bernhard Goetz boarded this subway train at 14th Street in Manhattan and sat down on a bench toward

(continues)

(continued)

the rear section of the same car occupied by the four youths. Goetz was carrying an unlicensed .38-caliber pistol loaded with five rounds of ammunition in a waistband holster. The train left the 14th Street station and headed toward Chambers Street.

Canty approached Goetz, possibly with Allen beside him, and stated, "Give me five dollars." Neither Canty nor any of the other youths displayed a weapon. Goetz responded by standing up, pulling out his handgun, and firing four shots in rapid succession. The first shot hit Canty in the chest; the second struck Allen in the back; the third went through Ramseur's arm and into his left side; the fourth was fired at Cabey, who apparently was then standing in the corner of the car, but missed, deflecting instead off of a wall of the conductor's cab.

After Goetz briefly surveyed the scene around him, he fired another shot at Cabey, who then was sitting on the end bench of the car. The bullet entered the rear of Cabey's side and severed his spinal cord.

All but two of the other passengers fled the car when, or immediately after, the shots were fired. The conductor, who had been in the next car, heard the shots and instructed the motorman to radio for emergency assistance. The conductor then went into the car where the shooting occurred and saw Goetz sitting on a bench, the injured youths lying on the floor or slumped against a seat, and two women who had apparently taken cover, also lying on the floor.

Goetz told the conductor that the four youths had tried to rob him. While the conductor was aiding the youths, Goetz headed toward the front of the car. The train had stopped just before the Chambers Street station and Goetz went between two of the cars, jumped onto the tracks, and fled.

Police and ambulance crews arrived at the scene shortly thereafter. Ramseur and Canty, initially listed in critical condition, have fully recovered. Cabey remains paralyzed and has suffered some degree of brain damage.

On December 31, 1984, Goetz surrendered to police in Concord, New Hampshire, identifying himself as the gunman being sought for the subway shootings in New York nine days earlier.

Later that day, after receiving *Miranda* warnings, he made two lengthy statements, both of which were tape recorded with his permission. In the statements, which are substantially similar, Goetz admitted that he had been illegally carrying a handgun in New York City for three years. He stated that he had first purchased a gun in 1981 after he had been injured in a mugging. Goetz also revealed that twice between 1981 and 1984 he had successfully warded off assailants simply by displaying the pistol.

According to Goetz's statement, the first contact he had with the four youths came when Canty, sitting or lying on the bench across from him, asked, "How are you?" to which he replied, "Fine." Shortly thereafter, Canty, followed by one of the other youths, walked over to the defendant and stood to his left, while the other two youths remained to his right, in the corner of the subway car.

Canty then said, "Give me five dollars." Goetz stated that he knew from the smile on Canty's face that they wanted to "play with me." Although he was certain that none of the youths had a gun, he had a fear, based on prior experiences, of being "maimed."

Goetz then established "a pattern of fire," deciding specifically to fire from left to right. His stated intention at that point was to "murder, to hurt them, to make them suffer as much as possible." When Canty again requested money, Goetz stood up, drew his weapon, and began firing, aiming for the center of the body of each of the four.

Goetz recalled that the first two he shot "tried to run through the crowd but they had nowhere to run." Goetz then turned to his right to "go after the other two." One of these two "tried to run through the wall of the train, but...he had nowhere to go." The other youth (Cabey) "tried pretending that he wasn't with [the others]," by standing still, holding on to one of the subway hand straps, and not looking at Goetz. Goetz nonetheless fired his fourth shot at him.

He then ran back to the first two youths to make sure they had been "taken care of." Seeing that they had both been shot, he spun back to check on the latter two. Goetz noticed that the youth who had been standing still was now sitting on a bench and seemed unhurt. As Goetz told the police, "I said, 'you seem to be all right, here's another,'" and he then fired the shot which severed Cabey's spinal cord. Goetz added that "If I was a little more under self-control...I would have put the barrel against his forehead and fired." He also admitted that "If I had had more [bullets], I would have shot them again, and again, and again."

After waiving extradition, Goetz was brought back to New York and arraigned on a felony complaint charging him with attempted murder and criminal possession of a weapon. The matter was presented to a grand jury in January 1985, with the prosecutor seeking an indictment for attempted murder, assault, reckless endangerment, and criminal possession of a weapon. Neither the defendant nor any of the wounded youths testified before this grand jury.

On January 25, 1985, the grand jury indicted Goetz on one count of criminal possession of a weapon in the third degree (Penal Law § 265.02) for possessing the gun used in the subway shootings, and two counts of criminal possession of a weapon in the fourth degree (Penal Law § 265.01) for possessing two other guns in his apartment building. It dismissed, however, the attempted murder and other charges stemming from the shootings themselves.

Several weeks after the grand jury's action, the People, asserting that they had newly available evidence, moved for an order authorizing them to resubmit the dismissed charges to a second grand jury. Supreme Court, Criminal Term, after conducting an in camera [in the judge's chambers] inquiry, granted the motion. Presentation of the case to the second Grand Jury began on March 14, 1985. Two of the four youths, Canty and Ramseur, testified. Among the other witnesses were four passengers from the seventh car of the subway who had seen some portions of the incident.

Goetz again chose not to testify, though the tapes of his two statements were played for the grand jurors, as had been done with the first grand jury.

On March 27, 1985, the second grand jury filed a ten-count indictment, containing four charges of attempted murder (Penal Law §§ 110.00, 125.25[1]), four charges of assault in the first degree (Penal Law § 120.10[1]), one charge of reckless endangerment in the first degree (Penal Law § 120.25), and one charge of criminal possession of a weapon in the second degree (Penal Law § 265.03 [possession of a loaded firearm with intent to use it unlawfully against another]). Goetz was arraigned on this indictment on March 28, 1985, and it was consolidated with the earlier three-count indictment.

On October 14, 1985, Goetz moved to dismiss the charges contained in the second indictment, alleging, among other things, that the prosecutor's instructions to that grand jury on the defense of justification were erroneous and prejudicial to the defendant so as to render its proceedings defective.

On November 25, 1985, while the motion to dismiss was pending before Criminal Term, a column appeared in the *New York Daily News* containing an interview which the columnist had conducted with Darryl Cabey the previous day in Cabey's hospital room. The columnist claimed that Cabey had told him in this interview that the other three youths had all approached Goetz with the intention of robbing him.

The day after the column was published, a New York City police officer informed the prosecutor that he had been one of the first police officers to enter the subway car after the shootings and that Canty had said to him, "We were going to rob [Goetz]." The prosecutor immediately disclosed this information to the Court and to defense counsel, adding that this was the first time his office had been told of this alleged statement and that none of the police reports filed on the incident contained any such information.

In an order dated January 21, 1986, the Court, after inspection of the grand jury minutes held that the prosecutor, in a supplemental charge elaborating upon the justification defense, had erroneously introduced an objective element into this defense by instructing the grand jurors to consider whether Goetz's conduct was that of a "reasonable man in [Goetz's] situation."

The Court concluded that the statutory test for whether the use of deadly force is justified to protect a person should be wholly subjective, focusing entirely on the defendant's state of mind when he used such force. It concluded that dismissal was required for this error because the justification issue was at the heart of the case. [We disagree.]

OPINION

Penal Law article 35 recognizes the defense of justification, which "permits the use of force under certain circumstances." One such set of circumstances pertains to the use of force in defense of a person, encompassing both self-defense and defense of a third person (Penal Law § 35.15). Penal Law § 35.15(1) sets forth the general principles governing all such uses of force:

> A person may use physical force upon another person when and to the extent he reasonably believes such to be necessary to defend himself or a third person from what he *reasonably* [emphasis added] believes to be the use or imminent use of unlawful physical force by such other person.

(continues)

(continued)

Section 35.15(2) sets forth further limitations on these general principles with respect to the use of "deadly physical force":

> A person may not use deadly physical force upon another person under circumstances specified in subdivision one unless
>
> a. He *reasonably believes* [emphasis added] that such other person is using or about to use deadly physical force or
>
> b. He *reasonably believes* [emphasis added] that such other person is committing or attempting to commit a kidnapping, forcible rape, forcible sodomy or robbery.

Section 35.15(2)(a) further provides, however, that even under these circumstances a person ordinarily must retreat if he knows that he can with complete safety to himself and others avoid the necessity of using deadly physical force by retreating.

Thus, consistent with most justification provisions, Penal Law § 35.15 permits the use of deadly physical force only where requirements as to triggering conditions and the necessity of a particular response are met. As to the triggering conditions, the statute requires that the actor "reasonably believes" that another person either is using or about to use deadly physical force or is committing or attempting to commit one of certain enumerated felonies, including robbery.

As to the need for the use of deadly physical force as a response, the statute requires that the actor "reasonably believes" that such force is necessary to avert the perceived threat. While the portion of section 35.15(2)(b) pertaining to the use of deadly physical force to avert a felony such as robbery does not contain a separate "retreat" requirement, it is clear from reading subdivisions (1) and (2) of section 35.15 together, as the statute requires, that the general "necessity" requirement in subdivision (1) applies to all uses of force under section 35.15, including the use of deadly physical force under subdivision (2)(b).

Because the evidence before the second Grand Jury included statements by Goetz that he acted to protect himself from being maimed or to avert a robbery, the prosecutor correctly chose to charge the justification defense in section 35.15 to the Grand Jury. The prosecutor properly instructed the grand jurors to consider whether the use of deadly physical force was justified to prevent either serious physical injury or a robbery, and, in doing so, to separately analyze the defense with respect to each of the charges. He elaborated upon the prerequisites for the use of deadly physical force essentially by reading or paraphrasing the language in Penal Law § 35.15. The defense does not contend that he committed any error in this portion of the charge.

When the prosecutor had completed his charge, one of the grand jurors asked for clarification of the term "reasonably believes." The prosecutor responded by instructing the grand jurors that they were to consider the circumstances of the incident and determine "whether the defendant's conduct was that of a reasonable man in the defendant's situation." It is this response by the prosecutor—and specifically his use of "a reasonable man"—which is the basis for the dismissal of the charges by the lower courts. As expressed repeatedly in the Appellate Division's plurality opinion, because section 35.15 uses the term "he reasonably believes," the appropriate test, according to that court, is whether a defendant's beliefs and reactions were "reasonable to him."

Under that reading of the statute, a jury which believed a defendant's testimony that he felt that his own actions were warranted and were reasonable would have to acquit him, regardless of what anyone else in defendant's situation might have concluded. Such an interpretation defies the ordinary meaning and significance of the term "reasonably" in a statute, and misconstrues the clear intent of the Legislature, in enacting section 35.15, to retain an objective element as part of any provision authorizing the use of deadly physical force.

Penal statutes in New York have long codified the right recognized at common law to use deadly physical force, under appropriate circumstances, in self-defense. These provisions have never required that an actor's belief as to the intention of another person to inflict serious injury be correct in order for the use of deadly force to be justified, but they have uniformly required that the belief comport with an *objective notion of reasonableness* [emphasis added]....plurality below agreed with defendant's argument that the change in the statutory language from "reasonable ground," used prior to 1965, to "he reasonably believes" in Penal Law § 35.15 evinced a legislative intent to conform to the subjective standard.

We cannot lightly impute to the Legislature an intent to fundamentally alter the principles of justification to allow the perpetrator of a serious crime to go free simply because that person believed his actions were reasonable and necessary to prevent some perceived harm. To completely exonerate such an individual, no matter how aberrational or bizarre his thought patterns, would allow citizens to set their own standards for the permissible use of force. It would also allow a legally competent defendant suffering from delusions to kill or perform acts of violence with impunity, contrary to fundamental principles of justice and criminal law.

We can only conclude that the Legislature retained a reasonableness requirement to avoid giving a license for such actions. Statutes or rules of law requiring a person to act "reasonably" or to have a "reasonable belief" uniformly prescribe conduct meeting an objective standard measured with reference to how "a reasonable person" could have acted.

Goetz argues that the introduction of an objective element will preclude a jury from considering factors such as the prior experiences of a given actor and thus require it to make a determination of "reasonableness" without regard to the actual circumstances of a particular incident. This argument, however, falsely presupposes that an objective standard means that the background and other relevant characteristics of a particular actor must be ignored. To the contrary, we have frequently noted that a determination of reasonableness must be based on the "circumstances" facing a defendant or his "situation." Such terms encompass more than the physical movements of the potential assailant.

As just discussed, these terms include any relevant knowledge the defendant had about that person. They also necessarily bring in the physical attributes of all persons involved, including the defendant. Furthermore, the defendant's circumstances encompass any prior experiences he had which could provide a reasonable basis for a belief that another person's intentions were to injure or rob him or that the use of deadly force was necessary under the circumstances.

Accordingly, a jury should be instructed to consider this type of evidence in weighing the defendant's actions. The jury must first determine whether the defendant had the requisite beliefs under section 35.15, that is, whether he believed deadly force was necessary to avert the imminent use of deadly force or the commission of one of the felonies enumerated therein. If the People do not prove beyond a reasonable doubt that he did not have such beliefs, then the jury must also consider whether these beliefs were reasonable. The jury would have to determine, in light of all the "circumstances," as explicated above, if a reasonable person could have had these beliefs.

The prosecutor's instruction to the second Grand Jury that it had to determine whether, under the circumstances, Goetz's conduct was that of a reasonable man in his situation was thus essentially an accurate charge.

The order of the Appellate Division should be REVERSED, and the dismissed counts of the indictment reinstated.

QUESTIONS

1. Consider the following:
   a. New York tried Goetz for attempted murder and assault. The jury acquitted him of both charges. The jury said Goetz "was justified in shooting the four men with the silver-plated .38-caliber revolver he purchased in Florida." They did convict him of illegal possession of a firearm, for which the court sentenced Goetz to one year in jail.
   b. Following the sentencing, Goetz told the court: "This case is really more about the deterioration of society than it is about me. . . . I believe society needs to be protected from criminals."

Criminal law professor George Fletcher followed the trial closely. After the acquittal, he commented:

> The facts of the Goetz case were relatively clear, but the primary fight was over the moral interpretation of the facts. . . . I am not in the slightest bit convinced that the four young men were about to mug Goetz. If he had said, "Listen buddy, I wish I had $5, but I don't," and walked to the other side of the car the chances are 60–40 nothing would have happened. Street-wise kids like that are more attuned to the costs of their behavior than Goetz was. (qtd. in Roberts 1989)

If Professor Fletcher is right, was Goetz justified in shooting?

2. Under what circumstances can people use deadly force, according to the New York statutes cited in the opinion?
3. Do you agree with those circumstances?
4. Would you add more? Remove some? Which ones? Why?
5. Were Goetz's shots a preemptive strike? Retaliation? Necessary for self-protection? Defend your answer.

LO4

RETREAT

What if you can avoid an attack by escaping? Do you have to retreat? Or can you stand your ground and fight back? According to Richard Maxwell Brown (1991), the leading modern authority on American violence, "As far back as the thirteenth century, English common law dealt harshly with the act of homicide" (3). The burden was on defendants to prove their innocence, and no one could prove innocence unless he (all homicides were committed by men) proved he'd "retreated to the wall." The English common law "retreat to the wall" survived in a minority of American states:

> But one of the most important transformations in American legal and social history occurred in the nineteenth century when the nation as a whole repudiated the English common-law tradition in favor of an American theme of no duty to retreat: that one was legally justified in standing one's ground to kill in self-defense.
>
> Recognized at the time as a crucial change in the "American mind," it was a combination of Eastern legal authorities and Western judges who wrought the legal transformation from an English law that, as they saw it, upheld cowardice to an American law suited to the bravery of the "true man." The centuries-long English legal severity against homicide was replaced in our country by a proud new tolerance for killing in situations where it might have been avoided by obeying a legal duty to retreat. (5)

stand-your-ground rule if you didn't start a fight, you can stand your ground and kill to defend yourself without retreating from any place you have a right to be

retreat rule you have to retreat from an attack if you reasonably believe (1) that you're in danger of death or serious bodily harm; and (2) that backing off won't unreasonably put you in danger of death or serious bodily harm

castle exception when attacked in your home, you have no duty to retreat and can use deadly force to fend off an unprovoked attack, but only if you reasonably believe the attack threatens death or serious bodily injury

Who was this "true man"? According to Jeannie Suk (2008), various social meanings contributed to the definition. A true man was honest; he made decisions based on what he believed to be true, and he shouldn't have to flee from attack because he'd done nothing wrong to provoke or deserve the attack. The "true" man also did whatever he had to do to provide for his wife and children; he was the source of strength for his vulnerable dependents. The true man's duty to his family extended to his country:

> True men were patriots and protectors of the nation who would fight if necessary... to safeguard the legal rights fundamental to freedom. They had a sense of civic responsibility tied to the duty to ensure the rule of law and leadership of the nation. (Suk 2008, 245)

Relying on these meanings, judges and legislators generalized the right to self-defense into the majority **stand-your-ground rule**; namely, if he didn't start the fight, he could stand his ground and kill to "defend himself without retreating from any place he had a right to be" (245).

The minority rule, the **retreat rule**, says you have to retreat, if you reasonably believe that

1. you're in danger of death or serious bodily harm; and
2. backing off won't unreasonably put you in danger of death or serious bodily harm.

LO5

States that require retreat have carved out an exception to the retreat doctrine. According to this **castle exception** to the retreat rule, when you're attacked in your home, you can stand your ground and use deadly force to fend off an unprovoked attack, but only if you reasonably believe the attack threatens death or serious bodily injury (*State v. Kennamore* 1980, 858).

Later on in this chapter, we explore the adoption of new statutes that significantly expand ordinary people's power to defend themselves in their homes *and* in public places. But for now, let's look at how the elements of self-defense apply to domestic violence, especially battered women.

Domestic Violence

> It is not now and never has been the law that a man assailed in his own dwelling is bound to retreat. If assailed there, he may stand his ground and resist the attack. He is under no duty to take to the fields and the highways, a fugitive from his own home.
>
> —*People v. Tomlins* (1914)

COHABITANT RULE

LO5

The Connecticut Supreme Court relied on family violence to back up its creation of the **cohabitant exception** to the Connecticut retreat rule, even though it involved male roommates (*State v. Shaw* 1981). James Shaw Jr. rented one of two bedrooms in Wilson's owner-occupied house. They got into an argument, which escalated into a fistfight. (Each claimed that the other started the fight.) Wilson went to his bedroom and grabbed his .30-30 Winchester rifle, intending to order Shaw to leave. Shaw went to his bedroom and got his .22 revolver. Weapons in hand, they both entered the kitchen from their bedrooms. Shaw fired five or six shots hitting Wilson three times (562).

cohabitant exception in the jurisdictions that follow the retreat rule, people who live in the same home don't have to retreat

The timing of the case coincided with the growing public recognition that domestic violence was a "serious and widespread crime." The feminist movement had convincingly argued that women were victims of violence at home. Law enforcement was beginning to treat domestic violence as a crime and not a private family matter (Suk 2008, 250). According to the court:

> In the great majority of homicides the killer and the victim are relatives or close acquaintances. We cannot conclude that the Connecticut legislature intended to sanction the reenactment of the climactic scene from "High Noon" in the familial kitchens of this state. (*State v. Shaw* 1981, 566)

BATTERED WOMEN WHO KILL THEIR ABUSERS

LO5

By the late 1990s, the recognition that battered women cases fit the "real man" protecting-his-castle frame had definitely influenced the law of self-defense. Courts in several castle doctrine states have adopted rules that allow women to "stand their ground and kill their batterers." All of these courts supported their decisions with a "sympathetic understanding of the dynamics of domestic violence and its victims" (Suk 2008, 252).

Notice that husbands and boyfriends murder their wives and girlfriends more than ten times as often as women who murder their husbands and boyfriends. This lopsidedness translates into small numbers of women. But, these small numbers are important because they often take place in abusive relationships. As a result, the domestic violence reform movement has included on its agenda a self-defense for women charged with murdering their batterers. (Kinports 2004, 161)

First, there used to be problems even introducing expert testimony on **battered woman's syndrome** (BWS) to prove self-defense. Recall that the heart of self-defense is reasonableness. Reasonableness requires defendants to prove *both* that

battered woman's syndrome (BWS) mental disorder that develops in victims of domestic violence as a result of serious, long-term abuse

1. She had a reasonable belief that at the moment she killed, she was in *imminent* danger of death or great bodily harm; *and*
2. She reasonably believed that she needed to use that *amount* of force to repel it.

Now, every state allows expert witnesses to explain BWS to judges and juries. Some courts have gone further. They changed the element of "reasonable belief" that force was necessary, to a "reasonable battered woman" believed that force was necessary. (Kinports 2004, 161–62; our next case excerpt *State v. Stewart*; and Criminal Law in Focus Box)

Reasonableness and the Battered Woman

Donna Lee Bechtel v. Oklahoma

Standards of reasonableness has been traditionally characterized as either "objective" or "subjective." Under the objective standard of reasonableness, the trier of fact is required to view the circumstances, surrounding the accused at the time of the use of force, from the standpoint of hypothetical reasonable person. Under the subjective standard of reasonableness, the fact finder is required to determine whether the circumstances, surrounding the accused at the time of the use of force, are sufficient to induce in the accused an honest and reasonable belief that he or she must use force to defend himself or herself against imminent harm.

Oklahoma's standard of reasonableness may be gleaned from past decisions of this Court and is set forth in OUJI–CR 743, which reads as follows:

> A person is justified in using deadly force in self-defense if that person reasonably believed that use of deadly force was necessary to protect herself from imminent danger of death or great bodily harm. Self-defense is a defense although the danger to life or personal security may not have been real, if a reasonable person, in the circumstances and from the viewpoint of the defendant, would reasonably have believed that she was in imminent danger of death or great bodily harm.

The aforesaid instruction was given in this case. While the instruction explicitly states that the fact finder should assume the viewpoint and circumstances of the defendant in assessing the reasonableness of his or her belief, i.e. subjective, it also requires the defendant's viewpoint to be that of a reasonable person, in similar circumstances and with the same perceptions, i.e., objective. Thus, Oklahoma's standard is a hybrid, combining both the objective and subjective standards.

This Court has considered the issue of the clarity of this instruction on several occasions.... However, in light of the jury's inquiry we believe that the instruction in question served to confuse the jury who submitted the following inquiry:

> OUJI–746 reads: [The jury instruction]
>
> Self-defense is permitted a person solely because of necessity. Self-defense is not available to a person who [was the aggressor] [provoked another with intent to cause the altercation] [voluntarily entered into mutual combat], no matter how great the danger to personal security became during the altercation unless the right of self-defense is reestablished.
>
> "Self-defense is permitted a person solely because of necessity.
>
> [Jury Question] (1) Does this mean or imply when no other options are available;
>
> or from
>
> (2) Defendant's viewpoint & circumstances."

[Also, in view of] our decision today to allow testimony on the Battered Woman Syndrome in appropriate cases, we deem it necessary to modify OUJI–CR 743 by striking the words "reasonably" and "reasonable" from such instruction. Under our present instructions, a fact finder conceivably may ponder whether the battered woman's perception should be viewed from the standpoint of a *reasonable person in the circumstances of the battered woman* or from the standpoint of a *reasonable battered woman*. (italics added) We hereby adopt a new OUJI–CR 743A instruction that will be given in all Battered

Woman Syndrome cases. Such modified instruction shall read as follows:

> A person is justified in using deadly force in self-defense if that person believed that use of deadly force was necessary to protect herself from imminent danger of death or great bodily harm. Self-defense is a defense although the danger to life or personal security may not have been real, if a person, in the circumstances and from the viewpoint of the defendant, would reasonably have believed that she was in imminent danger of death or great bodily harm.

Imminence and the Battered Woman Syndrome

Under our "hybrid" reasonableness standard, the meaning of imminent must necessarily envelope the battered woman's perceptions based on all the facts and circumstances of his or her relationship with the victim. The battered woman learns to recognize the small signs that precede periods of escalated violence. She learns to distinguish subtle changes in tone of voice, facial expression, and levels of danger. She is in a position to know, perhaps with greater certainty than someone attacked by a stranger, that the batterer's threat is real and will be acted upon. Thus,...an abused woman may kill her mate during the period of threat that precedes a violent incident, right before the violence escalates to the more dangerous levels of an acute battering episode. Or, she may take action against him during a lull in an assaultive incident, or after it has culminated, in an effort to prevent a recurrence of the violence. And so, the issue is not whether the danger was in *fact* imminent, but whether, given the circumstances as she perceived them, the defendant's *belief was reasonable that the danger was imminent.*

In our next case excerpt, *State v. Stewart* (1988), the Supreme Court of Kansas ruled that Peggy Stewart, a battered woman, was not justified in killing her husband while he was asleep in their home.

CASE

*In **State v. Stewart (1988),** Peggy Stewart was charged with murder in the first degree of her husband.*

Did she shoot him dead in self-defense?

State v. Stewart

763 P.2d 572 (Kans. 1988)

HISTORY

Peggy Stewart (Defendant) was charged with murder in the first degree of her husband. The Butler District Court, entered verdict of not guilty. The prosecution appealed with a question reserved. The Supreme Court (5–2) held that the statutory justification for the use of deadly force in self-defense did not excuse a homicide committed by a battered wife where there was no evidence of deadly threat or imminent danger contemporaneous with killing, sustained the Appeal.

LOCKETT, J.

(continues)

(continued)

FACTS

Following an annulment from her first husband and two subsequent divorces in which she was the petitioner, Peggy Stewart married Mike Stewart in 1974. Evidence at trial disclosed a long history of abuse by Mike against Peggy and her two daughters from one of her prior marriages. Laura, one of Peggy's daughters, testified that early in the marriage Mike hit and kicked Peggy, and that after the first year of the marriage Peggy exhibited signs of severe psychological problems. Subsequently, Peggy was hospitalized and diagnosed as having symptoms of paranoid schizophrenia; she responded to treatment and was soon released. It appeared to Laura, however, that Mike was encouraging Peggy to take more than her prescribed dosage of medication.

In 1977, two social workers informed Peggy that they had received reports that Mike was taking indecent liberties with her daughters. Because the social workers did not want Mike to be left alone with the girls, Peggy quit her job. In 1978, Mike began to taunt Peggy by stating that Carla, her 12-year-old daughter, was "more of a wife" to him than Peggy.

Later, Carla was placed in a detention center, and Mike forbade Peggy and Laura to visit her. When Mike finally allowed Carla to return home in the middle of summer, he forced her to sleep in an un-air conditioned room with the windows nailed shut, to wear a heavy flannel nightgown, and to cover herself with heavy blankets. Mike would then wake Carla at 5:30 A.M. and force her to do all the housework. Peggy and Laura were not allowed to help Carla or speak to her.

When Peggy confronted Mike and demanded that the situation cease, Mike responded by holding a shotgun to Peggy's head and threatening to kill her. Mike once kicked Peggy so violently in the chest and ribs that she required hospitalization. Finally, when Mike ordered Peggy to kill and bury Carla, she filed for divorce. Peggy's attorney in the divorce action testified in the murder trial that Peggy was afraid for both her and her children's lives.

One night, in a fit of anger, Mike threw Carla out of the house. Carla, who was not yet in her teens, was forced out of the home with no money, no coat, and no place to go. When the family heard that Carla was in Colorado, Mike refused to allow Peggy to contact or even talk about Carla.

Mike's intimidation of Peggy continued to escalate. One morning, Laura found her mother hiding on the school bus, terrified and begging the driver to take her to a neighbor's home. That Christmas, Mike threw the turkey dinner to the floor, chased Peggy outside, grabbed her by the hair, rubbed her face in the dirt, and then kicked and beat her.

After Laura moved away, Peggy's life became even more isolated. Once, when Peggy was working at a cafe, Mike came in and ran all the customers off with a gun because he wanted Peggy to go home and have sex with him right that minute. He abused both drugs and alcohol, and amused himself by terrifying Peggy, once waking her from a sound sleep by beating her with a baseball bat. He shot one of Peggy's pet cats, and then held the gun against her head and threatened to pull the trigger. Peggy told friends that Mike would hold a shotgun to her head and threaten to blow it off, and indicated that one day he would probably do it.

In May 1986, Peggy left Mike and ran away to Laura's home in Oklahoma. It was the first time Peggy had left Mike without telling him. Because Peggy was suicidal, Laura had her admitted to a hospital. There, she was diagnosed as having toxic psychosis as a result of an overdose of her medication. On May 30, 1986, Mike called to say he was coming to get her. Peggy agreed to return to Kansas. Peggy told a nurse she felt like she wanted to shoot her husband. At trial, she testified that she decided to return with Mike because she was not able to get the medical help she needed in Oklahoma.

When Mike arrived at the hospital, he told the staff that he "needed his housekeeper." The hospital released Peggy to Mike's care, and he immediately drove her back to Kansas. Mike told Peggy that all her problems were in her head and he would be the one to tell her what was good for her, not the doctors. Peggy testified that Mike threatened to kill her if she ever ran away again. As soon as they arrived at the house, Mike forced Peggy into the house and forced her to have oral sex several times.

The next morning, Peggy discovered a loaded .357 magnum. She testified she was afraid of the gun. She hid the gun under the mattress of the bed in a spare room. Later that morning, as she cleaned house, Mike kept making remarks that she should not bother because she would not be there long, or that she should not bother with her things because she could not take them with her. She testified she was afraid Mike was going to kill her.

Mike's parents visited Mike and Peggy that afternoon. Mike's father testified that Peggy and Mike were affectionate with each other during the visit. Later, after Mike's parents had left, Mike forced Peggy to perform oral sex. After watching television, Mike and Peggy went to bed at 8:00 P.M. As Mike slept, Peggy thought about suicide and heard voices in her head repeating over and over, "kill or be killed." At this time, there were two vehicles in the driveway and Peggy had access to the car keys. About 10:00 P.M., Peggy went to the spare bedroom and removed the gun from under the mattress, walked back to the bedroom, and killed her husband while he slept. She then ran to the home of a neighbor, who called the police.

When the police questioned Peggy regarding the events leading up to the shooting, Peggy stated that things had not gone quite right that day, and that when she got the chance she hid the gun under the mattress. She stated that she shot Mike to "get this over with, this misery and this torment." When asked why she got the gun out, Peggy stated to the police:

"I'm not sure exactly what…led up to it…and my head started playing games with me and I got to thinking about things and I said I didn't want to be by myself again.…I got the gun out because there had been remarks made about me being out there alone. It was as if Mike was going to do something again like had been done before. He had gotten me down here from McPherson one time and he went and told them that I had done something and he had me put out of the house and was taking everything I had. And it was like he was going to pull the same thing over again."

Two expert witnesses testified during the trial. The expert for the defense, psychologist Marilyn Hutchinson, diagnosed Peggy as suffering from "battered woman syndrome," or post-traumatic stress syndrome. Dr. Hutchinson testified that Mike was preparing to escalate the violence in retaliation for Peggy's running away. She testified that loaded guns, veiled threats, and increased sexual demands are indicators of the escalation of the cycle. Dr. Hutchinson believed Peggy had a repressed knowledge that she was in a "really grave lethal situation."

The State's expert, psychiatrist Herbert Modlin, neither subscribed to a belief in the battered woman syndrome nor to a theory of learned helplessness as an explanation for why women do not leave an abusive relationship. Dr. Modlin testified that abuse such as repeated forced oral sex would not be trauma sufficient to trigger a post-traumatic stress disorder. He also believed Peggy was erroneously diagnosed as suffering from toxic psychosis. He stated that Peggy was unable to escape the abuse because she suffered from schizophrenia, rather than the battered woman syndrome.

At defense counsel's request, the trial judge gave an instruction on self-defense to the jury. The jury found Peggy not guilty.

…

Although the State may not appeal an acquittal, it may reserve questions for appeal. We will not entertain an appeal by the prosecution merely to determine whether the trial court committed error. The appeal by the prosecution must raise a question of statewide interest, the answer to which is essential to the just administration of criminal law. The question reserved is whether the trial judge erred in instructing on self-defense when there was no imminent threat to the defendant and no evidence of any argument or altercation between the defendant and the victim contemporaneous with the killing. We find this question and the related question of the extent to which evidence of the battered woman syndrome will be allowed to expand the statutory justification for the use of deadly force in self-defense are questions of statewide importance.

The State claims that under the facts the instruction should not have been given because there was no lethal threat to defendant contemporaneous with the killing. The State points out that Peggy's annulment and divorces from former husbands, and her filing for divorce after leaving Mike, proved that Peggy knew there were non-lethal methods by which she could extricate herself from the abusive relationship.

Early Kansas cases held that killing in self-defense was justifiable when the defendant had reasonable grounds to believe that an aggressor (1) had a design to take the defendant's life, (2) attempted to execute the design or was in an apparent situation to do so, and (3) induced in the defendant a reasonable belief that he intended to do so immediately. *State v. Horne*, 15 Kan. 547, 554 (1875).

These common-law principles were codified in K.S.A. 21–3211, which provides:

> A person is justified in the use of force against an aggressor when and to the extent it appears to him and he reasonably believes that such conduct is necessary to defend himself or another against such aggressor's imminent use of unlawful force.

(continues)

(continued)

The traditional concept of self-defense has posited one-time conflicts between persons of somewhat equal size and strength. When the defendant claiming self-defense is a victim of long-term domestic violence, such as a battered spouse, such traditional concepts may not apply. Because of the prior history of abuse, and the difference in strength and size between the abused and the abuser, the accused in such cases may choose to defend during a momentary lull in the abuse, rather than during a conflict. However, in order to warrant the giving of a self-defense instruction, the facts of the case must still show that the spouse was in imminent danger close to the time of the killing.

A person is justified in using force against an aggressor when it appears to that person and he or she reasonably believes such force to be necessary. A reasonable belief implies both an honest belief and the existence of facts which would persuade a reasonable person to that belief. A self-defense instruction must be given if there is any evidence to support a claim of self-defense, even if that evidence consists solely of the defendant's testimony.

Where self-defense is asserted, evidence of the deceased's long-term cruelty and violence towards the defendant is admissible. In cases involving battered spouses, expert evidence of the battered woman syndrome is relevant to a determination of the reasonableness of the defendant's perception of danger. In order to instruct a jury on self-defense, there must be some showing of an imminent threat or a confrontational circumstance involving an overt act by an aggressor. There is no exception to this requirement where the defendant has suffered long-term domestic abuse and the victim is the abuser. In such cases, the issue is not whether the defendant believes homicide is the solution to past or future problems with the batterer, but rather whether circumstances surrounding the killing were sufficient to create a reasonable belief in the defendant that the use of deadly force was necessary. In three recent Kansas cases where battered women shot their husbands, the women were clearly threatened in the moments prior to the shootings. [Summary of these cases omitted here.] Each case involved a threat of death to the wife and a violent confrontation between husband and wife, contemporaneous with the shooting.

Here, however, there is an absence of imminent danger to defendant: Peggy told a nurse at the Oklahoma hospital of her desire to kill Mike. She later voluntarily agreed to return home with Mike when he telephoned her. She stated that after leaving the hospital Mike threatened to kill her if she left him again. Peggy showed no inclination to leave. In fact, immediately after the shooting, Peggy told the police that she was upset because she thought Mike would leave her. Prior to the shooting, Peggy hid the loaded gun. The cars were in the driveway and Peggy had access to the car keys. After being abused, Peggy went to bed with Mike at 8 P.M. Peggy lay there for two hours, then retrieved the gun from where she had hidden it and shot Mike while he slept.

Under these facts, the giving of the self-defense instruction was erroneous. Under such circumstances, a battered woman cannot reasonably fear imminent life-threatening danger from her sleeping spouse.

Finally, our legislature has not provided for capital punishment for even the most heinous crimes. We must, therefore, hold that when a battered woman kills her sleeping spouse when there is no imminent danger, the killing is not reasonably necessary and a self-defense instruction may not be given. To hold otherwise in this case would in effect allow the execution of the abuser for past or future acts and conduct.

One additional issue must be addressed. In its *amicus curiae* brief, the Kansas County and District Attorney Association contends the instruction given by the trial court improperly modified the law of self-defense to be more generous to one suffering from the battered woman syndrome than to any other defendant relying on self-defense. We agree....

Here, the trial judge gave the instruction, stating:

> The defendant has claimed her conduct was justified as self-defense. A person is justified in the use of force against an aggressor when and to the extent it appears to him and he reasonably believes that such conduct is necessary to defend himself or another against such aggressor's imminent use of unlawful force. Such justification requires both a belief on the part of the defendant and the existence of facts that would persuade a reasonable person to that belief.

The trial judge then added the following:

> You must determine, from the viewpoint of the defendant's mental state, whether the defendant's belief in the need to defend herself was reasonable in light of her subjective impressions and the facts and circumstances known to her.

This addition was apparently encouraged by the following language in *State v. Hodges*, 239 Kan. 63, Syl. ¶ 4, 716 P.2d 563:

> Where the battered woman syndrome is an issue in the case, the standard for reasonableness concerning an accused's belief in asserting self-defense is not an objective, but a subjective standard. The jury must determine, from the viewpoint of defendant's mental state, whether defendant's belief in the need to defend herself was reasonable.

The statement that the reasonableness of defendant's belief in asserting self-defense should be measured from the defendant's own individual subjective viewpoint conflicts with prior law. Our test for self-defense is a two-pronged one. We first use a subjective standard to determine whether the defendant sincerely and honestly believed it necessary to kill in order to defend. We then use an objective standard to determine whether defendant's belief was reasonable—specifically, whether a reasonable person in defendant's circumstances would have perceived self-defense as necessary.... [I]n cases involving battered spouses, "the objective test is how a reasonably prudent battered wife would perceive the aggressor's demeanor."

... [I]t was error for the trial court to instruct the jury to employ solely a subjective test in determining the reasonableness of defendant's actions.

The appeal is sustained.

DISSENT

PRAGER, CJ, dissents [without opinion].

HERD, J:

...It is not within the scope of appellate review to weigh the evidence. An appellate court's function is to merely examine the record and determine if there is *any* evidence to support the theory of self-defense. If the record discloses any competent evidence upon which self-defense could be based, then the instruction must be given. In judging the evidence for this purpose, all inferences should be resolved in favor of the defendant.

It is evident from prior case law... [omitted] Peggy met her burden of showing some competent evidence that she acted in self-defense, thus making her defense a jury question. She testified she acted in fear for her life, and Dr. Hutchinson corroborated this testimony. The evidence of Mike's past abuse, the escalation of violence, his threat of killing her should she attempt to leave him, and Dr. Hutchinson's testimony that Peggy was indeed in a "lethal situation" more than met the minimal standard of "any evidence" to allow an instruction to be given to the jury.

Peggy introduced much uncontroverted evidence of the violent nature of the deceased and how he had brutalized her throughout their married life. It is well settled in Kansas that when self-defense is asserted, evidence of the cruel and violent nature of the deceased toward the defendant is admissible. The evidence showed Mike had a "Dr. Jekyll and Mr. Hyde" personality. He was usually very friendly and ingratiating when non-family persons were around, but was belligerent and domineering to family members. He had a violent temper and would blow up without reason.

Mike was cruel to his two stepdaughters, Carla and Laura, as well as to the Peggy. He took pride in hurting them or anything they held dear, such as their pets. Mike's violence toward Peggy and her daughters caused Peggy to have emotional problems with symptoms of paranoid schizophrenia. He would overdose Peggy on her medication and then cut her off it altogether. Mike's cruelty would culminate in an outburst of violence, and then he would suddenly become very loving and considerate. This was very confusing to Peggy. She lived in constant dread of the next outburst.

Peggy became progressively more passive and helpless during the marriage but finally became desperate enough to confront Mike and tell him the cruelty to her daughters had to stop. Mike responded by holding a shotgun to her head and threatening to kill her in front of the girls. The violence escalated. At one point, Mike kicked Peggy so violently in the chest and ribs that she required hospitalization.

Mike threw twelve-year-old Carla out of the house without resources, and Laura left home as soon as she could. Mike would not let Peggy see her daughters and ran Laura off with a shotgun when she tried to visit. Peggy's life became even more isolated. Towards the end, both the phone and utilities were disconnected from the house.

Peggy finally took the car and ran away to Laura's home in Oklahoma. It was the first time she had ever left Mike without telling him. She was suicidal and again hearing voices, and Laura had her admitted to a hospital. She was diagnosed as having

(continues)

(continued)

toxic psychosis from a bad reaction to her medication. She soon felt better, but was not fully recovered, when Mike found out where she was and called her to say he was coming to get her. She told a nurse she felt like she wanted to shoot him, but the nurse noted her major emotion was one of hopelessness.

The hospital nevertheless released Peggy to Mike's care, and he immediately drove her back to Kansas, telling her on the way she was going to have to "settle down now" and listen to him because he was the boss. *He said if she ever ran away again, he would kill her.*

When they reached the house, Mike would not let Peggy bring in her suitcases and forced her to have oral sex four or five times in the next 36 hours, with such violence that the inside of her mouth was bruised. The next morning, Peggy found a box of bullets in the car that had not been there before. She then discovered a loaded .357 magnum. This frightened her, because Mike had promised to keep his guns unloaded. She did not know how to unload the gun, so she hid it under the mattress of the bed in a spare room. As she cleaned house, Mike remarked she should not bother, because she would not be there long. He told her she should not bother with her things, because she could not take them with her. She took these statements to mean she would soon be dead and she grew progressively more terrified. Throughout the day Mike continued to force her to have oral sex, while telling her how he preferred sex with other women.

The sexual abuse stopped when Mike's parents came to visit. Mike's father testified everything seemed normal during their stay. After the visit, Mike again forced Peggy to perform oral sex and then demanded at 8:00 P.M. she come to bed with him. The cumulative effect of Mike's past history, coupled with his current abusive conduct, justified Peggy's belief that a violent explosion was imminent. As he slept, Peggy was terrified and thought about suicide and heard voices in her head repeating over and over, "kill or be killed." The voices warned her there was going to be killing and to get away.

She went to the spare bedroom and removed the gun from under the mattress, walked back to the bedroom, and fatally shot Mike. After the first shot, she thought he was coming after her so she shot again and fled wildly outside, barefoot, wearing only her underwear. Ignoring the truck and car outside, although she had the keys in her purse inside, she ran over a mile to the neighbors' house and pled with them to keep Mike from killing her. She thought she had heard him chasing her. The neighbor woman took the gun from Peggy's hand and gave her a robe while her husband called the sheriff. The neighbor testified Peggy appeared frightened for her life and was certain Mike was alive and looking for her.

Psychologist Marilyn Hutchinson qualified as an expert on the battered woman syndrome and analyzed the uncontroverted facts for the jury. She concluded Peggy was a victim of the syndrome and reasonably believed she was in imminent danger. In *State v. Hodges*, 716 P.2d 563 (1986), we held it appropriate to permit expert testimony on the battered woman syndrome to prove the reasonableness of the defendant's belief she was in imminent danger. Most courts which have addressed the issue are in accord.

The majority implies its decision is necessary to keep the battered woman syndrome from operating as a defense in and of itself. It has always been clear the syndrome is not a defense itself. Evidence of the syndrome is admissible only because of its relevance to the issue of self-defense. The majority of jurisdictions have held it beyond the ordinary jury's understanding why a battered woman may feel she cannot escape, and have held evidence of the battered woman syndrome proper to explain it. The expert testimony explains how people react to circumstances in which the average juror has not been involved. It assists the jury in evaluating the sincerity of the defendant's belief she was in imminent danger requiring self-defense and whether she was in fact in imminent danger.

Dr. Hutchinson explained to the jury at Peggy's trial the "cycle of violence" which induces a state of "learned helplessness" and keeps a battered woman in the relationship. She testified Peggy was caught in such a cycle. The cycle begins with an initial building of tension and violence, culminates in an explosion, and ends with a "honeymoon." The woman becomes conditioned to trying to make it through one more violent explosion with its battering in order to be rewarded by the "honeymoon phase," with its expressions of remorse and eternal love and the standard promise of "never again." After all promises are broken time after time and she is beaten again and again, the battered woman falls into a state of learned helplessness where she gives up trying to extract herself from the cycle of violence. She learns fighting back only delays the honeymoon and escalates the violence. If she tries to leave the relationship, she is located and returned and the violence increases. She is a captive. She begins to believe her husband is omnipotent, and resistance will be futile at best.

It is a jury question to determine if the battered woman who kills her husband as he sleeps fears he will find and kill her if she leaves, as is usually claimed. Under such circumstances the battered woman is not under actual physical attack when she kills but such attack is imminent, and as a result she believes her life is in imminent danger. She may kill during the tension-building stage when the abuse is apparently not as severe as it sometimes has been, but nevertheless has escalated so that she is afraid the acute stage to come will be fatal to her. She only acts on such fear if she has some survival instinct remaining after the husband-induced "learned helplessness."

Dr. Hutchinson testified the typical batterer has a dichotomous personality, in which he only shows his violent side to his wife or his family. A batterer's major characteristic is the need to blame all frustration on someone else. In a typical battering relationship, she said, the husband and wife are in traditional sex roles, the wife has low self-esteem, and the husband abuses drugs or alcohol. The husband believes the wife is his property and what he does to her is no one's business. There is usually a sense of isolation, with the woman not allowed to speak with friends or children. Overlying the violence is the intimation of death, often created by threats with weapons.

It was Dr. Hutchinson's opinion Mike was planning to escalate his violence in retaliation against Peggy for running away. She testified that Mike's threats against Peggy's life, his brutal sexual acts, and Peggy's discovery of the loaded gun were all indicators to Peggy the violence had escalated and she was in danger. Dr. Hutchinson believed Peggy had a repressed knowledge she was in what was really a gravely lethal situation. She testified Peggy was convinced she must "kill or be killed."

The majority claims permitting a jury to consider self-defense under these facts would permit anarchy. This underestimates the jury's ability to recognize an invalid claim of self-defense. Although this is a case of first impression where an appeal by the State has been allowed, there have been several similar cases in which the defendant appealed on other grounds. In each of these cases where a battered woman killed the sleeping batterer, a self-defense instruction has been given when requested by the defendant.

The majority bases its opinion on its conclusion Peggy was not in imminent danger, usurping the right of the jury to make that determination of fact. The majority believes a person could not be in imminent danger from an aggressor merely because the aggressor dropped off to sleep. This is a fallacious conclusion. For instance, picture a hostage situation where the armed guard inadvertently drops off to sleep and the hostage grabs his gun and shoots him. The majority opinion would preclude the use of self-defense in such a case.

The majority attempts to buttress its conclusion Peggy was not in imminent danger by citing 19th Century law. The old requirement of "immediate" danger is not in accord with our statute on self-defense, K.S.A. 21–3211, and has been emphatically overruled by case law. Yet this standard permeates the majority's reasoning. A review of the law in this state on the requirement of imminent rather than immediate danger to justify self-defense is therefore required.

[Summary of cases purportedly supporting this conclusion omitted here.]

I would deny this appeal.

QUESTIONS

1. List all the facts and circumstances relevant to deciding whether Peggy Stewart was in "imminent" danger.
2. Summarize the court majority's arguments against imminent danger. Summarize the dissent's arguments for imminent danger.
3. Consider the following comments:
   a. Retaliation, as opposed to defense, is a common problem in cases arising from wife battering and domestic violence. The injured wife waits for the first possibility of striking against a distracted or unarmed husband. The man may even be asleep when the wife finally reacts.
   b. Retaliation is the standard case of "taking the law into your own hands." There is no way, under the law, to justify killing a wife batterer or a rapist in retaliation or revenge, however much sympathy there may be for the wife wreaking retaliation. Private citizens cannot act as judge and jury toward each other. They have no authority to pass judgment and to punish each other for past wrongs (Fletcher 1988, 21–22).

(continues)

(continued)

c. "The right to use force in the defense of one's person, family, habitation, lands, or goods is one of the unalienable rights of man. As it is a right not granted by any human code, no human code can take it away. It was recognized by the Roman law, declared by that law to be a natural right, and part of the law of nations. It is no doubt recognized by the code of every civilized State" (Thompson 1880, 546).

d. "A man is not born to run away. The law must consider human nature and make some allowance for the fighting instinct at critical moments. In Texas it is well settled, as you might imagine, that a man is not born to run away" (DeWolfe Howe 1953, 1:331).

Are any of the statements relevant to battered woman domestic violence cases? Do you agree with the statements? Explain your answer.

4. In your opinion, did Peggy Stewart kill Mike Stewart in self-defense? As a preemptive strike? Or as retaliation? Or something else? Defend your answer.

DEFENSE OF OTHERS

LO6

The law must consider human nature and make some allowance. Historically, self-defense meant protecting yourself and the members of your immediate family. Although several states still require a special relationship, the trend is in the opposite direction. Many states have abandoned the special relationship requirement altogether, replacing it with the defense of anyone who needs immediate protection from attack.

Several states that retain the requirement have expanded it to include lovers and friends. The "others" must have the right to defend themselves before someone else can claim the defense. This is important in cases involving abortion rights protestors. In *State v. Aguillard* (1990, 674), protestors argued they had the right to prevent abortions by violating the law because they were defending the right of unborn children to live. In rejecting the defense of others, the court said:

> The "defense of others" specifically limits the use of force or violence in protection of others to situations where the person attacked would have been justified in using such force or violence to protect himself. In view of *Roe v. Wade* and the provisions of the Louisiana abortion statute, defense of others as justification for the defendants' otherwise criminal conduct is not available in these cases. Since abortion is legal in Louisiana, the defendants had no legal right to protect the unborn by means not even available to the unborn themselves. (676)

DEFENSE OF HOME AND PROPERTY

LO6

> The right to use force in the defense of one's person, family, habitation, lands, or goods is one of the natural and unalienable rights of man. As it is a right not granted by any human code, no human code can take it away. It was recognized by the Roman law; it was declared by that law to be a natural right and a part of the law of nations. It is no doubt recognized by the code of every civilized State.
>
> —*Thompson* (1880, 546)

The right to use force to defend your home is rooted deeply in the common law idea that "a man's home is his castle." As early as 1604, Sir Edward Coke, the great common law judge, in his report of Semayne's Case, wrote:

> The house of everyone is to him his castle and fortress, as well for his defense against injury and violence, as for his repose; and although the life of a man is a thing precious and favored in law...if thieves come to a man's house to rob him, or murder, and the owner or his servants kill any of the thieves in defense of himself and his house, it is not felony and he shall lose nothing. (*State v. Mitcheson* 1977, 1122)

The most impassioned statement of the supreme value placed on the sanctity of homes came from the Earl of Chatham during a debate in the British Parliament in 1764:

> The poorest man may in his cottage bid defiance to all the forces of the Crown. It may be frail; its roof may shake; the wind may blow through it; the storm may enter; the rain may enter; but the King of England may not enter; all his force dares not cross the threshold of the ruined tenement. (qtd. in Hall 1991, 2:4)

Don't let the Earl of Chatham's moving words lure you into thinking you can automatically kill an intruder to defend the sanctity of your home. Sir William Blackstone (1769), in his eighteenth-century Commentaries (the best-known—and often the only known—law book to American lawyers at that time), argues that the right is broad but limited. He writes:

> If any person attempts to break open a house in the nighttime and shall be killed in such attempt, the slayer shall be acquitted and discharged. This reaches not to the breaking open of any house in the daytime, unless it carries with it an attempt of robbery. (180)

You can see that the defense was limited to nighttime invasions, except for breaking into homes to commit daytime *robberies*. Most modern statutes limit the use of deadly force to cases where it's reasonable to believe intruders intend to commit crimes of violence (like homicide, assault, rape, and robbery) against occupants.

Statutes vary as to the area that the use of deadly force covers. Most require entry into the home itself. This doesn't include the **curtilage**, the area immediately surrounding the home. Many require entry into an occupied home. This means you can't set some automatic device to shoot whoever trips the switch when you're not home.

curtilage the area immediately surrounding the home

Homes are special places; they're not in the same category as our "stuff." Can you use force to protect your "stuff"? Not deadly force. But you can use the amount of nondeadly force you reasonably believe is necessary to prevent someone from taking your stuff. You also can run after and take back what someone has just taken from you.

But, as with all the justifications based on necessity, you can't use force if there's time to call the police. For example, O. J. Simpson and his friends burst into a Las Vegas hotel room, with guns drawn and O. J. demanding, "I want my stuff! I want my stuff!" At his trial later for armed robbery and burglary, his argument that he was justified didn't work. He had time to call the police (ABC News, 2007).

New "Castle Laws"

LO7

Self-defense is undergoing an epochal transformation. Between 2005 and 2015, more than 40 states have passed or proposed new "Castle Doctrine" legislation intended to expand the right to use deadly force in self-defense (Suk 2008, 237). The first castle doctrine law passed the Florida legislature in October 2005, unanimously in the state senate and by a hefty majority, 94 to 20, in the state house of representatives. The Florida Personal Protection Law (2009) became the model for most of the new castle laws.

"RIGHT TO DEFEND" OR "LICENSE TO KILL"?

Supporters and opponents of the castle laws see them in fundamentally different ways. Supporters hail them as the public reasserting fundamental rights. Marion Hammer, the first woman president of the National Rifle Association, says the castle law codifies the "right of the people to use any manner of force to protect their home and its inhabitants." She contends this right goes back to the 1400s, and that Florida prosecutors and courts took away that right by requiring that "law-abiding citizens who are attacked by criminals" have to retreat:

> When they take away your basic rights and freedoms, every once in a while you have to take them back. No law abiding citizen should be forced to retreat from an attacker in their homes or any place they have a legal right to be. Under the existing law [before the castle law was enacted] you had a duty to try to run and maybe get chased down, and beat to death. Now, if you have a knife, firearm or pepper spray, you can use force to protect yourself. (Kleindienst 2005)

Gun control advocates, on the other hand, decry the castle laws, warning that they're "ushering in a violent new era where civilians may have more freedom to use deadly force than even the police." They're not a "right to defend"; they're a "license to kill" (Rather 2009). The Brady Campaign to Prevent Gun Violence strongly opposes the new castle laws. (The late Jim Brady, President Reagan's press secretary, was badly wounded and paralyzed during John Hinckley's attempt to assassinate President Reagan [see Chapter 6].) According to Peter Hamm, communications director for the campaign:

> The biggest myth in Florida is that this is about protecting people who use legitimate self-defense. This law sends a message to people who are potentially dangerous and have an itchy trigger finger that as long as they can make a reasonable case they were in fear, they can use deadly force against somebody. It's a particular risk faced by travelers coming to Florida for a vacation because they have no idea it's going to be the law of the land. If they get into a road-rage argument, the other person may feel he has the right to use deadly force. (Kleindienst 2005)

Given the above, don't confuse the U.S. Supreme Court cases *District of Columbia v. Heller* (2008) and *McDonald v. City of Chicago* (2010), discussed in Chapter 2, with the castle laws. *Heller* and *McDonald* both dealt with the Second Amendment guaranteed right to *have* a gun. The castle laws authorize individuals to *use* the guns they have the right to have.

WHY THE SPREAD OF CASTLE LAWS NOW?

There's no empirical research to help explain why so many states have adopted the "new castle laws." There was no similar reaction in the 1980s when Colorado's "make-my-day" law, enacted in 1985, expanded traditional self-defense to resemble in most respects the new laws. There was also no pulling back on new castle laws following the Sandy Hook school massacre in 2012, either in the states or by federal legislation.

But there's plenty of *speculation* as to why these laws have proliferated now. Two commonly mentioned reasons are Americans' heightened consciousness and concern about their security since 9/11 and the lack of enough police officers to protect the public. Florida and Mississippi are examples:

- During the series of hurricanes that battered Florida in 2005, "In a lot of these devastated areas, law enforcement would tell communities, 'You're on your own, we can't get to you.' So we needed to be sure that when people protected themselves, their families and their property, that they weren't gonna be prosecuted by some criminal-coddling prosecutor" (Rather 2009).

- With the cuts in law enforcement officers in Jackson, Mississippi, Police Chief McMillin "says he's waging a battle of attrition with a force that's nearly 200 officers short of the 600 the city needs." So he says it's no wonder that civilians are taking up the fight and using tools like the castle doctrine to help protect themselves:

> People are sick and tired of being victims. They're tired of being robbed. They're tired of their houses being broken into. They think that they have to take matters into their own hands if they're gonna be safe. (Rather 2009)

Cliff Cargill, a firearms instructor certified by the National Rifle Association (NRA), says business has been booming with Jackson's crime on the rise and the new laws on the books. "If I'm in my home, my place of business or my vehicle, I don't have to justify my existence in my surroundings. If somebody breaks into my house to rob and/or do me harm, then I should be presumed innocent by anybody that comes to investigate that situation." Cargill says, "Packing heat is not paranoia, but common sense." There's an old saying, "When seconds count, the police are only minutes away. Well in the meantime, the clock's running. What's that intruder doing to you?" That's especially true in Jackson, where locals say the police are badly out-gunned (Rather 2009).

CASES UNDER NEW CASTLE LAWS

LO7

Let's look at some of the cases illustrating how citizens are using the new laws and how police, prosecutors, and courts are responding to citizens' actions under the laws (CLIF "Expansion of 'New Castle' Laws" see Table 5.1).

TABLE 5.1 Expansion of New "Castle Laws"

STATE	YEAR	NAME	FACTS	DISPOSITION
Florida	2006	Jacqueline Galas, 23	Prostitute shot and killed 72-year-old client with his gun	Not charged
Florida	2006	Robert Lee Smiley, Jr., 56	Taxi driver shot and killed drunk passenger outside cab after altercation	Charged with first-degree murder; trial jury deadlocked 9–3
Mississippi	2008	Sarbrinder Pannu, 31	Convenience store clerk followed shoplifter outside store and shot him twice	Charged with murder and acquitted
Mississippi	2008	Unidentified clerk in gas mart	Terrence Prior, 23, wearing a clown mask, shot after bursting through the door of a gas mart waving a gun, demanding money from the register; clerk followed him out the door, shot, and killed him outside the station; store had been robbed three times in recent weeks by a masked man	Not charged
Texas	2007	Joe Horn, 62	Retired computer consultant shot two men in the back and killed two men from his front porch, as they were leaving his neighbor's house with money and jewelry	Grand jury refused to indict
Arizona	2004	Harold Fish, 59	Retired teacher on a hike fatally shot Grant Kuenzli, 43, claiming the man and his dogs charged at him	Convicted and sentenced to ten years in prison before Arizona passed a castle law to protect people like Fish

JACQUELINE GALAS A New Port Richey prostitute, Jacqueline Galas, 23, said that a longtime client, Frank Labiento, 72, threatened to kill her and then kill himself last month. A suicide note he had left and other evidence supported her contention. The law came into play when Ms. Galas grabbed Mr. Labiento's gun and chose not to flee but to kill him. "Before that law," Mr. Halkitis said, "before you could use deadly force, you had to retreat. Under the new law, you don't have to do that." The decision not to charge Ms. Galas was straightforward, Mr. Halkitis said. "It would have been a more difficult situation with the old law," he said, "much more difficult" (Liptak 2006).

ROBERT LEE SMILEY, JR. In November 2004, before the new law was enacted, Robert Lee Smiley Jr., then 56, a cabdriver in West Palm Beach, killed a drunken passenger in an altercation after dropping him off. Mr. Smiley killed Jimmie Morningstar, 43 years old. A sports bar had paid Mr. Smiley $10 to drive Mr. Morningstar home in the early morning of November 6, 2004. Mr. Morningstar was apparently reluctant to leave the cab once it reached its destination, and Mr. Smiley used a stun gun to hasten his exit. Once outside the cab, Mr. Morningstar flashed a knife, Mr. Smiley testified at his first trial that, once outside the cab, Mr. Morningstar flashed a knife. (A knife was never found.) Mr. Smiley, who had gotten out of his cab, reacted by shooting at his passenger's feet and then into his body, killing him.

Cliff Morningstar, the dead man's uncle, said he was baffled by the killing. "He had a radio," Mr. Morningstar said of Mr. Smiley. "He could have gotten in his car and left. He could have shot him in his knee." Carey Haughwout, the public defender who represents Mr. Smiley, conceded that no knife was found. "However," Ms. Haughwout said, "there is evidence to support that the victim came at Smiley after Smiley fired two warning shots, and that he did have something in his hand."

Smiley was charged and tried for murder. The jury deadlocked 9 to 3 in favor of convicting him. According to Henry Munnilal, the jury foreman, a 62-year-old accountant, "Mr. Smiley had a lot of chances to retreat and to avoid an escalation. He could have just gotten in his cab and left. The thing could have been avoided, and a man's life would have been saved." Mr. Smiley tried to invoke the new law, which does away with the duty to retreat and would almost certainly have meant his acquittal, but an appeals court refused to apply it retroactively.

In April 2006, a Florida appeals court indicated that the new law, had it applied to Mr. Smiley's case, would have affected its outcome. "Prior to the legislative enactment, a person was required to 'retreat to the wall' before using his or her right of self-defense by exercising deadly force," Judge Martha C. Warner wrote, for the new law abolished that duty (Liptak 2006).

SARBRINDER PANNU The owner of the Mississippi BP station, Surinder Singh, where Sarbrinder Pannu worked told Dan Rather:

Rather: It was just after ten on a hot Mississippi night in August 2008 at a gas mart on the outskirts of Jackson. A man in a black SUV pulled into the lot, walked inside, grabbed a case of beer from the cooler, and walked right out the door. Without paying. A single case of beer wasn't going to break the bank, but according to the property owner, Mr. Surinder Singh, who operates several sister stores nearby, the man was just the latest of a seemingly endless stream of thieves.

Singh: They come, they take stuff.... By the time we call the police they are already gone. And they know that. So when... when the police come, they say, "Well, call us if they come back."

Rather: But the clerk manning the counter that night wasn't willing to wait for anyone to come back. According to police, he ran outside with a .357 magnum, aimed at the man in the black SUV, and fired three shots.

Singh: Somebody got to stop him. The police cannot be there 24 hours. The only person who was there to stop him was the clerk. And he stopped him, whatever means he could.

Rather: Thirty-six-year-old James Hawthorne Jr. was pronounced dead at the hospital. (Rather 2009)

Pannu was charged with murder and acquitted.

UNIDENTIFIED GAS MART CLERK "Dan Rather Reports" continued, describing yet another incident that didn't even go to trial. The shooter—an unidentified gas station–convenience store clerk—wasn't charged with the shooting:

Rather: Just a few nights later, there was another shooting at a gas mart a few miles away; police say a man in a clown mask burst through the door waving a gun, demanding money from the register. It was the third time in recent weeks the store was robbed by a man in a clown mask, as captured on this surveillance video. But when the masked man ran out with the cash, this time the clerk didn't let him get away.

Reporter, WJTV Live Broadcast: The clerk went after him and shot him outside the store....

Rather: Ten rounds, according to the police report. Twenty-three-year-old Terrence Prior was pronounced dead at the hospital. (Rather 2009)

YOU *DECIDE*

Do the New Castle Laws protect the right to defend or provide a license to kill?

The following dialogue is from *Dan Rather Reports*.

Marion Hammer, executive director of Unified Sportsmen of Florida, representative of the Florida chapter of the NRA: When you are prosecuting law-abiding people for defending themselves against criminals, it's wrong and it has to be fixed. And the castle doctrine laws fixed that.

Gregory Hicks, an attorney in Warren City, Florida: I believe in protecting one's property. I believe in the fact that your home is your castle. But I don't believe you have the right to use that kind of deadly force on a prank. I'm sorry, that's not the way an ordered society acts.

Dan Rather: To shoot or not to shoot? For even the most seasoned police officer, it's the ultimate dilemma. A split-second choice that could prevent a violent crime or be a fatal mistake. But it's no longer just police who are deciding whether or not to pull the trigger. There's a new breed of laws that's expanding the rights of civilians to use deadly force. They are called the "castle doctrine" laws, and since 2005, they've been passed or proposed in more than 35 states.

The new laws are not about the right to bear arms, but the right to use them. The National Rifle Association says the castle doctrine is restoring a tradition of self-defense that dates back to medieval England, when a man's home was considered his castle. But others say these laws are ushering in a violent new era where civilians may have more freedom to use deadly force than even the police. (Rather 2009)

Question

- After reading about the castle law cases in this section, would you say the new castle laws are a right to defend or a license to kill?

"CHOICE OF EVILS"

LO8

choice-of-evils defense also called the *general defense of necessity,* it justifies the choice to commit a lesser crime to avoid the harm of a greater crime

The core of the **choice-of-evils defense** is the necessity to prevent imminent danger; in that respect, it's like all the defenses we've discussed up to now. And it's the reason it's also called the **general defense of necessity**. The justifications based on the necessity of defending yourself, other people, and your home aren't controversial. Why? Because we see those who attack ourselves, our families, and our homes as evil and the defenders as good. However, in the general choice-of-evils defense, the line between good and evil isn't always drawn as clearly as it is in self-defense and the defense of home.

The choice-of-evils defense justifies the choice to commit a lesser crime to avoid the *harm* of a greater crime. The defense enjoys a long history in the law of Europe and the Americas.

And throughout that history, the defense has generated heated controversy. Bracton, the great thirteenth-century jurist of English and Roman law, declared that what "is not otherwise lawful, necessity makes lawful." Other distinguished English commentators, such as Sir Francis Bacon, Sir Edward Coke, and Sir Matthew Hale in the sixteenth and seventeenth centuries, agreed with Bracton. The influential seventeenth-century English judge Hobart expressed the argument this way: "All laws admit certain cases of just excuse, when they are offended in letter, and where the offender is under necessity, either of compulsion or inconvenience."

On the other side of the debate, the distinguished nineteenth-century English historian of criminal law Judge Sir James F. Stephen believed that the defense of necessity was so vague that judges could interpret it to mean anything they wanted. A similar observation was made in the mid-1950s by the distinguished professor of criminal law Glanville Williams. "It is just possible to imagine cases in which the expediency of breaking the law is so overwhelmingly great," wrote Williams, "that people may be justified in breaking it, but these cases cannot be defined beforehand" (1961, 724–25).

Early cases record occasional instances of defendants who successfully pleaded the necessity defense. In 1500, a prisoner successfully pleaded necessity to a charge of prison break; he was trying to escape a fire that burned down the jail. The most common example in the older cases is destroying houses to stop fires from spreading. In 1912, a man was acquitted on the defense of necessity when he burned a strip of the owner's heather to prevent a fire from spreading to his house (Hall 1960, 425).

The most famous case of imminent necessity is *The Queen v. Dudley and Stephens* (1884). Thomas Dudley and Edwin Stephens, two adults with families, Edmund Brooks, and Richard Parker a seventeen-year-old man without any family responsibilities, were lost in a lifeboat on the high seas. They had no food or water except for two cans of turnips and a turtle they caught in the sea on the fourth day. After twenty days (the last eight without food), perhaps a thousand miles from land with virtually no hope of rescue, Dudley and Stephens—after failing to get Brooks to cast lots—and without consulting Parker, told Brooks that if no rescue vessel appeared by the next day, they were going to kill Parker for food. They explained to Brooks that his life was the most expendable because they each had family responsibilities and he didn't.

The following day, no vessel appeared. After saying a prayer for Parker, Dudley, with Stephens's assent, killed Parker who was unconscious from lack of food and water. Dudley, Stephens, and Brooks survived on Parker's flesh and blood for four days, when they were finally rescued.

Dudley and Stephens were prosecuted, convicted, and sentenced to death for murder. They appealed, pleading the defense of necessity. Lord Coleridge, in this famous passage, rejected the defense of necessity:

> The temptation to act here was not what the law ever called necessity. Nor is this to be regretted. Though law and morality are not the same, and many things may be immoral which are not necessarily illegal, yet the absolute divorce of law from morality would be of fatal consequence; and such divorce would follow if the temptation to murder in this case were to be held by law an absolute defense of it. It is not so.
>
> To preserve one's life is generally speaking a duty, but it may be the plainest and the highest duty to sacrifice it. War is full of instances in which it is a man's duty not to live, but to die. The duty, in case of shipwreck, of a captain to his crew, of the crew to the passengers, of soldiers to women and children; these duties impose on men the moral necessity, not of the preservation, but of the sacrifice of their lives for others. It is not correct, therefore, to say that there is any absolute or unqualified necessity to preserve one's own life.
>
> It is not needful to point out the awful danger of admitting the principle contended for.
>
> Who is to be the judge of this sort of necessity? By what measure of the comparative value of lives to be measured? Is it to be strength, or intellect, or what? It is plain that the principle leaves to him who is to profit by it to determine the necessity which will justify him in deliberately taking another's life to save his own.
>
> In this case, the weakest, the youngest, the most unresisting, was chosen. Was it more necessary to kill him than one of the grown men? The answer must be "No"—"So spake the Fiend, and with necessity, The tyrant's plea, executed his devilish deeds." It is not suggested that in this particular case, the deeds were "devilish," but it is quite plain that such a principle once admitted might be made the legal cloak for unbridled passion and atrocious crime.

Lord Coleridge sentenced them to death, but expressed his hope that Queen Victoria would pardon them. The queen didn't pardon them, but she almost did—she commuted their death penalty to six months in prison.

The choice-of-evils defense consists of proving that the defendant made the right choice, the only choice—namely, the necessity of choosing now to do a lesser evil to avoid a greater evil. The Model Penal Code choice-of-evils provision sets out the elements in three steps:

1. Identify the evils.
2. Rank the evils.
3. Choose based on the reasonable belief that the greater evil is imminent; namely, it's going to happen right now. (ALI 1985, 1:2, 8–22)

Simply put, the choice-of-evils defense justifies choosing to commit a lesser crime to avoid the *harm* of a greater crime. The choice of the greater evil has to be both imminent and necessary. Those who choose to do the lesser evil have to believe reasonably that their only choice is to cause the lesser evil to avoid the imminent greater harm.

The Model Penal Code lists all of the following "right" choices:

- Destroying property to prevent spreading fire
- Violating a speed limit to get a dying person to a hospital

- Throwing cargo overboard to save a sinking vessel and its crew
- Dispensing drugs without a prescription in an emergency
- Breaking into and entering a mountain cabin to avoid freezing to death (ALI 1985, 1:2, 8)

The right choices are life, safety, and health over property. Why? Because according to the American Law Institute, the values of life, safety, and health always trump property interests (1985, 12).

Notice that the MPC doesn't leave the ranking of evils to individuals; it charges legislatures or judges and juries at trial with the task. Once an individual has made the "right" choice, she's either acquitted or it's considered a mitigating circumstance that can lessen the punishment. Courts rarely uphold choice-of-evils claims by defendants.

In our next case excerpt, *Toops v. State* (1994), the court ruled that Terry Toops was entitled to a jury instruction on the defense of necessity in a drunk-driving case.

CASE

In ***Toops v. State* (1994),** *Terry Toops was convicted of operating a vehicle while intoxicated, operating a vehicle with 10 percent or more alcohol in the blood, operating a vehicle while intoxicated with a prior offense of operating a vehicle while intoxicated, and operating a vehicle with 10 percent or more alcohol in the blood with a prior offense of operating a vehicle while intoxicated.*

Was driving drunk a lesser evil than a car out of control?

Toops v. State

643 N.E.2d 387 (Ind. App. 1994)

HISTORY

Terry Toops (Defendant) was convicted in the Cass Superior Court of operating a vehicle while intoxicated, operating a vehicle with 10 percent or more alcohol in the blood, operating a vehicle while intoxicated with a prior offense of operating a vehicle while intoxicated, and operating a vehicle with 10 percent or more alcohol in the blood with a prior offense of operating a vehicle while intoxicated. Toops appealed. The Court of Appeals reversed and remanded.

RUCKER, J.

FACTS

In the late evening hours of October 30, 1992, Terry Toops, Warren Cripe, and Ed Raisor were at Toops's home in Logansport, Indiana, drinking beer. Around 3:00 A.M. the following morning the trio decided to drive to a store in town. Because he was intoxicated, Toops agreed to allow Cripe to drive Toops's car. Toops sat in the front passenger seat and Raisor sat in the rear. Toops began to feel ill during the drive and stuck his head out the window for fresh air.

In the meantime, Sheriff's Deputy Michael Day and Town Marshall Gary Layer were on routine patrol when they observed a person later identified as Toops hanging out the car window. The officers decided to investigate and made a u-turn to follow the car. Cripe saw the patrol car turn around and panicked because he was a minor and had been drinking. He let go of the steering wheel and jumped into the back seat of the car. The car began to careen out of control, leaving its lane, veering into the northbound lane of traffic, then veering back into the southbound lane. Toops finally slid into the driver's seat and brought the car under control.

The officers overtook the car and noted that Toops, whom they had originally seen hanging out of the car window, was now seated behind the steering wheel. The officers also noted that Cripe and Raisor were seated in the back seat of the car. At the officers' request, Toops submitted to a breath test that revealed a BAC of .21%. As a result Toops was arrested and charged with various alcohol-related traffic offenses. He was also charged with Criminal Recklessness, Operating a Vehicle Without a Seat Belt, and Driving Left of Center, all of which the State dismissed prior to trial. After a trial by jury, Toops was convicted on all remaining counts.

At the close of evidence, Toops tendered the proposed jury instruction:

> The Defendant in this case has raised the defense of "Necessity" to excuse his assuming the controls of the vehicle at a time when he was intoxicated. "Necessity" involves a choice between two admitted evils where other options are unavailable. "Necessity" justifies illegal conduct if that conduct was the sole reasonable alternative available to Defendant given the circumstances of the case.
>
> In this case, the Defendant, Terry Toops, has admitted that he assumed control of the vehicle at a time when he was intoxicated. If you find that the Defendant's illegal conduct was justified by the circumstances, then you should find the Defendant "Not Guilty."

The trial court refused to give the instruction indicating "I cannot find that necessity is a recognized defense in the State of Indiana."

OPINION

The origins of the necessity defense are lost in antiquity. At least one writer advances the notion that it may be traced to the Bible itself, the analogy being the destruction of property to save human lives: "Then the mariners were afraid, and cried every man unto his god, and cast forth the wares that were in the ship into the sea, to lighten it of them."

The defense of necessity arose in the common law to excuse criminal conduct when a defendant was confronted with two evils and chose to engage in the prohibited conduct because it represented the lesser of the two evils. The underlying rationale is that to impose punishment upon a person who acted reasonably to avoid the greater harm serves neither to rehabilitate that person nor to deter others presented with a similar situation.

One of the leading decisions in this country recognizing the defense of necessity in a criminal law context is found in the landmark case of *United States v. Holmes*, 26 Fed. Cas. 360 (No. 15,383) (C.C.E.D. Pa. 1842). In that case a ship sank at sea forcing the survivors to crowd into a leaking lifeboat. The crew decided to throw 16 passengers overboard to prevent the boat from sinking. Holmes, a crew member who participated in tossing passengers into the sea, was convicted of manslaughter and sentenced to six months' imprisonment. On appeal Holmes argued that his conduct was justified given the choices confronting him. Although rejecting Holmes's argument because the method of determining who was to live or die was not fair, the court nonetheless accepted the principle that committing a harm, even the taking of human life, could sometimes be justified because it avoided the loss of even more lives, which was a greater harm.

The common law defense of necessity has evolved over the years and is often referred to as the "choice of evils" defense. The central element involves the emergency nature of the situation. Under the force of extreme circumstances, conduct that would otherwise constitute a crime is justifiable and not criminal because of the greater harm which the illegal act seeks to prevent. Neither this court nor our supreme court has had occasion to discuss the parameters or the applicability of the common law necessity defense in a criminal context. However, our supreme court has recognized the existence of the defense. In any event, contrary to the State's argument, to say that the common law defense of necessity is not a recognized defense in the State of Indiana is incorrect.

While there are no common law crimes in this State, the same is not true for common law defenses. The law in this jurisdiction is well settled that a defendant in a criminal case is entitled to have the jury instructed on any theory or defense which has some foundation in the evidence. There is no question that the evidence presented in this case raised a jury question as to whether Toops's control of the car while intoxicated, an illegal act, was necessary to prevent a greater harm, namely: an automobile collision potentially resulting in personal injury or property damage. Because the trial judge has a statutory duty to state to the jury "all matters of law which are necessary for their information in giving their verdict" the failure to give any instruction on the necessity defense in this case was error.

(continues)

(continued)

However, having determined error does not mean that we endorse the wording of Toops's proposed instruction. The instruction represents an incomplete statement of the law. That incompleteness is understandable however because no Indiana case has specifically set forth the elements of the necessity defense. In that regard we agree with the California court's holding in *People v. Pena* (1983), 197 Cal. Rptr. 264, 271, that the following requirements have traditionally been held to be prerequisites in establishing a necessity defense:

1. the act charged as criminal must have been done to prevent a significant evil;
2. there must have been no adequate alternative to the commission of the act;
3. the harm caused by the act must not be disproportionate to the harm avoided;
4. the accused must entertain a good-faith belief that his act was necessary to prevent greater harm;
5. such belief must be objectively reasonable under all the circumstances; and
6. the accused must not have substantially contributed to the creation of the emergency.

In the event of retrial on remand, the foregoing elements should be incorporated into any tendered instruction on the defense of necessity.

Reversed and remanded.

QUESTIONS

1. List all the facts and circumstances relevant to deciding whether Terry Toops was justified in driving while he was drunk.
2. State the elements of the defense as the court identifies them. How do they compare with the elements stated in the text?
3. In your opinion, was Toops entitled to the necessity defense? Defend your answer with case and opinion details and the text section on the defense.

YOU DECIDE

Was burglary the lesser evil?

State v. Celli

263 N.W.2d 145 (S.D. 1978)

Facts

On a cold winter day, William Celli and his friend, Glynis Brooks, left Deadwood, South Dakota, hoping to hitchhike to Newcastle, Wyoming, to look for work. The weather turned colder, they were afraid of frostbite, and there was no place of business open for them to get warm. Their feet were so stiff from the cold that it was difficult for them to walk.

They broke the lock on the front door and entered the only structure around, a cabin. Celli immediately crawled into a bed to warm up, and Brooks tried to light a fire in the fireplace. They rummaged through drawers to look for matches, which they finally located, and started a fire. Finally, Celli came out of the bedroom, took off his wet moccasins, socks, and coat; placed them near the fire; and sat down to warm himself. After warming up somewhat they checked the kitchen for edible food. That morning, they had shared a can of beans but had not eaten since. All they found was dry macaroni, which they could not cook because there was no water.

A neighbor noticed the smoke from the fireplace and called the police. When the police entered the cabin, Celli and Brooks were warming themselves in front of the fireplace. The police searched them but turned up nothing belonging to the cabin owners.

Question

- The trial court convicted Celli and Brooks of fourth-degree burglary. The appellate court reversed on other grounds. If you were deciding the case, would you allow the defense of necessity? In other words, was burglary the lesser evil? Defend your answer, applying all of the steps in the choice-of-evils defense.

CONSENT

LO9

defense of consent the justification that competent adults voluntarily consented to crimes against themselves and knew what they were consenting to

Consent has nothing to do with necessity. Nevertheless, it can be a justification. The defense of consent is based on the idea that competent adults voluntarily consented to crimes against themselves *and* knew what they were consenting to. The heart of the defense of consent is the high value placed on individual autonomy in a free society. If mentally competent adults want to be crime victims, so the argument for the justification of consent goes, no paternalistic (or maternalistic if you prefer) government should get in their way.

Consent may make sense in the larger context of individual freedom and responsibility, but the criminal law is hostile to consent as a justification for committing crimes. For all the noise about choice, you know already that except for the voluntary act requirement (discussed in Chapter 3), there are many examples of crimes where the freedom to choose one course of action instead of another is either a total fiction or very limited. We've seen some major examples in the chapters so far. There's the void-for-vagueness doctrine discussed in Chapter 2. Other examples were the mental state of negligence and the absence of mental fault in strict liability discussed in Chapter 4.

Individuals can take their own lives and inflict injuries on themselves, but in most states they can't authorize others to kill them or even wound or injure them. Let's look at how confined choice is in the defense of consent and examine some of the reasons. See the Criminal Law in Focus Box below for a typical example.

Alabama Criminal Code Consent Law: Alabama Criminal Code (1977) Section 13a-2–7

1. *In general.* The consent of the victim to conduct charged to constitute an offense or to the result thereof is a defense if such consent negatives a required element of the offense or precludes the infliction of the harm or evil sought to be prevented by the law defining the offense.
2. *Consent to bodily harm.* When conduct is charged to constitute an offense because it causes or threatens bodily harm, consent to such conduct or to the infliction of such harm is a defense only if:
   a. The bodily harm consented to or threatened by the conduct consented to is not serious; or
   b. The conduct and the harm are reasonably foreseeable hazards of joint participation in a lawful athletic contest or competitive sport.
3. *Ineffective consent.* Unless otherwise provided by this Criminal Code or by the law defining the offense, assent does not constitute consent if:
   a. It is given by a person who is legally incompetent to authorize the conduct; or
   b. It is given by a person who by reason of immaturity, mental disease or defect, or intoxication is manifestly unable and known by the actor to be unable to make a reasonable judgment as to the nature or harmfulness of the conduct; or
   c. It is given by a person whose consent is sought to be prevented by the law defining the offense; or
   d. It is induced by force, duress, or deception.

In most states, the law recognizes only four situations where consent justifies otherwise criminal conduct:

- No serious injury results from the consensual crime.
- The injury happens during a sporting event.
- The conduct benefits the consenting person, such as when a patient consents to surgery.
- The consent is to sexual conduct. (Fletcher 1978, 770)

voluntary consent consent was the product of free will, not of force, threat of force, promise, or trickery

knowing consent the person consenting understands what she's consenting to; she's not too young or insane to understand

authorized consent the person consenting has the authority to give consent

Fitting into one of these four exceptions is necessary, but it's not enough to entitle defendants to the defense. They also have to prove that the consent was voluntary, knowing, and authorized. **Voluntary consent** means consent was the product of free will, not of force, threat of force, promise, or trickery. Forgiveness after the commission of a crime doesn't qualify as voluntary consent. **Knowing consent** means the person consenting understands what she's consenting to; she's not too young or insane to understand. **Authorized consent** means the person consenting has the authority to give consent; I can't give consent for someone else for whom I'm not legally responsible.

In our next case, *State v. Shelley* (1997), the court dealt with the sporting event exception.

CASE

*In **State v. Shelley (1997),** Jason Shelley was convicted of second-degree assault, arising out of an incident in which Shelley intentionally punched another basketball player during a game.*

Did he consent to the attack?

State v. Shelley

929 P.2d 489 (Wash. App. 1997)

HISTORY

Jason Shelley was convicted in the Superior Court, King County, of second-degree assault, arising out of an incident in which Shelley intentionally punched another basketball player during a game. Shelley appealed. The Court of Appeals affirmed the conviction.

GROSSE, J.

FACTS

On March 31, 1993, Jason Shelley and Mario Gonzalez played "pickup" basketball on opposing teams at the University of Washington Intramural Activities Building (the IMA). Pickup games are not refereed by an official; rather, the players take responsibility for calling their own fouls.

During the course of three games, Gonzalez fouled Shelley several times. Gonzalez had a reputation for playing overly aggressive defense at the IMA. Toward the end of the evening, after trying to hit the ball away from Shelley, he scratched Shelley's face and drew blood. After getting scratched, Shelley briefly left the game and then returned.

Shelley and Gonzalez have differing versions of what occurred after Shelley returned to the game. According to Gonzalez, while he was waiting for play in the game to return to Gonzalez's side of the court, Shelley suddenly hit him. Gonzalez did not see Shelley punch him. According to Shelley's version of events, when Shelley rejoined the game, he was running down the court and he saw Gonzalez make "a move towards me as if he was maybe going to prevent me from getting the ball."

The move was with his hand up "across my vision." Angry, he "just reacted" and swung. He said he hit him because he was afraid of being hurt, like the previous scratch. He testified that Gonzalez continually beat him up during the game by fouling him hard.

A week after the incident, a school police detective interviewed Shelley and prepared a statement for Shelley to sign based on the interview. Shelley reported to the police that Gonzalez had been "continually slapping and scratching him" during the game. Shelley "had been getting mad" at Gonzalez, and the scratch on Shelley's face was the "final straw."

As the two were running down the court side by side, "I swung my right hand around and hit him with my fist on the right side of his face." Shelley asserted that he also told the detective that Gonzalez waved a hand at him just before Shelley threw the punch and that he told the detective that he was afraid of being injured.

Gonzalez required emergency surgery to repair his jaw. Broken in three places, it was wired shut for six weeks. His treating physician believed that a "significant" blow caused the damage.

During the course of the trial, defense counsel told the court he intended to propose a jury instruction that: "A person legally consents to conduct that causes or threatens bodily harm if the conduct and the harm are reasonably foreseeable hazards of joint participation in a lawful, athletic contest or competitive sport."

Although the trial court agreed that there were risks involved in sports, it stated that "the risk of being intentionally punched by another player is one that I don't think we ever do assume." The court noted, "In basketball you consent to a certain amount of rough contact. If they were both going for a rebound and Mr. Shelley's elbow or even his fist hit Mr. Gonzalez as they were both jumping for the rebound and Mr. Gonzalez's jaw was fractured in exactly the same way then you would have an issue."

Reasoning that "our laws are intended to uphold the public peace and regulate behavior of individuals," the court ruled "that as a matter of law, consent cannot be a defense to an assault." The court indicated that Shelley could not claim consent because his conduct "exceeded" what is considered within the rules of that particular sport:

> Consent is a contract that is contemplated within the rules of the game and that is incidental to the furtherance of the goals of that particular game. If you can show me any rule book for basketball at any level that says an intentional punch to the face in some way is a part of the game, then I would take another look at your argument. I don't believe any such rule book exists.

Later, Shelley proposed jury instructions on the subject of consent:

> An act is not an assault, if it is done with the consent of the person alleged to be assaulted. It is a defense to a charge of second degree assault occurring in the course of an athletic contest if the conduct and the harm are reasonably foreseeable hazards of joint participation in a lawful athletic contest or competitive sport.

The trial court rejected these, and Shelley excepted. The trial court did instruct the jury about self-defense.

OPINION

First, we hold that consent is a defense to an assault occurring during an athletic contest. This is consistent with the law of assault as it has developed in Washington. A person is guilty of second-degree assault if he or she "intentionally assaults another and thereby recklessly inflicts substantial bodily harm."

One common law definition of assault recognized in Washington is "an unlawful touching with criminal intent." At the common law, a touching is unlawful when the person touched did not give consent to it, and it was either harmful or offensive. As our Supreme Court stated in *State v. Simmons*, "Where there is consent, there is no assault." The State argues that because Simmons was a sexual assault case, the defense of consent should be limited to that realm. We decline to apply the defense so narrowly.

Logically, consent must be an issue in sporting events because a person participates in a game knowing that it will involve potentially offensive contact and with this consent the "touchings" involved are not "unlawful." The rationale that courts offer in limiting consent as a defense is that society has an interest in punishing assaults as breaches of the public peace and order, so that an individual cannot consent to a wrong that is committed against the public peace.

Urging us to reject the defense of consent because an assault violates the public peace, the State argues that this principle precludes Shelley from being entitled to argue the consent defense on the facts of his case. If consent cannot be a defense to assault, then most athletic contests would need to be banned because many involve "invasions of one's physical integrity." Because society has chosen to foster sports competitions,

(continues)

(continued)

players necessarily must be able to consent to physical contact and other players must be able to rely on that consent when playing the game. This is the view adopted by the drafters of the Model Penal Code:

> There are, however, situations in which consent to bodily injury should be recognized as a defense to crime. There is the obvious case of participation in an athletic contest or competitive sport, where the nature of the enterprise often involves risk of serious injury. Here, the social judgment that permits the contest to flourish necessarily involves the companion judgment that reasonably foreseeable hazards can be consented to by virtue of participation.

The more difficult question is the proper standard by which to judge whether a person consented to the particular conduct at issue. The State argues that when the conduct in question is not within the rules of a given sport, a victim cannot be deemed to have consented to this act. The trial court apparently agreed with this approach.

Although we recognize that there is authority supporting this approach, we reject a reliance on the rules of the games as too limiting. Rollin M. Perkins in Criminal Law explains:

> The test is not necessarily whether the blow exceeds the conduct allowed by the rules of the game. Certain excesses and inconveniences are to be expected beyond the formal rules of the game. It may be ordinary and expected conduct for minor assaults to occur. However, intentional excesses beyond those reasonably contemplated in the sport are not justified.

Instead, we adopt the approach of the Model Penal Code which provides:

> 2. *Consent to Bodily Injury*. When conduct is charged to constitute an offense because it causes or threatens bodily injury, consent to such conduct or to the infliction of such injury is a defense if:
>   a. the conduct and the injury are reasonably foreseeable hazards of joint participation in a lawful athletic contest or competitive sport or other concerted activity not forbidden by law.

The State argues the law does not allow "the victim to 'consent' to a broken jaw simply by participating in an unrefereed, informal basketball game." This argument presupposes that the harm suffered dictates whether the defense is available or not. This is not the correct inquiry. The correct inquiry is whether the conduct of defendant constituted foreseeable behavior in the play of the game.

Additionally, the injury must have occurred as a byproduct of the game itself. In *State v. Floyd*, a fight broke out during a basketball game and the defendant, who was on the sidelines, punched and severely injured several opposing team members. The defense did not apply because the statute "contemplated a person who commits acts during the course of play." There is a "continuum, or sliding scale, grounded in the circumstances under which voluntary participants engage in sport which governs the type of incidents in which an individual volunteers (i.e., consents) to participate."

The New York courts provide another example. In a football game, while tackling the defendant, the victim hit the defendant. After the play was over and all of the players got off the defendant, the defendant punched the victim in the eye....Initially it may be assumed that the very first punch thrown in the course of the tackle was consented to by defendant. The act of tackling an opponent in the course of a football game may often involve "contact" that could easily be interpreted to be a "punch." Defendant's response after the pileup to complainant's initial act of "aggression" cannot be mistaken. This was not a consented to act. *People v. Freer*, 381 N.Y.S.2d 976, 978 (1976).

The State may argue that the defendant's conduct exceeded behavior foreseeable in the game. Although in "all sports players consent to many risks, hazards and blows," there is "a limit to the magnitude and dangerousness of a blow to which another is deemed to consent." This limit, like the foreseeability of the risks, is determined by presenting evidence to the jury about the nature of the game, the participants' expectations, the location where the game has been played, as well as the rules of the game.

Here, taking Shelley's version of the events as true, the magnitude and dangerousness of Shelley's actions were beyond the limit. There is no question that Shelley lashed out at Gonzalez with sufficient force to land a substantial blow to the jaw, and there is no question but that Shelley intended to hit Gonzalez. There is nothing in the game of basketball, or even rugby or hockey, that would permit consent as a defense to such conduct. Shelley admitted to an assault and was not precluded from arguing that the assault justified self-defense; but justification and consent are not the same inquiry.

We affirm.

QUESTIONS

1. According to the court, why can participants in a sporting event consent to conduct that would otherwise be a crime?
2. Why should they be allowed to consent to such conduct when in other situations (such as those enumerated in the Exploring Further cases that follow) they can't consent?
3. Should individuals be allowed to knowingly and voluntarily consent to the commission of crimes against themselves? Why or why not?
4. Why was Shelley not allowed the defense of consent in this case?
5. Do you agree with the court's decision? Relying on the relevant facts in the case, defend your answer.

YOU *DECIDE*

Can she consent to being assaulted?

State v. Brown

364 A.2d 27 (N.J. 1976)

Facts

Mrs. Brown was an alcoholic. On the day of the alleged crime she had been drinking, apparently to her husband Reginald Brown's displeasure. Acting according to the terms of an agreement between the defendant Reginald Brown and his wife, he punished her by beating her severely with his hands and other objects.

Brown was charged with atrocious assault and battery. He argued he wasn't guilty of atrocious assault and battery because he and Mrs. Brown, the victim, had an understanding to the effect that if she consumed any alcoholic beverages (and/or became intoxicated), he would punish her by physically assaulting her. The trial court refused the defense of consent.

Was Mr. Brown justified because of Mrs. Brown's consent?

Decision

No, said the New Jersey Appellate Court:

The laws are simply and unequivocally clear that the defense of consent cannot be available to a defendant charged with any type of physical assault that causes appreciable injury. If the law were otherwise, it would not be conducive to a peaceful, orderly and healthy society.

This court concludes that, as a matter of law, no one has the right to beat another even though that person may ask for it. Assault and battery cannot be consented to by a victim, for the State makes it unlawful and is not a party to any such agreement between the victim and perpetrator. To allow an otherwise criminal act to go unpunished because of the victim's consent would not only threaten the security of our society but also might tend to detract from the force of the moral principles underlying the criminal law.

Thus, for the reasons given, the State has an interest in protecting those persons who invite, consent to and permit others to assault and batter them. Not to enforce these laws which are geared to protect such people would seriously threaten the dignity, peace, health and security of our society.

Can he consent to being shot?

State v. Fransua

510 P.2d 106 (N.M. Ct. App. 1973)

Facts

Daniel Fransua and the victim were in a bar in Albuquerque. Fransua had been drinking heavily that day and the previous day. Sometime around 3:00 P.M., after an argument, Fransua told the victim he'd shoot him if he had a gun. The victim got up, walked out of the bar, went to his car, took out a loaded pistol, and went back in the bar. He came up to Fransua, laid the pistol on the bar, and said, "There's the gun. If you want to shoot me, go ahead."

(continues)

(continued)

Fransua picked up the pistol, put the barrel next to the victim's head, and pulled the trigger, wounding him seriously.

Was the victim's consent a justification that meant Fransua wasn't guilty of aggravated battery?

Decision

No, said the New Mexico Court of Appeals:

> It is generally conceded that a state enacts criminal statutes making certain violent acts crimes for at least two reasons: One reason is to protect the persons of its citizens; the second, however, is to prevent a breach of the public peace. While we entertain little sympathy for either the victim's absurd actions or the defendant's equally unjustified act of pulling the trigger, we will not permit the defense of consent to be raised in such cases.
>
> Whether or not the victims of crimes have so little regard for their own safety as to request injury, the public has a stronger and overriding interest in preventing and prohibiting acts such as these. We hold that consent is not a defense to the crime of aggravated battery, irrespective of whether the victim invites the act and consents to the battery.

Summary

LO1 Criminal conduct alone isn't enough to establish criminal liability if the defendant's conduct was justified or excused. In justification defenses, defendants admit they were *responsible* for their acts but claim that, under the circumstances, what they did was *right*. In excuse defenses, defendants admit what they did was *wrong* but claim that, under the circumstances, they weren't *responsible* for their actions.

LO1 Both justifications and excuses are affirmative defenses, which require defendants to start matters off by putting forth some evidence in support of their justification or excuse. Perfect defenses, if successful, result in acquittal while imperfect defenses result in the defendant being found guilty of a lesser charge. Mitigating circumstances convince fact finders that the defendant does not deserve the maximum penalty for the crime they committed.

LO2 According to the rule of law, the government has a monopoly on the use of force. Self-defense is a limited exception to the government monopoly on the use of force. To justify the use of deadly force in self-defense, the defendant must reasonable believe that they're faced with the choice kill or be killed, right now!

LO3 The four elements of self-defense are: (1) nonaggressor, meaning that the defender didn't start or provoke the attack; (2) necessity, requiring that the defender reasonably believes deadly force is necessary to repel an *imminent*, deadly attack; (3) proportionality, meaning that deadly force was used only if nondeadly force isn't enough; and (4) a *reasonable* belief that it's necessary to use deadly force to repel the imminent, deadly attack.

LO4 The English common law put the burden on defendants to prove they "retreated to the wall" before acting in self-defense. The American majority "stand-your-ground rule" is based on the idea that a "true man" shouldn't have to flee from attack because he's done nothing wrong to provoke or deserve the attack. This rule gives him the right to protect his family and country, stand his ground, and kill to "defend himself without retreating from any place he has a right to be."

LO5 In the minority of states that follow the retreat rule, two exceptions usually exist: (1) the castle exception allows a defender to stand her ground and use deadly force to fend off an unprovoked attack in the home and; and (2) the cohabitant exception allows people who live in the same home to stand their ground as well. By the late 1990s, battered women were recognized as fitting the "true man protecting his caste" frame; now, every state allows expert witnesses to explain "battered women's syndrome" to judges and juries in cases of self-defense in the home.

LO6 Historically, self-defense meant protecting yourself and the members of your immediate family and, although some states still require this sort of special relationship, the trend is headed in the opposite direction as many states have extended the right to use force to defend *anyone* who needs immediate protection from attack. The defense of home is rooted deeply in the common law idea that "a man's home is his castle" and limited the use of deadly force to nighttime invasions or daytime robberies. Modern statutes limit the use of deadly force to defend occupied homes if it's reasonable to believe the intruders intend to commit violent crimes against the occupants. Deadly force is generally not allowed to protect other property, but nondeadly force can be used to protect our "stuff."

LO7 The new "castle doctrine" laws vastly expand ordinary people's power to defend themselves in their homes, in public places, or anywhere else they have a legal right to be. Supporters of the laws consider them to be a public reassertion of a fundamental right to defend, while critics fear these laws are a "license to kill" rather than a right to self-defense. The new castle doctrine laws have dramatically altered the outcome of cases involving the use of deadly force.

LO8 Like most other defenses, the heart of the choice-of-evils defense is the necessity to prevent imminent danger. Unlike other affirmative defenses, the choice-of-evils defense justifies choosing to commit a lesser crime to avoid a greater harm.

LO9 The defense of consent is rooted in individual autonomy: if mentally competent adults want to be crime victims, no paternalistic government should get in their way. The consent has to voluntary, knowing, and authorized to use consent as a defense to criminal liability.

Key Terms

criminal conduct, p. 164
justification defenses, p. 164
excuse defenses, p. 164
affirmative defenses, p. 164
perfect defenses, p. 164
competency hearings, p. 164
imperfect defense, p. 164
mitigating circumstances, p. 165
initial aggressor, p. 166
withdrawal exception, p. 166
necessity, p. 168
imminence requirement, p. 168
stand-your-ground rule, p. 176
retreat rule, p. 176
castle exception, p. 176
cohabitant exception, p. 177
battered woman's syndrome (BWS), p. 177
curtilage, p. 187
choice-of-evils defense, p. 192
defense of consent, p. 197
voluntary consent, p. 198
knowing consent, p. 198
authorized consent, p. 198

Learning Objectives

1 To understand that defendants who plead an excuse defense admit what they did was wrong but claim that, under the circumstances, they weren't responsible for their actions.

2 To appreciate the long history of the insanity defense, and to know the popular myths and empirical realities surrounding the insanity defense.

3 To understand the difference between insanity and competency when proving the affirmative defense of insanity.

4 To know the four different tests of insanity and which elements of mental capacity, reason, and/or will form the basis of each test.

5 To understand the difference between diminished capacity and diminished responsibility and appreciate how they apply only to homicide.

6 To understand how the law handles the excuse of age and that juvenile court judges can use their discretion to transfer a juvenile to adult criminal court.

7 To know the four elements of duress and appreciate the problem with blaming people *who* are forced to commit crimes.

8 To understand that voluntary intoxication is no excuse for committing a crime but involuntary intoxication is.

9 To understand that entrapment is used in all societies even though it violates a basic purpose of government in free societies: to prevent crime rather than encourage it.

10 To understand why, despite their criticisms, syndrome excuses are, and should be, taken seriously.

6 Defenses to Criminal Liability II

Excuses

Chapter Outline

Starting in young adulthood, Donald Myers III was treated at hospitals in Indiana and Alabama for his mental health issues and was prescribed various anti-psychotic medications. Towards the end of April 2004, Myers's mother, Judy Wininger, noticed that Myers was no longer taking his anti-psychotic medications, and she contacted Northeastern Center, a counseling center where Myers had previously been treated. The hospital prepared a bed for Myers to be admitted upon Wininger's request on April 28, 2004. However, Myers refused to go.

On the evening of April 29, 2004, David Brown was driving in the Silver Lake Trailer Court with his wife, Vicki Brown, and young grandson in the car. Brown heard a loud boom, and when he looked into the rearview mirror, there was a man running towards the vehicle pointing a long gun in the direction of their vehicle. Myers fired the gun in Brown's direction. Brown called 911. Shortly thereafter, Desmond Augenstein saw Myers walking down the middle of the road and saw that Myers was holding a gun. Myers raised the gun and shot twice in Augenstein's direction. Augenstein called 911 to notify police.

Several police officers were dispatched to the area to investigate. As Trooper Smith approached the scene, he saw Myers begin tracking his vehicle with a gun. Myers fired the gun directly at the driver's side window. Trooper Smith ordered Myers to stop. Myers ignored this order and kept walking. Indiana State Police Trooper Kerry Ghent saw Myers with a long gun and yelled for Myers to stop, but Myers appeared to

TABLE 6.1 Three Analytical Steps of Criminal Liability
1. Was there criminal conduct? (Chapters 3 and 4)
2. If there was criminal conduct, was it justified? (Chapter 5)
3. If it wasn't justified, was it excused? (That's where we are now.)

merely look through him and continue walking. Trooper Ghent fired at Myers and knew that Myers was hit near his shoulder when he saw Myers react and turn away.

Trooper Smith and Deputy Knott heard the gunshots and fired upon Myers. Myers retreated into a wooded area along the roadside. The officers immediately established a perimeter around Myers's location to prevent him from exiting out the opposite side. Other law enforcement officials arrived. A negotiator attempted to convince Myers to surrender. Gas was eventually fired into Myers's location in an attempt to force him out into an open space, but Myers remained in the brush.

An armored vehicle was finally utilized to approach Myers, and two members of the tactical team apprehended him. Myers was immediately taken to the hospital due to gunshot wounds to his left shoulder and groin area. The next day, Myers was charged with multiple counts of attempted murder and criminal recklessness.

LO1

In Chapter 5, you learned that defendants who plead defenses of justification accept responsibility for their actions but claim that, under the circumstances (necessity and consent), what they did was justified (Table 6.1, step 2). In this chapter, you learn about defendants who plead excuse. They admit what they did was wrong but claim that, under the circumstances, they weren't responsible for what they did. The best-known excuse is insanity, but you'll learn about others in this chapter, too (Table 6.1, step 3).

Excuse defenses are presented after the *prosecution* has proved its case beyond a reasonable doubt (Table 6.1, step 1) and the *defendant* has *not* proved that her conduct was justified (Table 6.1, step 2). Now, she claims she's excused (Table 6.1, step 3). Legally, she's pleading an affirmative defense. (Recall that in affirmative defenses, defendants have to carry some of the burden of proving they have an excuse that will relieve them of criminal responsibility (see Chapter 2, "The Burden of Proof," pp. 47–48).)

THE INSANITY DEFENSE

Contrary to what most people think, the insanity defense is not a "get out of jail free" pass, a way for fakers to get away with murder. That's the widespread myth. Here's the reality:

- Defendants offer an insanity defense in less than 1 percent of all felony cases, and are successful only about one-quarter of the time.
- Defendants found not guilty by reason of insanity are often confined in mental institutions for many years, and in some cases for a longer time than they would have been incarcerated had they been found guilty.
- Few offenders "fake" insanity; most defendants who plead insanity have a long history of mental illness and prior hospitalizations.
- In the large majority of cases, prosecution and defense expert psychiatrists agree on whether defendants are legally insane.

In this section, we'll look at the history of the insanity defense, the myths and reality surrounding it, and the tests used to determine legal insanity.

History of the Insanity Defense

LO2

In about 350 B.C.E., when the Greek philosopher Plato was old, he recommended in *Laws* that "if anyone be insane, let him not be seen openly in the town, but let his kinfolk watch over him as best they may, under a penalty of a fine" (Walker 1985, 26). By 1350, the English kings were granting pardons to insane criminals, leaving them in the care of guardians to protect them from harming themselves and the neighborhood from their potential wrongdoing. For example, in one case Professor Nigel Walker found, the jury's verdict said that the madman killed his daughter but not "feloniously or with malice aforethought" (27).

A number of high-profile cases, involving attacks on the monarchs or people in their service, led to various tests of insanity. Most focused on impaired reason (mental diseases or defects that impaired the ability to know "good from evil" and later "right from wrong"). In *Rex v. Arnold* (1724), the delusional Edward Arnold attempted to assassinate one of King George III's courtiers. The judge instructed the jury that to succeed in a plea of insanity, Arnold had to prove that he was "a man that is totally deprived of his understanding and memory, and does not know what he is doing, no more than an infant, than a brute, or a wild beast" (765).

Another high-profile case, *Regina v. McNaughtan* (1843), had far and away the most influence on English and U.S. insanity defense law. From 1843, when it was decided, to present U.S. law, with few exceptions and interruptions, it remains the law in the majority of the states and the federal government.

Like almost all the high-profile insanity defense cases, it involved an attack on a powerful political figure. The intended victim was the English Prime Minister, Sir Robert Peel. The attacker was a young Scottish Chartist, Daniel McNaughtan. Chartism was a mid-Victorian activist reform movement with strong support in Scotland. It was feared and hated by the middle and upper classes that viewed Chartists as dangerous radicals and terrorists fomenting class warfare.

McNaughtan was afraid, too. According to his lawyer, he was suffering from the "fierce and fearful delusion" that Sir Robert and his Tory party were his enemies. On January 20, 1843, mistaking Peel's private secretary Edward Drummond for the prime minister, McNaughtan fatally shot Drummond in the back. He was instantly apprehended, locked up in Newgate prison, and put on trial on March 4. He was backed by an enormously competent team of four trial lawyers, nine prominent medical experts, and eight lay witnesses from Glasgow (Moran 1985, 37–38).

Both the defense and the Crown agreed that McNaughtan "was sane on all matters except politics"; the case boiled down to what was a valid defense of insanity. The defense argued that suffering from partial insanity should qualify for the defense. Specifically, McNaughtan acted out of a delusion, and any act during that delusion excused him. The Crown argued that the insane are criminally responsible unless "they're totally incapable of knowing right from wrong" (38) ("wild beasts").

The Crown decided not to rebut the medical testimony claiming that McNaughtan suffered from insane delusions that caused his act of shooting Drummond. At this point, Chief Justice Nicholas Tindal stopped the trial abruptly. The chief justice was impressed with the impartial medical testimony from two medical experts, impartial because neither side paid for their services. The Crown was probably also impressed—in his closing statement to the jury, he withdrew the case. Tindal essentially gave the jury a directed verdict: "If you find the prisoner not guilty...on the ground of insanity...proper care will be taken of him" (39).

After deliberating "less than two minutes, the jury declared, 'We find the defendant not guilty, on the ground of insanity'" (Hermann and Sor 1983, 510). The verdict caused great consternation. The public feared that madmen could kill without fear of punishment. This poem written shortly after captures the public reaction brilliantly:

> Ye people of England: exult and be glad,
> For you're now at the will of the merciless mad.
>
> Why say you that but three authorities reign—
> Crown, Commons, and Lords! You omit the insane!
>
> They're a privileged class, whom no statute controls,
> And their murderous charter exists in their souls.
>
> Do they wish to spill blood—they have only to play
> A few pranks—get asylumed a month and a day
>
> Then heigh! to escape from the mad-doctor's keys,
> And to pistol or stab whomsoever they please.
>
> (Thomas Campbell 1843; qtd. in Hermann and Sor 1983, 500)

Queen Victoria displayed her own consternation when she pressed the prime minister to get Parliament to *force* the judges to "follow the law" (39–40).

> We have seen the trials of Oxford [who almost assassinated the queen] and McNaughtan conducted by the ablest lawyers of the day and they allow and advise the jury to pronounce the verdict of not guilty on account of insanity, whilst everybody is morally convinced that both malefactors were perfectly conscious and aware of what they did! Could not the legislature lay down the [right–wrong] rule that the Lord Chancellor does in his paper, and why could the judges not be bound to interpret the law in this and no other sense in their charges to the Juries? (Herman and Sor 1983, 510)

The queen's consternation reflected the growing public anger expressed in the poem. The muddled state of the insanity defense prompted the House of Lords to ask the common law judges to attend one of their sessions and advise them on exactly what the law of insanity was. This would enable them to pass adequate legislation to codify the insanity defense. On June 19, just five months after Daniel McNaughtan shot Edward Drummond, the judges obliged. The *McNaughtan rules*, which codified the insanity defense, comprise the elements of the right–wrong test that remain the law in most states and the federal government today. (See "Right–Wrong Test" later.)

Before we turn to the right–wrong and other insanity tests, we need to note that these high-profile insanity defense trials were attacks on royal and legislative power during times of war and domestic unrest. In other words, they were clearly the product of their times. Medical and legal arguments were mere props in morality plays, of good and evil, right and wrong, social peace and chaos. Professor Moran (1985), the acclaimed authority on the insanity defense and McNaughtan's case, writes:

> Formal legal doctrine and actual courtroom decisions are often shaped by the same social forces that influence all other human endeavors. The view that the insanity defense is a legal loophole through which the guilty defendant often escapes punishment seems too narrow, for it can also be a powerful mechanism by which the court retains the authority to confine a defendant who is otherwise beyond the reach of the criminal law. James Hadfield, although he was acquitted spent the last 41 years of his

life in confinement. And Daniel McNaughtan spent his last 22 years in confinement following his acquittal by reason of insanity. (42)

The Insanity Defense: Myths and Reality

LO2

The public badly misunderstands "insanity," the defense of insanity, and how the defense actually works today—just as they have throughout its history (see Criminal Law in Focus, "The Insanity Defense: Popular Myths and Empirical Reality"). Let's clear up some misunderstandings and then look at some of the myths and the realities about the defense of insanity.

First, insanity doesn't mean "mental disease or mental defect." *Mental disease* (also called "mental illness") and *mental defect* are medical terms; *insanity* is a legal term. But—and here's one source of confusion and misunderstanding—mental disease and mental defect are part of the definition of insanity. What psychiatry calls "mental disease" or "mental defect" might, or might not, be insanity. Mental disease and mental defect are legal **insanity** only when the disease or defect affects a person's reason. In a few states, they're legal insanity when they affect a person's will (willpower)—namely, the power to control your actions.

insanity the legal term that refers to a mental disease or defect that impairs the reason and/or will to control actions

The Insanity Defense

Popular Myths and Empirical Reality

MYTH	REALITY
The insanity defense is overused.	All empirical analyses are consistent: "the public, legal profession and—specifically—legislators 'dramatically' and 'grossly' overestimate both the frequency and the success rate of the insanity plea" (Perlin 1990). Less than one percent (0.87%) of defendants plead insanity, and a mere 23.55 percent of those who do plead, succeed (Valdes 2005, 1723).
The use of the insanity defense is limited to murder cases.	In one jurisdiction where the data have been closely studied, slightly fewer than one-third of the successful insanity pleas entered over an eight-year period were reached in cases involving a victim's death. Further, individuals who plead insanity in murder cases are no more successful at being found "Not Guilty by Reason of Insanity" (NGRI) than persons charged with other crimes (Perlin 1990).
There's no risk to the defendant who pleads insanity.	Defendants who asserted an insanity defense at trial and who were ultimately found guilty of their charges served significantly longer sentences than defendants tried on similar charges who didn't assert the insanity defense (Perlin 1990).
NGRI acquittees are quickly released from custody.	Of all the individuals found NGRI over an eight-year period in one jurisdiction, only 15 percent had been released from all restraints; 35 percent remained in institutional custody; and 47 percent were under partial court restraint following conditional release (Perlin 1990).
NGRI acquittees spend much less time in custody than do defendants convicted of the same offenses.	NGRI acquittees actually spend almost double the amount of time that defendants convicted of similar charges spend in prison settings and often face a lifetime of post-release judicial oversight (Perlin 1990).

(continues)

(continued)

Criminal defendants who plead insanity are usually faking.	Of 141 individuals found NGRI in one jurisdiction over an eight-year period, there was no dispute that 115 were schizophrenic (including 38 of the 46 cases involving a victim's death), and in only 3 cases was the diagnostician unable to specify the nature of the patient's mental illness (Perlin 1990).
Criminal defense attorneys employ the insanity defense plea solely to "beat the rap."	First, the level of representation afforded to mentally disabled defendants is frequently substandard. Second, the few studies that have been done paint an entirely different picture: lawyers may enter an insanity plea to obtain immediate mental health treatment for their client, as a plea-bargaining device to ensure that their client ultimately receives mandatory mental health care, and to avoid malpractice litigation. Third, the best available research suggests that jury biases exist relatively independent of lawyer functioning and are generally "not induced by attorneys" (Perlin 1990).

Sources: Perlin 1990, 648–55; Valdes 2005, 1722–25.

Another source of confusion, and a dominant myth, is that the consequences resulting from the "not guilty by reason of insanity" (NGRI) verdict are too lenient or nonexistent. It's widely believed that not guilty by reason of insanity means that defendants go home. Where do they get this idea? From a few high-profile cases, such as John Hinckley. The world watched as television cameras caught Hinckley stepping out of a crowd, pulling out a revolver, shooting, wounding, and almost killing President Reagan. Hinckley also shot and permanently disabled James Brady, the president's press secretary. Months later, the world watched as Hinckley was found not guilty by reason of insanity. What the world doesn't see on camera or hear any talk about is that Hinckley remains tightly secured in St. Elizabeth's Hospital. Similarly, you know—but very few do—that Daniel McNaughtan also never went free, and neither did most of the other high-profile defendants who attacked powerful people.

Contrary to widespread belief, few defendants plead the insanity defense (only a few thousand a year in the United States, or less than 1 percent of all criminal cases). Of those few who do plead insanity, only about 25 percent ever succeed.

civil commitment a noncriminal (civil) proceeding in which courts have the power to decide if defendants who were insane when they committed their crimes are still insane

The few who "succeed" don't go free. In a noncriminal (civil) proceeding, called civil commitment, courts have to decide if defendants who were insane when they committed their crimes are still insane. If they are—and courts almost always decide they are—they're locked up in maximum-security prisons called "hospitals." And, like John Hinckley, they stay there for a long time—until they're no longer "mentally ill and dangerous"—often for the rest of their lives.

The case of John Hinckley is an excellent example. Hinckley shot and almost killed President Reagan in an attempt to assassinate him to impress the actress Jodie Foster. (Hinckley was obsessed with Foster, whom he'd never met.) Hinckley was found not guilty by reason of insanity. The public was outraged, believing that Hinckley "walked" for attempting to assassinate the president, but Hinckley still isn't free.

LO3 Proving Insanity

The defense of insanity not only poses definition problems but also gives rise to difficulties in proving insanity at two critical times:

1. When the crime was committed (sanity).
2. When the defendant is charged and tried (competency).

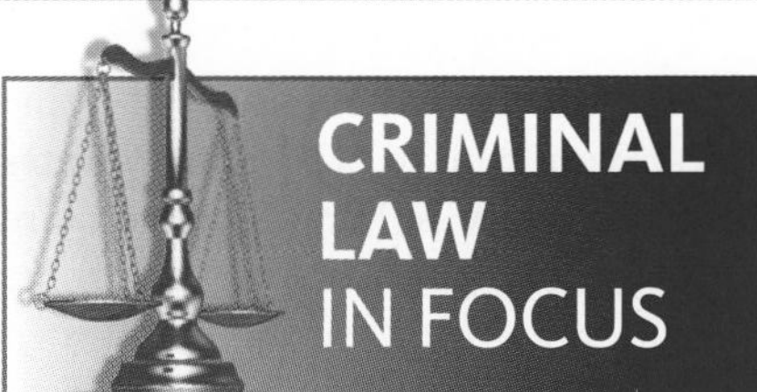

Competence and Sanity: Critical Differences

	COMPETENCE	SANITY
Definition	Whether the defendant has the mental capacity to (1) understand the legal proceedings and (2) to consult with her lawyer and aid in her defense.	Depends on whether the defendant satisfies the elements of the state's definition of insanity, namely the right–wrong; irresistible impulse; MPC substantial capacity; or *Durham* test
Decision Maker	Judge	Jury (or judge in bench trials)
Time of determination	Before court proceedings start	At the end of the trial with verdict
Raising issue	Defendant, prosecutor, or judge	Defendant by affirmative defense rules
Legal Basis	Due process clause, U.S. Constitution, and federal statutes	Each state has its own definition.
Timeframe	Defendant's state of mind at the time of pre-trial and trial proceedings	Defendant's state of mind when the crime was committed
Consequences	Interruption in court proceedings until defendant's sanity is restored. During the delay defendants are expected to receive treatment. In serious crimes, this treatment will take place in a psychiatric hospital.	Defendants found insane don't get a "get out of jail free" ticket. Commitment proceedings following trial order them confined in psychiatric hospitals where they may remain for longer than if they'd gone to prison and served their full sentence.

Those writing and talking about the insanity defense are often sloppy in separating these two critical times and making their significance clear. (I plead guilty to committing this offense in earlier editions of this book.) I hope the "Criminal Law in Focus" pays my debt to my readers.

States vary as to who has to prove insanity at each of these times and how convincingly they have to do so. [See *Myers III v. State* excerpt earlier on proof of insanity, and *State v. Belew* excerpt later under post-traumatic stress syndrome (PTSD).] The Hinckley trial made these questions the subject of heated debate and considerable legislative "reform" in the 1980s.

Federal law required the government to prove Hinckley's sanity beyond a reasonable doubt. So if Hinckley's lawyers could raise a doubt in jurors' minds about his sanity, the jury had to acquit him. That means that even though the jury thought Hinckley was sane, if they weren't convinced beyond a reasonable doubt that he was, they had to acquit him.

And that's just what happened: the jury did believe Hinckley was sane but had their doubts, so they acquitted him. In 1984, the federal Comprehensive Crime Control Act (Federal Criminal Code and Rules 1988, § 17[b]) shifted the burden of proof from the government having to prove sanity beyond a reasonable doubt to defendants having to prove they were insane by clear and convincing evidence.

Most states don't follow the federal standard; they call insanity an affirmative defense. As an affirmative defense, sanity and, therefore, responsibility are presumed. The practical reason for the presumption saves the government the time and effort to prove sanity in the vast number of cases where insanity isn't an issue. In that sense, it's like concurrence: it's necessary but practically never an issue (*Clark v. Arizona* 2006).

To overcome the sanity presumption, the defense has the burden to offer some evidence of insanity. If they do, the burden shifts to the government to prove sanity. States differ as to how heavy the government's burden to prove sanity is. Some states require proof beyond a reasonable doubt; some require clear and convincing evidence; and some require a preponderance of the evidence. There's a trend in favor of shifting the burden to defendants and making that burden heavier. This is both because Hinckley's trial generated antagonism toward the insanity defense and because of growing hostility toward rules that the public believes coddle criminals (ALI 1985 [3], 226; Perlin 1989–90).

LO4 Tests of Insanity

It might be used only rarely, but the insanity defense stands for two important moral ideals—familiar to you by now: (1) it's right to blame only people who are responsible, and (2) if we can't blame them, it's wrong to punish them. Four tests determine whether people with mental disease or defects aren't responsible enough to blame and punish. In other words, they're excused from criminal liability:

1. *Right–wrong test (the McNaughtan rule)*. The oldest rule, it's used in 28 states and the federal courts (*Clark v. Arizona* 2006, slip opinion, majority 9).
2. *Irresistible impulse test*. Only a few jurisdictions use this rule (LaFave 2003b, 389).
3. *Product test (Durham rule)*. It's followed only in New Hampshire.
4. *Substantial capacity test (the MPC test)*. This was the majority rule until John Hinckley attempted to murder President Reagan in 1981. It's still the rule in 14 jurisdictions (*Clark v. Arizona* 2006, slip opinion, majority, 10) but not in federal courts, where it was abolished in 1984 and replaced with a return to the right–wrong test.

reason psychologists call it "cognition"; the capacity to tell right from wrong

will psychologists call it "volition," most of us call it "willpower"; in the insanity tests, it refers to defendants' power to control their actions

All four tests look at defendants' mental capacity, but they differ in what they're looking for. The right–wrong test focuses exclusively on reason—psychologists call it "cognition"—that is, on the capacity to tell right from wrong. The other tests focus on reason and/or will. Will—psychologists call it "volition"—is what most of us call "willpower"; in the insanity tests, it refers to defendants' power to control their actions.

LO4 THE RIGHT–WRONG TEST (*McNAUGHTAN* RULE)

right–wrong test (also called the **McNaughtan rule**) the defendant suffered a defect of reason caused by a disease of the mind, and, consequently, at the time of the act didn't know what she was doing or that the act was wrong

Boiled down to its essence, there are two elements to the right–wrong test (the McNaughtan rule) created in *McNaughtan*:

1. The defendant suffered a defect of reason caused by a disease of the mind.
2. Consequently, at the time of the act she did not know:
   a. the nature and quality of the act (she didn't know what she was doing) *or*
   b. that the act was wrong.

Although the right–wrong test was adopted quickly and has been followed almost exclusively in the United States for over a century, it has always had strong critics among both lawyers and psychiatrists. According to both, cognition is only *part* of the human psyche and can't alone determine human behavior (Hermann and Sor 1983, 512).

mental disease most courts define it as psychosis, mostly paranoia and schizophrenia

There's also lots of back and forth in the courts about just what the words in the test, namely "disease," "defect," "know," and "wrong," mean. Statutes rarely give the courts much guidance, leaving them to "legislate" judicially on the matter. Most courts say that mental disease refers to two psychoses, paranoia and schizophrenia. It doesn't include personality disorders, such as psychopathic and sociopathic personalities that lead to criminal or antisocial conduct. Mental defect refers to mental retardation or brain damage severe enough to make it impossible to know what you're doing, or if you know, you don't know that it's wrong.

mental defect refers to mental retardation or brain damage severe enough to make it impossible to know what you're doing, or if you know, you don't know that it's wrong

In most states, "know" means cognition, which means "intellectual awareness." Some states require more—that defendants understand or "appreciate" (grasp the true significance of) their actions (Freud's "There's knowing, and there's *knowing*"). Most courts don't define the term, leaving juries to define it by applying it to the facts of specific cases as they see fit. The "nature and quality of the act" means you don't know what you're doing (ALI 1985 1:2, 174–76). (To use an old law school example, "If a man believes he's squeezing lemons when in fact he's strangling his wife," he doesn't know the "nature and quality of his act.")

Deciding what "wrong" means has created problems. Some states require that defendants didn't know their conduct was legally wrong; others say it means morally wrong. In *People v. Schmidt* (1915), Schmidt confessed to killing Anna Aumuller by slitting her throat. He pleaded insanity, telling physicians who examined him that

> he had heard the voice of God calling upon him to kill the woman as a sacrifice and atonement. He confessed to a life of unspeakable excesses and hideous crimes, broken, he said, by spells of religious ecstasy and exaltation. In one of these moments, believing himself, he tells us, in the visible presence of God, he committed this fearful crime. (325)

The trial judge instructed the jury that Schmidt had to know that slitting Aumuller's throat was a crime. The New York Court of Appeals disagreed: "We are unable to accept the view that the word 'wrong'...is to receive such a narrow construction." The Court of Appeals recommended this as a suitable jury instruction:

> Knowledge of the nature and quality of the act has reference to its physical nature and quality, and that knowledge that it is wrong refers to its moral side; that to know that the act is wrong, the defendant must know that it is "contrary to law, and contrary to the accepted standards of morality, and then he added...that it must be known to be contrary to the laws of God and man." (336)

In our next case excerpt *Myers III v. State* (2015), the Indiana Supreme Court upheld Donald W. Myers III (Defendant)'s conviction of four counts of attempted murder. The jury found him guilty but mentally ill.

CASE

*In **Myers III v. State (2015),** Donald W. Myers III was convicted and found guilty but mentally ill, of four counts of attempted murder. Myers appealed.*

Was he guilty but mentally ill?

Myers III v. State

Indiana Supreme Court (2015)
No. 76S03–1407-CR-493

HISTORY

Donald W. Myers III (Defendant) was convicted and found guilty but mentally ill, following a jury trial in the Circuit Court, Steuben County, Allen N. Wheat, J., of four counts of attempted murder on the basis that he was guilty, but mentally ill. Myers appealed.

(continues)

(continued)

The Indiana Supreme Court, David, J., held that (1) the verdict was supported by the evidence;...(3) the sentence of 30 years consecutive on each count was not inappropriate, and Affirmed.

DAVID, J., joined by RUSH, CJ., DICKSON and MASSA, JJ.

Donald W. Myers, III, has a history of mental illness, and has been diagnosed with paranoid schizophrenia. Unprovoked, Myers fired a shotgun several times at multiple vehicles, including a police cruiser. Myers was ultimately convicted on four counts of attempted murder. The jury found Myers guilty but mentally ill. Myers claims that no reasonable jury could have reached this conclusion and that he should have been found not guilty by reason of insanity....

We seek to emphasize the great adherence our judicial system affords to the right of a trial by jury and the verdicts reached by those juries. The U.S. Supreme Court has declared that "the basic purpose of a trial is the determination of truth...and it is the jury to whom we have entrusted the responsibility...." *Brown v. Louisiana*, 447 U.S. 323, 334 (1980) This Court has also acknowledged that the jury trial is a "fundamental right in our democratic judicial system that must be scrupulously guarded against encroachment." Having completed our review, we affirm the jury's verdict finding Myers guilty but mentally ill.

FACTS

In 2000, Donald W. Myers, III, was diagnosed with paranoid schizophrenia. Starting in young adulthood, Myers was treated at hospitals in Indiana and Alabama for his mental health issues and was prescribed various anti-psychotic medications. In 2004, Myers was living with his mother at the Silver Lake Trailer Court off of U.S. 20. Towards the end of April 2004, Myers's mother, Judy Wininger, noticed that Myers was no longer taking his anti-psychotic medications, and she contacted Northeastern Center, a counseling center where Myers had previously been treated. The hospital prepared a bed for Myers to be admitted upon Wininger's request on April 28, 2004. However, Myers refused to go.

On the evening of April 29, 2004, David Brown was driving in the Silver Lake Trailer Court with his wife, Vicki Brown, and young grandson in the car. Brown heard a loud boom, and when he looked into the rearview mirror, there was a man running towards the vehicle pointing a long gun in the direction of their vehicle. Then, another gunshot was fired in the direction of Brown's vehicle. Brown drove the vehicle out of Silver Lake onto U.S. 20, and saw the man who fired the weapon running alongside the road. Brown called 911 and gave a description of the man. The man firing the weapon was later identified as Myers.

Shortly thereafter, Desmond Augenstein was driving westbound on U.S. 20 when he saw Myers walking down the middle of the road heading eastbound. Augenstein saw a vehicle coming the opposite direction and turned around to check on Myers's well-being. Augenstein then saw that Myers was holding a gun, and he quickly turned the vehicle back around. Myers raised the gun and shot twice in Augenstein's direction. Augenstein was driving with the windows down and heard bullets flying by the window. He also called 911 to notify police.

Several police officers were dispatched to the area to investigate. Indiana State Police Trooper Lionel Smith located Myers standing partially submerged in a ditch along U.S. 20 on the opposite side of the road from where Trooper Smith was driving. As Trooper Smith got closer, he saw Myers approach the white fog line of the road and begin tracking his vehicle with a gun. Once Myers was parallel to the police cruiser, he fired the gun directly at the driver's side window. Trooper Smith turned his vehicle around, and once he stopped his police cruiser behind Myers, he got out of the vehicle and ordered Myers to stop. However, Myers ignored this order and kept walking at a normal pace. During this time, Steuben County Deputy Sheriff Phillip Knott joined Trooper Smith, and the two together continued to follow behind Myers, ordering him to stop.

Indiana State Police Trooper Kerry Ghent was approaching the area from the opposite direction, and after hearing over dispatch that shots had been fired at Trooper Smith, he pulled his vehicle across the westbound lanes of U.S. 20 to block traffic. He got out of his vehicle and saw Myers with a long gun walking towards him. Trooper Ghent yelled for Myers to stop, but Myers appeared to merely look through him and continue walking. After Myers refused to stop and drop his weapon, Trooper Ghent fired at Myers and knew that Myers was hit near his shoulder when he saw Myers react and turn away. Trooper Smith and Deputy Knott heard the gunshots and did not know whether Myers or Trooper Ghent had fired. Both officers fired upon Myers when he turned and started approaching them, at which time Myers retreated into a wooded area along the roadside.

The officers immediately established a perimeter around Myers's location to prevent him from exiting out the opposite side. The police vehicles were repositioned to shine spotlights in the direction where Myers was hiding to get better visibility. As other law enforcement officials arrived, a visual was kept on Myers while a negotiator attempted to convince him to surrender. Gas was eventually fired into Myers's location in an attempt to force him out into an open space, but Myers remained in the brush. An armored vehicle was finally utilized to approach Myers, and two members of the tactical team apprehended him. Myers was immediately taken to the hospital due to gunshot wounds to his left shoulder and groin area.

At the hospital, a police officer was stationed outside Myers's hospital room. Myers did not want to talk to police, and made some statements to his mother indicating that he wanted an attorney. Specifically, Myers told his mother that he wanted to sue the police for shooting at him.

The next day, Myers was charged with multiple counts of attempted murder and criminal recklessness. Shortly thereafter, defense counsel filed a notice of defense of mental disease or defect. After psychological evaluations were conducted, Myers was determined to lack the capacity to understand the nature of his criminal charges or to assist in his defense. Myers was placed in the custody of the Division of Mental Health & Addiction Services and was assigned to be institutionalized at the Logansport State Hospital to receive further treatment and evaluation.

In July 2009, the Logansport State Hospital indicated that Myers had regained competency enough to stand trial. However, after two designated medical experts conducted another competency evaluation of Myers, he was again found to be incompetent to stand trial. It was not until April 16, 2013, that Myers's jury trial finally commenced. The jury returned verdicts of guilty but mentally ill on the four counts of Class A felony attempted murder.

Myers was sentenced to thirty (30) years on each count to be served consecutively, for an aggregate sentence of one hundred and twenty (120) years. Myers appealed his convictions and sentence.

I. INSANITY DEFENSE

To be convicted of a criminal offense, the State must prove each element of the offense beyond a reasonable doubt. Criminal responsibility can be avoided if the defendant can successfully raise and establish the insanity defense. To successfully assert this defense, an individual must prove by a preponderance of the evidence: "(1) that he or she suffers from a mental illness and (2) that the mental illness rendered him or her unable to appreciate the wrongfulness of his or her conduct at the time of the offense." Thus, proof of mental illness alone is insufficient.

In the case before us, Myers asserted an insanity defense, and the jury found him guilty but mentally ill. It is not disputed that Myers suffered from a mental illness. Since 2000, Myers has been diagnosed with schizophrenia. Therefore, the only remaining question for the purposes of Myers's insanity defense is whether his mental illness prevented him from understanding the wrongfulness of his conduct at the time of the offense.

It is for the trier of fact to determine whether the defendant appreciated the wrongfulness of his conduct at the time of the offense. The defendant is in the position of having to appeal a negative judgment. A reviewing court will reverse *only when the evidence is without conflict* and *leads only to the conclusion* that the defendant was insane when the crime was committed. The reviewing court will not reweigh the evidence or assess the credibility of witnesses but will consider only the evidence most favorable to the judgment and the reasonable and logical inferences to be drawn therefrom.

At trial, the experts who conducted psychological evaluations of Myers unanimously agreed that Myers's mental illness made him incapable of understanding the wrongfulness of his conduct at the time of the offense.

Wininger, Myers's mother, did not see Myers on the day of the offense, but she testified that the day before the shooting took place he was not in his right mind.

Thus, only the experts gave an opinion on Myers's mental state at the time of the offense....

Indiana precedent has clearly established that unanimous expert testimony alone is not determinative where there is conflicting lay opinion testimony or demeanor evidence also presented at trial. This Court has addressed several cases where insanity defenses were unsuccessful, even in light of nonconflicting expert testimony that the defendants were insane at the time of the offense....

In each instance, there has been other sufficient probative evidence from which a conflicting inference of sanity reasonably could be drawn. For example,

(continues)

(continued)

demeanor evidence, when considered in light of the other evidence can permit a jury to draw a reasonable inference of sanity. This is true because testimony regarding behavior before, during, and after a crime may be more indicative of actual mental health at the time of the crime than mental exams conducted weeks or months later.

Although Myers had a history of mental illness, he had seemingly been coping better with his mental illness over the past several years. He had been stable on his medications and had not been hospitalized for three years. Furthermore, Wininger denied that Myers suffered from delusions. Myers had never met the individuals who he shot at, and nothing in the record indicates that he had ever attacked any other individuals due to delusions regarding his believed involvement in the military or CIA. Most significantly, Myers did nothing during the incident itself that explicitly demonstrated he was suffering from a delusion at that time. Consideration of the specific evidence presented at this trial is necessary to determine whether a conflicting inference of sanity could have been made.

The State presented testimony from victims and multiple eyewitnesses describing how the incident unfolded. Both of the Browns testified to Myers running after their vehicle, pointing a long gun directly at them and firing. Augenstein also testified that Myers pointed a gun directly at his vehicle and fired. Trooper Smith explained in even greater detail that Myers walked up to the fog line and tracked his police cruiser with a gun as he drove closer to Myers. Then, Myers held the gun at waist level, which was directly in line with Trooper Smith's head, and fired when the police cruiser was directly parallel to him. Trooper Smith heard the pellets from the gun hitting the driver-side window of the police cruiser.

Multiple law enforcement officers also testified to Myers's refusal to obey orders instructing him to stop and put his weapon down. When Myers was eventually fired upon by police due to his refusal to put his weapon down, he fled into a brushy wooded area near the road. Myers remained hidden for over two hours while a police negotiator tried to convince him to surrender. Even after gas was fired into the area where Myers was hiding, he remained. A tactical team finally approached Myers in an armored vehicle.

Additionally, when law enforcement instructed Myers to put his hands up, Myers responded in a rational manner by explaining that he could only raise one arm because he had been shot in the shoulder. Myers was eventually apprehended and taken to the hospital where he was treated for his gunshot injuries. While at the hospital, Myers did not want to talk to police and alluded to his mother that he wanted an attorney in order to sue the police for shooting at him. Upon further investigation, shotgun shells were found in Myers's vest pocket. The State argued that Myers had consciously picked up the casings after they were fired in order to conceal evidence linking his weapon to the shooting.

Based upon the circumstantial evidence provided above, it would be possible for a reasonable jury to conclude that Myers was able to appreciate the wrongfulness of his conduct at the time of the offense.

Some of Myers's behaviors have even been recognized by this Court as demonstrating consciousness of wrongdoing. First, evidence of flight may be considered as circumstantial evidence of consciousness of guilt. Additionally, evidence of an attempt to avoid arrest also tends to show guilt. Furthermore, Myers's rational communication with police immediately before his apprehension could serve to corroborate a reasonable inference by the jury that Myers was aware of the wrongfulness of his conduct.

The defense relied upon expert testimony, which was based upon evaluations of Myers that were conducted months after the incident occurred. Dr. Herbert Trier evaluated Myers on one occasion, six years after the incident occurred. Dr. David Lombard conducted two evaluations of Myers, one which was approximately two months after the incident and another approximately six years after the incident. Dr. Lombard explained that because Myers claimed that he never had a gun or fired a weapon that night, he could not say how the defendant's delusions were affecting his thoughts at the time he shot the gun. Furthermore, Dr. Lombard did not interview any police or eyewitnesses, and Dr. Trier also testified that he did not review police reports or any written statements regarding the incident. It was within the province of the jury to give less weight to expert testimony that relied upon evaluations of Myers months and years after the incident than to the testimony of individuals actually present at the time of the offense.

Wininger did provide some lay opinion testimony that Myers was not in his right mind the day before, that he had stopped taking his medication, and that she had called his doctor to arrange a bed for him at the hospital. However, her testimony at trial indicated inconsistencies. Wininger testified that she had noticed that Myers was responding slowly, but did not think that he was having delusions. Moreover, in her testimony regarding a prior deposition, she stated that she had noticed nothing different about Myers leading up to the incident.

Despite the evidence presented by the State, reasonable minds could interpret a conflict in the evidence regarding Myers's sanity at the time of the offense. Myers's actions could be interpreted as calculated and deliberate when he aimed a gun and fired directly at multiple victims. Additionally, Myers's fleeing from police and attempts to avoid arrest could also indicate a level of consciousness that he had done something punishable. Furthermore, Myers's only verbal communication with law enforcement prior to his apprehension was seemingly rational and cognizant of what was being requested of him. Myers sensibly explained that he was unable to comply with the police request to raise both arms because he had been shot.

Finally, Myers's demeanor after the incident at the hospital could also lead an individual to believe Myers was cognizant of the wrongfulness of his conduct. Even though Myers made statements that he wanted an attorney so he could sue the police for shooting at him, a jury could still determine that this demonstrated some understanding that shooting at people is wrong.

Though there was evidence that could also support the conclusion that Myers was insane at the time of the crime, it is not necessary that the court find the circumstantial evidence excludes every reasonable hypothesis of innocence. It need only be demonstrated that inferences may reasonably be drawn which support the finding of guilt. It is not within the purview of this Court to reverse the jury's verdict simply because a more reasonable inference could be made. Rather, the fact that a conflicting inference can be made is controlling. For example, while fleeing and hiding from the police could be consistent with the fact that Myers was suffering from a delusion at the time of the offense, a jury could also infer that this is evidence demonstrating Myers's understanding of the wrongfulness of his conduct.

It is not the role of this Court to reweigh the evidence presented at trial and make a determination on which of those inferences the jury should have made, or to determine what reasonable inferences could have been drawn by the jury. Based on the evidence presented at trial, it is possible for a jury to have made a reasonable inference that Myers was mentally ill but still able to understand the wrongfulness of his conduct at the time of the offense. Therefore, Myers's convictions on four counts of attempted murder are affirmed.

III. APPROPRIATENESS OF SENTENCE

Under Indiana Appellate Rule 7(B), a reviewing court may revise a sentence upon determining that the sentence is "inappropriate in light of the nature of the offense and the character of the offender." This determination "turns on our sense of the culpability of the defendant, the severity of the crime, the damage done to others, and myriad other factors that come to light in a given case." We recognize that "the principal role of appellate review should be to attempt to leaven the outliers but not to achieve a perceived 'correct' result in each case."

In the present case, Myers was convicted of four counts of Class A felony attempted murder. The possible sentence that can be assigned for a Class A felony ranges from twenty to fifty years, with thirty years being the advisory sentence. *See* Ind.Code § 35-50-2-4. Myers was sentenced to thirty years for each count of attempted murder to be served consecutively, making his aggregate sentence one hundred and twenty years.

After reviewing the aggravating factors pronounced by the trial court, and in consideration of the fact that the advisory sentence was imposed, it is our collective judgment that the sentence imposed by the trial court was not inappropriate.

Furthermore, with a few exceptions, it is within the trial court's discretion whether to order sentences be served concurrently or consecutively. Whether the counts involve one or multiple victims is highly relevant to the decision to impose consecutive sentences.... Here, multiple victims were fired upon, one of which was a young child and another a police officer. We cannot conclude that the trial court abused its discretion in deciding that Myers's sentences should be served consecutively.

CONCLUSION

There was sufficient evidence for a jury to draw a reasonable inference that the defendant was able to appreciate the wrongfulness of his conduct at the time of the offense. The admission of testimony

(continues)

(continued)

regarding Myers's convoluted request for counsel and refusal to speak to police did not constitute a due process violation. In addition, Myers's sentence is not inappropriate given the nature of the offense and his character, nor was it inappropriate for the trial court to order his sentences to be served consecutively. Therefore, we affirm Myers's convictions of guilty but mentally ill, and affirm his sentence of one hundred and twenty years for four counts of Class A felony attempted murder.

DISSENT

RUCKER, J.

Where there is no conflict among the expert opinions that the defendant was insane at the time of the offense, there must be other evidence of probative value from which a conflicting inference of sanity can be drawn. Such probative evidence is usually in the form of lay opinion testimony that conflicts with the experts or demeanor evidence that, when considered in light of the other evidence, permits a reasonable inference of sanity to be drawn.

The majority acknowledges, "the experts who conducted psychological evaluations of Myers unanimously agreed that Myers's mental illness made him incapable of understanding the wrongfulness of his conduct at the time of the offense." And except for Myers's mother who said the day before the shootings Myers was "not in his right mind," there was no other lay or expert testimony that gave an opinion as to Myers's mental state at the time of the offense. As such there must then exist other evidence of probative value from which a conflicting inference of sanity can be drawn.

And the only other evidence left in this case is that of demeanor. Even where there is no conflict among the experts and the lay witnesses, a finding that a defendant was sane at the time of the crime still may be sustained by probative *demeanor evidence* from which a conflicting inference of sanity may be drawn. Demeanor is useful because a defendant's behavior before, during, and after a crime may be more indicative of actual mental health at the time of the crime than mental exams conducted weeks or months later.

While not saying so in express terms the majority appears to rely on such evidence pointing out for example the testimony of multiple witnesses describing how the incident unfolded. However, although demeanor evidence often is useful, there are limits to its probative value. First, demeanor evidence is of more limited value when the defendant has a long history of mental illness with psychosis....

The proposition that a jury may infer that a person's actions before and after a crime are indicative of his actual mental health at the time of the crime is logical when dealing with a defendant who is not prone to delusional or hallucinogenic episodes. However, when a defendant has a serious and well-documented mental disorder, such as schizophrenia, one that causes him to see, hear, and believe realities that do not exist, such logic collapses.

Myers has a long mental illness history of paranoid schizophrenia. As one of the experts summed up in his report:

> Based on Mr. Myers documented history of schizophrenic symptoms, his history of thought disorder, hallucinations and delusions, and his symptom pattern on the day of the incidents in question, it is this evaluator's clinical opinion that Mr. Myers was suffering from a mental health condition at the time of his offenses and that mental health condition (schizophrenia) incapacitated his understanding of right and wrong and his ability to control his actions.

All other experts presented similar evaluations. I agree with my colleagues on the Court of Appeals that "the jury clearly erred in rejecting Myers's insanity defense." Accordingly I would reverse Myers's four Class A felony attempted murder convictions.

QUESTIONS

1. State the elements of Indiana's version of the right–wrong test.
2. List all the facts relevant to each element of the test.
3. Summarize the trial court's reasons for ruling that Donald Myers was not insane at the time of the crime.
4. Summarize the majority's arguments that Myers was "Guilty but mentally ill."
5. Summarize why the dissenters reasons why the trial court judge's verdict should not be overturned.
6. Which is the *best* argument? Defend your answer.

THE IRRESISTIBLE IMPULSE TEST

LO4

Just because you know something is wrong—even if you fully appreciate its wrongfulness—doesn't mean you can stop yourself from doing it. (I used to be fat. I knew and fully appreciated the "wrongfulness" of overeating. I can remember so many times knowing those french fries were really bad for me, but I just couldn't stop myself from shoving them in.) Critics who faulted the narrow cognitive bent of the right–wrong test recommended bringing will, or volition, into the picture (it was an equal part of the picture during the Middle Ages). According to the irresistible impulse test, we can't blame or deter people who, because of a mental disease or defect, know that what they're doing is "wrong" but can't bring their actions into line with their knowledge of right and wrong.

irresistible impulse test we can't blame or deter people who, because of a mental disease or defect know, that what they're doing is "wrong" but can't bring their actions into line with their knowledge of right and wrong

Only a few jurisdictions have supplemented the right–wrong test with a test that takes volition into account. According to the test, even if defendants know what they're doing, and know it's wrong, they can qualify for a verdict of not guilty by reason of insanity if they suffer from a mental disease that damages their volition (willpower).

In 1877, the court in *Parsons v. State* spelled out the application of the right–wrong test with its irresistible impulse supplement:

1. At the time of the crime, was the defendant afflicted with "a disease of the mind"?
2. If so, did the defendant know right from wrong with respect to the act charged? If not, the law excuses the defendant.
3. If the defendant did have such knowledge, the law will still excuse him if two conditions concur:
   a. If the mental disease caused the defendant to so far lose the power to choose between right and wrong and to avoid doing the alleged act that the disease destroyed his free will and
   b. If the mental disease was the sole cause of the act

Georgia's Criminal Code (2006, Title 16, Section 16–3–3) provides:

> A person shall not be found guilty of a crime when, at the time of the act, because of mental disease, injury, or congenital deficiency, [he] acted as he did because of a delusional compulsion as to such act which overmastered his will to resist committing the crime.

Some critics say the irresistible impulse supplement doesn't go far enough. First, they argue that it should include not just sudden impulses but also conduct "characterized by brooding and reflection." Others claim that the irresistible requirement requires that defendants lack total control over their actions. Still others maintain that it's impossible to distinguish between irresistible impulses and those that are simply unresisted. In other words, it allows too much room for fakers.

Other critics reject volition utterly. They argue that allowing people who lack self-control to escape punishment cripples both retribution and deterrence. They point to the high-profile case of John Hinckley Jr., acquitted because the jury found him insane when, in 1981, he attempted to assassinate President Ronald Reagan to get actress Jodie Foster's attention.

After the "river of fury" that followed Hinckley's trial (Perlin 1989–90, 637), the federal government and several states abolished the irresistible impulse defense on the ground that juries can't distinguish between irresistible impulses beyond the power to control and those that aren't. The federal statute (U.S. Code 2003) abolishing the irresistible impulse test in federal cases provides as follows:

> It is an affirmative defense to a prosecution under any Federal statute that, at the time of the commission of the acts constituting the offense, the defendant, as a result of a severe mental disease or defect, was unable to appreciate the nature and quality or the wrongfulness of his acts. Mental disease or defect does not otherwise constitute a defense.

LO4

THE PRODUCT OF MENTAL ILLNESS TEST (*DURHAM* RULE)

As the science of psychiatry and psychology advanced, the right–wrong test generated increasing criticism. One line of criticism began in the 1950s, when many social reformers thought that Freudian psychology could cure individual and social "diseases." *Durham v. U.S.* (1954) reflects the influence of that psychology. According to the Court:

> The science of psychiatry now recognizes that a man is an integrated personality and that reason, which is only one element in that personality, is not the sole determinant of his conduct. The right–wrong test, which considers knowledge or reason alone, is therefore an inadequate guide to mental responsibility for criminal behavior. (871)

product-of-mental-illness test also known as the ***Durham* rule,** acts that are the "products" of mental disease or defect excuse criminal liability

Based on these insights, the U.S. Circuit Court for the District of Columbia replaced the right–wrong test with the **product-of-mental-illness test**, also known as the *Durham* **rule**. According to this "new" test (New Hampshire adopted it in 1871), acts that are the "products" of mental disease or defect excuse criminal liability. So, with this test, the court stretched the concept of insanity beyond the purely intellectual knowledge examined by the right–wrong test into deeper areas of cognition and will.

Disillusionment with Freudian psychology, a major shift in public opinion from rehabilitation to punishment, and the anger and disgust following the verdict in John Hinckley's trial for attempting to kill President Reagan prompted the U.S. Congress to replace the product test with the right–wrong test. That legislation did away with the product test in the District of Columbia, where Durham was decided. Only two states, New Hampshire and Maine, ever adopted the product test. Maine abandoned the test. That leaves the product test in effect only in New Hampshire, where it was created in 1871.

LO4

THE SUBSTANTIAL CAPACITY TEST (MODEL PENAL CODE TEST)

substantial capacity test a person is not responsible for criminal conduct if at the time of such conduct as a result of mental disease or defect he lacks substantial capacity either to appreciate the criminality [wrongfulness] of his conduct or to conform his conduct to the requirements of law.

The **substantial capacity test**, adopted in the MPC, is supposed to remove the objections to the right–wrong test, its irresistible impulse supplement, and the psychiatric-oriented Durham rule. It emphasizes both of the qualities in insanity that should determine culpability: reason and will (Schopp 1988).

The MPC test changes the McNaughtan right–wrong/irresistible impulse supplement tests in several ways. First, as the name of the test indicates, defendants need not lack total mental capacity; the test adds the words "*substantial* capacity" to remove the possibility of requiring "*total* lack of reason" (the "wild beast") cognition test. And it removes the possibility that "*irresistible*" in "irresistible impulse" means total lack of knowledge and control. So people who can tell right from wrong only modestly and/or who have only a feeble will to resist are insane.

Most substantial capacity test states follow the MPC's definition of "substantial capacity":

> A person is not responsible for criminal conduct if at the time of such conduct as a result of mental disease or defect he lacks substantial capacity either to appreciate the criminality [wrongfulness] of his conduct or to conform his conduct to the requirements of law. (ALI 1985 [3], 163)

Second, the use of "appreciate" instead of "know" makes clear that intellectual awareness by itself isn't enough to create culpability; emotional (affective) components of understanding are required. The phrase "conform his conduct" removes the requirement of a "sudden" lack of control. In other words, the code provision eliminates the suggestion that losing control means losing it on the spur of the moment, as the "impulse" in "irresistible impulse test" can be read to mean. The MPC's definition of "mental disease or defect" excludes psychopathic personalities, habitual criminals, and antisocial personalities from the defense (Hermann and Sor 1983, 522).

Third, the word "wrong" was changed twice, first to "criminality" and then finally to "wrongfulness." The drafters took the position that the insanity defense deals with an impaired "moral sense," stemming from a broader application of the guilty mind (*mens rea*), rather than a strict criminal mind. Supporters of the MPC test believe that the simpler, plain language will help jurors to avoid feeling forced to rely on experts so they can "reason to its own conclusions about the criminal responsibility of the defendant based on whether he was insane at the time the crime was committed" (522–23).

The MPC test has its critics. Some claim that "substantial impairment" is "vague" and that it allows too many defendants to escape criminal responsibility. But the strongest criticism is that it "continues the faults of the *McNaughten* [sic] rules and the irresistible impulse tests by providing separate knowledge and control tests; in doing so, this test seems to rest on a bifurcated (two-part) rather than an integrated view of the human personality" (524).

THE DEFENSE OF DIMINISHED CAPACITY

LO5

"**Diminished capacity**" is an unfortunate term. First, it's not an affirmative defense in the sense that it excuses criminal conduct. It's a failure-of-proof defense (discussed at the beginning of the chapter), "a rule of evidence that allows the defense to introduce evidence to negate...specific intent" in a very narrow set of cases—premeditation in first-degree murder. "It is an attempt to prove that the defendant, incapable of the requisite intent of the crime charged, is innocent of that crime but may well be guilty of a lesser one" (*State v. Phipps* 1994, 143)—second-degree murder instead of first-degree murder.

diminished capacity a failure-of-proof defense in which the defendant attempts to prove that the defendant, incapable of the requisite intent of the crime charged, is innocent of that crime but may well be guilty of a lesser one

Second, diminished capacity isn't the same as diminished responsibility, with which it's often confused. "**Diminished responsibility**" is a defense of excuse; it's a variation on the defendant's argument, "What I did was wrong, but under the circumstances I'm not responsible." In diminished responsibility, the defendant argues, "What I did was wrong, but under the circumstances I'm less responsible." According to *State v. Phipps* (1994; excerpted later in "The Syndrome Defenses"):

diminished responsibility an excuse defense in which the defendant argues, "What I did was wrong, but under the circumstances I'm less responsible"

> A defendant pleading diminished responsibility does not seek relief from punishment by justification or excuse. Instead, she seeks to be punished for a lesser offense that

> she generally admits that she committed. In contrast, diminished capacity focuses on a defendant's capacity to commit a specific intent crime. If specific intent is established it doesn't excuse punishment. Instead, punishment is based on the general intent crime the defendant was capable of committing. Evidence to demonstrate such a lack of specific intent is not equivalent to evidence to establish diminished responsibility. (144)

Most states reject both types of diminished capacity. California is one example. The legislature abolished diminished capacity, mostly because of public hostility to it:

> The defense of diminished capacity is hereby abolished. In a criminal action . . . evidence concerning an accused person's . . . mental illness, disease, or defect shall not be admissible to show or negate capacity to form the particular purpose, intent, motive, malice aforethought, knowledge, or other mental state required for the commission of the crime charged. . . . (California Penal Code 2003, § 25)

The statute doesn't eliminate diminished capacity altogether. It provides that "diminished capacity or a mental disorder may be considered by the court [but] only at the time of sentencing."

In practice, diminished capacity and diminished responsibility apply only to homicide. Most of the cases involve reducing first- to second-degree murder. In very few cases, defendants are allowed to introduce evidence to reduce murder to manslaughter. In other words, diminished capacity and diminished responsibility are very rare issues in criminal law (LaFave 2003a, 453). How often do defendants succeed in reducing their liability when they're allowed to introduce "diminishment" evidence? Unfortunately, we don't know.

THE EXCUSE OF AGE

LO6 The common law divided children into three categories for the purpose of deciding their capacity to commit crimes:

1. *Under age 7.* Children had no criminal capacity.
2. *Ages 7–14.* Children were presumed to have no criminal capacity, but the presumption could be overcome.
3. *Over age 14.* Children had the same capacity as adults.

Today, statutes determine when young people can be convicted of crimes. These statutes come in several varieties, and they vary as to the age of capacity to commit crimes. One type of statute identifies a specific age, usually 14, but sometimes as young as 10 and as old as 18. These statutes usually provide that children under the specified age are subject to juvenile delinquency proceedings, even very young children. Another type of statute grants exclusive jurisdiction to juvenile courts up to a certain age but makes exceptions for a list of serious crimes. A third type of statute simply states that juvenile court jurisdiction isn't exclusive (LaFave 2003a, 487).

All states have established juvenile justice systems to handle juvenile delinquency. One kind of delinquency, and the one we're concerned with here, is conduct that violates the criminal law. Most juvenile court statutes place no lower age limit on delinquency; they all place an upper age limit, almost always 18. Don't misunderstand this to mean that all juvenile cases will be handled in juvenile court. Every state has a statute that provides for the transfer of juveniles to adult criminal court. The technical term for this transfer is "waiver to adult criminal court," meaning the juvenile court gives up its jurisdiction over the case and turns it over to the adult criminal court.

waiver to adult criminal court meaning the juvenile court gives up its jurisdiction over the case and turns it over to the adult criminal court

The shift from the philosophy of rehabilitation to retribution has led to more juveniles at younger ages being tried as adults (see "Criminal Law in Focus" box).

Juveniles Tried as Adults

- In New York, two 15-year-old private school students stand accused of savagely slashing to death a 44-year-old real estate agent and dumping his body in the lake at midnight in Central Park.
- In New Jersey, a 15-year-old awaits trial for the murder, sexual assault, and robbery of an 11-year-old who had been going door to door collecting for his school's PTA fundraiser.
- In Mississippi, a 16-year-old slit the throat of his own mother before going to Pearl High School to hunt down the girl who had just broken up with him—killing her, killing another girl, and wounding seven of his high school classmates.
- In Arizona, three teenagers (out of a believed ten), ages 13, 14, and 16, face prosecution for the 18-hour abduction and gang rape of a 14-year-old.
- In California, three Satan-worshipping high school students, ages 15, 16, and 17, stand charged with drugging, raping, torturing, and murdering a 15-year-old, reportedly in hopes that a virgin sacrifice would earn them "a ticket to hell." (Gordon 1999, 193–94)

Waivers to adult court come in three varieties: judicial, prosecutorial, and legislative. By far, the most common is **judicial waiver**; that's when a juvenile court judge uses her discretion to transfer a juvenile to adult criminal court. Most states have adopted the criteria for making the waiver decision approved by the U.S. Supreme Court (*Kent v. United States* 1966) for the District of Columbia. These include:

judicial waiver when juvenile court judges use their discretion to transfer a juvenile to adult criminal court

- The seriousness of the offense
- Whether the offense was committed in an aggressive, violent, premeditated, willful manner
- Whether the offense was against a person
- The amount of evidence against the juvenile
- The sophistication and maturity of the juvenile
- The prior record of the juvenile
- The threat the juvenile poses to public safety (LaFave 2003a, 490)

CASE

*In **State v. K.R.L. (1992)**, the Washington State Supreme Court rejected the state's argument that an eight-year-old boy had the capacity to form the intent to commit burglary.*

Was he too young to commit burglary?

State v. K.R.L.

840 P.2d 210 (Wash. App. 1992)

HISTORY

K.R.L., an eight-year-old boy, was convicted of residential burglary by the Superior Court, Clallam County, and he appealed. The Court of Appeals reversed.

ALEXANDER, J.

FACTS

In July 1990, K.R.L., who was then 8 years and 2 months old, was playing with a friend behind a business building in Sequim. Catherine Alder, who lived near the business, heard the boys playing and she instructed them to leave because she believed the area was dangerous. Alder said that K.R.L.'s response was belligerent, the child indicating that he would leave "in a minute." Losing patience with the boys, Alder said "no, not in a minute, now, get out of there now." The boys then ran off. Three days later, during daylight hours, K.R.L. entered Alder's home without her permission. He proceeded to pull a live goldfish from her fishbowl, chopped it into several pieces with a steak knife, and "smeared it all over the counter." He then went into Alder's bathroom and clamped a "plugged in" hair curling iron onto a towel.

Upon discovering what had taken place, Alder called the Sequim police on the telephone and reported the incident.

A Sequim police officer contacted K.R.L.'s mother and told her that he suspected that K.R.L. was the perpetrator of the offense against Alder. K.R.L.'s mother confronted the child with the accusation and he admitted to her that he had entered the house. She then took K.R.L. to the Sequim Police Department where the child was advised of his constitutional rights by a Sequim police officer.

This took place in the presence of K.R.L.'s mother, who indicated that she did not believe "he really understood." K.R.L. told the police officer that he knew it was wrong to enter Alder's home. The statement given by K.R.L. to the officer was not offered by the State to prove guilt. Initially, the State took the position that K.R.L. fully understood those rights and that he had made a free and voluntary waiver of rights. Defense counsel objected to the admission of the statements and eventually the State withdrew its offer of the evidence, concluding that the evidence was cumulative in that K.R.L.'s admissions were already in evidence through the testimony of his mother. K.R.L. was charged in Clallam County Juvenile Court with residential burglary, a class B felony. Residential burglary is defined in RCW 9A.52.025 as:

> A person is guilty of residential burglary if, with intent to commit a crime against a person or property therein, the person enters or remains unlawfully in a dwelling....

At trial, considerable testimony was devoted to the issue of whether K.R.L. possessed sufficient capacity to commit that crime. The juvenile court judge heard testimony in that regard from K.R.L.'s mother, Catherine Alder, two school officials, a Sequim policeman who had dealt with K.R.L. on two prior occasions as well as the incident leading to the charge, one of K.R.L.'s neighbors, and the neighbor's son. K.R.L.'s mother, the neighbor, the neighbor's son, and the police officer testified to an incident that had occurred several months before the alleged residential burglary.

This incident was referred to by the police officer as the "Easter Candy Episode." Their testimony revealed that K.R.L. had taken some Easter candy from a neighbor's house without permission. As a consequence, the Sequim police were called to investigate. K.R.L.

responded to a question by the investigating officer, saying to him that he "knew it was wrong and he wouldn't like it if somebody took his candy."

The same officer testified to another incident involving K.R.L. This was described as the "Joyriding Incident," and it occurred prior to the "Easter Candy Episode." It involved K.R.L. riding the bicycles of two neighbor children without having their permission to do so. K.R.L. told the police officer that he "knew it was wrong" to ride the bicycles.

The assistant principal of K.R.L.'s elementary school testified about K.R.L.'s development. He said that K.R.L. was of "very normal" intelligence. K.R.L.'s first grade teacher said that K.R.L. had "some difficulty" in school. He said that he would put K.R.L. in the "lower age academically."

K.R.L.'s mother testified at some length about her son and, in particular, about the admissions he made to her regarding his entry into Alder's home. Speaking of that incident, she said that he admitted to her that what he did was wrong "after I beat him with a belt, black and blue." She also said that her son told her "that the Devil was making him do bad things."

The juvenile court rejected the argument of K.R.L.'s counsel that the State had not presented sufficient evidence to show that K.R.L. was capable of committing a crime. It found him guilty, saying:

> From my experience in my eight, nine years on the bench, it's my belief that the so-called juvenile criminal system is a paper tiger and it's not going to be much of a threat to Mr. [K.R.L.], so I don't think that for that reason there is a whole lot to protect him from.

OPINION

There is only one issue—did the trial court err in concluding that K.R.L. had the capacity to commit the crime of residential burglary? RCW 9A.04.050 speaks to the capability of children to commit crimes and, in pertinent part, provides:

> Children under the age of eight years are incapable of committing crime. Children of eight and under twelve years of age are presumed to be incapable of committing crime, but this presumption may be removed by proof that they have sufficient capacity to understand the act or neglect, and to know that it was wrong.

This statute applies in juvenile proceedings. Because K.R.L. was 8 years old at the time he is alleged to have committed residential burglary, he was presumed incapable of committing that offense. The burden was, therefore, on the State to overcome that presumption and that burden could only be removed by evidence that was "clear and convincing." Thus, on review we must determine if there is evidence from which a rational trier of fact could find capacity by clear and convincing evidence.

There are no reported cases in Washington dealing with the capacity of 8-year-old children to commit crimes. That is not too surprising in light of the fact that up to age 8, children are deemed incapable of committing crimes.

The State emphasizes that K.R.L. appeared to appreciate that what he did at Alder's home and on prior occasions was wrong. When K.R.L. was being beaten "black and blue" by his mother, he undoubtedly came to the realization that what he had done was wrong. We are certain that this conditioned the child, after the fact, to know that what he did was wrong. That is a far different thing than one appreciating the quality of his or her acts at the time the act is being committed.

In arguing that it met its burden, the State placed great reliance on the fact that K.R.L. had exhibited bad conduct several months before during the so-called "Easter Candy" and "Joyriding" incidents. Again, we do not know much about these incidents, but it seems clear that neither of them involved serious misconduct and they shed little light on whether this child understood the elements of the act of burglary or knew that it was wrong.

Here, we have a child of very tender years—only two months over 8 years. While the State made a valiant effort to show prior bad acts on the part of the child, an objective observer would have to conclude that these were examples of behavior not uncommon to many young children.

Furthermore, there was no expert testimony in this case from a psychologist or other expert who told the court anything about the ability of K.R.L. to know and appreciate the gravity of his conduct. Although two school officials testified, one of them said K.R.L. was of an age lower than 8, "academically." In short, there is simply not enough here so that we can say that in light of the State's significant burden, there is sufficient evidence to support a finding of capacity.

Reversed.

(continues)

(continued)

QUESTIONS

1. Was the trial judge or the Supreme Court of Washington right in the ruling on the capacity of K.R.L. to form criminal intent? Back up your answer with facts from the case.
2. Did K.R.L. know what he was doing intellectually yet not sufficiently appreciate what he was doing? What facts support this conclusion?
3. Should it matter whether he appreciated what he did as long as he knew what he did was wrong? Explain your answer.

YOU *DECIDE*

Is it ethical policy to try an eight-year-old for murder?

An eight-year-old boy faces double-murder charges in the shooting death of his father and another man while residents in the bucolic community of St. Johns try to make sense of the chilling crime. "This is precedent-setting. We're going to charge an eight-year-old with two counts of homicide," Police Chief Roy Melnick said. "We haven't had anything like this in Apache County in my 23 years as a prosecutor," County Attorney Criss Candelaria said. "We need to figure out what was going on in this boy's head."

The child's father, 29, and a boarder, Tim Romans, 39, were found dead at the family residence about 5 P.M. Wednesday, shortly after neighbors reported the sound of gunfire. The *Arizona Republic* is withholding the father's and child's names to avoid identifying a juvenile. Melnick said police discovered one of the bodies outside the front door, the other in an upstairs room.

Question

- Should the prosecutor charge the boy with first-degree murder? Back up your answer with the information you got from the "The Excuse of Age" section in this chapter (p. 222).

Source: Dennis Wagner, "St. Johns boy, 8, suspected of double murder," *Arizona Republic*, November 8, 2008.

THE DEFENSE OF DURESS

LO7

defense of duress when defendants use the excuse that they were forced to do what they did

"Sometimes people are forced to do what they do," writes Professor Hyman Gross (1978). What if what they're forced to do is a crime? Should they be excused? The defense of duress is about answering these questions. According to Professor Gross, "It seems that the compulsion ought to count in their favor. After all, we say, such a person wasn't free to do otherwise—he couldn't help himself" (276).

On the other hand, he continues:

> There are times...when we ought to stand firm and run the risk of harm to ourselves instead of taking a way out that means harm to others. In such a situation we must expect to pay the price if we cause harm when we prefer ourselves, for then the harm is our fault even though we did not mean it and deeply regret it. (276)

Let's take a closer look at duress and its elements.

The Problem with the Duress Defense

LO7

Professor Gross's comments strike at the heart of the problem of duress: it's hard to blame someone who's forced to commit a crime, but should we excuse people who harm innocent people to save themselves? The positions taken by three of the last two centuries' great authorities on criminal law show how different the answers can be. At one extreme is the great historian of the criminal law and judge, Sir James Stephen (1883, 108), who maintained that duress is never an excuse for crime. (Stephen did say, however, that duress should mitigate the punishment.) At the other extreme is Professor Glanville Williams (1961, 755). Author of a highly respected treatise on criminal law, he says the law should excuse individuals if they're so "in thrall[ed] to some power" the law can't control their choice. Professor Jerome Hall (1960, 448), author of yet another distinguished treatise, took the middle position that duress shouldn't excuse the most serious crimes, but it should be an excuse when the choice is "Commit a minor crime or die—now!"

The Elements of Duress

LO7

There are four elements in the defense of duress:

1. *Nature of the threat.* Death threats are required in some states. Threats of "serious bodily injury" qualify in several. Others don't specify what threats qualify.
2. *Immediacy of the threats.* In some states, the harm has to be "instant." In others, "imminent" harm is required. In Louisiana, duress is an excuse only if the defendant reasonably believed the person making the threats would "immediately carry out the threats if the crime were not committed."
3. *Crimes the defense applies to.* In the majority of states, duress isn't a defense to murder. In other states, it's a defense to all crimes. Some states are silent on the point.
4. *Level of belief regarding the threat.* Most states require a reasonable belief the threat is real. Others demand the threat actually be real. Some say nothing on the point.

Duress Statutes in Three States

New York Penal Code, § 40.00

In any prosecution for an offense, it is an affirmative defense that the defendant engaged in the proscribed conduct because he was coerced to do so by the use or threatened imminent use of unlawful physical force upon him or a third person, which force or threatened force a person of reasonable firmness in his situation would have been unable to resist.

Minnesota Criminal Code, § 609.08 (3)

When any crime is committed or participated in by two or more persons, any one of whom participates only under compulsion by another engaged therein, who by threats creates a reasonable apprehension in the mind of such participator that in case of refusal that participator is liable to instant death, such threats and apprehension constitute duress which will excuse such participator from criminal liability.

(continues)

(continued)

Alabama Penal Code, Section 13A-3-30 (a)

It is a defense to prosecution that the actor engaged in the proscribed conduct because he was compelled to do so by the threat of imminent death or serious physical injury to himself or another....

1. The defense provided by this section is unavailable in a prosecution for:

a. murder; or

b. any killing of another under aggravated circumstances.

THE DEFENSE OF INTOXICATION

LO8 Johnny James went quietly to his death by lethal injection...inside the Texas prison system's Huntsville Unit. His crimes were disgusting. He abducted two women, forced them to have sex with each other, raped them, and then shot them both in the head. One died, but the other lived to identify him at trial. The Texas courts turned a deaf ear to James's plea that he was too drunk to know what he was doing when he abducted, raped, and shot his victims.

According to Professor George Fletcher (1978), the defense of intoxication is "buffeted between two conflicting principles":

1. *Accountability*. Those who get drunk should take the consequences of their actions. Someone who gets drunk is liable for the violent consequences.
2. *Culpability*. Criminal liability and punishment depend on blameworthiness (846).

The common law approach focused on the first principle:

> As to artificial, voluntarily contracted madness, by drunkenness or intoxication, which, depriving men of their reason, puts them in a temporary frenzy; our law looks upon this as an aggravation of the offense, rather than as an excuse for any criminal misbehavior. (Blackstone 1769, 25–26)

The Johnny James case is only one dramatic example that the common law principle is alive and well today. John Gibeaut (1997), who wrote about the James case in the article "Sobering Thoughts," notes the contemporary emphasis on accountability in the subtitle: "Legislatures and courts increasingly are just saying no to intoxication as a defense or mitigating factor." Section 13–03 of the Arizona Criminal Code (2003) is a typical accountability statute:

> Temporary intoxication resulting from the voluntary ingestion, consumption, inhalation or injection of alcohol, an illegal substance under chapter 34 of this title or other psychoactive substances or the abuse of prescribed medications does not constitute insanity and is not a defense for any criminal act or requisite state of mind.

involuntary intoxication an excuse to criminal liability in all states; it includes cases in which defendants don't know they're taking intoxicants or know but are forced to take them

Between November 1996 and May 1997, at least ten states introduced bills similar to the Arizona statute. According to a member of the Prosecution Function Committee of the American Bar Association's Criminal Justice Section, "The fight goes back to the ancient struggle over just how much free will one has" (Gibeaut 1997, 57).

What we have said so far applies only to *voluntary* intoxication. **Involuntary intoxication** is an excuse to criminal liability in all states. Involuntary intoxication includes cases in which defendants don't know they're taking intoxicants or know but are forced to take them. In *People v. Penman* (1915), a man took what his friend told him were "breath perfumer" pills; in fact, they were cocaine tablets. While under their influence, he killed someone. The court allowed the defense of intoxication.

Involuntary intoxication applies only under extreme conditions. According to one authority (Hall 1960), "A person would need to be bound hand and foot and the liquor literally poured down his throat, or...would have to be threatened with immediate serious injury" (540). In another case, *Burrows v. State* (1931), where the defendant claimed involuntary intoxication, an eighteen-year-old man was traveling with an older man across the desert. The older man insisted that the young man drink some whiskey with him. When he said no, the older man got abusive. Afraid that the older man would throw him out of the car in the middle of the desert without any money, he drank the whiskey, got drunk, and killed the older man. The court rejected his defense of involuntary intoxication, because the older man had not compelled the youth "to drink against his will and consent."

The reason the law excuses involuntary intoxication and not voluntary intoxication is that we can blame voluntarily intoxicated persons and hold them accountable for their actions. Why? They chose to put themselves in a state where they either didn't know or couldn't control what they were doing. We can't blame involuntarily intoxicated persons for their actions. Why not? Because people forced or tricked into an intoxicated state didn't choose to put themselves out of control. (Review Chapter 3, p. 97, on voluntarily induced involuntary conditions that qualify as *actus reus*.)

Alcohol isn't the only intoxicant covered by the defense of intoxication. In most states, it includes all "substances" that disturb mental and physical capacities. In *State v. Hall* (1974), Hall's friend gave him a pill, telling him it was only a "little sunshine" to make him feel "groovy." In fact, the pill contained LSD (lysergic acid diethylamide). A car picked up Hall while he was hitchhiking. The drug caused Hall to hallucinate that the driver was a rabid dog, and, under this sad delusion, Hall shot and killed the driver. The court said that criminal responsibility recognizes no difference between alcohol and other intoxicants.

THE DEFENSE OF ENTRAPMENT

LO9

Ancient tyrants and modern dictators alike have relied on secret agents as a law enforcement tool. From the days of Henry VIII to the era of Hitler and Stalin, to Slobodan Milošević, and Saddam Hussein, to Moammar Gadhafi, and Kim Jong-un in our own time, the world's police states have relied on persuading people to commit crimes, so they could catch and then crush their opponents.

But government persuasion isn't only a dictator's tool. All societies rely on it, even though it violates a basic purpose of government in free societies. The great Victorian British Prime Minister William Gladstone was referring to this purpose when he advised government to make it easy to do right and difficult to do wrong. Persuading people to commit crimes also flies in the face of the entreaty of the Lord's Prayer to "lead us not into temptation, but deliver us from evil" (Carlson 1987).

entrapment excuse that argues government agents got people to commit crimes they wouldn't otherwise commit

For a long time, U.S. courts rejected the idea that **entrapment** (government agents getting people to commit crimes they wouldn't otherwise commit) excused criminal liability. In *Board of Commissioners v. Backus* (1864), the New York Supreme Court explained why:

> Even if inducements to commit crime could be assumed to exist in this case, the allegation of the defendant would be but the repetition of the pleas as ancient as the world, and first interposed in Paradise: "The serpent beguiled me and I did eat." That defense was overruled by the great Lawgiver, and whatever estimate we may form, or whatever judgment pass upon the character or conduct of the tempter, this plea has never since availed to shield crime or give indemnity to the culprit, and it is safe to say that under any code of civilized, not to say Christian ethics, it never will. (42)

The court in *People v. Mills* (1904) summed up the acceptance of entrapment this way:

> We are asked to protect the defendant, not because he is innocent, but because a zealous public officer exceeded his powers and held out a bait. The courts do not look to see who held out the bait, but to see who took it. (791)

The earlier attitude was based on indifference to government encouragement to commit crimes. After all, "once the crime is committed, why should it matter what particular incentives were involved and who offered them?" However, attitudes have shifted from indifference to both a "limited sympathy" toward entrapped defendants and a growing intolerance of government inducements to entrap otherwise law-abiding people (Marcus 1986).

The practice of entrapment arose because of the difficulty in enforcing laws against consensual crimes, such as drug offenses, pornography, official wrongdoing, and prostitution. There's no constitutional right not to be entrapped. Entrapment is an affirmative defense created by statutes; that is, defendants have to show some evidence they were entrapped. If they do this, the burden shifts to the prosecution to prove defendants weren't entrapped. The jury—or the judge in trials without juries—decides whether officers in fact entrapped defendants. The courts have adopted two types of tests for entrapment; one is subjective and the other objective.

LO9 Subjective Entrapment Test

subjective test of entrapment asks whether the intent to commit the crime originated with the defendant

The majority of state and all federal courts have adopted a **subjective test of entrapment**. The subjective test of entrapment focuses on the predisposition of defendants to commit crimes. According to the test, the defense has to prove the government pressured the defendants to commit crimes they wouldn't have committed without the pressure.

The crucial question in the subjective test is: "Where did the criminal intent originate?" If it originated with the defendant, then the government didn't entrap the defendant. If it originated with the government, then the government did entrap the defendant. For example, in a leading U.S. Supreme Court entrapment case, *Sherman v. U.S.* (1958), Kalchinian, a government informant and undercover agent, met Sherman in a drug treatment center. He struck up a friendship with Sherman and eventually asked Sherman to get him some heroin. Sherman (a heroin addict) refused. Following weeks of persistent begging and pleading, Sherman finally gave in and got Kalchinian some heroin. The police arrested Sherman. The U.S. Supreme Court found that the intent originated with the government. According to the Court, Sherman was hardly predisposed to commit a drug offense given that he was seriously committed to a drug treatment program to cure his addiction.

After defendants present some evidence that the government persuaded them to commit crimes they wouldn't have committed otherwise, the government can prove disposition to commit the crimes in one of the following ways:

- Defendants' prior convictions for similar offenses
- Defendants' willingness to commit similar offenses
- Defendants' display of criminal expertise in carrying out the offense
- Defendants' readiness to commit the crime

Consensual crimes, especially drug offenses, are the usual target of law enforcement inducement tactics, but some police departments have also used them to combat street muggings.

In our next two excerpts, *Oliver v. State* (1985) and *DePasquale v. State* (1988), the Nevada Supreme Court dealt with two street mugging decoy cases operating in an area of Las Vegas with a high population of "street people."

CASE

In ***Oliver v. State*** **(1985) and** ***DePasquale v. State*** **(1988),** *Ernest Oliver and Vincent DePasquale were convicted of larceny from the person.*

Were they entrapped?

Oliver v. State

703 P.2d 869 (Nev. 1985)

HISTORY

Ernest Oliver was convicted of larceny from the person in the Eighth Judicial District Court and sentenced to ten years in prison. He appealed. The Supreme Court reversed.

GUNDERSON, J.

FACTS

On the night of Oliver's arrest, three policemen undertook to conduct a "decoy operation" near the intersection of Main and Ogden in Las Vegas. That corner is in a downtown area frequented by substantial numbers of persons commonly characterized as "street people," "vagrants," and "derelicts." It appears Oliver, a black man, is one of these.

Disguised as a vagrant in an old Marine Corps jacket, the decoy officer slumped against a palm tree, pretending to be intoxicated and asleep. His associates concealed themselves nearby. The decoy prominently displayed a ten-dollar bill, positioning it to protrude from the left breast pocket of his jacket. This was done, the decoy later testified, "to provide an opportunity for a dishonest person to prove himself." Oliver, who had the misfortune to come walking down the street, saw the decoy and evidently felt moved to assist him. Shaking and nudging the decoy with his foot, Oliver attempted to warn the decoy that the police would arrest him if he did not move on. The decoy did not respond, and Oliver stepped away. Up to this point, Oliver had shown no predisposition whatever to commit any criminal act.

Then, Oliver saw the ten-dollar bill protruding from the decoy's pocket. He reached down and took it. "Thanks, Home Boy," he said. Thereupon, he was arrested by the decoy and the two other officers. Following the trial, a jury convicted Oliver of larceny from the person, and he has been sentenced to ten years' imprisonment.

(continues)

(continued)

OPINION

Oliver's counsel contends he was entrapped into committing the offense in question. We agree. Government agents or officers may not employ extraordinary temptations or inducements. They may not manufacture crime.

We have repeatedly endorsed the following concept: Entrapment is the seduction or improper inducement to commit a crime for the purpose of instituting a criminal prosecution, but if a person in good faith and for the purpose of detecting or discovering a crime or offense furnishes the opportunity for the commission thereof by one who has the requisite criminal intent, it is not entrapment.

Thus, because we discern several facts which we believe combined to create an extraordinary temptation, which was inappropriate to apprehending merely those bent on criminal activity, we feel constrained to reverse Oliver's conviction. We note, first of all, that the decoy portrayed himself as completely susceptible and vulnerable. He did not respond when Oliver attempted to wake him, urging him to avoid arrest by moving to another location. Moreover, the decoy displayed his ten dollar bill in a manner calculated to tempt any needy person in the area, whether immediately disposed to crime or not.

In the case of Oliver, the police succeeded in tempting a man who apparently did not approach the decoy with larceny in mind, but rather to help him. Even after being lured into petty theft by the decoy's open display of currency and apparent helplessness, Oliver did not go on to search the decoy's pockets or to remove his wallet.

He appealed and the Nevada Supreme Court reversed.

DePasquale v. State

757 P.2d 367 (Nev. 1988)

YOUNG, J.

FACTS

In DePasquale, four officers on the LVMPD's S.C.A.T. Unit (Street Crime Attack Team) were performing a decoy operation near the intersection of Fremont Street and Casino Center Blvd. in Las Vegas on April 30, 1983, at 11:45 P.M. Officer Debbie Gautwier was the decoy, and Officers Shalhoob, Young, and Harkness were assigned to "backup." Officer Gautwier was dressed in plain clothes and was carrying a tan shoulder bag draped over her left shoulder.

Within one of the side, zippered pockets of the bag, she had placed a \$5 bill and \$1 bill wrapped with a simulated \$100 bill. The money, including the numbers of the simulated \$100 bill, were exposed so as to be visible to persons near by; however, the zipper was pulled tight against the money so as to require a concentrated effort to remove it.

Officer Young, also in plain clothes, was standing approximately six to seven feet away from Officer Gautwier (the decoy), near the entrance of the Horseshoe Club, when Randall DeBelloy approached Officer Gautwier from behind and asked if he could borrow a pen. Officer Gautwier stated that she did not have a pen, and DeBelloy retreated eight to ten feet. Within a few seconds he approached a second time, asking for a piece of paper. Again the response was "no." During these approaches Officer Young observed DeBelloy reach around Officer Gautwier toward the exposed cash.

DeBelloy again retreated eight to ten feet from Officer Gautwier. He then motioned with his hand to two men who were another eight to ten feet away, and the trio huddled together for 15 to 30 seconds. As DeBelloy talked with the two men, he looked up and over in the direction of Officer Gautwier. Vincent DePasquale was one of the two men who joined DeBelloy in this huddle.

While this trio was conversing, Officer Gautwier had been waiting for the walk signal at the intersection. When the light changed, she crossed Fremont Street and proceeded southbound on the west sidewalk of Casino Center Blvd. DePasquale and DeBelloy followed her, 15 to 20 feet behind. After crossing the street, Officer Gautwier looked back briefly and saw DeBelloy following her. DePasquale was four to seven feet behind DeBelloy and to his right.

As they walked in this formation, DePasquale yelled out, "Wait lady, can I talk to you for a minute."

As Officer Gautwier turned to her right in response—seeing DePasquale whom she identified in court—DeBelloy took a few quick steps to her left side, took the money with his right hand, and ran.

DeBelloy was arrested, with the marked money in his possession, by Officers Harkness and Shalhoob. DePasquale was arrested by Officers Gautwier and Young. Both were charged with larceny from the person and convicted by a jury.

OPINION

DePasquale argues that he was entrapped, that the district court erred in its instruction to the jury on the law of entrapment, that the evidence fails to support the verdict, and that the sentence of ten years is disproportionate and, therefore, cruel and unusual.

Upon these facts, the decoy simply provided the opportunity to commit a crime to anyone who succumbed to the lure of the bait. Entrapment encompasses two elements:

1. an opportunity to commit a crime is presented by the state
2. to a person not predisposed to commit the act.

Thus, this subjective approach focuses upon the defendant's predisposition to commit the crime. In the present case, the cash, although exposed, was zipped tightly to the edge of a zippered pocket, not hanging temptingly from the pocket of an unconscious derelict. Admittedly, the money was exposed; however, that attraction alone fails to cast a pall over the defendant's predisposition. The exposed valuables (money) were presented in a realistic situation, an alert and well-dressed woman walking on the open sidewalks in the casino area.

The fact that the money was exposed simply presented a generally identified social predator with a logical target. These facts suggest that DePasquale was predisposed to commit this crime. Furthermore, the fact that DePasquale had no contact with the decoy but rather succumbed to the apparent temptation of his co-defendant to systematically stalk their target evidences his predisposition.

Lastly, DePasquale complains that his sentence was disproportionate to the crime and, therefore, cruel and unusual punishment. A sentence is unconstitutional if it is so disproportionate to the crime for which it is inflicted that it shocks the conscience and offends fundamental notions of human dignity. While the punishment authorized in Nevada is strict, it is not cruel and unusual.

Accordingly, we AFFIRM the judgment of conviction.

QUESTIONS

1. State the test for entrapment according to Nevada law.
2. What facts led the Court to conclude that Oliver was entrapped but DePasquale wasn't?

Objective Entrapment Test

LO9

objective test of entrapment if the intent originates with the government and their actions would tempt an "ordinarily law-abiding" person to commit the crime, the court should dismiss the case

A minority of courts follows an objective test of entrapment. The objective test focuses not on the predisposition of defendants but instead on the actions that government agents take to induce individuals to commit crimes. According to the objective test, if the intent originates with the government and their actions would tempt an "ordinarily law-abiding" person to commit the crime, the court should dismiss the case even if the defendant was predisposed to commit the crime. This test is a prophylactic rule aimed to deter "unsavory police methods" (ALI 1985 1:2, 406–7).

SYNDROME DEFENSES

LO10

syndrome a group of symptoms or signs typical of a disease, disturbance, or condition

Since the 1970s, a range of syndromes, describing affected mental states, has led to novel defenses in criminal law. Webster defines a syndrome as "a group of symptoms or signs typical of a disease, disturbance, or condition." Law professor and famous defense attorney Alan Dershowitz (1994) has written a book about these novel defenses. Its title, *The Abuse Excuse and Other Cop-Outs, Sob Stories, and Evasions of Responsibility*, makes clear his opinion of them.

Dershowitz's book includes discussions of the policeman's love, fear, chronic brain, and holocaust syndromes. He worries these excuses are "quickly becoming a license to kill and maim" (3). His is probably a needless worry because defendants rarely plead these excuses, and, except for a few notorious cases picked up by television, the newspapers, and more on the Web, defendants rarely succeed when they do plead syndromes and other "abuse excuses."

LO10 Premenstrual Syndrome (PMS)

premenstrual syndrome (PMS) excuse that PMS led to the defendant committing the criminal acts

Some syndromes are (and should be) taken seriously as excuses. For example, some women have claimed the battered woman syndrome to justify killing spouses in self-defense, even though they weren't in imminent danger (Chapter 7). Occasionally, women also have used the **premenstrual syndrome (PMS)** to excuse their crimes. In a New York case, Shirley Santos called the police, telling them, "My little girl is sick." The medical team in the hospital emergency room diagnosed the welts on her little girl's legs and the blood in her urine as the results of child abuse. The police arrested Santos, who explained, "I don't remember what happened. I would never hurt my baby. I just got my period" (qtd. in Press and Clausen 1982, 111).

At a preliminary hearing, Santos asserted PMS as a complete defense to assault and endangering the welfare of a child, both felonies. She admitted beating her child but argued that she had blacked out because of PMS; hence, she couldn't have formed the intent to assault or endanger her child's welfare. After lengthy plea bargaining, the prosecutor dropped the felony charges, and Santos pleaded guilty to the misdemeanor of harassment. She received no sentence, not even probation or a fine, even though her daughter spent two weeks in the hospital from the injuries. The plea bargaining prevented a legal test of the PMS defense in this case. Nevertheless, the judge's leniency suggests that PMS affected the outcome informally.

There are three obstacles to proving the PMS defense (Carney and Williams 1983):

1. Defendants have to prove that PMS is a disease; little medical research exists to prove that it is.
2. The defendant has to suffer from PMS; rarely do medical records document the condition.
3. PMS has to cause the mental impairment that excuses the conduct; too much skepticism still surrounds PMS to expect ready acceptance that it excuses criminal conduct.

LO10 Post-Traumatic Stress Disorder (PTSD)

From October 2001 to 2008, about 1.64 million U.S. troops were deployed to fight the wars in Afghanistan and Iraq. The pace of the deployments was "unprecedented in the history of the all-volunteer force." Not only that, but deployments to combat were longer, and redeployment (sometimes several times) was common while at the same time breaks between deployments were less frequent. Despite these intense periods of combat, both wars employed fewer troops and the casualty rates of troops killed and wounded were *lower* than in other long wars like Vietnam and Korea. Why? Dramatic advances in medical technology and body armor translated into more survivors and fewer deaths than the previous wars (Tanielian and Jaycox 2008, xix).

Unfortunately, different kinds of casualties emerged, "invisible wounds" brought about by "multiple deployments per individual service member and exposure to difficult threats, such as improvised explosive devices (IEDs)." These invisible wounds took the form of mental health and cognitive impairments. The most frequent are post-traumatic stress disorder (PTSD), depression, and traumatic brain injury (TBI), resulting from blasts or other head injuries (xix).

post-traumatic stress disorder (PTSD) defense excuse that argues the defendant wasn't responsible because of PTSD

> Unfortunately, these conditions are often invisible to the eye. Unlike like the physical wounds of war that maim and disfigure, these conditions remain invisible to other service members, to family members, and to society in general. All three conditions affect mood, thoughts, and behavior; yet these wounds often go unrecognized and unacknowledged. (xx)

A telephone study involving 1,965 of the 1.64 million service members previously deployed to Afghanistan and Iraq found "substantial rates of mental health problems in the last 30 days" (xxi). (See Figure 6.1 on mental health and cognitive issues faced by Afghanistan and Iraq war vets.) Notice that the study's authors Tanielian and Jaycox (2008) include major depression as one of the post-deployment mental health consequences, even though it's often not considered a combat-related injury. They include it because their analyses suggest that it's "highly associated with combat exposure." (xxi)

The authors conclude that, assuming their study represents the 1.64 million service members returning from Afghanistan and Iraq, as of October 2007, there were about 300,000 individuals suffering from PTSD or major depression and that 320,000 probably experienced TBI during their deployment. About a third have at least one of the three conditions, and about 5 percent suffer from all three.

Our interest here is how do these conditions lead to involvement with the criminal justice system, especially as an excuse for otherwise criminal conduct? In other words, when can defendants support the contention that "What I did was a crime, but under the circumstances I wasn't responsible for committing it. It was my PTSD or major depression, or TBI that I can't control." In our next case excerpt, *State v. Belew* (2014), the Ohio Supreme Court rejected Jeffrey Belew's PTSD defense.

Figure 6.1

Percent of Afghanistan/Iraq War Vets Suffering from PTSD, Depression, and Traumatic Brain Injuries (TBI)

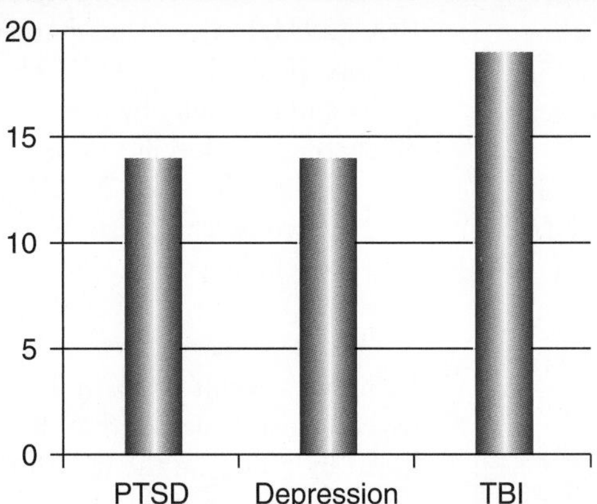

Source: Data reported in Invisible Wounds of War: Psychological and Cognitive Injuries, Their Consequences, and Services to Assist Recovery, edited by Terri Tanielian and Lisa Jaycox, © RAND corporation (can be downloaded from free from RAND: http://www.rand.org/pubs/monographs/MG720.html)

CASE

*In **State v. Belew (2014),** Jeffrey Belew was convicted and sentenced to 27 years in prison.*

Were his "hidden wounds" an excuse for shooting police officers?

State v. Belew

17 N.E.3d 515 (Ohio 2014)

PFEIFER, O'DONNELL, KENNEDY, and FRENCH, JJ., concur.
O'CONNOR, CJ., and LANZINGER and O'NEILL, JJ., dissent.

HISTORY

Jeffrey Belew was convicted and sentenced to 27 years in prison. The Ohio Court of Appeals affirmed his conviction. A majority of the Ohio Supreme Court let the conviction and sentence stand without opinion. But, one justice dissented, and wrote the following opinion.

LANZINGER, J., dissenting.

I respectfully dissent from the court's decision to dismiss this case as having been improvidently accepted. Amici curiae in support of appellant, Jeffery Belew, filed two memoranda in support of jurisdiction asserting that this case involves a matter of great general interest and public importance and filed two supporting merit briefs.[1] And although the state does not disagree with Belew's proposition that "when credibly diagnosed, a trial court must consider combat-related post-traumatic stress disorder and other service-related disabilities as mitigation when imposing sentence on a military veteran," it argues that the trial court here did properly consider those factors when sentencing him.

I believe that we should render an opinion on how post-traumatic stress disorder ("PTSD") must be considered by a court when it sentences a military veteran. And just as important, we should clarify the standard that an appellate court must use in reviewing a sentence of this type. It is my position that only a full opinion by this court will clarify both the appellate court's standard of review and the trial court's need to support the record for a felony sentence.

[1] One brief was filed by Ohio Suicide Prevention Foundation, Disability Rights Ohio, National Disability Rights Network, National Alliance on Mental Illness of Ohio, and Ohio Empowerment Coalition, Inc. The other brief was filed by the Arms Forces.

FACTS

On April 10, 2011 Belew fired at least four shots at police officers who were responding to a domestic-disturbance call in Oregon, Ohio. Belew's shots struck an arriving police car twice, and he did not respond to commands to cease fire until he was wounded by shots fired by the officers. He was arrested and received hospital care.

Belew was indicted on April 20, 2011, for two counts of attempted aggravated murder of a law-enforcement officer and two counts of felonious assault, which were first-degree felonies under R.C. 2903.11(D)(1) because the shots were fired at peace officers. Each count contained specifications that he both displayed, brandished, indicated possession of, or used a firearm (R.C. 2941.145) and discharged his firearm at peace officers (R.C. 2941.1412). He entered pleas of not guilty and not guilty by reason of insanity ("NGRI") to all charges and specifications.

As a result of his NGRI plea, Belew was evaluated by two psychologists, who provided reports to the court concluding that he did not qualify for the insanity defense. One of the psychologists diagnosed him with alcohol dependence, persistent major depression, and PTSD as a result of his military service in Iraq. That psychologist believed that Belew was hoping to be killed by police on the day of the shooting. The other psychologist found evidence of possible malingering or a personality disorder.

After plea negotiations, Belew changed his plea to guilty and the state dismissed certain counts and specifications. He was sentenced to 27 years in prison: two consecutive ten-year terms for each count of felonious assault to be served consecutively to two concurrent seven-year terms for the firearm specifications. He appealed his sentence to the Sixth District Court of Appeals, which affirmed the trial court's order, holding that the trial court appropriately weighed statutory factors in imposing his sentence. We then accepted a discretionary appeal.

The trial court in this case received the psychological reports and the presentence-investigation report into evidence. Psychologist Dr. Wayne Graves, who testified at the sentencing hearing, opined specifically about the diagnosis of PTSD, which resulted from Belew's military service in Iraq, and about the consequences of PTSD. Defense counsel and the prosecuting attorney also spoke. Afterwards, the sentencing judge stated:

> I have reviewed the presentence report that has been prepared, I've reread the report prepared by Dr. Charlene Cassel of the Court Diagnostic and Treatment Center, I've reread Dr. Wayne Graves's report, I have read two letters from the Defendant's mother, and I've listened very carefully to the testimony of Dr. Wayne Graves here today, as well as listened to what Counsel and Defendant has had to say, and I've balanced all of that information in sentencing this afternoon.

She then addressed the defendant directly:

> Mr. Belew, you claim that you suffer from post-traumatic stress disorder as a result of being in the military and you provide that as an excuse for your actions. There is no excuse, Mr. Belew. I have to—I feel that I'm compelled because of my concerns of why you entered the military, to weigh that. And your words to Dr. Charlene Cassel were, I joined the Marines to see how many people I could kill. That's, generally—if I'm not mistaken, people don't join the military to see how many people they can kill. You were continually in trouble and constantly drunk and under the influence of alcohol and drugs, and you received a bad conduct discharge after being court martialed for stealing government property.

Turning to the offenses, the judge then stated:

> These offenses are extremely serious, Mr. Belew, these officers could have been killed, because you intended to kill them. They responded to a call of a fight between you and your brother because you were in possession of a handgun and were extremely intoxicated. And you don't remember what happened that night, as you said, because you were suffering from an alcohol blackout. And according to Dr. Charlene Cassel, people who are suffering alcohol blackouts do not do things that are uncharacteristic of things that they wouldn't normally do. You shot at Officer Martin when he stopped his vehicle, you shot at him several times, and when the other two officers came to assist they gave several commands to you to stop and put down your weapon, but you continued to walk toward them with your gun pointed at them. And it was only after you were wounded that you stopped. You are lucky to be standing here today, Mr. Belew, because they very well could have killed you.

The judge next stated: "You do have a minimal criminal history." However, she also stated, "because of your actions I believe you are a danger to this community."

Belew did not receive a maximum 34-year sentence for the offenses and specifications for which he was convicted. The sentencing judge's entry stated that the prison terms were ordered to be served consecutively because consecutive sentences were "necessary to fulfill the purposes of R.C. 2929.11,2 and not disproportionate to the seriousness of the offender's

[2](A) A court that sentences an offender for a felony shall be guided by the overriding purposes of felony sentencing. The overriding purposes of felony sentencing are to protect the public from future crime by the offender and others and to punish the offender using the minimum sanctions that the court determines accomplish those purposes without imposing an unnecessary burden on state or local government resources. To achieve those purposes, the sentencing court shall consider the need for incapacitating the offender, deterring the offender and others from future crime, rehabilitating the offender, and making restitution to the victim of the offense, the public, or both.

(B) A sentence imposed for a felony shall be reasonably calculated to achieve the two overriding purposes of felony sentencing set forth in division (A) of this section, commensurate with and not demeaning to the seriousness of the offender's conduct and its impact upon the victim, and consistent with sentences imposed for similar crimes committed by similar offenders.

(C) A court that imposes a sentence upon an offender for a felony shall not base the sentence upon the race, ethnic background, gender, or religion of the offender.

(continues)

(continued)

conduct or the danger the offender poses" and that the "harm caused was great or unusual." The record here did not allow the Sixth District Court of Appeals to clearly and convincingly find that the record does not support the sentencing court's findings.

Although different judges may have weighed the statutory factors at issue here differently, the relevant statutes did not allow the appellate court to substitute its own judgment for that of the trial judge. All findings of the trial judge have record support and the required findings were made. I would therefore affirm the judgment of the court of appeals. I respectfully dissent from the order that dismisses this case as improvidently accepted.

O'NEILL, J., dissenting.

The United States Marine Corps took a marginal recruit from an abusive family and turned him into a fighting machine. They sent him to Iraq to defend all of us, and in the process they turned him into a confused alcoholic with a clear diagnosis of post-traumatic stress disorder ("PTSD") and possibly a traumatic brain injury.

Once home, and still on active duty, he became a misfit alcoholic who was, essentially, no longer of any use to the Marine Corps. He was often drunk, did not obey orders, and most significantly, received no treatment whatsoever for the PTSD that he had sustained in the fog of war.

Not too surprisingly, on one drunken day while on active duty, he and a friend "borrowed" a Humvee and went on a joyride. They were quickly apprehended by the officer of the day, and from that point forward, it was clear that the Marines no longer needed the product they had created.

He was demoted and given a bad-conduct discharge for the Humvee incident. Significantly, his less-than-honorable discharge deprived him of the medical assistance from the federal Department of Veterans Affairs that he so desperately needed.

As a civilian he simply did not fit in, and, still suffering from untreated and undiagnosed PTSD, his antisocial behavior predictably escalated.

We are here today because of the tragic events that led to his conviction. It is without question, and well supported in the record, that this troubled throwaway from society wanted to commit "suicide by cop." There is no other explanation for why an individual would open fire on two approaching, well-trained, well-armed police officers. He failed. Rather than dying, Belew received a nonfatal bullet to the chest—and not one of the officers was struck. He took responsibility for his actions and pled guilty to several offenses but received an aggregate sentence of 27 years in prison that was far harsher than it should have been.

Incredibly, the trial court and the court of appeals have locked onto the phrase "no excuse." The trial court stated, "Mr. Belew, you claim that you suffer from post-traumatic stress disorder as a result of being in the military and you provide that as an excuse for your actions. There is no excuse, Mr. Belew."

I would respectfully suggest that one trial court judge, three appellate court judges, and the majority of this court simply do not get it. PTSD is not an excuse. It is an explanation.

Mr. Belew's disability was not an "excuse." He was and is suffering from a well-known and definable disease, which was diagnosed by Dr. Wayne Graves, whose testimony was admitted into evidence without objection and presented in the sentencing hearing.

After the date of the trial court's sentencing of Belew in this case, the General Assembly enacted the following language: "The sentencing court shall consider the offender's military service record and whether the offender has an emotional, mental, or physical condition that is traceable to the offender's service in the armed forces of the United States." R.C. 2929.12(F).

This case is clearly the poster child for implementation of the new statute, and today this court has the rare opportunity to lead with clarity. The record is before us. There is more at stake here than garden-variety excuses for criminal culpability. Belew was a marginal Marine recruit; he developed PTSD while on active duty; and he was turned out of the service with a bad-conduct discharge and little or no capacity to function safely in society.

Tragically, he is not the only member of the armed forces to arrive at this juncture. He has been diagnosed with PTSD as a result of his time in the Marine Corps—a condition that remains untreated. It is inexcusable that he cannot access federal benefits for his PTSD. We can and should do better. I would reverse the judgment of the court of appeals and remand this case to the trial court for a new sentencing hearing and decision that properly takes into consideration Belew's military-service record and his diagnosis of PTSD. Anything else is unreasonable.

QUESTIONS

1. List the facts relevant to deciding whether Jeffrey Belew suffered from PTSD.
2. Summarize the trial judge's reasons for rejecting Belew's claim that his PTSD excused his otherwise criminal conduct.
3. Summarize Justice Lanzinger's reasons why he believes that PTSD deserves more attention.
4. Why does dissenting Justice O'Neill "suggest that one trial court judge, three appellate court judges, and the majority of this court simply do not get it. PTSD is not an excuse. It is an explanation."? Do you agree? Defend your answer.

Summary

Defendants who plead excuse admit what they did was wrong but claim that, under the circumstances, they weren't responsible for their actions. Excuse defenses are affirmative defenses, which require the defendant to carry some of the burden of proving their excuse will relieve them of criminal liability. **LO1**

Contrary to popular belief, the excuse defense of insanity is rarely used or successful, and insane defendants usually are confined in mental institutions for many years. The long history of the insanity defense in high-profile cases during times of political turmoil reflects the idea that we can only blame people who are responsible for their actions. **LO2**

Proving insanity happens during two separate, critical times. Insanity refers to the defendants mental capacity at the time the crime was committed, while competence refers to the defendant's mental capacity to understand the legal proceedings and work with her lawyer to aid in her own defense. Because the excuse of insanity is an affirmative defense in most states, sanity and responsibility are presumed unless the defendant proves otherwise. **LO3**

Four tests are used to determine whether people with mental diseases or defects aren't responsible enough to blame and punish. The right–wrong test of insanity (*McNaughtan* rule) focuses only on defect in reason and is used in federal and most state courts. The irresistible impulse test is followed in a few jurisdictions and focuses only on defect in will. The product-of-mental-illness test (*Durham* rule) focuses on criminal acts resulting from mental disease and is only followed in New Hampshire. The substantial capacity test (the MPC test) focuses on both reason and will when determining legal sanity. **LO4**

Diminished capacity is a failure-of-proof defense attempting to show that the defendant is guilty of a lesser crime by negating specific intent. Diminished responsibility is an affirmative excuse defense in which defendants admit what they did was wrong but claim that, under the circumstances, they are less responsible for their actions. In practice, diminished capacity and diminished responsibility apply only to homicide. **LO5**

LO6 The common law divided children into three categories for the purpose of deciding their capacity to commit crimes: (1) under age 7, children had no criminal capacity; (2) aged 7–14, children were presumed to have no criminal capacity, but the presumption could be overcome; (3) over age 14, children had the same capacity as adults. Modern statutes focus on when young people can be convicted of crimes. These statutes come in several varieties, and they vary as to the age of capacity to commit crimes. Every state has a statute that provides for the transfer (waiver) of juveniles to adult criminal court.

LO7 The problem of duress is that it's hard to blame someone who's forced to commit a crime, but excusing people who harm innocents to save themselves causes debate. The defense of duress consists of four elements: the (1) nature of the threat, (2) immediacy of the threats, (3) crimes the defense applies to, and (4) level of belief regarding the threat.

LO8 The defense of voluntary intoxication is buffeted between two conflicting principles: (1) accountability: those who get drunk and commit a crime should take the consequences of their actions, and (2) culpability: criminal liability and punishment depend on blameworthiness. Involuntary intoxication, on the other hand, is an excuse to criminal liability in all states.

LO9 For a long time, U.S. courts rejected the idea that entrapment excused criminal liability, based on the idea that once the crime is committed it didn't matter what particular incentives were involved and who offered them. However, attitudes have shifted from indifference to both a limited sympathy toward entrapped defendants and a growing intolerance of government inducements to entrap otherwise law-abiding people.

LO10 Since the 1970s, a range of syndromes has led to novel defenses in criminal law. Though there's criticism because of a few notorious cases, some syndromes are taken seriously as excuses. Defendants rarely plead these excuses, and they rarely succeed when they do plead syndromes. Premenstrual symptom (PMS) and post-traumatic stress disorder (PTSD) are examples of these syndromes.

Key Terms

insanity, p. 209
civil commitment, p. 210
reason, p. 212
will, p. 212
right–wrong test (also called the McNaughtan rule), p. 212
mental disease, p. 212
mental defect, p. 213
irresistible impulse test, p. 219
product-of-mental-illness test (also called the *Durham* rule), p. 220
substantial capacity test (the MPC test), p. 220
diminished capacity, p. 221
diminished responsibility, p. 221
waiver to adult criminal court, p. 223

judicial waiver, p. 223
defense of duress, p. 226
involuntary intoxication, p. 228
entrapment, p. 229
subjective test of entrapment, p. 230
objective test of entrapment, p. 233
syndrome, p. 233
premenstrual syndrome (PMS), p. 234
post-traumatic stress disorder (PTSD) defense, p. 235

Learning Objectives

1. To know the different parties to crime and appreciate the difference between complicity and vicarious liability.

2. To appreciate that participants before and during the commission of a crime (accomplices) are guilty of the crime itself.

3. To know that mere presence or inaction isn't enough to establish accomplice *actus reus*; the defendant had to take some positive act to aid the commission of the offense.

4. To appreciate that courts are divided over whether knowledge is sufficient to prove accomplice *mens rea*.

5. To understand that participants after the commission of crimes (accessories) are guilty of a separate, less serious offense.

6. To understand that vicarious liability transfers the *actus reus* and *mens rea* from one person to another because of their relationship.

7. To understand that vicarious liability can apply either to enterprises (mostly businesses) or to individuals.

7 Parties to Crime and Vicarious Liability

Chapter Outline

Was She an Accomplice?

Carol Hoffman, Helen Ulvinen's daughter-in-law, was murdered late on the evening of August 10 or the very early morning of August 11 by her husband, David Hoffman. She and David had spent an amicable evening together playing with their children, and when they went to bed David wanted to make love to his wife.

When she refused him he lost his temper and began choking her. While he was choking her, he began to believe he was "doing the right thing" and that to get "the evil out of her" he had to dismember her body.

After his wife was dead, David called down to the basement to wake his mother, asking her to come upstairs to sit on the living room couch. From there she would be able to see the kitchen, bathroom, and bedroom doors and could stop the older child if she awoke and tried to use the bathroom.

Mrs. Ulvinen didn't respond at first but after being called once, possibly twice more, she came upstairs to lie on the couch. In the meantime, David had moved the body to the bathtub. Mrs. Ulvinen was aware that while she was in the living room her son was dismembering the body but she turned her head away so that she could not see.

After dismembering the body and putting it in bags, Hoffman cleaned the bathroom, took the body to Weaver Lake, and disposed of it. On returning home, he told his mother to wash the cloth covers from the bathroom toilet and tank, which she did. David fabricated a story about Carol leaving the house the previous night after an argument, and Helen agreed to corroborate it. David phoned the police with a missing person report, and during the ensuing searches and interviews with the police, he and his mother continued to tell the fabricated story.

The principle of *actus reus* stands on the fundamental idea that we punish people for what they do, not for who they are. The principle of *mens rea* stands on the fundamental idea that we can only punish people we can blame. This chapter affirms another basic idea of our criminal law: that one person can be liable for someone else's crimes. This liability arises in two ways:

1. When an actor is liable for someone else's conduct (*complicity*)
2. When the relationship between two parties makes one party criminally liable for another party's conduct (*vicarious liability*)

In this chapter, we'll look more closely at parties to crimes; participation before, during, and after the commission of a crime; and vicarious liability.

PARTIES TO CRIME

LO1

complicity establishes when *you* can be criminally liable for someone *else's* conduct; applies criminal liability to accomplices and accessories

vicarious liability establishes when a party can be criminally liable for someone else's conduct because of a relationship; transfers the criminal conduct of one party to another because of their relationship

agency theory the idea that we're autonomous agents with the freedom to choose our actions and become accountable for someone else's actions when we voluntarily "join in and identify with those actions"

forfeited personal identity theory the idea that when you choose to participate in crime, you forfeit your right to be treated as an individual; "your acts are my acts"

accomplices participants before and during the commission of crimes

accessories participants after crimes are committed

"Two heads are better than one." "The whole is greater than the sum of its parts." These popular sayings express the positive side of teamwork, an ordinary phenomenon under ordinary circumstances. When, under extraordinary circumstances, teamwork turns malicious, then benign "teamwork" can become "complicity" in criminal law. A group of young men playing football generates no criminal liability; a gang rape—teamwork turned malicious—is aggravated rape.

Complicity establishes when *you* can be criminally liable for someone *else's* conduct. It applies criminal liability to accomplices and accessories because they participate in crimes.

Vicarious liability establishes when a party can be criminally liable because of a relationship. Vicarious liability transfers the criminal conduct of one party to another because of their relationship. By far the most common relationships are business relationships, such as employer–employee, corporation–manager, buyer–seller, producer–consumer, and service provider–recipient. Vicarious liability, however, can also arise in other situations, such as making the owner of a car liable for the driver's traffic violations and holding parents liable for their children's crimes.

Why should you be held to account for someone else's crimes? Two theories explain why. First, the agency theory of accomplice liability assumes that we're autonomous agents with the freedom to choose our actions. We become accountable for someone else's actions when we voluntarily "join in and identify with those actions" (Kadish 1985, 355). Underlying the second theory, forfeited personal identity theory, is the idea that when you choose to participate in crime, you forfeit your right to be treated as an individual. In effect, you say, "Your acts are my acts" (Dressler 2012, 459).

The Criminal Law in Focus box defines the four common law parties to crime. These four distinct categories used to be important because of the common law rule that the government couldn't try accomplices until principals in the first degree were convicted. This ban applied even if there was absolute proof of guilt. Why? Probably because all felonies were capital offenses. But as the number of capital crimes shrank, so did the need for the complicated law of principals and accessories.

Today, there are two parties to criminal complicity:

1. Accomplices, participants before and during the commission of crimes
2. Accessories, participants after crimes are committed

Common Law Parties to Crime

1. **Principals in the first degree** persons who actually commit the crime
2. **Principals in the second degree** persons present when the crime is committed and who help commit it (lookouts and getaway drivers)
3. **Accessories before the fact** persons not present when the crimes are committed but who help before the crime is committed (for example, someone who provided a weapon used in a murder)
4. **Accessories after the fact** persons who help after the crime is committed (harboring a fugitive)

principals in the first degree persons who actually commit the crime

principals in the second degree persons present when the crime is committed and who help commit it (lookouts and getaway drivers)

accessories before the fact persons not present when the crimes are committed but who help before the crime is committed (for example, someone who provided a weapon used in a murder)

accessories after the fact persons who help after the crime is committed (harboring a fugitive)

PARTICIPATION BEFORE AND DURING THE COMMISSION OF A CRIME

LO2

All participants before and during the commission of a crime (accomplices) are prosecuted for the crime itself (for example, accomplices to murder are prosecuted as murderers). So participation before and during a crime (accomplice liability) is a very serious business, because the punishment for being an accomplice is the same as for the person who actually committed the crime.

accomplice liability liability that attaches for participation before and during a crime (prosecution for the crime itself)

Participation *after* crimes are committed (accessory liability) is prosecuted as a separate, minor offense (for example, accessory to murder). Accessories are punished for misdemeanors, a much less serious offense, because accessories are considered obstructers of justice, not felons.

accessory liability liability that attaches for participation after crimes are committed (prosecution for a minor offense other than the crime itself)

We need to clear up a problem before we get further into accomplice liability. Accomplices are often confused with co-conspirators (Chapter 8), because both accomplice and conspiracy cases have more than one participant, but they're two completely different crimes. Conspiracy is an agreement to commit some other crime. A conspiracy to commit murder is not murder; it's the lesser offense of agreeing to commit murder (Chapter 8). Participating in a murder is the crime of murder itself. For example, two people agree to commit a murder. At this point, they've committed conspiracy to murder. Now they go to a gun shop, buy a gun, and drive together to the victim's house. One acts as a lookout while the other shoots the victim, who dies instantly. They drive away together. They're both murderers. They've committed two separate crimes—the less serious crime of conspiracy to commit murder and the crime of murder.

conspiracy an agreement to commit some other crime

The rule that the crime of conspiracy and the crime the conspirators agree to commit are separate offenses is called the *Pinkerton* rule. The name comes from a leading U.S. Supreme Court case, *Pinkerton v. U.S.* (1946). The two Pinkerton brothers conspired to evade taxes. They were found guilty of both conspiracy to evade taxes and tax evasion itself. According to Justice Douglas, who wrote the opinion for the Court: "It has been long and consistently recognized by the Court that the commission of the offense and a conspiracy to commit it are separate and distinct offenses" (643).

***Pinkerton* rule** the crime of conspiracy and the crime the conspirators agree to commit are separate offenses

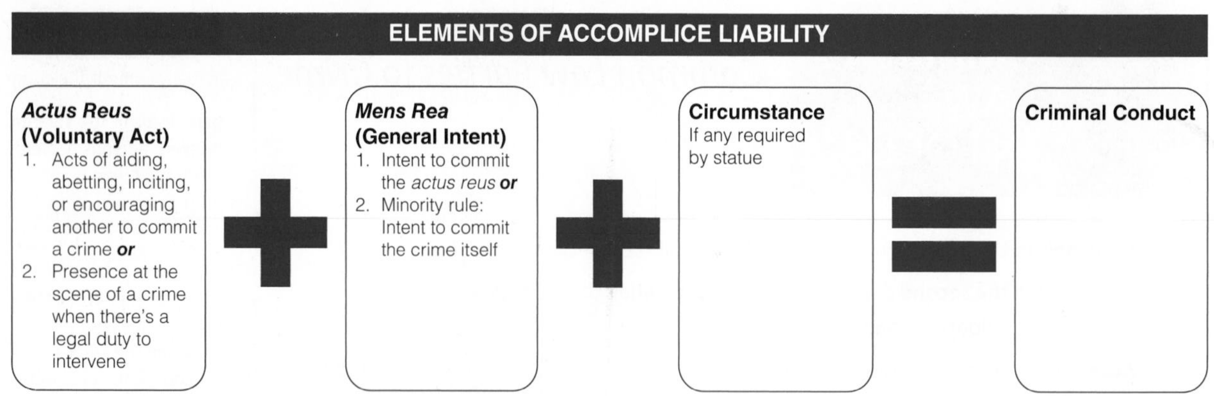

LO2 Accomplice *Actus Reus*

accomplice *actus reus* defendant took "some positive act in aid of the commission of the offense"

You'll usually see words borrowed from the old common law of principals and accessories to define **accomplice *actus reus*** in modern accomplice statutes. The words "aid," "abet," "assist," "counsel," "procure," "hire," or "induce" are widespread. The meaning of these words boils down to one core idea: The actor took "some positive act in aid of the commission of the offense." How much aid is enough? It's not always easy to decide, but here are a few acts that definitely qualify:

- Providing guns, supplies, or other instruments of crime
- Serving as a lookout
- Driving a getaway car
- Sending the victim to the principal
- Preventing warnings from getting to the victim (ALI 1953, 43)

mere presence rule a person's presence at, and flight from, the scene of a crime aren't enough to satisfy the *actus reus* requirement of accomplice liability

Words can also qualify as accomplice *actus reus* if they encourage and approve the commission of the crime. Mere presence at the scene of a crime is not enough to qualify as accomplice *actus reus*. According to the **mere presence rule**, even presence at the scene of a crime followed by flight isn't enough action.

For example, in *Bailey v. U.S.* (1969), Bailey spent most of the afternoon shooting craps with another man. Then, when a man carrying cash walked by, Bailey's craps partner pulled a gun and robbed the man with the cash. Both Bailey and his craps partner fled the scene. Bailey was caught; his partner never was. The court held that, although flight from the scene of a crime can be taken into account, it's not enough to prove accomplice *actus reus*.

According to the court:

> We no longer hold tenable the notion that "the wicked flee when no man pursueth, but the righteous are as bold as a lion." The proposition that "one flees shortly after a criminal act is committed or when he is accused of something does so because he feels some guilt concerning the act" is not absolute as a legal doctrine "since it is a matter of common knowledge that men who are entirely innocent do sometimes fly from the scene of a crime through fear of being apprehended as guilty parties or from an unwillingness to appear as witnesses." (1114)

There's one major exception to the mere presence rule: when defendants have a legal duty to act, presence alone is enough to satisfy the *actus reus* requirement. In *State v. Walden* (1982), George Hoskins beat Aleen Walden's one-year-old son Lamont "repeatedly over an extended period of time," with a leather belt, until he was bloody. Walden "looked on the entire time the beating took place but did not say anything or do anything to stop the 'Bishop' [Hoskins] from beating Lamont or to otherwise deter such conduct" (783).

A jury found Walden guilty as an accomplice to assault. On appeal, the court said that

> the trial court properly allowed the jury to consider a verdict of guilty of assault upon a theory of aiding and abetting, solely on the ground that the defendant was present when her child was brutally beaten. A person who so aids or abets under another in the commission of a crime is equally guilty with that other person as a principal. (787)

One final point about accomplice *actus reus*: actions taken *after* crimes are committed aren't themselves accomplice *actus reus*, but juries can use participation after the crime to prove defendants participated before or during the commission of the crime. In our next case excerpt, *State v. Ulvinen* (1981)—involving a grisly murder—the Minnesota Supreme Court dealt with these issues in connection with Helen Ulvinen's participation before and after her son David murdered his wife, Carol.

CASE

In ***State v. Ulvinen* (1981),** *Helen Ulvinen was convicted of first-degree murder pursuant to Minn. Stat. § 609.05, subd. 1 (1980), which imposes criminal liability on one who "intentionally aids, advises, hires, counsels, or conspires with or otherwise procures" another to commit a crime.*

Was she an accomplice to murder?

State v. Ulvinen

313 N.W.2d 425 (Minn. 1981)

HISTORY

Helen Ulvinen was convicted of first-degree murder pursuant to Minn. Stat. § 609.05, subd. 1 (1980), which imposes criminal liability on one who "intentionally aids, advises, hires, counsels, or conspires with or otherwise procures" another to commit a crime. The Minnesota Supreme Court reversed.

OTIS, J.

FACTS

Carol Hoffman, Helen Ulvinen's daughter-in-law, was murdered late on the evening of August 10, or in the very early morning of August 11 by her husband, David Hoffman. She and David had spent an amicable evening together playing with their children, and when they went to bed David wanted to make love to his wife. When she refused him he lost his temper and began choking her. While he was choking her, he began to believe he was "doing the right thing" and that to get "the evil out of her" he had to dismember her body.

After his wife was dead, David called down to the basement to wake his mother, asking her to come upstairs to sit on the living room couch. From there she would be able to see the kitchen, bathroom, and bedroom doors and could stop the older child if she awoke and tried to use the bathroom.

(continues)

(continued)

Mrs. Ulvinen didn't respond at first but after being called once, possibly twice more, she came upstairs to lie on the couch. In the meantime, David had moved the body to the bathtub. Mrs. Ulvinen was aware that while she was in the living room her son was dismembering the body but she turned her head away so that she could not see.

After dismembering the body and putting it in bags, Hoffman cleaned the bathroom, took the body to Weaver Lake, and disposed of it. On returning home, he told his mother to wash the cloth covers from the bathroom toilet and tank, which she did. David fabricated a story about Carol leaving the house the previous night after an argument, and Helen agreed to corroborate it. David phoned the police with a missing person report, and during the ensuing searches and interviews with the police, he and his mother continued to tell the fabricated story.

On August 19, 1980, David confessed to the police that he had murdered his wife. In his statement, he indicated that not only had his mother helped him cover up the crime, but she had known of his intent to kill his wife that night. After hearing Hoffman's statement the police arrested Mrs. Ulvinen and questioned her with respect to her part in the cover up. Police typed up a two-page statement, which she read and signed. The following day a detective questioned her further regarding events surrounding the crime, including her knowledge that it was planned.

Mrs. Ulvinen's relationship with her daughter-in-law had been a strained one. She moved in with the Hoffmans on July 26, two weeks earlier to act as a live-in babysitter for their two children. Carol was unhappy about having her move in and told friends that she hated Helen, but she told both David and his mother that they could try the arrangement to see how it worked.

On the morning of the murder, Helen told her son that she was going to move out of the Hoffman residence because "Carol had been so nasty to me." In his statement to the police, David reported the conversation that morning as follows:

> Sunday morning I went downstairs and my mom was in the bedroom reading the newspaper and she had tears in her eyes, and she said in a very frustrated voice, "I've got to find another house." She said, "Carol don't want me here," and she said, "I probably shouldn't have moved in here." And I said then, "Don't let what Carol said hurt you. It's going to take a little more period of readjustment for her." Then, "I told mom that I've got to do it tonight so that there can be peace in this house."

Q: What did you tell your mom that you were going to have to do that night?

A: I told my mom I was going to have to put her to sleep.

Q: Dave, will you tell us exactly what you told your mother that morning, to the best of your recollection?

A: I said I'm going to have to choke her tonight, and I'll have to dispose of her body so that it will never be found. That's the best of my knowledge.

Q: What did your mother say when you told her that?

A: She just—she looked at me with very sad eyes and just started to weep. I think she said something like "it will be for the best."

David spent the day fishing with a friend of his. When he got home that afternoon he had another conversation with his mother. She told him at that time about a phone conversation Carol had in which she discussed taking the children and leaving home. David told the police that during the conversation with his mother that afternoon he told her, "Mom, tonight's got to be the night."

Q: When you told your mother, "Tonight's got to be the night," did your mother understand that you were going to kill Carol later that evening?

A: She thought I was just kidding her about doing it. She didn't think I could.

Q: Why didn't your mother think that you could do it?

A: Because for some time I had been telling her I was going to take Carol scuba diving and make it look like an accident.

Q: And she said?

A: And she always said, "Oh, you're just kidding me."

Q: But your mother knew you were going to do it that night?

A: I think my mother sensed that I was really going to do it that night.

Q: Why do you think your mother sensed you were really going to do it that night?

A: Because when I came home and she told me what had happened at the house, and I told her, "Tonight's got to be the night," I think she said, again I'm not certain, that "it would be the best for the kids."

OPINION

In this state, presence, companionship, and conduct before and after the offense are circumstances from which a person's participation in the criminal intent may be inferred. The evidence is undisputed that Ulvinen was asleep when her son choked his wife. She took no active part in the dismembering of the body but came upstairs to intercept the children, should they awake, and prevent them from going into the bathroom.

She cooperated with her son by cleaning some items from the bathroom and corroborating David's story to prevent anyone from finding out about the murder. She is insulated by statute from guilt as an accomplice after-the-fact for such conduct because of her relation as a parent of the offender. (See Minn. Stat. § 609.495, subd. 2 (1980).)

The jury might well have considered Ulvinen's conduct in sitting by while her son dismembered his wife so shocking that it deserved punishment. Nonetheless, these subsequent actions do not succeed in transforming her behavior prior to the crime to active instigation and encouragement. Minn. Stat. § 609.05, subd. 1 (1980) implies a high level of activity on the part of an aider and abettor in the form of conduct that encourages another to act. Use of terms such as "aids," "advises," and "conspires" requires something more of a person than mere inaction to impose liability as a principal.

The evidence presented to the jury at best supports a finding that Ulvinen passively acquiesced in her son's plan to kill his wife. The jury might have believed that David told his mother of his intent to kill his wife that night and that she neither actively discouraged him nor told anyone in time to prevent the murder. Her response that "it would be the best for the kids" or "it will be the best" was not, however, active encouragement or instigation. There is no evidence that her remark had any influence on her son's decision to kill his wife.

Minn. Stat. § 609.05, subd. 1 (1980) imposes liability for actions which affect the principal, encouraging him to take a course of action which he might not otherwise have taken. The state has not proved beyond a reasonable doubt that appellant was guilty of anything but passive approval. However morally reprehensible it may be to fail to warn someone of their impending death, our statutes do not make such an omission a criminal offense. We note that mere knowledge of a contemplated crime or failure to disclose such information without evidence of any further involvement in the crime does not make that person liable as a party to the crime under any state's statutes.

David told many people besides appellant of his intent to kill his wife but no one took him seriously. He told a co-worker, approximately three times a week, that he was going to murder his wife, and confided two different plans for doing so. Another co-worker heard him tell his plan to cut Carol's air hose while she was scuba diving, making her death look accidental, but did not believe him. Two or three weeks before the murder, David told a friend of his that he and Carol were having problems and he expected Carol "to have an accident sometime." None of these people has a duty imposed by law to warn the victim of impending danger, whatever their moral obligation may be.

Her conviction must be reversed.

QUESTIONS

1. List all the facts (including words) surrounding Mrs. Ulvinen's behavior before or during the murder that might make her an accomplice.
2. List all the facts after the murder that a jury could infer proved Mrs. Ulvinen participated before or during the murder itself.
3. According to the court, why isn't Mrs. Ulvinen guilty of murder?
4. Do you agree with the court that, however morally reprehensible her behavior, she, nonetheless, wasn't an accomplice? Defend your answer.

Figure 7.1

ACCOMPLICE *MENS REA*

Examples of knowingly but not purposely helping someone:

- I lease an apartment to someone I know is going to use it for prostitution.
- A gun dealer sells me a gun she knows I'm going to use to shoot someone.
- A telephone company provides service to a customer it knows is going to use it for illegal gambling.
- A farmer leases 200 acres of farmland to a renter he knows is going to grow marijuana for sale. (ALI 1985 I:2, 316)

LO4

Accomplice *Mens Rea*

My friend Steve: Lend me your gun.

Me: What for?

Steve: So I can rob the grocery store.

Me: OK, but only if you give me half the take.

My intent is clear in this scenario (as it is in most complicity cases): my purpose in lending Steve my gun is to help him rob the grocery store, and I definitely want the robbery to succeed. So we can say my mental attitude is "purposely"; I'm acting for the very purposes of (1) helping Steve and (2) committing a robbery. Cases like this scenario don't give courts much trouble. Others do—like knowingly helping someone who is going to commit a crime but not for the very purpose of benefiting from the criminal venture (Figure 7.1).

Early court decisions ruled that knowingly helping someone was enough to prove the mental element required for accomplice liability. For example, in *Backun v. United States* (1940), Max Backun sold silver to Zucker, silver that he knew was stolen. But Backun didn't sell the silver for the purpose of sharing any profits with Zucker. Still, according to the court, knowingly selling the stolen property was good enough:

> Guilt depends, not on having a stake in the outcome of crime but on aiding and assisting the perpetrators; and those who make a profit by furnishing to criminals, whether by sale or otherwise, the means to carry on their nefarious undertakings, aid them just as truly as if they were actual partners with them, having a stake in the fruits of their enterprise. (637)

In another famous federal case, *U.S. v. Peoni* (1938, 401), decided by the well-known and enormously respected Judge Learned Hand, the outcome was the opposite. Joseph Peoni sold counterfeit money to Dorsey in the Bronx. Dorsey was caught trying to pass the fake money in Brooklyn. Peoni was indicted as an accomplice to Dorsey. At the trial, the prosecution relied on the words "aids, abets, counsels, commands, induces, or procures" in the U.S. Criminal Code's accomplice statute. The prosecution argued that Peoni knew Dorsey possessed counterfeit money and that knowledge was enough to convict him. The jury convicted Peoni, but, on appeal, Judge Hand didn't buy the prosecution's argument. According to Judge Hand, if someone were suing Peoni for damages, knowledge would be good enough, but this was a criminal case, where all the words in the statute

> demand that he in some sort associate himself with the venture, that he participate in it as in something that he wishes to bring about, that he seek by his action to make it succeed. All the words used—even the most colorless, "abet"—carry an implication of purposive attitude towards it. (402)

U.S. v. Peoni is cited over and over again as defining the *mens rea* of accomplice liability. If only it were that clear, but it's not. In a 2002 survey of only federal court cases, Assistant U.S. Attorney Baruch Weiss (2002) cited "a few examples" illustrating the confusion. Here are some answers to the question, Is simple knowledge enough?

1. Yes, said the Supreme Court in 1870
2. No, said Judge Learned Hand in 1938
3. Yes, implied the Supreme Court in 1947
4. No, said the Supreme Court in 1949
5. Yes, if it's accompanied by an act that substantially facilitates the commission of the underlying offense, said the Supreme Court in 1961
6. Usually, said the Second Circuit in 1962
7. Only if knowledge is enough for the underlying offense, said the Second Circuit in another case in 1962
8. Sometimes, said the Seventh Circuit in 1985
9. Always, implied the Seventh Circuit in 1995
10. No, said the Second Circuit in 1995 and the Seventh Circuit in 1998 (1351–52)

PARTICIPATION AFTER THE COMMISSION OF A CRIME

LO5

In common law, accessories after the fact were punished like accomplices: they were treated as if they'd committed the crime itself. So, if you gave a burglar a place to hide after he'd committed burglary, you were also guilty of burglary. But accessories aren't really burglars; they don't come on the scene until the burglary is over. That's why they used to be called "accessories *after* the fact." Furthermore, so the thinking goes, it's not as bad to help someone who's already committed a crime as it is to help her commit the crime in the first place.

Modern statutes have reduced the punishment to fit this less serious offense. Accessory after the fact (now called simply "**accessory**") is a separate offense, usually a misdemeanor. Sometimes it even has a different name, such as "obstructing justice," "interfering with prosecution," and "aiding in escape."

accessory accessory after the fact; usually a misdemeanor

Most accessory-after-the-fact statutes have four elements, which includes one *actus reus*, two *mens rea*, and one circumstance element:

1. The accessory personally aided the person who committed the crime (the *actus reus* element).
2. The accessory knew the felony was committed (*mens rea* element).
3. The accessory aided the person who committed the crime for the purpose of hindering the prosecution of that person (*mens rea* element).
4. Someone besides the accessory actually committed a felony (the circumstance element).

In our next case excerpt, the bizarre *State v. Chism* (1983), the Supreme Court of Louisiana dealt with the state's accessory statute.

ELEMENTS OF ACCESSORY-AFTER-THE-FACT LIABILITY

***Actus Reus* (Voluntary Act)** Aiding a felon to avoid arrest, prosecution, or conviction	+	***Mens Rea* (General Intent)** Intent to aid a felon to avoid arrest, prosecution, or conviction	+	**Circumstance** If any required by statute	=	**Criminal Conduct**

CASE

*In **State v. Chism (1983),** Brian Chism was convicted of being an accessory after the fact and was sentenced to three years in Parish Prison, with two and one-half years suspended.*

Was he an accessory after the fact?

State v. Chism

436 So.2d 464 (La. 1983)

HISTORY

Brian Chism (the defendant) was convicted before the First Judicial District Court, Caddo Parish, of being an accessory after the fact, and was sentenced to three years in Parish Prison, with two and one-half years suspended, and the defendant appealed. The Louisiana Supreme Court affirmed the conviction, vacated the sentence, and remanded the case for resentencing.

DENNIS, J.

FACTS

On the evening of August 26, 1981, in Shreveport, Tony Duke gave Brian Chism a ride in his automobile. Brian Chism was impersonating a female, and Duke was apparently unaware of Chism's disguise. After a brief visit at a friend's house, the two stopped to pick up some beer at the residence of Chism's grandmother.

Chism's one-legged uncle, Ira Lloyd, joined them, and the three continued on their way, drinking as Duke drove the automobile. When Duke expressed a desire to have sexual relations with Chism, Lloyd announced that he wanted to find his ex-wife Gloria for the same purpose. Shortly after midnight, the trio arrived at the St. Vincent Avenue Church of Christ and persuaded Gloria Lloyd to come outside. As Ira Lloyd stood outside the car attempting to persuade Gloria to come with them, Chism and Duke hugged and kissed on the front seat as Duke sat behind the steering wheel.

Gloria and Ira Lloyd got into an argument, and Ira stabbed Gloria with a knife several times in the stomach and once in the neck. Gloria's shouts attracted the attention of two neighbors, who unsuccessfully tried to prevent Ira from pushing Gloria into the front seat of the car alongside Chism and Duke. Ira Lloyd climbed into the front seat also, and Duke drove off. One of the bystanders testified that she could not be sure but she thought she saw Brian's foot on the accelerator as the car left.

Lloyd ordered Duke to drive to Willow Point, near Cross Lake. When they arrived, Chism and Duke, under Lloyd's direction, removed Gloria from the vehicle and placed her on some high grass on the side of the roadway, near a wood line. Ira was unable to help the two because his wooden leg had come off. Afterward, as Lloyd requested, the two drove off, leaving Gloria with him.

There was no evidence that Chism or Duke protested, resisted, or attempted to avoid the actions which Lloyd ordered them to take. Although Lloyd was armed with a knife, there was no evidence that he threatened either of his companions with harm.

Duke proceeded to drop Chism off at a friend's house, where he changed to male clothing. He placed the bloodstained women's clothes in a trash bin. Afterward, Chism went with his mother to the police station at 1:15 a.m. He gave the police a complete statement, and took the officers to the place where Gloria had been left with Ira Lloyd. The police found Gloria's body in some tall grass several feet from that spot.

An autopsy indicated that stab wounds had caused her death. Chism's discarded clothing disappeared before the police arrived at the trash bin.

OPINION

According to Louisiana statute 14:25:

> An accessory after the fact is any person who, after the commission of a felony, shall harbor, conceal, or aid the offender, knowing or having reasonable ground to believe that he has committed the felony, and with the intent that he may avoid or escape from arrest, trial, conviction, or punishment…
>
> Whoever becomes an accessory after the fact shall be fined not more than five hundred dollars, or imprisoned, with or without hard labor, for not more than five years, or both; provided that in no case shall his punishment be greater than one-half of the maximum provided by law for a principal offender.

Chism appealed from his conviction and sentence and argues that the evidence was not sufficient to support the judgment. Consequently, in reviewing the defendant's assigned error, we must determine whether, after viewing the evidence in the light most favorable to the prosecution, any rational trier of fact could have found beyond a reasonable doubt that:

1. a completed felony had been committed by Ira Lloyd before Brian Chism rendered him the assistance described below; and
2. Chism knew or had reasonable grounds to know of the commission of the felony by Lloyd; and
3. Chism gave aid to Lloyd personally under circumstances that indicate either that he actively desired that the felon avoid or escape arrest, trial conviction, or punishment or that he believed that one of these consequences was substantially certain to result from his assistance.

There was clearly enough evidence to justify the finding that a felony had been completed before any assistance was rendered to Lloyd by the defendant. The record vividly demonstrates that Lloyd fatally stabbed his ex-wife before she was transported to Willow Point and left in the high grass near a wood line. Thus, Lloyd committed the felonies of attempted murder, aggravated battery, and simple kidnapping, before Chism aided him in any way. A person cannot be convicted as an accessory after the fact to a murder because of aid given after the murderer's acts but before the victim's death, but under these circumstances the aider may be found to be an accessory after the fact to the felonious assault.

The evidence overwhelmingly indicates that Chism had reasonable grounds to believe that Lloyd had committed a felony before any assistance was rendered. In his confessions and his testimony Chism indicates that the victim was bleeding profusely when Lloyd pushed her into the vehicle, that she was limp and moaned as they drove to Willow Point, and that he knew Lloyd had inflicted her wounds with a knife.

The Louisiana offense of accessory after the fact deviates somewhat from the original common law offense in that it does not require that the defendant actually know that a completed felony has occurred. Rather, it incorporates an objective standard by requiring only that the defendant render aid "knowing or having reasonable grounds to believe" that a felony has been committed.

The closest question presented is whether any reasonable trier of fact could have found beyond a reasonable doubt that Chism assisted Lloyd under circumstances that indicate that either Chism actively desired that Lloyd would avoid or escape arrest, trial, conviction, or punishment, or that Chism believed that one of these consequences was substantially certain to result from his assistance.

In this case we conclude that a trier of fact reasonably could have found that Chism acted with at least a general intent to help Lloyd avoid arrest because:

1. Chism did not protest or attempt to leave the car when his uncle, Lloyd, shoved the mortally wounded victim inside;
2. he did not attempt to persuade Duke, his would-be lover, to exit out the driver's side of

(continues)

(continued)

the car and flee from his uncle, whom he knew to be one-legged and armed only with a knife;

3. he did not take any of these actions at any point during the considerable ride to Willow Point;
4. at their destination, he docilely complied with Lloyd's directions to remove the victim from the car and leave Lloyd with her, despite the fact that Lloyd made no threats and that his wooden leg had become detached;
5. after leaving Lloyd with the dying victim, he made no immediate effort to report the victim's whereabouts or to obtain emergency medical treatment for her;
6. before going home or reporting the victim's dire condition he went to a friend's house, changed clothing and discarded his own in a trash bin from which the police were unable to recover them as evidence;
7. he went home without reporting the victim's condition or location;
8. and he went to the police station to report the crime only after arriving home and discussing the matter with his mother.

Chism asserted that he helped to remove the victim from the car and to carry her to the edge of the bushes because he feared that his uncle would use the knife on him. However, fear as a motivation to help his uncle is inconsistent with some of Chism's actions after he left his uncle. Consequently, we conclude that despite Chism's testimony, the trier of fact could have reasonably found that he acted voluntarily and not out of fear when he aided Lloyd and that he did so under circumstances indicating that he believed that it was substantially certain to follow from his assistance that Lloyd would avoid arrest, trial, conviction, or punishment.

For the foregoing reasons, it is also clear that the judge's verdict was warranted. There is evidence in this record from which a reasonable trier of fact could find a defendant guilty beyond a reasonable doubt. Therefore, we affirm the defendant's conviction.

We note, however, that the sentence imposed by the trial judge is illegal. The judge imposed a sentence of three years. He suspended two and one-half years of the term. The trial judge has no authority to suspend part of a sentence in a felony case. The correct sentence would have been a suspension of all three years of the term, with a six-month term as a condition of two years' probation. We therefore vacate the defendant's sentence and remand the case for resentencing.

Conviction AFFIRMED; sentence vacated; REMANDED.

DISSENT

DIXON, CJ.

I respectfully dissent from what appears to be a finding of guilt by association. The majority lists five instances of inaction, or failure to act, by defendant:

1. did not protest or leave the car;
2. did not attempt to persuade Duke to leave the car;
3. did neither (1) nor (2) on ride to Willow Point;...
4. made no immediate effort to report crime or get aid for the victim;...
5. failed to report victim's condition or location after changing clothes.

The three instances of defendant's action relied on by the majority for conviction were stated to be:

1. complying with Lloyd's direction to remove the victim from the car and leave the victim and Lloyd at Willow Point;
2. changing clothes and discarding bloody garments; and...
3. discussing the matter with defendant's mother before going to the police station to report the crime.

None of these actions or failures to act tended to prove defendant's intent, specifically or generally, to aid defendant avoid arrest, trial, conviction or punishment.

QUESTIONS

1. Identify the elements of accessory after the fact according to the Louisiana statute.
2. List all the facts stated by the court, and then match them to each of the elements of the statute.
3. Summarize the court's conclusions regarding the evidence of each of the elements.
4. Do you agree with the court that Chism is guilty of being an accessory after the fact? Back up your answer with facts in the case.
5. Summarize the reasons the dissent couldn't go along with the majority. Do you agree with the dissent? Defend your answer.

VICARIOUS LIABILITY

LO6

Recall that vicarious liability refers to liability that is imposed for someone else's acts. It transfers the *actus reus* and the *mens rea* from one person to another person—or from one or more persons to an enterprise—because of their relationship.

Most vicarious liability involves business relationships, such as employer–employee, manager–corporation, buyer–seller, producer–consumer, and service provider–recipient. But it can also apply to other enterprises, such as the college fraternity (*Zeta Chi* case excerpt, p. 259), and relationships between individuals, such as making the owner of a car liable for the driver's traffic violations and holding parents liable for their children's crimes.

Let's look first at the vicarious criminal liability of corporations based on their relationships with those employed by the corporation.

Corporate Liability

LO7

> Did you ever expect a corporation to have a conscience when it has no soul to be damned, and no body to be kicked?
>
> —Lord Chancellor Edward Thurlow (1731–1806, qtd. in Weismann 2009)

> Since a corporation acts by its officers and agents, their purposes, motives, and intent are just as much those of the corporation as are the things done. If, for example, the invisible, intangible essence or air which we term a corporation can level mountains, fill up valleys, lay down iron tracks, and run railroad cars on them, it can intend to do it, and can act therein as well viciously as virtuously.
>
> —New York Central & Hudson River Railroad Company v. U.S. (1909)

Now let's discuss the history of corporate liability and the effects of making a corporation an "artificial being" that can commit crimes and be held responsible for those committed by employees.

HISTORY

Criminologist Edwin Sutherland introduced us to the "white collar criminal" and "white collar crime" in 1939, but as the introductory quotations demonstrate, concern about corporate crime is centuries old. The history of corporations began with the charters the English monarchs granted as a privilege exchanged for money. In other words, they were government entities. The Industrial Revolution dramatically changed the nature of corporations from government entities controlled by government to private business operated by internal management.

Corporate criminal law began as (and still is) the creature of *federal* law, stemming from the "contracts" and "commerce" clauses in the U.S. Constitution. The contracts clause (Article 1, Section 10, paragraph 1) provides: "No State shall... pass any... law impairing the Obligation of Contracts...." The interstate commerce clause (Article I, Section 8) provides: "The Congress shall have power to... regulate Commerce with foreign Nations, and among the several States, and with the Indian Tribes."

As corporate business increasingly affected interstate commerce in the late nineteenth century, Congress stepped in to legislate, and U.S. attorneys to prosecute, corporate crime.

During most of the twentieth century, the belief that self-regulation is the best model to make sure that corporations are meeting their obligations to shareholders and the public prevailed. That belief continues today.

Speaking to the Hartford Bond Club in 1938, then chairman of the Securities and Exchange Commission (SEC), and later Supreme Court Justice, William O. Douglas told the audience:

> Self-discipline is always more welcome than discipline imposed from above. From the broad public viewpoint, such regulation can be far more effective... and persuasive and subtle in its conditioning over business practices and business morality. By and large, the government can operate satisfactorily only by proscription. That leaves untouched large areas of conduct and activity; some of it susceptible of government regulation but in fact too minute for satisfactory control, some of it lying beyond the periphery of the law in ethics and morality. Into these large areas, self-regulation is by far the preferable course from all viewpoints. (qtd. in Seligman 2004, 1361–62)

Earlier the same year, Douglas told a congressional committee that if self-regulation of the stock market was to succeed, the Securities and Exchange Commission had to play an important, but residual, role. In Douglas's typically blunt words:

> Government would keep the shotgun, so to speak, behind the door, loaded, well-oiled, cleaned, ready to use, but with hope that it would never have to be used. (1361)

According to Professor Joel Seligman (2004), the leading expert on the history of the SEC, after seventy years, "stock market self-regulation remains a work in progress" (1348). The same can be said for all corporate regulation (Weismann 2009, 2). The weaknesses of self-regulation are well recognized, as this list in 1973 still demonstrates:

- Lack of enthusiasm for regulation by the regulated group
- Temptation to use a corporate façade of regulation as a "shield to ward off meaningful regulation"
- Businesspeople's "tendency to use collective action to advance their interests through the imposition of purely anticompetitive restraints as opposed to those justified by regulatory needs"
- Resistance to regulatory changes because of the economic interest in preserving the current status (Seligman 2004, 1347)

Writing after the subprime crisis, the collapse of the financial corporate giants, and the ensuing recession in 2008, here's how former white-collar-crime defense attorney and then prosecutor Professor Miriam Weismann (2009) sums up the history and current state of corporate regulation:

> Corporate regulation is, therefore, dependent for the most part on self-restraint and ethical corporate governance within the regulatory environment mandated by Congress. The role of the regulators and law enforcement is proscriptive in nature as opposed to proactive. This means that the government is not in a meaningful position to prevent misconduct. Instead, its role is largely reactive, punishing and/or prosecuting once the misconduct is uncovered. (2)

Let's look now at the legal and policy bases for vicarious corporate criminal liability—namely, the doctrine of *respondeat superior* ("let the master answer").

RESPONDEAT SUPERIOR ("LET THE MASTER ANSWER")

We begin with a legal fiction created by the U.S. Supreme Court in *Trustees of Dartmouth College v. Woodward* (1918). According to the Court, "A corporation is an artificial being, invisible, intangible." So a corporation can sue, be sued, and enter into contracts. And, most important for us—corporations can commit crimes. The Supreme Court decided that in *New York Central & Hudson River Railroad Company v. U.S.* (1909).

The New York Central & Hudson River Railroad Company was convicted and fined $180,000 for paying "kickbacks" to the American Sugar Refining Company for shipments of sugar from New York City to the city of Detroit, Michigan. The railroad fixed the shipping rate for sugar at 23 cents per 100 pounds from New York City to Detroit. The railroad's general traffic manager and assistant traffic manager entered into an unlawful agreement with the shippers—the American Sugar Refining Company of New York and the American Sugar Refining Company of New Jersey—and the consignees of the sugar, W. H. Edgar & Son, of Detroit. Pursuant to the agreement, the shippers paid the full rate, and the railroad "kicked back" to the shippers 5 cents for each 100 pounds.

The purpose of the kickback was to "prevent them from resorting to transportation by the water route between New York and Detroit, thereby depriving the roads interested of the business, and to assist Edgar & Son in meeting the severe competition with other shippers and dealers" (490–91).

The railroad attacked the constitutional validity of certain features of the Elkins Act, the law the railroad was convicted under. According to the act:

> Anything done or omitted to be done by a corporation common carrier subject to the act to regulate commerce, and the acts amendatory thereof, which, if done or omitted to be done by any director or officer thereof, or any receiver, trustee, lessee, agent, or person acting for or employed by such corporation, would constitute a misdemeanor under said acts, or under this act, shall also be held to be a misdemeanor committed by such corporation; and, upon conviction thereof, it shall be subject to like penalties as are prescribed in said acts, or by this act, with reference to such persons, except as such penalties are herein changed.
>
> In construing and enforcing the provisions of this section, the act, omission, or failure of any officer, agent, or other person acting for or employed by any common carrier, acting within the scope of his employment, shall, in every case, be also deemed to be the act, omission, or failure of such carrier, as well as that of the person. (491–92)

The railroad argued that

> these provisions of the law are unconstitutional because Congress has no authority to impute to a corporation the commission of criminal offenses, or to subject a corporation to a criminal prosecution by reason of the things charged. The argument is that to thus punish the corporation is in reality to punish the innocent stockholders, and to deprive them of their property without opportunity to be heard, consequently without due process of law. (492)

The Court rejected the argument and relied on the doctrine of *respondeat superior* ("let the master answer"), borrowed from tort (noncriminal wrongs) law.

According to *respondeat superior*, corporate employees' acts are imputed to the corporation.

respondeat superior a doctrine in tort law that makes a master liable for the wrong of a servant; in modern terms, an employer may be liable for the wrong of an employee

> The general freight traffic manager and the assistant freight traffic manager were authorized to establish rates at which freight should be carried over the line of the New York Central & Hudson River Company, and were authorized to unite with other companies in the establishing, filing, and publishing of through rates, including the through rate or rates between New York and Detroit referred to in the indictment. Thus, the subject-matter of making and fixing rates was within the scope of the authority and employment of the agents of the company, whose acts in this connection are sought to be charged upon the company.
>
> Thus clothed with authority, the agents were bound to respect the regulation of interstate commerce enacted by Congress, requiring the filing and publication of rates and punishing departures therefrom. Applying the principle governing civil liability, we go only a step farther in holding that the act of the agent, while exercising the authority delegated to him to make rates for transportation, may be controlled, in the interest of public policy, by imputing his act to his employer and imposing penalties upon the corporation for which he is acting. (494)

The Court's rationale for extending vicarious liability by the doctrine of *respondeat superior* was the "history of the times":

> It is a part of the public history of the times that statutes against rebates could not be effectually enforced so long as individuals only were subject to punishment for violation of the law, when the giving of rebates or concessions inured to the benefit of the corporations of which the individuals were but the instruments. This situation… was no doubt influential in bringing about the enactment of the Elkins law, making corporations criminally liable. (495)
>
> …
>
> While the law should have regard to the rights of all, and to those of corporations no less than to those of individuals, it cannot shut its eyes to the fact that the great majority of business transactions in modern times are conducted through these bodies, and particularly that interstate commerce is almost entirely in their hands, and to give them immunity from all punishment because of the old and exploded doctrine that a corporation cannot commit a crime would virtually take away the only means of effectually controlling the subject-matter and correcting the abuses aimed at.
>
> … It would be a distinct step backward to hold that Congress cannot control those who are conducting this interstate commerce by holding them responsible for the intent and purposes of the agents to whom they have delegated the power to act in the premises. (495–96)

Those were the "good old days," when the typical corporate crime case involved "slush funds," fraudulent billing schemes, and tax cheats. Corporate crime was an "inside job," and the corporate criminals hid misconduct from their accountants and lawyers. Now, there's a whole new kind of corporate crime and criminal. Corporate "watchdogs" (law firms, accounting firms, auditors, investment advisors, banks, and even regulators) who were supposed to "bark" when the public interest was threatened were silent; even worse, they were part of the "runaway organizational corporate behavior that injected chaos into America's capital markets" (Weismann 2009, xvii–xviii).

U.S. v. Arthur Andersen, LLP (2004) is the story of how Arthur Andersen, one of the largest accounting and consulting firms in the world, was brought down as a member of the "supporting cast" in the "rubble" of Enron Corporation. (Andersen was Enron's auditor. It audited Enron's publicly filed financial statements and provided internal audit and consulting services to it.) Enron switched its business from operating natural gas pipelines to an energy conglomerate, coupled with "aggressive accounting practices and rapid growth" (*Arthur Andersen LLP v. U.S.* 2005, 2).

Enron's financial performance began to decline in 2000. In August, an Enron senior accountant warned Kenneth Lay, CEO, that Enron "could implode in a wave of accounting scandals." An SEC investigation soon loomed. Before the SEC investigation formally began, Enron began to destroy documents pursuant to its documents "retention" policy. On October 16, SEC notified Enron that it had opened an investigation in August and requested certain information and documents. On October 19, Enron forwarded a copy to Andersen (3–4).

On the same day, Enron sent an e-mail to Andersen's internal team of accounting experts and attached a copy of its documents retention policy to Andersen. On October 23, after a conference call with Kenneth Lay, Enron CEO, David Duncan, head of Andersen's internal team of accounting experts, instructed everyone to "make sure to follow the document policy." Substantial destruction of paper and electronic documents followed. On October 26, a senior Andersen partner warned in an e-mail that "the problems are just beginning and we will be in the cross hairs. The marketplace is going to keep the pressure on this and is going to force SEC to be tough" (4).

Throughout this period, Andersen continued to destroy documents. In March 2002, Andersen was indicted. "The indictment alleged that, between October 10 and November 9, 2001, Andersen 'did knowingly, intentionally and corruptly persuade… Andersen's employees, with intent to cause them to withhold documents from, and alter documents for use in, 'official proceedings, namely: regulatory and criminal proceedings and investigations'" (3–4).

The case went to trial, and the jury convicted Andersen. The U.S. Circuit Court affirmed. The U.S. Supreme Court overturned the verdict (4–5). But Arthur Andersen has all but disappeared. It has shrunk from a worldwide firm of enormous prestige and reputation to a small Chicago firm devoted mostly to handling the scores of civil suits against it arising out of the Enron debacle.

Not all corporate vicarious criminal liability arises out of giant businesses and their giant "watchdogs" in finance. Even college fraternities that incorporate may find themselves in criminal court. In our next case excerpt, *State v. Zeta Chi Fraternity* (1997), Zeta Chi was charged with and convicted of recklessly selling alcohol to minors and knowingly permitting prostitution.

CASE

In ***State v. Zeta Chi Fraternity* (1997),** *Zeta Chi Fraternity was convicted of selling alcohol to a person under the age of 21, and of prostitution.*

Did the fraternity sell alcohol to a minor and allow prostitution?

State v. Zeta Chi Fraternity

686 A.2d. 530 (N.H. 1997)

(continues)

(continued)

HISTORY

Zeta Chi (Defendant), a college fraternity, was convicted, following trial in the Superior Court, Strafford County, of selling alcohol to a person under the age of 21, and of prostitution. Defendant appealed. The Supreme Court affirmed the convictions.

HORTON, J.

FACTS

Zeta Chi, a New Hampshire corporation and fraternity at the University of New Hampshire in Durham, held a "rush" at its fraternity house to attract new members. In order to encourage people to attend the rush, Zeta Chi hired two female strippers to perform at the event. Fraternity brothers encouraged guests to give the strippers dollar bills so that they would continue to perform. The brothers also told guests that the more money the strippers were given, the more that they would do. One of the members of the fraternity was providing change for larger bills.

As part of the performance, the dancers lay on a mattress brought out by members of the fraternity and simulated oral sex on each other. At one point, a guest gave five dollars to one of the strippers who sat on the guest's lap. When a brother moved the dancer along, the guest complained that he had given five dollars. The stripper took the guest to the mattress and pushed his head into her crotch. Two witnesses testified at trial that they saw guests being led to the mattress after they gave money, at which point the guests then performed oral sex on the dancer.

In addition, Andrew Strachan, a nineteen-year-old guest at the fraternity party, testified that at some point during the evening he learned that beer was available from a soda machine. He made his way to an apartment in another part of the fraternity house where the machine was located, waited in line with three or four other people, and purchased three to five cans of beer. Strachan also testified that he noticed someone making change for the machine.

The fraternity's secretary testified that the fraternity members voted not to provide alcohol at the rush and that they moved the vending machine that contained beer to a separate apartment in another part of the fraternity house for the rush. He also testified, however, that the fraternity had control over the vending machine and its proceeds and that only fraternity members would have an interest in making change for the machine.

OPINION

I. SUFFICIENCY OF EVIDENCE

A. Illegal Sale Of Alcohol

Zeta Chi argues that the State failed to prove that it caused alcohol to be sold to Strachan. See RSA 179:5:

> I. No licensee, salesperson, direct shipper, common carrier, delivery agent, nor any other person, shall sell or give away or cause or allow or procure to be sold, delivered or given away any liquor or beverage to a person under the age of 21 or to an intoxicated individual.
>
> II. No licensee, manager or person in charge of a licensed premises shall allow or permit any individual, who is under the age of 21, to possess or consume any liquor or beverage on the licensed premises.

Zeta Chi asserts that because the fraternity voted not to provide beer at the rush and the soda machine was moved from the main area in the fraternity house to a separate apartment at the back of the house, Zeta Chi did not have control over the machine, and, therefore, could not have caused the sale of alcohol from the machine. Essentially, Zeta Chi is arguing that the individuals responsible for making the beer available for sale to Strachan were not acting on behalf of the corporation or within the scope of their authority.

We begin by noting that the only defendant in this case is a corporate entity. A corporation is a jural person, but not a person in fact. It is an artificial creature, acting only through agents.... A corporation may be held criminally liable for criminal acts performed on its behalf by agents or employees acting within the scope of their authority or employment. The criminal conduct need not have been performed, authorized, ratified, adopted or tolerated by the corporation's directors, officers or other high managerial agents in order to be chargeable to the corporation.

In fact, a corporation can be convicted for actions of its agents even if it expressly instructed the agents not to engage in the criminal conduct. The agents, however, must have been acting within the scope of their actual or apparent authority. Express authority exists when the principal explicitly manifests its authorization for the agent to act. Implied authority is the reasonable incident or construction of the terms of express authority or results from acquiescence by the principal in a course of dealing by the agent. Apparent authority, on the other hand, exists where the principal so conducts itself as to cause a third party to reasonably believe that the agent is authorized to act.

It is the rare case in which the corporate leadership explicitly authorizes its agents to engage in criminal conduct. Of necessity, the proof of authority to so act must rest on all the circumstances and conduct in a given situation and the reasonable inferences to be drawn therefrom.

Evidence at trial indicates that Zeta Chi had control over the apartment in which the vending machine was located, even though it had voted to make the apartment separate from the fraternity house. More importantly, however, witnesses testified that Zeta Chi had control over the soda machine; that only Zeta Chi had an interest in the proceeds from the machine; that only fraternity members had keys to the apartment in which the machine was located; that someone was making change for the machine; and that no one would have an interest in making change except a member of the fraternity. We believe that from these facts the jury could reasonably have found that an agent of Zeta Chi sold beer from the vending machine and that this agent was acting on behalf of the corporation and within the scope of his authority.

Zeta Chi next argues that the evidence was insufficient for the jury to find that Zeta Chi acted recklessly, the *mens rea* charged in the indictment. Because Zeta Chi is a corporation, its mental state depends on the knowledge of its agents. The corporation is considered to have acquired the collective knowledge of its employees and is held responsible for their failure to act accordingly.

A person acts recklessly with respect to a material element of an offense when he is aware of and consciously disregards a substantial and unjustifiable risk that the material element exists or will result from his conduct. The risk must be of such a nature and degree that, considering the circumstances known to him, its disregard constitutes a gross deviation from the conduct that a law-abiding person would observe in the situation.

In this case, the jury could reasonably have found that Zeta Chi acted recklessly from the facts that about 150 guests, many of them under the age of twenty-one, were at the rush party that had been widely publicized on campus; that it was Zeta Chi's vending machine; that only fraternity members had keys to the apartment in which the machine was located; that party guests gained access to the machine; that someone was making change; and that a number of people were waiting in line to use the machine.

B. Prostitution

Zeta Chi contends that the State failed to prove that it knowingly allowed the prostitution and that if prostitution occurred, the individuals who allowed it were not acting within the scope of their authority.

We will first address the issue of agency. As noted above, in the context of corporate criminal liability, the corporation acts through its agents and those agents must be acting within the scope of either their actual or apparent authority in order for the corporation to be liable for their actions. Zeta Chi asserts that because the members of the fraternity announced that guests were not allowed to touch the dancers and that, if the dancer stayed too long with one guest, members of the fraternity would move her along, this indicated the lack of actual or apparent authority.

Whether an agent has acted within his actual or apparent authority… is a question for the trier of fact. Apparent authority can result when the principal fails to disapprove of the agent's act or course of action so as to lead the public to believe that his agent possesses authority to act… in the name of the principal. In this case, there was testimony that the guests were told that if they paid more money the dancers would do more; that on more than one occasion guests were led to the mattress that was brought into the room by the brothers to perform oral sex in exchange for money; and that at least one guest performed oral sex on the dancer for "quite a while."

From these facts the jury could reasonably have found that members of the fraternity acted within the scope of their authority and on behalf of the corporation in allowing oral sex to be performed in exchange for money.

Zeta Chi argues that the State failed to prove the requisite *mens rea* with regard to the prostitution

(continues)

(continued)

charge, that is, that Zeta Chi knowingly permitted oral sex to occur at the party. "A person acts knowingly with respect to conduct or to a circumstance that is a material element of an offense when he is aware that his conduct is of such nature or that such circumstances exist." Zeta Chi argues that the material element to which the "knowingly" *mens rea* applies is permission. Zeta Chi contends that there was no opportunity for Zeta Chi to manifest its lack of permission before the oral sex occurred because the dancer's actions were unexpected.

Based on the facts of this case, Zeta Chi's argument is without merit. As noted above, because Zeta Chi is a corporation, and a corporation acts through its agents, the knowledge obtained by the agents of the corporation acting within the scope of their agency is imputed to the corporation. There was testimony that several guests performed oral sex on the dancer and that on at least one occasion it occurred for several minutes. Moreover, the fraternity president testified that he "was very well in control" of the party. Therefore, even if the first act caught members of the fraternity by surprise, the jury could reasonably have inferred that Zeta Chi knowingly permitted oral sex to occur from Zeta Chi's failure to prevent the subsequent conduct.

A corporation is not insulated from criminal liability merely because it published instructions and policies which are violated by its employee; the corporation must place the acts outside the scope of an employee's employment by adequately enforcing its rules.

Convictions affirmed.

QUESTIONS

1. State the elements of vicarious liability according to New Hampshire law.
2. List all the facts relevant to deciding whether Zeta Chi, through its officers, was acting within its authority in each of the crimes.
3. Summarize the court's arguments upholding the trial court's conviction in each of the offenses.
4. In your opinion, was Zeta Chi guilty of selling alcohol to a minor? Of prostitution? Back up your answer with facts and arguments from the court's opinion.

LO7 Individual Vicarious Liability

Vicarious liability cases that attract the most attention involve large national corporations like Enron and their derivatives, like Arthur Andersen LLP, in trials that are tried in federal courts. But *Zeta Chi* shows us that not every vicarious liability involves federal cases against huge corporations. Individuals are vicariously liable for their agents' actions in state cases; most don't attract our attention. Most common are cases of employees' crimes, committed within the scope of their employment but without the approval or knowledge of their employers.

Because state individual vicarious liability, like federal corporate vicarious criminal liability, depends on statutes, the issue in most vicarious liability cases is interpreting whether the statute actually imposes vicarious liability. In our next case excerpt, *City of Waukesha v. Boehnen* (2015), bar owner Robert Boehnen challenged his vicarious liability under a Waukesha, Wisconsin, city underage drinking ordinance.

CASE

In ***City of Waukesha v. Boehnen* (2015),** *Robert Boehnen was charged with violating a Waukesha, Wisconsin, ordinance that makes it illegal for a person who holds a liquor license or one of his or her employees to serve alcohol to anyone not of legal age.*

Was the owner criminally liable for selling liquor to minors?

City of Waukesha v. Boehnen

2015 WL 1914727 (Wis. App.)

BROWN, CJ.

HISTORY

Robert Boehnen was charged with violating a Waukesha, Wisconsin, ordinance that makes it illegal for a person who holds a liquor license or one of his or her employees to serve alcohol to anyone not of legal age. The Waukesha Municipal Court convicted Boehnen and ordered him to pay a fine. The Wisconsin Court of Appeals affirmed.

FACTS

Robert Boehnen owns Fox Run Lanes and holds a license to sell alcohol in that establishment. One of the bartenders he employs sold a beer to an underage volunteer participating in a sting operation conducted by the Waukesha police. Boehnen was not present at the time of this sale. However, the police cited Boehnen, and not the bartender, for serving the underage person under WAUKESHA, WIS., MUN. CODE § 9.16(2). The City has a policy of always citing the business owner, as opposed to his or her employees, when enforcing this law.

OPINION

Boehnen claims that his due process rights were violated because the City did not prove intent, which he argues is an element of the violation, and the circuit court wrongly found vicarious liability as a result. Claiming that intent must be an element of the ordinance as a matter of due process, is a constitutional question that we review *de novo*. We presume that ordinances are constitutional. The party challenging the ordinance must prove it unconstitutional beyond a reasonable doubt.

Boehnen relies primarily on *Morissette v. United States* (1956) to make his argument. In *Morissette*, the appellant was convicted under a federal statute of "knowingly" stealing and converting government property, but the trial court did not require the prosecutor to prove intent as an element of the crime. The United States Supreme Court reversed, holding that even if a statute contains no explicit mention of intent it may still be an element of the crime. Because the statute at issue in *Morissette* outlawed "knowingly" stealing and converting government property, the Court held that the legislature required the prosecutor to prove intent.

However, the Court also held that if the word "knowingly" had not been present, the defendant could have been found guilty of the crime regardless of his mental state. Boehnen argues that the ordinance at issue here unconstitutionally imputes vicarious liability by not requiring the prosecutor to prove his intent to break the law. But he misunderstands the holding in *Morissette*. First, *Morissette* discusses a federal statute. Therefore, the principles in that case are not necessarily transferable to the ordinance at issue here. Also, *Morissette* does not require that prosecutors prove intent for every offense, all of the time. Strict liability offenses do still exist and are appropriate in certain instances. Whether a law imposes strict liability depends on legislative intent, meaning we must evaluate the statute's language, purpose, and practical requirements for effective law enforcement.

The law is quite clear on this matter. In *State v. Beaudry*, 365 N.W.2d 593 (1985), our supreme court deliberated whether a bar owner could be held vicariously liable for the illegal actions of an employee. The court acknowledged a long history of strict liability offenses for persons that violate a statute regarding the illegal sale of alcohol which contains no language about intent. The legislature imposes strict liability in such instances because "protection of the public interest warrants the imposition of liability unhindered by examination of the subjective intent of each accused."

The theory of vicarious liability does not require that the charged person commit an illegal act, but rather it transfers liability from an employee to his or her employer. We must look at the language of the statute itself to determine whether it imposes vicarious liability. Because the ordinance at issue adopts a state statute verbatim, the principles we have discussed form a basis for our analysis.

(continues)

(continued)

The City charged Boehnen under WAUKESHA, WIS., MUN. CODE § 9.16(2), which states: "No licensee or permittee may sell, vend, deal or traffic in alcoholic beverages to or with any underage person not accompanied by his or her parent, guardian or spouse who has attained the legal drinking age." The ordinance is clearly different from the statute in *Morissette*. Here, the ordinance contains no language even hinting about intent, and it clearly imposes strict liability on any offender, regardless of mental state. Therefore, Boehnen's intent, or lack thereof, is irrelevant, as a specific mental state is not required for the court to find him guilty.

Furthermore, the law contemplates liability for either the person holding the liquor license or one of his or her employees. This language indicates that the ordinance considers both bar owners and their employees as potential violators. While the ordinance does not explicitly say bar owners are liable for the actions of their employees, we see nothing to indicate that an employer should be insulated from the illegal conduct of his or her staff in situations like this one. Therefore, we hold that the circuit court properly imputed vicarious liability to Boehnen for the actions of his bartender.

Judgment affirmed.

QUESTIONS

1. List the facts relevant to deciding whether bar owner Robert Boehnen is guilty of violating the ordinance.
2. Summarize Boehnen's argument that he's not liable for his bartender selling liquor to the police sting volunteer.
3. Summarize the Wisconsin Court of Appeal's arguments supporting its decision to affirm Boehnen's conviction.
4. In your opinion, should the bartender, Boehnen, or both be held liable? Support your answer with points regarding vicarious liability made in the opinion, in the vicarious liability section, and in Chapter 4, "Strict Liability," pp. 142–145 of your text.

Virtually all vicarious liability statutes involve the employer–employee relationship. But not all do, as we saw in *State v. Zeta Chi*. Also, in some states and municipalities, registered vehicle owners are liable for some traffic violations involving their vehicles, regardless of who violated the law. So if you let your friend drive your car to go shopping, and he didn't feed the parking meter, you're liable for paying the fine.

Another nonbusiness relationship subject to individual vicarious criminal liability is parents' criminal liability for their kids' crimes. For example, in 1995, Salt Lake City enacted an ordinance that made it a crime for parents to fail to "supervise and control their children." By 1997, seventeen states and cities had adopted one of these parental responsibility laws.

The idea of holding parents responsible for their children's crimes is nothing new. Contributing to the delinquency of a minor is an old offense. Contributing to the delinquency of minors statutes mandate that the acts of minor children were done at the direction of or with the consent of their parents. So, in one case, a father was found guilty for "allowing his child to violate a curfew ordinance," and, in another, a mother was convicted for "knowingly" permitting her children "to go at large in violation of a valid quarantine order."

One disturbing case involved the Detroit suburb of St. Clair Shores, which has an ordinance making it a crime to fail to "exercise reasonable control" to prevent children from committing delinquent acts. Alex Provenzino, 16, committed a string of seven burglaries. The local police ordered his parents to "take control" of Alex. When his father tried to discipline him, Alex "punched his father." When he tried to restrain him, Alex escaped by pressing his fingers into his father's eyes. When Alex tried to attack him with a golf club, his father called the police. The parents were charged with, but acquitted of, both vicariously committing the seven burglaries and failing to supervise their son (Siegel 1996, A1).

Traditional **parental responsibility statutes** aren't the same as vicarious liability. Parental responsibility statutes are based on parents' acts and omissions; vicarious liability statutes are based on the parent–child relationship. Vicarious liability statutes grew out of public fear, frustration, and anger over juvenile violence and parents' failure to control their kids. However, there are only a few cases in the appellate courts based on these vicarious liability statutes that make the crimes of kids the crimes of their parent solely on the basis of the parent–child relationship (DiFonzo 2001). One of these rare cases is now more than thirty years old.

parental responsibility statutes based on parents' acts and omissions; differ from vicarious liability statutes, which are based on the parent–child relationship

In our next case excerpt, *State v. Akers* (1979), the New Hampshire Supreme Court dealt with a state statute making parents liable for their children's illegal snowmobile driving.

CASE

In ***State v. Akers* (1979),** *parents were found guilty of violating a snowmobile statute which makes parents vicariously liable for the acts of their children simply because they occupy the status of parents. The parents waived all right to an appeal* de novo *("new trial") to superior court. The parents objected to the constitutionality of the parental responsibility statute.*

Are the parents guilty of illegal snowmobiling?

State v. Akers

400 A.2d 38 (N.H. 1979)

HISTORY

Parent defendants were found guilty of violating a snowmobile statute which makes parents vicariously liable for the acts of their children simply because they occupy the status of parents. The parents waived all right to an appeal *de novo* ("new trial") to superior court. The parents objected to the constitutionality of the parental responsibility statute. The New Hampshire Supreme Court sustained the objections.

GRIMES, J.

FACTS

The defendants are fathers whose minor sons were found guilty of driving snowmobiles in violation of RSA 269-C:6—a II (operating on public way) and III (reasonable speed) (Supp. 1977). RSA 269-C:24 IV, which pertains to the operation and licensing of Off Highway Recreational Vehicles (OHRV), provides that "the parents or guardians or persons assuming responsibility will be responsible for any damage incurred or for any violations of this chapter by any person under the age of 18." Following a verdict of guilty for violating RSA 269-C:24 IV the two defendants waived all right to an appeal *de novo* to the superior court and all questions of law were reserved and transferred by the District Court to the New Hampshire Supreme Court.

OPINION

The defendants argue that (1) RSA 269-C:24 IV, the statute under which they were convicted, was not intended by the legislature to impose criminal responsibility, and (2) if in fact the legislative intention was to impose criminal responsibility, then the statute would

(continues)

(continued)

violate N.H. Const. pt. 1, art. 15 and U.S. Const. amend. XIV, § 1.

The language of RSA 269-C:24 IV, "Parents will be responsible for any violations of this chapter by any person under the age of 18," clearly indicates the legislature's intention to hold the parents criminally responsible for the OHRV violations of their minor children. It is a general principle of this State's Criminal Code that "a person is not guilty of an offense unless his criminal liability is based on conduct that includes a voluntary act or the voluntary omission to perform an act of which he is physically capable." RSA 269-C:24 IV seeks to impose criminal liability on parents for the acts of their children without basing liability on any voluntary act or omission on the part of the parent. Because the statute makes no reference at all to parental conduct or acts it seeks to impose criminal responsibility solely because of their parental status contrary to the provisions of RSA 626:1.

The legislature has not specified any voluntary acts or omissions for which parents are sought to be made criminally responsible and it is not a judicial function to supply them. It is fundamental to the rule of law and due process that acts or omissions which are to be the basis of criminal liability must be specified in advance and not ex post facto. N.H. Const. pt. 1, art. 23.

It is argued that liability may be imposed on parents under the provisions of RSA 626:8 II(b), which authorizes imposing criminal liability for conduct of another when "he is made accountable for the conduct of such other person by the law defining the offense." This provision comes from the Model Penal Code § 2.04(2)(b). The illustrations of this type of liability in the comments to the Code all relate to situations involving employees and agents, and no suggestion is made that it was intended to authorize imposing vicarious criminal liability on one merely because of his status as a parent.

Without passing upon the validity of statutes that might seek to impose vicarious criminal liability on the part of an employer for acts of his employees, we have no hesitancy in holding that any attempt to impose such liability on parents simply because they occupy the status of parents, without more, offends the due process clause of our State constitution.

Parenthood lies at the very foundation of our civilization. The continuance of the human race is entirely dependent upon it. It was firmly entrenched in the Judeo-Christian ethic when "in the beginning" man was commanded to "be fruitful and multiply" (Genesis I). Considering the nature of parenthood, we are convinced that the status of parenthood cannot be made a crime. This, however, is the effect of RSA 269-C:24 IV. Even if the parent has been as careful as anyone could be, even if the parent has forbidden the conduct, and even if the parent is justifiably unaware of the activities of the child, criminal liability is still imposed under the wording of the present statute.

There is no other basis for criminal responsibility other than the fact that a person is the parent of one who violates the law. One hundred and twenty seven years ago the justices of this court in giving their opinions regarding a proposed law that would have imposed vicarious criminal liability on an employer for acts of his employee stated, "(b)ut this does not seem to be in accordance with the spirit of our Constitution…" Because the net effect of the statute is to punish parenthood, the result is forbidden by substantive due process requirements of N.H. Const. pt. 1, art. 15.

Exceptions sustained.

DISSENT

BOIS, J.

The majority read RSA 269-C:24 IV in isolation. They conveniently ignore RSA 626:8 (Criminal Liability for Conduct of Another), which provides in subsection II that "(a) person is legally accountable for the conduct of another person when: (b) he is made accountable for the conduct of such other person by the law defining the offense." RSA 269-C:24 IV is such a law. Imposing criminal liability based on status for certain violations of a *mala prohibitum* nature does not offend constitutional requirements.

Even if I were to accept the majority's conclusion that the vicarious imposition of criminal liability on parents of children who have committed an OHRV [Off Highway Recreational Vehicles] violation under RSA ch. 269-C is constitutionally impermissible, I would still uphold the validity of RSA 269-C:24 IV. A closer reading of this State's Criminal Code belies the majority's reasoning that RSA 269-C:24 IV holds parents of minor offenders criminally responsible for their children's offenses solely on the basis of their parental status. RSA 626:1 I, enunciating the fundamental principle of the Criminal Code, states that all criminal liability must be based on a "voluntary act" or "voluntary omission."

When RSA 269-C:24 IV is read in conjunction with RSA 626:1 I, a parental conviction can result only when the State shows beyond a reasonable doubt that a minor child has committed a violation under a provision of chapter 269-C, and that his parent voluntarily performed or omitted to perform an act such as participating in the minor's conduct, or entrusting, or negligently allowing his minor child to operate an OHRV.

When RSA 269-C:24 IV is construed to require a voluntary act or voluntary omission in accordance with RSA 626:1 I, there are no due process infirmities, either under N.H.Const. pt. 1, art. 15 or U.S. Const. amend. XIV, § 1. Culpable intent is not required to impose criminal penalties for minor infractions. "It is well settled in this jurisdiction that the Legislature may declare criminal a certain act or omission to act without requiring it to be done with intent." When the legislature imposes criminal responsibility without requiring intent, we will override it only when such imposition violates concepts of fundamental fairness.

In the present case, there is a demonstrable public interest to assure the safe operation of OHRVs, and the minor penalties imposed upon violators of RSA 269-C:24 IV are insubstantial. In such circumstances, we will not second guess the wisdom of the legislature.

Public welfare offenses requiring no criminal intent have also been held consistent with the due process requirements of U.S. Const. amend. XIV, § 1. "There is wide latitude in the lawmakers to declare an offense and to exclude elements of knowledge and diligence from its definition.... In vindicating its public policy a State in punishing particular acts may provide that "he shall do them at his peril."

QUESTIONS

1. Exactly what does the New Hampshire statute prohibit?
2. Summarize all of the arguments of the majority and dissenting opinions. Which side do you agree with? Defend your answer.
3. Apart from the legal and constitutional arguments, do you think it's good public policy to make parents criminally liable for their children's crimes? Defend your answer.

YOU *DECIDE*

Is it wise public policy to make parents guilty for their children's crimes?

Susan and Anthony Provenzino of St. Clair Shores, Michigan, knew their 16-year-old son, Alex, was troubled. His first arrest occurred in May 1995, and in the year that followed, he continued his delinquent behavior by committing burglary, drinking alcohol, and using and selling marijuana. Alex was difficult at home as well, verbally abusing his parents and once attacking his father with a golf club. Although the Provenzinos were disturbed by Alex's behavior, they supported his release from juvenile custody during the fall of 1995, fearing he would be mistreated in the youth facility where he was detained—a facility where juveniles charged with more violent crimes were housed.

It is unlikely that the Provenzinos expected to be the first parents tried and convicted of violating a two-year-old St. Clair Shores ordinance that places an affirmative responsibility on parents to "exercise reasonable control over their children." On May 5, 1996, however, after a jury deliberated only 15 minutes, the Provenzinos were convicted of violating the parental accountability ordinance. They were each fined $100 and ordered to pay an additional $1,000 in court fees.

Instructions

1. Go to the Office of Juvenile Justice and Delinquency Prevention's essay, "Parental Responsibility Laws," at http://www.ojjdp.gov/pubs/reform/ch2_d.html.
2. Read the section "Juvenile Justice Reform Initiatives in the States 1994–1996: Parental Responsibility Laws." Pay special attention to parents' responsibility for their children's *crimes*.
3. Compile a list of the various responses—criminal, civil, and private—to parental responsibility for their children's crimes.
4. Based on these materials, which of the alternatives is the wisest ethical public policy?

Summary

LO1 Although both complicity and vicarious liability involve more than one party, they differ critically. Complicity establishes when you can be held criminally liable for someone else's conduct. Vicarious liability establishes when a party can be criminally liable because of a relationship. Today, there are two parties to criminal complicity: (1) accomplices, participants before and during the commission of crimes and, (2) accessories, participants after crimes are committed.

LO2 Accomplice liability is very serious business and results in prosecution for the crime itself; for example, accomplices to murder are prosecuted as murderers. Accomplices are often confused with co-conspirators, but they're two completely different crimes. Conspiracy is an agreement to commit a crime; for example, conspiracy to commit murder is not murder but a lesser offense of agreeing to murder.

LO3 Accomplice *actus reus* boils down to one core idea: the actor took "some positive act in aid of the commission of the offense". Mere presence when a crime is committed isn't enough to satisfy the *actus reus* requirement of accomplice liability, even if it is followed by flight from the crime. Failing to act or stop the crime also fails to meet the requirement unless there was a duty to act.

LO4 Accomplice *mens rea* is clear in cases in which the mental attitude is "purposely." Courts remain divided, however, over the question of whether knowledge is enough to establish accomplice *mens rea*.

LO5 Accessory liability is less blameworthy than participation in the crime itself; it is usually a misdemeanor offense.

LO6 Vicarious liability transfers the *actus reus* and *mens rea* of one person to another person—or from one or more persons to an enterprise—because of their relationship. Vicarious liability can only be created by statute.

LO7 Most vicarious liability involves business relationships, such as employer–employee, manager–corporation, buyer–seller, producer–consumer, and service provider–recipient. Sometimes, individuals are vicariously liable for their agents' actions.

Key Terms

complicity, p. 244
vicarious liability, p. 244
agency theory, p. 244
forfeited personal identity theory, p. 244
accomplices, p. 244
accessories, p. 244
principals in the first degree, p. 245
principals in the second degree, p. 245
accessories before the fact, p. 245
accessories after the fact, p. 245
accomplice liability, p. 245
accessory liability, p. 245
conspiracy, p. 245
Pinkerton rule, p. 245
accomplice *actus reus*, p. 246
mere presence rule, p. 246
accessory, p. 251
respondeat superior, p. 257
parental responsibility statutes, p. 265

Learning Objectives

1 To understand that inchoate offenses punish people for taking some steps towards a criminal purpose, but not enough steps to complete the intended crime.

2 To appreciate the long history of attempt law and to understand that criminal attempt liability is based on two rationales: preventing dangerous conduct and neutralizing dangerous people.

3 To know the *mens rea* of criminal attempt is always the purpose or specific intent to commit a specific crime.

4 To understand that the *actus reus* of attempt is an act that goes beyond mere preparation but not far enough to complete the crime.

5 To understand the difference between legal and factual impossibility and to know that legal impossibility is a defense to criminal liability but factual possibility is not.

6 To know that voluntary and complete abandonment of an attempt in progress is a defense to criminal liability in about half the states.

7 To understand that punishing conspiracy is based on preventing crimes by recognizing the special danger of group criminality.

8 To understand that conspiracy *actus reus* consists of two parts: an agreement to commit a crime and an overt act in furtherance of the agreement.

9 To understand the relationship between the parties to conspiracy and to know that large-scale conspiracies fall into two major categories: wheel conspiracies and chain conspiracies.

10 To understand the Racketeer Influenced and Corrupt Organizations (RICO) Act and how it works against organized crime.

11 To understand that punishing solicitation, or trying to get someone else to commit a crime, is based on the same idea as punishing conspiracy: to prevent crimes before they start by anticipating the dangers of group criminality.

8 Inchoate Crimes

Chapter Outline

Marjory Damms and her husband Ralph were separated. Marjory had recently instituted an action for divorce against Ralph. She was 39 years old and he 33. Ralph talked Marjory into getting in his car, telling her he'd drive her to work. (Ralph had a handgun in the car, which he showed to Marjory.) Instead of driving Marjory to work, he drove in another direction, telling Marjory he was going to take her "up North" to talk about reconciliation.

As they approached a roadside restaurant, Ralph asked Marjory if she would like something to eat. She replied that she wasn't hungry but would drink some coffee. Damms then drove the car off the highway beside the restaurant and parked it with the front facing, and in close proximity to, the restaurant wall.

Marjory opened the car door and started to run around the restaurant building screaming, "Help!" Damms pursued her with a pistol in his hand. Mrs. Damms's cries for help attracted the attention of the persons inside the restaurant, including two officers of the state traffic patrol who were eating their lunch. One officer rushed out of the front door and the other the rear door. In the meantime, Mrs. Damms had run nearly around three sides of the building. In seeking to avoid colliding with a child, who was in her path, she turned, slipped, and fell. Damms crouched down, held the pistol at her head, and pulled the trigger, but nothing happened. He then exclaimed, "It won't fire. It won't fire."

LO1

We all know that a man who chases his wife around a restaurant parking lot and shoots her in the head and kills her with a loaded gun in his hand when she trips and falls commits murder. However, what if the man does the same thing, but the gun isn't loaded? Is that a crime? That's what this chapter is about—criminal liability for:

criminal attempts trying but failing to commit crimes

criminal conspiracy making an agreement to commit a crime

criminal solicitation trying to get someone else to commit a crime

inchoate offenses from the Latin "to begin"; crimes that satisfy the *mens rea* of purpose or specific intent and the *actus reus* of taking some steps toward accomplishing the criminal purpose—but not enough steps to complete the intended crime

- **Criminal attempts**, trying to commit crimes but failing to complete them
- **Criminal conspiracy**, making agreements to commit crimes
- **Criminal solicitation**, trying to get someone else to commit a crime

We call these three crimes **inchoate offenses**. The word "inchoate" comes from Latin *incohare* (to begin). Each inchoate offense has some of its own elements, but they all share two elements: the *mens rea* of purpose or specific intent (Chapter 4) and the *actus reus* of taking some steps toward accomplishing the criminal purpose—but not enough steps to complete the intended crime.

Just to keep your bearings about where we are in the "big picture" of criminal law—and in your book—the inchoate offenses stand partly in the general and partly in the special part. Unlike the principles in the general part, they're specific crimes, such as attempted robbery. But, like the general part, they apply to many crimes, such as in the mental attitude of specific intent or purpose and the voluntary acts that fall short of completing the intended crime. That's why the Model Penal Code designates them "offenses of general application" (Dubber 2002, 142).

Incomplete criminal conduct poses a dilemma: whether to punish someone who's done no harm or to set free someone who's determined to commit a crime. Inchoate crimes asks the question: How far should criminal law go to prevent crime by punishing people who haven't accomplished their criminal purpose?

Creating criminal liability for uncompleted crimes flies in the face of the notion that free societies punish people for what they've *done*, not for what they *might* do. On the other hand, the doctrine of inchoate crimes reflects the widely held belief that "an ounce of prevention is worth a pound of cure." The law of inchoate crimes resolves the dilemma by three means:

1. Requiring a specific intent or purpose to commit the crime or cause a harm
2. Requiring some action to carry out the purpose
3. Punishing inchoate crimes less severely than completed crimes (ALI 1985, 3:293–98; Perkins and Boyce 1982, 611–58)

ATTEMPT

Failure is an unwelcome part of everyday life that we'd like to avoid. But in criminal law, we *want* those who try to hurt others, to fail. So, we're relieved when a would-be murderer shoots and misses his target. In this section, we'll look at how attempt law has evolved over more than two thousand years; the rationales for attempt law; the elements of criminal attempt; and how failures to complete crimes due to either impossibility or voluntary abandonment are treated within the law.

Attempt Law History

LO2

> One who has a purpose and intention to slay another and only wounds him should be regarded as a murderer.
>
> —Plato, *Laws*, 360 BCE

> For what harm did the attempt cause, since the injury took no effect?
>
> —Henry of Bracton, about 1300
> (Qtd. in Bracton 1968–77, 3:21)

These quotes, separated by about a thousand years, underscore how long philosophers and judges have struggled with how the criminal law should respond to criminal attempts. Until the 1500s, the English common law sided with Bracton; in attempts, "a miss was as good as a mile" (Hall 1960, 560). A few cases of attempted murder in the 1300s adopted Plato's view according to the maxim, "The intent shall be taken for the deed." One was a servant who cut his master's throat and ran off with his goods; the other was a man who attacked his lover's husband, leaving him for dead (561). But according to the great scholars of medieval English law, Sir Frederick Pollock and William Maitland (1898), "The adoption of this perilous saying was but a momentary aberration" provoked by excessive leniency in these "murderous assaults which did not cause death" (II, 476, n. 3).

Modern attempt law began in 1500s England out of frustration with this "excessive leniency" in a violent society where tempers were short and hot, and everyone was armed. The famous royal court (a special court of the monarch not bound by common law rules) that met in the Star Chamber started punishing a wide range of potential harms, hoping to nip violence in the bud. Typical cases included lying in wait, threats, challenges, and even words that "tended to challenge." Surviving records are full of efforts to punish budding violence that too often erupted into serious injury and death (Elton 1972, 170–71).

In the early 1600s, stressing the need to prevent the serious harms spawned by dueling, Francis Bacon maintained that "all the acts of preparation should be punished" (Samaha 1974; 1981, 189).

By the late 1700s, the English common law courts had created a full-fledged law of attempt. In the great case of *Rex v. Scofield* (1784), a servant put a lighted candle in his master's house, intending to burn the house down. The house didn't burn, but the servant was punished anyway. According to the court, "The intent may make an act, innocent in itself, criminal; nor is the completion of an act, criminal in itself, necessary to constitute criminality."

By the 1800s, common law attempt was well-defined:

> All attempts whatever to commit indictable offenses, whether felonies or misdemeanors are misdemeanors, unless by some special statutory enactment they are subjected to special punishment. (Stephen 1883, 2:224)

Some jurisdictions still follow the common law of attempt. In 1979, a Maryland judge confidently wrote that "the common law is still alive and well in Maryland" and that the common law of attempt "still prospers on these shores" (*Gray v. State* 1979, 854). As of May 2015, it was still good law. In our next case excerpt, *State v. Dabney* (2004), the Maryland Court of Special Appeals reversed Franklin Roosevelt Dabney's conviction of fourth-degree burglary.

CASE

*In **Dabney v. State (2004),** Franklin Roosevelt Dabney (Defendant) was convicted, after a jury trial in the Circuit Court, Baltimore County, of attempted fourth-degree burglary. Defendant appealed. The Court of Special Appeals reversed.*

Did he attempt to commit burglary?

Dabney v. State

858 A.2d 1084 (2004)

HISTORY

Franklin Roosevelt Dabney (Defendant) was convicted, after a jury trial in the Circuit Court, Baltimore County, of attempted fourth-degree burglary. Defendant appealed. The Court of Special Appeals reversed.

MOYLAN, J., JOINED BY HOLLANDER, AND SHARER, JJ.

The Baltimore County Police Department charged Franklin Roosevelt Dabney (Appellant) with attempted fourth-degree burglary. Attempted fourth-degree burglary? It smacks of convicting Al Capone, after Elliot Ness had been on his trail for a decade, of income tax evasion. It is perfectly legal, of course, but there remains the lingering aftertaste of overkill. Dabney was convicted by a Baltimore County jury of attempted burglary in the fourth degree, punishable by up to 3 years in prison. Dabney appealed on the ground that he was convicted of a non-existent crime, to wit, an attempt to commit an attempt.

FACTS

At approximately midnight on the evening of January 19–20, 2003, Dabney left his apartment in northwestern Baltimore County, got into his black Infiniti, and drove out of his neighborhood. For reasons unexplained to us in this record, a police surveillance team, consisting of six or seven unmarked police cars, was on station, waiting to monitor Dabney's every move. They monitored him as he stopped at a service station and purchased gasoline. As the appellant then approached the Reisterstown Road entrance to the Baltimore Beltway (I-695) and turned east on it toward Towson, a police helicopter joined the surveillance.

On his way around the Beltway, the appellant first took the Dulaney Valley Road exit and detoured through a residential neighborhood just off Dulaney Valley Road. Apparently finding nothing to his liking, he returned to the Beltway and resumed his journey east and south. Without a single traffic infraction, the appellant followed the Beltway to the southeastern corner of the county, where he left the Beltway and proceeded into a residential neighborhood in White Marsh.

Using a thermal imaging camcorder, Officer Connolly described the appellant's behavior once inside the residential neighborhood: "[He] just did a lot of driving around all of these little side streets." Dabney parked his car on Ballygar Road, around the corner from the home of Vendel and Patricia Ann Katona, who lived on the perpendicular Kilbride Road. When he got out of his vehicle, he walked up Ballygar Road to its intersection with Kilbride. He turned right on Kilbride and walked to the Katona home, which is the second house in from the intersection.

Mr. and Mrs. Katona did not know Dabney, had neither met him nor heard of him, and did not give him permission to enter onto their property. The light was on in the Katona living room. Mrs. Katona was still up, reading and watching television, although Mr. Katona had gone to bed at around 11:30. Two cars were parked in the Katonas's front driveway. Dabney walked up that driveway, paused for about ten seconds between the two parked cars, walked back down the driveway to the street, and then crossed the lawn to the front porch of the house. After standing on the porch for a short time, Dabney walked around the side of the house and then to the rear of the house.

Then he came back around from the rear of the house and up along the side of the house.

Then, a car came down the street, pulled up and stopped, approximately, in front of the house that he was at. He then ran down behind the house, ran down behind the neighbor's house, and went down to the house at the corner, and hid behind the house here at the corner. He stayed there, approximately, maybe 20 seconds or so. Then, he ran straight from this house back to his car.

Approximately five seconds later, Dabney's car drove off. He drove immediately away from the White Marsh neighborhood. The police didn't stop him. Indeed, he wasn't arrested until a month later, at which time he was charged with attempted fourth degree burglary. The thermal imaging tape was played for the jury. Dabney didn't testify. The odyssey was never explained.

OPINION

Dabney wasn't convicted of a consummated fourth-degree burglary, but only of an attempted fourth-degree burglary. "Ay, there's the rub."

Of the various forms of criminal behavior covered by the umbrella crime of fourth-degree burglary, the attempted sub variety for which the appellant was primarily, if not exclusively, tried was a type of criminal behavior that had earlier been one of the two ways in which an accused could be found guilty of being a rogue and vagabond. Maryland Code, Criminal Law Article, § 6-205(c) provides, in pertinent part: "A person, with the intent to commit theft, may not be in or on . . . a yard, garden, or other area belonging to the dwelling . . . of another."

Dabney was clearly guilty of a consummated fourth-degree burglary of that particular subvariety and not of a mere attempt. As the case was ready to go to the jury, the prosecutor was aware of a looming problem as he addressed the court. "We have to address the verdict sheet, because *it's not attempted burglary in the fourth degree, it's burglary in the fourth degree*—he was on that property with the intent to steal." (Emphasis supplied.)

The court reminded the prosecutor of the obvious and prominent impediment to correcting the verdict sheet. The appellant had never been charged with a consummated fourth-degree burglary and consequently could not be convicted of it. The verdict sheet, in a word, could not be corrected. The prosecutor responded, "the State's argument regarding that would be that he attempted to have an intent to commit a theft," whatever that may mean. There may be a subtlety there beyond our comprehension, but we have no idea what it may be. The court subsequently instructed the jury on the law of attempt and on fourth-degree burglary of the rogue and vagabond subvariety. The jury returned a verdict of guilty of attempted fourth-degree burglary.

The problem is not that proof of consummation would not also support a conviction for the attempt, because the attempted crime is, as a matter of logical necessity, a lesser included crime within the consummated crime. Some attempts fail and others succeed, but they are attempts in either event. The attempt simply lacks one element possessed by the consummated crime, and it has no independent element of its own. The problem is that an attempt to commit this particular predicate crime (a fourth-degree burglary of the rogue and vagabond subvariety) may carry in its genes a different but innate impediment all of its own, and thereon hangs the tale that follows.

THE COMMON LAW MISDEMEANOR OF ATTEMPT

In *Gray v. State*, 43 Md. App. 238, 239, 403 A. 2d 853 (1979), this Court traced the early development of the common law misdemeanor [in England]. We then turned to the firm implementation of attempt law into the soil of Maryland.

> It is, furthermore, clear that the common law misdemeanor of criminal attempt, notwithstanding its post-Revolutionary final crystallization, has always been recognized as part of the common law of Maryland.
>
> From the beginning, it has been indisputably established that the common law misdemeanor consists of two elements: 1) the *mens rea* of intending to commit a particular crime and 2) the *actus reus* of taking a substantial step, beyond mere preparation, toward the commission of the targeted crime.

BURGLARY IN THE FOURTH DEGREE

Fourth-degree burglary is an umbrella statute, embracing no less than four subvarieties of now criminal behavior. What is true of some of those subvarieties, moreover, is not true of others. The first two, for instance, are mere general intent crimes, whereas the latter two are specific intent crimes. The first two are recent statutory inventions, whereas the latter two were already venerable at the time of Blackstone and Hale. It is a miscellaneous collection, with its common denominator or organizing principle being that the various offenses share, if nothing else, the same level of appropriate punishment of being "subject to imprisonment not exceeding 3 years." § 6-205(e).

(continues)

(continued)

[Only the third subvariety applies here.]

(c) *Prohibited—Being in or on dwelling, storehouse, or environs.* A person, with the intent to commit theft, may not be in or on:

(1) the dwelling or storehouse of another; or

(2) a yard, garden, or other area belonging to the dwelling or storehouse of another.

[Subvariety (c)] does not require the breaking and entering of a structure. It does demand, however, the enhanced *mens rea* of a specific intent, "to commit theft." [It was] formerly constituted the independent rogue and vagabond statute. Art. 27, § 490.

ROGUES AND VAGABONDS

Whereas subvarieties (a) and (b) of fourth-degree burglary are of recent vintage (dating from 1973 and 1979, respectively), subvarieties (c) and (d) enjoy an ancient lineage. Interesting insight into the common law's attitude toward rogues and vagabonds may be gleaned from Part IV (Of Public Wrongs) of Sir William Blackstone's *Commentaries on the Law of England* (Robert Malcolm Kerr edition, 1962), first published in 1765.

Aimed at persons of disreputable status or character, his introduction to the category is enlightening. [See Chapter 1, p. 8, "Offences against public police."] Of the thirteen categories of rogues and vagabonds that he describes, it is category 10 and 11 that eventually made it to Maryland. [Category 11 refers to subvariety (c): "Persons being found in or upon any dwelling-house, warehouse, or out-house, or in any enclosed yard, garden, or area, for any unlawful purpose."

THE ROAD NOT TAKEN

Of the four subvarieties of fourth-degree burglary, only two of them, on the facts of this case, might arguably have qualified as the predicate or target crime for the attempt that was charged. Subvariety (b) was inapplicable because no "storehouse" was involved. Subvariety (d) was inapplicable because no "burglar's tool" was involved. On these facts, the predicate crime attempted, assuming the sufficiency of the proof of intent, might have been subvariety (a), the breaking and entering of the dwelling of the Katonas. It might also have been subvariety (c), being in the yard or other area belonging to the dwelling of the Katonas with the intent to commit a theft. It might easily have been both.

It appears to us that the overall strategy of the prosecution was not carefully planned. This is ironic in view of the massive investigative effort that had preceded it. If subvariety (c) of fourth-degree burglary was going to be relied upon, the appellant should have been charged with a consummated fourth-degree burglary, and not merely with an attempt.

WAS THIS A COGNIZABLE ATTEMPT?

[Omitted]

A. Statement No. 1: "There is No Such Crime as an Attempted Assault"

[Omitted]

B. Statement No. 2: "There Is No Such Crime as an Attempted Attempt"

[Omitted]

C. Statement No. 4: "There Is No Such Crime as an Attempt to Commit an Inchoate Crime"

[Omitted]

D. Statement No. 3: "There Is No Such Crime as an Attempt to Commit a Crime in the Nature of an Attempt"

It is important to keep in mind that *prosecution for attempt is only one of several ways in which the criminal law can reach conduct merely tending toward the doing of some harm otherwise proscribed by law.* The crimes of assault and burglary, which served as a means of dealing with the most common forms of attempt prior to recognition of attempt as a distinct crime, are still very much with us. In addition, even *the most modern codes include crimes defined in terms of conduct* which is arguably of itself harmless but *which has been made criminal because it is* (or is very likely to be) *a step toward the doing of harm.* For example, one modern code includes not only a host of possession-type crimes (e.g., possession of obscene material with intent to disseminate it, possession of a forged instrument with intent to issue or deliver same, *possession of burglary tools with intent to commit a burglary*, possession of explosives or incendiary devices with intent to use them in committing an offense, possession of any instrument adapted for the use of narcotics by subcutaneous injection, possession of weapons with intent to use same against another unlawfully, possession of a gambling device), but also other substantive offenses defined in terms of using certain items for a particular purpose, offering to do something, attracting an intended victim, *or even being in a certain place for a bad purpose.* (Emphasis added by the court.)

Many (but not all) of these statutes reach conduct which is merely preparatory in nature and which thus would not be encompassed within the general law of attempts. A fourth-degree burglary of subvariety (c) might well be deemed "conduct…which has been made criminal because it is…a step toward the doing of harm."

We are satisfied that subvariety (c) of fourth-degree burglary (and subvariety (d) for that matter) is a crime in the nature of an attempt. Its *actus reus* of being on the property belonging to the dwelling of another has no criminal significance in its own right absent the *mens rea* of an intent to commit theft. The requirement of that *mens rea* makes the defendant's presence at that location a substantial step in attempting a theft.

To be sure, the same observation might also be made about burglary in the first degree and perhaps the two phenomena are simply at different points along the same continuum. That does not mean, however, that being at different points on the same continuum may not have critical significance. The critical difference may be between 1) a very serious *actus reus* with a coincidental intent to commit some further criminal act and 2) a relatively far less serious *actus reus* with a primary intent to commit some further criminal act.

Whether a crime qualifies as being in the nature of an attempt may ultimately depend on how much of its collective criminality is wrapped up in its attempt component. The critical difference may be whether the attempt component of a larger crime is its major theme, giving it its essential identity, or only a minor theme.

The term "a crime in the nature of an attempt" may, indeed, require finer tuning in the future on a case-by-case basis. It would seem that it should not be held to embrace major crimes, capable of full consummation in their own right, simply because they might, coincidentally, contemplate the achievement of some further purpose. The drawing of a final line between Statement # 3 of the proposition under analysis and Statement # 4, however, may have to await *ad hoc* resolution as the cases develop.

OUR HOLDING

We hold that the rogue and vagabond subvariety of fourth-degree burglary that was the target of the attempt in this case was itself a crime in the nature of an attempt. We further hold that there is no such cognizable crime as an attempt to commit a crime in the nature of an attempt. The appellant, therefore, was convicted of a non-existent crime, and the conviction must be reversed.

QUESTIONS

1. List all of the facts relevant to deciding whether Franklin Roosevelt Dabney committed subvariety rogue and vagabond attempted fourth-degree burglary.
2. Summarize the trial court's holding that Dabney committed attempted fourth-degree burglary.
3. Summarize the Special Court of Appeals' arguments that Dabney could not commit attempted fourth-degree burglary.
4. In your opinion, should it be possible to commit attempted fourth-degree burglary? Explain your answer.

The Rationales for Criminal Attempt Law

LO2

Why do we punish people who haven't hurt anyone? There are two old and firmly entrenched rationales. One focuses on dangerous acts (*actus reus*), the other on dangerous persons (*mens rea*). The **dangerous act rationale** looks at how close defendants came to completing their crimes. The **dangerous person rationale** concentrates on how fully defendants have developed their intent to commit their crime.

dangerous act rationale looks at how close defendants came to completing their crimes

dangerous person rationale concentrates on how fully defendants have developed their intent to commit their crime

Both rationales measure dangerousness according to actions, but they do so for different reasons. The dangerous act rationale aims to prevent harm from dangerous conduct, so its concern is how close to completion the crime was. The dangerous person rationale aims to neutralize dangerous people, so it looks at how developed the defendant's criminal purpose was (Brodie 1995, 237–38).

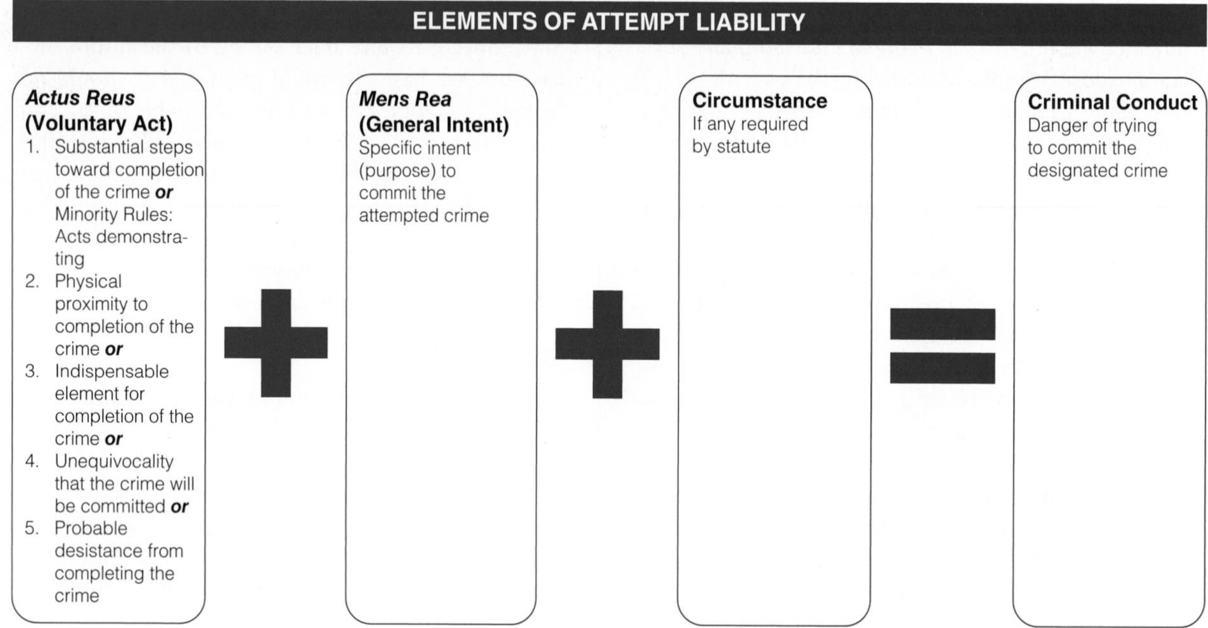

The Elements of Criminal Attempt Law

The crime of attempt consists of two elements:

1. Intent or purpose to commit a specific crime and
2. An act, or acts, to carry out the intent

general attempt statute a single statute that applies to the attempt to commit any crime in the state's criminal code

specific attempt statutes separate statutes that define attempts in terms of specific crimes in the criminal code, such as attempted murder, attempted robbery, and attempted rape—crimes that involved a specific intent

See the Elements of Attempt Liability illustration of these requirements.

There are two types of attempt statutes, general attempt and specific intent. A **general attempt statute** is a single statute that applies to the attempt to commit *any* crime in the state's criminal code. Alabama's attempt statute is a typical general attempt statute: "A person is guilty of an attempt to commit a crime if, with the intent to commit a specific offense, he does any overt act towards the commission of such offense" (Alabama Criminal Code 1975). **Specific attempt statutes** define attempts in terms of specific crimes in the criminal code, such as attempted murder, attempted robbery, and attempted rape in separate statutes.

Let's look at each of the two elements the prosecution has to prove beyond a reasonable doubt in criminal attempt cases, attempt *mens rea* and *actus reus*.

LO3

ATTEMPT *MENS REA*

attempt *mens rea* the specific intent to commit a crime

You can't "blunder into an attempt," because attempt is a crime of purpose (Sayre 1928, 841). "Attempt" means to try, and you can't try to do what you don't specifically intend to do. As one authority put it, "An attempt without intent is unthinkable; it cannot be" (Enker 1977, 847). So, when it comes to attempt *mens rea*, you don't have to worry about the difficult task of figuring out whether it was knowing, reckless, negligent, or strict liability. Why? Because **attempt *mens rea*** always requires the specific intent to commit a crime.

In *State v. King* (2015), our next case excerpt, the South Carolina Court of Appeals decided whether attempted murder requires the specific intent to kill the victim.

CASE

*In **State v. King (2004),** Rakeem D. King (Defendant) was convicted in the Circuit Court, Charleston County, of attempted murder, armed robbery, and possession of a firearm during the commission of a violent crime. King appealed. The SC Court of Appeals reversed.*

Did he intend to kill?

State v. King

2015 WL 1913949 (2015 S.C. App.)

HISTORY

Rakeem D. King (Defendant) was convicted in the Circuit Court, Charleston County, J.C. Nicholson, Jr., J., of attempted murder, armed robbery, and possession of a firearm during the commission of a violent crime. King appealed. The SC Court of Appeals reversed.

WILLIAMS, J., CONCURRED IN RESULT ONLY.

FEW, CJ.

FACTS

On November 26, 2010, at 4:06 A.M., a customer called Yellow Cab requesting to be picked up at 1808 Carlton Street in North Charleston. The operator recorded the customer's telephone number from Yellow Cab's caller identification. At 4:11 A.M., Yellow Cab dispatched Dario Brown to that location. Brown was familiar with the Carlton Street area because his aunt had lived at 1809 Carlton—directly across the street from 1808 Carlton.

Brown testified he expected the customer to be his cousin because he lived in the area, and Brown had picked him up at the same location and time of night in the past. Brown saw a person coming from the yard of 1809 Carlton—his aunt's old house, which was abandoned at the time. When the person got into the back of the cab, Brown realized it was not his cousin. Brown turned around, looked the man in the face, and asked why he came from the abandoned house. Brown and the man began to argue about whether the man lived at 1809 Carlton.

Brown testified he drove toward the dead-end of Carlton Street so he could make a U-turn and take the man to his destination. Brown stated that before he reached the end of the street, "I heard his cocking a pistol. When I looked back he had raised the gun to my face and told me to give him the money." Brown handed the man "give away money." The man told Brown it was not enough, however, and pointed the gun at the back of Brown's head. Brown testified, "I made an attempt to move [the gun] with my elbow and my forearm trying to move it out of the way telling him he doesn't have to rob me." The man demanded more money. Brown opened the door to the cab and had "one foot on the ground and [his] other foot on the brake." Brown testified the gun was "[s]till placed at the back of my neck." With his hands over his head, Brown "gave him a look in his eye" and testified the man "looked as if he was going to shoot me." When Brown tried again "to move the gun away from [his] face," the man shot Brown in the arm.

Brown testified he jumped from the cab and ran toward the dead-end of Carlton Street. "I looked back and I saw him in pursuit behind me"—"maybe two steps behind me." Brown explained he tried to jump over a fence at the end of the street, "but my arm gave out so I kind of flipped head first over [the fence] and landed on my back." Brown testified, "When I hit the ground...he was...holding the gate with one hand and reaching over with his other hand with the gun in it." Brown testified the man fired another shot at him. Brown crawled behind a van, and the man fired more shots. Brown testified the man was "still outside the gate saying that he is not going to shoot me anymore if I just give him the money." Brown stated, "I want to say in all I heard maybe six or seven shots but I can't be exact."

Brown eventually called the police from his cell phone. Officer Jennifer Butler testified she arrived at 4:21 A.M. and saw Brown's empty cab "that had run

(continues)

(continued)

into a pole on the side of the road." Shortly thereafter, she made contact with Brown and called emergency medical services. She did not see anyone else. After Brown was taken to the hospital, Officer Butler and a detective walked door-to-door "in the immediate area...to speak with the people to see if they heard anything or happened to see anything." Over King's hearsay objection, Officer Butler testified she "learned there was more than one shot"—"approximately three or four shots" were fired.

Kelly Murphy—a crime scene technician—testified she found "a .25 auto shell casing" in the cab. Murphy also testified she and four other officers searched the Carlton Street area for two hours and found no other shell casings. Murphy conceded on cross-examination that "if there were shells there I needed to find them," and "if there were any of those anywhere I would have collected those."

[Eyewitness ID section omitted.]

The jury found King guilty of attempted murder, armed robbery, and possession of a firearm during the commission of a violent crime. The trial court sentenced King to thirty years in prison for armed robbery and five years for possession of a firearm, with those sentences to run consecutive. For the attempted murder conviction, the trial court sentenced King to ten years in prison, concurrent with the other sentences. [Only attempted murder included in this excerpt.]

OPINION

King argues the State must prove as an element of attempted murder that King acted with specific intent to kill Brown. We agree, and thus we find the trial court erred when it charged the jury, "A specific intent to kill is not an element of attempted murder but it must be a general intent to commit serious bodily harm."

Section 16-3-29 of the South Carolina Code (Supp. 2014) defines attempted murder: "A person who, with intent to kill, attempts to kill another person with malice aforethought, either expressed or implied, commits the offense of attempted murder." Because the crime is defined by statute, we first look to the language of the statute to determine what the Legislature intended the elements of the crime to be—including the level of intent required.

If the language of a statute is unambiguous and conveys a clear meaning, the court must determine the intent of the Legislature exclusively from that language, and other rules of statutory interpretation are not needed. The phrase "with intent to kill" in section 16-3-29 does not clearly indicate what level of intent the Legislature meant to require the State to prove because the word "intent" can mean anything from purpose to negligence. The required [intent] for a particular crime can be classified into a hierarchy of culpable states of mind in descending order of culpability, as purpose, knowledge, recklessness, and negligence. Therefore, we must look beyond the words of the statute and use our rules of statutory construction to determine what the Legislature intended.

Section 16-3-29 was enacted in 2010 as part of the Omnibus Crime Reduction and Sentencing Reform Act. Before 2010, our courts held attempt crimes require the State to prove the defendant had specific intent to complete the attempted crime. In *State v. Sutton*, 532 S.E.2d 283, 285 (2000), decided before the Legislature enacted section 16-3-29—our supreme court faced the question "whether attempted murder was an offense in this state." To answer the question, the court compared the elements of assault and battery with intent to kill (ABWIK) and the elements of attempted murder. Though the court "declined to recognize a separate offense of attempted murder." "Attempted murder would require the specific intent to kill," and "specific intent means that the defendant consciously intended the completion of acts comprising the attempted offense."

With this history of our courts requiring the State to prove specific intent as an element of attempt crimes, the Legislature chose to include the phrase "with intent to kill" in section 16-3-29. The Legislature is presumed to know how the terms and phrases it uses in a statute have been interpreted in the past.

The Legislature's use of the phrase "with intent to kill," considered in light of our courts' prior rulings that specific intent is required for attempt crimes—particularly the supreme court's statement in *Sutton*, "Attempted murder would require the specific intent to kill" indicates the Legislature intended to require the State to prove the specific intent to kill as an element of attempted murder.

The State argues, however, the Legislature intended to codify the common law crime of ABWIK [Assault and Battery With Intent to Kill] when it enacted section 16-3-29, and because a specific intent to kill was not an element of ABWIK, the Legislature did not intend to require a specific intent to kill as an element of attempted murder. To support its argument that section 16-3-29 is a codification of ABWIK, the State points to the following language in the Omnibus Crime Reduction and Sentencing Reform Act: "The common law offenses of [ABWIK and others] are abolished," and, "[W]herever in the 1976 Code reference is made to [ABWIK], it means attempted murder as defined in Section 16-3-29."

We disagree with the State's argument. We find the Legislature intended to require the State to prove specific intent to commit murder as an element of attempted murder, and therefore the trial court erred by charging the jury that attempted murder is a general intent crime.

The State contends the trial court's errors did not prejudice King and were harmless beyond a reasonable doubt. Whether an error is harmless depends on the circumstances of the particular case. No definite rule of law governs this finding; rather, the materiality and prejudicial character of the error must be determined from its relationship to the entire case. Error is harmless when it could not reasonably have affected the result of the trial. Engaging in this harmless error analysis, we question whether beyond a reasonable doubt the trial error did not contribute to the guilty verdict.

We find the trial court's errors prejudiced King as to his attempted murder conviction, affected the result of his trial on that charge, and thus were not harmless beyond a reasonable doubt. One of the key issues at trial was whether King continued to shoot at Brown after they exited the cab. Brown testified "six or seven" shots were fired, all but one of which were fired outside the cab. However, there are specific facts in this case that could lead a jury to find King fired only one shot. In particular, Brown was dispatched to Carlton Street at 4:11 A.M. He testified it took him "a minute, two minutes" to get there. Officer Butler testified she arrived on the scene at 4:21 A.M. Officers searched the area for hours and found only one shell casing. Under these circumstances, it seems highly unlikely King could have robbed and shot Brown in the cab, chased him down Carlton Street while shooting at him, and then retrieved all the shell casings in the dark before Officer Butler arrived.

Brown's testimony that he repeatedly pushed King's gun away supports the inference that when King shot Brown in the cab, he did so in a struggle and did not intend to kill Brown. It is more difficult to imagine, however, that King could have chased Brown down Carlton Street while shooting at him unless he specifically intended to kill Brown. Thus, the State presented a stronger case for attempted murder from the shots fired during the chase. These circumstances made Officer Butler's testimony as to the number of shots fired critical to the State's ability to prove King continued to shoot at Brown after they exited the cab, and thus made her testimony important to the State's ability to prove King guilty of attempted murder.

Therefore, we find Officer Butler's inadmissible testimony as to the number of shots King fired affected the jury's verdict on attempted murder, and we cannot say that either the admission of the evidence or the erroneous jury charge are harmless beyond a reasonable doubt.

We find the trial court erred in charging the jury that a specific intent to kill is not an element of attempted murder and in admitting Officer Butler's hearsay testimony. Because we find these errors prejudiced King as to his conviction for attempted murder, we reverse and remand for a new trial.

QUESTIONS

1. List all the facts relevant to deciding Rakeem King's state of mind regarding attempted murder.
2. The trial judge instructed the jury that, "A specific intent to kill is not an element of attempted murder but it must be a general intent to commit serious bodily harm." Why did the Court of Appeals rule that the instruction was reversible error?
3. Should attempted murder require the specific intent to kill?

ATTEMPT *ACTUS REUS*

LO4

You're sitting in your apartment, planning in detail when, how, and where you're going to kill your boyfriend and your best friend because they cheated on you with each other. You decide to do it tonight with your roommate's gun. You get up, go to her room, get the gun, pick up your car keys, and go to your car. Then, the enormity of what you're going to do hits you. You say to yourself, "What's wrong with me? What am I doing? I can't kill them." You go back and turn on the TV.

I don't believe anyone would think you committed attempted murder. Why? First, because, as we learned in Chapters 3 and 4, we don't punish people for their bare intentions. Justice Oliver Wendell Holmes (1963) in a famous passage wrote, "There is no law against a man's intending to commit a murder the day after tomorrow" (54). Of course, there's no more than bare intention in our example. You got the gun, picked up your car keys, and went to your car. But we have a deeply entrenched rule that preparing to carry out your intention to commit a crime doesn't qualify as an attempt to commit a crime. Attempt *actus reus* requires that you take *some* steps toward completing the crime.

attempt *actus reus* taking some steps toward completing a crime

What if you went into your room, took the gun, loaded it, got your car keys, got in your car, and drove to your boyfriend's apartment. When he answered the door, you took out the gun, and pulled the trigger, but your hands were shaking so much you missed? I believe everybody would think you attempted to murder your boyfriend. Why? Because you did everything you could to kill him. This version of the example represents the strictest rule of attempt *actus reus* called the last act rule—namely, that someone has committed all but the last act necessary to complete the crime.

last act rule attempt *actus reus* requires all but the last act needed to complete the crime

Most real cases aren't so easy. They fall somewhere between mere intent and "all but the last act" necessary to complete the crime. The toughest question in attempt law may be, "How close to completing a crime is close enough to satisfy the criminal act requirement of attempt?" The general answer is somewhere on a continuum between preparation and the last act. This general answer is so general that it's useless as a guide for deciding (and for us, understanding) real cases. So courts and attempt statutes have established proximity tests that help decision makers decide when defendants' acts have taken them further than mere preparation, and brought them close enough to completing crimes to satisfy the attempt *actus reus* requirement.

proximity tests help courts decide when defendants' acts have taken them further than just getting ready to attempt and brought them close enough to completing crimes to qualify as attempt *actus reus*

The tests focus on two theories of attempt: dangerous conduct and dangerous people. Dangerous proximity tests focus on dangerous conduct; they look at what *remains for actors to do* before they hurt society by completing the crime. (Proximity here means the act closest to the act that completes the crime.) Dangerous person tests look at what *actors have already done* to demonstrate that they're a danger to society, not just in this crime but, more important, in crimes they might commit in the future if they're not dealt with now.

dangerous proximity tests focus on dangerous conduct; they look at what remains for actors to do before they hurt society by completing the crime

dangerous person tests look at what actors have already done to demonstrate that they're a danger to society, not just in this crime but, more important, in crimes they might commit in the future if they're not dealt with now

As we examine the main tests of dangerous conduct (*actus reus*) and dangerous persons (*mens rea*), keep in mind that the approaches of the tests aren't mutually exclusive.

As you work your way through the tests, don't look at them as conflicting definitions of the one single "true" test. Instead, think of them as a variety of approaches available to describe more definitely the acts that are enough to fall within the spectrum between the end of preparation yet short of the completed crime and/or that demonstrate a clear mental determination to commit the crime.

The Florida Court of Appeals offers this guidance to decision makers, "It does not appear that Florida has ever expressly adopted one of the approaches." It went on to note that "adopting one approach to the exclusion of the others may not be advisable" (*State v. Hudson* 1999, 1000). Why doesn't a one-size-fits-all approach advisable? Because only treating tests as flexible instruments that best fit the countless variations in facts among individual cases. Now, let's look at the tests.

The proximity tests ask, "Were the defendant's acts close enough to the intended crime to count as the criminal act in the attempt?" Before we can answer that, we have to answer the question, "How close is close enough?" We'll look at six tests that try to answer this question:

1. All but the last act test
2. Dangerous proximity to success

3. Indispensable element test
4. Unequivocality test
5. Probable desistance test
6. Substantial steps test

ALL BUT THE LAST ACT TEST No cases or statutes have limited attempt *actus reus* to the last act. Of course, "all but the last act" satisfies the proximity test. The problem with this strict test is that it excludes dangerous conduct that falls short of the last proximate act that should be included. For example, the first dose of poison in a case of intended killing by small doses of poison wouldn't satisfy the last proximate act test for attempted murder *actus reus*. But it *should*. (LaFave 2010, 624). According to widely cited and quoted criminal law Professor Joshua Dressler (2012), "Today, there is general agreement that an attempt occurs *at least* by the time of the last act, but no jurisdiction *requires* it" (392; emphasis in the original).

Some courts have adopted broader proximity tests to help judges decide whether the facts that juries have found the prosecution has proven beyond a reasonable doubt are enough. That is, they help to decide whether the defendant's acts fall within the spectrum between preparation (which clearly doesn't satisfy the proximity test) and the last proximate act, which clearly does. Let's look at two of these broader proximity tests: the dangerous proximity to success and indispensable element tests.

"DANGEROUS PROXIMITY TO SUCCESS" TEST The **dangerous proximity to success test** (also called the **physical proximity test**) asks whether defendants have come "dangerously close" to completing the crime. In Justice Holmes's words, "There must be a dangerous proximity to success" (*Hyde v. U.S.* 1912, 388).

dangerous proximity to success test (the physical proximity test) asks whether defendants have come "dangerously close" to completing the crime

This test focuses on what actors still have to do to carry out their purpose to commit crimes, not on what they've done already to commit them. For example, if you plan to rob a bank messenger, and you're driving around checking out places where you think she might be, but you haven't found her yet, have you attempted to rob her? No, according to the court that decided the famous case of *People v. Rizzo* (1927):

> These defendants had planned to commit a crime, and were looking around the city for an opportunity to commit it, but the opportunity fortunately never came. Men would not be guilty of attempt at burglary if they planned to break into a building while they were hunting about the streets for the building not knowing where it was. Neither would a man be guilty of an attempt to commit murder if he armed himself and started out to find the person he intended to kill but could not find him. So here these defendants were not guilty of an attempt to commit robbery... when they had not found or reached the presence of the person they intended to rob. (888)

"INDISPENSABLE ELEMENT" TEST The **indispensable element test** asks whether defendants have reached a point where they've gotten control of everything they need to complete the crime. For example, a drug dealer can't attempt to sell Ecstasy until she gets some Ecstasy, even if she has a customer right there, ready, and waiting to buy it. Once she's got the Ecstasy, she's close (proximate) enough to completing the crime to satisfy the attempt criminal act requirement.

indispensable element test asks whether defendants have reached a point where they've gotten control of everything they need to complete the crime

Now, let's turn to two dangerous person tests that look at what defendants have already done, not at what they still have to do: the unequivocality and substantial steps tests.

unequivocality test, also called **the *res ipsa loquitur* test** ("the act speaks for itself"), examines whether an ordinary person who saw the defendant's acts without knowing her intent would believe she was determined to commit the intended crime

"UNEQUIVOCALITY" TEST The **unequivocality test**, also called the ***res ipsa loquitur*** **test** ("the act speaks for itself"), examines whether an ordinary person who saw the defendant's acts without knowing his intent would believe he was determined to commit the intended crime. Notice, it's the *intended* crime, not any crime. Here's a frequently used example to describe the test:

> It is as though a cinematograph film, which had so far depicted the accused person's act without stating what was his intention, had been suddenly stopped, and the audience were asked to say to what end those acts were directed. If there is only one reasonable answer to this question then the accused has done what amounts to an "attempt" to attain that end. (Turner 1934, 238)

Walter Lee Stewart passed the "stop the film test" in *State v. Stewart* (1988, 50). Here's the story:

> Scott Kodanko was waiting for a bus on a Saturday afternoon after leaving work. He was alone in a three-sided Plexiglas bus shelter open to the street in downtown Milwaukee. Two men, Mr. Moore and Walter Lee Stewart, the defendant, entered the bus shelter while a third man, Mr. Levy, remained outside.
>
> Moore and the defendant stood one to two feet from Kodanko. Kodanko was in a corner of the shelter, his exit to the street blocked by the two men. Moore asked Kodanko if he wanted to buy some cigarettes. Kodanko responded that he did not. Moore then said, "Give us some change." When Kodanko refused, the defendant said "Give us some change, man." The defendant repeated this demand in an increasingly loud voice three to four times. Kodanko still refused to give the two men change.
>
> The defendant then reached into his coat with his right hand at about the waist level, whereupon Moore stated something to the effect of "put that gun away." At that point Levy, who had been waiting outside the bus shelter, entered and said to the defendant and Moore "Come on, let's go." Levy showed Kodanko some money, stating, "I don't want your money, I got lots of money." (45–46)

According to the Court:

> If the defendant had been filmed in this case and the film stopped just before Levy entered the bus stop and the three men departed, we conclude that a trier of fact could find beyond a reasonable doubt that the defendant's acts were directed toward robbery. The film would show the defendant demanding money and appearing to reach for a gun. This evidence is sufficient to prove that the defendant had taken sufficient steps for his conduct to constitute an attempted robbery. (50)

The distinguished Professor Glanville Williams (1961) criticizes the unequivocality test because in ambiguous cases, it "would acquit many undoubted criminals." For example:

> D goes up to a haystack, fills his pipe, and lights a match. The act of lighting a match, even to a suspicious-minded person, is ambiguous. It may indicate only that D is going to light his pipe; but, perhaps on the other hand, the pipe is only a "blind" and D is really bent on setting fire to the stack. We do not know. Therefore, on the equivocality test, the act is not proximate. (630)

probable desistance test determines if defendants have gone far enough toward completing the crime that it's unlikely they'll turn back

"PROBABLE DESISTANCE" TEST The **probable desistance test**, another dangerous person test, focuses on how far defendants have gone, not on what's left for them to do to complete the crime. The test determines if defendants have gone far enough toward completing the crime that it's unlikely they'll turn back.

THE MODEL PENAL CODE (MPC) "SUBSTANTIAL STEPS" TEST The **Model Penal Code's substantial steps test** (also called the "**MPC test**") was designed to accomplish three important goals:

MPC substantial steps test test that requires that attempters take enough steps toward completing the crime to prove that they're determined to commit it

1. Replace (or at least drastically reform) the proximity and unequivocality tests with a clearer and easier to understand and apply test.
2. Draw more sharply (and push back further toward preparation) the line between preparation and beginning to attempt the crime.
3. Base the law of attempt firmly on the theory of neutralizing dangerous persons, not just on preventing dangerous conduct.

In line with these goals, the MPC's substantial steps test for attempt *actus reus* includes two elements:

1. "Substantial steps" toward completing the crime
2. Steps that "strongly corroborate the actor's criminal purpose"

In other words, the code requires that attempters take enough steps toward completing the crime not to show that a crime is about to occur but to prove that the attempters are determined to commit it.

The Line Between "Preparation" and "Attempt"

To sharpen the line between preparation and attempt, push it back closer to preparation, and make clear the commitment to neutralizing dangerous people, the code lists seven acts (most of which would qualify as mere preparation in traditional attempt statutes) that can amount to "substantial steps" if they strongly corroborate the actor's criminal purpose to commit the intended crime:

- Lying in wait, searching for, or following the contemplated victim of the crime
- Enticing, or seeking to entice, the contemplated victim of the crime to go to the place contemplated for its commission
- Reconnoitering [or "casing"] the place contemplated for the commission of the crime
- Unlawful entry of a structure, vehicle, or enclosure in which it is contemplated that the crime will be committed
- Possession of materials to be employed in the commission of the crime that are specially designed for such unlawful use or that can serve no lawful purpose of the actor under the circumstances
- Possession, collection, or fabrication of materials to be employed in the commission of the crime, at or near the place contemplated for its commission, if such possession, collection, or fabrication serves no lawful purpose of the actor under the circumstances
- Soliciting an innocent agent to engage in conduct constituting an element of the crime (ALI 1985, 3:296)

The "vast majority" of current criminal codes have adopted the MPC "substantial steps" language, but most have not included the MPC seven facts that push attempt back into what traditionally and still are considered acts of preparation, not of attempt (LaFave 2003a, 594). It's probably as true now as it was in 1967 that:

> Much ink has been spilt in an attempt to arrive at a satisfactory standard for telling where preparations [sic] ends and attempt begins, but the tests adopted in the various jurisdictions fall somewhere between the two extremes represented respectively by the old common law guide and the one suggested by the Model Penal Code of the American Law Institute. (*Mims v. U.S.* 1967, 148)

In our next case excerpt, *Mims v. U.S.* (1967), the U.S. Fifth Circuit Court of Appeals sent the case back to the trial court to determine whether George Lee Mims Sr. attempted or only prepared to rob the Madeira Beach Bank.

CASE

*In **Mims v. U.S. (1967)**, the U.S. Fifth Circuit Court of Appeals sent the case back to the trial court to determine whether George Lee Mims Sr. attempted or only prepared to rob the Madeira Beach Bank.*

Did he attempt to rob the bank?

George Lee Mims, Sr. v. U.S.

375 F.2d 135 (5th Cir. 1967)

HISTORY

George Lee Mims, Sr. was prosecuted for an attempt to enter the Madeira Beach Bank with intent to rob it by force and violence and by intimidation. The United States District Court for the Middle District of Florida entered a judgment of conviction, and Mims appealed. The Court of Appeals reversed and sent the case back for retrial.

BREWSTER, J.

FACTS

George Lee Mims, Sr. (Appellant) was a middle-aged mechanic who had been employed at the municipal garage in Treasure Island, Florida, near Madeira Beach, for several years prior to the incidents here involved. His wife died in March, 1962, leaving him with two children by their marriage. One of them was George Lee Mims, Jr., 13 years of age, and the other was a daughter several years older. Within less than 60 days after the death of his wife, he and a married woman with two children had agreed to marry each other if she could persuade her husband to get a divorce. There was some delay about the divorce, and she moved into appellant's house with her children in the middle of June, and continued to live there with him without benefit of clergy until they married shortly before the trial in the following year.

The additions to the appellant's household brought on financial difficulties, even though he was moonlighting on a filling station job three evenings a week and was handling a little repair work on his friends' personal cars on some weekends. He was also having some serious problems with his children. The nature of them was not disclosed. He apparently tried to solve his problems by drinking, and during June and July he frequently drank to excess. Some calls to the Madeira Beach Bank prior to June for the purpose of repairing adding machines had given him access to and familiarity with the area of the bank where the money was kept and he began to consider robbing it.

In early June, he implicated Willie Joe Henderson, a 22-year-old Negro with an eleventh grade education who worked under him at the garage. He also involved his son, George Lee Mims, Jr., Dennis O'Connor, a

15-year-old boy who had run away from home and moved into appellant's house, and Stephen O'Connor, 14 years old.

Guns and ammunition were procured, so that at the time of the two trips to the bank each participant was armed with a loaded pistol, a shotgun or a rifle. For disguises, they had coveralls, sailor hats and face masks. Appellant explained to his companions that the advantage of the coveralls was that they could be put on over street clothes and taken off quickly. By virtue of knowledge gained while working on the adding machines in the bank, the appellant gave each of his companions a definite assignment to do while in the bank. He had also concluded that the fewest customers would be in the bank around closing time, so he planned to enter it just before it closed its doors to the public for the day.

The first trip to the bank for the purpose of robbing it was Saturday, July 7th. At that time Thomas Napper was not involved. All the other participants met at the garage where appellant and Henderson worked at a time when it was closed for business that day. They put on their coveralls and disguises, got into a car and drove to the bank, intending to reach there about five minutes before closing time. However, they miscalculated the time, and got there a few minutes after it had closed. When they arrived and saw the situation, they left without making any attempt to go into the bank.

The next visit to the bank was on Wednesday, July 11th. On the previous day, the appellant rented from the King Car Rentals Service in Treasure Island a Ford Galaxie [sic] bearing Florida license plates for use in going to and from the bank. Before going to the bank he put some stolen out-of-state license plates over the Florida plates. He also rented an apartment with a private garage in an area that could be reached quickly after leaving the bank. The rented car was put in the garage at the apartment on July 10th and left there until it was used for transportation to the bank. The plan was that the participants could come to the apartment in their own cars, put on their disguises there, go to the bank in the rented car, rob the bank and return to the apartment before police began to watch the cars on the streets, shed their disguises, hide the getaway car, guns and disguises in the apartment and garage, and then leave in their regular clothes in small groups in the other cars.

Willie Joe Henderson brought his cousin, Thomas Napper, to the apartment and had him included in the group that was to rob the bank. The appellant was under the influence of whiskey when he appeared that day, and brought two bottles of whiskey with him. When all the parties had put on their disguises and were ready to go, appellant suggested to them that a drink of whiskey would settle their nerves. Some of them took a drink. They drove to the bank parking lot in the rented car, and sent Henderson around to see if the bank was still open. It was, but he was getting reluctant to go through with the robbery and went back and told them the bank was closed. They knew that he had been wavering, and began to doubt his statement after a few minutes; so all of them went around to the bank entrance with intention to go in and commit the robbery, if the bank was still open.

The proof indicates that they had no more intention of forcing their way in if the bank was closed, than they had when they went to the bank on the preceding Saturday. By the time they got to the entrance, the bank had actually closed for the day. A Mrs. Barkiewicz was at the door shaking it to attract the attention of one of the bank employees to get him to let her in to correct an error in a deposit she had made a few minutes before closing time. One of the boys placed the muzzle of his pistol at the side of her head, and another one told her that they were going to rob the bank. She thought it was a prank. When she replied that it was too late, as the bank had already closed, one of appellant's party said, "Let's get out of here" and they ran back to their car and fled.

OPINION

The court instructed the jury that they need not spend any time debating as to whether or not an attempt was made to rob the bank, as the evidence showed such attempt as a matter of law. Counsel for the appellant did not object to that instruction, even though he had indicated in his opening statement at the beginning of the trial that the charge would be contested... on the ground "that there was never a valid attempt, an actual attempt to commit the crime as alleged...." The instruction was so peremptory in nature that the error must be noticed without an objection having been made.

The appellant was entitled to have the question of whether there was an attempt to enter the bank for the purpose of robbing it submitted to the jury under appropriate instructions covering, among other things, for determining whether the conduct of the participants had gone beyond the intent and

(continues)

(continued)
preparation stage and had reached the point where an overt act had been committed directly tending to effect the commission of the substantive offense.

Much ink has been spilt in an attempt to arrive at a satisfactory standard for telling where preparations ends and attempt begins, but the tests adopted in the various jurisdictions fall somewhere between the two extremes represented respectively by the old common law guide and the one suggested by the Model Penal Code of the American Law Institute. The question has not been decided by this Court; but, in the event of another trial, help can be obtained from the few federal cases on it.

The *Buffum* case states a test that has been frequently approved:

> Preparation alone is not enough, there must be some appreciable fragment of the crime committed, it must be in such progress that it will be consummated unless interrupted by circumstances independent of the will of the attempter, and the act must not be equivocal in nature.

The *Gregg* case approves that test laid down by Cardozo, Jr.,...[that] the act must "carry the project forward within dangerous proximity to the criminal end to be attained."

The *Coplon* case quoted with approval the following from the opinion of Holmes, J., in the *Peaslee* case,

> Preparation is not an attempt. But some preparations may amount to an attempt. It is a question of degree. If the preparation comes very near to the accomplishment of the act, the intent to complete it renders the crime so probable that the act will be a misdemeanor, although there is still the need of a further exertion of the will to complete the crime.

In discussing the same question in the *Kennedy* case, Holmes, J., said: "Every question of proximity must be determined by its own circumstances, and analogy is too imperfect to give much help."

The conviction...is reversed and remanded.

QUESTIONS

1. List all of the facts and circumstances relevant to deciding whether George Lee Mims Sr. attempted to rob the bank.
2. Assume you're the prosecutor. On the facts and circumstances available from the excerpt, argue that the case went far enough beyond preparation to satisfy the *actus reus* element.
3. Now, assume you're the defense attorney. On the facts and circumstances available from the excerpt, argue that the case went no further than preparation.
4. Now, you be the judge. Write an opinion deciding the case, relying on your answers to 2 and 3.

Defenses to Attempt Liability

Remember that "attempts are cases of failure" (Fletcher 1978, 131). Failure can be due to several causes: police officers might show up; victims might resist and escape; a passerby might appear. These are all circumstances beyond the attempter's control, and they're not defenses to a charge of attempt. We'll look at two that can be (1) legally impossible attempts and (2) abandoned attempts. Both are affirmative defenses. (Recall that defendants have to prove affirmative defenses, in most states by a preponderance of the evidence—Chapter 2, p. 48.)

LO5 LEGAL IMPOSSIBILITY

legal impossibility occurs when actors intend to commit crimes, and do everything they can to carry out their criminal intent, but the criminal law doesn't ban what they did

To avoid paying customs, a man sneaks an antique book past customs, not knowing that there's an exception in the law for antique books. Has he attempted to evade customs laws? No. A woman stabs her batterer husband repeatedly, thinking he's asleep. In fact, he had died of a heart attack two hours before she stabbed him. Has she committed attempted murder? No.

The first scenario is an example of **legal impossibility**. A legal impossibility occurs when actors intend to commit crimes, and do everything they can to carry out their

1. *Did they get "very near" to robbing the clerk?*

People v. Rizzo, 158 N.E. 888 (N.Y.App. 1927)

Facts

Charles Rizzo, Anthony J. Dorio, Thomas Milo, and John Thomasello were driving through New York City looking for a payroll clerk they intended to rob. While they were still looking for their victim, the police apprehended and arrested them. They were tried and convicted of attempted robbery. Rizzo appealed. Did their acts add up to attempt *actus reus*?

Decision

The trial court said yes. The New York Court of Appeals (New York's highest court) reversed:

The Penal Law, § 2, prescribes that:

> An act, done with intent to commit a crime, and tending but failing to effect its commission, is "an attempt to commit that crime." The word "tending" is very indefinite. It is perfectly evident that there will arise differences of opinion as to whether an act in a given case is one tending to commit a crime. "Tending" means to exert activity in a particular direction. Any act in preparation to commit a crime may be said to have a tendency toward its accomplishment. The procuring of the automobile, searching the streets looking for the desired victim, were in reality acts tending toward the commission of the proposed crime.
>
> The law, however, had recognized that many acts in the way of preparation are too remote to constitute the crime of attempt. The line has been drawn between those acts which are remote and those which are proximate and near to the consummation. The law must be practical, and therefore considers those acts only as tending to the commission of the crime which are so near to its accomplishment that in all reasonable probability the crime itself would have been committed, but for timely interference. The cases which have been before the courts express this idea in different language, but the idea remains the same. The act or acts must come or advance very near to the accomplishment of the intended crime.

2. *Was it "preparation" or "all but the last act"?*

Commonwealth v. Peaslee, 59 N.E. 55 (Mass. 1901)

Facts

Lincoln Peaslee had made and arranged combustibles in a building he owned so they were ready to be lighted and, if lighted, would have set fire to the building and its contents. He got within a quarter of a mile of the building, but his would-be accomplice refused to light the fire. Did Peaslee attempt to commit arson?

Decision

No, said the court:

> A mere collection and preparation of materials in a room, for the purpose of setting fire to them, unaccompanied by any present intent to set the fire, would be too remote and not all but "the last act" necessary to complete the crime.

criminal intent, but the criminal law doesn't ban what they did. So even though he wanted to evade customs laws, and did all he could to commit the crime of tax evasion, it's legally impossible to commit a crime that doesn't exist. If the law were different, he'd be guilty; but it isn't, so legal impossibility is a defense to criminal liability.

factual impossibility occurs when actors intend to commit a crime and try to but it's physically impossible because some fact or circumstance unknown to them interrupts or prevents the completion of the crime

Stabbing an already dead victim is an example of **factual impossibility**. A factual impossibility occurs when actors intend to commit a crime and try to but it's physically impossible due to some fact or circumstance unknown to them. The woman intended to murder her battering husband. She did all she could to commit it by stabbing him; if the facts had been different—that is, if her victim had been alive—she would have murdered him.

Legal impossibility requires a different law to make the conduct criminal; factual impossibility requires different facts to complete the crime. In most jurisdictions, legal impossibility is a defense to criminal attempt; factual impossibility isn't. The main reason for the difference is that to convict someone for conduct that the law doesn't prohibit, no matter what the actor's intentions, violates the principle of legality—no crime without a law, no punishment without a crime (see Chapter 1). Factual impossibility, on the other hand, would allow chance to determine criminal liability. A person who's determined to commit a crime, and who does enough to succeed in that determination, shouldn't escape responsibility and punishment because of a stroke of good luck.

In our next case excerpt, *State v. Damms* (1960), the Wisconsin Supreme Court affirmed Ralph Damms's conviction for attempting to murder his wife because his unloaded gun was considered a "stroke of luck."

CASE

In ***State v. Damms* (1960),** *the Wisconsin Supreme Court affirmed Ralph Damms's conviction for attempting to murder his wife because his unloaded gun was considered a "stroke of luck."*

Was the unloaded gun a "stroke of luck"?

State v. Damms

100 N.W.2d 592 (Wis. 1960)

HISTORY

The defendant, Ralph Damms, was charged by information [a criminal charge by the prosecutor without a grand jury] with the offense of attempt to commit murder in the first degree. The jury found the defendant guilty as charged, and the defendant was sentenced to imprisonment in the state prison at Waupun for a term of not more than ten years. Damms appealed to the Wisconsin Supreme Court. The Wisconsin Supreme Court affirmed the conviction.

CURRIE, J.

FACTS

The alleged crime occurred on April 6, 1959, near Menomonee Falls in Waukesha County. Prior to that date Marjory Damms, wife of the defendant, had instituted an action for divorce against him and the parties lived apart. She was 39 years old and he 33 years of age. Marjory Damms was also estranged from her mother, Mrs. Laura Grant.

That morning, a little before eight o'clock, Damms drove his automobile to the vicinity in Milwaukee where he knew Mrs. Damms would take the bus to go to work. He saw her walking along the sidewalk, stopped, and induced her to enter the car by falsely stating that Mrs. Grant was ill and dying. They drove to Mrs. Grant's home. Mrs. Damms then discovered that her mother was up and about and not seriously ill. Nevertheless, the two Damms remained there nearly two hours conversing and drinking coffee. Apparently, it was the intention of Damms to induce a reconciliation between mother and daughter, hoping it would result in one between himself and his wife, but not much progress was achieved in such direction.

At the conclusion of the conversation, Mrs. Damms expressed the wish to phone for a taxicab to take her to work. Damms insisted on her getting into his car, and said he would drive her to work. They again entered his car, but instead of driving south toward her place of employment, he drove in the opposite direction. Some conversation was had in which he stated that it was possible for a person to die quickly and not be able to make amends for anything done in the past, and he referred to the possibility of "judgment day" occurring suddenly.

Mrs. Damms' testimony as to what then took place is as follows: "When he was telling me about this being judgment day, he pulled a cardboard box from under the seat of the car and brought it up to the seat and opened it up and took a gun out of a paper bag. He aimed it at my side and he said, 'This is to show you I'm not kidding.' I tried to quiet him down. He said he wasn't fooling. I said if it was just a matter of my saying to my mother that everything was all right, we could go back and I would tell her that."

They did return to Mrs. Grant's home and Mrs. Damms went inside and Damms stayed outside. In a few minutes he went inside and asked Mrs. Damms to leave with him. Mrs. Grant requested that they leave quietly so as not to attract the attention of the neighbors. They again got into the car, and this time drove out on Highway 41 toward Menomonee Falls. Damms stated to Mrs. Damms that he was taking her "up north" for a few days, the apparent purpose of which was to effect a reconciliation between them.

As they approached a roadside restaurant, he asked her if she would like something to eat. She replied that she wasn't hungry but would drink some coffee. Damms then drove the car off the highway beside the restaurant and parked it with the front facing, and in close proximity to, the restaurant wall.

Damms then asked Mrs. Damms how much money she had with her and she said "a couple of dollars." He then requested to see her checkbook and she refused to give it to him. A quarrel ensued between them. Mrs. Damms opened the car door and started to run around the restaurant building screaming, "Help!" Damms pursued her with the pistol in his hand.

Mrs. Damms's cries for help attracted the attention of the persons inside the restaurant, including two officers of the state traffic patrol who were eating their lunch. One officer rushed out of the front door and the other the rear door. In the meantime, Mrs. Damms had run nearly around three sides of the building. In seeking to avoid colliding with a child, who was in her path, she turned, slipped, and fell. Damms crouched down, held the pistol at her head, and pulled the trigger, but nothing happened. He then exclaimed, "It won't fire. It won't fire."

Damms testified that at the time he pulled the trigger the gun was pointing down at the ground and not at Mrs. Damms's head. However, the two traffic patrol officers both testified that Damms had the gun pointed directly at her head when he pulled the trigger. The officers placed Damms under arrest. They found that the pistol was unloaded. The clip holding the cartridges, which is inserted in the butt of the gun to load it, was later found in the cardboard box in Damms's car together with a box of cartridges.

That afternoon, Damms was questioned by a deputy sheriff at the Waukesha county jail, and a clerk in the sheriff's office typed out the questions and Damms's answers as they were given. Damms later read over such typed statement of questions and answers, but refused to sign it. In such statement Damms stated that he thought the gun was loaded at the time of the alleged attempt to murder. Both the deputy sheriff and the undersheriff testified that Damms had stated to them that he thought the gun was loaded. To the contrary, though, Damms testified at the trial that he knew at the time of the alleged attempt that the pistol was not loaded.

OPINION

The two questions raised on this appeal are:

1. Did the fact that it was impossible for the accused to have committed the act of murder because the gun was unloaded preclude his conviction of the offense of attempt to commit murder?
2. Assuming that the foregoing question is answered in the negative, does the evidence establish the guilt of the accused beyond a reasonable doubt?

Sec. 939.32(2), Stats., provides as follows:

> An attempt to commit a crime requires that the actor have an intent to perform acts and attain a result which, if accomplished, would constitute such crime and that he does acts toward the commission of the crime which demonstrate unequivocally, under all the circumstances, that he formed that intent and would *commit the crime except for the intervention of another person or some other extraneous factor*. [emphasis added, see definition on p. 294]

The issue with respect to the first of the aforestated two questions boils down to whether the impossibility of accomplishment due to the gun being unloaded falls within the statutory words "except for the intervention of some other extraneous factor." We conclude that it does.

(continues)

(continued)

An article in 1956 *Wisconsin Law Review*, by Assistant Attorney General Platz, points out that "attempt" [in the Wisconsin statute] is more intelligible fashion than using such tests as "beyond mere preparation," the place at which the actor may repent and withdraw, or "dangerous proximity to success." Quoting the author:

> Emphasis upon the dangerous propensities of the actor as shown by his conduct, rather than upon how close he came to succeeding, is more appropriate to the purposes of the criminal law to protect society and reform offenders or render them temporarily harmless.

Sound public policy would seem to support the majority view that impossibility not apparent to the actor should not absolve him from the offense of attempt to commit the crime he intended. An unequivocal act accompanied by intent should be sufficient to constitute a criminal attempt. Insofar as the actor knows, he has done everything necessary to insure the commission of the crime intended, and he should not escape punishment because of the fortuitous circumstance that by reason of some fact unknown to him it was impossible to effectuate the intended result.

It is our considered judgment that the fact that the gun was unloaded when Damms pointed it at his wife's head and pulled the trigger did not absolve him of the offense charged, if he actually thought at the time that it was loaded.

We do not believe that the further contention raised in behalf of the accused, that the evidence does not establish his guilt of the crime charged beyond a reasonable doubt, requires extensive consideration on our part.

The jury undoubtedly believed the testimony of the deputy sheriff and undersheriff that Damms told them on the day of the act that he thought the gun was loaded. This is also substantiated by the written statement constituting a transcript of his answers given in his interrogation at the county jail on the same day.

The gun itself, which is an exhibit in the record, is the strongest piece of evidence in favor of Damms's present contention that he at all times knew the gun was unloaded. Practically the entire bottom end of the butt of the pistol is open. Such opening is caused by the absence of the clip into which the cartridges must be inserted in order to load the pistol. This readily demonstrates to anyone looking at the gun that it could not be loaded. Because the unloaded gun with this large opening in the butt was an exhibit which went to the jury room, we must assume that the jury examined the gun and duly considered it in arriving at their verdict.

We are not prepared to hold that the jury could not come to the reasonable conclusion that, because of Damms's condition of excitement when he grabbed the gun and pursued his wife, he so grasped it as not to see the opening in the end of the butt which would have unmistakably informed him that the gun was unloaded. Having so concluded, they could rightfully disregard Damms's testimony given at the trial that he knew the pistol was unloaded.

Judgment affirmed.

DISSENT

DIETERICH, J.

I disagree with the majority opinion in respect to their interpretations and conclusions of sec. 939.32(2), Stats. The issue raised on this appeal: Could the defendant be convicted of murder, under sec. 939.32(2), Stats., when it was impossible for the defendant to have caused the death of anyone because the gun or pistol involved was unloaded? Sec. 939.32(2), Stats., provides:

> An attempt to commit a crime requires that the actor have an intent to perform acts and attain a result which, if accomplished, would constitute such crime and that he does acts toward the commission of the crime which demonstrate unequivocally, under all the circumstances, that he formed that intent and would commit the crime except for the intervention of another person or some *other extraneous factor*. [emphasis added]

In view of the statute, the question arising under sec. 939.32(2), is whether the impossibility of accomplishment due to the pistol being unloaded falls within the statutory words "except for the intervention of...or some other extraneous factor." It does not.

In interpreting the statute we must look to the ordinary meaning of words. Webster's *New International Dictionary* defines "extraneous" as not belonging to or dependent upon a thing, originated or coming from without. The plain distinct meaning of the statute is: A person must form an intent to commit a particular crime and this intent must be coupled with sufficient preparation on his part and with overt acts from which it can be determined clearly, surely and absolutely the crime would be committed except for the intervention of some independent thing or something originating or coming from someone or something over which the actor has no control.

As an example, if the defendant actor had formed an intent to kill someone, had in his possession a loaded pistol, pulled the trigger while his intended victim was within range and the pistol did not fire because the bullet or cartridge in the chamber was defective or because someone unknown to the actor had removed the cartridges or bullets or because of any other thing happening which happening or thing was beyond the control of the actor, the actor could be guilty under sec. 339.32(2), Stats.

But when as in the present case (as disclosed by the testimony) the defendant had never loaded the pistol, although having ample opportunity to do so, then he had never completed performance of the act essential to kill someone, through the means of pulling the trigger of the pistol. This act, of loading the pistol, or using a loaded pistol, was dependent on the defendant himself. It was in no way an extraneous factor since by definition an extraneous factor is one which originates or comes from without.

Under the majority opinion the interpretations of the statute are if a person points an unloaded gun (pistol) at someone, knowing it to be unloaded and pulls the trigger, he can be found guilty of an attempt to commit murder. This type of reasoning I cannot agree with.

He could be guilty of some offense, but not attempt to commit murder. If a person uses a pistol as a bludgeon and had struck someone, but was prevented from killing his victim because he (the actor) suffered a heart attack at that moment, the illness would be an extraneous factor within the statute and the actor could be found guilty of attempt to commit murder, provided the necessary intent was proved.

In this case, there is no doubt that the pistol was not loaded. The defendant testified that it had never been loaded or fired. The following steps must be taken before the weapon would be capable of killing:

1. To load pistol requires pulling of slide operating around barrel toward holder or operator of pistol.
2. After pulling slide to rear, safety latch is pushed into place by operator of pistol to hold pistol in position for loading.
3. A spring lock is located at one side of opening of magazine located at the bottom grip or butt of gun.
4. This spring is pulled back and the clip is inserted into magazine or bottom of pistol and closes the bottom of the grip or butt of the pistol.
5. The recoil or release of the safety latch on the slide loads the chamber of the pistol and it is now ready to fire or be used as a pistol.

The law judges intent objectively. It is impossible to peer into a man's mind particularly long after the act has been committed. Viewing objectively the physical salient facts, it was the defendant who put the gun, clip and cartridges under the car seat. It was he, same defendant, who took the pistol out of the box without taking clip or cartridges. It is plain he told the truth—he knew the gun would not fire; nobody else knew that so well. In fact his exclamation was "It won't fire. It won't fire."

The real intent showed up objectively in those calm moments while driving around the county with his wife for two hours, making two visits with her at her mother's home, and drinking coffee at the home. He could have loaded the pistol while staying on the outside at his mother-in-law's home on his second trip, if he intended to use the pistol to kill, but he did not do this required act.

The majority states:

> The gun itself, which is an exhibit in the record, is the strongest piece of evidence in favor of Damms's present contention that he at all times knew the gun was unloaded. Practically the entire bottom end of the butt of the pistol is open. This readily demonstrates to anyone looking at the gun that it could not be loaded.

They are so correct. The defendant had the pistol in his hand several times before chasing his wife at the restaurant and it was his pistol. He, no doubt, had examined this pistol at various times during his period of ownership—unless he was devoid of all sense of touch and feeling in his hands and fingers it would be impossible for him not to be aware or know that the pistol was unloaded. He could feel the hole in the bottom of the butt, and this on at least two separate occasions for he handled the pistol by taking it out of the box and showing it to

(continues)

(continued)

his wife before he took her back to her mother's home the second time, and prior to chasing her at the restaurant.

Objective evidence here raises reasonable doubt of intent to attempt murder. It negatives [sic] intent to kill. The defendant would have loaded the pistol had he intended to kill or murder or used it as a bludgeon. The Assistant Attorney General contends and states in his brief:

> In the instant case, the failure of the attempt was due to lack of bullets in the gun but a loaded magazine was in the car. If defendant had not been prevented by the intervention of the two police officers, or possibly someone else, or conceivably by the flight of his wife from the scene, he could have returned to the car, loaded the gun, and killed her. Under all the circumstances the jury were justified in concluding that that is what he would have done, but for the intervention.

If that conclusion is correct, and juries are allowed to convict persons based on speculation of what might have been done, we will have seriously and maybe permanently, curtailed the basic rights of our citizenry to be tried only on the basis of proven facts. I cannot agree with his contention or conclusion.

The total inadequacy of the means (in this case the unloaded gun or pistol) in the manner intended to commit the overt act of murder, precludes a finding of guilty of the crime charged under sec. 939.32(2), Stats.

QUESTIONS

1. List all the facts relevant to deciding whether Ralph Damms intended to murder Marjory Damms.
2. List all the facts relevant to deciding whether Damms had taken enough steps to attempt to murder Marjory Damms according to the Wisconsin statute.
3. Summarize the majority's arguments that the unloaded gun was an extraneous factor, a stroke of luck Damms shouldn't benefit from.
4. Summarize the dissent's arguments that the unloaded gun wasn't an extraneous factor but an impossibility that prevents Damms from attempting to murder Marjory Damms.
5. In your opinion, is the majority or dissent right? Explain your answer in terms of what effect impossibility should have on liability for criminal attempt.
6. Should it matter why the gun was unloaded? Explain your answer.
7. What if Damms knew the gun was unloaded? Should he still be guilty of attempted murder? Explain your answer.
8. Is the Wisconsin rule punishing attempts that are about half the actions needed to complete the crime a good idea?
9. Some states punish attempts at the same level as completed crimes because people bent on committing crimes shouldn't benefit at all from a stroke of luck. Do you agree? Defend your answer with arguments from the case excerpt and the text.

LO6 VOLUNTARY ABANDONMENT

We know from the last section that those bent on committing crimes *and* have taken steps to carry out their criminal plans can't escape criminal liability just because an outside force or person interrupted them, namely an **extraneous factor**. But what about people who clearly intend to commit crimes, take enough steps to carry out their intent, and then change their mind and voluntarily abandon the scheme? Should the law benefit those who themselves are the force that intercepts the crimes they wanted to commit and are marching toward completing? The answer depends on which jurisdiction they're in.

extraneous factor a "stroke of luck"—namely, a circumstance beyond the attempter's control that prevents the completion of the crime

According to the **voluntary abandonment defense** (also called **voluntary renunciation defense**), defendants who voluntarily and completely renounce their criminal purpose can avoid criminal liability.

voluntary abandonment defense (also called **voluntary renunciation defense**) defendants who voluntarily and completely renounce their criminal purpose can avoid criminal liability

Michigan has a typical voluntary abandonment statute:

> It is an affirmative defense...that, under circumstances manifesting a voluntary and complete renunciation of his criminal purpose, the actor avoided the commission of the offense attempted by abandoning his criminal effort.

A renunciation is not "voluntary and complete" within the meaning of this chapter if it is motivated in whole or in part by either of the following:

1. A circumstance which increases the probability of detection or apprehension of the defendant or another participant in the criminal operation or which makes more difficult the consummation of the crime.
2. A decision to postpone the criminal conduct until another time or to substitute another victim or another but similar objective.

According to the Model Penal Code, voluntary abandonment means:

> A change in the actor's purpose not influenced by outside circumstances, what may be termed repentance or change of heart. Lack of resolution or timidity may suffice. A reappraisal by the actor of the criminal sanctions hanging over his conduct would presumably be a motivation of the voluntary type as long as the actor's fear of the law is not related to a particular threat of apprehension or detection. (ALI 1985, 3:356)

Supporters of the voluntary abandonment defense favor it for two reasons. First, those who voluntarily renounce their criminal attempts in progress (especially during the first acts following preparation) aren't the dangerous people the law of attempt is designed to punish; they probably weren't even bent on committing the crime in the first place. Second, at the very end of the progress to completing the crime, it prevents what we most want—the harm the completed crime is about to inflict on victims.

This defense encourages would-be criminals to give up their criminal designs by the promise of escaping punishment. Opponents say the defense encourages bad people to take the first steps to commit crimes because they know they can escape punishment (1989, 1).

The drafters of the Model Penal Code claim that the "prevailing view" favors the voluntary abandonment defense. But Professor LaFave (2010) notes that the

> American cases cited in support of allowing voluntary desistance for the most part contain such statements *in dictum* [comments not part of the law of the case] or in concurring or dissenting opinions. Cases in which the defendant's claim of voluntary withdrawal was plausible enough to make failure to instruct on the defense reversible error are extremely rare. (643)

Nevertheless, he concludes that, "On balance" arguments in favor of the defense are "more persuasive than the arguments against the defense" (643).

The arguments supporting the defense include:

1. Complete and voluntary renunciation of criminal purpose shows the defendant isn't dangerous.
2. Those "who have crossed the threshold of attempt will still be encouraged to desist and thereby escape punishment."

The counterargument is that the defense may "embolden" those who are thinking about committing a crime to take the first steps toward committing the crime when they know they can withdraw without negative consequences (643–44).

In *Le Barron v. State* (1966), our next case excerpt, the court rejected David Le Barron's defense that he voluntarily abandoned his plan to rape Jodean Randen.

CASE

*In **Le Barron v. State** (**1966**), David Le Barron was convicted of attempted rape and sentenced to not more than fifteen years in prison. He appealed. The Wisconsin Supreme Court affirmed the conviction.*

Did he voluntarily abandon his attempt to rape?

Le Barron v. State

145 N.W.2d 79 (Wis. 1966)

HISTORY

David Le Barron was convicted of attempted rape and sentenced to not more than 15 years in prison. He appealed. The Wisconsin Supreme Court affirmed the conviction.

CURRIE, J.

FACTS

On March 3, 1965, at 6:55 P.M., the complaining witness, Jodean Randen, a housewife, was walking home across a fairly well-traveled railroad bridge in Eau Claire, Wisconsin. She is a slight woman whose normal weight is 95 to 100 pounds. As she approached the opposite side of the bridge, she passed a man who was walking in the opposite direction.

The man turned and followed her, grabbed her arm, and demanded her purse. She surrendered her purse and at the command of the man began walking away as fast as she could. Upon discovering that the purse was empty, he caught up with her again, grabbed her arm, and told her that if she did not scream he would not hurt her.

He then led her—willingly, she testified, so as to avoid being hurt by him—to the end of the bridge. While walking he shoved her head down and warned her not to look up or do anything and he would not hurt her.

On the other side of the bridge along the railroad tracks there is a coal shack. As they approached the coal shack he grabbed her, put one hand over her mouth, and an arm around her shoulder and told her not to scream or he would kill her. At this time Mrs. Randen thought he had a knife in his hand.

He then forced her into the shack and up against the wall. As she struggled for her breath he said, "You know what else I want," unzipped his pants and started pulling up her skirt. She finally succeeded in removing his hand from her mouth, and after reassuring him that she would not scream, told him she was pregnant and pleaded with him to desist or he would hurt her baby.

He then felt her stomach and took her over to the door of the shack, where in the better light he was able to ascertain that, under her coat, she was wearing maternity clothes. He thereafter let her alone and left after warning her not to scream or call the police, or he would kill her.

OPINION

The material portions of the controlling statutes provide:

> § 944.01(1), Stats. Any male who has sexual intercourse with a female he knows is not his wife, by force and against her will, may be imprisoned not more than 30 years.
>
> § 939.32(2), Stats. An attempt to commit a crime requires that the actor have an intent to perform acts and attain a result which, if accomplished, would constitute such crime and that he does acts toward the commission of the crime which demonstrate unequivocally, under all the circumstances, that he formed that intent and would commit the crime except for the intervention of another person or some other extraneous factor.

The two statutory requirements of intent and overt acts which must concur in order to have attempt to rape are as follows:

1. The male must have the intent to act so as to have intercourse with the female by overcoming or preventing her utmost resistance by physical violence, or overcoming her will to resist by the use of threats of imminent physical violence likely to cause great bodily harm;
2. the male must act toward the commission of the rape by overt acts which demonstrate unequivocally, under all the circumstances, that he formed the intent to rape and would have committed the rape except for the intervention of another person or some other extraneous factor.

The thrust of defendant's argument, that the evidence was not sufficient to convict him of the crime of attempted rape, is two-fold: first, defendant desisted from his endeavor to have sexual intercourse with complainant before he had an opportunity to form an intent to accomplish such intercourse by force and against her will; and, second, the factor which caused him to desist, viz., the pregnancy of complainant, was intrinsic and not an "extraneous factor" within the meaning of sec. 939.32(2), Stats.

It is difficult to consider the factor of intent apart from that of overt acts since the sole evidence of intent in attempted rape cases is almost always confined to the overt acts of the accused, and intent must be inferred therefrom. In fact, the express wording of sec. 939.32(2), Stats. recognizes that this is so.

We consider defendant's overt acts, which support a reasonable inference that he intended to have sexual intercourse with complainant by force and against her will, to be these:

1. He threatened complainant that he would kill her if she refused to cooperate with him;
2. he forced complainant into the shack and against the wall; and
3. he stated, "You know what else I want," unzipped his pants, and started pulling up her skirt.

The jury had the right to assume that defendant had the requisite physical strength and weapon (the supposed knife) to carry out the threat over any resistance of complainant.

We conclude that a jury could infer beyond a reasonable doubt from these overt acts of defendant that he intended to have sexual intercourse with defendant by force and against her will. The fact that he desisted from his attempt to have sexual intercourse as a result of the plea of complainant that she was pregnant would permit of the opposite inference. However, such desistance did not compel the drawing of such inference nor compel, as a matter of law, the raising of a reasonable doubt to a finding that defendant had previously intended to carry through with having intercourse by force and against complainant's will.

The argument that the pregnancy which caused defendant's desistance does not qualify as an "extraneous factor" is in conflict with our holding in *State v. Damms*. [See case excerpt under "Legal Impossibility."]

Affirmed.

QUESTIONS

1. List all the facts relevant to deciding whether Le Barron had the intent to rape Jodean Randen.
2. At what point, if any, did his acts cross the line from preparation to the *actus reus* of attempt under Wisconsin law?
3. Describe the details surrounding Le Barron's decision to abandon the attempted rape of Randen.
4. Why did Le Barron abandon his attempt to rape Randen? Because he believed it was morally wrong to rape a pregnant woman? Or did the pregnancy simply repel him sexually? Does it matter? Explain your answer.
5. Is Le Barron equally dangerous, whichever reason led to interrupting the rape? Explain.
6. The court said a jury could have concluded Randen's pregnancy was either an extraneous factor he couldn't benefit from or an intrinsic factor that caused Le Barron to renounce voluntarily his intention to rape. If you were a juror, how would you have voted on whether the pregnancy was an extraneous or an intrinsic factor?

YOU DECIDE

Should Both Women Be Treated Equally?

In the heat of an argument, a woman grabs a gun and fires at her spouse, trying to kill him. She misses. Realizing the horror of what she has tried to do, she throws down the gun and embraces her husband. Another woman, also arguing with her spouse, grabs a gun and shoots at him. She, too, misses on the first shot. She fires again and again, a total of four times. Three of the bullets strike her husband and cause serious injury, but he is eventually able to run away from her and escape to safety.

Instructions

Is the defense of abandonment ethical public policy if it applies to the first woman, who shot at her husband, but not to the second woman? Be sure to include the rationales for abandonment from this section to support your answer.

CONSPIRACY

LO7

> The core of conspiracy is an agreement to commit a crime. It's this agreement that gives rise to criminal liability, by transforming a lonely criminal thought hatched in the mind of a single, powerless individual into an agreement with another person. I reveal myself as one of those persons who suffer from an abnormal disposition to engage in criminal conduct, by distinguishing myself from those untold millions who harbor criminal thoughts, but never share them with others, never mind act on them in any way. But my decision to seek out likeminded proto criminals, and to join hands with them in the pursuit of a common criminal goal is symptomatic of my extraordinary dangerousness. By combining forces with another similarly dangerous person, I multiply my already considerable dangerousness through the magic of cooperation. (Dubber 2002, 163)

conspiracy the crime of agreeing with one or more people to commit a crime

Conspiracy, the crime of agreeing with one or more people to commit a crime, is further removed from actually committing a crime than attempts to commit crimes. In fact, there are two public policy justifications for attaching criminal liability to actions further away from completion than attempts:

1. Conspiracy works hand in hand with attempts to nip criminal purpose in the bud.
2. Conspiracy strikes at the special danger of group criminal activity. (ALI 1985, 3:377–78)

conspiracy *actus reus* consists of two parts: (1) an agreement to commit a crime and (2) an overt act in furtherance of the agreement

In this section, we'll look at what's necessary to prove the *actus reus* and *mens rea* of conspiracy, how the law treats the circumstance elements of parties to conspiracies, and the objectives of conspiracies. (See the Elements of Conspiracy illustration.) Then, we look at large-scale conspiracies, gang conspiracies, and RICO-related conspiracies.

LO8

Conspiracy *Actus Reus*

Conspiracy *actus reus* consists of two parts: (1) an agreement to commit a crime (in all states) and (2) an overt act in furtherance of the agreement (in about half the states). Let's look at each part.

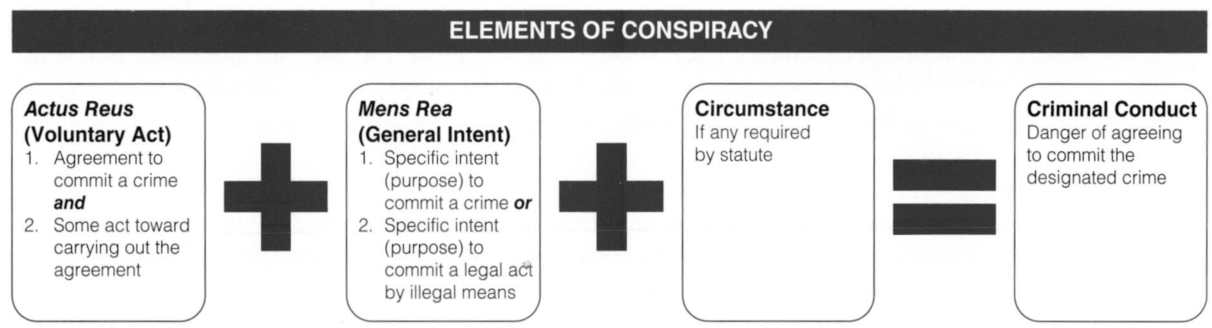

THE AGREEMENT

The heart of the crime of conspiracy is the act of agreement between two or more people to commit a crime. The agreement doesn't have to be a signed written contract. It's "not necessary to establish that the defendant and his coconspirators signed papers, shook hands, or uttered the words 'we have an agreement'" (*State v. Vargas* 2003, 208–9). Facts and circumstances that point to an unspoken understanding between the conspirators are good enough to prove the conspirators agreed to commit a crime. This rule makes sense because conspirators rarely put their agreements in writing.

The rule might make sense, but it encourages vague definitions of "agreement" that can lead to injustice. In one famous trial during the Vietnam War, the government tried the well-known baby doctor turned war protestor, Dr. Benjamin Spock, for conspiracy to avoid the draft law. Videotapes showed several hundred spectators clapping while Dr. Spock urged young men to resist the draft. Spurred on by antagonism to antiwar protestors, the prosecutor in the case made the ridiculous assertion that any person seen clapping on the videotape was a co-conspirator. According to the prosecutor, these people were aiding Spock, and that made them parties to a conspiracy to violate the draft law (Mitford 1969, 70–71).

THE OVERT ACT

In about half the states, the agreement itself satisfies the *actus reus* of conspiracy. The other half and the federal courts require the act of agreeing to commit a crime plus another act to further the agreement; the second act is called the **overt act requirement**.

overt act requirement the requirement of an act that furthers the agreement in conspiracy

Why the requirement of an "overt act"? To verify the firmness of the agreement. The overt act doesn't have to amount to much. In the words of the American Law Institute's commentator (1985, [3] 387), it may "be of very small significance." And according to the U.S. Supreme Court Justice Oliver Wendell Holmes (*Hyde v. U.S.* 1912):

> If the overt act is required, it does not matter how remote the act may be from accomplishing the [criminal] purpose, if done to effect it; that is, I suppose, in furtherance of it in any degree. (388)

Conspiracy *Mens Rea*

conspiracy *mens rea* the mental element in conspiracy, frequently identified as specific intent by authorities, but it's not defined clearly in statutes and it's defined inconsistently by courts

Conspiracy *mens rea*, the mental element in conspiracy, wasn't defined clearly at common law, and most modern legislatures haven't made it any clearer. This leaves the courts to define it. The courts in turn have taken imprecise, widely divergent, and inconsistent approaches to the *mens rea* problem. According to former Supreme Court Justice Robert Jackson, "The modern crime of conspiracy is so vague that it almost defies definition" (*Krulewitch v. U.S.* 1949, 445–46).

Authorities frequently call conspiracy a specific-intent crime. But what does that mean? Does it mean that conspiracy involves intent to enter an agreement to commit a crime? Or does conspiracy also have to include an intent to attain a specific criminal objective? A **criminal objective** is the criminal goal of an agreement to commit a crime.

criminal objective the criminal goal of an agreement to commit a crime

For example, if two men agree to burn down a building, they intend to commit arson. But if they don't intend to hurt anyone and someone dies, did they also conspire to commit murder? Not if the conspiracy *mens rea* means the specific intent to achieve a particular criminal objective.

This example demonstrates an important distinction between, on one hand, the intent to make agreements and, on the other hand, the intent to achieve a criminal objective. If the objective is to commit a specific crime, it has to satisfy that crime's *mens rea*. So conspiring to take another's property isn't conspiring to commit larceny unless the conspirators intended to deprive the owner of possession permanently (see Chapter 11).

Courts further complicate conspiracy *mens rea* by not clarifying whether it requires purpose. Consider cases involving suppliers of goods and services, such as doctors who order drugs from pharmaceutical companies that they then use or sell illegally. At what point do the suppliers become co-conspirators, even though they haven't agreed specifically to supply drugs for illegal distribution?

Do prosecutors have to prove the suppliers agreed specifically to further the buyers' criminal purposes? Most courts say yes, even though that kind of proof is difficult to obtain, because as we've already seen, conspirators aren't foolish enough to put proof of their crimes in writing. So purpose has to be inferred from circumstances surrounding the agreement, such as quantities of sales, the continuity of the supplier–recipient relationship, the seller's initiative, a failure to keep records, and the relationship's clandestine nature. Some argue that knowing, or conscious, wrongdoing ought to satisfy the conspiracy *mens rea* (*Direct Sales Co. v. U.S.* 1943).

LO9 Parties to Conspiracy

The traditional definition of "conspiracy" includes the attendant circumstance element that agreements involve "two or more parties agreeing or combining to commit a crime" (ALI 1985, 3:398). Most modern statutes have replaced this traditional definition with a **unilateral approach to conspiracy parties** that doesn't require that all conspirators agree—or even know—the other conspirators. For example, if one of two conspirators secretly has no intention to go through with the agreement, the other conspirator is still a party.

unilateral approach to conspiracy parties the rule that not all conspirators have to agree with—or even know—the other conspirators

When there's more than one party, failure to convict one party doesn't prevent conviction of other parties to the conspiracy. Typically, statutes are similar to the Illinois Criminal Code (Illinois Criminal Law and Procedure 1988), which provides:

> It shall not be a defense to conspiracy that the person or persons with whom the accused is alleged to have conspired:

1. Has not been prosecuted or convicted, or
2. Has been convicted of a different offense, or
3. Is not amenable to justice, or
4. Has been acquitted, or
5. Lacked the capacity to commit an offense. (chap. 38, § 8-4)

The Criminal Objective of the Conspiracy

Conspiracy is an agreement but an agreement to do what? In the old days, the **criminal objective of the conspiracy** was defined to cover a broad spectrum. The objective could be as narrow as an agreement to commit a felony or as broad as agreements to

criminal objective of the conspiracy the object of conspiracy agreements has to be to commit crimes

- commit "any crime"
- do "anything unlawful"
- commit "any act injurious to the public health, or for the perversion of or obstruction of justice, or due administration of the laws" (ALI 1985, 3:395)
- do even "lawful things by unlawful means"

In most modern statutes, the criminal objective of the conspiracy is almost always limited to agreements to commit crimes. The vague definitions of the elements in conspiracy offer considerable opportunity for prosecutorial and judicial discretion. At times, this discretion borders on abuse, leading to charges that conspiracy law is unjust. First, a general criticism is that conspiracy law punishes conduct too far remote from the actual crime. Second, labor organizations, civil liberties groups, and large corporations charge that conspiracy is a weapon against their legitimate interests of, respectively, collective bargaining and strikes, dissent from accepted points of view and public policies, and profit making.

Critics say that when prosecutors don't have enough evidence to convict for the crime itself, they turn, as their last hope, to conspiracy. Conspiracy's vague definitions greatly enhance the chance for a guilty verdict. Not often mentioned, but extremely important, is that intense media attention to conspiracy trials can lead to abuse. This happened in the conspiracy trials of Dr. Benjamin Spock, the Chicago Eight, and others involving radical politics during the 1960s.

It also occurred in the Watergate conspiracy trials involving President Nixon's associates during the 1970s, in the alleged conspiracies surrounding the sale of arms to Iran for hostages and the subsequent alleged diversion of funds during the 1980s, and in the alleged conspiracy of Osama bin Laden's chauffer and the various alleged conspiracies of officials in the White House during the early 2000s. Several states have made efforts to overcome these criticisms by defining conspiracy elements more narrowly. The definitions of "agreement or combination" (two or more parties combining to commit crimes) are no longer as vague as they once were.

The Model Penal Code has adopted the overt act requirement (acts in furtherance of the act of agreement), and about half the states are following that lead. Those states have refined *mens rea* to include only purposeful conduct—that is, a specific intent to carry out the objective of the agreement or combination. Knowledge, recklessness, and negligence are increasingly attacked as insufficient culpability for an offense as remote from completion as conspiracy. Furthermore, most recent legislation restricts conspiratorial objectives to criminal ends. Phrases such as "unlawful objects," "lawful objects by unlawful means," and "objectives harmful to public health, morals, trade, and commerce" are increasingly regarded as too broad and, therefore, unacceptable.

wheel conspiracies one or more defendants participate in every transaction (the hub of the wheel) and others participate in only one transaction (the spokes in the wheel)

Large-Scale Conspiracies

LO9

The relationship of parties to conspiracies can get intricate, particularly when they involve large operations. Most of these large-scale conspiracies fall into two major patterns: "wheel" and "chain" conspiracies. In **wheel conspiracies**, one or more defendants participate in every transaction. These participants make up the hub of the wheel

chain conspiracies participants at one end of the chain may know nothing of those at the other end, but every participant handles the same commodity at different points, such as manufacture, distribution, and sale

conspiracy. Others participate in only one transaction; they are the spokes in the wheel. In chain conspiracies, participants at one end of the chain may know nothing of those at the other end, but every participant handles the same commodity at different points, such as manufacture, distribution, and sale.

Chain conspiracies often involve the distribution of some commodity, such as illegal drugs. In one famous old case still relevant today, *U.S. v. Bruno* (1939), smugglers brought narcotics into New York, middlemen purchased the narcotics, and two groups of "retailers" (one operating in New York and the other in Louisiana) bought narcotics from the middlemen.

In our next case excerpt, *Griffin v. Gipson* (2015), the U.S. Magistrate Judge for Eastern District of California found that the prosecutor proved beyond a reasonable doubt that David Griffin, gang name "Baby Attitude," a member of the "29th Street Crips" gang based in South Sacramento, and several other members of the gang conspired to murder Destiny Doe. The conspiracy to commit murder in California requires prosecutors to prove four elements beyond a reasonable doubt:

1. Griffin and other defendant gang members and associates entered into an agreement to unlawfully kill Doe.
2. Each defendant specifically intended to enter into an agreement to kill a human being.
3. Each of them harbored a specific intent to kill.
4. One of more of them committed an overt act in furtherance of the agreement.

CASE

*In **Griffin v. Gipson** (2015), the U.S. Magistrate Judge for Eastern District of California found that the prosecutor proved beyond a reasonable doubt that David Griffin, gang name "Baby Attitude," a member of the "29th Street Crips" gang based in South Sacramento, and several other members of the gang conspired to murder Destiny Doe.*

Did he conspire to commit murder?

Griffin v. Gipson

U.S. District Court, Eastern District California. No. 2:13-cv-02516-MCE-GGH (2015)

HOLLOWS, U.S. MAGISTRATE JUDGE

HISTORY

David Griffin (Petitioner) is a state prisoner proceeding *pro se* with a petition for a writ of habeas corpus pursuant to 28 U.S.C. § 2254. Petitioner was convicted of robbery in concert, burglary, aggravated kidnapping, *conspiracy to commit murder*, and attempted murder; each included enhancements for firearm use and committing the offenses for the benefit of a criminal street gang. He was also convicted of active participation in a criminal street gang. Petitioner was sentenced to a prison term of 19 years 8 months, plus 65 years to life. Petitioner challenges his conviction on due process grounds as follows: 1) prosecutorial misconduct in rebuttal closing argument; 2) prosecutorial misconduct regarding alleged misstatements of law; and 3) insufficient evidence of a conspiracy to commit murder.

Upon careful consideration of the record and the applicable law, the undersigned [U.S. Magistrate Judge Gregory G. Hollows] will recommend that petitioner's application for habeas corpus relief be denied. [This case excerpt includes only the parts dealing with "conspiracy to commit murder."]

FACTS

Defendants Zachary Tyler ("Smash"), David Griffin ("Baby Attitude") and Lashea Merritt ("Lady Smash") were members of a criminal street gang called the 29th Street Crips, which is based in South Sacramento. Tyler's gang name was "Smash," Merritt was called "Lady Smash," and Griffin went by the name of "Baby Attitude." Defendant Jordan Kidd was a member of the Valley High Crips, which is an "ally" of the 29th Street Crips. His gang name was "Five." Defendant Kimberly Knorr was an "associate" of the 29th Street Crips who was in a dating relationship with Kidd. Her gang name was "Lady Five."

In January 2007, Destiny Doe and Knorr were living at the residence of Nate E. in Sacramento. Doe worked as an assistant preschool teacher while also moonlighting as a prostitute for Nate's "escort" service. Knorr also worked for Nate. While they lived together, Knorr often bragged to Doe about things she and her "Crip homies" did together.

On the evening of January 22, 2007, Doe and Knorr were returning home in Doe's car when Doe received a call from Nate telling her Knorr had been kicked out of the residence and not to bring her to Nate's house. Doe dropped Knorr off at a gas station on the corner of Fruitridge and Franklin Boulevard.

Knorr's sister, B.K., was dating Tyler at around this time and, on the evening of January 22, was with him at the home of A.S., who was Merritt's mother and was known by the gang name of "Mama Solo." Also present were A.S., Griffin, Kidd, Merritt, and Merritt's brother, L.M., who is known as "Baby Solo."

After Knorr was dropped off, she called B.K. and told her she had argued with Nate and was moving out of his residence. Knorr said she had been dropped off by Doe and needed a ride to pick up her things. Tyler drove to Knorr's location and brought her back to the A.S. residence.

When Knorr arrived, she was upset and said Nate had insulted the gang. In particular, Knorr told them Nate had said, "fuck them—fuck Smash and them. They're not no 29th Street Garden Block Crips." Garden Block Crips is another name for the 29th Street Crips.

The others in the room jumped up and "started talking shit to one another about it." Tyler said, "fuck that nigga, let's go smoke him." In gang culture, to "smoke" means to kill. Tyler also said they should rob Nate. Tyler, Kidd, Griffin, Knorr, Merritt and L.M. departed in two cars, a white and a blue Buick.

Meanwhile, Doe had returned to Nate's residence and was resting in her room. Nate was also present. Later, Doe heard a disturbance in front of the residence caused by a prior girlfriend of Nate named Mia. When Doe first moved into the house, Knorr and Mia were also living there, but Mia had since moved out. On this evening, Mia was banging on the window and trying to get Nate to come outside and talk with her. Doe got up and moved to what had been Knorr's bedroom, which was toward the back of the residence. She fell asleep on Knorr's bed.

Some time later, Doe awoke and saw a silhouette outside the bedroom window. She then saw four or five people wearing bandanas enter the bedroom through the window. They pointed guns at her and told her not to say anything. Doe was held at gunpoint while others searched the residence for Nate, who had fled upon seeing what was happening. Doe was told to get dressed and was taken into the living room. Meanwhile, the intruders took off their bandanas and rummaged through the house looking for things to steal. Doe heard the names Smash and Five mentioned and saw the intruders put clothes and a stereo inside a sheet which they later took with them.

When the intruders departed, they took Doe as well. She got into the blue Buick with three of them, and they followed the white Buick away from the scene. Doe later identified the three in the car with her as the one called "Five" along with Griffin and Merritt.

They all stopped at an apartment complex on 29th Street that had been the birthplace of the gang. Tyler took Doe aside and said to her that "you're with us now and I'll take care of you, and why don't you work for me?" They later got back in the cars and drove away, telling Doe they are the "mob" and this is the "mob life" and "you're with the mob now."

They eventually arrived at the home of A.S., where Doe was taken inside. She saw Knorr, B.K., A.S., another woman and a young boy, as well as the others from the home invasion. Doe was taken to a bedroom, where Tyler, Kidd and Griffin talked about "running a train" on her and forcing her to perform oral sex. Tyler yelled at Doe, "you're gonna suck up all my homies," and Kidd and Merritt ordered her to orally copulate "Little Homie." Merritt further said, "give my little homie some head, you're a ho anyway."

(continues)

(continued)

Tyler told Doe she was going to go out and start making money for him. Doe was eventually told she had to orally copulate L.M. and was left alone in the room with him. She did as directed and, after eight minutes or so, L.M. departed. Tyler then came in the room and forced Doe to orally copulate him as well.

Later that evening, Doe was again placed in the white Buick and departed with Tyler, Kidd, Griffin, and Knorr. It is unclear whether Merritt accompanied them on this trip. Kidd and Griffin were both armed with handguns. Before leaving, B.K. overheard Kidd and Tyler say, "If somethin' is gonna be done, the bitch has gotta be iced." She also heard Tyler say something to A.S. like, "we brought the bitch here so she couldn't tell."

After stopping at another residence for 15 or 20 minutes, they drove to an area near railroad tracks and an empty field. Doe was told to get out of the car and to start walking through the field. She did as directed. After a while, Doe started hearing gunshots. She began walking faster and then running and continued to hear gunshots. She also saw bullets hit the ground around her. One of the shots hit Doe in the back just below the shoulder blade. Doe ran toward the light of a house and eventually reached the house, where she yelled for help. A man came outside, saw Doe and carried her onto the porch. He called 9-1-1 for help. Doe told the man the 29th Street Crips had shot her.

According to the prosecution's gang expert, all of the foregoing actions of the defendants were for the benefit of the 29th Street Crips.

On February 3, 2007, police officers contacted Tyler and Merritt in a hotel room. They found a handgun and ammunition in the room. On February 13, police officers found Griffin in a residence along with a gun and ammunition. On February 28, police officers discovered Kidd in a residence with a handgun and ammunition. All five defendants were charged with robbery in concert, burglary, aggravated kidnapping, conspiracy to commit murder, and attempted murder. On each offense, they were further charged with enhancements for firearm use and committing the offenses for the benefit of a criminal street gang. They were also charged with a separate offense for active participation in a criminal street gang.

[Only the part of the opinion dealing with the "conspiracy to commit murder" charge, is included here]

The case was tried to two juries, one for Kidd alone and the other for the remaining defendants. After his arrest, Kidd had been interviewed by police, and the videotape of that interview was played to his jury alone. In that interview, Kidd first denied any involvement in the matter. However, he eventually admitted he went to Nate's house, but only to steal something and not to kidnap or shoot anyone. He denied kidnapping or shooting anyone. He also denied having a gun and claimed that he departed with Knorr before the others came out of the house and did not know Doe had been taken with them. He denied accompanying the others to the home of A.S.

Tyler was the only defendant to testify at trial. He acknowledged that he went with Knorr to Nate's residence that night, but claimed he went there only to allow Knorr to pick up her things.

Tyler claimed he waited in the car while Knorr went inside and that Doe came out with Knorr and departed with them voluntarily. Tyler asserted that, when they left, Doe asked to be taken to a school where she met up with some of her "homeboys." Doe got out and spoke with four men. Tyler overheard her say "fuck Nate" and told the guys they could go to his house and take whatever they wanted because she left the front door unlocked.

Tyler then drove them to the residence of A.S. and hung out there for a while. Later, Tyler took Doe to meet up with a "date" she had that evening. According to Tyler, that was the last time he saw Doe.

Tyler, Griffin and Kidd were convicted on all charges, and all enhancements were found true. For conspiracy to commit murder, Griffin received an indeterminate term of 25 years to life.

On October 21, 2013, Griffin filed a petition for writ of habeas corpus in the Sacramento Superior Court, which was denied on November 14, 2013. Griffin filed his federal petition for writ of habeas corpus in this court on December 5, 2013.

OPINION

Griffin contends that his due process rights had been violated because his conspiracy to commit murder conviction was not supported by sufficient evidence. The Court of Appeal rejected this claim on direct appeal as follows:

> Griffin contends there is insufficient evidence he entered into a conspiracy to murder Doe. Griffin acknowledges there was an agreement among the defendants to commit a robbery but

"the codefendants were not of a single mind about the rest of the evening." Doe testified that Griffin, unlike the others, was quieter and more polite to her. Thus, he argues, "one cannot infer from his behavior after the robbery that he necessarily was in agreement with the other co-defendants for the rest of the evening."

In fact, Doe testified that when they left the home of A.S., Tyler and Griffin told her they were taking her home. She also told Detective Nutley that Tyler and Griffin were opposed to hurting or killing her. Griffin further points out that Doe's testimony was uncertain as to who actually shot at her. According to Griffin, while the jury could have found he joined at the last minute in the attempt to murder Doe, "the evidence does not support the inference beyond a reasonable doubt that he joined in an agreement to kill before-hand."

A conspiracy is an agreement between two or more people to commit a public offense. It requires not only a specific intent to agree to commit a public offense but a further specific intent to commit the offense itself. It also requires proof of an overt act committed by one or more of the conspirators in furtherance of the object of the agreement.

The agreement or the unlawful design of [the] conspiracy may be proved by circumstantial evidence without the necessity of showing that the conspirators met and actually agreed to commit the offense which was the object of the conspiracy. While mere association does not prove a criminal conspiracy, common gang membership may be part of circumstantial evidence supporting the inference of a conspiracy. The circumstances from which a conspiratorial agreement may be inferred include the conduct of defendants in mutually carrying out a common illegal purpose, the nature of the act done, the relationship of the parties and the interests of the alleged conspirators."

Here, in addition to a common gang membership among the alleged conspirators, the evidence showed defendants got together to discuss what was to be done with Doe. Although there may have been disagreement among them, eventually they embarked on a course of action that involved taking Doe to a field, releasing her and then taking shots at her as she attempted to flee. From this evidence alone, a reasonable jury could infer defendants agreed to kill Doe before they ever left the home of A.S. Hence, substantial evidence supports Griffin's conviction for conspiracy to commit murder.

When a challenge is brought alleging insufficient evidence, federal habeas corpus relief is available if it is found that upon the record evidence adduced at trial, viewed in the light most favorable to the prosecution, no rational trier of fact could have found the essential elements of the crime proven beyond a reasonable doubt. (*Jackson v. Virginia*, 443 U.S. 307, 319 (1979). *Jackson* established a two-step inquiry for considering a challenge to a conviction based on sufficiency of the evidence.

First, a reviewing court must consider the evidence presented at trial in the light most favorable to the prosecution. When faced with a record of historical facts that supports conflicting inferences a reviewing court must presume—even if it does not affirmatively appear in the record—that the trier of fact resolved any such conflicts in favor of the prosecution, and must defer to that resolution.

Second, after viewing the evidence in the light most favorable to the prosecution, the reviewing court must determine whether this evidence, so viewed, is adequate to allow any rational trier of fact to find the essential elements of the crime beyond a reasonable doubt. At this second step, we must reverse the verdict if the evidence of innocence, or lack of evidence of guilt, is such that all rational fact finders would have to conclude that the evidence of guilt fails to establish every element of the crime beyond a reasonable doubt.

Superimposed on these already stringent insufficiency standards is the AEDPA requirement that even if a federal court were to initially find on its own that no reasonable jury should have arrived at its conclusion, the federal court must also determine that the state appellate court could not have affirmed the verdict under the *Jackson* standard in the absence of an unreasonable determination.

A federal habeas court determines sufficiency of the evidence in reference to the substantive elements of the criminal offense as defined by state law. To show that petitioner was guilty of conspiracy to commit murder under California law, the prosecution was required to show that: (1) petitioner and his codefendants entered into an agreement to unlawfully kill Doe; (2) each specifically intended to enter into an agreement to kill a human being; (3) each of them harbored a specific

(continues)

(continued)

intent to kill; and (4) one or both of them committed an overt act in furtherance of the agreement.

Petitioner concedes that there was an agreement to commit robbery at Belleau Woods but contends that the co-defendants were not in agreement about the rest of the evening, in particular with respect to what to do with Ms. Doe. Petitioner notes Ms. Doe described his treatment of her as more polite, less verbally abusive and less aggressive than the other co-defendants. Ms. Doe also reported to Detective Nutley that petitioner was opposed to hurting or killing Ms. Doe.

Petitioner also notes that the record does not indicate whether the parties reached any agreement at the last house and that Ms. Doe was unclear whether she saw two shooters or one shooter and whether one of the shooters was co-defendant Kidd or someone else. In sum, petitioner contends that his relative kindness to Ms. Doe prior to the shooting, the lack of direct evidence of an agreement to kill Ms. Doe, and Ms. Doe's inability to identify whether there were one or two shooters do not support the inference that petitioner joined in an agreement to kill Ms. Doe. To the contrary, based on the evidence in the record as more fully discussed below, a rational trier of fact could find the essential elements of conspiracy to commit murder beyond a reasonable doubt.

Respondent contends that the Court of Appeal's rejection of petitioner's sufficiency of evidence claim was neither contrary to, nor an unreasonable application of *Jackson*. The undersigned agrees. The Court of Appeal identified the elements of the crime of conspiracy to commit murder and explained how circumstantial evidence, including common gang membership, the conduct of the defendants, the nature of the act done, the relationship of the parties and the interests of the alleged conspirators, could be used to prove an agreement or unlawful design.

The evidence shows that petitioner and his co-defendants were either members, associates, or allies of a criminal street gang called the 29th Street Crips. (Gang expert opined petitioner was a member of the 29th Street Crips); (gang expert opined defendant Jordan Kidd was a member of the Valley High Crips); (gang expert opined defendant Kimberly Knorr was an associate of the 29th Street Crips); (gang expert opined defendant Zachary Tyler was a member of the 29th Street Crips).

The record also supports the inference that the group, through their conduct, reached an agreement to murder Ms. Doe. As Ms. Doe testified, petitioner, Tyler, and Kidd took her and put her back in the car, after she had been sexually assaulted. She testified that petitioner and Kidd were holding guns. They took her to another house, had her sit in a recliner, and went into another room to talk. After several minutes, they took Ms. Doe and placed her in the backseat of the car between petitioner and Kidd.

Tyler drove the group to an empty field and parked. Petitioner and Kidd exited the car and told Ms. Doe to get out and walk home, pointing towards the field. As Ms. Doe walked through the field, she heard gunshots. She testified that she looked back toward the car and saw two men pointing their guns at her. Based on this testimony, a reasonable jury could infer that at the last house they visited, petitioner reached an agreement with his codefendants to kill Ms. Doe. Petitioner's sufficiency of the evidence claim should be denied.

For all the foregoing reasons, the petition should be denied. Pursuant to Rule 11 of the Federal Rules Governing Section 2254 Cases, this court must issue or deny a certificate of appealability when it enters a final order adverse to the applicant. A certificate of appealability may issue only "if the applicant has made a substantial showing of the denial of a constitution right." 28 U.S.C. § 2253(c)(2). For the reasons set forth in these findings and recommendations, a substantial showing of the denial of a constitutional right has not been made in this case.

Accordingly, IT IS HEREBY RECOMMENDED that:

1. Petitioner's application for a writ of habeas corpus be denied; and
2. The District Court decline to issue a certificate of appealability.

These findings and recommendations are submitted to the United States District Judge assigned to the case, pursuant to the provisions of 28 U.S.C. § 636(b)(1). Within fourteen days after being served with these findings and recommendations, any party may file written objections with the court and serve a copy on all parties. Such a documents should be captioned "Objections to Magistrate Judge's Findings and Recommendations." Any reply to the objections shall be served and filed within fourteen days after service of the objections. Failure to file objections within the specified time may waive the right to appeal the District Court's order. *Martinez v. Ylst*, 951 F.2d 1153 (9th Cir. 1991).

QUESTIONS

1. List the four elements of conspiracy to commit murder.
2. List all the facts relevant to the four elements.
3. Summarize the magistrate's arguments to support the finding that Griffin and others conspired to murder Destiny Doe.
4. Summarize Griffin's argument that there's reasonable doubt that he conspired to murder Doe.
5. In your opinion, did Griffin conspire to murder Doe? Did he attempt to murder her? Back up your answer.

THE RACKETEER INFLUENCED AND CORRUPT ORGANIZATIONS ACT (RICO)

Despite efforts to restrict the reach of conspiracy, the **Racketeer Influenced and Corrupt Organizations Act** (RICO) demonstrates the continued vitality of conspiracy law. RICO reflects the need for effective means to meet the threat of racketeering posed by organized crime. It imposes enhanced penalties for "all types of organized criminal behavior, that is, enterprise criminality—from simple political to sophisticated white-collar schemes to traditional Mafia-type endeavors" (Blakely and Gettings 1980, 1013–14). **Racketeering** originally referred to the extortion of money or advantage by threat or force. Today, the meaning has expanded to encompass a pattern of illegal activity (such as extortion and murder) carried out in the furtherance of an enterprise owned or controlled by those engaged in the activity.

The clumsy title Racketeer Influenced Corrupt Organization Act—universally called by its acronym RICO—refers to a controversial federal statute that originated under President Lyndon Johnson in 1968 and was signed into law by President Richard Nixon in 1970. RICO created several new crimes, reinstated property forfeiture as punishment for crime, and introduced a new civil action that allows RICO victims to sue RICO offenders (Lynch 2002, 1343).

RICO grew out of fear that organized crime was infiltrating legitimate businesses, a problem widely publicized after President Johnson's Crime Commission highlighted the problem in 1967. The original idea was to make it a crime to invest money gotten by crime in legitimate businesses. But RICO as enacted created a series of crimes that went far beyond organized crime's investing their ill-gotten money to infiltrate legitimate businesses. RICO's broadest and most often prosecuted crime consists of three elements:

1. conducting the affairs of any "**enterprise**" (defined as "just about any form of human endeavor")
2. by means of a "**pattern of racketeering activity**" (defined as committing two or more of a huge list of related crimes)
3. that do or threaten to continue for a period of time. (Lynch 2002, 1343)

Notice that RICO crimes aren't like the crimes governed by the principles of criminal liability we covered in Chapter 3 (criminal conduct) and Chapter 4 (criminal conduct that causes a harmful result). In fact, it's not clear that RICO involves any conduct at all. Judge Lynch has called RICO crimes "the crime of being a criminal" (Lynch 1987, 661). Probably more accurately, RICO is akin to accomplice and vicarious criminal liability (see Chapter 7) and to conspiracy. But it's broader; it depends on "abstract relationships: the "enterprise"' is a structure of relationships among individuals, and the "pattern of racketeering" is a form of relationship among crimes.

LO10

Racketeer Influenced and Corrupt Organizations Act (RICO) imposes enhanced penalties for "all types of organized criminal behavior, that is, enterprise criminality—from simple political to sophisticated white-collar schemes to traditional Mafia-type endeavors"

racketeering original meaning was the extortion of money or advantage by threat or force; now the meaning has expanded to include a pattern of illegal activity (such as extortion and murder) carried out in the furtherance of an enterprise owned or controlled by those engaged in the activity

enterprise just about any form of human endeavor

pattern of racketeering activity committing two or more of a huge list of related crimes

RICO's broad definitions make it a crime for anyone with a "significant role in operating a business, government office, labor union, social or political organization, or informal grouping" to commit a series of crimes (two is enough) either to further the organization's or informal group's goals or simply by using its resources.

RICO raises the question: Why create crimes out of conduct and relationships that are already criminal? Let's look at three types of RICO cases that may help to answer that question and give you a better understanding of how the U.S. government uses RICO: organized crime, white-collar crime, and government corruption.

LO10 Prosecuting Organized Crime

RICO's most dramatic success story is its use in organized crime cases. Its success is due to the relational nature of RICO that we noted earlier. Almost all murder, rape, robbery, and other "traditional" trials focus on a single defendant who's committed a single crime. The rules are established to keep each crime and each defendant separate from one another. It's the opposite in RICO prosecutions.

The operation of an enterprise—say a "criminal gang"—through a pattern of racketeering (at least two separate crimes) is defined in RICO as a single crime. RICO trials look and feel different. Here's how:

1. Evidence that the defendant associates with disreputable people isn't prejudicial like it is in a traditional trial; it's essential to the government's proof of the "enterprise" element.
2. Multiple crimes, even crimes very different in nature, are relevant to prove the pattern element.
3. Mass trials of large numbers of defendants charged with the same RICO enterprise are expected. (Lynch 1990, 786–91)

Why Prosecute Organized Crime under RICO?

One reason is that organized crime operates in more than one state, which under ordinary law would require a separate prosecution for each individual crime. RICO's "pattern" element allows these crimes to be tried as only one case. (There are other procedural advantages for prosecutors that we won't get into here.) The pattern element has facilitated trying large numbers of organized crime defendants like the Mafia in a single trial. Critics have attacked these "mega trials" for several reasons, including:

1. They weaken defendants' protections against wrongful convictions by complicating the jury's job of finding the facts.
2. They drag out trials, making it more expensive for defendants.
3. They foster unfair "spillover" of inferences of guilt in other crimes and to other defendants where the evidence is weak. (Lynch 2002, 1344)

Prosecuting White-Collar Crime

LO10

RICO's broad definition has also made RICO an "attractive tool for prosecutors in serious white-collar criminal cases." These prosecutions have their critics too. Most RICO white-collar crime prosecutions rely on federal mail and wire fraud statutes. These laws ban the use of the mail and interstate electronic communications to aid a "scheme to defraud." And, they're "almost infinitely adaptable to cover a wide range of financial and business misconduct." But, they, as well as securities law violations, also count as the predicate offenses ("pattern offenses") that trigger RICO prosecution. Every use of the mails, for example, counts as a separate crime. So mailing two letters to further a scheme to defraud a single victim is two crimes—and RICO's pattern element is satisfied.

United States v. Porcelli (1989) is a good example of how this works. The defendant owned a chain of gas stations. He regularly understated his New York sales tax. (This wasn't even a crime at the time in New York.) Federal prosecutors charged him with RICO violations because he committed mail fraud by mailing in his phony sales tax returns. The penalty—forfeiture of his business, worth many times more than the $5 million in unpaid taxes.

Destruction of someone's business, not to mention, reputation—both of which white-collar criminals value highly—is a severe penalty. It's often enough to intimidate them into pleading guilty. But is it worse than what "street criminals" face? Judge Lynch (1990) has his doubts:

> Try telling an accused street seller of drugs about the excessive leverage RICO gives the U.S. Attorney to "force" guilty pleas from rich and powerful financial institutions, after he has been detained pretrial in lieu of bail in an overcrowded jail, offered a guilty plea with a sentence of time served, and confronted with the reality that if he goes to trial he not only risks a much longer sentence, but faces certain confinement until the overcrowded court reaches his case. RICO gives wealthy white-collar defendants, who have the resources to fight the system that most defendants lack, a taste of the realities of plea bargaining justice as it is experienced every day by less well-healed defendants. (784–85)

Prosecuting Government Corruption

Government corruption cases make up the largest number of RICO cases under RICO Section 1962(c). Government employees are charged in these cases with conducting the affairs of a government agency through a pattern of bribery, corruption, and mail fraud. Notice that these cases—the most numerous—have nothing to do with organized crime, for example, the Mafia.

Many of these cases involve state and local government officials' corruption in their own state, county, or city. Why? Not because there's more state- and local-level corruption or that state and local corruption is more serious. It's because there's no federal statute making state and local government corruption a federal crime. But RICO fills this gap, allowing federal prosecutors to prosecute state and local officials—with much more severe penalties and without the hesitation local prosecutors might feel about prosecuting fellow officials (777–78).

Critics aren't pleased with this federal "meddling" in local political affairs. There's also a problem of fairness. Under RICO, "racketeering" doesn't have to involve serious offenses. For example, taking small bribes is a misdemeanor in all localities. But taking two small bribes satisfies the "pattern" element of RICO and triggers its severe criminal sentence and civil forfeiture provisions. RICO permits prosecutors to decide to seek harsher penalties without proving any aggravating circumstances (Lynch 1990, 779–80).

LO10 Punishing RICO Offenders

RICO authorizes high maximum fines ($250,000 for *each* violation) and long maximum prison sentences (imprisonment for 25 years, and for life, if one of the predicate crimes is murder). In addition, RICO imposes a mandatory penalty of forfeiture to the U.S. government of not only any money and property derived from the crime but any interest the defendant holds in the enterprise or any property of any kind that "provides a source of influence over the enterprise." Forfeiture aims not only to punish the offender but to "deny continuing power over an enterprise to anyone who has corrupted it to criminal ends" (Lynch 2002, 344).

In our next case excerpt, *Alexander v. U.S.* (1993), Ferris Alexander found out just how harsh forfeiture can be after he was convicted of selling pornography, sentenced to six years in prison; fined $100,000; ordered to pay the cost of prosecution, incarceration, and supervised release; *and* ordered to forfeit his interest in ten pieces of commercial real estate and thirty-one current or former businesses.

CASE

In ***Alexander v. U.S.* (1993),** *Ferris Alexander was convicted of selling pornography, sentenced to six years in prison; fined $100,000; ordered to pay the cost of prosecution, incarceration, and supervised release; and ordered to forfeit his interest in ten pieces of commercial real estate and thirty-one current or former businesses.*

Was the forfeiture an excessive fine?

Alexander v. U.S.

510 U.S. 909 (1993)

HISTORY

Ferris Alexander, Sr. (Defendant, now Petitioner) was convicted in the United States District Court for the District of Minnesota, of tax offenses, obscenity offenses, and Racketeer Influenced and Corrupt Organizations Act (RICO) violations, and he appealed. The Eighth Circuit Court of Appeals affirmed. Certiorari was granted. The Supreme Court remanded. The U.S. District Court, Minnesota reaffirmed after remand. The U.S. Seventh Circuit Court of Appeals affirmed.

REHNQUIST, CJ, JOINED BY WHITE, O'CONNOR, SCALIA, AND THOMAS, JJ.

After a full criminal trial, petitioner Ferris J. Alexander, owner of more than a dozen stores and theaters dealing in sexually explicit materials, was convicted on 17 obscenity counts and 3 counts of violating the Racketeer Influenced and Corrupt Organizations Act (RICO). The obscenity convictions, based on the jury's findings that four magazines and three videotapes sold at several of petitioner's stores were obscene, served as the predicates for his three RICO convictions.

In addition to imposing a prison term and fine, the District Court ordered petitioner to forfeit, pursuant to 18 U.S.C. § 1963 (1988 ed. and Supp. III), certain assets that were directly related to his racketeering activity as punishment for his RICO violations. Petitioner argues that this forfeiture violated the First and Eighth Amendments to the Constitution. We reject petitioner's claims under the First Amendment but remand for reconsideration of his Eighth Amendment challenge.

FACTS

Ferris Alexander was in the so-called "adult entertainment" business for more than 30 years, selling pornographic magazines and sexual paraphernalia, showing sexually explicit movies, and eventually selling and renting videotapes of a similar nature. He received shipments of these materials at a warehouse in Minneapolis, Minnesota, where they were wrapped in plastic, priced, and boxed. He then sold his products through some 13 retail stores in several different Minnesota cities, generating millions of dollars in annual revenues. In 1989, federal authorities filed a 41-count indictment against petitioner and others, alleging operation of a racketeering enterprise in violation of RICO. The indictment charged 34 obscenity counts and 3 RICO counts, the racketeering counts being predicated on the obscenity charges. The indictment also charged numerous counts of tax evasion and related offenses that are not relevant to the questions before us.

Following a 4-month jury trial in the United States District Court for the District of Minnesota, petitioner was convicted of 17 substantive obscenity offenses: 12 counts of transporting obscene material in interstate commerce for the purpose of sale or distribution, in violation of 18 U.S.C. § 1465; and 5 counts of engaging in the business of selling obscene material, in violation of 18 U.S.C. § 1466 (1988 ed. and Supp. III).

He also was convicted of 3 RICO offenses that were predicated on the obscenity convictions: one count of receiving and using income derived from a pattern of racketeering activity, in violation of 18 U.S.C. § 1962(a); one count of conducting a RICO enterprise, in violation of § 1962(c); and one count of conspiring to conduct a RICO enterprise, in violation of § 1962(d). As a basis for the obscenity and RICO convictions, the jury determined that four magazines and three videotapes were obscene. Multiple copies of these magazines and videos, which graphically depicted a variety of "hard core" sexual acts, were distributed throughout petitioner's adult entertainment empire.

Petitioner was sentenced to a total of six years in prison, fined $100,000, and ordered to pay the cost of prosecution, incarceration, and supervised release. In addition to these punishments, the District Court reconvened the same jury and conducted a forfeiture proceeding pursuant to § 1963(a)(2). At this proceeding, the Government sought forfeiture of the businesses and real estate that represented petitioner's interest in the racketeering enterprise, § 1963(a)(2)(A), the property that afforded petitioner influence over that enterprise, § 1963(a)(2)(D), and the assets and proceeds petitioner had obtained from his racketeering offenses, §§ 1963(a)(1), (3).

The jury found that petitioner had an interest in 10 pieces of commercial real estate and 31 current or former businesses, all of which had been used to conduct his racketeering enterprise. Sitting without the jury, the District Court then found that petitioner had acquired a variety of assets as a result of his racketeering activities. The court ultimately ordered petitioner to forfeit his wholesale and retail businesses (including all the assets of those businesses) and almost $9 million in moneys acquired through racketeering activity. Not wishing to go into the business of selling pornographic materials—regardless of whether they were legally obscene—the Government decided that it would be better to destroy the forfeited expressive materials than sell them to members of the public.

OPINION

Petitioner also argues that the forfeiture order in this case—considered atop his 6-year prison term and $100,000 fine—is disproportionate to the gravity of his offenses and therefore violates the Eighth Amendment, either as a "cruel and unusual punishment" or as an "excessive fine." The Court of Appeals, though, failed to distinguish between these two components of petitioner's Eighth Amendment challenge. Instead, the court lumped the two together, disposing of them both with the general statement that the Eighth Amendment does not require any proportionality review of a sentence less than life imprisonment without the possibility of parole. But that statement has relevance only to the Eighth Amendment's prohibition against cruel and unusual punishments. Unlike the Cruel and Unusual Punishments Clause, which is concerned with matters such as the duration or conditions of confinement, "[t]he Excessive Fines Clause limits the government's power to extract payments, whether in cash or in kind, as punishment for some offense." The criminal forfeiture at issue here is clearly a form of monetary punishment no different, for Eighth Amendment purposes, from a traditional "fine." Accordingly, the forfeiture in this case should be analyzed under the Excessive Fines Clause.

Petitioner contends that forfeiture of his entire business was an "excessive" penalty for the Government to exact "[o]n the basis of a few materials the jury ultimately decided were obscene." It is somewhat misleading, we think, to characterize the racketeering crimes for which petitioner was convicted as involving just a few materials ultimately found to be obscene.

(continues)

(continued)

Petitioner was convicted of creating and managing what the District Court described as "an enormous racketeering enterprise." It is in the light of the extensive criminal activities which petitioner apparently conducted through this racketeering enterprise over a substantial period of time that the question whether the forfeiture was "excessive" must be considered. We think it preferable that this question be addressed by the Court of Appeals in the first instance.

For these reasons, we hold that the Court of Appeals should have considered whether they resulted in an "excessive" penalty within the meaning of the Eighth Amendment's Excessive Fines Clause. Accordingly, we vacate the judgment of the Court of Appeals and remand the case for further proceedings consistent with this opinion.

It is so ordered.

QUESTIONS

1. List all of the specific items in the forfeiture.
2. Summarize Ferris Alexander Sr.'s arguments that the forfeiture was an excessive fine.
3. Summarize the U.S. Supreme Court's arguments supporting the forfeiture.
4. Do you think the forfeiture was excessive?

SOLICITATION

LO11

Suppose I want to murder my wife, but I'm afraid to do it. If I ask a friend to kill her and she does, we're both murderers. If she tries to kill her and fails because her gun isn't loaded, then we've committed attempted murder. If she agrees to kill her and buys the gun but doesn't follow through, we've committed conspiracy to commit murder.

solicitation the crime of trying to get someone else to commit a crime.

But what if I try to get my friend to kill my wife by offering her $5,000, and she turns me down? That's a crime, too. It's called solicitation, the crime of trying to get *someone else* to commit a crime. The crime is complete the instant the solicitor communicates the solicitation to the other person. Against the objection that to punish the bare act of solicitation was punishing the "intent to commit evil," which isn't a crime, the Connecticut Supreme Court wrote, "The solicitation is an act; and God forbid that it should not be considered as an offense (Michael and Wechsler 1940, 607).

There's disagreement about whether trying to get someone else to commit a crime, even though they don't comply, is dangerous enough to be a crime. Those in the "not dangerous enough" group make two arguments to support their position. First, solicitation isn't dangerous enough *conduct* because an independent moral agent (the person solicited) stands between solicitors and their criminal objectives. Second, solicitors aren't dangerous enough *people*. They prove it by turning to someone else to do what they're too timid to do themselves.

Those in the "dangerous enough" group have their own arguments. First, they say solicitation is just another form of the danger created by group participation in crime (Chapter 7), only more removed from the completed crime than conspiracy—kind of like an attempted conspiracy. Second, solicitors are intelligent, artful masters at manipulating others to do their dirty work.

Let's look at the elements of solicitation—the *actus reus*, *mens rea*, and the attendant circumstance of the criminal objective of the solicitation. (See the Elements of Solicitation illustration.)

Solicitation *Actus Reus*

solicitation *actus reus* acts that include some kind of inducement to commit the solicited crime

The criminal act in criminal solicitation consists of words, but the law only imprecisely tells us what words qualify as solicitation *actus reus.* Courts agree that statements that merely favor committing a crime aren't enough to qualify as criminal acts. So someone who says, "I think it'd be great if someone killed that terrorist" hasn't solicited murder.

ELEMENTS OF SOLICITATION

***Actus Reus* (Voluntary Act)**		***Mens Rea* (General Intent)**		**Circumstance**		**Criminal Conduct**
Words commanding, urging, or encouraging another person to commit a crime	+	Specific intent (purpose) to induce another person to commit a crime	+	If any required by statute	=	Danger of trying to get someone to commit or participate in a crime

There has to be some kind of inducement to commit a crime. The typical words we see in the statutes and court opinions are like the ones we saw in accomplice liability (Chapter 7): "advises," "commands," "counsels," "encourages," "entices," "entreats," "importunes," "incites," "induces," "instigates," "procures," "requests," "solicits," or "urges." In other words, the criminal act in solicitation consists of the effort to get another to commit a crime, whether or not the solicitation ever ripens into a completed crime (LaFave 2003a, 573–74).

Does the solicitor have to address the words to precise individuals? Not necessarily. Soliciting "audiences" can be precise enough. One speaker was convicted for urging his audience to commit murder and robbery. But, in another case, a New York court dismissed solicitation charges against Robert Quentin and John Garcia. The pamphlet they distributed was "a general solicitation (however reprehensible) to a large indefinable group to commit a crime" (*People v. Quentin* 1968, 448). The pamphlet contained these paragraphs:

> America is carnivorous. She eats the world for desert. Behind slick pictures of pretty-suburban-middle-class-churchgoing-family lie hamburgers seasoned with napalm, race crimes too brutal to recall, cultures plundered, and triviality elevated into a way of life. The rich are rich because they are thieves, the poor because they are victims, and the future will condemn those who accept the present as reality.
>
> Break down the family, church, nation, city, economy. Subversiveness saves us. Our professors are spies; let us close the schools and flow into the streets. Grow hair long and become too freaky to fit into the machine culture.
>
> What's needed is a generation of people who are freaky, crazy, irrational, sexy, angry, irreligious, childish and mad: people who burn draft cards, burn high school and college degrees: people who say: "To hell with your goals"; people who lure the youth with music, pot and acid: people who re-define reality, who re-define the normal;* * * The white youth of America have more in common with Indians plundered, than they do with their own parents. Burn their house down, and you will be free. (445)

This was followed by a paragraph entitled "How to make a fire bomb, and a recipe for Tryptamine, a psychedelic agent." The recipe ends with the statements:

> Tetrahydrofurane is a very powerful reducing agent; wear safety glasses, add very cautiously, and perform this step with ventilation, away from flames (H[2] is evolved). The yield is about 40 grams of DMT, in tetrahydrofurane solution. This cannot be drunk or injected, but may be smoked by sprinkling on mint or cannabis leaves and letting the solution evaporate. It's evaporated when it starts smelling like DMT instead of tetrahydrofurane. (445)

Solicitation *Mens Rea*

solicitation *mens rea* requires words that convey that their purpose is to get someone to commit a specific crime

Solicitation is a specific-intent crime; that is, it's a crime of purpose. The solicitation *mens rea* requires words that convey that their purpose is to get someone to commit a specific crime. If I urge my friend who works in an expensive jewelry shop to take a gold chain for me, I've solicited her to steal the chain. If, on the other hand, I ask another friend who works in a clothing shop to get a coat for me to use for the evening, and I plan to return the coat the next morning before anyone knows it's missing, I haven't solicited her to steal the coat because I don't intend to steal the coat, only to use it for the night (Chapter 11).

In *State v. Schleifer* (1923), our next case excerpt, the Connecticut Supreme Court ruled that the labor leader Ernest Schleifer was talking to every individual in the large audience gathered to hear him when he called for violence against the railroad management and its property.

CASE

*In **State v. Schleifer (1923),** the Connecticut Supreme Court ruled that the labor leader Ernest Schleifer was talking to every individual in the large audience gathered to hear him when he called for violence against the railroad management and its property.*

Did he "solicit" his audience to destroy their employers' homes and businesses?

State v. Schleifer

121 A. 805 (Conn. 1923)

HISTORY

Ernest Schleifer was charged in an information with solicitation to commit crimes. The trial court granted Schleifer's motion to dismiss the charge. The State appealed the dismissal. The Connecticut Supreme Court of Errors reversed.

WHEELER, CJ.

Ernest Schleifer by oral address to [a large crowd, spoke] in language in substance as follows:

> You will never win the strike with soft methods. You young men ought to go out on the bridge. Don't use eggs; use coal or indelible ink. Break foremen's windows at their homes. Watch the scabs when they come from work, lay for them, especially on pay day. Take them in a dark alley and hit them with a lead pipe. That is the softest thing you can use.
>
> Reimburse yourselves for what we have sacrificed for five months. Don't forget to bump off a few now and then, so Mr. Pearson will know that you are not getting cold feet. You car men know how to take a brake shoe off. Take the brake shoe and put it under something that will put the cars off the irons. A little sand or emery in the journal boxes will help greatly.
>
> Don't be satisfied with trimming the engines. Put some of the cars on the bum. Also, if convenient, put something in between the frames and rods of engines on sidings. Get busy, young fellows, and trim these scabs. Things are running too smooth on the New Haven Road, but let me hear from you while I am here. Go ahead and rip things, and don't let the injunction stop you from trimming these scabs. Don't forget to tie them up with derailments. You boys ought to cut them all up.

To this information, Schleifer filed a motion to quash, which the trial court sustained upon the grounds as stated in part therein, viz.:

2. That the information fails to set forth any offense or crime....
8. That the information merely charges the defendant with having uttered certain words set forth in said information, and such utterances do not constitute a crime by virtue of any statute of this state, or at common law.
9. That the information merely states that the defendant entertained certain intentions, as evidenced by certain expressions made by him, and such intentions do not either at common law or by virtue of any statute constitute crime.

In his memorandum on the motion to quash the court held that in the common-law crime of solicitation "the inducement or invitation must have been directed to one individual soliciting the accomplishment of some particular act which, if complied with, would result in the commission of some specific offense." The trial court further held:

> While it cannot be seriously denied that the public utterance in a promiscuous assembly of such entreaties and exhortations as are charged in this information is highly prejudicial to the public peace, and ought to be seriously penalized, it is a situation that should be met by appropriate legislation. I do not feel warranted in view of all the authorities in undertaking to extend the present limitations of the common law crime of solicitation so as to include the acts of the accused now under consideration.

The accused supports his motion to quash and the ruling of the trial court thereon by maintaining that solicitation alone is not a crime under the common law, and has never been treated as such except in cases where the solicitation was in fact the crime of an attempt. It is necessary that we meet this proposition directly.

If the law be as counsel for the accused claim, we might well say, as Lord Kenyon, the Chief Justice of the court of King's Bench, said in *King v. Higgins*:

> The offense imputed to this defendant is of the most serious kind, no less than that for his own wicked gains he solicited and incited a servant to rob his master; and can it be a question in a country professing to have laws subservient to justice and morality whether this be an offense?

The crimes which the state charges the accused intended by his oral address to urge his hearers to commit were felonies or aggravator crimes akin to felonies, to wit, murder, robbery, aggravated assault with deadly or dangerous weapons, assault with intent to murder, and assault with intent to rob. The language alleged to have been used by this accused does advise, incite, and urge those to whom it was directed to the commission of these crimes, as well as the crime of breach of the peace.

It would be difficult to conceive of an evil minded and desperate criminal urging a more dangerous and dastardly course of action. It invited and commanded not alone deeds of violence towards the railroad employees who remained on their jobs and the members of their households, but also the most serious injury and in all probability death to the innocent travelers upon the railroad and to the crew hands.

The immediate question for us to decide is whether our law is remediless to punish the individual who, with wanton disregard of life and property, incites and commands not one, but many, to the commission of gravest crimes. We determined in 1828 in *State v. Avery*, that the solicitation to another, by letter, to commit adultery was a high crime and misdemeanor nearly allied and equal in guilt to felony, and that an information charging this offense was sufficient under our common law. It was urged that such a solicitation was not a crime because it was no more than an intent to commit evil. We disposed of the claim in these words:

> But it is argued, that a mere intent to commit evil is not indictable, without an act done; but is there not an act done, when it is charged, that the defendant solicited another to commit adultery? The solicitation is an act; and God forbid, that it should not be considered as an offense.

The trial court criticizes the information because it does not charge that any particular person was

(continues)

(continued)

solicited to the commission of any particular crime in any specified place, and the state assigns this among its other alleged errors. It was not necessary to make such an allegation. The solicitation was directed to each one present in the assemblage. It would not have been more direct or more compulsive if each one in the assemblage had been called by name by the accused.

The law of criminal pleading is settled upon this point. [According to Lord Chief Justice Coleridge:]

> The argument has been well put that an orator who makes a speech to 2,000 people does not address it to any one individual amongst those 2,000; it is addressed to the whole number. It is endeavoring to persuade the whole number or large portions of that number, and if a particular individual amongst that number addressed by the orator is persuaded, or listens to it and is encouraged, it is plain that the words of this statute are complied with; because according to well-known principles of law, the person who addresses those words to a number of persons, must be taken to address them to the persons who he knows hear them, who he knows will understand them in a particular way, do understand them in that particular way, and do act upon them.

Aside from the conclusion which we think should have been "and may act upon them," instead of "and do act upon them," we coincide with this statement. To the argument in behalf of the accused that the existence of statutes to punish solicitation to crime as an independent offense shows that there was no such common-law offense, hence the statutory offense was created, it is enough to say that these statutes are as a rule declaratory of the common law, as has been quite frequently pointed out, or they have been adopted for the purpose of adding to or taking from the penalty under the common law.

The [argument]...that the information merely states that the defendant entertained certain intentions may be answered briefly. The mere intention, unexpressed, of the accused does not, and is not claimed to, subject the accused to criminal punishment. But when the intention be expressed in the form of a solicitation, or incitement, or a command to another to commit a crime, and that crime a felony or a high crime and misdemeanor akin to felony, it is a crime under our common law.

Our consideration of the case has led to the approval of a rule somewhat broader than that of some of these authorities, but one which the consideration of this case has shown as to be necessary for the public safety. Suppose the accused had carefully incited and commanded his hearers to the commission of crimes against the public peace and safety which were neither felonies nor aggravated crimes; he could not under the rule of these authorities be informed against, for he would have committed no crime. Yet who can doubt that his inflamed hearers, if they acted upon his words, would not distinguish between the high and aggravated crime and the lesser crime of his specific advice and command, and that their beginning of a breach of the public peace and safety, and of the destruction of property, would inevitably lead to consequences of serious harm alike to the individual and to the state?

The judgment is set aside, and the cause remanded, to be proceeded with according to law.

The other Judges concurred.

QUESTIONS

1. List the facts and circumstances relevant to deciding whether Ernest Schleifer is guilty of criminal solicitation.
2. Summarize the arguments of the trial court and the prosecution in favor of criminal solicitation.
3. Summarize the arguments of the defendant and the Connecticut Supreme Court against criminal solicitation.
4. Which side do you agree with? Back up your answer with specific facts and circumstances and the arguments in the case and the text.

Solicitation Criminal Objective

Some statutes restrict the circumstance element of the **criminal objective of the solicitation** to committing felonies—in some cases, to committing violent felonies. In other jurisdictions, it's a crime to solicit another to commit any crime, whether it's a felony, misdemeanor, or violation. Furthermore, solicitation doesn't have to include an inducement to commit a criminal act at all. For example, suppose a robber urges a friend to borrow money and lend it to him for a plane ticket to escape from the jurisdiction. The robber has solicited escape or aiding and abetting a robbery. Although borrowing money isn't a crime, and lending money to a robber isn't by itself a crime, both escape and aiding and abetting robbers are crimes. Someone who urges another to commit those crimes has committed the crime of solicitation.

criminal objective of the solicitation circumstance element that the objective of the solicitation is law breaking; the seriousness varies by jurisdiction from any violation to violent felony

Summary

Each inchoate offense has some of its own elements, but they all share two elements: the *mens rea* of purpose or specific intent and the *actus reus* of taking some steps toward accomplishing the criminal purpose—but not enough steps to complete the intended crime. Incomplete criminal conduct poses a dilemma: whether to punish someone who's done no harm or to set free someone who's determined to commit a crime. **LO1**

For more than two thousand years, philosophers and judges have struggled with how the criminal law should respond to attempted crimes. Liability for criminal attempt offenses is based on two old and firmly entrenched rationales. One focuses on dangerous acts (*actus reus*), the other on dangerous persons (*mens rea*). **LO2**

The *mens rea* of criminal attempt is always purpose, the intent to commit a specific crime. **LO3**

Attempt *actus reus* is based on two theories of attempt: the social harm from dangerous conduct and the social harm from dangerous people. Attempt *actus reus* requires something beyond mere preparation, but less than all the steps required to complete the intended crime. Six different tests are used to answer the question, "How close is close enough to deserve punishment?" in criminal attempt law. **LO4**

A legal impossibility occurs when actors intend to commit crimes and do everything they can to carry out their criminal intent, but the criminal law doesn't ban what they did. A factual impossibility occurs when actors intend to commit a crime and try to but some fact or circumstance—an extraneous factor—interrupts them to prevent the completion of the crime. Legal impossibility is a defense to criminal attempt, but factual impossibility is not. **LO5**

A little more than half the states and the U.S. government accept the affirmative defense of voluntary abandonment to attempt liability. According to the Model **LO6**

Penal Code, voluntary abandonment means a change in the actor's purpose not influenced by outside circumstances, what may be termed "repentance" or "change of heart."

LO7 Conspiracy, the crime of agreeing with one or more people to commit a crime, is further removed from actually committing a crime than attempts to commit crimes. In fact, one can become guilty of conspiracy long before his act has come so dangerously near to completion as to make him criminally liable for the attempted crime. The law punishes conspirators to nip in the bud the dangers posed by group criminality.

LO8 Conspiracy *actus reus* consists of two parts: (1) an agreement to commit a crime (in all states) and; (2) an overt act in furtherance of the agreement (in about half the states).

LO9 There are two types of large-scale conspiracies: wheel and chain. Wheel conspiracies involve parties differently, with some participating in every transaction and others participating only in one. Chain conspiracies involve parties equally, with each participant handling the same commodity at different points through the process of manufacture, distribution, and sale.

LO10 RICO (Racketeer Influenced and Corrupt Organizations Act) makes criminal enterprise or illicit activity that is run like a business illegal. It applies harsh penalties to those engaged in such activity.

LO11 Solicitation is the crime of trying to get someone else to commit a crime. The *actus reus* of solicitation requires words that actually try to get someone to commit a crime. Solicitation *mens rea* requires purpose or specific intent to get someone to commit a crime. Solicitation is punished similarly to conspiracy, with the notion that nipping this activity in the bud helps to prevent the dangers of group criminality.

Key Terms

criminal attempts, p. 272
criminal conspiracy, p. 272
criminal solicitation, p. 272
inchoate offenses, p. 272
dangerous act rationale, p. 277
dangerous person rationale, p. 277
general attempt statute, p. 278
specific attempt statutes, p. 278
attempt *mens rea*, p. 278
attempt *actus reus*, p. 282
last act rule, p. 282
proximity tests, p. 282
dangerous proximity tests, p. 282
dangerous person tests, p. 282
dangerous proximity to success test (the physical proximity test), p. 283
indispensable element test, p. 283
unequivocality test, p. 284
probable desistance test, p. 284
MPC substantial steps test, p. 285
legal impossibility, p. 288
factual impossibility, p. 289
extraneous factor, p. 294
voluntary abandonment defense, p. 294

conspiracy, p. 298
conspiracy *actus reus*, p. 298
overt act requirement, p. 299
conspiracy *mens rea*, p. 299
criminal objective, p. 300
unilateral approach to conspiracy parties, p. 300
criminal objective of the conspiracy, p. 301
wheel conspiracies, p. 301
chain conspiracies, p. 302
Racketeer Influenced and Corrupt Organizations Act (RICO), p. 307
racketeering, p. 307
enterprise, p. 307
pattern of racketeering activity, p. 307
solicitation, p. 312
solicitation *actus reus*, p. 312
solicitation *mens rea*, p. 314
criminal objective of the solicitation, p. 317

1. To understand that most of the law regarding criminal homicide is about grading the seriousness of the offense. Grading criminal homicide is important because only first-degree murder qualifies for capital punishment.

2. To appreciate that the meaning of "person" is central to homicide law and to understand how it presents problems at both ends of the life course.

3. To appreciate how degrees of murder developed throughout history and to understand their relation to capital punishment.

4. To know and understand the elements of murder.

5. To learn the degrees of murder that presently exist in the United States.

6. To understand that most criminal homicide statutes can be applied to corporations, but prosecutions and convictions are very rare.

7. To understand that the heart of voluntary manslaughter is an intentional killing, in the heat of anger, triggered by an adequate provocation.

8. To understand that adequate provocation is not an excuse to criminal liability for homicide; it only reduces the seriousness of the crime and the punishment to allow for human frailty.

9. To know that the key elements of involuntary manslaughter are the *actus reus* of a voluntary act or omission and the *mens rea* of intentionally killing that cause the criminal harm of death.

10. To appreciate the moral, ethical, and legal dilemmas surrounding euthanasia, and to know the primary arguments in support of, and against, doctor-assisted suicide.

9 Crimes against Persons I

Murder and Manslaughter

Chapter Outline

Ray Snowden had been playing pool and drinking in a Boise pool room early in the evening. Snowden and a companion visited a club near Boise, then went to nearby Garden City. They visited several bars. Snowden had several drinks. Their last stop was the HiHo Club. While Snowden was in the HiHo Club he met and talked to Cora Lucyle Dean. He said he hadn't been acquainted with Mrs. Dean prior to that time, but he had "seen her in a couple of the joints up town." He danced with Mrs. Dean while at the HiHo Club. Snowden and Dean left together.

Snowden said after they left the club Mrs. Dean wanted him to find a cab and take her back to Boise. He refused because he didn't feel he should pay her fare. After some words, he related, "she got mad at me so I got pretty hot and I don't know whether I back handed her there or not. And, we got calmed down and decided to walk across to the gas station and call a cab."

They crossed the street, and began arguing again. Snowden said, "She swung and at the same time she kneed me again. I blew my top." Snowden said he pushed Dean over beside a pickup truck which was standing near a business building. There he pulled his knife—a pocket knife with a two-inch blade—and cut her throat.

The body, which was found the next morning, was viciously and sadistically cut and mutilated. An autopsy surgeon testified the voice box had been cut, and that this would have prevented the victim from making any intelligible outcry. There were other wounds inflicted while she was still alive—one in her neck, one in her abdomen, two in the face, and two on the back of the neck. The second neck wound severed the spinal cord and caused death. There were other wounds all over her body, and her clothing had been cut away. The nipple of the right breast was missing. (Snowden ate it.)

There was no evidence of a sexual attack on the victim; however, some of the lacerations were around the breasts and vagina of the deceased. A blood test showed Mrs. Dean was intoxicated at the time of her death.

Snowden took Dean's wallet. He hailed a passing motorist and rode back to Boise with him. There he went to a bowling alley and changed clothes. He dropped his knife into a sewer, and threw the wallet away. Then he went to his hotel and cleaned up again. He put the clothes he had worn that evening into a trash barrel.

"Death is different," the U.S. Supreme Court said about capital punishment. Killing is different, too—it's the most serious of all crimes. In 1769, Blackstone, the great eighteenth-century commentator on the criminal law, introduced his chapter on homicide with words that are pretty close to describing the crimes you'll be learning about in this chapter:

> Of crimes injurious to persons, the most important is the offence of taking away that life, which is the immediate gift of the great creator; and which therefore no man can be entitled to deprive another of. The subject therefore of the present chapter will be, the offense of homicide or destroying the life of man, in its several stages of guilt, arising from the particular circumstances of mitigation or aggravation. (4:177)

Of course, raping, assaulting, and kidnapping harm people, too; but however awful they may be, they leave their victims alive (Chapter 10). Crimes against homes and property (Chapter 11) and crimes against public order and morals (Chapter 12) also hurt their victims and society, but these are injuries to worldly things. According to the distinguished professor of criminal law George P. Fletcher (1978):

> Killing another human being is not only a worldly deprivation; in the Western conception of homicide, killing is an assault on the sacred, natural order. In the Biblical view, the person who slays another was thought to acquire control over the blood—the life force—of the victim. The only way that this life force could be returned to God, the origin of all life, was to execute the slayer himself. In this conception of crime and punishment, capital execution for homicide served to expiate the desecration of the natural order. (235–36)

CRIMINAL HOMICIDE IN CONTEXT

LO1 Criminal homicide in the context of the crimes that you'll be studying throughout the rest of the book are rare events. In 2013 (the most recent official numbers), there were 14,196 murders reported to the FBI compared with 1,163,146 total violent felonies. The total

VIOLENT CRIMES, 2013

Figure 9.1

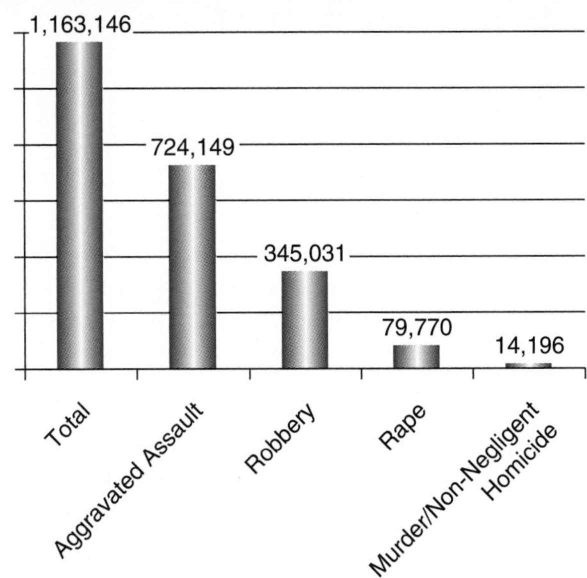

Source: *Crime in the United States* (September 2013), Table 1.

number of all crimes in the FBI index of serious crimes (homicide, forcible rape, robbery, aggravated assault, burglary, theft, motor vehicle theft, and arson) was 8,632,512 (FBI 2014). Figure 9.1 breaks down the 2013 totals from the FBI's index of violent crimes.

These numbers aren't meant to diminish the seriousness of killing another person—an act that stands alone in its awfulness. However, there are more reasons than raw numbers why we study criminal homicide. Much of what you've learned in the earlier chapters grew out of the law of criminal homicide. This is especially true of the mental element, or *mens rea*, and the justification of self-defense. But there's more: the three-step analysis of criminal liability—(1) criminal conduct, (2) without justification, or (3) excuse—grew out of the great work on the law of criminal homicide written by the principal drafter of the Model Penal Code (MPC), Professor Herbert Wechsler at Columbia Law School (Michael and Wechsler 1937; Dubber and Kelman 2005, 846).

Most of the law of homicide is devoted to answering questions like: Is this murder first or second degree? Is that killing murder or manslaughter? Is this manslaughter voluntary or involuntary? Students ask: "Does it really matter?" Certainly not to the victim—who's already and always dead! But it does make a big *legal* and *practical* difference. Why? Because the punishment for criminal homicide depends on the degree of murder or the type of manslaughter committed.

Three elements of criminal homicide—*actus reus*, *mens rea*, and special mitigating and aggravating circumstances—are used to define the kinds and grade the seriousness of the criminal homicides you'll learn about in this chapter. Defining what kind of criminal homicide a particular killing is and grading its seriousness will make you think about deep philosophical questions regarding crime and punishment. This is good and proper.

But there's more than a *philosophical* question here. There's the *policy* question of the kind and amount of punishment to inflict on people who kill other people. Should we kill them? Lock them up for the rest of their lives? Lock them up for a certain number of years? Fine them? All of these are provided for in the state and federal criminal codes. And they vary not only from one criminal homicide to another but also from state to state, sometimes drastically. For the most striking example, first-degree murder is the only crime you can die for, and, in non–death penalty states, it's the only crime for which you can get life in prison without a chance of parole.

As you read the chapter, keep in focus both the moral or ethical dimension and the policy dimension of criminal homicide and their importance in shaping the definition, grading, and punishment of how and why one person kills another.

In this chapter, we'll examine the history of the law of criminal homicide and the elements of murder and manslaughter—namely, the (1) *actus reus*, (2) the *mens rea*, and (3) the circumstance elements—and how they affect the punishment of the various degrees of murder and voluntary manslaughter. Then, we'll turn to the lesser offenses of involuntary manslaughter and criminal negligence homicide. But before we do, let's examine the important preliminary question: What does "person" or "human being" mean in criminal homicide law?

THE MEANING OF "PERSON" OR "HUMAN BEING"

LO2 Killing another "person" is central to criminal homicide liability because it defines who's a victim. "Person" seems like a simple concept to understand. However, it raises deep philosophical questions and hot controversy. We won't get deeply into the broad controversy, except as a preliminary matter to understanding the elements of criminal homicide. The definition of "person" for purposes of criminal homicide presents problems at both ends of the life cycle—when life begins and when it ends. When life begins tells us when a potential victim becomes a real victim; when life ends tells us when a real victim is no longer a victim.

LO2 When Does Life Begin?

> The person killed must be a reasonable creature in being…at the time of the killing….To kill a child in its mother's womb, is now no murder, but a great felony. But if the child be born alive, and dies by reason of the potion or bruises it received in the womb, it is murder in such as administered or gave them.
>
> —Blackstone (1769, 198)

born-alive rule the rule that to be a person, and therefore a homicide victim, a baby had to be "born alive" and capable of breathing and maintaining a heartbeat on its own

Throughout most of its history, homicide law has followed the **born-alive rule**. The opening quote from Blackstone's *Commentaries on the Laws of England* (1769) stated the rule in its common law form. To be a person, and therefore a homicide victim, a baby had to be "born alive" *and* capable of breathing and maintaining a heartbeat on its own. Eighteen states still follow the "born alive" rule (Smith 2000, 1848).

Some courts in states that follow the born-alive rule have interpreted their statutes to include deaths caused by prenatal injuries if the fetus dies after it's born alive. (Notice that was also the law in 1769!) For example, in *State v. Cotton* (2000), Lawrence Cotton accidentally shot his girlfriend, L.W., in the back of the head. L.W. was eight and a half months pregnant at the time. Although L.W. died shortly after arriving at the hospital, her daughter was delivered alive. But the fatal injury to L.W. had so decreased the baby's blood supply that the infant died the following day (920). Cotton was convicted on two counts of reckless homicide, one for L.W. and one for the infant. Cotton argued that the cause of death, his accidental shot that killed his girlfriend, occurred before the fetus was born. The Arizona Court of Appeals rejected Cotton's argument:

> That the shooting in this case occurred while the infant was in utero does not preclude her post-birth status as a "person" for purposes of Arizona's homicide statutes.

> While the homicide statutes require that the victim be a "person," they do not limit the nature or timing of the injury that causes the death of the "person." Because the infant here was undeniably a "person" at the time of her death a day after the shooting, it is irrelevant that the injuries that led to her death were inflicted while she was still in utero. (922–23)

In 24 states, it's a crime to kill a fetus (Smith 2000, 1851). They've done in three ways:

1. Revise their existing homicide statutes to include fetuses as homicide victims.
2. Create new homicide statutes aimed exclusively at fetuses.
3. Create statutes that punish attacks on pregnant women that cause death to the fetuses they're carrying.

The California legislature added just three words ("or a fetus") to its existing murder statute in order to overturn *Keeler v. Superior Court* (1970). In *Keeler*, the California Supreme Court refused to push back the definition of "person" to include fetuses before the birth process. Keeler was convicted of manslaughter for causing the death of his wife's unborn fetus by kicking her in the stomach. Before *Keeler*, the statute read, "Murder is the unlawful killing of a human being with malice aforethought." Now it reads "Murder is the unlawful killing of a human being, *or a fetus*, with malice aforethought" [emphasis added] [California Penal Code 2006, § 187(a)].

Other state legislatures have left their homicide statutes intact and created the new crime of feticide, specifically directed at the killing of fetuses. These special feticide statutes vary as to when in the gestational development criminal liability attaches. Some say it's at viability; some say at "quickening"; some specify the number of weeks; and some say criminal liability attaches at "conception" or "fertilization" (Smith 2000, 1851; LaFave 2010, 770).

feticide the crime of killing a fetus

The nearby Criminal Law in Focus box shows the breakdown of states and the stage of development their statutes adopt. I've arranged them from the latest to the earliest stage of development; the first is the narrowest definition of life for the purpose of the law of criminal homicide, and the last is the broadest definition.

Stages of Fetal Development in Feticide Statutes

STAGE OF DEVELOPMENT	DEFINITION	STATES
Born alive	Fully outside the mother, with an "independent circulation"	(18 states) Alabama, Alaska, Colorado, Connecticut, Hawaii, Idaho, Kentucky, Maryland, Maine, Montana, Nebraska, New Jersey, New York, North Carolina, Oregon, Texas, Vermont, West Virginia
Viability	End of the second trimester when the fetus can live outside the womb; usually at 28 weeks of pregnancy	(6 states) Indiana, Massachusetts, Michigan, Oklahoma, South Carolina, Tennessee

(continues)

(continued)

Quickening	When the mother first feels the fetus moving in the womb (i.e., quickening), usually between the 16th and 18th week of pregnancy	(5 states) Florida, Mississippi, Nevada, Rhode Island, Washington
12 weeks		Arkansas
7 to 8 weeks		California
Fertilization/conception		(7 states) Illinois, Louisiana, Minnesota, Missouri, North Dakota, Pennsylvania, Wisconsin
No stage of development designated		(3 states) Arizona, South Dakota, Utah

Source: Constructed from Smith (2000).

YOU DECIDE

Is partial birth abortion murder?

Dilation and Extraction for Late Second Trimester Abortion

The surgical method described in this paper differs from classic D&E in that it does not rely upon dismemberment to remove the fetus. Nor are inductions or infusions used to expel the intact fetus. Rather, the surgeon grasps and removes a nearly intact fetus through an adequately dilated cervix. The author has coined the term Dilation and Extraction or D&X to distinguish it from dismemberment-type D&Es. This procedure can be performed in a properly equipped physician's office under local anesthesia. It can be used successfully in patients 20–26 weeks in pregnancy. The author has performed over 700 of these procedures with a low rate of complications.

DESCRIPTION OF DILATION AND EXTRACTION METHOD (D&X)

Dilation and extraction takes over three days. In a nutshell, D&X can be described as follows: dilation; more dilation; real-time ultrasound visualization; version (as needed); intact extraction; fetal skull decompression; removal; clean-up; recovery.

Day 1—Dilation

In the operating room, the cervix is prepped, anesthetized and dilated to 9–11 mm. Five, six, or seven large Dilapan hydroscopic dilators are placed in the cervix. The patient goes home or to a motel overnight.

Day 2—Dilation

The patient returns to the operating room where the previous day's Dilapan are removed. The cervix is scrubbed and anesthetized. Between 15 and 25 Dilapan are placed in the cervical canal. The patient returns home or to a motel overnight.

Day 3—The Operation

The patient returns to the operating room where the previous day's Dilapan are removed. The surgical assistant administers 10 IU Pitocin intramuscularly. The cervix is scrubbed, anesthetized and grasped with a tenaculum. The membranes are ruptured, if they are not already. The surgical assistant places an ultrasound probe on the patient's abdomen and scans the fetus, locating the lower extremities. This scan provides the surgeon information about the orientation of the fetus and approximate location of the lower extremities. The transducer is then held in position over the lower extremities.

The surgeon introduces a large grasping forcep, such as a Bierer or Hern, through the vaginal and cervical canals into the corpus of the uterus. Based upon his knowledge of fetal orientation, he moves the tip of the instrument carefully towards the fetal lower extremities. When the instrument appears on the sonogram screen, the surgeon is able to open and close its jaws to firmly and reliably grasp a lower extremity. The surgeon then applies firm traction to the instrument causing a turning of the fetus (if necessary) and pulls the extremity into the vagina.

By observing the movement of the lower extremity and version of the fetus on the ultrasound screen, the surgeon is assured that his instrument has not inappropriately grasped a maternal structure. With a lower extremity in the vagina, the surgeon uses his fingers to deliver the opposite lower extremity, then the torso, the shoulders and the upper extremities. The skull lodges at the internal cervical opening. Usually there is not enough dilation for it to pass through. The fetus is oriented dorsum or spine up.

At this point, the right-handed surgeon slides the fingers of the left had along the back of the fetus and "hooks" the shoulders of the fetus with the index and ring fingers (palm down). Next he slides the tip of the middle finger along the spine towards the skull while applying traction to the shoulders and lower extremities. The middle finger lifts and pushes the anterior cervical lip out of the way.

While maintaining this tension, lifting the cervix and applying traction to the shoulders with the fingers of the left hand, the surgeon takes a pair of blunt curved Metzenbaum scissors in the right hand. He carefully advances the tip, curved down, along the spine and under his middle finger until he feels it contact the base of the skull under the tip of his middle finger. Reassessing proper placement of the closed scissors tip and safe elevation of the cervix, the surgeon then forces the scissors into the base of the skull or into the foramen magnum. Having safely entered the skull, he spreads the scissors to enlarge the opening.

The surgeon removes the scissors and introduces a suction catheter into this hole and evacuates the skull contents. With the catheter still in place, he applies traction to the fetus, removing it completely from the patient. The surgeon finally removes the placenta with forceps and scrapes the uterine walls with a large Evans and a 14 mm suction curette. The procedure ends.

Recovery

Patients are observed a minimum of 2 hours following surgery. A pad check and vital signs are performed every 30 minutes. Patients with minimal bleeding after 30 minutes are encouraged to walk about the building or outside between checks. Intravenous fluids, Pitocin and antibiotics are available for the exceptional times they are needed.

Patients with severe cramps with Dilapan dilation are provided Phenergan 25 mg suppositories rectally every 4 hours as needed. Rare patients require Synalogos DC in order to sleep during Dilapan dilation. Patients with a hemoglobin less than 10 g/dl prior to surgery receive packed red blood cell transfusions.

Follow-up

All patients are given a 24-hour physician's number to call in case of a problem or concern. At least three attempts to contact each patient by phone one week after surgery are made by the office staff. All patients are asked to return for check-up three weeks following their surgery.

THIRD TRIMESTER

The author is aware of one other surgeon who uses a conceptually similar technique. He adds additional changes of Dilapan and/or lamineria in the 48 hour dilation period. Coupled with other refinements and a slower operating time, he performs these procedures up to 32 weeks or more.

SUMMARY

In conclusion, Dilation and Extraction is an alternative method for achieving late second trimester abortions to 26 weeks. It can be used in the third trimester. Among its advantages are that it is a quick, surgical outpatient method that can be performed on a scheduled basis under local anesthesia.

Among its disadvantages are that it requires a high degree of surgical skill, and may not be appropriate for a few patients.

Source: Martin Haskell, M.D. Presented at the National Abortion Federation Risk Management Seminar, September 13, 1992.

(continues)

(continued)

Here's how one nurse who attended the abortion of a 26½-week-old fetus performed by Dr. Haskell described the procedure:

> Dr. Haskell went in with forceps and grabbed the baby's legs and pulled them down into the birth canal. Then he delivered the baby's body and the arms—everything but the head. The doctor kept the head right inside the uterus.... The baby's little fingers were clasping and unclasping, and his little feet were kicking. Then the doctor stuck the scissors in the back of his head, and the baby's arms jerked out, like a startle reaction, like a flinch, like a baby does when he thinks he is going to fall. The doctor opened up the scissors, stuck a high-powered suction tube into the opening, and sucked the baby's brains out. Now the baby went completely limp.... He cut the umbilical cord and delivered the placenta. He threw the baby in a pan, along with the placenta and the instruments he had just used.

Source: *Gonzales v. Carhart*, 500 U.S. 124, at 138–39.

Instructions

Abortion politics focuses on extremes. At one end is the deeply held belief that intentionally terminating a pregnancy from the moment of conception is murder. At the other end is the deeply held belief that "The embryo is not a child. It is not a baby. It is not yet a human being." (Ramsey 2006, 722, n. 4) The enactment and the aftermath of the federal Partial-Birth Abortion Ban Act of 2003 is a prime example. Even in the U.S. Supreme Court case that upheld its validity, *Gonzales v. Carhart* (2007) (5–4) generated sharp and unusually emotionally charged exchanges between the five at oral arguments and in the majority, concurring, and dissenting opinions. After reading the excerpts above, listening to the oral arguments and Justices Kennedy (majority) and Ginsburg's (dissent) announcement of the opinions at http://www.oyez.org/cases/2000-2009/2006/2006_05_380, and the section "When Does Life Begin?" pp. 324–325, do you believe statutes that make partial birth abortions murder or feticide are wise public policy? Explain your answer.

LO2 When Does Life End?

It used to be easy to define "death": when the heart and breathing stop. Not anymore. Determining when life ends has become increasingly complex as organ transplants and sophisticated artificial life support mechanisms make it possible to maintain vital life signs. Still, to kill a dying person, to accelerate a person's death, or to kill a "worthless" person is clearly homicide under current law. In *State v. Fiero* (1979, 77–78), a doctor who removed a vital organ too soon committed criminal homicide. And anyone who kills another by purposely disconnecting a respirator has also committed criminal homicide.

The concept of brain death has complicated the simple definition as to when the heart and breathing stop. This complication has implications not just for medicine and morals but also for criminal law. If artificial supports alone maintain breathing and the heartbeat while brain waves remain minimal or flat, brain death has occurred. The Uniform Brain Death Act provides that an individual who has suffered irreversible cessation of all brain functions, including those of the brain stem, is dead (ALI 1985, 2:1, 10–11).

More difficult cases involve individuals with enough brain functions to sustain breathing and a heartbeat but nothing more, such as patients in a deep coma. They may breathe and their hearts may beat on their own, but are they alive according to the criminal law? Troubling cases arise in which patients in a deep coma have been described by medical specialists as "vegetables" but regain consciousness and live for a considerable time afterward, such as the Minneapolis police officer who was shot and written off for dead after more than a year in a deep coma. He regained consciousness and lived for several more years.

MURDER

LO3

The common law divided homicides into two kinds, and so do modern criminal codes, the MPC, and this chapter. The two kinds are:

1. murder, killing a person with "malice aforethought," which we'll define and discuss in this section
2. manslaughter, killing a person without malice aforethought, which we'll discuss in the "Manslaughter" section

murder killing a person with "malice aforethought"

manslaughter killing a person without malice aforethought

According to Blackstone, writing in 1769, malice aforethought was the "grand criterion, which now distinguishes murder from other killing" (188–89). (See the Elements of Common Law Murder illustration.) These two divisions were in turn divided into several kinds of murder and manslaughter, and, eventually, some special kinds of homicide, such as vehicular homicide (which we'll discuss later in the chapter), were added.

A long history of criminal homicides preceded the publication of Blackstone's classic work in 1769. Part of this we'll discuss in this section. We also examine the elements of murder, the kinds and degrees of murder, first-degree murder, second-degree murder, and corporation murder.

History of Murder Law

LO3

Our modern law of criminal homicide took centuries to develop. Over several centuries, the English common law judges had developed two broad kinds of homicide, criminal and noncriminal. By the 1550s, the common law judges, with the help of a growing number of statutes, had further divided criminal homicide into murder and manslaughter and noncriminal homicide into justifiable and excusable homicide (Chapters 5 and 6).

By 1700, the English common and statute laws of homicide and the American colonies' law recognized three kinds of homicide:

1. justifiable homicide, killing in self-defense (Chapter 5), capital punishment, and law enforcement use of deadly force
2. excusable homicide, killings done by someone "not of sound memory and discretion" (insane and immature) (Chapter 6)
3. criminal homicide, all homicides that are neither justified nor excused

justifiable homicide killing in self-defense

excusable homicide killings done by someone "not of sound memory and discretion"

criminal homicide all homicides that are neither justified nor excused

We'll examine manslaughter later in the chapter. For now, let's concentrate on murder. In the early 1600s, Sir Edward Coke wrote that common law murder occurred when a person "of sound memory and discretion, unlawfully killeth any reasonable

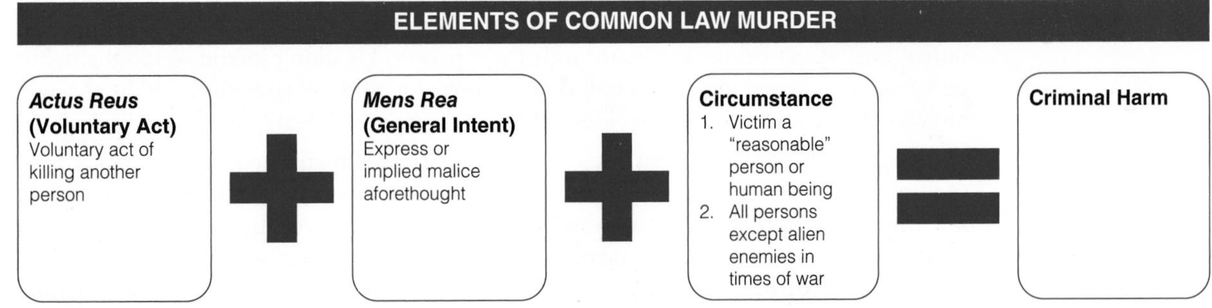

creature in being and under the king's peace, with malice aforethought, either express or implied" (Blackstone 1769, 4:195, quoting from Coke 1628, 3:47).

Here's how Blackstone defined the elements of common law murder in 1769:

1. *Sound memory and discretion* excused "lunatics and infants" from criminal liability.
2. *"Unlawfully"* meant killing without justification (Chapter 5) or excuse (Chapter 6).
3. *Killeth* included causing death by "poisoning, striking, starving, drowning, and a thousand other forms of death, by which human nature may be overcome" (196).
4. *Reasonable creature in being* was someone already born alive and breathing at the time of the killing (198).
5. *Under the king's peace* meant "to kill an alien, a Jew, or an outlaw, who are all under the king's protection, is as much murder as to kill the most regular Englishman; except he be an alien enemy in time of war" (198).
6. *With malice aforethought, express or implied.*

malice aforethought originally the mental state of intentional killing, with some amount of spite, hate, or bad will, planned in advance of the killing

Let's take a closer look at the mental element—killing with **malice aforethought**. At first, "malice" meant with specific intent or killing on purpose—and probably with some amount of spite, hate, or bad will. "Aforethought" meant the acts were planned in advance of the killing. The English homicide statutes in the 1550s defined "murder" as killing someone intentionally by "poison" or "lying in wait," classic examples of acts planned in advance. So the only kind of murder was intentional, premeditated killing—in other words, killing with malice aforethought.

After that, the judges invented new kinds of murder. First, they added intentional (malicious) killings that weren't premeditated. These included sudden killings during the heat of passion, "unreasonably" provoked by the victim's conduct. We'll discuss "unreasonably" provoked when we get to voluntary manslaughter, but it's enough for now to think of it this way: if a reasonable person would have cooled off between the provocation and the killing, the killing was murder, even though it wasn't premeditated. For example, suppose Pete, a student in my Criminal Law class, doesn't like being touched by men. As he's leaving class, Nick comes up, puts his arm around Pete, and says, "Boring class, huh?" Very offended, Pete pulls away, saying "Back off, jerk." Nick responds with, "Oh, come on, I'm just being friendly" and approaches Pete again. Pete pulls out his gun and shoots Nick; Nick dies. Pete was "unreasonably" provoked.

Next, the judges added unintended killings if they occurred during the commission of felonies. For example, an arsonist set fire to a house when she believed no one was at home. Unfortunately, someone was at home, and he burned to death. She didn't intend to kill him, and because she didn't intend to kill him, obviously she couldn't have planned to kill him before she set fire to the house.

depraved heart murder extremely reckless killings

Then came **depraved heart murder**, defined as extremely reckless killings. Recall here the definition of "recklessly" (Chapter 4): knowingly creating a substantial and unjustifiable risk. In the case of a depraved heart murder, the risk is of death. For example, a roofer on a tall building, without bothering to look, throws a heavy board onto a busy street below; the board kills three people. He didn't intend to kill them, but he knew he was creating a high risk that the board would kill someone, and he threw it anyway. These are extremely reckless killings, or depraved heart murders.

intent to cause serious bodily injury murder no intent to kill is required when a victim dies following acts triggered by the intent to inflict serious bodily injury short of death

The judges took one last step away from the premeditated, intentional killing requirement. They created **intent to cause serious bodily injury murder**. No intent to kill was required when a victim died following acts triggered by the intent to inflict serious bodily injury short of death. Suppose a parent has a seventeen-year-old son who regularly drinks heavily, cuts school, and steals to buy alcohol; he's just generally out of control. Talking to him, grounding him, taking away his car, sending him to counseling—nothing works. So his father, angry and frustrated, decides to "beat him within an inch of his life." He does, and his son dies. He commits an intent to cause serious bodily injury murder.

serious bodily injury bodily injury that involves a substantial risk of death; protracted unconsciousness; extreme physical pain; protracted or obvious disfigurement; or protracted loss or substantial impairment of a function of a bodily member, organ or mental faculty

Serious bodily injury has a technical meaning. Some states define it by statute. Here's Tennessee's (Tennessee Criminal Code 2005, 39-11-106(a)(34)) definition, which is similar to other states' definitions: "Serious bodily injury" means bodily injury that involves:

1. A substantial risk of death;
2. Protracted unconsciousness;
3. Extreme physical pain;
4. Protracted or obvious disfigurement; or
5. Protracted loss or substantial impairment of a function of a bodily member, organ or mental faculty.

"express" malice aforethought the mental element of killings that fit the original meaning of "murder"—intentional killings planned in advance

Throughout the centuries when judges were expanding the definition of "murder" to include these very different kinds of killings, they continued to call them all by the same name—"killing another with malice aforethought." But they added the critical phrase "express or implied." **"Express" malice aforethought** was reserved for killings that fit the original meaning of "murder"—intentional killings planned in advance.

According to Blackstone (1769):

> Express malice is when one, with a sedate deliberate mind and formed design, doth kill another, which formed design is evidenced by external circumstances discovering that inward intention; as lying in wait, antecedent menaces, former grudges, and concerted schemes to do him some bodily harm. (199)

"implied" malice aforethought the mental element of intentional killings without premeditation or reasonable provocation; unintentional killings during the commission of felonies; depraved heart killings; and intent to inflict grievous bodily harm killings

"Implied" malice aforethought referred to the four additional kinds of murder we just discussed:

1. Intentional killings without premeditation or reasonable provocation
2. Unintentional killings during the commission of felonies
3. Depraved heart killings
4. Intent to inflict grievous bodily harm killings

Elements of Murder

LO4

Murder is a result crime. (Recall from Chapter 3 that result crimes consist of criminal conduct that causes a criminal harm.) Therefore, proving murder requires proof beyond a reasonable doubt of these elements:

1. Murder *actus reus*, the act of killing
2. Murder *mens rea*, intentional, knowing, or extremely reckless killing
3. Causation, the act caused
4. Death
5. Attendant circumstances, if there are any

See the Elements of Murder Illustration of these requirements.

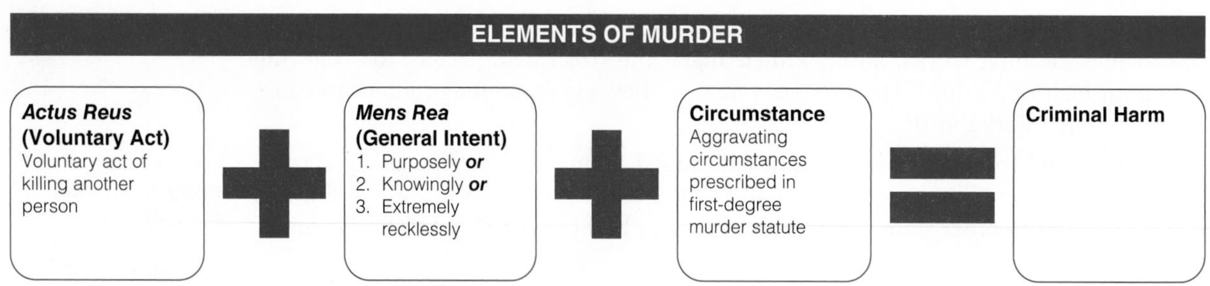

Before we go any further, it's important to keep in mind throughout the following discussion that the required criminal acts, mental attitudes, tests of causation, and attendant circumstances vary from state to state. So if you're interested in finding out what the elements of murder (or any of the specific kinds of homicide, or for that matter, any of the crimes in the rest of the book) are in your state, you can find them online free. (One of the several links to your state's code is https://www.law.cornell.edu/wex/table_criminal_code. They're also available on apps for tablets and smartphones.)

Now, let's turn to the elements of murder. We won't discuss causation here because Chapter 4 and the "Doctor-Assisted Suicide" sections later in this chapter cover all you need to know about it. As for the result, the death of a person, we said all that was necessary in the "The Meaning of 'Person' or 'Human Being'" section earlier. Finally, we'll leave the discussion of the circumstance element to the places in the text where there's a circumstance element. We'll focus on how the general principles of *actus reus* and *mens rea* apply to the criminal act and mental attitude elements of criminal homicide.

MURDER *ACTUS REUS*

murder *actus reus* the act of killing by poisoning, striking, starving, drowning, and a thousand other forms by which human nature can be overcome

"Killing" or "causing death" is the heart of murder *actus reus*, and it's easy to define. We can't improve on Blackstone's (1769) words: "The killing may be by poisoning, striking, starving, drowning, and a thousand other forms by which human nature can be overcome" (196). It can also result from failures to act—such as a husband who stands by and watches his blind wife, whom he hates, walk off the edge of a cliff. It can result from words—such as a wife who sneaks up behind her husband, whom she hates, who is standing at the edge of the Grand Canyon and yells, "Boo!" causing him to fall over the edge.

Notice that *how* the murderer kills someone doesn't matter in most cases. But it can be a circumstance element in first-degree murder or an aggravating circumstance in death penalty cases. Even though there were no degrees of murder at the time, Blackstone (1769) teaches us that it's murder if a victim dies after "one beats another in a cruel and unusual manner":

> As when a park keeper tied a boy, that was stealing wood, to a horse's tail and dragged him along the park; when a master corrected his servant with an iron bar; and a schoolmaster stamped on his scholar's belly, so that each of the sufferers died. These were justly held to be murders because, the correction being excessive and such as could not proceed but from a bad heart, it was equivalent to an act of slaughter. (199–200)

MURDER *MENS REA*

murder *mens rea* can include purposeful, knowing, or reckless as the mental element in killing

Murder *mens rea* can include every state of mind included in the concept of malice aforethought (discussed in the last section). In the language of the Model Penal Code (discussed in Chapter 4), purpose, knowledge, and recklessness can qualify as the mental element in murder. We'll have more to say about the mental element in each of the degrees of murder, which we'll turn to now.

KINDS AND DEGREES OF MURDER

LO5

The English judges never formally divided murder into degrees. All murders were capital offenses. But the judges had enormous discretion to free all convicted felons by means of "benefit of clergy," a practice that began with a rule that allowed priests to be tried only in ecclesiastical courts. To get transferred from the common law to the ecclesiastical courts, priests had to prove they were clerics by reading a passage from the Bible. At first, this was a reliable test because only clerics could read. Eventually, "reading the book" became a pure formality, for two reasons. First, the passage in the "book" convicted felons had to "read" was always the same few words; and second, literacy increased well beyond the clergy.

The judges manipulated the formality to mitigate *informally* the harshness of the common law, which mandated that all felons, from cold-blooded murderers to petty thieves, should hang. By the reign of Henry VIII (1509–37), successful pleas of clergy were so widely granted by the judges that Parliament enacted a form of mandatory sentencing to curb judicial discretion; it banned the plea in all cases of premeditated murder (Samaha 1974). The list of "nonclergyable" offenses would grow in the centuries that followed.

Dividing murder into degrees expanded the idea that not all felons—in this case, not all murderers—should be executed. In the new United States, degrees of murder were created by legislatures, not judges. Pennsylvania was the first state to depart from the common law, enacting a statute in 1794 that divided murder into first and second degrees. The Pennsylvania statute provided that

> all murder, which shall be perpetrated by means of poison, lying in wait, or by any other kind of willful, deliberate or premeditated killing, or which shall be committed in the perpetration, or attempt to perpetrate any arson, rape, robbery or burglary shall be deemed murder in the first degree; and all other kinds of murder shall be deemed murder in the second degree. (Pennsylvania Laws 1794, chap. 257, §§ 1–2)

So under the statute, premeditated intent to kill murders and some felony murders were capital offenses, just as they were under the old common law. And they still are. All other murders (depraved heart and intent to cause serious bodily injury) were second-degree murders, just as they were under the old law. *Sometimes*, they still are. The Model Penal Code doesn't use the term "degrees," but, since its publication in 1960, state criminal codes have increasingly used the MPC's scheme of dividing murder according to mental attitude—purposely, knowingly, and extremely recklessly.

Most states quickly followed Pennsylvania's example. Behind this quick adoption of the statutes was the first of numerous waves of opposition to the death penalty throughout U.S. history. Three results followed, results that influenced the criminal law you're studying in this book profoundly:

1. The gradual peeling away of layers of criminal homicides that were thought not to deserve the death penalty
2. The emergence of more detailed grading schemes, placing various types of criminal homicide along the spectrum of available criminal punishments
3. The development of various justifications and excuses making certain homicides noncriminal (Low 1990, 335)

Today, most states divide homicide into two degrees, and a few divide it into three degrees. We'll look at first-degree and second-degree murder.

LO5

First-Degree Murder

first-degree murder the only crime today in which the death penalty can be imposed, consisting of (1) premeditated, deliberate intent to kill murders and (2) felony murders

Almost all states that divide murder into degrees establish two kinds of first-degree murder: (1) premeditated, deliberate intent to kill murders and (2) felony murders. First-degree murder is the only crime today in which the death penalty can be imposed (Chapter 2). Because of a series of U.S. Supreme Court cases, death penalty cases are complicated proceedings. So we need to look at first-degree murder and the death penalty before we go further.

DEATH PENALTY AND FIRST-DEGREE MURDER

The death penalty is discretionary in all states that authorize it. To guide judges' and juries' decisions whether to execute or sentence to life in prison a person convicted of first-degree murder, the U.S. Supreme Court, in a series of decisions since the 1970s, has completely revised the procedures for imposing capital punishment. The matter is highly complicated, and the Court's cases haven't always made it clear just what's required, but here's a list of the main practices the Constitution bans, requires, and allows:

1. *Mandatory* death sentences are banned. States can't require the death penalty in *all* first-degree murders.
2. *Unguided* discretionary death penalty decisions are banned. Judges and juries can't impose the death penalty without a list of specific criteria for and against the death penalty to guide their decision.
3. *Mitigating factors are required.* States can't limit the range of mitigating factors that might favor life imprisonment instead of death.
4. *Additional aggravating factors are allowed.* Jurors and/or judges are allowed to consider factors in favor of death not specifically included in statutory lists of aggravating factors.

capital cases death penalty cases in death penalty states and "mandatory life sentence without parole" cases in non–death penalty states

Most states have adopted the MPC's two recommended procedures—bifurcation and the criteria for guiding the decision to impose the death sentence in capital cases. (We define "capital cases" as death penalty cases in death penalty states and "mandatory life sentence without parole" cases in non–death penalty states.)

bifurcation procedure the requirement that the death penalty decision be made in two phases: a trial to determine guilt and a second separate proceeding, after a finding of guilt, to consider the aggravating factors for, and mitigating factors against, capital punishment

The bifurcation procedure mandates that the death penalty decision be made in two phases: a trial to determine guilt and a second separate proceeding, after a finding of guilt, to consider the aggravating factors for, and mitigating factors against, capital punishment. At the penalty phase, prosecutors get the opportunity to present evidence not presented at the trial phase, and defendants can offer evidence in mitigation.

The criteria for decision in death penalty cases must be limited by the criteria established and announced *before* the decision to sentence the defendant to death. Juries, or judges where state law authorizes judges to decide, have to consider aggravating and mitigating factors before making their decision. They can't actually impose the death penalty unless they find "one of the aggravated circumstances and further find that there are no mitigating circumstances sufficiently substantial to call for leniency" (ALI 1985, Art. 210.6).

The list of aggravating circumstances includes:

1. The murder was committed by a convict under sentence of imprisonment.
2. The defendant was previously convicted of another murder or of a felony involving the use or threat of violence to the person.

3. At the time the murder was committed, the defendant also committed another murder.
4. The defendant knowingly created a great risk of death to many persons.
5. The murder was committed while the defendant was engaged or was an accomplice in the commission, or an attempt to commit, or flight after committing or attempting to commit, robbery, rape, or deviant sexual intercourse by force or threat of force, arson, burglary, or kidnapping.
6. The murder was committed for the purpose of avoiding or preventing a lawful arrest or effecting an escape from lawful custody.
7. The murder was committed for pecuniary gain.
8. The murder was especially heinous, atrocious, or cruel, manifesting exceptional depravity.

The list of mitigating factors includes:

1. The defendant has no significant history of criminal activity.
2. The murder was committed while the defendant was under the influence of extreme mental or emotional disturbance.
3. The victim was a participant in the defendant's homicidal conduct or consented to the homicidal act.
4. The murder was committed under circumstances that the defendant believed to provide a moral justification or extenuation for his conduct.
5. The defendant was an accomplice in a murder committed by another person and his participation in the homicidal act was relatively minor.
6. The defendant acted under duress or under the domination of another person.
7. At the time of the murder, the capacity of the defendant to appreciate the criminality [wrongfulness] of his conduct or to conform his conduct to the requirements of law was impaired as a result of mental disease or defect or intoxication.
8. The defendant was a young age at the time of the crime.

FIRST-DEGREE MURDER *MENS REA*

"All murder which is perpetrated by...willful, deliberate, and premeditated killing...is murder of the first degree" (California Penal Code 2006, §189). This is the broad, even vague, definition of "first-degree murder" often found in criminal codes.

Let's look at these terms. "Willful" means the intent to kill. "If an intention to kill exists, it is willful," a judge instructed the jury in a Pennsylvania murder trial just after the Civil War (*Commonwealth v. Drum* 1868, 6). The same isn't true of "deliberate" and "premeditated." They're frequently issues in the cases, and the courts define them differently, sometimes radically so.

Most courts say that "premeditated" and "deliberate" mean something more than the intent to kill. In other words, they refine the mental attitude of the MPC's "purposely" and "knowingly" and the common law's "specific intent." Judges understand that the purpose of the refinement is to distinguish between murders so awful that they deserve the harshest punishment the law allows from murders that don't deserve the worst punishment.

But just what the refinement consists of varies greatly, and there's often disagreement, sometimes among judges on the same court, not just on the definitions but whether they apply to the facts of the case they're deciding. Unfortunately, some courts blur the line between intentional killings and the more refined deliberate, premeditated intentional killings. The result is that there's no meaningful difference between first and second-degree murder. This is serious business, not just theoretically but practically, too, because it could mean, literally, the difference between life and death.

Professor Wayne LaFave (2010) teaches us (and many judges too!) that it's "not easy to give a meaningful definition of the words 'premeditate' and 'deliberate'" (809). He tries to help us with this example:

> For premeditation the killer asks himself the question, "Shall I kill him?" The intent to kill aspect of the crime is found in the answer, "Yes I shall." The deliberation part of the crime requires a thought like, "Wait, what about the consequences? Well, I'll do it anyway." (809, n. 4)

And then he adds,

> Perhaps the best that can be said of "deliberation" is that it requires a cool mind that is capable of reflection, and of "premeditation" that it requires that one with the cool mind did in fact reflect, at least for a short period of time, before killing. (809–10)

Blackstone (1769) called "willful, premeditated, deliberate killings" the "grand criterion" of murder because they reflect "the dictate of a wicked, depraved, and malignant heart" (199). Modern court opinions display a far broader spectrum of definitions. At one extreme are those that fit the definitions of the original "grand criterion"—killings planned in advance and then committed in "cold blood" that we've just reviewed.

A good example is *People v. Anderson* (1968):

> We have repeatedly pointed out that the legislative classification of murder into two degrees would be meaningless if "deliberation" and "premeditation" were construed as requiring no more reflection than may be involved in the mere formation of a specific intent to kill. A verdict of murder in the first degree (on a theory of a willful, deliberate, and premeditated killing) is proper only if the slayer killed as a result of careful thought and weighing of considerations; as a deliberate judgment or plan; carried on coolly and steadily. (948)

Proving "Premeditation" and "Deliberation"

States that adopt this specific-intent-plus-real-premeditation-deliberation definition rely on three categories of evidence to prove murders really were premeditated and deliberate:

Category 1. Facts about how and what defendant did prior to the actual killing which show that the defendant was engaged in activity directed toward, and explicable as intended to result in, the killing—what may be characterized as planning activity;

Category 2. Facts about the defendant's prior relationship and/or conduct with the victim from which the jury could reasonably infer a "motive" to kill the victim, which inference of motive, together with facts of type (1) or (3), would in turn support an inference that the killing was the result of "a pre-existing reflection and careful thought and weighing of considerations rather than mere unconsidered or rash impulse hastily";

Category 3. Facts about the nature of the killing from which the jury could infer that the manner of killing was so particular and exacting that the defendant must have intentionally killed according to a preconceived design to take his victim's life in a particular way for a reason which the jury can reasonably infer from facts of type (1) or (2). (949)

The following table highlights cases that demonstrate each of the three categories.

PROVING PREMEDITATED, DELIBERATE INTENT		
CATEGORY 1	**CATEGORY 2**	**CATEGORY 3**
• *U.S. v. Blue Thunder* (1979): brought the murder weapon, a knife, to the murder scene • *People v. Kemp* (1961): entered the house through a bedroom window • *U.S. v. Downs* (1995): arranged to meet the victim at home when no one would be home	• *State v. Crawford* (1996): prior threats to kill the victim • *State v. Thomas* (1999): starving the child to death would conceal a prior killing • *State v. Hamlet* (1984): victim had bragged about knocking out the defendant in a prior fight	• *U.S. v. Treas-Wilson* (1993): precise and fatal injury; 4-inch incision *severing* the esophagus, trachea, and large veins of the neck and extended into the fifth vertebra • *People v. Steele* (2002): stabbed victim eight times in the chest • *State v. Taylor* (2002): eight blows to the head with a heavy object

At the other extreme are courts that define "willful, premeditated, deliberate" killing as the equivalent of the specific intent to kill. A good example is *Macias v. State* (1929):

> There need be no appreciable space of time between the intention to kill and the act of killing. They may be as instantaneous as successive thoughts of the mind. It is only necessary that the act of killing be preceded by a concurrence of will, deliberation, and premeditation on the part of the slayer, and, if such is the case, the killing is murder in the first degree. (715)

There's considerable criticism in court decisions and among commentators that this equivalent of specific intent definition renders the difference between first- and second-degree murder meaningless. That's serious because it means there's no real difference between capital murder that can lead to execution in death penalty states or to life in prison without the chance of parole in non–death penalty states.

In *State v. Snowden* (1957), Ray Snowden picked up Cora Dean in a bar. They danced, drank, fought, and Snowden stabbed Dean to death. He was convicted of first degree, premeditated murder. His appeal is the subject of our next case excerpt.

PROVING "INTENT TO KILL": THE DEADLY WEAPON DOCTRINE

However the statutes define and judges interpret the intent to kill requirement, how do prosecutors prove that the defendant acted with the required intent? Rarely will defendants announce to witnesses, "See this slime bag who slept with the love of my life? Well, it's payback time. Watch me pay him back with the bullets in this gun in my hand." In fact, most will do it secretly, and silently, so there won't be witnesses. So prosecutors have to make their case by the circumstantial evidence they gather to present in court.

deadly weapon doctrine one who intentionally uses a deadly weapon on another human being and thereby kills him is presumed to have formed the intent to kill

The deadly weapon doctrine is one of these circumstances. According to the **deadly weapon doctrine**, "one who intentionally uses a deadly weapon on another human being and thereby kills him presumably intends to kill him" (LaFave 2010, 775). The doctrine was hinted at as early as 1675, in a case reported by Sir Matthew Hale. A was sitting

CASE

*In **State v. Snowden,** Snowden was convicted by a jury of first-degree premeditated murder. The Idaho Supreme Court affirmed.*

Did he premeditate and deliberately murder?

State v. Snowden

313 P.2d 706 (Idaho 1957)

HISTORY

Raymond Alien Snowden, Defendant, pleaded guilty to murder in the first degree. The District Court, 3rd Judicial District, Ada County, entered judgment and the sentence of death, and Snowden appealed. The Supreme Court, held that where it appeared that upon being struck by Cora Lucyle Dean, Snowden deliberately opened up his pocket knife, cut the woman's throat, and then hacked and cut until he killed her, and expended himself, imposition of the death sentence was not an abuse of discretion by the trial court. Affirmed.

MCQUADE, J.

FACTS

The victim, Cora Lucyle Dean, was stabbed to death September 22, 1956, in Garden City, Idaho. Defendant Snowden had been playing pool and drinking in a Boise pool room early in the evening. With a companion, one Carrier, he visited a club near Boise, then went to nearby Garden City. There the two men visited a number of bars, and defendant had several drinks. Their last stop was the HiHo Club.

Witnesses related that while Snowden was in the HiHo Club he met and talked to Cora Lucyle Dean. He said he hadn't been acquainted with Mrs. Dean prior to that time, but he had "seen her in a couple of the joints up town." He danced with Mrs. Dean while at the HiHo Club. Upon departing from the tavern, the two left together.

In statements to police officers that were admitted in evidence, Snowden said after they left the club Mrs. Dean wanted him to find a cab and take her back to Boise, and he refused because he didn't feel he should pay her fare. After some words, he related, "she got mad at me so I got pretty hot and I don't know whether I back handed her there or not. And, we got calmed down and decided to walk across to the gas station and call a cab.

They crossed the street, and began arguing again. Snowden said, "She swung and at the same time she kneed me again. I blew my top." Snowden said he pushed Dean over beside a pickup truck which was standing near a business building. There he pulled his knife—a pocket knife with a two-inch blade—and cut her throat.

The body, which was found the next morning, was viciously and sadistically cut and mutilated. An autopsy surgeon testified the voice box had been cut, and that this would have prevented the victim from making any intelligible outcry. There were other wounds inflicted while she was still alive—one in her neck, one in her abdomen, two in the face, and two on the back of the neck. The second neck wound severed the spinal cord and caused death. There were other wounds all over her body, and her clothing had been cut away. The nipple of the right breast was missing. (Snowden ate it.)

There was no evidence of a sexual attack on the victim; however, some of the lacerations were around the breasts and vagina of the deceased. A blood test showed Mrs. Dean was intoxicated at the time of her death.

Snowden took Dean's wallet. He hailed a passing motorist and rode back to Boise with him. There he went to a bowling alley and changed clothes. He dropped his knife into a sewer, and threw the wallet away. Then he went to his hotel and cleaned up again. He put the clothes he had worn that evening into a trash barrel.

After hearing the testimony of police officers and other witnesses, the trial court determined the killing was murder in the first degree and there were no circumstances in mitigation of the offense or of the punishment to be inflicted. Snowden was sentenced to death.

OPINION

By statute, murder is defined as the unlawful killing of a human being with malice aforethought. I.C. § 18-4001. In the present case Snowden killed a human being, and his actions indicate malice aforethought. *There was no considerable provocation shown, and the circumstances attending the killing show an abandoned and malignant heart* [emphasis added]. The rule is malice is implied for any deliberate and cruel act against another, however sudden, which shows an abandoned and malignant heart, and the facts show there was malice in the acts of the defendant at the time of the killing.

Snowden's principal argument pertaining to malice aforethought is that he did not have sufficient time to develop a desire to take the life of the deceased, but rather his action was instantaneous and a normal reaction to the physical injury which she had dealt him. Inasmuch as Snowden took the life of Cora Lucyle Dean, and did so with malice aforethought, it necessarily must follow that he is guilty of murder.

Degrees of murder are defined by statute as follows:

> All murder which is perpetrated by means of poison, or lying in wait, torture, or by any other kind of willful, deliberate and premeditated killing, or which is committed in the perpetration of, or attempt to perpetrate arson, rape, robbery, burglary, kidnapping or mayhem, is murder of the first degree. All other kinds of murder are of the second degree. I.C. § 18-4003.

[The trial court] found...that Snowden's acts in taking the life of Cora Dean were willful, deliberate, and premeditated. I.C. § 18-4003 requires first degree homicide to be perpetrated by any kind of willful, deliberate, and premeditated killing....The test to determine if the killing was willful, deliberate, and premeditated has been set out in *State v. Shuff*:

> The unlawful killing must be accompanied with a deliberate and clear intent to take life, in order to constitute murder of the first degree. The intent to kill must be the result of deliberate premeditation. It must be formed upon the pre-existing reflection, and not upon a sudden heat of passion sufficient to preclude the idea of deliberation.

The court further stated in this case while approving an instruction:

> ...Any unlawful killing of a human being, with malice aforethought, is murder; but if nothing further characterizes the offense it is murder of the second degree. To constitute the higher offense there must be superadded, to the general definition above given, willfulness, deliberation, and premeditation. By willfulness is meant that it was of purpose, with the intent that, by the given act, the life of the party should be taken. It must be deliberate and premeditated.

By this it is not meant that the killing must have been conceived or intended for any particular length of time. It is sufficient if it was done with reflection and conceived beforehand. And in this view, as I have said before, the deliberate purpose to kill and the killing may follow each other as rapidly as successive impulses or thoughts of the mind.

In the present case, the trial court had no other alternative than to find the defendant guilty of willful, deliberate, and premeditated killing with malice aforethought in view of the defendant's acts in deliberately opening up a pocket knife, next cutting the victim's throat, and then hacking and cutting until he had killed Cora Lucyle Dean and expended himself. The full purpose and design of defendant's conduct was to take the life of the deceased.

[Snowden also contended that the trial court erred in its]...imposition of the penalty of death. Punishment for murder is set out in I.C. § 18-4004:

> Every person guilty of murder in the first degree shall suffer death or be punished by imprisonment in the state prison for life, and the jury may decide which punishment shall be inflicted.

It was stated in *State v. Powell*, 227 P.2d 582, 585:

> Upon a plea of guilty, the trial judge is clothed by the statute with the power and duty of fixing the punishment. It is within his sound discretion to determine whether the punishment shall be life imprisonment or death. Unless such discretion is abused, it will not be disturbed by this court.

(continues)

(continued)

The trial court could have imposed life imprisonment, or, as in the instant case, sentenced the defendant to death. It is abuse of discretion we are dealing with, and in particular the alleged abuse of discretion in prescribing the punishment for murder in the first degree as committed by the defendant. To choose between the punishments of life imprisonment and death there must be some distinction between one homicide and another. This case exemplifies an abandoned and malignant heart and sadistic mind, bent upon taking human life. It is our considered conclusion, from all the facts and circumstances, the imposition of the death sentence was not an abuse of discretion by the trial court.

The judgment is affirmed.

QUESTIONS

1. How does the court define the terms "willful," "deliberate," and "premeditated"?
2. Sort and arrange the facts of the case according to the definitions of the three terms in (1).
3. In your opinion, did Ray Snowden commit first-degree murder?
4. Assuming Snowden is guilty of first-degree murder, should he be sentenced to death? Consider the lists of aggravating and mitigating circumstances in the "The Death Penalty" section (pp. 334–35). Which items on the list might apply to him? Explain your answer, based on the facts in the case.

and drinking in an alehouse. B, a woman, called him a "son of a whore." He picked up a broomstick and threw it at her; it hit her and she died. Was the killing murder or manslaughter? The judges rejected the argument that her words were adequate provocation to reduce murder to manslaughter (see "Adequate Provocation," p. 356).

But the judges had a problem with malice aforethought because of the broomstick. If it was a "striking with such an instrument as necessarily would have caused death, as stabbing with a sword, or pistoling," it would definitely not be manslaughter; they could imply malice from the yet unformed deadly weapon doctrine. But whether "this striking, that was so improbable to cause death," could be the basis for malice aforethought, they couldn't agree. So they recommended that the king pardon him, which he did (Oberer 1962, 1572, n. 38).

The doctrine grew out of widely accepted proposition in both civil and criminal cases that individuals are presumed to intend the natural and probable consequences of their acts. Here's an example of the deadly weapon presumption: Suppose that, if without a word, and with no one in sight, Hannah loads her Ruger .357 revolver, carefully aims it at Zack, and pulls the trigger to get him for giving her a bad grade, and the bullet hits him in the head and kills him. It's logical to conclude that Hannah intended to kill Zack. Hence, the deadly weapon presumption.

Be careful not to conclude that the presumption is mandatory. In fact, in homicide, it's more a permissible inference than a mandatory presumption. In Professor LaFave's (2010) words, "The conclusion *may* be drawn, rather than *must* be drawn, in the absence of counter proof" that because the killer intentionally used a deadly weapon, the killer intended to kill the victim (775) (emphasis added). In other words, the use of a deadly weapon that kills isn't automatically murder. The shooter still has a chance to convince a jury (or a judge in a trial without a jury) that although she shot intentionally she didn't intend to kill, as where she intended to scare or inflict a minor wound (776).

Let's return to the broomstick in Lord Hale's report of the alehouse killing: What's a deadly weapon? "One which, from the manner used, is calculated or likely to produce death or serious bodily injury" (*Wilson v. State* 1909, 1015).

Not everyone agrees that premeditated, deliberate killings—even if they're truly planned and committed in cold blood—are the worst kind of murders. According to the nineteenth-century English judge and criminal law reformer James F. Stephen (1883):

> As much cruelty, as much indifference to the life of others, a disposition at least as dangerous to society, probably even more dangerous, is shown by sudden as by premeditated murders. The following cases appear to me to set this in a clear light. A man, passing along the road, sees a boy sitting on a bridge over a deep river and, out of mere wanton barbarity, pushes him into it and so drowns him. A man makes advances to a girl who repels him. He deliberately but instantly cuts her throat. A man civilly asked to pay a just debt pretends to get the money, loads a rifle and blows out his creditor's brains. In none of these cases is there premeditation unless the word is used in a sense as unnatural as "aforethought" in "malice aforethought," but each represents even more diabolical cruelty and ferocity than that which is involved in murders premeditated in the natural sense of the word. (94)

Could an especially brutal *actus reus* be one of these other kinds of first-degree murder? Let's look for the answer in first-degree murder *actus reus*.

FIRST-DEGREE MURDER *ACTUS REUS*

As you've already learned, how a murderer kills doesn't matter, at least not most of the time. As Blackstone taught us in 1769: "The killing may be by poisoning, striking, starving, drowning, and a thousand other forms by which human nature can be overcome." But first-degree murder *actus reus* can be critical when it comes to deciding whether to sentence a person convicted of first-degree murder to death, to prison for life without parole in states without the death penalty, or to a lesser penalty. Killing by means of "heinous, atrocious, or cruel" acts, meaning especially brutal murders or torture murders intended to cause lingering death, appears on the list of aggravating factors that qualifies a murderer for the death penalty.

CASE

*In **Duest v. State (1985),** the Florida Supreme Court applied the state's "heinous, atrocious, or cruel" aggravating circumstance provision to approve the death penalty for Lloyd Duest, who was convicted of first-degree murder in a "gay bashing" killing during a robbery.*

Was the murder heinous, atrocious, or cruel?

Duest v. State

462 So.2d 446 (Fla. 1985)

HISTORY

Lloyd Duest (the defendant) was convicted in the Circuit Court, Broward County, Patricia W. Cocalis, J., of first-degree murder, for which the sentence of death was imposed, and the defendant appealed. The Supreme Court, Adkins, J., held that evidence was sufficient to support the conviction; and evidence was sufficient to support the findings on challenged aggravating circumstances.

ADKINS, J. BOYD, CJ., AND OVERTON, JOINED BY ALDERMAN, MCDONALD, HRLICH AND SHAW, JJ., CONCUR.

(continues)

(continued)

FACTS

On February 15, 1982, the defendant was seen by witnesses carrying a knife in the waistband of his pants. Subsequently, he told a witness that he was going to a gay bar to "roll a fag." The defendant was later seen at a predominantly gay bar with John Pope, the victim. The two of them then left the bar in Pope's gold Camaro. Several hours later, Pope's roommate returned home and found the house unlocked, the lights on, the stereo on loud, and blood on the bed. The sheriff was contacted. Upon arrival, the deputy sheriff found Pope on the bathroom floor in a pool of blood with multiple stab wounds. The defendant was found and arrested on April 18, 1982.

OPINION

Defendant contends that there was insufficient evidence of premeditated murder to convict him as charged in the indictment. Premeditation, like other factual circumstances, may be established by circumstantial evidence. Such circumstantial evidence must not only be consistent with the defendant's guilt, but must also be inconsistent with any reasonable hypothesis of innocence.

The record reflects that defendant had stated he gets his money by "rolling gay guys" and that he intended to do the same on the day that the victim was murdered. Defendant was seen with the victim at a gay bar immediately prior to the murder and was seen leaving the bar with the victim in the victim's car. Shortly thereafter, defendant was seen driving the victim's car alone. At that time, witnesses saw blood stains on the sleeve of his jogging suit. The victim's stolen jewelry case was also seen in the car, which was being driven by defendant after the murder. Moreover, on the day of the murder, defendant had in his possession a seven-inch knife. The cause of death in this case was multiple stab wounds. We find that there was sufficient circumstantial evidence to sustain defendant's conviction of premeditated murder.

Defendant objects to the trial court's findings with respect to the aggravating and mitigating circumstances. The trial court found the following aggravating circumstances:

1. the defendant had been previously convicted of armed robbery and assault with intent to commit murder, section 921.141(5)(b);
2. the capital felony was committed while the defendant was engaged in the commission of a robbery, section 921.141(5)(d);
3. the capital felony was committed for pecuniary gain, section 921.141(5)(f);
4. the capital felony was especially heinous, atrocious, or cruel, section 921.141(5)(h);
5. the capital felony was a homicide which was committed in a cold, calculated, and premeditated manner without any pretense of moral or legal justification, section 921.141(5)(i).

The trial court considered circumstances 2 and 3 as one circumstance because of overlapping facts and legal definitions. Therefore, four aggravating circumstances were applicable. As to mitigating circumstances, none were applied to this case.

Defendant only challenges two of the aggravating circumstances. He asserts that the murder was not particularly heinous, atrocious or cruel. We disagree with the defendant. The evidence presented at trial shows that the victim received eleven stab wounds, some of which were inflicted in the bedroom and some inflicted in the bathroom. The medical examiner's testimony revealed that the victim lived some few minutes before dying.

This case is similar to *Morgan v. State*, 415 So.2d 6 (Fla. 1982), where the evidence showed that the death was caused by one or more of ten stab wounds. In that case, this Court approved the finding that the homicide was especially heinous, atrocious, or cruel. Under the totality of the circumstances and applying our previous decisions to the facts of the instant case, we find that trial court properly applied this aggravating circumstance.

Defendant also challenges the finding that the homicide was committed in a cold, calculated, and premeditated manner. In finding that this aggravating circumstance applied, the trial court found:

> Evidence adduced at trial indicated that defendant informed witness Demezio some two days prior to the murder that he brings homosexuals back to their apartments, beats them up, and takes their money or jewelry. Defendant on the day of the murder went to his temporary residence with the victim, went into the closet where Demezio kept a dagger and left the residence with John Pope, Jr., the victim. The dagger was later discovered missing, and John Pope, Jr. was later discovered at his home, dead. His car and jewelry box were missing.

We find that the evidence supports the finding that the homicide was committed in a cold, calculated, and premeditated manner. In the instant case, even if we were to find that one or two of the aggravating circumstances found by the trial judge, was inapplicable, it would still be appropriate to maintain the death penalty.

For the reasons expressed, we affirm the defendant's conviction and the imposition of the death sentence.

It is so ordered.

QUESTIONS

1. How does the court define "heinous, atrocious, or cruel"?
2. List the facts in the case that are relevant to deciding whether this was a "heinous, atrocious, or cruel" murder.
3. Summarize the arguments in favor of and against classifying this as a "heinous, cruel, and atrocious" murder.

YOU *DECIDE*

Was beating him to death with a baseball bat atrocious first-degree murder?

Commonwealth v. Golston, 249, 366 N.E.2d 744 (Mass. 1977)

Opinion

The Ohio Revised Code vehicular homicide statute (Section 2903.06) About 2:00 P.M. on Sunday, August 24, 1975, a white man about 34 years old came out of a store and walked toward his car. Siegfried Golston, a 19-year-old African American man, tiptoed up behind the victim and hit him on the head with a baseball bat. A witness testified to the sound made by Golston's blow to the victim's head: "Just like you hit a wet, you know, like a bat hit a wet baseball; that's how it sounded." Golston then went into a building, changed his clothes, and crossed the street to the store, where he worked. When asked why he had hit the man, Golston replied, "For kicks." The victim later died. Was this "atrocious murder" a form of first-degree murder that qualified Golston for the death penalty?

Decision

According to the Court:

> There was evidence of great and unusual violence in the blow, which caused a four-inch cut on the side of the skull. There was also evidence that after he was struck the victim fell to the street, and that five minutes later he tried to get up, staggered to his feet and fell again to the ground. He was breathing very hard and a neighbor wiped vomit from his nose and mouth. Later, according to the testimony, the defendant said he did it, "For kicks." There is no requirement that the defendant know that his act was extremely atrocious or cruel, and no requirement of deliberate premeditation. A murder may be committed with extreme atrocity or cruelty even though death results from a single blow. Indifference to the victim's pain, as well as actual knowledge of it and taking pleasure in it, is cruelty; and extreme cruelty is only a higher degree of cruelty.

Instructions

Do you agree with the court that this was first-degree murder? When you're defending your answer, consider James F. Stephen's, English Judge and criminal law reformer, comments on p. 341.

Second-Degree Murder

LO5

As you learned earlier in the chapter, the reason for creating first and second-degree murders, beginning with Pennsylvania in 1794, was to separate murders that deserved the death penalty from those that didn't. The goal was to *limit* capital punishment

second-degree murders murders that aren't first-degree murders, including intentional murders that weren't premeditated or deliberate, felony murders, intent to inflict serious bodily injury murders, and depraved heart murders

without *eliminating* it. Second-degree murders included intentional murders that weren't premeditated or deliberate. But not all second-degree murders required intentional killing. These are "implied malice" murders, created by the common law judges, which still exist in common law states and by statute today. They include felony murders, intent to inflict serious bodily injury murders, and depraved heart murders.

Sometimes, second-degree murder is treated as a default murder category, meaning it includes all murders that aren't first-degree murders. Some state statutes make this default definition explicit. Michigan's statute (Michigan Criminal Code 2006, § 750.317) is a good example. After defining first-degree murder, the Michigan second-degree murder section provides:

> All other kinds of murder shall be murder of the second degree, and shall be punished by imprisonment in the state prison for life, or any term of years, in the discretion of the court trying the same.

CASE

In ***People v. Thomas*** **(1978),** *the Michigan Court of Appeals interpreted Michigan's second-degree murder statute to include Daniel Thomas's conduct.*

Did he commit second-degree murder?

People v. Thomas

272 N.W.2d 157 (Mich. App. 1978)

HISTORY

Charged with second-degree murder, M.C.L. § 750.317; M.S.A. § 28.549, Daniel Lindley Thomas (the defendant) was convicted by a jury of involuntary manslaughter, M.C.L. § 750.321; M.S.A. § 28.553. Thereafter, sentenced to a prison term of 5 to 15 years, the defendant appeals as of right. The Court of Appeals affirmed.

HOLBROOK, J.

FACTS

The victim, a 19-year-old male "catatonic schizophrenic," was at the time of his death a resident of Oak Haven, a religious practical training school. When it appeared he was not properly responding to ordinary treatment, Daniel Thomas (the defendant), the work coordinator at Oak Haven, obtained permission from the victim's parents to discipline him if such seemed necessary.

Thereafter Thomas, together with another supervisor at Oak Haven, took decedent to the edge of the campus, whereupon decedent's pants were taken down, following which he was spanked with a rubber hose. Such disciplinary session lasted approximately 15 to 30 minutes. During a portion thereof the decedent's hands were tied behind his back for failure to cooperate.

Following the disciplinary session, Thomas testified that the young man improved for a while but then commenced to backslide. Thomas received permission from the decedent's parents to subject him to further discipline. On September 30, 1976, Thomas again took the decedent to the approximate same location, removed his pants, bound his hands behind him with a rope looped over a tree limb, and proceeded to beat him with a doubled-over rubber hose.

This beating lasted approximately 45 minutes to an hour. While the evidence conflicted, it appears that the victim was struck between 30 to 100 times. The beating resulted in severe bruises ranging from the victim's waist to his feet. The decedent's roommate testified that the decedent had open bleeding sores on his thighs. On the date of death, which was nine days after the beating, the decedent's legs were immobile. At no time did Thomas obtain medical attention for the victim.

Thomas admitted he had exercised poor judgment, after seeing the bruises, in continuing the discipline. He further testified that in the two days following the discipline, the decedent seemed to be suffering from the flu, but by Sunday was up and walking and was in apparent good health until one week following the beating, when the decedent became sick with nausea and an upset stomach. These symptoms continued for two days, when the decedent died.

As a result of the autopsy, one Dr. Clark testified that the bruises were the result of a trauma and that the decedent was in a state of continuous traumatization because he was trying to walk on his injured legs. Dr. Clark testified that the decedent's legs were swollen to possibly twice their normal size. He further testified that the actual cause of death was acute pulmonary edema, resulting from the aspiration of stomach contents. The aspiration caused a laryngeal spasm, causing the decedent to suffocate on his own vomit. Although pulmonary edema was the direct cause of death, Dr. Clark testified that said condition usually had some underlying cause and that, while there were literally hundreds of potential underlying causes, it was his opinion that in the instant case the underlying cause was the trauma to the decedent's legs. In explaining how the trauma ultimately led to the pulmonary edema, Dr. Clark testified that the trauma to the legs produced "crush syndrome" or "blast trauma," also known as "tubular necrosis."

"Crush syndrome" is a condition caused when a part of the body has been compressed for a long period of time and then released. In such cases, there is a tremendous amount of tissue damage to the body part that has been crushed. When the compression is relieved, the tissues begin to return to their normal position, but due to the compression, gaps appear between the layers of tissues, and these areas fill up with blood and other body fluids, causing swelling.

In the present case, Dr. Clark estimated that about 10 to 15 percent of the decedent's entire body fluids were contained in the legs, adding an additional ten pounds in weight to the normal weight of the legs and swelling them to twice their normal size. This extra blood and body fluid decreased the amount of blood available for circulation in the rest of the body and would cause the person to become weak, faint, and pass out if he attempted to sit up or do other activities. The decedent was sitting up when he died. It was Dr. Clark's opinion that the causal connection between the trauma and death was more than medically probable and that it was "medically likely." He further testified he could say with a reasonable degree of medical certainty that the trauma to the legs was the cause of death.

Agatha Thrash, a pathologist called by the defense, offered testimony to refute that of Dr. Clark, although she did admit that pulmonary edema could have been the final cause of death and that Dr. Clark was correct in finding acute tubular necrosis. She concluded that death was probably caused by "encephalomyocarditas," which is an acute swelling of the brain and heart.

OPINION

Appellant (Thomas) claims that the prosecution failed to establish the malice element of second-degree murder. We disagree. Malice or intent to kill may be inferred from the acts of the defendant. The intent to kill may be implied where the actor actually intends to inflict great bodily harm or the natural tendency of his behavior is to cause death or great bodily harm. In the instant case defendant's savage and brutal beating of the decedent is amply sufficient to establish malice. He clearly intended to beat the victim and the natural tendency of defendant's behavior was to cause great bodily harm.

Next Thomas claims that the trial court erred by allowing evidence of the first beating to be admitted. We hold such to have been properly admitted as a like act tending to show defendant's motive, intent, the absence of mistake or accident on defendant's part.

Affirmed.

QUESTIONS

1. List all the facts relevant to proving Daniel Thomas's mental attitude.
2. According to the court, what's the mental element required for second-degree murder?
3. In your opinion, is Thomas guilty of murder? If so, what degree—first or second degree? Explain your answer.
4. If he's not guilty, should he be guilty of some lesser degree of criminal homicide? Give a preliminary answer now; then, when we get to manslaughter, you can give a more informed answer.

Intent to inflict serious bodily injury murders, like the one in *People v. Thomas*, are often called depraved heart murders and treated as a subset of second-degree murders. Let's turn to two varieties of second-degree murder, depraved heart and felony murder.

LO5 Depraved Heart Murder

Depraved heart murders are unintentional but extremely reckless murders. Recall that the reckless mental attitude consists of consciously creating a substantial risk of criminal harm, in this case death. (There are also reckless manslaughters, which are difficult to distinguish from depraved heart murders. You'll encounter some in the "Manslaughter" section.) For now, let's put the difference crudely: reckless manslaughter is killing very recklessly, and reckless murder (depraved heart murder) is killing very, very, very recklessly.

Some states have specific depraved heart second-degree murder statutes. California's provision reads, "Malice is implied, when the circumstances attending the killing show an abandoned and malignant heart" (quoted in *People v. Protopappas* 1988, 922).

LO5 Felony Murder

> If A meaning to steal a deer in the park of B, shooteth at the deer, and by the glance of the arrow killeth a boy that is hidden in a bush, this is murder, for that the act was unlawful, although A had no intent to hurt the boy, nor knew not of him. But, if B the owner of the park has shot at his own deer, and without any ill intent had killed the boy by the glance of his arrow, this had been homicide by misadventure [mistake], and no felony.
>
> —Kadish, Schulhofer, and Steiker (2007, 436, qtd. from Coke 1644)

felony murder rule derives unintentional deaths that occur during the commission of some felonies are murders

From this hypothetical in Sir Edward Coke's *Third Institute*, the great seventeenth-century English judge and commentator on the laws of England, the modern U.S. **felony murder rule derives.** According to the doctrine, unintentional deaths that occur during the commission of another felony are murders. The court in *People v. Stamp* (1969) stated the doctrine in an armed robbery case where the owner of the business being robbed died of a heart attack during the robbery:

> A felon is held strictly liable for all killings committed by him or his accomplices in the course of the felony. As long as the homicide is the direct causal result of the robbery, the felony-murder rule applies whether or not the death was a natural or probable consequence of the robbery. (603)

In other words, felony murder is a "sweeping doctrine holding felons strictly liable for any death resulting from any felony" (Binder 2004, 60), with a long history stretching back more than three hundred years. In this sweeping rule, all the prosecution has to do is prove two elements: (1) the commission of the predicate or underlying felony, such as the robbery in *Stamp*, and (2) a death during the commission of the felony.

Criminal law teachers, scholars, lawyers, and courts have accepted—but hotly criticized—the sweeping rule known as the default felony murder rule. Thanks to Professor Guyora Binder's (2004) painstaking research, we now know that despite Lord Coke's rule that accidental deaths resulting from unlawful acts were murders, "English common law had no felony murder rule at the time of the American Revolution." And, if Lord Coke was stating a general rule of law, it was "emphatically rejected by English courts and commentators" (201).

In the United States, less strict felony murder statutes were common during the nineteenth century. In the "great bulk" of state statutes, and the "great bulk" of court cases, "felony murder liability was predicated on the dangerous felonies of robbery, burglary, rape, arson, or murder." In Professor Binder's report of his analysis of the cases:

> Apart from one case predicated on a bungled suicide and four cases predicated on putatively consensual abortions, none of the known felony murders punished in nineteenth-century America could plausibly be described as accidental. In almost all of these cases, death resulted from the deliberate infliction of violence. In a few cases defendants knowingly imposed a great risk of death on their victims in pursuit of their criminal ends. In short, the felony murder rules put into practice in nineteenth-century America had requirements of culpability built into the requisite felonies. (202)

The same holds true today in most jurisdictions (Binder 2000, 770). The law varies widely, due mainly to efforts to limit the rule in one of the following ways:

1. Limit the crimes the rule applies to
2. Strict interpretation of the cause of death
3. Limit on the time period that commission of the predicate crime includes
4. Underlying crime has to be independent of the death (LaFave 2010, 785)

Let's look at each.

Many states limit the rule to felonies committed, or *attempted*, that are inherently dangerous to human life. Others limit the rules to a short list of the common law felonies, including rape, sodomy, robbery, burglary, arson, mayhem, and larceny. Still others include only felonies *malum in se* (Chapter 1).

Statutes take two approaches to the "inherently dangerous to human life" limit. Under one approach, followed by a minority of the states, the question is whether the facts and circumstances of the particular case create a foreseeable danger to human life. For example, although false imprisonment (detention without victim's consent) isn't inherently dangerous, death was considered foreseeable in *State v. Harrison* (1977).

Frank Harrison and his friend Emmett Cunejo were driving in their car with guns and ammunition to go prairie dog hunting. They stopped to pick up Susan Brown walking along the road. They picked her up and kept her in the car against her will. Cunejo fired the gun, pulled the trigger thinking the gun was unloaded. It was loaded, and the bullets hit Brown in the head, killing her instantly. He was charged and convicted of felony murder, the predicate felony being false imprisonment. In upholding the conviction, the court wrote that to qualify for felony murder the false imprisonment "must be inherently dangerous or committed under circumstances that are inherently dangerous." It was up to the jury to decide whether those circumstances were inherently dangerous (1324).

The other approach limits the rule to inherently dangerous predicate crimes. Under this approach the elements of the crime in the abstract determine whether the rule applies. So when a chiropractor convinced an eight-year-old girl's Christian Science parents that he could cure her eye cancer without surgery and she died, he was acquitted because the underlying felony—grand theft—wasn't inherently dangerous.

The nearby Criminal Law in Focus box cites cases that have been held inherently dangerous to life and those held not to be inherently dangerous to life.

Inherently Dangerous to Life in the Abstract Felonies

Felonies that have been held inherently dangerous to life include:

- Shooting at an inhabited dwelling (*People v. Hansen*, 885 P.2d 1022 [1994])
- Poisoning with intent to injure (*People v. Mattison*, 481 P.2d 193 [1971])
- Arson of a motor vehicle (*People v. Nichols*, 474 P.2d 6733 [1970])
- Grossly negligent discharge of a firearm (*People v. Clem*, 78 Cal.App.4th 346 [2000])
- Manufacturing methamphetamine (*People v. James*, 62 Cal.App.4th 244 [1998])
- Kidnapping (*People v. Greenberger*, 58 Cal.App.4th 298, 377, 68 Cal.Rptr.2d 61 [1997]); (*People v. Pearch*, 229 Cal. App.3d 1282, 1299, 280 Cal.Rptr. 584 [1991])
- Reckless or malicious possession of a destructive device (*People v. Morse*, 2 Cal.App.4th 620 [1992])

Felonies that have been held not inherently dangerous to life in the abstract include:

- Practicing medicine without a license under conditions creating a risk of great bodily harm, serious physical or mental illness, or death (*People v. Burroughs*, 678 P.2d 894 [1984])
- False imprisonment by violence, menace, fraud, or deceit (*People v. Henderson*, 560 P.2d 1180 [1977])
- Possession of a concealable firearm by a convicted felon (*People v. Satchell*, 489 P.2d 1361 [1971])
- Possession of a sawed-off shotgun (*People v. Satchell*, 489 P.2d 1361 [1971])
- Escape (*People v. Lopez*, 489 P.2d 1372 [1971])
- Grand theft (*People v. Phillips*, 414 P.2d 353 [1966])
- Conspiracy to possess methedrine (*People v. Williams*, 406 P.2d 647 [1965])
- Extortion (*People v. Smith*, 62 Cal.App.4th 1233 [1998])
- Furnishing phencyclidine (*People v. Taylor*, 6 Cal. App.4th 1084 [1992])
- Child endangerment or abuse (*People v. Lee*, 234 Cal. App.3d 1214 [1991])

How do we justify substituting the *mens rea* of lesser offenses for the *mens rea* of murder? The lesser offense accompanying the felony has its own punishment. How does that lesser offense add to the "criminality of the killing (as by making an otherwise noncriminal [accidental] killing criminal), or to the grade of the criminal killing (as by making murder what otherwise would be manslaughter)"? (Kadish, Schulhofer, and Steiker 2007, 439).

Three reasons say supporters of the felony murder rule:

1. It encourages felons to "exercise maximum care during felonies.
2. It "prompts potential felons to refrain from committing felonies in the first place."
3. "It warns prospective felons that they will not be able to hide behind false claims of accident or mere negligence." (Tomkovicz 1994, 1454)

The problem, says Professor Tomkovicz, is that the rule rests on "unproven and highly questionable assumptions." Why? Because the number of killings during felonies is "relatively low." Adding a "small risk" of punishment for these few killings is "probably not a major influence on" these would-be killers' behavior. And a "good number" of those whom the rule somehow affects "probably" wouldn't have killed anyway (1456).

Tomkovicz concedes that "it would be difficult, if not impossible to prove" that the rule doesn't save considerable numbers of lives every year:

> Nonetheless, nonetheless, in a world in which the evidence is uncertain (or nonexistent) and in which it seems unlikely that felons actually hear the rule's deterrent message in the ways that courts presume that they do, common sense would suggest putting the burden of proof upon those who contend that deterrent gains are sufficient to outweigh the infringement of our fundamental philosophy of fault and punishment. (1456–57)

Professor George Fletcher (1981) criticizes the "unrefined ways of thinking about criminal responsibility" that underlie the rule: "That someone who engages in a felony lowers the threshold of moral responsibility for the resulting death. If there is a principle behind this way of thinking, it is that a wrongdoer must run the risk that things will turn out worse than she expects" (426). This thinking "violates a basic principle of just punishment. Punishment must be proportional to wrongdoing."

> When the felony-murder rule converts an accidental death into first-degree murder, then punishment is rendered disproportionate to the wrong for which the offender is personally responsible. The principle that the wrongdoer must run the risk explicitly obscures the question of actual responsibility for the harmful result. (427–28)

The attacks on the justice of the rule and the lack of empirical research demonstrating that the rule deters dangerous felons and reduces the number of deaths during the commission of felonies probably explain why four states—Ohio, Hawaii, Michigan, and Kentucky—have abolished felony murder—and why most others have restricted felony murder to deaths that were foreseeable during the commission of the underlying felony.

Corporation Murder

LO6

Can corporations commit murder? Yes, according to a few prosecutors who've prosecuted corporations for murder (Cullen, Maakestad, and Cavender 1987). Probably the most publicized corporate murder case involved the deaths of three young women who were killed on an Indiana highway in 1978 when their Ford Pinto exploded after being struck from behind by another vehicle.

The explosion followed several other similar incidents involving Pintos that led to grisly deaths. Published evidence revealed that Ford might have known that the Pinto gas tanks weren't safe but took the risk that they wouldn't explode and injure or kill anyone. Following the three young women's deaths, the state of Indiana indicted Ford Motor Company for reckless homicide, charging that Ford had recklessly authorized, approved, designed, and manufactured the Pinto and allowed the car to remain in use with defectively designed fuel tanks. These tanks, the indictment charged, killed the three young women in Indiana. For a number of reasons not related directly to whether corporations can commit murder, the case was later dismissed.

In another case that drew wide public attention during the 1980s, Autumn Hills Convalescent Centers, a corporation that operated nursing homes, went on trial for charges that it had murdered an eighty-seven-year-old woman by neglect. David Marks, a Texas assistant attorney general, said, "From the first day until her last breath, she was unattended to and allowed to lie day and night in her own urine and waste."

The case attracted attention because of allegations that as many as sixty elderly people had died from substandard care at the Autumn Hills nursing home near

Galveston, Texas. The indictment charged that the company had failed to provide nutrients, fluids, and incontinent care for the woman, Mrs. Breed, and neglected to turn and reposition her regularly to combat bedsores. One prosecution witness testified that Mrs. Breed's bed was wet constantly and the staff seldom cleaned her. The corporation defended against the charges, claiming that Mrs. Breed had died from colon cancer, not improper care (Reinhold 1985, 17).

Most state criminal codes apply to corporate criminal homicide in the same way that they apply to other crimes committed for the corporation's benefit. Specifically, both corporations and high corporate officers acting within the scope of their authority and for the benefit of a corporation can commit murder. In practice, however, prosecutors rarely charge corporations or their officers with criminal homicide, and convictions rarely follow.

The reluctance to prosecute corporations for murder, or for any homicide requiring the intent to kill or inflict serious bodily injury, is due largely to the hesitation to view corporations as persons. Although, theoretically, the law clearly makes that possible, in practice, prosecutors and courts have drawn the line at involuntary manslaughter, a crime whose *mens rea* is negligence and occasionally recklessness.

As for corporate executives, the reluctance to prosecute stems from vicarious liability and the questions it raises about culpability (see Chapter 4). It has been difficult to attribute deaths linked with corporate benefit to corporate officers who were in charge generally but didn't order or authorize a killing, didn't know about it, or even didn't want it to happen.

Only in outrageous cases that receive widespread public attention, such as the Pinto and nursing home cases, do prosecutors risk acquittal by trying corporations and their officers for criminal homicide. In these cases, prosecutors aren't hoping to win the case in traditional terms, meaning to secure convictions. Prosecutors consider just getting these cases into court to be a "win." Of course, you can't send a corporation to jail, but you can punish its officers as representatives of the corporation. Don't confuse this with punishing corporate officers for official criminal behavior. Here, they go to jail for their individual criminal conduct—and for the corporation's.

CASE

In ***People v. O'Neil*** **(1990),** *a jury convicted corporate and individual officers of murder, but the appellate court reversed their convictions.*

Did they "murder" their employee?

People v. O'Neil

550 N.E.2d 1090 (Ill. App. 1990)

HISTORY

Following a joint bench trial [trial by a judge without a jury], Steven O'Neil, Charles Kirschbaum, and Daniel Rodriguez, agents of Film Recovery Systems, Inc. (Film Recovery), were convicted of the murder of Stefan Golab, a Film Recovery employee, from cyanide poisoning stemming from conditions in Film Recovery's plant in Elk Grove Village, Illinois. Corporate defendants Film Recovery and its sister corporation Metallic Marketing Systems, Inc. (Metallic

Marketing), were convicted of involuntary manslaughter in the same death.

O'Neil, Kirschbaum, and Rodriguez each received sentences of 25 years' imprisonment for murder. O'Neil and Kirschbaum were also each fined $10,000 with respect to the murder convictions. Corporate defendants Film Recovery and Metallic Marketing were each fined $10,000 with respect to the convictions for involuntary manslaughter.

The defendants appealed, and the Appellate Court reversed the convictions.

LORENZ, J.

FACTS

In 1982, Film Recovery occupied premises at 1855 and 1875 Greenleaf Avenue in Elk Grove Village. Film Recovery was there engaged in the business of extracting, for resale, silver from used X-ray and photographic film. Metallic Marketing operated out of the same premises on Greenleaf Avenue and owned 50 percent of the stock of Film Recovery. The recovery process was performed at Film Recovery's plant located at the 1855 address and involved "chipping" the film product and soaking the granulated pieces in large open bubbling vats containing a solution of water and sodium cyanide. The cyanide solution caused silver contained in the film to be released. A continuous flow system pumped the silver-laden solution into polyurethane tanks, which contained electrically charged stainless steel plates to which the separated silver adhered. The plates were removed from the tanks to another room where the accumulated silver was scraped off. The remaining solution was pumped out of the tanks and the granulated film, devoid of silver, shoveled out.

On the morning of February 10, 1983, shortly after he disconnected a pump on one of the tanks and began to stir the contents of the tank with a rake, Stefan Golab became dizzy and faint. He left the production area to go rest in the lunchroom area of the plant. Plant workers present on that day testified that Golab's body had trembled and he had foamed at the mouth. Golab eventually lost consciousness and was taken outside of the plant. Paramedics summoned to the plant were unable to revive him. Golab was pronounced dead upon arrival at Alexian Brothers Hospital.

The Cook County medical examiner performed an autopsy on Golab the following day. Although the medical examiner initially indicated that Golab could have died from cardiac arrest, he reserved final determination of death pending examination of results of toxicological laboratory tests on Golab's blood and other body specimens. After receiving the toxicological report, the medical examiner determined that Golab died from acute cyanide poisoning through the inhalation of cyanide fumes in the plant air.

The defendants were subsequently indicted by a Cook County grand jury. The grand jury charged defendants O'Neil, Kirschbaum, Rodriguez, Pett, and Mackay with murder, stating that, as individuals and as officers and high managerial agents of Film Recovery, they had, on February 10, 1983, knowingly created a strong probability of Golab's death.

The indictment stated the individual defendants failed to disclose to Golab that he was working with substances containing cyanide and failed to advise him about, train him to anticipate, and provide adequate equipment to protect him from, attendant dangers involved.

The grand jury charged Film Recovery and Metallic Marketing with involuntary manslaughter stating that, through the reckless acts of their officers, directors, agents, and others, all acting within the scope of their employment, the corporate entities had, on February 10, 1983, unintentionally killed Golab. Finally, the grand jury charged both individual and corporate defendants with reckless conduct as to 20 other Film Recovery employees based on the same conduct alleged in the murder indictment, but expanding the time of that conduct to "on or about March 1982 through March 1983."

Proceedings commenced in the circuit court in January 1985 and continued through the conclusion of trial in June of that year. In the course of the 24-day trial, evidence from 59 witnesses was presented, either directly or through stipulation of the parties. That testimony is contained in over 2,300 pages of trial transcript. The parties also presented numerous exhibits including photographs, corporate documents, and correspondence, as well as physical evidence.

On June 14, 1985, the trial judge pronounced his judgment of the defendants' guilt. The trial judge found that "the mind and mental state of a

(continues)

(continued)

corporation is the mind and mental state of the directors, officers and high managerial personnel because they act on behalf of the corporation for both the benefit of the corporation and for themselves." Further, "If the corporation's officers, directors and high managerial personnel act within the scope of their corporate responsibilities and employment for their benefit and for the benefit of the profits of the corporation, the corporation must be held liable for what occurred in the work place." The defendants filed timely notices of appeal, the matters were consolidated for review, and arguments were had before this court in July 1987. ...

OPINION

The Criminal Code of 1961 defines murder as follows:

> A person who kills an individual without lawful justification commits murder if, in performing the acts which cause the death: He knows that such acts create a strong probability of death or great bodily harm to that individual. (Ill.Rev.Stat.1981, ch. 38, par.9-1(a)(2).)

Involuntary manslaughter is defined as:

> A person who unintentionally kills an individual without lawful justification commits involuntary manslaughter if his acts whether lawful or unlawful which cause the death are such as are likely to cause death or great bodily harm to some individual, and he performs them recklessly. (Ill.Rev.Stat.1981, ch. 38, par. 9-3(a).)

Reckless conduct is defined as:

> A person who causes bodily harm to or endangers the bodily safety of an individual by any means, commits reckless conduct if he performs recklessly the acts which cause the harm or endanger safety, whether they otherwise are lawful or unlawful. (Ill.Rev.Stat.1981, ch. 38, par. 12-5(a).)

In Illinois, a corporation is criminally responsible for offenses "authorized, requested, commanded, or performed by the board of directors or by a high managerial agent acting within the scope of his employment." A high managerial agent is defined as "an officer of the corporation, or any other agent who has a position of comparable authority for the formulation of corporate policy or the supervision of subordinate employees in a managerial capacity" (Ill. Rev.Stat. 1981, ch. 38, par. 5-4(c)(2)). Thus, a corporation is criminally responsible whenever any of its high managerial agents possess the requisite mental state and is responsible for a criminal offense while acting within the scope of his employment.

Evidence at trial indicated Golab died after inhaling poisonous cyanide fumes while working in a plant operated by Film Recovery and its sister corporation Metallic Marketing where such fumes resulted from a process employed to remove silver from used X-ray and photographic film. The record contains substantial evidence regarding the nature of working conditions inside the plant. Testimony established that air inside the plant was foul smelling and made breathing difficult and painful. Plant workers experienced dizziness, nausea, headaches, and bouts of vomiting.

There is evidence that plant workers were not informed they were working with cyanide. Nor were they informed of the presence of, or danger of breathing, cyanide gas. Ventilation in the plant was poor. Plant workers were given neither safety instruction nor adequate protective clothing.

Finally, testimony established that defendants O'Neil, Kirschbaum, and Rodriguez were responsible for operating the plant under those conditions. For purposes of our disposition, we find further elaboration on the evidence unnecessary.

Moreover, although we have determined evidence in the record is not so insufficient as to bar retrial, our determination of the sufficiency of the evidence should not be in any way interpreted as a finding as to defendants' guilt that would be binding on the court on retrial.

Reversed and remanded.

QUESTIONS

1. List all the evidence for and against the corporations' and the individuals' liability for murder and involuntary manslaughter.
2. Why did the court reverse and remand the case?
3. On remand, would you find the defendants guilty of murder? Explain your answer.
4. Do you agree that it's inconsistent to find that the corporation had one state of mind and the individuals another?

5. Consider the following remarks made after the convictions in the original trial:

   a. Following the conviction in the original trial, then attorney Richard M. Daley said the verdicts meant that employers who knowingly expose their workers to dangerous conditions leading to injury or even death can be held criminally responsible for the results of their actions.
   b. Ralph Nader, consumer advocate lawyer, said, "The public is pretty upset with dangerously defective products, bribery, toxic waste, and job hazards. The polls all show it. The verdict today will encourage other prosecutors and judges to take more seriously the need to have the criminal law catch up with corporate crime."
   c. Professor John Coffee, Columbia Law School, said, "When you threaten the principal adequately, he will monitor the behavior of his agent."
   d. A California deputy district attorney put it more bluntly: "A person facing a jail sentence is the best deterrent against wrongdoing."
   e. Joseph E. Hadley Jr., a corporate lawyer who specializes in health and safety issues, said the decision would not send shockwaves through the corporate community: "I don't think corporate America should be viewed as in the ballpark with these folks. This was a highly unusual situation, but now people see that where the egregious situation occurs, there could be a criminal remedy."
   f. Robert Stephenson, a lawyer defending another corporation, said, "I don't believe these statutes [murder and aggravated battery] were ever meant to be used in this way."
   g. Utah's governor, Scott M. Matheson, refused to extradite Michael T. McKay, a former Film Recovery vice president then living in Utah, because he was an "exemplary citizen who should not be subjected to the sensational charges in Illinois." (Greenhouse 1985, 1)

   Which of the statements best describes what you think is proper policy regarding prosecutions of corporate executives for murder? Defend your answer.

MANSLAUGHTER

LO7

> Manslaughter arises from the sudden heat of the passions, murder from the Wickedness of the heart.
>
> —Blackstone (1769, 190)

manslaughter an ancient common law crime created by judges, not by legislators, consisting of two crimes: voluntarily or involuntarily killing another person

Manslaughter, like murder, is an ancient common law crime created by judges, not by legislators. Manslaughter was originally one crime. Later, it became two crimes—voluntary manslaughter (intentional killing) and involuntary manslaughter (unintentional killing). Eventually, involuntary manslaughter developed, and is still developing, into various and often inconsistent and confusing types. We'll get into this later in the chapter (LaFave 2010, 837).

But let's start with the eighteenth-century division. According to eighteenth-century commentator Blackstone (1769):

> Manslaughter is...the unlawful killing of another, which may be either voluntarily upon a sudden heat, or involuntarily...where one had no intent to do another any personal mischief. (191–92)

Blackstone's definition is more than three centuries old, but it goes straight to *mens rea*—the heart of manslaughter, as it is in most murder classifications: "Was it intentional (voluntary) or unintentional (involuntary)?"

YOU DECIDE

Murder or manslaughter?

Commonwealth v. Carl Vatcher, 438 Mass. 584 (2003)

Carl E. Vatcher fatally shot his 11-year-old son, James. A Superior Court jury convicted him of murder in the first degree on a theory of deliberate premeditation. On the morning of the shooting James's mother left for work shortly before 8 A.M., leaving the defendant and James alone together. James had a number of physical and developmental disorders, including hypotonia[1] and attention deficit disorder. He was a third grader who participated in a special needs program, could not read, bathe himself, or tie his shoes, and had some difficulty climbing stairs and walking. At trial, James's teachers described him as a "very easygoing, lovable child" who got along well with other children at school. He "enjoyed being with people and people enjoyed being with him."

Some time after James's mother left for work, an argument erupted between father and son, the details of which we reserve for later discussion. The argument escalated, culminating with the defendant firing one shot from a bolt-action .22 caliber rifle into James's abdomen.[2] James said, "You shot me, it hurts." The child tried to run upstairs, but the defendant caught him. The defendant later told police that he "wanted [his son] to die quick," and so, as James "wheezed," "gasped," and "struggled," the defendant tried to cover his son's nose and mouth with his hand. When that "wasn't working," the defendant took a shoelace from a boot and wrapped it around his son's neck.[3] As James was dying, the defendant "kept telling him how he was going to heaven and that no one was going to kick him or yell at him anymore."[4]

After the shooting, the defendant covered James's body with trash bags and blankets and left the body in the cellar. The defendant left the house around 2 P.M. after unsuccessfully trying to asphyxiate himself.[5] James's mother returned home at about 4 P.M. When she discovered and began to play an audiotape recording in which the defendant admitted to killing James, she telephoned the police.[6]

When officers arrived, James's mother directed them to the audiotape recording, which they played in full. Among other things, the defendant admitted that he "bought a rifle and he shot James," then "strangled him cuz he wasn't dead." He stated that James's body was in the basement. The defendant explained that, "I was gonna do this a long time ago, but I kept putting it off. I couldn't put it off anymore.... All I wanted was a normal kid, an average kid, but no, I didn't get that." He also stated, "The only way I could've done this is if I lost control and I did. I lost control this morning."[7]

An officer found James's body in the cellar, and shortly thereafter an emergency medical technician confirmed that James was dead. After obtaining a search warrant, police collected several pieces of evidence from the Vatcher residence.[8]

---

[1] James's mother testified that "hypotonia" is a condition that causes low muscle tone throughout the body.

[2] The defendant acquired the rifle in May, 1999, in exchange for a semi-automatic rifle he had purchased in March, 1999. The defendant was not known to his family or his neighbors to be interested in guns or hunting or to own a gun.

[3] The evidence at trial was that the defendant was over one foot taller than James and more than double his weight.

[4] In various statements introduced at trial, the defendant stated that he had not wanted a child, that he considered James "an intrusion" into his married life, and that he did not believe he was or could be a good father. Evidence at trial showed that James had been the frequent target of his mother's verbal abuse and his father's physical abuse. Over the years, the defendant had banged James's head on the floor, struck James in the chest, and hit James's head against the bathroom door. The defendant told police that on one occasion he had hit James so hard that he, the defendant, broke his own finger. In a "suicide" note introduced in evidence, the defendant described himself as "the kind of guy who strikes back when struck," and wrote that he could "hit harder" than James could. The medical examiner who conducted the autopsy testified that he observed a number of bruises on James's body and limbs that were of different ages and varieties.

[5] The record indicates that the defendant tried to kill himself on two other occasions prior to his arrest the next day.

[6] In addition to the statement on the audiotape recording, the defendant made several other statements admitted in evidence, including statements in a suicide note written the day of the killing and a statement to police made after his arrest. The defendant filed various motions to suppress these statements, all of which were denied, except that his statement to police was redacted in part.

[7] The quotations are from a transcript of the audiotape recording admitted in evidence.

[8] The evidence consisted of two notes in the defendant's handwriting, a discharged cartridge casing, a spent projectile, and traces of blood. A few days later, the police secured a second warrant and retrieved a gun box and a shoelace or bootlace from the home. In a separate search, officers retrieved from the defendant's automobile a suicide note, a box of live rounds of .22 caliber ammunition, a gun lock, and a rifle which an expert subsequently determined discharged the casing found in the Vatchers' home. All the items of physical evidence were admitted at trial.

The Supreme Judicial Court held that: (1) the evidence did not support defendant's claim of sudden provocation adequate to support an instruction on voluntary manslaughter; (2) a voluntary manslaughter instruction was not warranted; and (3) the evidence did not support reducing defendant's conviction to a second-degree murder conviction.

Instructions

Did Carl Vatcher commit murder or voluntary manslaughter? Defend your answer with points made in the sections, "Kinds and Degrees of Murder;" "First-Degree Murder;" and "Second-Degree Murder." Then, review the Massachusetts Supreme Judicial Court's opinion of the case at http://masscases.com/cases/sjc/438/438mass584.html. Did reading the opinion change your mind? Explain your answer.

Voluntary Manslaughter

LO7

> If upon a sudden quarrel two persons fight, and one of them kills the other, this is [voluntary] manslaughter. And, so it is, if they upon such an occasion go out and fight in a field, for this is one continued act of passion and the law pays that regard to human frailty, as not to put a hasty and a deliberate act upon the same footing with regard to guilt. So also a man be greatly provoked, as by pulling his nose, or other great indignity, and immediately kills the aggressor, though this is not excusable, since there is no absolute necessity for doing so to preserve himself, yet neither is it murder for there is no previous malice.
>
> —Blackstone (1769, 191)

Blackstone's description of voluntary manslaughter in the late 1700s is an excellent way to begin our discussion of today's voluntary manslaughter. **Voluntary manslaughter** is about letting your anger get the best of you in the worst possible way—killing another person. The law of voluntary manslaughter (as in all criminal homicides) requires proof of the *actus reus*, *mens rea*, causation, and death. One additional element has to be proved: the circumstance element of *adequate provocation* (discussed next). (See the Elements of Voluntary Manslaughter illustration.)

voluntary manslaughter suddenly and intentionally killing another person in the heat of anger following adequate provocation; elements include murder *actus reus*, *mens rea*, causation, and death

ELEMENTS OF VOLUNTARY MANSLAUGHTER

***Actus Reus* (Voluntary Act)**		***Mens Rea* (General Intent)**		**Circumstance**		**Criminal Harm**
Voluntary act of killing another person	+	1. Intent to kill ***or*** 2. Intent to inflict serious bodily harm	+	1. Killing in sudden heat of passion ***and*** 2. Adequate provocation ***or*** 3. Honest (but not reasonable) belief that the killing was in self-defense	=	

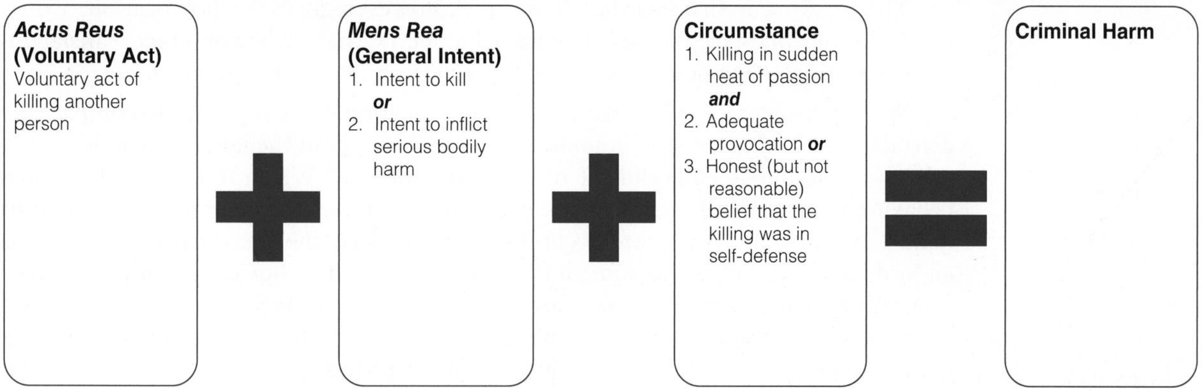

Criminal law aims to bridle passions and build self-control, but it also recognizes the frailty of human nature. The law of voluntary manslaughter takes into account both the seriousness of this felony and the reality of human frailty. So although a sudden intentional killing in anger is a very serious felony, it's not the most serious; that's reserved for murder. Let's be clear that the law of voluntary manslaughter doesn't reward individuals who give in to their rages by letting them walk; it punishes them severely, but it punishes them less than they'd get for murder. Why? Because it recognizes the effect that adequate provocation can have. But what is adequate provocation, the circumstance element of voluntary manslaughter?

LO8 ADEQUATE PROVOCATION

Voluntary manslaughter has one element not present in murder, and one we haven't discussed, namely, the circumstance element of adequate provocation. In voluntary manslaughter, adequate provocation is the trigger that sets off the sudden killing of another person.

Not everyone who is provoked to fly into a rage and suddenly kills has committed voluntary manslaughter instead of murder. The law requires adequate provocation. Adequate provocation has three elements:

adequate provocation the requirement that the provocation for killing in anger has to be something the law recognizes, the defendant himself had to be provoked, and that a reasonable person would have been provoked

1. It has to be a provocation that the law recognizes.
2. The defendant himself has to be provoked (subjective provocation)
3. The provocation has to be one that would provoke a reasonable person under the circumstances in this case (objective provocation).

The Maryland Court of Appeals put it this way in *Dennis v. State* (1995):

> For a provocation to be "adequate," it must be "calculated to inflame the passion of a reasonable person and tend to cause *that person* to act for the moment from passion rather than reason." [emphasis added]

The Maryland Court describes one aspect of "adequacy." There is another,

> which flows from the requirement that the passion be that of a reasonable person; the provocation must be one the law is prepared to recognize as minimally sufficient, in proper circumstances, to overcome the restraint normally expected from reasonable persons. There are many "slings and arrows of outrageous fortune" that people either must tolerate or find an alternative way, other than homicide, to redress. (695)

The thinking is that *reasonable persons*, however great the provocation, would never kill someone except in self-defense (Chapter 5). That's why voluntary manslaughter isn't *justifiable* homicide; it's only a lesser version of intentional murder.

Who is this "reasonable person" whose provocation we're supposed to compare the defendant's to? "Reasonable" sounds odd here. Throughout the law, reasonable person refers to "the public embodiment of rational behavior." When you think of rational behavior, the picture of a provoked killer probably doesn't come immediately to your mind's eye, does it? It's "more accurate...to describe...the [reasonable person]...as an 'ordinary' person...who sometimes, unfortunately, acts out of uncontrolled emotion rather than reason" (Dressler 2009, 538). English and U.S. courts have described the reasonable person variously, in phrases like a person of "average disposition, i.e. not exceptionally belligerent; sober at the time of provocation; and of normal mental capacity" (539).

Four "Adequate" Provocations

1. *Mutual combat (fighting).* Only serious fights qualify as adequate provocation; scuffles don't. Some batteries—but not all offensive touching (see Chapter 10)—are adequate provocation. Being pistol whipped on the head, being struck hard in the face by fists, or enduring "staggering" body blows qualify. Being slapped or shoved doesn't.
2. *Assault and battery* (Chapter 10). Assault without body contact is sometimes adequate provocation. In *Beasley v. State* (1886), a man shot at Beasley and missed him. Beasley was so enraged he shot his attacker in the back as the assailant ran away. The court ruled the shot in the back wasn't justified as self-defense, but the initial incident was provocative enough to reduce murder to manslaughter.

   Insulting gestures by themselves aren't adequate provocation, but if they indicate an intent to attack with deadly force, they are. So "flipping someone the bird" isn't adequate provocation, but waving a gun around in a threatening manner can be.
3. *Trespass* (see Chapter 11). Trespassing is adequate provocation only if the trespassers invade a home and threaten someone with death.
4. *Adultery.* Almost everywhere spouses who catch their spouse in an act of adultery are reasonably provoked. In most states, the law extends to spouses who reasonably believe their spouses are committing adultery, even though they don't see it happening, or it's not true.

"SUDDEN HEAT OF PASSION" WITH NO "COOLING-OFF" PERIOD

LO8

Voluntary manslaughter requires killing in the "sudden heat of passion" with no "cooling-off" period (Perkins and Boyce 1982, 95–96). Whether the actual time between the provocation and the killing—seconds, hours, or even days—qualifies as the "sudden heat of passion" depends upon the facts of the individual case. Courts apply an objective test of cooling-off time; namely, would a reasonable person under the same circumstances have had time to cool off? If defendants have a reasonable time for their murderous rages to subside, the law views their killings as murders even if they take place immediately following the provocations.

objective test of cooling-off time requires that a reasonable person under the same circumstances would have had time to cool off

The court applied the objective test in a famous old case, *State v. Flory* (1929). E. T. Ostrum (age sixty-five to seventy) stayed with his daughter Daisy Flory (age twenty-one) and her husband Charles Flory (age twenty-two), at their farm in Montana, while Flory left to go trapping. (Flory was a farmer in summer and a trapper in winter). When Flory returned just before Christmas, Ostrum went back to his own farm in Campbell County, Wyoming, about fifty miles from Charles and Daisy's farm. After Ostrum left, Daisy told Charles that her father had raped her. Charles left their farm with his gun, which he always carried with him, and walked all day, staying overnight at a Mr. Hudsonpillar's house. The next morning he walked the rest of the way, arriving at his father-in-law's at about 11 A.M. They exchanged angry words, and Flory shot Ostrum, who was unarmed. According to Charles, "I was mad on the way over [from Mr. Hudsonpillar's] but not any madder than anyone else under the circumstances" (460).

A jury convicted Charles of second-degree murder. He appealed. The appeals court ruled that although the incest and rape couldn't justify the killing, they could be used to reduce Charles Flory's crime to voluntary manslaughter because a jury could find that Flory's passion hadn't reasonably cooled. The court said that the heinous combination of incest and rape was more than enough to keep a reasonable person in a murderous rage for at least several days (464).

LO8

CAUSATION

To prove voluntary manslaughter, the prosecution has to prove that the provocation caused the passion and the killing. Suppose Sonny intends to kill his wife Carly because she lied to him. He goes to her bedroom, finds her in bed with his worst enemy, and shoots her to death. Is it voluntary manslaughter or murder? It's murder, because Carly's lie, not her adultery, provoked Sonny to kill her.

Let's look more closely at causation, or triggers, the law considers adequate provocation. Is provocation by words enough? How about provocation by spouses and other intimates? Should nonviolent advances by a gay person or "gay panic" by the killer be viewed as adequate provocation? We'll examine each of these questions next.

"words can never provoke" rule the rule that words are never adequate provocation to reduce murder to manslaughter

PROVOCATION BY WORDS It's often said that words are never adequate provocation. That was true when the **"words can never provoke" rule** was created in the days of the common law. It's still the rule in most states but not everywhere. For example, the Minnesota Criminal Code provides:

> § 609.20 Manslaughter in the First Degree
>
> Whoever does any of the following is guilty of manslaughter in the first degree and may be sentenced to imprisonment for not more than 15 years or to payment of a fine of not more than $30,000, or both: intentionally causes the death of another person in the heat of passion provoked by such words or acts of another as would provoke a person of ordinary self-control under like circumstances, provided that the crying of a child does not constitute provocation.

"last-straw" rule also called the **"long smoldering"** or **"slow burn" rule**, defines adequate provocation as "a smoldering resentment or pent-up rage resulting from earlier insults or humiliating events culminating in a triggering event that, by itself, might be insufficient to provoke the deadly act"

extreme mental or **emotional disturbance manslaughter** a homicide committed under the influence of extreme mental or emotional disturbance for which there is reasonable explanation or excuse. The reasonableness of such explanation or excuse shall be determined from the viewpoint of the person in the actor's situation under the circumstances as he believes them to be

There are more signs besides the Minnesota provision that the bright-line rule "words can never provoke" isn't as bright as it used to be. Some courts have adopted a more flexible approach that "words can sometimes amount to adequate provocation" (LaFave 2010, 823–24). California and Pennsylvania courts have adopted the **"last-straw" rule** (also called the **"long smoldering"** or **"slow burn" rule**) of adequate provocation. It's defined as "a smoldering resentment or pent-up rage resulting from earlier insults or humiliating events culminating in a triggering event that, by itself, might be insufficient to provoke the deadly act" (*Dennis v. State* 1995, 689).

Probably the most significant development is the adoption by several states of the Model Penal Code (MPC) **extreme mental** or **emotional disturbance manslaughter** provision:

> Section 210.3 *Manslaughter*
>
> Criminal homicide constitutes manslaughter when:
>
> (a) it is committed recklessly; or
>
> (b) a homicide which would otherwise be murder is committed under the influence of extreme mental or emotional disturbance for which there is reasonable explanation or excuse. The reasonableness of such explanation or excuse shall be determined from the viewpoint of the person in the actor's situation under the circumstances as he believes them to be. (ALI 1985, Model Penal Code)

Other states (probably most) continue to follow the words-can-never-provoke rule. Maryland is one. In *Dennis v. State* (1995), for example, the Maryland Court of Appeals rejected the last-straw rule. John Patrick Dennis married his high school sweetheart Robin when she became pregnant with their child. According to Dennis, he worked hard to support his family, but they ran into money problems because of Robin's illegal drug use and spending habits.

Robin moved out of their house and in with her boyfriend, Dantz. After learning that Robin and Dantz did drugs in front of their son, Dennis became really agitated. He went to confront them at Dantz's. When he got there, he saw Robin and Dantz through the window; they were hugging and maybe getting "sexual." Dennis claims to have blacked out at that point. Robin called the police, screaming that Dantz was dead (690).

Dennis was convicted of first degree murder. The trial court rejected his claim that he was adequately provoked. He appealed. The Court of Appeals affirmed, rejecting the last-straw rule, and held that "rejected taunts and verbal assaults" aren't "adequate provocation, even when taking on their humiliating and enraging character from antecedent events" (689).

PROVOCATION BY INTIMATES According to the common law **paramour rule**, a husband who caught his wife in the act of adultery had adequate provocation to kill. (Some state statutes went even further than the common law rule; they called paramour killings justifiable homicide.) In the early days, the rule was only available to husbands. Today, it applies to both. Many cases have held that it's voluntary manslaughter for a spouse to kill the adulterous spouse, the paramour, or both, if the killing took place in the first heat of passion following the sight of the adultery.

paramour rule the common law rule that a husband who caught his wife in the act of adultery had adequate provocation to kill; today, it applies to both parties of a marriage

Many voluntary manslaughter cases in states that have rejected the paramour rule and adopted the MPC rule don't involve "sordid affairs and bedside confrontations." According to Professor Victoria Nourse (1997), significant numbers of cases in her empirical study of states who've adopted the MPC extreme mental or emotional disturbance manslaughter provision (quoted earlier)

> involved no sexual infidelity whatsoever, but only the desire of the killer's victim to leave a miserable relationship. Reform has permitted juries to return a manslaughter verdict in cases where the defendant claims passion because the victim left, moved the furniture out, planned a divorce, or sought a protective order.

Even infidelity has been transformed under reform's gaze into something quite different from the sexual betrayal we might expect—it is the infidelity of a fiancé who danced with another, of a girlfriend who decided to date someone else, and of the divorcee found pursuing a new relationship months after the final decree. (1332–33)

PROVOCATION BY NONVIOLENT HOMOSEXUAL ADVANCE (NHA)

> Mike, an honors student at the local junior college, plays quarterback on the football team. Good-looking and well-liked by his classmates, Mike prides himself on being an All-American guy. One day, Mike takes a hard fall on his shoulder during football training. After practice, Mike decides to relax in the school's sauna where he finds his friend and fellow teammate Gary. Gary asks him about his shoulder. Mike tells him that it's pretty sore. Gary, who is openly gay, asks if Mike wants him to massage his shoulder. Mike says that would be great.
>
> Mike, clad only in a short white towel, lies face down on a nearby bench. Gary starts to massage Mike's shoulders and back. Mike tries to muffle a groan of pleasure. The massage feels good, almost too good. Mike starts to feel uneasy. What if another

CASE

*In **Commonwealth v. Schnopps (1983),** the trial court rejected George Schnopps's provocation argument and he was convicted of first degree murder. At a retrial, Schnopps was convicted again of first degree murder. The Massachusetts Supreme Judicial Court affirmed.*

Did he commit first-degree murder?

Commonwealth v. Schnopps

459 N.E.2d 98 (Mass. 1983)

HISTORY

George Schnopps, the defendant, was convicted before the Superior Court, Berkshire County, Massachusetts, of first-degree murder of his estranged wife and of unlawfully carrying a firearm. At a retrial, the defendant, Schnopps, again was convicted of first-degree murder, and he appealed again. The Massachusetts Supreme Judicial Court affirmed.

ABRAMS, J.

FACTS

On October 13, 1979, George Schnopps fatally shot his wife (Marilyn) of 14 years. The victim and Schnopps began having marital problems approximately six months earlier when Schnopps became suspicious that his wife was seeing another man. Schnopps and his wife argued during this period over his suspicion that she had a relationship with a particular man, whom Schnopps regarded as a "bum." On a few occasions Schnopps threatened to harm his wife with scissors, with a knife, with a shotgun, and with a plastic pistol.

A few days prior to the slaying, Schnopps threatened to make his wife suffer as "she had never suffered before." However, there is no evidence that Schnopps physically harmed the victim prior to October 13.

On October 12, 1979, while at work, Schnopps asked a coworker to buy him a gun. He told the coworker he had been receiving threatening telephone calls. After work, Schnopps and the coworker went to Pownal, Vermont, where the coworker purchased a .22-caliber pistol and a box of ammunition for the defendant. Schnopps stated he wanted to protect himself and his son, who had moved back with him.

Schnopps and his coworker had some drinks at a Vermont bar. The coworker instructed Schnopps in the use of the .22-caliber pistol. Schnopps paid his coworker for the gun and the ammunition. While at the bar Schnopps told the coworker that he was "mad enough to kill." The coworker asked Schnopps "if he was going to get in any trouble with the gun." Schnopps replied that "a bullet was too good for her, he would choke her to death." Schnopps testified that his wife had left him three weeks prior to the slaying. He claims that he first became aware of problems in his 14-year marriage at a point about six months before the slaying. According to Schnopps, on that occasion he took his wife to a club to dance, and she spent the evening dancing with a coworker.

On arriving home, Schnopps and his wife argued over her conduct. She told him that she no longer loved him and that she wanted a divorce. Schnopps became very upset. He admitted that he took out his shotgun during the course of this argument, but he denied that he intended to use it.

During the next few months, Schnopps argued frequently with his wife. Schnopps accused her of seeing another man, but she steadfastly denied the accusations. On more than one occasion Schnopps threatened his wife with physical harm. He testified he never intended to hurt his wife but only wanted to scare her so that she would end the relationship with her coworker.

One day in September 1979, Schnopps became aware that the suspected boyfriend used a "signal" in telephoning Schnopps's wife. Schnopps used the signal, and his wife answered the phone with "Hi, Lover." She hung up immediately when she recognized Schnopps's voice. That afternoon she did not return home. Later that evening, she informed Schnopps by telephone that she had moved to her mother's house and that she had the children with her. On that day she moved to her mother's home and took their three children with her.

(The children were two daughters, age thirteen and age four, and a son, age eleven.)

On October 6, the son returned to his father's home. She told Schnopps she would not return to their home. Thereafter she "froze me out" and would not talk to him. During this period, Schnopps spoke with a lawyer about a divorce and was told that he had a good chance of getting custody of the children due to his wife's "desertion and adultery."

On the day of the slaying, Schnopps told a neighbor he was going to call his wife and have her come down to pick up some things. He said he was thinking of letting his wife have the apartment. This was the first time Schnopps indicated he might leave the apartment. He asked the neighbor to keep the youngest child with her if his wife brought her so he could talk with his wife.

Schnopps told his wife that he wanted his children at home and that he wanted the family to remain intact. Schnopps cried during the conversation, and begged his wife to let the children live with him and to keep their family together.

His wife replied, "No, I am going to court, you are going to give me all the furniture, you are going to have to get the Hell out of here, you won't have nothing." Then, pointing to her crotch, she said, "You will never touch this again, because I have got something bigger and better for it."

Schnopps said that these words "cracked" him. He explained that everything went "around" in his head, that he saw "stars." He went "toward the guns in the dining room." He asked his wife, "Why don't you try" (to salvage the marriage). He told her, "I have nothing more to live for," but she replied, "Never, I am never coming back to you."

The victim jumped up to leave and Schnopps shot her. He was seated at that time. He told her she would never love anyone else. After shooting the victim, Schnopps said, "I want to go with you," and he shot himself.

Shortly before 3:00 P.M., Schnopps called a neighbor and said he had shot his wife and also had tried to kill himself. Schnopps told the first person to arrive at his apartment that he shot his wife "because of what she had done to him."

Neighbors notified the police of the slaying. On their arrival, Schnopps asked an officer to check to see if his wife had died. The officer told him that she had, and he replied, "Good." A police officer took Schnopps to a hospital for treatment of his wounds. The officer had known Schnopps for 29 years. Schnopps said to the officer that he would not hurt a fly. The officer advised Schnopps not to say anything until he spoke with a lawyer.

Schnopps then said, "The devil made me do it." The officer repeated his warning at least three times. Schnopps said that he "loved his wife and his children." He added, "Just between you and I, I did it because she was cheating on me." The victim died of three gunshot wounds to the heart and lungs. Ballistic evidence indicated that the gun was fired within two to four feet of the victim. The evidence also indicated that one shot had been fired while the victim was on the floor.

The defense offered evidence from friends and coworkers who noticed a deterioration in Schnopps's physical and emotional health after the victim had left Schnopps. Schnopps wept at work and at home; he did not eat or sleep well; he was distracted and agitated. On two occasions, he was taken home early by supervisors because of emotional upset and agitation. He was drinking.

Schnopps was diagnosed at a local hospital as suffering from a "severe anxiety state." He was given Valium. Schnopps claimed he was receiving threatening telephone calls. Schnopps and the Commonwealth each offered expert testimony on the issue of criminal responsibility.

Schnopps's expert claimed Schnopps was suffering from a "major affective disorder, a major depression," a "psychotic condition," at the time of the slaying. The expert was of the opinion Schnopps was not criminally responsible.

The Commonwealth's expert claimed that Schnopps's depression was a grief reaction, a reaction generally associated with death. The expert was of the opinion Schnopps was grieving over the breakup of his marriage, but that he was criminally responsible.

The judge instructed the jurors on every possible verdict available on the evidence. The jurors were told they could return a verdict of murder in the first degree on the ground of deliberately premeditated malice aforethought; murder in the second degree; manslaughter; not guilty by reason of insanity; or not guilty.

OPINION

On appeal, Schnopps does not now quarrel with that range of possible verdicts nor with the instruction which the trial court gave to the jury. Nor does Schnopps now dispute that there may be some view of some of the evidence which might support the verdict returned in this matter.

(continues)

(continued)

Rather, Schnopps claims that his case is "not of the nature that judges and juries, in weighing evidence, ordinarily equate with murder in the first degree." Schnopps therefore concludes that this is an appropriate case in which to exercise our power under G.L. c. 278, § 33E. We do not agree.

Pursuant to G.L. c. 278, § 33E, we consider whether the verdict of murder in the first degree was against the weight of the evidence, considered in a large or nontechnical sense. Our power under § 33E is to be used with restraint.

Moreover, "We do not sit as a second jury to pass anew on the question of Schnopps's guilt." Schnopps argues that the evidence as a whole demonstrates that his wife was the emotional aggressor, and that her conduct shattered him and destroyed him as a husband and a father. Schnopps points to the fact that he was not a hoodlum or gangster, that he had no prior criminal record, and that he had a "good relationship" with his wife prior to the last six months of their marriage. Schnopps concludes these factors should be sufficient to entitle him to a new trial or the entry of a verdict of a lesser degree of guilt.

The Commonwealth argues that the evidence is more than ample to sustain the verdict. The Commonwealth points out that at the time of the killing there was not a good relationship between the parties; that Schnopps had threatened to harm his wife physically on several occasions; and that he had threatened to kill his wife. Schnopps obtained a gun and ammunition the day before the killing.

Schnopps arranged to have his younger child cared for by a neighbor when his wife came to see him. The jury could have found that Schnopps lured his wife to the apartment by suggesting that he might leave and let her live in it with the children. The evidence permits a finding that the killing occurred within a few minutes of the victim's arrival at Schnopps's apartment and before she had time to take off her jacket.

From the facts, the jury could infer that Schnopps had planned to kill his wife on October 13, and that the killing was not the spontaneous result of the quarrel but was the result of a deliberately premeditated plan to murder his wife almost as soon as she arrived.

Ballistic evidence indicated that as the victim was lying on the floor, a third bullet was fired into her. From the number of wounds, the type of weapon used, as well as the effort made to procure the weapon, the jurors could find that Schnopps had "a conscious and fixed purpose to kill continuing for a length of time."

If conflicting inferences are possible, "it is for the jury to determine where the truth lies." There was ample evidence which suggested the jurors' conclusion that Schnopps acted with deliberately premeditated malice aforethought.

On appeal, Schnopps complains that the prosecutor's summation, which stressed that premeditated murder requires "a thought and an act," could have confused the jurors by suggesting that if "at any time earlier Schnopps merely thought about killing that person," that was sufficient to constitute deliberately "premeditated malice aforethought."

We do not read the prosecutor's argument as suggesting that conclusion. The prosecutor focused on the Commonwealth's evidence of deliberately premeditated malice aforethought throughout his argument. There was no error.

In any event, the argument, read as a whole, does not create a "substantial likelihood of a miscarriage of justice." Schnopps's domestic difficulties were fully explored before the jury. The jurors rejected Schnopps's claim that his domestic difficulties were an adequate ground to return a verdict of a lesser degree of guilt. The degree of guilt, of course, is a jury determination. The evidence supports a conclusion that Schnopps, angered by his wife's conduct, shot her with deliberately premeditated malice aforethought.

The jurors were in the best position to determine whether the domestic difficulties were so egregious as to require a verdict of a lesser degree of guilt. We conclude, on review of the record as a whole, that there is no reason for us to order a new trial or direct the entry of a lesser verdict.

Judgment affirmed.

QUESTIONS

1. If you were a juror, could you in good conscience say that Schnopps was adequately provoked? Explain your answer, relying on the facts in the case, the court's opinion, and the text prior to the excerpt.
2. If so, was it the adultery that provoked him or the provocative words his wife used to describe her adulterous relationship?
3. Do you think the prohibition against provocative words makes sense?
4. If you were writing a voluntary manslaughter law, state the elements of the offense as you believe they should be.

> teammate comes in and sees Gary touching his body? What if this teammate tells others that he is gay? What if Gary tries to make a pass at him?
>
> As these thoughts are racing through his mind, Mike feels Gary's hands move down to his legs, then up his thighs, underneath the small white towel. Gary starts to rub Mike's buttocks. Mike jumps up and yells, "You pervert! What the f— do you think you're doing!" Mike starts punching and kicking until Gary falls to the ground. Even though Gary is not fighting back, Mike continues to beat and stomp on him until he stops moving. Gary dies the next day. (Lee 2003, 1–2)

Most men and women—gay and straight—would justifiably get angry if someone touched their genitals without their consent. According to Professor Joshua Dressler (1995), most NHA cases that find their way into the appellate courts demonstrate that "unwanted sexual advance is a basis for justifiable indignation" (754). Professor Dressler offers the following general statements about NHA cases:

1. Indignation in response to a violation of one's sexual privacy or autonomy is justifiable.
2. Anger, one possible manifestation of such indignation, is justifiable or excusable.
3. Any resulting killing is wholly unjustifiable. (So self-defense doesn't apply—you can't kill in response to an unwanted, *nonviolent* sexual advance.)
4. But, if the invasion of privacy is significant, ordinary, fallible human beings might become so upset that their out-of-control reaction deserves mitigated punishment (754).

Although he was referring to cases involving homosexual strangers, the points in Professor Dressler's list should apply to all acquaintance *nonviolent* advances—homosexual and heterosexual. In other words, "there's a partial excuse in many sexual-advance cases." And this "partial excuse" for the "impassioned killing" spawned by an unwanted sexual advance might reduce the killing from murder to manslaughter (754–55).

"GAY PANIC" Mike might take a different road to getting a murder prosecution reduced to voluntary manslaughter—"gay panic." The gay panic claim is based on "the theory that a person with latent homosexual tendencies will have an extreme and uncontrollably violent reaction when confronted with a homosexual proposition" (1542). Mike might succeed if he can prove that (1) he's a latent homosexual and (2) this "condition" (sometimes labeled a psychological disorder) caused him to react violently to homosexual sexual advances (Note 1989). Gay panic is sometimes considered one form of the excuse of diminished capacity (which we discussed in Chapter 6). Here we treat it as an adequate provocation.

gay panic adequate provocation based on "the theory that a person with latent homosexual tendencies will have an extreme and uncontrollably violent reaction when confronted with a homosexual proposition"

In *Commonwealth v. Carr* (1990), our next case excerpt, Stephen Roy Carr argued that his mother's lesbian relationship when he was a boy, along with the sexual abuse against him while he was in prison, was behind his homicidal rage set off when he saw Claudia Brenner and Rebecca Wight having sex.

THE EMOTION–ACT DISTINCTION

LO8

All of us can empathize with Mike's emotions when Gary made his unwanted advances. Who wouldn't feel indignant, violated, outraged? In other words, any reasonable person (I mean here any ordinary person) could feel similarly. But what about Mike's acts in response to Gary's advances? Would a reasonable person stomp Gary to death? Proponents of the emotion–act distinction make the sensible claim that we should separate the reasonableness of lethal action from the emotions that led to the killing

emotion–act distinction separating the emotions that led to a killing from the question of whether the killing itself was reasonable

CASE

*In **Commonwealth v. Carr,** Stephen Roy Carr was convicted of first murder and was sentenced life in prison. He appealed and the Superior Court affirmed.*

Did seeing the lesbian lovemaking cause a "gay panic"?

Commonwealth v. Carr

580 A.2d 1362 (Penn. Supp. 1990)

HISTORY

Stephen Roy Carr (Defendant) was convicted of murder in the first degree before the Court of Common Pleas of Adams County, Criminal Division, and he was sentenced to life imprisonment. He appealed. The Superior Court affirmed.

WIEAND, J.

On May 13, 1988, Claudia Brenner and Rebecca Wight were hiking along the Appalachian Trail in Adams County, when they found an appropriate campsite and stopped for the night. There, they were resting and engaging in lesbian lovemaking when Claudia Brenner was shot in the right arm. After a short pause, additional shots were fired, as a result of which Brenner was struck four additional times in and about her face, neck and head. Rebecca Wight ran for cover behind a tree and was shot in the head and back. Brenner attempted to help Wight, who was unable to walk, but was unable to rouse her. Brenner thereupon went for help, but by the time help arrived, Wight was dead. Suspicion subsequently focused on Stephen Roy Carr. He was arrested and taken into custody on a fugitive warrant from the State of Florida. He was subsequently tried without a jury and found guilty of murder in the first degree.

OPINION

Carr defended at trial on grounds that he had shot Brenner and Wight in the heat of passion caused by the serious provocation of their nude homosexual lovemaking. In support of this defense and to show the existence of passion, Carr offered to show a history of constant rejection by women, including his mother who may have been involved in a lesbian relationship, sexual abuse while in prison in Florida, inability to hold a job, and retreat to the mountains to avoid further rejection. This was relevant, he contended, to show that he was impassioned when provoked by the "show" put on by the women, including their nakedness, their hugging and kissing and their oral sex. The trial court refused to allow evidence of Carr's psychosexual history, finding it irrelevant.

The crime of voluntary manslaughter is defined by the Pennsylvania Crimes Code as follows:

> A person who kills an individual without lawful justification commits voluntary manslaughter if at the time of the killing he is acting under a sudden and intense passion resulting from serious provocation....

The passion which will reduce an unlawful killing to voluntary manslaughter must be caused by legally adequate provocation. The test for determining the existence of legally adequate provocation is an objective test. In making the objective determination as to what constitutes sufficient provocation reliance may be placed upon the cumulative impact of a series of related events. The ultimate test for adequate provocation remains whether a reasonable man, confronted with this series of events, became impassioned to the extent that his mind was "incapable of cool reflection."

If and when sufficient provocation is found, then the focus of inquiry shifts to the defendant's response to that provocation. If sufficient provocation exists, the fact finder must also determine whether the defendant actually acted in the heat of passion when he committed the homicide and thus whether the provocation led directly to the killing or whether there was sufficient "cooling" period so that a reasonable man would have regained his capacity to reflect.

The sight of naked women engaged in lesbian lovemaking is not adequate provocation to reduce an unlawful killing from murder to voluntary manslaughter. It is not an event which is sufficient to cause a reasonable person to become so impassioned as to be incapable of cool reflection. Whatever a person's views about homosexuality, the law does not condone or excuse the killing of homosexuals any more than it condones the killing of heterosexuals. Similarly, it does not recognize homosexual activity between two persons as legal provocation sufficient to reduce an unlawful killing of one or both of the actors by a third person from murder to voluntary manslaughter.

A trial court must make an initial determination whether sufficient evidence has been presented of serious provocation. In the instant case, the judge was both court and jury. Carr was permitted to show the nature of the activities in which his victims were engaged when he came upon them in the woods. In a provocation defense, the actions of the victim establishing provocation are relevant. Those are the victim's actions on the [day] in question because the provocation must lead directly to the killing.

After it had been determined that these activities were inadequate to provoke a heat of passion response, however, Carr's rejection by women and his mother's sexual preference were irrelevant. Carr's history of misfortunes is not events which are in any way related to the events which he claims provoked him on May 13, 1988. An accused cannot, by recalling some past injury or insult, establish a foundation for a manslaughter verdict. The trial court did not err when it excluded evidence of appellant's psychosexual history.

The judgment of sentence is affirmed.

QUESTIONS

1. List all of the relevant facts and circumstances that provoked Stephen Roy Carr to kill Rebecca Wight.
2. Summarize the reason why Carr claims he committed voluntary manslaughter.
3. State the court's definition of provocation.
4. Summarize the court's reasons for rejecting Carr's claim.
5. In your opinion, was Carr guilty of murder or voluntary manslaughter? Back up your answer with details and arguments from the excerpt.

(Lee 2003, 261). Why? Because, according to Professor Cynthia Lee (2003), there's a "big difference between reasonable emotions (fear, anger, outrage) and reasonable action. Even if a particular *emotion* is reasonable under the circumstances, this does not mean that acting on that emotion by using deadly force is also reasonable" (261).

act reasonableness meaning "a finding that a reasonable person in the defendant's shoes would have responded as violently as the defendant did"

Just because the distinction makes sense doesn't mean the law recognizes it. Professor Lee examined model jury instructions to determine whether states required **act reasonableness**, meaning "a finding that a reasonable person in the defendant's shoes would have responded as violently as the defendant did" (262). Only two states followed this approach.

emotional reasonableness a finding that "the defendant's emotional outrage or passion was reasonable"

Most states adopt an **emotional reasonableness** approach, meaning a finding that "the defendant's *emotional* outrage or *passion* was reasonable." A few states require both act and emotional reasonableness (262–63). Professor Lee recommends implementation of the emotion–act distinction in voluntary manslaughter law (268; Criminal Law in Focus box, "Provocation Jury Instruction").

Involuntary Manslaughter

LO9

> The second branch, or involuntary manslaughter...is where a person does an act lawful in itself, but in an unlawful manner and without due caution and circumspection: as when a workman flings down a stone or piece of timber into the street and kills a man....
>
> —Blackstone (1769, 192)

involuntary manslaughter an unintentional killing (*mens rea*) by a voluntary act or omission (*actus reus*)

The central elements in **involuntary manslaughter** are its *actus reus* (killing by a voluntary act or omission) and its *mens rea* (an unintentional killing). Of course, as in

Provocation Jury Instruction

Voluntary manslaughter. An individual who kills in response to legally adequate provocation is guilty of voluntary manslaughter rather than murder. Legally adequate provocation is defined as provocation which would provoke the reasonable person in the defendant's shoes into a state of uncontrolled passion. Before you may return a verdict of voluntary manslaughter, you must be satisfied that the following three requirements are met:

1. *Actual heat of passion*. The defendant was actually provoked into a heat of passion.
2. *Emotional reasonableness*. The defendant's emotions were reasonable. A defendant's emotions may be considered reasonable if the reasonable (i.e., ordinary) person in the defendant's shoes would have been provoked into a heat of passion.
3. *Act reasonableness*. The defendant's acts were also normatively reasonable. A defendant's acts may be considered normatively reasonable if the defendant's response bears a reasonable relationship to the provoking act or incident.

Source: Lee 2003, 268.

all crimes of criminal conduct causing criminal harm, involuntary manslaughter also includes the elements of causation and resulting harm (death here). We won't repeat our discussion of causation from Chapter 4 here. (See the Elements of Involuntary Manslaughter illustration.)

All states have punished involuntary manslaughter from their earliest days, but they didn't define it, and if they did, they did so vaguely. For example, most statutes used terms like "culpable negligence," "criminal negligence," or "gross negligence" but left in doubt the meaning of the terms. Most comprehensive modern criminal codes have adopted at least some of the Model Penal Code (MPC) homicide sections in the nearby Criminal Law in Focus box, "Model Penal Code Homicide Sections" (LaFave 2003, 794–95).

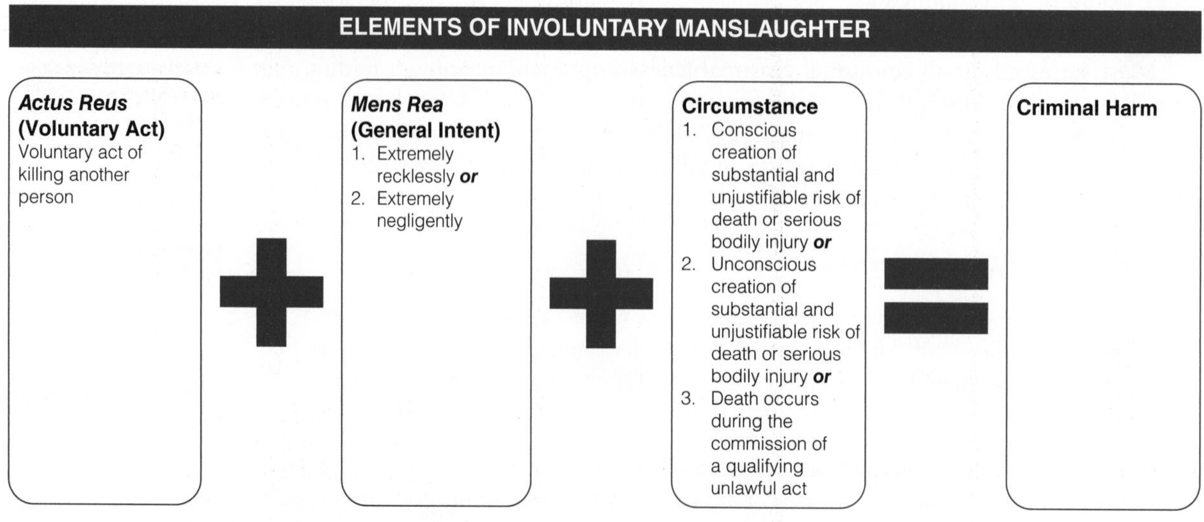

Model Penal Code Homicide Sections

Article 210. § 210.1. Criminal Homicide

1. A person is guilty of criminal homicide if he purposely, knowingly, recklessly or negligently causes the death of another human being.
2. Criminal homicide is murder, manslaughter or negligent homicide.

§ 210.3. Manslaughter

1. Criminal homicide constitutes manslaughter when:
   a. it is committed recklessly; or
   b. a homicide which would otherwise be murder is committed under the influence of extreme mental or emotional disturbance for which there is reasonable explanation or excuse. The reasonableness of such explanation or excuse shall be determined from the viewpoint of a person in the actor's situation under the circumstances as he believes them to be.
2. Manslaughter is a felony of the second degree.

§ 210.4. Negligent Homicide

1. Criminal homicide constitutes negligent homicide when it is committed negligently.
2. Negligent homicide is a felony of the third degree.

Source: Model Penal Code (MPC).

Most state codes have not adopted the MPC general criminal reckless and negligence provisions. Instead, they've created criminal liability for deaths caused by a variety of circumstances, including deaths from failures to furnish medical care for helpless, sick, or injured persons they have a duty to care for; permitting overcrowded conditions; failure to provide adequate fire exits in public entertainment places; delivery of dangerous drugs; and conducting dangerous blasting operations. But two—operating motor vehicles and handling firearms—"lead the list" (LaFave 2010, 840–41).

CRIMINAL NEGLIGENCE MANSLAUGHTER

Involuntary manslaughter goes by the name of criminal negligence manslaughter in some statutes and cases. In practice, **criminal negligence manslaughter** consists of two elements:

criminal negligence manslaughter death caused by a person who is aware that her acts create a substantial and unjustifiable risk of death or serious bodily injury, but acts anyway

1. *Actus reus*. The defendant's acts create a high (substantial and unjustifiable) risk of death or serious bodily injury.
2. *Mens rea*. The defendant is aware that the risk of death or serious bodily injury is high but commits the acts anyway.

Recall that when you're acting recklessly, you *know* you're creating a high risk of harm (see Chapter 4); when you're acting negligently, you *should*, but don't, know you're creating the high risk. There's often confusion in the labels (and in the minds of legislators and judges), but the reality is that most of the time, the mental element is recklessness. So, if you find it difficult to keep the difference clear in your mind, you have company in high places. When there's a doubt about the meaning, criminal negligence probably means criminal recklessness in involuntary manslaughter cases.

In our next case excerpt, *State v. Mays* (2000), 19-year-old Nicholas Mays killed Michael Boumer in a grocery store parking lot, when Mays "messed with" him by "nudging" Boumer with his car.

CASE

*In **State v. Mays,** Nicholas Mays pleaded guilty and was sentenced to five years in prison for aggravated vehicular homicide. He appealed, and the Ohio Court of Appeals affirmed in part, and reversed and remanded in part.*

Did he commit aggravated vehicular homicide?

State v. Mays

743 N.E.2d 447 (Ohio App. 2000)

HISTORY

Upon convictions entered pursuant to guilty pleas, Nicholas Mays, the defendant, was sentenced by the Hamilton County Court of Common Pleas to five years' incarceration for aggravated vehicular homicide. He appealed. The Ohio Court of Appeals affirmed in part, and reversed and remanded in part.

DOAN, J.

FACTS

On August 19, 1999, 19-year-old Mays was operating an automobile in which his cousin was a passenger. At approximately 1:45 A.M., they saw a pedestrian, later identified as Michael Boumer, in a grocery store parking lot. According to Mays, Boumer appeared to be intoxicated. (Investigating officers confirmed that Boumer had consumed some alcohol. However, the record also indicates that Boumer was mentally handicapped.) The two young men decided that they would "mess with" Boumer by appearing to offer him a ride. Mays intended to nudge Boumer with the vehicle and then drive away.

Mays did drive the vehicle in the direction of Boumer, but instead of merely nudging him, he inadvertently ran over him, causing him fatal injuries. Upon seeing that Boumer was injured, Mays drove to another location and called for emergency aid. He then went to a car wash, where he cleaned the vehicle to remove evidence of the fatal collision.

On the day after the incident, Mays took a planned trip to Florida, during which his mother convinced him that he should report his involvement in the crime. Mays did so, returning to Cincinnati and giving a full confession to the police.

OPINION

The Ohio Revised Code vehicular homicide statute (Section 2903.06) reads in part:

> (A) No person, while operating or participating in the operation of a motor vehicle, motorcycle, snowmobile, locomotive, watercraft, or aircraft, shall cause the death of another or the unlawful termination of another's pregnancy in any of the following ways:
>
> . . .
>
> (2) Recklessly;
>
> (3) Negligently;
>
> (1) Whoever violates division (A)(2) of this section is guilty of aggravated vehicular homicide and shall be punished as provided in divisions (B)(1)(b) of this section.
>
> . . .
>
> (b) Except as otherwise provided in this division, aggravated vehicular homicide committed in violation of division (A)(2) of this section is a felony of the third degree. In addition to any other sanctions imposed, the court shall suspend the offender's driver's license, commercial driver's license, temporary instruction permit,

probationary license, or nonresident operating privilege for a definite period of three years to life.

(2) Whoever violates division (A) (3) of this section is guilty of vehicular homicide. Except as otherwise provided in this division, vehicular homicide is a misdemeanor of the first degree.

Mays first argues that the court erred in imposing terms of incarceration greater than the minimum. To impose a prison term more than the minimum for the offender's first prison term, the court must find that the minimum sentence would demean the seriousness of the offense or not adequately protect the public from future crime. Here, the trial court found both to be applicable.

We hold that the trial court's finding with respect to the seriousness of the offenses is supported by the record. Mays conceded that his intention was to "mess with" a person whom he perceived to be impaired in some way, and in doing so, he deprived the thirty-nine-year-old victim of his life. Mays did not immediately seek help for Boumer, but instead thought first of his own interest in evading detection for the crime. His concealment of the crime was compounded when he washed the car and left the jurisdiction. Under these circumstances, the trial court reasonably concluded that the minimum term would demean the seriousness of the offenses. Because the trial court's finding with respect to the seriousness of the offenses was proper, we need not address Mays's argument concerning the adequate protection of the public.

In his second argument, Mays claims that the trial court erred in imposing the maximum sentence for aggravated vehicular homicide. Before imposing the maximum term of incarceration for an offense, the court must find that the offender has committed the worst form of the offense, poses the greatest likelihood of recidivism, or is of a certain class of repeat offenders. In the case at bar, the court found that Mays had committed the worst form of aggravated vehicular homicide. We disagree.

In past cases, this court has grappled with the somewhat vague concept of what constitutes the "worst form" of an offense. And while the concept is difficult to define in concrete terms, we hold that Mays's conduct in the case at bar did not constitute the worst form of aggravated vehicular homicide. Though the evidence certainly indicates that Mays exercised extremely poor judgment in carrying out his wish to "mess with" Boumer, there is no indication that he harbored any malice toward the victim.

Instead, the record indicates that Mays's conduct started as a reckless, poorly conceived prank and ended in tragedy. And while we in no way wish to minimize the loss of a human life or to condone Mays's actions, this is not the type of conduct for which the legislature has reserved the maximum sentence.

Furthermore, although he admittedly thought of his own interests before seeking help for Boumer, Mays did take steps to ensure that emergency personnel were notified promptly. His actions therefore did not reflect an utter lack of concern for Boumer or otherwise demonstrate a perversity of character that would justify the imposition of the maximum sentence.

Further, there is no indication that the victim suffered for a prolonged period of time before he died or suffered to a greater degree than any other victim of a vehicular homicide.

Finally, Mays surrendered to authorities and confessed to the crimes. Under these circumstances, we cannot say that Mays committed the worst form of the offense within the meaning of R.C. 2929.14(C). We therefore hold that the trial court erred in imposing the maximum term for that offense.

Mays next argues that the trial court erred in imposing consecutive sentences. To impose consecutive terms of imprisonment, the court must find that consecutive sentences are necessary to protect the public from future crime and that consecutive sentences are not disproportionate to the offender's conduct and to the danger the offender poses to the public.

The trial court must also find one of the following:

1. that the offenses occurred while the offender was under community control;
2. that the harm caused was great or unusual; or
3. that the offender's criminal history requires consecutive sentences.

Of the latter factors, the court in the instant case found that the harm caused was unusual or great.

We agree with Mays that the trial court's findings with respect to consecutive sentences are not supported by the record. Concerning the protection of the public from future crime, Mays's criminal record included no adult convictions and only one

(continues)

(continued)

juvenile delinquency adjudication. Thus, there is little indication that Mays is likely to recidivate.

Also, the trial court revoked Mays's operator's license, thereby reducing the likelihood that future vehicular offenses would occur.

Further, as to the finding that consecutive terms were not disproportionate to Mays's conduct and to the danger that he posed to the public, we have already noted that Mays's conduct, while reckless and ill-conceived, was not the product of malice.

Given the revocation of Mays's license, his confession, and his demonstrated remorse, the conduct also appears not likely to be repeated. The investigating officers and the author of the presentence-investigation report indicated that Mays was genuinely remorseful.

Finally, the harm caused by the offense, while senseless and tragic, was not greater than the harm caused in every other aggravated-vehicular-homicide case. Under these circumstances, we hold that the trial court erred in imposing consecutive sentences.

Having held that the trial court erred in imposing the maximum sentence for the aggravated vehicular homicide and in otherwise imposing consecutive sentences, we hereby reverse those parts of the trial court's judgment and remand the cause for resentencing in accordance with law.

Judgment affirmed in part, reversed in part and cause remanded.

DISSENT

HILDEBRANDT, PJ.

Mays senselessly took the life of the victim because he wished to "mess with" him. The wantonness of that conduct alone could have justified the trial court in imposing the maximum sentence. However, Mays compounded his misconduct by leaving the scene of the collision, thereby making it clear that he valued his own interest in evading detection above the life of Boumer. The majority concedes as much, yet persists in holding that Mays did not commit the worst form of the offense. His eventual call for emergency aid and his subsequent remorse for his actions did not erase the fact that his conduct was egregious and deserving of the greatest punishment.

For many of the same reasons, I believe that the imposition of consecutive sentences was proper. The utter lack of regard for human life that Mays exhibited by using his automobile to "mess with" a person whom he believed to be impaired provided ample support for the trial court's conclusion that consecutive sentences were necessary to prevent future crimes and to protect the public. Moreover, the fact that death is caused in all aggravated-vehicular-homicide cases should not prevent a finding that the harm caused in the instant case was great or unusual.

Mays's taking of a life in such a wanton manner justified the court in finding that the harm done was great or unusual. . . . In my view, nine years of incarceration is not excessive when weighed against the taking of a human life under these circumstances. I therefore respectfully dissent in part.

QUESTIONS

1. How does the Ohio statute define "vehicular homicide"?
2. Relying on the evidence in the case and referring to the Ohio provision, explain why Nicholas Mays was guilty of aggravated vehicular homicide.
3. How would you define "vehicular homicide"? Defend your definition.
4. Do you agree with the majority opinion's reasons for reversing the sentence? Or do the dissent and the trial court have the better arguments? Back up your answer.

UNLAWFUL ACT MANSLAUGHTER

unlawful act manslaughter or **misdemeanor manslaughter** unintended deaths occurring during the commission of nonhomicide offenses

In 1260, long before the common law judges created a division between murder and manslaughter, the great jurist Bracton wrote that unintended deaths that occur during unlawful acts are criminal homicides. In today's statutes and court opinions, they're called unlawful act manslaughter or misdemeanor manslaughter.

Some time after the judges created the offense of manslaughter, unlawful act manslaughters became a form of involuntary manslaughter. In modern times, statutes have restricted unlawful act manslaughter because the penalty is considered too harsh.

In fact, there's a trend to abolish unlawful act manslaughter, leaving criminal negligence manslaughter as the only kind of involuntary manslaughter.

Unlawful acts taken literally could include everything, including felonies, misdemeanors, and even traffic violations, city ordinances, administrative crimes, and even noncriminal wrongs, such as civil trespass and other torts (see Chapter 1). Misdemeanors are certainly included among these possibly unlawful acts; that's why the unlawful act manslaughter is often called "misdemeanor manslaughter." The most common misdemeanors that come up in the cases are speeding, drunk driving, and battery, mostly hitting someone who dies from the blow (see Chapter 10).

This is what happened in *People v. Datema* (1995). Greg and Pamela Datema were sitting around in their living room with friends talking, smoking pot, and drinking. The conversation turned to their previous romances. Pam and Greg started arguing about the people they'd slept with. Pam claimed she'd had sex with some of her paramours in front of their sons. Greg slapped her in the face—once. Pam slumped back; the other three thought she'd passed out. After 10 minutes, they got worried. When they shook her and she didn't wake up, they called for an ambulance. Pam never regained consciousness.

The medical examiner found that Pam Datema had a blood-alcohol level between 0.03 and 0.05 percent. He stated that death was caused by a tear in an artery in the head that occurred as a result of Greg's slap:

> Most people, when slapped, reflexively stiffen their necks and avoid serious injury. Occasionally, however, when a person is intoxicated, the reflexes do not react quickly enough, and a blow could result in a tearing. Generally, a higher blood-alcohol level is necessary, but the ingested marijuana, which was not able to be tested, was undoubtedly a contributing factor. (274)

As mentioned earlier, there's a trend toward abolishing unlawful act manslaughter; about half of the states have already done so (LaFave 2010, 844). Where it still exists, the states have placed limits on it. Most states limit the underlying offense to *mala in se* offenses. (Recall that *mala in se* offenses are inherently evil—for example, the battery in *People v. Datema* and the "nudge" in *State v. Mays*.)

To count as a *malum prohibitum* crime, death has to be a foreseeable consequence of the unlawful act. Recall from Chapter 1 that a *malum prohibitum* crime is a crime only because a specific statute or ordinance prohibits it. In *Todd v. State* (1992), Todd ran off with the church collection plate. A congregation member jumped in his car and pursued the thief. He suffered a heart attack, hit a tree, and died of cardiac arrest. The court held this wasn't a case of unlawful act manslaughter because death isn't a foreseeable risk in petty theft.

***malum prohibitum* crime** death has to be a foreseeable consequence of the unlawful act; the act is unlawful only because it's prohibited by a specific statute or ordinance

DOCTOR-ASSISTED SUICIDE

LO10

> Whoever no longer wishes to live shall state his reasons to the senate [ancient Greek government], and after having received permission shall abandon life. If your existence is hateful to you, die; if you are overwhelmed by fate, drink the hemlock.
>
> If you are bowed with grief, abandon life. Let the unhappy man recount his misfortune, let the magistrate supply him with the remedy, and his wretchedness will come to an end.
>
> —Libanius, ancient Greek philosopher (qtd. in Messinger 1993, 183)

> It would seem unlawful to kill any living thing. For the Apostle says (Romans 13:2): "They that resist the ordinance of God purchase to themselves damnation." Now Divine providence has ordained that all living things should be preserved, according to Psalm 146:8–9, "Who maketh grass to grow on the mountains... Who giveth to beasts their food." Therefore it seems unlawful to take the life of any living thing.
>
> —St. Thomas Aquinas, *Summa Theologica* (1265–1268)

> The sick they see to with great affection, and let nothing at all pass concerning either physic or good diet whereby they may be restored again to their health. Them that be sick of incurable diseases they comfort with sitting by them, with talking with them, and to be short, with all manner of helps that may be.
>
> But if the disease be not only incurable, but also full of continual pain and anguish; then the priests and the magistrates exhort the man, seeing his is not able to do any duty of life, and by outliving his own death is noisome and irksome to others and grievous to himself, that he will determine with himself no longer to cherish that pestilent and painful disease.
>
> And seeing his life is to him but a torment, that he will not be unwilling to die, but rather take a good hope to him, and either dispatch himself out of that painful life, as out of a prison, or a rack of torment, or else suffer himself willingly to be rid of it by others. And in so doing they tell him he shall do so wisely, seeing by his death he shall lose no commodity, but end his pain. But they cause none such to die against his will, nor they use no less diligence and attendance about him, believing this to be an honorable death.
>
> —Sir Thomas More, *Utopia* (1516)

> Medical jurisprudence is subordinate to medical ethics which expresses the moral order willed by God. Medical jurisprudence cannot, therefore, in any circumstances permit a doctor or patient to carry out euthanasia directly, nor may a doctor ever perform it upon himself or anyone else.
>
> —Pope Pius XII (1956)

euthanasia helping another person to die

These samples from history, philosophy, religion, and law make clear that the subject of helping others die has confronted societies throughout history with "the troubling dilemma of defining the meaning of death and the value of life" (Messinger 1993, 175). In our time, we call helping others die (assisted suicide) **euthanasia.** The *Oxford English Dictionary*'s (2009) eloquent definition: "a gentle and easy death" or "the means of bringing about a gentle and easy death" hides the deep, emotional, and irreconcilable division over helping others die.

In our look at doctor-assisted suicide, we'll discuss the kinds of euthanasia in our society, arguments against and for doctor-assisted suicide, where criminal law stands on the issue, and the public's opinion of doctor-assisted suicide.

Kinds of Euthanasia

Euthanasia exists in several forms. It can be passive (failing to take any extraordinary measures to keep someone alive) or active (deliberate acts to cause death). It can be voluntary, whereby a dying person can make a rational request and be examined to guarantee the validity of the request, or involuntary. Involuntary euthanasia can be beneficent (a family and court decision with good intentions) or malevolent (purposeful disregard of legal process or by co-opting the legal process) (Messinger 1993, 180–81). We concentrate on active voluntary euthanasia through doctor-assisted suicide.

Arguments against Doctor-Assisted Suicide

LO10

There are two primary arguments against doctor-assisted suicide: First, it's intrinsically immoral and wrong; second, unacceptable consequences will follow from it ("the slippery slope" argument) (Messinger 1993, 215). Let's look at each.

THE INTRINSICALLY IMMORAL AND WRONG ARGUMENT

The intrinsically immoral and wrong argument stems from the Judeo-Christian heritage's asserting the immorality of bringing about "premature" death. The Sixth Commandment, "Thou shalt not kill," leaves no doubt where the Judeo-Christian God stands on the issue. Humans are banned from killing in all circumstances. Why? The sanctity of human life and the merits of suffering. Either obey the divine will or take the consequences. In other words, divine will trumps human suffering, no matter how extreme that suffering is (Messinger 1993, 214–15).

THE "SLIPPERY SLOPE" ARGUMENT

According to the "slippery slope" argument, honest mistakes and malevolent motives can happen, and we can't control them. The potential for wrong diagnoses and the threat of nonmercy killings are too great to justify any exceptions to a total ban on doctor-assisted suicides. In addition, society's interest, not just the individual's, are at stake. When it runs amok, it can wreak great havoc, such as the Nazi atrocities, opponents point out (Messinger 1993, 215).

Mary Senander (1988), of the Anti-Euthanasia Task Force, makes this argument for the impact on society:

> If you want to commit suicide, you can do that. It's not illegal. If you want to hang yourself with a velvet cord from the rafters of your garage—I'm not recommending it and I wish you wouldn't—you *can* do that. If you want to blow your brains out with a diamond-studded pistol—I hope you won't, for your sake and for your family's—you can *do* that. If you want to save up pills and poison yourself—I'd try to talk you out of it—you *could* do it. But what you're asking for—what proponents of euthanasia are demanding—is my *approval* and *acceptance* of your actions. What's more you expect—and proponents of "aid dying" demand—someone *else* to help.
>
> When you ask for social and legal approval of killing, you're asking ME to participate in YOUR death, to share a communal responsibility and burden. And guilt. And blame. And I *won't do it*! Now, you're meddling with MY choices and MY conscience. Don't expect me to be silent when those issues of public policy are debated; I have my rights too.

Arguments in Favor of Doctor-Assisted Suicide

LO10

> Darkling I listen; and for many a time
> I have been half in love with easeful Death,
> Call'd him soft names in many a mused rhyme,

To take into the air my quiet breath;
Now more than ever seems it rich to die,
To cease upon the midnight with no pain …

—John Keats, "Ode to a Nightingale" (1819)

Supporters say that the argument for doctor-assisted suicide isn't so much an argument *for* euthanasia. It's an argument *against* "insufferable and unending pain; in a word, it's about compassion" (Messinger 1993, 223). But they don't stop with compassion. They maintain that there's a constitutional right to assisted suicide. According to proponents of the right to doctor-assisted suicide, the "right" is closely linked to the principle of personal autonomy embodied in the Court-created and controversial right to privacy (Chapter 2).

presumption of bodily integrity a state can't exercise power over individual members of society except to prevent harm to others

Resting the right to assisted suicide on the shaky controversial right to privacy has led proponents to look elsewhere and rely on a **presumption of bodily integrity**. This argument relies on the English philosopher John Stuart Mill's statement that a state can't exercise power over individual members of society except to prevent harm to others (Messinger 1993, 236). While the right to privacy is controversial, the right to bodily integrity is difficult to raise technically because of the judicial restrictions on "creating" law and rights (Chapters 1 and 2).

Others have argued that the "liberty interest" guaranteed in the due process clauses of the Fifth and Fourteenth Amendments to the U.S. Constitution includes the right to die and to seek assistance in exercising the right. But the U.S. Supreme Court upheld Washington State's ban on assisting another to commit suicide because recognizing a right to doctor-assisted suicide would require the reversal of "centuries of legal doctrine and practice" (*Washington v. Glucksberg* 1997, 723).

Washington v. Glucksberg leaves to state legislatures the decision to criminalize doctor-assisted suicide. In a decisive Washington State ballot initiative on election day in 2008, three out of five Washington State voters approved an initiative to decriminalize doctor-assisted suicide. Washington used as its model Oregon's Death with Dignity Act, which allows individuals to get a doctor to help them commit suicide. The Oregon act was upheld by the U.S. Supreme Court in *Gonzalez v. Oregon* (2005).

CRIMINAL LAW IN FOCUS

Oregon Death with Dignity Act

Written Request for Medication to End One's Life in a Humane and Dignified Manner 127.805 s.2.01. Who may initiate a written request for medication.

1. An adult who is capable, is a resident of Oregon, and has been determined by the attending physician and consulting physician to be suffering from a terminal disease, and who has voluntarily expressed his or her wish to die, may make a written request for medication for the purpose of ending his or her life in a humane and dignified manner in accordance with ORS 127.800 to 127.897.
2. No person shall qualify under the provisions of ORS 127.800 to 127.897 solely because of age or disability. [1995 c.3 s.2.01; 1999 c.423 s.2]

127.897 s.6.01. Form of the request

A request for a medication as authorized by ORS 127.800 to 127.897 shall be in substantially the following form:

Request for Medication to End My Life in a Humane and Dignified Manner

I, ______________________________, am an adult of sound mind.

I am suffering from ______________________________,
which my attending physician has determined is a terminal disease and which has been medically confirmed by a consulting physician.

I have been fully informed of my diagnosis, prognosis, the nature of medication to be prescribed and potential associated risks, the expected result, and the feasible alternatives, including comfort care, hospice care and pain control.

I request that my attending physician prescribe medication that will end my life in a humane and dignified manner.

Initial one:

__________ I have informed my family of my decision and taken their opinions into consideration.

__________ I have decided not to inform my family of my decision.

__________ I have no family to inform of my decision.

I understand that I have the right to rescind this request at any time.

I understand the full import of this request and I expect to die when I take the medication to be prescribed. I further understand that although most deaths occur within three hours, my death may take longer and my physician has counseled me about this possibility.

I make this request voluntarily and without reservation, and I accept full moral responsibility for my actions.

Signed: ______________________________

Dated: ______________________________

Declaration of Witness

We declare that the person signing this request:

(a) Is personally known to us or has provided proof of identity;

(b) Signed this request in our presence;

(c) Appears to be of sound mind and not under duress, fraud or undue influence;

(d) Is not a patient for whom either of us is attending physician.

______________________________ Witness 1/Date

______________________________ Witness 2/Date

NOTE: One witness shall not be a relative (by blood, marriage or adoption) of the person signing this request, shall not be entitled to any portion of the person's estate upon death and shall not own, operate or be employed at a health care facility where the person is a patient or resident. If the patient is an inpatient at a health care facility, one of the witnesses shall be an individual designated by the facility.

LO10 Doctor-Assisted Suicide and the Criminal Law

To justify doctor-assisted suicide runs up against the subject of this chapter—criminal homicide. The law of criminal homicide makes it difficult to distinguish doctor-assisted suicide from first-degree murder. Proponents argue that murder is condemned because it both violates a person's interest in continuing to live and is a destructive force in society. Neither of these is present in doctor-assisted suicide. The disruption to society has already taken place by the loss of a productive member of society. And violation of the right to live is obviously lacking—the person has decided she doesn't want to live (Messinger 1993, 237–38).

It should be clear that the positions on doctor-assisted suicide are irreconcilable because they reflect opposing strongly held beliefs about the meaning of life. Professor Thane Josef Messinger (1993) wrote words still applicable today:

> People view "life" as either sacrosanct, in which case any infinitesimally minute portion always has positive value, or as relative, in which case life can become negative at some variable point in the future, the only question being when. (224)

LO10 Public Opinion and Doctor-Assisted Suicide

The public, like the criminal law, is divided on the question of doctor-assisted suicide. The key finding of the 2007 Gallup annual Values and Beliefs poll reflects this division. Even so, 56 percent of respondents answered "should" and 38 percent answered "should not" to the question: "When a person has a disease that cannot be cured and is living in severe pain, do you think doctors should or should not be allowed by law to assist the patient to commit suicide if the patient requests it?" (Carroll 2007).

YOU *DECIDE*

Should doctor-assisted suicide be considered murder?

Just hours before they died, Sherry Miller, Marjorie Wantz, and their family members met with Kevorkian at the home of Sherry Miller's parents on October 22, 1991. Miller, 43, had advanced multiple sclerosis and had approached Kevorkian a year earlier. She kept pursuing him and told her story several times on television. Marjorie Wantz, 58, also had sought Kevorkian's help for years. Although not terminally ill, she suffered excruciating pain after many surgeries to remove benign vaginal tumors. She had tried to kill herself several times. Psychiatrists said she was depressed and suicidal and some felt her pain was psychosomatic. (Later, when the medical examiner conducted her autopsy he found no physical cause for her pain.) The day after this interview, they committed suicide in a rustic cabin. Wantz used a machine Kevorkian invented, which injected a fatal substance; Miller inhaled carbon monoxide because her veins were too weak for a needle.

He called the machine the Thanatron—"death machine" in Greek. It was devised so that the patient could pull the trigger. It started with an intravenous drip of saline solution. Then the patient would press a button starting a device that stopped the saline solution and started releasing a drug of thiopental with a 60-second timer. This would put the patient into a deep coma. Finally, the timer's click would begin a lethal dose of potassium chloride, which, in minutes, would stop the heart. The patient would die of a heart attack while asleep.

The Thanatron was made from odd bits and pieces of household tools and toy parts, magnets, and electrical switches. It had an electric clock motor with a pulley axle, and a chain and two coils acting as electric bar magnets. Kevorkian showed it off, including an appearance on *The Donahue Show*. He called it "dignified, humane, and painless, and the patient can do it in the comfort of their own home at any time they want."

Everyone who has known Jack Kevorkian first talks about his brain. "He could tell you any major league baseball player's batting average," his boyhood chum Richard Dakesian told me, his voice tinged with awe. "He probably could have graduated from high school when he was 13 or 14. He's the smartest man I ever knew. I think he was born ahead of his time."

Instructions

1. Consult the Frontline website "The Kevorkian Verdict" at http://www.pbs.org/wgbh/pages/frontline/kevorkian/tindex.html.
2. Write an essay answering the question, "Is it ethical public policy to make doctor-assisted suicide criminal homicide?" Support your answer with points made in the section on "Doctor-Assisted Suicide," and the Frontline website content.

Source: Frontline. 1996 (May 14). "The Kevorkian Verdict." http://www.pbs.org/wgbh/pages/frontline/kevorkian/interviews/.

Summary

Criminal homicide is the most serious of all crimes, but it's rare. Most of the law of homicide is devoted to answering the questions: Is killing first or second-degree murder? Is killing murder or manslaughter? Is manslaughter voluntary or involuntary? First-degree murder is the only crime you can be executed for, and in non–death penalty states, it's the only crime for which you can get life in prison without a chance of parole. **LO1**

Killing another "person" is central to criminal homicide liability because it defines who's a victim. The definition of "person" for purposes of criminal homicide presents problems at both ends of the life cycle—when life begins and when it ends. **LO2**

The reason for creating first and second-degree murders was to separate murders that deserved the death penalty from those that didn't. The death penalty is discretionary in all states in which the penalty is authorized. **LO3**

Proving murder requires proof beyond a reasonable doubt of (1) murder *actus reus*, the act of killing; (2) murder *mens rea*, intentional, knowing, or extremely reckless killing; (3) causation, the act caused; (4) death, the harm or result; and (5) attendant circumstances, if there are any. **LO4**

First-degree murder *mens rea* includes willful, deliberate, and premeditated killing by means of "heinous, atrocious, or cruel" acts. Second-degree murder is a catchall **LO5** offense that includes killings that are neither manslaughter nor first-degree murder. Felony murders are unintentional deaths that occur during the commission of some felonies.

LO6 Most state criminal codes apply to corporate criminal homicide in the same way that they apply to other crimes committed for the corporation's benefit, but prosecutions and convictions for corporation murder are very rare.

LO7 Voluntary manslaughter consists of the intentional, sudden killing of another triggered by adequate provocation.

LO8 Adequate provocation has to trigger the sudden killing of another person. Adequate provocation isn't an excuse for criminal homicide; it only reduces the seriousness of, and the punishment for, murder. The reduction is done to allow for human frailty.

LO9 The central elements in involuntary manslaughter are its *actus reus* (voluntary act or omission) and its *mens rea* (unintentional killing), resulting in the criminal harm of death. Criminal negligence homicide statutes cover a broad spectrum of behavior. The most common are unintentional deaths caused by operating vehicles and firearms, but the statutes also include unintentional deaths caused by practicing medicine illegally, handling explosives, delivering dangerous drugs, allowing vicious animals to run free, failing to care for a sick child, and not providing fire exits in businesses.

LO10 Euthanasia, or helping another person die, presents irreconcilable moral, ethical, and legal dilemmas about the meaning and value of human life. Voluntary euthanasia through doctor-assisted suicide exemplifies the divisive views on euthanasia. Arguments against doctor-assisted suicide rely on the ideas that: (1) killing is intrinsically immoral and wrong; and (2) the potential for abuse on a "slippery slope." Supporters of doctor-assisted suicide contend that the argument is not for euthanasia; rather, it is an argument against "insufferable and unending pain."

Key Terms

born-alive rule, p. 324
feticide, p. 325
murder, p. 329
manslaughter, p. 329
justifiable homicide, p. 329
excusable homicide, p. 329
criminal homicide, p. 329
malice aforethought, p. 330
depraved heart murder, p. 330
intent to cause serious bodily injury murder, p. 330
serious bodily injury, p. 331
"express" malice aforethought, p. 331
"implied" malice aforethought, p. 331
murder *actus reus*, p. 332
murder *mens rea*, p. 332
first-degree murder, p. 334
capital cases, p. 334
bifurcation procedure, p. 334
deadly weapon doctrine, p. 337
second-degree murders, p. 344
felony murder rule, p. 346
manslaughter, p. 353
voluntary manslaughter, p. 355
adequate provocation, p. 356

objective test of cooling-off time, p. 357

"words can never provoke" rule, p. 358

"last-straw" rule, p. 358

extreme mental or emotional disturbance manslaughter, p. 358

paramour rule, p. 359

gay panic, p. 363

emotion–act distinction, p. 363

act reasonableness, p. 365

emotional reasonableness, p. 365

involuntary manslaughter, p. 365

criminal negligence manslaughter, p. 367

unlawful act or misdemeanor manslaughter, p. 370

malum prohibitum crime, p. 371

euthanasia, p. 372

presumption of bodily integrity, p. 374

Learning Objectives

1. To understand the seriousness of rape and the grave, often invisible, harms it inflicts upon victims, but appreciate that voluntary and knowing consensual sexual behavior between two adults is legal, healthy, and desired.

2. To know that crimes against persons boil down to four types: taking a life, unwanted sexual invasions, bodily injury, and personal restraint.

3. To know that the requirements of common law rape have been dramatically altered in modern rape statutes; and to appreciate that during the 1970s and 1980s, sexual assault reform changed the face of criminal sexual assault law to confront the reality that most victims are raped by people they know.

4. To understand and appreciate the legal and cultural reasons that sexual assault reforms have failed to reduce the amount of acquaintance rapes.

5. To know the elements of modern rape law and understand that force beyond the degree required to complete sexual penetration or contact isn't always required to satisfy the force requirement in rape.

6. To understand and appreciate how cultural values and social norms influence the perception of rape at all stages of the criminal justice system.

7. To understand that rape can be accomplished without any actual force; and know that threats of force are enough if the victim experienced both subjective and objective fear.

8. To know that rape is a general-intent crime; that statutory rape is a strict liability crime in most states; and that sex offenses are graded based on several criteria.

9. To know that assault and battery are two separate crimes.

10. To appreciate that since the early 1970s, domestic violence crimes have been transformed from a private concern to a criminal justice problem.

11. To remember that stalking, although an ancient practice, is a new crime that's based on causing fear.

12. To know that kidnapping and false imprisonment violate the right of locomotion.

10 Crimes Against Persons II

Sex Offenses, Bodily Injury, and Personal Restraint

Chapter Outline

Did he commit a felony sex offense?

Peter Triestman and N.P. were both employed at a furniture store in Newark, New Jersey. Triestman was N.P.'s boss. According to an incident report filed with the Newark Police Department, Triestman asked N.P. to prepare a bed at the store so he could place pictures of the bed online to sell it. On May 22, 2008, Triestman asked N.P. to examine the bed with him in an upstairs room.

Once upstairs, Triestman and N.P. began changing the bedding. While doing so, Triestman told N.P. that the bed would look better with her laying on it naked. While saying this, Triestman moved closer to N.P., placed his left hand on her shoulder, put his right hand on her breast over her clothes, and tried to kiss her. She exclaimed, "Peter!" pulled away from Triestman, and walked away. She gathered her belongings, punched out her time card, and told her mother, who also worked in the store, which she was leaving.

Triestman followed N.P. before she left, apologized for touching her, and told her not to tell anyone. After leaving, N.P. informed her sister and father about what had happened. She and her sister then retrieved their mother from the store. Later that same evening, Triestman called N.P.'s home and informed her and her mother that they were fired. N.P. then filed an incident report.

LO1

Rape ranks second only to murder as the most serious crime in U.S. law and society. Reflecting its seriousness, rape was punishable by death in several states from colonial times until 1977. That was the year when the U.S. Supreme Court ruled that it was cruel and unusual punishment to execute a convicted rapist (see Chapter 2; *Coker v. Georgia* 1977).

The seriousness of rape isn't measured only by the *physical* injury it inflicts. According to existing law, rape doesn't have to leave any visible marks, not even so much as a minor cut or bruise. Two rape victims speak to a deeper injury that no one can see from the outside—these are injuries to the heart and soul:

> When he went for the buttons on my dress, I tried to stop him. Tried to yell. Nothing worked. He ripped my dress, my stockings, panties.... He ripped my soul out of me. (Pillsbury 2002, 878)
>
> My rapist stole me from me. He ripped my personality out of me—who I was—the same as if he ripped out my heart. (893)

LO1

Even sexually triggered touching, such as pinching buttocks, or fondling breasts, or kissing are felonies. Rape and other sexual assaults differ from all other felonies in three very important respects. Under other circumstances, they're healthy, wanted, and legal. One of the most critical problems in sex offenses is distinguishing flirting and seduction from sexual assault. In prosecuting these grave crimes against individual autonomy, we don't want to inhibit desirable and healthy lawful sexual activity between consenting adults.

LO2

In addition to rape and other sexual assaults, you'll learn about two other kinds of crimes against persons—nonsexual assault without actual body contact and its close relative stalking; battery (offensive nonsexual contact and physical injury); and kidnapping and false imprisonment (criminal restraints on liberty). Finally, we pay special attention to these nonsexual crimes within families.

As we did in criminal homicide, we'll leave discussion of the elements of causation and result to what you've already learned in the "Causation" section of Chapter 4, because although it's a required element in many crimes against person, it's rarely a contested issue in individual cases. Far more important are the issues we concentrate on here, and which are contested, often heatedly: *actus reus*; *mens rea*; attendant circumstance elements in actual sex and nonsexual assaults. ■

SEX OFFENSES

LO3

common law rape intentional, forced, nonconsensual, heterosexual vaginal penetration between a man and a woman not his wife

common law sodomy anal intercourse between two males

Originally, the criminal law recognized only two sex crimes—rape and sodomy. Common law rape was strictly limited to intentional, forced, nonconsensual, heterosexual vaginal *penetration*. It was aimed at the traditional view of rape: a *male* stranger leaps from the shadows at night and sexually attacks a defenseless *woman* he's never seen before, and forcibly penetrates her vagina. Men couldn't rape their wives. Common law sodomy, the other traditional sex offense, referred only to anal intercourse between two males.

In 1769, William Blackstone, the leading eighteenth-century authority on the common law in both England and the colonies, defined common law rape as the "carnal knowledge of a woman forcibly and against her will" (210).

This definition boiled down to four elements:

carnal knowledge vaginal sexual intercourse

- Sexual intercourse by force, or a threat of severe bodily harm (*actus reus*)
- Intentional vaginal intercourse (*mens rea*)
- Intercourse between a man and a woman not his wife (attendant circumstance)
- Intercourse without the woman's consent (attendant circumstance)

The common law required proof beyond a reasonable doubt of all four elements because, as Sir Matthew Hale (1847), the highly regarded seventeenth-century chief justice and legal scholar of the criminal law, noted:

> It is true that rape is a most detestable crime, and therefore ought severely and impartially to be punished; but it must be remembered, that it is an accusation easy to be made, hard to be proved, and harder to be defended by the party accused, though innocent. (634)

Blackstone (1769), the Americans' favorite authority, added:

> The heinousness of the offence many times transporting the judge and jury with so much indignation, that they are overhastily carried to the conviction of the person accused thereof, by the confident testimony of sometimes false and malicious witnesses. (215)

In common law trials, rape victims were allowed to testify against accused rapists; it was up to the jury to decide whether to believe them. But the victim's credibility depended on proof of three conditions, always difficult (and often impossible) to satisfy:

- The victim's chastity
- Prompt reporting of the rape
- Other witnesses corroborated the rape

Blackstone (1769) *talked* tough enough when he asserted that even prostitutes could be of good fame, but took it almost all back in this warning about victim's credibility:

> If the ravished be of evil fame, and stand unsupported by others; if she concealed the injury for any considerable time after she had opportunity to complain; if the place where the fact was alleged to be committed, was where it was possible she might have been heard, and she made no outcry; these and the like circumstances carry a strong, but not conclusive, presumption that her testimony is false or feigned. (213–14)

Times are dramatically different, at least in the formal criminal law definition of rape, if not in the social reality of sex offenses. This is especially true of acquaintance or "date" rape and sexual assault.

Before we get to the present definitions of these offenses, it's very important that you to understand and appreciate the legal distinction between the far more serious crimes involving sexual *penetration* (rape) and the less serious crimes involving sexual *contact* (criminal sexual assault and battery). Both court opinions and legislation recognize this distinction, and grade the crimes and prescribe and administer the punishments for them accordingly. Penetrations are always felonies with harsher (most of the time a *lot* harsher) penalties than contacts, most of which are misdemeanors.

LO3 The New Criminal Sexual Conduct Regime

Court opinions have relaxed these narrow definitions of rape and sodomy. Also, legislatures enacted criminal sexual conduct statutes in the 1970s and the 1980s that expanded the definition of "sex offenses" to embrace a wide range of nonconsensual penetrations and contacts, even if they fall far short of violent (pp. 404–407).

These reforms in sex offense law were brought about because reformers, popular culture, scholars, and increasingly state legislatures "outed" a dirty secret: in the vast majority of rapes, men rape women (and sometimes men) they know. In this chapter, we'll distinguish between two kinds of rape. In **aggravated rape**, strangers (and *sometimes* individuals they know) shoot, stab, or otherwise seriously injury and sometimes kill their victims. In **unarmed acquaintance rape**, rapists are "the men a woman knows, dates, works with, meets at a bar and drives home with [and] who come from good families" (Estrich 1992, 7). As one White female juror told Gary LaFree (1989), the defendant was a "nice looking young fellow, nicely dressed like a college boy. I couldn't believe he could be involved in something like this." Another juror, a White male, said the "defendant didn't match the stereotype of a rapist. He was quiet. An average person intellectually. He looked like a stock boy at the local grocery store." (219). These men mostly use words and nondeadly violent coercion to overpower their victims and gratify their sexual appetite. Table 10.1 depicts the characteristics of rape and sexual assault offenders that victims report they perceived during the years 1995–2013, the latest numbers available when this book went to press.

aggravated rape rape by strangers or individuals with weapons who physically injure their victims

unarmed acquaintance rape nonconsensual sex between individuals who are known to one another

Under this new regime of criminal law, the criminal justice system has reduced the number of aggravated rapes *somewhat*, although mistaken eyewitness identification remains a major problem in obtaining rape convictions in aggravated rapes by *strangers*.

It shouldn't surprise you to know that most acquaintance rapists are adolescents who (like most others in their age group) often—sometimes *very* often—have sex on their minds.

Professor Katharine Baker put it well in "Once a Rapist?" (1997):

> Rapists are young.... Research documents that coercive behavior in college men is positively correlated with immaturity, irresponsibility, and lack of social conscience. Youth probably commit a disproportionate number of all crimes, but what is important in analyzing rapist motivation is that youthful predisposition for irresponsible criminal activity coincides with male coming of age. The experimenting can become coercive because many boys are taught that power, dominance, and violence, can be arousing to women. (600–01)

Before we move on, let's be absolutely clear on one point. Neither the law of rape, nor the biology of the acquaintance rapist, nor cultural norms regarding male and female sex roles justifies or excuses sex without consent, let alone condones it!

We'll concentrate on acquaintance rape where the new regime of criminal sexual conduct has failed miserably to reduce unarmed acquaintance rapes. Let's look at two possible reasons for this failure: the law and the culture.

LO4 THE LAW

Acquaintance rape cases face two legal obstacles in the criminal justice system: proving guilt beyond a reasonable doubt with only the words of the accuser and the accused to prove it. (It's only in the movies and occasionally in social media where people have

TABLE 10.1 Perceived Offender Characteristics in Rape and Sexual Assault Victimizations against Females Ages 18–24 (by post-secondary enrollment status of victim), 1995–2013

OFFENDER CHARACTERISTIC	STUDENTS[a]	NONSTUDENTS[b]
Number of offenders		
One	95%	92%
Two or more	5%[g]	5%
Unknown	—[f, g]	3%[g]
Age[c]		
18–20	17%	13%
21–29	51%	53%
30 or older	23%	23%
Mixed group	2%[g]	3%
Unknown	7%	7%
Sex		
Male	97%	91%[h]
Female	1%[g]	3%[g,h]
Mixed group/unknown	2%[g]	5%[g,h]
Race[d]		
White	63%	60%
Black	19%	22%
Other/mixed group[e]	10%	12%
Unknown	8%	7%
Alcohol/drug use		
Yes	47%	40%
No	25%	36%[h]
Don't know/unknown	28%	24%

[a] Includes female victims ages 18 to 24 enrolled part time or full time in a post-secondary institution (i.e., college or university, trade school, or vocational school).
[b] Includes female victims ages 18 to 24 not enrolled in a post-secondary institution.
[c] Detail may not sum to total due to small portion of offenders age 17 or younger.
[d] Prior to 2012, victims were not asked about perceived Hispanic origin of offenders, so Hispanic offenders make up an unknown portion of the white, black, and other race of offender categories.
[e] American Indian, Alaska Native, Asian, Native Hawaiian, and other Pacific Islander, persons of two or more races, and mixed groups that may include persons of any race.
[f] Less than 0.5%.
[g] Interpret with caution; estimate based on 10 or fewer sample cases, or coefficient of variation is greater than 50%.
[h] Nonstudent estimates are significantly different from student estimates at the 95% confidence level.

Source: Bureau of Justice Statistics, National Crime Victimization Survey, 1995–2013.

sex in public or while being spied on or caught in the act. For most, sex in real time is a most private affair, to talk and brag about to others before and after but not during.) Let's look at each.

PROOF BEYOND A REASONABLE DOUBT Recall here the meaning of the constitutional requirement that the prosecution has to prove every element of a crime "beyond a reasonable doubt:" (*Victor v. Nebraska* 1994, 1, 8, 12) Reasonable doubt is often used but hard to define. The great English criminal law expert, Glanville Williams, suggested one possible solution: Don't define it, leave it to the jury's "common sense." But "[t]here's probably no harm in telling the jury… that a reasonable doubt is one for which a sensible reason can be supplied (1961, 873; also Chapter 2 of your text, pp. 47–48). LO4

Also helpful: Keep in mind that it's the highest level of proof recognized by our law and it's reserved for criminal cases.

Now let's see how this is a problem for acquaintance rape victims. First, notice what are *not* issues. There's no physical evidence to introduce, like rape kits, because both complainant and defendant agree they had sex. There's no weapon to trace because they agree none was used. There's no mistaken identity because they know each other. A single issue remains: Did the complainant consent to the sex? That single issue is a huge problem because of the kind of evidence needed to prove consent: words and nonverbal communication.

LO4 PROOF BY WORDS AND NONVERBAL COMMUNICATION It's extremely difficult to tell who's telling the truth, but that's what the consent issue boils down to. It's even more difficult if we remind ourselves that acquaintance rape defendants enjoy the presumption of innocence. So juries have to begin the trial "disbelieving the victim's claim she did *not* consent." (Baker 1999, 691, italics added)

As if this is not difficult enough, only the victim is subject to cross-examination, during which defense counsel will inevitably uncover inconsistencies. Jurors should realize that no one's memory is perfect. Acquaintance rape victims, like all of us, can't remember who said what to whom. But jurors in acquaintance rape cases are "highly suspicious of both parties" (Baker 1999, 692).

The bottom line: Acquaintance rape defendants, like all defendants in criminal cases, have the advantage. Juries don't have to believe that the complainant willingly had sex. In most of these cases, it's reasonable to believe that she *might* have consented. Victims may even have the preponderance of the evidence on their side. But that's not enough. Even if they believe the victims story, they (quite rightly) conclude that they *have* to acquit because they reasonably doubted the defendant's guilt.

THE CULTURE

That said, we need to explain why what the new regime of rape law formally calls rape, acquaintance rapists say—and often believe—is only "bad sex" or "bad romance" (Pillsbury 2002, 856).

According to law professor David P. Bryden's excellent article "Redefining Rape" (2000):

> An acquaintance rapist is most likely to escape justice if his victim violated traditional norms of female morality and prudence: for example, by engaging in casual sex, drinking heavily, or hitchhiking. When the victim is a norm-violating woman, people often blame her rather than the rapist. (318)

The criminal justice system's poor performance in dealing with unarmed acquaintance rapes is a serious problem, but it's made worse by these social realities:

1. The overwhelming number of rapes are acquaintance rapes (Robinson 2008, 628 n. 12), 80 percent in 2013 (Bureau of Justice Statistics December 2014, Table 6).
2. Acquaintance rape victims are far less likely to report their rapes to the police.
3. Prosecutors and jurors are less likely to convict.

Another aspect of the social reality of rape is the substantial number of rapes committed against men (McMullen 1990). It's almost impossible to get details about male rape victims. The FBI's Uniform Crime Reports, the most widely cited statistics of crimes reported to the police, don't break down the numbers of rape victims by sex. The National Crime Victim Survey, the most thorough government victimization survey, reported that between 1995 and 2013, in 2010, 78 percent of male rape/sexual assault victims knew their assailant. The survey notes warned "Interpret with Caution!" because of the small numbers of respondents. That is, about 15,000 men contrasted with 169,000 females responded in 2010, which works out to less than one tenth of one (0.01) percent of all women in the general population.

To learn more about how the law treats rape, in this section we study the history of modern rape law statutes defining criminal sexual conduct; the elements of modern rape law; statutory rape; and how the law grades the seriousness of sex offenses and the penalties it prescribes for them.

Criminal Sexual Conduct Statutes

LO3

During the late 1960s and '70s a wave of feminist advocacy swept across the country, challenging most institutions and women's position in public and private life. Rape law reform was close to the top of the feminist agenda. Feminists were not alone. From the beginning, some social scientists and legal scholars joined them. At the heart of their critique was that in existing rape law, the victim, not the rapist, was on trial. Police, prosecutors, and courts asked, "What was the victim doing?" "What was she wearing?" "Did she resist as much as she could?" "Could someone back up her story?" "What's her sex life like?" They *didn't* ask, "How serious was she injured?" "How much force did the rapist use?" "Did he threaten her?"

Professor Susan Estrich (1992) calls it the **"assumption of risk" approach** to rape cases:

> No one I've talked to—Radio callers, prosecutors, and judges alike—would extend the assumption of risk approach to people who walk alone on dangerous streets at night and get mugged, or people who forgot to lock their cars or leave the back windows of the house wide open. What makes sex different is the unstated assumption that a wallet or a car or household belongings are yours unless you actually give them away, whereas a woman's body may be presumed available; that when she acts foolishly, she gives up her right to bodily integrity, whereas foolish homeowners and car owners are still entitled to their property. (10)

"assumption of risk" approach to rape cases view of rape cases that holds the victim accountable for their manner of dress, sexual history, amount of resistance to the attack, and other behaviors deemed socially unacceptable

In the late 1970s, amid growing public concern about increasing reports of rape, the anti-rape campaign turned to lobbying state legislatures to revise the rape laws. In this effort, they gained powerful allies from crime control advocates, particularly police and prosecutors. (Spohn 1999, 120–21)

On paper, the campaign was a stunning success. By the mid-1980s, every state and the District of Columbia had changed at least some parts of their old law. Figure 10.1 depicts the first of these statutes in 1974.

Some essentially ripped up their old rape law, banishing even the word "rape," and adopted comprehensive **criminal sexual conduct statutes** that adopted the following items on the anti-rape coalition's agenda:

criminal sexual conduct statutes comprehensive statutes that replaced the single crime of rape with a series of graded offenses, eliminated the resistance and corroboration requirements, restricted the use of evidence regarding the victim's sexual history, and removed the marital rape exception

- *Definition.* Replace the single crime of rape with a series of graded offenses
- *Nonconsent, force, and resistance.* Eliminate the requirement that victims have to prove their nonconsent by physically resisting their attacker
- *Corrobation.* Eliminate the requirement that the prosecutor has to corroborate the victim's testimony

Figure 10.1

MICHIGAN CRIMINAL SEXUAL CONDUCT STATUTE

First degree This consists of "sexual penetration," defined as sexual intercourse, cunnilingus, fellatio, anal intercourse, "or any other intrusion, however slight, of any part of a person's body or of any object into the genital or anal openings of another person's body." In addition one of the following must have occurred:

1. The defendant must have been armed with a weapon.
2. Force or coercion was used, and the defendant was aided by another person.
3. Force or coercion was used, and personal injury to the victim was caused.

Second degree This consists of "sexual contact," defined as the intentional touching of the victim's or actor's personal parts or the intentional touching of the clothing covering the immediate area of the victim's intimate parts for purposes of sexual arousal or gratification.

"Intimate parts" is defined as including the primary genital area, groin, inner thigh, buttock, or breast. In addition, one of the circumstances required for first-degree criminal sexual conduct must have existed.

Third degree This consists of sexual penetration accomplished by force or coercion.

Fourth degree This consists of sexual contact accomplished by force or coercion.

- *Victim sexual history*. Restrict the introduction of evidence of the victim's prior sexual activity
- *Marital rape exception*. Eliminate the rule that the rape doesn't apply to husbands

Let's look at each of these provisions.

DEFINITION AND GRADING

The new statutes commonly dropped the name "rape" with its emphases on force and resistance to penile–vaginal penetration. In its place, the statutes created degrees of "sexual assault" and "sexual battery." The degrees depended on the seriousness of the offense:

- Type of conduct. Penetration is more serious than contact
- Type of coercion. In order of seriousness: Use of weapons, physical attack, restraint, threat
- Amount of injury to the victim
- Whether assailant committed another felony besides the rape, for example, the rape plus robbery of the victim
- Assailant didn't act alone but had accomplices
- Age of the victim and age gap between victim and rapist

Most statutes also redefined "penetration." Minnesota's definition is typical of the most comprehensive statutes: Sexual penetration includes any of the following acts committed without the victim's consent "whether or not the emission of semen occurs":

(1) sexual intercourse, cunnilingus, fellatio, or anal intercourse; or

(2) any intrusion however slight into the genital or anal openings:

(i) of the complainant's body by any part of the actor's body or any object used by the actor for this purpose;

(ii) of the complainant's body by any part of the body of the complainant, by any part of the body of another person, or by any object used by the complainant or another person for this purpose, when effected by a person in a

position of authority, or by coercion, or by inducement if the child is under 13 years of age or mentally impaired; or
(iii) of the body of the actor or another person by any part of the body of the complainant or by any object used by the complainant for this purpose, when effected by a person in a position of authority, or by coercion, or by inducement if the child is under 13 years of age or mentally impaired. (Section 609.31, Subd 12)

NONCONSENT, FORCE, AND RESISTANCE

Ancient rape law consisted of unlawful penile–vaginal intercourse with a woman without her consent and against her will. The heart of the crime was the woman's nonconsent; the focus was on the woman's state of mind at the time of the rape, namely did she consent. No one seems to know when or how or why the element of force crept into the definition, but one thing is clear: it led to the unfortunate resistance requirement. So, the heart of the offense became the burden on women to "resist to the utmost," or at least to in order to prove she didn't consent to the sexual intercourse. (Burger 1977, 8)

Police and rape counselors pointed out that the rule increased the chances victims would suffer serious injury. Feminists and legal scholars argued that the rule required rape victims to do what no other victim of violent crimes had to do. In response, some states eliminated the resistance requirement. Others retained the consent defense but defined consent as freely given agreement to the act of penetration, which in effect also removed the resistance requirement. (Spohn 1999, 124).

CORROBORATION

Rape convictions can't rest on the victim's testimony alone. The prosecution had to produce other evidence to prove the elements of the rapist's identity, the penetration, and the victim's nonconsent. Critics pointed to the obvious—it's difficult (probably impossible) to corroborate so private an act. Most states eliminated the corroboration requirement (Spohn 1999, 125–26).

corroboration requirement an element in rape that the prosecution had to prove rape by the testimony of witnesses other than the victim

VICTIM'S SEXUAL HISTORY

The old law allowed the defense to present the victim's previous sexual conduct to prove that she consented, and to impeach her as a witness. Most of this evidence boiled down to relying on the assumption that "if she did it once, she'll do it again. (For fuller discussion of the critique of the sexual history rule, see Spohn 1999, 126–27; Berger 1977, 55–58.) By 1985, the federal courts and almost all states had adopted rape shield laws, either entirely eliminating or limiting the use of the victim's past sexual conduct. (Spohn 1999, 127)

rape shield laws statutes that prohibit introducing evidence of victims' past sexual conduct

MARITAL EXCEPTION

In my 2014 Criminal Law class, on learning about the marital rape exception, one student exclaimed, "It made my blood boil!" The anti-rape reform coalition agreed; it recommended abolishing it. As of 2009, it's a crime in all 50 states for husbands and all other men and women to rape their husbands, wives, and unmarried "partners." But, is it really? Well, sort of. Some states have abolished the exemption entirely. But, in many others, remnants remain. Some states, like California, define marital rape as a separate crime from stranger rape.

marital rape exception provided that husbands could not legally rape their wives

Here are some others:

- Twenty states grant immunity to a husband who has sex with his wife while she's unconscious or otherwise incapable of giving consent.
- In the states whose laws have maintained the distinction between marital and nonmarital rape, the prosecution is confronted with elevated levels of proof built into these laws.
- Some of the states that still treat marital rape differently from nonmarital rape require that marital rape victims report the crime within a shorter period of time than is required of nonmarital rape victims.
- Some of these states impose less severe sentences upon rapists who are married to their victims than on those who are not, including allowing for dismissal of charges if the victim-spouse agrees and if the spouse-rapist undergoes counseling.
- Some states even require that the prosecution make a greater showing that force or violence was used during marital rape than is required in a nonmarital rape case. (England 2014)

These legal limits to the abolition of the exemption may in part explain this tragic story. In 2006, after Regan Martin refused to have sex with her husband, John Samolis tied her hands behind her back, brutally beat and raped her, and walked out, leaving her bloody and severely injured on the floor of their Crete, Illinois, home. (Polisi 2009) After serving 19 months, he was released (Twohey 2008).

Despite these advances in rape law, keep in mind Professor David Bryden's (2000) assessment of the reality of current sexual assault law:

> Most legislatures and courts still define rape narrowly. In acquaintance rape cases, in most states, nonconsensual sex is not rape unless the perpetrator employs force or a threat of force, or the victim is unconscious, badly drunk, underage, or otherwise incapacitated. Even if the victim verbally declines sex, the encounter is not rape in most states unless the man employs "force." Sex obtained by nonviolent threats ("you'll lose your job," etc.), or by deception, usually is not a crime. (321)

Professor Bryden's assessment is 15 years old now. But it still holds. Countless later research and court cases still rely on it.

LO5 The Elements of Modern Rape Law

Most traditional rape statutes, and the newer criminal sexual assault laws, define "rape" as intentional sexual penetration by force without consent. There are many variations in the statutes, but in most jurisdictions, rape today boils down to three elements:

- *Actus reus*. Sexual penetration by force or threat of force
- *Mens rea*. Intentional sexual penetration
- *Circumstance*. Nonconsent by the victim

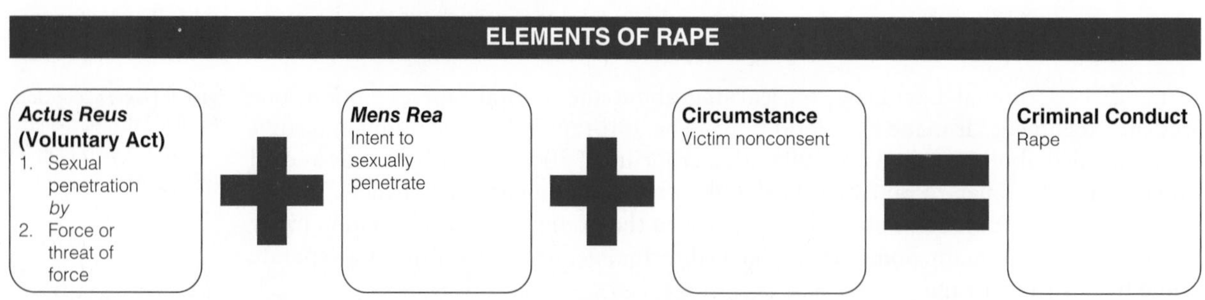

RAPE *ACTUS REUS*: THE FORCE AND RESISTANCE RULE

force and resistance rule provided that victims had to prove to the courts that they didn't consent to rape by demonstrating that they resisted the force of the rapist

Rape is a crime of violence; its *actus reus* is sexual intercourse by force. For most of its history, rape *actus reus* was governed by the **force and resistance rule**. The "force" part of the rule wasn't satisfied if victims consented to sexual intercourse. In practice, the prosecution didn't have to prove that victims consented; victims had to prove they didn't consent. This is where the "resistance" part of the rule comes in. Victims had to prove they didn't consent by proving they resisted the force of the accused rapist.

According to an early frequently cited case, *Reynolds v. State* (1889):

> Voluntary submission by the woman, while she has power to resist, no matter how reluctantly yielded, removes from the act an essential element of the crime of rape if the carnal knowledge was with the consent of the woman, no matter how tardily given, or how much force had theretofore been employed, it is not rape. (904)

Proof of nonconsent by resistance is peculiar to the law of rape. In no other crime where lack of consent is an element of the crime does the law treat passive acceptance as consent. Robbery requires taking someone's property by force or threat of force, but it's outrageous even to think that the element of force puts the burden on victims to prove they resisted. Entering an unlocked apartment house without consent to commit a crime is burglary, but it would be absurd to demand that residents prove they didn't consent to the entry.

The same is true of theft. According to Lani Anne Remick (1993):

> A common defense to a charge of auto theft is that the car's owner consented to the defendant's use of the vehicle. A mere showing that the owner never gave the defendant permission to take the car is enough to defeat this defense; no showing that the owner actually told the defendant not to take the car is necessary. (1111)

In rape law, however, the "default" position is consent. Proof of the absence of affirmative indications by the victim is not enough to defeat a consent defense; instead, the prosecution must show that the alleged victim indicated to the defendant through her overt actions and/or words that she did not wish to participate in sexual activity with him.

Thus, "the law presumes that one will not give away that which is his to a robber, but makes no similar presumption as to the conduct of women and rapists." In fact, quite the opposite is true: in the context of sexual activity the law presumes consent. For example, proving both that a woman did not verbally consent and that her actions consist of lying still and not moving does not raise a presumption of nonconsent but of consent. Only through evidence of some sort of overt behavior such as a verbal "no" or an attempt to push away the defendant can the prosecution meet its burden of proving nonconsent (1111).

Factors that have influenced courts' view of nonconsent include the amount of resistance the victim offered, the threat of force, and the danger to the victim if she resisted. We'll look at each of these and exceptions to the force and resistance rule.

LO9

utmost resistance standard requirement that rape victims had to use all the physical strength they had to prevent penetration

The amount of resistance required to prove lack of consent has changed over time. From the 1800s until the 1950s, the **utmost resistance standard** prevailed. According to the standard, to show they didn't consent, victims had to resist with all the physical power they possessed. In *Brown v. State* (1906), a 16-year old virgin testified that her neighbor grabbed her, tripped her to the ground, and forced himself on her:

> I tried as hard as I could to get away. I was trying all the time to get away just as hard as I could. I was trying to get up; I pulled at the grass; I screamed as hard as I could,

and he told me to shut up, and I didn't, and then he held his hand on my mouth until I was almost strangled. (538)

The jury convicted the neighbor of rape, but, on appeal, the Wisconsin Supreme Court reversed, deciding the victim hadn't resisted enough:

> Not only must there be entire absence of mental consent or assent, but there must be the most vehement exercise of every physical means or faculty within the woman's power to resist the penetration of her person, and this must be shown to persist until the offense is consummated. (538)

The Nebraska Supreme Court's language was even tougher in *Casico v. State* (1947):

> The general rule is that a mentally competent woman must in good faith resist to the utmost with the most vehement exercise of every physical means or faculty naturally within her power to prevent carnal knowledge, and she must persist in such resistance as long as she has the power to do so until the offense is consummated. (900)

reasonable resistance rule provides that the amount of force required to repel rapists shows nonconsent in rape prosecutions

In the 1950s, most courts softened the utmost resistance definition to the reasonable resistance rule, the rule followed in almost all states today. According to the rule, the amount of resistance depends on the totality of circumstances in each case. For example, in *Jones v. State* (1984), Marvin Jones ran N.M. off the road while she was on the way to a fast-food store with her daughters. Jones opened the door, grabbed her arm, choked her, and forced her toward his car.

Fearing for her life, N.M. got into the car with her daughters. Jones drove to a secluded spot, threatened her, and forced her to commit oral sodomy. Then, he took her out on the road and raped her. At his first-degree rape and oral sodomy trial, Jones argued that N.M. consented. He was convicted and sentenced to 50 years in prison. He appealed, arguing there wasn't enough evidence that N.M. submitted because of "the threat of immediate and great bodily harm." The Oklahoma Court of Criminal Appeals affirmed his conviction and sentence:

> In Oklahoma, a woman threatened with rape is not required to resist to the uttermost; instead, she is not required to do more than her age, strength, and the surrounding circumstances make reasonable. In light of the facts of this case, as recited above, we find that there was more than ample evidence to establish that the prosecutrix submitted due to the threats of great bodily harm. (757)

extrinsic force in rape cases, requires some physical effort in addition to the amount needed to accomplish the penetration

intrinsic force in rape cases, requires only the amount of force necessary to accomplish the penetration

Many of the new rape and sexual assault statutes have dropped the resistance requirement entirely—at least in formal law. This has had little or no effect in practice in stranger rape cases because it's pretty clear that these rapists use force against victims they don't know. Unarmed acquaintance rapes are a different matter; evidence of reasonable resistance is often critical. In practical terms, force implies resistance. This is because acquaintance rapists don't use force unless victims resist their advances. In other words, force and resistance are two sides of the same coin; if force is an element, then so is resistance (Bryden 2000, 356).

LO5

Courts today have adopted either of two definitions of "force." Extrinsic force requires some act of force in addition to the effort needed to accomplish penetration. The amount of force required varies according to the circumstances of particular cases. Intrinsic force requires only the amount of physical effort necessary to accomplish penetration.

EXTRINSIC FORCE The Pennsylvania Supreme Court adopted and applied the extrinsic force standard in our next case excerpt in a highly controversial and widely debated in and out of the courts, *Commonwealth v. Berkowitz* (1994).

CASE

In ***Commonwealth v. Berkowitz*** **(1992),** *Robert Berkowitz was convicted of rape, and the intermediate court of appeals affirmed. The Pennsylvania Supreme Court reversed, holding that the evidence didn't support a finding of "forcible compulsion" but did support a finding of the lesser offense of "indecent assault."*

Did he have sexual intercourse by force and without consent?

Commonwealth v. Berkowitz

609 A. 2d 1338 (Penn. Sup. 1992)
641 A. 2d 1161 (Penn. 1994)

HISTORY

Robert Berkowitz (defendant) was charged with and convicted of rape in the Court of Common Pleas, Monroe County, of rape. He was sentenced to one to four years. The intermediate court of appeals (The Pennsylvania Superior Court) affirmed the conviction. The Pennsylvania Supreme Court, in a unanimous decision ruled that the evidence at trial didn't support finding of "forcible compulsion." But—the court found that the evidence did support a finding of the lesser offense of "indecent assault." Indecent assault required proof that Berkowitz engaged in "indecent contact—any touching of the sexual or other intimate parts of another person—without the consent of the other person. [Indecent assault is a misdemeanor. Berkowitz was sentenced to six months to a year, and was granted parole after serving the minimum six months.]

PER CURIAM [BY THE WHOLE COURT]

FACTS

609 A. 2d 1338 (Penn. Sup. 1992)

In the spring of 1988, Robert Berkowitz and the victim were both college sophomores at East Stroudsburg State University, ages 20 and 19 years old, respectively. They had mutual friends and acquaintances. On April 19 of that year, the victim went to Berkowitz's dormitory room. What transpired in that dorm room between Berkowitz and the victim thereafter is the subject of the instant appeal.

During a one-day jury trial held on September 14, 1988, the victim gave the following account during direct examination by the Commonwealth. At roughly 2:00 on the afternoon of April 19, 1988, after attending two morning classes, the victim returned to her dormitory room. There, she drank a martini to "loosen up a little bit" before going to meet her boyfriend, with whom she had argued the night before. Roughly 10 minutes later she walked to her boyfriend's dormitory lounge to meet him. He had not yet arrived.

Having nothing else to do while she waited for her boyfriend, the victim walked up to Berkowitz's room to look for Earl Hassel, Berkowitz's roommate. She knocked on the door several times but received no answer. She therefore wrote a note to Mr. Hassel, which read, "Hi Earl, I'm drunk. That's not why I came to see you. I haven't seen you in a while. I'll talk to you later, [Victim's name]." She did so, although she had not felt any intoxicating effects from the martini, "for a laugh."

After the victim had knocked again, she tried the knob on Berkowitz's door. Finding it open, she walked in. She saw someone lying on the bed with a pillow over his head, whom she thought to be Earl Hassel. After lifting the pillow from his head, she realized it

(continues)

(continued)

was Berkowitz. She asked him which dresser was his roommate's. He told her, and the victim left the note.

Before the victim could leave Berkowitz's room, however, he asked her to stay and "hang out for a while." She complied because she "had time to kill" and because she didn't really know Berkowitz and wanted to give him "a fair chance." Berkowitz asked her to give him a back rub but she declined, explaining that she did not "trust" him. He then asked her to have a seat on his bed. Instead, she found a seat on the floor, and conversed for a while about a mutual friend.

On cross-examination, the victim testified that during this conversation she had explained she was having problems with her boyfriend. No physical contact between the two had, to this point, taken place.

Thereafter, however, Berkowitz moved off the bed and down on the floor, and "kind of pushed [the victim] back with his body. It wasn't a shove, it was just kind of a leaning-type of thing." Next Berkowitz "straddled" and started kissing the victim. The victim responded by saying, "Look, I gotta go. I'm going to meet [my boyfriend]." Then Berkowitz lifted up her shirt and bra and began fondling her. The victim then said "no."

After roughly 30 seconds of kissing and fondling, Berkowitz "undid his pants and he kind of moved his body up a little bit." The victim was still saying "no" but "really couldn't move because Berkowitz was shifting her body so he was over me." Berkowitz then tried to put his penis in her mouth. The victim did not physically resist, but rather continued to verbally protest, saying "No, I gotta go, let me go," in a "scolding" manner.

Ten or 15 more seconds passed before the two rose to their feet. Berkowitz disregarded the victim's continual complaints that she "had to go," and instead walked two feet away to the door and locked it so that no one from the outside could enter. The victim testified that she realized at the time that the lock was not of a type that could lock people inside the room.

Then, in the victim's words, "He put me down on the bed. It was kind of like—he didn't throw me on the bed. It's hard to explain. It was kind of like a push but no…." She did not bounce off the bed. "It wasn't slow like a romantic kind of thing, but it wasn't a fast shove either. It was kind of in the middle."

Once the victim was on the bed, Berkowitz began "straddling" her again while he undid the knot in her sweatpants. He then removed her sweatpants and underwear from one of her legs. The victim did not physically resist in any way while on the bed because Berkowitz was on top of her, and she "couldn't like go anywhere." She did not scream out at anytime because "it was like a dream was happening or something."

Berkowitz then used one of his hands to "guide" his penis into her vagina. At that point, after Berkowitz was inside her, the victim began saying "no, no to him softly in a moaning kind of way because it was just so scary." After about 30 seconds, Berkowitz pulled out his penis and ejaculated onto the victim's stomach.

Immediately thereafter, Berkowitz got off the victim and said, "Wow, I guess we just got carried away." To this the victim retorted, "No, we didn't get carried away, you got carried away." The victim then quickly dressed, grabbed her school books, and raced downstairs to her boyfriend who was by then waiting for her in the lounge. Once there, the victim began crying. Her boyfriend and she went up to his dorm room where, after watching the victim clean off Berkowitz's semen from her stomach, he called the police.

Defense counsel's cross-examination elicited more details regarding the contact between Berkowitz and the victim before the incident in question. The victim testified that roughly two weeks prior to the incident, she had attended a school seminar entitled, "Does 'no' sometimes mean 'yes'?" Among other things, the lecturer at this seminar had discussed the average length and circumference of human penises. After the seminar, the victim and several of her friends had discussed the subject matter of the seminar over a speaker-telephone with Berkowitz and his roommate, Earl Hassel. The victim testified that during that telephone conversation, she had asked Berkowitz the size of his penis. According to the victim, Berkowitz responded by suggesting that the victim "come over and find out." She declined.

When questioned further regarding her communications with Berkowitz prior to the April 19, 1988, incident, the victim testified that on two other occasions, she had stopped by Berkowitz's room while intoxicated. During one of those times, she had laid down on his bed. When asked whether she had asked Berkowitz again at that time what his penis size was, the victim testified that she did not remember.

Berkowitz took the stand in his own defense and offered an account of the incident and the events leading up to it which differed only as to the consent involved. According to Berkowitz, the victim had begun communication with him after the school seminar by asking him of the size of his penis and of whether he would show it to her. Berkowitz had suspected that the victim wanted to pursue a sexual relationship with him because she had stopped by his room twice after the phone call while intoxicated, lying down on his bed with her legs spread and again asking to see his penis. He believed that his suspicions were confirmed when she initiated the April 19, 1988, encounter by stopping by his room (again after drinking) and waking him up.

Berkowitz testified that, on the day in question, he did initiate the first physical contact, but added that the victim warmly responded to his advances by passionately returning his kisses. He conceded that she was continually "whispering no's," but claimed that she did so while "amorously... passionately" moaning. In effect, he took such protests to be thinly veiled acts of encouragement. When asked why he locked the door, he explained that "that's not something you want somebody to just walk in on you doing."

According to Berkowitz, the two then lay down on the bed, the victim helped him take her clothing off, and he entered her. He agreed that the victim continued to say "no" while on the bed, but carefully qualified his agreement, explaining that the statements were "moaned passionately." According to Berkowitz, when he saw a "blank look on her face," he immediately withdrew and asked "is anything wrong, is something the matter, is anything wrong." He ejaculated on her stomach thereafter because he could no longer "control" himself. Berkowitz testified that after this, the victim "saw that it was over and then she made her move. She gets right off the bed... she just swings her legs over and then she puts her clothes back on." Then, in wholly corroborating an aspect of the victim's account, he testified that he remarked, "Well, I guess we got carried away," to which she rebuked, "No, we didn't get carried, you got carried away."

OPINION

641 A. 2d 1161 (Penn. 1994)

CAPPY, J. FOR A UNANIMOUS COURT

The crime of rape is defined as follows:

§ 3121. Rape

A person commits a felony of the first degree when he engages in sexual intercourse with another person not one's spouse:

1. by forcible compulsion;
2. by threat of forcible compulsion that would prevent resistance by a person of reasonable resolution;
3. who is unconscious; or
4. who is so mentally deranged or deficient that such person is incapable of consent.

The victim of a rape need not resist.

The force necessary to support a conviction of rape need only be such as to establish lack of consent and to induce the victim to submit without additional resistance. The degree of force required to constitute rape is relative and depends on the facts and particular circumstance of the case.

In regard to the critical issue of forcible compulsion, the complainant's testimony is devoid of any statement which clearly or adequately describes the use of force or the threat of force against her. In response to defense counsel's question, "Is it possible that [when Appellee lifted your bra and shirt] you took no physical action to discourage him," the complainant replied, "It's possible." When asked, "Is it possible that Berkowitz was not making any physical contact with you aside from attempting to untie the knot in the drawstrings of complainant's sweatpants," she answered, "It's possible." She testified that "He put me down on the bed. It was kind of like—He didn't throw me on the bed. It's hard to explain. It was kind of like a push but not—I can't explain what I'm trying to say."

She concluded that "it wasn't much" in reference to whether she bounced on the bed, and further detailed that their movement to the bed "wasn't slow like a romantic kind of thing, but it wasn't a fast shove either. It was kind of in the middle." She agreed that Appellee's hands were not restraining her in any manner during the actual penetration, and that the weight of his body on top of her was the only force applied.

She testified that at no time did Berkowitz verbally threaten her. The complainant did testify that she sought to leave the room, and said "no"

(continues)

(continued)

throughout the encounter. As to the complainant's desire to leave the room, the record clearly demonstrates that the door could be unlocked easily from the inside, that she was aware of this fact, but that she never attempted to go to the door or unlock it. As to the complainant's testimony that she stated "no" throughout the encounter with Berkowitz, we point out that, while such an allegation of fact would be relevant to the issue of consent, it is not relevant to the issue of force. Where there is a lack of consent, but no showing of either physical force, a threat of physical force, or psychological coercion, the "forcible compulsion" requirement under 18 Pa. C.S. § 3121 is not met.

The degree of physical force, threat of physical force, or psychological coercion required under 18 Pa. C.S. § 3121 must be sufficient to prevent resistance by a person of reasonable resolution, but the "peculiar situation" of the victim and other subjective factors should be considered by the court in determining "resistance," "assent," and "consent."

Reviewed in light of the above described standard, the complainant's testimony simply fails to establish that Berkowitz forcibly compelled her to engage in sexual intercourse as required under 18 Pa. C.S. § 3121. Thus, even if all of the complainant's testimony was believed, the jury, as a matter of law, could not have found Berkowitz guilty of rape. Accordingly, we hold that the Superior Court did not err in reversing Berkowitz's conviction of rape.

Accordingly, the order of the Superior Court reversing the rape conviction is affirmed.

QUESTIONS

1. Explain how the court came to the conclusion that the Pennsylvania rape statute required extrinsic force.
2. List all the facts relevant to deciding whether Robert Berkowitz's actions satisfy the extrinsic force requirement.
3. Assume you're the prosecutor, and argue that Robert Berkowitz did use extrinsic force to achieve sexual penetration.
4. Now, assume you're the Berkowitz's lawyer, and argue that he didn't use extrinsic force to achieve sexual penetration.
5. Was Superior Court "right" to reverse Robert Berkowitz's rape conviction? Explain your answer.
6. Did the complainant share no/little, some, equal, most of the responsibility for the sexual intercourse? The indecent sexual contact? Defend your answers.

LO4 DOES "NO" ALWAYS MEAN "NO"? Ever since *Commonwealth v. Berkowitz* (1994) homed in on the question whether women have *really* consented to sexual intercourse, the case has generated heated debate in law reviews, law school classrooms, criminal justice professionals, courts, juries, legislatures and elected public officials.

The case also generated debate outside three criminal justice system. One editorial, referring to the "all-male Pennsylvania Supreme Court," called the decision "one of the worst setbacks for the sexual assault movement in the last several years." A *St. Louis Post-Dispatch* editorial entitled "When 'No' means nothing," asked, "What is it about the word 'no' they don't understand?" (Cited in Kahan 2010, 741).

The debate extended even further, exploring the connection between law and social norms, namely the social meaning of rape and how to change the culture that fosters it (Kahan 2010, 731). We'll turn to empirical research regarding the debate shortly.

Critics maintain that the *Berkowitz* court may include words that speak the language of sex, but in reality they're only a cover for an antique culture of male domination and female submission that speaks the language of force. As a result, "real rapists" avoid punishment, which puts other women at risk of their attack. Unfortunately, rape victims doubt their own innocence, leading them in some cases to believe they weren't *really* raped; or to blame themselves for what happened. For these and other reasons, many rape victims don't report the event to the police (see Table 10.2).

TABLE 10.2 Rape or Sexual Assault Victimizations against Females Ages 18 to 24 (reported and not reported to police and reasons for not reporting, by post-secondary enrollment status), 1995–2013

	STUDENTS[a]	NONSTUDENTS[b]
Reported[c]	20%	32%[f]
Not reported	80%	67%[f]
Reason for not reporting		
Reported to different official	4%[e]	14%[f]
Personal matter	26%	23%
Not important enough to respondent	12%	5%[f]
Police would not or could not do anything to help	9%	19%[f]
Did not want to get offender in trouble with law	10%	10%
Advised not to report	—[d,e]	1%[e]
Fear of reprisal	20%	20%
Other reason	31%	35%

Note: Detail may not sum to total due to multiple reasons for not reporting. About 0.4% of student and 0.6% of nonstudent victims did not know or did not report whether the victimization was reported to police.

[a]Includes female victims ages 18 to 24 enrolled part time or full time in a post-secondary institution (i.e., college or university, trade school, or vocational school).
[b]Includes female victims ages 18 to 24 not enrolled in a post-secondary institution.
[c]Includes only reports to the police, not to other officials or administrators. The NCVS does not collect information on victim reporting to parties other than law enforcement.
[d]Less than 0.5%.
[e]Interpret with caution; estimate based on 10 or fewer sample cases, or coefficient of variation is greater than 50%.
[f]Nonstudent estimates are significantly different from student estimates at the 95% confidence level.

Source: Bureau of Justice Statistics, National Crime Victimization Survey, 1995–2013.

The low reporting accounts for many reformers strongly support the "No means no" rule, some of them going further to call for a "No *always* means no" bright line rule. *Berkowitz* at least interrupted, and probably was a backward step from the reform statutes.

Defenders, on the other hand, maintain that the traditional definition reflects social reality. They dismiss the critics' complaints as unrealistic and ideology driven political correctness aimed at destroying legitimate gender differences in social roles. When it comes to consent, the reality is that "'No' doesn't *always* mean 'no'." According to writer Gregg Easterbrook, "Maybe half the sex in world history has followed an initial no, or more than one "no." What ends up as consensual sex, however unsatisfying, often begins with the woman saying "no." (Quoted in Kahan 2010, n. 53.) It can often mean "'yes" or "maybe," or, "I'm still making up my mind."

Adopting a broad version of "no mean no" rule, and removing its Siamese twin, the "force" or "threat of force" requirement, has a boomerang effect, say critics. Here's how it works. Harsh punishment and permanent stigma attaches to a rape conviction. Even an arrest or charge can bring major hardship to rape suspects. These brutal realities aren't lost on criminal justice officials who can use their enormous discretion to soften this harshness. In some number of cases, police will refuse to arrest, prosecutors to prosecute, and judges and juries to convict.

cultural cognition how group values influence individuals' perceptions of facts

LO6

THE KAHAN *BERKOWITZ* EXPERIMENT The passionate rape reform debate has produced a large body of empirical research on all elements of the controversy. We'll focus here on Professor Dan Kahan's experimental research testing *cultural cognition theory*. **Cultural cognition** refers to how group values influence individuals' perceptions of facts. One of the Cultural Cognition's many projects is Kahan's study, "Culture, Cognition, and Consent: Who Perceives What, and Why, in Acquaintance Rape." It relies on a slightly edited version of the rich facts in *Berkowitz*, regarding whether the complainant consented to sexual intercourse. Kahan designed a mock-juror experiment that analyzed participants' perceptions of the facts and their judgments about the possible outcomes in the case. The sample consisted of a diverse national sample of 1,500 Americans, 18 years and older, representative of the general population (52 percent female, 74 percent White, and 11 percent Black; average income between $40,000 and $50,000; average education level of "some college.") (Kahan 2010, 765)

Participants read a slightly edited version of the facts in *Berkowitz*, including the accounts of Berkowitz and the complainant who were "described as agreeing that complainant had repeatedly said 'no' before and during sexual intercourse" (765). Then, participants were assigned to one of five groups, according to five definitions of rape:

1. *No definition group*. Members received no definition of rape before they responded to the case facts or outcome.
2. *Common law group*. A man is guilty of rape if he (a) uses force or the threat of force (b) to engage in sexual intercourse with a woman (c) without the woman's consent and (d) knows or can reasonably or be reasonably expected to know that the woman does not consent.
3. *Strict liability group*. A man is guilty of rape if he (a) uses force or the threat of force (b) to engage in sexual intercourse with a woman (c) without the woman's consent. Members were advised that "a mistaken belief that the woman consented is not a defense."
4. *Reform group*. A man is guilty of rape if he (a) uses force or the threat of force (b) to engage in sexual intercourse with a woman (c) without the woman's consent. Members were advised that "a mistaken belief that the woman consented is not a defense." In addition, consent was defined explicitly: "Consent means words or overt actions indicating a freely given agreement to have sexual intercourse." (768)
5. *"No means no" group*. A man is guilty of rape if he (a) engages in sexual intercourse with a woman (b) without the woman's consent. Members were advised that "Sexual intercourse is without the woman's consent if the woman communicates by actions or by words, including the uttering of the word 'no,' that she does not consent to sexual intercourse. If the man knows that the woman has said 'no,' a mistaken belief that the woman has consented is not a defense." (769)

After they read the *Berkowitz* story, and the legal definition (except, of course for group one which received no definition), members were asked to indicate how intensely they agreed or disagreed with the following statements:

- "Despite what she said or might have felt after, "Lucy" (the story name for the complainant in *Berkowitz*) really did consent to sexual intercourse with "Dave" (Berkowitz's story name)."
- "Lucy would have tried to push Dave off of her if she really meant not to consent to sexual intercourse."
- "Dave believed that Lucy consented to sexual intercourse."
- "Given all the circumstances, it would have been reasonable for Dave to believe Lucy consented to the intercourse."

- "By saying "no" several times, Lucy made it clear to Dave that she did not consent to sexual intercourse."
- "It would be unfair to convict Dave of a crime as serious as rape."
- "Dave should be found guilty of rape."

LO6

The results suggest two main conclusions that support the cultural cognition theory that values precede facts in both normative and cognitive ways. First, beliefs about resistance to sexual intercourse are polarized culturally. The more egalitarian a person's view of the world, the more likely they will believe that Dave raped Lucy; the more hierarchical their world view, the more likely they are to say he didn't rape her.

Cultural differences also reflect differences in perceptions of the facts. Hierarchical individuals are more likely to believe that Lucy did consent and that Dave honestly and reasonably believed that she consented. Hierarchical individuals are also more likely to believe that Dave didn't use force against Lucy, or to put her in fear. These cultural disagreements over consent *don't* reflect a conflict between male and female points of view. In fact, the most pro-defendant group is that of hierarchical *women*, particularly older ones.

According to Kahan, in the hierarchs' view of the world, women who want casual sex use token resistance to sex ("no means yes") to disguise their lack of virtue. Strongly hierarchical women are more likely to perceive that "women are saying 'no' while meaning 'yes'"—and to condemn them for it because they have the greatest stake in the law affirming hierarchical norms. Thus, "far from reflecting a dispute among women and men," contesting "the significance of the word 'no' in cases like *Berkowitz* features a conflict primarily *among* women on how the indulgence of the desire for sex outside of the relationships sanctioned by hierarchical norms should affect women's social status" (794).

The second major finding from the study is that the legal definitions of rape had a minimum effect on the participants' judgment that Dave raped Lucy. The two most common reforms in the wave of laws passed in the 1970s and 1980s—eliminating the force and resistance requirements, and the reasonable mistake defense elements of traditional rape had no effect.

> There was no meaningful difference in the outcome judgments of subjects instructed to apply the "strict liability," "reform," or "common law" formulation… and those furnished no definition of rape at all. (795) This result is consistent with the general finding that legal definitions exert less force than do lay prototypes of common crimes. (Smith 1991)

There was a slight increase (about 10 percent) in those in the "no means no" group (a reform not adopted in any state) who believed Dave raped Lucy. Remember, Lucy said "no" repeatedly during the encounter so there was no reason to doubt Dave raped Lucy under the definition. Yet, more than a third of the "no means no" group continued to believe Dave was *not* guilty in the face of all those "no's." (796)

INTRINSIC FORCE Recall that Robert Berkowitz was charged with rape under the extrinsic force rule, but was convicted of the misdemeanor of criminal sexual contact, largely because the victim repeatedly said "no." Now, we look at another case, one that involved a juvenile whose victim also said no several times and was found guilty under a judicially created no means no rule.

CASE

*In **State in the Interest of S.M.I (2012),** Juvenile, S.M.I. (16 years old) appeals from an adjudication of delinquency on a charge that, if committed by an adult, would constitute second-degree sexual assault.*

Did he force her to have sexual intercourse?

STATE in the Interest of S.M.I.

2012 WL 1473326 (N.J. Super. A.D. 2012) Superior Court of New Jersey, Appellate Division.

A.A. RODRÍGUEZ, ASHRAFI AND FASCIALE, JJ.

PER CURIAM.

HISTORY

Juvenile S.M.I. (16 years old) appeals from an adjudication of delinquency on a charge that, if committed by an adult, would constitute second-degree sexual assault, *N.J.S.A.* 2C:14–2c(1). We have reviewed the record and now affirm. The juvenile was originally charged with the first-degree offenses of kidnapping, *N.J.S.A.* 2C:13–1b(1), and aggravated sexual assault, *N.J.S.A.* 2C:14–2a(3). At a trial conducted on four dates in November and December 2010, the State presented testimony from five witnesses including the 13-year-old girl, and the defense presented testimony from six witnesses including the juvenile. Several of the witnesses were teenage acquaintances and relatives of the girl and the juvenile, but there were no eyewitnesses to the incident. The girl's testimony was crucial to prove the circumstances of the sexual activity.

FACTS

The juvenile (age 16) and the girl (age 13) lived on the same street. The girl testified that she first met him on the date of the alleged sexual assault. However, the juvenile and other witnesses testified that the two were previously acquainted, albeit only for a few days or weeks. The girl testified that in the late afternoon of July 18, 2010, the juvenile came to her door when she was home alone. She did not invite him in, but she did not stop him from stepping into the house, and later from following her upstairs to her bedroom. She testified that she told him he must leave because her father would soon arrive home from work and would be displeased with his presence in the house, but the juvenile did not leave.

In the bedroom, according to the girl, the juvenile pressed her for sexual activity, telling her that she was pretty and similar words of flattery. She told him several times and in different ways that she did not want to engage in sexual activity with him and that she was concerned about her father coming home and finding them. He persisted, not accepting her declinations. At one point, she left the bedroom and went downstairs to use a bathroom but then returned to the bedroom because she did not want to leave the juvenile alone in her house.

According to the girl, the juvenile undressed himself and her and engaged in several forms of sexual activity short of intercourse. She did not resist him physically, but she attempted to communicate her discomfort verbally and through passive failure to cooperate with his conduct. She testified that she told him several times that she was too young and did not want to do the things he was doing or suggesting. The juvenile continued to pursue his aims. He lay on top of her, holding her wrists above her head, and eventually he penetrated her in sexual intercourse, using a condom.

After he left, the girl's father came home and saw a mark on her neck, raising his suspicions. The sexual conduct was revealed more directly by the girl herself to her friends. Immediately after the incident, she communicated with friends in person or by means of text messages such that the incident became known within her circle within a matter of days. The parents also obtained information leading them to suspect that their daughter had been involved sexually with the juvenile and possibly another boy. Eight days after the incident, the girl's father and grandmother took her to the police station, where she gave a statement accusing the juvenile of sexually assaulting her.

The witnesses at trial gave testimony that was potentially relevant to the veracity of the girl's accusation. For example, the girl's mother testified that she confronted the juvenile and he admitted he had engaged in sexual intercourse with her daughter. The girl's father testified that he confronted both the juvenile and the other boy and that the other boy admitted romantic conduct but no sexual impropriety while the juvenile denied his accusations.

The several teenage relatives and acquaintances provided testimony about the prior acquaintance of the juvenile and the girl, her relationship with the other boy, and the activities of the teenage group on or near the date of the incident. The other boy testified, and he produced photographs taken of two text messages on his cell phone that the juvenile had sent him after the date of the incident. The text messages demanded that he take responsibility for sexual conduct with the girl but arguably suggested admission of guilt by the juvenile.

The State had no forensic evidence of a sexual assault, apparently because the police only learned about the incident eight days after it occurred, and also because the juvenile had allegedly used a condom, thus making it unlikely that his DNA could be recovered from bedding or clothing.

At the end of the State's case, the judge granted the juvenile's motion to dismiss the first-degree charges of kidnapping and aggravated sexual assault. The judge denied defendant's motion to dismiss a second-degree charge of sexual assault.

In his testimony, the juvenile denied outright that he had engaged in any sexual conduct with the girl and, in fact, denied that he had been to her house. At the end of all testimony, the judge found the juvenile guilty of the second-degree charge. The judge evaluated the testimony in detail, focusing most prominently on the opposing versions of the girl and the juvenile. While finding that the girl was not truthful in all respects as to the relationships she had with the group of teenagers and her conduct near the time of the incident, the judge found that her testimony about the incident itself was credible. The judge understood the elements of sexual assault, and he explained why the testimony was sufficient to prove beyond a reasonable doubt that the juvenile forced and coerced the girl into having sexual intercourse and other sexual conduct.

At a disposition hearing, the judge imposed a term of three years at the Training School for Boys but suspended the term on condition that the juvenile successfully complete two years of probation and complete the Capital Academy Program.

The sexual assault statute provides in relevant part:

> An actor is guilty of sexual assault if he commits an act of sexual penetration with another person under any one of the following circumstances:
>
> (1) The actor uses physical force or coercion, but the victim does not sustain severe personal injury.
>
> [*N.J.S.A.* 2C:14–2c.]

OPINION

To sustain a charge of second-degree sexual assault under this statute, the State must prove the following essential elements:

1. That [the juvenile] committed an act of sexual penetration with another person.
2. That [the juvenile] acted knowingly.
3. That [the juvenile] used physical force or coercion.
4. That the victim did not sustain severe personal injury.

[*Model Jury Charge (Criminal)*, "Sexual Assault (Force/Coercion)" (2005).]

The juvenile argues the State did not prove beyond a reasonable doubt that he engaged in sexual activity through force or coercion. He contends that the evidence was insufficient to refute his reasonable belief that the girl had consented to the sexual activity. He also contends that the judge's decision on the element of force and coercion was against the weight of the evidence.

The weight of the evidence argument only applies to jury trials. In a non-jury trial, the standard is whether there is sufficient credible evidence in the record to support the judge's determination.

We exercise a limited scope of review from a trial judge's findings of fact and the conclusions that flow from those findings. We must give due regard to the trial judge's credibility determinations based upon the opportunity of the judge to see and hear the witnesses. Appellate courts accord particular deference to fact-finding in family cases, and to the conclusions that logically flow from those findings.

(continues)

(continued)

The judge explained, and both sides agree, that the controlling case as to sufficient evidence of physical force or coercion is *State in the Interest of M.T.S.*, 129 *N.J.* 422 (1992). In *M.T.S.*, the Supreme Court equated "physical force" in the sexual offense statutes with an act of sexual contact or penetration and the absence of affirmative and freely given consent by the alleged victim. The Court held that the State was not required to prove physical force "extrinsic to the sexual act." *M.T.S., supra*, 129 *N.J.* at 444. The State satisfies its burden if it proves that the other person did not affirmatively consent to the sexual conduct.

The juvenile emphasizes that the State bears the burden of proving force or coercion beyond a reasonable doubt. He quotes the following passage from *M.T.S.* as particularly relevant to this case and in support of his contention that the State did not meet its burden of proof with the evidence it presented:

> In a case such as this one, in which the State does not allege violence or force extrinsic to the act of penetration, the factfinder must decide whether the defendant's act of penetration was undertaken in circumstances that led the defendant reasonably to believe that the alleged victim had freely given affirmative permission to the specific act of sexual penetration. Such permission can be indicated either through words or through actions that, when viewed in the light of all the surrounding circumstances, would demonstrate to a reasonable person affirmative and freely given authorization for the specific act of sexual penetration.

Here, the juvenile argues that the mixed messages communicated by the girl led him to believe reasonably that she was a willing sexual partner. His reasonable belief arose from her allowing him into her house and bedroom, kissing him, returning to the bedroom after she left to use the bathroom, and staying when she had multiple opportunities to leave or to order him out of her house. The juvenile argues that the girl never attempted to stop his conduct, which together with the ambivalence of her communications and conduct caused him to believe that her only concern was her father coming home and not the sexual activity itself.

We discern no error in the Family Part judge's rejection of the juvenile's factual argument. The evidence permitted the judge to find that the girl said "no" a number of times, but the juvenile would not cease his efforts. The judge concluded that the juvenile's persistence amounted to coercion in the circumstances of this case, and that the State proved that the girl did not voluntarily consent. As the trial judge said: "the bottom line... is that no means no."

Additionally, the evidence permitted a finding of extrinsic physical force in that the juvenile, significantly bigger than the girl, lay on top of her and held her wrists, thus causing her to believe, according to her testimony as credited by the judge, that she was under his control and had no recourse.

We conclude the evidence was sufficient for a finding beyond a reasonable doubt that the sexual penetration occurred through the use of force and coercion as those terms were defined in *M.T.S.*

Affirmed.

QUESTIONS

1. List all the evidence relevant to determining whether M.T.S.'s actions satisfied the intrinsic force requirement.
2. Summarize the court's reasoning for adopting the intrinsic force rule.
3. Taking into account the evidence, decision, and reasoning in *Berkowitz*, which do you believe is the better approach to the force requirement—extrinsic or intrinsic force? Explain your answer.
4. Should legislatures or courts decide which rule to adopt? Explain your answer.

LO7 THE THREAT OF FORCE

threat-of-force requirement requires the prosecution to prove that the victim experienced both subjective and objective fear in rapes involving threats of force

The force requirement doesn't require actual force; threatening to use force is enough. To satisfy the threat-of-force requirement, the prosecution has to prove the victim experienced two kinds of fear:

1. Subjective fear. The victim honestly feared imminent and serious bodily harm.
2. Objective fear. The fear of imminent and serious bodily harm was reasonable under the circumstances.

Brandishing a weapon satisfies the requirement. So do verbal threats—such as threats to kill, seriously injure, or kidnap. But the threat doesn't have to include showing weapons or using specifically threatening words. Courts can consider all of the following in deciding whether the victim's fear was reasonable (Edwards 1996, 260–61):

- The respective ages of the perpetrator and the victim
- The physical sizes of the perpetrator and the victim
- The mental condition of the perpetrator and the victim
- The physical setting of the assault
- Whether the perpetrator had a position of authority, domination, or custodial control over the victim

subjective fear means that the victim honestly feared imminent and serious bodily harm

objective fear means that the fear was reasonable under the circumstances

RAPE *MENS REA*

LO8

Rape is a general-intent crime. Recall from Chapter 4 that one common meaning of "general intent" is that defendants intended to commit the act defined in the crime—in the case of rape, the act is forcible sexual penetration. This, of course, doesn't mean there can't be a different state of mind regarding circumstance elements, specifically nonconsent. These circumstance elements center around mistakes—mistakes about age in the cases involving underage victims or mistakes about the consent to sexual penetration by competent adult victims.

It's impossible to purposely, or even knowingly, make a mistake. That leaves three possibilities: reckless mistakes, negligent mistakes, or no-fault mistakes (strict liability). The states are divided as to which mental element to require.

At one extreme are states that adopt strict liability. An example of strict liability regarding consent is *Commonwealth v. Fischer* (1998). Kurt Fischer and another Lafayette College freshman gave "grossly divergent" stories regarding their encounter in Fischer's dorm room. The victim testified that when they went to his room, Fischer locked the door, pushed her onto the bed, straddled her, held her wrists above her head, and forced his penis into her mouth. She struggled through the whole encounter, warned him that "someone would find out," told him she had to be at a class, and didn't want to have sex with him. Fischer ignored all this, forced his hands inside a hole in her jeans, pushed his penis through the hole, removed it, and ejaculated on her face, hair, and sweater (1112–13).

Fischer testified that when they got to his room, the victim told him it would have to be a "quick one." Fischer admitted he held the victim's arms above her head, straddled her, and put his penis in her mouth, and said, "I know you want my dick in your mouth." When she replied, "no," Fischer said, "no means yes." After Fischer insisted again that she "wanted it," and she replied, "No, I honestly don't," he stopped trying. Then they just lay on the bed fondling and kissing each other (1113).

The jury found Fischer guilty of involuntary deviate sexual intercourse and aggravated indecent assault; he was sentenced to five years in prison. On appeal, Fischer argued that he honestly, but mistakenly, believed the victim consented. The Pennsylvania Superior Court expressed approval of an **honest and reasonable mistake rule**—that is, a negligence mental element—because of changing sexual habits, particularly on college campuses (1114).

honest and reasonable mistake rule a negligence mental element in rape cases in which the defendant argues that he honestly, but mistakenly, believed the victim consented to sex

Nevertheless, the court ruled, it didn't have the authority to replace the state's strict liability rule with a negligence rule on its own. Quoting from a rape case involving two Temple University students, the court said the reasonable and honest mistake of fact rule regarding consent…

> is not now and has never been the law of Pennsylvania. When one individual uses force or the threat of force to have sexual relations with a person not his spouse and without the person's consent he has committed the crime of rape. *If the element of the defendant's belief as to the victim's state of mind is to be established as a defense to the crime of rape then it should be done by the legislature which has the power to define crimes and defenses. We refuse to create such a defense.* (1114) [emphasis in original]

A few courts have adopted a recklessness requirement, requiring that the defendant has to be aware that there's a risk the victim hasn't consented to sexual intercourse. Critics argue that rape is too serious a charge and the penalties are too severe to allow convictions based on a negligent or even a reckless mistake. They demand that defendants have to know their victims didn't consent before they can be subjected to the stigma of such a heinous crime and such severe punishment.

Law professor Susan Estrich (1987), a rape law scholar and herself a rape victim, disagrees:

> If inaccuracy or indifference to consent is "the best that this man can do" because he lacks the capacity to act reasonably, then it might well be unjust and ineffective to punish him for it. More common is the case of the man who could have done better but did not; heard her refusal or saw her tears, but decided to ignore them.
>
> The man who has the inherent capacity to act reasonably but fails to has, through that failure, made a blameworthy choice for which he can justly be punished. The law has long punished unreasonable action which leads to the loss of human life as manslaughter—a lesser crime than murder, but a crime nonetheless. The injury of sexual violation is sufficiently great, the need to provide that additional incentive pressing enough, to justify negligence liability for rape as for killing. (97–98)

LO8

STATUTORY RAPE

statutory rape to have carnal knowledge of a person under the age of consent whether or not accomplished by force

Statutory rape means having sex with minors. The law doesn't require statutory rapists to use force; the victim's immaturity substitutes for force. Furthermore, nonconsent isn't an element, nor is consent a defense, because minors can't legally consent to sex. In other words, statutory rape is a strict liability crime in most states.

A few states, such as California and Alaska, however, do permit the defense of reasonable mistake of age. In those states, the defense applies if a man reasonably believes his victim is over the age of consent. In other words, negligence is the required *mens rea* regarding the circumstance element of age.

LO8

CRIMINAL SEXUAL CONTACT

defense of reasonable mistake of age a defense to statutory rape in California and Alaska if the defendant reasonably believed his victim was at or over the age of consent

Now let's look at the sexual contact crimes. Recall that they're less serious than rape, unless of course there are weapons, punching, and kicking involved. We're referring here to employers, classmates, health-care workers, dates and other people you know who hug, fondle, stroke, kiss or otherwise touch you when you don't want them to. In our next case excerpt, Paul Triestman, a "boss" kissed, put his arm around an employee, and fondled her breast. The court had to decide whether these were criminal sexual contacts.

CASE

*In **State v. Triestman (2010),** Peter Triestman was charged with fourth-degree criminal sexual contact.*

Did he commit criminal sexual contact?

State v. Triestman

3 A. 3d 634 (2010)

CUFF, CL. MINIMAN AND WAUGH, JJ

HISTORY

Peter Triestman was charged with fourth-degree criminal sexual contact. He filed a motion to dismiss indictment. The Superior Court, Law Division, Essex County, denied the motion. Triestman appealed. The Superior Court, Appellate Division, Miniman, J.A.D., held that:

(1) instructions to the grand jury were sufficiently misleading as to warrant dismissal of indictment, but

(2) physical force in addition to sexual contact is not required for conviction for criminal sexual contact.

Reversed and remanded.

FACTS

MINIMAN, J.A.D.

Peter Triestman and N.P. were both employed at a furniture store in Newark, New Jersey. Triestman was N.P.'s boss. According to an incident report filed with the Newark Police Department, Triestman asked N.P. to prepare a bed at the store so he could place pictures of the bed online to sell it. On May 22, 2008, Triestman asked N.P. to examine the bed with him in an upstairs room. Once upstairs, Triestman and N.P. began changing the bedding. While doing so, Triestman told N.P. that the bed would look better with her laying on it naked. While saying this, Triestman moved closer to N.P., placed his left hand on her shoulder, put his right hand on her breast over her clothes, and tried to kiss her. She exclaimed, "Peter!" pulled away from Triestman, and walked away. She gathered her belongings, punched out her time card, and told her mother, who also worked in the store, that she was leaving.

Triestman followed N.P. before she left, apologized for touching her, and told her not to tell anyone. After leaving, N.P. informed her sister and father about what had happened. She and her sister then retrieved their mother from the store. Later that same evening, Triestman called N.P.'s home and informed her and her mother that they were fired. N.P. then filed an incident report.

Triestman was subsequently arrested on June 17, 2008,... [He was charged under *N.J.S.A.* 2C:14–3b] with one count of... fourth-degree criminal sexual contact....

OPINION

The legislative history of *N.J.S.A.* 2C:14–3b begins in October 1971 when the New Jersey Criminal Law Revision Commission issued its final report in which it engaged in a "complete reexamination of [New Jersey criminal] law." The purpose of the Commission's suggested revisions to the New Jersey Criminal Code was "to modernize the criminal law of this State so as to embody principles representing the best in modern statutory law, to eliminate inconsistencies, ambiguities, outmoded and conflicting, overlapping and redundant provisions and to revise and codify the law in a logical, clear and concise manner."

...

The final version of the Code as enacted in 1978 included the crime of criminal sexual contact. [According to] *N.J.S.A.* 2C:14–3b, [liability depends on one or more of the following] four circumstances:

(1) The actor uses physical force or coercion, but the victim does not sustain severe personal injury;

(2) The victim is one whom the actor knew or should have known was physically helpless, or mentally incapacitated;

(continues)

(continued)

(3) The victim is on probation or parole, or is detained in a hospital, prison or other institution or is mentally defective and the actor has supervisory or disciplinary power over the victim by virtue of the actor's legal, professional or occupational status;

(4) *The victim is at least 16 but less than 18 years old and the actor is a member of the victim's household with supervisory or disciplinary power over the victim.* [Emphasis added; this is the provision relevant to this case excerpt.]

The definition of "sexual contact"... stated:

> "Sexual contact" means an intentional touching by the victim or actor, either directly or through clothing, of the victim's or actor's intimate parts for the purpose of degrading or humiliating the victim or sexually arousing or sexually gratifying the actor. Sexual contact of the actor with himself must be in view of the victim whom the actor knows to be present.

The Supreme Court had occasion to consider this legislative history in *M.T.S.*, 129 *N.J.* 422, 609 *A.*2d 1266. There, the issue under *N.J.S.A.* 2C:14–2c(1) was "whether the element of 'physical force' is met simply by an act of non-consensual penetration involving no more force than necessary to accomplish that result." The juvenile "engaged in consensual kissing and heavy petting with a fifteen-year-old girl and thereafter engaged in actual sexual penetration of the girl to which she had not consented." *There was no evidence of any extra force or threats to accomplish penetration.* [Italics added]

The Court [in *M.T.S.*] observed, "an unconstrained reading of the statutory language indicates that both the act of 'sexual penetration' and the use of 'physical force or coercion' are separate and distinct elements of the offense." The trial court concluded that physical force was established by the penetration without consent....

The Court then reasoned that interpreting the crime of sexual assault "to require physical force in addition to that entailed in an act of involuntary or unwanted sexual penetration would be fundamentally inconsistent with the legislative purpose to eliminate any consideration of whether the victim resisted or expressed non-consent." The Court rejected a requirement that "the element of force need be extrinsic to the sexual act" because it "would not only reintroduce a resistance requirement into the sexual assault law, but also would immunize many acts of criminal sexual contact short of penetration."

The Court recognized that "the standard defining the role of force in sexual penetration must prevent the possibility that the establishment of the crime will turn on the alleged victim's state of mind or responsive behavior."

...

The Court [then]... concluded:

> That understanding of the crime of sexual assault fully comports with the public policy sought to be effectuated by Legislature. In redefining rape law as sexual assault, the Legislature adopted the concept of sexual assault as a crime against the bodily integrity of the victim. Although it is possible to imagine a set of rules in which persons must demonstrate affirmatively that sexual contact is unwanted or not permitted, such a regime would be inconsistent with modern principles of personal autonomy. The Legislature recast the law of rape as sexual assault to bring that area of law in line with the expectation of privacy and bodily control that long has characterized most of our private and public law. In interpreting "physical force" to include any touching that occurs without permission we seek to respect that goal.

The Court determined that any other interpretation of the law "would directly undermine the goals sought to be achieved by its reform."... Triestman and the ACDL-NJ... urge that the State must prove Triestman used some physical force beyond the mere sexual contact.

We conclude that the judge did not abuse his discretion in denying Triestman's motion to dismiss the indictment based on his entirely correct interpretation and application of *M.T.S.* Indeed, *M.T.S.* is controlling here. The Supreme Court specifically stated that sexual contact is criminal when "physical force" demonstrates that it is unauthorized and offensive, and any unauthorized sexual contact is a crime under the law of criminal sexual contact.

Contrary to Triestman's argument here, the Court rejected the concept that "physical force" in addition to the sexual contact is required for sexual contact to be criminal. Perhaps most salient is the Supreme Court's reasoning that an interpretation of the statute requiring "physical force" extrinsic from and independently additional to the sexual act would "immunize many acts of criminal sexual contact short of penetration," and that "[t]he characteristics that make a sexual contact unlawful are the same as those that make a sexual penetration unlawful."

Reversed and remanded for further proceedings consistent with this opinion.

BODILY INJURY AND THREATS OF BODILY INJURY CRIMES

LO9

Assault and battery, although combined in many modern statutes, are two separate crimes. A **battery** is an unwanted and unjustified offensive touching. Body contact is central to the crime of battery. An **assault** is either an attempted or a threatened battery, depending on how the statute defines it. The essential difference between assault and battery is that assault requires no physical contact; an assault is complete before the offender touches the victim. (Stalking involves intentionally scaring another person by following, tormenting, or harassing him or her, see p. 415).

battery unwanted and unjustified offensive touching

assault an attempt to commit battery or intentionally putting another in fear

In this section, we'll look at the bodily injury crime of battery and the threats of bodily injury crimes of assault and stalking.

Battery

The battery *actus reus* is unlawful touching, but not every offensive physical contact is unlawful. Spanking children is offensive, at least to the children, but it's not battery. Why? Because the law recognizes it as the lawful act of disciplining children. Unlawful touching includes a broad spectrum of acts but usually means any unjustified touching without consent. Some courts have even included spitting in the face of someone you want to insult (*State v. Humphries* 1978).

Statutes don't always spell out the battery *mens rea*. At common law, battery was an intentionally inflicted injury. Modern courts and statutes extend battery *mens rea* to reckless and negligent contacts. The MPC (ALI 1953, no. 11) defines "battery *mens rea*" as "purposely, recklessly, or negligently causing bodily injury," or "negligently causing bodily injury... with a deadly weapon."

Some state statutes call this expanded offense by a different name. Louisiana (Louisiana Statutes Annotated 1974, 17-A, 14.39), for example, provides that "inflicting any injury upon the person of another by criminal negligence" is "negligent injuring." (See the Elements of Battery Box.)

Battery requires *some* injury. Batteries that cause minor physical injury or emotional injury are misdemeanors in most states. Batteries that cause serious bodily injury are felonies. Some code provisions are directed at injuries caused by special circumstances.

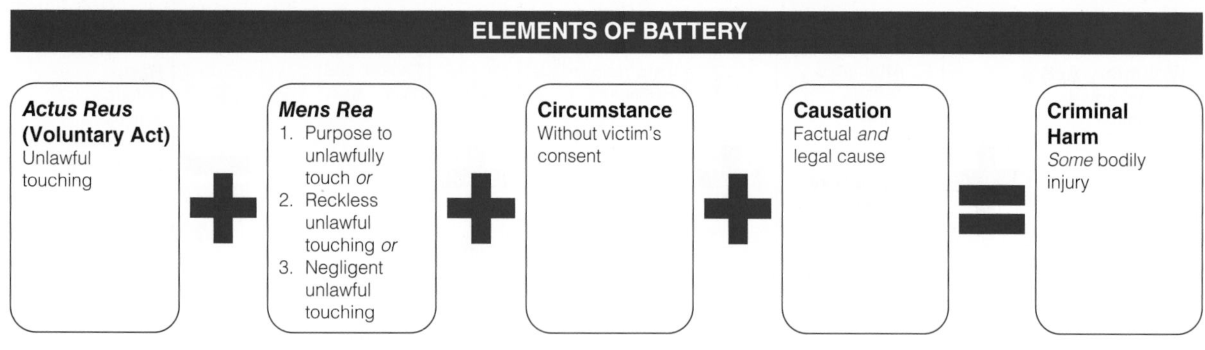

For example, injuries caused by pit bulls prompted the Minnesota legislature (Minnesota Statutes Annotated 1989, § 609.26) to enact the following provision:

> Section 609.26. A person who causes great or substantial bodily harm to another by negligently or intentionally permitting any dog to run uncontrolled off the owner's premises, or negligently failing to keep it properly confined is guilty of a petty misdemeanor....
>
> Subd. 3. If proven by a preponderance of the evidence, it shall be an affirmative defense to liability under this section that the victim provoked the dog to cause the victim's bodily harm.

Injuries and deaths resulting from drug abuse led the same legislature to enact this provision:

> 609.228 Whoever proximately causes great bodily harm by, directly or indirectly, unlawfully selling, giving away, bartering, delivering, exchanging, distributing, or administering a controlled substance... may be sentenced to imprisonment for not more than ten years or to payment of a fine of not more than $20,000, or both.

The MPC grades bodily harm offenses as follows:

> § 211.1 2.
>
> Bodily injury is a felony when such injury is inflicted purposely or knowingly with a deadly weapon; or
>
> serious bodily injury is inflicted purposely, or knowingly or recklessly under circumstances manifesting extreme indifference to the value of human life.
>
> Except as provided in paragraph (2), bodily injury is a misdemeanor, unless it was caused in a fight or scuffle entered into by mutual consent, in which case it is a petty misdemeanor.

attempted battery assault having the specific intent to commit battery and taking substantial steps toward carrying it out without actually completing the battery

threatened battery assault intentional scaring requiring only that actors intend to frighten their victims, thus expanding assault beyond attempted battery

Assault

Assaults are either attempted batteries or threatened batteries, depending on the state. (Notice both kinds are complete crimes without touching the victim.) **Attempted battery assault** consists of having the specific intent to commit a battery and taking substantial steps toward carrying it out without actually completing the attempt. **Threatened battery assault**, sometimes called the crime of "intentional scaring," requires only that actors intend to frighten their victims, thus expanding assault beyond attempted battery. Threatened battery doesn't require actually having the intent to injure their victims physically; the intent to frighten victims into believing the actor will hurt them is enough. (See the Elements of Assault Box.)

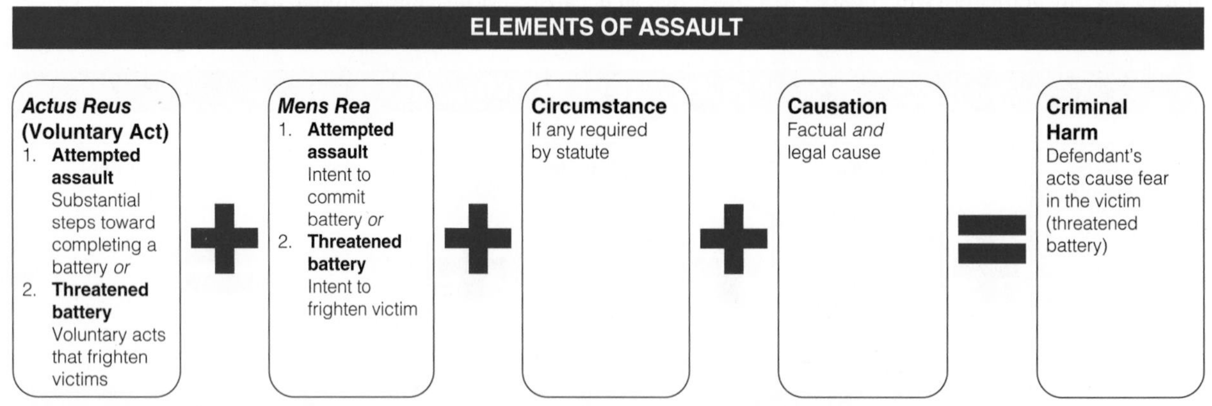

Victims' awareness is critical to proving threatened battery assault. Specifically, victims' fear of an immediate battery has to be reasonable. Words alone aren't assaults; threatening gestures have to accompany them. But this requirement isn't always fair. For example, what if an assailant approaches from behind a victim, saying, "Don't move, or I'll shoot!" These words obviously are reasonable grounds to fear imminent injury, but they aren't assault because they are, after all, only words.

Conditional threats, threats based upon the existence of specified conditions that don't yet exist, aren't enough either because they're not immediate. The conditional threat "I'd punch you out if you weren't a kid" isn't immediate because it depends on the victim's age. In a few jurisdictions, a present ability to carry out the threat has to exist. In most, however, even a person who approaches a victim with a gun she knows is unloaded, points the gun at the victim, and pulls the trigger (intending only to frighten her victim) has committed threatened battery (Encyclopedia of Crime and Justice 1983, 1:89).

Conditional threats threats that are not immediate but based upon the existence of certain conditions that don't presently exist

Attempted and threatened battery assaults are aimed at separate harms. Attempted battery assault deals with an incomplete physical injury. Threatened battery assault is directed at a present psychological or emotional harm—namely, putting a victim in fear. So in attempted battery assault, a victim's awareness doesn't matter; in threatened battery assault, it's indispensable.

The MPC deals with threatened and attempted battery assaults as follows:

> § 211.1 Simple Assault
>
> A person is guilty of assault if he:attempts to cause... bodily injury to another; or
>
> attempts by physical menace to put another in fear of imminent serious bodily harm.
>
> Simple assault is a misdemeanor unless committed in a fight or scuffle entered into by mutual consent, in which case the assault is a petty misdemeanor (ALI 1985).

Historically, all assaults were misdemeanors. However, modern statutes have created several aggravated or felonious assaults. Most common are assaults with the intent to commit violent felonies (murder, rape, and robbery, for example), assaults with deadly weapons (such as guns and knives), and assaults on police officers.

The MPC includes a comprehensive assault and battery statute that integrates, rationalizes, and grades assault and battery. It takes into account *actus reus*, *mens rea*, circumstance elements, and intended harm. Note the careful attention paid to these elements:

> § 211.2
>
> A person is guilty of aggravated assault if he:
>
> a. attempts to cause serious bodily injury to another, or causes such injury purposely, knowingly or recklessly under circumstances manifesting extreme indifference to the value of human life; or
>
> b. attempts to cause or purposely or knowingly causes bodily injury to another with a deadly weapon.

Aggravated assault under paragraph (a) is a felony of the second degree; aggravated assault under paragraph (b) is a felony of the third degree.

> § 211.3
>
> A person commits a misdemeanor if he recklessly engages in conduct which places or may place another person in danger of death or serious bodily injury. Recklessness and danger shall be presumed where a person knowingly points a firearm at or in the direction of another, whether or not the actor believed the firearm to be loaded. (ALI 1985)

LO10 Domestic Violence Crimes

Since the early 1970s, the criminal law has transformed violence in the family from a private concern to a criminal justice problem. Violence in intimate relationships is extensive and isn't limited to one socioeconomic group, one society, or one period of time. Every type and form of family and intimate relationship has the potential of being violent (Gelles 2002, 671).

Numerous case excerpts in earlier chapters show how pervasive domestic violence is in the cases in this book: Chapter 4 (*mens rea* of purposely, knowingly, recklessly, and negligently); Chapter 5 (justifications, domestic violence, and self-defense; domestic violence and consent); Chapter 6 (excuse of post-traumatic stress syndrome); Chapter 7 (accomplice to murder, mother and son; vicarious liability of parents for their children's crimes); Chapter 8 (attempted murder, husband and wife); and Chapter 9 (voluntary manslaughter, husband and wife). We'll see it again in Chapter 11 (burglary and identity theft).

The Ohio Domestic Violence statute (Figure 10.2) is an example of how the law of assault and battery affects the definition and application of domestic violence. Study the provisions of the Ohio statute before you read the case excerpt following it.

Figure 10.2

OHIO DOMESTIC VIOLENCE ACT

2919.25 Domestic Violence.

A. No person shall knowingly cause or attempt to cause physical harm to a family or household member.
B. No person shall recklessly cause serious physical harm to a family or household member.
C. No person, by threat of force, shall knowingly cause a family or household member to believe that the offender will cause imminent physical harm to the family or household member.
D. (1) Whoever violates this section is guilty of domestic violence, and the court shall sentence the offender as provided in divisions (D)(2) to (6) of this section.
    (2) A violation of division (C) of this section is a misdemeanor of the fourth degree, and a violation of division (A) or (B) of this section is a misdemeanor of the first degree (up to 6 months in jail and/or up to $1,000 fine).
    (3) If the offender previously has pleaded guilty to or been convicted of domestic violence, or any offense of violence if the victim of the offense was a family or household member at the time of the commission of the offense, a violation of division (A) or (B) of this section is a felony of the fourth degree (6–18 months incarceration and/or a fine up to $5,000), and a violation of division (C) of this section is a misdemeanor of the second degree.
    (4) If the offender previously has pleaded guilty to or been convicted of two or more offenses of domestic violence, or any offense of violence if the victim of the offense was a family or household member at the time of the commission of the offense, a violation of division (A) or (B) of this section is a felony of the third degree (1–5 years in prison and/or a fine up to $10,000), and a violation of division (C) of this section is a misdemeanor of the first degree.

[(E) is irrelevant for our discussion.]

F. As used in this section and sections 2919.251 and 2919.26 of the Revised Code:
    (1) "Family or household member" means any of the following:
    (a) Any of the following who is residing or has resided with the offender:
        i. A spouse, a person living as a spouse, or a former spouse of the offender;
        ii. A parent or a child of the offender, or another person related by consanguinity or affinity to the offender;
        iii. A parent or a child of a spouse, person living as a spouse, or former spouse of the offender, or another person related by consanguinity or affinity to a spouse, person living as a spouse, or former spouse of the offender.
    (b) The natural parent of any child of whom the offender is the other natural parent or is the putative other natural parent.
    (2) "Person living as a spouse" means a person who is living or has lived with the offender in a common law marital relationship, who otherwise is cohabiting with the offender, or who otherwise has cohabited with the offender within five years prior to the date of the alleged commission of the act in question.

Effective Date: 11-09-2003; 2008 HB280 04-07-2009

FELONY PUNISHMENTS

DEGREE	PRISON TIME	MAXIMUM FINE
1st	3–10 years	$20,000
2nd	2–8 years	$15,000
3rd	1–5 years	$10,000
4th	6–18 months	$5,000
5th	6–12 months	$2,500

MISDEMEANOR PUNISHMENTS

DEGREE	MAXIMUM JAIL TIME	MAXIMUM FINE
1st	6 months	$1,000
2nd	90 days	$750
3rd	60 days	$500
4th	30 days	$250
5th	No jail	$150

Source: Reynard 2008.

CASE

*In **Hamilton v. Cameron (1997),** our next case excerpt, the Ohio Court of Appeals overturned a trial court's guilty verdict because the state failed to prove the elements of domestic violence.*

Was he guilty of domestic violence?

Hamilton v. Cameron

700 N.E. 2d 336 (Ohio App. 3d 1997)

HISTORY

Bobby J. Cameron (the defendant) was found guilty in the Municipal Court, Hamilton County, of committing domestic violence. The Municipal Court judge sentenced Cameron for a violation of "R.C. 2919.25." Cameron was fined $50 plus court costs, and Cameron's shotguns were confiscated. The defendant appealed. The Court of Appeals, Walsh, J., held that the defendant did not commit domestic violence by telling his wife "I'd probably have to blow your head off to get you to shut up," and reversed the Municipal Judge's decision.

WALSH, J.

Cameron and his wife, Darlene Cameron ("Darlene"), had an argument on February 22, 1996. Darlene wanted to discuss matters involving their 12-year-old son. Darlene testified that Cameron did not want to discuss the matters at the time and that she continued to "push the issue." During the argument, Cameron claims that he said, "I'd probably have to blow your head off to get you to shut up."

Darlene testified, "He was telling me to shut up. He said something about blowing my head off that would necessitate, be necessary in order for that to occur, to get me to shut up." Deputy Michael Jacobs testified that Darlene told him that Cameron said that he was going to blow her head off.

After the argument had finished, Darlene went into another room of the house and called her mother because she was "still upset and angry." Darlene told

(continues)

(continued)

her mother about the argument with Cameron. After the call, Darlene's mother called Darlene's sister, and then Darlene's sister called the police and reported that Cameron had threatened to shoot Darlene.

Officers arrived at Cameron's home approximately 45 minutes after the argument and found no disturbance at the home. The officers found Cameron in the living room working on a computer with their 12-year-old son, and Darlene in the back bedroom watching their 6-year-old son play Nintendo. The officers noticed a shotgun on a gun rack in the home and asked if Cameron had any more weapons. Cameron told the officers that there was another shotgun in the closet. Both of the shotguns were loaded.

A complaint was filed against Cameron, which was signed by Darlene. The complaint states that Cameron violated R.C. 2919.25(A) [or] (B) by threatening "to shoot his wife, Darlene, with a shotgun. Two shotguns were loaded and in reach of the couple's children." On the back of the complaint was a written statement that reads: "Mr. Cameron did threaten to shoot his wife, Darlene, with a shotgun. Two shotguns were loaded and available and in reach of couple's children." During Cameron's trial, Darlene testified as to why she signed the complaint against Cameron.

Q. Did you then subsequently come down [to the police station] and sign a complaint?
A. After the fact, [Cameron] and I [were] talking together, we were told someone had to go. There was I guess [a] new law because I had read it in the journal. But like, if they are called on a domestic violence call, someone gets arrested. We were told that someone had to go and I heard my husband say in the living room, "No, I don't want to sign a complaint against my wife." So, I know one officer came in and asked [Officer] Jacobs will she sign a complaint, and he said yes. I said nothing.
Q. And you subsequently ended up signing it?
A. I did, but I didn't know I had the choice between doing it and not doing it.
Q. Did your complaint say that he threatened to shoot you with a loaded shotgun on February 22, 1996, at 9:30 P.M.?
A. Yes it does.
Q. That is your signature on the bottom of that correct?
A. That is my signature.
Q. You read that both the front and back where you signed that complaint twice with the same allegations?
A. Actually, I didn't read it. It was prepared. I believe that was the desk sergeant at the police station next door. My children and I waited in the lobby for over an hour and a half. We were very tired, very thirsty. Very upset, everyone. The kids, because of their tiredness. They were very testy. And when I [was] finally call[ed] in to sign it, I can recall the person who presented it to me saying that he just wrote down what was in the report. I just signed it. I just wanted to go home. I knew [what] I was there for and I just signed it. I didn't read it.

Darlene also testified that she signed a restraining order against Cameron because "I was just thinking separation, distance at my control. If that's what it took, then I wanted time to think. I just wanted time." Darlene testified that at the time she was not in fear of Cameron and that he never made a movement toward the shotgun on the gun rack.

Darlene did not testify that she believed that Cameron intended to carry out the threat of shooting her, or that she believed that she was in imminent physical harm. No evidence was presented of prior acts by Cameron showing that he had harmed or had threatened to harm Darlene before the incident. Cameron claims that he did not make the statement intending to threaten Darlene.

OPINION

Cameron presents one assignment of error: "The trial court erred to the prejudice of Cameron in finding Cameron guilty of domestic violence when an essential element of the crime is lacking."

The judgment entry states that Cameron violated "R.C. 2919.25." R.C. 2919.25 reads as follows:

> No person shall knowingly cause or attempt to cause physical harm to a family or household member.
>
> No person shall recklessly cause serious physical harm to a family or household member.
>
> No person, by threat of force, shall knowingly cause a family or household member to believe that the offender will cause imminent physical harm to the family or household member.

The elements of the crime of domestic violence (R.C. 2919.25[A]) are that a charged defendant must have "knowingly caused, or attempted to cause, physical harm to a family or household member." Physical harm is defined as "any injury, illness, or other physiological impairment, regardless of its gravity or duration" R.C. 2901.01(C). After reviewing the record, we cannot find any evidence that Cameron caused physical harm to Darlene, or even an allegation by Darlene that she had been physically harmed.

A violation of R.C. 2919.25(A) can also be demonstrated by a showing that Cameron attempted to commit physical harm. The evidence in the record shows that the only act Cameron committed was the statement "I'd probably have to blow your head off to get you to shut up." No evidence was presented to show that Cameron knowingly attempted to carry out the threat. Accordingly, we hold that the trial court erred in finding Cameron had committed domestic violence by violating R.C. 2919.25(A) or (B). R.C. 2919.25(B) substitutes the culpable mental state of "recklessly" for "intentionally" as described in paragraph (A). The analysis of the harm element is the same.

Although the complaint does not state that Cameron had violated R.C. 2919.25(C), the language of the complaint does state one of the elements of R.C. 2919.25(C) by stating that Cameron "threatened to shoot his wife." However, in order to show that a person violated R.C. 2919.25(C), it must be shown by the prosecution that "the victim believed the offender would cause her imminent physical harm at the time the incident took place." The state of mind of the victim is an essential element of this crime. While it is true that victims may change their testimony to protect a spouse, there must be some evidence either that a victim stated, or that from other evidence it could be inferred, that the victim thought that the accused would cause imminent physical harm.

Under the facts of this case, we find no violation of R.C. 2919.25(C). The record shows that Darlene did not call the police and that she remained in the house. Further, when the police arrived, Darlene was watching the six-year-old play Nintendo, and the twelve-year-old was with Cameron. The only evidence presented is that Cameron uttered a statement which could at best be described as a conditional threat, and that the means to carry out the threat were available to Cameron. No evidence was presented that Cameron ever made a motion toward a shotgun, or that he took any other action or made any other statement in furtherance of the threat which would cause the victim to believe she would suffer imminent physical harm. The victim in fact stated that she did not believe the threat.

Further, R.C. 2919.25(C) is not a lesser offense of R.C. 2919.25(A) or (B) because R.C. 2919.25(A) or (B) can be violated without the victim believing that the offender "will cause imminent physical harm." Because R.C. 2919.25(C) is not a lesser offense of R.C. 2919.25(A) or (B), the complaint against Cameron cannot be amended to show a violation of R.C. 2919.25(C) because it would change the identity of the crime, and would be a violation of Crim.R. 7(D). Id. at 628, 656 N.E. 2d at 373–374. The court's order is hereby vacated.

Accordingly, the judgment of the trial court is reversed. All fines paid and/or property confiscated is to be returned to Cameron. Judgment is entered for Cameron.

Judgment reversed.

DISSENT

POWELL, J.

I must respectfully dissent. The record in this case shows simply that the defendant threatened to blow his wife's head off to get her to shut up; that the threat worked and the victim "shut up"; that the victim called her family, who in turn called the police; that the police arrived at the victim's home forty-five minutes later and found the victim in the bedroom with her child, still "visibly shaken"; that the officers found loaded firearms in the room with the defendant; that defendant acknowledged making the statement; and that the victim signed the complaint and the restraining order so she would have time to think.

Applying the standard advanced by the Ohio Supreme Court, I feel that there is ample evidence upon which the trial court could rely to find the essential elements of the crime proven beyond a reasonable doubt. The trial court judge is the fact finder, not this court. The trial judge clearly did not believe the victim's testimony that would protect her spouse, but rather chose to believe the disinterested police officer's testimony as to the victim's state when they found her still "visibly shaken" forty-five minutes later. This evidence is sufficient for the fact finder to infer that the victim thought that the accused would cause her imminent physical harm.

(continues)

(continued)

QUESTIONS

1. State the elements of the offense of domestic violence that Bobby J. Cameron was convicted of.
2. List the facts relevant to deciding whether Cameron is guilty of domestic violence.
3. Summarize the arguments of the majority opinion reversing the guilty verdict.
4. Summarize the dissent's argument in favor of upholding the trial court's judgment.
5. Which opinion do you think is "right"? Defend your answer.

YOU *DECIDE*

Is criminal law the best response to promote ethical domestic violence public policy?

On the night of June 23, 1993, John Wayne Bobbitt arrived at the couple's Manassas, Virginia, apartment highly intoxicated after a night of partying and, according to testimony by Lorena Bobbitt in a 1994 court hearing, raped his wife. (John was tried and acquitted for this alleged spousal rape in 1994; he was prosecuted by the same district attorney who prosecuted Lorena for allegedly attacking John.)

Afterward, Lorena Bobbitt got out of bed and went to the kitchen for a drink of water. According to an article in the National Women's Studies Association Journal, in the kitchen she noticed a carving knife on the counter and "memories of past domestic abuses raced through her head." Grabbing the knife, Lorena Bobbitt entered the bedroom where John was asleep, and she proceeded to cut off more than half of his penis.

After assaulting her husband, Lorena left the apartment with the severed penis. After driving a short while, she rolled down the car window and threw the penis into a field. Realizing the severity of the incident, she stopped and called 911. After an exhaustive search, the penis was located, packed in ice, and brought to the hospital where John was located. The two-and-a-half-inch penis was reattached by Dr. David Berman during a nine-and-a-half-hour operation.

Lorena was taken into custody. During the trial, the couple revealed details of their volatile relationship and the events leading up to the assault. Lorena stated that John sexually, physically, and emotionally abused her during their marriage. She also stated that John flaunted his infidelities and forced her to have an abortion. Several witnesses provided testimony supporting Lorena's claims. Lorena's defense attorneys maintained that John's constant abuse caused Lorena to eventually "snap" as she was suffering from clinical depression and a possible bout of post-traumatic stress disorder due to the abuse.

John denied the allegations of abuse. However, when he was cross-examined, his statements often conflicted with known facts, severely weakening the prosecution's case. After seven hours of deliberation, the jury found Lorena "not guilty" due to insanity causing an irresistible impulse to sexually wound her husband. As a result, she could not be held liable for her actions. Under state law, the judge ordered Lorena to undergo a 45-day evaluation period at a mental hospital, after which she would be released.

Instructions

Watch "Lorena Bobbitt, 15 Years Later," http://www.cbsnews.com/news/lorena-bobbitt-15-years-later/ and read the selections concerning the response to domestic violence that best promotes the best ethical public policy.

Based on the video and readings, write an essay that (a) lists and briefly describes the criminal and noncriminal responses described and discussed on the video and in the articles and (b) takes a position on which one most effectively promotes the best ethical public policy.

Source: "Lorena Bobbitt, 15 Years Later," *CBS News*, 2008.

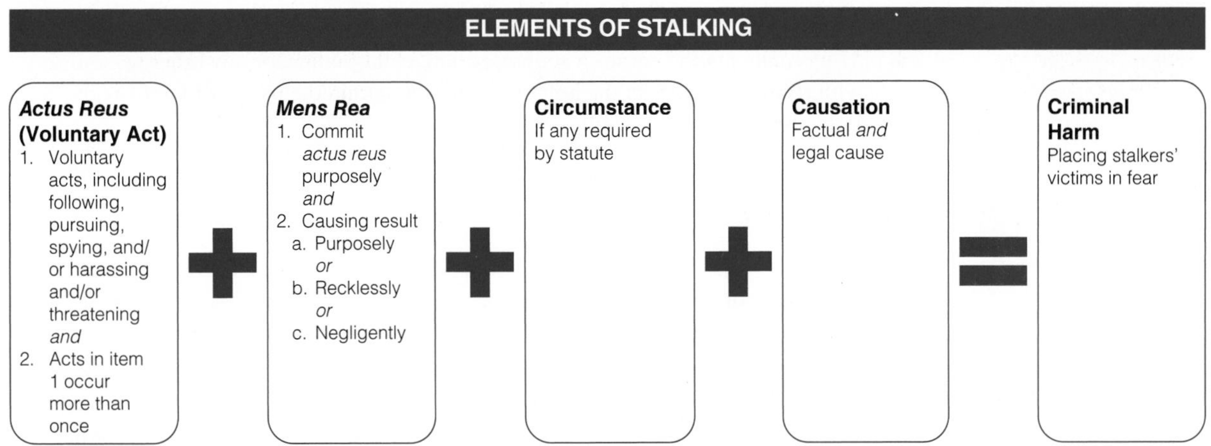

Stalking

LO11

stalking intentionally scaring another person by following, tormenting, or harassing

Stalking is an ancient practice but it's a modern crime that involves intentionally scaring another person by following, tormenting, or harassing him or her. Statutes criminalizing stalking "intended to fill gaps in the law by criminalizing conduct that fell short of assault or battery… by insuring that victims did not have to be injured or threatened with death before stopping a stalker's harassment" (LaFave 2010).

Statutes making stalking a crime began in California, after an obsessed fan murdered actress Rebecca Schaeffer in her Los Angeles apartment, after he stalked her for two years. Within a five-week period, stalkers murdered four other women they stalked in Orange County—*after* they got restraining orders against them! (Bradfield 1998, 243–44). California enacted its path-breaking antistalking statute in 1990.

Other states quickly followed California's example; today, every state and the U.S. government have stalking statutes. The laws reflect widespread concern over the "stalking phenomenon" (LaFave 2003a, 828–29). Although many victims are celebrities like Rebecca Schaeffer, the vast majority are "ordinary" people, most of them women. Nearly 1.5 million people are stalked every year. Seventy-five to eighty percent involve men stalking women. Stalking has major negative effects on its victim, including depression, substance abuse, phobias, anxiety, obsessive-compulsive behaviors, and dissociative disorders (829). We'll look more closely at antistalking statutes, stalking *actus reus* and *mens rea*, the bad result in stalking, and cyberstalking.

ANTISTALKING STATUTES

Antistalking statutes vary enormously from state to state and the U.S. statute. Let's begin with the National Institute of Justice Research Report, *Domestic Violence, Stalking, and Anti-Stalking Legislation* (1996). Appendix B includes a model stalking law for the states. Many states have adopted parts of it:

> Section 1
>
> For purposes of this code:
>
> 1. "*Course of conduct*" means repeatedly maintaining a visual or physical proximity to a person or repeatedly conveying verbal or written threats or threats implied by conduct or a combination thereof directed at or toward a person;

2. "*Repeatedly*" means on two or more occasions; and
3. "*Immediate family*" means a spouse, parent, child, sibling, or any other person who regularly resides in the household or who within the past six months regularly resided in the household.

Section 2

Any person who

1. Purposely engages in a course of conduct directed at a specific person that would cause a reasonable person to fear bodily injury to himself or herself or a member of his or her immediate family or to fear the death of himself or herself or a member of his or her immediate family; and
2. Has knowledge or should have knowledge that the specific person will be placed in reasonable fear of bodily injury to himself or herself or a member of his or her immediate family or to fear the death of himself or herself or his or her immediate family; and
3. Whose acts induce fear in the specific person of bodily injury to himself or herself or a member of his or her immediate family or induce fear in the specific individual of the death of himself or herself or a member of his or her immediate family; is guilty of stalking. (National Institute of Justice)

STALKING *ACTUS REUS*

Despite great diversity from state to state, the stalking statutes all share some common requirements when it comes to the criminal act of stalking. First, as in the model code, all 50 states require that the act happen more than once (LaFave 2003a, 831). Some codes use the word "repeatedly"; others, as in the model code, say there has to be a "course of conduct."

As to the kind of conduct that has to be repeated, all states require some variation of the model code's "maintaining a visual or physical proximity." These acts include following, pursuing, spying, and/or harassing. About half the states require some kind of threat, including the model code's "verbal or written threats or threats implied by conduct," "threat," "terroristic threat," or "credible threat" (LaFave 2003a, 832).

Other statutes list very specific acts, including one or more of the following: interfering with the victim; approaching or confronting the victim; appearing at the victim's job or home; placing objects on the victim's property; causing damage to the victim's pet; calling the victim on the phone, or sending letters or e-mail to the victim (832).

STALKING *MENS REA*

Stalking is a result crime. All statutes require a specific intent to commit the acts discussed in the *actus reus* section. They also require some mental attitude causing the bad result, but the exact mental attitude varies considerably among the states (836).

Slightly more than half the states require some level of subjective fault; recall that "subjective fault" refers to purpose, knowledge, or recklessness. Most of these states require that the actor's purpose was to cause the bad result. A few of these subjective fault states require either that stalkers know their acts will cause the bad result or that they act recklessly; that is, they know their acts create a substantial and unjustifiable risk of causing the bad result (837).

About one-third of the states require only objective fault—namely, negligence. In other words, the requirement is objective reasonableness: actors don't know their acts are creating a substantial and unjustifiable risk of causing the bad result, but they should know. The remaining states require no mental attitude; they provide for strict liability. The only requirement is a voluntary act (837).

STALKING BAD RESULT

The bad result in stalking is placing stalkers' victims in fear. States take four different approaches to the fear caused. Most states adopt a subjective and objective fear test. The model code is a good example. The defendant's acts "induce fear in the specific person"; this is subjective fear. It also requires objective fear; that is, the defendant's acts "would cause a reasonable person to fear." The second is the subjective fear only test: the victim was actually afraid. The third is the objective fear only test; a reasonable person would be afraid. The fourth is the intent to instill fear test. Here, the actor's intent to instill fear is enough, whether the acts actually caused fear or would have caused fear in a reasonable person (LaFave 2003a, 835–36).

CYBERSTALKING

The Internet is a "fertile ground for stalking" (Merschman 2001, 275). This "dark side of the Web" provides cheap and powerful tools for instilling fear in their victims. Email was the primary tool at the turn of the century. (See case excerpt, *State v. Hoying* 2005.) However, after 2000, texting and social networking sites rapidly took over; the explosive growth of cell phones, tablets, and Facebook provided the opportunity for **cyberstalking**, "the use of the Internet, and other electronic communications devices to stalk another person through threatening behavior" (Mishler 2000, 117), or to harass, humiliate, embarrass, or torment using digital technology. In 1999, the Los Angeles and Manhattan District Attorneys reported that 20 percent of its stalking victims were cyberstalked (Attorney General 1999).

cyberstalking the use of the Internet, email, or other electronic communication devices to stalk another person through threatening behavior

Cyberstalking reaches victims in their homes, where they feel safest; what's worse, stalkers can stalk from the comfort of their homes. "Make no mistake: this kind of stalking can be as frightening and as real as being followed and watched in your neighborhood or in your home" (Mishler 2000, 117).

CASE

In ***State v. Hoying* (2005),** *Ted Hoying insisted his endless e-mails didn't cause his coworker Kelly Criswell either physical or mental harm. The court applied the elements of stalking to Hoying's e-mail cyberstalking setting.*

Did he cyberstalk her?

State v. Hoying

WL 678989 (Ohio App. 2005)

HISTORY

Ted Hoying, the defendant, was convicted by a jury in the Court of Common Pleas, of menacing by stalking and intimidation of a victim. He was sentenced to a total of six and one-half years in prison. The defendant appealed. The Ohio Court of Appeals affirmed.

BROGAN, J.

(continues)

(continued)

FACTS

Ted Hoying met the victim, Kelly Criswell, when they both worked at a local restaurant. In June 2002, Hoying asked Criswell for a date and became quite angry when she declined. When Hoying persisted in contacting Ms. Criswell after she left her employment with the restaurant, Ms. Criswell obtained a civil protection order against Hoying in February 2003. Subsequently, between August 15, 2003, and September 7, 2003, Hoying sent 105 e-mails to Ms. Criswell in violation of the protection order.

In the first e-mail, which is dated August 15, 2003, Hoying acknowledged that he could get in trouble for writing. He then asked Ms. Criswell to remove the civil protection order. Ms. Criswell did not reply to any of Hoying's e-mails, which became increasingly agitated.

The first threatening e-mail is dated August 16. This e-mail states, "Maybe I still have your picture and I will post it on the Net. Fair is fair. Ted." Subsequently, Hoying wrote, "Why don't you tell the authorities I shot three boxes of shells at clay birds yesterday? I'm going to do that the rest of my life at least once a week. I don't give a rat's ass what number eight says on that civil protection order. Ted." That e-mail is also dated August 16, 2003.

In another e-mail dated August 16, 2003, Hoying threatened to come to Ms. Criswell's place of employment unless she met with him. The same day, in another e-mail message, Hoying indicated that he would persist in sending e-mails until Ms. Criswell agreed to talk to him.

In an e-mail dated August 17, 2003, Hoying made a significant threat to Ms. Criswell. Specifically, he said:

> Kelly, set me free. I'm no longer a man. I'm shackled like a beast. What is a man if he is not free? Let me take away your freedom and you feel the sting. Also, it's not pleasant. Set me free. Ted H.

In another e-mail written on the same day, Hoying again threatened to go to Ms. Criswell's place of employment. He reiterated that threat in another e-mail, which was also written on August 17, 2003.

As a result of receiving these e-mails, Ms. Criswell filed charges in Xenia Municipal Court, alleging that Hoying had violated the civil protection order. Hoying acknowledged receiving the charge in an e-mail dated August 28, 2003. In that e-mail, Hoying said, "Kelly, why did you do that at Xenia? All I wanted was for things to be normal. I thought you could be nice." The same day, Hoying threatened to file criminal charges against Ms. Criswell's boyfriend, whom Hoying thought was named "Grinstead."

Subsequently, on August 30, 2003, Hoying sent Ms. Criswell another message. In that e-mail, Hoying threatened that "If the stuff in Xenia is not handled then some things are going to happen." The next day, Hoying sent a message, which said:

> Ms. Criswell, tell your old man to get rid of the Xenia stuff or the hammer is going to fall heavy on him. It will take three years to get all of this stuff straightened out. If not, remember you are going to be subpoenaed for the thefts since you supplied some of the info, so you might as well say good bye to your job. I've been nice to you. I don't deserve to be paid back like this. I don't want to hurt you, but if you choose their side then that is that. This is such high school shit. I'm not coming to court anyway. I have an important doctor's appointment. My life is just as important as yours. If it is not handled and they come for me, they better bring an army. Ted.

As a result of the e-mails, Ms. Criswell changed her address, changed her license plate, changed employment, and eventually moved away. (Ms. Criswell's current living arrangement was not revealed in court, for her protection.) Ms. Criswell also testified that she could possibly need psychiatric or psychological assistance in the future because of everything Hoying had done.

OPINION

Hoying claims that his conviction for menacing by stalking was based on insufficient evidence. As support for this contention, Hoying notes that he did not cause physical harm to Ms. Criswell and she did not seek professional help for mental distress. He also notes a lack of evidence that he was aware that Ms. Criswell believed he would cause her physical harm or mental distress.

The essential elements of menacing by stalking are found in R.C. 2903.211, which provides, in pertinent part, that:

> No person by engaging in a pattern of conduct shall knowingly cause another person to believe that the offender will cause physical

> harm to the other person or cause mental distress to the other person....
>
> Whoever violates this section is guilty of menacing by stalking.

Menacing by stalking is a felony of the fourth degree if any of the following applies:

> At the time of the commission of the offense, the offender was the subject of a protection order issued under section 2903.213 or 2903.214 of the Revised Code, regardless of whether the person to be protected under the order is the victim of the offense or another person.

After reviewing the evidence, we agree with the State that a reasonable jury could have inferred from the content of the e-mails that Hoying knew Ms. Criswell would consider the messages to be a threat to her physical safety or to that of her father. A reasonable jury could also have found that the messages would cause Ms. Criswell mental distress. The fact that Ms. Criswell previously sought a civil protection order was some evidence that she was afraid of the defendant, and the e-mails were sent after the protection order was issued to the defendant. Ms. Criswell also testified that she was "scared to death" of Hoying and that he had caused her much mental distress.

As an additional matter, Hoying's conduct in court did not help his case, as he interrupted Ms. Criswell's testimony several times with inappropriate comments, including calling her a liar. In one outburst, Hoying made what could be interpreted as a threat, stating, "She'd better start telling the truth and quit lying, that's for sure."

Hoying did not present any evidence to counteract the victim's testimony, or to prove that she was lying. Accordingly, any rational trier of fact had more than an ample basis for finding Hoying guilty of menacing by stalking.

Hoying also challenges the trial court's action in sentencing Hoying to the maximum term for the conviction of menacing by stalking, which is a fourth-degree felony, at least under the circumstances of this case. See R.C. 2903.211(B)(2)(g). Although community control sanctions are available for fourth-degree felonies, Hoying admits that they are not guaranteed. Hoying further concedes that he probably forfeited the ability to obtain community control by his conduct during trial and the sentencing hearing, and by his refusal to participate in the presentence investigation process. Having reviewed the record, we fully agree with that statement.

Nonetheless, Hoying contends that he should not have received the maximum sentence for menacing by stalking because the record does not support a finding that he poses the greatest likelihood of recidivism. We disagree.

Under R.C. 2929.14(A)(4), the potential term for a fourth-degree felony is six to eighteen months. R.C. 2929.14(C) additionally states that: Except as provided in division (G) of this section or in Chapter 2925. of the Revised Code, the court imposing a sentence upon an offender for a felony may impose the longest prison term authorized for the offense pursuant to division (A) of this section only upon offenders who committed the worst forms of the offense, upon offenders who pose the greatest likelihood of committing future crimes, upon certain major drug offenders under division (D)(3) of this section, and upon certain repeat violent offenders in accordance with division (D)(2) of this section.

When a trial court imposes maximum sentences, it must state its findings and reasoning at the sentencing hearing. Also, when a trial court states its reasons for imposing a maximum sentence, it must connect those reasons to the finding which the reason supports. The court cannot merely pronounce causes that objectively may be its reasons. The court must also identify which of those causes are the particular reasons for each of the statutory findings that the court made.

In the present case, the trial court complied with the requirement of making findings at the sentencing hearing. The court also adequately connected its reasons for imposing a maximum sentence to the finding that the reason supported. At the sentencing hearing, the court stated that it found that Hoying had the greatest likelihood to re-offend, and that Hoying had committed the worst form of the offense.

Before reciting the court's specific reasons for these findings, we should note that the very night the jury verdict was issued, Hoying attempted to contact the victim. According to the State, Hoying attempted to contact Ms. Criswell five times. Hoying denied making five attempts, but did admit that he tried to contact the victim after the verdict to ask for help with his appeal. In view of the nature of the crime (menacing by stalking) and the jury verdict of "guilty," an attempt to contact the victim of the crime shows either a disconnection from reality or an obstinate refusal to submit to the authority of the law.

(continues)

(continued)

Hoying also refused to cooperate in any way with the presentence investigation. In addition, Hoying disrupted the sentencing process, showering foul language and abuse on the victim, her family, and even the court, to the point that Hoying eventually had to be removed from the courtroom. Ultimately, in discussing the length of the sentence, the trial court specifically connected the following reasons to its findings, by stating that:

> when the victim in this case testified, the Defendant's conduct as to her testimony was absolutely parallel to the conduct of the crime in which he was charged, beginning with his sense of enjoyment of the presence of the victim as she testified, and as her testimony became less beneficial to the Defendant, he proceeded to become more aggravated and agitated, writing notes, ultimately basically yelling at the victim during the course of that testimony, clearly, giving an indication as to his attitude and conduct toward the victim in this matter which brought this case forward in the first place.

For that reason, the Court finds that the shortest prison term would not protect the public from future crimes, and the court has the greatest fear for Kelly Criswell, which the record will reflect, has moved from the immediate area and has taken extraordinary steps to prevent her location from being identified by this Defendant.

The Court notes for the record that testimony in this case and the information subsequently received indicates that the particular victim in this case had no relationship whatsoever with the Defendant, can't even suggest there ever was a scintilla of a relationship, yet the Defendant's attitude toward her is just a classic stalking attitude, and the harm caused to her is so significant that it is necessary to take extreme measures so the Court can protect her, as well as others from future crime.

The Court clearly feels the Defendant's conduct as demonstrated at his arrest, at his arraignment, during the conduct of this matter, the trial, and the sentencing here demonstrates an attitude on his part of failure to comply with authority, the failure to respect the integrity of other individuals, and quite candidly, makes this Defendant a very dangerous individual.

The shortest prison term will demean the seriousness of the Defendant's conduct.

The Court further finds based upon the facts stated herein and the information provided, which will be made a part of the record in this matter, that the Defendant's conduct has, to a great degree, established the worst form of the offense. I do not discount Counsel's statement that a first time offender is one in which there is an indication from the legislature that the least restrictive setting should apply; however, this Court can say unequivocally, in all the time that I've been on the Bench, I've never seen a Defendant that I'm more sure of is a serious threat to society and to the public.

The Court also finds the Defendant clearly poses the greatest likelihood to commit future crimes in this matter, and as such, the Court makes reference particularly to the competency report prepared earlier this year where the Defendant indicated in his evaluation, quote, I know I'm not crazy. I knew what I was doing when I contacted her knowing I was violating the order, end quote.

We find that the above discussion by the trial court fully complies with requirements for imposing maximum sentences. We also agree with the trial court that a maximum sentence was warranted. The record in this case is quite troubling, since it portrays an individual who either has no remorse for his actions, or refuses to admit he needs mental health treatment. Even though Hoying was found competent to stand trial, that does not mean that he is free of mental health problems that should be addressed, hopefully while he is in the prison system.

The judgment of the trial court is affirmed.

QUESTIONS

1. State the elements of stalking according to the Ohio stalking statute.
2. List all the facts relevant to deciding whether the prosecution proved each of the elements.
3. Assume you're the prosecutor. Relying on the facts of the case and the reasoning of the trial and the appellate court, argue that Hoying was guilty of stalking.
4. Assume you're Hoying's attorney. Relying on the facts of the case and Hoying's arguments, argue that Hoying wasn't guilty of stalking.
5. In your opinion, do the facts support a guilty verdict? Was the six-and-one-half-year sentence too harsh? Explain your answers.

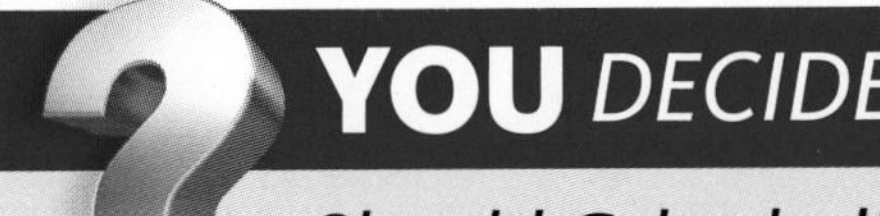

Should Cyberbullying be a crime?

Read "Should bullies be treated as criminals?" available at http://usatoday30.usatoday.com/news/nation/story/2012-06-12/bullying-crime-schools-suicide/55554112/1.

1. List and summarize the solutions to cyberbullying problem proposed in the article.
2. Summarize the arguments in favor and against making cyberbullies criminals.
3. Is making cyberbullies criminals the wise ethical public policy?

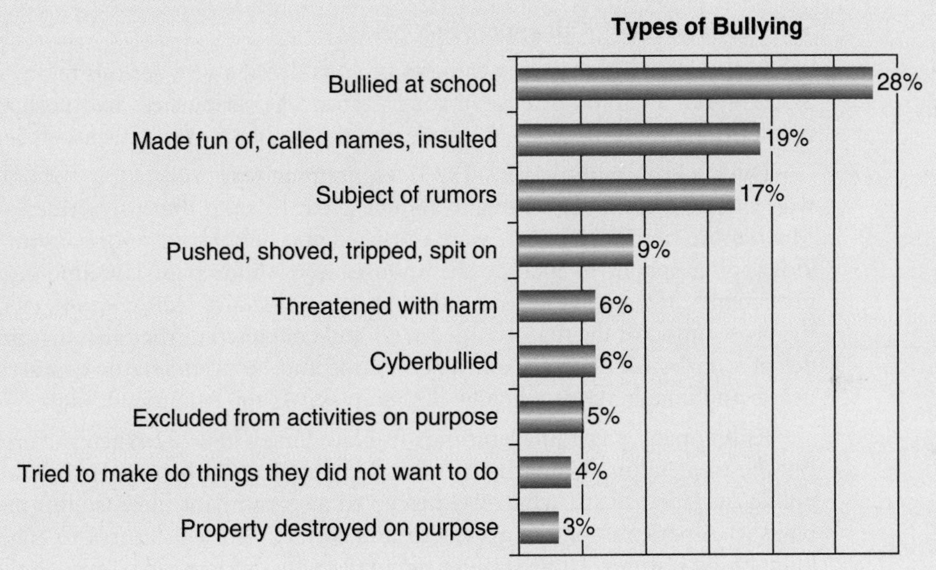

PERSONAL RESTRAINT CRIMES

One of the greatest things about living in a free society is the right to control our freedom of movement, even though we may not appreciate it until it's taken away from us. In the eighteenth century, they called it the right of locomotion—the right to come and go as we please, to stay if we don't want to move, and to move if we don't want to stay.

right of locomotion the right to come and go without restraint

I'm reminded of how precious this right is every time we get several inches of snow (which can be pretty often here in Minnesota). My house has a long driveway that needs plowing before I can get out. As much as I love my house, I feel trapped if the snowplow doesn't get there within an hour. This is a silly example, but it underscores the issues of the two crimes against personal liberty we'll look at in this section: kidnapping and false imprisonment.

Kidnapping

kidnapping the taking and carrying away of another person with the intent to deprive the other person of personal liberty

Kidnapping is an ancient result crime that originally involved holding the king's relatives for ransom. Of course, it was considered a serious offense because it interfered with the personal liberty of members of royal families. **Kidnapping** is taking and carrying away another person with the intent to deprive that person of personal liberty.

At common law, kidnapping consisted of six elements:

1. seizing
2. carrying away (asportation of), and
3. confining,
4. by force, threat of force, fraud, or deception,
5. another person,
6. with the intent to deprive the other person of his or her liberty.

See the Elements of Kidnapping Box below.

In the 1900s, kidnapping came to be considered a very serious felony in the United States—even a capital offense in some states. The seriousness had nothing to do with royalty but a lot to do with events during the first half of the twentieth century.

During Prohibition (1919–1933), kidnapping was prevalent in the organized crime world. One gang member might abduct a rival, "take him for a ride," and kill him. Much more frequently, rivals were captured and held hostage for ransom. Before long, kidnapping spread to include the spouses and children of law-abiding wealthy and prominent citizens. The most famous case was *State v. Hauptmann* (1935), involving the prosecution of the man charged with and convicted of the ransom kidnap and murder of Charles Lindbergh's son. The famous and beloved aviator captured Americans' hearts and imaginations when he flew solo across the Atlantic Ocean.

Kidnapping was a misdemeanor in New Jersey in 1932 when the crime occurred. But the tremendous sympathy that Lindbergh's popular hero status generated, and the public outrage toward what was perceived as a rampant increase in random kidnappings of America's "pillars of wealth and virtue," led legislatures to enact harsh new kidnapping statutes. These statutes remain largely in force today, even though they were passed in an emotional overreaction to a few notorious cases.

In 1974, another widely publicized case breathed new life into these harsh statutes when Patricia Hearst, heiress to newspaper tycoon William Randolph Hearst, was kidnapped. The case met with public outrage, not only because of sympathy for the prominent Hearst family but also because of shock at the psychological and physical dimensions of the crime. The kidnappers were self-styled revolutionaries calling themselves the Symbionese Liberation Army (SLA). One of the SLA's first demands was that

ELEMENTS OF KIDNAPPING

***Actus Reus* (Voluntary Act)**	+	***Mens Rea***	+	**Circumstance**	=	**Criminal Conduct**
1. Seizing *and* 2. Carrying away (asportation) the victim		Specific intent to 1. Confine *or* 2. Significantly restrain *or* 3. Hold victims in secret		If any required by statute		Kidnapping

Hearst's father, Randolph, distribute $1 million in food to the poor of California. Later on, much to her parents' and the public's horror, Patricia Hearst was accused of converting to the SLA and was later convicted of participating in bank robberies to raise money for the "revolution."

All this took place during a time when radicalism and violence were very much feared and when the Vietnam War protest and airline hijackings for terrorist political purposes were very much on the public's mind. The public saw Patty Hearst's capture and her family's deep trauma not just as one family's suffering but a threat to destroy American society.

The Hearst case focused attention on how monstrous kidnapping can be. It drew together in one story capture, detention, terror, violence, and political radicalism. The details were trumpeted every day in newspapers and on radio and television. Hope that existing harsh and sweeping kidnapping legislation would be reassessed calmly vanished in this inflamed, emotional atmosphere.

President Nixon expressed his hope—a hope that many others shared—that the Supreme Court wouldn't declare capital punishment for kidnapping unconstitutional. California governor Ronald Reagan reflected the deep public outrage against kidnapping when he wished aloud that the kidnappers' demand for a free food program would set off a botulism epidemic among the poor.

Let's look at the *actus reus* and *mens rea* elements of kidnapping and at how the law grades the seriousness of acts of kidnapping.

KIDNAPPING *ACTUS REUS*

The heart of kidnapping *actus reus* consists of seizing and carrying away—the asportation of—the victim. Since at least the eighteenth century, carrying a victim into a foreign country where no friends or family could give her aid and comfort, and the law couldn't offer protection, added a terrifying dimension to kidnapping.

asportation the act of carrying away or physically moving a victim of kidnapping

In those early days, the victim had to be carried at least as far as another country and usually across its border. Modern interpretations have made the asportation requirement meaningless.

The notorious case of *People v. Chessman* (1951) is the best example. Caryl Chessman was a serial rapist who, in one instance, forced a young woman to leave her car and get into his, which was only 22 feet away. The Court held that the mere fact of moving the victim, not how far she was moved, satisfied the asportation requirement. So moving his victim 22 feet was enough to convict and sentence Chessman to the gas chamber.

CASE

*In **People v. Allen (1997),** the California Supreme Court ruled that it's not the number of feet the carjacker moved the victims but the "quality and character" of his movement that matters in asportation.*

Did he move her a "substantial" distance?

People v. Allen

64 Cal. Rptr. 2d 497 (1997)

(continues)

(continued)

HISTORY

Tyrone Allen was convicted in the Superior Court, City and County of San Francisco, of the kidnapping of a person under the age of 14. He appealed. The Court of Appeal affirmed.

RUVOLO, J.

FACTS

On August 7, 1995, May SunYoung and her family lived at 2951 Treat Street in San Francisco. That morning, Ms. SunYoung was on her way to take her seven-year-old daughter, Kirstie, to summer camp and stopped her automobile briefly in the driveway to close her garage door manually as she was backing out onto the street.

As Ms. SunYoung closed her garage door, a man approached her from behind and said, "Excuse me, can you do me a favor?" While turning around she saw Tyrone Allen getting into her vehicle, whose engine was still running. He then locked the car doors. Kirstie was still in the vehicle with her seatbelt on and began crying. Because the driver's side window was rolled down about seven inches, Ms. SunYoung put her arms through the window and struggled with Allen in an attempt to reach the ignition key and turn off the engine.

Allen then released the parking brake, put the vehicle in reverse, and backed out of the driveway with Kirstie inside and Ms. SunYoung running alongside the vehicle still attempting to reach the ignition key. The vehicle backed across Treat Street, which was a two-lane road with two parking lanes, until it hit the opposite curb and came to a stop. Allen estimated the vehicle movement was 30 to 40 feet. While Allen now claims this estimate to be "speculation," both sides at different times suggested that the distance moved was approximately five car lengths, or 50 feet.

Allen exited the vehicle, threw the car keys onto the ground, shoved Ms. SunYoung against a fence, and ran down the street carrying her purse, which had been left in the vehicle. Shortly thereafter, a neighbor on Treat Street several blocks away saw a man run by. In response to the neighbor's attempts to stop the man, the fleeing suspect stated, "Stay back, I got a gun." After a brief struggle, the man ran off but was later apprehended by San Francisco police officers and identified as Allen.

The jury instruction given regarding the simple kidnapping count was CALJIC No. 9.52, which sets forth the elements of kidnapping of a person under 14 years of age as follows:

> Every person who unlawfully and with physical force or by any other means of instilling fear moves any other person under 14 years of age without her consent for a substantial distance, that is, a distance more than slight or trivial, is guilty of the crime of kidnapping.... (Pen. Code, § 208, subd. (b); all further statutory references are to the Penal Code unless otherwise indicated.)

OPINION

The only element of the crime for which Allen asserts there was insufficient evidence and inadequate jury instructions is asportation. For "simple" kidnapping, that is, a kidnapping not elevated to a statutory form of "aggravated" kidnapping, the movement needed must be "substantial," or a distance that is more than "trivial, slight, or insignificant."

Allen argues that his conviction for simple kidnapping must be reversed because the minimum distance requirement for asportation is not met. He asserts the movement of Ms. SunYoung's vehicle 30–50 feet down her driveway and across Treat Street with Kirstie inside as a matter of law cannot be "substantial," or a distance that is more than "trivial, slight, or insignificant."

Allen is correct that under most cases decided pre-1981 which have examined only the actual distance involved, the movement here would not meet the legal test of substantiality. Those cases which have considered the quality and character of the movement in addition to its absolute distance have weighed the purpose for the movement, whether it posed an increased risk of harm to the victim, and the context of the environment in which the movement occurred.

Purposes for movement found to be relevant have been those undertaken to facilitate the commission of a further crime, to aid in flight, or to prevent detection. We believe these factors are appropriate considerations.

"Substantiality" implies something more than only measured distance. While "slight" is consistent with a quantitative analysis, the term "trivial" is a qualitative term suggestive of the conclusion that more is envisioned in determining whether a kidnapping occurs than simply how far the victim is moved. The legal requirement for asportation is satisfied by a finding of either.

In so holding, we conclude that while in absolute footage the distance moved here may have been empirically short, it was of a character sufficient to justify a finding of "substantiality" by the jury. The movement, in part, was plainly made to prevent Ms. SunYoung from regaining possession of her vehicle and to facilitate Allen's flight from the area with Kirstie. In addition to evasion of capture, the vehicle was moved from a position of relative safety onto a thoroughfare. The boundary crossed was significant because it placed Kirstie at greater risk of injury.

We confirm these factors, coupled with the distance traveled, are sufficient to satisfy the "substantial movement" requirement for the crime of simple kidnapping....

Affirmed.

DISSENT

KLINE, J.

Movement as short a distance as that shown here—30 to 40 feet—has never been held to satisfy the asportation requirement of kidnapping. Indeed, considerably greater distances have often been held insufficient. As the majority opinion points out, movement of 90 feet, nearly three times the distance the victim in this case was moved, was held insufficient. The shortest distance this court has ever held to be "substantial" for this purpose was a full city block.

I agree that by moving the child in the vehicle across the street Allen committed a crime other than carjacking and the various other offenses of which he was properly convicted; that crime was not kidnapping, however, but false imprisonment (Pen. Code, § 236), which does not require any movement.

Because the asportation in this case was trivial within the meaning of the applicable case law, I would reverse the judgment of conviction of simple kidnapping for lack of evidentiary support. I agree that in all other respects the judgment should be affirmed.

QUESTIONS

1. What test did the court establish to determine how far defendants have to move victims to satisfy the asportation element of kidnapping *actus reus*?
2. What reasons does the majority give to support its definition of "asportation"?
3. How does the dissent's definition of "asportation" differ from that of the majority's?
4. What reasons does the dissent give for its definition?
5. Do you agree with the majority or the dissent's definition of "asportation"? Defend your answer.

KIDNAPPING *MENS REA*

Kidnapping *mens rea* means the specific intent to confine, significantly restrain, or hold victims in secret. The Wisconsin statute, for example, defines a "kidnapper" as one who "seizes or confines another without his consent and with intent to cause him to be secretly confined." Whatever the exact wording of the statutes, the heart of the kidnapping mental attitude remains to "isolate the victim from the prospect of release or friendly intervention" (Wisconsin Criminal Code 2006, § 940.31).

kidnapping *mens rea* the mental element of kidnapping requiring the specific intent to confine, significantly restrain, or hold victims in secret

GRADING KIDNAPPING SERIOUSNESS

Kidnapping is usually divided into two degrees: simple and aggravated. The most common aggravating circumstances include kidnapping for the purpose of:

- Sexual invasions
- Obtaining a hostage
- Obtaining ransom

- Robbing the victim
- Murdering the victim
- Blackmailing
- Terrorizing the victim
- Achieving political aims

The penalty for aggravated kidnapping is usually life imprisonment and, until recently, occasionally even death.

LO12 False Imprisonment

false imprisonment depriving others of their personal liberty without the asportation requirement

False imprisonment is a lesser form of personal restraint than kidnapping, but the heart of the crime remains depriving others of their personal liberty. It's a lesser offense because there's no asportation requirement; the deprivation of liberty is brief; and the detention is less stressful. "False imprisonment" was succinctly defined as compelling a person "to remain where he does not wish to remain" (*McKendree v. Christy* 1961, 381).

Most forcible detentions or confinements, however brief, satisfy the *actus reus* of false imprisonment. This doesn't include restraints authorized by law—for example, when parents restrict their children's activities or victims detain their victimizers.

The Model Penal Code (MPC) requires the restraint to "interfere *substantially* with the victim's liberty," but, in most state statutes, any interference with another person's liberty is enough. For example, here's the way the Florida statute defines the *actus reus* of false imprisonment:

> False imprisonment means forcibly, by threat, or secretly confining, abducting, imprisoning, or restraining another person without lawful authority and against her or his will. (Florida Criminal Code 2006)

Although physical force often accomplishes the detention, it doesn't have to; threatened force is enough. So the threat "If you don't come with me, I'll drag you along" is enough. Even nonthreatening words can qualify, such as when a police officer who has no right to do so orders someone on the street into a squad car, asserting, "You're under arrest."

False imprisonment is a specific-intent crime. According to a typical statute: "False imprisonment consists of intentionally confining or restraining another person without his consent." (New Mexico Criminal Code 2006). The motive for the detention doesn't matter. For example, if police officers make unlawful arrests, they can be prosecuted for false imprisonment even if they believed the arrests were lawful.

Summary

LO1 Rape is second only to murder as the most serious crime in U.S. law and society. Though it is no longer punishable by death, rape causes grave, often invisible, injuries to victims. Rape and other sexual assaults are different from all other felonies in that, in other circumstances, some of the behaviors connected with them are legal, healthy, and desired.

Crimes against persons boil down to four types: taking a life; unwanted sexual invasions; bodily injury; and personal restraint. LO2

Common law rape was very narrowly defined as intentional, forced, nonconsensual, heterosexual vaginal penetration by a man of a woman who isn't his wife. Victim credibility in common law trials relied upon the victim's chastity, prompt reporting of the rape, and other witnesses corroborating the rape. Common law definitions of rape were altered dramatically in modern-day rape law. Many states abolished the corroboration rule that required witnesses to back up rape victims' testimony. Most also passed rape shield statutes that banned or limited prosecutors from introducing evidence of victims' past sexual conduct. The prompt-reporting rule was also relaxed, allowing rape crimes to be prosecuted even if the victim did not report it right away. Statutes recognize rape by husbands as a crime. Modern court opinions have also relaxed the strict definitions of "rape." Sexual assault, or criminal sexual conduct, statutes enacted in the 1970s and the 1980s were aimed at changing the existing "assumption of risk" approach to rape cases and have expanded the definition of "sex offenses" to embrace a wide range of nonconsensual penetrations and contacts, even if they fall far short of violent contact. LO3

Despite the criminal sexual assault reforms, the new regime of criminal sexual conduct has failed to reduce unarmed acquaintance rapes. It's exceedingly difficult to prove every element of acquaintance rape beyond a reasonable doubt based only on words and nonverbal communication. Further, most rapes are acquaintance rapes, acquaintance rape victims are far less likely to report their rapes to the police, and prosecutors and juries are less likely to convict acquaintance rapists. LO4

The elements of modern rape law include the *actus reus* of sexual penetration for force or threat, the *mens rea* of intent to penetrate, and nonconsent by the victim. Courts today have adopted either of two definitions of "force": (1) extrinsic force and (2) intrinsic force. Extrinsic force requires force additional to that required for penetration; intrinsic force only requires the force to accomplish penetration. LO5

Cultural cognition, or how group values influence individuals' interpretations of facts, impacts the society's view of what qualifies as rape. Even under a "no means no" definition of rape, many people believe that "no" can often mean "yes" or "maybe" when consenting to sexual contact. LO6

The force requirement of modern rape law doesn't require actual, physical force; threats of force can satisfy this requirement. According to the threat-of-force requirement, prosecutors have to prove that the victim experienced both subjective and objective fear of imminent, serious bodily harm. LO7

Rape is a general-intent crime: defendants intended to commit the act of forcible sexual penetration. Statutory rape is a strict liability crime in most states. Statutory LO8 rapists don't have to use force; the victim's immaturity takes the place of force. Minors can't legally consent to sexual conduct. Only Alaska and California allow for a reasonable mistake of age as a defense. The seriousness of sex offenses under the reform laws of the 1970s and 1980s is graded according to several criteria, including (1) penetrations and contacts; (2) forcible and nonconsensual; (3) physical injury to the victim or not; and (4) "gang rapes" and single rapist rapes. Most traditional rape statutes, and the newer criminal sexual assault laws, define "rape" as intentional sexual penetration by force without consent.

LO9 The essential difference between assault and battery is that assault requires no physical contact; an assault is complete before the offender touches the victim.

LO10 Since the early 1970s, domestic violence crimes have been transformed from a private concern to a criminal justice problem. Violence in intimate relationships is extensive and isn't limited to one socioeconomic group, one society, or one period of time.

LO11 Stalking involves intentionally scaring another person by following, tormenting, or harassing him or her. Victims need not be injured or threatened. Cyberstalking is the use of the Internet, e-mail, or other electronic communications devices to stalk another person through threatening behavior.

LO12 Kidnapping is an ancient result crime that consisted of holding the monarch's relatives for ransom. False imprisonment is a lesser form of personal restraint than kidnapping, but the heart of the crime remains depriving others of their right to locomotion.

Key Terms

common law rape, p. 382
common law sodomy, p. 382
carnal knowledge, p. 382
aggravated rape, p. 384
unarmed acquaintance rape or "date rape", p. 384
"assumption of risk" approach to rape cases, p. 387
criminal sexual conduct statutes, p. 387
corroboration requirement, p. 389
rape shield laws, p. 389
marital rape exception, p. 389
force and resistance rule, p. 391
utmost resistance standard, p. 391
reasonable resistance rule, p. 392
extrinsic force, p. 392
intrinsic force, p. 392
cultural cognition, p. 397
threat-of-force requirement, p. 402
subjective fear, p. 402
objective fear, p. 402
honest and reasonable mistake rule, p. 403
statutory rape, p. 404

defense of reasonable mistake of age, p. 404
battery, p. 407
assault, p. 407
attempted battery assault, p. 408
threatened battery assault, p. 408
conditional threats, p. 409
stalking, p. 415
cyberstalking, p. 417
right of locomotion, p. 421
kidnapping, p. 422
asportation, p. 423
kidnapping *mens rea*, p. 425
false imprisonment, p. 426

Learning Objectives

1 To know that crimes against other people's property consist of taking, damaging or destroying, and invading property, either physically or using the Internet and other wireless networks.

2 To understand that the general social concern with violent crimes against persons led to the creation of the different "taking" crimes—larceny, embezzlement, false pretenses, white-collar crime, robbery, and receiving stolen property.

3 To understand that consolidated theft statutes combined the laws of larceny, embezzlement, and false pretenses into one offense called "theft."

4 To know that federal mail fraud and Ponzi schemes are white-collar crimes against property.

5 To understand that the heart of robbery is the use of actual or threatened force to obtain another's property right now.

6 To know that the crime of receiving stolen property targets professional fences and ordinary people who know, or should know, they're buying stolen things.

7 To know the elements of arson and appreciate that it is a serious felony.

8 To understand that criminal mischief is the damage or destruction of tangible property.

9 To understand that the heart of burglary and trespass is invading other people's property, not taking, destroying, or damaging it.

10 To appreciate the devastating losses, monetary and otherwise, caused by the widespread crime of identity theft.

11 To understand and appreciate that personal computing and the Internet has greatly enhanced the opportunity for cybercrimes against intellectual property and using the dark net.

11 Crimes Against Property

Chapter Outline

Was it theft?

Store Detective Lauryna Petrauskiene observed the defendant, while inside the store, remove one (1) handbag, one (1) pair of tights and one (1) jacket from a rack and conceal one (1) handbag, one (1) pair of tights and one (1) jacket by placing said items inside defendant's bag and then Store Detective Lauryna Petrauskiene observed the defendant walk past more than one open register and move to another floor in the store in possession of the property and without paying for it. Thereafter, defendant was stopped and Store Detective Lauryna Petrauskiene recovered said items, valued at $944.00, from defendant's bag, property which belonged to the store and for which the defendant had no receipt.

—People v. Lai Lee (2009)

LO1

There are many specific crimes against property—too many to list here, let alone discuss. To simplify, we look at three categories of crimes against property and a few representative crimes within each. The three categories are:

1. Taking other people's property
2. Damaging or destroying other people's property
3. Invading other people's property

First, we look at four crimes that consist of taking someone else's property:

1. *Theft.* Sneaking away with an iPad left unattended in the library
2. *Fraud.* Abuse of trust: Bernard Madoff's Ponzi scheme that took billions of dollars from investors who trusted him with their fortunes; Navy Commander Charles E. Coughlin who was charged with and convicted of fraudulently trying to collect over $150,000 from the 9-11 victims' funds
3. *Robbery.* Sticking a gun in someone's side and demanding the $100 she just withdrew from an ATM machine
4. *Receiving stolen property.* Buying a new notebook computer for $75 that you know is stolen

Second, we'll look at two crimes involving destroying and damaging someone else's property:

1. *Arson.* Setting a house on fire
2. *Criminal mischief.* Damaging someone else's property (such as driving your car up on an obnoxious neighbor's new sod and spinning the wheels)

Third, we'll look at two criminal invasions of someone else's property:

1. *Burglary.* Unlawfully entering someone else's house with the intent to steal a TV inside
2. *Criminal trespass.* Entering your neighbor's yard where a "no trespassing" sign is posted

cybercrime crimes aimed at the valuable information contained in computers and wireless devices, especially computer databases accessible through the Internet

All of these offenses represent the *traditional* ways to take, destroy or damage, and invade other people's property. **Cybercrime**, defined as crimes committed by means of the Internet or some other wireless network, is a serious and rapidly growing problem. There are four types of cybercrimes (Yang and Hoffstadt 2006, 203–4):

1. *Crimes against information brokers.* Data collectors (credit reporting agencies) and data aggregators (Westlaw)
2. *Crimes against manufacturers and distributors of digital media.* Movie, recording, and software companies
3. *Crimes against online product and service sales.* Businesses that offer their products and services for sale on the Internet
4. *Crimes against business computer systems.* Internal computer systems connected to the Internet, used to conduct daily business affairs, and house companies' asset data, including their trade secrets

We often call cybercrimes "new crimes." But they're really just new ways (admittedly sometimes very complex and sophisticated ways) to commit the three ancient kinds of property crimes: taking it, damaging or destroying it, and invading it. According to *The Electronic Frontier* (2000):

> Advances in technology—the advent of the automobile and the telephone for instance—have always given wrongdoers new means for engaging in unlawful conduct. The Internet is no different: it is simply a new medium through which traditional crimes can now be committed. ■

HISTORY OF CRIMINALLY TAKING OTHER PEOPLE'S PROPERTY

LO2

The long history of criminal taking began as part of the social concern with violent crimes against the person (Chapters 9 and 10). That concern led to the creation of the common law felony of robbery—taking property by force or the threat of force—which is a violent crime against persons and their property.

robbery taking property by force or the threat of force—a violent crime against persons and their property

Then, criminal law expanded to include taking property without consent, even if the thief used no force. The first nonconsensual, nonviolent taking felony was larceny, the ancient common law crime of stealing. Larceny consisted (and still consists) of three elements:

larceny taking and carrying away a person's property without the use of force and with the intent to permanently deprive the owner of possession

1. taking, *and*
2. carrying away someone else's property without their consent (most of the time, even without their knowledge), *and*
3. with the intent to permanently deprive victims of possession.

Larceny was born as the common law tool to protect the Anglo-Saxons' most valuable possession (livestock) from dishonest or untrustworthy thieves (LaFave and Scott 1986, chap. 8; Perkins and Boyce 1982, chap. 4).Larceny didn't protect the property of those who voluntarily handed it over to a caretaker—for example, a carrier who delivered property to someone else or a bank that held depositors' money. Larceny required that thieves "take *and* carry away" the property. Caretakers did neither; what they did was "convert" property that was lawfully in their possession to their own use. In criminal law, conversion means "wrongfully possessing or disposing of someone else's property as if it were yours."

conversion wrongfully possessing or disposing of someone else's property as if it were yours

As society advanced, the failure of larceny to protect adequately against conversion by caretakers created a growing gap in the criminal law. This was especially true in a society with exploding quantities and kinds of valuable and easily portable possessions. These possessions included both tangible property (personal property items like jewelry) and intangible property (stocks, bonds, and promissory notes)—namely, *paper* worth nothing by itself but which was proof of (it represented) something of value.

tangible property personal property, not real estate

intangible property property worth nothing by itself but is proof of something of value (such as stock options, bonds, notes, trademarks, licenses, and patents)

As society became more complex, caretakers who converted property that owners voluntarily handed over to them became an enormous problem. Legislatures responded to this problem of unlawful conversion of property by creating the felony of embezzlement.

The earliest embezzlement statutes were directed at occupations handling other people's *money*, such as bank clerks. Eventually, statutes reached broadly to include all kinds of property obtained by breaches of trust. According to the MPC reporter (ALI 1985, 2:223.1):

embezzlement the crime of lawfully gaining possession of someone else's property and later converting it to one's own use

> A few American legislatures enacted fraudulent-conversion statutes penalizing misappropriation by anyone who received or had in his possession or control the property of another, or property which someone else "is entitled to receive and have." Indeed, some modern embezzlement statutes go so far as to penalize breach of faith without regard to whether anything is misappropriated. Thus, the fiduciary who makes forbidden investments, the official who deposits public funds in an unauthorized depository, the financial advisor who betrays his client into paying more for a property than fair market value, may be designated an embezzler. (129)

abuse-of-trust crimes crimes growing out of opportunities to get someone else's property that was entrusted to the perpetrators because of their occupation, now known as white-collar crimes today

Embezzlement was the first of what we call the **abuse-of-trust crimes**. They're also called white-collar crimes—crimes growing out of opportunities to get someone else's property that was entrusted to the perpetrators because of their occupation (see White-Collar Crime, p. 438).

Although the term at first referred only to crimes committed by *business executives*, it now includes property crimes that grow out of opportunities created by any lawful occupation (for example, if I take the MacBook Air the university provided to help me teach my classes, and I use it, instead, to promote the sales of the book you're reading, I'd be a "white-collar criminal"). Or to secretaries who take office supplies for their personal use. Or, workers who take home tools and other items connected with their work. (We call them *blue-collar crimes*.) Statutes and courts are still creating new crimes to combat the same old evil of satisfying the desire to get other people's property by the new methods, such as stealing their identities from computers and the Internet.

To recap: Robbery applied to taking or threatening to take someone else's property by force; larceny applied to sneaking away someone else's property; and embezzlement applied to keeping permanently property that keepers had only a temporary right to possess. Moving on, what about crafty scam artists who tricked owners into giving up possession or ownership? The deceivers hadn't "taken" the property, because the owners willingly gave it to them. They hadn't converted it either, because they didn't have even a temporary right to possess it.

fraud a general term that means getting property by deception

They got it by **fraud**, a general term that means getting property by deception. Influenced by the doctrine of *caveat emptor* ("let the buyer beware"), common law fraud, obtaining another's property by "simple deception," wasn't a crime. The English common law court, in *Regina v. Jones* (1703), put it succinctly: "Making a fool of another is not a crime" (330). It was, however, a common law misdemeanor to cheat, which in criminal law was limited to using false weights and other "tokens" to cheat the general public.

In 1753, the English Parliament enacted a statute that expanded cheating to include a new misdemeanor, which was defined as obtaining "'money, goods, wares or merchandizes by false pretenses with intent to cheat or defraud" (Kadish, Schulhofer, and Steiker 2007, 956). This statute became the prototype for the modern felony of **obtaining property by false pretenses**, which filled the gap left by larceny and embezzlement when it came to fraudulently getting ownership (not just possession) of other people's property.

obtaining property by false pretenses in modern law, often called "theft by deceit"; making false representations concerning past or present facts with the intent to defraud another

In false pretenses *actus reus*, "deceiving" (defrauding) replaces "taking" in larceny and "converting" in embezzlement. Deception requires a lie, such as promising you that if you give me $100 I'll get you an iPad, a promise I know I can't keep or don't intend even to try to keep.

So, with history and law to help us, we'll start our study of crimes related to misappropriating other people's property. These include the ancient "taking" felony of larceny and its modern descendant, theft; white-collar crimes, focusing on federal mail fraud and Ponzi schemes; taking property by force (robbery); and receiving property someone else has stolen.

LO3 Larceny and Theft

The logic of social and economic history lies behind the separation of the three ways to get other people's property into separate crimes. But the distinctions still make sense. As we saw earlier, when society changed, embezzlement supplemented larceny, and then

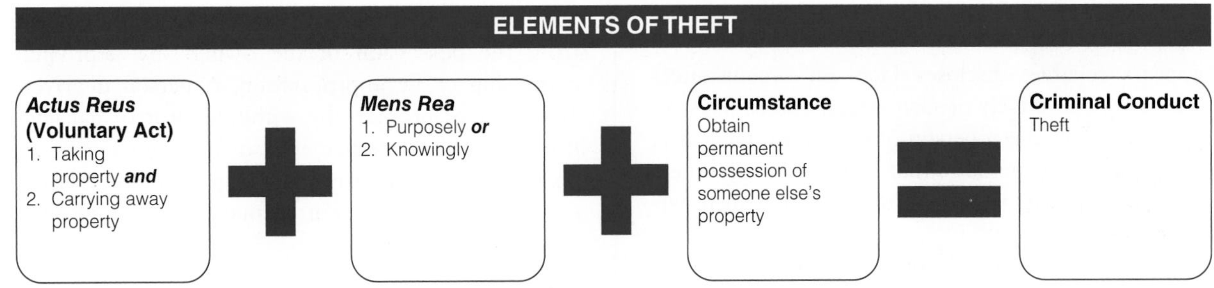

theft by deceit (false pretenses) supplemented both larceny and embezzlement to fight the new ways of unlawfully taking other people's money.

Most states have consolidated the old crimes of larceny, embezzlement, and false pretenses into one offense called **theft**. They accept the social reality that all these ancient crimes were aimed at the same evil—intentionally getting control of someone else's property.

theft intentionally getting control of someone else's property, includes larceny, embezzlement, and false pretense crimes

Consolidated theft statutes eliminate needlessly separating theft into distinct offenses according to their *actus reus*. Thus, modern theft statute *actus reus* comprises "taking and carrying away," "converting," or "swindling" to obtain possession of someone else's property. The *mens rea* in modern theft statutes remains as it always was—acquiring someone else's property "purposely" or "knowingly" in MPC language, or "intentionally" in non-MPC states, for the purpose of permanently depriving the owner of her possession.

In our next case excerpt, *People v. Lai Lee* (2009), the Criminal Court, City of New York, ruled that the facts did not add up to a reasonable belief that Lai Lee "with intent to deprive" the store of property, by "withholding" it "permanently or for some extended period of time."

CASE

*In **People v. Lai Lee (2009)**, the Criminal Court, City of New York, ruled that the facts did not add up to a reasonable belief that Lai Lee "with intent to deprive" the store of property, by "withholding" it "permanently or for some extended period of time."*

Was it purse snatching or shoplifting?

People v. Lai Lee

24 Misc.3d12333(A) (Criminal Court, City of New York 2009)

WHITEN, J.

The defendant, Lai Lee, is charged with one count of Petit Larceny (PL § 155.25), and has filed a motion seeking dismissal of the complaint as facially insufficient. In order to be facially sufficient..., the facts and any accompanying depositions of an information must provide reasonable cause to believe the defendant committed the offense charged, as well as non hearsay factual allegations of an evidentiary character which, if true, establish every element of the offense charged and defendant's commission thereof. "Reasonable cause to believe that a person has committed an offense" exists when evidence or information, which

(continues)

(continued)

appears reliable, discloses facts or circumstances which are collectively of such weight and persuasiveness as to convince a person of ordinary intelligence, judgment and experience that it is reasonably likely that such offense was committed and that such person committed it.

The requirement of nonhearsay allegations has been described as "much more demanding standard" than showing reasonable cause alone." However, it is nevertheless a much lower threshold than the burden of proof beyond a reasonable doubt. Thus, the law does not require that the information contain the most precise words or phrases most clearly expressing the charge, only that the crime and the factual basis therefore be sufficiently alleged.

Finally, where the allegations of facts contained in information "give an accused sufficient notice to prepare a defense and are adequately detailed to prevent a defendant from being tried twice for the same offense, they should be given a fair and not overly restrictive or technical reading."

FACTS

Store Detective Lauryna Petrauskiene observed the defendant, while inside the store, remove one (1) handbag, one (1) pair of tights and one (1) jacket from a rack and conceal one (1) handbag, one (1) pair of tights and one (1) jacket by placing said items inside defendant's bag and then Store Detective Lauryna Petrauskiene observed the defendant walk past more than one open register and move to another floor in the store in possession of the property and without paying for it. Thereafter, defendant was stopped and Store Detective Lauryna Petrauskiene recovered said items, valued at $944.00, from defendant's bag, property which belonged to the above named store and for which the defendant had no receipt.

Store Detective Lauryna Petrauskiene is a custodian of said property and defendant did not have permission or authority to take or possess the property.

The defendant is charged with one count of violating PL § 155.25, Petit Larceny. A person is guilty of Petit Larceny when he or she steals property. (PL § 155.25). "A person steals property...when, with intent to deprive another of property or to appropriate the same to himself...,[he or she] wrongfully takes, obtains or withholds such property from an owner thereof." To support the offense charged, "there must be a taking or severance of the goods from the possession of the owner" by depriving ownership or by appropriation. A person deprives an owner of property by withholding it or causing it to be withheld permanently or for some extended period. A person appropriates property of another by exercising control over it permanently or for some extended period.

OPINION

Defendant contends the complaint is facially insufficient because it fails to allege nonhearsay factual allegations, which, if true, support every element of the crimes charged. Defendant's argument is twofold. First, defendant argues the allegations that she placed items in a bag, without a description of the type of bag fails to support the charge, inasmuch as, it fails to establish a concealment. Second, defendant argues the allegations that she moved within the store with the items fails to support that she exercised dominion and control wholly inconsistent with the continued rights of the owner, inasmuch as, the alleged facts fail to establish larcenous conduct supporting the allegation that she did not intend to pay for the items, such as her walking towards the exit or other conduct inconsistent with the continued rights of the owner.

In support of her contention, the defendant relies upon two post-trial decisions, *People v. Parrett* (90 Misc.2d 541 [Dist. Ct. Nassau Co. 1977]) and *People v. Olivo*, 52 N.Y.2d 309 [1981]. In *Parrett*, the defendant was stopped at the top of an escalator after allegedly being observed placing two items in her handbag on the main floor of the store. The court held that until a defendant left the premises there was no proof that the defendant committed larceny, since there was no proof that defendant intended to deprive the owner of the property. Accordingly, defendant argues that since she did not leave the premises the complaint fails to support that she intended to deprive the owner of the property.

In *People v. Olivo*, 52 N.Y.2d 309, the Court of Appeals held that a person caught with goods while still inside a store may be convicted of larceny for shoplifting where it is established that he or she exercised dominion and control wholly inconsistent with the rights of the owner, and other elements of the crime are present. The *Olivo* court set forth factors that would support a finding that a defendant exercised dominion and control inconsistent with the rights of the owner. These factors include

1. whether the defendant conceals the merchandise in a way deemed an exercise of dominion and control inconsistent with the owner's continued rights,
2. whether there is evidence of larcenous behavior,
3. the proximity to or movement towards one of the exits,
4. possession of secreted goods a few steps from the door or moving in that direction, and
5. possession of a known shoplifting device actually used to conceal merchandise, such as specially designed outer garment or a false bottom carrying case.

It is a sad commentary on our merchandising structure that some large store owners deem it necessary to sequester patrons by floor, requiring that transactions be completed on one floor before traveling to a second floor. These retailers seem oblivious to the clear inconvenience occasioned by causing visits to multiple checkout lines on multiple floors of an establishment where desired accessorizing apparel are distributed throughout the many floors of the store.

This hyper security, which complicates intra-store commerce also presents challenges to the store owner's related claims in a charged crime such as Petit Larceny. The question of when a "taking" has occurred is a primary consideration in evaluating the facial sufficiency of claims supported by non-specific behavior.

The German novelist, poet and scientist, Johann Wolfgang von Goethe (1749–1832) wrote "Behavior is a mirror in which every one displays his image". The image or behavior of a defendant who does not attempt to leave store premises or conceal merchandise in a manner which exercises dominion and control to the exclusion of the owner creates in the first instance, an unacceptable ambiguity when only non-specific behavior is alleged, which does not on its face rise to the level of a "taking". If such behavior does not on its face rise to the level of a "taking" then a defendant's insufficiency argument must be seriously considered.

Applying the *Olivo* factors to the present case, the court finds the allegations fail to provide sufficient facts to support that the defendant exercised dominion and control inconsistent with the owner's continued rights by placing the merchandise in a bag. Other than the accusation that the defendant placed items in a bag, the allegations fail to provide some other conduct to support the claim that defendant's actions were consistent with that of a shoplifter.

As stated in *Olivo*, a shoplifter, unlike customers with implied consent to possess merchandise while shopping, treats merchandise in a manner inconsistent with the implied rights granted to consumers, so much so that the unusual behavior by the defendant would allow the trier of facts to find a taking. (Self-serve stores invite the customer both to come on the premises and to take physical possession of merchandise.) Although, the items were placed in a "bag" dominion and control is not established since the placement of the merchandise in a bag is not by definition "concealment". The allegations fail to allege facts, such as the description of the bag or that the security tags were removed, that support the items were concealed or detached from the owner. Mere movement of an item merely tends to support the idea of control and not necessarily the actions needed to gain possession and control.

Given the environmental or Earth movement, as well as the sale by various stores of "earth bags" or "recyclable bags" the placement of items in a bag is becoming common place to the average shopper. Therefore, the placement of an item in "a bag" without more, fails to support a concealment or detachment.

Proof of larcenous behavior and intent can be supported with additional conduct, such as the removal of garment security device, or whether the bag was of a type typically used to conceal merchandise, such as a false bottom carrying case or a "booster" bag. *People v. Banister*, 13 Misc.3d 764, 765 [Crim. Ct. N.Y. Co. 2006] identified a "Booster bag" as an altered shopping bag lined with gray electrical tape utilized to steal merchandise to which security devices are affixed in that the electrical tape prevents store theft detectors from sensing security devices inside the bag.

Accordingly, the allegations fail to establish conduct inconsistent with a customer's implied rights while shopping. There is no claim of an abridgement of the shopper's right to free movement asserted here. The allegations do not assert there existed signage preventing customers from moving items from one floor to another floor or decreeing that items must be purchased on the level where displayed. Furthermore, unlike the defendants in *Olivo*, who were in proximity to or moving toward the exits, Ms. Lee is alleged to have been moving toward a second floor escalator when she was apprehended. The court takes judicial

(continues)

(continued)

notice that unless a notice to the contrary is posted, the alleged behavior of moving items within a department store is common, inasmuch as, department store customers commonly wait until all shopping or browsing is complete to make a final purchase. For the reasons set forth, defendant's motion to dismiss the accusatory instrument as facially insufficient is granted.

This constitutes the decision and order of the court.

QUESTIONS

1. State the elements of larceny.
2. Summarize the court's arguments to support the proof of each of the elements of larceny.
3. Did the court stretch the original meaning of the elements? Explain.
4. Is the decision good public policy? Explain.
5. Should the court, or the legislature, change the meaning of the elements of larceny to fit modern conditions? Explain your answer.

White-Collar Crime

> This paper...is a comparison of crime in the upper or white-collar class, composed of respectable or at least respected business and professional men, and crime in the lower classes, composed of persons of low socioeconomic status....The criminal statistics show unequivocally that crime, as popularly conceived and officially measured, has a high incidence in the lower class and a low incidence in the upper class. Less than two percent of the persons committed to prisons in a year belong to the upper class. These statistics refer to criminals handled by police, the criminal and juvenile courts, and the prisons, and to such crimes as murder, assault, burglary, larceny, sex offenses, and drunkenness.
>
> —Sutherland (1940, 1)

LO4 The quote is taken from criminologist Edwin Sutherland's Presidential Address to the American Sociological Association in 1940, "White-Collar Criminality." He was referring to two kinds of business and professional crime:

1. *Fraud and swindling*. For example, misrepresentation in corporate financial statements and tax fraud
2. *Double cross*. For example, a corporation director, acting on insider information, buys land the corporation needs, and sells it at a "fantastic profit" to his corporation. (3)

They're what the racketeer "Al Capone called 'the legitimate rackets'" (3).

Sutherland was calling attention to a large and growing variety of criminal behavior that criminologists had ignored. Although his language may sound out of date, and may even grate on the ears of the politically correct, "his instinct was right, even in the context of a basic criminal law context. Whatever white-collar crime may be, exactly, it is important to recognize that crimes are committed on a regular basis, by those who qualify as white-collar workers, including among others—lawyers" (Dubber and Kelman 2009, 917).

white-collar crime criminal behavior committed by the white-collar class, including fraud, swindling, and "double crossing"

But this is a criminal *law* book, not a book about white-collar *criminals*. So we'll focus on Sutherland's fraud and swindling crimes against property with a special emphasis on mail fraud and Ponzi schemes.

FEDERAL MAIL FRAUD

> To federal prosecutors of white-collar crime, the mail fraud statute is our Stradivarius, our Colt 45, Louisville Slugger, our Cuisinart—our true love. We may flirt with RICO...and call the conspiracy "darling," but we always come home to the virtues

> of 18 U.S.C. § 1341 with its simplicity, adaptability, and comfortable familiarity. It understands us, and like many a foolish spouse we like to think we understand it.
>
> —O'Sullivan (2014, 419)

Combined with the wire fraud statutes, **mail fraud statutes** are the most frequently charged federal statutes for three reasons:

mail fraud statutes includes "schemes to defraud or for obtaining money or property" using the U.S. mail

1. They're inchoate offenses so they apply to fraudulent schemes that haven't taken place or caused any loss.
2. They consist of just two elements:
   a. *Actus reus*. Sending mail or communicating by wire (fax, telephone calls, e-mails, and presumably text messages and social networking).
   b. *Mens rea*. With the intent to carry out the fraudulent schemes.
3. They have "seemingly infinite malleability." They include not only "consumer frauds, stock frauds, land frauds, bank frauds, insurance frauds, and commodity frauds, but have extended even to... blackmail, counterfeiting, election fraud, and bribery." Moreover, they can serve as a basis for "more complex charges such as money laundering and RICO offenses," and civil or criminal forfeiture. (O'Sullivan 2012, 420)

In our next case excerpt, *U.S. v. Maze*, the U.S. Supreme Court upheld the U.S. Government's reliance on the mail fraud statute to prosecute a thief.

CASE

*In **U.S. v. Maze (1974)**, the U.S. government relied on the mail fraud statute to prosecute Thomas Maze for stealing his roommate's BankAmericard and using it to pay his bills for a cross-national road trip to California in his roommate's car, which he also stole.*

Did he commit federal mail fraud?

U.S. v. Maze

414 U.S. 395, 94 S.Ct. 645 (1974)

HISTORY

Thomas Maze, Defendant, was convicted in the United States District Court for the Western District of Kentucky at Louisville on four counts of mail fraud. The Court of Appeals reversed. The Supreme Court affirmed.

REHNQUIST, J.

FACTS

Thomas E. Maze moved to Louisville, Kentucky, and there shared an apartment with Charles L. Meredith. In the spring of that year Maze's fancy lightly turned to thoughts of the sunny Southland, and he thereupon took Meredith's BankAmericard and his 1968 automobile and headed for Southern California. By presenting the BankAmericard and signing Meredith's name, Maze obtained food and lodging at motels located in California, Florida, and Louisiana. Each of these establishments transmitted to the Citizens Fidelity Bank & Trust Co. in Louisville, which had issued the BankAmericard to Meredith, the invoices representing goods and services furnished to Maze. Meredith, meanwhile, on the day after Maze's departure from Louisville, notified the Louisville bank that his credit card had been stolen.

(continues)

(continued)

Upon Maze's return to Louisville he was indicted on four counts of violation of the federal mail fraud statute (18 U.S.C. § 1341).

The mail fraud counts of the indictment charged that Maze had devised a scheme to defraud the Louisville bank, Charles L. Meredith, and several merchants in different States by unlawfully obtaining possession of the BankAmericard issued by the Louisville bank to Meredith, and using the card to obtain goods and services. The indictment charged that Maze had obtained goods and services at four specified motels by presenting Meredith's BankAmericard for payment and representing himself to be Meredith, and that Maze knew that each merchant would cause the sales slips of the purchases to be delivered by mail to the Louisville bank which would in turn mail them to Meredith for payment. The indictment also charged that the delay in this mailing would enable Maze to continue purchasing goods and services for an appreciable period of time.

Maze was tried by a jury in the United States District Court for the Western District of Kentucky. At trial, representatives of the four motels identified the sales invoices from the transactions on Meredith's BankAmericard which were forwarded to the Louisville bank by their motels. An official of the Louisville bank testified that all of the sales invoices for those transactions were received by the bank in due course through the mail, and that this was the customary method by which invoices representing BankAmericard purchases were transmitted to the Louisville bank.

The jury found Maze guilty as charged on all counts, and he appealed the judgment of conviction to the Court of Appeals for the Sixth Circuit. That court reversed the judgment as to the mail fraud statute. Because of an apparent conflict among the courts of appeals as to the circumstances under which the fraudulent use of a credit card may violate the mail fraud statute, we granted the Government's petition for certiorari. For the reasons stated below, we affirm the judgment of the Court of Appeals.

OPINION

The applicable parts of the mail fraud statute provide as follows:

> Whoever, having devised or intending to devise any scheme or artifice to defraud, or for obtaining money or property by means of false or fraudulent pretenses, representations, or promises…for the purpose of executing such scheme or artifice or attempting so to do…knowingly causes to be delivered by mail according to the direction thereon, or at the place at which it is directed to be delivered by the person to whom it is addressed, any (matter or thing whatever to be sent or delivered by the Postal Service) shall be fined not more than $1,000 or imprisoned not more than five years, or both. 18 U.S.C. § 1341.

We assume, as did the Court of Appeals, that the evidence would support a finding by the jury that Maze "caused" the mailings of the invoices he signed from the out-of-state motels to the Louisville bank. But the more difficult question is whether these mailings were sufficiently closely related to Maze's scheme to bring his conduct within the statute.

Under the statute, the mailing must be for the purpose of executing the scheme, as the statute requires, but it is not necessary that the scheme contemplate the use of the mails as an essential element. (*Pereira v. United States*). The Government relies on *Pereira*, supra, and *United States v. Sampson*, 371 U.S. 75, 83 S.Ct. 173, 9 L.Ed.2d 136 (1962), to support its position, while Maze relies on *Kann v. United States*, and *Parr v. United States*, 363 U.S. 370 (1960).

In *Kann*, corporate officers and directors were accused of having set up a dummy corporation through which to divert profits of their own corporation to their own use. As a part of the scheme, the defendants were accused of having fraudulently obtained checks payable to them which were cashed or deposited at a bank and then mailed for collection to the drawee bank. This Court held that the fraud was completed at the point at which defendants cashed the checks.

The Government, however, relying on *United States v. Sampson*, argues that essential to the success of any fraudulent credit-card scheme is the "delay" caused by use of the mails "which aids the perpetrator…in the continuation of a fraudulent credit card scheme and the postponement of its detection." In *Sampson*, various employees of a nationwide corporation were charged with a scheme to defraud businessmen by obtaining advance fees on the promise that the defendants would either help the businessmen to obtain loans or to sell their businesses.

Even after the checks representing the fees had been deposited to the accounts of the defendants, however, the plan called for the mailing of the accepted application together with a form letter assuring the victims that the services for which they had contracted would be performed. The Court found that *Kann* did not preclude the application of the mail fraud statute to "a deliberate, planned use of the mails after the victims' money had been obtained."

We do not believe that *Sampson* sustains the Government's position. The subsequent mailings there were designed to lull the victims into a false sense of security, postpone their ultimate complaint to the authorities, and therefore make the apprehension of the defendants less likely than if no mailings had taken place. But the successful completion of the mailings from the motel owners here to the Louisville bank increased the probability that Maze would be detected and apprehended. There was undoubtedly delay in transmitting invoices to the Louisville bank, as there is in the physical transmission of any business correspondence between cities separated by large distances.

Mail service as a means of transmitting such correspondence from one city to another is designed to overcome the effect of the distance which separates the places. But it is the distance, and not the mail service, which causes the time lag in the physical transmission of such correspondence. (Since we are admonished that we may not as judges ignore what we know as men, we do not wish to be understood as suggesting that delays in mail service are solely attributable to the distance involved. If the Postal Service appears on occasion to be something less than a 20th century version of the wingfooted Mercury, the fact remains that the invoices were mailed to and were ultimately received by the Louisville bank.)

Congress could have drafted the mail fraud statute so as to require only that the mails be in fact used as a result of the fraudulent scheme. But it did not do this; instead, it required that the use of the mails be "for the purpose of executing such scheme or artifice. . . ." Since the mailings in this case were not for that purpose, the judgment of the Court of Appeals is

Affirmed.

DISSENT

WHITE, J., JOINED BY BURGER CJ, AND BRENNAN AND BLACKMUN JJ.

Until today the acts charged in the indictment in this case—knowingly causing four separate sales invoices to be mailed by merchants to the bank that had issued the stolen BankAmericard in furtherance of a scheme to defraud the bank by using the credit card without authorization and by falsely securing credit—would have been a criminal offense punishable as mail fraud under 18 U.S.C. § 1341. But no more. By misreading this Court's prior decisions and giving an unambiguous federal criminal statute an unrealistic reading, the majority places beyond the reach of the statute a fraudulent scheme that by law is not consummated until after the mails have been used, that utilizes the mails as a central, necessary instrumentality in its perpetration, and that demands federal investigatory and prosecutorial resources if it is to be effectively checked. Because I cannot subscribe to the majority's reasoning or the result it reaches, I dissent.

The majority's decision has ramifications far beyond the mere reversal of a lone criminal conviction. In this era of the "cashless" society, Americans are increasingly resorting to the use of credit cards in their day-to-day consumer purchases. Today well over 300 million credit cards are in circulation, and annual charges exceed $60 billion. In 1969 alone, 1.5 million credit cards were lost or stolen, resulting in fraud losses exceeding $100 million. Current estimates of annual credit card fraud losses are put as high as $200 million. Under the result reached by the majority, only those credit card frauds exceeding $5,000 covered by 15 U.S.C. 1644 will be subject to federal criminal jurisdiction.

Yet this burgeoning criminal activity, as evidenced by the very facts of this case, does not recognize artificial state boundaries. In the future, nationwide credit card fraud schemes will have to be prosecuted in each individual State in which a fraudulent transaction transpired. Here, for example, Maze must now be charged and tried in California, Louisiana, and Florida. This result, never intended by Congress, may precipitate a widespread inability to apprehend and/or prosecute those who would hijack the credit card system.

I dissent.

(continues)

(continued)

QUESTIONS

1. State the elements of the federal mail fraud statute relevant to deciding whether Thomas Maze was guilty of mail fraud.
2. List the facts relevant to deciding whether Thomas Maze violated the statute.
3. Summarize the arguments for the majority's opinion reversing Maze's conviction.
4. Summarize the dissent's arguments in favor of upholding Maze's conviction.
5. Which position do you favor? Defend your answer.
6. Is the dissent's worry over the social problem the Mail Fraud Act is aimed at misplaced? Is it still a problem? Defend your answer with arguments made by the majority and dissent, and the text in the section "Federal Mail Fraud."

LO4 PONZI SCHEMES

Ponzi schemes a fraudulent investment operation that pays returns to investors from their own money or money paid by subsequent investors rather from any actual profit earned

The "great recession" that began in 2007 hurt legitimate industries—automobiles, real estate, and banking. We're all aware of these casualties. What you probably don't know is that the downturn also hurt an old form of false pretenses—Ponzi schemes (named after a con artist who ripped off millions from gullible victims in 1920). In **Ponzi schemes**, schemers tell investors they're buying assets such as real estate, stocks and bonds, or consumer products. In fact, they're buying nothing. Instead, Ponzi schemers use the money to pay earlier investors. Eventually, the money dries up and everything collapses.

During this recession, Ponzi schemes have collapsed at record rates. The FBI has about five hundred open Ponzi investigations nationwide, up from three hundred in 2006.

Why the increase in Ponzi schemes? In order to answer that question, we need to put *increase* in perspective. Traditionally, Ponzis were small scams spread by "word of mouth, direct mail and advertisements in magazines" (Wilber 2009). The Internet and modern communications dramatically changed that. These technology advances, and the economic boom of the 1990s and early 2000s, enabled Ponzi schemers to lure institutional investors into handing over billions of dollars, and small ones into using their home equity loans to cash in on the bonanza.

Enter the "Great Recession of 2009." Ponzi scheme investors demanded their money back. When they couldn't get it, they reported the schemers to federal agents. Also, wary *potential* investors in increasing numbers reported investment opportunities that seemed too good to be true. This seriously wounded the Ponzis. But, Professor William K. Black, former executive director of the Institute for Fraud Prevention, believes that when good times return, so will Ponzis. "The crooks know that potential investors, some desperate for a quick return, will not always be so wary" (qtd.in Wilber 2009).

In 2009, Bernie Madoff pleaded guilty to eleven felony charges stemming from running a massive Ponzi scheme for years. Madoff defrauded his victims of more than $65 billion. The government entered a $170 billion legal judgment against him, and he was sentenced to 150 years in prison for his crimes. But the court also issued a forfeiture order that called for "forfeiture of all property, real and personal, that…is derived from proceeds traceable to the commission of the said offenses."See the Criminal Law in Focus box, "Madoff Forfeiture Order."

Madoff Forfeiture Order

UNITED STATES DISTRICT COURT
SOUTHERN DISTRICT OF NEW YORK

UNITED STATES OF AMERICA

- v. -

BERNARD L. MADOFF,

Defendant.

SECOND FINAL ORDER OF FORFEITURE
(1st Pub. Group–Selected Assets; 2nd Pub. Group)

09 Cr. 213 (DC)

USDC SDNY
DOCUMENT
ELECTRONICALLY FILED
DOC #:
DATE FILED: 09/22/10

BACKGROUND

The Criminal Proceedings

WHEREAS, on or about June 26, 2009, the Court entered a Preliminary Order of Forfeiture (Final as to the Defendant) (the "Preliminary Order") as to BERNARD L. MADOFF, the defendant ("MADOFF" or the "defendant"), which is incorporated herein by reference as if set out in full;

WHEREAS, on June 29, 2009, the Court sentenced the defendant to, *inter alia*, 150 years' imprisonment and criminal forfeiture in accordance with the terms of the Preliminary Order;

WHEREAS, in the Preliminary Order, the Court imposed an aggregate money judgment upon the defendant in the amount of $170.799 billion ($170 billion as to the First Forfeiture Allegation and $799 million as to the Second Forfeiture Allegation), and ordered the defendant to forfeit all of his right, title and interest in any and all property and other interests belonging to, owed to or controlled in whole or in part by the defendant, and all property traceable to such property, including, but not limited to, all right, title and interest of the defendant in the property listed in Exhibit A to the Preliminary Order (the "Specific Property");

WHEREAS, pursuant to 21 U.S.C. § 853(n)(7), the United States is therefore entitled to have clear title to the Subject Property and to warrant good title to any subsequent purchaser or transferee.

NOW, THEREFORE, on the application of Preet Bharara, United States Attorney for the Southern District of New York, Barbara A. Ward and Matthew L. Schwartz, Assistant United States Attorneys, of counsel,

IT IS ORDERED, ADJUDGED AND DECREED THAT:

1. All right, title and interest in the Subject Property is hereby forfeited to the United States of America for disposition according to law.

2. All right, title and interest in any and all interest and/or income ("Interest") accrued on the Subject Property (or the proceeds of its sale, where applicable) while on deposit in the Seized Assets Deposit Account is hereby forfeited to the United States of America for disposition according to law. The United States Marshals Service shall calculate such Interest, accruing from the dates of deposit in the Seized Assets Deposit Account, and transfer any and all such Interest to the Department of Justice Assets Forfeiture Fund along with the forfeited property, in anticipation of remission proceedings for the benefit of victims to be conducted by the Department of Justice pursuant to 21 U.S.C. § 853(i) and 28 C.F.R. Part 9.

3. The net proceeds from the sale of the Subject Property, together with Interest (as defined in the next preceding paragraph), shall be applied to the Money Judgments imposed upon the defendant, in partial satisfaction thereof.

4. Nothing in this Order shall affect any property subject to the Preliminary Order of Forfeiture other than the Subject Property, or any petition asserting an interest in any such property.

5. The Court retains jurisdiction to take additional action, enter further orders, and amend this and any future orders as necessary to implement and enforce this Order.

6. The Clerk of the Court shall forward certified copies of this Order to Assistant United States Attorney Barbara A. Ward, One St. Andrew's Plaza, New York, New York, 10007.

Dated: New York, New York
September 22, 2010

DENNY CHIN
United States ~~District~~ Circuit Judge,
Sitting by Designation

Source: Second Final Order of Forfeiture in United States v. Madoff. Some material has been deleted.

CIVIL LIABILITY

In our emphasis on the centuries-old *criminal* response to protect property from swindlers, we can't overlook that thefts, frauds, and swindles are also civil wrongs. "The history of larceny and fraud is also the history of supplementing civil actions with criminal punishment." What was once a tort is now also a crime (Dubber and Kelman 2005, 919).

The case of Navy Commander Charles E. Coughlin is an excellent example of a case pursued simultaneously on both tracks. A jury found Coughlin guilty of filing a false claim with the September 11th Victim Compensation Fund and stealing $151,000 from the government. Coughlin collected money for a neck injury that he said he suffered during the 9-11 attacks. In fact, the injury had occurred three years before the attack. He was sentenced to 41 months in federal prison. The civil suit, in which the U.S. government hopes to recoup the money Commander Coughlin was convicted of taking, was ongoing as of this writing.

YOU *DECIDE*

Should he forfeit his property even if a jury didn't convict him?

The U.S. military granted Navy commander Charles E. Coughlin a Purple Heart and the government awarded him $331,000 for neck and other injuries he claimed to have suffered when American Airlines Flight 77 crashed into the Pentagon on September 11, 2001. Now government lawyers have concluded that Coughlin lied about his injuries—and they are seeking to seize his $1 million house in Severna Park, his Mercedes-Benz, and his minivan. The U.S. attorney's office has filed a civil suit alleging that the now-retired commander falsely claimed he suffered "a partial permanent disability" after falling debris struck him on the head at the Pentagon, where 184 people were killed.

Question

- "Is it wise public policy to continue its *civil* action to seize Coughlin's house and car, even though he's serving his time in prison for his fraud?" To answer the question, consider the sections on "Crimes and Noncriminal Legal Wrongs," and "Criminal Punishment in U.S. Society" in Chapter 1.

Robbery

LO5

Now that you've seen the ancient crime of larceny brought up to date by modern fraud, let's turn to robbery, the other ancient property crime modern robbery statutes and case law have brought up to date. *Robbery* consists of theft accomplished by force, violence, or intimidation (*State v. Robertson* 1999). What we're saying here is that robbery is really two crimes, theft and battery or assault (Chapter 10). But the criminal law has never treated it that way, because robbery is considered more serious than the sum of its parts. The MPC reporter explains why:

> The violent petty thief operating in the streets and alleys of big cities—the "mugger"—is one of the main sources of insecurity and concern in the population at large. There is a special element of terror in this kind of depredation. The ordinary citizen does not

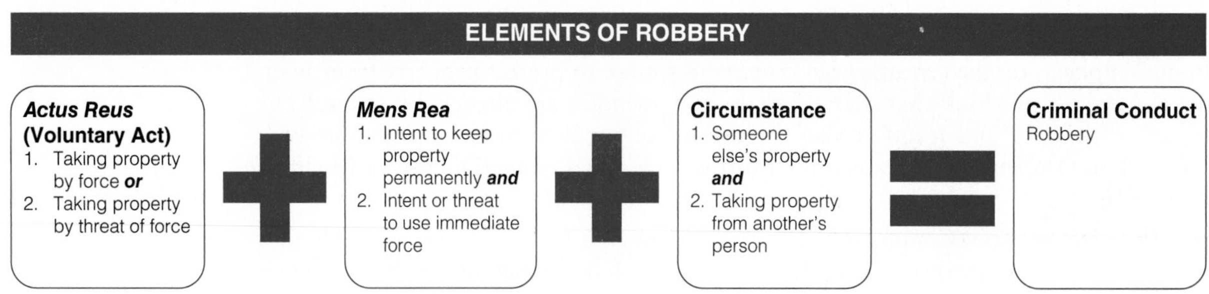

> feel particularly threatened by the surreptitious larceny, embezzlement, or fraud. But there is understandable abhorrence of the robber who accosts on the streets and who menaces his victims with actual or threatened violence against which there is a general sense of helplessness. Fears and detests such behavior, the offender exhibits himself as seriously deviated from community norms, thus justifying more serious sanctions. The robber may be distinguished from the stealthy thief by the hardihood that enables him to carry out his purpose in the presence of his victim and over his opposition—obstacles that might deter ordinary sneak thieves and that justify the feeling of special danger evoked by the robber. (98)

As a victim of 5 (or was it 6?) muggings on Chicago streets, I can vouch for the fear, anger, and sense of violation that goes along with losing something valuable, like the watch my mother gave me as a high school graduation present. But it's more than the monetary value of what I lost that signifies. It's the personal violation that accompanied fear and humiliation, even when the threat isn't real. During the second mugging, I gave up my money because the mugger showed me his "weapon" bulging in his coat pocket. After I handed over the money, he pulled the "weapon" out of his pocket—a comb—and ran his thumb down the teeth, sneering, "Hey man, you should be more careful in the future," snickering as he swaggered away.

Let's look at the elements of robbery: its *actus reus*, *mens rea*, and required attendant circumstances.

ROBBERY *ACTUS REUS* (CRIMINAL ACT)

robbery *actus reus* an act or threat of force beyond the amount needed to take and carry away someone else's property

An act of force is the essence of the robbery *actus reus*. But how much force? *Any* amount beyond the amount needed to take and carry away someone else's property is enough. Picking a pocket isn't robbery because "picking pockets" is defined as requiring only enough force to remove the contents of the pocket. But even slightly mishandling the victim, like a push, turns the pickpocket into a robber. Robbery doesn't even require the use of *actual* force; threatened force (a drawn gun or knife) is enough.

Owens v. State (2001) illustrates this. Bernard Owens, sneaked up behind the victim while she was talking on a pay telephone, and "ripped my purse off my shoulder," which "pulled on her and left a mark on her shoulder." When he "grabbed and snatched it," it "hurt." But Owens didn't "threaten her or try to injure her." The trial court jury convicted him of robbery. Owens appealed, arguing that the evidence didn't "establish the force necessary to prove robbery, and that the charge should be reduced to theft." The Florida Court of Appeals agreed because "the victim did not resist at all, nor was she held or struck. While the snatching produced a mark, her testimony established that the mark resulted merely from the force Owens employed to remove the purse" (144).

"Purse Snatching" vs. "Robbery"

- *Owens v. State*, 787 So.2d 143 (2001). Purse snatching that left a mark on the victim's shoulder from a purse strap was *not* a robbery.
- *West v. State*, 539 A.2d 231 (1988). Purse snatched from a woman's hand was not a robbery.
- *State v. Curley*, 939 P.2d 1103 (1997). Although the victim felt a shove on her shoulder, the purse snatching was not necessarily robbery.
- *Wash v. State*, 408 N.E.2d 634 (1980). Evidence of violence or force was sufficient when the defendant assaulted the victim and took her purse while he was fleeing her apartment.
- *State v. Johnson*, 411 So.2d 439 (1982). Defendant's taking of a purse dropped by a woman who fought him as he beat and attempted to rob her was properly found to be theft by use of force.

Source: State v. Rolon, 45 A.3d 518 (2012).

Our next case excerpt, *State v. Rolon* (2012), grapples with the distinction between purse-snatching and robbery. The lively majority and dissenting opinions demonstrate the importance of the facts of each case in deciding whether the prosecution proved the force element.

CASE

In **State v. Rolon (2012)***, sufficient evidence existed that would justify a reasonable juror in finding that Nelson Rolon robbed 87-year-old Irene Joseph.*

Did he rob or steal from the victim?

State v. Rolon

45 A.3d 518 (RI 2012)

HISTORY

On August 27, 2007, an 87-year-old woman's purse was stolen in a supermarket parking lot. As a result, the defendant, Nelson Rolon, was charged with, and ultimately convicted of, first-degree robbery. He was sentenced to 25 years in prison, with twelve years to serve and the remainder suspended, with probation. He now appeals his conviction to this Court, arguing that the trial justice erred in denying his motion for a judgment of acquittal because the evidence produced at trial was legally insufficient to prove the element of force. For the reasons set forth in this opinion, we affirm (5–1) the judgment of the Superior Court.

SUTTELL, C.J., JOINED BY GOLDBERG, FLAHERTY, ROBINSON, AND INDEGLIA, JJ.

FACTS

On September 28, 2007, a grand jury indicted defendant for the first-degree robbery of Irene Joseph, an elderly person, in violation of G.L.1956 § 11-39-1(a).

(continues)

(continued)

Although § 11-39-1 sets forth the penalties for the different degrees of robbery, it does not define the elements of that crime. Consequently, we long have held that § 11-39-1 incorporates the common-law definition of robbery, that definition being the felonious and forcible taking from the person of another of goods or money of any value by violence or by putting the victim in fear.[1] The defendant's trial took place in December 2008. The state did not present Ms. Joseph as a witness at the trial because, at that time, she was eighty-nine years old and confined to a nursing home. The state did, however, present six witnesses against defendant, the substance of whose testimonies we review below. [Only testimony of witnesses regarding the element of force is included in this excerpt.]

The first witness to testify was Lorraine Martin, an employee of the Stop & Shop on Smithfield Road in the Town of North Smithfield. At around one o'clock in the afternoon on August 27, 2007, Ms. Martin was eating lunch in her car in the Stop & Shop parking lot when she heard a woman yelling: "Help me. He stole my pocketbook. Stop him. Somebody help me." Ms. Martin testified that when she looked to her right, she saw a "skinny, frail," elderly woman "going after" a man who was "jumping" into a vehicle. She then witnessed the man back the vehicle out of its parking spot, such that the elderly woman "had to jump out of the way, because he would have hit her." At that point, Ms. Martin testified, she decided that she "had to do something," so she pulled her car out of its parking spot, started following the vehicle, and called 911. She followed the vehicle for approximately five minutes, never losing sight of it, and eventually was able to see the vehicle's license plate as it was turning around in a cul-de-sac.

Melanie Ruiz, who has a child with defendant, was the third witness to testify at his trial. Ms. Ruiz testified that at some point while she was with defendant on August 27, 2007, he gave her a plastic bag and "told her to hold it for him for a day or two" and not to "leave it in the car." Ms. Ruiz kept the bag in a closet in her house, but she gave it to the police the next day. She testified that she did not add or remove anything from the bag while it was in her possession, and that she believed it to contain "a hat, sunglasses, and a shirt." The bag was admitted into evidence as a full exhibit; when asked by the state to look at the contents of the bag, Ms. Ruiz did so, noting that the bag contained a hat, sunglasses, a shirt, *and a knife*. [emphasis added]

Glenn Lamoureux, a sergeant in the North Smithfield Police Department, testified next at defendant's trial. He testified that on August 27, 2007, he responded to the Stop & Shop on Smithfield Road after receiving "a call from dispatch to respond to that location for a robbery that had just taken place." Upon arrival, Sgt. Lamoureux learned that a "purse snatching" had occurred in the parking lot. He then took photographs of the "immediate area" where the snatching occurred and "attempted to locate some evidence." Sergeant Lamoureux located a piece of a "black leather strap" that "appeared to be from a purse" in the same area of the parking lot; he also retrieved another piece of a purse strap that, he testified, Ms. Joseph had been "clutching in her hand." Both strap pieces were entered into evidence as full exhibits. According to Sgt. Lamoureux, when he spoke to Ms. Joseph, "she was visibly shaken," and he "could tell she was nervous because of what had taken place."

Finally, Sgt. Lamoureux testified that later in the day on August 28, 2007, he called defendant and asked him to come to the police station "for an additional statement." At the station, after being advised of his rights, defendant denied meeting Ms. Figueroa [defendant's wife] for lunch the previous day, asking Ms. Ruiz to lie to the police, or giving her a bag to hide. At one point, according to Sgt. Lamoureux, defendant said "I'm guilty of this," and then immediately said, "but I didn't do this." Sergeant Lamoureux testified that defendant also asked "about the victim and how old she was, and if he would be able to see the victim."

Sharon Pagliarini, a detective in the North Smithfield Police Department, was the last witness to testify at defendant's trial; she testified about the bag that was obtained from Ms. Ruiz's closet. Detective Pagliarini identified the bag and its contents, stating that all of the items in the bag—a T-shirt, a "white

[1] "Every person who shall commit: (1) robbery by use of a dangerous weapon; (2) robbery where a victim is injured; or (3) robbery where the victim is a person who is severely impaired or an elderly person; shall be guilty of first degree robbery and shall be imprisoned for not less than ten (10) years and may be imprisoned for life, or fined not more than fifteen thousand dollars ($15,000), or both."

hat," sunglasses, and "a knife with the description of Nelson"—were "in the same or substantially the same condition as when she found them in the closet of Ms. Ruiz's house."

After the state rested, defendant indicated that he would not call any witnesses and moved for a judgment of acquittal. In so moving, defendant argued that "even drawing every inference favorable to guilt in the light most favorable to the state, a jury still could not find beyond reasonable doubt that the element of force has been met in this case." The defendant suggested that because there was no testimony at trial with respect to the actual interaction between defendant and Ms. Joseph at the moment the purse was stolen, the purse very well could have been "caught in the handles of a carriage and the strap cut free," with Ms. Joseph being on the other side of her car.

The defendant admitted that such circumstances would be enough to convict him of larceny, but he asserted that they would be insufficient to convict him of robbery—a crime that requires a finding that the taking of goods was "by violence or by putting the victim in fear." The defendant argued that to make such a finding, the jury would have to make "an assumption"—"passing into the realm of speculation"—and that simply would not be sufficient to sustain the requisite burden of proof.

The state, in response, agreed that the element of force is essential to the crime of robbery, but it argued that it had presented sufficient evidence of force in this case. Specifically, the state pointed to the physical evidence in this case: the knife found in the plastic bag that defendant had asked Ms. Ruiz to hold on to and the two pieces of the purse strap, one found in the Stop & Shop parking lot and the other recovered from Ms. Joseph. The state asserted that an inference could be drawn from those pieces of evidence "that the straps had been cut." The state also argued that the way the straps had been cut shows that defendant took the purse "by force with that knife cutting those straps away from Ms. Joseph."[2]

In ruling on defendant's motion for a judgment of acquittal, the trial justice stated that the evidence presented at trial, "when viewed in the light most favorable to the state, and when reasonable inferences are drawn therefrom," was sufficient to allow the jury to find beyond a reasonable doubt that defendant had a knife, that he cut Ms. Joseph's purse with the knife, and that he thereby took her purse "by force, violence, or intimidation."

The trial justice also stated that Ms. Joseph's age, her plea for help immediately after her purse was snatched, and her "nervous" state after the incident, as testified to by Sgt. Lamoureux, further supported the inference that she was placed in fear at the time of the theft. Ultimately, the trial justice denied defendant's motion for a judgment of acquittal.

The jury found defendant guilty of first-degree robbery. Thereafter, defendant filed a motion for a new trial, which the trial justice denied on December 17, 2008. On February 25, 2009, defendant was sentenced to twenty-five years at the Adult Correctional Institutions, with twelve years to serve and the remainder suspended, with probation. He appealed on March 5, 2009, and a judgment of conviction and commitment was entered thereafter.

OPINION

On appeal, defendant argues that the trial justice erred in denying his motion for a judgment of acquittal because the evidence presented at trial "was legally insufficient to prove the element of force as is required for robbery." According to defendant, the state did not present any evidence "to suggest that force greater than the amount needed to effectuate the taking of the handbag was employed," nor, he argues, was any evidence presented that Ms. Joseph "was intimidated or put in fear while the taking occurred." The defendant concedes that "at best, the state's case merely amounted to proof of larceny from the person."

In *State v. Robertson*, 740 A.2d at 333–34, this Court adopted the rule that "a snatching involves sufficient force to support a conviction of robbery if the article taken is so attached to the person or the clothes of the victim as to afford resistance." In so doing, we noted that "robbery is punished more severely than larceny because the crime presents the risk of harm to the person of the victim and not solely to the victim's property," and that this "risk of bodily injury * * * is present when the item that is being snatched is attached to the body or the clothing of the victim." It bears repeating that "the force used in a robbery 'makes the violation of the person more atrocious than privately stealing.'"

(continues)

[2]The state noted that the piece of strap retrieved from Ms. Joseph "has a slice mark about an inch above the cut that was made."

(continued)

Because defendant's sole contention on appeal is that the state presented insufficient evidence of force, we review only that evidence from which a jury could have inferred that defendant used force in stealing Ms. Joseph's purse. At defendant's trial, the following pieces of physical evidence were admitted as full exhibits: (1) two pieces of a purse strap with cut and slice marks on them, one that was found at the scene of the crime and another that the victim, Ms. Joseph, had been "clutch[ing] in her hand"; and (2) a plastic bag containing, among other things, a knife "with the description [*sic*] of Nelson," which defendant asked Ms. Ruiz to hide for him. When viewing this evidence in the light most favorable to the state, a reasonable inference could be drawn that defendant had a knife at the time that he took Ms. Joseph's purse and, further, that he used that knife to cut the straps of her purse to effectuate the taking.

We do not agree with defendant's assertion that the evidence presented does not "suggest that force greater than the amount needed to effectuate the taking of the handbag was employed." The record indicates that, not only were the two strap pieces cut, but there also are slice marks on the straps. The presence of these marks counters defendant's claim that "the purse was taken swiftly and by stealth" because it suggests that a struggle for the purse ensued. Consequently, we are of the opinion that a reasonable inference could be drawn that at the time when defendant took the purse from Ms. Joseph, she was aware of the taking and resisted it, or, at the very least, the purse was "so attached" to her "as to afford resistance." Therefore, we are satisfied that the state produced sufficient evidence from which a jury could infer beyond a reasonable doubt that defendant used force to take Ms. Joseph's purse.

Upon our review of the record in the light most favorable to the state, drawing all reasonable inferences consistent with guilt, we are satisfied that sufficient evidence existed that would justify a reasonable juror in finding that the defendant robbed Ms. Joseph on August 27, 2007. For this reason, we affirm the trial justice's denial of the defendant's motion for a judgment of acquittal.

For the reasons stated in this opinion, we affirm the judgment of the Superior Court. The record of this case shall be remanded to the Superior Court.

DISSENT

FLAHERTY, J.

Our well-settled law defines robbery as "the felonious taking of money or goods of any value from the person of another, or in his presence, against his will, by violence, or putting him in fear." Indeed, we have said that "the gist of the crime of robbery is the taking by force and fear." As noted by defendant, scores of pages in legal reporters are devoted to the details of purse-snatching cases; this appears to reflect how the crime of purse snatching, and its relationship to robbery, has proven to be somewhat vexatious to courts around the country. (See Criminal Law in Focus, "Purse Snatching v. Robbery.")

In my opinion, the record is clear that there was utterly no evidence that Ms. Joseph was in fear, or even that she was aware that her purse was being stolen at the precise moment that the crime occurred. As the majority relates, Ms. Joseph was in a nursing home at the time of trial and was unable to testify, but her out-of-court statement to an independent witness that a man "stole her pocketbook" was admitted. Her statement, however, does not reasonably reflect that she was afraid at the time her purse was taken. The same is true of her demeanor after the crime took place. Indeed, the fact that the intrepid Ms. Joseph actually chased the thief into the parking lot of the restaurant undercuts any suggestion that she was relieved of her purse by means of fear or intimidation.

Because the state introduced no evidence of fear, it necessarily must have relied on the theory that defendant accomplished the theft by force. To that end, I disagree with the majority's conclusion that force or violence against the person reasonably can be inferred by a finder of fact when the only evidence introduced was that of force against the property, at least under the circumstances before us here. The majority rests its conclusion on three factors: (1) the cut purse straps; (2) the defendant's knife, which was presumably used to cut the straps; and (3) what the majority has determined—without citation to testimony or evidentiary support in the record beyond the exhibit itself—are additional "slice marks" on the strap segments that suggest that a "struggle for the purse ensued." The fact that the thief cut the straps is evidence of force directed at the property. However, the record is bereft of evidence that any force or violence was brought to bear on Ms. Joseph in an attempt to obtain the purse. Again, there were no eyewitnesses to the theft, and Ms. Joseph's statement sheds no light on the use of force or violence against her person.

With all due respect to the majority, the state presented no evidence suggesting that the knife ever was brandished before Ms. Joseph, or that any "struggle" occurred between defendant and Ms. Joseph whatsoever. These are speculative assertions that have no foundation in fact, and this Court has firmly held that a conviction may not rest on conjecture and surmise. Moreover, the facts here are remote from those that confronted this Court in *Robertson*, 740 A.2d at 332. In that case, the state introduced evidence that a defendant made the victim feel "nervous" by asking him questions; the defendant then unexpectedly reached into the victim's car and ripped two gold chains from his neck. I have no quarrel with the holding of the Court in that case that "a snatching involves sufficient force to support a conviction of robbery if the article taken is so attached to the person or the clothes of the victim as to afford resistance." In *Robertson*, however, there was evidence that the chains were clasped around the victim's neck and had to be torn off, which necessarily implies a significant degree of force against the person.

Also, in that case the defendant was face-to-face with his victim, and he placed his hands on his victim's person while relieving him of his necklace. Here, there is simply no evidence in the record suggesting that the snatching itself was so violent that it necessarily implied the use of force or fear against Ms. Joseph's person.

I need not gild the lily: in my opinion, under these facts, the mere fact that the thief cut the straps of Ms. Joseph's purse does not lead to an inference that the defendant used more force than was necessary to remove the purse from her possession, or that any fear whatsoever was brought to bear upon her.

Therefore, I respectfully dissent.

QUESTIONS

1. List all the facts relevant to deciding whether Nelson Rolon robbed 87-year-old Irene Joseph.
2. Summarize the majority's argument upholding Rolon's conviction.
3. Summarize the dissent's argument that Rolon committed theft not robbery.
4. In your opinion did Rolon rob Joseph? Defend your answer.

ROBBERY *MENS REA* (INTENT)

Robbery *mens rea* is the same as theft *mens rea* (the intent to take another person's property and keep it permanently) but with the additional intent to use immediate force, or the threat of immediate force, to get it. So it's not robbery to take an iPod away from someone if you honestly, but mistakenly, believe it's yours. Of course, it's still a crime (battery if you use force or assault if you threaten to use it); it's just not robbery (LaFave and Scott 1986, 778–79).

robbery *mens rea* the intent to take another person's property and keep it permanently with the additional intent to use immediate force, or the threat of immediate force, to get it

THE DEGREES OF ROBBERY

Most states have divided robbery into degrees, based on three circumstances:

1. Whether robbers are armed
2. Whether the robber acted alone or with accomplices
3. The kind and degree of injury robbers inflict on their victims

New York's Penal Code (2003, § 160.00) is typical. First-degree robbers (§ 160.15) carry deadly weapons (or "play weapons" that look real) and seriously injure their victims. Second-degree robbers (§ 160.10) have accomplices or display play weapons and inflict some injury on their victims. Third-degree robbers (§ 160.05) are unarmed, and they inflict no injury on their victims.

LO6

Receiving Stolen Property

receiving stolen property benefiting from the theft of someone else's property without having participated in the wrongful acquisition in the first place

It's not only a crime to take someone else's property by theft, it's also a crime to "receive" property that someone else has stolen. Called "receiving stolen property," the purpose of making it a crime is to prevent and to punish individuals who benefit from someone else's theft, even though they didn't have anything to do with the original theft.

Although "receiving" is primarily directed at fences (professionals who sell stolen property for profit), it also targets people who know, or should know, they're buying stolen stuff because the prices are too low.

fences receivers of stolen goods or places where stolen goods are bought

RECEIVING STOLEN PROPERTY *ACTUS REUS*

receiving stolen property *actus reus* the act of receiving and controlling at least temporarily (but not necessarily possessing) the property

Receiving stolen property *actus reus* is the act of receiving the property. Receiving requires that the receiver control the property, at least briefly. But the receiver doesn't have to possess the property physically. So if I buy a stolen set of Bose mini speakers from a fence for a friend, and the fence hands them over directly to my friend, I've received the stolen speakers, even though I've never seen or touched them. If my friend gives the speakers to her friend, her friend also has received them. Also, anyone who temporarily hides stolen goods for someone else has received the stolen goods.

RECEIVING STOLEN PROPERTY *MENS REA*

receiving stolen property *mens rea* depending on the jurisdiction, knowing or believing that received goods are stolen

Receiving stolen property *mens rea* varies. In some states, receivers have to *know* the goods are stolen. In others, *believing* the goods are stolen is enough. In all jurisdictions, knowledge may be inferred from surrounding circumstances, such as receiving goods from a known thief or buying goods at a fraction of their real value (like buying a new top-of-the-line42-inchSmart 3DTV for $75). Some jurisdictions require only that receivers were reckless or negligent about whether the property was stolen. Recklessness and negligence as to whether the property was stolen are often directed at likely fences, usually junk dealers and pawnshop operators. (See the Elements of Receiving Stolen Property illustration.)

Receivers have to intend to keep the property permanently. This excludes police officers who knowingly accept stolen property and secretly place it in the hands of suspected fences to catch them. They haven't received stolen property because they don't intend to keep it, only to use it as bait.

Texas is one state that requires that receivers know that the property they control is stolen. The state has to prove actual knowledge beyond a reasonable doubt, but the prosecution can use circumstantial evidence to meet its burden.

CASE

*In **Sonnier v. State (1992),** a Texas bench trial court convicted Olga Sonnier of receiving stolen property and sentenced her to fifteen years in prison for knowingly pawning four stolen Peavy amplifier speakers for $275 that were worth $1,400. The Texas Court of Appeals reversed.*

Did she know the speakers were stolen?

Sonnier v. State

849 S.W.2d 828 (Tex. App. 1992)

HISTORY

Olga Lee Sonnier, the defendant, was convicted after a bench trial in the 230th District Court, Harris County, of theft. She was sentenced to 15 years confinement, and she appealed. The Court of Appeals reversed and judgment of acquittal was ordered.

MIRABAL, J.

FACTS

On November 2, 1989, John L. Clough, the complainant, discovered several items missing from his establishment, the Houstonian Club. Among the items missing were four amplifier speakers, known as "P.V." or "Peavey" speakers. The speakers are the type that are connected to an amplifier system when bands play at the club. When the four speakers are stacked and connected, they stand about four feet tall and three feet wide. The speakers were valued at $1,400 when purchased, and could not be replaced for less than $2,000.

The complainant last saw the speakers on the night of November 1, 1989. He did not know the appellant, she was not his employee, and he did not give anyone permission to take the speakers from his club. An employee, Gaylord or "Ricky" Burton, worked for him a couple of months, but vanished at the same time the speakers did. Burton was supposed to be at the club on the morning the speakers disappeared.

The complainant reported the theft to the police. He told them he believed Burton had stolen the speakers. One of the complainant's employees had seen Burton take the speakers the morning of November 2, 1989. The speakers were found in a pawn shop. The complainant identified the speakers by their serial numbers.

Two employees of the pawn shop said two men came into the shop on November 2, 1989, and tried to pawn the speakers. The men had no identification, and the employees could not accept the speakers without some identification. The men came back later with the appellant (Olga Sonnier), who had a driver's license, and she pawned the four speakers for $225.

The police, after an investigation, were unable to locate Burton, but did locate the appellant because her name, address, and signature were on the pawn tickets. The appellant was charged with theft. A pawn shop employee positively identified the appellant as the woman who pawned the speakers. The appellant called two witnesses, an employee of the pawn shop, Anthony Smith, and Sergeant Graves of the Houston Police Department. The appellant did not testify.

Smith testified two men tried to pawn the speakers. When he would not accept the speakers without some identification, the men left, but came back later with the appellant. She presented a driver's license and pawned the speakers. Sergeant Graves testified that the appellant phoned him and said she pawned the speakers for some friends who did not have a driver's license.

(continues)

(continued)

OPINION

Sonnier asserts that the evidence is insufficient to show she had actual knowledge that the speakers were stolen. The essential elements of theft by receiving are:

1. that a theft occurred by another person;
2. the defendant received the stolen property; and
3. when the defendant received the stolen property she knew it was stolen.

TEXAS CRIMINAL CODE
SEC. 31.03. THEFT

1 A person commits an offense if he unlawfully appropriates property with intent to deprive the owner of property.

2. Appropriation of property is unlawful

a. if it is without the owner's effective consent;

b. the property is stolen and the actor appropriates the property knowing it was stolen by another....

Under the statute and the indictment, the State had the burden to prove beyond a reasonable doubt that appellant had actual subjective knowledge that the speakers were stolen. The evidence, viewed in the light most favorable to the prosecution, shows:

1. On the same day the speakers were stolen, two men brought them to a pawn shop to hock them.
2. When the pawn shop refused to accept the speakers because neither man would offer identification, the two men left, and then returned with appellant.
3. Appellant pawned the four speakers for the two men. She used her driver's license, giving her correct name and address. She received $225 for the four speakers, about $56 for each, while they were worth at least $350 each.

The State emphasized in the trial court, and on appeal, that the sheer value of the speakers is enough for the trial court to find appellant knew they were stolen. The State argues that selling stolen property for less than market value is some evidence that the seller knew the property was stolen.

However, here the speakers were pawned, not sold, and the evidence does not indicate that the pawn shop paid an unusually low amount to pawn the speakers. Further, the evidence does not show that appellant, or any reasonable person of common experience, would likely even know the market value of the speakers.

We cannot say that the circumstances in this case exclude every other reasonable hypothesis except the hypothesis that appellant knew the speakers were stolen when she pawned them. We find, under the circumstances, appellant just as reasonably could have been doing a favor for her friends or acquaintances when she accompanied them to the pawn shop and used her own ID so the speakers could be pawned. We sustain appellant's point of error one.

Sonnier asserts the evidence was also insufficient to support her conviction under the "straight theft" paragraph of the indictment which alleged appellant:

1. unlawfully appropriated the speakers by acquiring them and otherwise exercising control over them,
2. with the intent to deprive the owner of the property,
3. without the effective consent of the owner. Tex. Penal Code Ann. § 31.03(a), (b)(1)....

The evidence before the trial court placed appellant in possession of the speakers on the day they were stolen. The unexplained possession of stolen property may be sufficient to sustain a conviction for theft. To warrant such an inference of guilt from the circumstances of possession alone, the possession must be personal, recent, unexplained, and must involve a distinct and conscious assertion of a right to the property by the defendant.

When the party in possession gives a reasonable explanation for having the recently stolen property, the State must prove the explanation is false. Whether the explanation is reasonable and true is a question of fact. The fact finder is not bound to accept a defendant's explanation for possession of recently stolen property. A trial judge, sitting without a jury, is authorized to accept or reject any or all of the evidence.

Sonnier was in possession of the speakers when she pledged them at the pawn shop. This was a distinct and conscious assertion of a right to the property. She pawned the speakers on the day they were stolen, a "recent" possession. The explanation for appellant's possession of the speakers came from the State's witnesses, as well as appellant's. The evidence is uncontradicted that two men possessed the speakers and tried to pawn them. It was only when the two men were not allowed to pawn the speakers that they left, and then returned to the same pawn shop accompanied by appellant.

The explanation for Sonnier's possession or control over the speakers is clear and uncontested—the two men requested her help in getting the speakers pawned. There is no evidence of what the two men told Sonnier in order to get her help. We find nothing in the record to contradict the hypothesis that Sonnier may have believed the speakers belonged to one of the two men. There is not one shred of evidence placing Sonnier at the complainant's club at the time the speakers were removed; the evidence, instead, points only to complainant's prior employee, Burton, as the likely thief.

In addition to the inference of guilt raised by possession of recently stolen property, the evidence when viewed as a whole must still be sufficient under normal standards of appellate review, and if the evidence supports a reasonable hypothesis other than the guilt of Sonnier, a finding of guilt beyond a reasonable doubt is not a rational finding.

When viewed in its totality, we find the evidence in this case does not support a guilty verdict.

We reverse the judgment and order a judgment of acquittal.

QUESTIONS

1. State the elements of theft without consent of the owner and the elements of receiving stolen property in the Texas theft statute.
2. List all the facts relevant to deciding each of the elements of theft without consent and receiving stolen property.
3. Assume you're the prosecutor. Argue that Olga Sonnier is guilty of theft without consent and receiving stolen property. Back up your answer with the facts you listed in (2).
4. Assume you're the defense counsel. Argue that Olga Sonnier should be acquitted of theft without consent and receiving stolen property. Back up your answer with the facts you listed in (2).

Now let's turn to the second category of property crimes: damaging and destroying other people's property, which includes the specific crimes of arson and criminal mischief.

DAMAGING AND DESTROYING OTHER PEOPLE'S PROPERTY

In this section, we'll discuss two crimes of destroying property: **arson** (damaging or destroying buildings by burning) and **criminal mischief** (damaging or destroying personal property).

arson damaging or destroying buildings by burning

criminal mischief damaging or destroying personal property

Arson

LO7

In the 1700s, "arson" was defined as "the malicious and willful burning of the house or outhouses of another." Blackstone (1769) called it an "offense of very great malignity, and much more serious than simple theft." According to Blackstone, here's why:

> Because, first, it is an offence against that right, of habitation, which is acquired by the law of nature as well as the laws of society. Next, because of the terror and confusion that necessarily attends it. And, lastly, because in simple theft the thing stolen only changes its master, but still remains in essence for the benefit of the public, whereas by burning the very substance is absolutely destroyed. (220)

Arson has grown far beyond its origins in burning houses to include burning almost any kind of building, vessel, or vehicle. Also, the property burned doesn't have to be someone else's. Today, arson is a crime against possession and occupancy, not just

TABLE 11.1 National Estimates of Intentionally Set Fires and Losses in Residential Buildings

YEAR	FIRES	DEATHS	INJURIES	DOLLAR LOSS
2008	18,300	310	825	$694,200,000
2009	16,200	265	775	$597,100,000
2010	16,000	260	750	$489,000,000

Source: U.S. Department of Homeland Security, U.S. Fire Administration, *National Estimates of Intentionally Set Fires in Residential Buildings* (2008–2010), http://www.usfa.fema.gov/downloads/pdf/statistics/v13i10.pdf (accessed May 29, 2015).

against ownership. So even where owners aren't in possession of, or don't occupy, their own property, arson can still be committed against it. For example, if I lease my house and become its landlord, and I set fire to it to collect insurance on it, I've committed arson because I transferred occupancy to my tenant.

One thing hasn't changed; arson is still a very serious crime against property and persons. Arson kills hundreds and injures thousands of people every year, and damages and destroys hundreds of millions of dollars' worth of property and costs millions in lost taxes and jobs. (See Table 11.1.)

Most states prescribe harsh penalties for arson. For example, in Texas and Alabama, arson is punishable by life imprisonment. Let's look further at the *actus reus*, *mens rea*, and degrees of arson.

ARSON *ACTUS REUS*: BURNING

burning criminal act of setting a building on fire

At common law, burning had its obvious meaning—setting a building on fire. However, just setting the fire wasn't enough; the fire had to reach the structure and burn it. But burning didn't mean burning to the ground. Once the building caught on fire, the arson was complete, however slight the actual burning was.

Modern statutes have adopted the common law rule, and the cases pour lots of effort into deciding whether the smoke from the fire only blackened or discolored buildings, whether the fire scorched them, or whether the fire burned only the outside wall or the wood under it. The MPC (ALI 1985, 2:2, 3) tries to clear up many of the technical questions in common law arson by providing that "burning" means "starting a fire," even if the fire never touches the structure it was meant to burn. The drafters justify this expansion of common law burning on the ground that there's no meaningful difference between a fire that has already started but hasn't reached the structure and a fire that's reached the structure but hasn't done any real damage to it. Burning also includes explosions, even though the phrase "set on fire" doesn't usually mean "to explode." (See the Elements of Arson illustration see below.)

In *Williams v. State* (1992), when Tonyia Williams, one of the guests at a New Year's Eve party, started a fire, "the only physical damage caused by fire was smoke throughout

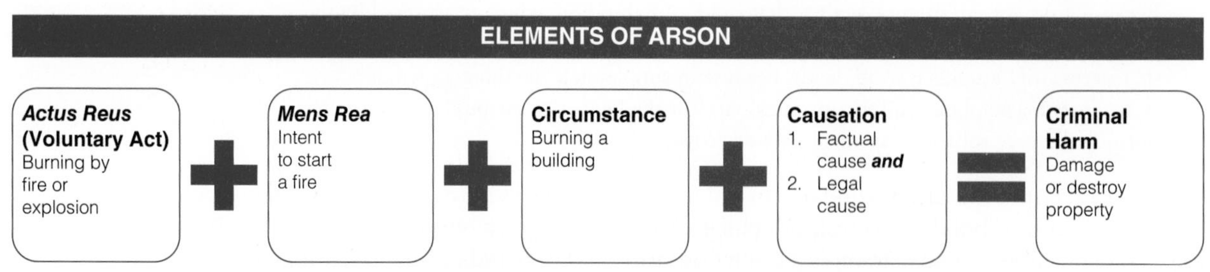

the house and soot and smoke damage to one of the walls in the basement" (963). Indiana's arson statute defined arson as: "A person who, by means of fire or explosive, knowingly or intentionally damages: (1) a dwelling of another person without his consent" (964). Williams argued that the "soot and smoke damage to the wall of the basement do not constitute 'damages' within the meaning of the arson statute." She argued that arson "requires proof of burning or charring as was the case at common law" (964).

The state argued that

> damages in our present statute is not tied to the common law definition of the word "burning" and should therefore be construed in its plain and ordinary sense. Any damage, even smoke damage, would therefore be enough to satisfy the requirements of the statute. (964)

Williams was convicted, and she appealed. According to the Indiana Appeals Court:

> Traditionally the common law rigidly required an actual burning. The fire must have been actually communicated to the object to such an extent as to have taken effect upon it. In general, any charring of the wood of a building, so that the fiber of the wood was destroyed, was enough to constitute a sufficient burning to complete the crime of arson.

However, merely singeing, smoking, scorching, or discoloring by heat weren't considered enough to support a conviction (964). The Indiana Appeals Court agreed with the state: "We find that the smoke damage and the soot on the basement wall were enough to support a conviction for arson" (965).

ARSON *MENS REA*

Most statutes follow the common law **arson *mens rea*** requirement that arsonists have to "maliciously and willfully" burn or set fire to buildings. Some courts call arson *mens rea* general intent. According to the general-intent definition, purpose refers to the act in arson (burning or setting fire to buildings), not to the resulting harm (damaging or destroying them). So a prisoner who burned a hole in his cell to escape was guilty of arson because he purposely started the fire. So was a sailor who lit a match to find his way into a dark hold in a ship to steal rum. The criminal intent in arson is general—an intent to start a fire, even if there is no intent to burn a specific structure.

arson *mens rea* requires a malicious and willful intent to burn or set fire to buildings in most statutes; in some jurisdictions, requires only the general-intent to start a fire

THE DEGREES OF ARSON

Typically, there are two degrees of arson. The most serious, **first-degree arson**, is burning homes or other occupied structures (such as schools, offices, and churches) where there's danger to human life. **Second-degree arson** includes burning unoccupied structures, vehicles, and boats.

first-degree arson burning homes or other occupied structures (such as schools, offices, and churches) where there's danger to human life

second-degree arson includes burning unoccupied structures, vehicles, and boats

The MPC divides arson into two degrees, based on defendants' blameworthiness. The most blameworthy are defendants who intend to destroy buildings, not merely set fire to or burn them; these are first-degree arsonists. Second-degree arsonists set buildings on fire for other purposes. For example, if I burn a wall with an acetylene torch because I want to steal valuable fixtures attached to the wall, I'm guilty of second-degree arson for "recklessly" exposing the building to destruction even though I intended only to steal fixtures.

Statutes don't grade arson according to motive, but it probably ought to play some part, if not in formal degrees, then in sentencing. Why? Because arsonists act for a variety of motives. Some are so consumed by rage they burn down their enemies' homes. Then there are the pyromaniacs, whose psychotic compulsion drives them to set buildings on fire for thrills. And there are the rational, but equally deadly, arsonists who burn down their own buildings or destroy their own property to collect insurance. Finally, and most deadly and difficult to catch, the professional torch commits arson for hire.

LO8

Criminal Mischief

malicious mischief common law crime of intentionally damaging or destroying another's tangible property

Arson under the common law was, and still is, the serious felony of intentionally burning occupied buildings. Criminal mischief descends from another common law crime, the misdemeanor called "malicious mischief." Malicious mischief consisted of destroying or damaging tangible property ("anything of value" that you can see, weigh, measure, or feel).

The modern counterpart of malicious mischief (the MPC calls it "criminal" mischief) includes three types of harm to tangible property:

1. Destruction or damage by fire, explosives, or other "dangerous acts" (the original malicious mischief)
2. Tampering with tangible property so as to endanger property
3. Deception or threat that causes someone to suffer money loss

All three forms of damage and destruction usually are defined as felonies but less serious felonies than the more serious crime of arson. (Elements of Malicious Mischief Box)

CRIMINAL MISCHIEF *ACTUS REUS*

criminal mischief *actus reus* in destruction or damage criminal mischief, the criminal act is burning, exploding, flooding, or committing some other dangerous act; in tampering, it's any act that threatens or endangers property; in deception or threat, it's causing harm through deception or threats

Criminal mischief *actus reus* mirrors the three types of criminal mischief. In destruction or damage criminal mischief, the *actus reus* is burning, exploding, flooding, or committing some other dangerous act. Tampering is any act that creates a danger to property, even if it doesn't actually cause any damage to the property. So a cross burning on the lawn of an interracial couple's house wasn't "tampering" with the property, because the burning cross by itself created no damage and it didn't pose a threat of damage to the property (*Commonwealth v. Kozak* 1993).

Deception or threat *actus reus* usually consists of "expensive practical jokes," such as "sending a false telegram notifying the victim that his mother is dying so that he spends several hundred dollars on a vain trip" or "misinforming a neighboring farmer that local tests of a particular seed variety have been highly successful, so that he wastes money and a year's work planting that seed" (ALI 1985, 2:2, 49).

CRIMINAL MISCHIEF *MENS REA*

Generalizations about criminal mischief *mens rea* are impossible because the statutes are all over the place, including whether they contain all the mental states we've encountered throughout the book (purposely, knowingly, recklessly, and negligently). So you need to check the malicious (or criminal) mischief statute of an individual state

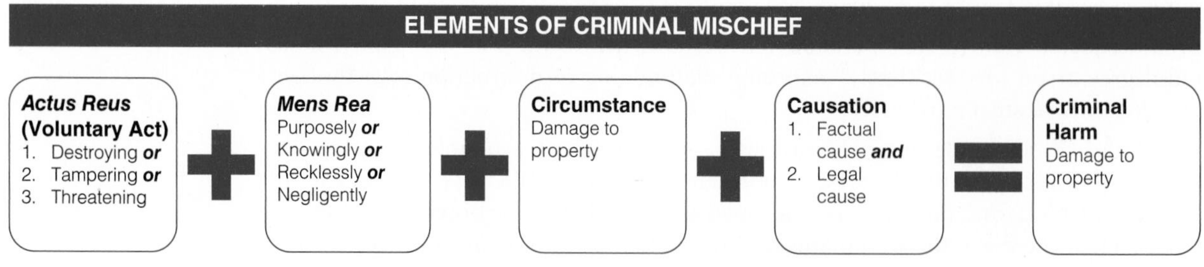

to find out how it defines the element of criminal intent. (The MPC criminal mischief's *actus reus* and *mens rea* requirements set out in the CLIF make a lot of sense, *and* they're comprehensive.)

CRIMINAL LAW IN FOCUS

MPC Criminal Mischief Provision

§ 220.3 Criminal Mischief

1. *Offense Defined.* A person is guilty of criminal mischief if he
   a. damages tangible property of another purposely, recklessly, or by negligence in the employment of fire, explosives, or other dangerous means; *or*
   b. purposely or recklessly tampers with tangible property of another so as to endanger person or property; *or*
   c. purposely or recklessly causes another to suffer pecuniary loss by deception or threat.
2. *Grading.* Criminal mischief is a felony of the third degree if the actor purposely causes pecuniary loss in excess of $5,000, or a substantial interruption or impairment of public communication, transportation, supply of water, gas or power, or other public service. It is a misdemeanor if the actor purposely causes pecuniary loss in excess of $100, or a petty misdemeanor if he purposely or recklessly causes pecuniary loss in excess of $25. Otherwise criminal mischief is a violation.

CASE

In ***Commonwealth v. Mitchell* (1993)**, *the Pennsylvania Superior court affirmed Duane Mitchell's conviction for criminal mischief by means of painting "nigger," "KKK," and other racial slurs on Betty Jo and James Johnson's House.*

Was he guilty of malicious mischief?

Commonwealth v. Mitchell

645 A. 2d (Penn Superior Court 1993)

HISTORY

Following a nonjury trial, held on December 22, 1992, Duane Mitchell (the defendant) was convicted of the criminal mischief...graded as a misdemeanor of the third degree. The defendant filed timely post-trial motions, which were denied, and the defendant was sentenced to pay a fine of $150. The Superior Court affirmed the trial court's denial of the motions.

CRONIN, J.

FACTS

Following a report to the Upper Darby Police Department on Sunday, June 21, 1992, at 9:49 P.M., Lieutenant Michael Kenney and Officer Mark Manley of the Upper Darby Police Department proceeded to 7142 Stockley Road, Upper Darby, Pennsylvania. Upon arriving at the above location, both officers observed the following: painted on the front walk the word "nigger," the letters "KKK," and a cross painted under three

(continues)

(continued)

dark marks; on each of the steps leading to the house was spray painted the word "nigger"; the front screen door had a painted cross with three marks above it; the patio was painted with the word "nigger" and a cross with three dark marks; the front walk had the word "nigger" and a cross with three dark marks; the front walk had the words "nigger get out" painted on it; the rear wall had painted the words "nigger get out or else" and a cross with the letters "KKK"; and the rear door had the words "KKK Jungle Fever Death" and a cross painted on it.

The owners of 7142 Stockley Road, Upper Darby, Pennsylvania, are James and Betty Jo Johnson, who had made settlement on the property on June 15, 1992, but had not occupied the home with their seven-year-old daughter, Zena. The Johnsons are an interracial couple, James Johnson being Afro-American and Betty Jo Johnson being Caucasian. The Johnsons had not given the defendant or any other person permission to spray paint on their property.

On June 25, 1992, the defendant, Duane Mitchell, was taken into custody by the Upper Darby Police Department. The defendant voluntarily waived, in writing, his right to counsel and his right to remain silent and freely gave a statement to the police. The defendant told the Upper Darby Police that he, the defendant, alone spray painted the above-mentioned words and symbols on the Johnson property located at 7142 Stockley Road, Upper Darby, Pennsylvania; at the time that he did the spray painting, he had been drinking.

Following a nonjury trial, held on December 22, 1992, the defendant was convicted of the summary offense of criminal mischief and the offense of ethnic intimidation, graded as a misdemeanor of the third degree in accordance with 18 Pa.C.S. § 2710(B). The defendant filed timely post-trial motions, which were denied by the order of trial court dated May 17, 1993.

OPINION

Criminal mischief is defined at 18 Pa.C.S. § 3304 as follows:

§ 3304. CRIMINAL MISCHIEF

1 Offense Defined—A person is guilty of criminal mischief if he:

a. damages the tangible property of another intentionally, recklessly, or by negligence in the employment of fire, explosives, or other dangerous means listed in section 3302(A) of this title (relating to causing or risking catastrophe);

b. intentionally or recklessly tampers with tangible property of another so as to endanger person or property; or

c. intentionally or recklessly causes another to suffer pecuniary loss by deception or threat. 18 Pa.C.S. § 3304(A)

The defendant argues that the evidence was insufficient to prove that tangible property was damaged in the employment of fire, explosion, or other dangerous means. 1 Pa.C.S. § 1903 states that "(A) Words and phrases shall be construed according to rules of grammar and according to their common usage;…" Section 1 of 18 Pa.C.S. § 3304 makes a person guilty of the crime of criminal mischief if that person either intentionally damages the tangible property of another; recklessly damages the tangible property of another; or negligently damages the tangible personal property of another in the employment of fire, explosives or other dangerous means listed in section 3302(A) of title 18.

In this case it is abundantly clear that the defendant spray painted the phrases and words mentioned herein on the Johnsons' home located at 7142 Stockley Road, Upper Darby, Pennsylvania and that the defendant did so without the permission of the Johnsons. Sufficient evidence exists to support a verdict if the evidence, when viewed in a light most favorable to the verdict winner along with all reasonable inferences drawn therefrom, allows a fact finder to find that all elements of a crime have been established beyond a reasonable doubt.

The evidence was sufficient to prove beyond a reasonable doubt that the defendant intentionally damaged the tangible property of the Johnsons.

A court must interpret a statute to ascertain the intent of the legislature. It is clear from the use of the conjunctive "or" in Section 1 of 18 Pa.C.S. § 3304 that the legislature intended to punish either the intentional or the reckless or the negligent damaging of the tangible property of another person. The intentional spray painting of graffiti on the walls of a building is factually sufficient to support a conviction for criminal mischief.

It is equally clear that the commission of any of the other acts specified in either Section 1 or Section 2 or Section 3 of 18 Pa.C.S. § 3304 is sufficient to support a conviction for criminal mischief since the conjunctive "or" is used between Sections 2 and 3 of 18 Pa.C.S. § 3304 and the conjunctive "or" is to be given the same meaning and legislative intent as "or" is given with the states of mind (intent, reckless or negligent) in Section 1 of 18 Pa.C.S. § 3304. See 1 Pa.C.S. § 1903(A), 1 Pa.C.S. § 1921(A)(B). For the foregoing reasons the defendant's post-trial motions were denied.

QUESTIONS

1. State the elements of *actus reus* and *mens rea* as the Pennsylvania criminal mischief statute defines them.
2. List the facts relevant to each of the elements.
3. Assume you're Duane Mitchell's lawyer and argue that the facts don't prove the elements beyond a reasonable doubt.
4. Assume you're the state's prosecutor and argue that the facts prove the elements beyond a reasonable doubt.

INVADING OTHER PEOPLE'S PROPERTY: BURGLARY AND CRIMINAL TRESPASS

The heart of burglary and criminal trespass is invading others' property, not taking, receiving, destroying, or damaging it. Invasion itself is the harm. So the two main crimes of invading someone else's property—their home, or other occupied structure (burglary) or invading other property (criminal trespass)—are crimes of criminal conduct (see Chapter 3); they don't require causing a bad result. So they're crimes even if no property is taken, damaged, or destroyed during the invasion. LO9

Burglary

> Burglary, or nighttime housebreaking, has always been looked upon as a very heinous offense, not only because of the abundant terror that it naturally carries with it, but also as it is a forcible invasion and disturbance of that right of habitation, which every individual might acquire in a state of nature. And the law of England has so particular and tender regard to the immunity of a man's house, that it styles it a castle and will never suffer it to be violated. (Blackstone 1769, 223)

Blackstone's definition of burglary written just before the American Revolution emphasizes the special nature of homes. Why are they special? For many people, their homes are their most valuable if not their only material asset. But homes are more than property that's worth money. The novelist Sinclair Lewis (1922) described this difference between homes as things with money value and homes as special places ("castles") that can't be measured by money alone: LO9

> The Babbitts' house was five years old. It had the best of taste, the best of inexpensive rugs, a simple and laudable architecture, and the latest conveniences. Throughout, electricity took the place of candles and slatternly hearth-fires. Along the bedroom baseboard were three plugs for electric lamps, concealed by little brass doors. In the halls were plugs for the vacuum cleaner, and in the living-room plugs for the piano lamp, for the electric fan. The trim dining-room (with its admirable oak buffet, its leaded-glass cupboard, its creamy plaster walls, its modest scene of a salmon expiring upon a pile of oysters) had plugs which supplied the electric percolator and the electric toaster.
>
> In fact there was but one thing wrong with the Babbitt house: *It was not a home.* (chap. 2; emphasis added)

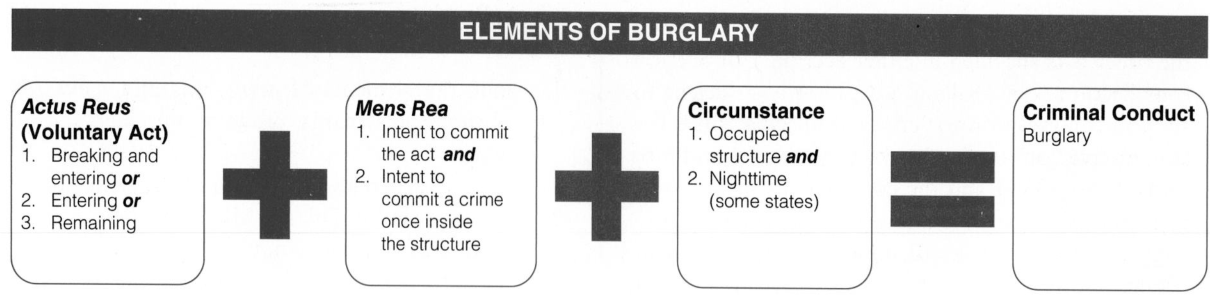

Lewis means that a house is the material thing worth money, but a home is the haven of refuge where we seek security and privacy from the outside world.

burglary breaking and entering a building or structure with intent to commit a crime inside the building

Burglary consists of breaking and entering a building with intent to commit a crime inside the building. The elements of common law burglary from which our modern law of burglary descends included:

a. Breaking and entering (*actus reus*)
b. The dwelling of another (circumstance element)
c. In the nighttime (circumstance element)
d. With the intent to commit a felony inside (*mens rea*)

Modern burglary has outgrown its common law origin of protecting only homes. Now, you can "burglarize" all kinds of structures, even vehicles, at any time of the day or night. Definitions such as "any structure" or "any building" are common in many statutes. One writer (Note 1951, 411) who surveyed the subject concluded that any structure with "four walls and a roof" was included. Here's California's list of "structures" you can burglarize:

> any house, room, apartment, tenement, shop, warehouse, store, mill, barn, stable, outhouse or other building, tent, vessel, floating home, locked or sealed cargo container, whether or not mounted on a vehicle, trailer coach, any house car, inhabited camper, vehicle, when the doors are locked, aircraft, or mine or any underground portion thereof. (California Penal Code 2015, § 459)

Let's look at the elements needed to prove burglary and then the degrees of burglary.

BURGLARY *ACTUS REUS*

breaking part of the *actus reus* of common law burglary, requiring an unlawful, frequently destructive, entry into someone else's building

entering part of the *actus reus* of burglary, meaning to come or go into the building or structure

Until the 1900s, burglary *actus reus* consisted of two actions—breaking and entering. In the early days of the common law, **breaking** meant making a violent entry, usually knocking down doors and smashing windows.

By 1900, the common law element of breaking had become a mere technicality, and most statutes today have eliminated it entirely, leaving entering as the only element. Entering, like breaking, has a broad meaning. The **entering** of burglary *actus reus* refers to coming or going into the building or structure.

Even as early as 1650, partial entry was enough to satisfy burglary. One court (*Rex v. Bailey* 1818) ruled that a burglar "entered" a house because his finger was inside the windowsill when he was caught. Today, some statutes have completely removed the entering element by providing that "remaining" in a structure lawfully entered is enough. So it's burglary to go into a store during business hours and hide in a restroom until the store closes with the intent to steal.

Some states don't even require burglars to get inside at all; it's enough if they try to enter. In *State v. Myrick* (1982), a man who got a door ajar but never set foot inside was convicted because the state's burglary statute didn't require entering or remaining. To some criminal law reformers, substituting "remaining" for "breaking and entering" badly distorts burglary's core idea—nighttime invasions into homes.

The MPC and several states take a middle ground between the old common law requirement of actual entry and eliminating entering completely. They've adopted a **surreptitious remaining element**, which means the burglar entered lawfully (for example, going into a bank during business hours and waiting inside until after the bank closed) with the intent to remain and commit a crime inside.

surreptitious remaining element the entering of a structure lawfully with the intent to remain and commit a crime inside

CIRCUMSTANCE ELEMENTS

The MPC's (ALI 1985, 2:2, 60) definition limits burglary to occupied structures, because they're the "intrusions that are typically the most alarming and dangerous." According to the code, "**occupied structure**" means "any structure, vehicle, or place adapted for overnight accommodations of persons, or for carrying on business therein, whether or not a person is actually present" (72). Most states take occupancy into account either as an element or as part of grading burglary as "aggravated burglary."

occupied structure "any structure, vehicle, or place adapted for overnight accommodations of persons, or for carrying on business therein, whether or not a person is actually present"

Another circumstance element of common law burglary was that burglars had to break and enter the **dwelling "of another"**—that is, anyplace where other people live. Modern law has expanded the common law definition from the victim's home to include homes that burglars own; for example, landlords can burglarize their tenants' apartments.

dwelling "of another" anyplace where other people live

In our next case excerpt, *Jewell v. State* (1996), the Indiana Court of Appeals affirmed a conviction for burglarizing one's own house.

CASE

In ***Jewell v. State* (1996)**, *the Indiana Court of Appeals affirmed Barry Jewell's conviction for burglarizing his house.*

Did he burglarize his own home?

Jewell v. State

672 N.E.2d 417 (Ind. App. 1996)

HISTORY

Barry L. Jewell, after a jury trial, was convicted of burglary with a deadly weapon resulting in serious bodily injury, a class A felony, and battery resulting in serious bodily injury, a class C felony. Jewell was sentenced to an aggregate term of 48 years imprisonment. After a retrial, Jewell appealed. The Indiana Court of Appeals affirmed.

ROBERTSON, J.

FACTS

In 1989, Bridget Fisher, who later married Jewell and changed her name to Bridget Jewell, purchased a home on contract in her maiden name from her relatives. Bridget and Jewell lived in the house together on and off before and after they married in 1990. Jewell helped fix the house up and therefore had some "sweat equity" in the house.

Jewell and Bridget experienced marital difficulties and dissolution proceedings were initiated.

(continues)

(continued)

Jewell moved out of the house, and Bridget changed the locks so that Jewell could not reenter. At a preliminary hearing in the dissolution proceedings, Bridget's attorney informed Jewell that Bridget wanted a divorce and wanted Jewell to stop coming by the house. Jewell moved into a friend's house, agreeing to pay him $100 per month in rent and to split the utility expenses.

Bridget resumed a romantic relationship with her former boyfriend, Chris Jones. Jewell told a friend that he wanted to get Jones in a dark place, hit him over the head with a two-by-four, and cut his "dick" off. Jewell confronted Jones at his place of employment and threatened to kill him if he were to continue to see Bridget.

Jewell was observed on numerous occasions watching Bridget's house. Jewell used a shortwave radio to intercept and listen to the phone conversations on Bridget's cordless phone.

At approximately 4:00 A.M. on the morning of June 13, 1991, Jewell gained entry to Bridget's house through the kitchen window after having removed a window screen.

Bridget and Jones were inside sleeping. Jewell struck Jones over the head with a two-by-four until he was unconscious, amputated Jones's penis with a knife, and fed the severed penis to the dog. Jones's severed penis was never found and he underwent reconstructive surgery. His physicians fashioned him a new penis made from tissue and bone taken from his leg. Jones experienced complications, and the result was not entirely satisfactory.

OPINION

Jewell attacks the sufficiency of evidence supporting his conviction of Burglary, which is defined as: A person who breaks and enters the building or structure of another person, with intent to commit a felony in it, commits burglary. (Ind. Code 354321.) Jewell argues he was improperly convicted of breaking into his own house.

The burglary statute's requirement that the dwelling be that "of another person" is satisfied if the evidence demonstrates that the entry was unauthorized. In the present case, Bridget had purchased the house in her own name before the marriage. When she and Jewell experienced marital difficulties, Jewell moved out and Bridget changed the locks to prevent Jewell from reentering the house. Bridget alone controlled access to the house. Jewell entered the house at 4:00 A.M. through the kitchen window after having removed the screen.

The evidence supports the conclusion that the entry was unauthorized; and, therefore, we find no error.

Judgment AFFIRMED.

QUESTIONS

1. List all of the facts relevant to determining whether Barry Jewell burglarized his own home.
2. How does the state of Indiana define the "dwelling of another" element?
3. How did the court arrive at the conclusion that Barry Jewell burglarized his own home?
4. What's the reason for the "unauthorized entry" requirement?
5. Do you agree with it? Defend your answer.

At common law, another circumstance element was "in the nighttime." Why? Nighttime intrusions frighten victims more than daytime intrusions. At least eighteen states retain the nighttime requirement. Some make it a circumstance element; others treat it as an aggravating circumstance. The rest have eliminated the nighttime requirement entirely.

BURGLARY *MENS REA*

Burglary is a specific-intent crime. The prosecution has to prove two *mens rea* elements:

1. The intent to commit the *actus reus* (breaking, entering, or remaining)
2. The intent to commit a crime once inside the structure broken into, entered, or remained in

The intended crime doesn't have to be serious. Intent to steal is usually good enough, but some states go further to include "any crime," "any misdemeanor," or even "any public offense" (Note 1951, 420).

Remember another important point: it's not necessary to complete *or* even attempt to commit the intended crime (see Chapter 8). Suppose I sneak into my rich former student Patrick's luxurious condo in Kona, Hawaii, while he's out making more money, with the intent steal one of his three wireless notebook computers that he doesn't need or use. Right after I get inside the front door, and not even close to where the notebooks are, my conscience gets the better of me. I say to myself, "I can't do this, even if Pat does have three notebook computers he doesn't need or use." So, I slink back out the front door. I still committed burglary because the burglary was complete the moment I was inside with the intent to steal one of the notebooks.

THE DEGREES OF BURGLARY

Because burglary is defined so broadly, many states divide it into several degrees. Alabama's burglary statute is typical (see Criminal Law in Focus, "Grading Burglary").

Despite efforts to grade burglary according to seriousness, the broad scope of the offense invites injustices. This is true in large part because burglary punishes the invasion and not the underlying crime—namely, the crime the burglar entered to commit. In many cases, the penalty for burglary is a lot harsher than the penalty for the

Grading Burglary

Alabama Criminal Code

§ 13A-7–5. Burglary in the First Degree

a. A person commits the crime of burglary in the second degree if he knowingly enters or remains unlawfully in a building with intent to commit theft or a felony therein and, if in effecting entry or while in the building or in immediate flight therefrom, he or another participant in the crime:
   1. Is armed with explosives or a deadly weapon; or
   2. Causes physical injury to any person who is not a participant in the crime; or
   3. Uses or threatens the immediate use of a dangerous instrument.

Sentence: 10 years to life

§ 13A-7–6. Burglary in the Second Degree

a. A person commits the crime of burglary in the second degree if he knowingly enters or remains unlawfully in a building with intent to commit theft or a felony therein and, if in effecting entry or while in the building or in immediate flight therefrom, he or another participant in the crime:
   1. Is armed with explosives or a deadly weapon; or
   2. Causes physical injury to any person who is not a participant in the crime; or
   3. Uses or threatens the immediate use of a dangerous instrument.
b. In the alternative to subsection (a) of this section, a person commits the crime of burglary in the second degree if he unlawfully enters a lawfully occupied dwelling house with intent to commit a theft or a felony therein.

Sentence: 2–20 years

§ 13A-7–7.Burglary in the Third Degree

a. A person commits the crime of burglary in the third degree if he knowingly enters or remains unlawfully in a building with intent to commit a crime therein.

Sentence: 1–10 years

intended crime. The difference between a five-year sentence and a twenty-year sentence sometimes depends upon the philosophical question of whether a thief forms the intent to steal before or after entering a building.

LO9

Criminal Trespass

criminal trespass the unwanted, unauthorized invasion of another person's property

Criminal trespass is the crime of invading another person's property without authorization. It's a broader but less serious crime than burglary. It's broader because it's not limited to invasions of occupied buildings, and the trespasser doesn't have to intend to commit a crime in addition to the trespass. The heart of criminal trespass is *unwanted presence*. The ancient misdemeanor called "trespass" referred to unwanted presence on (invasion of) another person's land. Not all unwanted presence was (or is) criminal trespass; only unauthorized presence qualifies. So, of course, law enforcement officers investigating a crime or gas company employees reading the meter, no matter how unwanted they are, aren't trespassers because they're authorized to be there.

Trespass used to be limited to unauthorized invasions of *physical* property. At first, only entry onto land was included. Then, entering and *remaining* on land *and* in buildings were added. Since the explosion of computers and the Internet, unauthorized access to electronic information systems has been included.

Let's look at the elements and degrees of criminal trespass and at the special trespassing offense of computer trespass.

THE ELEMENTS OF CRIMINAL TRESPASS

The *actus reus* of criminal trespass is the unauthorized entering of or remaining on the premises of another person (ALI 1985, 2:2, 87). The *mens rea* varies. Here are three variations:

1. The defendant knowingly enters or remains without authority or by invitation, license, privilege, or legality (most states).
2. The defendant has the specific intent to enter or remain without authority for some unlawful purpose (a few states).
3. The defendant bears strict liability for entering or remaining (Missouri, enters "unlawfully") (88).

THE DEGREES OF CRIMINAL TRESPASS

The MPC created three degrees of criminal trespass:

1. Misdemeanor entering or remaining in an occupied dwelling at night
2. Petty misdemeanor entering or remaining in any occupied building or structure
3. Violation entering or remaining in any place where a "no trespass" notice is given (warning to person, "no trespassing" sign, or fence)

ELEMENTS OF CRIMINAL TRESPASS

***Actus Reus* (Voluntary Act)**
1. Unauthorized entering ***or***
2. Unauthorized remaining

+

Mens Rea
1. Knowingly (majority rule) ***or***
2. Specific intent (a few states) ***or***
3. Strict liability (Missouri)

+

Circumstance
Someone else's premises

=

Criminal Conduct
Criminal trespass

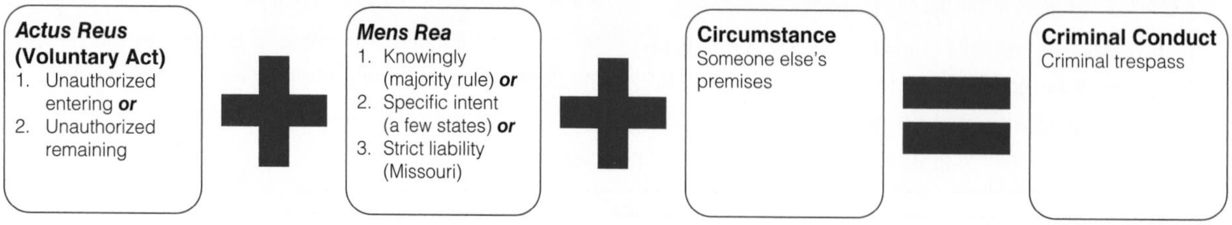

IDENTITY THEFT

> Often a thief needs only a name and Social Security number to open up a credit card account or to access an existing account. (Rustad 2001, 628)

LO10

identity theft stealing another person's identity for the purpose of getting something of value

Identity theft consists of stealing another person's identity for the purpose of getting something of value. Except for ordinary theft, identity theft claims more than twice as many victims in the United States as all other crimes of taking other people's property combined (see Figure 11.1). This isn't surprising, given the enormous range of personal information contained in business, nonprofit organization, and government electronic databases. These organizations collect, update, and use "masses of computerized information" about anyone who "voluntarily or involuntarily" deals with their institutions (see Table 11.2).

The consequences of wrongful access to personal information can be devastating, and they go beyond the money victims lose to identify thieves. The more than 9 million annual identity theft victims spend an average of 600 hours over two to four years and $1,400 to clear their names (V. Johnson 2005, 257, n. 7). Victims may also lose job opportunities;

Figure 11.1

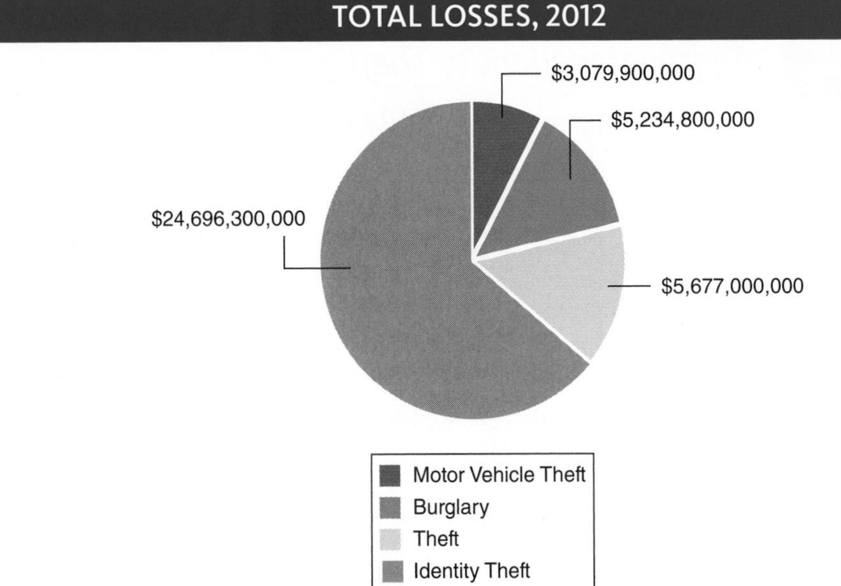

Source: Bureau of Justice Statistics, Victims of Identity Theft, 2012 (December 2013), constructed from Table 4, page 6.

TABLE 11.2 Types of Information Collected by Government, Business, and Nonprofit Organizations

TYPES	EXAMPLES OF THE INFORMATION COLLECTED
Names	First, middle, and last names
Relationships	Family members and employers
Contact information	Phone, physical addresses, e-mail addresses, websites
Personal information	Birthday, medical information, physical description, educational records
Official identifiers	Social security, driver's license, passport numbers
Financial records	Bank, credit card, frequent fliers, and investment accounts

Source: V. Johnson (2005, 256).

be refused loans, education, housing, or cars; and be arrested for crimes they didn't commit. In extreme cases, victims are blackmailed (for example, a former chemistry graduate student found a security flaw in a commercial website and demanded ransom from the company to keep his mouth shut, Rustad 2001, 63); stalked (Chapter 10, case excerpt, *State v. Hoying*); or even murdered (*Remsburg v. Docusearch, Inc.* 2003).

The motivations for stealing other people's identity vary. They may be jilted lovers (*Remsburg v. Docusearch*, Inc., 2003); "bored juveniles, disgruntled employees, corporate spies, or organized crime networks" (Rustad 2001, 65); or just your "run-of-the-mill" thieves (V. Johnson 2005, 257).

Whatever their reasons for stealing identities, identity thieves are extremely hard to catch. And when they *are* caught, they're hard to convict (McMahon 2004). The U.S. Congress attempted to protect people's identities by creating several identity theft laws. One of these laws is the *Aggravated Identity Theft Act of 2004* excerpted in the Criminal Law in Focus box, "Aggravated Identity Theft."

Aggravated Identity Theft

§ 1028A. Aggravated identity theft
Effective: July 15, 2004

a. **Offenses.**
   1. **In general**. Whoever, during and in relation to any felony violation enumerated in subsection (c), knowingly transfers, possesses, or uses, without lawful authority, a means of identification of another person shall, in addition to the punishment provided for such felony, be sentenced to a term of imprisonment of 2 years.

b. **Consecutive sentence**. Notwithstanding any other provision of law
   1. a court shall not place on probation any person convicted of a violation of this section;
   2. except as provided in paragraph (4), no term of imprisonment imposed on a person under this section shall run concurrently with any other term of imprisonment imposed on the person under any other provision of law, including any term of imprisonment imposed for the felony during which the means of identification was transferred, possessed, or used;
   3. in determining any term of imprisonment to be imposed for the felony during which the means of identification was transferred, possessed, or used, a court shall not in any way reduce the term to be imposed for such crime so as to compensate for, or otherwise take into account, any separate term of imprisonment imposed or to be imposed for a violation of this section; and
   4. a term of imprisonment imposed on a person for a violation of this section may, in the discretion of the court, run concurrently, in whole or in part, only with another term of imprisonment that is imposed by the court at the same time on that person for an additional violation of this section, provided that such discretion shall be exercised in accordance with any applicable guidelines and policy statements issued by the Sentencing Commission pursuant to section 994 of title 28.

c. **Definition**. For purposes of this section, the term "felony violation enumerated in subsection (c)" means any offense that is a felony violation of
   1. section 641 (relating to theft of public money, property, or rewards), section 656 (relating to theft, embezzlement, or misapplication by bank officer or employee), or section 664 (relating to theft from employee benefit plans);

2. section 911 (relating to false personation of citizenship);
3. section 922(a)(6) (relating to false statements in connection with the acquisition of a firearm);
4. any provision contained in this chapter (relating to fraud and false statements), other than this section or section 1028(a)(7);
5. any provision contained in chapter 63 (relating to mail, bank, and wire fraud);
6. any provision contained in chapter 69 (relating to nationality and citizenship);
7. any provision contained in chapter 75 (relating to passports and visas);
8. section 523 of the Gramm-Leach-Bliley Act (15 U.S.C. 6823) (relating to obtaining customer information by false pretenses);
9. section 243 or 266 of the Immigration and Nationality Act (8 U.S.C. 1253 and 1306) (relating to willfully failing to leave the United States after deportation and creating a counterfeit alien registration card);
10. any provision contained in chapter 8 of title II of the Immigration and Nationality Act (8 U.S.C. 1321 et seq.) (relating to various immigration offenses); or
11. section 208, 811, 1107(b), 1128B(a), or 1632 of the Social Security Act (42 U.S.C. 408, 1011, 1307(b), 1320a-7b(a), and 1383a) (relating to false statements relating to programs under the Act).

The U.S. Supreme Court reviewed the *mens rea* requirement in our next case excerpt, *Flores-Figueroa v. U.S.* (2009).

CASE

In ***Flores-Figueroa v. U.S.* (2009),** *Ignacio Carlos Flores-Figueroa (Defendant) was convicted in the United States District Court for the Southern District of Iowa of aggravated identity theft. The U.S. Supreme Court reversed and remanded because the government had failed to establish that he acted with requisite guilty knowledge that numbers on the alien registration cards that he presented to his employer belonged to another person, as opposed to merely being counterfeit.*

Did he "knowingly" use someone else's identification cards?

Flores-Figueroa v. U.S.

566 U.S. 646 (2009)

HISTORY

Ignacio Carlos Flores-Figueroa (Defendant) was convicted in the United States District Court for the Southern District of Iowa of aggravated identity theft. Flores-Figueroa appealed on the ground that the government had failed to establish that he acted with requisite guilty knowledge that numbers on the alien registration cards that he presented to his employer belonged to another person, as opposed to merely being counterfeit. The Eighth Circuit Court of Appeals, affirmed on the theory that government did not have to make such a showing to satisfy *mens rea*

(continues)

(continued)

requirement of the aggravated identity theft statute. The U.S. Supreme Court granted certiorari, and reversed and remanded.

BREYER, J., JOINED BY ROBERTS, CJ., AND STEVENS, KENNEDY, SOUTER, AND GINSBURG, JJ., SCALIA, THOMAS, AND ALITO, JJ., CONCURRED IN THE JUDGMENT.

A federal criminal statute forbidding "aggravated identity theft" imposes a mandatory consecutive 2-year prison term upon individuals convicted of certain other crimes *if*, during (or in relation to) the commission of those other crimes, the offender "*knowingly* transfers, possesses, or uses, without lawful authority, *a means of identification of another person*."18 U.S.C. § 1028A(a)(1) [emphasis added]. The question is whether the statute requires the Government to show that the defendant *knew* that the "means of identification" he or she unlawfully transferred, possessed, or used, in fact, belonged to "another person." We conclude that it does.

The statutory provision in question references a set of predicate crimes, including, for example, theft of government property, fraud, or engaging in various unlawful activities related to passports, visas, and immigration. § 1028A(c). It then provides that if any person who commits any of those other crimes (in doing so) "knowingly transfers, possesses, or uses, without lawful authority, a means of identification of another person," the judge must add two years' imprisonment to the offender's underlying sentence. § 1028A(a)(1). All parties agree that the provision applies only where the offender knows that he is transferring, possessing, or using *something*. And the Government reluctantly concedes that the offender likely must know that he is transferring, possessing, or using that *something* without lawful authority. But they do not agree whether the provision requires that a defendant also know that the *something* he has unlawfully transferred is, for example, a real ID belonging to another person rather than, say, a fake ID (*i.e.*, a group of numbers that does not correspond to any real Social Security number).

Petitioner Ignacio Flores-Figueroa argues that the statute requires that the Government prove that he *knew* that the "means of identification" belonged to someone else, *i.e.*, was "a means of identification *of another person*." The Government argues that the statute does not impose this particular knowledge requirement. The Government concedes that the statute uses the word "knowingly," but that word, the Government claims, does not modify the statute's last phrase ("a means of identification of another person") or, at the least, it does not modify the last three words of that phrase ("of another person").

FACTS

Ignacio Flores-Figueroa is a citizen of Mexico. In 2000, to secure employment, Flores gave his employer a false name, birth date, and Social Security number, along with a counterfeit alien registration card. The Social Security number and the number on the alien registration card were not those of a real person. In 2006, Flores presented his employer with new counterfeit Social Security and alien registration cards; these cards (unlike Flores' old alien registration card) used his real name. But this time the numbers on both cards were in fact numbers assigned to other people.

Flores' employer reported his request to U.S. Immigration and Customs Enforcement. Customs discovered that the numbers on Flores' new documents belonged to other people. The United States then charged Flores with two predicate crimes, namely, entering the United States without inspection, and misusing immigration documents. And it charged him with aggravated identity theft, the crime at issue here.

Flores moved for a judgment of acquittal on the "aggravated identity theft" counts. He claimed that the Government could not prove that he *knew* that the numbers on the counterfeit documents were numbers assigned to other people. The Government replied that it need not prove that knowledge, and the District Court accepted the Government's argument. After a bench trial, the court found Flores guilty of the predicate crimes and aggravated identity theft. The Court of Appeals upheld the District Court's determination. And we granted certiorari to consider the "knowledge" issue—a matter about which the Circuits have disagreed.

OPINION

There are strong textual reasons for rejecting the Government's position. As a matter of ordinary English grammar, it seems natural to read the statute's word "knowingly" as applying to all the subsequently listed elements of the crime. The Government cannot easily claim that the word "knowingly" applies only to the statutes first four words, or even its first seven.

It makes little sense to read the provision's language as heavily penalizing a person who "transfers, possesses, or uses, without lawful authority" a *something*, but does not know, at the very least, that the "something" (perhaps inside a box) is a "means of identification." Would we apply a statute that makes it unlawful "*knowingly* to possess drugs" to a person who steals a passenger's bag without knowing that the bag has drugs inside?

The Government claims more forcefully that the word "knowingly" applies to all but the statute's last three words, *i.e.*, "of another person." The statute, the Government says, does not require a prosecutor to show that the defendant *knows* that the means of identification the defendant has unlawfully used in fact belongs to another person. But how are we to square this reading with the statute's language?

In ordinary English, where a transitive verb has an object, listeners in most contexts assume that an adverb (such as knowingly) that modifies the transitive verb tells the listener how the subject performed the entire action, including the object as set forth in the sentence. Thus, if a bank official says, "Smith knowingly transferred the funds to his brother's account," we would normally understand the bank official's statement as telling us that Smith knew the account was his brother's. Nor would it matter if the bank official said "Smith knowingly transferred the funds to the account of his brother." In either instance, if the bank official later told us that Smith did not know the account belonged to Smith's brother, we should be surprised.

Similar examples abound. If a child knowingly takes a toy that belongs to his sibling, we assume that the child not only knows that he is taking something, but that he also knows that what he is taking is a toy *and* that the toy belongs to his sibling. If we say that someone knowingly ate a sandwich with cheese, we normally assume that the person knew both that he was eating a sandwich and that it contained cheese.

At the same time, dissimilar examples are not easy to find. The Government says that "knowingly" modifies only the verbs in the statute, while remaining indifferent to the subject's knowledge of at least part of the transitive verb's object. In certain contexts, a listener might understand the word "knowingly" to be used in that way. But the Government has not provided us with a single example of a sentence that, when used in typical fashion, would lead the hearer to believe that the word "knowingly" modifies only a transitive verb without the full object, *i.e.*, that it leaves the hearer gravely uncertain about the subject's state of mind in respect to the full object of the transitive verb in the sentence. The likely reason is that such sentences typically involve special contexts or themselves provide a more detailed explanation of background circumstances that call for such a reading.

We conclude that § 1028A(a)(1) requires the Government to show that the defendant knew that the means of identification at issue belonged to another person. The judgment of the Court of Appeals is reversed, and the case is remanded for further proceedings consistent with this opinion.

It is so ordered.

QUESTIONS

1. List all the facts relevant to deciding whether Flores-Figueroa acted "knowingly."
2. Summarize the government's arguments that Flores-Figueroa acted "knowingly."
3. Summarize Flores-Figueroa's arguments that he did *not* act "knowingly."
4. Which argument is the best *mens rea* policy regarding identity theft? Defend your answer.

CYBERCRIMES

LO11

We may be "digital people" living in an "Information Age," but data collection isn't new. When mass markets began to replace the relationships between small shop owners and customers who knew each other personally, advertising was aimed at customers most likely to buy their products. The General Motors sales department tried out this new "targeted marketing" in the 1920s. Ford owners became the target. GM learned that first-time Ford owners still owned their Fords after two years. So GM targeted these Ford owners and sent them a brochure on GM cars. Then, they sent out questionnaires asking for input on GM cars. They thought this would be a good marketing device—showing that here's a big corporation that cared enough to listen to ordinary people. It worked. (Solve 2006, 16–17).

Today, computers, "smartphones," "tablets," and the Internet have exponentially enhanced the capacity to exploit information about *individuals* and about *ideas*. "Life is built upon computerized data bases" (V. Johnson 2005, 255) that can be used for good and for ill. Personal information about our health, our finances, and our likes and dislikes helps doctors, banks, and merchants help us. But it also helps identity thieves take our money and wreck our lives (V. Johnson 2005, 256–57) and, in extreme cases, even kill us and the people we love (*Remsburg v. Docusearch, Inc.*, 2003). Let's look at two kinds of cyber property crimes: Intellectual property and *dark net* or *digital underworld* crimes.

LO11 Intellectual Property Crimes

intellectual property ideas and their practical application owned by an individual, a business, or a society

Intellectual property can be the most valuable property of any individual, business, or society (U.S. Department of Justice 2006, 13).

The importance of intellectual property wasn't lost on our nation's founders. They wrote it into the Constitution.

> The Congress shall have power to promote the progress of science and useful arts, by securing for limited times to authors and inventors the exclusive right to their respective writings and discoveries. (U.S. Constitution, Article I, Section 8)

We recognize it today in the copyright laws that protect against unauthorized copying and distribution of books, films, music compositions, sound recordings, and software programs. Other laws protect intellectual property from infringement on trademarks, trade secrets, and patents and thefts, damage, and destruction of intellectual property. Intellectual property definitely needs protection; intellectual property theft costs at least $250 billion every year (U.S. Department of Justice 2006, 13). The cost may be a lot higher because businesses don't report these thefts, fearing it will hurt business. It's also difficult to catch cybercriminals. Cybercriminals are smart, skilled, and highly motivated, not just by money but by the darker and dangerous side of our nature—revenge, hate, ideology, and the powerful, seductive, addictive thrill of hacking (Rustad 2001, 65).

A whole new vocabulary has grown to describe the ways hackers commit cybercrimes. In addition to viruses and wiretapping, methods known even to functional computer illiterates like me, here's a list of some others compiled by Professor Michael Rustad (2001, 64):

- *Spoofing*. When an attacker compromises routing packets to direct a file or transmission to a different location.
- *Piggybacking programs*. When hackers piggyback onto other programs to enter computer systems.
- *Data diddling*. The practice by employees and other knowledgeable insiders of altering or manipulating data, credit limits, or other financial information.
- *Salami attack*. A series of minor computer crimes—slices of a larger crime—that are difficult to detect. (For example, a hacker finds a way to get into a bank's computers and quietly skims off a penny or so from each account. Once he has $200,000, he quits.)
- *E-mail flood attack*. When so much e-mail is sent to a target that the transfer agent is overwhelmed, causing other communication programs to destabilize and crash the system.
- *Password sniffing*. Using password-sniffing programs to monitor and record the name and password of network users as they log in and impersonating the authorized users to access restricted documents.

- *Worm.* Uses a network to send copies of itself to other systems and it does so without any intervention. In general, worms harm the network and consume bandwidth, whereas viruses infect or corrupt files on a targeted computer. Viruses generally do not affect network performance, because their malicious activities are mostly confined within the target computer itself.

In our next case excerpt, *U.S. v. Ancheta* (2006), twenty-year-old cyberthief Jeanson Ancheta, got caught and pleaded guilty to multiple counts of cybercrime fraud and damaging computers protected by the "Fraud and Related Activity in Connection with Computers" (U.S. Code 2006, Title 18, Part I, Chapter 47 §1030(a)(5)(A)(i), 1030(a)(5)(B)(i), and 1030(b)). Ancheta worked in an Internet café in Downey, California. According to his aunt, he had modest ambitions—to join the military reserves—but he lived a luxurious lifestyle as an Internet café employee. He was often seen driving his BMW and spending more than $600 a week on new clothes and car parts.

The explanation was the profits he made from the results of a worm he authored. The worm allowed him to infect as many computers on the Internet as he could with off-the-shelf remote access Trojans (RATs) (Vamosi 2006). Ancheta pleaded guilty to multiple counts of cybercrime fraud; he received fifty-seven months in prison—the longest prison cybercrime theft sentence to date—and had to forfeit his BMW.

Ancheta pleaded guilty to the federal cybercrime of "Fraud and Related Activity in Connection with Computers." That statute defines the crime as follows:

> Whoever knowingly causes [or attempts to cause] the transmission of a program, information, code, or command, and as a result of such conduct, intentionally causes damage without authorization, to a protected computer... [affecting] 1 or more persons during any 1-year period... [and] affecting 1 or more other protected computers aggregating at least $5,000 in value....

The punishment under the statute is a fine and/or imprisonment for up to twenty years.

CASE

*In **U.S. v. Ancheta (2006)**, twenty-year-old cyberthief Jeanson Ancheta got caught and pleaded guilty to multiple counts of computer fraud.*

Did he commit computer fraud?

U.S. v. Ancheta

(C.D. Cal. 2006)

AQUILINA, J.

Concluding the first prosecution of its kind in the United States, a well-known member of the "botmaster underground" was sentenced this afternoon to nearly five years in prison for profiting from his use of "botnets"—armies of compromised computers—that he used to launch destructive attacks, to send huge quantities of spam across the Internet, and to receive surreptitious installations of adware.

Jeanson James Ancheta, 21, of Downey, California, was sentenced to 57 months in federal prison by U.S.

(continues)

(continued)

District Judge R. Gary Klausner in Los Angeles. During the sentencing hearing, Judge Klausner characterized Ancheta's crimes as "extensive, serious and sophisticated." The prison term is the longest known sentence for a defendant who spread computer viruses.

Ancheta pleaded guilty in January to conspiring to violate the Computer Fraud Abuse Act, conspiring to violate the CAN-SPAM Act, causing damage to computers used by the federal government in national defense, and accessing protected computers without authorization to commit fraud. When he pleaded guilty, Ancheta admitted using computer servers he controlled to transmit malicious code over the Internet to scan for and exploit vulnerable computers. Ancheta caused thousands of compromised computers to be directed to an Internet Relay Chat channel, where they were instructed to scan for other computers vulnerable to similar infection, and to remain "zombies" vulnerable to further unauthorized accesses.

Ancheta further admitted that, in more than 30 separate transactions, he earned approximately $3,000 by selling access to his botnets. The botnets were sold to other computer users, who used the machines to launch distributed denial of service (DDOS) attacks and to send unsolicited commercial e-mail, or spam.

Ancheta acknowledged specifically discussing with the purchasers the nature and extent of the DDOS attacks or proxy spamming they were interested in conducting. Ancheta suggested the number of bots or proxies they would need to accomplish the specified acts, tested the botnets with them to ensure that the DDOS attacks or proxy spamming were successfully carried out, and advised them on how to properly maintain, update, and strengthen their purchased armies.

In relation to the computer fraud scheme, Ancheta admitted generating for himself and an unindicted coconspirator more than $107,000 in advertising affiliate proceeds by downloading adware to more than 400,000 infected computers that he controlled. By varying the download times and rates of the adware installations, as well as by redirecting the compromised computers between various servers equipped to install different types of modified adware, Ancheta avoided detection by the advertising affiliate companies who paid him for every install. Ancheta further admitted using the advertising affiliate proceeds he earned to pay for, among other things, the multiple servers he used to conduct his illegal activity.

Following the prison term, Ancheta will serve three years on supervised release. During that time, his access to computers and the Internet will be limited, and he will be required to pay approximately $15,000 in restitution to the Weapons Division of the U.S. Naval Air Warfare Center in China Lake and the Defense Information Systems Agency, whose national defense networks were intentionally damaged by Ancheta's malicious code. The proceeds of Ancheta's illegal activity—including more than $60,000 in cash, a BMW automobile, and computer equipment—have been forfeited to the government.

Addressing the defendant at the conclusion of the sentencing hearing, Judge Klausner said: "Your worst enemy is your own intellectual arrogance that somehow the world cannot touch you on this." This case was investigated by the Los Angeles Field Office of the Federal Bureau of Investigation, which received assistance from the Southwest Field Office of the Naval Criminal Investigative Service and the Western Field Office of the Defense Criminal Investigative Service.

QUESTIONS

1. State the *actus reus*, *mens rea*, attendance circumstance(s), and "bad result" elements of the federal "Fraud and Related Activity in Connection with Computers" statute.
2. List the relevant facts Ancheta admitted, and match them up with the elements you stated in (1).
3. What purposes of punishment do the forfeiture and sentence reflect? Recall the purposes of punishment laid out in Chapter 1: punishment requires (a) condemnation and hard treatment; (b) retribution; (c) a means of prevention (general and special deterrence, incapacitation, and rehabilitation); and (d) restitution. Back up your answer using these purposes of punishment requirements.
4. Was the sentence fair? Too harsh? Too lenient? Explain your answer.

The Dark Net

> There's a part of the Internet most people have never gone to because it's an encrypted, hidden underworld that's home to pornography, black markets, trolls, criminals and extremists.
>
> —Teri Gross, *Fresh Air* (2015)

You can't get on this hidden encrypted Internet with browsers like Firefox, Chrome, or Safari. The people on this hidden network of about 50,000 sites don't reveal their location or their identity, or anything else about themselves. It amounts to what Jamie Bartlett (2014) calls a "Wild West" of "anonymous users that can't be censored. So anybody with something to hide, whether it's for good reasons or ill, finds a very natural home there." Even though you can't get on the digital dark net with the "normal," browsers, you don't have to buy anything to get on it. All you need to do is go to a Tor browser. Tor is the acronym for *The Onion Router*. Just download the software from the Internet, and you can go to any website—*anonymously*. (U.S. Naval Intelligence created Tor to allow their intelligence officers to browse the Internet without revealing their identity.)

Tor browser created by U.S. Naval intelligence, *The Onion Router*, or Tor browser, allows users to access the dark web and any website anonymously

> When you go online with it, you can go to any website. You can go to cnn.com with this browser. But, it bounces your request to access a website via several different computers around the world, encrypting and decrypting your request as it goes, which means by the time it gets to the CNN website, no one really knows where that request has come from. (Gross 2015)

As I write this (June 6, 2015), the most famous digital underworld site is Silk Road, a black market Amazon or eBay. Ross Ulbricht created and ran Silk Road's billion-dollar anonymous black market. According to the Assistant U.S. Attorney Preet Bharara (2015):

> Silk Road was an online black market of unprecedented scope. By the time it was shuttered in October 13, over 13,000 offerings were listed on its homepage for illegal drugs of every conceivable variety. A wide variety of other illicit goods and services were sold on the site as well, including fake IDs and passports, computer-hacking tools and services, counterfeit goods and pirated media, criminal guidebooks and instruction manuals, and money-laundering services.
>
> In total, over 1.5 million transactions were conducted over Silk Road, involving over 100,000 buyer accounts and nearly 4,000 seller accounts. Those transactions had a total value of nearly $214 million in U.S. currency. . . . The buyers and sellers involved in these transactions were spread across the world, from Argentina to Australia, from the United States to the Ukraine. (2)

The Silk Road in Operation

Ulbricht specifically designed Silk Road for the purpose of facilitating black-market transactions. He hosted the site on the Tor network to enable users to conduct business anonymously. He implemented a Bitcoin-based payment system to enable them to make payments and cash out proceeds without leaving behind a traditional

(continues)

(continued)

money trail. He provided instruction on "stealth" shipping methods and other ways to evade detection by law enforcement. And he created a slick user interface aimed at making the illicit commerce on the site as simple and frictionless as ordinary online shopping.

The effect of Ulbricht's conduct was to dramatically lower the entry barriers into the underground economy—for both buyers and sellers alike. As illustrated by the trial testimony of Michael Duch, a significant heroin dealer on Silk Road, the site's plug-and-play platform enabled someone like Mr. Duch—who had never dealt drugs before in his life—to develop a bustling heroin-trafficking business in just a few weeks, all from the comfort of his own living room. Mr. Duch merely had to procure a supply of drugs (which he bought from his existing personal supplier on the street), and Silk Road provided the rest: an anonymous online sales portal, a huge preexisting customer base, how-to advice from the "Seller's Guide" and Silk Road discussion forum, and an escrow system enabling him to collect payment from his customers remotely. As Mr. Duch testified, he never would have been able to become a drug dealer so easily and surreptitiously in real space; he was only able to do so online, through the facilitating technology of Silk Road.

By the same token, Silk Road made it simple for anyone anywhere to buy any drug of their choosing. They needed only a computer and a shipping address. With the click of a mouse, a Silk Road user could circumvent all of the physical obstacles that might otherwise prevent or deter one from obtaining drugs locally. Someone who might not know where to find drugs in his or her area, or feel comfortable searching them out, could find and buy drugs effortlessly on Silk Road. Again, Mr. Duch's testimony is instructive. He was able to sell heroin on Silk Road at double the price he paid for it on the street in the New York metropolitan area, in part because he was re-shipping it to less populous locations across the country where heroin was harder to come by. In the same way, Silk Road made it easy for existing users of one drug to find and abuse more serious drugs. The site provided a one-stop online shopping mall where the supply of drugs was virtually limitless.

Source: U.S. v. Ross Ulbricht (2015, 2–3).

Our next case excerpt, *U.S. v. Ulbricht* (2015) is a little unusual—it's not an appellate court opinion. Why? Because the trial court just sentenced Ross Ulbricht, and his lawyers have not yet appealed Judge Forrest's sentence. This excerpt includes excerpts from the criminal complaint, Ross Ulbricht's letter to Judge Forrest, and excerpts from Judge Forrest's emotionally charged three-hour sentencing hearing.

CASE

*In **U.S. v. Ulbricht (2015)**, the U.S. District Court convicted Ross Ulbricht of seven counts of connected to the ownership and operation of online hidden black market website, "Silk Road," a/k/a "Dread Pirate Roberts."*

Is he a libertarian hero or calculating drug lord?

U.S. v. Ulbricht, a/k/a "Dread Pirate Roberts," a/k/a "DPR," a/k/a "Silk Road"

U.S. District Court, Southern District of New York (2015)

1.

"ROSS ULBRICHT GUILTY," U.S. ATTORNEY'S OFFICE, PRESS RELEASE FEBRUARY 5, 2015

Preet Bharara, the United States Attorney for the Southern District of New York, announced today that ROSS WILLIAM ULBRICHT, a/k/a "Dread Pirate Roberts," a/k/a "DPR," a/k/a "Silk Road," was found guilty yesterday on all seven counts in connection with his operation and ownership of Silk Road, a hidden website designed to enable its users to buy and sell illegal drugs and other unlawful goods and services anonymously and beyond the reach of law enforcement, following a four-week trial before U.S. District Judge Katherine B. Forrest.

Manhattan U.S. Attorney Preet Bharara said: "As a unanimous jury has found, Ross William Ulbricht operated Silk Road—a clandestine global marketplace that offered buyers and sellers of illegal goods and services a promise of anonymity. Ulbricht built this black market bazaar to exploit the dark web and the digital currency Bitcoin to allow users to conduct illegal business beyond the reach of law enforcement. Ulbricht's arrest and conviction—and our seizure of millions of dollars of Silk Road Bitcoins—should send a clear message to anyone else attempting to operate an online criminal enterprise. The supposed anonymity of the dark web is not a protective shield from arrest and prosecution."

According to the Complaint, the Superseding Indictment, and the evidence presented at trial:

- ULBRICHT created Silk Road in approximately January 2011, and owned and operated the underground website until it was shut down by law enforcement authorities in October 2013. Silk Road emerged as the most sophisticated and extensive criminal marketplace on the Internet, serving as a sprawling black-market bazaar where unlawful goods and services, including illegal drugs of virtually all varieties, were bought and sold regularly by the site's users. While in operation, Silk Road was used by thousands of drug dealers and other unlawful vendors to distribute hundreds of kilograms of illegal drugs and other unlawful goods and services to well over a hundred thousand buyers, and to launder hundreds of millions of dollars deriving from these unlawful transactions.
- ULBRICHT deliberately operated Silk Road as an online criminal marketplace intended to enable its users to buy and sell drugs and other illegal goods and services anonymously and outside the reach of law enforcement.
- ULBRICHT sought to anonymize transactions on Silk Road in two principal ways.
- First, ULBRICHT operated Silk Road on what is known as "The Onion Router," or "Tor" network, a special network of computers on the Internet, distributed around the world, designed to conceal the true IP addresses of the computers on the network and thereby the identities of the networks' users.
- Second, ULBRICHT designed Silk Road to include a Bitcoin-based payment system that served to facilitate the illegal commerce conducted on the site, including by concealing the identities and locations of the users transmitting and receiving funds through the site.
- The vast majority of items for sale on Silk Road were illegal drugs, which were openly advertised as such on the site. As of September 23, 2013, Silk Road had nearly 13,000 listings for controlled substances, listed under such categories as "Cannabis," "Dissociatives," "Ecstasy," "Intoxicants," "Opioids," "Precursors," "Prescription," "Psychedelics," and "Stimulants." From November 2011 to September 2013, law enforcement agents made more than 60 individual undercover purchases of controlled substances from Silk Road vendors. These purchases included heroin, cocaine, ecstasy, and LSD, among other illegal drugs, and were filled by vendors believed to be located in more than ten different countries, including the United States, Germany, the Netherlands, Canada, the United Kingdom, Spain, Ireland, Italy, Austria, and France.
- In addition to illegal narcotics, other illicit goods and services were openly bought and sold on Silk Road as well. For example, as of September 23, 2013, there were: 159 listings under the category "Services," most of which offered computer hacking services, such as a listing by a vendor offering to hack into social networking accounts of the customer's choosing; 801 listings under the category "Digital goods," including malicious software, hacked accounts at various online services, and pirated media content; and 169 listings under the category "Forgeries," including offers to produce fake driver's licenses, passports, Social Security cards, utility bills, credit card statements, car insurance records, and other forms of false identification documents.
- Using the online moniker "Dread Pirate Roberts," or "DPR," ULBRICHT controlled and oversaw every aspect of Silk Road, and managed a staff of paid, online administrators and computer programmers who assisted with the day-to-day operation of the site. Through his ownership and operation of Silk Road, ULBRICHT reaped commissions worth over $13 million generated

(continues)

(continued)

from the illicit sales conducted through the site. ULBRICHT also demonstrated a willingness to use violence to protect his criminal enterprise and the anonymity of its users. ULBRICHT even solicited six murders-for-hire in connection with operating the site, although there is no evidence that these murders were actually carried out.

* * *

ULBRICHT, 30, of San Francisco, California, was found guilty of:

1. one count of distributing narcotics, one count of distributing narcotics by means of the Internet, and one count of conspiring to distribute narcotics, each of which carries a maximum sentence of life in prison and a mandatory minimum sentence of 10 years;
2. one count of engaging in a continuing criminal enterprise, which carries a maximum sentence of life in prison and a mandatory minimum sentence of 20 years in prison;
3. one of count of conspiring to commit computer hacking, which carries a maximum sentence of five years in prison;
4. one count of conspiring to traffic in false identity documents, which carries a maximum sentence of 15 years; and
5. one count of conspiring to commit money laundering, which carries a maximum sentence of 20 years in prison.

The maximum sentences are prescribed by Congress and are provided for informational purposes only, as the sentence will be determined by the judge. ULBRICHT is scheduled to be sentenced on May 15, 2015.

Source: http://www.fbi.gov/newyork/press-releases/2015/ross-ulbricht-the-creator-and-owner-of-the-silk-road-website-found-guilty-in-manhattan-federal-court-on-all-counts (accessed June 6, 2015).

2.

ROSS ULBRICHT LETTER TO JUDGE FORREST MAY 26, 2015

Dear Judge Forrest,

I am writing you this letter in anticipation of my upcoming sentencing. This is a challenging letter to write because, as one who faces punishment, I have a strong incentive to say anything I think might result in leniency. But I have endeavored to be honest and forthright throughout this process, and so I will be in this letter as well.

My incarceration for the past year and half has given me a lot of time to reflect on the actions I took which led to my arrest and conviction, and my motivations for those actions.

When I created and began to work on Silk Road I wasn't seeking financial gain. I was, in fact, in fairly good financial shape at the time. I was the head of a startup company, Good Wagon Books, that was growing and had potential. I held two degrees that could land me an excellent job I could fall back on should the company fail. I created Silk Road because I thought the idea for the website itself had value, and that bringing Silk Road into being was the right thing to do.

I believed at the time that people should have the right to buy and sell whatever they wanted so long as they weren't hurting anyone else. However, I've learned since then that taking immediate actions on one's beliefs, without taking the necessary time to really think them through, can have disastrous consequences. Silk Road turned out to be a very naive and costly idea that I deeply regret.

Silk Road was supposed to be about giving people the freedom to make their own choices, to pursue their own happiness, however they individually saw fit. What it turned into was, in part, a convenient way for people to satisfy their drug addictions. I do not and never have advocated the abuse of drugs. I learned from Silk Road that when you give people freedom, you don't know what they'll do with it. While I still don't think people should be denied the right to make this decision for themselves, I never sought to create a site that would provide another avenue for people to feed their addictions. Had I been more mature, or more patient, or even more worldly then, I would have done things differently.

I was naive in other ways as well. Before this case, I had never been arrested, let alone jailed. Imprisonment was an abstract concept for me. I knew it was undesirable, but I didn't have a firm grasp on what it would actually be like. I have now learned that the absolute worst aspect is separation from my family and loved ones and the grief it has caused them.

If I had realized the impact my creation of Silk Road would ultimately have on the people I care about most, I never would have created Silk Road. I created it for what I believed at the time to be selfless reasons, but in the end it turned out to be a very selfish thing to do.

In creating Silk Road, I ruined my life and destroyed my future. I squandered the enviable upbringing my family provided me, all of the opportunities I have been given, and the ones I have earned, and my talents. I could have done so much more with my life. I see that now, but it is too late. You are charged with sentencing me to at least 20 years. In 20 years I could have made a positive contribution to society, without breaking the law. In 20 years I could have raised a family, and celebrated countless milestones in the lives of my friends, parents and siblings. I tell you these things because I want you to know that while I miss the comforts and joys of freedom, the most painful loss is the loss of my ability to support the people I care about and to be a daily part of their lives, and to be a productive member of society. For these reasons, if you find that my conviction warrants a sentence that allows for my eventual release, I will not lose my love for humanity during my years of imprisonment, and upon my release I will do what I can to make up for not being there for the people I love, and to make the world a better place, but within the limits of the law.

As I see it, a life sentence is more similar in nature to a death sentence than it is to a sentence with a finite number of years. Both condemn you to die in prison, a life sentence just takes longer. If I do make it out of prison, decades from now, I won't be the same man, and the world won't be the same place. I certainly won't be the rebellious risk taker I was when I created Silk Road. In fact, I'll be an old man, at least 50, with the additional wear and tear prison life brings. I will know firsthand the heavy price of breaking the law and will know better than anyone that it is not worth it. Even now I understand what a terrible mistake I made. I've had my youth, and I know you must take away my middle years, but please leave me my old age. Please leave a small light at the end of the tunnel, an excuse to stay healthy, an excuse to dream of better days ahead, and a chance to redeem myself in the free world before I meet my maker.

3.

SILK ROAD CREATOR ROSS ULBRICHT SENTENCED TO LIFE IN PRISON KATE VINTON, MAY 29, 2015

A year and a half after he was arrested in a San Francisco library—and four years after he first created the online drug marketplace Silk Road—Ulbricht is now looking at spending the rest of his life in prison.

In court, Ulbricht expressed remorse and asked for a lenient sentence. "I wish I could go back and convince myself to take a different path," he told Judge Katherine Forrest. "If given the chance, I would never breach the law again."

Judge Forrest, however, was not convinced. "There's no way Silk Road could be reasonably expected to reduce violence," she said. "You are a no better person than any other drug dealer. Your education doesn't make you different, and makes this morning inexplicable. Silk Road's creation showed that you thought you were better than the law," she added.

In addition to life in prison, Ulbricht also owes the government almost $200 million for all illegal drug and fake ID sales in Bitcoin on the Silk Road. "Ulbricht is liable for a money judgment in the amount of all the criminal proceeds laundered through Silk Road, regardless of the extent he personally retained those funds."

After the trial, Ulbricht's mother said she felt the ruling was based on emotion. "They have their war on drugs, and they are going to have their example. And Ross is that example," she said.

As one of the first court cases dealing with questions of privacy and anonymity online, the fallout of the Silk Road takedown will set precedent. "Ulbricht went from hiding his cybercrime identity to becoming the face of cybercrime and as today's sentence proves, no one is above the law," said U.S. Attorney Preet Bharara in a statement after the sentencing.

The debate over the length of Ulbricht's sentence in the past few weeks has hinged on a few central questions—was Ulbricht a (perhaps misguided) hero and former Boy Scout following acting on his libertarian convictions, or was he a calculating drug lord getting rich off of others' drug addictions and ruin? Was the Silk Road a safer way for drug transactions to happen or a platform for dangerous, untraceable criminal activity on Tor?

(continues)

(continued)

Earlier this week, the prosecution asked for a lengthy sentencing and presented victim impact statements from the families of two of six people who allegedly died of Silk Road-related drug overdoses. Meanwhile the defense argued for leniency, presenting a remorseful letter from Ulbricht and letters of support from friends and family. In the end, the prosecution got its way, with Ulbricht getting the maximum possible sentence for his seven charges.

On Wednesday, the government presented Judge Forrester with an 18-page letter, urging the judge to give Ulbricht a lengthy sentence to "send a clear message to anyone tempted to follow his example that the operation of these illegal enterprises comes with severe consequences." The government argued that Ulbricht "understood that his business was fueling drug abuse and addiction." According to the letter, Ulbricht made a huge profit from the Silk Road and "was willing to use violence to protect his enterprise, as evidenced by his solicitation of multiple murders for hire in attempts to eliminate perceived threats." (Ulbricht was never actually charged for these alleged murder-for-hires, which were allegedly faked by a corrupt undercover DEA agent.)

The victim impact statements also asked the judge for a harsh sentence, arguing that the writers' loved ones might still be alive without the ease of access to drugs provided by the Silk Road. At the trial itself, the families of two of these victims testified, and their testimony brought Ulbricht to tears. "I never wanted that to happen," he said in apology.

Source: http://www.forbes.com/sites/katevinton/2015/05/29/ulbricht-sentencing-silk-road/1/ (accessed June 6, 2015).

QUESTIONS

1. Summarize the U.S. government's case against Ross Ulbricht.
2. Summarize the reasons Judge Forrest sentenced Ross Ulbricht to life in prison without parole the appropriate punishment for Ross Ulbricht. Do you agree? Defend your answer.
3. Was Ulbricht "a (perhaps misguided) hero and former Boy Scout acting on his libertarian convictions"? Or, "Was he a calculating drug lord getting rich off of others' drug addictions and ruin"? "Was the Silk Road a safer way for drug transactions to happen or a platform for dangerous, untraceable criminal activity on Tor [The Onion Router]"?
4. Would Ross Ulbricht's letter move you to show some leniency? Move you to "throw the book at him"? Have no effect on your decision? Defend your answer.
5. In his fascinating interview with Teri Gross on "Fresh Air," Jamie Bartlett, author of *The Dark Net*, observed:

> If you try too hard to undermine those systems of privacy and encryption that are being used by the bad guys because you're only worried about them, you are also going to adversely affect all the people that use it for social benefit. And that's one of the reasons why in the end, we are going to have to work out a way of living with some of this bad stuff. Because the benefits of Internet freedom and of Internet privacy are so enormous—not just in this country, not just in democracies but especially in brutal dictatorships all around the world. And so if we want those people to have protection and privacy, unfortunately it means that some bad people are going to use it for ill as well. But we shouldn't destroy the whole system simply as a result of the behavior of the bad guys.

Do you agree? Defend your answer.

Summary

LO1 There are three categories of crimes against property: (1) taking other people's property (theft, fraud, robbery, and receiving stolen property); (2) damaging or destroying other people's property (arson, criminal mischief); and (3) invading other people's property (burglary, criminal trespass).

LO2 The different "taking" property crimes are larceny, embezzlement, false pretenses, white-collar crimes, robbery, and receiving stolen property. The concern with violent crimes against the person led to the creation of the common law felony of robbery, which involves the use of force or the threat of the use of force. The history of larceny and fraud is also the history of supplementing civil actions with criminal punishment. Common law false pretenses *mens rea* requires the purpose or specific intent to obtain property by deceit and lies.

LO3 Consolidated theft statutes are a modern approach to certain "taking" crimes (larceny, embezzlement, and false pretenses). These statutes eliminate the artificial need to separate theft into distinct offenses according to the *actus reus*. Under modern theft statutes, *actus reus* includes taking and carrying away, converting, or swindling to obtain possession of someone else's property.

LO4 White-collar crime is criminal behavior committed by the white-collar class, including fraud, swindling, and "double crossing" and includes federal mail fraud and Ponzi schemes. Federal mail fraud statutes are an exceptionally powerful tool for prosecuting white-collar criminals because they are: (1) inchoate offenses; (2) comprised of just two elements and; (3) very broad and malleable. Ponzi schemes are fraudulent investment operations that fluctuate with the health of the economy.

LO5 The core of robbery is theft accomplished under circumstances intended to terrorize the victim by actual injury or the threat of immediate injury to the victim. The use of force, or the threat of force, is the essence of the robbery criminal act. Most states have divided robbery into degrees.

LO6 Receiving stolen property requires that the receiver control the property, at least briefly. In some states, receivers of stolen property have to know the goods are stolen; in others, believing the goods are stolen is enough.

LO7 Arson is a felony and an example of a "damaging or destroying" property crime. Arson includes burning almost any kind of building, vessel, or vehicle; it's a very serious crime against property and persons.

LO8 Criminal mischief is another example of a "damaging or destroying" property crime and is usually a felony, but it's less serious than arson. There are three kinds of criminal mischief: (1) destruction or damage criminal mischief, (2) tampering, and (3) deception or threat. The *mens rea* requirement varies, but generally it looks at whether the person purposely, knowingly, or negligently caused damage to or pecuniary loss of property.

LO9 The heart of burglary is invading others' property with the intent to commit a crime once inside. Criminal trespass is a broader but less serious invasion type of property crime than burglary. The heart of criminal trespass is unwanted presence.

LO10 More people are victims of identity theft than burglary, vehicle theft, and robbery combined in the United States—only ordinary theft claims more victims than identity theft. The consequences of wrongful access to personal information can be devastating, costly, and time-consuming.

LO11 Besides traditional ways to take, destroy or damage, and invade other people's property, cybercrime—crimes committed through the Internet or some other computer network—is a serious and rapidly growing new problem. Computers and the Internet have greatly enhanced the capacity to exploit information about individuals and steal ideas. Intellectual property is particularly vulnerable to cyberattacks, and the dark web provides a unique, anonymous opportunity for criminal activity.

Key Terms

cybercrime, p. 432
robbery, p. 433
larceny, p. 433
conversion, p. 433
tangible property, p. 433
intangible property, p. 433
embezzlement, p. 433
abuse-of-trust crimes, p. 434
fraud, p. 434
obtaining property by false pretenses, p. 434
theft, p. 435
white-collar crime, p. 438
mail fraud statutes, p. 439
Ponzi scheme, p. 442
robbery *actus reus*, p. 446
robbery *mens rea*, p. 451
receiving stolen property, p. 452
fences, p. 452
receiving stolen property *actus reus*, p. 452
receiving stolen property *mens rea*, p. 452
arson, p. 455
criminal mischief, p. 455
burning, p. 456
arson *mens rea*, p. 457
first-degree arson, p. 457
second-degree arson, p. 457
malicious mischief, p. 458
criminal mischief *actus reus*, p. 458
burglary, p. 462
breaking, p. 462
entering, p. 462
surreptitious remaining element, p. 463
occupied structure, p. 463
dwelling "of another," p. 463
criminal trespass, p. 466
identity theft, p. 467
intellectual property, p. 472
Tor browser, p. 475

Learning Objectives

1 To understand and appreciate that the efforts to control bad manners in public create a tension between order and liberty in constitutional democracies.

2 To know the definition of disorderly conduct and its widespread impact on criminal justice system.

3 To know and understand how our present "quality of life" offenses aimed at controlling "bad manners" in public grew out of the ancient offense of disorderly conduct.

4 To know and understand why the "broken windows" theory claims that "quality of life" crimes are linked to serious crime.

5 To know the difference between vagrancy and loitering and to appreciate the history of laws that address these crimes.

6 To know the definition of panhandling and understand how laws to restrict it have led to claims that they violate the First Amendment ban on free speech.

7 To understand that widespread fear of gangs has led state and city governments to enact criminal laws that allow them to obtain civil gang injunctions that regulate gang behavior.

8 To understand that the link between violent video games and criminal behavior is based on the "broken windows theory" of disorderly conduct.

9 To know that "victimless crimes" against public decency (the ancient "crimes against public morals") generate heated disagreement and debate between those who believe that criminal law should enforce morality and those who believe the nonviolent behavior of competent adults is none of the law's business.

10 To know that prostitution is a "victimless crime" with a long history of punishing women more than men.

11 To understand and appreciate the ethical dilemmas posed by discretionary decision making in the enforcement of crimes against public morals.

12 Crimes Against Public Order and Morals

Chapter Outline

> The last species of offenses which especially affect the commonwealth are . . . the due regulation and domestic order of the kingdom. The individuals of the state, like members of a well-governed family, are bound to conform their general behavior to the rules of propriety, good neighborhood, and good manners; and to be decent, industrious, and inoffensive. This head of offenses must therefore be very miscellaneous, as it comprises all such crimes as especially affect public society. (Blackstone 1769, 162)

LO1

Blackstone's eighteenth-century introduction to his chapter on crimes related to the "regulation and domestic order of the kingdom" is a good way to introduce you to the subject of this chapter, crimes against public order and morals. These crimes cover two vast areas of criminal law that involve mostly very minor crimes: disorderly conduct and "quality of life" crimes. Nonetheless, they affect many more people than the crimes against persons and their property we've already discussed (see Chapters 9–11 and Table 12.1) and the crimes against the state we'll discuss in Chapter 13.

Throughout most of our history, "bad manners" crimes have been called **crimes against public order**. Today, we call them **"quality of life" crimes**. The list of quality-of-life offenses is long, including public drinking and drunkenness; begging and aggressive panhandling; threatening behavior and harassment; blocking streets and public places; graffiti and vandalism; street prostitution; public urination and defecation; unlicensed vending; and even jaywalking.

Significant numbers of people across the spectrums of age, sex, race, ethnicity, and class believe strongly that "bad manners" in public places create disorder and threaten

crimes against public order formerly called "bad manners" crimes; today called **"quality of life" crimes**, they include public drinking, aggressive panhandling, harassment, graffiti and vandalism, and street prostitution, among others

order acting according to ordinary people's standard of "good manners"

liberty the right of individuals to come and go as they please without government interference

the quality of life of ordinary people (Skogan 1990). Others believe just as strongly that making bad manners a crime denies individuals their liberty without due process of law (see Fifth and Fourteenth Amendments to the U.S. Constitution; Chapter 2).

Constitutional democracy can't survive without both order and liberty. But there's a natural tension between them because they're values in conflict. Recall that the U.S. Supreme Court has recognized the need to balance order and liberty by holding repeatedly that our constitutional system requires "*ordered* liberty" (Chapter 2). In this chapter, "**order**" refers to acting according to ordinary people's standard of "good manners." "**Liberty**" refers to the right of individuals to come and go as they please without government interference.

In this chapter, we'll look first at *disorderly conduct* crimes. We'll examine in depth the application of disorderly conduct laws to what are now called "*quality of life*" crimes. These are crimes of "bad manners" in public.

Then, in our look at quality-of-life crimes surrounding gang activity, we'll examine the facts and myths about youth gang activity enforcement tactics. Specifically, we'll learn what the empirical research on the effectiveness of the noncriminal preventive response—namely, the *civil gang injunction* (CGI)—tells us.

We'll also examine the ban on violent video games and the empirical research that led a U.S. district court (*Interactive Digital Software Association v. St. Louis County* 2002) to find that

> exposure of children to graphic and lifelike violence contained in some video games has been correlated to violent behavior, and in fact the perpetrators of recent school shootings in Columbine, Colorado; Jonesboro, Arkansas; and Paducah, Kentucky were reported to be avid fans of such games. (1129)

TABLE 12.1 Estimated Number of Arrests, 2013

Offense	Number
All other offenses	3,282,651
Property crime[3]	1,559,284
Drug abuse violations	1,501,043
Driving under the influence	1,166,824
Violent crime[3]	480,360
Disorderly conduct	467,993
Drunkenness	443,527
Liquor laws	354,872
Vandalism	201,168
Weapons; carrying, possessing, etc.	137,779
Offenses against the family and children	101,247
Sex offenses (except rape and prostitution)	57,925
Curfew and loitering law violations	56,371
Prostitution and commercialized vice	48,620
Vagrancy	25,755
Gambling	6,024
Suspicion	1,096

[3]Violent crimes in this table are offenses of murder and nonnegligent manslaughter, rape (revised and legacy definitions), robbery, and aggravated assault. Property crimes are offenses of burglary, larceny-theft, motor vehicle theft, and arson.

Source: FBI Uniform Crime Reports (UCR), *Crime in the United States 2013*, Table 29.

Next, we'll examine separately another type of quality-of-life crime: "victimless crimes." These crimes involve willing participants or participants who don't see themselves as victims.

Finally, we'll return to a topic introduced you in Chapter 1—the social reality that criminal justice officials *create* a lot of law by exercising their discretionary power to apply the law in the criminal codes to daily life activities. But there we described generally how police power to arrest and prosecutors' power charge and plea bargain are sources of criminal law. Here, we home in on *municipal* police, prosecutor, and court law making.

More precisely, we'll focus on an aspect of local criminal justice thrust coincidentally into public attention as a back story to police shootings in a handful of cities. (FYI, there are 16,000+ local law enforcement agencies in the United States.) We put aside this important debate over the justification and fairness of the discretionary power of the police to use *deadly* force, a debate that reflects passionate, heartfelt debate on all sides. Our business here is to explore the use (and abuse) of local police, prosecutors, and municipal court discretionary power to arrest, charge, and fine *minor offense* violators for purposes that go beyond maintaining public order and morals, namely to provide income to operate city government, and which are enforced disproportionately according to race.

We begin with a look at disorderly conduct generally in our society.

DISORDERLY CONDUCT

LO2

Disorderly conduct crimes are offenses against public order and morals. They're minor crimes that legislators, judges, and scholars didn't pay much attention to until the 1950s when the Model Penal Code (MPC) was adopted by the American Law Institute (ALI). Why the lack of attention? The punishment was minor (small fines or a few days in jail); most defendants were poor; most never got to court, and in those that did, most were pleaded out, and trial convictions were rarely appealed. But disorderly conduct offenses are an important part of the criminal justice system for three reasons: they "affect large numbers of defendants, involve a great proportion of public activity, and powerfully influence the view of public justice held by millions of people" (ALI 1985, Part II, Vol. 3, Art. 250, 251, 309).

disorderly conduct crimes offenses against public order and morals

Let's look first at the ancient common law offense, "breach of the peace," from which the modern disorderly conduct statutes descend.

History of Disorderly Conduct

LO3

Disorderly conduct statutes grew out of the ancient common law crime known as "breach of the peace" (see Chapter 2, "Right to 'Freedom of Speech'" section). It included both the misdemeanors of **actual disorderly conduct** (e.g., fighting in public, making unreasonable noise) and **constructive disorderly conduct**, which was conduct that "tends to provoke or excite others to break it [the peace]" (Blackstone 1769, 148).

actual disorderly conduct breach-of-the-peace misdemeanor that includes fighting in public and making unreasonable noise

constructive disorderly conduct conduct that "tends to provoke or excite others to break the peace"

Wisconsin's "disorderly conduct" statute, for example, follows Blackstone:

> Whoever, in a public or private place, engages in violent, abusive, indecent, profane, boisterous, unreasonably loud or otherwise disorderly conduct under circumstances in which the conduct tends to cause or provoke a disturbance is guilty of a Class B misdemeanor. (Wisconsin Criminal Code 2003, § 947.01)

The problem with Wisconsin's statute, and those of most states with similar statutes, is twofold. First, they're too vague to give individuals and law enforcement officers notice of what the law prohibits (see Chapter 2, "The Void-for-Vagueness Doctrine" section). Second, neither requires *mens rea* (Chapter 4). The Model Penal Code (Section 250.2(1)) requires a mental attitude of subjective fault, namely knowing or reckless. So conscious risk creation is the minimum level of culpability; negligence isn't good enough (see Chapter 4, "The Model Penal Code (MPC) Levels of Culpability" section). MPC confines *actus reus* to three actions:

1. Fighting in public
2. Making "unreasonable noise" or using "abusive language" (see Chapter 2, "Right to 'Freedom of Speech'" section)
3. Creating a "hazardous or physically offensive condition," such as strewing garbage, setting off "stink bombs," or turning off lights in crowded public places

In practice, the most common use of disorderly conduct statutes is the ban on fighting in public. Fighting can cause two harms: (1) disturbing community peace and quiet and (2) disturbing or endangering innocent bystanders. The MPC also includes several "special" sections devoted to other specifically defined acts of disorderly conduct (see the Criminal Law in Focus box "Model Penal Code Elements of Special Disorderly Conduct Sections"). The majority of states have adopted the *actus reus* and the *mens rea* provisions of the MPC.

Model Penal Code Elements of Special Disorderly Conduct Sections

OFFENSE	ELEMENT	DESCRIPTION
False public alarms (250.3)	*Mens rea*	Knowingly
	Actus reus	Initiating or circulating a report or warning of a bombing or a catastrophe
	Harm	Likely to cause evacuation or public inconvenience or alarm
Public drunkenness (250.5)	*Actus reus*	Appearing in a public place "manifestly under the influence of alcohol, narcotics, or other drug, not therapeutically administered"
	Harm	To the degree it may "endanger himself or other persons or property, or annoy persons in his vicinity"
Loitering or prowling (250.6)	*Actus reus*	Loitering or prowling
	Circumstances	"In a place, at a time, or in a manner not usual for law-abiding individuals"
	Harm	Warrant "alarm for the safety of persons or property in the vicinity"
Obstructing highways or other public passages (250.7)	*Mens rea*	Purposely or recklessly
	Actus reus	Obstructs highway or public passage (except if exercising lawful First Amendment rights) (Chapter 2)
Disrupting meetings and processions (250.8)	*Mens rea*	Purposely
	Actus reus	Prevent or disrupt a lawful meeting, procession, or gathering either physically or by words, gestures, or displays designed to "outrage the sensibilities of the group"

"QUALITY OF LIFE" CRIMES

LO3, LO4

"Quality of life" crimes are "bad manners" crimes that threaten to disrupt public order. In the 1980s, two prominent scholars sensed a deep public yearning for recovering what they called a lost sense of public "good manners," especially in our largest cities. Professors James Q. Wilson and George L. Kelling (1982) suggested that what were labeled "petty crimes" weren't just "bothering" law-abiding people and creating a yearning for a more polite past; they were connected to serious crime. They called this connection between disorderly conduct and serious crime the broken-windows theory.

"quality of life" crimes "bad manners" crimes that threaten to disrupt public order

broken-windows theory first espoused by James Q. Wilson and George L. Kelling, the theory that minor offenses or disorderly conduct can lead to a rise in serious crime

According to Kelling, research conducted since his 1982 article has demonstrated "a direct link between disorder and crime." But in 1996, Wilson described the broken-windows theory more cautiously. In the foreword to a book written by Kelling and Catherine M. Coles, *Fixing Broken Windows* (1996), Wilson wrote:

> We used the image of broken windows to explain how neighborhoods might decay into disorder and even crime if no one attends faithfully to their maintenance. If a factory or office window is broken, passersby observing it will conclude that no one cares or no one is in charge. In time, a few will begin throwing rocks to break more windows. Soon all the windows will be broken, and now passersby will think that, not only is no one in charge of the building no one is in charge of the street on which it faces. Only the young, the criminal, or the foolhardy have any business on an unprotected avenue, and so more and more citizens will abandon the street to those they assume prowl it. Small disorders lead to larger and larger ones, and perhaps even to crime. (xiv)

Professor Wesley G. Skogan (1990), the author of some of the research on which Kelling relies, characterized his and others' research more cautiously than Kelling:

> Our concern with common crime is limited to whether disorder is a cause of it. Neighborhood levels of disorder are closely related to crime rates, to fear of crime, and the belief that serious crime is a neighborhood problem. This relationship could reflect the fact that the link between crime and disorder is a *causal* one, or that both are dependent on some third set of factors (such as poverty or neighborhood instability). (10) [emphasis added]

Despite the caution, Skogan still asserted that the data "support the proposition that disorder needs to be taken seriously in research on neighborhood crime and that, both directly and through crime, it plays an important role in neighborhood decline" (75).

Professor Bernard Harcourt (2001), then at the University of Chicago Law School, replicated Skogan's research and found a weak-to-no causal link between disorder and serious crime (8–9). The best recent research strongly suggests that disorder and serious crime have common causes, but they don't cause each other, at least not directly (Sampson and Raudenbush 1999, 637–38).

Most of the national debate over crime, criminal law books (this one included), and criminal justice courses concentrate on the serious crimes we've analyzed in Chapters 9 through 11. But there's a disconnect between this national focus on one side and local concern on the other. Mayors and local residents do worry about murder, rape, burglary, and theft, but they also care a lot about order on their streets, in their parks, and in other public places.

In one extensive survey of a representative sample of high- and low-crime neighborhoods in major cities, public drinking, followed closely by loitering youths, topped the list of worries among all classes, races, and ethnic groups, among both men and women.

Survey participants also listed begging, street harassment, noisy neighbors, vandalism, street prostitution, and illegal vending (Skogan 1990, 2).

Prosecutor Karen Hayter found this out when she created Kalamazoo, Michigan's Neighborhood Prosecutor Program. When Hayter "asked residents what crimes worried them the most, she thought it would be the big ones: murder, assault, breaking and entering," but that's not what she was told. Instead, said Hayter, "Loud noise, littering, loitering, curfew violations, junk autos, rundown houses—those are considered quality-of-life crimes, and they're very important to residents in an area" (National Public Radio 2003).

Any examination of criminal law has to recognize quality-of-life crimes as part of early twenty-first-century life. Since the 1980s, state statutes and city ordinances have reinvigorated and molded the old crimes against public order and morals to fit the public's demand that criminal justice preserve, protect, and even restore the quality of life in their communities. The courts have assumed the burden of balancing the social interest in public order against the social interest in individual liberty and privacy (Skogan 1990, 21).

Let's examine how states and localities have shaped traditional public order and morals laws to control the behavior of some "street people" (the homeless, youth gangs, and sex workers) and the quality-of-life crimes commonly associated with them: vagrancy, loitering, panhandling, and gang activity. We'll also examine recent concerns with violent video games and the new statutes that criminalize giving unrestricted access to them by minors. Prostitution is a quality-of-life crime, but we'll discuss it and important issues it raises about equal treatment before the law later in our discussion of "victimless crimes."

LO5 Vagrancy and Loitering

vagrancy the ancient crime of poor people wandering with no visible means of support

loitering the crime of remaining in one place with no apparent purpose

For at least 600 years, it's been a crime for poor people to roam without visible means of support (vagrancy) or to stand around with no apparent purpose (loitering). The Articles of Confederation specifically denied to paupers the freedom to travel from state to state. In 1837, in *Mayor of New York v. Miln*, the U.S. Supreme Court approved the efforts by the state of New York to exclude paupers arriving by ship. According to the Court, it's as necessary for a state to provide precautionary measures against the moral pestilence of paupers, vagabonds, and possibly convicts as it is to guard against physical pestilence, which may arise from unsound and infectious articles. Every state in the union had and enforced vagrancy and loitering statutes that wrote the Court's view into law (Simon 1992, 631).

VAGRANCY

Laws targeting poor people's behavior, and the attitudes behind these laws, began to change during the Great Depression of the 1930s. In 1941, the U.S. Supreme Court struck down a vagrancy statute that prohibited the importation of paupers into California. In response to the argument that the regulation of paupers enjoyed a long history, the Court dismissed the earlier decisions as out of date. According to the Court, "We do not think that it will now be seriously contended that because a person is without employment and without funds he constitutes a 'moral pestilence.'" In a concurring opinion, Justice Robert Jackson encouraged the Court to "say now, in no uncertain terms, that a mere property status, without more, cannot be used by a state to test, qualify, or limit his rights as a citizen of the United States" (*Edwards v. California* 1941, 184).

During the 1960s and 1970s, courts began to strike down vagrancy laws because they unfairly discriminated against the poor. The following excerpt from an opinion written by Chief Justice Thompson of the Nevada Supreme Court in *Parker v. Municipal Judge* (1967) reflects this trend:

> It is simply not a crime to be unemployed, without funds, and in a public place. To punish the unfortunate for this circumstance debases society. The comment of [U.S. Associate Supreme Court] Justice Douglas is relevant: "How can we hold our heads high and still confuse with crime the need for welfare or the need for work?"

In *Papachristou v. City of Jacksonville* (1972), the U.S. Supreme Court struck down the Jacksonville, Florida, vagrancy ordinance, which was nearly identical to virtually every other vagrancy law in the country. Writing for a unanimous Court, Justice Douglas declared the ordinance void for vagueness because it both failed to give adequate notice to individuals and it encouraged arbitrary law enforcement (Chapter 2). The Court warned that criminal statutes aimed at the poor

> teach that the scales of justice are so tipped that even-handed administration of the law is not possible. The rule of law, evenly applied to minorities as well as majorities, to the poor as well as the rich, is the great mucilage that holds society together. (169)

LOITERING

In *Kolender v. Lawson* (1983), the U.S. Supreme Court tightened the constitutional restrictions on loitering statutes. The counterpart to vagrancy, which means to *roam* with no visible means of support, loitering means to "*remain* in one place with no apparent purpose." In *Kolender*, the Court struck down a California statute that combined ancient vagrancy and loitering into a new crime defined as "wandering the streets and failing to produce credible identification" when a police officer asked for it. As it did with the vagrancy statute in *Papachristou*, the Court ruled that the statute was void for vagueness.

According to Harry Simon (1992), staff attorney for the Legal Aid Society in Santa Ana, California:

> With the Supreme Court's decisions in *Papachristou* and *Kolender*, loitering and vagrancy laws ceased to be effective tools to punish and control the displaced poor. While judicial attitudes on vagrancy and loitering laws had changed, local officials perceived the invalidation of these laws as a dangerous assault on their authority to enforce social order. (645)

According to Robert C. Ellickson (1996), professor of Property and Urban Law at the Yale Law School:

> Many judges at the time seemed blind to the fact that their constitutional rulings might adversely affect the quality of urban life and the viability of city centers. It is one thing to protect unpopular persons from wrongful confinement; it is another to imply that these persons have no duty to behave themselves in public places. In addition, federal constitutional rulings are one of the most centralized and inflexible forms of law making.
>
> In a diverse and dynamic nation committed to separation of powers and federalism, there is much to be said for giving state and local legislative bodies substantial leeway to tailor street codes to city conditions, and for giving state judges ample scope to interpret the relevant provisions of state constitutions. (1213–14)

At the same time these decisions were easing up on control over the behavior of poor people in public, other events were creating a rapidly—and, to many, a frightening—growth of an *underclass*. At the same time, state mental hospitals were deinstitutionalizing the mentally ill; family breakdowns and breakups were increasing steeply; crack cocaine was becoming more available on the streets; hard economic times were upon us; and budgets for social programs were tightening.

By the late 1980s, this rising underclass and its public presence and behavior led many city dwellers to conclude that things had gone too far. Liberal columnist Ellen Goodman, in "Swarms of Beggars Cause 'Compassion Fatigue,'" captured this attitude when she wrote, "Today at least, this tourist, walking from one block to another, one cup to another, one city to another, wants to join in a citizens' chorus: 'Enough's enough'" (Simon 1992, 1218).

Municipal codes reflected this growing intolerance of street people's behavior. By the late 1990s, Juliette Smith (1996) found that "at least thirty-nine American cities had initiated or continued policies that criminalize activities associated with homelessness" (29).

San Francisco is one of many cities whose officials enforced the quality-of-life laws against the "bad public manners" of street people. The Matrix Program "condemned quality of life violations" as "type of behavior [which] tends to make San Francisco a less desirable place in which to live, work or visit." It directed the

> vigorous enforcement of 18 specified code sections, including prohibitions against trespassing, public inebriation, urinating or defecating in public, removal and possession of shopping carts, solicitation on or near a highway, erection of tents or structures in parks, obstruction and aggressive panhandling.

Deputy Chief Thomas Petrini made clear Matrix's "intended nondiscriminatory policy of enforcement:

> All persons have the right to use the public streets and places so long as they are not engaged in specific criminal activity. Factors such as race, sex, sexual preference, age, dress, unusual or disheveled or impoverished appearance do not alone justify enforcement action. Nor can generalized complaints by residents or merchants or others justify detention of any person absent such individualized suspicion.

Bobby Joe Joyce, Timothy E. Smith, Thomas O'Halloren, and Jim Tullah, homeless people, didn't see Matrix that way. To them, police actions were "calculated to punish the homeless." It "targets hundreds of homeless persons who are guilty of nothing more than sitting on a park bench or on the ground with their possessions, or lying or sleeping on the ground covered by or on top of a blanket or cardboard carton." They sued the City and County of San Francisco, asking for a preliminary injunction against Matrix. In *Joyce v. City and County of San Francisco* (1994), U.S. District Judge Lowell Jensen rejected their claims that Matrix denied them equal protection of the laws and due process of law.

Panhandling

> Many City Councils have been convinced to adopt new and innovative controls on antisocial behavior to maintain minimal standards of public conduct and to keep public spaces safe and attractive.... One of the most common examples of these efforts are ordinances aimed at aggressive begging. (Tier 1993, 286)

LO6

These "new and innovative controls" rely on ancient laws against begging, or panhandling. Panhandling consists of stopping people on the street to ask them for food or money. Keep in mind that these antibegging ordinances don't apply to organized charities. So, although it's a crime for a private beggar to panhandle for money, it's legal for the Salvation Army to ring their bells to get contributions.

panhandling stopping people on the street to ask them for food or money

Why the distinction? Supporters of the distinction say the rights revolution has simply gone too far. It's reached the point, they say, where the rights of a minority of offensive individuals trump the quality of life of the whole community. Associate Supreme Court Justice Clarence Thomas (1996) commenting on "how judicial interpretations of the First Amendment and of 'unenumerated' constitutional rights have affected the ability of urban communities to deal with crime, disorder, and incivility on their public streets," told the Federalist Society:

> Vagrancy, loitering, and panhandling laws were challenged [during the rights revolution] because the poor and minorities could be victims of discrimination under the guise of broad discretion to ensure public safety. Moreover, as a consequence of the modern tendency to challenge society's authority to dictate social norms, the legal system began to prefer the ideal of self-expression without much attention to self-discipline or self-control.
>
> What resulted was a culture that declined to curb the excesses of self-indulgence—vagrants and others who regularly roamed the streets had rights that could not be circumscribed by the community's sense of decency or decorum. (269)

"Hey, buddy, can you spare some change?" is clearly speech. And, of course, the First Amendment guarantees individuals freedom of speech. But recall that free speech doesn't mean you can say anything you want anywhere at anytime (Chapter 2). The U.S. Supreme Court has "rejected the notion that a city is powerless to protect its citizens from unwanted exposure to certain methods of expression which may legitimately be deemed a public nuisance" (Scheidegger 1993, 7).

The Court has established a number of tests to determine whether ordinances violate the First Amendment guarantee of free speech. One is to look at the place where the speech takes place. In traditional public forums—streets, sidewalks, and parks—where people have since ancient times expressed their views, the freedom to solicit is virtually unrestricted. In designated public forums—places the government chooses to make available to the public—the government has more leeway to regulate solicitation. In nonpublic forums—airports, bus stations, railroad stations, subways, and shopping malls—the government has broad power to restrict and even prohibit solicitation (Scheidegger 1993, 7–9).

The First Amendment free speech clause also permits time, place, and manner regulations. According to the U.S. Supreme Court (*R.A.V. v. City of St. Paul* 1992; see Chapter 2), to be constitutional, restrictions have to satisfy three elements of a time, place, and manner test:

time, place, and manner test to be constitutional, restrictions on free speech can't be based on the content of the speech, must serve a significant government interest, and leave open other channels of expression

1. They're not based on the content of the speech.
2. They serve a significant government interest—for example, maintaining the free flow of pedestrian traffic.
3. They leave open other channels of expression.

The first element in the test bars the use of the regulation to suppress any message about social conditions that panhandlers are trying to convey. The second element is hotly contested. Advocates for panhandlers argue that the regulation of panhandling is really a government policy of removing "unsightly" poor people from public view. Others maintain that the "purpose is to permit people to use the streets, sidewalks, and public transportation free from the borderline robbery and pervasive fraud which characterizes so much of today's panhandling" (Scheidegger 1993, 10–11). The third element requires the regulation to allow panhandlers to beg in other ways. So a panhandling ordinance that prohibits "aggressive panhandling" leaves panhandlers free to beg peaceably. So do bans on fraudulent panhandling or panhandling in subways. Panhandlers can beg honestly on streets and in parks (10–11).

In addition to forum and time, place, and manner restrictions, the First Amendment gives the government considerable leeway to regulate nonverbal expression (expressive conduct; Chapter 2). This would allow direct efforts to stop panhandlers from approaching people or blocking the sidewalk to beg or receiving the money they solicited.

Finally, the First Amendment grants commercial speech (advertising and other means of "asking for" money) less protection than other types of speech. Because begging relies on talking listeners into handing over their money, panhandling is commercial speech. Jimmy Gresham, a homeless person, took that argument to the U.S. District Court and asked for an injunction against the enforcement of the Indianapolis ban on aggressive panhandling. The District Court rejected his commercial speech argument and denied his request for the injunction. The U.S. Court of Appeals for the Seventh Circuit affirmed the District Court's decision in *Gresham v. Peterson* (2000).

LO7 Gang Activity

"Bands of loitering youth" seriously threaten their quality of life, say many city residents (Skogan 1990, 23). Gangs can include everything from casual groups of kids who are just hanging out drinking a little bit all the way to "organized fighting squads" who terrorize neighborhoods. The casual groups do little more than "bother" residents. According to one observer, "They are neighborhood kids, and they sometimes make a nuisance of themselves. Actually they stand there because they have no place to go" (23). Gangs composed of older, rowdier members are more threatening.

According to a resident in a neighborhood with one of these gangs:

> Sometimes I walk out of my house and start to try to walk down the street, and a gang will cross the street and try to scare me and my mother. A gang used to sit and drink beer and smoke pot in front of our stairs. My mom used to come out and tell them to get off; they would, and then when she would go into the house they'd come back, sit down, and look at us. Actually we're afraid to walk around in the neighborhood after it gets dark. I stay right in front of the house where my mom can see me. (24)

Let's look at some criminal law and civil law efforts to control gang activities and then review the latest research on the effectiveness of these efforts.

CRIMINAL LAW RESPONSES TO GANG ACTIVITY

A number of state and city governments have passed criminal laws to regulate gang behavior. In some places, it's a crime to participate in a gang. Some statutes and ordinances have stiffened the penalties for crimes committed by gang members. Others make it a crime to encourage minors to participate in gangs. Some have applied organized crime statutes to gangs. A few have punished parents for their children's gang activities. Cities have also passed ordinances banning gang members from certain public places, particularly city parks.

In 1992, Chicago was facing a skyrocketing increase in crime rates that many outspoken people blamed on street gangs. But unlike the sweeping antiloitering injunction approved in California, the Chicago City Council passed a modern version of the ancient loitering ordinances (discussed in the "Loitering" section). Chicago's ordinance gave its police the power to order groups of loiterers (people who "remain in one place with no apparent purpose") to disperse or face arrest if officers reasonably believed that one of the loiterers was a gang member (Poulos 1995, 379–81).

No one was surprised when the ordinance set off an angry debate. Mayor Richard Daley Jr. expressed one view: "In some areas of the city, street gangs are terrorizing residents and laying claim to whole communities." Bobbie Crawford, a waitress, expressed another view: "When kids reach a certain age they hang around on street corners. I sure wouldn't like my children taken to a police station for hanging around." And Joan Suglich, mother of six, asked, "What if somebody asks his boys to walk him home so gang members don't jump him. Are police going to arrest them?"

No one was surprised when the debate ended up in the U.S. Supreme Court. In *City of Chicago v. Morales* (1999), a divided Court decided that the ordinance was void for vagueness. Several justices, but not a majority, also argued that the ordinance violated the right to come and go as you please without unreasonable government interference.

CASE

In ***City of Chicago v. Morales* (1999),** *a divided Supreme Court decided that the ordinance that gave the police the power to order groups of loiterers to disperse or face arrest was void for vagueness.*

Was the loitering ordinance void for vagueness?

City of Chicago v. Morales

527 U.S. 41 (1999)

HISTORY

Jesus Morales and other defendants in several separate cases were charged in the Circuit Court of Cook County with violating the Chicago antigang ordinance. Morales and the defendants in one case moved to dismiss the actions against them. The Circuit Court, Cook County, granted the motion. The city appealed. The Illinois Appellate Court affirmed.

The defendants in a second case were charged with violating the ordinance. The Circuit Court dismissed the charges. The Appellate Court affirmed. The city petitioned for leave to appeal, which the Appellate Court granted.

In a third case, the defendants were charged, in the Circuit Court, with violating the ordinance, were convicted, and were sentenced to jail terms. The defendants appealed. The Appellate Court reversed. The city petitioned for leave to appeal.

After granting the petitions to appeal in all three cases, and consolidating the cases for one hearing, the Supreme Court of Illinois affirmed. The U.S. Supreme Court granted certiorari and affirmed the judgment of the Illinois Supreme Court.

STEVENS, J.

FACTS

In 1992, the Chicago City Council enacted the Gang Congregation Ordinance, which prohibits "criminal street gang members" from "loitering" with one another or with other persons in any public place. The ordinance creates a criminal offense punishable by a fine of up to $500, imprisonment for not more than six months, and a requirement to perform up to 120 hours of community service. Commission of the offense involves four elements.

1. First, the police officer must reasonably believe that at least one of the two or more persons present in a "public place" is a "criminal street gang member."
2. Second, the persons must be "loitering," which the ordinance defines as "remain[ing] in any one place with no apparent purpose."
3. Third, the officer must then order "all" of the persons to disperse and remove themselves "from the area."
4. Fourth, a person must disobey the officer's order. If any person, whether a gang member or not, disobeys the officer's order, that person is guilty of violating the ordinance.

(continues)

(continued)

Two months after the ordinance was adopted, the Chicago Police Department promulgated General Order 92-4 to provide guidelines to govern its enforcement. That order purported to establish limitations on the enforcement discretion of police officers "to ensure that the antigang loitering ordinance is not enforced in an arbitrary or discriminatory way."

The limitations confine the authority to arrest gang members who violate the ordinance to sworn "members of the Gang Crime Section" and certain other designated officers and establish detailed criteria for defining street gangs and membership in such gangs.

In addition, the order directs district commanders to "designate areas in which the presence of gang members has a demonstrable effect on the activities of law abiding persons in the surrounding community," and provides that the ordinance "will be enforced only within the designated areas." The city, however, does not release the locations of these "designated areas" to the public.

During the three years of its enforcement, the police issued over 89,000 dispersal orders and arrested over 42,000 people for violating the ordinance. In the ensuing enforcement proceedings, two trial judges upheld the constitutionality of the ordinance, but 11 others ruled that it was invalid.

The city believes that the ordinance resulted in a significant decline in gang-related homicides. It notes that in 1995, the last year the ordinance was enforced, the gang-related homicide rate fell by 26 percent. In 1996, after the ordinance had been held invalid, the gang-related homicide rate rose 11 percent. However, gang-related homicides fell by 19 percent in 1997, over a year after the suspension of the ordinance.

Given the myriad factors that influence levels of violence, it is difficult to evaluate the probative value of this statistical evidence, or to reach any firm conclusion about the ordinance's efficacy.

OPINION

The basic factual predicate for the city's ordinance is not in dispute. The very presence of a large collection of obviously brazen, insistent, and lawless gang members and hangers-on on the public ways intimidates residents, who become afraid even to leave their homes and go about their business. That, in turn, imperils community residents' sense of safety and security, detracts from property values, and can ultimately destabilize entire neighborhoods.

We have no doubt that a law that directly prohibited such intimidating conduct…[as described in the facts] would be constitutional, but this ordinance broadly covers a significant amount of additional activity. Uncertainty about the scope of that additional coverage provides the basis for respondents' claim that the ordinance is too vague.

The freedom to loiter for innocent purposes is part of the "liberty" protected by the Due Process Clause of the Fourteenth Amendment. We have expressly identified this "right to remove from one place to another according to inclination" as "an attribute of personal liberty" protected by the Constitution. Indeed, it is apparent that an individual's decision to remain in a public place of his choice is as much a part of his liberty as the freedom of movement inside frontiers that is "a part of our heritage" or the right to move "to whatsoever place one's own inclination may direct" identified in Blackstone's *Commentaries*.

Vagueness may invalidate a criminal law for either of two independent reasons. First, it may fail to provide the kind of notice that will enable ordinary people to understand what conduct it prohibits; second, it may authorize and even encourage arbitrary and discriminatory enforcement.

A law fails to meet the requirements of the Due Process Clause if it is so vague and standardless that it leaves the public uncertain as to the conduct it prohibits. It is difficult to imagine how any citizen of the city of Chicago standing in a public place with a group of people would know if he or she had an "apparent purpose." If she were talking to another person, would she have an apparent purpose? If she were frequently checking her watch and looking expectantly down the street, would she have an apparent purpose?

Since the city cannot conceivably have meant to criminalize each instance a citizen stands in public with a gang member, the vagueness that dooms this ordinance is not the product of uncertainty about the normal meaning of "loitering," but rather about what loitering is covered by the ordinance and what is not.

The Illinois Supreme Court emphasized the law's failure to distinguish between innocent conduct and conduct threatening harm. Its decision followed the precedent set by a number of state courts that have upheld ordinances that criminalize loitering combined with some other overt act or evidence of criminal intent (ordinance criminalizing loitering with purpose to engage in drug-related activities; ordinance criminalizing loitering for the purpose of engaging in or soliciting lewd act).

The city's principal response to this concern about adequate notice is that loiterers are not subject to sanction until after they have failed to comply with an officer's order to disperse. "Whatever problem is created by a law that criminalizes conduct people normally believe to be innocent is solved when persons receive actual notice from a police order of what they are expected to do." We find this response unpersuasive for at least two reasons.

1. First, the purpose of the fair notice requirement is to enable the ordinary citizen to conform his or her conduct to the law. No one may be required at peril of life, liberty or property to speculate as to the meaning of penal statutes. Such an order cannot retroactively give adequate warning of the boundary between the permissible and the impermissible applications of the law.
2. Second, the terms of the dispersal order compound the inadequacy of the notice afforded by the ordinance. It provides that the officer "shall order all such persons to disperse and remove themselves from the area." This vague phrasing raises a host of questions. After such an order issues, how long must the loiterers remain apart? How far must they move? If each loiterer walks around the block and they meet again at the same location, are they subject to arrest or merely to being ordered to disperse again? As we do here, we have found vagueness in a criminal statute exacerbated by the use of the standards of "neighborhood" and "locality."...Both terms are elastic and, dependent upon circumstances, may be equally satisfied by areas measured by rods or by miles.

The Constitution does not permit a legislature to set a net large enough to catch all possible offenders, and leave it to the courts to step inside and say who could be rightfully detained, and who should be set at large. This ordinance is therefore vague "not in the sense that it requires a person to conform his conduct to an imprecise but comprehensible normative standard, but rather in the sense that no standard of conduct is specified at all."

The broad sweep of the ordinance also violates the requirement that a legislature establish minimal guidelines to govern law enforcement. There are no such guidelines in the ordinance. In any public place in the city of Chicago, persons who stand or sit in the company of a gang member may be ordered to disperse unless their purpose is apparent.

The mandatory language in the enactment directs the police to issue an order without first making any inquiry about their possible purposes. It matters not whether the reason that a gang member and his father, for example, might loiter near Wrigley Field is to rob an unsuspecting fan or just to get a glimpse of Sammy Sosa leaving the ballpark; in either event, if their purpose is not apparent to a nearby police officer, she may—indeed, she "shall"—order them to disperse. Recognizing that the ordinance does reach a substantial amount of innocent conduct, we turn, then, to its language to determine if it "necessarily entrusts law making to the moment-to-moment judgment of the policeman on his beat."

The principal source of the vast discretion conferred on the police in this case is the definition of loitering as "to remain in any one place with no apparent purpose." [That definition] provides absolute discretion to police officers to determine what activities constitute loitering.

It is true that the requirement that the officer reasonably believes that a group of loiterers contains a gang member does place a limit on the authority to order dispersal. That limitation would no doubt be sufficient if the ordinance only applied to loitering that had an apparently harmful purpose or effect, or possibly if it only applied to loitering by persons reasonably believed to be criminal gang members. Not all of the respondents in this case, for example, are gang members.

The city admits that it was unable to prove that Morales is a gang member but justifies his arrest and conviction by the fact that Morales admitted "that he knew he was with criminal street gang members." But this ordinance requires no harmful purpose and applies to non-gang members as well as suspected gang members. It applies to everyone in the city who may remain in one place with one suspected gang member as long as their purpose is not apparent to an officer observing them. Friends, relatives, teachers, counselors, or even total strangers might unwittingly engage in forbidden loitering if they happen to engage in idle conversation with a gang member.

We recognize the serious and difficult problems testified to by the citizens of Chicago that led to the enactment of this ordinance. We are mindful that the

(continues)

(continued)

preservation of liberty depends in part on the maintenance of social order. However, in this instance the city has enacted an ordinance that affords too much discretion to the police and too little notice to citizens who wish to use the public streets.

Accordingly, the judgment of the Supreme Court of Illinois is AFFIRMED.

DISSENT

THOMAS, J. JOINED BY REHNQUIST, CJ. AND SCALIA, J.

The duly elected members of the Chicago City Council enacted the ordinance at issue as part of a larger effort to prevent gangs from establishing dominion over the public streets. By invalidating Chicago's ordinance, I fear that the Court has unnecessarily sentenced law-abiding citizens to lives of terror and misery. The ordinance is not vague. Any fool would know that a particular category of conduct would be within its reach. Nor does it violate the Due Process Clause. The asserted "freedom to loiter for innocent purposes" is in no way "deeply rooted in this Nation's history and tradition."

The human costs exacted by criminal street gangs are inestimable. In many of our Nation's cities, gangs have "virtually overtaken certain neighborhoods, contributing to the economic and social decline of these areas and causing fear and lifestyle changes among law-abiding residents."

Ordinary citizens like Ms. D'Ivory Gordon explained that she struggled just to walk to work:

> When I walk out my door, these guys are out there. They watch you. They know where you live. They know what time you leave, what time you come home. I am afraid of them. I have even come to the point now that I carry a meat cleaver to work with me. I don't want to hurt anyone, and I don't want to be hurt. We need to clean these corners up. Clean these communities up and take it back from them.

Eighty-eight-year-old Susan Mary Jackson echoed her sentiments, testifying:

> We used to have a nice neighborhood. We don't have it anymore. I am scared to go out in the daytime, you can't pass because they are standing. I am afraid to go to the store. I don't go to the store because I am afraid. At my age if they look at me real hard, I be ready to holler.

Another long-time resident testified:

> I have never had the terror that I feel everyday when I walk down the streets of Chicago. I have had my windows broken out. I have had guns pulled on me. I have been threatened. I get intimidated on a daily basis, and it's come to the point where I say, well, do I go out today? Do I put my ax in my briefcase? Do I walk around dressed like a bum so I am not looking rich or got any money or anything like that?

Today, the Court focuses extensively on the "rights" of gang members and their companions. It can safely do so—the people who will have to live with the consequences of today's opinion do not live in our neighborhoods. Rather, the people who will suffer from our lofty pronouncements are people like Ms. Susan Mary Jackson; people who have seen their neighborhoods literally destroyed by gangs and violence and drugs.

They are good, decent people who must struggle to overcome their desperate situation, against all odds, in order to raise their families, earn a living, and remain good citizens. As one resident described, "There is only about maybe 1 or 2 percent of the people in the city causing these problems maybe, but it's keeping 98 percent of us in our houses and off the streets and afraid to shop."

By focusing exclusively on the imagined "rights" of the 2 percent, the Court today has denied our most vulnerable citizens the very thing that Justice STEVENS elevates above all else—the "freedom of movement." And that is a shame.

QUESTIONS

1. List the four elements in the Chicago antigang ordinance.
2. List the specific arguments the majority gave to support its conclusion that the ordinance was vague.
3. Explain specifically all of the reasons why the dissenting judges disagreed.
4. Would "any fool" know what conduct this ordinance prohibited? Defend your answer.
5. Did the majority properly balance the interest in community order with the individual liberty? Explain your answer.
6. If the majority didn't properly strike the balance, how would you do it differently? Explain your answer.

CIVIL LAW RESPONSES TO GANG ACTIVITY

In addition to criminal penalties, cities have also turned to civil remedies to control gang activity. For example, in the ancient civil remedy, the **injunction to abate public nuisances** (which is still used), city attorneys ask courts to declare gang activities and gang members public nuisances. They ask the courts to issue public nuisance injunctions, which are court orders to eliminate the particular nuisance.

injunction to abate public nuisances court orders to eliminate the particular nuisance

According to the California Supreme Court, in *People ex rel. Gallo v. Acuna* (1997), "a public nuisance may be any act which alternatively is injurious to health or is indecent, or offensive to the senses; the result of the act must interfere with the comfortable enjoyment of life or property; and those affected by the act may be an entire neighborhood or a considerable number of people."

Injunctions, like crimes that outlaw gang activities, call for balancing community and individual rights. The community interest in the quality of life requires peace, quiet, order, and a sense of security. At the same time, even members of street gangs have the right to associate, express themselves, travel freely, and be free from vague laws (see Chapter 2, "The Void-for-Vagueness Doctrine" section).

REVIEW OF EMPIRICAL RESEARCH ON GANGS AND GANG ACTIVITY

Youth crime in the United States remains near the lowest levels seen in the past three decades, yet public concern and media coverage of gang activity has skyrocketed since 2000. Fear has spread from neighborhoods with long-standing gang problems to communities with historically low levels of crime, and some policy makers have declared the arrival of a national gang "crisis." Yet many questions remain unanswered. How can communities and policy makers differentiate between *perceived threats* and *actual challenges* presented by gangs? Which communities are most affected by gangs, and what is the nature of that impact? How much of the crime that plagues poor urban neighborhoods is attributable to gangs? And what methods work to promote public safety?

In this section, we'll focus on the latest available research on the effectiveness of civil injunctions to control gangs. **Civil gang injunctions** (CGI) are a growing gang suppression strategy. They're noncriminal lawsuits brought by cities seeking restraining orders to bar gang members from gang activities, which can include interacting with one another, entering specific sections of the city, and wearing gang colors.

civil gang injunctions (CGI) noncriminal lawsuits brought by cities seeking restraining orders to bar gang members from gang activities

Sociologists Cheryl Maxson, Karen Hennigan, and David Sloane (2005) conducted the first scientific assessment of CGIs in San Bernardino, California. They surveyed residents in five neighborhoods about their perceptions and experience of crime, gang activity, and neighborhood quality eighteen months before and six months after the injunction was issued. They found positive evidence of short-term effects in the disordered, primary injunction area, including less gang presence, fewer reports of gang intimidation, and less fear of confrontation with gang members, but no significant changes in intermediate or long-term outcomes except for less fear of crime (577).

Professor Jeffrey Grogger (2002) also evaluated the effectiveness of CGIs. Grogger developed an extensive database of neighborhood-level reported crime counts from four police jurisdictions within Los Angeles County. He constructed two different comparison samples of neighborhoods not covered by injunctions to control for underlying trends that could cause an overstatement of the CGIs' effects. The analysis indicates that, in the first year after the injunctions are imposed, they lead the level of violent crime to decrease by 5 to 10 percent (69).

Saint Paul, Minnesota, is an excellent example of the cycle of news coverage, the findings from the investigations reported in the Gang Wars report (Grogger 2002), and the adoption of the city's CGI (see our next case excerpt).

CASE

***City of Saint Paul v. East Side Boys and Selby Siders* (2009)** *involves the 2009 civil gang injunctions in the city of Saint Paul, Minnesota.*

Should members of the gang be banned from attending the Rondo Days celebration?

City of Saint Paul v. East Side Boys and Selby Siders

(City of Saint Paul 2009[1])

HISTORY

On June 30, 2009, Saint Paul, Minnesota, initiated two CGI lawsuits against the East Side Boys and the Selby Siders, two local gangs with a long history of violent criminal conduct, including a recent murder and numerous recent confrontations involving gunfire.

FACTS

"As we have clearly stated, criminal gangs are not welcome in our community. The public has a right to be free from criminal gang violence and intimidation, and as the home of some of the most prominent community festivals in the country like Rondo Days, we are doing everything we can to protect our community from gang activity. Saint Paul is a safe city, and these injunctions are an innovative tool to send a clear message to gangs that we will not tolerate any violence in our community," Mayor Chris Coleman said.

"These civil injunctions have proven to be worthwhile tools, as they specifically focus on those gangs who have repeatedly demonstrated purpose and action that tears at the safety and fabric of the community events like Rondo," Saint Paul Police Chief John Harrington said. "In addition to the benefits of enforceability, these injunctions speak to Saint Paul's historical standards of community safety."

The civil legal actions are intended to help prevent criminal gang activity from occurring during the Rondo Days festival on July 18. [The Rondo Days Festival is an annual celebration to remember the African-American neighborhood of Rondo, which was split by the construction of Interstate 94 in the mid-1960s.] City Attorney John Choi said the two civil actions are a part of an important law enforcement strategy to proactively disrupt criminal gang activity in Saint Paul's neighborhoods. "We had great public safety results because of the civil gang injunction against the Sureño 13 earlier this year, and we have every expectation that this proactive effort will work again with the Selby Siders and East Side Boys," Choi said.

The Civil Gang Injunction Statute (Minn. Stat. §§ 617.91–617.97) authorizes a city attorney, county attorney or the attorney general to commence a civil action against criminal gangs to enjoin criminal gang activity. The civil lawsuit filed by Choi seeks injunctive relief pursuant to the Civil Gang Injunction Statute that was developed by the Community Prosecution Unit of the Saint Paul City Attorney's Office and passed by the Minnesota Legislature in 2007. In May, the Ramsey County District Court issued Minnesota's first civil gang injunction against a criminal gang in *City of Saint Paul v. Sureño* 13 (Ramsey County District Court Case Number 62-CV-09-3113).

Among other things, the City of Saint Paul is seeking a court order prohibiting the known leaders of the East Side Boys and Selby Siders from associating with known gang members anywhere near the Rondo Days Festival.

"From our city attorney's office to our police department to our Second Shift initiative, much of what we do in Saint Paul is about public safety and improving the lives of our residents," Mayor Coleman said. "The civil lawsuits filed demonstrate the proactive approach Saint Paul is taking to prevent gangs from taking root in Saint Paul."

QUESTIONS

1. Assume you're an aide to the city. Would you recommend that the city go forward with the injunction?
2. Relying on the information in your text, what specifically would you want the mayor, police chief, city attorney, and the public to know about CGIs?

[1]This case excerpt is based on information from the city of Saint Paul, Minnesota, website.

VIOLENT VIDEO GAMES

> Finding that a young man who committed a violent crime also played a popular video game, such as *Call of Duty*, *Halo*, or *Grand Theft Auto*, is as pointless as pointing out that the criminal also wore socks. (Markey, Markey, and French 2014, 16)

> I am a published poet who, in the 1980s, viewed university as a place to "play video games, chase girls, and play guitar." (qtd. in Van Cleave 2010)

LO8

On Tuesday, April 20, 1999, two students at Columbine High School in Colorado, murdered twelve students and one teacher, wounded twenty-four others, and then committed suicide. Eric Harris and Dylan Klebold enjoyed playing the first-person shooter video game *Doom*. Similarly, the Virginia Tech shooter, Seung-Hui Cho, who murdered 32 people and wounded 17 others on April 16, 2007, was a fan of the violent video first-person shooter game *Counterstrike*. More recently, shooter Adam Lanza, who murdered 20 elementary school kids and six teachers and other adults at an elementary school in Sandy Hook, Connecticut, on December 12, 2012, played *Call of Duty*, another first-person shooter game that mimics wartime violence.

A number of cities reacted by enacting municipal ordinances banning violent video games from arcades because, it was *contended* (not *proven*), that playing the games *can* cause violent behavior in youths who play them (Markey, Markey, and French 2014).

One that has received lots of political, public, and scholarly attention is the Indianapolis ordinance. Here's the Preamble:

> Exposure of children to graphic and lifelike violence contained in some video games has been correlated to violent behavior, and in fact the perpetrators of recent school shootings in Columbine, Colorado; Jonesboro, Arkansas; and Paducah, Kentucky were reported to be avid fans of such games. (*Interactive Digital Software Association v. St. Louis County* 2002, 1129)

The *scientific* link between violent video games and criminal behavior is modern, but the idea behind it echoes the ancient common law offense known as "breach of the peace," which included both actual disorderly conduct and conduct that "*tends* to provoke or excite others to break it [the peace]" (p. 448, Blackstone 1769, 148, emphasis added). It also reflects the *contested* broken windows theory that minor disorder leads to serious crimes (p. 489).

President Obama was obviously interested in the link. After the Sandy Hook murders, he called on "scientists" to study the link, and several state and federal legislatures introduced bills, including the federal "Video Games Enforcement Act," to regulate the sale of violent video games. Legislators expressed their concern. Tennessee Senator Lamar Alexander went as far as to say that "video games are a bigger problem than guns, because video games affect people" (Linkins 2013).

But does the *empirical* evidence support that claim? One comprehensive analysis identified 74 studies (based on "best practices," namely valid measurement and sound methodologies) "concluded that exposure to violent video games is a causal risk factor for increased cognitions, aggressive affect, and aggressive behaviors." (Markey, Markey, and French 2014, 1). Amid continuing debate spawned by the claims of a causal link, an American Psychological Association (APA) task force conducted a comprehensive review of research on violence in video games and interactive media (Markey, Markey, and French 2014).

They took issue with the claims of a causal link between violent video games and "aggressive assaults and homicides," and the Task Force's analysis of the best practices research found "no evidence to suggest" that playing the games "was a major (or minor) contributing cause of violence in the United States" (14). Instead,

> Annual trends in video game sales for the past 33 years were unrelated to violent crime both concurrently and up to 4 years later. Unexpectedly, monthly sales of video games were related to concurrent *decreases* in aggravated assaults and unrelated to homicides.

How can this be? The Task Force suggests a few reasons. First is the *carthartsis theory*: "When people play violent games, they are able to release their aggression in the virtual world instead of the real world." Some research has found that adolescent boys say they feel less angry after playing violent video games, and even play the games for the very purpose of controlling their aggression. To be fair, other research finds little evidence that venting your anger on a "safe target" reduces aggression (15).

More cautious and less contentious is *innate motivational disposition*: "Individuals who are prone to aggression and violence tend to seek out violent media games to provide them with models that express behaviors and desires consistent with their own innate motivational system." For example, when the latest first-person shooter game is released, they're likely to go out and buy it, and play it. "In other words, because violent individuals are playing violent video games in their homes, there may be a decrease in violent crime when violent video games are released" (15).

The Task Force takes pains to point out that playing violent video games is only one of many risk factors for violent behavior. ("No scientist has suggested that violent video games are the only cause of violent behavior, just as no scientist has suggested that heat is the only cause of violent crime or smoking is the only cause of lung cancer" (15).)

Let's close this discussion with these words of wisdom and caution:

> When the media, politicians, or researchers link the murderous rampages of male adolescents with violent video games, they are conveying a classic illusory correlation. These individuals are ignoring that 90% of young males play video games. Finding that a young man who committed a violent crime also played a popular video game like *Call of Duty, Halo*, or *Grand Theft Auto*, is as pointless as pointing out that the criminal also wore socks. The rhetoric about violent video games does not match the data. (16)

Furthermore, they warn us that what they say in the previous paragraph in no way means that playing violent video games has *no* effect. There's plenty of evidence that violent videos "*do* increase aggressive cognition, aggressive affect, and *some* aggressive behaviors, such a bullying, spreading gossip, minor fights at school, pushing and shoving, or hurling insults." Finally, the current research does not address how exposure to violent video games at a young age might affect later behavior (16).

They conclude with these wise words:

> We need to be clear with our peers and the general audience about the claims we make that are backed up by research and those that are speculation. In short, as scientists, we need to be careful that we do not blur the line between our scientific results and our scientific conjecture.

"VICTIMLESS CRIMES"

LO9 Victimless crimes are crimes involving willing participants. Let's be clear about how we're going to use this term in this section. First, it applies only to consenting adults, not minors. Second, it refers to crimes committed by adults who don't see themselves as

TABLE 12.2 Victimless Crimes
Substance abuse (see Chapters 2 and 3)
Internet censorship
Loitering
Prostitution
Sodomy (*Lawrence v. Texas*, see Chapter 2)
Seat-belt law violations
Helmet law violations
Violating bans on bungee jumping
Assisted suicide

victimless crimes crimes involving willing adult participants who don't see themselves as victims

victims of their behavior. Referring to many crimes in which the perpetrators don't see themselves as victimized as "victimless crimes" is controversial; Table 12.2 lists some of these crimes.

We've already covered the crimes associated with illegal drugs in a constitutional democracy (see Chapters 2 and 3, *Robinson v. California* and *Powell v. Texas*). Furthermore, we've discussed the application of the principles of *actus reus* and *mens rea* to drug crimes (see Chapters 3 and 4). Let's look at the controversy surrounding the issue and then focus on **prostitution**, engaging in sex in exchange for money or its equivalent.

prostitution engaging in sex in exchange for money or its equivalent

History of Victimless Crimes

In medieval days, when the Church was more powerful than kings and queens, ecclesiastical courts had total power to try and punish crimes against "family and morals," including all nonviolent sexual behavior and marital relations breaches. As monarchs grew stronger, royal courts eventually gained control over most of these offenses. Once the monarch's courts took them over, they became the crimes against public morals, most of which would be on the list of anyone who subscribes to the idea of victimless crimes (Morris and Hawkins 1970, chap. 1).

Controversy makes it tough to balance public good and individual privacy in these cases. There's broad agreement that the crimes against persons and property you read about in Chapters 9 through 11 deserve punishment. However, no such agreement exists when it comes to whether those listed in Table 12.2 should be crimes. In fact, there's a deep rift between those who believe criminal law should enforce morals to "purify" society and those who believe just as deeply that consenting adults' nonviolent sexual conduct is none of the criminal law's business (Morris and Hawkins 1970).

Perhaps no issue in criminal policy has caused more acrimonious debate over a longer time than that of the role law should play in enforcing public morals. Two English Victorian scholars, the philosopher John Stuart Mill and the historian Sir James F. Stephen, started the debate. Their two major positions were summed up in the widely known and debated Wolfenden Report, an English document recommending the decriminalization of private sexual conduct of two types, between adult consenting male homosexuals and between adult sex workers and their customers.

Here's the summary of the majority of the commission's position:

> There remains one additional argument which we believe to be decisive, namely, the importance which society and the law ought to give to individual freedom of choice and action in matters of private morality. Unless a deliberate attempt is to be made by society, acting through the agency of the law, to equate the sphere of crime with

> that of sin, there must remain a realm of private morality and immorality which is, in brief and crude terms, not the law's business. To say this is not to condone or encourage private immorality. On the contrary, to emphasize the personal private nature of moral or immoral conduct is to emphasize the personal and private responsibility of the individual for his own actions, and that is a responsibility which a mature agent can properly be expected to carry for himself without the threat of punishment from the law. (Wolfendon Report 1957, 20–21)

Here's English jurist Sir Patrick Devlin's rebuttal to the majority position:

> Society is entitled by means of its laws to protect itself from dangers....There is disintegration when no common morality is observed and history shows that the loosening of moral bonds is often the first state of disintegration, so that society is justified in taking the same steps to preserve its moral code as it does to preserve its government and other essential institutions. The suppression of vice is as much the law's business as the suppression of subversive activities; it is no more possible to define a sphere of private morality than it is to define one of private subversive activity. (Wolfendon Report 1957, 48)

For most of U.S. history, prostitution was discussed solely within the framework of victimless crimes—whether it's the law's business to interfere with adults' rights to buy and sell sex. Until the eleventh edition of your book, we did the same. But prostitution is so much more than that, so we'll discuss it in the larger context that it deserves. That larger context is the unequal treatment of men and women in the United States in the twenty-first century.

Prostitution

> The law's desire to punish "bad girls" has often been moderated by its wish to save "nice boys" from harm, inconvenience or embarrassment. (Lefler 1999, 13)

LO10 Prostitution involves at least two people—the prostitute who provides the sexual service and the client ("john," "trick," or patron) who buys the service. Frequently, there's also a third party—the promoter (pimp) who controls the prostitute, finds johns, and takes a cut of prostitute's earnings. We'll concentrate in this section on the double standard in law and social reality for prostitutes and johns. Vice squad officers accost prostitutes on the street, or act as decoys to catch them offering sex for money, and arrest them. The same officers allow their clients to remain anonymous and leave. (That's where the catchall name "john" originated.) In this section, we'll examine the history of this ancient crime; the double standard today; and two remedies for the double standard—equal protection lawsuits and local government programs that target johns.

THE HISTORY OF PROSTITUTION LAWS

From colonial times, prostitution was the common law crime of "selling one's body for money." In the 1800s, states passed statutes that made prostitution a crime. By 1900, there were anti-prostitution statutes in every state (Kandel 1992, 341). (That remains true today, except for seven counties in Nevada.) The criminal law moved from a "hands off" approach to enforcing these laws during most of the 1800s to an aggressive "swift and harsh" punishment response by 1900. The aggressive response went beyond targeting women for actually "selling one's body for money." Police officers arrested women who were on the street after dark on the assumption that "any woman on the street at that time intended to solicit money for sex" (Kandel 1992, 341).

Inside the courtroom, the harsh treatment continued; judges sentenced women based on their sexual history, not on the elements of prostitution—selling sex for money. But, while women were hauled into court to answer charges, no johns were in sight to answer for buying sex, let alone having to answer for their sexual history. "Thus, men satisfied their sexual desires with no consequences while women alone paid the price" (Lefler 1999, 14).

Why did the double standard persist throughout so much of U.S. history? Most scholars point to two beliefs with deep roots in Victorian culture and society:

1. "While males were viewed as reformable, even though they committed an immoral sexual act," women were "lost causes, incapable of redemption" (Lefler 1999, 4).
2. Men can't control their sex drive, but women don't even have a sex drive. So the justice system didn't punish the men, treating prostitutes as necessary (14–15). (Of course, they were necessary evils.)

THE DOUBLE STANDARD TODAY

The solution to the double standard required two major changes. First, legislatures had to enact statutes to provide for punishing the prostitute and the john. These laws are necessary, but they're not enough to reach true equal treatment without a second change—namely, that law enforcement, prosecutors, and courts have to enforce the statutes equally against prostitutes and johns.

At present, there are three types of prostitution statutes—those that

1. punish the prostitute but not the john.
2. punish both but punish the prostitute more severely.
3. punish both the prostitute and the john equally.

A few states retain the double standard in its traditional form (number 1). Those that punish both but punish the prostitute more (number 2) follow the MPC § 251.2 (ALI 1985). Johns can never go to jail, only be fined, no matter how many times they're arrested. Prostitutes can do time for multiple offenses. MPC reporters justify the difference on the ground that, because prostitutes receive money, their involvement in the crime is greater and, therefore, they deserve harsher punishment. Courts often agree with the reporters' double standard rationale. Many state statutes now follow 3; they provide for full equality of punishment for both prostitutes and johns.

Let's turn our attention from the law on the books to the law in action—namely, the equality of enforcement, where the available statistics show that the double standard is far from dead. The FBI collects numbers of arrests for "Prostitution and Commercialized Vice," which it defines as:

> The unlawful promotion of or participation in sexual activities for profit, including attempts. To solicit customers or transport persons for prostitution purposes; to own, manage, or operate a dwelling or other establishment for the purpose of providing a place where prostitution is performed; or to otherwise assist or promote prostitution.

In 2013, the FBI reported 35,562 prostitution arrests nationwide. Figure 12.1 depicts the percentages of those arrests by sex.

Look at this gap between men and women with some caution. We don't know how many men are johns because we don't know how many men are pimps and prostitutes. And we don't know how many women are madams (e.g., Heidi Fleiss). Furthermore, and more important, we don't know how many prostitution arrests are hidden in the

Figure 12.1

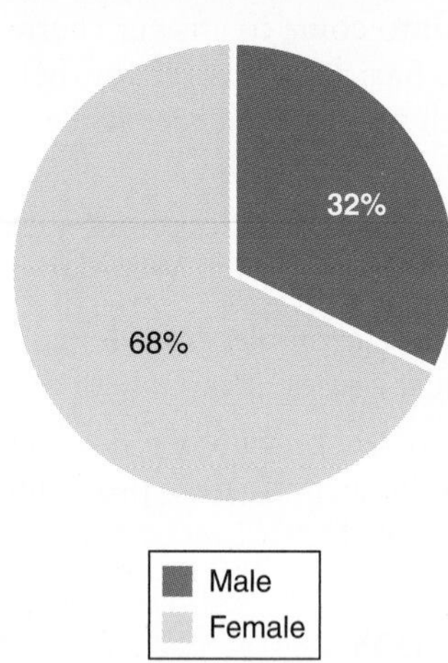

Source: FBI Uniform Crime Reports, Arrests, Table 29.

"disorderly conduct" numbers (see FBI UCR 2013, Table 33) because of officer discretion and department policy to arrest prostitutes (but not johns) for disorderly conduct (Kandel 1992, 332).

What accounts for this persistent double standard, whatever the size of the gender gap? One explanation is that police decoys arrest prostitutes; therefore, there are no johns to arrest (Lefler 1999, 20). Another is that by arresting prostitutes, they're catching the "profiteer." But one lawyer wondered, if that's true why don't they go after the pimps? They're the ones who "exploit women for profit" (21).

COURT REMEDIES FOR THE DOUBLE STANDARD

Some individual judges have acted to fight discriminatory enforcement. For example, former Boston Municipal Court Judge Sarah Hunt, who heard prostitution cases daily, refused to hear cases against prostitutes unless officers had arrested the john, too (Kandel 1992, 340). Some prostitutes argue that the no-johns-to-arrest problem created by decoys denies them equal protection of the law. It's extraordinarily difficult to succeed in equal protection challenges.

LOCAL GOVERNMENT PROGRAMS TARGETING "JOHNS"

Some local governments have created new programs directed at johns. They differ from the traditional policy of incarcerating only prostitutes. They may deter johns, but are programs directed only at johns discriminatory and, therefore, no better than the double standard that punishes only prostitutes? Think about that in connection with three john-focused policies: car forfeiture, driver's license revocation, and publishing the names of arrested johns in local newspapers and online.

CAR FORFEITURE Men who police arrest for paying to have sex in their cars have their cars impounded automatically. Some statutes require the return of the cars if johns pay heavy fines. Others go further and sell the impounded cars. There's no empirical data to tell us whether these laws reduce the amount of prostitution. But, even if they do deter prostitution-related activities, they're not enough to solve the problem. They only apply to johns arrested in their cars. Also, the johns don't always own the cars they're driving. In addition, some courts have ruled that seizing johns' cars before they're convicted denies them the right to due process. Cities such as Oakland, California, have solved this problem by providing for an immediate civil forfeiture hearing (Lefler 1999, 28–29).

DRIVER'S LICENSE REVOCATION This proposal allows police officers to revoke johns' driver's licenses if they're caught in their cars having sex with a prostitute. Minnesota has adopted a variation on this type of law, placing a notation on the driver's license of any john convicted of prostitution-related crimes committed in his car. Section 609.324 of the Minnesota Criminal Code, Penalties for Patrons, Subdivision 5, "Use of motor vehicle to patronize prostitutes; driving record notation," provides that, "When a court sentences a person convicted of violating this section while acting as a patron, the court shall determine whether the person used a motor vehicle during the commission of the offense and whether the person has previously been convicted of violating this section."

If the court finds that the person used a motor vehicle during the commission of the offense, it shall forward its finding along with an indication of whether the person has previously been convicted of a prostitution offense to the commissioner of public safety who shall record the finding on the person's driving record. If the person has previously been convicted of a violation of this section, the finding becomes public data (Minnesota Criminal Code 2011, § 609.324).

Revocation, like forfeiture, is only a partial solution. It targets only johns who commit the offense while they're in their cars. Critics such as Julie Lefler (1992) recommend that states should pass statutes that mandate revocation for all johns, whether cars are involved or not. "This would provide police with another weapon in their arsenal to deter johns from these offenses." Lefler concedes that it won't affect johns who don't have licenses. She also points out that revoking johns' driver's licenses who weren't arrested in their cars might be unconstitutional. She argues, however, that

> having a driver's license is a privilege rather than a right. If prostitutes can be forced to give up their entire freedom by being incarcerated for their offense, it is more than fair that johns in turn be forced to give up a mere privilege as a consequence of their crimes. (Lefler 1992, 30)

PUBLISHING NAMES IN VARIOUS MEDIA "No one entering La Mesa, Calif., can miss the billboards that announce 'Attention johns: We take pictures.' La Mesa Mayor Art Madrid says the signs—and the promise to print those pictures in local papers—have reduced prostitution. 'If we have no johns, we'll have no hookers,' he says" (Larrabee 1995, A3). According to attorney Courtney Guyton Persons (1996), the secrecy of anonymous sex "has been slapped on billboards as communities, desperate to disinfect their crime-ridden streets, expose solicitors' secret sins to sunlight" (1526–27):

> Critics question its effectiveness and its cost. They point to a New Jersey paper that listed a young engineer who had just lost his wife and three children. When he saw his name in the paper, he killed himself. City attorneys and defense lawyers worry about its constitutionality. Newspapers worry about getting sued. Editorials call it inhumane and disproportionate. But law enforcement "insists that nothing else has worked, and community groups figure it's worth a try." (1527)

Persons is wary of the wisdom of choosing the policy of shaming johns:

> Unlike other types of penalties, shame punishments are explicitly designed to make a public spectacle of the offender's conviction and punishment, and to trigger a

negative, downward change in the offender's self-concept. Colonial society's sense of community and common faith may once have imbued shame penalties with some power to reinforce normative consensus. Today, however, in a climate of increasing normative fragmentation, that function seems unlikely. Instead, shame punishments may sacrifice individuals' dignity with little discernible impact on prostitution. Whatever their meaning, shame punishments' qualitative distinction from other sanctions raises humaneness concerns that form a possible cost of selecting shaming. (1570)

MINOR OFFENSES: PUBLIC ORDER OR CASH COWS?

Investigation of Ferguson MO Police Officer Darren Wilson

Based on this investigation, the Department has concluded that Darren Wilson's actions do not constitute prosecutable violations under the applicable federal criminal civil rights statute, which prohibits uses of deadly force that are "objectively unreasonable," as defined by the United States Supreme Court. The evidence, when viewed as a whole, does not support the conclusion that Wilson's uses of deadly force were "objectively unreasonable" under the Supreme Court's definition. Accordingly, under the governing federal law and relevant standards set forth in the USAM, it is not appropriate to present this matter to a federal grand jury for indictment, and it should therefore be closed without prosecution. (U.S. Department of Justice, Civil Rights Division, 2015)

Investigation of the Ferguson MO Police Department (FPD)

Ferguson's law enforcement practices are shaped by the City's focus on revenue rather than by public safety needs. This emphasis on revenue has compromised the institutional character of Ferguson's police department, contributing to a pattern of unconstitutional policing, and has also shaped its municipal court, leading to procedures that raise due process concerns and inflict unnecessary harm on members of the Ferguson community. (U.S. Department of Justice, Civil Rights Division, Criminal Section, March 4, 2015)

LO11 (A preliminary note on this section: The materials here are intended to help you decide for yourself whether these police practices promote public order or only generate income for city governments. There's still too much research yet to do, and developments are still unfolding to make any final judgments.)

These vignettes are part of two U.S. Department of Justice (DOJ) reports released the same day—March 4, 2015. One clears Officer Darren Wilson; the other condemns the Ferguson Police Department (FPD). If you're culture warriors—and watch, listen, and read only "news" and "commentary" of your side in the culture wars—you know (or cared) about only one of the stories. But, if you're reading this book, I hope you'll give *both* reports a fair shot. The Darren Wilson story doesn't relate to our topic, but I included an excerpt from it in the next Criminal Law in Focus box from conservative Leon Wolf's *Diary*, "Many Conservatives are blowing it on the Ferguson DOJ Report," which appeared on the conservative website *RedState*. As an additional "good advice" piece, it will prevent you from dismissing out of hand the Ferguson Police Department report.

"Many Conservatives Are Blowing It on the DOJ Ferguson Report"

It's unfortunate, the way news is consumed and interpreted in the age of twitter. Everyone feels tremendous pressure to form an opinion quickly and state it loudly and with certainty. Once this has been done, people are highly resistant to changing their minds and they become impervious to new evidence.

Perhaps nowhere has this phenomenon been more obvious (or regrettable) than in Ferguson, Missouri, in the wake of the shooting death of Michael Brown. Interpreting the news out of Ferguson has become a part of ideological tribalism in which, if you are a conservative you stand for the Ferguson PD and if you are a liberal you stand against them.

The report, taken as a whole, even in terms of material collected exclusively from FPD documents, is incredibly damning of police and municipal court practices in Ferguson...The practices of the FPD and Municipal Court are destructive to freedom and in blatant violation of our constitutional rights, and they depend for sufferance on the fact that most people are not willing (or, in the case of most of Ferguson's residents, able) to mount an expensive legal fight for relatively trivial amounts of money.

I am singularly unimpressed with the argument that the report should be dismissed because it is the product of the Holder DOJ's dissatisfaction at the resolution of the Michael Brown case. The implicit admission in such an argument is that many police departments are worse; if so, the proper response is not to excuse the Ferguson PD but rather to acknowledge that there are, in fact, systemic problems that...should also be solved.

Many municipal police departments face increasing and unrelenting pressure from city hall to fill increasingly wide gaps in revenue with money from fines and citations. Even a well-intentioned police officer who respects freedom, the citizenry, and vulnerable populations can succumb to temptation when his paycheck and his ability to feed his family is put on the line. And in those cases, where legitimate offenses do not occur, he will be sorely tempted to create them...among the portion of the populace that is least likely to complain and least likely to be believed when they do complain: non-wealthy black citizens.

Until we, as a people, are willing to understand and address the problem, it will never get better. Until we are willing to hold our municipal officials accountable for using the police force to suck money out of people's pockets instead of legitimately protecting the public safety, the problem will get worse. But most importantly, until and unless we are able to emotionally detach ourselves from the horrible Michael Brown situation and see that what has been exposed, even according to the (probably whitewashed) FPD records, is a travesty, there is no hope for improvement.

I categorically reject and condemn the claim that this report or President Obama's comments upon it led to the shooting of those two officers in Ferguson. Like everyone else, I deplore and condemn these acts of unjust violence. But the fact that they occurred does not mean that the truth behind the report caused them. It is possible to condemn unjust and oppressive policing and also the unprovoked murder of police.

We can do better than our response to the Ferguson DOJ report. And our country deserves better from us.

Source: Leon Wolf, "Many Conservatives Are Blowing It on the Ferguson DOJ Report: Their reaction is neither fair, accurate, nor good for America, *RedState*, June 3, 2015, http://www.redstate.com/2015/03/15/many-conservatives-blowing-it-ferguson-doj-report/.

Then, there's an extended excerpt from the FPD Report. It's in the format of a Case Excerpt, but it's not typical because it's at the investigation stage.

CASE

From the ***U.S. D.O.J. Investigation of the Ferguson MO Police Department (FPD),*** **March 4, 2015,** *the use of minor offense fines to pay for Ferguson city government personnel and operations.*

Investigation of the Ferguson Police Department

U.S. Department of Justice v. Civil Rights Division

March 4, 2015

INTRODUCTION

Ferguson's law enforcement practices are shaped by the City's focus on revenue rather than by public safety needs. This emphasis on revenue has compromised the institutional character of Ferguson's police department, contributing to a pattern of unconstitutional policing, and has also shaped its municipal court, leading to procedures that raise due process concerns and inflict unnecessary harm on members of the Ferguson community.

POLICE PRACTICES

The City's emphasis on revenue generation has a profound effect on FPD's approach to law enforcement. Patrol assignments and schedules are geared toward aggressive enforcement of Ferguson's municipal code, with insufficient thought given to whether enforcement strategies promote public safety or unnecessarily undermine community trust and cooperation. Officer evaluations and promotions depend to an inordinate degree on "productivity," meaning the number of citations issued. Partly as a consequence of City and FPD priorities, many officers appear to see some residents, especially those who live in Ferguson's predominantly African-American neighborhoods, less as constituents to be protected than as potential offenders and sources of revenue.

Even relatively routine misconduct by Ferguson police officers can have significant consequences for the people whose rights are violated. For example, in the summer of 2012, a 32-year-old African-American man sat in his car cooling off after playing basketball in a Ferguson public park. An officer pulled up behind the man's car, blocking him in, and demanded the man's Social Security number and identification. Without any cause, the officer accused the man of being a pedophile, referring to the presence of children in the park, and ordered the man out of his car for a pat-down, although the officer had no reason to believe the man was armed. The officer also asked to search the man's car. The man objected, citing his constitutional rights. In response, the officer arrested the man, reportedly at gunpoint, charging him with eight violations of Ferguson's municipal code. One charge, Making a False Declaration, was for initially providing the short form of his first name (e.g., "Mike" instead of "Michael"), and an address which, although legitimate, was different from the one on his driver's license. Another charge was for not wearing a seat belt, even though he was seated in a parked car. The officer also charged the man both with having an expired operator's license, and with having no operator's license in his possession. The man told us that, because of these charges, he lost his job as a contractor with the federal government that he had held for years.

MUNICIPAL COURT PRACTICES

Ferguson has allowed its focus on revenue generation to fundamentally compromise the role of Ferguson's municipal court. The municipal court does not act as a neutral arbiter of the law or a check on unlawful police conduct. Instead, the court primarily uses its judicial authority as the means to compel the payment of fines and fees that advance the City's financial interests. This has led to court practices that violate the Fourteenth Amendment's due process and equal protection requirements. The court's practices also impose unnecessary harm, overwhelmingly on African-American individuals, and run counter to public safety.

We spoke, for example, with an African-American woman who has a still-pending case stemming from 2007, when, on a single occasion, she parked her car illegally.

She received two citations and a $151 fine, plus fees. The woman, who experienced financial difficulties and periods of homelessness over several years, was charged with seven Failure to Appear offenses for missing court dates or fine payments on her parking tickets between 2007 and 2010. For each Failure to Appear, the court issued an arrest warrant and imposed new fines and fees. From 2007 to 2014, the woman was arrested twice, spent six days in jail, and paid $550 to the court for the events stemming from this single instance of illegal parking. Court records show that she twice attempted to make partial payments of $25 and $50, but the court returned those payments, refusing to accept anything less than payment in full. One of those payments was later accepted, but only after the court's letter rejecting payment by money order was returned as undeliverable. This woman is now making regular payments on the fine. As of December 2014, over seven years later, despite initially owing a $151 fine and having already paid $550, she still owed $541.

RACIAL BIAS

Ferguson's police and municipal court practices both reflect and exacerbate existing racial bias, including racial stereotypes. Ferguson's own data establish clear racial disparities that adversely impact African Americans. The evidence shows that discriminatory intent is part of the reason for these disparities. Over time, Ferguson's police and municipal court practices have sown deep mistrust between parts of the community and the police department, undermining law enforcement legitimacy among African Americans in particular.

Ferguson's law enforcement practices overwhelmingly impact African Americans. Data collected by the Ferguson Police Department from 2012 to 2014 shows that African Americans account for 85% of vehicle stops, 90% of citations, and 93% of arrests made by FPD officers, despite comprising only 67% of Ferguson's population. African Americans are more than twice as likely as white drivers to be searched during vehicle stops even after controlling for non-race based variables such as the reason the vehicle stop was initiated, but are found in possession of contraband 26% less often than white drivers, suggesting officers are impermissibly considering race as a factor when determining whether to search.

African Americans are more likely to be cited and arrested following a stop regardless of why the stop was initiated and are more likely to receive multiple citations during a single incident. From 2012 to 2014, FPD issued four or more citations to African Americans on 73 occasions, but issued four or more citations to non-African Americans only twice.

FPD appears to bring certain offenses almost exclusively against African Americans. For example, from 2011 to 2013, African Americans accounted for 95% of Manner of Walking in Roadway charges, and 94% of all Failure to Comply charges. Notably, with respect to speeding charges brought by FPD, the evidence shows not only that African Americans are represented at disproportionately high rates overall, but also that the disparate impact of FPD's enforcement practices on African Americans is 48% larger when citations are issued not on the basis of radar or laser, but by some other method, such as the officer's own visual assessment.

Our investigation indicates that this disproportionate burden on African Americans cannot be explained by any difference in the rate at which people of different races violate the law. Rather, our investigation has revealed that these disparities occur, at least in part, because of unlawful bias against and stereotypes about African Americans. We have found substantial evidence of racial bias among police and court staff in Ferguson. For example, we discovered emails circulated by police supervisors and court staff that stereotype racial minorities as criminals, including one email that joked about an abortion by an African-American woman being a means of crime control.

City officials have frequently asserted that the harsh and disparate results of Ferguson's law enforcement system do not indicate problems with police or court practices, but instead reflect a pervasive lack of "personal responsibility" among "certain segments" of the community. Our investigation has found that the practices about which area residents have complained are in fact unconstitutional and unduly harsh.

But the City's personal-responsibility refrain is telling: it reflects many of the same racial stereotypes found in the emails between police and court supervisors. This evidence of bias and stereotyping, together with evidence that Ferguson has long recognized but failed to correct the consistent racial disparities caused by its police and court practices, demonstrates that the discriminatory effects of Ferguson's conduct are driven at least in part by discriminatory intent in violation of the Fourteenth Amendment.

At times, the constitutional violations are even more blatant. An African-American man recounted to us an experience he had while sitting at a bus stop near Canfield Drive. According to the man, an FPD

(continues)

(continued)

patrol car abruptly pulled up in front of him. The officer inside, a patrol lieutenant, rolled down his window and addressed the man:

Lieutenant: Get over here.
Bus Patron: Me?
Lieutenant: Get the f*** over here. Yeah, you.
Bus Patron: Why? What did I do?
Lieutenant: Give me your ID.
Bus Patron: Why?
Lieutenant: Stop being a smart ass and give me your ID.

The lieutenant ran the man's name for warrants. Finding none, he returned the ID and said, "get the hell out of my face." These allegations are consistent with other, independent allegations of misconduct that we heard about this particular lieutenant, and reflect the routinely disrespectful treatment many African Americans say they have come to expect from Ferguson police. That a lieutenant with supervisory responsibilities allegedly engaged in this conduct is further cause for concern.

EFFECT ON PEOPLE LIVING IN OR NEAR POVERTY

In lieu of proportioning a fine to a particular individual's ability to pay or allowing a process by which a person could petition the court for a reduction, the court offers payment plans to those who cannot afford to immediately pay in full. But such payment plans do not serve as a substitute for an ability-to-pay determination, which, properly employed, can enable a person in some cases to pay in full and resolve the case.

Moreover, the court's rules regarding payment plans are themselves severe. Unlike some other municipalities that require a $50 monthly payment, Ferguson's standard payment plan requires payments of $100 per month, which remains a difficult amount for many to pay, especially those who are also making payments to other municipalities.

Further, the court treats a single missed, partial, or untimely payment as a missed appearance. In such a case, the court immediately issues an arrest warrant without any notice or opportunity to explain why a payment was missed—for example, because the person was sick, or the court closed its doors early that day.

The court reportedly has softened this rule during the course of our investigation by allowing a person who has missed a payment to go to court to seek leave for not paying the full amount owed. However, even this softened rule provides minimal relief, as making this request requires a person to appear in court the first Wednesday of the month at 11:00 A.M. If a person misses that session, the court immediately issues an arrest warrant.

UNDUE HARSHNESS PENALTIES FOR MISSED PAYMENTS OR APPEARANCES

The procedural deficiencies identified above work together to make it exceedingly difficult to resolve a case and exceedingly easy to run afoul of the court's stringent and confusing rules, particularly for those living in or near poverty. That the court is at least in part responsible for causing cases to protract and result in technical violations has not prevented it from imposing significant penalties when those violations occur.

Although Ferguson's court—unlike many other municipal courts in the region—has ceased imposing the Failure to Appear charge, the court continues to routinely issue arrest warrants for missed appearances and missed payments. The evidence we have found shows that these arrest warrants are used almost exclusively for the purpose of compelling payment through the threat of incarceration.

The evidence also shows that the harms of the court's warrant practices are exacerbated by the court's bond procedures, which impose unnecessary obstacles to clearing a warrant or securing release after being arrested on a warrant and often function to further prolong a case and a person's involvement in the municipal justice system. These practices—together with the consequences to individuals and communities that result—raise significant due process and equal protection concerns.

BOND PRACTICES IMPOSE UNDUE HARDSHIPS

Despite the fact that those arrested by FPD for outstanding municipal warrants can be held for several days if unable to post bond, the Ferguson municipal court does not give credit for time served. As a result, there have been many cases in which a person has been arrested on a warrant, detained for 72 hours or more, and released owing the same amount as before the arrest was made. Court records do not even track the total amount of time a person has spent in jail as part of a case. When asked why this is not tracked, a member of court staff told us: "It's only three days anyway."

DISPROPORTIONATE HARM TO FERGUSON AFRICAN AMERICANS

Ferguson's police and municipal court practices disproportionately harm African Americans. Further, our investigation found substantial evidence that this harm stems in part from intentional discrimination in violation of the Constitution.

African Americans experience disparate impact in nearly every aspect of Ferguson's law enforcement system. Despite making up 67% of the population, African Americans accounted for 85% of FPD's traffic stops, 90% of FPD's citations, and 93% of FPD's arrests from 2012 to 2014. Other statistical disparities, set forth in detail below, show that in Ferguson:

- African Americans are 2.07 times more likely to be searched during a vehicular stop but are 26% less likely to have contraband found on them during a search. They are 2.00 times more likely to receive a citation and 2.37 times more likely to be arrested following a vehicular stop.
- African Americans have force used against them at disproportionately high rates, accounting for 88% of all cases from 2010 to August 2014 in which an FPD officer reported using force. In all 14 uses of force involving a canine bite for which we have information about the race of the person bitten, the person was African American.
- African Americans are more likely to receive multiple citations during a single incident, receiving four or more citations on 73 occasions between October 2012 and July 2014, whereas non-African Americans received four or more citations only twice during that period.
- African Americans account for 95% of Manner of Walking charges; 94% of all Fail to Comply charges; 92% of all Resisting Arrest charges; 92% of all Peace Disturbance charges; and 89% of all Failure to Obey charges.
- African Americans are 68% less likely than others to have their cases dismissed by the Municipal Judge, and in 2013 African Americans accounted for 92% of cases in which an arrest warrant was issued.
- African Americans account for 96% of known arrests made exclusively because of an outstanding municipal warrant.

While FPD's data collection and retention practices are deficient in many respects, the data that is collected by FPD is sufficient to allow for meaningful and reliable analysis of racial disparities. These data—collected directly by police and court officials—reveals racial disparities that are substantial and consistent across a wide range of police and court enforcement actions.

Ferguson's police and municipal court practices not only disproportionately harm African Americans. Our investigation also found substantial evidence that this harm stems in part from intentional discrimination in violation of the Constitution.

Of all stopped black drivers, 91%, or 8,987, received citations, while 87%, or 1,501, of all stopped white drivers received a citation. 891 stopped black drivers—10% of all stopped black drivers—were arrested as a result of the stop, whereas only 63 stopped white drivers—4% of all stopped white drivers—were arrested. This disparity is explainable in large part by the high number of black individuals arrested for outstanding municipal warrants issued for missed court payments and appearances. As we discuss below, African Americans are more likely to have warrants issued against them than whites and are more likely to be arrested for an outstanding warrant than their white counterparts. Notably, on 14 occasions, FPD listed the only reason for an arrest following a traffic stop as "resisting arrest." In all 14 of those cases, the person arrested was black.

These disparities in the outcomes that result from traffic stops remain even after regression analysis is used to control for non-race-based variables, including driver age; gender; the assignment of the officer making the stop; disparities in officer behavior; and the stated reason the stop was initiated. Upon accounting for differences in those variables, African Americans remained 2.07 times more likely to be searched; 2.00 times more likely to receive a citation; and 2.37 times more likely to be arrested than other stopped individuals. Each of these disparities is statistically significant and would occur by chance less than one time in 1,000. The odds of these disparities occurring by chance together are significantly lower still.

INADEQUATE DATA COLLECTION ON PEDESTRIAN STOPS

Although available data enables an assessment of the disparate impact of many FPD practices, many other practices cannot be assessed statistically because of FPD's inadequate data collection. FPD does not reliably collect or track data regarding pedestrian stops, or FPD officers' conduct during those stops. Given

(continues)

(continued)

this lack of data, we are unable to determine whether African Americans are disproportionately the subjects of pedestrian stops, or the rate of searches, arrests, or other post-pedestrian stop outcomes.

We note, however, that during our investigation we have spoken with not only black community members who have been stopped by FPD officers, but also non-black community members and employees of local businesses who have observed FPD conduct pedestrian stops of others, all of whom universally report that pedestrian stops in Ferguson almost always involve African-American youth. Even though FPD does not specifically track pedestrian stops, other FPD records are consistent with those accounts. Arrest and other incident reports sometimes describe encounters that begin with pedestrian stops, almost all of which involve African Americans.

Our investigation uncovered direct evidence of racial bias in the communications of influential Ferguson decision makers. In email messages and during interviews, several court and law enforcement personnel expressed discriminatory views and intolerance with regard to race, religion, and national origin. The content of these communications is unequivocally derogatory, dehumanizing, and demonstrative of impermissible bias.

We have discovered evidence of racial bias in emails sent by Ferguson officials, all of whom are current employees, almost without exception through their official City of Ferguson email accounts, and apparently sent during work hours. These email exchanges involved several police and court supervisors, including FPD supervisors and commanders. The following emails are illustrative:

- A November 2008 email stated that President Barack Obama would not be President for very long because "what black man holds a steady job for four years."
- A March 2010 email mocked African Americans through speech and familial stereotypes, using a story involving child support. One line from the email read: "I be so glad that dis be my last child support payment! Month after month, year after year, all dose payments!"
- An April 2011 email depicted President Barack Obama as a chimpanzee.
- A May 2011 email stated: "An African-American woman in New Orleans was admitted into the hospital for a pregnancy termination. Two weeks later she received a check for $5,000. She phoned the hospital to ask who it was from. The hospital said, 'Crimestoppers.'"
- A June 2011 email described a man seeking to obtain "welfare" for his dogs because they are "mixed in color, unemployed, lazy, can't speak English and have no frigging clue who their Daddies are."
- An October 2011 email included a photo of a bare-chested group of dancing women, apparently in Africa, with the caption, "Michelle Obama's High School Reunion."
- A December 2011 email included jokes that are based on offensive stereotypes about Muslims.

Our review of documents revealed many additional email communications that exhibited racial or ethnic bias, as well as other forms of bias. Our investigation has not revealed any indication that any officer or court clerk engaged in these communications was ever disciplined. Nor did we see a single instance in which a police or court recipient of such an email asked that the sender refrain from sending such emails, or any indication that these emails were reported as inappropriate. Instead, the emails were usually forwarded along to others.

This documentary evidence of explicit racial bias is consistent with reports from community members indicating that some FPD officers use racial epithets in dealing with members of the public. We spoke with one African-American man who, in August 2014, had an argument in his apartment to which FPD officers responded, and was immediately pulled out of the apartment by force. After telling the officer, "you don't have a reason to lock me up," he claims the officer responded: "N*****, I can find something to lock you up on." When the man responded, "good luck with that," the officer slammed his face into the wall, and after the man fell to the floor, the officer said, "don't pass out motherf****r because I'm not carrying you to my car." Another young man described walking with friends in July 2014 past a group of FPD officers who shouted racial epithets at them as they passed.

Several Ferguson officials told us during our investigation that it is a lack of "personal responsibility" among African-American members of the Ferguson community that causes African Americans to experience disproportionate harm under Ferguson's approach to law enforcement. Our investigation suggests that this explanation is at odd with the facts. While there are people of all races who may lack personal responsibility, the harm of Ferguson's approach to law enforcement is largely due to the myriad systemic deficiencies discussed above.

Our investigation revealed African Americans making extraordinary efforts to pay off expensive tickets for minor, often unfairly charged, violations, despite systemic obstacles to resolving those tickets. While our investigation did not indicate that African Americans are disproportionately irresponsible, it did reveal that, as the above emails reflect, some Ferguson decision makers hold negative stereotypes about African Americans, and lack of personal responsibility is one of them. Application of this stereotype furthers the disproportionate impact of Ferguson's police and court practices. It causes court and police decision makers to discredit African Americans' explanations for not being able to pay tickets and allows officials to disown the harms of Ferguson's law enforcement practices.

The common practice among Ferguson officials of writing off tickets further evidences a double standard grounded in racial stereotyping. Even as Ferguson City officials maintain the harmful stereotype that black individuals lack personal responsibility—and continue to cite this lack of personal responsibility as the cause of the disparate impact of Ferguson's practices—white City officials condone a striking lack of personal responsibility among themselves and their friends. Court records and emails show City officials, including the Municipal Judge, the Court Clerk, and FPD supervisors assisting friends, colleagues, acquaintances, and themselves in eliminating citations, fines, and fees. For example:

- In October 2013, Judge Brockmeyer sent Ferguson's Prosecuting Attorney an email with the subject line "City of Hazelwood vs. Ronald Brockmeyer." The Judge wrote: "Pursuant to our conversation, attached please find the red light camera ticket received by the undersigned. I would appreciate it if you would please see to it that this ticket is dismissed." The Prosecuting Attorney, who also serves as prosecuting attorney in Hazelwood, responded: "I worked on red light matters today and dismissed the ticket that you sent over. Since I entered that into the system today, you may or may not get a second notice – you can just ignore that."
- In August 2013, an FPD patrol supervisor wrote an email entitled "Oops" to the Prosecuting Attorney regarding a ticket his relative received in another municipality for traveling 59 miles per hour in a 40 miles-per-hour zone, noting "[h] aving it dismissed would be a blessing." The Prosecuting Attorney responded that the prosecutor of that other municipality promised to nolle pros (decline to prosecute) the ticket. The supervisor responded with appreciation, noting that the dismissal "[c]ouldn't have come at a better time."
- Also in August 2013, Ferguson's Mayor emailed the Prosecuting Attorney about a parking ticket received by an employee of a non-profit day camp for which the Mayor sometimes volunteers. The Mayor wrote that the person "shouldn't have left his car unattended there, but it was an honest mistake" and stated, "I would hate for him to have to pay for this, can you help?" The Prosecuting Attorney forwarded the email to the Court Clerk, instructing her to "NP [nolle prosequi, or not prosecute] this parking ticket."
- In November 2011, a court clerk received a request from a friend to "fix a parking ticket" received by the friend's coworker's wife. After the ticket was faxed to the clerk, she replied: "It's gone baby!"
- In March 2014, a friend of the Court Clerk's relative emailed the Court Clerk with a scanned copy of a ticket asking if there was anything she could do to help. She responded: "Your ticket of $200 has magically disappeared!" Later, in June 2014, the same person emailed the Court Clerk regarding two tickets and asked: "Can you work your magic again? It would be deeply appreciated." The Clerk later informed him one ticket had been dismissed and she was waiting to hear back about the second ticket.

City officials' application of the stereotype that African Americans lack "personal responsibility" to explain why Ferguson's practices harm African Americans, even as these same City officials exhibit a lack of personal—and professional—responsibility in handling their own and their friends' code violations, is further evidence of discriminatory bias on the part of decision makers central to the direction of law enforcement in Ferguson.

Based on this evidence, it is apparent that FPD requires better training, limits on officer discretion, increased supervision, and more robust accountability systems, not only to ensure that officers act in accordance with the Fourth Amendment, but with the Fourteenth Amendment as well. FPD has failed to take any such

(continues)

(continued)

corrective action, and instead has actively endorsed and encouraged the perpetuation of the practices that have led to such stark disparities. This, together with the totality of the facts that we have found, evidences that those practices exist, at least in part, on account of an unconstitutional discriminatory purpose.

CONCLUSION: DISPARITY, DISCRIMINATION, AND LEGITIMACY

A growing body of research, alongside decades of police experience, is consistent with what our investigation found in Ferguson: that when police and courts treat people unfairly, unlawfully, or disrespectfully, law enforcement loses legitimacy in the eyes of those who have experienced, or even observed, the unjust conduct. Further, this loss of legitimacy makes individuals more likely to resist enforcement efforts and less likely to cooperate with law enforcement efforts to prevent and investigate crime. To improve community trust and police effectiveness, Ferguson must ensure not only that its officers act in accord with the Constitution, but that they treat people fairly and respectfully.

Even where lawful, many discretionary FPD enforcement actions increase distrust and significantly decrease the likelihood that individuals will seek police assistance even when they are victims of crime, or that they will cooperate with the police to solve or prevent other crimes. Chief Jackson told us "we don't get cooperating witnesses" from the apartment complexes. Consistent with this statement, our review of documents and our conversations with Ferguson residents revealed many instances in which they are reluctant to report being victims of crime or to cooperate with police, and many instances in which FPD imposed unnecessary negative consequences for doing so.

Our investigation indicates that Ferguson as a City has the capacity to reform its approach to law enforcement. A small municipal department may offer greater potential for officers to form partnerships and have frequent, positive interactions with Ferguson residents, repairing and maintaining police-community relationships. These reform efforts will be well worth the considerable time and dedication they will require, as they have the potential to make Ferguson safer and more united.

QUESTIONS

1. Summarize the evidence the DOJ report presents to support its claim that the major purpose of enforcing the minor public order offenses is to pay for the personnel and operation of city government.
2. Do you believe the DOJ made its case? Defend your answer.
3. Do you believe the evidence supports the claims that the enforcement proved disparity against Black residents of Ferguson? Support your answer.
4. Do you believe the evidence also proves that the evidence proves discrimination against Black residents? Back up your answer with details from the report.
5. Do you agree with Leon Wolf's *Diary*, "Many Conservatives are blowing it on the Ferguson DOJ Report"? Explain your answer.

Summary

LO1 "Quality of life" crimes refer to the laws that are meant to control "bad manners" in public places. They underscore the tension between liberty and order in a constitutional democracy. These very minor crimes affect many more people than the crimes against persons and their property, and most people are more worried by quality of life crimes than serious crimes.

LO2, LO3 Disorderly conduct crimes are crimes against public order and morals. Disorderly conduct grew out of the ancient crime known as "breach of the peace," which included both actual disorderly conduct and constructive disorderly conduct (provoking others to break the peace).The Model Penal Code has limited modern disorderly conduct to three actions triggered by subjective fault: (1) fighting in public; (2) making unreasonable noise or using abusive language and; (3) creating a hazardous or physically offensive condition. Most states have adopted the MPC's provisions on disorderly conduct.

LO4 The "broken windows" theory states there's a link between minor quality-of-life offenses and more serious crimes. The empirical findings as to whether there's a link are mixed.

LO5 For at least 600 years, it's been a crime for poor people to roam without visible means of support (vagrancy) or to stand around with no apparent purpose (loitering).

LO6 New and innovative controls against aggressive begging by street people rely on ancient laws against begging, or panhandling. States can control the time, place, and manner of panhandling but not the content of panhandling.

LO7 There's wide consensus within high and low-crime neighborhoods in major cities that public drinking, followed closely by loitering youths, tops the worries among all classes, races, and ethnic groups, among both men and women. These "bands of loitering youth" have led to number of state and city governments have passed criminal laws to regulate gang behavior. Antigang ordinances meet due process and liberty requirements if they define "loitering" more specifically than just hanging out with no apparent purpose, but the effectiveness of these civil gang injunctions in controlling gang behavior is mixed.

LO8 The scientific link between violent video games and criminal behavior is modern, but the idea behind it reflects the crime of disorderly conduct as well as the "broken windows theory." The empirical research on the connection between violent video games and criminal behavior is mixed, however.

LO9, LO10 The term "victimless crime" applies to (1) consenting adults, not minors and (2) to crimes committed by adults who don't see themselves as victims of their behavior. An example is prostitution. Prostitution is an ancient business that has historically punished females much more harshly than male "johns."

LO11 Discretionary decision making in the enforcement of minor crimes poses several ethical issues. Racial discrimination and profit-oriented criminal justice practices have generated much controversy over the enforcement of these minor offenses.

Key Terms

crimes against public order, p. 485
"quality of life" crimes, p. 485
order, p. 486
liberty, p. 486
disorderly conduct crimes, p. 487
actual disorderly conduct, p. 487
constructive disorderly conduct, p. 487
"quality of life" crimes, p. 489
broken-windows theory, p. 489
vagrancy, p. 490
loitering, p. 490
panhandling, p. 492
time, place, and manner test, p. 493
injunction to abate public nuisances, p. 499
civil gang injunctions (CGI), p. 499
victimless crimes, p. 502
prostitution, p. 503

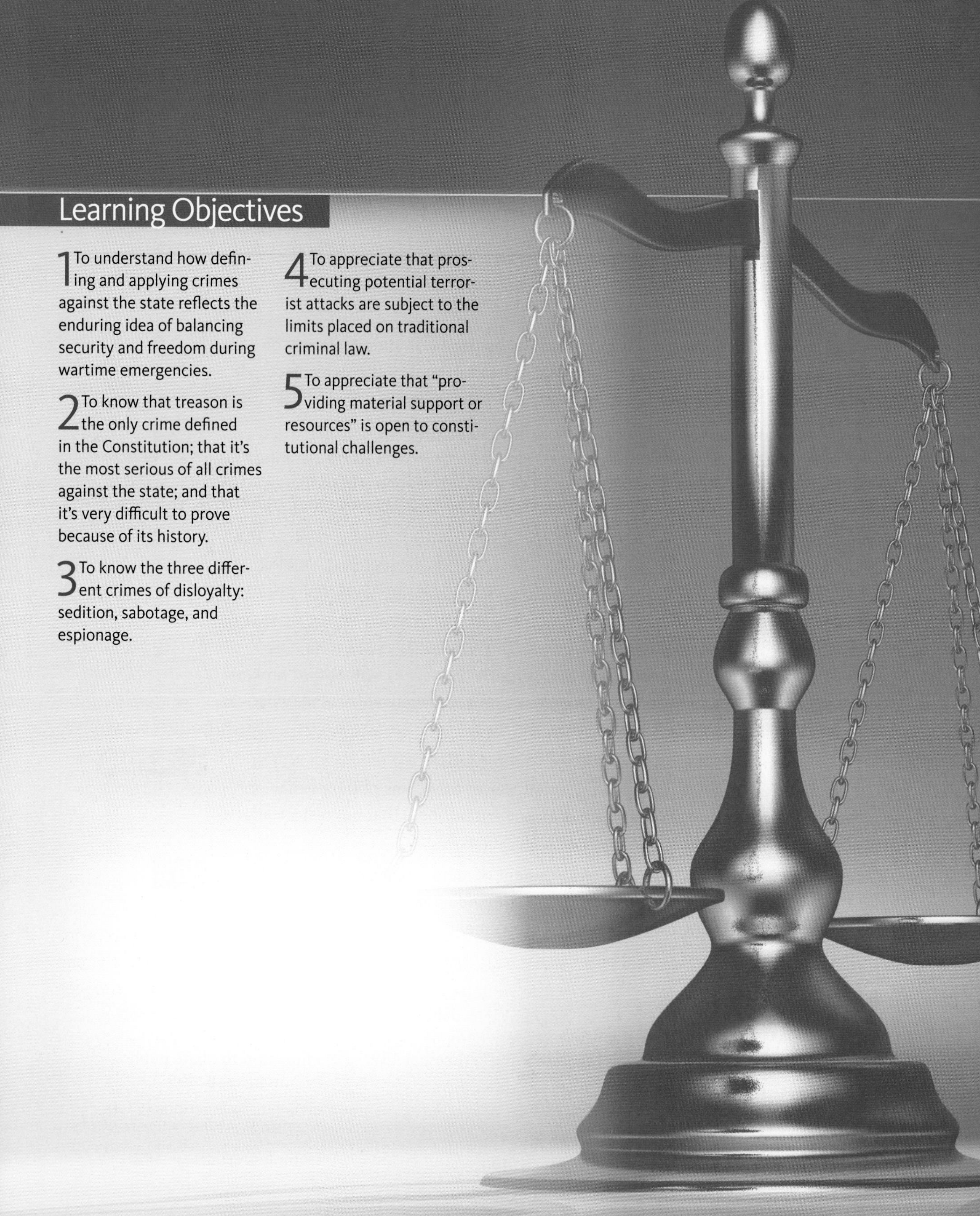

Learning Objectives

1 To understand how defining and applying crimes against the state reflects the enduring idea of balancing security and freedom during wartime emergencies.

2 To know that treason is the only crime defined in the Constitution; that it's the most serious of all crimes against the state; and that it's very difficult to prove because of its history.

3 To know the three different crimes of disloyalty: sedition, sabotage, and espionage.

4 To appreciate that prosecuting potential terrorist attacks are subject to the limits placed on traditional criminal law.

5 To appreciate that "providing material support or resources" is open to constitutional challenges.

13 Crimes Against the State

Chapter Outline

We know that foreign cyber actors are probing America's critical infrastructure networks. They target the computer control systems that operate chemical, electricity and water plants and those that guide transportation throughout this country. We know of specific instances where intruders have successfully gained access to these control systems. We also know that they are seeking to create advanced tools to attack these systems and cause panic and destruction and even the loss of life.

Let me explain how this could unfold. An aggressor nation or extremist group could use these kinds of cyber tools to gain control of critical switches. They could, for example, derail passenger trains or even more dangerous, derail trains loaded with lethal chemicals. They could contaminate the water supply in major cities or shutdown the power grid across large parts of the country. The most destructive scenarios involve cyber actors launching several attacks on our critical infrastructure at one time, in combination with a physical attack on our country. Attackers could also seek to disable or degrade critical military systems and communication networks.

The collective result of these kinds of attacks could be a cyber Pearl Harbor; an attack that would cause physical destruction and the loss of life. In fact, it would paralyze and shock the nation and create a new, profound sense of vulnerability.

—Secretary of Defense Leon Panetta, 2012

As director of the CIA and now Secretary of Defense, I have understood that cyber attacks are every bit as real as the more well-known threats like terrorism, nuclear weapons proliferation and the turmoil that we see in the Middle East.

—Secretary of Defense Leon Panetta, October 11, 2012

> Discourse around cyber security and cyber terrorism is changing. It is evolving, slowly but perceptibly, from anxiety about a single catastrophic event—a "cyber Pearl Harbor"—to a conversation about how to manage a digital threat landscape that includes a large number of smaller incidents directed against a wide range of targets. Some of these episodes, to be sure, may prove catastrophic to individual victims. The strategic impact of proliferating cyber challenges, however, is more likely to be felt in their accumulated effect on our economic interests over time than in a single catastrophic event targeting American infrastructure.
>
> —*Zachary K. Goldman, April 17, 2015*

LO1

Both the threat of single catastrophic attacks and a large number of smaller incidents directed against a wide range of targets reflect the tension between two core values in U.S. constitutional democracy—the need for safety and security and the desire for privacy and liberty. This chapter is about how we apply the enduring principles of criminal law (see Chapters 1–4) to protect the core values of security and freedom in a time of testing by threats from individuals and groups who are prepared to kill innocent individuals both in the United States and around the world. However, grave as the threat may be today, we need to understand and appreciate that the U.S. Constitution, too, was adopted during a time of threats to our nation's security.

We'll examine the history and modern law of treason, the other ancient crimes of disloyalty (sedition, sabotage, and espionage), and how the specific crimes against domestic and international terrorism, enacted after the Oklahoma City bombing in 1993, were strengthened after the attacks on the World Trade Center and the Pentagon on September 11, 2001.

TREASON

LO2

treason the crime of levying war against the United States or of giving aid and comfort to its enemies

Treason is the only crime defined in the U.S. Constitution. This is how Article III, Section 3, defines this most serious of all crimes against the state:

> Treason against the United States shall consist only in levying War against them, or, in adhering to their Enemies, giving them Aid and Comfort. No Person shall be convicted of Treason unless on the Testimony of two Witnesses to the same overt Act, or on Confession in open Court.

There's also a treason statute (Treason Act 2006) that includes the constitutional definition and adds this penalty provision:

> Whoever, owing allegiance to the United States, levies war against them or adheres to their enemies, giving them aid and comfort within the United States or elsewhere, is guilty of treason and shall suffer death, or shall be imprisoned not less than five years and fined under this title but not less than $10,000; and shall be incapable of holding any office under the United States. (Title 18, § 2381)

Let's look at how treason laws were viewed both before and after the Revolution.

Treason Laws and the American Revolution

LO2

The revolutionaries who wrote the U.S. Constitution knew that the new government they were about to create couldn't survive without the active support (or at least the passive submission) of most of the people. They also wisely surmised that it was going to be some time before this new republican form of government took hold among the people.

The people's allegiance was especially important to the newborn nation's survival in the early years following the Revolution, a time of perilous threats from enemies inside and outside the new country. From within, Benedict Arnold's betrayal of General Washington was fresh in their minds, and royalists among them remained loyal to King George III. From without, hostile old countries had designs on the new country's territory. To the north in Canada, the British hovered, smarting from the loss of their American colonies and looking for payback. Spain to the south had just taken back Florida and claimed the whole Mississippi Valley. Colonists had only recently thrown France out of the Ohio Valley. These unfriendly nations formed alliances with Native American nations by taking advantage of deep injustices the colonists continued to inflict on the tribes.

These threats led the authors of the Constitution to take a tough stand against individuals who broke their allegiance in the face of these dangers. But there was a flipside to their tough stand. Many of the drafters' ancestors had fled to the colonies for the very purpose of escaping persecution for heresy and prosecution for treason. More to the point, they were traitors themselves under English law. English treason consisted either of levying war against the king or giving aid and comfort to the king's enemies. They'd done plenty of both. They'd levied war against the King of England by fighting the Revolutionary War, and they'd given aid and comfort to the British's bitterest enemy, France.

Everything they did to further the interests of the colonies was done under threat of prosecution for treason. English prosecutions for treason weren't pretty. Thomas Jefferson referred to the English law of treason as a "deadly weapon in the hands of tyrannical kings" and "weak and wicked Ministers which had drawn the blood of the best and honestest men in the kingdom" (Jefferson 1853, 1:215). Benjamin Franklin probably had treason in mind at the signing of the Declaration of Independence when he quipped, "We must all hang together, or most assuredly we shall all hang separately" (qtd. in Lederer 1988, 27).

What were they worried about? The existing British law defined treason as "adherence to the enemy." *Adherence* here means breaking allegiance to your own country by forming an "attachment to the enemy." Criminalizing attachment—joining the enemy's military forces—wasn't an issue; everybody agreed that was treason. But what about "giving aid and comfort to the enemy"? With this loose phrase, "attachment" could lead to attacks on thoughts and feelings. Suppose "disloyalty" took the forms of sympathy for our enemies or even apathy toward our own cause. Were they treason, too? (They were under British law.) Would zealous patriotism, so needed in troubled times, tempt the government to bend the rules in its attempt to protect the country? (It did under British law.)

adherence to the enemy the definition of treason under English common law, meaning breaking allegiance to your own country by forming an "attachment to the enemy"

The worries that treason law would be abused boiled down to two concerns:

1. That peaceful opposition to the government, not just rebellion, would be repressed.
2. That innocent people might be convicted of treason because of perjury, passion, and/or insufficient evidence. The authors of the Constitution were determined that disloyal feelings or opinions and the passions of the time wouldn't be a part of the law of treason.

So, as much as the Constitution's authors recognized the need for allegiance to the new government, their fear of abusive prosecutions for treason led them to adopt "every limitation that the practice of governments had evolved or that politico-legal philosophy to that time had advanced" (*Cramer v. U.S.* 1945, 23–24). By the time the Constitution was adopted, the new government and current thinking among the governing class came

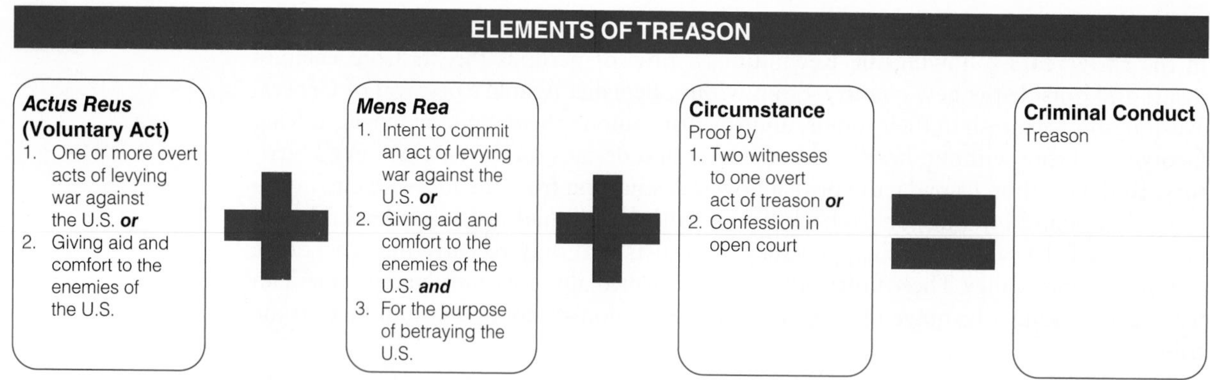

to limit treason to two disloyal behaviors: (1) levying war against your own country and (2) giving aid and comfort to the enemy.

The authors of the Constitution adopted these two acts and then, for more protection, added three more limits to the reach of treason:

1. They banned legislatures and courts from creating new treasons.
2. They required two witnesses to at least one overt (unconcealed) act of treason or a confession in open court.
3. They wrote these limits into the body of the U.S. Constitution, where it would be very tough to tamper with them because of the intentionally cumbersome constitutional amendment process.

treason *actus reus* consists of either levying war against the United States or giving aid and comfort to the enemies of the United States

treason *mens rea* consists of intentionally giving aid and comfort for the very purpose of betraying the United States

proof of treason requires either two witnesses to the *actus reus* or confession in open court

Treason has three elements. First, treason *actus reus* requires either levying war against the United States or giving aid and comfort to the enemies of the United States. Second, treason *mens rea* requires intentionally giving aid and comfort for the very purpose of betraying the United States. Third, proof of treason requires either two witnesses to the *actus reus* or confession in open court. (See the Elements of Treason illustration.)

Associate U.S. Supreme Court Justice Robert Jackson stated the elements of treason in this straightforward language in one of the very few treason cases in U.S. history, *Cramer v. U.S.* (1945):

> The crime of treason consists of two elements: adherence to the enemy; and rendering him aid and comfort. A citizen intellectually or emotionally may favor the enemy and harbor sympathies or convictions disloyal to this country's policy or interest, but so long as he commits no act of aid and comfort to the enemy, there is no treason. On the other hand, a citizen may take actions, which do aid and comfort the enemy—making a speech critical of the government or opposing its measures, profiteering, striking in defense plants or essential work, and the hundred other things which impair our cohesion and diminish our strength—but if there is no adherence to the enemy in this, if there is no intent to betray, there is no treason. (29)

Treason Laws since the Adoption of the U.S. Constitution

LO2

Distrust of treason prosecutions didn't end with the adoption of the Constitution. Throughout U.S. history, the government has charged only about 30 people for treason, and presidents have pardoned or at least mitigated death sentences of most of those few who've been found guilty. The only exception was President Eisenhower's refusal to stop the execution of Ethel Rosenberg, convicted of conspiring to give atomic bomb secrets to the Soviet Union. She and her husband, Julius, were executed in 1951. There's still plenty of controversy surrounding the Rosenbergs' executions (Meerpol 2003).

In 1945, six years before the Rosenbergs' executions, the U.S. Supreme Court dealt with disloyalty—giving aid and comfort to Nazi Germany for the purpose of betraying the United States—and proving it, in *Cramer v. U.S.* (1945). This case was part of the fallout from the darkest days of World War II. Early in June 1942, when the war was going badly for the Allies, German submarines were able to get close enough to the East Coast of the United States to allow eight Germans to get ashore, four on Long Island and four in Florida. They managed to bring along several crates of dynamite and lots of cash. The plan was to blow up bridges, factories, and maybe a department store owned by Jews. The object of the plot was, first, to sabotage the war effort by destroying strategic places. Second, they planned to demoralize the American public by terror—namely, by the brazen act of coming right onto U.S. soil and blowing up our places of defense and business. In 1943, one of the eight, Cramer, was arrested and charged with treason. At Cramer's treason trial, two FBI agents testified they had witnessed his meetings with two other of the eight, and that the three ate, drank, and "engaged long and earnestly in conversation."

The government claimed these acts amounted to "giving aid and comfort to the enemy" and that the FBI agents' testimony satisfied the constitutional requirement of two witnesses. The trial judge and jury agreed; Cramer was convicted (*Cramer v. U.S.*, 1945). However, the U.S. Supreme Court, by a vote of 5–4, disagreed and reversed Cramer's conviction. According to Justice Jackson, writing for the majority, two witnesses to the dinner wasn't good enough to prove treason (38).

SEDITION, SABOTAGE, AND ESPIONAGE

LO3

The lesson of *Cramer v. U.S.* is clear: It's very hard to convict someone of treason—and as you've already learned, that's just exactly what the authors intended. But treason isn't the only crime aimed at combating disloyalty and keeping the allegiance of our citizens. Let's look at three of these crimes, which are very much like ancient crimes with the same names—sedition, sabotage, and espionage. Then, we'll examine some specific antiterrorist laws that borrowed from these three ancient crimes. Finally, we'll turn to the cyber terrorism brought boldly into relief by the spate of cyber-attacks during 2014, including those against Sony Pictures, Apple iCloud, Google, Home Depot, and others.

sedition the crime of advocating the violent overthrow of the government

seditious speech advocating the overthrow of the government in speeches

Sedition

LO3

For centuries, it's been a crime against the state not just to commit treason but to "stir up" others to overthrow the government by violence. Advocating the violent overthrow of the government was called sedition. The "stirring up" could be done by speeches (seditious speech), writings (seditious libel), or agreement (seditious conspiracy).

seditious libel advocating the overthrow of the government in writings

seditious conspiracy conspiring to the violent overthrow of the government

In 1798, during the French Revolution and impending war with France, the U.S. Congress enacted the country's first sedition act. This highly contested law banned a lot more than stirring up the violent overthrow of the government. It made it a crime to "unlawfully combine or conspire together with intent to oppose any measure or measures of the government of the United States, or to impede the operation of any law of the United States, or to intimidate or prevent any [official] from undertaking, performing, or executing his duty." (Urofsky and Finkelman 2002a, 1:141)

The Sedition Act also made it a crime to

> write, print, utter, or publish any false, scandalous and malicious writing or writings with intent to "defame" the U.S. Government or excite the hatred of the good people [against the U.S. Government]. (142)

The U.S. Code (Seditious Conspiracy 2006) definition of "seditious conspiracy" sticks to conspiracies that advocate violence. It provides:

> If two or more persons in any State or Territory, or in any place subject to the jurisdiction of the United States, conspire to overthrow, put down, or to destroy by force the Government of the United States, or to levy war against them, or to oppose by force the authority thereof, or by force to prevent, hinder, or delay the execution of any law of the United States, or by force to seize, take, or possess any property of the United States contrary to the authority thereof, they shall each be fined under this title or imprisoned not more than twenty years, or both. (Title 18, § 2384)

No one has been charged under this law, and we'll not spend more time on it here.

Sabotage

LO3

sabotage the crime of damaging or destroying property for the purpose of hindering preparations for war and national defense during national emergencies

Sabotage is the crime of damaging or destroying property for the purpose of interfering with and hindering preparations for war and defense during national emergencies. Here's how the U.S. Code (Sabotage Act 2012) defines the criminal sabotage of war and defense materials, buildings, and utilities:

> Whoever, with intent to injure, interfere with, or obstruct the national defense of the United States, willfully injures, destroys, contaminates or infects, or attempts to so injure, destroy, contaminate or infect any national-defense material, national-defense premises, or national-defense utilities, shall be fined under this title or imprisoned not more than 20 years, or both.

Sabotage *actus reus* consists of injuring, destroying, contaminating or infecting (or attempting to) any war material, war premises, or war utilities. (See the Elements of Sabotage illustration.)

Other sections of Chapter 105 apply to similar acts against forts, harbors, and sea areas (§ 2152); production of defective war (§ 2154) or national defense (§ 2155)

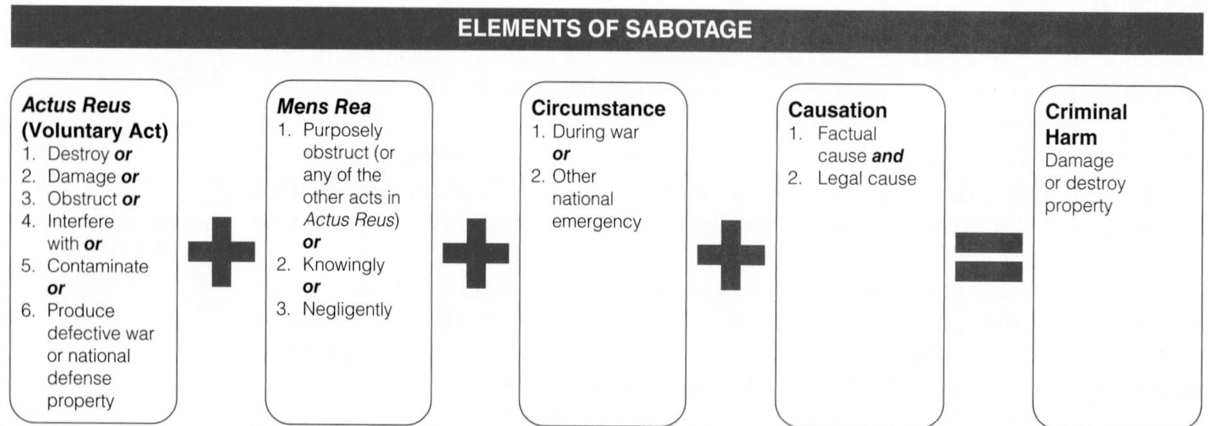

material, premises, and utilities; and destruction of national defense materials, premises, and utilities. Utilities include this copious list:

> railroads, railways, electric lines, roads of whatever description, any railroad or railway fixture, canal, lock, dam, wharf, pier, dock, bridge, building, structure, engine, machine, mechanical contrivance, car, vehicle, boat, aircraft, airfields, air lanes, and fixtures or appurtenances thereof, or any other means of transportation whatsoever, whereon or whereby such war material or any troops of the United States, or of any associate nation, are being or may be transported either within the limits of the United States or upon the high seas or elsewhere; and all air-conditioning systems, dams, reservoirs, aqueducts, water and gas mains and pipes, structures and buildings, whereby or in connection with which air, water or gas is being furnished, or may be furnished, to any war premises or to the Armed Forces of the United States, or any associate nation, and all electric light and power, steam or pneumatic power, telephone and telegraph plants, poles, wires, and fixtures, and wireless stations, and the buildings connected with the maintenance and operation thereof used to supply air, water, light, heat, power, or facilities of communication to any war premises or to the Armed Forces of the United States, or any associate nation. (§ 2151)

The sabotage *mens rea*, or level of culpability, varies in the statute. Most often, it's "willfully," sometimes "with intent to," and at least once "with reason to believe." Whatever the exact words, it's probably closest to the highest levels of culpability—purposely and/or knowingly (Chapter 4).

The first You Decide box, "Did they commit sabotage?" is an excellent example from a case in involving what the *Daily Beast* described as

> the setup for a bad joke: armed with flashlights and bolt cutters, an 82-year-old nun and two accomplices—a carpenter and a Vietnam War veteran—break into one of the most secure nuclear weapons facilities in the country. The trio dodge barbed wire, motion sensors, video cameras and sleepy guards to get to the heart of the plant, where they splatter human blood and spray paint biblical references on the main uranium storage building. When a guard finally arrives on the scene, they break into song and offer him food. (Crocker 2014)

YOU *DECIDE*

Did they commit sabotage?

U.S. v. Michael R. Walli, Megan Rice, and Greg Boertje-Obed

U.S. Attorney's Office, Eastern District Tennessee

785 F.3d 1080 (CA 6 2015)

History

According to the U.S. Attorney's Office, Eastern District Tennessee:

On February 18, 2014, Michael Walli, Megan Rice, and Greg Boertje-Obed were sentenced in U.S. District Court by the Honorable Amul Thapar, U.S. District Judge. Sister Megan Rice was sentenced to serve 35 months in prison. Walli and Boertje-Obed were each sentenced to serve 62 months in prison. All three will serve three years' supervised release upon their release from prison. Additionally, these individuals were ordered to pay $52,953 in restitution to the Department of Energy.

(continues)

(continued)

These individuals were convicted in May 2013 of one count of injuring national defense premises, that is, the Y-12 National Security Complex, with the intent to interfere with the national defense of the United States and another count of depredation against property of the United States.

U.S. Attorney William C. Killian commended the sentences and said he hoped it would send a strong message. "The Y-12 National Security Complex plays a critical role in our country's national defense. People cannot take the law into their own hands and unlawfully intrude upon sensitive government facilities. Those who violate the law and compromise the security of the Y-12 National Security Complex will be vigorously prosecuted."

Facts (according to the U.S. Court of Appeals, Sixth Circuit majority)

In the dark of night on July 28, 2012, in Oak Ridge, Tennessee, an 82 year-old nun and two Army veterans, ages 57 and 63, cut their way through four layers of fences and reached a building where the Department of Energy stores enriched uranium. There the trio spray-painted antiwar slogans, hung crime tape and banners with biblical phrases, splashed blood, and sang hymns. When a security guard finally arrived, the group offered him bread and read aloud a prepared message about "transforming weapons into real life-giving alternatives to build true peace." Then the group surrendered to the guard's custody.

The group's actions caused about $8,000 of damage to government property. The government eventually charged them with trespassing in violation of 42 U.S.C. § 2278a(c) and injuring government property in violation of 18 U.S.C. § 1361. When the defendants refused to plead guilty to those charges, however, the government pulled the trespassing count (which was only a misdemeanor) and instead charged them with violating the peacetime provision of the Sabotage Act, 18 U.S.C. § 2155(a), which Congress enacted during World War II. That provision applies only if the defendant acted "with intent to injure, interfere with, or obstruct the national defense," and authorizes a sentence of up to 20 years. A jury convicted the defendants on the sabotage count and the injury-to-property count. After the defendants' convictions, the district court sentenced Michael Walli and Greg Boertje–Obed (the Army veterans) to 62 months' imprisonment on each count and Megan Rice (the nun) to 35 months' imprisonment on each count, all to run concurrently. On appeal, the defendants argue that they lacked the intent necessary to violate the Sabotage Act.

Questions

1. *Do you agree with the defendants?*

Before you answer, read these excerpts from the majority and dissenting opinions, and the section "Sabotage" in your text. Pay special attention to the Sabotage Act of 2012.

Majority

Therefore, proof that they acted knowingly is proof enough that they acted intentionally. Hence the question before us is this: whether the jury could rationally find that, when the defendants cut their way into Y-12 and engaged in their protest activities there, they consciously desired to interfere with the national defense or knew that such interference was practically certain to result. We must affirm the defendants' convictions if, based upon the evidence admitted at trial, any rational jury could find beyond a reasonable doubt that they acted with intent to interfere with the national defense when they injured Y-12's premises.

No rational jury could find that the defendants had that intent when they cut the fences; they did not cut them to allow al Qaeda to slip in behind. Nor could a rational jury find that the defendants had that intent when they engaged in their protest activities outside the HEUMF. True, their ultimate goal in engaging in those activities was to advance the cause of disarmament, by persuading Y-12's employees to abandon their pursuits there. But "the ultimate end" that "compel[s] the defendant to act ... is more properly labeled a 'motive.'" And the defendants' immediate purpose in hanging the banners themselves, and in otherwise erecting their shrine outside the HEUMF, was simply to protest.

Dissent

I believe that a rational jury could convict defendants. As the majority correctly states, we must affirm if a rational jury could find that "the defendants' actions were consciously meant to impair the nation's capacity to wage war." Testimony as to each defendant specified their intent:

Walli: "I wanted all the criminal activities to stop," and "I hoped to institute the rule of law" in answering the question did you hope "to interfere with the operations at Y-12"; and Walli had stated that nuclear weapons were unlawful.

Boertje-Obed: "we went to ... oppose nuclear weapons directly ... [t]hrough direct action";

Rice: "we were able to ... begin the work of disarmament";

Their intent to obstruct and interfere, however couched and however quixotic, was thus something that a rational juror could find existed. Defendants clearly stated that their intent was to impede, in any way that they could, the production of nuclear weapons, which they regarded as illegal, undesirable and counterproductive. The existence and degree of intent to obstruct was presented to the jury, and I would not override its judgment by declaring as a matter of law that no rational jury could find the intent to obstruct, simply because the obstruction here was by disrupting the general operation of the facility, rather than destroying a specific item.

Finally, I agree that creating bad publicity for the government is not chargeable as "obstruction" or "interference" under the Sabotage Act. However, because invading a facility involved in the production of nuclear weapons, with the intent of stopping "all the criminal activities," even if the possibility of achieving that objective is quite minimal, is a crime, and the jury so found. I would affirm the convictions and I therefore respectfully dissent.

2. *Should they be released from prison?*

Although the Court of Appeals threw out the sabotage convictions and sentences, it let stand a conviction and fine for "injuring government property." Then, "suddenly and unexpectedly, they were released from federal prison." (Schlosser 2015) Based on the majority and dissent's opinions, do you agree with the release from prison? There was lots of public reaction to the release but basically it all boiled down to the question of whether the trio had "interfered with national security when they cut through fences to break into the Y-2 National Security Complex in Oak Ridge in July 2012." (Associated Press, May 8 2015)

You can easily sample this reaction using your favorite search engine.

Espionage

espionage the crime of spying for the enemy

Espionage is the crime of spying for the enemy. The U.S. Code (Espionage and Censorship Act 2006) separates espionage into two crimes: (1) espionage during peace and (2) espionage during war.

espionage during peace turning or attempting to turn over information about national defense to any foreign country with "intent or with reason to believe" the information is "to be used" to either hurt the United States or help any foreign country

The code defines espionage during peace as turning or attempting to turn over information about national defense to any foreign country with "intent or with reason to believe" the information is "to be used" to either hurt the United States or help any foreign country. The penalty is any term of imprisonment up to life or, if someone died as a result of the espionage, death (§ 794[a]).

espionage during war consists of collecting, recording, publishing, or communicating (or attempting to do any of these) "any information" about troop movements, ships, aircraft, or war materials and any other information "which might be useful to the enemy"

The crime of espionage during war consists of collecting, recording, publishing, or communicating (or attempting to do any of these) "any information" about troop movements, ships, aircraft, or war materials and any other information "which might be useful to the enemy." The penalty is death or any term of imprisonment up to life (§ 794[b]).

THE HISTORY OF THE ESPIONAGE ACT

I am one of those who believe that when my country is at war, engaged in deadly strife with an enemy, as a matter of policy, we ought to surrender our individual views and get behind the government if we can possibly do so. In such times we ought to reconcile ourselves to our government's successful conduct of the war. But while that is my belief, it is also my contention, grounded in the deepest principles of free government, that if a man thinks a war is unjust or improvident, or that it is being carried on in a corrupt manner, it is his absolute right to say so. Indeed, if it is a question of

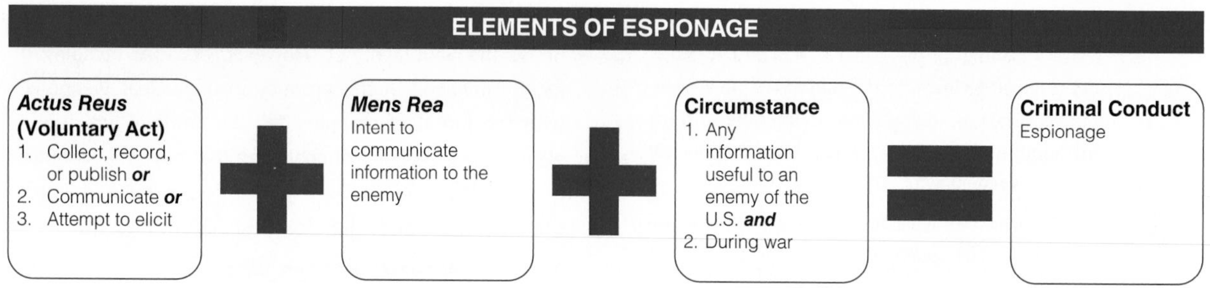

> the method of carrying on the war and he believes it is unwise or unjust, it is his duty to say so.
>
> —Senator William Borah on the "Espionage Act," 1923 (qtd. in Spartacus Educational, 2014)

In the second quote that begins this section, Senator Borah referred to the hundreds of individuals still locked up for violating the Espionage Act of 1917. This isn't the place for a detailed history of those turbulent times, but here are a few highlights we should note. By 1915, President Woodrow Wilson was moving the government from neutrality toward Great Britain's side in World War I. Moving the country wasn't so easy. At the same time, there were significant opponents to U.S. involvement in the war. There were the pacifists opposed to all wars; the socialists who opposed "profiteering" wars; and the "hyphenated" U.S. Americans, especially the vocal German-Americans, supporting Germany.

President Wilson was greatly concerned about pro-German sentiment and played on the general public's anxiety about "strangers in the land," especially those who supported the Kaiser. In his Third Annual Message to Congress on December 7, 1915, President Wilson played to this anxiety when he delivered these lines:

> There are citizens of the United States, I blush to admit, born under other flags but welcomed by our generous naturalization laws to full freedom and opportunity of America, who have poured the poison of disloyalty into the very arteries of our national life; who have sought to bring the authority and good name of our Government into contempt, to destroy our industries wherever they thought it effective for their vindictive purposes to strike at them, and to debase our politics to the uses of foreign intrigue.... A little while ago such a thing would have seemed incredible. But the ugly and incredible thing has actually come about and we are without adequate federal laws to deal with it. I urge you to enact such laws at the earliest possible moment and feel that in doing so I am urging you to do nothing less than save the honor and self-respect of the nation. Such creatures of passion, disloyalty, and anarchy must be crushed out. (Wilson 1915)

The Espionage Act became law just after the United States entered World War I. Most of it, like the provisions that made espionage and sabotage crimes, was noncontroversial. It was Section 3, amended in 1918 to become the Sedition Act of 1918 that generated over two thousand cases, in which the government obtained over one thousand convictions. The amended Section 3 provided:

> Whoever, when the United States is at war, shall willfully utter, print, write, or publish any disloyal, profane, scurrilous, or abusive language about the form of government of the United States, or the Constitution of the United States, or the military or naval forces of the United States, or the flag or the uniform of the Army or Navy of the United States, or any language intended to bring the form of government, or the Constitution or the military or naval forces or the flag of the United States into contempt, scorn, contumely, or disrepute or shall willfully display the flag of any foreign enemy,

> or shall willfully urge, incite, or advocate any curtailment of production in this country of any thing or things necessary to the prosecution of the war and whoever shall advocate, teach, or defend, or suggest the doing of any of the acts or things in this section enumerated and whoever shall by word or act support or favor the cause of any country with which the United States is at war or by word or act oppose the cause of the United States shall be punished by a fine of not more than $10,000 or imprisonment of not more than twenty years, or both. (Sedition Act 1918, § 3)

The broad sweep of Section 3 became apparent within a month of U.S. entry into the war, when the film *The Spirit of* '76 premiered in May. The U.S. government seized the film, arrested the producer, German immigrant Robert Goldstein, and tried and convicted him under Section 3 of the Espionage Act. The judge sentenced him to ten years in prison (*U.S. v. Motion Picture Film*, "The Spirit of '76" 1917).

By far, the largest sedition trials were the three International Workers of the World (IWW) trials in Chicago, Sacramento, and Wichita. Of these, Chicago's was surely the most sensational. But they all started on September 5, 1917, when U.S. Justice Department agents simultaneously raided forty-eight IWW local halls across the country and seized five tons of documents. Based partly on these documents, a federal grand jury in Chicago indicted 101 IWW leaders—"principal organizers, speakers, editors, and executives of the IWW" (Taft 1962, 76). (Forty-six members were tried and convicted in Sacramento and twenty-six in Wichita.)

In the Chicago trial, each defendant was charged with conspiring with thousands of others to obstruct the war effort by sabotage and by speaking and writing against the war and the draft (Taft 1962, 57). The Chicago U.S. attorney opened the trial with the words, "It is the IWW that is on trial here" (Renshaw 1968, 67). All 101 IWW leaders were convicted; William ("Big Bill") Haywood, the IWW Secretary Treasurer, and fourteen other defendants were fined $30,000 each; thirty-three received ten-year sentences; thirty-five received five-year sentences; and the rest under five years (Renshaw, 68).

By the middle of the 1920s, large-scale sedition prosecutions under the Espionage Act largely disappeared. But they didn't die. This is especially true during times like World War II, the Cold War, the Vietnam War, and now in Iraq and Afghanistan, when U.S. troops are engaged in combat and dangerous peacekeeping operations abroad. The Espionage Act then aims mainly at U.S. government employees who leak information they're sworn to keep secret because it's related to national security.

The U.S. government has occasionally prosecuted these employees. To cite one sensational example, in 1971, at the height of the Vietnam War, the government charged the whistleblowers Pentagon military analyst Daniel Ellsberg and Anthony Russo under the Espionage Act for leaking the Pentagon Papers to the *New York Times*. Up to that point, it was the largest leak in U.S. history. The case ended in a mistrial. The government also failed in its attempt to block the *New York Times* from publishing the documents.

THE ESPIONAGE ACT TODAY

Now, the Espionage Act is back. Since 2009, the U.S. government has charged ten U.S. government employees under the act. Let's look at each:

- *Daniel Ellsberg and Anthony Russo (1973)*. Famous national security whistleblowers prosecuted for releasing the Pentagon Papers.

  Sentence: Charges dropped after revelations that President Nixon's henchmen burglarized Ellsberg's psychoanalyst looking for dirt and tried to bribe the judge in their case with the directorship of the FBI.

- *Samuel Morison (1985)*. Naval analyst who sent pictures of the Soviet navy to *Jane's Fighting Ships*, a reference book on the world's warships.

  Sentence: Twenty-four months. He was subsequently pardoned by President Clinton.
- *Larry Franklin (2005)*. Pentagon analyst charged with leaking ran-related intelligence material to lobbyists for the American Israel Public Affairs Committee.

  Sentence: Ten months (four at a halfway house) and 100 hours of community service.
- *Chelsea Manning (2010)*. Private Bradley Manning was arrested in May 2010 as part of the fallout from the largest leak in U.S. history—the documents given to "WikiLeaks," the website that proclaims it's dedicated to making secret information public. (Critics say it's devoted to attacking the U.S. government.) Private Manning, a U.S. Army intelligence analyst, was convicted of providing more than 700,000 government files to WikiLeaks, a gigantic leak that lifted the veil on American military and diplomatic activities around the world. Depending on your point of view, Private Manning is either a "premeditated traitor" or an "accidental hero" (Liebelson 2012).

  Sentence: Thirty-five years. This sentence is "the longest ever handed down in a case involving a leak of United States government information for the purpose of having the information reported to the public. Private Manning, 25, will be eligible for parole in about seven years, his lawyer said" (Savage and Heutmann 2013).
- *Thomas Drake (2010)*. Drake, a former senior executive in the National Security Agency (NSA), was charged in 2010 under the Espionage Act with retaining top-secret national defense documents for the purpose of unauthorized disclosure. (To Drake's defenders, he was a whistleblower who was a key witness in a Defense Department Inspector General audit that found that the NSA spent $1.2 billion on an ineffective private contract when it could've done the work in-house for $3 million!) Drake pleaded guilty to a misdemeanor in exchange for dropping the Espionage Act charges (Liebelson 2012).

  Sentence: One-year probation.
- *Shamai Leibowitz (2010)*. Orthodox Jewish translator (dual Israeli–U.S. citizen), revealed to a blogger, information about U.S. spying against Israeli diplomats. Leibowitz released the transcripts because he was concerned about Israel's "aggressive efforts to influence public opinion, and fears that Israel might strike nuclear facilities in Iran, a move he saw as potentially disastrous" (Shane 2011).

  Sentence: Twenty months in prison
- *Stephen Jin-Woo Kim (2014)*. U.S. State Department advisor convicted of leaking to Fox News, information about North Korea's plans to test a nuclear bomb.

  Sentence: Thirteen months.
- *Jeffrey Sterling (2015)*. Convicted of sharing classified secrets with *New York Times* reporter James Risen. Sterling provided information to Risen that appeared in Risen's *State of War* (2006) in a chapter about the CIA's Operation Merlin, which in 2000 provided Iran with flawed design information for a nuclear weapon component.

  Sentence: Forty-two months.
- *John Kiriakou (2013)*. Convicted of revealing the CIA's secret interrogation program to journalists.

  Sentence: Thirty months.
- *Edward Snowden (pending)*. Revealed secret allowing wholesale, covert surveillance of innocent people by the NSA.

  Sentence: Possible long prison term.

The espionage cases, especially the U.S. government employee whistleblowing/leaks cases, have drawn lots of (probably disproportionate) attention in the national press and in the world of blogs and tweets (and, yes, even in the book you're reading). Notice that we've covered 100 percent of the U.S. government's leak cases. Now, let's turn to the specific antiterrorist crimes.

ANTITERRORIST CRIMES

LO4

"Congress has given prosecutors a formidable arsenal of criminal statutes to deploy in criminal prosecutions" (Zabel and Benjamin 2009, 13). They include the specific terrorism crimes in the U.S. Code in Chapter 113B, §§ 2331–2339 (see Criminal Law in Focus "Selected Provisions and Definitions of Terrorism in the United States Code"), which we'll discuss, as well as the traditional crimes of murder (see Chapter 9), financial fraud (see Chapter 11), false statements, banned firearms training and possession (see Chapter 3), and general conspiracy (see Chapter 8).

Before we get to specific crimes, let's establish what we mean by terrorism in this book: the use of violence or intimidation to achieve political or ideological aims. The U.S. Code (Terrorism Act 2012) breaks down terrorism into international terrorism crimes and domestic terrorism crimes (Table 13.1).

terrorism the use of violence or intimidation in the pursuit of political aims

The specific antiterrorist crimes are included in U.S. Code, Chapter 113B, Terrorism (Title 18, Part I), under the sections frequently referred to as the USA PATRIOT Act (2001), an acronym for the Uniting and Strengthening America by Providing Appropriate Tools Required to Intercept and Obstruct Terrorism Act.

LO4

USA PATRIOT Act passed by Congress after the September 11, 2001, attacks, creating some new (and enhancing the penalties for existing) crimes of domestic and international terrorism

These sections include the following crimes:

1. Use of certain weapons of mass destruction (§ 2332a)
2. Acts of terrorism transcending national boundaries (§ 2332b)
3. Harboring or concealing terrorists (§ 2339)
4. Providing material support or resources to terrorists (§ 2339A)
5. Providing material support or resources to designated foreign terrorist organizations (§ 2339B)
6. Providing financial support for terrorism (§2339C)
7. Receiving training from a foreign terrorist organization (§2339D)

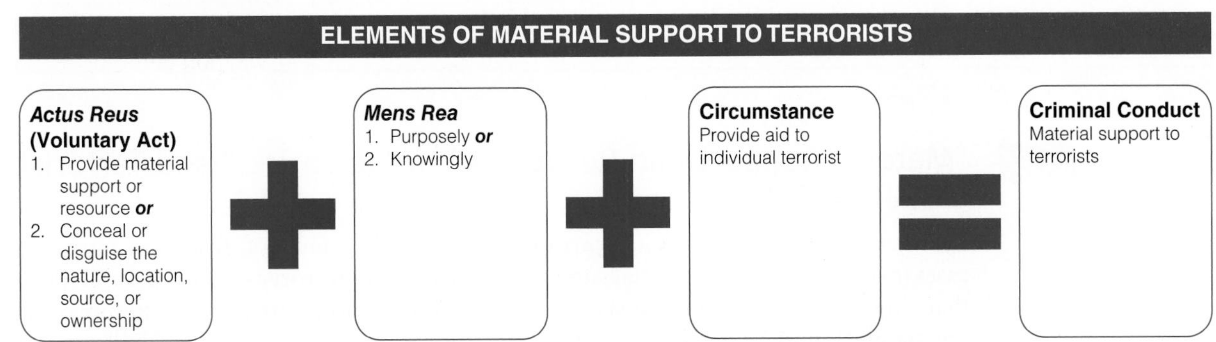

ELEMENTS OF MATERIAL SUPPORT TO TERRORIST ORGANIZATIONS

***Actus Reus* (Voluntary Act)**
1. Provide support or resources ***or***
2. Attempt to provide support or resources ***or***
3. Conspire to provide support or resources

Mens Rea
Knowingly commit *Actus Reus*

Circumstance
Designated foreign terrorist organization

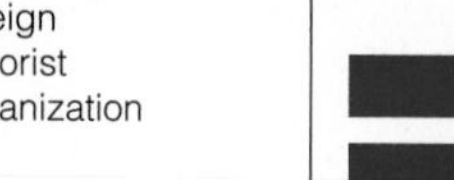

Criminal Conduct
Material support to terrorist organizations

CRIMINAL LAW IN FOCUS

Selected Provisions and Definitions of Terrorism in the United States Code

§ 2331. Definitions

As used in this chapter—

(1) the term "international terrorism" means activities that—

(A) involve violent acts or acts dangerous to human life that are a violation of the criminal laws of the United States or of any State, or that would be a criminal violation if committed within the jurisdiction of the United States or of any State;

(B) appear to be intended—

(i) to intimidate or coerce a civilian population;

(ii) to influence the policy of a government by intimidation or coercion; or

(iii) to affect the conduct of a government by mass destruction, assassination, or kidnapping; and

(C) occur primarily outside the territorial jurisdiction of the United States, or transcend national boundaries in terms of the means by which they are accomplished, the persons they appear intended to intimidate or coerce, or the locale in which their perpetrators operate or seek asylum;

(2) the term "domestic terrorism" means activities that—

(A) involve acts dangerous to human life that are a violation of the criminal laws of the United States or of any State;

(B) appear to be intended—

(i) to intimidate or coerce a civilian population;

(ii) to influence the policy of a government by intimidation or coercion; or

(iii) to affect the conduct of a government by mass destruction, assassination, or kidnapping; and

(C) occur primarily within the territorial jurisdiction of the United States.

LO5 "Material Support and Resources" to "Terrorists" and Terrorist Organizations

There's wide agreement (but a surprising lack of precise numbers) that most terrorism cases involve providing "material support" to terrorists or terrorist organizations. Notice that although they're almost always called "material support" offenses, the statute reads "material support or resources." A number of lower courts have decided challenges to the constitutionality of the "material support" sections—namely, the First Amendment rights of free speech and assembly and the Fifth and Fourteenth Amendments' denial of due process (vagueness). (See Chapter 2 for discussion of the application of these constitutional limits on criminal law generally.) They've reached conflicting results.

"material support" offenses the federal crime of providing "training," "expert advice or assistance," "service," and "personnel to terrorists or terrorist organizations

U.S. Criminal Code "Material Support and Resources" Provisions

U.S. Code (§ 2339A)

(a) Offense.—Whoever provides material support or resources or conceals or disguises the nature, location, source, or ownership of material support or resources, knowing or intending that they are to be used in preparation for, or in carrying out, a violation of section [list of numerous other U.S. Code violations] or in carrying out, the concealment of an escape from the commission of any such violation, or attempts or conspires to do such an act, shall be fined under this title, imprisoned not more than 15 years, or both, and, if the death of any person results, shall be imprisoned for any term of years or for life. A violation of this section may be prosecuted in any Federal judicial district in which the underlying offense was committed, or in any other Federal judicial district as provided by law.

(b) Definitions.—As used in this section—

(1) the term "material support or resources" means any property, tangible or intangible, or service, including currency or monetary instruments or financial securities, financial services, lodging, training, expert advice or assistance, safehouses, false documentation or identification, communications equipment, facilities, weapons, lethal substances, explosives, personnel (1 or more individuals who may be or include oneself), and transportation, except medicine or religious materials;

(2) the term "training" means instruction or teaching designed to impart a specific skill, as opposed to general knowledge; and

(3) the term "expert advice or assistance" means advice or assistance derived from scientific, technical or other specialized knowledge.

(§ 2339B)

(a) Prohibited Activities.—

(1) Unlawful conduct.—Whoever knowingly provides material support or resources to a foreign terrorist organization, or attempts or conspires to do so, shall be fined under this title or imprisoned not more than 15 years, or both, and, if the death of any person results, shall be imprisoned for any term of years or for life. To violate this paragraph, a person must have knowledge that the organization is a designated terrorist organization, that the organization has engaged or engages in terrorist activity (as defined in section 212(a)(3)(B) of the Immigration and Nationality Act), or that the organization has engaged or engages in terrorism (as defined in section 140(d)(2) of the Foreign Relations Authorization Act, Fiscal Years 1988 and 1989).

(2) Financial institutions.—Except as authorized by the Secretary, any financial institution that becomes aware that it has possession of, or control over, any funds in which a foreign terrorist organization, or its agent, has an interest, shall—

(A) retain possession of, or maintain control over, such funds; and

(B) report to the Secretary the existence of such funds in accordance with regulations issued by the Secretary.

(b) Civil Penalty.—Any financial institution that knowingly fails to comply with subsection (a)(2) shall be subject to a civil penalty in an amount that is the greater of—

(A) $50,000 per violation; or

(continues)

(continues)

(B) twice the amount of which the financial institution was required under subsection (a)(2) to retain possession or control.

(c) Injunction.—Whenever it appears to the Secretary or the Attorney General that any person is engaged in, or is about to engage in, any act that constitutes, or would constitute, a violation of this section, the Attorney General may initiate civil action in a district court of the United States to enjoin such violation.

HOLDER V. HUMANITARIAN LAW PROJECT (2010)

Then, in 2010, the U.S. Supreme Court decided that "as applied to the facts of the case" in *Holder v. Humanitarian Law Project* that the "material support or resources" for terrorist organization was neither constitutionally vague nor did it violate First Amendment speech and assembly rights.

The story of the case centers on two foreign dissident groups, and their supporters in the United States (the plaintiffs in the case). The dissidents are the Kurdistan Workers' Party (also known as the Partiya Karkeran Kurdistan, or PKK) and the Liberation Tigers of Tamil Eelam (LTTE). Founded in 1974, PKK aimed to establish an independent Kurdish state in southeastern Turkey. Founded in 1976, LTTE aimed to create an independent Tamil state in Sri Lanka. The District Court in this action found that both PKK and the LTTE engage in political and humanitarian activities. However, both groups are on the U.S. list of terrorist organizations, and the Government presented evidence that both groups have "also committed numerous terrorist attacks, some of which have harmed American citizens."

The plaintiffs are the groups' supporters, namely the Humanitarian Law Project (HLP) (a human rights organization with consultative status to the United Nations); Ralph Fertig (HLP's president, and a retired administrative law judge); Nagalingam Jeyalingam (a Tamil physician, born in Sri Lanka and a naturalized U.S. citizen); and five nonprofit groups "dedicated to the interests of persons of Tamil descent."

- The plaintiffs argued that the First Amendment protects the following activities are protected:Training PKK members on how to use humanitarian and international law to peacefully resolve disputes;
- Political advocacy on behalf of Kurds who live in Turkey;
- Teaching PKK members how to petition various representative bodies such as the United Nations for relief;
- Political advocacy on behalf of Tamils who live in Sri Lanka.

The U.S. Supreme Court (6–3) held that the material support and resources provision is constitutional *but* only as applied to the particular forms of support in the bulleted list. First, according to Chief Justice Roberts writing for the majority, as applied to this case, the statute is not vague. "Training," "expert advice or assistance," "service," and "personnel" aren't like "annoying" and "indecent" that the Court has struck down because they're too vague. Maybe the statute won't be clear in every case, but it's clear enough regarding these plaintiffs in this case.

Justice Stephen G. Breyer, joined by Justices Ruth Bader Ginsburg and Sonia Sotomayor, disagreed. He agreed that the statute was not unconstitutionally vague. But, he disagreed that the Constitution permits the government to prosecute the plaintiffs criminally for engaging in coordinated teaching and advocacy furthering the designated organizations' lawful political objectives. He reasoned that the government had not met its burden to show that the speech prohibited by the statute served a compelling governmental interest.

SOCIAL MEDIA AND "MATERIAL SUPPORT AND RESOURCES"

> Alex, a 23-year-old Sunday school teacher and babysitter, was trembling with excitement the day she told her Twitter followers that she had converted to Islam. For months, she had been growing closer to a new group of friends online—the most attentive she had ever had—who were teaching her what it meant to be a Muslim. Increasingly, they were telling her about the Islamic State and how the group was building a homeland in Syria and Iraq where the holy could live according to God's law. One in particular, Faisal, had become her nearly constant companion, spending hours each day with her on Twitter, Skype, and email, painstakingly guiding her through the fundamentals of the faith. But, when she told him that she had found a mosque just five miles from the home she shared with her grandparents in rural Washington state, he suddenly became cold. (Callimachi 2015)

Alex's experience highlights how social media has blurred even further the definition of "material support" in *Holder v. Humanitarian Law Project*. You should note that social media activity "has become an increasingly prominent consideration for law enforcement." (Hong 2015) Our next case excerpt, *U.S. v. Asher Abid Khan*, a twenty-year-old man indicted for "conspiracy to provide material support to the Islamic State of Iraq and the Levant (ISIL)".[1] The evidence is largely obtained from a search of Khan's friend S.R.G.'s Facebook account. The S.R.G. Facebook account contained several pictures depicting S.R.G. dressed in camouflage sitting in front of and handling what appeared to be AK-47-style rifles. It also contained communications between S.R.G., Khan, and others wherein S.R.G. discusses his travel planning to Syria, his joining ISIL, and his desire to recruit others to join ISIL. Keep in mind that this is not a typical case excerpt because the social media cases material support cases related to ISIS and ISIL are all in their early stages. So, what you're about to read is based on the affidavit accompanying the complaint, and the indictment in the case.

[1] On August 29, 2014, a United States magistrate judge in the Southern District of Texas issued a search and seizure warrant authorizing a search of S.R.G.'s Facebook account.

CASE

U.S. v. Asher Abid Khan *was charged with conspiracy to provide material support to Islamic State of Iraq and Levant (ISIL).*

U.S. v. Asher Abid Khan

2014

I make this affidavit in support of an application for a complaint and arrest warrant for Asher Abid Khan ("Khan"), a 20-year old Houston area resident, who conspired to provide himself and his friend, S.R.G. ("S.R.G."), as fighters for a designated foreign terrorist organization, namely the Islamic State in the Levant ("ISIL"), with known aliases: Islamic State of Iraq and al-Sham, the Islamic State of lraq and Syria, ad-Dawla al-Islamiyya fial-'lraq wa-sh-Sham, Daesh, and Dawla al Islamiya. Based on my training and experience, and the facts as set forth in this affidavit, there is probable cause to believe that Khan committed a violation of 18 U.S.C. § 2339B (Conspiracy to

(continues)

(continued)

Provide Material Support and Resources to a Foreign Terrorist Organization).

On October 15, 2004, the United States Secretary of State designated Al-Qa'ida in Iraq ("AQI") as a Foreign Terrorist Organization ("FTO"). On May 15, 2014, the Secretary of State amended the designation of AQI as a FTO to add the alias Islamic State of Iraq and the Levant ("ISIL") as its primary name. The Secretary also added the following aliases to the ISIL listing: the Islamic State of Iraq and al-Sham ("ISIS"), the Islamic State of Iraq and Syria ("ISIS"), ad-Dawla al-Islamiyya fl al-'lraq wa-sh-Sham, Daesh, Dawla al Islamiya, and A1-Furqan Establishment for Media Production. Although the group has never called itself "Al-Qaeda in Iraq," this name has frequently been used to describe it through its history. In an audio recording publicly released on June 29, 2014, ISIL announced a formal change of ISIL's name to Islamic State ("IS"). To date, ISIL remains a designated FTO.

FACTS

This is an investigation of two Texas-based friends, S.R.G. and Khan, both of whom attempted to travel to Syria to join ISIL. S.R.G. eventually made it to Syria and ISIL with the assistance of Khan, and an Unnamed Co-Conspirator ("CC-1"), a Turkish-based foreign terrorist fighter facilitator discovered initially by Khan, and others. And, while Khan made it to Turkey in the same quest, he decided to immediately return home to Texas because of information he received from his family regarding his mother's health. S.R.G. and Khan's ISIL-related plans and actions, CC-1's involvement, and the knowledge of S.R.G. and Khan's friends and associates are captured in their electronic communications with each other, including on social media platforms like Facebook.

THE CONSPIRACY AS TOLD THROUGH FACEBOOK MESSAGES

In or about October 2014, the FBI became aware of Khan based on a search of S.R.G.'s Facebook account.[2] The S.R.G. Facebook account contained several pictures depicting S.R.G. dressed in camouflage sitting in front of and handling what appeared to be AK-47-style rifles. It also contained communications between S.R.G., Khan, and others wherein S.R.G. discusses his travel planning to Syria, his joining ISIL, and his desire to recruit others to join ISIL.

Although S.R.G. made it to Syria and fought with ISIL, Khan, a United States citizen, was tricked into returning home to Texas after he reached Turkey, and he did not continue to Syria.[3] Khan, however, put S.R.G. into direct contact with CC-1, so S.R.G. could accomplish his goal of joining ISIL and engaging in violent jihad in Syria. Khan currently resides in Spring, Texas, with his family.

CC-1, a 24-year-old foreign national believed to be currently residing in Turkey, travels between Syria and Turkey on a regular basis. He also used Facebook on a regular basis, creating at least four known accounts. One of those accounts communicated extensively with Khan and S.R.G. about ISIL. This affidavit sets forth a series of Facebook messages between Khan and S.R.G.; Khan and CC-1; CC-1 and S.R.G.; and Khan and his Houston area-based associates occurring primarily from January 2014 through February 2014. The messages reveal Khan's and S.R.G.'s plans to join and provide material support to ISIL and their execution of those plans. The messages also reveal CC-1's role as a foreign terrorist fighter facilitator. Finally, the messages show how Khan confided in others about his plans, and shed light on his views as late as September 2014.

JANUARY 2014—PLANNING

While living in Australia with relatives, where Khan had resided since October 2013,[4] Khan used his Facebook account to send a "Friend Request" to S.R.G.'s Facebook account. S.R.G. accepted the request on or about January 6, 2014. That same day, Khan had a conversation with S.R.G. in which Khan informed S.R.G. that: (1) he had moved to Australia; and, (2) he was "planing [sic] to go to Iraq soon to join the Islamic state of Iraq and sham. In shaa Allah." ("God willing" in Arabic) Khan continued their Facebook conversation by inviting S.R.G. to join him and advised: "I'll send you a couple of lectures tomorrow as well to get you familiar with fighting in Islam and all that." After

[2] On August 29, 2014, a United States magistrate judge in the Southern District of Texas issued a search and seizure warrant authorizing a search of S.R.G.'s Facebook account.

[3] In order to convince Khan to return home, concerned family members falsely told him that his mother was hospitalized.

[4] Khan departed the United States on October 18, 2013, from Houston, Texas to Dubai International Airport, and arrived in Australia on October 19, 2013.

S.R.G. agreed to join Khan, Khan stated: "Love for shahada (the Islamic declaration of faith) is so strong. Okay well do some research on ISIS (islamic state of Iraq and sham)."

On or about January 10, 2014, Khan and S.R.G. discussed, among other things, travel logistics and the impact that leaving would have on family. The next day, on or about January 11, 2014, Khan reached out, apparently for the first time, to CC-1. After explaining he was in Sydney, Australia, he stated "I wana join ISIS can you help?"

Between January 11, 2014, and January 13, 2014, Khan and S.R.G. continued to discuss travel logistics and whether they should travel to Iraq or Syria. Khan weighed the pros and cons of each destination, and indicated that traveling to Syria required that they first go to Turkey and cross the border, which could be dangerous, whereas travel to Iraq would require that they "make our way ourselves to the ISIS HQ." Khan's desire to fight is made clear by his subsequent statement, "and then after taking training with them we can go on the front lines in damascas." Khan also indicated that he was trying to get everything done in order to travel by February 2014.

On or about January 13, 2014, Khan contacted CC-1 via Facebook and gave him more background about who he (Khan) is and why he was seeking to join ISIL. He explained how he grew up in the "west" and recently came to Australia because he didn't like living in the west anymore, and that he is "sad" because he sits in Australia "comfortably while [his] brothers are in so much hardship." As a result, he wanted to help his "brothers and sister" to seek his "maker's mercy." In response, CC-1 stated that he could help Khan once he [Khan] reached Turkey. Khan replied that he will "make plans for turkey, then contact you."

On or about January 19, 2014, Khan forwarded to S.R.G. multiple screen shots of what purported to be messages between Khan and an unidentified subject in which Khan appeared to be asking for help from the individual to meet up with ISIL in Fallujah. The following statements were included in the exchange:

KHAN: I saw the picture of sharia court established in Falluja. So if i went to Baghdad and went to Falluja from there, could I meet up with ISIS?

USER 2: bro are you really serious abt this? sorry to ask you again ... as now there are fitna there ... and many muhajireen have been martyred by the secular rebels.[5]

KHAN: All I know is that I want to fight fisabillah ["for the sake of Allah"].... Who knows how long this fitna [division between brothers that ultimately leads to fighting] will last? What if I miss my chance? I don't want to fight for war booty or for nationalism. I want to just rise the laws of Allah and be a shaheed [to die a martyr] in his cause. I don't want to be fighting with the wrong group, and so far all I see is ISIS fighting for Khilafah [a Muslim state].

KHAN: Wallahi ["I swear to Allah"] if I spoke Arabic, I'd be there already.

USER 2: ok give me time ... and if i dont come back to you keep reminding me - not every day but once a week will do

On or about January 16, 2014, the U.S. State Department issued passport number 512162275 to Khan. And, on January 29, 2014, Khan informed S.R.G., "My new passport has arrived."

2. FEBRUARY 2014—PLANNING CONTINUED, TRAVEL & CC-1'S FACILITATION OF S.R.G.'S TRAVEL TO SYRIA

On or about February 4, 2014, Khan contacted CC-1 via Facebook and engaged in a lengthy conversation. After confirming that CC-1 would be able to help Khan "on arrival," the two discussed where they should meet in Turkey, including the most economical way (both price and route) to get to Turkey. CC-1 told Khan that "there is a bus from Istanbul to Adana and then Antakya," and that he (CC-1) will come to Khan when Khan is in Antakya. Antakya is a city in Southern Turkey close to Turkey's border with Syria.

On or about February 11, 2014, Khan and S.R.G. discussed their travel plans over Facebook. Khan stated, "Salam akhi! ["Peace my brother"] Ok so far our plan is, INSA ["God willing"], we go to Istanbul, catch a bus (around 15 hours) to Adana and then to Antakya." Khan then continued by offering to pay for, and print out, a visa for S.R.G. S.R.G.

[5] The Arabic term "fitna" is likely a reference to a division between brothers that ultimately leads to fighting. And the Arabic term "Muhajireen" means immigrants and is likely a reference to foreign fighters.

(continues)

(continued)

ultimately refused Khan's offer, and likely obtained a visa on his own.

On or about February 13, 2014, Khan provided S.R.G. detailed instructions over Facebook on how to purchase the appropriate "one way" United Airlines ticket to travel from "houston intercontinental" to "Istanbul-Ataturk" on "the 24th of February." On that same day, Khan contacted CC-1 via Facebook and sought advice about whether he should trim his beard. The next day CC-1 responded that Khan should definitely trim his beard, and CC-1 suggested how short Khan should trim it. Khan then asked how long it would take for CC-1 to reach him in Antakya, and CC-1 replied "not long" because he was already in Antakya.

On or about February 15, 2014, Khan and S.R.G. discussed the need to have a plausible cover for their travel to Turkey. Khan mentioned how they could have problems in the "turkey airport when they ask us why we are here and what not in which case we need to state a whole tourist plan."

Three days later, on or about February 18, 2014, Khan told CC-1 that he "will be traveling in a couple days," and then asked how he can reach CC-1 once he arrived in Turkey, and if there was a number he could call to reach CC-1. CC-1 instructed Khan to "purchase a Turkcell sim card and cheap mobile phone" when he reached Istanbul. CC-1 then provided a telephone number per Khan's request.

On or about February 22, 2014, Khan had a conversation with S.R.G. in which Khan asked S.R.G.: "Have you reached Houston safely? And did you get your visa?" Khan also reminded S.R.G. to, "make sure you print your ticket." and "forward me your ticket as well. Just so I know your flight numbers." S.R.G. indicated that he was nervous stating: "If I could I would destroy all the butterfly's in my stomach," And, Khan reminded S.R.G. of their cover story stating: "LOL, bro chill and have fun. This is an experience so enjoy it and learn from it. You're a tourist and tourist are never nervous. They are curious." S.R.G. also asked Khan "to check his Facebook often."

According to U.S. Customs and Border Protection ("CBP"), S.R.G. traveled on February 23, 2014, from George Bush International Airport in Houston, Texas to London Heathrow. On February 24, 2014, Khan left Australia for Turkey on a Malaysia Airlines flight.

On or about February 24, 2014, Khan had the following exchange with S.R.G. in which S.R.G. explained to Khan: "I'm here in London now," and "I gotta find out if my bag went str8 to turkey." Khan, while in Malaysia, responded by telling S.R.G., "My parents are tippin bro. I hers my moms in the hospital." After a 166-second telephone call between the two men, S.R.G. wrote and complained to Khan: "Dude you can't pull shit like that, I didn't come with all that much cash, I have no connections I've got no clue wtf." Then, after S.R.G. pleaded with Khan to not leave him stranded, Khan stated, "I'm coming to turkey don't worry iA. ["Insha Alla", or "God Willing"] He also gave S.R.G. some advice: "When you get to turkey, they might ask if you have enough money back from turkey for like a return ticket. Tell them your friend will be paying or something. Just make an excuse that you have the money to go back. If you have your card, show them it and say you have like 2 grand in there."

S.R.G. flew from London to Turkey on or about February 24, 2014, and Khan flew from Malaysia to Turkey on February 24, 2014. Khan then flew to the United States on February 25, 2014.

On or about February 26, 2014, S.R.G. informed Khan, who, by this time, had returned to Houston, that the contact number for "Mohammad" [CC-1] did not work. In response, Khan explained to S.R.G., "I messaged him telling him about you." Khan then sent S.R.G. what appeared to be a copy of the message he [Khan] sent to "Mohammad" (CC-1):

> Asalam o alaikum bro. Came all the way to Istanbul and my family deceived me by saying my mom was in the ICU so I rushed back. My friend however is decided to carry on without me and is now in Antakya, I have him your number and he treys calling but he said it didn't work. ... Can you please talk to him? I think he messaged you on fb. His name is Abdullah Ali, he is a Mexican convert.

On or about February 26, 2014, S.R.G. and CC-1 then had the following conversation, where CC-1 instructed S.R.G. on which hotel to go to, where to meet him, and how to recognize him:

S.R.G: Please pick me up I'm in the bus station a Antakya
Call me
5078754164
I tried calling your number but I think I'm missing some thing There's guys asking me if I Im tryna go to syria

They backed down a Lil bit but I can tell there still talking about me

CC-1: Assalaam aleikum bro, go to a hotel, hotel Antakya is preferred

S.R.G.: Ok
Will do,
I'll just ask them for a taxi?

CC-1: Yep

S.R.G: Ok dose that hotel have WiFi?

CC-1: Yes it most probably should

S.R.G.: I will go to hotel antakya

CC-1: I'll be there in a few hours, don't talk to anyone about Syria
If anyone brings it up reject it like it's a foolish thing to ask you

S.R.G: Yep Ok. ia

CC-1: Let me know when u are in the hotel

S.R.G: I'm at the hotel, take your time

CC-1: ok sweet

S.R.G: :)

CC-1: Akhi I'm coming shortly Please pick up your phone

S.R.G.: Hey
My bad my done isn't working

S.R.G: I'm on my tablet it died but I'm charging it now, should I check out and walk with my language
And walk towards you?

CC-1: No stay for now. When does your check in expire

S.R.G.: Tmrw 12 pm

CC-1: Ok akhi come to the Palladium mall, it is on the opposite side of the river
You cross the river and go left, it is a big whiteish building maybe 1 km away
Don't check out

S.R.G.: What do I take to the mall?
All my baggage?

CC-1: Nothing

S.R.G.: OK

CC-1: We are just meeting up Akhi

S.R.G.: Ok

CC-1: Once you get there go to the food court on the top level

S.R.G.: Ok I am wearing whit glasses on top of my black hat, blue sweater white Jordan's and black pant, and a very shirt under my sweater

CC1: You got your phone with you?

S.R.G. No, did it ring when you called it?

CC-1: Yep

S.R.G.: Ok I'll take it with me then, Just give me a few min

CC-1: I'll be in front of a food shop called pidem

S.R.G.: Ok

The next day, on or about February 27, 2014, S.R.G. and CC-1 had the following conversation:

S.R.G. Did you get home safely last night?

CC-1: Yes Alhamdullilah. I'll be at yours soon. I just need to have breakfast and do one little thing and I'll be at yours.
Maybe at around 11am max

S.R.G.: Ok
I will be ready IA
Ghjbfssf [sic]
Assalamwalikum

On that same day, S.R.G. confirmed to Khan that he had "been delivered :)," that he was still with "Mohammad" (CC-1). In response, Khan asked, "And are you with dawla. Like ISIS?" S.R.G. replied, "No not yet." Khan also offered: "Aye if you ever need money, ask me!" And, S.R.G. stated that he feels like he "belongs" and that his "entire life was ment [sic] for this."

3. MARCH TO AUGUST 2014–S.R.G. FINDS HIS WAY TO ISIL

A little over a month later, on or about March 29, 2014, S.R.G. explained to Khan that "Dawla" [ISIL] [sic] "left," that he is in a place akin to "boot" [likely a reference to boot camp], and that he had an "ak" [likely a reference to an AK-47 assault rifle] that he had shot it and had even fought a "lil bit." Khan wrapped up this conversation with the following message:

> I'm happy for you and you are always in my prayer. I don't want you getting in trouble so im a wrap this up real quick. Just a few things! Be careful who you kill, don't neglect salah, recite qur'an and make tones of dua for guidance. And then trust in Allah. Don't curse ppl you don't know stuff about. And just take care, always.

On or about April 11, 2014, S.R.G. informed Khan he was not with "Dwl" [ISIL?] but he, instead, had been training with a group that just formed up. S.R.G. stated that when his training was over, he

(continues)

(continued)

would "try to go with Dwl." S.R.G. also sent a picture of what appeared to be an AK-47 and stated, "That's my baby," and that "You can have one too if you'd like."

Between on or about July 1, 2014, and July 15, 2014, Khan and S.R.G. engaged in several conversations over Facebook. During one of those conversations, Khan emphasized that S.R.G. should try getting to "dawla." During another one of those conversations, S.R.G. sent Khan a photograph of himself holding an AK-47 and a Qur'an, and confirmed that the photograph was taken recently. Khan then inquired: "How's the land of sham [Syria] bro? The land of the sahabi?" ["followers of Islam"] And, S.R.G. replied: "Wallah ["I swear to Allah"] its amazing," and "I wish you where [sic] here."

Khan continued by re-offering S.R.G. money and food. And, in response, S.R.G. replied that he had everything he needed. Khan concluded by telling S.R.G. that everyone from the masjid missed him, but that "they're all afraid to message you though cuz they think they might get arrested lol."

On or about August 11, 2014, S.R.G. informed Khan that he was with "ISIS" and he "wanted to be with them in the first place, "to which Khan responded by instructing S.R.G. to "make sure they [presumably S.R.G. and his fellow fighters] are doing everything according to Islam you know, not killing innocent ppl and all that."

Besides S.R.G. and CC-1, Khan also discussed his plans with others, including "Individual 1." Individual 1 is a female who lives in Spring, Texas. Khan has known Individual 1 since at least his freshman year of high school, and Khan's Facebook account shows that Khan and Individual 1 had many long and detailed conversations over Facebook. Those Facebook messages make clear that Individual 1 was not supportive of Khan's decision to travel to Syria, but they also make clear that Khan had a special relationship with Individual 1 such that he confided in her more so than he did in others.

KHAN DISCUSSES HIS PLANS TO DIE SHAHEED

Because of that special relationship, and prior to his and S.R.G.'s departures, Khan revealed to Individual 1 his thoughts on the Islamic State and becoming a shaheed (dying a martyr), his and S.R.G.'s plans to travel to Syria to help establish the Islamic State, and the use of an unidentified contact to help them in their quest.

These disclosures by Khan are found in his Facebook communications with "Individual 1." In addition, those communications also revealed who was aware of Khan's plans or parts of his plans.

A review of Facebook records associated with Khan's account revealed that, on or about January 24, 2014, Individual 1 and Khan engaged in a lengthy conversation related to Khan's intent to travel to Iraq and Syria to help establish an Islamic State, revive the Caliphate, and die a shaheed. Specifically, Khan indicated that he intended to go to "Iraq in shaa Allah, maybe Syria," to "study sharia" in Iraq and "help the refugees in Syria." Khan stated that he probably would not come back to the United States or Australia because he would "be acting against their troops and agenda."

In response, Individual 1 questioned whether Khan's parents knew of Khan's plan, and Individual 1 noted that Khan was the one that Khan's parents "used to depend on" and that he [Khan] did not think "they'd be okay with it." Khan replied that he felt compelled to go because his "brothers and sisters" are being "raped, tortured and killed." Khan also indicated that he found someone to meet him in Iraq and that he wants to "help establish an Islamic state, and iA ("Insha Allah," "God Willing") revive the Khilafah :)."

Individual 1 responded by questioning Khan's intent, asking whether "this" was something Khan intended to do for the rest of his life and whether he would eventually "settle down and live a normal life."

Individual 1 then continued by suggesting that Khan "should take some time to like calm down and think this whole thing through," that "maybe acting on impulse isn't such a good idea," and "maybe you should like talk to people at your masjid or your aunt and uncle or something before you do anything drastic." Individual 1 also suggested that Khan "wait a couple of years and see if [his] perspective changes," and "see if [he] maybe could find a better way to help out."

Later, after Individual 1 continued to implore Khan to reconsider his plans, Khan indicated that he was going to "be straight forward, I wana die as a Shaheed," and that he was "looking forward to dying in Allah's cause and meeting Allah."

Individual 1 responded by continuing to attempt to convince Khan that his plans were ill conceived. Individual 1 argued that: "I just think you're being impulsive or maybe you're not thinking this whole thing through. I can understand why you want to go help out and everything, but like I said there are other methods that may be equally beneficial."

Individual 1 also threatened to tell Khan's family about Khan's plans. Ultimately, however, Individual 1 agreed not to tell Khan's family and agreed to talk about "normal stuff" moving forward.

On or about January 31, 2014, Khan sent a message to Individual 1 indicating that he had "honestly done what [he] could," that his 'job is to remind ... Not force ... IA a Shaheed is granted 70 intersessions [a prayer that pleads with God for your needs and the needs of others]. And that he is "kinda doing this for them too ..."

On or about February 2, 2014, in a discussion initiated by Khan where he asked Individual 1 "what like do you love doing that you are good at??" Khan, when asked the same question by Individual l, answered his own question with "haha mines has to do with the Islamic state ... so first that needs to be established but IA I can work to progress it too lol."

On or about February 14, 2014, Khan and Individual 1 had the following conversation about a YouTube video:

KHAN:	https://m.youtube.com/watch?v=oXKSnVzcy2E (Tribute to Sheikh Anwar Al –Awlaki) I love him" May Allah give him the highest place in jannah ("heaven") 18
Individual 1:	Ameen I've never heard any of his lectures
KHAN:	He was a man, killed for his knowledge. Literally He has THE BEST LECTURES An American born, perfect English like us I wish I could inject everything I know about him into you. And creat the same love I have for him in you. And every other Muslim
Individual 1:	Aww I'll watch one his lectures soon iA
KHAN:	I'll send you a great one. He gives you a tour of jannah, way better than I did.
Individual 1:	Alright (:

On that same day, after Khan pleaded with Individual 1 to understand his "feelings" because she was the "one that always did," Khan again reaffirms his desire to become a "shaheed."

B. KHAN'S DISCUSSIONS WITH INDIVIDUAL 1 RE: TURKEY, S.R.G., AND A CONTACT IN TURKEY

On or about January 31, 2014, Khan asked Individual 1 about S.R.G. when he asked if she knows "Abdullah Ali? A Mexican convert from our masjid?" Individual 1 replied that "I've heard of him, I've never met him." A little over two weeks later, however, it's clear that she knew Abdullah (i.e., S.R.G.) was traveling with Khan. On or about February 17, 2014, Khan mentioned that he (Abdullah/S.R.G.) is "getting his ticket," an apparent reference to his impending purchase of a ticket to Turkey. He then told Individual l that "all my stuff is going smoothly but Abdullah's card isn't working right now." A few minutes later, he explained that he wasn't buying the ticket yet because he is waiting for Abdullah, to which Individual 1 asked "what if abdullah decides not to go." And after Khan bought his ticket later that day, he asked Individual 1 for "instant prayers ... for me and abdullah."

On or about February 17, 2014, after Khan bought his ticket to Turkey, Individual l understood that Khan would be working with others once he arrived in Turkey. She asked Khan how he could trust the people picking him up, to which Khan responded "he seems legit lol."

Individual 1 was apparently not convinced, and stated "He seems legit?? What if it's a trap or something O.O."

Khan acknowledged there are many traps and then stated "i was referred to this guy by a brother over here ... and when i asked him directly he flipped out ... like i was suppose to ask him in code lol ... idk he seem legit ... iA."

Individual 1, still not convinced, told Khan that he should wait a while until he can confirm that the "guy is 100% legit," and after explaining that he would lose "lk" (apparently a reference to cancelling his trip to Turkey, Khan stated that "i trust Allah, that's enough for me :)"

On or about February 20, 2014, Khan sent a message to Individual 1 indicating that "after I leave for turkey iA, when ever I message you, I will start the message with 'Salamm' with 2 m's" and "if you get a message besides that, don't reply." Khan apparently wanted to institute a way for Individual l to recognize that it was only him, and not some

(continues)

(continued)

imposter, communicating with her after he reached Turkey.

On or about February 26, 2014, after Khan returned to the United States leaving S.R.G. in Turkey, Khan sent a message to Individual 1 indicating that "Abdullah found the guy," and that Individual 1 "should [k]eep him in your prayers."

CONCLUSION

Based on the foregoing, which I affirm is true and correct to the best of my knowledge and belief, I respectfully submit that probable cause exists to support a charge of 18 U.S.C. § 23398 (Conspiracy to Provide Material Support and Resources to a Foreign Terrorist Organization), and that the nature of this crime combined with other facts and circumstances.

QUESTIONS

1. Based on a review of the elements of conspiracy (Chapter 8, p. 299), has Khan committed conspiracy? Has S.R.G. (CC-1)? Has Individual 1? Back up your answer with details from the Facebook evidence.
2. Do you believe that Khan intended to provide material support to ISIL? Did S.R.G.? Did Individual 1? Back up your answer with details from the Facebook evidence.
3. Assuming Khan, S.R.G., and Individual 1 are guilty, what punishment would you impose? Under present law, the charges could result in 15 years imprisonment and a $250,000 fine. Is this too harsh? Too lenient? Just about right? Defend your answer.
4. How serious a threat to our national security, do you believe social networking like that in this case is? Explain your answer.

YOU *DECIDE*

Which should be banned as "material support and resources" to terrorists?

- Former President Jimmy Carter, while he monitored elections in Lebanon, met with leaders of all the parties, including designated terrorist organization Hezbollah, to advise them on fair election procedures.
- A reporter published an interview with a terrorist fighter.
- A social media platform included accounts claiming to be from the Somalian-designated terrorist group al Shabab.
- The *New York Times* and *Washington Post* published an op-ed from representatives of the designated terrorist organization.

Instructions

Read the following:

- David Cole, "The Roberts Court's Free Speech Problem," *The New York Review of Books Blog*, June 28, 2010, http://www.nybooks.com/blogs/nyrblog/2010/jun/28/roberts-courts-free-speech-problem/.
- Glenn Greenwald, "Can the U.S. Government close social media accounts?" *Salon*, December 20, 2011, http://www.salon.com/2011/12/20/the_u_s_government_targets_twitter_terrorism/.

Even if the incidents described in the links don't violate the First Amendment, or other provisions in the Constitution, what would be the ethical thing to do regarding their publication?

Summary

The revolutionaries who wrote the U.S. Constitution knew that the new government they were about to create couldn't survive without the active support of most of the people. The people's allegiance would be especially important to the nation's survival in the early years following the Revolution, a time of great threats from enemies inside (traitor, spies, and other disloyal individuals) and outside the new country. This need to balance individual freedom against national security is still reflected in modern law. **LO1**

Treason is the only crime defined in the U.S. Constitution and is the most serious of all crimes against the State. Treason is very difficult to prove, and throughout U.S. history, the government has prosecuted only a handful of people for treason. Furthermore, presidents have pardoned or at least mitigated death sentences of most of those few who have been found guilty. **LO2**

Other ancient crimes of disloyalty still exist today, specifically sedition, sabotage, and espionage. Sedition is the crime of advocating the violent overthrow of the government. Sabotage is the crime of damaging or destroying property for the purpose of hindering preparations for war and national defense during national emergences. Espionage is the crime of spying for the enemy. All of the definitions of these crimes have evolved to accommodate changes in society and technology. **LO3**

A number of sections of the U.S. Code make available crimes related to terrorists and terrorist organizations for prosecuting offenders. The most comprehensive law developed to fight terror is the USA PATRIOT Act, passed by Congress soon after the terrorist attacks on the United States on September 11, 2001. **LO4**

The most-argued issues in material support cases include: (1) Due process—"Is the term 'material support' void for vagueness?" and the (2) First Amendment—"Does providing material support violate the right to free speech and association?" We see in our ongoing current events the same struggle that the drafters of the Constitution witnessed and addressed: the "push-and-pull" between individual liberties versus the role of government to protect and preserve its people and the country in which they live. Balancing these conflicting values is further complicated by the widespread use of social media for both free speech and criminal purposes. **LO5**

Key Terms

treason, p. 520
adherence to the enemy, p. 521
treason *actus reus*, p. 522
treason *mens rea*, p. 522
proof of treason, p. 522
sedition, p. 523
seditious speech, p. 523
seditious libel, p. 523
seditious conspiracy, p. 523
sabotage, p. 524
espionage, p. 527
espionage during peace, p. 527
espionage during war, p. 527
terrorism, p. 531
USA PATRIOT Act, p. 531
"material support" offenses, p. 532

Glossary

abuse-of-trust crimes crimes growing out of opportunities to get someone else's property that was entrusted to the perpetrators because of their occupation, now known as white-collar crimes today

accessories after the fact persons who help after the crime is committed (harboring a fugitive)

accessories before the fact persons not present when the crimes are committed but who help before the crime is committed (for example, someone who provided a weapon used in a murder)

accessories participants after crimes are committed

accessory accessory after the fact; usually a misdemeanor

accessory liability liability that attaches for participation after crimes are committed (prosecution for a minor offense other than the crime itself)

accomplice *actus reus* defendant took "some positive act in aid of the commission of the offense"

accomplice liability liability that attaches for participation before and during a crime (prosecution for the crime itself)

accomplices participants before and during the commission of crimes

act reasonableness meaning "a finding that a reasonable person in the defendant's shoes would have responded as violently as the defendant did"

actual disorderly conduct breach-of-the-peace misdemeanor that includes fighting in public and making unreasonable noise

actual possession physical control of banned items on my person, for example, marijuana in my pocket ***actus reus*** the requirement that all crimes have to include a voluntary criminal act, which is the physical element of a crime and the first principle of criminal liability

adequate provocation the requirement that the provocation for killing in anger has to be something the law recognizes, the defendant himself had to be provoked, and that a reasonable person would have been provoked

adherence to the enemy the definition of treason under English common law, meaning breaking allegiance to your own country by forming an "attachment to the enemy"

administrative agencies appointed participants in creating criminal law that assist the U.S. Congress

administrative crimes violations of federal and state agency rules that make up a controversial but rapidly growing source of criminal law

affirmative defenses defendants have to "start matters off by putting in some evidence in support" of their defenses of justification and excuse

affirmative defenses defendants have to "start matters off by putting in some evidence in support" of their justification or excuse defenses

agency theory the idea that we're autonomous agents with the freedom to choose our actions and become accountable for someone else's actions when we voluntarily "join in and identify with those actions"

aggravated rape rape by strangers or individuals with weapons who physically injure their victims

American bystander rule there's no legal duty to rescue or summon help for someone who's in danger, even if the bystander risks nothing by helping

appellate courts in most states and the federal government, the two levels of appeals courts: an intermediate court of appeals and a supreme court

Apprendi rule other than the fact of prior conviction, any fact that increases the penalty for a crime beyond the prescribed statutory maximum must be submitted to a jury and proved beyond a reasonable doubt

arson damaging or destroying buildings by burning

arson *mens rea* requires a malicious and willful intent to burn or set fire to buildings in most statutes; in some jurisdictions, requires only the general intent to start a fire

asportation the act of carrying away or physically moving a victim of kidnapping

assault an attempt to commit battery or intentionally putting another in fear

"assumption of risk" approach to rape cases view of rape cases that holds the victim accountable for their manner of dress, sexual history, amount of resistance to the attack, and other behaviors deemed socially unacceptable

attempt *actus reus* taking some steps toward completing a crime

attempt *mens rea* the specific intent to commit a crime

attempted battery assault having the specific intent to commit battery and taking substantial steps toward carrying it out without actually completing the battery

attendant circumstances element a "circumstance" connected to an act, an intent, and/or a bad result

authorized consent the person consenting has the authority to give consent

automatism unconscious bodily movements

bad result crimes (result crimes) crimes that include five elements: (1) a voluntary act, (2) the mental element, (3) circumstantial elements, (4) causation, and (5) a criminal harm

barbaric punishments punishments considered no longer acceptable to civilized society

battered woman's syndrome (BWS) mental disorder that develops in victims of domestic violence as a result of serious, long-term abuse

battery unwanted and unjustified offensive touching

bifurcation procedure the requirement that the death penalty decision be made in two phases: a trial to determine guilt and a second separate proceeding, after a finding of guilt, to consider the aggravating factors for, and mitigating factors against, capital punishment

born-alive rule the rule that to be a person, and therefore a homicide victim, a baby had to be "born alive" and capable of breathing and maintaining a heartbeat on its own

breaking part of the *actus reus* of common law burglary, requiring an unlawful, frequently destructive, entry into someone else's building

broken-windows theory first espoused by James Q. Wilson and George L. Kelling, the theory that minor offenses or disorderly conduct can lead to a rise in serious crime

burden of persuasion defendants have to prove their justification or excuse defenses by a preponderance of the evidence

burden of production to make defendants responsible for presenting evidence in their own justification or excuse defense

burden of proof to have to prove beyond a reasonable doubt "every fact necessary to constitute the crime charged"

burglary breaking and entering a building or structure with intent to commit a crime inside the building

burning criminal act of setting a building on fire

capital cases death penalty cases in death penalty states and "mandatory life sentence without parole" cases in non–death penalty states

carnal knowledge vaginal sexual intercourse

case citation the numbers, letters, and punctuation that tell you where to locate the full case report; they follow the title of a case in the excerpts or in the bibliography at the end of the book

castle exception when attacked in your home, you have no duty to retreat and can use deadly force to fend off an unprovoked attack, but only if you reasonably believe the attack threatens death or serious bodily injury

causation holding an actor criminally accountable for the results of her conduct

chain conspiracies participants at one end of the chain may know nothing of those at the other end, but every participant handles the same commodity at different points, such as manufacture, distribution, and sale

choice-of-evils defense also called the general defense of necessity, it justifies the choice to commit a lesser crime to avoid the harm of a greater crime

civil commitment a noncriminal (civil) proceeding in which courts have the power to decide if defendants who were insane when they committed their crimes are still insane

civil gang injunctions (CGI) noncriminal lawsuits brought by cities seeking restraining orders to bar gang members from gang activities

classical deterrence theory rational human beings won't commit crimes if they know that the pain of punishment outweighs the pleasure gained from committing crimes

clear and present danger doctrine allows the government to punish words that "produce a clear and present danger of a serious substantive evil that rises far above public inconvenience, annoyance, or unrest"

codified written definitions of crimes and punishment enacted by legislatures and published

cohabitant exception in the jurisdictions that follow the retreat rule, people who live in the same home don't have to retreat

common law rape intentional, forced, nonconsensual, heterosexual vaginal penetration between a man and a woman not his wife

common law sodomy anal intercourse between two males

compensatory damages damages recovered by tort plaintiffs for their actual injuries

competency hearings special hearings to determine if defendants who have used the insanity excuse defense are still insane

complicity establishes when you can be criminally liable for someone else's conduct; applies criminal liability to accomplices and accessories

concurrence the principle of criminal liability that requires that a criminal intent has to trigger the criminal act

concurring opinion agrees with the conclusions of either the majority or the dissenting opinion but provides different reasons for reaching the conclusion

conditional threats threats that are not immediate but based upon the existence of certain conditions that don't presently exist

conduct crimes requiring a criminal act triggered by criminal intent

conspiracy *actus reus* consists of two parts: (1) an agreement to commit a crime and (2) an overt act in furtherance of the agreement

conspiracy the crime of agreeing with one or more people to commit a crime

conspiracy *mens rea* the mental element in conspiracy, frequently identified as specific intent by authorities, but it's not defined clearly in statutes and it's defined inconsistently by courts

constitutional democracy the majority can't make a crime out of conduct protected by the fundamental rights in the U.S. Constitution

constitutional right to privacy a right that bans "all governmental invasions of the sanctity of a man's home and the privacies of life"

constructive disorderly conduct conduct that "tends to provoke or excite others to break the peace"

constructive possession banned items not on my person but in places I control, for example, in my car or apartment

conversion wrongfully possessing or disposing of someone else's property as if it were yours ***corpus delicti*** Latin for "body of the crime"; it refers to the body of victims in homicides and to the elements of the crime in other crimes

corroboration requirement an element in rape that the prosecution had to prove rape by the testimony of witnesses other than the victim

court's holding the legal rule the court has decided to apply to the facts of the cases

court's reasoning the reasons the court gives to support its holding

crimes against public order formerly called "bad manners" crimes; today called "*quality of life*" crimes, they include public drinking, aggressive panhandling, harassment, graffiti and vandalism, and street prostitution, among others

criminal acts voluntary bodily movements

criminal attempts trying but failing to commit crimes

criminal conduct a criminal act triggered by criminal intent (*mens rea*)

criminal conspiracy making an agreement to commit a crime

criminal court opinions create criminal law by interpreting state and municipal criminal codes

criminal homicide all homicides that are neither justified nor excused

criminal homicide conduct that causes another person's death

criminal law enforcement agencies create criminal law through informal discretionary law making to decide how the criminal law process works on a day-to-day basis

criminal law imagination the contributions of law, history, philosophy, the social sciences, and sometimes biology to explain the moral desires we wish to impose on the world

criminal liability conduct that unjustifiably and inexcusably inflicts or threatens substantial harm to individual or public interests

criminal mischief *actus reus* in destruction or damage criminal mischief, the criminal act is burning, exploding, flooding, or committing some other dangerous act; in tampering, it's any act that threatens or endangers property; in deception or threat, it's causing harm through deception or threats

criminal mischief damaging or destroying personal property

criminal negligence manslaughter death caused by a person who is aware that her acts create a substantial and unjustifiable risk of death or serious bodily injury, but acts anyway

criminal objective of the conspiracy the object of conspiracy agreements has to be to commit crimes

criminal objective of the solicitation circumstance element that the objective of the solicitation is law breaking; the seriousness varies by jurisdiction from any violation to violent felony

criminal objective the criminal goal of an agreement to commit a crime

criminal omission the failure to act when there's a legal duty to act

criminal punishment penalties that meet four criteria: (1) inflict pain or other unpleasant consequences; (2) prescribe a punishment in the same law that defines the crime; (3) administered intentionally; (4) administered by the state

criminal sexual conduct statutes comprehensive statutes that replaced the single crime of rape with a series of graded offenses, eliminated the resistance and corroboration requirements, restricted the use of evidence regarding the victim's sexual history, and removed the marital rape exception

criminal solicitation trying to get someone else to commit a crime

criminal trespass the unwanted, unauthorized invasion of another person's property

cruel and unusual punishments "barbaric" punishments and punishments that are disproportionate to the crime committed

culpability only someone who intends to harm her victim deserves punishment; accidents don't qualify

culpability or blameworthiness the idea that it's fair and just to punish only people we can blame

cultural cognition how group values influence individuals' perceptions of facts

curtilage the area immediately surrounding the home

cybercrime crimes aimed at the valuable information contained in computers and wireless devices, especially computer databases accessible through the Internet

cyberstalking the use of the Internet, email, or other electronic communication devices to stalk another person through threatening behavior

dangerous act rationale looks at how close defendants came to completing their crimes

dangerous person rationale concentrates on how fully defendants have developed their intent to commit their crime

dangerous person tests look at what actors have already done to demonstrate that they're a danger to society, not just in this crime but, more important, in crimes they might commit in the future if they're not dealt with now

dangerous proximity tests focus on dangerous conduct; they look at what remains for actors to do before they hurt society by completing the crime

dangerous proximity to success test (the physical proximity test) asks whether defendants have come "dangerously close" to completing the crime

deadly weapon doctrine one who intentionally uses a deadly weapon on another human being and thereby kills him is presumed to have formed the intent to kill

defense of consent the justification that competent adults voluntarily consented to crimes against themselves and knew what they were consenting to

defense of duress when defendants use the excuse that they were forced to do what they did

defense of reasonable mistake of age a defense to statutory rape in California and Alaska if the defendant reasonably believed his victim was at or over the age of consent

depraved heart murder extremely reckless killings

deterrence the use of punishment to prevent or reduce future crimes

diminished capacity a failure-of-proof defense in which the defendant attempts to prove that the defendant was incapable of the requisite intent of the crime charged, is innocent of that crime but may well be guilty of a lesser one

diminished responsibility an excuse defense in which the defendant argues, "What I did was wrong, but under the circumstances I'm less responsible"

disorderly conduct crimes offenses against public order and morals

dwelling of another anyplace where other people live

elements of a crime to convict, the prosecution must prove beyond a reasonable doubt: (1) a criminal act (in all crimes), (2) criminal intent (in some crimes), (3) concurrence (in all crimes), (4) attendant circumstances (in some crimes), and (5) that criminal conduct caused a criminal harm (in bad result crimes only)

embezzlement the crime of lawfully gaining possession of someone else's property and later converting it to one's own use

emotion-act distinction separating the emotions that led to a killing from the question of whether the killing itself was reasonable

emotional reasonableness a finding that "the defendant's emotional outrage or passion was reasonable"

entering part of the *actus reus* of burglary, meaning to come or go into the building or structure

enterprise just about any form of human endeavor

entrapment excuse that argues government agents got people to commit crimes they wouldn't otherwise commit

espionage the crime of spying for the enemy

espionage during peace turning or attempting to turn over information about national defense to any foreign country with "intent or with reason to believe" the information is "to be used" to either hurt the United States or help any foreign country

espionage during war consists of collecting, recording, publishing, or communicating (or attempting to do any of these) "any information" about troop movements, ships, aircraft, or war materials and any other information "which might be useful to the enemy"

euthanasia helping another person to die

"evolving standards" test standards of decency that mark the progress of a maturing society

***ex post facto* law** a retroactive law that does one of three things: (1) criminalizes an act that wasn't a crime when it was committed, (2) increases the punishment for a crime after the crime was committed, or (3) takes away a defense that was available to a defendant when the crime was committed

excusable homicide killings done by someone "not of sound memory and discretion"

excuse defenses defendants admit what they did was wrong but claim that, under the circumstances, they weren't responsible for what they did

"express" malice aforethought the mental element of killings that fit the original meaning of "murder"—intentional killings planned in advance

expressive conduct nonverbal actions that communicate ideas and feelings

extraneous factor a "stroke of luck"—namely, a circumstance beyond the attempter's control that prevents the completion of the crime

extreme mental or emotional disturbance manslaughter a homicide committed under the influence of extreme mental or emotional disturbance for which there is reasonable explanation or excuse. The reasonableness of such explanation or excuse shall be determined from the viewpoint of the person in the actor's situation under the circumstances as he believes them to be

extrinsic force in rape cases, requires some physical effort in addition to the amount needed to accomplish the penetration

factual cause also called "but for" cause or "cause in fact"; if it weren't for an actor's conduct, the result wouldn't have occurred

factual impossibility occurs when actors intend to commit a crime and try to but it's physically impossible because some fact or circumstance unknown to them interrupts or prevents the completion of the crime

failure to intervene not actively preventing or interrupting injuries and death to persons or damage and destruction of property

failure to report not providing information when you're legally required to

failure-of-proof defenses mistake defenses in which defendants usually present enough evidence to raise a reasonable doubt that the prosecution has proved the *mens rea* required for criminal liability

fair notice in vague laws, it isn't whether the defendant knows there's a law against the act but whether an ordinary, reasonable person would know that the act is a crime

false imprisonment depriving others of their personal liberty without the asportation requirement

fault-based defenses defenses based on creating a reasonable doubt about the prosecution's proof of a voluntary act

federal system fifty-two criminal codes, one for each of the fifty states, one for the District of Columbia, and one for the U.S. criminal code

felonies against persons the core offenses of murder, manslaughter, rape, kidnapping, and robbery

felonies against property the core offenses of felonious theft, robbery, arson, and burglary

felonies crimes punishable by death or confinement in the state's prison for one year to life without parole

felony murder rule unintentional deaths that occur during the commission of some felonies are murders

fences receivers of stolen goods or places where stolen goods are bought

feticide the crime of killing a fetus

first-degree arson burning homes or other occupied structures (such as schools, offices, and churches) where there's danger to human life

first-degree murder the only crime today in which the death penalty can be imposed, consisting of (1) premeditated, deliberate intent to kill murders and (2) felony murders

force and resistance rule provided that victims had to prove to the courts that they didn't consent to rape by demonstrating that they resisted the force of the rapist

forfeited personal identity theory the idea that when you choose to participate in crime, you forfeit your right to be treated as an individual; "your acts are my acts"

fraud a general term that means getting property by deception

fundamental right to privacy a right that requires the government to prove that a compelling interest justifies invading it

gay panic adequate provocation based on "the theory that a person with latent homosexual tendencies will have an extreme and uncontrollably violent reaction when confronted with a homosexual proposition"

general attempt statute a single statute that applies to the attempt to commit any crime in the state's criminal code

general deterrence aims to reduce crime by the threat of punishment to convince criminal wannabes in the general population to not commit a crime in the future

general intent the intent to commit the criminal act forbidden by statute

"Good Samaritan" doctrine imposes a legal duty to help or call for help for imperiled strangers

"guilty" verdict legally, not necessarily factually, guilty; it means the government proved its case beyond a reasonable doubt

hard punishment a sentence of a year or more in prison

hedonism the natural law that human beings seek pleasure and avoid pain

honest and reasonable mistake rule a negligence mental element in rape cases in which the defendant argues that he honestly, but mistakenly, believed the victim consented to sex

identity theft stealing another person's identity for the purpose of getting something of value

ignorance maxim the presumption that defendants knew the law they were breaking

imminence requirement an element of self-defense requiring the danger to be "right now!"

imperfect defense when a defendant fails in the full defense but is found guilty of a lesser offense

"implied" malice aforethought the mental element of intentional killings without premeditation or reasonable provocation; unintentional killings during the commission of felonies; depraved heart killings; and intent to inflict grievous bodily harm killings

incapacitation prevents convicted criminals from committing future crimes by locking them up, or more rarely, by altering them surgically or executing them

inchoate offenses from the Latin "to begin"; crimes that satisfy the *mens rea* of purpose or specific intent and the *actus reus* of taking some steps toward accomplishing the criminal purpose—but not enough steps to complete the intended crime

indispensable element test asks whether defendants have reached a point where they've gotten control of everything they need to complete the crime

initial aggressor someone who provokes an attack can't then use force to defend herself against the attack she provoked

injunctions to abate public nuisances court orders to eliminate the particular nuisance

insanity the legal term that refers to a mental disease or defect that impairs the reason and/or will to control actions

intangible property property worth nothing by itself but is proof of something of value (such as stock options, bonds, notes, trademarks, licenses, and patents)

intellectual property ideas and their practical application owned by an individual, a business, or a society

intent to cause serious bodily injury murder no intent to kill is required when a victim dies following acts triggered by the intent to inflict serious bodily injury short of death

intervening cause an event that comes between the initial act in a sequence and the end result

intrinsic force in rape cases, requires only the amount of force necessary to accomplish the penetration

involuntary intoxication an excuse to criminal liability in all states; it includes cases in which defendants don't know they're taking intoxicants or know but are forced to take them

involuntary manslaughter an unintentional killing (*mens rea*) by a voluntary act or omission (*actus reus*)

irresistible impulse test we can't blame or deter people who, because of a mental disease or defect know, that what they're doing is "wrong" but can't bring their actions into line with their knowledge of right and wrong

judgment the court's judgment (sometimes called the court's "decision") is how the court disposes of the case

judicial waiver when juvenile court judges use their discretion to transfer a juvenile to adult criminal court

justice depends on culpability; only those who deserve punishment ought to receive it

justifiable homicide killing in self-defense

justification defenses defendants admit they were responsible for their acts but claim that, under the circumstances, what they did was right (justified)

kidnapping *mens rea* the mental element of kidnapping requiring the specific intent to confine, significantly restrain, or hold victims in secret

kidnapping the taking and carrying away of another person with the intent to deprive the other person of personal liberty

knowing consent the person consenting understands what she's consenting to; she's not too young or insane to understand

knowing possession items possessors are aware is either on their person or in places they control

knowingly the mental state of awareness in conduct crimes and, in result crimes, awareness that it's "practically certain" that the conduct will cause the bad result

larceny taking and carrying away a person's property without the use of force and with the intent to permanently deprive the owner of possession

last act rule attempt *actus reus* requires all but the last act needed to complete the crime

"last-straw" rule also called the "long smoldering" or "slow burn" rule, defines adequate provocation as "a smoldering resentment or pent-up rage resulting from earlier insults or humiliating events culminating in a triggering event that, by itself, might be insufficient to provoke the deadly act"

legal ("proximate") cause a subjective question that asks, "Is it fair to blame Defendant for the harm triggered by a chain of events her action(s) set in motion?"

legal duty an obligation created by a statute, contract, or special relationship, and enforceable by law

legal fiction pretending something is a fact when it's not, if there's a "good" reason for the pretense

legal impossibility occurs when actors intend to commit crimes, and do everything they can to carry out their criminal intent, but the criminal law doesn't ban what they did

liberty the right of individuals to come and go as they please without government interference

loitering the crime of remaining in one place with no apparent purpose

mail fraud statutes includes "schemes to defraud or for obtaining money or property" using the U.S. mail

majority opinion the law of the case; the opinion of the majority of the justices on the court who participated in the case

***mala in se* (inherently evil) crimes** offenses that require some level of criminal intent

***mala prohibita* offenses** offenses that are crimes only because a specific statute or ordinance prohibits them

malice aforethought originally the mental state of intentional killing, with some amount of spite, hate, or bad will, planned in advance of the killing

malicious mischief common law crime of intentionally damaging or destroying another's tangible property

***malum prohibitum* crime** death has to be a foreseeable consequence of the unlawful act; the act is unlawful only because it's prohibited by a specific statute or ordinance

manifest criminality the requirement that mental attitudes have to turn into actions for a "crime" to be committed

manslaughter an ancient common law crime created by judges, not by legislators, consisting of two crimes: voluntarily or involuntarily killing another person

manslaughter killing a person without malice aforethought

marital rape exception provided that husbands could not legally rape their wives

"material support" offenses the federal crime of providing "training," "expert advice or assistance," "service," and "personnel to terrorists or terrorist organizations

medical model of criminal law crime is a "disease," and criminals are "sick" in need of "treatment" and "cure"

mens rea Latin for guilty mind, the mental element (also called "criminal intent," "evil mind," "mental attitude," or "state of mind") in crime

mental defect refers to mental retardation or brain damage severe enough to make it impossible to know what you're doing, or if you know, you don't know that it's wrong

mental disease most courts define it as psychosis, mostly paranoia and schizophrenia

mere possession items you possess but you don't know what they are

mere presence rule a person's presence at, and flight from, the scene of a crime aren't enough to satisfy the *actus reus* requirement of accomplice liability

misdemeanors offenses punishable by fine and/or confinement in the local jail for up to one year

mistake of fact a defense to criminal liability whenever the mistake prevents the formation of any fault-based mental attitude—namely, purposely, knowingly, recklessly, or negligently

mitigating circumstances circumstances that convince fact finders (judges or juries) that defendants don't deserve the maximum penalty for the crime they're convicted of

Model Penal Code (MPC) proposed criminal code drafted by the American Law Institute and used to reform criminal codes

moral duty an obligation or norm created and enforced by society, conscience, and religion that's not enforceable by law

motive something that causes a person to act

MPC substantial steps test test that requires that attempters take enough steps toward completing the crime to prove that they're determined to commit it

municipal codes criminal law created by city and town councils elected by city residents

murder *actus reus* the act of killing by poisoning, striking, starving, drowning, and a thousand other forms by which human nature can be overcome

murder killing a person with "malice aforethought"

murder *mens rea* can include purposeful, knowing, or reckless as the mental element in killing

narrow lenity rule the requirement of courts to interpret ambiguous statutes in favor of defendants only in the core felony cases and other crimes requiring fault

necessity a defense that argues an imminent danger of attack was prevented

negligently the mental attitude that a person acts negligently with respect to a material element of an offense when he should be aware of a substantial and unjustifiable risk that the material element exists or will result from his conduct. The risk must be of such a nature and degree that the actor's failure to perceive it, considering the nature and purpose of his conduct and the circumstances known to him, involved a gross deviation from the standard of care that a reasonable person would observe in the actor's situation.

"not guilty" verdict doesn't mean "innocent"; it means that the government didn't prove its case beyond a reasonable doubt

objective fault requires no purposeful or conscious bad mind in the actor

objective fear means that the fear was reasonable under the circumstances

objective test of cooling-off time requires that a reasonable person under the same circumstances would have had time to cool off

objective test of entrapment if the intent originates with the government and their actions would tempt an "ordinarily law-abiding" person to commit the crime, the court should dismiss the case

obtaining property by false pretenses in modern law, often called "theft by deceit"; making false representations concerning past or present facts with the intent to defraud another

occupied structure "any structure, vehicle, or place adapted for overnight accommodations of persons, or for carrying on business therein, whether or not a person is actually present"

one-voluntary-act-is-enough rule conduct that includes a voluntary act satisfies the voluntary act requirement

opinion "the point of the story"; the court backs up its judgment by explaining how and why it applied the law (general principles and the elements of crimes) to the facts of the case

order acting according to ordinary people's standard of "good manners"

overt act requirement the requirement of an act that furthers the agreement in conspiracy

panhandling stopping people on the street to ask them for food or money

paramour rule the common law rule that a husband who caught his wife in the act of adultery had adequate provocation to kill; today, it applies to both parties of a marriage

parental responsibility statutes based on parents' acts and omissions; differ from vicarious liability statutes, which are based on the parent–child relationship

pattern of racketeering activity committing two or more of a huge list of related crimes

perfect defenses defenses in which defendants are acquitted if they're successful

***Pinkerton* rule** the crime of conspiracy and the crime the conspirators agree to commit are separate offenses

plurality opinion an opinion that represents the reasoning of the greatest number (but less than a majority) of justices

Ponzi scheme a fraudulent investment operation that pays returns to investors from their own money or money paid by subsequent investors rather from any actual profit earned

post-traumatic stress disorder (PTSD) defense excuse that argues the defendant wasn't responsible because of PTSD

premenstrual syndrome (PMS) excuse that PMS led to the defendant committing the criminal acts

preponderance of the evidence more than 50 percent of the evidence proves justification or excuse

presumption of bodily integrity a state can't exercise power over individual members of society except to prevent harm to others

presumption of innocence which means that the prosecution has the burden of proof when it comes to proving the criminal act and intent

preventionists punishment is only a means to a greater good, usually the prevention or at least the reduction of future crime

principals in the first degree persons who actually commit the crime

principals in the second degree persons present when the crime is committed and who help commit it (lookouts and getaway drivers)

principle of concurrence some mental fault has to trigger the criminal act in conduct crimes and the cause in result crimes

principle of legality no one can be convicted of, or punished for, a crime unless the law defined the crime and prescribed the punishment before the person engaged in the behavior that was defined as a crime

principle of proportionality the punishment has to fit the crime

principle of utility permits only the minimum amount of pain necessary to prevent the crime

probable desistance test determines if defendants have gone far enough toward completing the crime that it's unlikely they'll turn back

product-of-mental-illness test also known as the *Durham* rule, acts that are the "products" of mental disease or defect excuse criminal liability

proof beyond a reasonable doubt the highest burden of proof in the U.S. Criminal justice system reserved for criminal cases; the prosecution must prove every element of the crime charged to this standard.

proof of treason requires either two witnesses to the *actus reus* or confession in open court

prostitution engaging in sex in exchange for money or its equivalent

proximity tests help courts decide when defendants' acts have taken them further than just getting ready to attempt and brought them close enough to completing crimes to qualify as attempt *actus reus*

punishment intentionally inflicting pain or other unpleasant consequences on another person

punishment imagination crimes that fit within the criminal law imagination and that the law should punish by locking people up

police power all federal, state, and local governments' executive, legislative, and judiciary's power, including uniformed police officers, to carry out and enforce the criminal law

punitive damages damages recovered by tort plaintiffs to punish the defendant for their intentional "evil behavior"

purposely the most blameworthy mental state requiring the actor's "conscious object" to be to commit crimes or cause criminal results

"quality of life" crimes "bad manners" crimes that threaten to disrupt public order

racketeering original meaning was the extortion of money or advantage by threat or force; now the meaning has expanded to include a pattern of illegal activity (such as extortion and murder) carried out in the furtherance of an enterprise owned or controlled by those engaged in the activity

Racketeer Influenced and Corrupt Organizations Act (RICO) imposes enhanced penalties for "all types of organized criminal behavior, that is, enterprise criminality—from simple political to sophisticated white collar schemes to traditional Mafia-type endeavors"

rape shield laws statutes that prohibit introducing evidence of victims' past sexual conduct

rationalism the natural law that individuals can act to maximize pleasure and minimize pain, permitting human beings to apply natural laws mechanistically (according to rules) instead of having to rely on the discretionary judgment of individual decision makers

reason psychologists call it "cognition"; the capacity to tell right from wrong

reasonable resistance rule provides that the amount of force required to repel rapists shows nonconsent in rape prosecutions

receiving stolen property *actus reus* the act of receiving and controlling at least temporarily (but not necessarily possessing) the property

receiving stolen property benefiting from the theft of someone else's property without having participated in the wrongful acquisition in the first place

receiving stolen property *mens rea* depending on the jurisdiction, knowing or believing that received goods are stolen

recklessly conscious creation of a "substantial and unjustifiable" risk of criminal harm

rehabilitation aims to prevent future crimes by changing individual offenders so they'll want to play by the rules and won't commit any more crimes in the future ***respondeat***

superior a doctrine in tort law that makes a master liable for the wrong of a servant; in modern terms, an employer may be liable for the wrong of an employee

retreat rule you have to retreat from an attack if you reasonably believe (1) that you're in danger of death or serious bodily harm and (2) that backing off won't unreasonably put you in danger of death or serious bodily harm

retributionists inflicting on offenders physical and psychological pain ("hard treatment") so that they can pay for their crimes

right of locomotion the right to come and go without restraint

right-wrong test (also called the **McNaughtan rule**) the defendant suffered a defect of reason caused by a disease of the mind, and, consequently, at the time of the act didn't know what she was doing or that the act was wrong

robbery taking property by force or the threat of force—a violent crime against persons and their property

robbery *actus reus* an act or threat of force beyond the amount needed to take and carry away someone else's property

robbery *mens rea* the intent to take another person's property and keep it permanently with the additional intent to use immediate force, or the threat of immediate force, to get it

rule of law the idea that government power should be defined and limited by laws

rule of lenity the requirement of courts to resolve every ambiguity in a criminal statute in favor of the defendant

sabotage the crime of damaging or destroying property for the purpose of hindering preparations for war and national defense during national emergencies

Second Amendment "the right of law-abiding, responsible citizens to use arms in defense of hearth and home"

second-degree arson includes burning unoccupied structures, vehicles, and boats

second-degree murders murders that aren't first-degree murders, including intentional murders that weren't premeditated or deliberate, felony murders, intent to inflict serious bodily injury murders, and depraved heart murders

sedition the crime of advocating the violent overthrow of the government

seditious conspiracy conspiring to the violent overthrow of the government

seditious libel advocating the overthrow of the government in writings

seditious speech advocating the overthrow of the government in speeches

serious bodily injury bodily injury that involves a substantial risk of death; protracted unconsciousness; extreme physical pain; protracted or obvious disfigurement; or protracted loss or substantial impairment of a function of a bodily member, organ or mental faculty

social reality of U.S. criminal law the dual nature of U.S. criminal law divided into two categories: a small number of serious, core offenses and a large number of lesser crimes, or "everything else"

solicitation *actus reus* acts that include some kind of inducement to commit the solicited crime

solicitation *mens rea* requires words that convey that their purpose is to get someone to commit a specific crime

solicitation the crime of trying to get someone else to commit a crime

specific attempt statutes separate statutes that define attempts in terms of specific crimes in the criminal code, such as attempted murder, attempted robbery, and attempted rape—crimes that involved a specific intent

specific deterrence aims to reduce crime by inflicting the actual punishment to convince offenders not to commit crimes in the future

specific intent the general intent to commit the *actus reus* of a crime plus the intent to cause a criminally harmful result

stalking intentionally scaring another person by following, tormenting, or harassing

stand-your-ground rule if you didn't start a fight, you can stand your ground and kill to defend yourself without retreating from any place you have a right to be

state criminal codes criminal law created by elected representatives in state legislatures

status the character or condition of a person or thing

statutory rape to have carnal knowledge of a person under the age of consent whether or not accomplished by force

strict liability liability without either subjective or objective fault

subjective fault fault that requires a "bad mind" in the actor

subjective fear means that the victim honestly feared imminent and serious bodily harm

subjective test of entrapment asks whether the intent to commit the crime originated with the defendant

substantial capacity (MPC) test a person is not responsible for criminal conduct if at the time of such conduct as a result of mental disease or defect he lacks substantial capacity either to appreciate the criminality [wrongfulness] of his conduct or to conform his conduct to the requirements of law

surreptitious remaining element the entering of a structure lawfully with the intent to remain and commit a crime inside

syndrome a group of symptoms or signs typical of a disease, disturbance, or condition

tangible property personal property, not real estate

terrorism the use of violence or intimidation in the pursuit of political aims

theft intentionally getting control of someone else's property, includes larceny, embezzlement, and false pretense crimes

theories of criminal punishment ways of thinking about the purposes of criminal punishment

threatened battery assault intentional scaring requiring only that actors intend to frighten their victims, thus expanding assault beyond attempted battery

threat-of-force requirement requires the prosecution to prove that the victim experienced both subjective and objective fear in rapes involving threats of force

three-strikes laws intended to make sure that offenders who are convicted of a third felony get locked up for a very long time (sometimes for life)

time, place, and manner test to be constitutional, restrictions on free speech can't be based on the content of the speech, must serve a significant government interest, and leave open other channels of expression

Tor browser created by U.S. Naval intelligence, *The Onion Router,* or Tor browser, allows users to access the dark web and any website anonymously

torts private wrongs for which you can sue the party who wronged you and recover money

treason ***actus reus*** consists of either levying war against the United States or giving aid and comfort to the enemies of the United States

treason ***mens rea*** consists of intentionally giving aid and comfort for the very purpose of betraying the United States

treason the crime of levying war against the United States or of giving aid and comfort to its enemies

trial courts where the cases for the state and the defense are presented; their witnesses and the physical evidence are introduced; and the fact finders (juries in jury trials or judges in nonjury bench trials) decide what the "true" story is and whether the evidence all adds up to proof of guilt beyond a reasonable doubt

U.S. Criminal Code criminal law created by the U.S. Congress

unarmed acquaintance rape nonconsensual sex between individuals who are known to one another

unequivocality test also called the *res ipsa loquitur* test ("the act speaks for itself"), examines whether an ordinary person who saw the defendant's acts without knowing her intent would believe she was determined to commit the intended crime

unilateral approach to conspiracy parties the rule that not all conspirators have to agree with—or even know—the other conspirators

unlawful act or misdemeanor manslaughter unintended deaths occurring during the commission of nonhomicide offenses

USA Patriot Act passed by Congress after the September 11, 2001, attacks, creating some new (and enhancing the penalties for existing) crimes of domestic and international terrorism

utmost resistance standard requirement that rape victims had to use all the physical strength they had to prevent penetration

vagrancy the ancient crime of poor people wandering with no visible means of support

vicarious liability establishes when a party can be criminally liable for someone else's conduct because of a relationship; transfers the criminal conduct of one party to another because of their relationship

victimless crimes crimes involving willing adult participants who don't see themselves as victims

void-for-overbreadth doctrine protects speech guaranteed by the First Amendment by invalidating laws written so broadly that the fear of prosecution creates a "chilling effect" that discourages people from exercising that freedom

void-for-vagueness doctrine the principle that statutes violate due process if they don't define a crime and its punishment clearly enough for ordinary people to know what is lawful

voluntary abandonment defense (voluntary renunciation defense) defendants who voluntarily and completely renounce their criminal purpose can avoid criminal liability

voluntary consent consent was the product of free will, not of force, threat of force, promise, or trickery

voluntary manslaughter suddenly and intentionally killing another person in the heat of anger following adequate provocation; elements include murder *actus reus*, *mens rea*, causation, and death

waiver to adult criminal court meaning the juvenile court gives up its jurisdiction over the case and turns it over to the adult criminal court

wheel conspiracies one or more defendants participate in every transaction (the hub of the wheel) and others participate in only one transaction (the spokes in the wheel)

white-collar crime criminal behavior committed by the white-collar class, including fraud, swindling, and "double crossing"

will psychologists call it "volition," most of us call it "willpower"; in the insanity tests, it refers to defendants' power to control their actions

withdrawal exception if initial aggressors completely withdraw from attacks they provoke, they can defend themselves against an attack by their initial victims

"words can never provoke" rule the rule that words are never adequate provocation to reduce murder to manslaughter

Bibliography

ABC News. 2007. "Memorabilia Dealer and Former Friend Said Simpson Was in the Room during Robbery." *Good Morning America*, September 17. Accessed March 14, 2012. http://abcnews.go.com/GMA/story?id=3611324&page=1#.T2Cpwsw3_Gc.

Ainsworth, Bill. 2004. "Poll Finds Broad Support for Limits on 3-Strikes Laws." *San Diego Union*, June 10.

Alabama Criminal Code. 1975. Accessed July 24, 2012. http://alisondb.legislature.state.al.us/acas/CodeOfAlabama/1975/13297.htm.

Alexander v. U.S. 1993. 510 U.S. 909.

Allen, Francis A. 1993. *The Habits of Legality: Criminal Justice and the Rule of Law.* New York: Oxford University Press.

Alter, Adam L., Julia Kernochan, and John M. Darley. 2007. "Morality Influences How People Apply the Ignorance of Law Defense." *The Law & Society Review*: 41:819–64.

American Law Institute (ALI). 1953. *Model Penal Code Tentative Draft No. 1*. Philadelphia: ALI.

______. 1985. *Model Penal Code and Commentaries.* Philadelphia: ALI.

______. 2007. *Model Penal Code: Sentencing, Tentative Draft No. 1*. Philadelphia: ALI.

Andenæs, Johannes. 1983. "Deterrence." In *Encyclopedia of Crime and Justice*, edited by Sanford H. Kadish. New York: Free Press.

Apprendi v. New Jersey. 2000. 530 U.S. 466.

Aquinas, St. Thomas. [1265–68] 2012. *Summa Theologica.* 2nd ed. Edited and translated by the Dominican Friars. Los Angeles: Viewforth Press.

Arizona Criminal Code. 2003. Effect of Alcohol or Drug Use. Accessed July 24, 2012. http://www.azleg.state.az.us/ars/13/00503.htm.

Arthur Andersen LLP v. U.S. 2005. 544 U.S. 696.

Atkins v. Virginia. 2002. 536 U.S. 304.

Attorney General. 1999. *1999 Report on Cyberstalking: A New Challenge for Law Enforcement and Industry.* Washington, DC: U.S. Department of Justice.

Backun v. U.S. 1940. 112 F.2d 635 (4th Cir.).

Baker, Katharine K. 1997. "Once a Rapist?" *Harvard Law Review*: 110:563–624.

______. 1999. "Sex, Rape, and Shame." *Boston University Law Review*: 79:663–716.

Bailey v. U.S. 1969. 416 F.2d 1110 (D.C. Cir.).

Batey, Robert. 1997. "Vagueness and the Construction of Criminal Statutes—Balancing Act." *Virginia Journal of Social Policy and Law* 5:1.

*Beasley v. State. 1894.*38 N.E. 35

Beazell v. Ohio. 1925. 269 U.S. 167.

Benekos, Peter, and Alido Merlo. 1995. "Three Strikes and You're Out!: The Political Sentencing Game." *Federal Probation*, March.

Bentham, Jeremy. 1864. *Theory of Legislation*. London. 1864.

Bharara, Attorney Preet. 2015. https://www.scribd.com/doc/266723681/Ulbricht-Prosecution-Sentencing-Letter.

Binder, Guyora. 2000. "Meaning and Motive in the Law of Homicide." *Buffalo Criminal Law Review* 3:755–74.

______. 2004. "The Origins of American Felony Murder Rules." *Stanford Law Review* 57:59–208.

Bishop, Joel Bishop. 1907. *Commentaries on the Criminal Law*, Seventh edition, Volume I. Boston: Little, Brown, and Company.

Black, Henry Campbell. 1983. *Black's Law Dictionary*. 5th ed. St. Paul, MN: Thomson West.

Blackstone, Sir William. 1769. *Commentaries on the Laws of England, IV*. Oxford: Clarendon Press.

Blakely v. Washington. 2004. 542 U.S. 296.

Blakely, Richard, and Mark Gettings. 1980. "Racketeer Influenced and Corrupt Organizations (RICO): Basic Concepts—Criminal and Civil Remedies." *Temple Law Quarterly* 53.

Board of Commissioners v. Backus. 1864. 29 How. Pr. 33.

Bracton, Henry of. 1968. *On the Laws and Customs of England*. Translated by Samuel E. Thorne. Cambridge: Harvard University Press.

Bradfield, Jennifer L. 1998. "Anti-Stalking Laws: Do They Adequately Protect Stalking Victims?" *Harvard Women's Law Journal* 21:229, 249.

Brodie, Kyle S. 1995. "The Obviously Impossible Attempt: A Proposed Revision to the Model Penal Code. *Northern Illinois University Law Review* 15:237.

Brown v. State. 1906. 106 N.W. 536 (Wis.).

Brown, Richard Maxwell. 1991. *No Duty to Retreat: Violence and Values in American History and Society.* NY: Oxford University Press.

Bryden, David P. 2000. "Redefining Rape." *Buffalo Criminal Law Review* 3:318.

Bureau of Justice Statistics. 2014. *Rape and Sexual Assault Victimization Among College Age Females, 1995–2013*. Washington DC; U.S. Department of Justice.

Burger, Vivian. 1977. "Man's Trial: Woman's Tribulation: Rape Cases in the Courtroom." *Columbia Law Review* 77:1–103. Accessed December 21, 2014. http://www.chicagotribune.com/news/chi-regan-sidenov11-story.html.

Burrows v. State. 1931. 297 P. 1029.

California Penal Code. 2003. Accessed July 20, 2012. http://www.leginfo.ca.gov/.html/pen_table_of_contents.html.

______. 2006. Sections 187–99. Accessed July 20, 2012. http://www.leginfo.ca.gov/cgi-bin/displaycode?section=pen&group=00001–01000&file=187-199.

California Penal Code. 2015. Accessed September 3, 2015.

Callimachi, Rukimini. 2015. "ISIS and the Lonely American." *New York Times*, June 27.

Carey v. Population Services International. 1977. 431 U.S. 678.

Carney, Robert Mark, and Brian D. Williams. 1983. "Premenstrual Syndrome: A Criminal Defense." *Notre Dame Law Review* 59:263–69.

Carroll, Joseph. 2007. "Public Divided over Moral Acceptability of Doctor-Assisted Suicide." Gallup News Service, May 31. Accessed July 20, 2012. http://www.gallup.com/poll/27727/public-divided-over-moral-acceptability-doctorassisted-suicide.aspx.

Casico v. State. 1947. 25 N.W.2d 897 (Neb.).

Chambers v. Florida. 1940. 309 U.S. 227.

Chaplinsky v. New Hampshire. 1942. 315 U.S. 568.

Chicago v. Roman. 1998. 705 N.E.2d 81 (Ill.).

City of Chicago v. Morales. 1999. 527 U.S. 41.

City of Saint Paul. 2009. "Mayor Coleman Announces Civil Gang Injunction Lawsuit against the East Side Boys, Selby Siders." Saint Paul Minnesota Website, July 1. Accessed July 8, 2012. http://stpaul.gov/civicalerts.aspx?aid=529&arc=1060&preview=yes.

City of Waukesha v. Boehnen. 2015. Accessed July 29, 2015. http://law.justia.com/cases/wisconsin/court-of-appeals/2015/2014ap001386.html.

Clark v. Arizona. 2006. 548 U.S. 735.

Coffee, John C., Jr. 1992. "Paradigms Lost: The Blurring of the Criminal and Civil Law Models—and What Can Be Done about It." *Yale Law Journal* 101:1875.

Coke, Sir Edward. 1628. *Institutes of the Laws of England*. London: Flesher, Haviland, and Young.

______. 1644. *Third Part of the Institutes of the Laws of England: Concerning High Treason, and Other Pleas of the Crown, and Criminal Causes*. London: Flesher.

Coker v. Georgia. 1977. 433 U.S. 584.

Cole, David. 2010. "The Roberts Court's Free Speech Problem." *New York Review of Books*, June 28. http://www.nybooks.com/blogs/nyrblog/2010/jun/28/roberts-courts-free-speech-problem/.

Commonwealth v. Berkowitz. 1992. 609 A.2d 1338 (Pa.Super.).

______. 1994. 641 A.2d 1161 (Pa.).

Commonwealth v. Carr. 1990. 580 A.2d 1362 (Pa.Sup.).

Commonwealth v. Drum. 1868. WL 7210 (Pa.).

Commonwealth v. Fischer. 1998. 721 A.2d 1111 (Pa.Super.).

Commonwealth v. Golston. 1977. 249, 366 N.E.2d 744 (Mass.).

Commonwealth v. Mitchell. 1993. WL 773785 (Pa.Com.Pl.).

Commonwealth v. Peaslee. 1901. 59 N.E. 55 (Mass.).

Commonwealth v. Pestinikas. 1992. 617 A.2d 1339.

Commonwealth v. Rhodes. 1996. 920 S.W.2d 531 (Ky. App.).

Commonwealth v. Schnopps. 1983. 459 N.E.2d 98 (Mass.).

Comstock, G. D. 1989. "Developments—Sexual-Orientation and the Law." *Harvard Law Review* 102:1508-51.

Cook, Philip J., Jens Ludwig, and Adam Samaha. 2009. "Gun Control after *Heller*: Threats and Side Shows from a Social Welfare Perspective." *UCLA Law Review* 56:1041–93.

Corrado, Michael. 1994. "Is There an Act Requirement in the Criminal Law?" *University of Pennsylvania Law Review* 142:1529.

Cramer v. U.S. 1945. 325 U.S. 1.

Cullen, Francis T., William J. Maakestad, and Gray Cavender. 1987. *Corporate Crime under Attack: The Ford Pinto Case and Beyond*. Cincinnati: Anderson.

Crocker, Lizzie. 2014. "The Nuclear Nun Goes to Jail." *Daily Beast,* February 18. Accessed June 27, 2015. http://www.thedailybeast.com/articles/2014/02/18/nuclear-nun-to-be-sentenced.html.

D.C. Gun Laws. 2009. § 7–2502.01. http://dcguncase.com/blog/dc-gun-laws/.

DeGiorolami, Marc O. 2012. "Against Theories of Punishment: The Thought of Sir James Fitzjames Stephen." Accessed January 4, 2015. http://www.class.uh.edu/faculty/tsommers/against%20theories%20of%20punishment%20DeGirolami.pdf.

Dennis v. State. 1995. 105 Md.App. 687.

DePasquale v. State. 1988. 757 P.2d 367 (Nev.).

Dershowitz, Alan. 1994. *The Abuse Excuse and Other Cop-Outs, Sob Stories, and Evasions of Responsibility.* Boston: Little, Brown.

Diamond, John L. 1996. "The Myth of Morality and Fault in Criminal Law." *American Criminal Law* 34.

DiFonzo, James. 2001. "Parental Responsibility for Juvenile Crime." *Oregon Law Review* 80:1.

Direct Sales Co. v. U.S. 1943. 319 U.S. 703.

District of Columbia v. Heller. 2008. 554 U.S. 570.

______. 1995. "When 'Heterosexual Men' Men Kill 'Homosexual' Men: Sexual Advances, Provocation Law, Sexual Advances, and the 'Reasonable Man' Standard." *Journal of Criminal Law & Criminology* 85(3):726–63.

______. 2009. *Understanding Criminal Law*. 5th ed. Newark, N.J.: Matthew Bender & Company, Inc.

______. 2012. *Understanding Criminal Law*, 6th ed. Lexis-Nexis: New Providence, NJ.

Dressler, Joshua, and Alan C. Michaels. 2006. *Understanding Criminal Procedure*. Vol. II: *Adjudication*. Newark, N.J.: Matthew Bender & Company, Inc.

Dubber, Markus D. 2001. "Policing Possession: The War on Crime and the End of Criminal Law." *Journal of Criminal Law and Criminology* 91:829.

______. 2002. *Criminal Law: Model Penal Code*. New York: Foundation Press.

______. 2009. *Criminal Law*. 2nd ed. Eagan, MN: West.

Dubber, Markus D., and Mark G. Kelman. 2005. *American Criminal Law*. New York: Foundation Press.

Duest v. State. 1985. 462 So.2d 446 (Fla.).

Durham v. U.S. 1954. 214 F.2d 862 (D.C. Cir.).

Edwards v. California. 1941. 314 U.S. 162.

Edwards, Daphne. 1996. "Acquaintance Rape and the 'Force' Element: When 'No' Is Not Enough." *Golden Gate Law Review* 26:241.

Ehrlich, Isaac. 1975. "The Deterrent Effect of Capital Punishment: A Question of Life and Death." *American Economic Review* 65(3):414.

Eisenstadt v. Baird. 1972. 405 U.S. 438.

"Electronic Frontier: The Challenge of Unlawful Conduct Involving the Use of the Internet." 2000. Executive Summary. http://www.politechbot.com/docs/unlawful conduct.html.

Ellickson, Robert C. 1996. "Controlling Chronic Misconduct in City Spaces: Of Panhandlers, Skid Rows, and Public-Space Zoning." *Yale Law Journal* 105.

Elton, Geoffrey R. 1972. *The Tudor Constitution*. Cambridge, UK: Cambridge University Press.

England, Deborah. 2014. "The History of Marital Rape Laws." Defense Lawyer.com. Accessed December 21, 2014. http://www.criminaldefenselawyer.com /resources/criminal-defense/crime-penalties/marital-rape.htm.

Enker, Arnold. 1977. "*Mens Rea* in Criminal Attempt." *American Bar Foundation Research Journal* 845–79.

Epilepsy Therapy Project. 2011a. "Driving and the Law." Epilepsy.com. Accessed November 21, 2011. http://www.epilepsy.com/epilepsy/rights_driving.

———. 2011b. "Auras." *Epilepsy.com*. Accessed November 21, 2011. http://www.epilepsy.com/epilepsy/auras.

Estrich, Susan. 1992. "Palm Beach Stories." *Law & Philosophy* 11(1):5–33.

———. 1987. *Real Rape*. Cambridge, Mass.: Harvard University Press.

Ewing v. California. 2003. 538 U.S. 11.

Farnsworth, Clyde. 1994. "Mercy Killing in Canada Stirs Calls for Changes in Law." *New York Times*, November 21.

Farrand, Max, ed. 1929. "Introduction." *The Laws and Liberties of Massachusetts*. Cambridge, Mass.: Harvard University Press.

Fletcher, George. 1978. *Rethinking Criminal Law*. Boston: Little, Brown.

———. 1981. "Reflections on Felony Murder," *Southwestern University Law Review* 12:413–29.

———. 1988. *A Crime of Self-Defense: Bernhard Goetz and the Law on Trial*. New York: Free Press.

Figueroa v. U.S. 2009. 566 U.S. 646.

Florida Criminal Code. 2006. § 787.02. Accessed July 22, 2012. http://archive.flsenate.gov/statutes/.

Florida Personal Protection Law. 2009. Accessed July 24, 2012. http://www.jacksonvillelawyerhelp.com/2012 /07/florida-statute-776–012-use-of-force-in-defense-of-person/; http://www.jacksonvillelawyerhelp.com/2012 /07/florida-statute-776–013-home-protection-use-of-deadly-force/

Fox, Everett. 1995. *The Five Books of Moses*. New York: Schocken Books.

Fries, Jacob H. 2001. "4,000 Cars Seized in Effort to Halt Drunk Driving." *New York Times*, July 3.

Gall v. U.S. 2007. 552 U.S. 38.

Gaylin, Willard. 1982. *The Killing of Bonnie Garland*. New York: Simon & Schuster.

Gelles, Richard J. 2002. "Family Abuse and Crime." *Encyclopedia of Crime and Justice*. Eagan, MN: Thomson Learning.

Geoffrey A. Jackman et al., Seeing Is Believing: What Do Boys Do When They Find a Real Gun?, 107 PEDIATRICS 1247, 1247–48 (2001).

GeorgiaCarry.Org, Inc. v. Georgia. 2011. 764 F.Supp.2d 1306 (M.D.Ga.).

Gibeaut, John. 1997. "Sobering Thoughts." *American Bar Association Journal* 83.

Gitlow v. New York. 1925. 268 U.S. 652.

Goldman, Zachary K. 2015. "Terrorism 2.0? New Challenges in Cyberspace." *Georgetown Journal of International Affairs*. Accessed June 24, 2015. http://journal .georgetown.edu/terrorism-2–0-new-challenges-in-cyberspace/.

Gonzalez v. Carhart. 2007. 500 U.S. 124.

Gonzalez v. Oregon. 2005. 546 U.S. 243.

Gordon, Brenda. 1999. "A Criminal's Justice or a Child's Justice? Trends in the Waiver of Juvenile Court Jurisdiction and the Flaws in the Arizona Response." *Arizona Law Review* 41:193.

Graham v. Florida. 2010. 560 U.S. (Slip opinion).

Grayned v. City of Rockford. 1972. 408 U.S. 104.

Gray v. State. 1979. 403 A.2d 853.

Green, Stuart P. 1997. "Why It's a Crime to Tear the Tag Off a Mattress: Overcriminalization and the Moral Content of Regulatory Offenses." *Emory Law Journal* 46: 1533.

Greenhouse, Linda. 2003. "Justices Deny Appeal in Execution of Juveniles." *New York Times*, January 27.

Greenhouse, Steven. 1985. "Three Executives Convicted of Murder for Unsafe Workplace Conditions." *New York Times*, June 15.

Greenwald, Glenn. 2011. "Can the U.S. Government Close Social Media Accounts?" *Salon*, December 20. Accessed May 29, 2012. http://www.salon.com/2011/12/20 /the_u_s_government _targets_twitter_terrorism/.

Gresham v. Peterson. 2000. 225 F.3d 899 (7th Cir.).

Griffin v. Gipson. 2015. U.S. District Court, Eastern District California. No. 2:13-cv-02516-MCE-GGH. Accessed May 12, 2015. http://www.gpo.gov/fdsys/pkg /USCOURTS-caed-2_13-cv-02516/pdf/USCOURTS-caed-2_13-cv-02516–3.pdf.

Griswold v. Connecticut. 1965. 381 U.S. 479.

Grogger, Jeffrey. 2002. "The Effects of Civil Gang Injunctions on Reported Violent Crime: Evidence from Los Angeles County." *Journal of Law and Economics* VLV:69–90.

Gross, Hyman. 1978. *A Theory of Criminal Justice*. New York: Oxford University Press.

Gross, Teri. 2015. "Infiltrating the Dark Net, Where Criminals, Trolls and Extremists Reign." June 3. Accessed June 6, 2015. http://www.npr.org/sections/alltechconsidered/2015/06/03/411476653/infiltrating-the-dark-net-where-criminals-trolls-and-extremists-reign.

Hale, Sir Matthew. 1847. *The History of the Pleas of the Crown*. Philadelphia: R. H. Small.

Hall, Jerome. 1960. *The General Principles of Criminal Law*. 2nd ed. Indianapolis: Bobbs-Merrill.

Hall, John Wesley, Jr. 1991. *Search and Seizure*. 2nd ed. Deerfield, IL: Clark Boardman Callaghan.

Hamilton v. Cameron. 1997. 700 N.E.2d 336 (OhioApp.3d).

Harcourt, Bernard. 2013. "The Collapse of the Harm Principle Redux." Chicago, Public Law and Legal Theory Working Paper No. 437. August 16. Accessed July 20, 2014. http://papers.ssrn.com/sol3/papers.cfm?abstract_id=2311329.

______. 2001. *Illusions of Order*. Cambridge, MA: Harvard University Press.

______. 2005. "Carceral Imaginations." *Carceral Notebooks* 1:3–19.

Harper Rainey, William. 1900. "History of the University of Chicago Law School." Accessed July 19, 2014. http://www.law.uchicago.edu/school/history.

Hart, Henry M., Jr. 1958. "The Aims of the Criminal Law." *Law and Contemporary Problems* 23:401.

Hart, Herbert L. A., and Tony Honoré. 1995. *Causation in the Law*. 2nd ed. New York: Oxford University Press.

Haskill, Martin. 1992. "Dilation and Extraction for Late Second Trimester Abortion." National Abortion Federation. Accessed May 20, 2015. http://operationrescue.org/pdfs/NAFpaper091392.pdf.

Heritage Foundation. 2015. "Overcriminalization: An Explosion of Federal Criminal Law." Heritage Foundation. Accessed January 6, 2015. http://www.heritage.org/research/factsheets/2011/04/overcriminalization-an-explosion-of-federal-criminal-law.

Hermann, Donald H. J., and Yvonne S. Sor. 1983. "Convicting or Confining? Alternative Directions in Insanity Law Reform: Guilty But Mentally Ill Versus New Rules for Release of Insanity Acquittees." *Brigham Young Law Review* (1983):499, 508.

Holmes, Oliver Wendell. 1963. *The Common Law*. Boston: Little, Brown.

Hong, Nicole. 2015. "'Material Support' Statute Is Front and Center in Antiterror Push." *Wall Street Journal*, May 27.

Horton v. City of Oakland. 2000. 98 Cal.Rptr.2d 371.

Howe, Mark DeWolfe, ed. 1953. *Holmes-Laski Letters*. Cambridge, Mass: Harvard University Press.

Human Rights Watch. 2002. "World Report. U.S. Death Penalty." Accessed July 23, 2012. http://www.hrw.org/wr2k2/us.html#Death%20Penalty.

Hyde v. U.S. 1912. 225 U.S. 347.

Illinois Criminal Law and Procedure. 1988. St. Paul, MN: West.

In re Kemmler. 1890. 136 U.S. 436.

In re Medley. 1890. 134 U.S. 160.

In re Winship. 1970. 397 U.S. 358.

Interactive Digital Software Association v. St. Louis County. 2002. 200 Fed. Supp.2d 1126 (E.D.Mo.).

Jefferson, Thomas. 1853. *The Writings of Thomas Jefferson*. Edited by Albert Ellery Bergh. Washington, DC: Government Printing Office.

Jewell v. State. 1996. 672 N.E.2d 417 (Ind.App.).

Johnson, Vincent R. 2005. "Cybersecurity, Identity Theft, and the Limits of Tort Liability." *South Carolina Law Review* 57:255.

Jones v. State. 1984. 682 P.2d 757 (Okla.Crim.App.).

Joyce v. City and County of San Francisco. 1994. 846 F.Supp. 843 (N.D.Cal.).

Kadish, Sanford H. 1985. "Complicity, Cause, and Blame: A Study in the Interpretation of Doctrine." *California Law Review* 73:323–410.

______, ed. 1983. *Encyclopedia of Crime and Justice*. Vol. 1. New York: Free Press.

______. 1988. "The Model Penal Code's Historical Antecedents." *Law Journal* 19: 521–38.

Kadish, Sanford H., Stephen Schulhofer, and Carol Steiker. 2007. *Criminal Law and Its Processes*. 8th ed. New York: Aspen Publishers.

Kahan, Dan M. 2010. "Culture, Cognition, and Consent: Who Perceives What, and Why, in Acquaintance-Rape Cases." *University of Pennsylvania Law Review* 158:729.

Kahan, Dan M. 1994. "Lenity and Federal Common Law Crimes." *Supreme Court Review* 345.

______. 1996. "What Do Alternative Sanctions Mean? *University of Chicago Law Review* 63:591.

______. 2011. "What is motivated reasoning?" *Discover*, May 5. Accessed December 28, 2014. http://blogs.discovermagazine.com/intersection/2011/05/05/what-is-motivated-reasoning-how-does-it-work-dan-kahan-answers/#.VJ_piD8A.

Kandel, Minouche. 1992. "Whores in Court: Judicial Processing of Prostitutes in Boston Municipal Court in 1990." *Yale Journal of Law and Feminism* 4:329–52.

Kann, Mark E. 2008. "Limited Liberty, Durable Patriarchy." Markus Dubber and Mariana Valverde, eds., *Police and the Liberal State*. Stanford: Stanford University Press.

Keeler v. Superior Court. 1970. 470 P.2d 617 (Cal.).

Kelling, George L., and Catherine M. Coles. 1996. *Fixing Broken Windows*. New York: Free Press.

Kennedy v. Louisiana. 2008. 554 U.S. 407.

Kent v. United States. 1966. 383 U.S. 541.

Kinports, Kim. 2004. "So Much Activity, So Little Change: A Reply to Critics of the Battered Women's Self-Defense." *St. Louis University Public Law Review* 23:155–92.

Kleindienst, Linda. 2005. "Gun Foes to Warn Tourists on Law; Beginning Saturday, Floridians Can Use Deadly Force in Self-Defense." *Orlando Sentinel*, September 26.

Kolender v. Lawson. 1983. 461 U.S. 352.

Koppersmith v. State. 1999. 742 So.2d 206 (Ala.App.).

Krulewitch v. U.S. 1949. 336 U.S. 440.

LaFave, Wayne R. 2003a. *Criminal Law*. 4th ed. St. Paul, MN: Thomson West.

______. 2010. *Criminal Law*. 5th ed. St. Paul MN: Thompson West.

______. 2003b. *Substantive Criminal Law*. Vol. 1. 2nd ed. St. Paul, MN: Thomson West.

LaFave, Wayne R., and Austen Scott. 1986. *Criminal Law*. 2nd ed. St. Paul, MN: West.

LaFree, Gary D. 1989. *Rape and Criminal Justice: The Social Construction of Sexual Assault*. Belmont CA: Wadsworth.

Lanzetta v. New Jersey. 1939. 306 U.S. 451.

Larkin, Paul. 2014. "The Extent of America's Overcriminalization Problem." Washington DC: The Heritage Foundation. Accessed August 6, 2014. http://www.heritage.org/research/reports/2014/05/the-extent-of-americas-overcriminalization-problem.

Larrabee, John. 1995. "Fighting Crime with a Dose of Shame; in Some Communities, Old-Fashioned Public Humiliation Has Returned." *USA Today*, June 19.

Law Center to Prevent Gun Violence. 2014. "Post-*Heller* Litigation Summary. San Francisco: Law Center to Prevent Gun Violence. Accessed January 15, 2015. http://smartgunlaws.org/post-heller-litigation-summary/.

Lawrence v. Texas. 2003. 539 U.S. 558.

Le Barron v. State. 1966. 145 N.W.2d 79 (Wis.).

Lederer, Richard. 1988. *Get Thee to a Punnery*. New York: Bantam Doubleday.

Lee, Cynthia. 2003. *Murder and the Reasonable Man: Passion and Fear in the Criminal Courtroom*. New York. New York University Press.

Lefler, Julie. 1999. "Shining the Spotlight on Johns: Moving toward Equal Treatment of Male Customers and Female Prostitutes." *Hastings Women Law Journal* 10:11–35.

Legal Match. 2015. "Three-Strikes-Laws in Different States." Accessed January 26, 2015. *LegalMatch.com*. http://www.legalmatch.com/law-library/article/three-strikes-laws-in-different-states.html.

Lewin, Tamar. 1985. "Criminal Onus on Executives." *New York Times*, 5 March.

Lewis, C. S. 1953. "The Humanitarian Theory of Punishment." *Res Judicata* 6:224.

Lewis, Sinclair. 1922. *Babbitt*. New York: Harcourt Brace.

Liebelson, Dana. 2012. "Six Americans Obama and Holder Charged under the Espionage Act." *Project on Government Oversight (POGO)*, January 27. Accessed May 25, 2012. http://pogoblog.typepad .com/pogo/2012/01/six-americans-obama-and-holder-charged-under-the-espionage-act-and-one-bonus-whistleblower.html.

Linkins, Jason. 2013. "Lamar Alexander says video games are a bigger problem than guns but no, they aren't." *Huffington Post*, January 30. Accessed June 12, 2015. http://www.huffingtonpost.com/2013/01/30/lamar-alexander-video-games-guns_n_2584837.html.

Liptak, Adam. 2003. "Louisiana Sentence Renews Debate on the Death Penalty." *New York Times*, August 28.

______. 2006. "15 States Expand Right to Shoot in Self-Defense." *New York Times*, August 7.

Loewy, Arnold. 1987. *Criminal Law*. St. Paul, MN: West.

Logan, Wayne A. 2001. "The Shadow Criminal Law of Municipal Governance." *Ohio State Law Journal* 62:1409.

Louisiana Statutes Annotated. 1974. Rev. Stat. Title 17-A.

Low, Peter. 1990. *Criminal Law*. St. Paul, MN: West.

Luna, Erik. 2009. "Criminal Justice and the Public Imagination." *Ohio State Journal of Criminal Law*: 7:71–147.

______. 2004. "Overextending Criminal Law." Gene Healy, ed. *Go Directly to Jail*. Washington, DC: Cato Institute.

Lynch, Gerard E. 1987. "The Crime of Being a Criminal." *Columbia Law Review* 87:661–764; 920–84.

______. 1990. "A Conceptual, Practical, and Political Guide to RICO Reform." *Vanderbilt Law Review* 43:769–803.

______. 2002. "RICO (Racketeer Influenced and Corrupt Organizations) Act." *Encyclopedia of Crime and Justice*. Vol. 3. 2nd ed. New York: Gale Group/Thomson Learning.

Macias v. State. 1929. 283 P. 711.

Madison, James. [1787] 1961. "The Federalist No. 51." *The Federalist*, edited by Jacob E. Cooke. Middletown, CN: Wesleyan University Press.

Marcus, Paul. 1986. "The Development of Entrapment Law." *Wayne Law Review* 33:5.

Markey, Patrick M., Charlotte N. Markey, and Juliana E. French. 2014. *Violent Video Games and Real-World Violence: Rhetoric Versus Data*. American Psychological Association. Accessed June 11, 2015. http://dx.doi.org/10.1037/ppm0000030.

Maxson, Cheryl, Karen Hennigan, and David Sloane. 2005. "'It's Getting Crazy Out There': Can a Civil Gang Injunction Change a Community?" *Criminology and Public Policy* 4(3):577–606.

Mayer, Andre, and Michael Wheeler. 1982. *The Crocodile Man: A Case of Brain Chemistry and Criminal Violence*. Boston: Houghton-Mifflin.

Mayor of New York v. Miln. 1837. 36 U.S. (11 Pet.) 102.

McDonald v. City of Chicago. 2010. 130 S.Ct. 3020.

McKendree v. Christy. 1961. 172 N.E.2d 380.

McMahon, R. Bradley. 2004. "After Billions Spent to Comply with HIPPA and GBA Provisions, Why Is Identity Theft the Most Prevalent Crime in America?" *Villanova Law Review* 49:625.

McMullen, Richie. 1990. *Male Rape: Breaking the Silence on the Last Taboo.* London: Gay Men's Press.

Meerpol, Robert. 2003. *An Execution in the Family: One Son's Journey.* New York: St. Martin's Press.

Merschman, Joseph. 2001. "The Dark Side of the Web: Cyberstalking and the Need for Contemporary Legislation." *Harvard Women's Law Journal* 24:255.

Messinger, Thane Josef. 1993. "A Gentle and Easy Death: From Ancient Greece to beyond Cruzan toward a Reasoned Legal Response to the Societal Dilemma of Euthanasia." *Denver University Law Review* 71: 175–251.

Michael, Jerome, and Herbert Wechsler. 1937. "A Rationale of the Law of Homicide." *Columbia Law Review* 701, 1261.

Mills, David, and Michael Romano. 2014. "Proposition 36 Progress Report." Stanford CA: Stanford Law School Three Strikes Project.

Mims v. U.S. 1967. 375 F.2d 135 (5th Cir.).

Minnesota Criminal Code. 2005. *Definitions.* § 609.341. http://www.revisor.leg.state.mn.us/stats/609/341.html.

______. 2011. *Patrons; Prostitutes; Housing Individuals Engaged in Prostitution; Penalties.* § 609.324. https://www.revisor.mn.gov/statutes/?id=609.324.

______. 2014. *Criminal Sexual Conduct Definitions.* § 609.34. https://www.revisor.mn.gov/statutes/?id=609.341.

Minnesota Statutes Annotated. 1989. Cumulative Supplement.

Minturn T. Wright, III. 1951. *Note: Statutory Burglary: The Magic of Four Walls and a Roof,* 100. *University of Pennsylvania Law Review 411.*

Mishaga v. Monken, Director of Illinois State Police. 2010. 753 F.Supp.2d 750 (C.D. Ill.).

Mishler, Joanna Lee. 2000. "Cyberstalking: Can Communication via the Internet Constitute a Credible Threat, and Should an Internet Service Provider Be Liable If It Does?" *Santa Clara Computer and High Technology Law Journal* 17: 115.

Mitford, Jessica. 1969. *The Trial of Dr. Spock.* New York: Knopf.

M'Naghten's Case. 1843. 8 Eng.Rep. 718.

Model Penal Code and Commentaries. 1985. Philadelphia: American Law Institute (ALI).

Moran, Richard. 1985. "The Modern Foundation for the Insanity Defense: The Cases of James Hadfield (1800) and Daniel McNaughtan (1843)." *Annals of the American Academy of Political and Social Science* 477: 31–42.

More, Sir Thomas. 1516. *Utopia.* London: Reeves & Turner.

Morgan v. State. 1982. 415 So.2d 6 (Fla.).

Moriarty, Daniel G. 1989. "Extending the Defense of Renunciation." *Temple Law Review* 62.

Morissette v. U.S. 1952. 342 U.S. 246.

Morris, Herbert. 1976. *On Guilt and Innocence.* Los Angeles: University of California Press.

Morris, Norval. 1951. "Somnambulistic Homicide: Ghosts, Spiders, and North Koreans." *Res Judicata* 5.

______. 1974. *The Future of Imprisonment.* Chicago: University of Chicago Press.

Morris Norval, and Gordon Hawkins. 1970. *An Honest Politician's Guide to Crime Control.* Chicago: University of Chicago Press.

Myers III v. State. 2015. No. 76S03-1407-CR-493 (Indiana Supreme Court).

Nadler, Janice. 2005. "Flouting the Law." *Texas Law Review* 83:1399–1442.

National Institute of Justice. 1996. *Domestic Violence, Stalking, and Antistalking Legislation: An Annual Report to Congress under the Violence Against Women Act.* Washington DC: US. Department of Justice.

National Public Radio. 2003. *Morning Edition,* September 18.

National Research Council (NRC). 2014. *The Growth of Incarceration in the United States: Exploring Causes and Consequences.* Washington DC: National Academies Press.

New Mexico Criminal Code. 2006. *False Imprisonment.* § 30-4-3. http://law.justia.com/codes/new-mexico/2006/nmrc/jd_30-4-3-c297.html.

New York Central & Hudson River Railroad Company v. U.S. 1909. 212 U.S. 481.

New York Penal Code. 2003. http://public.leginfo.state.ny.us/menugetf.cgi?COMMONQUERY=LAWS.

Harvard Law Review. 2006. "The New Rule of Lenity." *Harvard Law Review* 119:2420–41. http://www.jstor.org/stable/4093511?seq=1#page_scan_tab_contents.

Nourse, Victoria. 1997. "Passion's Progress: Modern Law Reform and the Provocation Defense." *Yale Law Journal* 106:1331.

Novak, William J. 1996. *The People's Welfare: Law and Regulation in Nineteenth-Century America.* Chapel Hill: University of North Carolina Press.

Oberer, Walter E. 1962. "The Deadly Weapon Doctrine—Common Law Origin." *Harvard Law Review* 75: 1565.

Oliver v. State. 1985. 703 P.2d 869 (Nev.).

Olmstead v. U.S. 1928. 277 U.S. 438.

O'Sullivan, Julie R. 2014. *Federal White Collar Crime,* 5th ed. St. Paul MN: West Publishing.

Owens v. State. 2001. 787 So.2d 143.

Oxford English Dictionary. 2009. Edited by John Simpson. New York: Oxford University Press.

Oxford New American Dictionary. 2013. Accessed December 28, 2014. http://www.oxfordreference.com/view/10.1093/acref/9780195392883.001.0001/acref-9780195392883.

Packer, Herbert L. 1968. *The Limits of the Criminal Sanction.* Stanford, CA: Stanford University Press.

Palrgrave, Sir Francis. 1837. *Truths and Fictions of the Middle Ages: The Merchant and the Friar.* London. J. Parker.

Panetta, Leon. 2012. "Remarks by Secretary Panetta on Cybersecurity to the Business Executives for National Security, New York City." October 11, 2012. Accessed

June 24, 2015. http://www.defense.gov/transcripts/transcript.aspx?transcriptid=5136.

Papachristou v. City of Jacksonville. 1972. 405 U.S. 156.

Parr v. United States. 1960. 363 U.S. 370, 80 S.Ct. 1171, 4 L.Ed.2d 1277.

Parsons v. State. 1877. 2 So. 854 (Ala.).

Pennsylvania Laws. 1794. chap. 257, §§ 1–2.

Penry v. Lynaugh. 1989. 492 U.S. 302.

People ex rel. Gallo v. Acuna. 1997. 929 P.2d 596.

People v. Allen. 1997. 64 Cal.Rptr.2d 497.

People v. Anderson. 1968. 447 P.2d 942.

People v. Burroughs. 1984. 668 P.2d 894.

People v. Chessman. 1951. 238 P.2d 1001 (Cal.).

People v. Clem. 2000. 78 Cal.App. 4th 346.

People v. Datema. 1995. 533 N.W.2d 272 (Mich.).

People v. Goetz. 1986. 497 N.E.2d 41 (N.Y.).

People v. Greenberger. 1997. 58 Cal.App.4th 298, 377; 68 Cal.Rptr.2d 61.

People v. Henderson. 1977. 560 P.2d 1180.

People v. James. 1998. 62 Cal.App.4th 244.

People v. Kemp. 1961. 359 P.2d 913 (Cal.).

People v. Kibbe. 1974. 362 N.Y.S.2d 848.

People v. Kimball. 1981. 311 N.W.2d 343 (Mich.App.).

People v. Lai Lee. 2009. 24 Misc.3d 1233(A).

People v. Lee. 1991. 234 Cal.App.3d 1214.

People v. Levy. 2011. 936 N.Y.S 2d 835.

People v. Lopez. 1971. 489 P.2d 1372.

People v. Mattison. 1971. 481 P.2d 193.

People v. Mills. 1904. 70 N.E. 786.

People v. Nichols. 1970. 474 P.2d 6733.

People v. Oliver. 1989. 258 Cal.Rptr.138.

People v. O'Neil. 1990. 550 N.E.2d 1090 (Ill.App.).

People v. Penman. 1915. 110 N.E. 894.

People v. Phillips. 1966. 414 P.2d 353 (Cal.App.).

People v. Protopappas. 1988. 201 Cal.App.3d 152 (Cal.App.).

People v. Quentin. 1968. 296 N.Y.S.2d 443.

People v. Pearch. 1991. 229 Cal.App.3d 1282, 1299; 280 Cal.Rptr. 584.

People v. Rizzo. 1927. 158 N.E. 888 (N.Y.App.).

People v. Satchell. 1971. 489 P.2d 1361.

People v. Schmidt. 1915. 216 N.Y. 324.

People v. Smith. 1998. 62 Cal.App.4th 1233.

People v. Stamp. 1969. 2 Cal.App.3d 203.

People v. Steele. 2002. 47 P.3d 225. (Cal.).

People v. Taylor. 1992. 6 Cal.App.4th 1084.

People v. Thomas. 1978. 272 N.W.2d 157 (Mich.App.).

People v. Tomlins. 1914. 213 N.Y. 240, 107 N.E. 496.

People v. Williams. 1965. 205 N.E.2d 749 (Ill.App.).

Perkins, Rollin M., and Ronald N. Boyce. 1982. *Criminal Law*. 3rd ed. Mineola, NY: Foundation Press.

Perlin, Michael. 1990. "Unpacking the Myths: The Symbolism Mythology of Insanity Defense Jurisprudence." *Case Western Reserve Law Review* 40:599.

———. 1989–90. "Mythology of Insanity Defense Jurisprudence." *Case Western Reserve University* 40:599–731.

Persons, Courtney Guyton. 1996. "Sex in the Sunlight: The Effectiveness, Efficiency, and the Constitutionality and Advisability of Publishing Names and Pictures of Prostitutes' Patrons." *Vanderbilt Law Review* 49:1525–75.

Pillsbury, Samuel H. 2002. "Crimes against the heart: Recognizing the wrongs of forced sex. *Loyola of Los Angeles Law Review*: 35:845–960.

Pinkerton v. U.S. 1946. 328 U.S. 640.

Planned Parenthood v. Casey. 1991. 505 U.S. 833.

Plato. 1975. *Laws*. Translated by Trevor J. Saunders. Middlesex, England: Penguin Books.

Polisi, Caroline. 2009. "Spousal Rape Laws Continue to Evolve." *WENews*, July 1. Accessed December 21, 2014. http://womensenews.org/story/rape/090701/spousal-rape-laws-continue-evolve#.VJbqnDnkLg.

Pope Pius XII. 1956. "Discourse to Those Taking Part in the Second Naples World Congress on Fertility and Human Sterility." *AAS* 48:470.

Poulos, Peter W. 1995. "Chicago's Ban on Gang Loitering: Making Sense out of Vagueness and Overbreadth in Loitering Laws." *California Law Review* 83:379.

Powell v. Texas. 1968. 392 U.S. 514.

Press, Ann, and Peggy Clausen. 1982. "Not Guilty Because of PMS?" *Newsweek*, November 8.

Preyer, Kathryn. 1983. "Crime, the Criminal Law, and Reform in Post-Revolutionary Virginia." *Law and History Review* 1.

Queen v. Dudley and Stephens. 1884. 14 Q. B. 273.

Ramsey, Carolyn B. 2006. "Restructuring the Debate over Fetal Homicide Laws." *Ohio State Law Journal* 67:721–82.

Rather, Dan. 2009. "Dan Rather Reports, 'The Castle Doctrine.'" *Dan Rather Reports*, September 9. Episode 405. http://www.axs.tv/ui/inc/show_transcripts.php?ami=A5849&t=Dan_Rather_Reports&en=405.

R.A.V. v. City of St. Paul. 1992. 505 U.S. 377, 112 S.Ct. 2538.

Regina v. Jones. 1703. 91 Eng. Rep. 330.

Regina v. McNaughtan. 1843. 8 Eng. Rep. 718.

Reilly, Ryan J. 2014. "DEA Official: 'Every Single Parent' Opposes Marijuana Legalization." *Huffington Post*, March 5. Accessed August 4, 2014. http://www.huffingtonpost.com/2014/03/04/dea-tom-harrigan_n_4898585.html?page_version=legacy&view=print&comm_ref=false.

Reinhold, Robert. 1985. "Trial Opens in Death at Texas Nursing Home." *New York Times*, October 1.

Remick, Lani Anne. 1993. "Read Her Lips: An Argument for a Verbal Consent Standard in Rape." *University of Pennsylvania Law Review* 141:1103.

Remsburg v. Docusearch, Inc. 2003. 816 A.2d 1001 (N.H.).

Renshaw, Patrick. 1968. "The IWW and the Red Scare 1917–24." *Journal of Contemporary History* 3:63–72.

Rex v. Arnold. 1724. *Howell's State Trials* 16:695.

Rex v. Bailey. 1818. *Crown Cases Reserved*.

Rex v. Scofield. 1784. Cald. 397.

Reynolds v. State. 1889. 42 N.W. 903.

Rimer, Sara, and Raymond Bonner. 2000. "Whether to Kill Those Who Killed as Youths." *New York Times,* August 22.

Roberts. Sam. 1989. "Metro Matters; Exploring Laws and the Legacy of the Goetz Case. *New York Times* (January 23).

Robinson v. California. 1962. 370 U.S. 660.

Robinson, Paul, and Markus Dubber. 2004. "An Introduction to the Model Penal Code of the American Law Institute." Social Science Research Network. Accessed July 22, 2012. http://papers.ssrn.com/sol3/papers.cfm?abstract_id=661165.

Robinson, Paul. 2008. *Distributive Principles of Criminal Law: Who Should Be Punished How Much?* Accessed August 7, 2012. http://www.law.upenn.edu/fac/.../DP_full_SNT_rev_4_1_08_phr.pdf.

Robinson, Paul H., Robert Kurzban, Owen D. Jones. 2007. "The Origins of Shared Intuitions of Justice." *Vanderbilt Law Review* 60:1633–88.

Roe v. Wade. 1973. 410 U.S. 113.

Roper v. Simmons. 2005. 543 U.S. 551.

Rustad, Michael L. 2001. "Private Enforcement of Cybercrime on the Electronic Frontier." *Southern California Interdisciplinary Law Journal* 11:63.

Sabotage Act. 2012. *U.S. Code*. Title 18, § 2153. http://www4.law.cornell.edu/uscode/html/uscode18/usc_sup_01_18_10_I_20_105.html.

Samaha, Joel. 1974. *Law and Order in Historical Perspective*. New York: Academic Press.

______. 1978. "Hanging for Felony." *Historical Journal* 21.

Sampson, Robert J., and Stephen W. Raudenbush. 1999. "Deterrent Effect of the Police on Crime." *American Journal of Sociology* 105:163–89.

Savage, Charlie, and Emmarie Heutmann. 2013. "Manning Sentenced to 35 Years for a Pivotal Leak of U.S. Files. *New York Times*, August 21. Accessed June 27, 2015. http://www.nytimes.com/2013/08/22/us/manning-sentenced-for-leaking-government-secrets.html.

Savage, David G. 2010. "Activist's Case Will Test U.S. Anti-Terrorism Law." *Los Angeles Times*, February 18. Accessed May 29, 2012. http://articles.latimes.com/2010/feb/18/nation/la-na-court-terrorism18–2010feb18.

______. 1932. "*Mens Rea*." *Harvard Law Review* 45:974.

Scheidegger, Kent S. 1993. *A Guide to Regulating Panhandling*. Sacramento, Calif.: Criminal Justice Legal Foundation.

Schenck v. U.S. 1919. 249 U.S. 47.

Schlosser, Eric. 2015. "A Nun Walks Free: The Government's Sabotage Case Dismissed." *The New Yorker*, May 18. Accessed June 27, 2015. http://www.newyorker.com/news/news-desk/a-nun-walks-free-the-governments-sabotage-case-dismissed.

Schwartz, Richard. 1983. "Rehabilitation." *Encyclopedia of Crime and Justice*. New York: Free Press.

Sedition Act. 1918. "Primary Documents—U.S. Espionage Act, 7 May 1918." *FirstWorldWar.com*. Accessed May 23, 2012. http://www.firstworldwar.com/source/espionageact1918.htm.

Seligman, Joel. 2004. "Cautious Evolution or Perennial Irresolution: Stock Market Self-Regulation during the First Seventy Years of the Securities and Exchange Commission." *Business Lawyer* 59:1347–87.

Senander, Mary. 1988. International Anti-Euthanasia Task Force, Death on Demand: "Don't Count Me In!" Quoted in Thane Joseph Messinger, "A Gentle and Easy Death: From Ancient Greece to beyond Cruzan: Toward a Reasoned Legal Response to the Societal Dilemma of Euthanasia," *Denver University Law Review* 71 (1993): 219–20.

Shane, Scott. 2011. "Leak Offers Look at Efforts by U.S. to Spy on Israel." *New York Times*, September 5. Accessed May 25, 2012. http://www.nytimes.com/2011/09/06/us/06leak.html?pagewanted=all.

Shenon, Philip. 1985. "Dispute over Intent in Drug Cases Divided FDA and Justice Department." *New York Times,* September 19.

Shepherd, Joanna. 2002. "Fear of the First Strike: The Full Deterrent Effect of California's Two- and Three-Strikes Legislation." *Journal of Legal Studies* 31 (January): 159.

Sherman v. U.S. 1958. 356 U.S. 369.

Siegel, Barry. 1996. "Held Accountable for Son's Burglaries." *Los Angeles Times*, May 10.

Simon, Harry. 1992. "Towns without Pity: A Constitutional and Historical Analysis of Official Efforts to Drive Homeless Persons from American Cities." *Tulane Law Review* 66.

Singer, Richard G., and John Q. LaFond. 2013. *Criminal Law*. 6th ed. New York: Walters Kluwer Law & Business.

Skogan, Wesley G. 1990. *Disorder and Decline*. New York: Free Press.

Smallwood v. State. 1996. 680 A.2d 512 (Md.).

Smith, Juliette. 1996. "Arresting the Homeless for Sleeping in Public: A Paradigm for Expanding the *Robinson* Doctrine." *Columbia Journal of Law and Social Problems* 29.

Smith, Sandra. 2000. "Fetal Homicide: Woman or Fetus as Victim? A Survey of Current State Approaches and Recommendations for Future State Application." *William & Mary Law Review* 41:1845–84.

Solem v. Helm. 1983. 463 U.S. 277.

Sonnier v. State. 1992. 849 S.W.2d 828 (Tex.App.).

Spartacus Educational. 2014. "Espionage Act." Spartacus Educational. Accessed July 13, 2012. http://www.spartacus.schoolnet.co.uk/FWWespionage.htm.

Spohn, Cassia. 1999. "The Rape Reform Movement: The Traditional Common Law and Rape Law Reforms." *Jurimetrics* 39:119–30.

Stanford v. Kentucky. 1989. 492 U.S. 361.

Stanley v. Georgia. 1969. 394 U.S. 557.

State in the Interest of M.T.S. 1992. 609 A.2d 1266 (N.J.).

State v. Aguillard. 1990. 567 So.2d 674 (La.).

State v. Akers. 1979. 400 A.2d 38 (N.H.).

State v. Anderson. 1991. 566 N.E. 2d 1224 (Ohio).

State v. Batie. 2015. WL 929478 (OhioApp.).

State v. Bauer. 2014. 329P.3d 67 (WA).

State v. Belew. 2014. 17 N.E. 3d 515 (OhioApp.).
State v. Burrell. 1992. 509 .2d 571 (NH).
State v. Chism. 1983. 436 So.2d 464 (La.).
State v. Crawford. 1996. 472 S.E.2d 920 (N.C.).
State v. Curley. 1997. 939 P.2d 1103 (N.Mex.App.).
State v. Dabney. 2004. 858 A.2d 1084 (Md.App).
State v. Damms. 1960. 100 N.W.2d 592 (Wis.).
State v. Fiero. 1979. 603 P.2d 74.
State v. Fleck. 2012. 810 N.W.2d 303 (MN).
State v. Flory. 1929. 276 P. 458 (Wyo.).
State v. Hall. 1974. 214 N.W.2d 205.
State v. Hamlet. 1984. 321 S.E.2d 837 (N.C.).
State v. Harrison. 1977. 564 P.2d 1321 (N.M.).
State v. Hauptmann. 1935. 180 A.2d 809 (N.J.).
State v. Hoying. 2005. WL 678989 (OhioApp.).
State v. Hudson. 1999. 745 So. 2d. 997 (Fla.App.)
State v. Jacobson. 2005. 697 N.W. 2d 610 (MN).
State v. Jantzi. 1982. 56, 57, 641 P.2d 62 (Ore.App.).
State v. Jerrett. 1983. 307 S.E.2d 339.
State v. King. 2004. WL 1913949 (SC App.).
State v. K.R.L. 1992. 840 P.2d 210 (Wash.App.).
State v. Kuntz. 2000. 995 P.2d 951 (Mont.).
State v. Loge. 2000. 608 N.W.2d 152 (Minn.).
State v. Mays. 2000. 743 N.E.2d 447 (OhioApp.).
State v. Metzger. 1982. 319 N.W.2d 459 (Neb.).
State v. Miranda. 1998. 715 A.2d 680.
State v. Mitcheson. 1977. 560 P.2d 1120 (Utah).
State v. Myrick. 1982. 291 S.E.2d 577.
State v. Newman. 2013. 302 P.3d 435 (OR).
State v. Ninham. 2011. 797 N.W.2d 451 (Wis.).
State v. Phipps. 1994. 883 S.W.2d 138 (Tenn.App.).
State v. Powell. 1951. 227 P.2d 582, 585.
State v. Robertson. 1999. 740 A.2d 330 (RI).
State v. Rolon. 2012. 45 A.3d 518.
State v. Schleifer. 1923. 432 121 A. 805 (Conn.).
State v. Sexton. 1999. 733 A.2d 1125 (N.J.).
State v. Shaw. 1981. 185 Conn. 372, 441 A.2d 561.
State v. Shelley. 1997. 929 P.2d 489 (Wash.App.).
State v. Snowden. 1957. 313 P.2d 706 (Idaho).
State v. Stark. 1992. 832 P.2d 109 (Wash.App.).
State v. Stewart. 1988. 763 P.2d 572 (Kans.).
State v. Taylor. 2002. 650 N.W.2d 190 (Minn.).
State v. Thomas. 1999. 590 N.W.2d 755 (Minn.).
State v. Triestman. 2010. A3d 634.
State v. Ulvinen. 1981. 313 N.W.2d 425 (Minn.).
State v. Vargas. 2003. 812 A.2d. 205.
State v. Walden. 1982. 293 S.E.2d 780.
State v. Zeta Chi Fraternity. 1997. 686 A.2d. 530 (N.H.).
Stephen, Sir James F. 1883. *A History of the Criminal Law of England*. London: Macmillan.
Stuntz, William. 2001. "The Pathological Politics of Criminal Law." *Michigan Law Review* :100:505–600.
Suk, Jeannie. 2008. "The True Woman: Scenes from the Law of Self-Defense." *Harvard Journal of Law and Gender* 31(Summer): 237–75.
Sutherland, Edwin. 1940. "White-Collar Criminality." *American Sociological Review* 5(1):1–12. http://www.cooley.libarts.wsu.edu/criminology/Documents/sutherland.pdf.
Swann v. U.S. 1994. 648 A.2d 928.
"Symposium: Wrongful Convictions and Systemic Reform." 2005. *American Criminal Law Reform* 42:4.
Taft, Philip. 1962. "The Federal Trials of the IWW." *Labor History* 3(1): 57–91.
Tanielian, Terri and Lisa H. Jaycox. 2008. *Invisible Wounds of War: Psychological and Cognitive Injuries, Their Consequences, and Services to Assist Recovery*. Santa Monica, CA: Rand Corporation.
Tennessee Criminal Code. 2005. "Serious Bodily Injury." Title 39, Chapter 11, Section 106(a)(34). Accessed July 23, 2012. http://law.justia.com/codes/tennessee/2010/title-39/chapter-11/part-1/39–11–106/.
Thomas, Clarence. 1996. "Federalist Society Symposium: The Rights Revolution." *Michigan Law and Policy Review* 1:269.
Thompson v. Oklahoma. 1988. 487 U.S. 815.
Thompson, Seymour. 1880. "Homicide in Self-Defense." *American Criminal Law Review* 14:545.
Tier, Robert. 1993. "Maintaining Safety and Civility in Public Spaces: A Constitutional Approach to Aggressive Begging." *Louisiana Law Review* 54:285.
Todd v. State. 1992. 594 So.2d 802 (Fla.App.).
Toops v. State. 1994. 643 N.E.2d 387 (Ind.App.).
Tomkovicz, James J. 1994. "The Endurance of the Felony-Murder Rule." *Washington and Lee Law Review* 51:1429–80.
Tomlins, Christopher. 2008. "The Supreme Sovereignty of the State," in Markus Dubber and Mariana Valverde, eds., *Police and the Liberal State*. Stanford, CA: Stanford University Press.
Treason Act. 2006. *U.S. Code*. Title 18, § 2381.
Trop v. Dulles. 1958. 356 U.S. 86.
Turner, Michael, Jody Sundt, Brandon Applegate, and Francis Cullen. 1995. "'Three Strikes and You're Out' Legislation: A National Assessment." *Federal Probation 59(3):16–35*.
Twohey, Megan. 2008. "An abuser, in his own words." *Chicago Tribune* (November 11).
Tyler, Tom. 2006. *Why People Obey the Law*. Princeton NJ: Princeton University Press.
Urofsky, Melvin, and Paul Finkelman. 2002a. *Documents of American Constitutional and Legal History*. New York: Oxford University Press.
———. 2002b. *A March of Liberty*. New York: Oxford University Press.
U.S. Attorney's Office, Southern District of Texas. 2015. "Texas Resident Charged with Conspiracy to Provide Material Support to ISIL." May 26. Accessed June 19, 2015. https://www.fbi.gov/houston/press-releases/2015/texas-resident-charged-withconspiracy-to-provide-material-support-to-isil.
U.S. Department of Justice (USDOJ). 2015. *Department of Justice Report Regarding the Criminal Investigation*

into the Shooting Death of Michael Brown by Ferguson, Missouri Police Officer Darren Wilson. March 4. Accessed June 9, 2015. http://www.justice.gov/sites/default/files/opa/press-releases/attachments/2015/03/04/doj_report_on_shooting_of_michael_brown_1.pdf.

U.S. Department of Justice. 2015. *Investigation of the Ferguson Police Department*. Civil Rights Division. March 4. Accessed June 13, 2015. http://www.justice.gov/sites/default/files/opa/press-releases/attachments/2015/03/04/ferguson_police_department_report.pdf.

U.S. v. Ancheta. 2006. (C.D. Cal.).

U.S. v. Arthur Andersen, LLP. 2004. 544 U.S. 696.

U.S. v. Asher Abid Khan. http://www.ipqpubs.com/wp-content/uploads/2011/03/Consent-Decree-Deltex.pdf

U.S. v. Booker. 2005. 543 U.S. 220.

U.S. v. Blue Thunder. 1979. 604 F.2d 550 (8th Cir.).

U.S. v. Bruno. 1939. 105 F.2d 921.

U.S. v. Chester. 2010. 628 F.3d 673 (4th Circuit).

U.S. v. Cordoba-Hincapie. 1993. 825 F.Supp. 485.

U.S. v. Downs. 1995. 56 F.3d 973 (8th Cir.).

U.S. v. Gementera. 2004. 379 F.3d 596. Accessed October 31, 2011. http://law.justia.com/cases/federal/appellate-courts/F3/379/596/475040/.

U.S. v. Haynes. 1998. 143 F.3d 1089 (7th Cir., Wis.).

U.S. v. International Minerals & Chemical Corporation. 1971. 402 U.S. 558.

U.S. v. Maze. 1974. 414 U.S. 395, 94 S.Ct. 645.

U.S. v. Motion Picture Film, "The Spirit of '76." 1917. 252 F. 946.

U.S. v. Peoni. 1938. 100 F.2d 401 (2nd Cir.).

U.S. v. Porcelli. 1989. 865 F.2d 1352 (2nd Cir.).

U.S. v. R.L.C. 1992. 503 U.S. 291.

U.S. v. Ross Ulbricht. 2015. U.S. District Court, Southern District of New York. 14 Cr. 68 (KBF).

U.S. v. Sampson. 1962. 371 U.S. 75, 83 S.Ct. 173, 9 L.Ed.2d.

U.S. v. Treas-Wilson. 1993. 3 F.3d 1406 (10th Cir.).

U.S. v. Wiltberger. 1820. 18 U.S. 76.

U.S. Department of Justice. 2006. *Progress Report of the Department of Justice's Task Force on Intellectual Property*. Washington, DC: Department of Justice. http://www.justice.gov/opa/documents/ipreport61906.pdf.

U.S. Sentencing Commission. 2006. *Final Report on the Impact of* United States v. Booker *on Federal Sentencing*. Washington, DC: U.S. Sentencing Commission.

Valdes, Stephen G. 2005. "Frequency and Success: An Empirical Study of Criminal Law Defenses, Federal Constitutional Evidence Claims, and Plea Negotiations." *New York University Law Review* 153:1709–1814.

Vamosi, Robert. 2006. "An American Cybervillain." *CNET Reviews*. Accessed July 23, 2012. http://reviews.cnet.com/4520-3513_7-6427016-1.html.

Van Cleave, Ryan. 2010. *Unplugged: my journey into the dark world of video game addiction*. Deerfield Beach FL: Health Communications, Inc.

Victor v. Nebraska. 1994. 511 U.S. 1.

Von Hirsch, Andrew, and Andrew Ashworth. 2005. *Proportionate Sentencing*. New York: Oxford University Press.

Wash v. State. 1980. 408 N.E.2d 634.

Washington v. Glucksberg. 1997. 521 U.S. 702.

Weems v. U.S. 1910. 217 U.S. 349.

Weinstein, Judge Jack B., and Ian Dewsbury. 2006. "Comment on the meaning of 'proof beyond a reasonable doubt.'" *Law, Probability, and Risk* 5:167–73.

Weismann, Miriam, 2009. *Crime, Incorporated*. Chicago: American Bar Association.

Weiss, Baruch. 2002. "What Were They Thinking? The Mental States of Aider and Abettor, and the Causer under Federal Law." *Fordham Law Review* 70:1341.

West v. State. 1988. 408 N.E.2d 634.

Wheeler, Jacob D. 1854. *Reports of Criminal Law Cases Decided at the City-Hall of the City of New York*. Albany: Gould Banks & Co; New York: Banks Gould & Co.

Wilber, Del Quentin. 2009. "Economic Downturn Accelerates Collapse of Ponzi Schemes." *Washington Post*, June 12. Accessed June 1, 2015. http://www.washingtonpost.com/wp-dyn/content/article/2009/06/11/AR2009061103993.html.

Williams v. State. 1992. 600 N.E.2d 962 (Ind.App.).

Williams v. State. 2013. 110 So.3d 59 (Fla.App.).

Williams, Glanville. 1961. *Criminal Law*. 2nd ed. London: Stevens and Sons.

Wilson, James Q. 1975. *Thinking about Crime*. New York: Basic Books.

Wilson, James Q., and Richard Herrnstein. 1985. *Crime and Human Nature*. New York: Simon & Schuster.

Wilson, James Q., and George L. Kelling. 1982. "Broken Windows." *Atlantic Monthly*, March.

Wilson v. State. 1909. 38 S.W.2d 1013 (Tex.Cr.App.).

Wilson, Woodrow. 1915. "Third Annual Message, December 7, 1915." Miller Center. Accessed May 23, 2012. http://millercenter.org/president/speeches/detail/3794.

Wisconsin Criminal Code. 2003. § 947.01. http://folio.legis.state.wi.us/cgi-bin/om_isapi.dll?clientID=547736967&infobase=stats.nfo&jump=ch.%20947.

______. 2006. § 940.31. http://nxt.legis.state.wi.us/nxt/gateway.dll?f=templates&fn=default.htm&vid=WI:Default&d=stats&jd=ch.%20940.

Wolfenden Report. 1957. *Report of Committee on Homosexual Offences and Prostitution*. London: Stationer's Office.

Woolard v. Gallagher. 2013. 712 F.3d 865 (CA 4).

Xi Van Ha v. State. 1995. http://www.touchngo.com/ap/html/ap-1400.htm.

Yang, Debra Wong, and Brian M. Hoffstadt. 2006. "Countering the Cyber-Crime Threat." *American Criminal Law Review* 43:201.

Zabel, Richard B., and James J. Benjamin. 2009. *In Pursuit of Justice: Prosecuting Terrorism Cases in the Federal Courts. 2009 Update and Recent Developments*. Washington, DC: Human Rights First.

Case Index

T

U

V

W

X

Z

Index

Note: Page numbers in **boldface** denote glossary terms.

Appendix

Selected Amendments of the Constitution of the United States: The Bill of Rights and Amendment XIV

Amendment I Congress shall make no law respecting an establishment of religion, or prohibiting the free exercise thereof; or abridging the freedom of speech, or of the press; or the right of the people peaceably to assemble, and to petition the Government for a redress of grievances.

Amendment II A well regulated Militia, being necessary to the security of a free State, the right of the people to keep and bear Arms, shall not be infringed.

Amendment III No Soldier shall, in time of peace be quartered in any house, without the consent of the Owner, nor in time of war, but in a manner to be prescribed by law.

Amendment IV The right of the people to be secure in their persons, houses, papers, and effects, against unreasonable searches and seizures, shall not be violated, and no Warrants shall issue, but upon probable cause, supported by Oath or affirmation, and particularly describing the place to be searched, and the persons or things to be seized.

Amendment V No person shall be held to answer for a capital, or otherwise infamous crime, unless on a presentment or indictment of a Grand Jury, except in cases arising in the land or naval forces, or in the Militia, when in actual service in time of War or public danger; nor shall any person be subject for the same offence to be twice put in jeopardy of life or limb; nor shall be compelled in any criminal case to be a witness against himself, nor be deprived of life, liberty, or property, without due process of law; nor shall private property be taken for public use, without just compensation.

Amendment VI In all criminal prosecutions, the accused shall enjoy the right to a speedy and public trial, by an impartial jury of the State and district wherein the crime shall have been committed, which district shall have been previously ascertained by law, and to be informed of the nature and cause of the accusation; to be confronted with the witnesses against him; to have compulsory process for obtaining witnesses in his favor, and to have the Assistance of Counsel for his defence.

Amendment VII In Suits at common law, where the value in controversy shall exceed twenty dollars, the right of trial by jury shall be preserved, and no fact tried by a jury, shall be otherwise re-examined in any Court of the United States, than according to the rules of the common law.

Amendment VIII Excessive bail shall not be required, nor excessive fines imposed, nor cruel and unusual punishments inflicted.

Amendment IX The enumeration in the Constitution, of certain rights, shall not be construed to deny or disparage others retained by the people.

Amendment X The powers not delegated to the United States by the Constitution, nor prohibited by it to the States, are reserved to the States respectively, or to the people.